Contemporary Authors®

NEW REVISION SERIES

ISSN 0275-7176

Contemporary Authors®

A Bio-Bibliographical Guide to
Current Writers in Fiction, General Nonfiction,
Poetry, Journalism, Drama, Motion Pictures,
Television, and Other Fields

DEBORAH A. STRAUB
Editor

JAMES G. LESNIAK
DONNA OLENDORF
BRYAN RYAN
Associate Editors

THOMAS WILOCH
Senior Writer

NEW REVISION SERIES
volume 24

 Gale Research Inc.
Book Tower • Detroit, Michigan 48226

Copyright © 1988 by Gale Research Inc.

Library of Congress Catalog Card Number 81-640179
ISBN 0-8103-1978-0
ISSN 0275-7176

Computerized photocomposition by
Typographics, Incorporated
Kansas City, Missouri

Contents

Indexing note: All *Contemporary Authors New Revision Series* entries are indexed in the *Contemporary Authors* cumulative index, which is bound into the back of even-numbered *Contemporary Authors* original volumes (blue and black cover with orange bands) and available separately as an offprint.

Authors and Media People
Featured in This Volume

Kobo Abe (Japanese novelist, dramatist, and author of short stories)—Abe writes philosophical thrillers with existential themes that evoke comparisons with the work of Franz Kafka. Titles available in English translation include *Woman in the Dunes* and *The Ruined Map*.

Lloyd Alexander (American author of novels for children)—Alexander's fantasy fiction, such as *The High King* and *Westmark*, is noted for its blend of Welsh and Arthurian legend, humor, and adventure.

Margaret Atwood (Canadian novelist and poet)—Atwood explores themes of feminism, Canadian nationalism, isolation, and the search for self-identity in such novels as *The Edible Woman, Surfacing, Life before Man, Bodily Harm*, and *The Handmaid's Tale*. Two volumes of selected poems offer a representative sample of her verse. (Entry contains interview.)

Beryl Bainbridge (British novelist)—Bainbridge's satiric and darkly comic portraits of the English working class include *The Dressmaker*, which was published in the United States as *The Secret Glass, The Bottle Factory Outing*, and *Sweet William*.

James Baldwin (American novelist, essayist, and dramatist who died in 1987)—Baldwin explored the aspirations, disappointments, and coping strategies of American blacks in a hostile society. Among his best-known works are the essay collections *Nobody Knows My Name: More Notes of a Native Son* and *The Fire Next Time*, the novel *Go Tell It on the Mountain*, and the play "Blues for Mister Charlie."

Heinrich Boell (German short story writer, novelist, dramatist, and essayist who died in 1985)—Boell's efforts to revitalize post-World War II German literature earned him a 1972 Nobel Prize. Major fiction that has been translated into English includes *Traveller, If You Come to Spa, And Where Were You, Adam?, And Never Said a Word, Group Portrait with Lady*, and *A Soldier's Legacy*.

Michael Bond (British author of fiction for children and adults)—Bond introduced his most popular character in the 1958 book *A Bear Called Paddington*. He is also the creator of Monsieur Pamplemousse, a French food inspector and detective who appears in a series of adult mysteries. (Entry contains interview.)

David Brin (American science fiction writer)—Brin has achieved fame for "hard science" novels such as *Startide Rising* that examine the theory of evolution and the possibilities of genetic engineering. (Entry contains interview.)

William F. Buckley, Jr. (American political commentator, magazine editor, and novelist)—One of the most recognized and articulate spokesmen for American conservatives, Buckley has published a variety of nonfiction works on politics and sailing as well as a series of bestselling spy novels featuring CIA agent Blackford Oakes. Notable nonfiction titles are *God and Man at Yale, Cruising Speed*, and *Right Reason*. (Entry contains interview.)

Antonio Buero Vallejo (Spanish dramatist)—Buero Vallejo's plays, including "Historia de una escalera," "In the Burning Darkness," and "Sleep of Reason," are regarded as subtle protests against the regime of Spain's late dictator, Francisco Franco.

Ed Bullins (American dramatist)—A principal figure in the black arts movement of the 1960s, Bullins is the author of "Clara's Ole Man," "In New England Winter," "The Taking of Miss Janie," and other plays that examine the disillusionment and frustration of ghetto life.

Octavia E. Butler (American science fiction writer)—In her novels *Patternmaster, Kindred*, and *Dawn: Xenogenesis*, Butler examines such concepts as genetic engineering in terms of racial and sexual awareness.

Lucille Clifton (American poet and author of books for children)—Clifton emphasizes pride in black heritage and the importance of family in the poetry collection *Good Times*, the memoir *Generations*, and the Everett Anderson series for children.

Pat Conroy (American novelist)—Conroy's novels, including such bestsellers as *The Great Santini* and *The Prince of Tides*, offer bitterly humorous and often bizarre views of life and relationships in the modern South.

Robert Daley (American novelist and author of nonfiction)—Daley has drawn on his own experiences as a former deputy police commissioner to produce the nonfiction books *Target Blue: An Insider's View of the N.Y.P.D.* and *Prince of the City: The Story of a Cop Who Knew Too Much*, as well as the suspense novels *The Dangerous Edge* and *Hands of a Stranger*. (Entry contains interview.)

J. P. Donleavy (American expatriate novelist and dramatist)—Donleavy, who became an Irish citizen in 1967, is best known for his bawdy yet bleak first novel, *The Ginger Man*, which many consider a modern classic. (Entry contains interview.)

Ralph Ellison (American novelist, author of short stories, essayist, and critic)—Ellison's reputation rests primarily on the highly acclaimed novel *Invisible Man*, the story of a black man's search for personal and cultural identity.

Ernest J. Gaines (American novelist and author of short stories)—Gaines's fiction, which includes *The Autobiography of Miss Jane Pittman, In My Father's House*, and *A Gathering of Old Men*, recalls the black culture and storytelling traditions of the author's native Louisiana.

A. B. Guthrie, Jr. (American novelist)—Guthrie depicts the taming of the American frontier in novels such as *The Big Sky, The Way West*, and *These Thousand Hills*.

Michael S. Harper (American poet)—Harper draws from folk traditions and history to chronicle black life in America. *Images of Kin* contains representative samples of his verse.

Rona Jaffe (American novelist and author of short stories)—Noted for the skillful storytelling and multiple plots typical of her first and most famous novel, *The Best of Everything,* Jaffe writes of a generation of women who came of age in the 1950s. (Entry contains interview.)

Larry L. King (American journalist and dramatist)—King's articles and other works, including the successful Broadway musical "The Best Little Whorehouse in Texas," are characterized by highly personal observations about life in his native state.

Carolyn Kizer (American poet)—Influenced by Eastern traditions in poetry, Kizer writes simple, restrained verse with political and feminist undercurrents. Her collection *Yin* won a 1985 Pulitzer Prize.

Philip Larkin (British poet who died in 1985)—Larkin, who was often referred to as "England's *other* Poet Laureate," achieved acclaim on the strength of a small but distinguished body of work, including *The Less Deceived, The Whitsun Weddings,* and *High Windows.*

Haki R. Madhubuti (American poet, publisher, editor, critic and educator)—Madhubuti, formerly Don L. Lee, writes poetry and nonfiction that reflect his commitment to fostering black culture. Among his notable titles are the poems *Think Black* and *Black Pride* and the collections *Dynamite Voices I: Black Poets of the 1960s* and *Earthquakes and Sunrise Missions: Poetry and Essays of Black Renewal, 1973-1983.*

Paul Mazursky (American director, producer, and screenwriter)—Mazursky's films, which include such popular works as "Bob & Carol & Ted & Alice," "An Unmarried Woman," and "Down and Out in Beverly Hills," affectionately satirize members of the urban middle class and their trendy lifestyles.

Thomas McGuane (American novelist and screenwriter)—McGuane achieved fame as the author of *The Sporting Club, The Bushwacked Piano,* and *Ninety-two in the Shade,* three stylistically flamboyant novels that capture the disillusionment of the late 1960s. (Entry contains interview.)

James Alan McPherson (American author of short stories)—In collections such as *Hue and Cry* and the award-winning *Elbow Room,* McPherson depicts ordinary, working-class people struggling with universal human problems.

Ron Milner (American dramatist)—Milner's plays, which include "What the Wine-Sellers Buy," "Checkmates," and "Don't Get God Started," are marked by an appeal to black families and communities to overcome life's obstacles by uniting around basic moral principles.

Farley Mowat (Canadian author of fiction and nonfiction)—Mowat's scathing accounts of man's abuse of nature, animals, and even other humans, examined in books such as *People of the Deer, Never Cry Wolf,* and *Sea of Slaughter,* have brought him international recognition as an advocate of all life forms. (Entry contains interview.)

Charles Neider (Russian-born American editor, novelist, and author of nonfiction)—A well-known editor of Mark Twain's writings, Neider is also the author of several books on Antarctica, including the nonfiction titles *Edge of the World* and *Beyond Cape Horn* and the novel *Overflight.* (Entry contains interview.)

Jayne Anne Phillips (American novelist and author of short stories)—Among Phillips's powerful and disturbing short stories about alienated people and families are those in the collections *Black Tickets* and *Fast Lanes.* (Entry contains interview.)

Sonia Sanchez (American poet, dramatist, political activist, and educator)—Sanchez emphasizes the performance aspects of poetry, linking it to the oral traditions of her African ancestors. Representative work appears in *Homecoming, We a BaddDDD People, A Blues Book for Blue Black Magical Women,* and *homegirls & handgrenades.*

Barbara Tuchman (American historian)—Tuchman combines sound historical research with a strong narrative line in her bestselling works, among them *The Guns of August, The Proud Tower: A Portrait of the World before the War, 1890-1914, Stilwell and the American Experience in China, 1911-1945,* and *A Distant Mirror: The Calamitous Fourteenth Century.*

Morris L. West (Australian-born novelist)—In theological thrillers such as *The Devil's Advocate, The Shoes of the Fisherman,* and *The Clowns of God,* West features political turmoil, worldwide governmental corruption, and the internal workings of the Catholic Church.

Preface

The *Contemporary Authors New Revision Series* provides completely updated information on authors listed in earlier volumes of *Contemporary Authors (CA)*. Entries for active individual authors from *any* volume of *CA* may be included in a volume of the *New Revision Series*. The sketches appearing in *New Revision Series* Volume 24, for example, were selected from more than twenty previously published *CA* volumes.

As always, the most recent *Contemporary Authors* cumulative index continues to be the user's guide to the location of an individual author's listing.

Compilation Methods

The editors make every effort to secure information directly from the authors. Copies of all sketches in selected *CA* volumes published several years ago are routinely sent to the listees at their last-known addresses. Authors mark material to be deleted or changed and insert any new personal data, new affiliations, new writings, new work in progress, new sidelights, and new biographical/critical sources. All returns are assessed, more comprehensive research is done, if necessary, and those sketches requiring significant change are completely updated and published in the *New Revision Series*.

If, however, authors fail to reply or are now deceased, biographical dictionaries are checked for new information (a task made easier through the use of Gale's *Biography and Genealogy Master Index* and other Gale biographical indexes), as are bibliographical sources such as *Cumulative Book Index* and *The National Union Catalog*. Using data from such sources, revision editors select and revise nonrespondents' entries that need substantial updating. Sketches not personally reviewed by the biographees are marked with a dagger (†) to indicate that these listings have been revised from secondary sources believed to be reliable, but they have not been personally reviewed for this edition by the authors sketched.

In addition, reviews and articles in major periodicals, lists of prestigious awards, and, particularly, requests from *CA* users are monitored so that writers on whom new information is in demand can be identified and revised listings prepared promptly.

Format

CA entries provide biographical and bibliographical information in an easy-to-use format. For example, individual paragraphs featuring such rubrics as "Addresses," "Career," and "Awards, honors" ensure that a reader seeking specific information can quickly focus on the pertinent portion of an entry. In sketch sections headed "Writings," the title of each book, play, and other published or unpublished work appears on a separate line, clearly distinguishing one title from another. This same convenient bibliographical presentation is also featured in the "Biographical/Critical Sources" sections of sketches where individual book and periodical titles are listed on separate lines. *CA* readers can therefore quickly scan these often-lengthy bibliographies to find the titles they need.

Comprehensive Revision

All listings in this volume have been revised and/or augmented in various ways, though the amount and type of change vary with the author. In many instances, sketches are totally rewritten, and the resulting *New Revision Series* entries are often considerably longer than the authors' previous listings. Revised entries include additions of or changes in such information as degrees, mailing addresses, literary agents, career items, career-related and civic activities, memberships, awards, work in progress, and biographical/critical sources. They may also include extensive bibliographical additions and informative new sidelights.

Writers of Special Interest

CA's editors make every effort to include in each *New Revision Series* volume a substantial number of revised entries on active authors and media people of special interest to *CA*'s readers. Since the *New Revision Series* also includes sketches on noteworthy deceased writers, a significant amount of work on the part of *CA*'s editors goes into the revision of entries on important deceased authors. Some of the prominent writers, both living and deceased, whose sketches are contained in this volume are noted in the list on pages vii-viii headed Authors and Media People Featured in This Volume.

Exclusive Interviews

CA provides exclusive, primary information on certain authors in the form of interviews. Prepared specifically for *CA,* the never-before-published conversations presented in the section of the sketch headed "*CA* Interview" give users the opportunity to learn the authors' thoughts, in depth, about their craft. Subjects chosen for interviews are, the editors feel, authors who hold special interest for *CA*'s readers.

Authors and journalists in this volume whose sketches contain exclusive interviews are Margaret Atwood, Michael Bond, David Brin, William F. Buckley, Jr., Robert Daley, J. P. Donleavy, Rona Jaffe, Thomas McGuane, Farley Mowat, Charles Neider, and Jayne Anne Phillips.

Contemporary Authors Autobiography Series

Designed to complement the information in *CA* original and revision volumes, the *Contemporary Authors Autobiography Series* provides autobiographical essays written by important current authors. Each volume contains from twenty to thirty specially commissioned autobiographies and is illustrated with numerous personal photographs supplied by the authors. The range of contemporary writers describing their lives and interests in the *Autobiography Series* encompasses authors such as Dannie Abse, Vance Bourjaily, Doris Grumbach, Elizabeth Forsythe Hailey, Marge Piercy, Frederik Pohl, Alan Sillitoe, William Stafford, Diane Wakoski, and Elie Wiesel. Though the information presented in the autobiographies is as varied and unique as the authors, common topics of discussion include their motivations for writing, the people and experiences that shaped their careers, the rewards they derive from their work, and their impressions of the current literary scene.

Autobiographies included in the *Contemporary Authors Autobiography Series* can be located through both the *CA* cumulative index and the *Contemporary Authors Autobiography Series* cumulative index, which lists not only personal names but also titles of works, geographical names, subjects, and schools of writing.

Contemporary Authors Bibliographical Series

The *Contemporary Authors Bibliographical Series* is a comprehensive survey of writings by and about the most important authors since World War II in the United States and abroad. Each volume concentrates on a specific genre and nationality and features approximately ten major writers. Volume 1, for instance, covers the American novelists James Baldwin, John Barth, Saul Bellow, John Cheever, Joseph Heller, Norman Mailer, Bernard Malamud, Carson McCullers, John Updike, and Eudora Welty. *Bibliographical Series* entries consist of three parts: a primary bibliography that lists works written by the author, a secondary bibliography that lists works about the author, and an analytical bibliographical essay that thoroughly discusses the merits and deficiencies of major critical and scholarly works. Complementing the information in other *CA* volumes, the *Bibliographical Series* is a new key to finding and evaluating information on the lives and writings of those authors who have attracted significant critical attention.

Each author's entry in the *Contemporary Authors Bibliographical Series* can be located through both the *CA* cumulative index and, beginning with Volume 2, the *Contemporary Authors Bibliographical Series* cumulative author index. A cumulative critic index, citing critics discussed in the bibliographical essays, also appears in each *Bibliographical Series* volume.

CA Numbering System

Occasionally questions arise about the *CA* numbering system. Despite numbers like "97-100" and "123," the entire *CA* series consists of only 83 physical volumes with the publication of *CA New Revision Series* Volume 24. The following information notes changes in the numbering system, as well as in cover design, to help users better understand the organization of the entire *CA* series.

CA First Revisions	• 1-4R through 41-44R (11 books) *Cover:* Brown with black and gold trim. There will be no further *First Revisions* because revised entries are now being handled exclusively through the more efficient *New Revision Series* mentioned below.

CA Original Volumes	• 45-48 through 97-100 (14 books) *Cover:* Brown with black and gold trim. • 101 through 123 (23 books) *Cover:* Blue and black with orange bands. The same as previous *CA* original volumes but with a new, simplified numbering system and new cover design.
CA New Revision Series	• *CANR*-1 through *CANR*-24 (24 books) *Cover:* Blue and black with green bands. Includes only sketches requiring extensive change; **sketches are taken from any previously published *CA* volume.**
CA Permanent Series	• *CAP*-1 and *CAP*-2 (2 books) *Cover:* Brown with red and gold trim. There will be no further *Permanent Series* volumes because revised entries are now being handled exclusively through the more efficient *New Revision Series* mentioned above.
CA Autobiography Series	• *CAAS*-1 through *CAAS*-7 (7 books) *Cover:* Blue and black with pink and purple bands. Presents specially commissioned autobiographies by leading contemporary writers to complement the information in *CA* original and revision volumes.
CA Bibliographical Series	• *CABS*-1 and *CABS*-2 (2 books) *Cover:* Blue and black with blue bands. Provides comprehensive bibliographical information on published works by and about major modern authors.

Retaining *CA* Volumes

As new volumes in the series are published, users often ask which *CA* volumes, if any, can be discarded. The Volume Update Chart on page xiii is designed to assist users in keeping their collections as complete as possible. All volumes in the left column of the chart should be retained to have the most complete, up-to-date coverage possible; volumes in the right column can be discarded if the appropriate replacements are held.

Cumulative Index Should Always Be Consulted

The key to locating an individual author's listing is the *CA* cumulative index bound into the back of alternate original volumes (and available separately as an offprint). Since the *CA* cumulative index provides access to *all* entries in the *CA* series, the latest cumulative index should always be consulted to find the specific volume containing a listee's original or most recently revised sketch.

Those authors whose entries appear in the *New Revision Series* are listed in the *CA* cumulative index with the designation **CANR-** in front of the specific volume number. For the convenience of those who do not have *New Revision Series* volumes, the cumulative index also notes the specific earlier volumes of *CA* in which the sketch appeared. Below is a sample index citation for an author whose revised entry appears in a *New Revision Series* volume.

Sagan, Carl (Edward) 1934- CANR-11
Earlier sketch in CA 25-28R

For the most recent information on Sagan, users should refer to Volume 11 of the *New Revision Series,* as designated by "CANR-11"; if that volume is unavailable, refer to *CA* 25-28 First Revision, as indicated by "Earlier sketch in CA 25-28R," for his 1977 listing. (And if *CA* 25-28 First Revision is unavailable, refer to *CA* 25-28, published in 1971, for Sagan's original listing.)

Sketches not eligible for inclusion in a *New Revision Series* volume because the biographee or a revision editor has verified that no significant change is required will, of course, be available in previously published

CA volumes. Users should always consult the most recent *CA* cumulative index to determine the location of these authors' entries.

For the convenience of *CA* users, the *CA* cumulative index also includes references to all entries in these related Gale literary series: *Authors in the News, Children's Literature Review, Concise Dictionary of American Literary Biography, Contemporary Literary Criticism, Dictionary of Literary Biography, Something About the Author, Something About the Author Autobiography Series,* and *Twentieth-Century Literary Criticism.*

Acknowledgments

The editors wish to thank Judith S. Baughman for her assistance with copyediting.

Suggestions Are Welcome

The editors welcome comments and suggestions from users on any aspect of the *CA* series. If readers would like to suggest authors whose *CA* entries should appear in future volumes of the *New Revision Series,* they are cordially invited to write: The Editors, *Contemporary Authors New Revision Series,* Book Tower, Detroit, MI 48226; or, call toll-free at 1-800-521-0707.

Volume Update Chart

IF YOU HAVE:	YOU MAY DISCARD:
1-4 First Revision (1967)	1 (1962) 2 (1963) 3 (1963) 4 (1963)
5-8 First Revision (1969)	5-6 (1963) 7-8 (1963)

Both 9-12 First Revision (1974)
  AND *Contemporary Authors Permanent Series,*
  Volume 1 (1975)
	9-10 (1964)
	11-12 (1965)

Both 13-16 First Revision (1975)
  AND *Contemporary Authors Permanent Series,*
  Volumes 1 and 2 (1975, 1978)
	13-14 (1965)
	15-16 (1966)

Both 17-20 First Revision (1976)
  AND *Contemporary Authors Permanent Series,*
  Volumes 1 and 2 (1975, 1978)
	17-18 (1967)
	19-20 (1968)

Both 21-24 First Revision (1977)
  AND *Contemporary Authors Permanent Series,*
  Volumes 1 and 2 (1975, 1978)
	21-22 (1969)
	23-24 (1970)

Both 25-28 First Revision (1977)
  AND *Contemporary Authors Permanent Series,*
  Volume 2 (1978)
	25-28 (1971)

Both 29-32 First Revision (1978)
  AND *Contemporary Authors Permanent Series,*
  Volume 2 (1978)
	29-32 (1972)

Both 33-36 First Revision (1978)
  AND *Contemporary Authors Permanent Series,*
  Volume 2 (1978)
	33-36 (1973)

37-40 First Revision (1979)	37-40 (1973)
41-44 First Revision (1979)	41-44 (1974)
45-48 (1974) 49-52 (1975) ↓ ↓ 123 (1988)	NONE: These volumes will not be superseded by corresponding revised volumes. Individual entries from these and all other volumes appearing in the left column of this chart will be revised and included in the *New Revision Series*.
Volumes in the *Contemporary Authors New Revision Series*	NONE: The *New Revision Series* does not replace any single volume of *CA*. All volumes appearing in the left column of this chart must be retained to have information on all authors in the series.

† *Indicates that a listing has been revised from secondary sources believed to be reliable, but has not been personally reviewed for this edition by the author sketched.*

ABE, Kobo 1924-

PERSONAL: Born March 7, 1924, in Tokyo, Japan; son of Asakichi (a doctor) and Yorimi Abe; married Machi Yamada (an artist), March, 1947; children: Neri (daughter). *Education:* Tokyo University, M.D., 1948.

ADDRESSES: Home—1-22-10 Wakaba Cho, Chofu City, Tokyo, Japan.

CAREER: Novelist and playwright. Director and producer of the Kobo Theatre Workshop in Tokyo, Japan, 1973—.

AWARDS, HONORS: Post-war literature prize, 1950; Akutagawa prize, 1951, for *Kabe-S karumashi no hanzai;* Kishida prize for drama, 1958; Yomiuri literature prize, 1962; special jury prize from Cannes Film Festival, 1964, for film, "Woman in the Dunes"; Tanizaki prize for drama, 1967.

WRITINGS:

NOVELS IN ENGLISH TRANSLATION

Daiyon Kampyoki, Kodan-sha, 1959, translation by E. Dale Saunders published as *Inter Ice Age Four,* Knopf, 1970.

Suna no onna, Shincho-sha, 1962, translation by Saunders published as *Woman in the Dunes,* Knopf, 1964, adapted screenplay with Hiroshi Teshigahara published under same title, Phaedra, 1966, 2nd edition, 1971.

Tanin no kao, Kodan-sha, 1964, translation by Saunders published as *The Face of Another,* Knopf, 1966.

Moetsukita chizu, Shincho-sha, 1967, translation by Saunders published as *The Ruined Map,* Knopf, 1969.

Hakootoko, Shincho-sha, 1973, translation published as *The Box Man,* Knopf, 1975.

Mikkai, 1977, translation by Juliet W. Carpenter published as *Secret Rendezvous,* Knopf, 1979.

OTHER NOVELS

Owarishi michino shirubeni (title means "The Road Sign at the End of the Road"), Shinzenbi-sha, 1948.

Kabe-S karumashi no hanzai (title means "The Crimes of S. Karma"), Getsuyo-syobo, 1951.

Kiga domei (title means "Hunger Union"), Kodan-sha, 1954.

Kemonotachi wa kokyo o mezasu (title means "Animals Are Forwarding to Their Natives"), Kodan-sha, 1957.

Ishi no me (title means "Eyes of Stone"), Shincho-sha, 1960.

Omaenimo tsumi ga aru (title means "You Are Guilty Too"), Gakusyukenkyusha, 1965.

Enomoto Buyo (title means "Enomoto Buyo"), Tyuokaron-sha, 1965.

PLAYS IN ENGLISH TRANSLATION

Tomodachi, Enemoto Takeaki, Kawade-syobo, 1967, translation by Donald Keene published as *Friends,* Grove, 1969.

Bo ni natta otoko, Shincho-sha, 1969, translation by Keene published as *The Man Who Turned into a Stick* (produced in New York City at Playhouse 46, May, 1986), University of Tokyo Press, 1975.

OTHER PLAYS

Seifuku (title means "The Uniform"), Aokisyoten, 1955.

Yurei wa kokoniiru (title means "Here Is a Ghost"), Shincho-sha, 1959.

Abe Kobe gikyoku zenshu (title means "The Collected Plays of Kobo Abe"), Shincho-sha, 1970.

Mihitsu no koi (title means "Willful Negligence"), Shincho-sha, 1971.

Ai no megane wa irogarasu (title means "Love's Spectacles Are Colored Glass"), Shincho-sha, 1973.

Midoriiro no stocking (title means "Green Stocking"), Shincho-sha, 1974.

Ue (title means "The Cry of the Fierce Animals"), Shincho-sha, 1975.

OTHER WORKS

Suichu toshi (short stories; title means "The City in Water"), Togen-sha, 1964.

Yume no tobo (short stories; title means "Runaway in the Dream"),Tokuma-syoten, 1968.

Uchinaro henkyo (essays; title means "Inner Border"), Tyuokoron-sha, 1971.

Abe Kobo zensakuhin (title means "The Collected Works of Kobo Abe"), fifteen volumes, Shincho-sha, 1972-73.

Han gekiteki ningen (collected lectures; title means "Anti-Dramatic Man"), Tyuokoron-sha, 1973.

Hasso no shuhen (lectures; title means "Circumference of Inspiration"), Shincho-sha, 1974.

Warau Tsuki (short stories; title means "The Laughing Moon"), Shincho-sha, 1975.

Ningen sokkuri, Shincho hunko, 1976.

SIDELIGHTS: Kobo Abe's fiction bears little resemblance to the traditional literature of Abe's native country, Japan. With its existential themes and what *Saturday Review* contributor Thomas Fitzsimmons describes as its "bizarre situations loaded with metaphysical overtones," Abe's work has more in common with that of Samuel Beckett and Franz Kafka, to whom he is often compared. His preoccupation with modern man's sense of displacement originated during his childhood. Abe grew up in the ancient Manchurian city of Mukden, which was seized from China by the Japanese in 1931. According to the *Washington Post*'s David Remnick, Abe "was fascinated by the Chinese quality of the town and was appalled by the behavior of the Japanese army during occupation. As a testament to his ambivalence about Japan, he changed his name from Kimfusa to the more Chinese rendering, Kobo. Abe was in high school during the war and though he once said, 'I longed to be a little fascist,' he never accepted the perverse nationalism of his country in the '40s. When he heard of Japan's imminent defeat in late 1944, he was 'overjoyed.'" The author's strong feelings against nationalism remain with him to this day, and he told Remnick, "Place has no role for me. I am rootless." Many critics believe that Abe's alienation from his own country is also the key to his international popularity. As Hisaaki Yamanouchi says in his book *The Search for Authenticity in Modern Japanese Literature,* "It enabled him to create a literary universe which transcends the author's nationality. He is probably the first Japanese writer whose works, having no distinctly Japanese qualities, are of interest to the Western audience because of their universal relevance."

Abe's first novel to be translated into English was *Suna no onna (The Woman in the Dunes).* In this story, a schoolteacher and amateur entymologist goes to the country for a weekend of insect-hunting. He stumbles upon a primitive tribe living in sand pits and becomes their prisoner. Escape is his obsession for a time, but when it is finally possible, he has lost the desire to return to his former identity. Critics praise Abe for both his metaphysical insights and his engrossing description of life in the sand pits. "The story can be taken at many levels," reports a *Times Literary Supplement* reviewer. "It is an allegory, it shares elements with *Pincher Martin* and Kafka; . . . and it also has the suspense, the realism, and the obsessive regard for detail of a superb thriller. . . . It is a brilliantly original work, which cannot easily be fitted into any category or given any clear literary ancestors. The claustrophobic horror, the sense of physical degradation and bestiality, are conveyed in a prose as distinct and sharp as the sandgrains which dominate the book." Thomas Lask summarizes, "Mr. Abe put together a tale that combined a Crusoe-like fascination with survival with the larger issues of liberty and obligation."

The central theme of *The Woman in the Dunes*—loss of identity—reoccurs in most of Abe's subsequent novels. *Moetsukita chizu,* translated as *The Ruined Map,* uses the conventions of detective novels as a framework. Flight and pursuit merge as a private investigator gradually takes on the persona of the very man he has been hired to track down. Earl Mine finds *The Ruined Map*'s "combination of the macabre and the realistic" similar to that of *The Woman in the Dunes.* "Although less hallucinatory in its effect, *The Ruined Map* is in the end more terrifying, . . ." finds Miner. "Abe has a remarkable talent for creating fables of contemporary experience that manage to be at once rooted in minute detail and expressive of man's plight; but in none of his previous work have the detail and the larger meaning combined so perfectly. The sheer force of accumulating realities is what drives man to madness, what

leads him to abscond from himself since he cannot otherwise abscond from the modern world. It is astonishing how successfully Abe renders this effacing of human consciousness in the very mind that is lost." Shane Stevens also reserves high praise for *The Ruined Map,* calling it in the *New York Times Book Review* "a brilliant display of pyrotechnics, a compelling tour de force that seems to have been built lovingly, word by word, sentence by sentence, by a master jeweler of polished prose."

Although Abe's attitudes and concerns are far from those of a typical Japanese writer, some reviewers point out that the author's work is not completely outside his cultural tradition. *The Face of Another* and *Secret Rendezvous* are both presented in the form of journals and letters, a style that dates back to the 10th century in Japan. Furthermore, points out William Currie in *Approaches to the Modern Japanese Novel,* "Abe shows a meticulous care for concrete detail worthy of the most confirmed naturalist or realist. His precision and concreteness give the impression of reality to the dream or nightmare. In this regard, Abe, who is sometimes considered thoroughly Western in his approach to literature, is solidly in the Japanese tradition with his emphasis on the concrete and the particular."

A *New Republic* contributor refers to another aspect in which Abe's writing differs from most Western literature. "The Japanese seem to embrace the unspeakable openly, as a form of release, accepting the facets of the imagination Americans often skirt—even in the most lurid popular fiction," states the writer in his review of Abe's novel *Mikkai,* translated as *Secret Rendezvous. Secret Rendezvous* relates the story of a man's search for his wife, who has been taken to the hospital although she was not sick. The man discovers that the hospital is run by an "incestuous circle of rapists, voyeurs, 13-year-old nymphomaniacs, test-tube babies and centaurs." Abe's graphic descriptions of their activities drew negative reactions from many Western critics. Sidney DeVere Brown declares in *World Literature Today,* "The novel would be pornography but for the sterile laboratory in which the explicit scenes are placed." D. J. Enright protests in the *New York Review of Books:* "The paths whether of pursuit or of flight lead through turds, urine, phlegm, vomit, the stench of dead animals. A master of the seedy, Abe seems ambitious to erect it into a universal law." Concludes the *New Republic* reviewer: "Kobo Abe delights in the excessive and the perverse. With its surrealistic setting, its claustrophobic atmosphere, and its increasingly distressing scenes of sexual decadence and violence, *Secret Rendezvous* disturbs rather than titillates."

Doug Lang defends *Secret Rendezvous,* however. His *Washington Post Book World* review calls the plot incoherent, but continues, "fortunately, the novel does not depend on plot for its momentum. It depends much more on the ever-expanding circles of [the protagonist's] nightmarish experience, as Abe propels his main character to the outer perimeters of his existence, where he is confronted with the terrifying absurdity of his life. . . . The hospital is a metaphor for modern Japanese life. . . . *Secret Rendezvous* is very convincing. There is passion in it and a great deal of very bleak humor. Abe's view of things is not a pretty one, but it is well worth our attention." Howard Hibbitt concludes in *Saturday Review* that Abe is the master of the "philosophical thriller" and summarizes the strengths of his novels: "Brilliant narrative, rich description and invention, [and] vital moral and intellectual concerns."

BIOGRAPHICAL/CRITICAL SOURCES:

BOOKS

Contemporary Literary Criticism, Gale, Volume VIII, 1978, Volume XXII, 1982.
Janiera, Armando Martins, *Japanese and Western Literature*, Tuttle, 1970.
Tsurutu, Kinya, editor, *Approaches to the Modern Japanese Novel*, Sophia University, 1976.
Yamanouchi, Hisaaki, *The Search for Authenticity in Modern Japanese Literature*, Cambridge University Press, 1978.

PERIODICALS

Atlantic, October, 1979.
Chicago Tribune Book World, October 7, 1979.
Commonweal, December 21, 1979.
International Fiction Review, summer, 1979.
New Republic, September 22, 1979.
New York Review of Books, January 14, 1964, September 27, 1979.
New York Times, September 27, 1966, June 3, 1969, December 31, 1974, May 25, 1986.
New York Times Book Review, September 18, 1966, August 3, 1969, December 8, 1974, September 9, 1979.
New York Times Magazine, November 17, 1974.
Saturday Review, September 5, 1964, September 10, 1966, October 11, 1969, September 26, 1970.
Spectator, March 18, 1972.
Times Literary Supplement, March 18, 1965, March 6, 1969, September 3, 1971, March 17, 1972.
Washington Post, January 20, 1986.
Washington Post Book World, February 21, 1971, October 28, 1979.
World Literature Today, winter, 1981.†

—*Sketch by Joan Goldsworthy*

*   *   *

ABRAHAMS, Roger D(avid) 1933-

PERSONAL: Born June 12, 1933, in Philadelphia, Pa.; son of Robert David and Florence (Kohn) Abrahams; married third wife, Janet Anderson, March 13, 1977; children: (first marriage) Rodman David, Lisa. *Education:* Swarthmore College, B.A., 1955; Columbia University, M.A., 1958; University of Pennsylvania, Ph.D., 1961.

ADDRESSES: Home—Laverock, Pa. *Office*—University of Pennsylvania, Philadelphia, Pa. 19104.

CAREER: University of Texas at Austin, instructor, 1960-63, assistant professor, 1963-66, associate professor, 1966-69, professor of English and anthropology, 1969-79, chairman of English department, 1974-79, associate director, Center for Intercultural Studies in Folklore and Oral History, 1968-69, director, African and Afro-American Research Institute, beginning 1969; Claremont Colleges, Claremont, Calif., Alexander H. Kenan Professor of Humanities and Anthropology at Pitzer College and Scripps College, 1979-85; University of Pennsylvania, Philadelphia, professor of folklore and folklife, 1985—. Visiting faculty member, Folklore Institute, Indiana University, 1967, 1975; Andersen Professor of American Studies, Carleton College, 1969. Member of Social Science Research Council Committee on Afro-American Societies and Cultures and Texas Education Agency Consulting Committee on Confluence of Texas Cultures.

MEMBER: International Society for Folk Narrative Research, American Folklore Society (president, 1978-79), Phi Beta Kappa.

AWARDS, HONORS: Guggenheim fellow, 1965-66; National Institute of Mental Health fellow, 1968; American Folklore Society fellow, 1970; National Humanities Institute fellow, University of Chicago, 1976-77.

WRITINGS:

Deep Down in the Jungle: Negro Narrative Folklore from the Streets of Philadelphia, Folklore Associates, 1964, revised edition, Aldine, 1970.
(With George W. Foss, Jr.) *Anglo-American Folksong Style*, Prentice-Hall, 1968.
(Editor) *Jump Rope Rhymes: A Dictionary*, University of Texas Press, 1969.
Positively Black, Prentice-Hall, 1970.
(Editor) *A Singer and Her Songs; Almeda Riddle's Book of Ballads*, Louisiana State University Press, 1970.
(Editor with Rudolph C. Troike) *Language and Cultural Diversity in American Education*, Prentice-Hall, 1972.
Deep the Water, Shallow the Shore: Three Essays on Shantying in the West Indies (music transcribed by Linda Sobin), University of Texas Press, 1974.
(Editor with John F. Szwed) *Discovering Afro-America*, E. J. Brill, 1975.
Talking Black, Newbury House, 1976.
Afro-American Folk Culture: An Annotated Bibliography, Institute for the Study of Human Issues, 1977.
Between the Living and the Dead: Riddles Which Tell Stories, Academia Scientarium Fennica, 1980.
(Editor with Lois Rankin) *Counting-Out Rhymes: A Dictionary*, University of Texas Press, 1980.
(Editor with Richard Bauman) *And Other Neighborly Names*, University of Texas Press, 1981.
(Editor with Szwed) *After Africa*, Yale University Press, 1983.
The Man-of-Words in the West Indies, Johns Hopkins University Press, 1983.
(Compiler) *African Folktales: Traditional Stories of the Black World*, Pantheon, 1983.
(Editor) *Afro-American Folktales: Stories from Black Traditions in the New World*, Pantheon, 1985.
(Editor with Goldstein and Hand) *By Land and by Sea*, Legacy Books, 1985.
Folklore in the American Experience, Pantheon, 1988.
Preserving Even the Scraps: Almeda Riddle's Life and Songs, University of Illinois Press, in press.

Also editor of *Folktales of the World*, 1983.

WORK IN PROGRESS: A monograph on corn shuckings in the American South; editor with Marilyn Jorgenson of a dictionary of singing games in English.

SIDELIGHTS: According to D. J. Enright of the *Times Literary Supplement*, *Counting-Out Rhymes: A Dictionary* suffers from an excessively academic approach taken by editors Roger D. Abrahams and Lois Rankin. The work, explains Enright, consists of a theoretical introduction followed by the dictionary proper, a collection of rhymes children recite in order to choose a person to be "it" for a game. As an example of how the editors make an essentially simple subject seem complex, Enright cites the definition (given by the editors) of "counting out" as "a formulaic and ritualized way of focusing energies for those who wish to play games more complex than 'Tag,' but less coordinated in focus than team sports." Enright's reaction to the tone of the introduction is that "it could just as well be the strategies of global war . . . that Roger D. Abrahams [and Lois Rankin are] expounding and analysing. . . . To move from the introduction to the rhymes is not to descend from the adult to the childish but to exchange the creaking of rusty computers for the sound of recognizable human voices."

Enright notes the scope of the collection with enthusiasm, however: "The real surprise here—at any rate for those whose hours of play were regulated by 'eeny, meeny, miny, mo' or 'one potato, two potato'—is the abundance of ornate, sophisticated rhymes in evidence. . . . (One wonders about the propriety of including nursery rhymes like 'Hickory, dickory, dock' and 'This little piggy went to market,' . . . but the editors may have their reasons. In any case, we *are* grateful to them for bringing this material together.)"

Abrahams wrote to *CA:* "The gulf between the academy and the public remains too great. This is especially so in the field in which I work: folklore, Afro-American societies and cultures, ethnicity, and plural cultures. I have been trying for the last decade to discover some way around this problem, and have been encouraged to do so by my most recent publishers, Pantheon Books. Finding an appropriate style and voice for this effort is a struggle."

BIOGRAPHICAL/CRITICAL SOURCES:

PERIODICALS

Los Angeles Times Book Review, September 11, 1983.
New York Times Book Review, November 20, 1983.
Times Literary Supplement, December 19, 1980.
Village Voice, August 6, 1985.
Washington Post Book World, September 4, 1983.

*   *   *

ADAM, Cornel
See LENGYEL, Cornel Adam

*   *   *

ADAMEC, Ludwig W(arren) 1924-

PERSONAL: Born March 10, 1924, in Vienna, Austria; U.S. citizen; son of Ludwig and Emma (Kubitschek) Adamec; married Ena Vargas, June 9, 1962 (divorced May 8, 1975); children: Eric. *Education:* University of California, Los Angeles, B.A., 1960, M.A., 1961, Ph.D., 1966.

ADDRESSES: Home—3931 East Whittier, Tucson, Ariz. 85711. *Office*—Department of Oriental Studies, University of Arizona, Tucson, Ariz. 85721.

CAREER: University of California, Los Angeles, postdoctoral fellow, 1966, lecturer in history, 1966-67; University of Arizona, Tucson, assistant professor, 1967-69, associate professor, 1969-74, professor of Near Eastern studies, 1974—, director of Near Eastern Center, 1975-85. Research associate at University of Michigan, summer, 1967, and University of California, Los Angeles, 1968; Fulbright professor in Iran, 1973-74; visiting professor and Fulbright consultant, University of Baluchistan, Quetta, Pakistan, 1981-82. Member of board of governors, American Research Center in Egypt, Center for Arabic Study Abroad, American Research Institute in Turkey, and American Research Institute in Yemen, 1974-81; vice-president, American Institute of Iranian Studies, 1979-81; chief of Afghanistan Services, Voice of America, 1986-87.

MEMBER: Middle East Studies Association of North America (fellow), Middle East Institute, American Association of University Professors.

AWARDS, HONORS: Fulbright-Hays award for research in India and Afghanistan, 1964-65; Social Science Research Council grant, summer, 1968, 1975, and 1979; Foundation for the Humanities grant, summer, 1978.

WRITINGS:

Afghanistan, 1900-1923: A Diplomatic History, University of California Press, 1967.
(Editor with George L. Grassmuck, and contributor) *Afghanistan: Some New Approaches,* Center for Near Eastern and North African Studies, University of Michigan, 1969.
(Editor) *Political and Historical Gazetteer of Afghanistan,* Akademische Druck- und Verlagsanstalt (Graz), Volume I: *Badakhshan and Northeastern Afghanistan,* 1972, Volume II: *Farah and Southwestern Afghanistan,* 1973, Volume III: *Herat and Northwestern Afghanistan,* 1975, Volume IV: *Mazar-i-Sharif and North-Central Afghanistan,* 1978, Volume V: *Kandahar and South-Central Afghanistan,* 1979, Volume VI: *Kabul and Southeastern Afghanistan,* 1985.
Afghanistan's Foreign Affairs in the 20th Century: Relations with Russia, Germany, and Britain, University of Arizona Press, 1974.
(Editor) *Who's Who in Afghanistan,* Akademische Druck- und Verlagsanstalt, 1975.
Historical Gazetteer of Iran, Akademische Druck- und Verlagsanstalt, Volume I: *Tehran and Northwestern Iran,* 1976, Volume II: *Meshed and Northeastern Iran,* 1981, Volume IV: *Zahedan and Southeastern Iran,* 1987, Volume III: *Ahvaz and Shiraz and Southwestern Iran,* 1988.
Supplement to the Who's Who of Afghanistan: Democratic Republic of Afghanistan, Akademische Druck- und Verlagsanstalt, 1979.
Biographical Dictionary of Contemporary Afghanistan, Akademische Druck- und Verlagsanstalt, 1987.

Associate editor, *Afghanistan Journal,* 1974-76.

WORK IN PROGRESS: A history of political development of Afghanistan, 1880-1987.

SIDELIGHTS: Ludwig W. Adamec has lived for periods in Afghanistan, India, Iran, Europe, and the Arab Middle East. He is competent in German, French, Spanish, Persian, Arabic, and cognate languages.

*   *   *

ADAMS, Charles J(oseph) 1924-

PERSONAL: Born April 24, 1924, in Houston, Tex.; son of Joseph Edward (a barber) and Viola (Terry) Adams; married Joanna Zofia Teslar, August 18, 1963. *Education:* Baylor University, B.A., 1947; McGill University, graduate study, 1952-55; University of Chicago, Ph.D., 1955. *Religion:* Protestant.

ADDRESSES: Home—4398 Draper Ave., N.D.G., Montreal, Quebec, Canada H3A 2P2. *Office*—Institute of Islamic Studies, McGill University, Sherbrooke St., Montreal, Quebec, Canada.

CAREER: Princeton University, Princeton, N.J., instructor in the history of religions, 1953-54; McGill University, Institute of Islamic Studies, Montreal, Quebec, assistant professor, 1957-59, assistant director, 1959-63, professor and director, 1963—.

Visiting professor at University of California, Berkeley, summer, 1964, University of California, Santa Barbara, summer, 1967, University of Rochester, summer, 1970, University of Isphahan, winter and spring, 1977, and in Alexandria, Egypt, 1979; American Council of Learned Societies Lecturer in the History of Religions, 1971. Member of National Seminar on Pakistan, and UNESCO Commission for Establishment of an Institute of Higher Education in the Arab Countries, 1974-75. Trustee, Obor Foundation, 1976—. Consultant to National Selection Committee for Foreign Area Fellowship, Social Science Research Council, 1970, and American Council of Learned Societies Selection Committee for South Asia Awards, 1971. *Military service:* U.S. Army Air Forces, airborne radio operator, 1942-45.

MEMBER: American Society for the Study of Religion (treasurer; vice-president; president), American Oriental Society, American Academy of Religion, Middle East Studies Association (founding member; vice-president, 1971), Association for Asian Studies.

AWARDS, HONORS: Ford Foundation foreign training and research fellowship, 1954-57; Rockefeller Foundation research fellowship, 1958-59; Canada Council senior leave award, 1968-69.

WRITINGS:

(Editor) *A Reader's Guide to the Great Religions,* Free Press, 1965, 2nd edition, 1976.
(Editor) *The Ethico-Religious Concepts in the Qur'an,* McGill University Press, 1966.
(With Janet O'Dea and Thomas F. O'Dea) *Religion and Man: Judaism, Christianity and Islam,* Harper, 1972.
(Editor) *Iranian Civilization and Culture: Essays in Honor of the 2500th Anniversary of the Founding of the Persian Empire,* McGill-Queens University Press, 1973.
(Author of preface) Jean Rene Milot, *L'Islam et les Musulmans,* Fides, 1975.
(Author of foreword) Mihr Afroz Murad, *Intellectual Modernism of Shibli Nucmani: An Exposition of His Religious and Political Ideas,* Institute of Islamic Culture (Lahore), 1976.
(Author of foreword) Johannes J. G. Jansen, *The Neglected Duty,* Macmillan, 1986.

Also author of foreword, Abd al-Rabb, *Abu Yazid al-Bistani: His Life and Thought,* Iqbal Academy.

CONTRIBUTOR

Joseph M. Kitagawa, editor, *Modern Trends in World Religions,* Open Court, 1959.
Donald E. Smith, editor, *South Asian Politics and Religion,* Princeton University Press, 1966.
Kitagawa, editor, *History of Religions,* University of Chicago Press, 1967.
Aziz Ahmad and G. E. von Grunebaum, editors, *Muslim Self-Statement in India and Pakistan,* Otto Harrossowitz (Wiesbaden), 1970.
Joseph W. Elder, editor, *Lectures in Indian Civilization,* Kendall/Hunt, 1970.
Richard Comstock, editor, *Religion and Man,* Harper, 1971.
G. Parrinder, editor, *Man and His Gods: Encyclopedia of the World's Religions,* Hamlyn Publishing, 1971.
Proceedings of the Millenary of Shaykh al-Tusi, University of Mashhad, 1971.
Roger Savory, *History of Islamic Civilization,* Cambridge University Press, 1975.

Donald P. Little, editor, *Essays on Islamic Civilization Presented to Niyazi Berkes,* E. J. Brill, 1976.
Leonard Binder, editor, *The Study of the Middle East,* Wiley, 1976.
Jessie G. Lutz and Salah al-Shakhs, editors, *Tradition and Modernity,* University Press of America, 1982.
Earle Waugh and Regula Qureishi, editors, *The Muslim Community in North America,* University of Alberta Press, 1983.
John Esposito, editor, *Voices of Resurgent Islam,* Oxford University Press, 1983.
Savory and Dionisius A. Agius, editors, *Logos Islamikos,* Pontifical Institute of Mediaeval Studies (Toronto), 1984.
Richard C. Martin, editor, *Approaches to Islam in Religious Studies,* University of Arizona Press, 1985.
Nigel Biggar, Jamie S. Scott, and William Schweiker, editors, *Cities of God,* Greenwood Press, 1986.
L'Etat du Monde, Editions La Decouverte (Paris), 1986.

Also contributor to *Encyclopedia of Religion, World Book Encyclopedia, Encyclopedia Britannica, Encyclopedia Americana, Encyclopedia of World Biography,* and *Dictionary of World Biography;* also contributor to *Proceedings of the Table Ronde sur les Naqshbandis* and *Proceedings of the Conference on Qur'an Interpretation.*

OTHER

Editor of ''McGill Islamic Series''; co-editor of *Hikmat-i-Irani,* 16 volumes; member of editorial board, *Encyclopedia of Religion,* 16 volumes, Macmillan, 1987. Contributor to journals, including *International Journal, Christian Outlook, New Values, Arab Journal,* and *Islamic Order.* Editor, *Religious Studies Review.*

SIDELIGHTS: Charles J. Adams is proficient in Arabic, French, German, and Urdu.

AVOCATIONAL INTERESTS: Woodworking and travelling.

*   *   *

AEBY, Jacquelyn
(Jocelyn Carew, Vanessa Gray)

PERSONAL: Born in South Bend, Ind.; daughter of Ross (an educator) and Gladys (Kline) Aeby. *Education:* University of Chicago, B.A. *Religion:* Presbyterian.

ADDRESSES: Home—Howe, Ind.

CAREER: Has held secretarial positions in investment banking and real estate management.

MEMBER: Authors Guild, Authors League of America, P.E.O. Sisterhood.

WRITINGS:

Romance of the Turquoise Cat, Avalon, 1969.
Wait for the Dawn, Avalon, 1970.
Laurie's Legacy, Avalon, 1971.
No Gentle Love, Avalon, 1972.
The Trillium Cup, Avalon, 1972.
Linnet's Folly, Dell, 1973.
The Elusive Clue, Dell, 1974.
Flight of Fancy, Avalon, 1975.
Serena, Dell, 1975.
Counterfeit Love, Dell, 1975.
Diary of Danger, Dell, 1975.
Companion to Danger, Dell, 1975.

Sign of the Blue Dragon, Dell, 1976.
Never Look Back, Dell, 1976.
Falconer's Hall, Dell, 1976.
Cottage on Catherina Cay, Dell, 1976.
The Pipes of Margaree, Woodhill, 1978.

UNDER PSEUDONYM JOCELYN CAREW

The Golden Sovereigns, Avon, 1976.
Pavilion of Passion, Avon, 1983.

UNDER PSEUDONYM VANESSA GRAY

The Masked Heiress, New American Library, 1977.
The Lonely Earl, J. Curley, 1978.
The Wicked Guardian, J. Curley, 1978.
The Dutiful Daughter, J. Curley, 1979.
The Reckless Orphan, New American Library, 1981.
The Duke's Messenger, New American Library, 1982.
The Reckless Gambler, New American Library, 1985.
The Unruly Bride, New American Library, 1985.
The Errant Bridegroom, New American Library, 1986.
The Orphan's Disguise, New American Library, 1986.†

*   *   *

ALBANESE, Catherine L(ouise)   1940-

PERSONAL: Born August 21, 1940, in Philadelphia, Pa.; daughter of Louis and Theresa (Spiziri) Albanese. *Education:* Chestnut Hill College, A.B. (summa cum laude), 1962; Duquesne University, M.A. (history), 1968; University of Chicago, M.A. (history of Christianity), 1970, Ph.D., 1972.

ADDRESSES: Office—Religious Studies, University of California, Santa Barbara, Calif. 93117.

CAREER: St. Xavier College, Chicago, Ill., instructor in history of Christianity, 1969-70; University of Chicago Extension, Chicago, Ill., instructor in medieval culture, 1970; Wright State University, Dayton, Ohio, assistant professor, 1972-76, associate professor, 1977-81, professor of religion, 1981-87; University of California, Santa Barbara, professor of religious studies, 1987—. Visiting associate professor at Pennsylvania State University, 1976-77. Lecturer; has presented papers at scholarly conferences and participated in panel discussions at professional seminars. Editorial referee for several publishing companies.

MEMBER: American Academy of Religion, American Society of Church History, American Historical Association, American Studies Association, Organization of American Historians, Phi Alpha Theta.

AWARDS, HONORS: Wright State University grants, 1973-74, 1978-79, 1980-81; National Endowment for the Humanities, grants, 1975, 1977, fellowship for independent study and research, 1981-82; Fred Harris Daniels fellowship, American Antiquarian Society, 1977; American Philosophical Society grant, 1979.

WRITINGS:

Sons of the Fathers: The Civil Religion of the American Revolution, Temple University Press, 1976.
Corresponding Motion: Transcendental Religion and the New America, Temple University Press, 1977.
America: Religions and Religion, Wadsworth, 1981.
(Editor) *The Spirituality of the American Transcendentalists,* Mercer University Press, 1988.

CONTRIBUTOR

R. Pierce Beaver, editor, *Papers of the American Society of Missiology,* William Carey Library, 1976.
(With David L. Barr) Nicholas Peidiscalzi and William Collie, editors, *Teaching about Religion in Public Schools,* Argus Communications, 1977.
Beaver, editor, *American Missions in Bicentennial Perspective,* William Carey Library, 1977.
Joel Myerson, editor, *Dictionary of Literary Biography,* Volume III: *Antebellum Writers in New York and the South,* Gale, 1979.
Robert S. Ellwood, Jr., *Freedom of Religion in America: Historical Roots, Philosophical Concepts, and Contemporary Problems,* Transaction Books, 1982.

OTHER

Co-editor of ''Religion in North America'' series for Indiana University Press.

Contributor of more than twenty-five articles and reviews to academic journals. Member of editorial board, *Environmental Review,* 1976-78, *Journal of the American Academy of Religion,* 1979—, *Journal of Religion, Religious Studies Review,* and *Studies in Religion/Sciences Religieuses;* editorial referee for several journals, including *American Quarterly, Historian, Journal of American History,* and *Ohio Journal of Religious Studies.*

WORK IN PROGRESS: Nature Religion in America.

*   *   *

ALD, Roy A(llison)
(Omar Delphos, Michael Duball, Armand Kihl, A. Philo Mann)

PERSONAL—Education: Privately educated.

ADDRESSES: Home—75-51 187th St., Utopia Estates, N.Y. 11366.

CAREER: Free-lance writer of sports, Western, and science fiction material. Creator of *Alfred Hitchcock Mystery Magazine;* president and publisher of *Coupon;* publisher of *Photographer's Showplace, Underground Review,* and *Relax: Leisure Magazine for Men;* president of Creative Publications; editor for Fawcett World Library. Physical fitness authority, specializing in geriatric rehabilitation. Executive director of Creative Marketing and Merchandising Development (former president); co-owner of Strength and Health Gymnasiums; initiated federal efficiency program for Mental Industry for National Development. President of Council for the Investigation of Psionic Phenomena and of International Doll Museum. Consultant to Restaurant Cuisine Associates and Standard Reference Works Publishing Corp. *Military service:* U.S. Army, information specialist.

MEMBER: Societe des Gourmets Internationales (member of board of directors), National Jump-Rope Association (past executive director).

AWARDS, HONORS: Citation from Writers Newsletter, 1951, as highest earner in male adventure category, for writings under pseudonym Michael Duball; Golden Medallion Poetry Award, 1976, for writings under pseudonym Armand Kihl.

WRITINGS:

Favorite Recipes of Famous Men, foreword by Eddie Cantor, illustrated by Ald, Ziff-Davis, 1949.

(With Weegee) *Weegee's Creative Camera*, Doubleday, 1959.
Low Carbohydrate Diet Cookbook, Lancer Books, 1967.
Physical Fitness after Thirty-Five, Essandess, 1967.
The Cheerful Cat Cookbook, Essandess, 1968.
Cycling: The Rhythmic, Respiratory Way to Physical Fitness, Grosset, 1968.
The Happy Dog Cookbook, Essandess, 1968.
The Side Dish Cookbook, Essandess, 1968.
Rough Scrambles, Bantam, 1968.
The Case for an Afterlife, Lancer Books, 1968.
(Under pseudonym Omar Delphos) *Psychoastrology*, Tower, 1968.
(Under pseudonym A. Philo Mann) *The Kingdom of Fukkian*, Belmont, 1969.
Princess Pamela's Soul Food Cookbook, New American Library, 1969.
Sex Off Campus, Grosset, 1969.
The Complete Soup Cookbook, Prentice-Hall, 1969.
The Youth Communes, Tower, 1970.
The Skinnylook Cookbook, New American Library, 1970.
The Man Who Took Trips: A True Experience in Another Dimension, Delacorte, 1971.
Jump for Joy!, Geis, 1971.
Casseroles by Candlelight, Pyramid Publications, 1971.
Creative Wine Cookery, Pyramid Communications, 1972.
Jogging, Aerobics and Diet (original title, *The Aerobic Joggers' Guide and Diet Plan*), New American Library, 1973.

Also author of *Cycling for Fitness, Campus Relations, Celluloid Womb* (with Richard Hoffman, M.D.), and *The Trial of Pat Ward* (with Pat Ward, under pseudonym Michael Duball).

OTHER

Writer, director, and producer of "Weegee's Magic Camera," Castle Films, 1960.

WORK IN PROGRESS: The World Cancer: Experts Make Matters Worse; Robots of Consumption: The Shopping Addicts; Natural Lifetimekeeping: The Premature Aging Dilemma; six monographs under the heading *Philosophy of Physics: The Restabilization of Disordered Systems.*

SIDELIGHTS: Roy A. Ald comments that among his interests are investigations and lectures in the area of parapsychology as it relates to probability systems. Several communes have been established under his guidelines. Among his projects are the organization of "minimarkets," the "Pride in America" program, Housewives Sales Force, and *Sunday Junior News*.

*   *   *

ALDEN, Sue
See FRANCIS, Dorothy Brenner

*   *   *

ALEXANDER, Lloyd (Chudley) 1924-

PERSONAL: Born January 30, 1924, in Philadelphia, Pa.; son of Alan Audley (a stockbroker and importer) and Edna (Chudley) Alexander; married Janine Denni, January 8, 1946; children: Madeleine. *Education:* Attended West Chester State Teachers College and Lafayette College; earned degree at Sorbonne, University of Paris.

ADDRESSES: Home—1005 Drexel Ave., Drexel Hill, Pa. 19026. *Agent*—Brandt & Brandt, 1501 Broadway, New York, N.Y. 10036.

CAREER: Author of children's books; free-lance writer and translator, 1946—. Author-in-residence, Temple University, 1970-74. Also worked as cartoonist, layout artist, advertising copywriter, and editor of an industrial magazine. *Military service:* U.S. Army, Intelligence, 1942-46; became staff sergeant.

MEMBER: Authors Guild, Authors League of America, PEN, Amnesty International, Carpenter Lane Chamber Music Society (member of board of directors).

AWARDS, HONORS: Isaac Siegel Memorial Juvenile Award, 1959, for *Border Hawk: August Bondi;* American Library Association notable book citation, 1964, for *The Book of Three;* Newbery Honor Book Award, American Library Association, 1965, for *The Black Cauldron; School Library Journal* Best Books of the Year citation, 1967, for *Taran Wanderer,* Best Books for Spring citation, 1971, for *The King's Fountain,* Best Books for Young Adults citation, 1982, and Best of the Best Books, 1970-1983 citation, both for *Westmark;* American Institute of Graphic Arts Children's Books citation, 1967-68, for *The Truthful Harp;* Child Study Association of America Children's Books of the Year citation, 1968, for *The High King,* 1971, for *The King's Fountain,* 1973, for *The Cat Who Wished to Be a Man,* 1974, for *The Foundling and Other Tales of Prydain,* 1975, for *The Wizard in the Tree,* 1982, for *The Kestrel,* and 1985, for *The Black Cauldron* and *Time Cat;* National Book Award nomination and Newbery Medal, American Library Association, both 1969, both for *The High King;* Library of Congress Best Books of the Year citation, 1970, and National Book Award, 1971, both for *The Marvelous Misadventures of Sebastian;* Drexel Award, 1972 and 1976, for outstanding contributions to literature for children; *Boston Globe-Horn Book* award, 1973, for *The Cat Who Wished to Be a Man; New York Times* Outstanding Books of the Year Citation, 1973, for *The Foundling and Other Tales of Prydain;* Laura Ingalls Wilder Award nomination, 1975; CRABbery Award from Oxon Hill Branch of Prince George's County Library (Maryland), 1979, National Book Award nomination, 1979, Silver Pencil Award, 1981, and Austrian Children's Book Award, 1984, all for *The First Two Lives of Lukas-Kasha;* American Book Award nomination, 1980, for *The High King,* and 1982, for *The Wizard in the Tree;* American Library Association Best Books for Young Adults citation, 1981, for *Westmark,* 1982, for *The Kestrel,* and 1984, for *The Beggar Queen;* American Book Award, 1982, for *Westmark;* Parents' Choice Award, 1982, for *The Kestrel,* 1984, for *The Beggar Queen,* and 1986, for *The Illyrian Adventure;* Golden Cat Award, Sjoestrands Foerlag (Swedish publisher), 1984, for excellence in children's literature; Regina Medal, Catholic Library Association, 1986; Church and Synagogue Library Association Award, 1987; Field Award, Pennsylvania Library Association, 1987, for *The Illyrian Adventure.*

WRITINGS:

And Let the Credit Go, Crowell, 1955.
My Five Tigers, Crowell, 1956.
Janine Is French, Crowell, 1958.
My Love Affair with Music, Crowell, 1960.
(With Louis Camuti) *Park Avenue Vet*, Holt, 1962.
Fifty Years in the Doghouse, Putnam, 1963 (published in England as *Send for Ryan!*, W. H. Allen, 1965).

JUVENILES

Border Hawk: August Bondi (biography), Farrar, Straus, 1959.

Aaron Lopez and Flagship Hope (biography), Farrar, Straus, 1960.
Time Cat, Holt, 1963 (published in England as *Nine Lives,* Cassell, 1963).
Coll and His White Pig, Holt, 1965.
The Truthful Harp, Holt, 1967.
The Marvelous Misadventures of Sebastian, Dutton, 1970.
The King's Fountain, Dutton, 1971.
The Four Donkeys, Holt, 1972.
The Foundling and Other Tales of Prydain, Holt, 1973.
The Cat Who Wished to Be a Man, Dutton, 1973.
The Wizard in the Tree, Dutton, 1975.
The Town Cats and Other Tales, Dutton, 1977.
The First Two Lives of Lukas-Kasha, Dutton, 1978.

THE "PRYDAIN CHRONICLES" SERIES

The Book of Three, Holt, 1964.
The Black Cauldron, Holt, 1965.
The Castle of Llyr, Holt, 1966.
Taran Wanderer, Holt, 1967.
The High King, Holt, 1968.

THE WESTMARK TRILOGY

Westmark, Dutton, 1981.
The Kestrel, Dutton, 1982.
The Beggar Queen, Dutton, 1984.

THE VESPER HOLLY ADVENTURES

The Illyrian Adventure, Dutton, 1986.
The El Dorado Adventure, Dutton, 1987.
The Drackenberg Adventure, Dutton, 1988.

TRANSLATOR FROM THE FRENCH

Jean-Paul Sartre, *The Wall and Other Stories,* New Directions, 1948, published as *Intimacy and Other Stories,* Peter Nevill, 1949, New Directions, 1952.
Sartre, *Nausea,* New Directions, 1949 (published in England as *The Diary of Antoine Roquentin,* Lehmann, 1949).
Paul Eluard, *Selected Writings,* New Directions, 1951, published as *Uninterrupted Poetry: Selected Writings,* 1975.
Paul Vialar, *The Sea Rose,* Neville Spearman, 1951.

CONTRIBUTOR

Elinor Whitney Field, editor, *Horn Book Reflections on Children's Books and Reading,* Horn Book, 1969.
Cricket's Choice, Open Court, 1974.

OTHER

Also author of afterword to *Five Children and It* by E. Nesbit.

Work included in New Directions anthologies. Contributor to *Contemporary Poetry;* also contributor of articles to *School Library Journal, Harper's Bazaar, Horn Book,* and other periodicals. Member of editorial board, *Cricket.*

SIDELIGHTS: Lloyd Alexander's childhood fascination with Welsh and Arthurian legend is clearly reflected in many of his novels. Blending these and other early literary influences with his own brand of humor and adventure, Alexander has successfully created several of his own mythological worlds for young readers, leading *Dictionary of Literary Biography* contributor Laura Ingram to call him "a master in the field of modern children's literature."

Alexander's earliest literary ambition was to be a poet. He announced this on the eve of his high school graduation at the age of fifteen. His family was far from wealthy, and they were unimpressed with the idea. "Poetry, my father warned, was no practical career," Alexander told *CA.* "I would do well to forget it. My mother came to my rescue. At her urging, my father agreed I might have a try, on condition that I also find some sort of useful work."

Alexander worked as a messenger boy in a bank until he had saved enough money to enroll in West Chester State Teachers College. After only one term there, he decided that college was not the way for him to become a writer. A life of action seemed a more promising route; so, in 1942, Alexander enlisted in the army. To his disappointment, he was initially sent to Texas where he served as a cymbal player and chapel organist. Eventually, however, he was sent to Paris as part of a counterintelligence unit. He met and married his wife, Janine, during his stay in the French capital; he also earned a degree from the Sorbonne before the couple returned to settle near Alexander's hometown of Philadelphia, Pennsylvania.

Alexander's determination to be a published author remained strong, but the three novels he wrote in the next seven years only brought him rejection slips. He described this period to *CA:* "I had been writing grimly . . . , in a stubborn kind of hopeless hopefulness, ready to admit I was no writer at all." Eventually the cheerlessness of his attitude began to seem ridiculous to him. That change in attitude brought a change in his fortunes as well: "Looking back on those days, what seemed a catastrophe now struck me as deeply funny, I was able to laugh at it; and at myself. And enjoy it. I wrote a novel about it, as my fourth and last attempt. The novel was published." *And Let the Credit Go* appeared in 1955. Alexander followed this light, anecdotal account of his life with three more books in the same vein: *My Five Tigers, Janine Is French,* and *My Love Affair with Music.* His first books for children were *Border Hawk: August Bondi* and *Aaron Lopez and Flagship Hope,* biographies of two important though little-known Jewish-American patriots. The themes of faith and personal freedom Alexander emphasized in these biographies would also be important elements in the children's fantasies that soon would bring him national attention.

Alexander's first experiment with fantasy was *Time Cat,* a juvenile novel about a boy's adventures with his cat. "I realize now that *Time Cat* is an example of a fantasy perhaps more realistic than otherwise," reflects Alexander in an essay for *Horn Book.* "Basically, only one fantastic premise moved the story: that Gareth, a black cat, could take the young boy Jason into nine historical periods." Reviewers praised *Time Cat* as an entertaining introduction to history as well as an enjoyable tale. "Filled with excitement and humor the book also leaves the receptive reader with some interesting reflections on human conduct," notes *New York Times Book Review* writer Ellen Lewis Buell.

Time Cat was originally to have included a Welsh episode. While researching that chapter, however, the author rediscovered his strong childhood feelings for the old Welsh myths and decided to devote a whole book to their retelling. Despite his enthusiasm for the project, he found that it was slow to take shape. "Sifting the material, hoping to find whatever I was groping for, I accumulated box after box of file cards covered with notes, names, relationships, and I learned them cold," he remembers in *Horn Book.* "With great pains I began constructing a kind of family tree or genealogical chart of mythical heroes. . . . Nothing suited my purposes. At that point, the Muse in Charge of Fantasy, seductive in extremely filmy garments, sidled into my work room. 'Not making much headway, are you? How would it be,' she murmured huskily, 'if you invented your own mythology? Isn't that what you *really* want to do?'"

Alexander found that his research served him well even when he abandoned his original goal of faithfully retelling the Welsh stories. "It had given me roots, suggestions, possibilities," he writes in *Horn Book*. Once the author began the creation of his original fantasy, set in a land called Prydain, it grew to include five books: *The Book of Three*, *The Black Cauldron*, *The Castle of Llyr*, *Taran Wanderer*, and *The High King*. Despite the importance of the Welsh material to Alexander's work, "Prydain grew into something much more than a thinly disguised ancient Wales," asserts Ingram. "Undeniably, it was similar to that land, but reshaped by the addition of contemporary realism, modern values, and a generous dose of humor, as well as the special depth and insight provided by characters who not only act, but think, feel, and struggle with the same kinds of problems that confuse and trouble people in the twentieth century."

As *The Book of Three* opens, Alexander's young protagonist Taran is shown as an Assistant Pig-Keeper who longs for glory and heroism. He gets more excitement than he ever wished for when his search for a runaway pig leads him into a magical battle between the forces of good and evil. Taran learns much about the true nature of heroism during the course of his adventures. Humor is provided by his companions, including Fflewddur Fflam, the minstrel, and the sarcastic princess Eilonwy. Alexander's tone becomes increasingly serious in the subsequent Prydain novels. Taran and Eilonwy endure many trials, and in the process, they grow and mature until they are ready to lead Prydain into a new age in *The High King*. The authors of *Fantasy Literature: A Core Collection and Reference Guide* believe that on the merits of his Prydain novels, "Lloyd Alexander ranks as one of the best writers of high fantasy to emerge since Tolkien. . . . [He creates] a successful blend of tragedy and comedy with a resultant wisdom."

Many other reviewers also praise Alexander's deft, imaginative blend of action, humor, and philosophy. In her book *The Green and Burning Tree: On the Writing and Enjoyment of Children's Books*, Eleanor Cameron remarks, "Each episode of Taran's quest is absorbingly told and freshly seen (not an easy task considering that the tale of quest has such a long and distinguished tradition), and the truth of each episode brought out in such a way as to build strongly toward the moment of Taran's final illumination." *Washington Post Book World* contributor Houston L. Maples summarizes, "The author's total creation is a remarkable achievement, a rich and varied tapestry of brooding evil, heroic action and great natural beauty, vividly conceived, romantic in mood yet curiously contemporary in its immediacy and fast action."

Alexander followed his "Prydain chronicles" with several simple, lively tales for younger children. Some of these supplemented or retold stories of Prydain, including *Coll and His White Pig*, *The Truthful Harp*, and *The Foundling and Other Tales of Prydain*. Ingram finds that "Alexander's understated satire and valuable, if sometimes obvious morals are conveyed easily and effectively in . . . simple and engaging fashion." Jean Fritz recommends these stories for all readers in the *New York Times Book Review*, saying, "Read these tales before or

after the chronicles, or independently—no matter. The important thing is to go to Prydain."

In 1981 Alexander published what *Horn Book* reviewer Ethel L. Heins terms his "most inventive book in many years," *Westmark*. Like the Prydain books, *Westmark* combines a fast-paced plot, humor, and philosophical questions. Some reviewers suggest that in *Westmark*, the author even surpasses the narrative skill he displayed in his Prydain cycle. Fritz writes in another *New York Times Book Review* article: "Lloyd Alexander is obviously a bard who has traveled the roads of many kingdoms, perfecting the art of storytelling and becoming ever more wise in the ways of humankind. Like a juggler, he keeps four stories going at once in [*Westmark*]: tossing them lightly apart, calling them together, crisscrossing their paths until at last he has described a complete circle."

Alexander's kingdom of Westmark is described by Ingram as "an imaginary place which seems to be a cross between colonial America and feudal Europe." Other than that setting, there is no fantasy in *Westmark* or its two companion volumes, *The Kestrel* and *The Beggar Queen*. Instead, Alexander explores in these books the political evolution of Westmark. The three books have been as highly praised for their thoughtful content as for their lively storylines. Ingram writes that *Westmark*'s "adroitly controlled complex plot . . . often delves into the wide gray areas between good and evil." And *School Library Journal* contributor Hazel Rochman asserts, "The fast-paced plot, subtleties of character, ironic wit, quiet understatement and pervasive animal imagery—all work with superb concentration to undercut the heroics of war, its slogans, uniforms, and myths of comradeship and glory."

Ingram quotes Alexander as saying, "Writing realism or fantasy, my concerns are the same: how we learn to become genuine human beings." In writing fantasy, states Alexander in a *Horn Book* essay, one "presents the world as it should be. . . . Sometimes heartbreaking, but never hopeless, the fantasy world as it 'should be' is one in which good is ultimately stronger than evil, where courage, justice, love, and mercy actually function. Thus, it may often appear quite different from our own. In the long run, perhaps not. Fantasy does not promise Utopia. But if we listen carefully, it may tell us what we someday may be capable of achieving."

MEDIA ADAPTATIONS: The Cat Who Wished to Be a Man and *The Wizard in the Tree* have been produced on stage in Japan. *The Marvelous Misadventures of Sebastian* was produced as a television serial in Japan. "The Black Cauldron," an animated film produced by Walt Disney Productions in 1985, is based on parts of Alexander's Prydain novels.

AVOCATIONAL INTERESTS: Music (particularly violin, piano, and guitar), printmaking.

BIOGRAPHICAL/CRITICAL SOURCES:

BOOKS

Attebery, Brian, *The Fantasy Tradition in American Literature: From Irving to LeGuin*, Indiana University Press, 1980.

Cameron, Eleanor, *The Green and Burning Tree: On the Writing and Enjoyment of Children's Books*, Little, Brown, 1962.

Children's Literature Review, Gale, Volume I, 1976, Volume V, 1983.

Contemporary Literary Criticism, Volume XXXV, Gale, 1985.

Crouch, Marcus, *The Nesbit Tradition: The Children's Novel in England, 1945-1970*, Rowman, 1972.

Dictionary of Literary Biography, Volume LII: *American Writers for Children since 1960: Fiction,* Gale, 1986.

Field, Elinor Whitney, editor, *Horn Book Reflections on Children's Books and Reading,* Horn Book, 1969.

Fisher, Margery, *Who's Who in Children's Books: A Treasury of the Familiar Characters of Childhood,* Holt, 1975.

Hopkins, Lee Bennett, *More Books by More People,* Citation, 1974.

Livingston, Myra Cohn, *A Tribute to Lloyd Alexander,* Drexel Institute, 1976.

Sebesta, Sam Leaton and William J. Iverson, *Literature for Thursday's Child,* Science Research Associates, 1975.

Sutherland, Zena and others, *Children and Books,* 6th edition, Scott, Foresman, 1981.

Townsend, John Rowe, *Written for Children: An Outline of English Language Children's Literature,* revised edition, Lippincott, 1974.

Tymn, Marshall B. and others, *Fantasy Literature: A Core Collection and Reference Guide,* Bowker, 1979.

Wintle, Justin and Emma Fisher, editors, *The Pied Pipers: Interviews with the Influential Creators of Children's Literature,* Paddington Press, 1974.

PERIODICALS

Chicago Tribune Book World, November 26, 1967.
Christian Science Monitor, May 2, 1968, November 7, 1973.
Cricket, January, 1974, December, 1976, September, 1983.
Elementary English, December, 1971.
Horn Book, October, 1964, April, 1965, June, 1965, December, 1965, June, 1966, June, 1967, April, 1968, December, 1970, August, 1971, October, 1971, December, 1972, October, 1973, August, 1975, February, 1978, August, 1981, August, 1982, August, 1983, August, 1984, October, 1984.
Junior Bookshelf, October, 1966, June, 1967.
Language Arts, October, 1981, April, 1984.
Los Angeles Times, July 24, 1985, July 27, 1985.
National Observer, September 23, 1968.
New Statesman, November 8, 1963.
New Yorker, December 3, 1973.
New York Review of Books, December 3, 1964.
New York Times Book Review, March 23, 1958, April 14, 1963, December 3, 1964, June 19, 1966, April 9, 1967, March 24, 1968, November 15, 1970, July 25, 1971, November 5, 1972, September 30, 1973, November 4, 1973, May 4, 1975, November 13, 1977, December 10, 1978, May 10, 1981, April 25, 1982, June 7, 1987.
Philadelphia Sunday Bulletin, March 22, 1959.
Psychology Today, May, 1974.
Saturday Review, March 18, 1967, April 20, 1968, June 19, 1971.
School Library Journal, December, 1967, February, 1968, October, 1970, December, 1972, May, 1975, November, 1977, May, 1981, April, 1982.
Times Literary Supplement, November 24, 1966, May 25, 1967, October 3, 1968, April 6, 1973.
Top of the News, November, 1968.
Washington Post Book World, August 21, 1966, May 5, 1968, November 8, 1970, November 12, 1978, May 10, 1981, January 9, 1983.
Wilson Library Bulletin, October, 1970, June, 1974.
Writer, May, 1971.
Writer's Digest, April, 1973.

—*Sketch by Joan Goldsworthy*

ALEXANDER, Ric
See LONG, Richard A(lexander)

*　　*　　*

ANDERS, Jeanne
See ANDERSON, Joan Wester

*　　*　　*

ANDERSEN, Richard 1931-

PERSONAL: Born August 23, 1931, in Kansas City, Kan.; son of Marius Teodor (a carpenter) and Ellen K. (Christensen) Andersen; married Lois Jeannette Petersen (a music teacher), June 9, 1957; children: Kristyn Andersen Bova, Deryk, Jennifer Andersen Iaccino. *Education:* Dana College, B.A., 1953; Trinity Theological Seminary (now Wartburg Theological Seminary), B.D., 1960; California Graduate School of Theology, Ph.D., 1972.

ADDRESSES: Home—372 Colville Dr., San Jose, Calif. 95123. *Office*—St. Timothy's Lutheran Church, 5100 Camden Ave., San Jose, Calif. 95124.

CAREER: Dana College, Blair, Neb., public relations assistant, 1951-53; University of Dubuque, Dubuque, Iowa, public relations assistant, 1957-60; ordained Lutheran minister, 1960; associate pastor of Lutheran church in North Hollywood, Calif., 1960-62; founding pastor of Lutheran church in Ojai, Calif., 1962-64; senior pastor of Lutheran churches in Rancho Cordova, Calif., 1964-68, and La Habra, Calif., 1968-73; Community Church of Joy, Glendale, Ariz., founding pastor, 1973-78; Our Savior's Lutheran Church, Long Beach, Calif., senior pastor, 1978-86; St. Timothy's Lutheran Church, San Jose, Calif., senior pastor, 1986—. *Israel Today* correspondent to Lutheran World Federation Assembly, Budapest, 1984. Member of Lutheran campus council at Arizona State University; member of Office of Communication and Mission Support Standing Committee, American Lutheran Church, 1972-80; member of board of regents, Dana College, 1978-82. Founding chairman of Long Beach Mobilehome Mediation Board, 1986. Executive director of Lutheran schools in Hacienda Heights, Calif., 1973. *Military service:* U.S. Army, 1954-56.

MEMBER: National Conference of Christians and Jews (member of board and chairman of interreligious committee, Long Beach chapter, 1984-86).

AWARDS, HONORS: Named one of "20 Most Influential Lutherans in 1984" by *Lutheran Perspective;* honorable mention, *Lutheran Standard,* 1984, for article "Where Is Raoul Wallenberg?"; Medal of Honor, Daughters of the American Revolution, 1985; Long Beach (Calif.) City Council resolution, 1985, and citation, 1986; citation, Southern California region of National Conference of Christians and Jews, 1987.

WRITINGS:

PUBLISHED BY CONCORDIA

Loving in Forgiveness, 1973.
Your Keys to the Executive Suite, 1973.
Flights of Devotion, 1973.
Roads to Recovery, 1974.
For Those Who Mourn, 1974.
Now for the Good Wine, 1974.
The Love Formula: Living in Forgiveness, 1974.
Living Lenten Portraits, 1975.

(With Roy Barlag) *They Were There*, 1977.
(With Donald L. Deffner) *For Example*, 1977.
Devotions for Church School Teachers, 1979.
Inspirational Meditations for Sunday School Teachers, 1980.
A Little Library of Inspiration for Sunday School Teachers, 1982.
The Positive Power of Christian Partnership, 1982.

OTHER PUBLISHERS

Devotions along the Way, Augsburg, 1972.
A Plateau Above: The Story of Wallenberg and His Institute, Wallenberg Institute, 1985.

OTHER

Contributor to religion periodicals.

WORK IN PROGRESS: A book on Raoul Wallenberg.

SIDELIGHTS: Richard Andersen told *CA:* "I have written more sermons than books, yet it is the discipline of writing intelligible sermons that will be shared orally with worshiping congregations that has provided me the training for writing themes which will be published to be read. A person, it seems to me, must write for the ear as well as the eye, for then he writes for the mind and the soul. The reader will interpret the printed matter as something heard. Will it ring with such truth that empty words will be hastily rejected and pregnant thoughts welcomed? That's the objective. It's not just to fill the air-waves with clatter or the mind with clutter, but to share truth in such a way that what the eye perceives the ear hears and the heart comprehends. Writing is spiritual if it is truth framed in words. If it uplifts, then it is a spirituality that ennobles, but if it catapults you into an irretrievable mire, then it belongs to thoughtless eyes with an unwillingness to reason, let alone to hear truth."

AVOCATIONAL INTERESTS: International travel, reading novels, photography, "active concern for the release of honorary American Raoul Wallenberg from the Soviet Gulag."

*   *   *

ANDERSON, Jack 1935-

PERSONAL: Born June 15, 1935, in Milwaukee, Wis.; son of George William (a motion picture projectionist) and Eleanore (Forse) Anderson. *Education:* Northwestern University, B.S., 1957; Indiana University, M.A., 1958; University of California, Berkeley, additional graduate study, 1958-59.

ADDRESSES: Home—Apt. 1C, 110 Thompson St., New York, N.Y. 10012. *Office—New York Times*, 229 W. 43rd St., New York, N.Y., 10036.

CAREER: Oakland Tribune, Oakland, Calif., assistant drama critic, 1960-62; City of Berkeley, Calif., delivery truck driver, 1963; *Dance* (magazine), New York City, editorial assistant, 1964-69, associate critic, 1970-78; *Dancing Times*, London, England, New York correspondent, 1971—; *New York Times*, New York City, assistant dance critic, 1978—. Poet-in-residence, University of Kansas, 1970; program editor, Brooklyn Academy of Music, 1971-72.

AWARDS, HONORS: National Endowment for the Arts grant, 1968, for manuscript of *The Invention of New Jersey;* National Endowment for the Arts fellowship, 1973-74; de la Torre Bueno Award, 1980, for dance writing.

WRITINGS:

POETRY

The Hurricane Lamp, New/Books, 1969.
The Invention of New Jersey, University of Pittsburgh Press, 1969.
City Joys, Release Press, 1975.
The Dust Dancers, Bookmark, 1977.
Toward the Liberation of the Left Hand, University of Pittsburgh Press, 1977.
The Clouds of That Country, Hanging Loose Press, 1982.
Selected Poems, Release Press, 1983.

NONFICTION

Dance, Newsweek, 1974.
The Nutcracker Ballet, Mayflower, 1979.
The One and Only: The Ballet Russe de Monte Carlo, Dance Horizons, 1981.
Ballet and Modern Dance: A Concise History, Princeton Book, 1986.
The American Dance Festival, Duke University Press, 1987.
Choreography Observed, University of Iowa Press, 1987.

OTHER

Contributor of poems to *Nation, Transatlantic Review, Antioch Review, Prairie Schooner, Carleton Miscellany, Poetry*, and other journals, and of ballet and modern dance criticism to *Ramparts, London Daily Mail, Nation*, and other publications.

WORK IN PROGRESS: Poetry and dance history.

SIDELIGHTS: "Jack Anderson's *Selected Poems* and . . . *The Clouds of That Country*," says Diane Wakoski in the *American Book Review*, "represent a body of work by a significant original poet, one worthy of considerably more critical attention than he has been given." His art, she observes, is "imaginative autobiography" that "abandon[s] sentimentality," and "his technique has been . . . the elaborate but dramatic mocking of emotions and emotion-laden ideas." *Poetry* contributor Alan Williamson feels that the poems "fall into a few rather large categories" which he lists as "put-ons, . . . items of pop-art, verbal gamesmanship, and the Absurd disjunctively arranged after the manner of the New York School." A typical Anderson poem begins with "a statement of loneliness" and moves through fantasy until it takes on "the frame of an imaginary art work," states Philip Lopate in the *New York Times Book Review*. Anderson achieves "a quality of pathos" in such writing that makes it valuable, Williamson believes. It seems to Lopate that "the pathos of the need to fantasize" is the emotion Anderson means to share with his readers.

"Imaginary art happenings" appear often in the poems, perhaps because Anderson is also a dance critic, Lopate suggests. Beginning as a drama critic in Oakland, California, Anderson later became an associate critic for *Dance* magazine in New York. His reviews appear in London's *Dancing Times* and the *New York Times*, and his histories of ballet are widely admired. *Dance*, a one-volume history of the art, "unravels complex events with grace," Don McDonagh notes in the *New Republic. The One and Only: The Ballet Russe de Monte Carlo*, says Richard Buckle in the *Times Literary Supplement*, chronicles events in the life of an important "Russian" ballet company from the 1930s to the present. The story of the company's changes under directors Rene Blum, Serge Denham, Massine, and Balanchine eventuating in its Americanization after World War II is so complex, says Buckle, that "to have sorted it all out'' must have been for Anderson ''a remarkable labour of love.'' Reviewers consistently recommend both books to dance students and to general readers as well.

BIOGRAPHICAL/CRITICAL SOURCES:

PERIODICALS

American Book Review, September, 1983.
Ballet News, August, 1982.
Dance, May, 1975, November, 1981, January, 1982.
Georgia Review, fall, 1970.
New Republic, April 5, 1975.
New York Times Book Review, October 2, 1983.
Poetry, June, 1971.
Times Literary Supplement, July 30, 1982.
Village Voice, June 26, 1984.

*   *   *

ANDERSON, Joan Wester   1938-
(Jeanne Anders)

PERSONAL: Born August 12, 1938, in Evanston, Ill.; daughter of Theodore (an electronics engineer) and Monica (Noesges) Wester; married William H. Anderson (an insurance agent), August 20, 1960; children: Christopher, Timothy, William, Brian, Nancy. *Education:* Attended Mount Mary College. *Religion:* Roman Catholic.

ADDRESSES: Home—811 North Hickory, Arlington Heights, Ill. 60004.

CAREER: Free-lance writer, 1973—; lecturer. WIND-Radio, Chicago, Ill., music librarian, 1959-61. Performed in local little theater productions and directed and performed in a quartet accompanying vocalists on record albums, both 1959-61.

WRITINGS:

(With Ann Toland Serb) *Love, Lollipops and Laundry* (humor), Our Sunday Visitor Press, 1976.
(With Serb) *Stop the World—Our Gerbils Are Loose* (humor), Doubleday, 1979.
The Best of Both Worlds: A Guide to Home-Based Careers, Betterway Publications, 1982.
Dear World, Don't Spin So Fast . . . (humor), Abbey Press, 1983.
Teen Is a Four-Letter Word (inspirational), Betterway Publications, 1983.

UNDER PSEUDONYM JEANNE ANDERS

The Language of the Heart (Christian romance), Zondervan, 1985.
Leslie (Christian romance), Bethany House, 1987.

OTHER

Author of a monthly humor column in *Marriage and Family Living* and a monthly health feature in *True Confessions.* Contributor of over six hundred articles and short stories to a variety of publications, including *Ladies' Home Journal, Modern Bride, Modern Maturity, Christian Science Monitor,* and *Income Opportunities.*

WORK IN PROGRESS: A third romance novel.

SIDELIGHTS: Joan Wester Anderson recently told *CA:* ''Much of my current material is geared toward self-help material;

even in the novels and my speeches, I attempt to offer principles that will help readers to live fuller lives. My favorite 'helper' book, *Teen Is a Four-Letter Word,* encourages parents to love and affirm their adolescents' strong points, and explains that much of the kids' strange behavior is actually quite typical. I believe that writers can be a real force for good in our society if we look upon our talent as a means of bringing information, a good laugh and food for thought to those who look to us for guidance.''

*   *   *

ANDERSON, Rachel   1943-

PERSONAL: Born March 18, 1943, in Hampton Court, Surrey, England; daughter of Donald Clive (a writer and military historian) and Verily (a writer; maiden name, Bruce) Anderson; married David Bradby (a university lecturer in French and drama), June 19, 1965; children: Hannah, Lawrence, Nguyen Thanh Sang (adopted son), Donald. *Education:* Attended Hastings School of Art, 1959-60. *Politics:* Socialist. *Religion:* ''Church of England Christian.''

ADDRESSES: Home—Lower Damsells, Northrepps, Norfolk, England.

CAREER: Writer. Chatto & Windus Ltd., London, England, publicity assistant, 1963-64; worked for a brief period in editorial department of *Women's Mirror,* London, 1964, and for a very brief period (three days) in news department of British Broadcasting Corp., Bristol, England, 1966; these occupations ''preceded, interspersed, and followed by jobs as nursemaid, cleaning woman, van driver, gardener, etc., etc., and free-lance writer, and as broadcaster for BBC 'Woman's Hour.' ''

WRITINGS:

Pineapple (novel), J. Cape, 1965.
The Purple Heart Throbs (survey of romantic fiction), Hodder & Stoughton, 1974.
Dream Lovers, Hodder & Stoughton, 1978.
Moffatt's Road, Hodder & Stoughton, 1978.
The Poacher's Son, Oxford University Press, 1982.
Little Angel Comes to Stay, Oxford University Press, 1983.
The War Orphan, Oxford University Press, 1984.
Renard the Fox, Oxford University Press, 1986.
Tim Walks, CIO Publishing, 1986.
Little Angel, Bonjour, Oxford University Press, 1987.
French Lessons, Oxford University Press, 1988.
The Fruitcake Bus, Oxford University Press, 1988.

Also author of radio play, ''Tomorrow's Tomorrow,'' 1970. Contributor of articles to *Observer, Good Housekeeping, Homes & Gardens, Times* (London), *Weekend Telegraph, Punch, Guardian,* and other magazines and newspapers in England. Children's book page editor, *Good Housekeeping,* 1979—.

WORK IN PROGRESS: Ching Ching Cukoo, a novel based on the earlier life of her adopted son, Nguyen Thanh Sang; *Bonding,* a survey of adoptive practices.

SIDELIGHTS: Rachel Anderson told *CA:* ''[I was] brought up in a literary family. Am incapable of doing anything else so had to be a writer. Am [a] practicing Christian in an essentially heathen age. Speak French, Italian. Main interests are domestic bliss, travel, peace.'' In 1975, Anderson starred in ''Fateful Eclipse,'' a television drama by Nigerian writer Loalu Oguniyi, broadcast on Western Nigerian Television.

ANDREWS, Bart 1945-

PERSONAL: Original name, Andrew Stephen Ferreri; name legally changed in 1964; born February 25, 1945, in Brooklyn, N.Y.; son of Joseph (a businessman) and Camille (Sollecito) Ferreri; divorced. *Education:* New York University, B.A., 1964.

ADDRESSES: Office and agent—Andrews & Robb Agents, Sherry Robb, P.O. Box 727, Hollywood, Calif. 90078.

CAREER: Prospect House (resort hotel), Lake Bomoseen, Vt., social director, 1959-63; Columbia Broadcasting System (CBS), New York, N.Y., writer, 1963-64; free-lance television writer in Hollywood, Calif., 1964—; Andrews & Robb Agents, Hollywood, Calif., literary agent, 1982—.

MEMBER: American Society of Composers, Authors and Publishers, Authors Guild, Authors League of America, Writers Guild of America (West).

WRITINGS:

Different Spokes for Different Folks (humor), Serendipity Press, 1973.
Official TV Trivia Quiz Book, New American Library, 1975.
Yankee Doodle Dandies (humor), New American Library, 1975.
Official Movie Trivia Quiz Book, New American Library, 1976.
Official TV Trivia Quiz Book #2, New American Library, 1976.
(With Thomas J. Watson) *Lucy and Ricky and Fred and Ethel,* Dutton, 1976.
Star Trek Quiz Book, New American Library, 1977.
TV or Not TV, New American Library, 1977.
Star Wars Quiz Book, New American Library, 1977.
Fabulous Fifties Quiz Book, New American Library, 1978.
TV Addict's Handbook, New American Library, 1978.
Official TV Trivia Quiz Book #3, New American Library, 1978.
Tolkien Quiz Book, New American Library, 1979.
TV Picture Quiz Book, New American Library, 1979.
Super Sixties Quiz Book, New American Library, 1979.
(With Brad Dunning) *The Worst TV Shows Ever,* Dutton, 1980.
TV Fun Book, Scholastic Book Services, 1980.
(With Watson) *Loving Lucy: An Illustrated Tribute to Lucille Ball,* St. Martin's, 1980.
I Love Lucy Quiz Book, A. S. Barnes, 1981.
Double Lives, Doubleday, 1983.
The Cat's Meow, Dutton, 1984.
The I Love Lucy Book, Doubleday, 1985.
Holy Mackerel! The Amos 'n' Andy Story, Dutton, 1986.
The Cheers Scrapbook, New American Library, 1987.
(With Vanna White) *Vanna Speaks,* Warner Books, 1987.

Also author of about 150 television comedy scripts, including material for Bob Newhart, Carol Burnett, Soupy Sales, Paul Lynde, and Phyllis Diller, and for the television programs "Bewitched," "The Mary Tyler Moore Show," and "All in the Family." Co-author of libretto for musical comedy "Ape over Broadway," first produced Off-Broadway at Bert Wheeler Theatre, March 12, 1975.

WORK IN PROGRESS: A novel.

BIOGRAPHICAL/CRITICAL SOURCES:

PERIODICALS

Los Angeles Times Book Review, July 13, 1986.
New Republic, May 18, 1987.
Voice Literary Supplement, June, 1987.

*   *   *

ar C'HALAN, Reun
   See GALAND, Rene

*   *   *

ARNOLD, Caroline 1944-

PERSONAL: Born May 16, 1944, in Pittsburgh, Pa.; daughter of Lester L. (a social worker) and Catherine (a social worker; maiden name, Young) Schaeffer; married Arthur Arnold (a neuroscientist), June 24, 1967; children: Jennifer Elizabeth, Matthew William. *Education:* Grinnell College, B.A., 1966; University of Iowa, M.A., 1968.

ADDRESSES: Home and office—2700 Selby Ave., Los Angeles, Calif. 90064. *Agent*—Andrea Brown, Literary Agent, 319 East 52nd St., 2nd floor, New York, N.Y. 10022.

CAREER: Free-lance writer and artist. Art teacher in Yellow Springs and Xenia, Ohio, both 1968-69; New York Hospital, New York City, secretary, 1969-70; Rockefeller University, New York City, laboratory assistant, 1971-72, 1972-76; University of California, Los Angeles, laboratory assistant, 1976-79, extension teacher of writing course, 1982—.

MEMBER: Society of Children's Book Writers, Southern California Council on Literature for Children and Young People.

AWARDS, HONORS: Outstanding Science Trade Book citations, National Science Teachers Association-Children's Book Council Joint Committee, 1980, for *Five Nests* and *Electric Fish,* 1982, for *Animals That Migrate,* 1983, for *The Biggest Living Thing* and *Pets without Homes,* 1985, for *Saving the Peregrine Falcon,* and 1987, for *Genetics: From Mendel to Gene Splicing;* Children's Science Book Award honorable mention, 1983, for *Animals That Migrate;* Golden Kite Honor Book, Society of Children's Book Writers, 1984, for *Pets without Homes;* nonfiction award, Southern California Council on Literature for Children and Young People, 1985, for *Too Fat? Too Thin?: Do You Have a Choice?; Saving the Peregrine Falcon* was selected Children's Editors' Choice by *Booklist,* 1985, best book by *School Library Journal,* 1985, notable book by American Library Association, 1985, and received a special achievement award, PEN Los Angeles Center, 1986.

WRITINGS:

NONFICTION CHILDREN'S BOOKS

Five Nests, illustrated by Ruth Sanderson, Dutton, 1980.
Electric Fish, illustrated by George Gershinowitz, Morrow, 1980.
(And illustrator) *Sun Fun,* F. Watts, 1981.
Sex Hormones: Why Males and Females Are Different, illustrated by Jean Zallinger, Morrow, 1981.
Animals That Migrate, illustrated by Michele Zylman, Carolrhoda, 1982.
What Is a Community?, illustrated by Carole Bertol, F. Watts, 1982.
Where Do You Go to School?, illustrated by Bertol, F. Watts, 1982.
Who Works Here?, illustrated by Bertol, F. Watts, 1982.
Who Keeps Us Healthy?, illustrated by Bertol, F. Watts, 1982.
Who Keeps Us Safe?, illustrated by Bertol, F. Watts, 1982.
Why Do We Have Rules?, illustrated by Ginger Giles, F. Watts, 1983.
What Will We Buy?, illustrated by Giles, F. Watts, 1983.

How Do We Have Fun?, illustrated by Giles, F. Watts, 1983.
How Do We Travel?, illustrated by Giles, F. Watts, 1983.
How Do We Communicate?, illustrated by Giles, F. Watts, 1983.
(And illustrator) *The Biggest Living Thing*, Carolrhoda, 1983.
Pets without Homes, illustrated by Richard Hewett, Houghton, 1983.
Summer Olympics, F. Watts, 1983, 2nd updated edition, 1988.
Winter Olympics, F. Watts, 1983.
Measurements, F. Watts, 1984.
Maps and Globes, F. Watts, 1984.
Charts and Graphs, F. Watts, 1984.
Too Fat? Too Thin?: Do You Have a Choice?, Morrow, 1984.
Land Masses, F. Watts, 1985.
Bodies of Water, F. Watts, 1985.
Natural Resources, F. Watts, 1985.
Saving the Peregrine Falcon, Carolrhoda, 1985.
Music Lessons for Alex, photographs by Hewitt, Houghton, 1985.
(With Herma Silverstein) *Anti-Semitism*, Messner, 1985.
(With Silverstein) *Hoaxes That Made Headlines*, Messner, 1985.
Pain: What Is It? How Do We Deal with It?, illustrated by Frank Schwarz, Morrow, 1986.
Genetics: From Mendel to Gene Splicing, F. Watts, 1986.
The Golden Gate Bridge, F. Watts, 1986.
Everybody Has a Birthday, F. Watts, 1987.
How People Get Married, F. Watts, 1987.
What We Do When People Die, F. Watts, 1987.
Australia Today, F. Watts, 1987.
Coping with Disaster, Walker & Co., 1987.
Kangaroo, Morrow, 1987.
Giraffe, Morrow, 1987.
Zebra, Morrow, 1987.
A Walk on the Great Barrier Reef, Carolrhoda, 1987.
Trapped in Tar: Fossils from the Ice Age (Junior Literary Guild selection), Houghton, 1987.
Llama, Morrow, 1988.
Penguin, Morrow, 1988.
Saving the Tule Elk, Carolrhoda, 1988.
Juggler, Houghton, 1988.
Ole Swenson and the Hodag, Harcourt, 1988.
Dinosaur Mountain, Houghton, in press.

OTHER

My Friend from Outer Space (picture book), illustrated by Carol Nicklaus, F. Watts, 1981.
(Illustrator) Elizabeth Bremner and John Pusey, *Children's Gardens: A Field Guide for Teachers, Parents, and Volunteers*, Cooperative Extension, University of California, Los Angeles, 1982.

Also author of the television episode "Fire for Hire" for K-I-D-S series, KCET, Los Angeles, 1984. Contributor of articles and stories to magazines, including *Highlights for Children*, *Friend*, *Humpty Dumpty*, and *Cricket*.

SIDELIGHTS: Caroline Arnold commented to *CA:* "Like many writers of children's books, I began when my children were small. I thought I would write lovely stories for children and that because I was trained as a fine artist I would illustrate them myself. However, nearly all my books have been non-fiction, usually about scientific subjects, and most of them have been illustrated by other people. I have found that I enjoy the challenge of writing about complicated subjects in language that even a very young child can understand. My fascination with scientific subjects is reinforced by my own and other children's eagerness to know more about the world around them."

MEDIA ADAPTATIONS: My Friend from Outer Space has been made into a filmstrip, Westport Community Group, 1981.

*   *   *

ARNOLD, Elliott   1912-1980

PERSONAL: Born September 13, 1912, in New York, N.Y.; died after a brief illness, May 13, 1980, in New York, N.Y.; son of Jack and Gertrude (Frank) Arnold; married Helen Emmons (divorced, 1957); married Julie Kennedy, September, 1958 (divorced January, 1961); married Jacqueline Harris Stephens, February, 1961 (divorced, 1963); married Glynis Johns (an actress), October, 1964 (divorced, 1973); married Jeanne Shwam; children: (first marriage) Thomas Guy, Mary Jean. *Education:* New York University, graduate, 1934.

ADDRESSES: Agent—Robert H. Ginter & Co., 10889 Wilshire Blvd. Los Angeles, Calif. 90024.

CAREER: New York World-Telegram, New York, N.Y., newspaperman, 1934-42; *American Indian*, member of editorial staff, beginning 1948; writer. *Military service:* U.S. Army Air Forces, 1942-45; became captain; received Bronze Star.

MEMBER: The Players (New York).

AWARDS, HONORS: Commonwealth Club of California Silver Medals, 1948, for *Blood Brother*, 1960, for *Flight from Ashiya*, and 1968, for *A Night of Watching;* Screen Writers Guild prize, 1951, for "Broken Arrow"; William Allen White Children's Book Award for best juvenile fiction of the year, 1958, for *White Falcon;* National Conference of Christians and Jews Brotherhood Award, 1968, for *A Night of Watching*.

WRITINGS:

Two Loves, Greenburg, 1934.
Personal Combat, Greystone, 1936.
Finlandia: The Life of Sibelius (biography), Holt, 1938.
Only the Young, Holt, 1939.
The Commandos, Duell, Sloan & Pearce, 1942, published as *First Comes Courage*, Triangle, 1943.
(With Donald Hough) *Mediterranean Sweep* (nonfiction), Duell, Sloan & Pearce, 1944.
(With Richard Thruelsen) *Big Distance* (nonfiction), Duell, Sloan & Pearce, 1945.
Tomorrow Will Sing, Duell, Sloan & Pearce, 1945.
Blood Brother (also see below), Duell, Sloan & Pearce, 1947, reprinted, University of Nebraska Press, 1979.
Everybody Slept Here, Duell, Sloan & Pearce, 1948.
Deep in My Heart (biography of Sigmund Romberg), Duell, Sloan & Pearce, 1949.
Walk with the Devil, Knopf, 1950.
(With Michael Blankfort) "Broken Arrow" (film script; based on Arnold's novel *Blood Brother*), Twentieth Century-Fox, 1950.
Broken Arrow (juvenile), Duell, Sloan & Pearce, 1951.
Time of the Gringo, Knopf, 1953.
Rescue (nonfiction), Duell, Sloan & Pearce, 1956, abridged edition, Bantam, 1958.
White Falcon (juvenile), Knopf, 1958.
Flight from Ashiya (also see below), Knopf, 1959.
Brave Jimmy Stone (juvenile), Knopf, 1960.
(With James R. Webb) "Kings of the Sun" (film script), United Artists, 1963.

(With Waldo Salt) "Flight from Ashiya" (film script; based on Arnold's novel of the same title), United Artists, 1964.
A Night of Watching (Literary Guild selection), Scribner, 1967.
A Kind of Secret Weapon (juvenile), Scribner, 1969.
Code of Conduct, Scribner, 1970.
Forests of the Night, Scribner, 1971.
The Spirit of Cochise, Scribner, 1972.
Proving Ground, Scribner, 1973.
The Camp Grant Massacre, Simon & Schuster, 1976.
Quicksand: A Novel of the City, Simon & Schuster, 1977.

Also author of teleplays. Contributor of short stories to anthologies and magazines.

WORK IN PROGRESS: A film about the American Indian with Marlon Brando.

SIDELIGHTS: Elliott Arnold once wrote: "I must confess that I write books for young readers for a selfish reason. I write them to improve my writing. . . . I find an inclination to indulge myself in wordiness because I develop an affection for words . . . and I have found . . . that excesses and indulgences are total disaster if one wants to hold the interest of a young reader. You can't fake with those minds.

"A young reader has his mind and tastes and experiences untainted and he can smell a phony a mile off and you're on your guard. So, as it has come about, for me, writing for young people is a kind of purgative. It helps me shed the increments of bad taste, or most of them. It helps to restore purity and sight. Writing for young people is in its way going into a kind of artistic retreat, refinding the truths."

Fictionalizing historical events continually evokes critical response, such as that occasioned by Arnold's novel, *A Night of Watching.* While at first he considered writing a documentary about the evacuation of the Jews in Denmark, Arnold decided that "as exciting as fact may be it is very often not artistically exciting. There are two kinds of truth: factual and artistic. Fact tells you what happened. Art should tell you why it happened; it should say something permanent about experience. The historian is a journalist. The fiction writer creates characters—he plays God on paper."

MEDIA ADAPTATIONS: "First Comes Courage," produced by Columbia in 1943, was based on *The Commandos;* the film "Deep in My Heart," based on Arnold's novel of the same title, was produced by Metro-Goldwyn-Mayer in 1954; Arnold's novel *Blood Brother* was also adapted for television and broadcast as the series "Broken Arrow" by ABC-TV, 1956-58 and 1960; *A Night of Watching* was adapted into a television documentary.

BIOGRAPHICAL/CRITICAL SOURCES:

PERIODICALS

Books, summer, 1968.
Harper's, September, 1967.
New York Times Book Review, June 16, 1967.
Time, September 1, 1967.

OBITUARIES:

PERIODICALS

Chicago Tribune, May 15, 1980.
New York Times, May 14, 1980.
Publishers Weekly, May 30, 1980.†

ARONOFF, Myron J(oel) 1940-

PERSONAL: Born March 1, 1940, in Kansas City, Mo.; son of Harry J. (an engineer) and Rebecca (a speech and hearing therapist; maiden name, Copaken) Aronoff; married Rita Liedermooy (a teacher), December 21, 1962; children: Miriam Simone, Yael S. *Education:* Attended Northwestern University, 1958-60; Miami University, Oxford, Ohio, B.A., 1962; University of California, Los Angeles, M.A., 1965, Ph.D. (political science), 1976; Victoria University of Manchester, Ph.D. (social anthropology), 1969. *Politics:* Democrat. *Religion:* Jewish.

ADDRESSES: Home—610 Hoes Lane, Piscataway, N.J. 08865. *Office*—Department of Political Science, Rutgers University, New Brunswick, N.J. 08903.

CAREER: Tel Aviv University, Tel Aviv, Israel, visiting lecturer, 1969-70, lecturer, 1970-73, senior lecturer, 1973-76, associate professor of political science, 1976-77; Rutgers University, New Brunswick, N.J., associate professor, 1977-81, professor of political science, 1981—, chairman of department, 1979-81; vice chair for graduate studies, 1984—. Fellow-in-residence at Netherlands Institute for Advanced Studies in the Humanities and Social Sciences, 1974-75.

MEMBER: International Political Science Association, International Congress of Anthropological and Ethnological Sciences, American Political Science Association, American Anthropological Association, Israel Political Science Association, Israel Anthropological Association, Israel Sociological Association, Association of Social Anthropologists of the United Kingdom and the Commonwealth, Association for Political and Legal Anthropology (president, 1985-87), Association for Israel Studies (president, 1985-87).

AWARDS, HONORS: Grants from Bernstein Israel Research Trust, 1965-69, Social Science Research Council of the United Kingdom, 1969-71, Ford Foundation, 1973, and Social Science Research Council (United States), 1982-83.

WRITINGS:

Frontierstown: the Politics of Community Building in Israel, Manchester University Press, 1974.
(Editor, contributor, and author of introduction) *Freedom and Constraint: A Memorial Tribute to Max Gluckman,* Royal Van Gorcum, 1976.
Power and Ritual in the Israel Labor Party, Royal Van Gorcum, 1977.
(Editor and contributor) *Ideology and Interest: The Dialectics of Politics,* Transaction Books, 1980.
(Editor and contributor) *Culture and Political Change,* Transaction Books, 1982.
(Editor and contributor) *Religion and Politics,* Transaction Books, 1984.
(Editor and contributor) *Cross-Currents in Israeli Culture and Politics,* Transaction Books, 1984.
(Editor and contributor) *The Frailty of Authority,* Transaction Books, 1986.

CONTRIBUTOR

Allan Arian, editor, *The Elections in Israel: 1969,* Jerusalem Academic Press, 1972.
Michael Curtis and Mordecai Chertoff, editors, *Israel: Social Structure and Change,* Transaction Books, 1973.
Arian, editor, *The Elections in Israel: 1973,* Jerusalem Academic Press, 1975.

F. Belloni and Dennis Beller, editors, *Faction Politics,* American Bibliographical Center-Clio Press, 1978.

Henri J. M. Claessen and S. L. Seaton, editors, *Political Anthropology and the State of the Art,* Mouton, 1979.

Howard Penniman, editor, *Israel at the Polls: 1977,* American Enterprise Institute for Public Policy Research, 1979.

Emmanuel Marx, editor, *A Collective Portrait of Israel,* Academic Press, 1980.

Marx, Moshe Shokeid, and Shlomo Deshen, editors, *Readings in Social Anthropology,* Schocken, 1980.

Robert O. Freedman, editor, *Israel in the Begin Era,* Praeger, 1983.

Larissa Lomnitz, Laura Nader, and Fred Bailey, editors, *Power and Ideology in Organizations,* Academic Press, 1983.

OTHER

Contributor of about twenty-five articles and reviews to anthropology and political science journals. Editor of *Political Anthropology;* associate editor of *Society.*

WORK IN PROGRESS: Israeli Visions and Divisions: Cultural Change and Political Conflict.

SIDELIGHTS: Myron J. Aronoff lived in Israel for thirteen years; he spent two years in England and a year in the Netherlands. His Hebrew and Dutch are fluent. Other travel has taken him throughout Western Europe.

Aronoff told *CA:* "My primary interests are the relationship between culture (as patterns of humanly constructed meanings) and politics. I just completed a major project on cultural and political change in Israel that will focus on the changing dominant symbols, myths, and rituals which constitute Israeli civil religion in relation to major political change."

*   *   *

ASHLEY, Leonard R(aymond) N(elligan) 1928-

PERSONAL: Born December 5, 1928, in Miami, Fla.; son of Leonard Saville (a lawyer) and Sarah Anne Constance (Nelligan) Ashley. *Education:* McGill University, B.A. (first class honors in English), 1949, M.A., 1950; Princeton University, A.M., 1953, Ph.D., 1956. *Religion:* Episcopalian.

ADDRESSES: Home—1901 Avenue H, Brooklyn, N.Y. 11230. *Office*—Department of English, Brooklyn College of the City University of New York, Brooklyn, N.Y. 11210.

CAREER: University of Utah, Salt Lake City, instructor in English, 1953-55; University of Rochester, Rochester, N.Y., instructor in English, 1958-61; New School for Social Research, New York, N.Y., lecturer, 1961-72; Brooklyn College of the City University of New York, Brooklyn, N.Y., instructor, 1961-64, assistant professor, 1964-67, associate professor, 1967-71, professor of English, 1972—. Has presented papers at nearly one hundred scholarly conferences in the United States and abroad. Founder and director of an experimental theater at University of Rochester. Reader and consultant for several publishing companies, including Harper & Row. *Military service:* Royal Canadian Air Force, 1955-58; stationed in Canada, England, and France; became flying officer.

MEMBER: International Linguistic Association (secretary-treasurer, 1980-82; member of executive committee, 1982-87), International Congress of Onomastic Sciences (member of executive council, 1980-81), Modern Language Association of America, American Association of University Professors (vice-president of Brooklyn College Chapter, 1970-72; presi-

dent, 1972-74; member of executive council, 1974-75; secretary-treasurer of City University of New York Council, 1972-73; member of executive council, 1974-75), American Name Society (vice-president, 1976-78, 1986; president, 1979, 1987; member of board of managers, 1981-83), New England Modern Language Association, McGill Graduates' Society of New York (vice-president, 1970-71; president, 1971-75), American Society of Geolinguistics (member of board of directors, 1984—; president, 1985; conference director, 1985).

AWARDS, HONORS: Shakespeare Gold Medal; three fellowships from Princeton University; research grants from three universities.

WRITINGS:

(Contributor) F. F. Liu, *A Military History of Modern China,* Princeton University Press, 1956.

(Contributor) E. P. J. Corbett, *Classical Rhetoric for the Modern Student,* Oxford University Press, 1965.

Colley Cibber, Twayne, 1965.

George Peele, Twayne, 1966.

(Editor) *Nineteenth-Century British Drama: An Anthology of Representative Plays,* Scott Foresman, 1967.

(Editor with Stuart Astor) *British Short Stories: Classics and Criticism,* Prentice-Hall, 1967.

Authorship and Evidence in Renaissance Drama, Droz (Geneva), 1968.

(Editor) *Other People's Lives: Thirty-four Short Stories,* Houghton, 1970.

Mirrors for Man: Twenty-six Plays of the World Drama, Winthrop Publishing, 1974.

Tales of Mystery and Melodrama, Barron's, 1977.

Ripley's "Believe It or Not" Book of the Military, Simon & Schuster, 1977.

The Wonderful World of Superstition, Prophecy, and Luck, Dembner, 1984.

The Wonderful World of Magic and Witchcraft, Dembner, 1986.

Also author of military history books, including the *Air Defense of North America* (NORAD). Author of musical comedies, produced at McGill University, University of Rochester, and Brooklyn Colleges, and of radio programs and television scripts. Contributing editor, "Enriched Classics" series and "Collateral Classics" series, both published by Simon & Schuster, and of "Papertexts" series; editor of books for Scholars' Facsimiles and Reprints, including *Phantasms of the Living, Reliquies of Irish Poetry, A Narrative of the Life of Mrs. Charlotte Clarke, Shakespeare's Jest Book,* and *The Ballad Poetry of Ireland.*

Contributor to anthologies; contributor to numerous encyclopedias and reference books, including *History of the Theatre, Reader's Encyclopedia of World Drama,* Magill's *Encyclopedia of the Short Story, Great Writers of the English Language,* and *British Women Writers.* Contributor of more than one hundred articles to journals, including *Shakespeare Newsletter, College English, Verbatim, Maledicta,* and *Dracula Journals,* of reviews to *Educational Theatre Journal, Bibliotheque d'Humanisme et Renaissance* (Geneva), *Names* (a publication of the American Name Society), and other periodicals, of translations to magazines, including *Shenandoah,* and of poetry to *Western Humanities Review, Carleton Miscellany, Evidence,* and other journals. Member of editorial board of *Names.*

WORK IN PROGRESS: Nordic Folk Wisdom; Elizabethan Popular Culture; The Dictionary of Sex Slang for Stein & Day; a revised edition of *Colley Cibber.*

SIDELIGHTS: Leonard R. N. Ashley told *CA:* "As a reader for a number of university presses, I see many good books to recommend which do not reach print. As a reader for Harper & Row and other textbook publishers, I know how few proposals are actually marketed. Though I publish hundreds of pages of articles each year, I see that younger scholars are having an increasingly difficult time in the 'publish or perish' world of Academe (when they can find jobs at all). And I fear that, especially in the Humanities, opportunities are ever shrinking. With fewer electives and more unprepared graduate students, even senior professors find it more and more difficult to relate publication to teaching; moreover, the system requires those seeking promotion to slight the 'big book' (which takes years) and to churn out lots of smaller pieces, a habit which does not disappear when the top rank is reached.

"I am grateful for the Shakespeare Gold Medal, three Princeton fellowships, research grants from three universities, a full professorship in a municipal college with a distinguished fifty-year history and an exciting future under a vigorous and far-sighted president, but it is difficult to recommend the profession to would-be scholars just starting out. My own plans are to learn the new language (computers) and to adapt the old learning to new technologies (especially television), and I expect much of my future 'publication' to be in courses and materials for 'distance learning' and broadcasting.

"For some of us in academic pursuits, despite retrenchment and remediation and reduced income (the new Three R's), there is still the wonderful opportunity to study and write about whatever we like, and it is a marvel that a hard-pressed society is willing to pay even a favored few to do what they would do for nothing."

*   *   *

ASTOR, Gerald (Morton) 1926-

PERSONAL: Born August 3, 1926, in New Haven, Conn.; son of Louis (a sales executive) and Leah (Cohen) Astor; married Sonia Sacoder (a painter), November 23, 1949; children: Ted, Larry, Andrew. *Education:* Princeton University, A.B., 1949; attended Columbia University, 1949-51. *Politics:* Democrat. *Religion:* Jewish.

ADDRESSES: Home—50 Sprain Valley Rd., Scarsdale, N.Y. 10583. *Agent*—Toni Mendez, 141 East 56th St., New York, N.Y. 10022.

CAREER: Sports Illustrated, New York City, picture editor, 1954-62; *Look,* New York City, 1963-71, began as senior editor, became assistant managing editor; free-lance writer, 1971-80; executive editor of *Sport,* 1980-81; Columbia Broadcasting System (CBS), New York City, 1982—, project manager, *Time* magazine olympic games photography, 1983-84. *Military service:* U.S. Army, 1944-46; became sergeant.

MEMBER: Authors Guild, Authors League of America, Screen Writers Guild East.

AWARDS, HONORS: Albert Lasker Medical Journalism Award, 1965; Best Sports Stories Award, E. P. Dutton & Co., 1966, for *Look* magazine story "Mickey Mantle: Oklahoma to Olympus."

WRITINGS:

The New York Cops: An Informed History, Scribner, 1971.
"*. . . And a Credit to His Race": The Hard Life and Times of Joseph Louis Barrow, a.k.a. Joe Louis,* Saturday Re-

view Press, 1974, also published as *Gloves Off: The Joe Louis Story,* Pelham, 1975.
The Charge Is Rape (nonfiction), Playboy Press, 1974.
A Question of Rape (nonfiction), Pinnacle Books, 1974.
Hot Paper (nonfiction), Saturday Review Press, 1975.
(With Sean Callahan) *Photographing Sports: John Zimmerman, Mark Kauffman, and Neil Leifer,* Crowell, 1975.
(With Anthony Villano) *Brick Agent: Inside the Mafia for the FBI,* Quadrangle, 1977.
The Disease Detectives: Deadly Medical Mysteries and the People Who Solved Them, New American Library, 1983.
The "Last" Nazi: The Life and Times of Dr. Joseph Mengele, Donald I. Fine, 1985.
The Great American Pastime: Baseball through the Hall of Fame, Prentice-Hall, 1988.

Author with Saul Kapel of column on child psychology, "Growth, Conflict, and Hangups," in *New York Daily News, Houston Chronicle, Bridgeport Post,* and *Omaha World Herald.* Contributor of articles to magazines, including *Esquire, McCall's,* and *Playboy,* and newspapers, including *New York Times.*

SIDELIGHTS: Gerald Astor told *CA:* "Much of my work focuses on crime and medicine which are not so dissimilar. Both tend to involve life and death situations and there is frequently detective work to the cases (same word applies to both disciplines). Certainly both were involved in the book about Joseph Mengele, *The 'Last' Nazi: The Life and Times of Dr. Joseph Mengele.* The baseball book has been a pleasant shift from the Nazi doctor; but as a history of the game, it says much about the maturing of the United States."

Astor's *The "Last" Nazi,* according to Robert Blau in the *Chicago Tribune Book World,* "is a fast-paced documentary about the shielded movements of a killer, a sadist, and a loyal servant of the Reich." Finding the book an "informative account," Edwin M. Yoder, Jr. observes in the *Washington Post Book World* that "Astor resolutely declines to elevate or sensationalize [Mengele] into a storybook monster, a mad doctor, singularly abberational." Calling Astor's argument "provocative," Yoder states that "Astor's theory is that it was the madness of a society; that the personal evil was rooted in a social climate in which the line we would draw between legitimate scientific medicine and quack, dehumanizing experimentation was wavily and cloudily marked."

BIOGRAPHICAL/CRITICAL SOURCES:

PERIODICALS

Best Sellers, February 15, 1975.
Chicago Tribune Book World, November 10, 1985.
Los Angeles Times Book Review, February 9, 1986.
Washington Post Book World, November 17, 1985.

*   *   *

ATWOOD, Margaret (Eleanor) 1939-

PERSONAL: Born November 18, 1939, in Ottawa, Ontario, Canada; daughter of Carl Edmund (an entomologist) and Margaret (Killam) Atwood; married Graeme Gibson (a writer); children: Jess. *Education:* University of Toronto, B.A., 1961; Radcliffe College, A.M., 1962; Harvard University, graduate study, 1962-63, and 1965-67. *Politics:* "William Morrisite." *Religion:* "Immanent Transcendentalist."

ADDRESSES: Agent—Phoebe Larmore, 2814 Third St., Santa Monica, Calif. 90405.

CAREER: Writer. University of British Columbia, Vancouver, lecturer in English literature, 1964-65; Sir George Williams University, Montreal, Quebec, lecturer in English literature, 1967-68; York University, Toronto, Ontario, assistant professor of English literature, 1971-72; House of Anansi Press, Toronto, editor and member of board of directors, 1971-73; University of Toronto, Toronto, writer-in-residence, 1972-73; University of Alabama, Tuscaloosa, writer-in-residence, 1985; New York University, New York, N.Y., Berg Visiting Professor of English, 1986; Macquarie University, North Ryde, Australia, writer-in-residence, 1987.

MEMBER: Amnesty International, Writers' Union of Canada (vice-chairman, 1980-81), Canadian Civil Liberties Association (member of board, 1973-75), PEN International, Canadian Centre, Anglophone (president, 1984-85).

AWARDS, HONORS: E. J. Pratt Medal, 1961, for *Double Persephone;* President's Medal, University of Western Ontario, 1965; Governor General's Award, 1966, for *The Circle Game,* and 1986, for *The Handmaid's Tale;* first prize in Canadian Centennial Commission Poetry Competition, 1967; Union Prize, *Poetry,* 1969; Bess Hoskins Prize, *Poetry,* 1969 and 1974; D.Litt., Trent University, 1973, Concordia University, 1980, Smith College, 1982, University of Toronto, 1983, Mount Holyoke College, 1985, University of Waterloo, 1985, and the University of Guelph, 1985; LL.D., Queen's University, 1974; City of Toronto Book Award, 1977; Canadian Booksellers' Association Award, 1977; Periodical Distributors of Canada Short Fiction Award, 1977; St. Lawrence Award for fiction, 1978; Radcliffe Medal, 1980; *Life before Man* named notable book of 1980 by the American Library Association; Molson Award, 1981; Guggenheim fellowship, 1981; named Companion of the Order of Canada, 1981; International Writer's Prize, Welsh Arts Council, 1982; Book of the Year Award, Periodical Distributors of Canada and the Foundation for the Advancement of Canadian Letters, 1983; Ida Nudel Humanitarian Award, 1986; Toronto Arts Award for writing and editing, 1986; Governor General's Award and *Los Angeles Times* Book Award, both 1986, for *The Handmaid's Tale;* named *Chatelaine* magazine's Woman of the Year.

WRITINGS:

Survival: A Thematic Guide to Canadian Literature, House of Anansi Press, 1972.
Days of the Rebels, 1815-1840, Natural Science Library, 1976.
(Author of introduction) Catherine M. Young, *To See Our World,* GLC Publishers, 1979, Morrow, 1980.
Second Words: Selected Critical Prose, House of Anansi Press, 1982.
(Editor) *The New Oxford Book of Canadian Verse in English,* Oxford University Press, 1982.
(Editor with Robert Weaver) *The Oxford Book of Canadian Short Stories in English,* Oxford University Press, 1986.
(Editor) *The Canlit Foodbook,* Totem, 1987.

POEMS

Double Persephone, Hawkshead Press, 1961.
The Circle Game, Cranbrook Academy of Art (Bloomfield Hills, Mich.), 1964, revised edition, Contact Press, 1966.
Kaleidoscopes Baroque: A Poem, Cranbrook Academy of Art, 1965.
Talismans for Children, Cranbrook Academy of Art, 1965.
Speeches for Doctor Frankenstein, Cranbrook Academy of Art, 1966.

The Animals in That Country, Oxford University Press (Toronto), 1968, Atlantic-Little, Brown, 1969.
The Journals of Susanna Moodie, Oxford University Press, 1970.
Procedures for Underground, Atlantic-Little, Brown, 1970.
Power Politics, House of Anansi Press, 1971, Harper, 1973.
You Are Happy, Harper, 1974.
Selected Poems, 1965-1975, Oxford University Press, 1976, Simon & Schuster, 1978.
Marsh Hawk, Dreadnaught, 1977.
Two-Headed Poems, Oxford University Press, 1978, Simon & Schuster, 1981.
Notes Toward a Poem That Can Never Be Written, Salamander Press, 1981.
True Stories, Oxford University Press, 1981, Simon & Schuster, 1982.
Snake Poems, Salamander Press, 1983.
Interlunar, Oxford University Press, 1984.
Selected Poems II: Poems Selected and New, 1976-1986, Oxford University Press, 1986.

Also author of *Expeditions,* 1966, and *What Was in the Garden,* 1969.

NOVELS

The Edible Woman, McClelland & Stewart, 1969, Atlantic-Little, Brown, 1970.
Surfacing, McClelland & Stewart, 1972, Simon & Schuster, 1973.
Lady Oracle, Simon & Schuster, 1976.
Life before Man, McClelland & Stewart, 1979, Simon & Schuster, 1980.
Bodily Harm, McClelland & Stewart, 1981, Simon & Schuster, 1982.
Encounters with the Element Man, Ewert, 1982.
Unearthing Suite, Grand Union Press, 1983.
The Handmaid's Tale, McClelland & Stewart, 1985, Houghton, 1986.

STORY COLLECTIONS

Dancing Girls and Other Stories, McClelland & Stewart, 1977, Simon & Schuster, 1982.
Bluebeard's Egg and Other Stories, McClelland & Stewart, 1983.
Murder in the Dark: Short Fictions and Prose Poems, Coach House Press, 1983.

JUVENILES

Up in the Tree, McClelland & Stewart, 1978.
(With Joyce Barkhouse) *Anna's Pet,* James Lorimer, 1980.

TELEVISION SCRIPTS

''The Servant Girl,'' Canadian Broadcasting Corporation, 1974.
''Snowbird,'' CBC, 1981.
(With Peter Pearson) ''Heaven on Earth,'' CBC, 1986.

RADIO SCRIPTS

''The Trumpets of Summer,'' CBC Radio, 1964.

RECORDINGS

''The Poetry and Voice of Margaret Atwood,'' Caedmon, 1977.

CONTRIBUTOR

John Robert Colombo, editor, *How Do I Love Thee: Sixty Poets of Canada (and Quebec) Select and Introduce Their*

Favourite Poems from Their Own Work, M. G. Gurtig (Edmondton), 1970.

Eli Mandel, editor, *Five Modern Canadian Poets,* Holt (Toronto), 1970.

David Helwig and Joan Harcourt, editors, *72: New Canadian Stories,* Oberon Press, 1972.

Gwen Matheson, editor, *Women in the Canadian Mosaic,* PMA, 1976.

David Staines, editor, *The Canadian Imagination: Dimensions of a Literary Culture,* Harvard University Press, 1977.

Ann B. Shteir, editor, *Women on Women,* York University Press, 1978.

Contributor to *Atlantic, Poetry, Kayak, New Yorker, Harper's, New York Times Book Review, Saturday Night, Tamarack Review, Canadian Forum,* and other publications.

SIDELIGHTS: As a poet, novelist, story writer, and essayist, Margaret Atwood holds a unique position in contemporary Canadian literature. Her books have received critical acclaim in the United States, Europe, and her native Canada, and she has been the recepient of numerous literary awards. Ann Marie Lipinski, writing in the *Chicago Tribune,* describes Atwood as "one of the leading literary luminaries, a national heroine of the arts, the *rara avis* of Canadian letters." Atwood's critical popularity is matched by her popularity with readers. She is a frequent guest on Canadian television and radio, her books are best-sellers, and "people follow her on the streets and in stores," as Judy Klemesrud reports in the *New York Times.* Atwood, Roy MacGregor of *Maclean's* explains, "is to Canadian literature as Gordon Lightfoot is to Canadian music, more institution than individual." Atwood's popularity with both critics and the reading public has surprised her. "It's an accident that I'm a successful writer," she tells MacGregor. "I think I'm kind of an odd phenomenon in that I'm a serious writer and I never expected to become a popular one, and I never did anything in order to become a popular one."

Atwood first came to public attention as a poet in the 1960s with her collections *Double Persephone,* winner of the E. J. Pratt Medal, and *The Circle Game,* winner of a Governor General's Award. These two books marked out the terrain which all of Atwood's later poetry would explore. *Double Persephone* concerns "the contrast between the flux of life or nature and the fixity of man's artificial creations," as Linda Hutcheon explains in the *Dictionary of Literary Biography.* *The Circle Game* takes this opposition further, setting such human constructs as games, literature, and love against the instability of nature. Human constructs are presented as both traps and shelters, the fluidity of nature as both dangerous and liberating. Sherrill Grace, writing in her *Violent Duality: A Study of Margaret Atwood,* sees the central tension in all of Atwood's work as "the pull towards art on one hand and towards life on the other." This tension is expressed in a series of "violent dualities," as Grace terms it. Atwood "is constantly aware of opposites—self/other, subject/object, male/female, nature/man—and of the need to accept and work within them," Grace explains. "To create, Atwood chooses violent dualities, and her art re-works, probes, and dramatizes the ability to see double."

Linda W. Wagner, writing in *The Art of Margaret Atwood: Essays in Criticism,* believes that in Atwood's poetry "duality [is] presented as separation." This separation leads her characters to be isolated from one another and from the natural world, resulting in their inability to communicate, to break free of exploitive social relationships, or to understand their

place in the natural order. "In her early poetry, . . . ," Gloria Onley writes in the *West Coast Review,* "[Atwood] is acutely aware of the problem of alienation, the need for real human communication and the establishment of genuine human community—real as opposed to mechanical or manipulative; genuine as opposed to the counterfeit community of the body politic." Speaking of *The Circle Game,* Wagner writes that "the personae of those poems never did make contact, never did anything but lament the human condition. . . . Relationships in these poems are sterile if not destructive."

Atwood's sense of desolation, especially evident in her early poems, and her use of frequently violent images, moves Helen Vendler of the *New York Times Book Review* to claim that Atwood has a "sense of life as mostly wounds given and received." Speaking of *The Circle Game* and *Procedures for Underground,* Peter Stevens notes in *Canadian Literature* that both collections contain "images of drowning, buried life, still life, dreams, journeys and returns." In a review of *True Stories* for *Canadian Forum,* Chaviva Hosek states that the poems "range over such topics as murder, genocide, rape, dismemberment, instruments of torture, forms of torture, genital mutilation, abortion, and forcible hysterectomy," although Robert Sward of *Quill and Quire* explains that many reviewers of the book have exaggerated the violence and give "the false impression that all 38 poems . . . are about torture." Yet, Scott Lauder of *Canadian Forum* speaks of "the painful world we have come to expect from Atwood."

Suffering is common for the female characters in Atwood's poems, although they are never passive victims. In more recent works they take active measures to improve their situations. Atwood's poems, Onley states, concern "modern woman's anguish at finding herself isolated and exploited (although also exploiting) by the imposition of a sex role power structure." Speaking to Klemesrud, Atwood explains that her suffering characters come from real life: "My women suffer because most of the women I talk to seem to have suffered." By the early 1970s, this stance had made Atwood into "a cult author to faithful feminist readers," as Lipinski reports. Atwood's popularity in the feminist community was unsought. "I began as a profoundly apolitical writer," she tells Lindsy Van Gelder of *Ms.,* "but then I began to do what all novelists and some poets do: I began to describe the world around me."

Atwood's feminist concerns are evident in her novels as well, particularly in *The Edible Woman, Surfacing, Life before Man, Bodily Harm,* and *The Handmaid's Tale.* These novels feature female characters who are, Klemesrud reports, "intelligent, self-absorbed modern women searching for identity. . . . [They] hunt, split logs, make campfires and become successful in their careers, while men often cook and take care of their households." Like her poems, however, Atwood's novels "are populated by pained and confused people whose lives hold a mirror to both the front page fears—cancer, divorce, violence—and those that persist quietly, naggingly—solitude, loneliness, desperation," Lipinski writes.

The Edible Woman tells the story of Marian McAlpin, a young woman engaged to be married, who rebels against her upcoming marriage. Her fiance seems too stable, too ordinary, and the role of wife too fixed and limiting. Her rejection of marriage is accompanied by her body's rejection of food. Even a spare vegetarian diet cannot be eaten. Eventually Marian bakes a sponge cake in the shape of a woman and feeds it to her fiance because, she explains, "You've been trying to assimilate me.'' After the engagement is broken, she is able to eat some of the cake herself.

Reaction to *The Edible Woman* was divided, with some reviewers pointing to the flaws commonly found in first novels. John Stedmond of *Canadian Forum*, for example, believes that ''the characters, though cleverly sketched, do not quite jell, and the narrative techniques creak a little.'' Linda Rogers of *Canadian Literature* finds that ''one of the reasons *The Edible Woman* fails as a novel is the awkwardness of the dialogue.'' But other critics note Atwood's at least partial success. Tom Marshall, writing in his *Harsh and Lovely Land: The Major Canadian Poets and the Making of a Canadian Tradition*, calls *The Edible Woman* ''a largely successful comic novel, even if the mechanics are sometimes a little clumsy, the satirical accounts of consumerism a little drawn out.'' Millicent Bell of the *New York Times Book Review* calls it ''a work of feminist black humor'' and claims that Atwood's ''comic distortion veers at times into surreal meaningfulness.'' And Hutcheon describes *The Edible Woman* as ''very much a social novel about the possibilities for personal female identity in a capitalistic consumer society.''

Surfacing, Atwood's second novel, is ''a psychological ghost story,'' as Marshall explains it, in which a young woman confronts and accepts her past during a visit to her rural home. She comes to realize that she has repressed disturbing events from her memory, including an abortion and her father's death. While swimming in a local lake, she has a vision of her drowned father which ''drives her to a healing madness,'' Marshall states. Hutcheon explains that ''*Surfacing* tells of the coming to terms with the haunting, separated parts of the narrator's being . . . after surfacing from a dive, a symbolic as well as a real descent under water, where she has experienced a revealing and personally apocalyptic vision.''

Many of the concerns found in Atwood's poetry reappear in *Surfacing*. The novel, Roberta Rubenstein writes in *Modern Fiction Studies*, ''synthesizes a number of motifs that have dominated [Atwood's] consciousness since her earliest poems: the elusiveness and variety of 'language' in its several senses; the continuum between human and animal, human being and nature; the significance of one's heritage, . . . ; the search for a location (in both time and place); the brutalizations and victimizations of love; drowning and surviving.'' Margaret Wimsatt of *Commonweal* agrees. ''The novel,'' Wimsatt writes, ''picks up themes brooded over in the poetry, and knits them together coherently.'' Marshall believes that both *The Edible Woman* and *Surfacing* ''are enlargements upon the themes of [Atwood's] poems. In each of them a young woman is driven to rebellion against what seems to be her fate in the modern technological 'Americanized' world and to psychic breakdown and breakthrough.''

In *Life before Man*, Atwood dissects the relationships between three characters: Elizabeth, a married woman who mourns the recent suicide of her lover; Elizabeth's husband, Nate, who is unable to choose between his wife and his lover; and Lesje, Nate's lover, who works with Elizabeth at a museum of natural history. All three characters are isolated from one another and unable to experience their own emotions. The fossils and dinosaur bones on display at the museum are compared throughout the novel with the sterility of the characters' lives. As Laurie Stone notes in the *Village Voice*, *Life before Man* ''is full of variations on the theme of extinction.'' Similarly, Rubenstein writes in the *Chicago Tribune* that the novel is a ''su-

perb living exhibit in which the artifacts are unique (but representative) lives in progress.''

Although *Life before Man* is what Rosellen Brown of *Saturday Review* calls an ''anatomy of melancholy,'' MacGregor sees a tempering humor in the novel as well. *Life before Man*, MacGregor writes, ''is not so much a story as it is the discarded negatives of a family album, the thoughts so dark they defy any flash short of Atwood's remarkable, and often very funny, insight.'' Comparing the novel's characters to museum pieces and commenting on the analytical examination to which Atwood subjects them, Peter S. Prescott of *Newsweek* finds that ''with chilly compassion and an even colder wit, Atwood exposes the interior lives of her specimens.'' Writing in the *New York Times Book Review*, Marilyn French makes clear that in *Life before Man*, Atwood ''combines several talents—powerful introspection, honesty, satire and a taut, limpid style—to create a splendid, fully integrated work.''

The novel's title, French believes, relates to the characters' isolation from themselves, their history, and from one another. They have not yet achieved truly human stature. ''This novel suggests,'' French writes, ''that we are still living life before man, before the human—as we like to define it—has evolved.'' Prescott raises the same point. The novel's characters, he writes, ''do not communicate; each, in the presence of another, is locked into his own thoughts and feelings. Is such isolation and indeterminacy what Atwood means when she calls her story 'Life before Man'?'' This concern is also found in Atwood's previous novels, French argues, all of which depict ''the search for identity . . . a search for a better way to be—for a way of life that both satisfies the passionate, needy self and yet is decent, humane and natural.''

Atwood further explores this idea in *Bodily Harm*. In this novel Rennie Wilford is a Toronto journalist who specializes in light, trivial pieces for magazines. She is, Anne Tyler explains in the *Detroit News*, ''a cataloguer of current fads and fancies.'' Isabel Raphael of the London *Times* calls Rennie someone who ''deals only in surfaces; her journalism is of the most trivial and transitory kind, her relationship with a live-in lover limited to sex, and most of her friends 'really just contacts.''' Following a partial mastectomy, which causes her lover to abandon her, Rennie begins to feel dissatisfied with her life. She takes on an assignment to the Caribbean island of St. Antoine in an effort to get away from things for a while. Her planned magazine story—focusing on the island's beaches, tennis courts, and restaurants—is distinctly facile in comparison to the political violence she finds on St. Antoine. When Rennie is arrested and jailed, the experience brings her to a self-realization about her life. ''Death,'' Nancy Ramsey remarks in the *San Francisco Review of Books*, ''rather than the modern sense of ennui, threatens Rennie and the people around her, and ultimately gives her life a meaning she hadn't known before.''

Bodily Harm, Frank Davey of the *Canadian Forum* believes, follows the same pattern set in Atwood's earlier novels: ''Alienation from natural order . . . , followed by descent into a more primitive but healing reality . . . , and finally some reestablishment of order.'' Although Davey is ''troubled'' by the similarities between the novels and believes that ''Atwood doesn't risk much with this book,'' he concludes that ''these reservations aside, *Bodily Harm* is still a pleasure to read.'' But other critics have few reservations about the book. Anatole Broyard of the *New York Times*, for example, claims that ''the only way to describe my response to [*Bodily Harm*] is to say that it knocked me out. Atwood seems to be able to do just about everything: people, places, problems, a perfect ear, an exactly-right voice—and she tosses off terrific scenes with a casualness that leaves you utterly unprepared for the way these scenes seize you.'' Tyler calls Atwood ''an uncommonly skillful and perceptive writer,'' and goes on to state that, because of its subject matter, *Bodily Harm* ''is not always easy to read. There are times when it's downright unpleasant, but it's also intelligent, provocative, and in the end—against all expectations—uplifting.''

In *The Handmaid's Tale* Atwood turns to speculative fiction, creating the dystopia of Gilead, a future America in which Fundamentalist Christians have killed the president and members of congress and imposed their own dictatorial rule. In this future world, polluted by toxic chemicals and nuclear radiation, few women can bear children; the birthrate has dropped alarmingly. Those women who can bear children are forced to become Handmaids, the official breeders for society. All other women have been reduced to chattel under a repressive religious hierarchy run by men.

The Handmaid's Tale is a radical departure from Atwood's previous novels. Her strong feminism was evident in earlier books, but *The Handmaid's Tale* is dominated by the theme. As Barbara Holliday writes in the *Detroit Free Press,* Atwood ''has been concerned in her fiction with the painful psychic warfare between men and women. In 'The Handmaid's Tale,' a futuristic satire, she casts subtlety aside, exposing woman's primal fear of being used and helpless.'' Atwood's creation of an imaginary world is also new. As Mary Battiata notes in the *Washington Post, The Handmaid's Tale* is the first of Atwood's novels ''not set in a worried corner of contemporary Canada.''

Atwood was moved to write her story only after images and scenes from the book had been appearing to her for three years. She admits to Mervyn Rothstein of the *New York Times,* ''I delayed writing it . . . because I felt it was too crazy.'' But she eventually became convinced that her vision of Gilead was not far from reality. Some of the anti-female measures she had imagined for the novel actually exist. ''There is a sect now, a Catholic charismatic spinoff sect, which calls the women handmaids,'' Atwood tells Rothstein. ''A law in Canada,'' Battiata reports, ''[requires] a woman to have her husband's permission before obtaining an abortion.'' And Atwood, speaking to Battiata, points to repressive laws in Romania as well: ''No abortion, no birth control, and compulsory pregnancy testing, once a month.'' *The Handmaid's Tale,* Elaine Kendall explains in the *Los Angeles Times Book Review,* depicts ''a future firmly based upon actuality, beginning with events that have already taken place and extending them a bit beyond the inevitable conclusions. 'The Handmaid's Tale' does not depend upon hypothetical scenarios, omens, or straws in the wind, but upon documented occurrences and public pronouncements; all matters of record.'' Stephen McCabe of the *Humanist* calls the novel ''a chilling vision of the future extrapolated from the present.''

Yet, several critics voice a disbelief in the basic assumptions of *The Handmaid's Tale.* Mary McCarthy, in her review for the *New York Times Book Review,* complains that ''I just can't see the intolerance of the far right . . . as leading to a super-biblical puritanism.'' And although agreeing that ''the author has carefully drawn her projections from current trends. . . . ,'' McCarthy believes that ''perhaps that is the trouble: the projections are too neatly penciled in. The details . . . all raise

their hands announcing themselves present. At the same time, the Republic of Gilead itself, whatever in it that is not a projection, is insufficiently imagined.'' Richard Grenier of *Insight* objects that the Fundamentalist-run Gilead does not seem Christian: ''There seems to be no Father, no Son, no Holy Ghost, no apparent belief in redemption, resurrection, eternal life. No one in this excruciatingly hierarchized new clerical state . . . appears to believe in God.'' Grenier also finds it improbable that ''while the United States has hurtled off into this morbid, feminist nightmare, the rest of the democratic world has been blissfully unaffected.'' Writing in the Toronto *Globe and Mail,* William French states that Atwood's ''reach exceeds her grasp'' in *The Handmaid's Tale,* ''and in the end we're not clear what we're being warned against.'' Atwood seems to warn of the dangers of religious fanaticism, of the effects of pollution on the birthrate, and of a possible backlash to militant feminist demands. The novel, French states, ''is in fact a cautionary tale about *all* these things. . . . but in her scenario, they interact in an implausible way.''

Despite this flaw, French sees *The Handmaid's Tale* as being ''in the honorable tradition of *Brave New World* and other warnings of dystopia. It's imaginative, even audacious, and conveys a chilling sense of fear and menace.'' Prescott also compares *The Handmaid's Tale* to other dystopian novels. It belongs, he writes, ''to that breed of visionary fiction in which a metaphor is extended to elaborate a warning. . . . Wells, Huxley and Orwell popularized the tradition with books like 'The Time Machine,' 'Brave New World' and '1984'—yet Atwood is a better *novelist* than they.'' Christopher Lehmann-Haupt sees *The Handmaid's Tale* as a book that goes far beyond its feminist concerns. Writing in the *New York Times,* Lehmann-Haupt explains that the novel ''is a political tract deploring nuclear energy, environmental waste, and antifeminist attitudes. But it [is] so much more than that—a taut thriller, a psychological study, a play on words.'' Van Gelder agrees. The novel, she writes, ''ultimately succeeds on multiple levels: as a page-turning thriller, as a powerful political statement, and as an exquisite piece of writing.'' Lehmann-Haupt concludes that *The Handmaid's Tale* ''is easily Margaret Atwood's best novel to date.''

Just as *The Handmaid's Tale* is Atwood's most direct expression of her feminism, *Survival: A Thematic Guide to Canadian Literature* is the most direct presentation of her strong belief in Canadian nationalism. In the book Atwood discerns a uniquely Canadian literature, distinct from its American and British counterparts, and she discusses the dominant themes to be found in it. Canadian literature, she argues, is primarily concerned with victims and with the victim's ability to survive. Atwood, Onley explains, ''perceives a strong sado-masochistic patterning in Canadian literature as a whole. She believes that there is a national fictional tendency to participate, usually at some level as Victim, in a Victor/Victim basic pattern.'' But ''despite its stress on victimization,'' Hutcheon writes, ''this study is not a revelation of, or a reveling in, [masochism].'' What Atwood argues, Onley believes, is that ''every country or culture has a single unifying and informing symbol at its core: for America, the Frontier; for England, the Island; for Canada, Survival.''

Several critics find that Atwood's own work exemplifies this primary theme of Canadian literature. Her examination of destructive sex roles and her nationalistic concern over the subordinate role Canada plays to the United States are variations on the victor/victim theme. As Marge Piercy explains in the *American Poetry Review,* Atwood believes that a writer must consciously work within his or her nation's literary tradition. Atwood argues in *Survival*, Piercy writes, "that discovery of a writer's tradition may be of use, in that it makes available a conscious choice of how to deal with that body of themes. She suggests that exploring a given tradition consciously can lead to writing in new and more interesting ways." Because Atwood's own work closely parallels the themes she sees as common to the Canadian literary tradition, *Survival* "has served as the context in which critics have subsequently discussed [Atwood's] works," Hutcheon states.

Atwood's prominent stature in Canadian letters rests as much on her published works as on her efforts to define and give value to her nation's literature. "Atwood," Susan Wood states in the *Washington Post Book World*, "has emerged as a champion of Canadian literature and of the peculiarly Canadian experience of isolation and survival." Hutcheon notes Atwood's "important impact on Canadian culture" and believes that her books, "internationally known through translations, stand as testimony to Atwood's significant position in a contemporary literature which must deal with defining its own identity and defending its value."

Although she has been labelled a Canadian nationalist, a feminist, and even a gothic writer, Atwood incorporates and transcends these categories. Writing in *Saturday Night* of Atwood's several perceived roles as a writer, Linda Sandler concludes that "Atwood is all things to all people . . . a nationalist . . . a feminist or a psychologist or a comedian . . . a maker and breaker of myths . . . a gothic writer. She's all these things, but finally she's unaccountably Other. Her writing has the discipline of a social purpose but it remains elusive, complex, passionate. It has all the intensity of an act of exorcism." Atwood's work finally succeeds because it speaks of universal concerns. As Piercy explains, "Atwood is a large and remarkable writer. Her concerns are nowhere petty. Her novels and poems move and engage me deeply, can matter to people who read them."

CA INTERVIEW

CA interviewed Margaret Atwood by telephone on September 9, 1986, at her home in Toronto, Canada.

CA: Your latest novel, The Handmaid's Tale, *is set in an imaginary future society in which religious extremists have taken over and women are all relegated to specific roles, the most important being to produce babies. The book is horrifyingly believable. Was it difficult or depressing to sustain the imagination that carried you through its writing?*

ATWOOD: Not once I got started. I thought about it for about four years, and that part was difficult. But once I started writing it, it wasn't difficult—I suppose because I'd thought about it so much. In fact, I wrote it very quickly.

CA: You've said that during the writing you began to get all kinds of confirmation that the things in the book were really happening.

ATWOOD: Either they were really happening or something very like them was happening or had already happened. Even some of the things that were merely implied in the book—after I finished it, I got several clippings from various people that indicated such things had already happened.

CA: What were some of the scariest examples?

ATWOOD: Bottle funerals. A U.S. cult in which the women actually *are* called "Handmaids." Explicit anti-homosexual legislation in the U.S. A lot of stuff about secret-police-type surveillance in "religious" groups. That sort of thing.

CA: I couldn't help wondering if The Handmaid's Tale *is more frightening for women who grew up in the 1950s than for younger women. Have letters from readers indicated anything of the kind?*

ATWOOD: No, they've been right across the board. I think that it may, in fact, be a bit scarier for younger women because they haven't grown up in it, so it's even more unknown and more horrifying to them. Here they see it coming down the track towards them. And since the book was published, I think the United States has gone even more to the right.

CA: You told Le Anne Schreiber for Vogue *that all your novels begin with "a scene or visual image of some kind." Does the image nearly always simmer for a while, as with* The Handmaid's Tale, *before the whole idea follows?*

ATWOOD: Yes, I would say it does.

CA: Can you describe what happens during that process, and how you know when you're ready to start writing?

ATWOOD: If the image comes and then goes, nothing much happens—but if it keeps coming back, then I pay more attention to it. It's like looking at a moving painting and seeing a little more of it each time you look. But after that I have to find the "voice" of the book.

CA: Do your short stories and poems begin with an image as well?

ATWOOD: The poems begin with a phrase or a line. The short stories usually begin with an image, like the novels.

CA: You're also an artist—collage and cartoons and cover designs and maybe other things I don't know about.

ATWOOD: I'm not really an artist. I fool around with it, but I wouldn't call myself an artist. I paint privately, let's say.

CA: Do you suppose the fooling around with art, to use your modest description, is related to the visual beginnings of the written prose works?

ATWOOD: Probably it is. Some people say that their work begins with music or that the analogy is with music. Mine is definitely visual.

CA: Do dreams ever play a part in the writing?

ATWOOD: Certainly they do. They're primarily visual as well, and images come out of them.

CA: Are the poems often a long time in the making and subject to many revisions before you're happy with them?

ATWOOD: Not if I'm lucky. If I'm lucky I may get the whole thing in one session. But I can work on a poem for years and still not be satisfied with it.

CA: You've said you started writing at sixteen and you've been writing ever since. Were there people who gave special en-

couragement and help in the early stages, well before the prizes began coming?

ATWOOD: Yes. My high school English teachers, after I started writing, which was the last two years of high school. Several of my college teachers, definitely, and one of my aunts.

CA: Were you equally interested from the start in writing prose and poetry?

ATWOOD: I started both at the same time, and I seem to have been equally interested.

CA: There is an unpublished first novel, isn't there?

ATWOOD: Yes, there is.

CA: Is that likely ever to be published in any form?

ATWOOD: I hope not! All I can say about it is that it's an interesting first novel, but it was written by a twenty-three-year-old. Of course *The Edible Woman* was written by a twenty-four-year-old. But there is quite a difference.

CA: With the recognition came a lot of publicity, which perhaps got heavier with the publication of the controversial critical book Survival *in 1972. In retrospect, would you have had it otherwise, given a choice?*

ATWOOD: I wouldn't have had it otherwise, but I would have handled it differently. I wasn't aware of the image-making propensities of things like newspapers. And of course I was quite frank during my early interview. I don't think I would be quite that open if I were doing it again.

CA: But you don't think it hurt the writing in any way, do you?

ATWOOD: No, not at all. I think it was sometimes upsetting for me, and particularly in those days people tended to be frightened of or weird about young women of achievement. So a lot of that projection happened to me, which means that if you open up the papers you may find this person who has your face but the description isn't at all like what you think you are. That certainly happened a lot. It took me a while to figure out that what was coming out the other end had just as much to do with the reporter as it did with me. That's hard to keep in mind, especially when people come with their stories already written in their heads, and all they're looking for from you is something that will corroborate what they've decided in advance.

CA: And probably being a woman made you subject to certain kinds of silly treatment as well.

ATWOOD: I think there's no doubt about that. My very first interviews, for instance, were before the women's movement had penetrated people's heads very much, so that I really was asked things like "How do you manage to do all the house-work and write too?" and "When do you cook the lunch?" That all had to be lived through. (The answers, by the way, are, "If there's a choice the house stays dirty" and "I try to skip big lunches.")

CA: The female characters in your novels sometimes aren't sure about their own identity, but you seem to have them quite

in control creatively. Are they fully developed in your mind when you start a book, or are you uncertain about how they'll act until you're into the writing?

ATWOOD: I'm never entirely certain about how they're going to act. In fact, that's one of the things that keeps me writing along with the book. I'm willing to be surprised.

CA: Can you remember the image that Surfacing *began with?*

ATWOOD: There were two. One was the scene in the first chapter when they're driving towards the lake. It's the last couple of paragraphs of that chapter. The other was that part where the mother turns into a bird.

CA: Some critics have read Lady Oracle *as a parody of your other writing. Was it conceived as such?*

ATWOOD: I think there are touches of that in it. But I think it's mostly a parody of romantic writing of a certain kind.

CA: Lady Oracle *is partly a very funny book, as is* The Edible Woman. *Do you sometimes write a funny book deliberately as a kind of rest?*

ATWOOD: I think so, yes.

CA: Since you do different kinds of writing—novels, short stories, poems, critical writing—do they ever overlap and cause problems for you in managing them all?

ATWOOD: Not so far. I think all it means is that I tend to avoid writer's block. If you have several different forms and you come to a block in one of them, you can switch forms.

CA: Do you feel equally happy in all the kinds of writing you do?

ATWOOD: I dislike writing book reviews and speeches more than anything. I do it out of some twisted sense of duty which I may be getting old enough to feel I can forego.

CA: You've done a lot of traveling, much of it connected with your work. Does your perspective on what you're writing or planning to write change noticeably when you're away from home?

ATWOOD: It's a little bit hard to tell, but I think it does. The only light I can cast on that is that when you're not at home, it's a lot harder for people to get at you, and therefore it's easier to focus on the work.

CA: Did Bodily Harm *grow directly out of a trip?*

ATWOOD: It grew out of an acquaintance with the place. It was not one trip, but numerous trips.

CA: That was a most disturbing book in the way that the focus shifts so realistically from Rennie's loss of part of a breast through cancer and the possibility of a recurrence of the disease to the more immediate threat of death when she is imprisoned during the revolution she's caught up in. Was Bodily Harm *a disturbing book to write?*

ATWOOD: Yes, it was. That one was very disturbing.

CA: You've spoken out in the past about unfairness on the part of Canadian critics toward the country's writers. Are the writers themselves supportive of each other, and has the critical treatment improved?

ATWOOD: Among writers themselves, things are really very good. Writers are quite communally minded; they do a lot to help one another out and their behavior towards each other is really quite exemplary. As a community, I would say, it's unusually helpful towards its members. The reader is not a problem. My readership in Canada is large, loyal, positive, supportive. If I count the letters to see which are positive and which are negative, overwhelmingly they're positive. What we're talking about is media stuff. There you do get a certain amount of snideness, an attitude of let's cut down the author or the artist; it happens to people in all art forms. I think it has something to do with what we call the colonial mentality. Being part of a country that was recently a colony of Britain and is now, to a certain extent, an economic colony of the United States, means that we have certain problems that you just never encounter in the U.S. The equivalent there would be somebody from, say, Alabama to whom people immediately surrounding that person would say, "Well, if you're any good, why aren't you in New York?" It's that kind of thing. I think you would only really get that if you were in the American "provinces." And it would be in relation to New York or Los Angeles or San Francisco. Whereas we get it also in relation to New York or Los Angeles or San Francisco, but they're in a different country. It used to be London: "If you're any good, why aren't you in London?" When *The Handmaid's Tale* did so well in the States, it was Canadian media people—not Canadian writers, who all live here anyway—who would say, "When are you going to move to New York?"

CA: Is there a crossover readership between the French-language writing and the English-language writing in Canada?

ATWOOD: To a certain extent, yes. We're aware of one another. We read each other's books quite often in translation and sometimes in the original, and we have certain common ground. The writers never did have any fight going on with one another; it was the politicians who were doing that.

CA: There is a large and still-growing body of academic criticism on your work. What are your feelings about it generally?

ATWOOD: Mixed. On the one hand, critics are, as George Steiner has said, the postmen to the future. If your letter is going to be delivered, it's probably going to be the critics who are going to do it. But too, of course, there's a lot of what you would call in an animal substitution activity. That's when the chipmunk is faced with the cat and doesn't know which way to run so it scratches itself instead. There's a certain amount of verbal scratching going on just for the sake of doing something. But anybody who's spent any time in academia knows that. It's publish or perish, so publish what? Well, they have to scrabble around and find something. Of course a lot of people who write about my work do so because they're genuine enthusiasts. That's dandy. In that case, all the critic is is a kind of reader made visible.

CA: You have been writer-in-residence at various colleges, haven't you?

ATWOOD: Not very often. I did three months in Alabama in 1985 and three months at New York University in 1986. Be-

fore that time, I hadn't done anything of the kind except for one-night or one-week stands since 1972, which is a long time.

CA: I thought it was interesting that you started The Handmaid's Tale *in Berlin and finished it in Alabama. One associates both places with certain ideas of repression.*

ATWOOD: That's true. But actually Alabama was a darned good place to write. I was invited as an MFA chair and I only had to teach one class. The rest of the time I was free to write. And it was far enough away from Canada so that nobody called me unless they were desperate. The people in the English department were very nice, and I had a really good writing time. Living there would be a different story. But I think, on a certain level, a possible effort is being made there now, which wasn't always the case, as you'll remember.

CA: Having two writers in the household seems to work well for you and Graeme Gibson. Do you serve as first readers for each other?

ATWOOD: Absolutely not. We avoid that like the plague. *Never* would we do such a thing to one another. Those jobs should be done by professionals with whom you are not emotionally involved.

CA: In her Dictionary of Literary Biography *essay on your work, Linda Hutcheon wrote, "There seems little doubt that Atwood's own experience as a mother increased her interest in the particularity of the feminine imagination." Would you comment on that assessment?*

ATWOOD: I love being a mother. I'd do it some more if I weren't so elderly. But I can see that it could be a nightmare for other people or under other circumstances. I think that becoming one simply made me think about this condition in a less abstract way. I tend to be a particularist anyway—no *a priori* axioms, or not many.

CA: Are you still actively working with Amnesty International?

ATWOOD: I'm actively working right now with PEN, which has a Writers in Prison program that overlaps considerably with Amnesty.

CA: Toronto would seem to be a good place for a writer to live. There's a lot going on, and there are certainly some good writers there.

ATWOOD: Yes, and what a change! When I was growing up, we all felt that the first item on our agenda would have to be to get out of Toronto as fast as we could, shake the dust of Toronto from our feet. It's still a manageable city; you can have the experience here of living in a city without feeling you're living in a state of seige.

CA: Do you still keep a place in the country as well?

ATWOOD: Yes.

CA: I'm sure it's good to have both, so that you can get away from each to go to the other.

ATWOOD: Yes. I think it's necessary for us.

CA: Besides your work in PEN and Amnesty, you've been chairwoman of the Writers' Union of Canada. What are your greatest concerns for writers now?

ATWOOD: I think in the States and to a certain extent in Canada, one of the concerns that's going to be uppermost in the years immediately ahead of us if we don't blow up the world is the censorship issue. And I think that's going to go on for a while, so I believe it's going to be fairly high on the agenda.

CA: I think it's very bad here right now.

ATWOOD: It isn't really very bad there compared with lots of countries. If you think it's as bad as it's going to get, you're quite wrong. It can get a lot worse. There's an interesting publication called *Index on Censorship,* which gives a very good rundown on what's happening in the various countries. It's obvious that no repressive government wants freedom of speech. Whether they be of the Right or the Left or the Third World or whatever, if it's a repressive government, they will wish to shut up the writers. The artists and writers are like the canaries the miners used to carry down into coal mines. If the canaries became unconscious, it meant there was poison gas. Once a government starts shutting up its writers, you can figure that there are bad times ahead for the ordinary citizen.

BIOGRAPHICAL/CRITICAL SOURCES:

BOOKS

Atwood, Margaret, *The Edible Woman,* McClelland & Stewart, 1969, Atlantic-Little, Brown, 1970.
Contemporary Literary Criticism, Gale, Volume II, 1974, Volume III, 1975, Volume IV, 1975, Volume VIII, 1978, Volume XIII, 1980, Volume XV, 1980, Volume XXV, 1983, Volume XLIV, 1987.
Davidson, Arnold E. and Cathy N. Davidson, editors, *The Art of Margaret Atwood: Essays in Criticism,* House of Anansi Press, 1981.
Dictionary of Literary Biography, Volume LIII: *Canadian Writers since 1960,* Gale, 1986.
Gibson, Graeme, *Eleven Canadian Novelists,* House of Anansi Press, 1973.
Grace, Sherrill, *Violent Duality: A Study of Margaret Atwood,* Vehicule Press, 1980.
Grace, Sherrill, and Lorraine Weir, editors, *Margaret Atwood: Language, Text and System,* University of British Columbia Press, 1983.
Lecker, Robert and Jack David, editors, *The Annotated Bibliography of Canada's Major Authors,* ECW, 1980.
Marshall, Tom, *Harsh and Lovely Land: The Major Canadian Poets and the Making of a Canadian Tradition,* University of British Columbia Press, 1978.
Sandler, Linda, editor, *Margaret Atwood: A Symposium,* University of British Columbia, 1977.
Twigg, Alan, *For Openers: Conversations with 24 Canadian Writers,* Harbour, 1981.
Woodcock, George, *The Canadian Novel in the Twentieth Century,* McClelland & Stewart, 1975.

PERIODICALS

American Poetry Review, November/December, 1973, March/April, 1977, September/October, 1979.
Atlantic, April, 1973.
Book Forum, Volume IV, number 1, 1978.
Books in Canada, January, 1979, June/July, 1980, March, 1981.
Canadian Forum, February, 1970, January, 1973, November/December, 1974, December/January, 1977-78, June/July, 1981, December/January, 1981-82.
Canadian Literature, autumn, 1971, spring, 1972, winter, 1973, spring, 1974, spring, 1977.
Chicago Tribune, January 27, 1980, February 3, 1980, May 16, 1982.
Chicago Tribune Book World, January 26, 1986.
Christian Science Monitor, June 12, 1977.
Commonweal, July 9, 1973.
Communique, May, 1975.
Detroit Free Press January 26, 1986.
Detroit News, April 4, 1982.
Essays on Canadian Writing, spring, 1977.
Globe and Mail (Toronto), July 7, 1984, October 5, 1985, October 19, 1985, February 15, 1986, November 15, 1986, November 29, 1986, November 14, 1987.
Hudson Review, autumn, 1973, spring, 1975.
Humanist, September/October, 1986.
Insight, March 24, 1986.
Journal of Canadian Fiction, Volume I, number 4, 1972.
Los Angeles Times, March 2, 1982, April, 22, 1982, May 9, 1986, January 12, 1987.
Los Angeles Times Book Review, October 17, 1982, February 9, 1986, December 23, 1987.
Maclean's, January 15, 1979, October 15, 1979, March 30, 1981.
Malahat Review, January, 1977.
Manna, Number 2, 1972.
Meanjin, Volume 37, number 2, 1978.
Modern Fiction Studies, autumn, 1976.
Ms., January, 1987.
New Leader, September 3, 1973.
New Orleans Review, Volume 5, number 3, 1977.
Newsweek, February 18, 1980, February 17, 1986.
New York Times, December 23, 1976, January 10, 1980, February 8, 1980, March 6, 1982, March 28, 1982, September 15, 1982, January 27, 1986, February 17, 1986, November 5, 1986.
New York Times Book Review, October 18, 1970, March 4, 1973, April 6, 1975, September 26, 1976, May 21, 1978, February 3, 1980, October 11, 1981, February 9, 1986.
Observer, June 13, 1982.
Ontario Review, spring/summer, 1975.
Open Letter, summer, 1973.
Parnassus: Poetry in Review, spring/summer, 1974.
People, May 19, 1980.
Poetry, March, 1970, July, 1972, May, 1982.
Publishers Weekly, August 23, 1976.
Quill and Quire, April, 1981, September, 1984.
Room of One's Own, summer, 1975.
San Francisco Review of Books, January, 1982, summer, 1982.
Saturday Night, May 1971, July/August, 1976, September, 1976, May, 1981.
Saturday Review, September 18, 1976, February 2, 1980.
Saturday Review of the Arts, April, 1973.
Shenandoah, Volume 37, number 2, 1987.
Studies in Canadian Literature, summer, 1977.
This Magazine Is about Schools, winter, 1973.
Time, October 11, 1976.
Times (London), March 13, 1986, June 4, 1987, June 10, 1987.
Times Literary Supplement, March 21, 1986, June 12, 1987.
University of Toronto Quarterly, summer, 1978.
Village Voice, January 7, 1980.

Vogue, January, 1986.

Washington Post, April 6, 1986.

Washington Post Book World, September 26, 1976, December 3, 1978, January 27, 1980, March 14, 1982, February 2, 1986.

Waves, autumn, 1975.

West Coast Review, January, 1973.

—*Sketch by Thomas Wiloch*

—*Interview by Jean W. Ross*

*   *   *

AUERBACH, Stevanne 1938-
(Stevanne Auerbach Fink)

PERSONAL: Born September 22, 1938, in New York, N.Y.; daughter of Nathan and Jean (Rosen) Stockheim; married Arthur Auerbach, November 24, 1961 (divorced November, 1968); married Donald Fink (a physician), February 4, 1972 (divorced, 1979); children: (first marriage) Amy. *Education:* Queens College of the City of New York (now Queens College of the City University of New York), B.A., 1960; graduate study, University of Maryland, 1961-65; George Washington University, M.A., 1965; Union Graduate School, Ph.D., 1973.

ADDRESSES: Home—San Francisco, Calif. *Office*—Institute for Childhood Resources, 1005 Market St., San Francisco, Calif. 94103.

CAREER: Teacher of recreation and swimming in New York, N.Y., 1958-60; elementary school teacher in Silver Spring, Md., 1960-61; American Personnel and Guidance Association, Washington, D.C., professional assistant, 1961-63; B'nai B'rith Vocational Service, Washington, D.C., professional assistant, 1963-64; teacher of retarded children in Washington, D.C., 1965-66; Council for Exceptional Children, Washington, D.C., research associate, 1966-67; elementary school teacher in Washington, D.C., 1968; U.S. Department of Health, Education and Welfare, Washington, D.C., education program specialist, 1968-69, child care researcher, 1970-71; Far West Laboratory for Educational Research and Development, Berkeley, Calif., intern in childhood development, 1971-78; Institute for Childhood Resources, San Francisco, Calif., founder and director, 1978—. Lecturer and consultant throughout the United States.

MEMBER: Association for Childhood Education International, International Women's Writing Guild, National Writers Union, American Society of Journalists and Authors, Council for Exceptional Children, American Personnel and Guidance Association (life member), National Vocational Guidance Association, National Education Association, National Association for Education of Young Children, American Humanist Association, American Association of University Women, Washington Independent Writers Group, Media Alliance of San Francisco.

WRITINGS:

(Editor) *Counselor Education: A Progress Report on Standards,* American Personnel and Guidance Association, 1962.

(Editor) *NVGA Bibliography of Current Occupational Information,* American Personnel and Guidance Association, 1963.

(Contributor) Pamela Roby, editor, *Child Care—Who Cares?: Foreign and Domestic Infant and Early Childhood Development Policies,* Basic Books, 1973.

(Contributor) Roy Fairfield, editor, *Humanizing the Workplace,* Prometheus Press, 1974.

(Under name Stevanne Auerbach Fink) *Parents and Child Care,* Far West Laboratory for Educational Research and Development, 1974.

(Editor) *Child Care: A Comprehensive Guide,* four volumes, Human Sciences, 1975-76.

Confronting the Child Care Crisis, Beacon Press, 1979.

The Whole Child: A Sourcebook, Putnam, 1981.

Choosing Child Care: Parents' Guide to Child Care, Dutton, 1982.

The Toychest: A Sourcebook on Toys, Lyle Stuart, 1986.

The Alphabet Tree, Windswept House, 1986.

Also author of *Petals* (poems), 1974. Contributor to journals, newspapers, and magazines, including *Family Circle, Playthings, Parents Magazine, Day Care, Early Education, Young Children, Children's Business, Phi Delta Kappan, San Francisco Chronicle* and the *Detroit Free Press.* Editor, *Counselor's Information Service,* 1963-64, and *Physical Education for the Mentally Retarded.*

WORK IN PROGRESS: Book on war toys; new edition of *The Whole Child;* a novel; a collection of poetry; other publications.

SIDELIGHTS: Stevanne Auerbach told *CA:* "Writing has been a perfect way for me to synthesize learning, experience, and philosophy. I have been pleased to be able to develop 'breakthrough' books and articles in specific areas. I have worked to be a writer from undergraduate classes at Queens College where as an education major, inspired by many excellent professors, I wrote papers which continued to be consistent with my life's philosophy and work expression—service to children and families.

"While working in various professional activities in Washington, D.C., I helped produce publications: *Opportunities in the Peace Corps—A Fact Booklet, Physical Education for the Mentally Retarded, Counselor Education Standards,* and *The NVGA Guide to Occupational Literature,* and others in the Dramatic Arts in Education. While at HEW I produced reviews of model programs and many papers related to National Title I, child care, and other areas in education.

"During graduate school I began writing a personal journal, articles, and conducted a unique cross-cultural study on child care. Later I began writing books and found each one made a contribution which has resulted in great satisfaction. I did learn the art of producing a book by self-publishing one and later selling it to a major publisher. I now lecture and appear on television and radio throughout the United States on child-related topics and am pleased to be able to impact on helping to raise children in the '80s."

In *The Toy Chest: A Sourcebook of Toys for Children,* Auerbach surveys the vast toy marketplace and evaluates toys according to their various classifications: active, creative, or educational. The book contains interviews with individuals who represent all facets of toy production—manufacturers, advertising agencies, retailers, parents, and even the children. Lynn Kapplow writes in the *Christian Science Monitor:* "Reaching into this Toy Chest brings forth tips on safety, loads of information, and practical guidelines, all handled sensitively to help both parent and child choose toys of quality and long-lasting satisfaction. Auerbach indicated to *CA* that her plans include opening an international toy museum.

AVOCATIONAL INTERESTS: Collecting all resources (literature, arts, and poetry) about butterflies, with involvement in protecting them.

BIOGRAPHICAL/CRITICAL SOURCES:

PERIODICALS

Christian Science Monitor, July 24, 1986.

*   *   *

AVICE, Claude (Pierre Marie) 1925- (Pierre Barbet, David Maine, Olivier Sprigel)

PERSONAL: Born May 16, 1925, in Le Mans, France; son of Leon (a pharmacist) and Renee (Bardet) Avice; married Marianne Brunswick (a pharmacist), July 23, 1952; children: Brigitte Avice Newman, Patrick, Olivier. *Education:* University of Paris, Docteur en pharmacie, 1954.

ADDRESSES: Home—4 Square de l'Avenue du Bois, 75116 Paris, France.

CAREER: Science fiction writer. Pharmacist in Paris, France, 1952-81. Director of laboratory for medical analysis, 1955-58. Diplomate in bacteriology, serology, parasitology and hemotology.

MEMBER: Association Internationale des Critiques litteraires, World Science Fiction (member of the board, 1985), Societe francophone de Science-Fiction (vice-president, 1985), European Society of Science Fiction (coordinator, 1979), Science Fiction Writers of America (overseas director), Society of Doctors in Pharmacy (secretary).

AWARDS, HONORS: Gold medal from International Institute of Science Fiction (Poznan).

WRITINGS:

UNDER PSEUDONYM PIERRE BARBET

Vers un avenir perdu (title means "Towards a Lost Future"), Gallimard, 1962.
Babel 3,805, Gallimard, 1963.
Les Limiers de l'infini (title means "Bloodhounds of the Infinite"), Editions Fleuve Noir, 1966.
Les Cavernicoles de Wolf (title means "Cave Inhabitants of Wolf"), Editions Fleuve Noir, 1966.
L'Etoile du neant (title means "The Star of Nought"), Editions Fleuve Noir, 1967.
L'Enigme des quasars (title means "The Secret of Quasars"), Editions Fleuve Noir, 1967.
Hallali cosmique (title means "Cosmic Death"), Editions Fleuve Noir, 1967.
La Planete des cristophons (title means "Planet of Cristophons"), Editions Fleuve Noir, 1968.
Evolution magnetique (title means "Magnetic Evolution"), Editions Fleuve Noir, 1968.
Vikings de l'espace (title means "Space Vikings"), Editions Fleuve Noir, 1969.
Les Chimeres de Seginus (title means "The Chimeras of Seginus"), Editions Fleuve Noir, 1969.
L'Exile du temps (title means "Exile of Time"), Editions Fleuve Noir, 1969.

Etoiles en perdition (title means "Stars in Distress"), Editions Fleuve Noir, 1970.
Les Maitres des pulsars (title means "Masters of Pulsars"), Editions Fleuve Noir, 1970.
Les Grognards d'Eridan, Editions Fleuve Noir, 1970, translation by Stanley Hochman published as *The Napoleons of Eridanus*, DAW Books, 1976.
L'Agonie de la voie lactee (title means "The Agony of the Milky Way"), Editions Fleuve Noir, 1970.
Les Conquistadores d'Andromede (title means "The Conquistadors of Andromeda"), Editions Fleuve Noir, 1971.
Le Transmetteur de Ganymede (title means "Ganymede's Transmitter"), Editions Fleuve Noir, 1971.
Azraec de Virgo (title means "Azraec of Virgo"), Editions Fleuve Noir, 1971.
A quoi songent les psyborgs?, Editions Fleuve Noir, 1971, translation by Wendayne Ackerman published as *Games Psyborgs Play*, DAW Books, 1973.
L'Empire du Baphomet, Editions Fleuve Noir, 1972, translation by Bernand Kay published as *Baphomet's Meteor*, DAW Books, 1972.
Les Insurges de Laucor (title means "Insurgents of Laucor"), Editions Fleuve Noir, 1972.
La Planete empoisonnee (title means "Poisoned Planet"), Editions Fleuve Noir, 1972.
Tremplins d'etoiles (title means "Springboard of the Stars"), Editions Fleuve Noir, 1972.
La Planete enchantee, Editions Flueve Noir, 1973, translation by C. J. Richards published as *Enchanted Planet*, DAW Books, 1975.
Liane de Noldaz, Editions Fleuve Noir, 1973, translation by Hochman published as *The Joan-of-Arc Replay*, DAW Books, 1978.
Les Bioniques d'Atria (title means "Bionics of Atria"), Editions Fleuve Noir, 1973.
Le Batard d'Orion (title means "The Bastard of Orion"), Editions Fleuve Noir, 1973.
Magiciens galactiques (title means "Galactic Magicians"), Editions Fleuve Noir, 1974.
L'Univers des Geons (title means "The Universe of Geons"), Editions Fleuve Noir, 1974.
Croisade stellaire (title means "Stellar Crusade"), Editions Fleuve Noir, 1974.
Les Mercenaires de Rychna (title means "The Mercenaries of Rychna"), Editions Fleuve Noir, 1974.
La Nymphe de l'espace (title means "Nymph of Space"), Editions Fleuve Noir, 1975.
Patrouilleur du neant (title means "Patrol of Nought"), Editions Fleuve Noir, 1976.
A Problem in Bionics, DAW Books, 1977.
Commandos sur commande, Editions Fleuve Noir, 1978.
Odyssee galactique, Editions Fleuve Noir, 1978.
Trafic stellaire, Editions Fleuve Noir, 1979.
Oasis de l'espace, Editions Fleuve Noir, 1979.
Periple galactique, Editions Fleuve Noir, 1980.
Cite des asteroides, Editions Fleuve Noir, 1980.
Stellar Crusaders, DAW Books, 1980.
Le Marechal rebelle, Editions Fleuve Noir, 1981.
Les Psychos de Logir, Editions Fleuve Noir, 1981.
Survivants de l'apocalypse, Editions Fleuve Noir, 1982.
Cites stellaires, Editions Fleuve Noir, 1982.
L'Empereur d'Eridan, Editions Fleuve Noir, 1982, translation by Hochman published as *The Emperor of Eridanus*, DAW Books, 1983.
Les charognards de S'nien, Editions Fleuve Noir, 1983.

Rome doit etre detruite, Editions Fleuve Noir, 1983.
Les colons d'Eridan, Editions Fleuve Noir, 1984.
Carthage sera detruite, Editions Fleuve Noir, 1984.
Eldorado stellaire, Editions Fleuve Noir, 1985.
Cite biotique, Editions Fleuve Noir, 1985.
Teleclones, Editions Fleuve Noir, 1985.
Putsch galactique, Editions Fleuve Noir, 1985.
Glaciation nucleaire, Editions Fleuve Noir, 1986.
Croisade des assassins, Editions Fleuve Noir, 1986.
Temps changeants, Editions Fleuve Noir, 1986.
Defense spatiale, Editions Fleuve Noir, 1987.
Captifs de Corvus, Editions Fleuve Noir, 1987.
Un Reich de 1000 ans, Editions Fleuve Noir, 1987.

UNDER PSEUDONYM DAVID MAINE

Les Disparus du club Chronos (title means "Club Chronos is Missing"), Albin Michel, 1972.
Guerillero galactique (title means "Galactic Guerillas"), Albin Michel, 1976.
Renaissance planetaire, Albin Michel, 1980.
Invasion Cosmique, Albin Michel, 1982.

UNDER PSEUDONYM OLIVIER SPRIGEL

Crepuscule de futur, Librairie des Champs Elysees, 1975.
Venusine, Librairie des Champs Elysees, 1977.
Lendemains incertains, Librairie des Champs Elysees, 1978.

OTHER

(Contributor) Donald A. Wollheim, editor, *European Anthology,* Doubleday, 1976.

Also author (with others) of *La Grande Encyclopedie de la Science Fiction,* Del Drago (Italy) and *L'homme est-il seul dans l'univers?,* La Bionique. Contributor of science fiction short stories to anthologies and to French periodicals, including *Policier Mystere Magazine* and *Horizons du Fantastique.*

WORK IN PROGRESS: Two more science fiction works.

AVOCATIONAL INTERESTS: Sculpture, tennis.

SIDELIGHTS: Claude Avice's works have been published in Brazil, Hungary, Poland, Portugal, Italy, Switzerland and the United States.

B

BAINBRIDGE, Beryl 1933-

PERSONAL: Born November 21, 1933, in Liverpool, England; daughter of Richard (a salesman) and Winifred (Baines) Bainbridge; married Austin Davies (an artist), April 24, 1954 (divorced); children: Aaron Paul, Johanna Harriet, Ruth Emmanuella. *Education:* Attended Merchant Taylor's School, Great Crosby, England. *Politics:* Socialist. *Religion:* "Lapsed Catholic."

ADDRESSES: Home—42 Albert St., Camden Town, London NW1 7NU, England.

CAREER: Actress in England on radio and in repertory theatre, 1943-56; writer, 1956-68, 1972—. Also has worked in a wine-bottling factory, as a clerk for Gerald Duckworth & Company publishers, and as a host for the British Broadcasting Corporation series "English Journey," 1983, and "Forever England," 1986.

MEMBER: Royal Society of Literature (fellow).

AWARDS, HONORS: Booker Prize nomination, 1973, for *The Dressmaker;* Booker Prize nomination and Guardian Fiction Award, both 1974, both for *The Bottle Factory Outing;* Whitbread Award, 1977, for *Injury Time;* Litt.D. from University of Liverpool, 1986.

WRITINGS:

FICTION

A Weekend with Claud (novel), Hutchinson, 1967, revised edition published as *A Weekend with Claude,* Duckworth, 1981.
Another Part of the Wood (novel), Hutchinson, 1968, revised edition, Duckworth, 1979, Braziller, 1980.
Harriet Said (novel), Duckworth, 1972, Braziller, 1973.
The Dressmaker (novel), Duckworth, 1973, published as *The Secret Glass,* Braziller, 1973.
The Bottle Factory Outing (novel), Braziller, 1974.
Sweet William (novel), Braziller, 1975.
A Quiet Life (novel; also see below), Duckworth, 1976, Braziller, 1977.
Injury Time (novel; also see below), Braziller, 1977.
Young Adolf (novel), Duckworth, 1978, Braziller, 1979.
Winter Garden (novel), Duckworth, 1980, Braziller, 1981.
Watson's Apology (novel), Duckworth, 1984, McGraw, 1985.

Mum and Mr. Armitage (short stories), Duckworth, 1985.
Filthy Lucre, or The Tragedy of Andrew Ledwhistle and Richard Soleway (novel), Duckworth, 1986.

NONFICTION

English Journey, or The Road to Milton Keynes, Duckworth, 1984.
Forever England: North and South, Duckworth, 1987.

TELEVISION SCRIPTS

"Tiptoe through the Tulips," 1976.
"Blue Skies from Now On," 1977.
"The Warrior's Return," 1977.
"It's Lovely Day Tomorrow," 1977.
"Words Fail Me," 1979.
"Sweet William" (based on the novel of the same title), produced by British Broadcasting Corporation (BBC), 1979.
"A Quiet Life" (based on the novel of the same title), BBC, 1980.
(With Phillip Seville) "The Journal of Bridget Hitler," BBC, 1980.
"Somewhere More Central," 1981.

OTHER

(Contributor) Emma Tennant, editor, *Bananas,* Quartet Books, 1977.
(Contributor) A. D. Maclean, editor, *Winter's Tales 26,* Macmillan (London), 1980, St. Martin's, 1981.
(Editor) *New Stories 6* (anthology), Hutchinson, 1981.

Contributor to periodicals, including *Spectator, Listener, Times Literary Supplement,* and *Sunday Times Magazine.*

SIDELIGHTS: Beryl Bainbridge "is one of the half-dozen most inventive and interesting novelists working in Britain today," according to Julian Symons in the *New York Review of Books.* A native of Liverpool who now lives in London, Bainbridge has won critical acclaim and a wide readership on two continents for her black humor chronicles of the lives and neuroses of the English lower middle classes. Reviewers cite the unassuming author for her satiric but naturalistic portrayals of the drab and desperate British poor, of "the hidden springs of anarchy that bedevil the least adventurous of us, booby-trapping our lives and making them the occasion of violent and dangerous humor," in the words of *Spectator* contributor Harriet Waugh. Bainbridge's tales of urban wildness often stray into the realm of violence and nightmare, where trapped spirits collide with thwarted ambition and the bosom of the family offers more grief than relief. *Newsweek* correspondent Margo Jefferson writes, "Bainbridge's books are melancholy, provincial landscapes in which violence, like a thunderstorm, always threatens, sometimes strikes." *New York Times* columnist Anatole Broyard suggests that Bainbridge "has established herself as the high priestess of the rueful. She has opened a thrift shop in English literature, a home for frayed, faded, out-of-fashion and inexpensive people. The name of her shop might be Things Out of Joint. . . . Miss Bainbridge's people have all missed the train, or boat, the main chance. They are stranded in themselves, left behind by a world rushing toward the gratification of desire.''

Their dark subject matter notwithstanding, Bainbridge's novels have achieved a cult following, largely because the author juxtaposes horror and comedy with precision. As Anne Duchene notes in the *Times Literary Supplement*, reading a Bainbridge novel "has always been a special kind of experience, at once very funny, abrasive and intimate—rather like having a nasty sticking-plaster pulled off for you by an old friend: jokes, and the little unpleasantness briskly but tenderly dealt with, then drinks of relief all around." In the *Detroit News*, Anne Tyler writes: "Bainbridge addicts settle gleefully into her genteel parlors, knowing that shortly everything will fall apart. There'll be bodies in the hedge, baked apples behind the refrigerator. A grown man, in a fit of temper, will set fire to a chair arm. A woman will try to sleep while teenaged boys clamber over her bed in search of ping-pong balls. Like a schoolgirl fighting off the giggles, Beryl Bainbridge begins her stories with a determinedly straight face, plods virtuously forward—and then her sharp eye is snagged by some unlikely detail and all is lost. How can I stay serious, she seems to be asking, when people behave so absurdly?" *Books and Bookmen* reviewer James Brockway detects yet another level to Bainbridge's appeal. "The more I read her," he claims, "the more I suspect that the grip her work has taken on us, the ease with which she has won us, the enthusiasm with which the critics (most of them) greet her work,—the more I suspect that this is not merely due to her being an exquisite entertainer—a star performer, who can get away with anything, . . . a deliciously preposterous humorist and a very, very clever writer, but also to the powerful *subconscious* appeal of her subject matter: our present parlous postwar condition.''

Bainbridge told the *New York Times Book Review* that she writes in order to make sense of her own childhood experiences. "Childhood is a thing that happens so early you don't forget it," she said. "Everything else you grow out of, but you never recover from childhood. So I go over it again and again." By all accounts, Bainbridge's youth was spent in an extremely tense environment where bitter disputes between her parents developed frequently. *Dictionary of Literary Biography* contributor Barbara C. Millard notes that Bainbridge's mother's "preoccupation with class distinction" and her father's "manic temper" and financial insolvency precipitated quarrels during which Bainbridge defended her mother "by jumping on her father's back and bringing him to the ground." According to Willa Petschek in the *New York Times Book Review*, the family "stayed together for appearances' sake, but their tiny house was full of frightening emotions." It was this climate of strain, played out in the working-class neighborhoods of Liverpool, that Bainbridge has sought to duplicate in her fiction. She told the *Dictionary of Literary Biography*

that confronting the pain has helped her to exorcise it, although the process did not begin until she was nearing middle age. "Fortunately I did it late enough," she said. "If I had done it twenty years ago, I wouldn't have been neurotic for twenty years and so I wouldn't have written."

Fiction writing is indeed Bainbridge's second career; during her teen and early adult years she worked as an actress on the radio and in repertory theatres, and as late as 1972 she was still performing professionally. At sixteen she met and fell in love with her future husband, artist Austin Davies. They were married in 1954, although Bainbridge had misgivings about the match. While awaiting the birth of her first child in 1956, Bainbridge began to write a novel. She derived the plot from a newspaper story about two girls who had murdered their mother, but drew on her own childhood experiences to enhance and alter the details. The resulting work, *Harriet Said*, was completed in 1958 but went unpublished until 1972. Millard notes: "When Bainbridge submitted the manuscript to publishers in 1959, she received outraged response, including the comment that the book was 'too indecent and unpleasant even for these lax days.' " Editors were aghast at Bainbridge's tale of juvenile sexuality, voyeurism, and murder; their response so daunted Bainbridge that she returned to the stage. In 1959 her marriage ended, and she took her two young children back to Liverpool to live. Soon thereafter, however, she moved to London and started writing again. Her second novel, *A Weekend with Claud*, was published in 1967.

"Beryl Bainbridge's publishing history is perhaps the kind of thing you'd expect of a writer who is preoccupied with the idea of isolation," notes Karl Miller in the *New York Review of Books*. ". . . It may be that this portrayal of shyness and constraint, who appears to be no punctuator, found it difficult to cope with the embarrassment of a debut, and of getting herself properly published." Indeed, Bainbridge has since revised both of her first two books to go into print, *A Weekend with Claud* (revised as *A Weekend with Claude*) and *Another Part of the Wood*. In a piece for the London *Times*, Bainbridge attributes her success as an author to her acquaintance, in 1970, with Anna Haycraft, fiction editor for Gerald Duckworth & Company publishers. Bainbridge writes of Haycraft: "She had read my two published books, didn't like them all that much ('rotten' was the word she used) and wanted to know if I had written anything else. I showed her *Harriet Said*. . . . Duckworth published it, employed me in the office for a year, put me on a monthly salary—an arrangement that still exists—and suggested I write another novel as soon as possible." Bainbridge stresses that her editor's encouragement helped her to find her authorial voice: "It was she who told me to abandon the flowery and obscure style of my two later books and return to the simpler structure of the first. She pointed out that, in my case, clarity came from writing from my own experience. . . . I gradually learnt the best way, for me, of expressing what I wanted to say, and wrote a novel a year from then on.''

Critics suggest that although *A Weekend with Claud*, *Another Part of the Wood*, and *Harriet Said* lack the polish of later Bainbridge works, they nonetheless demonstrate a burgeoning talent at work. *New York Times Book Review* contributor Gail Godwin observes that *Harriet Said* "certainly ranks in content with the more celebrated thrillers of corrupt childhood, but it has literary and psychological virtues as well. The architecture of its narrative would have satisfied Poe: every incident advances the design. The language, though simple, often has the effect of poetry . . . [and] there are also several remarkable passages which reveal, so accurately, adolescence's frequent, unpredictable swing between mature and infantile behavior.'' Assessing *A Weekend with Claud,* Millard writes: ''In Claud, Bainbridge presents the first of her predatory men. He is tigerlike in his ruthless wooing and possession of women, and he creates what will become a familiar tension between the vulnerable female and the exploitative male. The novel lacks the author's characteristic crispness; its fuzzy prose is rescued only by the pointed imagery which projects an exact vision of the despair and folly of love and lovemaking.'' A *Washington Post* reviewer finds *Another Part of the Wood* ''a scrupulously detailed, wryly witty and ultimately harrowing study of manners in the British middle and working classes, of the effects of dependency on a variety of weak people and of the lies we all tell ourselves to make life bearable and the deadly passions that lie buried under the dull surface of our daily banalities.... This slow-moving book does acquire a cumulative momentum, pointing toward an effective, quietly powerful end, and much of the detail work is exquisite.''

Petschek contends that Bainbridge ''can date the onset of happiness back to the year she published the first of her . . . successful novels; what really happened, she says, is that . . . it dawned on her that the wretched tensions of childhood were not her fault, that her parents' unhappiness had not been caused by her.'' What Bainbridge also discovered was that her own life, past and present, could be mined for fiction. She began to mingle autobiography and imagination to depict, in *New York Times* reviewer Michiko Kakutani's words, a ''drab, depressing'' England ''where lives are circumscribed and expectations diminished. Families tend to be the source of suffocation rather than sustenance; and romance, too, has a way of dwindling into comedy instead of blossoming into hope.'' Judith Gies elaborates in the *New York Times Book Review:* ''When [Bainbridge's] characters are not meeting violent ends, their psyches are being pummeled. Drawn largely from the English lower middle class, they exist in a stifling and dangerous atmosphere of claustrophobic domesticity, crippling gentility and pretension. Her protagonists (generally women) make fumbling, gallant attempts to get out from under their bell jars—usually through love. But Bainbridge's characters never quite connect; they talk *through* each other.... The disturbing edge this produces is intensified by the author's use of naturalism—with its careful attention to detail—and the grotesque details she chooses to use. Her vision is as glittering and as narrow as a needle.''

Perhaps as an inevitable consequence of her perspective and aspirations, Bainbridge writes principally about love, or the lack thereof, between families or sexual partners. Miller suggests that her novels ''are adamant that intimacy and teaming-up conceal hostility, desperation, and an outcast condition. And yet they also contribute a good deal in the way of qualifying evidence, in the way of relief. There are occasions when people help each other, when need answers need.... Bleak as it can be at times, her fiction has in it ties of affection. It has saving instances, merciful exceptions, thoughtfully averted glances.'' *Times Literary Supplement* contributor Carol Rumens observes that Bainbridge's central characters, often though not always female, ''express, with the fragile authority of the wounded, the ravenous need of love that underlies adult pretensions and ideals.'' Millard explains how Bainbridge's microcosmic views of individuals can reveal wider cultural and emotional difficulties: ''The Bainbridgean female, alternately silly and wise, loving and self-absorbed, rebellious and conformist, deluded and perceptive—but always accommodating and vulnerable—has been interpreted as the image of a befud-

dled and helpless postwar England, and finally, as the image of modern humanity perplexed in the extreme. Her men and women are in the same modern fix—having escaped the old repressive rules of Victorian middle-class respectability, they yet seek normality but end up adrift in a sea of too many choices. Criticized early in her career for her 'dark view' of a violent world, Bainbridge is now credited with having identified, accurately, moral and cultural confusion as the contemporary malaise.'' Yet, Millard concludes, ''her characters have remained resilient, and the books have retained their good humor.''

Most critics agree that Bainbridge's prose style contributes significantly to the impact her novels make on readers. In the *New York Times Book Review,* Julia O'Faolain writes: ''It is Miss Bainbridge's style that makes her a seductive writer—her manner, not her matter, that is so good. Summaries do her no justice. Her genius is for a tapestry of ephemera. Detail is a component that she handles with a miniaturist's skill, often in a close-up so obsessive as to create a tension between her naturalistic accuracy and queerness of perspective.'' According to Mary Hope in *The Nation,* the ''*faux naivete,* one of the distinguishing marks of Bainbridge's writing, hides consummate technical comic skill. Bainbridge has you crying with laughter while the blood freezes in your veins. This close relationship between farce and horror often depends on extreme physical, as well as emotional, propinquity between the characters.... Her dialogue is always wildly funny, and she uses it most intricately to depict social anxiety and emotional turmoil or sterility. As in all great English writing, class discomfiture is used to pinpoint and give strength to the farcical situation.'' *Ms.* magazine reviewer Norma Rosen notes that Bainbridge ''writes brilliant detail into even the prettiest of her characters. It is all done with perfect timing and tone—though the language is resolutely plain.'' Edith Milton, in a *New Republic* essay, describes the cumulative effect of Bainbridge's prose: ''When the laughter is over, what remains is almost an abstraction, a rather novel view over a well-known landscape. The scale and clarity of its perspective are astonishing.''

The Dressmaker, published in America as *The Secret Glass,* remains one of Bainbridge's best-known works. Set in Liverpool during the Second World War, the novel explores the painful and claustrophobic existence of a young woman who lives with her two unmarried aunts. Millard suggests that the book ''depicts the cramped, impoverished lives of working-class Liverpudlians during the darker days of 1944. The psychological realism of the novel goes beyond reminiscence and proves Bainbridge a master of detail and atmosphere.'' Godwin feels that *The Dressmaker* ''will attract readers not for its suspense-entertainment but for its sharp character study and unrelenting Naturalism.... The author is painstaking in her evocation of era and perceptive about the world of manners in working-class Liverpool. She has much to tell us about those pressure cookers of family life and limited means. And she creates memorable portraits of her people.'' A *Times Literary Supplement* reviewer writes: ''To have disinterred so many nasty things in the woodshed and yet evoked a workaday image of Liverpudlian optimism and resilience, in so few claustrophobic pages, is a remarkable achievement. Miss Bainbridge's imagination pushes her towards nightmare, and her eye for detail is macabre; but because she writes with taut, matter-of-fact simplicity this seems as authentic as any contemporary image the camera has preserved of that mercifully vanished past.''

In recent years Bainbridge has moved away from the autobiographical ground situations that form such books as *The Dressmaker, The Bottle Factory Outing, Sweet William,* and *A Quiet Life,* and has instead let her imagination be piqued by history and travel. Her 1978 novel *Young Adolf,* for instance, describes a family reunion in Liverpool between Adolf Hitler and his half-brother Alois, who did indeed live in England. Broyard contends in a *New York Times* column that the book "has all the improbability of history. It is funny in a way that will make you shudder, sad in a way that will astonish you with unwanted feelings of sympathy. In making Hitler human, Miss Bainbridge has reminded us once again that it is persons, not abstract forces, that engender our disasters." *Christian Science Monitor* contributor Bruce Allen likewise asserts that the novel's best effects "rise out of Bainbridge's genius for finding latent menace in the dreariest everydayness.... Bainbridge's real subject is less a portrayal of an embryonic monster than a subtle revelation of the social enfeeblement that let him grow and prosper." *Winter Garden,* published in 1980, weaves a satirical tale of a group of artists who visit the Soviet Union by invitation. In the *New York Times Book Review,* Valerie Brooks comments that the work "is razor sharp, most appealing and somewhat resembles a quicksilver Stravinsky-Balanchine ballet. An unusual combination of characters and events creates mystery and tension." Marital discord proves the theme of *Watson's Apology,* Bainbridge's 1984 novel based on a notorious Victorian murder trial. According to Merle Rubin in the *Chicago Tribune Book World,* using the framework of documents surrounding the court case, "Bainbridge weaves her fictional fabrication: thickly detailed, redolent of the specific time and place, and suffused in the grimly desperate atmosphere of a misbegotten marriage."

Critics find much to praise in Bainbridge's many works of fiction. Edith Milton notes that the author "mocks at the same time our lives' drab imitation of fiction, and our fictions' bright imitation of life. Though her impact is that of satire, and though her joke is really very good, her method has the purity of certain photographs, where a closeness of focus, a magnification of detail, turns organic confusion and the ugliness of the familiar into geometry." *Times Literary Supplement* reviewer Diane Johnson writes of the Bainbridge novels: "Like a family of gifted eccentrics, they are diverse, yet there are strong similarities, as there always must be in the work of an original and accomplished writer.... The plots each with its lurking catastrophe are similar, the characters, each so memorable in his way, are similar too.... Her characters don't have illusions, they have bruises—always bruises of the spirit, often literal bruises, and sometimes lacerations." In *The Spectator,* Peter Ackroyd concludes that Bainbridge "observes the margins, she patrols the corners, where the great events of the day—where even 'life' itself—are seen only as a dusty and wayward reflection. This meant that her novels were always strikingly odd, and she has earned a well deserved reputation as one of our funniest writers."

Bainbridge has also adapted several of her novels for the screen and has served as a host-commentator on two British Broadcasting Corporation travel serials. Answering the demands of her growing readership, she has traveled widely in Great Britain, Europe, and the United States, always expressing a willingness to discuss the wellsprings from which her works have sprung. She once told *CA* that she writes to work out her own "personal obsessions," because she believes that writing, "like old photographs, gives a record by which past experience can be remembered." *New York Review of Books* essayist Frank

Kermode characterizes Bainbridge's ability as "an odd and in a muted way fantastic talent, as is perhaps necessary in modern English writers who manage to escape the rather stifling conditions of normal contemporary competence." In the *New York Times Book Review,* Guy Davenport makes the observation that Bainbridge "has her comic eye on cultural confusion. She makes us see that it goes deeper than we think and touches more widely than we had imagined. The most appalling muddles can still be laughed at, and laughter is a kind of understanding."

AVOCATIONAL INTERESTS: Painting.

BIOGRAPHICAL/CRITICAL SOURCES:

BOOKS

Contemporary Literary Criticism, Gale, Volume IV, 1975, Volume V, 1976, Volume VIII, 1978, Volume X, 1979, Volume XIV, 1980, Volume XVIII, 1981, Volume XXII, 1982.
Dictionary of Literary Biography, Volume XIV: *British Novelists since 1960,* Gale, 1983.

PERIODICALS

Albion, Volume XI, 1979.
Antioch Review, fall, 1979.
Atlantic, March, 1979.
Books and Bookmen, January, 1974, December, 1977, November, 1978, February, 1980.
Chicago Tribune Book World, April 8, 1979, January 12, 1986.
Christian Science Monitor, April 9, 1979.
Detroit News, April 29, 1979, April 27, 1980.
Encounter, February, 1975, February, 1976.
Hudson Review, winter, 1977-78.
Listener, November 29, 1973, November 20, 1980.
London Magazine, January, 1978, April-May, 1979.
London Review of Books, November 20-December 3, 1980.
Los Angeles Times, July 12, 1983.
Los Angeles Times Book Review, May 18, 1980, April 25, 1982, September 9, 1984, January 12, 1986.
Ms., December, 1974, August, 1977.
National Review, September 17, 1976.
New Leader, September 2, 1974, May 5, 1980.
New Republic, September 28, 1974, May 24, 1975, March 25, 1978, June 16, 1979.
New Review, November, 1977.
New Statesman, November 1, 1974, November 10, 1978, December 21-28, 1979, November 25, 1985.
Newsweek, August 12, 1974, March 19, 1979, April 7, 1979.
New Yorker, April 25, 1977.
New York Review of Books, May 16, 1974, July 15, 1976, April 5, 1979, July 17, 1980, October 26, 1984.
New York Times, August 21, 1974, May 26, 1975, March 17, 1976, March 1, 1978, March 7, 1979, May 18, 1979, March 5, 1980, March 13, 1981, September 6, 1984, July 11, 1987.
New York Times Book Review, September 30, 1973, September 15, 1974, June 8, 1975, May 16, 1976, March 20, 1977, February 26, 1978, March 11, 1979, April 13, 1980, March 1, 1981, March 21, 1982, September 23, 1984, October 20, 1985.
Publishers Weekly, March 15, 1976, April 9, 1979.
Saturday Review, July 26, 1975, April 2, 1977.
Spectator, November 2, 1974, October 11, 1975, October 9, 1976, October 1, 1977, November 11, 1978, December

8, 1979, November 1, 1980, April 28, 1984, November 3, 1984.

Sunday Times Magazine, February 17, 1980.

Time, November 11, 1974.

Times (London), September 3, 1981, April 5, 1984, August 17, 1984, October 4, 1984.

Times Literary Supplement, October 6, 1972, September 28, 1973, November 1, 1974, October 3, 1975, November 3, 1978, December 1, 1978, February 29, 1980, October 31, 1980, August 14, 1981, September 11, 1981, October 5, 1984, December 20, 1985, October 17, 1986, April 24, 1987.

Voice Literary Supplement, October, 1985.

Washington Post, April 8, 1980, March 5, 1981.

Washington Post Book World, December 4, 1977, August 20, 1978, April 15, 1979, September 23, 1984, November 17, 1985, July 26, 1987.

Yale Review, winter, 1978.†

—*Sketch by Anne Janette Johnson*

*   *   *

BAKER, William Joseph   1938-

PERSONAL: Born January 28, 1938, in Chattanooga, Tenn.; son of W. C. and Ethel (Seay) Baker; married Christina Lee Looper, June 5, 1961; children: Christina Joy, Cynthia Lee, Clara Ellen, Catherine Ann. *Education:* Furman University, B.A., 1960; Southeastern Seminary, B.D., 1963; Cambridge University, Ph.D., 1967.

ADDRESSES: Home—42 Grant St., Bangor, Me. 04401. *Office*—Department of History, University of Maine, Orono, Me. 04473.

CAREER: East Tennessee State University, Johnson City, assistant professor of history, 1966-67; Tusculum College, Greenville, Tenn., assistant professor of history and head of department, 1967-69; University of North Carolina, Charlotte, Bailey lecturer in history, 1970; University of Maine, Orono, assistant professor, 1970-73, associate professor of history, 1973-82, professor of history, 1982—. Visiting fellow, Institute for the Study of Social History, Warwick University, 1985. Member of Ford Foundation Medieval and Renaissance Institute, summer, 1968. Historical consultant to Paramount Pictures for "The Jesse Owens Story," 1984.

MEMBER: American Historical Association, Conference on British Studies.

AWARDS, HONORS: Grants from American Philosophical Society, 1969-70, 1977.

WRITINGS:

(Editor) *America Perceived: A View From Abroad in the Nineteenth Century,* Pendulum Press, 1974.

Beyond Port and Prejudice: Charles Lloyd of Oxford, 1784-1829, University of Maine Press, 1981.

Sports in the Western World, Rowman & Littlefield, 1982.

(Editor with James A. Rog) *Sports and the Humanities,* University of Maine Press, 1983.

Jesse Owens: An American Life, Free Press, 1986.

(Editor with Gerald P. Bodet, Peter N. Stearns, and Michael D. Richards) *Makers of Modern Europe,* Ginn Press, 1987.

(Editor with James A. Mangan) *Sport in Africa: Essays in Social History,* Holmes & Meier, 1987.

Contributor to academic journals. Member of editorial boards of *Journal of Sports History,* 1978-84, and *British Journal of*

Sports History, 1984-86. Executive editor of *International Journal of Sports History,* 1987—.

*   *   *

BALDWIN, James (Arthur)   1924-1987

PERSONAL: Born August 2, 1924, in New York, N.Y.; died of stomach cancer December 1 (some sources say November 30), 1987, in St. Paul de Vence, France; son of David (a clergyman and factory worker) and Berdis (Jones) Baldwin. *Education:* Graduate of De Witt Clinton High School, New York, N.Y., 1942.

ADDRESSES: Home—St. Paul de Vence, France. *Agent*—Edward Acton, Inc., 17 Grove St., New York, N.Y. 10014.

CAREER: Writer, 1944-87. Youth minister at Fireside Pentecostal Assembly, New York, N.Y., 1938-42; variously employed as handyman, dishwasher, waiter, and office boy in New York City, and in defense work in Belle Meade, N.J., 1942-46. Lecturer on racial issues at universities in the United States and Europe, 1957-87. Director of play, "Fortune and Men's Eyes," in Istanbul, Turkey, 1970, and film, "The Inheritance," 1973.

MEMBER: Congress on Racial Equality (member of national advisory board), American Academy and Institute of Arts and Letters, Authors League, International PEN, Dramatists Guild, Actors' Studio, National Committee for a Sane Nuclear Policy.

AWARDS, HONORS: Eugene F. Saxton fellowship, 1945; Rosenwald fellowship, 1948; Guggenheim fellowship, 1954; National Institute of Arts and Letters grant for literature, 1956; Ford Foundation grant, 1959; National Conference of Christians and Jews Brotherhood Award, 1962, for *Nobody Knows My Name: More Notes of a Native Son;* George Polk Memorial Award, 1963, for magazine articles; Foreign Drama Critics Award, 1964, for *Blues for Mister Charlie;* D.Litt. from the University of British Columbia, Vancouver, 1964; National Association of Independent Schools Award, 1964, for *The Fire Next Time;* American Book Award nomination, 1980, for *Just above My Head;* named Commander of the Legion of Honor (France), 1986.

WRITINGS:

FICTION

Go Tell It on the Mountain (novel), Knopf, 1953.

Giovanni's Room (novel; also see below), Dial, 1956, reprinted, Transworld, 1977.

Another Country (novel), Dial, 1962.

Going to Meet the Man (short stories), Dial, 1965.

(Contributor) *American Negro Short Stories,* Hill & Wang, 1966.

Tell Me How Long the Train's Been Gone (novel), Dial, 1968.

If Beale Street Could Talk (novel), Dial, 1974.

Little Man, Little Man: A Story of Childhood (juvenile), M. Joseph, 1976, Dial, 1977.

Just above My Head (novel), Dial, 1979.

Also author of *Harlem Quartet* (novel), 1987.

NONFICTION

Autobiographical Notes, Knopf, 1953.

Notes of a Native Son (essays), Beacon Press, 1955.

Nobody Knows My Name: More Notes of a Native Son (essays), Dial, 1961.

The Fire Next Time, Dial, 1963.

(Author of text) Richard Avedon, *Nothing Pesonal* (photographic portraits), Atheneum, 1964.

(With others) *Black Anti-Semitism and Jewish Racism,* R. W. Baron, 1969.

(With Kenneth Kaunda) Carl Ordung, editor, *Menschenwuerde und Gerechtigkeit* (essays delivered at the fourth assembly of the World Council of Churches), Union-Verlag, 1969.

(With Margaret Mead) *A Rap on Race* (transcripted conversation), Lippincott, 1971.

No Name in the Street (essays), Dial, 1972.

(With Francoise Giroud) *Cesar: Compressions d'or,* Hachette, 1973.

(With Nikki Giovanni) *A Dialogue* (transcribed conversation), Lippincott, 1973.

The Devil Finds Work (essays), Dial, 1976.

(With others) John Henrik Clarke, editor, *Harlem, U.S.A.: The Story of a City within a City,* Seven Seas [Berlin], 1976.

The Evidence of Things Not Seen, Holt, 1985.

The Price of the Ticket: Collected Nonfiction 1948-1985, St. Martin's, 1985.

(With others) Michael J. Weber, editor, *Perspectives: Angles on African Art,* Center for African Art, 1987.

PLAYS

The Amen Corner (first produced in Washington, D.C. at Howard University, 1955; produced on Broadway at Ethel Barrymore Theatre, April 15, 1965), Dial, 1968.

"Giovanni's Room" (based on novel of same title), first produced in New York City at Actors' Studio, 1957.

Blues for Mister Charlie (first produced on Broadway at ANTA Theatre, April 23, 1964), Dial, 1964.

One Day, When I Was Lost: A Scenario (screenplay; based on *The Autobiography of Malcolm X,* by Alex Haley), M. Joseph, 1972, Dial, 1973.

"A Deed for the King of Spain," first produced in New York City at American Center for Stanislavski Theatre Art, January 24, 1974.

Also author of "The Welcome Table," 1987.

OTHER

Jimmy's Blues: Selected Poems, M. Joseph, 1983, St. Martin's, 1985.

Contributor of book reviews and essays to numerous periodicals in the United States and abroad, including *Harper's, Nation, Esquire, Playboy, Partisan Review, Mademoiselle,* and *New Yorker.*

WORK IN PROGRESS: A study of the life of Martin Luther King, Jr.

SIDELIGHTS: A novelist and essayist of considerable renown, James Baldwin bore articulate witness to the unhappy consequences of American racial strife. Baldwin's writing career began in the last years of legislated segregation; his fame as a social observer grew in tandem with the civil rights movement as he mirrored blacks' aspirations, disappointments, and coping strategies in a hostile society. *Tri-Quarterly* contributor Robert A. Bone declared that Baldwin's publications "have had a stunning impact on our cultural life" because the author ". . . succeeded in transposing the entire discussion of American race relations to the interior plane; it is a major breakthrough for the American imagination." In his novels, plays,

and essays alike, Baldwin explored the psychological implications of racism for both the oppressed and the oppressor. Bestsellers such as *Nobody Knows My Name: More Notes of a Native Son* and *The Fire Next Time* acquainted wide audiences with his highly personal observations and his sense of urgency in the face of rising black bitterness. As Juan Williams noted in the *Washington Post,* long before Baldwin's death, his writings "became a standard of literary realism. . . . Given the messy nature of racial hatred, of the half-truths, blasphemies and lies that make up American life, Baldwin's accuracy in reproducing that world stands as a remarkable achievement. . . . Black people reading Baldwin knew he wrote the truth. White people reading Baldwin sensed his truth about the lives of black people and the sins of a racist nation."

Critics accorded Baldwin high praise for both his style and his themes. "Baldwin has carved a literary niche through his exploration of 'the mystery of the human being' in his art," observed Louis H. Pratt in *James Baldwin.* "His short stories, novels, and plays shed the light of reality upon the darkness of our illusions, while the essays bring a boldness, courage, and cool logic to bear on the most crucial questions of humanity with which this country has yet to be faced." In the *College Language Association Journal,* Therman B. O'Daniel called Baldwin "the gifted professor of that primary element, genuine talent. . . . Secondly he is a very intelligent and deeply perceptive observer of our multifarious contemporary society. . . . In the third place, Baldwin is a bold and courageous writer who is not afraid to search into the dark corners of our social consciences, and to force out into public view many of the hidden, sordid skeletons of our society. . . . Then, of course, there is Baldwin's literary style which is a fourth major reason for his success as a writer. His prose . . . possesses a crystal clearness and a passionately poetic rhythm that makes it most appealing." *Saturday Review* correspondent Benjamin De Mott concluded that Baldwin "retains a place in an extremely select group: That composed of the few genuinely indispensible American writers. He owes his rank partly to the qualities of responsiveness that have marked his work from the beginning. . . . Time and time over in fiction as in reportage, Baldwin tears himself free of his rhetorical fastenings and stands forth on the page utterly absorbed in the reality of the person before him, strung with his nerves, riveted to his feelings, breathing his breath."

Baldwin's central preoccupation as a writer lay in "his insistence on removing, layer by layer, the hardened skin with which Americans shield themselves from their country," according to Orde Coombs in the *New York Times Book Review.* The author saw himself as a "disturber of the peace"—one who revealed uncomfortable truths to a society mired in complacency. Pratt found Baldwin "engaged in a perpetual battle to overrule our objections and continue his probe into the very depths of our past. His constant concern is the catastrophic failure of the American Dream and the devastating inability of the American people to deal with that calamity." Pratt uncovered a further assumption in Baldwin's work; namely, that all of mankind is united by virtue of common humanity. "Consequently," Pratt stated, "the ultimate purpose of the writer, from Baldwin's perspective, is to discover that sphere of commonality where, although differences exist, those dissimilarities are stripped of their power to block communication and stifle human intercourse." The major impediment in this search for commonality, according to Baldwin, is white society's entrenched moral cowardice, a condition that through longstanding tradition equates blackness with dark impulses, carnality and chaos. By denying blacks' essential humanity so simplistically, the author argued, whites inflict psychic damage on blacks and suffer self-estrangement—a ''fatal bewilderment,'' to quote Bone. Baldwin's essays exposed the dangerous implications of this destructive way of thinking; his fictional characters occasionally achieve interracial harmony after having made the bold leap of understanding he advocated. In the *British Journal of Sociology,* Beau Fly Jones claimed that Baldwin was one of the first black writers ''to discuss with such insight the psychological handicaps that most Negroes must face; and to realize the complexities of Negro-white relations in so many different contexts. In redefining what has been called the Negro problem as white, he has forced the majority race to look at the damage it has done, and its own role in that destruction.''

Dictionary of Literary Biography essayist John W. Roberts felt that Baldwin's ''evolution as a writer of the first order constitutes a narrative as dramatic and compelling as his best story.'' Baldwin was born and raised in Harlem under very trying circumstances. His stepfather, an evangelical preacher, struggled to support a large family and demanded the most rigorous religious behavior from his nine children. Roberts wrote: ''Baldwin's ambivalent relationship with his stepfather served as a constant source of tension during his formative years and informs some of his best mature writings.... The demands of caring for younger siblings and his stepfather's religious convictions in large part shielded the boy from the harsh realities of Harlem street life during the 1930s.'' As a youth Baldwin read constantly and even tried writing; he was an excellent student who sought escape from his environment through literature, movies, and theatre. During the summer of his fourteenth birthday he underwent a dramatic religious conversion, partly in response to his nascent sexuality and partly as a further buffer against the ever-present temptations of drugs and crime. He served as a junior minister for three years at the Fireside Pentecostal Assembly, but gradually he lost his desire to preach as he began to question blacks' acceptance of Christian tenets that had, in essence, been used to enslave them.

Shortly after he graduated from high school in 1942, Baldwin was compelled to find work in order to help support his brothers and sisters; mental instability had incapacitated his stepfather. Baldwin took a job in the defense industry in Belle Meade, New Jersey, and there, not for the first time, he was confronted with racism, discrimination, and the debilitating regulations of segregation. The experiences in New Jersey were closely followed by his stepfather's death, after which Baldwin determined to make writing his sole profession. He moved to Greenwich Village and began to write a novel, supporting himself by performing a variety of odd jobs. In 1944 he met author Richard Wright, who helped him to land the 1945 Eugene F. Saxton fellowship. Despite the financial freedom the fellowship provided, Baldwin was unable to complete his novel that year. He found the social tenor of the United States increasingly stifling even though such prestigious periodicals as the *Nation, New Leader,* and *Commentary* began to accept his essays and short stories for publication. Eventually, in 1948, he moved to Paris, using funds from a Rosenwald Foundation fellowship to pay his passage. Most critics feel that this journey abroad was fundamental to Baldwin's development as an author.

''Once I found myself on the other side of the ocean,'' Baldwin told the *New York Times,* ''I could see where I came from very clearly, and I could see that I carried myself, which is my home, with me. You can never escape that. I am the grandson of a slave, and I am a writer. I must deal with both.'' Through some difficult financial and emotional periods, Baldwin undertook a process of self-realization that included both an acceptance of his heritage and an admittance of his bisexuality. Bone noted that Europe gave the young author many things: ''It gave him a world perspective from which to approach the question of his own identity. It gave him a tender love affair which would dominate the pages of his later fiction. But above all, Europe gave him back himself. The immediate fruit of self-recovery was a great creative outburst. First came two [works] of reconciliation with his racial heritage. *Go Tell It on the Mountain* and *The Amen Corner* represent a search for roots, a surrender to tradition, an acceptance of the Negro past. Then came a series of essays which probe, deeper than anyone has dared, the psychic history of this nation. They are a moving record of a man's struggle to define the forces that have shaped him, in order that he may accept himself.''

Many critics view Baldwin's essays as his most significant contribution to American literature. Works such as *Notes of a Native Son, Nobody Knows My Name, The Fire Next Time, No Name in the Street* and *The Evidence of Things Not Seen* ''serve to illuminate the condition of the black man in twentieth-century America,'' according to Pratt. Highly personal and analytical, the essays probe deeper than the mere provincial problems of white versus black to uncover the essential issues of self-determination, identity, and reality. ''An artist is a sort of emotional or spiritual historian,'' Baldwin told *Life* magazine. ''His role is to make you realize the doom and glory of knowing who you are and what you are. He has to tell, because nobody else *can* tell, what it is like to be alive.'' *South Atlantic Quarterly* contributor Fred L. Standley asserted that this quest for personal identity ''is indispensible in Baldwin's opinion and the failure to experience such is indicative of a fatal weakness in human life.'' C. W. E. Bigsby elaborated in *The Fifties: Fiction, Poetry, Drama:* ''Baldwin's central theme is the need to accept reality as a necessary foundation for individual identity and thus a logical prerequisite for the kind of saving love in which he places his whole faith. For some this reality is one's racial or sexual nature, for others it is the ineluctable fact of death.... Baldwin sees this simple progression as an urgent formula not only for the redemption of individual men but for the survival of mankind. In this at least black and white are as one and the Negro's much-vaunted search for identity can be seen as part and parcel of the American's long-standing need for self-definition.''

Inevitably, however, Baldwin's assessments of the ''sweet'' and ''bitter'' experiences in his own life led him to describe ''the exact place where private chaos and social outrage meet,'' according to Alfred Kazin in *Contemporaries.* Eugenia Collier described this confrontation in *Black World:* ''On all levels, personal and political . . . life is a wild chaos of paradox, hidden meanings, and dilemmas. This chaos arises from man's inability—or reluctance to face the truth about his own nature. As a result of this self-imposed blindness, men erect an elaborate facade of myth, tradition, and ritual behind which crouch, invisible, their true selves. It is this blindness on the part of Euro-Americans which has created and perpetuated the vicious racism which threatens to destroy this nation.'' In his essays on the 1950s and early 1960s, Baldwin sought to explain black experiences to a white readership as he warned whites about the potential destruction their psychic blindness might wreak. *Massachusetts Review* contributor David Levin noted that the author came to represent ''for 'white' Americans, the eloquent, indignant prophet of an oppressed people, a voice speaking . . . in an all but desperate, final effort to bring us out of what he calls our innocence before it is (if it is not already) too late. This voice calls us to our immediate duty for the sake of our own humanity as well as our own safety. It demands that we stop regarding the Negro as an abstraction, an invisible man; that we begin to recognize each Negro in his 'full weight and complexity' as a human being; that we face the horrible reality of our past and present treatment of Negroes—a reality we do not know and do not want to know.'' In *Ebony* magazine, Allan Morrison observed that Baldwin evinced an awareness ''that the audience for most of his non-fictional writings is white and he uses every forum at his disposal to drive home the basic truths of Negro-white relations in America as he sees them. His function here is to interpret whites to themselves and at the same time voice the Negro's protest against his role in a Jim Crow society.''

Because Baldwin sought to inform and confront whites, and because his fiction contains interracial love affairs—both homosexual and heterosexual—he came under attack from the writers of the Black Arts Movement, who called for a literature exclusively by and for blacks. Baldwin refused to align himself with the movement; he continued to call himself an ''American writer'' as opposed to a ''black writer'' and continued to confront the issues facing a multi-racial society. Eldridge Cleaver, in his book *Soul on Ice,* accused Baldwin of a hatred of blacks and ''a shameful, fanatical fawning'' love of whites. What Cleaver saw as complicity with whites, Baldwin saw rather as an attempt to alter the real daily environment with which American blacks have been faced all their lives. Pratt noted, however, that Baldwin's efforts to ''shake up'' his white readers put him ''at odds with current white literary trends'' as well as with the Black Arts Movement. Pratt explained that Baldwin labored under the belief ''that mainstream art is directed toward a complacent and apathetic audience, and it is designed to confirm and reinforce that sense of well-being. . . . Baldwin's writings are, by their very nature, iconoclastic. While Black Arts focuses on a black-oriented artistry, Baldwin is concerned with the destruction of the fantasies and delusions of a contented audience which is determined to avoid reality.'' As the civil rights movement gained momentum, Baldwin escalated his attacks on white complacency from the speaking platform as well as from the pages of books and magazines. *Nobody Knows My Name* and *The Fire Next Time* both sold more than a million copies; both were cited for their predictions of black violence in desperate response to white oppression. In *Encounter,* Colin MacInnes concluded that the reason ''why Baldwin speaks to us of another race is that he still believes us worthy of a warning: he has not yet despaired of making us *feel* the dilemma we all chat about so glibly, . . . and of trying to save us from the agonies that we too will suffer if the Negro people are driven beyond the ultimate point of desperation.''

Retrospective analyses of Baldwin's essays highlight the characteristic prose style that gives his works literary merit beyond the mere dissemination of ideas. In *A World More Attractive: A View of Modern Literature and Politics,* Irving Howe placed the author among ''the two or three greatest essayists this country has ever produced.'' Howe claimed that Baldwin ''has brought a new luster to the essay as an art form, a form with possibilities for discursive reflection and concrete drama. . . . The style of these essays is a remarkable instance of the way in which a grave and sustained eloquence—the rhythm of oratory, . . . held firm and hard—can be employed in an age

deeply suspicious of rhetorical prowess.'' ''Baldwin has shown more concern for the painful exactness of prose style than any other modern American writer,'' noted David Littlejohn in *Black on White: A Critical Survey of Writing by American Negroes.* ''He picks up words with heavy care, then sets them, one by one, with a cool and loving precision that one can feel in the reading. . . . The exhilarating exhaustion of reading his best essays—which in itself may be a proof of their honesty and value—demands that the reader measure up, and forces him to learn.''

Baldwin's fiction expanded his exploration of the ''full weight and complexity'' of the individual in a society prone to callousness and categorization. His loosely autobiographical works probed the milieus with which he was most familiar—black evangelical churches, jazz clubs, stifling Southern towns, and the Harlem ghetto. In *The Black American Writer: Fiction,* Brian Lee maintained that Baldwin's ''essays explore the ambiguities and ironies of a life lived on two levels—that of the Negro and that of the man—and they have spoken eloquently to and for a whole generation. But Baldwin's feelings about the condition—alternating moods of sadness and bitterness— are best expressed in the paradoxes confronting the haunted heroes of his novels and stories. The possible modes of existence for anyone seeking refuge from a society which refuses to acknowledge one's humanity are necessarily limited, and Baldwin has explored with some thoroughness the various emotional and spiritual alternatives available to his retreating protagonists.'' Pratt felt that Baldwin's fictive artistry ''not only documents the dilemma of the black man in American society, but it also bears witness to the struggle of the artist against the overwhelming forces of oppression. Almost invariably, his protagonists are artists. . . . Each character is engaged in the pursuit of artistic fulfillment which, for Baldwin, becomes symbolic of the quest for identity.''

Love, both sexual and spiritual, was an essential component of Baldwin's characters' quests for self-realization. John W. Aldridge observed in the *Saturday Review* that sexual love ''emerges in his novels as a kind of universal anodyne for the disease of racial separatism, as a means not only of achieving personal identity but also of transcending false categories of color and gender.'' Homosexual encounters emerged as the principal means to achieve important revelations; as Bigsby explained, Baldwin felt that ''it is the homosexual, virtually alone, who can offer a selfless and genuine love because he alone has a real sense of himself, having accepted his own nature.'' Baldwin did not see love as a ''saving grace,'' however; his vision, given the circumstances of the lives he encountered, was more cynical than optimistic. In his introduction to *James Baldwin: A Collection of Critical Essays,* Kenneth Kinnamon wrote: ''If the search for love has its origin in the desire of a child for emotional security, its arena is an adult world which involves it in struggle and pain. Stasis must yield to motion, innocence to experience, security to risk. This is the lesson that . . . saves Baldwin's central fictional theme from sentimentality. . . . Similarly, love as an agent of racial reconciliation and national survival is not for Baldwin a vague yearning for an innocuous brotherhood, but an agonized confrontation with reality, leading to the struggle to transform it. It is a quest for truth through a recognition of the primacy of suffering and injustice in the American past.'' Pratt also concluded that in Baldwin's novels, ''love is often extended, frequently denied, seldom fulfilled. As reflections of our contemporary American society, the novels stand as forthright indictments of the intolerable conditions that we have accepted unquestioningly as a way of life.''

Black family life—the charged emotional atmosphere between parents and children, brothers and sisters—provided another major theme in Baldwin's fiction. This was especially apparent in his first and best-known novel, *Go Tell It on the Mountain,* the story of a Harlem teenager's struggles with a repressive father and with religious conversion. According to Roberts, *Go Tell It on the Mountain* ''proved that James Baldwin had become a writer of enormous power and skill. [It] was an essential book for Baldwin. Although clearly a fictional work, it chronicles two of the most problematic aspects of his existence as a young man: a son's relationship to his stepfather and the impact of fundamentalist religion on the consciousness of a young boy.'' In her work entitled *James Baldwin,* Carolyn Wedin Sylvander praised Baldwin's family chronicle particularly because the author ''is dealing comprehensively and emotionally with the hot issue of race relations in the United States at a time . . . when neither white ignorance and prejudice nor black powerlessness is conducive to holistic depictions of black experience.'' Indeed, the overt confrontation between the races that characterizes Baldwin's later work was here portrayed as a peripheral threat, a danger greater than, but less immediate than, the potential damage inflicted by parents on children. Sylvander wrote: ''It is painfully, dramatically, structurally clear throughout *Go Tell It on the Mountain* that the struggles every individual faces—with sexuality, with guilt, with pain, with love—are passed on, generation to generation.'' Littlejohn described Baldwin's treatment of this essential American theme as ''autobiography-as-exorcism, . . .a lyrical, painful, ritual exercise whose necessity and intensity the reader feels.'' Pratt likewise stated that *Go Tell It on the Mountain* ''stands as an honest, intensive, self-analysis, functioning simultaneously to illuminate self, society, and mankind as a whole.''

In addition to his numerous books, Baldwin was one of the few black authors to have had more than one of his plays produced on Broadway. Both *The Amen Corner,* another treatment of storefront pentecostal religion, and *Blues for Mister Charlie,* a drama based on the racially-motivated murder of Emmett Till in 1955, had successful Broadway runs and numerous revivals. Standley commented in the *Dictionary of Literary Biography* that in both plays, ''as in his other literary works, Baldwin explores a variety of thematic concerns: the historical significance and the potential explosiveness in black-white relations; the necessity for developing a sexual and psychological consciousness and identity; the intertwining of love and power in the universal scheme of existence as well as in the structures of society; the misplaced priorities in the value systems in America; and the responsibility of the artist to promote the evolution of the individual and the society.'' In *The Black American Writer: Poetry and Drama,* Walter Meserve offered remarks on Baldwin's abilities as a playwright. ''Baldwin tries to use the theatre as a pulpit for his ideas,'' Meserve stated. ''Mainly his plays are thesis plays—talky, over-written, and cliche dialogue and some stereotypes, preachy, and argumentative. Essentially, Baldwin is not particularly dramatic, but he can be extremely eloquent, compelling, and sometimes irritating as a playwright committed to his approach to life.'' Meserve added, however, that although the author was criticized for creating stereotypes, ''his major characters are the most successful and memorable aspects of his plays. People are important to Baldwin, and their problems, generally embedded in their agonizing souls, stimulate him to write. . . . A humanitarian, sensitive to the needs and struggles of man,

he writes of inner turmoil, spiritual disruption, the consequence upon people of the burdens of the world, both White and Black.''

Baldwin's oratorical prowess—honed in the pulpit as a youth—brought him into great demand as a speaker during the civil rights era. Sylvander observed that national attention ''began to turn toward him as a spokesperson for blacks, not as much because of his novels as his essays, debates, interviews, panel discussions.'' Baldwin embraced his role as racial spokesman reluctantly and grew increasingly disillusioned as the American public ''disarmed him with celebrity, [fell] in love with his eccentricities, and institutionalized his outrage . . . into prime-time entertainment,'' to quote Aldridge. Nor was Baldwin able to feel that his speeches and essays were producing social change—the assassinations of three of his associates, Medgar Evers, Martin Luther King, Jr., and Malcolm X, shattered his remaining hopes for racial reconciliation. Kinnamon remarked that by 1972, the year Baldwin published *No Name in the Street,* ''the redemptive possibilities of love seemed exhausted in that terrible decade of assassination, riot, and repression. . . . Social love had now become for Baldwin more a rueful memory than an alternative to disaster.'' *London Magazine* contributor James Campbell also noted that by 1972 ''Baldwin the saviour had turned into Baldwin the soldier. What [observers] failed to notice was that he was still the preacher and the prophet, that his passion and rage were mingled with detachment, and that his gloomy prognostications were based on powerful observation and an understanding of the past which compelled their pessimism.''

Many critics took Baldwin to task for the stridency and gloom that overtook his writings. ''To function as a voice of outrage month after month for a decade and more strains heart and mind, and rhetoric as well,'' declared Benjamin DeMott in the *Saturday Review.* ''The consequence is a writing style ever on the edge of being winded by too many summonses to intensity.'' *New Republic* correspondent Nathan Glazer likewise stated that Baldwin had become ''an accusing voice, but the accusation is so broad, so general, so all-embracing, that the rhetoric disappears into the wind.'' Stephen Donadio offered a similar opinion in the *Partisan Review:* ''As his notoriety increased, his personality was oversimplified, appropriated, and consumed. . . . Mr. Baldwin created a situation in which the eye of the audience was fixed on the author as a performer, and the urgency of the race problem in America became a backdrop for elaborate rhetorical assaults which could be dutifully acknowledged but forgotten with a sigh.''

Baldwin's passionate detractors were offset by equally passionate defenders, however. Sylvander wrote: ''Wading through vehement and sometimes shallow reactions to the deep water of the statements and works themselves, one is struck repeatedly by the power of Baldwin's prose, and by our continuing need, as readers and as citizens, for his steadying apocalyptic vision. Finally, in his fantastic, experientially various, wide-ranging, searching, and committed life, one can find a vigorous model for venturing beyond charted areas.'' Charles Newman made two points in *James Baldwin: A Collection of Critical Essays.* First, Newman noted that Baldwin's experience is ''unique among our artists in that his artistic achievements mesh so precisely with his historical circumstances. He is that nostaglic type—an artist speaking for a genuinely visible revolution.'' Second, Newman maintained that as an observer of this painful revolution, ''almost alone [Baldwin] . . . continued to confront the unmanageable questions of modern society, rather than creating a nuclear family in which semantic fantasies may be enacted with no reference to the larger world except that it stinks.'' Kinnamon concluded: ''James Baldwin has always been concerned with the most personal and intimate areas of experience and also with the broadest questions of national and global destiny—and with the intricate interrelationships between the two. Whatever the final assessment of his literary achievement, it is clear that his voice—simultaneously that of victim, witness, and prophet—has been among the most urgent of our time.''

At the time of his death from cancer late in 1987, Baldwin was still working on two projects—a play, ''The Welcome Table,'' and a biography of Martin Luther King, Jr. Although he lived primarily in France, he had never relinquished his United States citizenship and preferred to think of himself as a ''commuter'' rather than as an expatriate. The publication of his collected essays, *The Price of the Ticket: Collected Nonfiction 1948-1985,* and his subsequent death sparked reassessments of his career and comments on the quality of his lasting legacy. ''Mr. Baldwin has become a kind of prophet, a man who has been able to give a public issue all its deeper moral, historical, and personal significance,'' remarked Robert F. Sayre in *Contemporary American Novelists.* ''. . . Certainly one mark of his achievement, . . . is that whatever deeper comprehension of the race issue Americans now possess has been in some way shaped by him. And this is to have shaped their comprehension of themselves as well.'' Sylvander asserted that what emerges from the whole of Baldwin's work is ''a kind of absolute conviction and passion and honesty that is nothing less than courageous. . . . Baldwin has shared his struggle with his readers for a purpose—to demonstrate that our suffering is our bridge to one another.''

Perhaps the most telling demonstration of the results of Baldwin's achievement came from other black writers. Orde Coombs, for instance, concluded: ''Because he existed we felt that the racial miasma that swirled around us would not consume us, and it is not too much to say that this man saved our lives, or at least, gave us the necessary ammunition to face what we knew would continue to be a hostile and condescending world.'' Playwright Amiri Baraka phrased a similar assessment even more eloquently in his funeral eulogy to Baldwin. ''This man traveled the earth like its history and its biographer,'' Baraka said. ''He reported, criticized, made beautiful, analyzed, cajoled, lyricized, attacked, sang, made us think, made us better, made us consciously human. . . . He made us feel . . . that we could defend ourselves or define ourselves, that we were in the world not merely as animate slaves, but as terrifyingly sensitive measurers of what is good or evil, beautiful or ugly. This is the power of his spirit. This is the bond which created our love for him.'' In a posthumous profile for the *Washington Post,* Juan Williams wrote: ''The success of Baldwin's effort as the witness is evidenced time and again by the people, black and white, gay and straight, famous and anonymous, whose humanity he unveiled in his writings. America and the literary world are far richer for his witness. The proof of a shared humanity across the divides of race, class and more is the testament that the preacher's son, James Arthur Baldwin, has left us.''

MEDIA ADAPTATIONS: The Amen Corner was adapted as a musical stage play, ''Amen Corner,'' by Garry Sherman, Peter Udell and Philip Rose, and produced on Broadway at the Nederlander Theater, November 10, 1983. *Go Tell It on the Mountain* was dramatized under the same title for the Public Broadcasting System's ''American Playhouse'' series, January 14, 1985.

BIOGRAPHICAL/CRITICAL SOURCES:

BOOKS

Balakian, Nona, and Charles Simmons, editors, *The Creative Present: Notes on Contemporary Fiction,* Doubleday, 1963.

Bigsby, C.W.E., *Confrontation and Commitment: A Study of Contemporary American Drama,* University of Missouri Press, 1967.

Bigsby, C.W.E., editor, *The Black American Writer,* Volume I: *Fiction,* Volume II: *Poetry and Drama,* Everett/Edwards, 1969.

Bone, Robert, *The Negro Novel in America,* Yale University Press, 1965.

Brustein, Robert, *Seasons of Discontent: Dramatic Opinions 1959-1965,* Simon & Schuster, 1965.

Burgess, Anthony, *The Novel Now: A Guide to Contemporary Fiction,* Norton, 1967.

Chapman, Abraham, editor, *Black Voices: An Anthology of Afro-American Literature,* New American Library, 1968.

Cleaver, Eldridge, *Soul on Ice,* McGraw-Hill, 1968.

Cohn, Ruby, *Dialogue in American Drama,* Indiana University Press, 1971.

Concise Dictionary of American Literary Biography: The New Consciousness 1941-1968, Gale, 1987.

Contemporary Authors Bibliographical Series, Volume I: *American Novelists,* Gale, 1986.

Contemporary Literary Criticism, Gale, Volume I, 1973, Volume II, 1974, Volume III, 1975, Volume IV, 1975, Volume V, 1976, Volume VIII, 1978, Volume XIII, 1980, Volume XV, 1980, Volume XVII, 1981, Volume XLII, 1987.

Cook, M. G., editor, *Modern Black Novelists: A Collection of Critical Essays,* Prentice-Hall, 1971.

Culture for the Millions, Van Nostrand, 1959.

Dance, Daryl, *Black American Writers: Bibliographical Essays,* St. Martin's, 1978.

Dictionary of Literary Biography, Gale, Volume II: *American Novelists since World War II,* 1978, Volume VIII: *Twentieth-Century American Dramatists,* 1981, Volume XXXIII: *Afro-American Fiction Writers after 1955,* 1984.

Eckman, Fern Marja, *The Furious Passage of James Baldwin,* M. Evans, 1966.

French, Warren, editor, *The Fifties: Fiction, Poetry, Drama,* Everett/Edwards, 1970.

Frost, David, *The Americans,* Stein & Day, 1970.

Gayle, Addison, Jr., *The Way of the World: The Black Novel in America,* Anchor Press, 1975.

Gibson, Donald B., editor, *Five Black Writers: Essays on Wright, Ellison, Baldwin, Hughes, and LeRoi Jones,* New York University Press, 1970.

Hesse, H. Ober, editor, *The Nature of a Humane Society,* Fortress, 1976.

Hill, Herbert, editor, *Anger and Beyond,* Harper, 1966.

Howe, Irving, *A World More Attractive: A View of Modern Literature and Politics,* Horizon Press, 1963.

Hyman, Stanley Edgar, *Standards: A Chronicle of Books for Our Time,* Horizon Press, 1966.

Kazin, Alfred, *Bright Book of Life: American Novelists & Storytellers from Hemingway to Mailer,* Little, Brown, 1973.

Kazin, Alfred, *Contemporaries,* Little, Brown, 1962.

King, Malcolm, *Baldwin: Three Interviews,* Wesleyan University Press, 1985.

Kinnamon, Kenneth, editor, *James Baldwin: A Collection of Critical Essays,* Prentice-Hall, 1974.

Klein, Marcus, *After Alienation: American Novels in Mid-Century,* World Publishing, 1964.

Littlejohn, David, *Black on White: A Critical Survey of Writing by American Negroes,* Viking, 1966.

Lumley, Frederick, *New Trends in 20th Century Drama: A Survey since Ibsen and Shaw,* Oxford University Press, 1967.

Macebuh, Stanley, *James Baldwin: A Critical Study,* Joseph Okpaku, 1973.

Major, Clarence, *The Dark and Feeling: Black American Writers and Their Work,* Joseph Okpaku, 1974.

Moeller, Karin, *The Theme of Identity in the Essays of James Baldwin,* Acta Universitatis Gotoburgensis, 1975.

Moore, Harry T., editor, *Contemporary American Novelists,* Southern Illinois University Press, 1964.

O'Daniel, Therman B., *James Baldwin: A Critical Evaluation,* Howard University Press, 1977.

Panichas, George A., *The Politics of Twentieth-Century Novelists,* Hawthorn, 1971.

Podhoretz, Norman, *Doings and Undoings,* Farrar, Straus, 1964.

Pratt, Louis Hill, *James Baldwin,* Twayne, 1978.

Rosenblatt, Roger, *Black Fiction,* Harvard University Press, 1974.

Sheed, Wilfrid, *The Morning After,* Farrar, Straus, 1971.

Simon, John, *Uneasy Stages: Chronicle of the New York Theatre,* Random House, 1975.

Sontag, Susan, *Against Interpretation and Other Essays,* Farrar, Straus, 1966.

Standley, Fred and Nancy Standley, *James Baldwin: A Reference Guide,* G. K. Hall, 1980.

Standley, Fred and Nancy Standley, editors, *Critical Essays on James Baldwin,* G. K. Hall, 1981.

Sylvander, Carolyn Wedin, *James Baldwin,* Frederick Ungar, 1980.

Turner, Darwin T., *Afro-American Writers,* Appleton, 1970.

Weatherby, William J., *Squaring Off: Mailer vs. Baldwin,* Mason/Charter, 1977.

Williams, John A. and Charles F. Harris, editors, *Amistad I: Writings on Black History and Culture,* Random House, 1970.

Williams, Sherley Anne, *Give Birth to Brightness: A Thematic Study in Neo-Black Literature,* Dial, 1972.

PERIODICALS

America, March 16, 1963.

Atlanta Constitution, May 19, 1976.

Atlantic, July, 1961, July, 1962, March, 1963, July, 1968, June, 1972.

Atlas, March, 1967.

Black Scholar, December, 1973-January, 1974.

Black World, June, 1972, December, 1974.

Books and Bookmen, August, 1968, September, 1972, December, 1979.

Book Week, May 31, 1964, September 26, 1965.

British Journal of Sociology, June, 1966.

Bulletin of Bibliography, January-April, 1965, May-August, 1968.

Chicago Tribune, September 16, 1979, October 10, 1979, November 15, 1985, December 16, 1987.

Christian Science Monitor, July 19, 1962.

College Language Association Journal, Number 7, 1964, Number 10, 1966, March, 1967.

Commentary, November, 1953, January, 1957, December, 1961, June, 1968, December, 1979, December, 1985.

Commonweal, May 22, 1953, December 8, 1961, October 26, 1962, December 7, 1962, October 12, 1973, June 24, 1977.

Critical Quarterly, summer, 1964.

Critique, winter, 1964-65.

Cross Currents, summer, 1961.

Ebony, October, 1961.

Ecumenical Review, October, 1968.

Encounter, August, 1963, July, 1965.

English Journal, May, 1973.

Esquire, July, 1968.

Freedomways, summer, 1963.

Globe & Mail (Toronto), January 11, 1986.

Harper's, March, 1963, September, 1968.

Hollins Critic, December, 1965.

Hudson Review, autumn, 1964, autumn, 1968.

Intellectual Digest, July, 1972.

Life, May 24, 1963, June 7, 1968, June 4, 1971, July 30, 1971.

Listener, July 25, 1974.

London Magazine, December, 1979-January, 1980.

Lone Star Book Review, January-February, 1980.

Look, July 23, 1968.

Los Angeles Times Book Review, December 1, 1985.

Mademoiselle, May, 1963.

Massachusetts Review, winter, 1964.

Midcontinent American Studies Journal, fall, 1963.

Muhammad Speaks, September 8, 1973, September 15, 1973, September 29, 1973, October 6, 1973.

Nation, July 14, 1962, November 17, 1962, March 2, 1963, December 13, 1965, April 10, 1972, June 10, 1968, July 3, 1976, November 3, 1979.

National Observer, March 6, 1967, June 3, 1968.

National Review, May 21, 1963, July 7, 1972.

Negro American Literature Forum, spring, 1969, winter, 1972.

Negro Digest, June, 1963, October, 1966, April, 1967.

New Leader, June 3, 1968, May 27, 1974, May 24, 1976.

New Republic, December 17, 1956, August 7, 1961, August 27, 1962, November 27, 1965, August 17, 1968, June 15, 1974, November 24, 1979, December 30, 1985.

New Statesman, July 13, 1962, July 19, 1963, December 4, 1964, November 3, 1972, June 28, 1974, February 25, 1977, November 29, 1985.

Newsweek, February 4, 1963, June 3, 1969, May 27, 1974.

New Yorker, June 20, 1953, November 25, 1961, August 4, 1962, July 8, 1974, November 26, 1979.

New York Herald Tribune Book Review, June 17, 1962.

New York Review of Books, May 28, 1964, December 17, 1964, December 9, 1965, June 29, 1972, June 13, 1974, December 6, 1979, January 21, 1988.

New York Times, May 3, 1964, April 16, 1965, May 31, 1968, February 2, 1969, May 21, 1971, May 17, 1974, June 4, 1976, September 4, 1977, September 21, 1979, September 23, 1979, November 11, 1983, January 10, 1985, January 14, 1985.

New York Times Book Review, February 26, 1956, July 2, 1961, June 24, 1962, December 12, 1965, June 2, 1968, June 23, 1968, May 28, 1972, May 19, 1974, May 2, 1976, September 23, 1979, May 24, 1984.

New York Times Magazine, March 7, 1965.

Nickel Review, February 27, 1970.

Observer, November 24, 1985, April 6, 1986.

Partisan Review, summer, 1963, winter, 1966.

People, January 7, 1980.

Progressive, August, 1972.

Queen's Quarterly, summer, 1965.

San Francisco Chronicle, June 28, 1962.

Saturday Review, December 1, 1956, July 1, 1961, July 7, 1962, February 2, 1963, February 8, 1964, May 2, 1964, November 6, 1965, June 1, 1968, May 27, 1972, June 15, 1974, January 5, 1980.

Sight and Sound, autumn, 1976.

South Atlantic Quarterly, summer, 1966.

Southern Humanities Review, winter, 1970.

Southern Review, summer, 1985.

Spectator, July 12, 1968, July 6, 1974, January 11, 1986, April 26, 1986.

Studies in Short Fiction, summer, 1975, fall, 1977.

Time, June 30, 1961, June 29, 1962, November 6, 1964, June 7, 1968, June 10, 1974.

Times (London), May 15, 1986, January 19, 1987, January 22, 1987.

Times Educational Supplement, December 27, 1985.

Times Literary Supplement, July 26, 1963, December 10, 1964, October 28, 1965, July 4, 1968, April 28, 1972, November 17, 1972, June 21, 1974, December 21, 1979, August 2, 1984, January 24, 1986, September 19, 1986.

Tri-Quarterly, winter, 1965.

Twentieth-Century Literature, April, 1967.

Village Voice, October 29, 1979, January 12, 1988.

Vogue, July, 1964.

Washington Post, September 23, 1979, October 15, 1979, September 9, 1983, September 25, 1983.

Washington Post Book World, September 11, 1977, September 23, 1979, October 27, 1985, December 9, 1987.

Western Humanities Review, spring, 1968.

World Literature Today, spring, 1980.

Yale Review, October, 1966.

OBITUARIES:

PERIODICALS

Chicago Tribune, December 2, 1987.

Detroit Free Press, December 2, 1987, December 8, 1987.

Los Angeles Times, December 2, 1987.

New York Times, December 2, 1987, December 9, 1987.

Philadelphia Inquirer, December 2, 1987, December 9, 1987, December 14, 1987.

Times (London), December 2, 1987.

Washington Post, December 2, 1987.†

—Sketch by Anne Janette Johnson

*　　*　　*

BALL, Desmond (John) 1947-

PERSONAL: Born May 20, 1947, in Nyah West, Victoria, Australia; son of John Selwyn and Dorothy Louisa (Cook) Ball. *Education:* Australian National University, B.Ec. (with first class honors), 1969, Ph.D., 1972. *Politics:* Labor. *Religion:* None.

ADDRESSES: Home—5 Gormanston Cres., Deakin, Australian Capital Territory, Australia. *Office*—Strategic and Defence Studies Centre, Australian National University, Canberra, Australian Capital Territory 2600, Australia.

CAREER: University of Sidney, Sidney, Australia, lecturer in international relations, 1972-74; Australian National University, Canberra, Strategic and Defense Studies Centre, research fellow, 1974-78, senior research fellow, 1978-79; International Institute for Strategic Studies, London, England, re-

search associate, 1979-80; Australian National University, Strategic and Defense Studies Centre, fellow, 1980-82, senior fellow, 1982-84, head, 1984—, Institute of Advanced Studies, special professor, 1987—. Visiting scholar at Institute of War and Peace Studies, Columbia University, 1970; research fellow at Center for International Affairs, Harvard University, 1972-73; senior research associate, Center for Strategic and International Affairs, University of California, Los Angeles. Lecturer at universities and military staff colleges in Australia and abroad, including Australian Staff College, Royal Australian Air Force Staff College, Royal Australian Naval Staff College, Joint Services Staff College, United States Air Force Academy, University of California, Los Angeles, University of California, San Diego, University of California, Berkeley, National War College, Columbia University, Cornell University, University of South Carolina, the American University, and Oxford University; lecturer at Wilson Center and Smithsonian Institution. Conducted field research in the United States, Belgium, Canada, Norway, Sweden, Finland, the Soviet Union, West Germany, France, the United Kingdom, India, Italy, Sri Lanka, the Philippines, South Korea, Pakistan, Thailand, Papua New Guinea, the Netherlands, Greece, Malaysia, New Zealand, People's Republic of China, Japan, Austria, and Indonesia. Strategy consultant, Joint Services Staff College; consultant to government bodies and authorities and to RAND Corporation and other public corporations. *Military service:* Australian Army, 1965-66.

MEMBER: United Services Institute, Returned Services League of Australia (member of defense committee, National Headquarters, 1981-86).

WRITINGS:

(Editor and contributor) *The Future of Tactical Airpower in the Defense of Australia,* Australian National University, 1977.

(With J. O. Langtry, Robert J. O'Neill, and Ross Babbage) *The Development of Australian Army Officers for the 1980's* (monograph), Strategic and Defense Studies Centre, Australian National University, 1978.

(With Langtry) *Controlling Australia's Threat Environment: A Methodology for Planning Australian Defense Force Development,* Australian National University, 1979.

Politics and Force Levels: The Strategic Missile Program of the Kennedy Administration, University of California Press, 1980.

A Suitable Piece of Real Estate: American Installations in Australia, Hale & Ironmonger, 1980.

(Editor with Langtry, and contributor) *Problems of Mobilization in Defense of Australia,* Phoenix Defense Publications, 1980.

Can Nuclear War Be Controlled? (monograph), International Institute for Strategic Studies, 1981.

Strategic Survey 1980-1981, International Institute for Strategic Studies, 1981.

(Editor) *Strategy and Defense: Australian Essays,* Allen & Unwin [Sidney], 1982, 2nd edition (with Cathryn Downes), 1987.

(Editor with Langtry, and contributor) *Civil Defense and Australia's Security in the Nuclear Age,* Strategic and Defense Studies Centre, Australian National University and Allen & Unwin [Sidney], 1983.

(Editor) *The ANZAC Connection,* Allen & Unwin, 1985.

(With Jeffrey T. Richelson) *The Ties That Bind: Intelligence Cooperation between the UKUSA Countries—the United*

Kingdom, the United States of America, Canada, Australia and New Zealand, Allen & Unwin, 1985.

(With Langtry and J. D. Stevenson) *Defend the North: The Case for the Alice Springs-Darwin Railway,* Allen & Unwin, 1985.

(With Ernest McNamara, Robin Ward, Langtry, and Richard Q. Agnew) *Australia's Defense Resources: A Compendium of Data,* Pergamon Press Australia, 1986.

(Editor with Langtry) *A Vulnerable Country? Civil Resources in the Defense of Australia,* Australian National University Press, 1986.

(Editor with Richelson) *Strategic Nuclear Targeting,* Cornell University Press, 1986.

(Editor with Andrew Mack) *The Future of Arms Control,* Australian National University Press, 1986.

(With Michael Brooks and Ian McNicol) *Star Wars,* Victorian Association for Peace Studies, 1986.

The Comprehensive Test Ban Treaty: A Role for Australia (monograph), Peace Research Centre, Australian National University, 1986.

(With Hans A. Bethe, Bruce G. Blair, Paul Bracken, and others) *Crisis Stability and Nuclear War* (report), American Academy of Arts and Sciences and Cornell University Peace Studies Program, 1987.

A Base for Debate: The U.S. Satellite Station at Nurrungar, Allen & Unwin, 1987.

(Editor) *Air Power in the Defense of Australia,* Pergamon Press [Sidney], 1987.

The Politics of Australian Defense Decision-Making, University of Queensland Press, 1987.

Secret Satellites Over Australia, Allen & Unwin (Sidney), 1987.

(Editor) *Aboriginals in the Defense of Australia,* Australian National University Press, 1987.

Pine Gap and the U.S. Geostationary SIGINT Satellite System, Allen & Unwin, 1987.

CONTRIBUTOR

O'Neill, editor, *The Strategic Nuclear Balance,* Australian National University, 1975.

Roger Scott and J. L. Richardson, editors, *The First Thousand Days of Labor,* Canberra College of Advanced Education, 1975.

H. G. Gelber, editor, *The Strategic Nuclear Balance,* University of Tasmania, 1976.

O'Neill, editor, *The Defense of Australia: Fundamental New Aspects,* Australian National University, 1977.

Strategic Survey 1977, International Institute for Strategic Studies, 1978.

Fedor Mediansky, editor, *The Military and Australia's Defence,* Longman Cheshire, 1979.

Jae Kyu Park, editor, *Prospects for Nuclear Proliferation in Developing Countries,* Institute for Far Eastern Studies, Kyungnam University, 1979.

Strategic Survey 1979, International Institute for Strategic Studies, 1980.

Coral Bell, editor, *Agenda for the Eighties,* Australian National University Press, 1980.

J. M. Roherty, editor, *Defense Policy Formation: Towards Comparative Analysis,* Carolina Academic Press, 1980.

Lawrence S. Hagen, editor, *The Crisis in Western Security,* Croom Helm, 1982.

O'Neill and D. M. Horner, editors, *Australia's Defense in the 1980's,* University of Queensland Press, 1982.

Bell, editor, *Academic Studies and International Politics,* Department of International Relations, Australian National University, 1982.

T. B. Millar, editor, *International Security in the Southeast Asian and Southwest Pacific Region,* University of Queensland Press, 1983.

John F. Reichart and Steven R. Sturm, editors, *American Defense Policy,* 5th edition, Johns Hopkins University Press, 1983.

Robert J. Art and Kenneth N. Waltz, editors, *The Use of Force: International Politics and Foreign Policy,* 2nd edition, University Press of America, 1983.

John Reeves and Kelvin Thompson, editors, *Labor Essays 1983: Policies and Programs for the Labor Government,* Drummond, 1983.

Report of Proceedings of a Study on the Protection of the Australian Public from Ionising Radiation, Australian Counter Disaster College, Natural Disasters Organisation, Department of Defense, 1983.

T. J. Hearn, editor, *Arms, Disarmament and New Zealand,* Department of University Extension, University of Otago, 1983.

Michael Denborough, editor, *Australia and Nuclear War,* Croom Helm, 1983.

Bernard Brodie, Michael D. Intriligator, and Roman Kolkowicz, editors, *National Security and International Stability,* Oelgeschlager, Gunn & Hain, 1984.

Hans Gunter Brauch, editor, *Kernwaffen und Rustungskontrolle: Ein Interdisciplinares Studienbuch,* Westdeutscher Verlag, 1984.

James A. Schear, editor, *Nuclear Weapons Proliferation and Nuclear Risk,* International Institute for Strategic Studies and Gower Publishing, 1984.

Kolkowicz and Neil Joeck, editors, *Arms Control and International Security,* Westview Press, 1984.

Paul Joseph and Simon Rosenblum, editors, *Search for Sanity: The Politics of Nuclear Weapons and Disarmament,* South End Press, 1984.

Steven E. Miller, editor, *Strategy and Nuclear Deterrence: An International Security Reader,* Princeton University Press, 1984.

George Edward Thibault, editor, *The Art and Practice of Military Strategy,* National Defense University, 1984.

Charles W. Kegley, Jr., and Eugene R. Wittkopf, editors, *The Nuclear Reader: Strategy, Weapons, War,* St. Martin's, 1985.

Ciro E. Zoppo and Charles Zorgbibe, editors, *On Geopolitics: Classical and Nuclear,* NATO Scientific Affairs Division and Martinus Nijhoff Publishers, 1985.

P. Edward Haley, David M. Keithly and Jack Merritt, editors, *Nuclear Strategy, Arms Control, and the Future,* Westview Press, 1985.

Claude A. Buss, editor, *National Security Interests in the Pacific Basin,* Hoover Institution Press, 1985.

Fred D. Byers, editor, *The C I Handbook,* EW Communications, 1986.

Kolkowicz and Ellen Propper Mickiewicz, editors, *The Soviet Calculus of Nuclear War,* Lexington Books, 1986.

Bruce L. Gumble, editor, *The International Countermeasures Handbook,* 12th edition, EW Communications, 1987, 13th edition, 1987.

Robert Travis Scott, editor, *The Race for Security: Arms and Arms Control in the Reagan Years,* Lexington Books, 1987.

Samuel F. Wells, Jr., and Robert S. Litwak, editors, *Strategic Defenses and Soviet-American Relations,* Ballinger Publishing, 1987.

OTHER

Also author of *The Ears of the Commissars: Soviet Signals Intelligence (SIGINT) Capabilities and Operations,* 1988; also author, with Rex Mortimer and Peter King, of *CORPOL-PLAN,* a political scenario for QANTAS Airways Ltd, 1973. Also editor with Langtry of *The Northern Territory in the Defense of Australia,* 1987, and, with Babbage, of *Geographic Information Systems and the Defense of Australia,* 1987. Contributor to *The Australian Encyclopedia.* Contributor to periodicals, including *Australian Outlook, Current Affairs Bulletin, Pacific Defense Reporter, Arms Control Today, Defense and Foreign Affairs, International Security* and others.

SIDELIGHTS: Desmond Ball told *CA:* "I believe very strongly that information on such critical public policy issues as strategy and defence should be much more accessible to the general public and that there should be much greater public debate on these issues. Information on defense matters is often unnecessarily cloaked in secrecy, while the academic literature is frequently filled with jargon and available only in specialized journals. Granted that defense is a highly technical subject, I believe that it remains possible to write about developments in national strategic policies and military capabilities in a way that is accessible to any interested person. Such accessibility on defense matters, no less than on other matters of public policy, is essential to the proper functioning of democracy."

BIOGRAPHICAL/CRITICAL SOURCES:

PERIODICALS

Times (London), November 26, 1986.
Times Literary Supplement, March 13, 1987.

*   *   *

BALL, Zachary
See JANAS, Frankie-Lee

*   *   *

BAMBARA, Toni Cade   1939-
(Toni Cade)

PERSONAL: Surname originally Cade, name legally changed in 1970; born March 25, 1939, in New York, N.Y.; daughter of Helen Brent Henderson Cade. *Education:* Queens College (now Queens College of the City University of New York), B.A., 1959; University of Florence, studied Commedia dell'Arte, 1961; student at Ecole de Mime Etienne Decroux in Paris, 1961, New York, 1963; City College of the City University of New York, M.A., 1964; additional study in linguistics at New York University and New School for Social Research. Also attended Katherine Dunham Dance Studio, Syvilla Fort School of Dance, Clark Center of Performing Arts, 1958-69, and Studio Museum of Harlem Film Institute, 1970.

ADDRESSES: Home—5720 Wissahickon Ave., Apt. E12, Philadelphia, Pa. 19144.

CAREER: Free-lance writer and lecturer. Social investigator, New York State Department of Welfare, 1959-61; director of recreation in psychiatry department, Metropolitan Hospital, New York City, 1961-62; program director, Colony House Community Center, New York City, 1962-65; English instruc-

tor in SEEK Program, City College of the City University of New York, New York City, 1965-69, and in New Careers Program of Newark, N.J., 1969; assistant professor, Livingston College, Rutgers University, New Brunswick, N.J., 1969-74; visiting professor of African American studies, Stephens College, Columbia, Mo., 1975; Atlanta University, visiting professor, 1977, research mentor and instructor, School of Social Work, 1977, 1979. Founder and director of Pamoja Writers Collective, 1976-85. Production artist-in-residence for Neighborhood Arts Center, 1975-79, Stephens College, 1976, and Spelman College, 1978-79. Production consultant, WHYY-TV, Philadelphia, Pa. Has conducted numerous workshops on writing, self-publishing, and community organizing for community centers, museums, prisons, libraries, and universities. Has lectured and conducted literary readings at many institutions, including the Library of Congress, Smithsonian Institute, Afro-American Museum of History and Culture and for numerous other organizations and universities. Humanities consultant to New Jersey Department of Corrections, 1974, Institute of Language Arts, Emory University, 1980, and New York Institute for Human Services Training, 1978. Art consultant to New York State Arts Council, 1974, Georgia State Arts Council, 1976, 1981, National Endowment for the Arts, 1980, and the Black Arts South Conference, 1981.

MEMBER: National Association of Third World Writers, Screen Writers Guild of America, African American Film Society, Sisters in Support of South African Sisterhood.

AWARDS, HONORS: Peter Pauper Press Award, 1958; John Golden Award for Fiction from Queens College (now Queens College of the City University of New York), 1959; Theatre of Black Experience award, 1969; Rutgers University research fellowship, 1972; Black Child Development Institute service award, 1973; Black Rose Award from *Encore,* 1973; Black Community Award from Livingston College, Rutgers University, 1974; award from the National Association of Negro Business and Professional Women's Club League; George Washington Carver Distinguished African American Lecturer Award from Simpson College; *Ebony*'s Achievement in the Arts Award; Black Arts Award from University of Missouri; American Book Award, 1981, for *The Salt Eaters;* Best Documentary of 1986 Award from Pennsylvania Association of Broadcasters and Documentary Award from National Black Programming Consortium, both 1986, for "The Bombing of Osage."

WRITINGS:

Gorilla, My Love (short stories), Random House, 1972.
The Sea Birds Are Still Alive (short stories), Random House, 1977.
The Salt Eaters (novel), Random House, 1980.
(Author of preface) Cecelia Smith, *Cracks,* Select Press, 1980.
(Author of foreword) Cherrie Moraga and Gloria Anzaldua, editors, *This Bridge Called My Back: Radical Women of Color,* Persephone Press, 1981.
(Author of foreword) *The Sanctified Church: Collected Essays by Zora Neale Hurston,* Turtle Island, 1982.
If Blessing Comes (novel), Random House, 1987.

SCREENPLAYS

"Zora," produced by WGBH-TV, 1971.
"The Johnson Girls," produced by National Educational Television, 1972.
"Transactions," produced by School of Social Work, Atlanta University, 1979.

"The Long Night," produced by American Broadcasting Co., 1981.

"Epitaph for Willie," produced by K. Heran Productions, Inc., 1982.

"Tar Baby" (based on Toni Morrison's novel), produced by Sanger/Brooks Film Productions, 1984.

"Raymond's Run," produced by Public Broadcasting System, 1985.

"The Bombing of Osage," produced by WHYY-TV, 1986.

"Cecil B. Moore: Master Tactician of Direct Action," produced by WHYY-TV, 1987.

EDITOR

(And contributor, under name Toni Cade) *The Black Woman*, New American Library, 1970.

(And contributor) *Tales and Stories for Black Folks*, Doubleday, 1971.

(With Leah Wise) *Southern Black Utterances Today*, Institute for Southern Studies, 1975.

CONTRIBUTOR

Addison Gayle, Jr., editor, *Black Expression: Essays by and about Black Americans in the Creative Arts*, Weybright, 1969.

Jules Chametsky, editor, *Black and White in American Culture*, University of Massachusetts Press, 1970.

Ruth Miller, *Backgrounds to Blackamerican Literature*, Chandler Publishing, 1971.

Janet Sternburg, editor, *The Writer on Her Work*, Norton, 1980.

Paul H. Connolly, editor, *On Essays: A Reader for Writers*, Harper, 1981.

Howe, editor, *Women Working*, Feminist Press, 1982.

Mari Evans, editor, *Black Women Writers (1950-1980): A Critical Evaluation*, Doubleday, 1984.

Baraka and Baraka, editors, *Confirmations*, Morrow, 1984.

Claudia Tate, editor, *The Black Writer at Work*, Howard University Press, 1984.

OTHER

Contributor to *What's Happnin, Somethin Else*, and *Another Eye*, all readers published by Scott, Foresman, 1969-70. Contributor of articles and book and film reviews to *Massachusetts Review, Negro Digest, Liberator, Prairie Schooner, Redbook, Audience, Black Works, Umbra, Onyx*, and other periodicals. Guest editor of special issue of *Southern Exposure*, summer, 1976, devoted to new southern black writers and visual artists.

SIDELIGHTS: Toni Cade Bambara is a well known and respected civil rights activist, professor of English and of African American studies, editor of two anthologies of black literature, and author of short stories and a novel. According to Alice A. Deck in the *Dictionary of Literary Biography*, "in many ways Toni Cade Bambara is one of the best representatives of the group of Afro-American writers who, during the 1960s, became directly involved in the cultural and sociopolitical activities in urban communities across the country." However, Deck points out that "Bambara is one of the few who continued to work within the black urban communties (filming, lecturing, organizing, and reading from her works at rallies and conferences), producing imaginative reenactments of these experiences in her fiction. In addition, Bambara established herself over the years as an educator, teaching in colleges and independent community schools in various cities on the East Coast."

Bambara's first two books of fiction, *Gorilla, My Love* and *The Sea Birds Are Still Alive*, are collections of her short stories. Susan Lardner remarks in the *New Yorker* that the stories in these two works, "describing the lives of black people in the North and the South, could be more exactly typed as vignettes and significant anecdotes, although a few of them are fairly long. . . . All are notable for their purposefulness, a more or less explicit inspirational angle, and a distinctive motion of the prose, which swings from colloquial narrative to precarious metaphorical heights and over to street talk, at which Bambara is unbeatable."

In a review of *Gorilla, My Love*, for example, a writer remarks in the *Saturday Review* that the stories "are among the best portraits of black life to have appeared in some time. [They are] written in a breezy, engaging style that owes a good deal to street dialect." A critic writing in *Newsweek* makes a similar observation, describing Bambara's second collection of short stories, *The Sea Birds Are Still Alive*, in this manner: "Bambara directs her vigorous sense and sensibility to black neighborhoods in big cities, with occasional trips to small Southern towns. . . . The stories start and stop like rapid-fire conversations conducted in a rhythmic, black-inflected, sweet-and-sour language." In fact, according to Anne Tyler in the *Washington Post Book World*, Bambara's particular style of narration is one of the most distinctive qualities of her writing. "What pulls us along is the language of [her] characters, which is startlingly beautiful without once striking a false note," notes Tyler. "Everything these people say, you feel, ordinary, real-life people are saying right now on any street corner. It's only that the rest of us didn't realize it was sheer poetry they were speaking."

In terms of plot, Bambara tends to avoid linear development in favor of presenting "situations that build like improvisations of a melody," as a *Newsweek* reviewer explains. Commenting on *Gorilla, My Love*, Bell Gale Chevigny observes in the *Village Voice* that despite the "often sketchy" plots, the stories are always "lavish in their strokes—there are elaborate illustrations, soaring asides, aggressive sub-plots. They are never didactic, but they abound in far-out common sense, exotic home truths."

Numerous reviewers have also remarked on Bambara's sensitive portrayals of her characters and the handling of their situations, portrayals that are marked by an affectionate warmth and pride. Laura Marcus writes in the *Times Literary Supplement* that Bambara "presents black culture as embattled but unbowed. . . . Bambara depicts black communities in which ties of blood and friendship are fiercely defended." Deck expands on this idea, remarking that "the basic implication of all of Toni Cade Bambara's stories is that there is an undercurrent of caring for one's neighbors that sustains black Americans. In her view the presence of those individuals who intend to do harm to people is counterbalanced by as many if not more persons who have a genuine concern for other people."

C. D. B. Bryan admires this expression of the author's concern for other people, declaring in the *New York Times Book Review* that "Bambara tells me more about being black through her quiet, proud, silly, tender, hip, acute, loving stories than any amount of literary polemicizing could hope to do. She writes about love: a love for one's family, one's friends, one's race, one's neighborhood and it is the sort of love that comes with maturity and inner peace." According to Bryan, "all of [Bambara's] stories share the affection that their narrator feels for the subject, an affection that is sometimes terribly painful, at other times fiercely proud. But at all times it is an affection that is so genuinely *genus homo sapiens* that her stories are not only *black* stories.''

In 1980, Bambara published her first novel, a generally well-received work entitled *The Salt Eaters*. Written in an almost dream-like style, *The Salt Eaters* explores the relationship between two women with totally different backgrounds and lifestyles brought together by a suicide attempt by one of the women. John Leonard, who describes the book as ''extraordinary,'' writes in the *New York Times* that *The Salt Eaters* ''is almost an incantation, poem-drunk, myth-happy, mud-caked, jazz-ridden, prodigal in meanings, a kite and a mask. It astonishes because Toni Cade Bambara is so adept at switching from politics to legend, from particularities of character to prehistorical song, from LaSalle Street to voodoo. It is as if she jived the very stones to groan.''

In a *Times Literary Supplement* review, Carol Rumens states that *The Salt Eaters* ''is a hymn to individual courage, a sombre message of hope that has confronted the late twentieth-century pathology of racist violence and is still able to articulate its faith in 'the dream'.'' And John Wideman notes in the *New York Times Book Review:* ''In her highly acclaimed fiction and in lectures, [Bambara] emphasizes the necessity for black people to maintain their best traditions, to remain healthy and whole as they struggle for political power. *The Salt Eaters*, her first novel, eloquently summarizes and extends the abiding concerns of her previous work.''

MEDIA ADAPTATIONS: Three of Bambara's short stories ''Gorilla, My Love,'' ''Medley,'' and ''Witchbird'' have been adapted for film.

BIOGRAPHICAL/CRITICAL SOURCES:

BOOKS

Contemporary Literary Criticism, Volume XXIX, Gale, 1984.
Dictionary of Literary Biography, Volume XXXVIII: *Afro-American Writers after 1955: Dramatists and Prose Writers*, Gale, 1985.
Parker, Bell and Beverly Guy-Sheftall, *Sturdy Black Bridges: Visions of Black Women in Literature*, Doubleday, 1979.
Prenshaw, Peggy Whitman, editor, *Women Writers of the Contemporary South*, University Press of Mississippi, 1984.
Tate, Claudia, editor, *Black Women Writers at Work*, Continuum, 1983.

PERIODICALS

Black World, July, 1973.
Books of the Times, June, 1980.
Chicago Tribune Book World, March 23, 1980.
Drum, spring, 1982.
First World, Volume II, number 4, 1980.
Los Angeles Times Book Review, May 4, 1980.
Ms., July, 1977, July, 1980.
National Observer, May 9, 1977.
Newsweek, May 2, 1977.
New Yorker, May 5, 1980.
New York Times, October 11, 1972, October 15, 1972, April 4, 1980.
New York Times Book Review, February 21, 1971, May 2, 1971, November 7, 1971, October 15, 1972, December 3, 1972, March 27, 1977, June 1, 1980, November 1, 1981.
Saturday Review, November 18, 1972, December 2, 1972, April 12, 1980.

Sewanee Review, November 18, 1972, December 2, 1972.
Times Literary Supplement, June 18, 1982, September 27, 1985.
Village Voice, April 12, 1973.
Washington Post Book World, November 18, 1973, March 30, 1980.†

—*Sketch by Margaret Mazurkiewicz*

*   *   *

BANDY, (Eugene) Franklin   1914-1987 (Eugene Franklin)

PERSONAL: Born December 15, 1914, in Atlanta, Ga.; died April 11, 1987, in White Plains, N.Y.; son of Eugene Franklin (a professional fund raiser) and Marjorie (Champion) Bandy; married Beth E. Leveson, August 27, 1948; children: Eugene Franklin III, John Champion. *Education:* University of Illinois, A.B., 1938.

ADDRESSES: Home—11 Lincoln Ave., Rye Brook, N.Y. 10573. *Agent*—Collier Associates, 2000 Flat Run Rd., Demain, Ohio 45679; and Anita Diamant, 310 Madison Ave., New York, N.Y. 10017.

CAREER: Cleveland Press, Cleveland, Ohio, reporter, 1936; World Book Publishing Co., Chicago, Ill., editor, 1938-42; Caples Co., New York City, vice-president, 1946-60; Geyer, Morey, Ballard, New York City, vice-president, 1960-63; Buchen Advertising, Inc., New York City, vice-president, 1963-70; Wyman Associates, Inc., New York City, executive vice-president, 1970-73; Pavilion Advertising Agency, New York City, president, 1974-87. *Military service:* U.S. Army, Signal Corps, 1942-46; became captain.

MEMBER: Mystery Writers of America, Authors Guild, Authors League of America, Crimewriter's Association of Great Britain, Private Eye Writers, Overseas Press Club, Overseas Yacht Club.

AWARDS, HONORS: Edgar Allan Poe Award, Mystery Writers of America, 1979, for *Deceit and Deadly Lies*.

WRITINGS:

The Shannonese Hustle, Avon, 1978.
Deceit and Deadly Lies, Charter Books, 1978.
The Blackstock Affair, Charter Books, 1980.
The Farewell Party, Charter Books, 1980.
(Contributor) Lucy Freeman, *The Murder Mystique: Crime Writers on Their Art*, Ungar, 1982.
Athena, Tor, 1987.

UNDER NAME EUGENE FRANKLIN

Murder Trapp, Stein & Day, 1971.
The Money Murders, Stein & Day, 1972.
The Bold House Murders, Stein & Day, 1973.

OTHER

Former staff editor, *World Book Encyclopedia* and Consolidated Book Publishers. Contributor to *Alfred Hitchcock Mystery Magazine*.

WORK IN PROGRESS: A novel.

SIDELIGHTS: Franklin Bandy once told *CA:* ''I've been writing professionally since, at age eleven, I won a dollar prize for the best essay on 'My Summer at Camp Cherokee.' A dollar went a long way in those days, but I was grossly underpaid. The camp used my letter in their advertising brochure for a number of years. To me, fiction seems to offer the greatest challenge, and I get great satisfaction, and much pleasure too, working at it and trying to improve my proficiency in the craft (or art).'' Popular in England, Bandy's books have also been translated into Italian, German, and Japanese.

During the course of his career, Bandy also worked as an editor, reporter, and an advertising and public relations executive. He once indicated that his most interesting public relations assignment was with the government of Ireland. Registered as an ''Agent of a Foreign Power'' with the Justice Department for eleven years, Bandy was primarily concerned with promoting the industrial development of Ireland. The assignment involved frequent travel to Ireland, England, and continental Europe, and afforded Bandy the opportunity to meet with Ireland's President Eamon De Valera.

At the time of his death, Bandy was in the process of completing another novel. His papers are collected at the University of Wyoming.

OBITUARIES:

PERIODICALS

Chicago Tribune, April 15, 1987.
Los Angeles Times, April 15, 1987.
New York Times, April 14, 1987.
Washington Post, April 15, 1987.
White Plains Reporter-Dispatch, April 12, 1987.

[Sketch reviewed by wife, Beth E. Bandy]

*   *   *

BANNER, Charla Ann Leibenguth 1942-
(Charla Ann Leibenguth)

PERSONAL: Born February 6, 1942, in Lafayette, Ind.; daughter of Charles Aaron (a utility storekeeper) and Myrtle (Cooley) Leibenguth; married Glen E. Banner (a newspaper editor), June 23, 1979. *Education:* Purdue University, B.S., 1965, M.S., 1966. *Politics:* Independent. *Religion:* Roman Catholic.

ADDRESSES: Home—1609 South Lafountain, Kokomo, Ind. 46902.

CAREER: Butler University, Indianapolis, Ind., instructor in pharmacy and pharmacy librarian, 1968-73, science librarian, 1973-81, adjunct assistant professor of pharmacy; instructor in pharmacology, Indiana University at Kokomo. Partner of Features Unlimited.

MEMBER: American Auto Racing Writers and Broadcasters Association, Rho Chi, Kappa Epsilon.

WRITINGS:

(Editor wth Susan Ebershoff-Coles; under name Charla Ann Leibenguth) *Motorsports: A Guide to Information Sources,* Gale, 1979.
Trading Post on the Wildcat, Windsor Press, 1987.
(Co-editor) *Automobile: Symbol of Pop Culture,* Oryx, 1988.

Author of ''Wine and Wedges,'' a column in *Zionsville Times,* 1980, and in *Community Messenger,* 1981-82, and of ''Above the Maddening Noise,'' a column in *Community Messenger,* 1981-82. Contributor of articles and reviews to magazines, including *Motor Trend, Health, Grit, Science Digest,* and *Modern People,* sometimes under name Charla Ann Leiben-

guth. Contributing editor, *Auto Racing News;* co-editor of several newsletters.

WORK IN PROGRESS: A novel with her brother, John Leibenguth.

SIDELIGHTS: Charla Banner told *CA:* ''Much of my freelance work now comes from writing for the newsletters we publish. I enjoy the challenge of writing on all aspects of life, but I haven't forgotten that creativity is important in nonfiction as well as fiction, and I strive to keep a fresh perspective in all my articles. I am also co-authoring a novel with my brother, John Leibenguth, and am filled with the joy and challenge of creating our characters and being altered by them.''

*   *   *

BARBET, Pierre
See AVICE, Claude (Pierre Marie)

*   *   *

BARRETT, N. S.
See BARRETT, Norman (S.)

*   *   *

BARRETT, Norman (S.)   1935-
(N. S. Barrett; pseudonyms: C. J. Norman, R. J. Stephen)

PERSONAL: Born August 27, 1935, in London, England; son of Philip Michael and Lily (Permutt) Barrett; married Alicia Cohen (a physical therapist), August 26, 1962; children: Simon, Vanessa. *Education:* St. Catherine's College, Oxford, B.A., 1957, M.A. (with honors), 1960.

ADDRESSES: Home—63 Edgwarebury Gardens, Edgware, Middlesex HA8 8LL, England. *Office*—11 The Quadrant, Manor Park Crescent, Edgware, Middlesex HA8 7LU, England.

CAREER: Furniture Development Council, London, England, research assistant, 1956-59; Pergamon Press Ltd., Oxford, England, sub-editor of scientific journals, 1959-61; Society of the Chemical Industry, London, sub-editor of scientific journals, 1961-62; Field Enterprises, London and Croyden, England, 1962-67, began as style editor of international edition of *World Book,* became copy editor; Publicare Ltd. (editorial services firm), London, founding director, 1967-79; free-lance writer, 1979—. Editorial director of Sackett Publicare Ltd. (publisher), 1977-79; consulting editor for Telegraph Publications, 1987—.

WRITINGS:

Fact Finder, Ward, Lock, 1980.
(With Don Howe) *Super Soccer Skills,* illustrated by Paul Buckle, Granada, 1981.
The Book of Football, Purnell, 1981.
(With Lawrie McMenemy) *Lawrie McMenemy's Book of Soccer,* edited by Wendy Hobson, designed by Richard Smoth, illustrated by James Ferguson, Purnell, 1981.
Football Champions, Purnell, 1982.
Great Moments in Sport, edited by Deborah Brammer, Purnell, 1982.
(With D. Howe) *World Cup '82: Guide to the Competition, the Teams, and the Players,* Daily Telegraph (London), 1982.

Young Footballer's Pocket Book, illustrated by P. Buckle, Purnell, 1982.

Soccer, illustrated by P. Buckle, Granada, 1983.

(With Mel Watman) *Daley Thompson,* Virgin Books, 1984.

(With M. Watman) *Steve Cram,* Virgin Books, 1984.

The All-Action Book of American Football, Century Hutchinson, 1987.

"PICCOLO PICTURE BAFFLERS" SERIES; PUBLISHED BY PAN BOOKS

Sport, designed by Keith Groom, illustrated by Terry Burton, 1978.

(With Lis Sackett and Christopher Tunney) *Super Baffler,* designed by K. Groom, illustrated by T. Burton, 1978.

The World We Live In, designed by K. Groom, illustrated by T. Burton, 1978.

Olympics 1980, designed and illustrated by David Nash, 1980.

"PICTURE LIBRARY" SERIES; PUBLISHED BY F. WATTS

(Under name N. S. Barrett) *Motorcycles,* 1984.

(Under name N. S. Barrett) *Helicopters,* 1984.

(Under name N. S. Barrett) *Trucks,* 1984.

(Under name N. S. Barrett) *Ships,* 1984.

(Under name N. S. Barrett) *Racing Cars,* 1985.

(Under name N. S. Barrett) *Airliners,* 1985.

(Under name N. S. Barrett) *Robots,* 1985.

(Under name N. S. Barrett) *TV and Video,* 1985.

(Under name N. S. Barrett) *Space Shuttle,* 1985.

(Under name N. S. Barrett) *Computers,* 1985.

(Under name N. S. Barrett) *Satellites,* 1985.

(Under name N. S. Barrett) *Lasers and Holograms,* 1985.

(Under name Norman Barrett) *The Moon,* 1985.

(Under name Norman Barrett) *Planets,* 1985.

(Under name Norman Barrett) *Sun and Stars,* 1986.

(Under name Norman Barrett) *Spacecraft,* 1986.

(Under name Norman Barrett) *Night Sky,* 1986.

(Under name Norman Barrett) *Astronauts,* 1986.

(Under pseudonym C. J. Norman) *Tanks,* 1986.

(Under pseudonym C. J. Norman) *Combat Aircraft,* 1986.

(Under pseudonym C. J. Norman) *Aircraft Carriers,* 1986.

(Under pseudonym C. J. Norman) *Warships,* 1986.

(Under pseudonym C. J. Norman) *Military Helicopters,* 1986.

(Under pseudonym R. J. Stephen) *Cranes,* 1987.

(Under pseudonym R. J. Stephen) *Earthmovers,* 1987.

(Under pseudonym R. J. Stephen) *Oil Rigs,* 1987.

(Under pseudonym R. J. Stephen) *Farm Machinery,* 1987.

(Under pseudonym R. J. Stephen) *Undersea Machines,* 1987.

(Under pseudonym R. J. Stephen) *Fire Engines,* 1987.

(Under name Norman Barrett) *BMX Bikes,* 1987.

(Under name Norman Barrett) *Custom Cars,* 1987.

(Under name Norman Barrett) *Trailbikes,* 1987.

(Under name Norman Barrett) *Stunt Riding,* 1987.

(Under name Norman Barrett) *Race Cars,* 1987.

Also author of other titles in this series, including *Dragsters, Windsurfing, Canoeing, Sailing, Hang Gliding, Skydiving, Snow Sports, Monkeys and Apes, Bears, Big Cats, Elephants, Pandas,* and *Polar Animals.*

EDITOR

Purnell's Encyclopedia of Association Football, Purnell, 1972, revised edition published as *Purnell's New Encyclopedia of Association Football,* 1978.

World Soccer from A to Z, Pan Books, 1973.

Purnell's Encyclopedia of Sport, Purnell, 1974.

(And compiler) *Fact Finder,* Hamlyn, 1976.

Purnell's Illustrated Nature Atlas, Purnell, 1977.

World of Knowledge Encyclopedia, Hamlyn, 1977.

Football Champions, Purnell, 1981.

The Battle for the Ashes, Telegraph Publications, 1985.

"I Was There," Telegraph Publications, 1985.

The Battle for the Ashes '87, Telegraph Publications, 1987.

Also editor of *The Game: The Marshall Cavendish Encyclopedia of World Sports, Telegraph Cricket Year Book,* 1982-87, and with Jack Rollin of *Sunday Telegraph Football Year Book,* 1983-86, and *Telegraph Football Year Book,* 1986—. Consulting editor, *The Gambler's Pocket Book,* 1980.

CONTRIBUTOR

Atlas of the Arab World, Daily Telegraph, 1983.

Atlas of the United States of America, Daily Telegraph, 1986.

Macmillan Children's Encyclopedia, Volume X: *Sport and Leisure,* Macmillan, 1986.

Also contributor to *Rothman's Football Yearbook, The Mitchell Beasley Joy of Knowledge Library: The Modern World,,* 1976, *The Hamlyn Pictorial Atlas of the World,* 1976, *Fact Index,* 1978, *Sunday Telegraph Canon Football Year Book,* 1983-86, and the *Telegraph Football Year Book,* 1986—.

OTHER

Author of volumes in the Walt Disney *Sport Goofy Encyclopedia* for Purnell/World Book Encyclopedia, including *The Olympic Games, Team Sports, Football Sports, Bat and Ball Sports, Soccer, Racket Sports, Adventure Sports, Running, Field Events, Water Sports, Combat, On Four Wheels, On Two Wheels, Golf and Target Sports,* and *Animals in Sport.*

SIDELIGHTS: Norman Barrett once told *CA:* "I have been virtually a free-lance editor since I helped to establish Publicare in 1967. I decided to go solo in 1979 and suddenly found myself writing full-time rather than editing and rewriting. Because of my publishing and editorial experience, I am now able to produce books for publishers almost single-handedly: originating, planning, writing, researching pictures, commissioning art work, doing layouts and basic typographical design, marking up copy, and proofreading. My major fields are soccer, the Olympics, sports in general, gambling, children's information books, and general reference works."

Barrett more recently added: "The direction of my writings took a sudden turn in 1984 when I agreed, almost reluctantly, to produce a series of six children's information books for a former colleague. I had not intended to do much writing, as most of the subjects were outside my major areas of interest. However, the nature of the series, picture books for six- to nine-year-olds, with about fifty words of text per page plus captions, demanded concise writing in simple language with a basic vocabulary. In addition, the content would have to be acceptable to both the U.K. and U.S. readers and educationists. I soon found that the only way to meet these requirements would be to write the material myself and have it authenticated by experts. The system worked very well. It has the added advantage that I am obliged to research each subject thoroughly before I write a sentence. The result is a basic manuscript that fits the layout requirements and contains a number of errors which are corrected by the authenticator (who also serves as a consultant during the planning and writing of the book), rather than a factually correct manuscript that has to be rewritten both to fit the layouts and to suit the age range, and which, in the process, may have errors introduced.

"I have now produced eight series, at the rate of twelve books a year, and this makes up about sixty percent of my output. For the last couple of years, I have been using a word processor and this has increased my productivity enormously. It is particularly helpful when I have, say, twelve lines at about thirty-six characters to produce and eleven or thirteen lines won't do."

＊　　＊　　＊

BARRON, Jerome A(ure) 1933-

PERSONAL: Born September 25, 1933, in Tewksbury, Mass.; son of Henry and Sadie (Shafmaster) Barron; married Myra Hymovich (a lawyer), June 18, 1961; children: Jonathan Nathaniel, David Jeremiah, Jennifer Leah. *Education:* Tufts University, A.B. (magna cum laude), 1955; Yale University, LL.B., 1958; George Washington University, LL.M., 1960. *Politics:* Democrat. *Religion:* Jewish.

ADDRESSES: Home—3231 Ellicott St. N.W., Washington, D.C. 20008. *Office*—National Law Center, George Washington University, 2121 Eye St., Washington, D.C. 20052.

CAREER: Admitted to Massachusetts Bar, 1959, and District of Columbia Bar, 1960. U.S. Court of Claims, Washington, D.C., law clerk, 1960-61; Cross, Murphy and Smith (law firm), Washington, D.C., associate, 1961-62; University of North Dakota, Grand Forks, assistant professor of law, 1962-64; University of New Mexico, Albuquerque, visiting associate professor of law, 1964-65; George Washington University, Washington, D.C., associate professor, 1965-68, professor of law, 1968-72; Syracuse University, Syracuse, N.Y., professor of law and dean of College of Law, 1972-73; George Washington University, professor of law, 1973-79, dean of National Center of Law, 1979—. *Military service:* U.S. Army, 1958-59.

MEMBER: American Bar Association, National Lawyers Club, Phi Beta Kappa.

AWARDS, HONORS: Frank Luther Mott research award from Kappa Tau Alpha, 1970, for *Mass Communication Law: Cases and Comment*.

WRITINGS:

(With Donald M. Gillmor) *Mass Communication Law: Cases and Comment*, West Publishing, 1969, supplement, 1971, 4th edition, 1984.
Freedom of the Press for Whom?: The Right of Access to the Mass Media, Indiana University Press, 1973.
(With C. Thomas Dienes) *Constitutional Law, Principles and Policy: Cases and Materials*, Bobbs-Merrill, 1975, supplements, 1976 and 1978, 3rd edition (with Dienes, Wayne McCormack, and Martin H. Redish), 1987.
(With others) *West's Review, Covering Multistate Subjects*, West Publishing, 1979.
(With Dienes) *Handbook of Free Speech and Free Press*, Little, Brown, 1979.
Public Rights and the Private Press, Butterworths, 1981.
(With Dienes) *Constitutional Law* ("Black Letter" series), West Publishing, 1983, 2nd edition, 1987.
(With Dienes) *Constitutional Law in a Nutshell*, West Publishing, 1986.

Contributor to *George Washington Law Review, Harvard Law Review, Northwestern University Law Review, Texas Law Review*. Member of advisory board, *Media Law Reporter*.

BARRY, James P(otvin) 1918-

PERSONAL: Born October 23, 1918, in Alton, Ill.; son of Paul A. (a U.S. Army officer) and Elder (Potvin) Barry; married Anne Jackson (an education librarian), April 16, 1966. *Education:* Ohio State University, B.A. (cum laude), 1940; U.S. Army Command and General Staff College, honor graduate, 1959.

ADDRESSES: Home—353 Fairway Blvd., Columbus, Ohio 43213; and Thunder Beach P.O., Penetanquishene, Ontario, Canada. *Office*—Ohioana Library Association, 1105 Ohio Departments Buildings, 65 South Front St., Columbus, Ohio 43215.

CAREER: U.S. Army, Artillery, 1940-66, with worldwide assignments ranging from adviser to Turkish Army to staff and editorial work in the Pentagon; became colonel; Capital University, Columbus, Ohio, administrator, 1967-71; free-lance writer and editor, 1971-77; Ohioana Library Association, Columbus, director, 1977—. Photographer and book illustrator, 1968—.

MEMBER: World Ship Society, Royal Canadian Yacht Club, Marine Historical Society, Great Lakes Historical Society, Ohio Historical Society, Phi Beta Kappa, University Club (Columbus), Columbus Country Club.

AWARDS, HONORS: Award from American Society for State and Local History, 1974, for *Ships of the Great Lakes: 300 Years of Navigation;* award from Society of Midland Authors, 1982, for *Wrecks and Rescues of the Great Lakes: A Photographic History*.

WRITINGS:

(And illustrator with photographs) *Georgian Bay: The Sixth Great Lake*, Clarke, Irwin, 1968, revised and enlarged edition, 1978.
The Battle of Lake Erie (young adult), F. Watts, 1970.
Bloody Kansas (young adult), F. Watts, 1972.
(And illustrator with photographs) *The Fate of the Lakes: A Portrait of the Great Lakes*, Baker Book, 1972.
The Louisiana Purchase (young adult), F. Watts, 1973.
Henry Ford and Mass Production (young adult), F. Watts, 1973.
(And illustrator with photographs) *Ships of the Great Lakes: 300 Years of Navigation* (Dolphin Book Club selection), Howell-North Books, 1973.
The Berlin Olympics 1936 (young adult), F. Watts, 1975.
(And illustrator with photographs) *The Great Lakes: A First Book* (young adult), F. Watts, 1976.
Wrecks and Rescues of the Great Lakes: A Photographic History (Dolphin Book Club selection), Howell-North Books, 1981.

Also author of booklet *Lake Erie* for Ohio EPA, 1980. Contributor of articles and reviews to journals and magazines. Former editor of military publications. Editor, *Ohioana Quarterly*, 1977—. Senior editor, *Inland Seas*, 1984—.

WORK IN PROGRESS: A photo book on the Great Lakes.

SIDELIGHTS: James P. Barry has been interested in writing since high school; two of his articles were published in *Yachting* while he was in college. Afterward, he wrote "technical military publications until [his] retirement from the army in

1966.'' Since then, he has returned to historical and regional writing.

A reviewer for *Financial Post* says of *The Fate of the Lakes: A Portrait of the Great Lakes,* ''Few documentations could prove as moving as this vivid, technically superior picture book.'' In *Yachting,* a reviewer writes of the same book: ''A project of this enormous scope requires of its narrator not only an intimate knowledge of a dozen subjects touching upon these large and famous bodies of water, but a style that will make the layman follow attentively in the author's footsteps. Mr. Barry happily possesses both these qualities and more.''

Of *Wrecks and Rescues of the Great Lakes: A Photographic History,* a reviewer in *Canadian Geographic Magazine* says, ''This book has been well researched and carefully produced—it will be of special interest to mariners, historians, and photographers.'' Another reviewer comments in the *Atlantic City Press* that *Wrecks and Rescues of the Great Lakes* is ''an eye-opener for those not acquainted with these bodies of water.''

BIOGRAPHICAL/CRITICAL SOURCES:

PERIODICALS

Atlantic City Press, January 31, 1982.
Canadian Geographic Magazine, April, 1982.
Financial Post, (Toronto), June 23, 1973.
Yachting, August, 1973.

*   *   *

BASS, Kingsley B., Jr.
    See BULLINS, Ed

*   *   *

BAUMOL, William J(ack)   1922-

PERSONAL: Born February 26, 1922, in New York, N.Y.; son of Solomon (a bookbinder) and Lillian (Itzkowitz) Baumol; married Hilda Missel, December 27, 1941; children: Ellen Francis, Daniel Aaron. *Education:* City College (now City College of the City University of New York), B.S.S., 1942; London School of Economics and Political Science, Ph.D., 1949.

ADDRESSES: Home—P.O. Box 1502, Princeton, N.J. 08542. *Office*—Department of Economics, Princeton University, Princeton, N.J. 08540.

CAREER: Affiliated wth U.S. Department of Agriculture, Washington, D.C., 1942-43, 1946; University of London, London School of Economics and Political Science, London, England, assistant lecturer in economics, 1947-49; Princeton University, Princeton, N.J., assistant professor, 1949-52, associate professor, 1952-54, professor of economics, 1954—; New York University, New York, N.Y., professor of economics, 1972—. Director of C. V. Starr Center for Applied Economics. Member, Consultants on Industry Economics, Inc. *Military service:* U.S. Army, 1943-46.

MEMBER: American Economic Association (vice-president, 1966-67; president, 1980), Econometric Society (fellow; member of council, 1960-61), Institute of Management Sciences, American Association of University Professors, Eastern Economic Association (president, 1978-79), Atlantic Economic Society (president, 1985-86).

AWARDS, HONORS: Guggenheim fellow, 1957-58; Ford faculty fellow, 1965-66; Dr. of Laws, Rider College, 1965; Dr. of Economics, Stockholm School of Economics, 1971; PSP Award, Professional and Scholarly Publishing Division, Association of American Publishers, 1986, for *Superfairness: Applications and Theory;* also received degrees from Knox College and University of Basel; honorary fellow, London School of Economics and Political Science.

WRITINGS:

Welfare Economics and the Theory of the State, Harvard University Press, 1951, 2nd edition, 1965.
Economic Dynamics, Macmillan, 1952, 3rd edition, 1970.
(With L. V. Chandler) *Economic Processes and Policies,* Harper, 1954.
Business Behavior, Value and Growth, Macmillan, 1959, revised edition, Harcourt, 1967.
Economic Theory and Operations Analysis, Prentice-Hall, 1961, 3rd edition, 1972.
(Editor with Klaus Knorr) *What Price Economic Growth?,* Prentice-Hall, 1962.
The Stock Market and Economic Efficiency, Fordham University Press, 1965.
(With W. G. Bowen) *Performing Arts—the Economic Dilemma: A Study of Problems Common to Theater, Opera, Music, and Dance,* Twentieth Century Fund, 1966.
(Editor) E. M. Lerner and W. T. Carleton, *A Theory of Financial Analysis,* Harcourt, 1966.
(Editor) E. Shapiro, *Macroeconomic Analysis,* Harcourt, 1966.
(Editor with S. M. Goldfeld) *Precursors in Mathematical Economics: An Anthology,* London School of Economics, 1968.
Portfolio Theory: The Selection of Asset Combinations, McCaleb-Seiler, 1970.
(With M. Marcus) *Economics of Academic Libraries,* American Council on Education, 1973.
(With W. E. Oates) *The Theory of Environmental Policy,* Prentice-Hall, 1975.
(With Oates and S.A.B. Blackman) *Economics, Environmental Policy, and the Quality of Life,* Prentice-Hall, 1979.
(With A. S. Blinder) *Economics: Principles and Policy,* Harcourt, 1979.
(Editor) *Public and Private Enterprise in a Mixed Economy,* St. Martin's, 1980.
(With Panzar and Willig) *Contestable Markets and the Theory of Industry Structure,* Harcourt, 1980.
Superfairness: Applications and Theory, MIT Press, 1986.

*   *   *

BEHRENS, June York   1925-

PERSONAL: Born April 25, 1925, in Maricopa, Calif.; daughter of Mark Hanna and Aline (Stafford) York; married Henry W. Behrens (a school principal), August 23, 1947; children: Terry Lynne, Denise. *Education:* University of California, Santa Barbara, B.A., 1947; University of Maryland (Overseas Program), Munich, Germany, additional study, 1955; University of Southern California, M.A., 1961; additional study at University of California, Los Angeles and University of London. *Religion:* Protestant.

ADDRESSES: Home—2732 San Ramon Dr., Rancho Palos Verdes, Calif. 90274.

CAREER: Elementary teacher in California, 1947-54, 1956-63, in overseas schools, 1954-56; vice-principal in Los Angeles, Calif., 1966; reading specialist in Los Angeles City Schools, 1966—.

MEMBER: National Education Association, American Association of University Women, California Teachers' Association.

AWARDS, HONORS: Distinguished achievement award from University of California, Santa Barbara.

WRITINGS:

Soo Ling Finds a Way (Junior Literary Guild Selection), Golden Gate, 1965.
A Walk in the Neighborhood, Elk Grove Press, 1968.
Who Am I?, Elk Grove Press, 1968.
Where Am I?, Elk Grove Press, 1969.
Air Cargo, Elk Grove Press, 1970.
Look at the Zoo Animals, Elk Grove Press, 1970.
Truck Cargo, Elk Grove Press, 1970.
Earth Is Home: The Pollution Story, Elk Grove Press, 1971.
Look at the Farm Animals, Elk Grove Press, 1971.
Ship Cargo, Elk Grove Press, 1971.
How I Feel, Elk Grove Press, 1973.
Look at the Desert Animals, Elk Grove Press, 1973.
Look at the Forest Animals, Elk Grove Press, 1974.
Train Cargo, Elk Grove Press, 1974.
Look at the Sea Animals, Elk Grove Press, 1975.
Together, Children's Press, 1975.
True Book of Metric Measurement, Children's Press, 1975.
What I Hear, Children's Press, 1976.
Can You Walk the Plank?, Children's Press, 1976.
Twisters, Children's Press, 1976.
Jimmy Carter (biography), Children's Press, 1977.
Whalewatch!, Children's Press, 1978.
Fiesta: Other Lands, Other Places, Children's Press, 1978.
The Manners Book, Children's Press, 1980.
Ronald Reagan (biography), Children's Press, 1981.
Powwow, Children's Press, 1981.
Sally Ride (biography), Children's Press, 1984.
I Can Be an Astronaut, Children's Press, 1984.
I Can Be a Truck Driver, Children's Press, 1985.
I Can Be a Pilot, Children's Press, 1985.
Miss Liberty, First Lady (biography), Children's Press, 1986.
Samoans!, Children's Press, 1986.
I Can Be a Nurse, Children's Press, 1986.
Whales of the World, Children's Press, 1987.

"ADVENTURES IN ART" SERIES

Looking at Horses, Children's Press, 1976.
Looking at Children, Children's Press, 1977.
Looking at Beasties, Children's Press, 1978.

"CHILDHOOD AWARENESS" SERIES

My Brown Bag Book, Children's Press, 1974.
My Favorite Thing, Children's Press, 1975.
What Is a Seal?, Children's Press, 1975.

"HOLIDAY PLAY" SERIES

Feast of Thanksgiving: The First American Holiday, Children's Press, 1975.
A New Flag for a New Country, Children's Press, 1975.
The Christmas Magic-Wagon, Children's Press, 1975.
Martin Luther King: The Story of a Dream, Children's Press, 1979.
Gung Hoy Fat Choy (Chinese New Year), Children's Press, 1982.
Hanukkah, Children's Press, 1983.
Passover, Children's Press, 1987.

"LIVING HERITAGE" SERIES

(With Pauline Brower) *Colonial Farm,* Children's Press, 1976.
(With Brower) *Algonquian Indians: At Summer Camp,* Children's Press, 1977.
(With Brower) *Pilgrims Plantation,* Children's Press, 1977.
(With Brower) *Canal Boats West,* Children's Press, 1978.
(With Brower) *Lighthouse Family,* Children's Press, 1979.
(With Brower) *Death Valley,* Children's Press, 1980.

OTHER

"Children of the World" (media series), Barr Films, 1978.
"The Mediterranean" (four filmstrips), 1978.
"Northern Africa" (four filmstrips), 1978.
"Asia" (four filmstrips), 1978.

SIDELIGHTS: June York Behrens wrote *CA:* "My need to write started in elementary school. Our fifth grade teacher Mrs. Otis was in love with books. That love spilled over into the classroom and touched those of us who adored her. I wrote my first book for Mrs. Otis. She said it was one of her favorite stories. The book was about horses, illustrated with cut-outs from magazines. Many years later I did another book, *Looking at Horses*. I thought about Mrs. Otis when the book came back from the printer.

"Writing plays for young children is an exciting new adventure for me. What a thrill to see children become the characters and change into completely different personalities!

"Whatever the form of written expression—manuscript, plays or scripting for filmstrips, my greatest joy comes from learning that the work has provided entertainment and learning experiences for young children."

*   *   *

BEISTLE, Shirley
   See CLIMO, Shirley

*   *   *

BELL, R(obert) C(harles)   1917-

PERSONAL: Born November 22, 1917, in Sudbury, Ontario, Canada; son of Robert Duncan (a farmer) and Violet Lydia (an actress; maiden name, Clarke) Bell; married Phyllis Pearl Hunter Codling, June 28, 1941; children: Robert Graham, Geoffrey Duncan, Diana Mary Hudson. *Education:* St. Bartholomew's Hospital Medical College, London, M.R.C.S. and L.R.C.P., 1941, F.R.C.S., 1949; University of London, M.B. and B.S., 1941. *Religion:* Church of England.

ADDRESSES: Home—20 Linden Rd., Gosforth, Newcastle-upon-Tyne, Northumberland NE3 4EY, England.

CAREER: Royal Infirmary, Newcastle-upon-Tyne, England, member of staff, 1950-52; plastic surgeon on board of Newcastle Regional Hospital, 1952-82. *Military service:* Royal Canadian Air Force, 1945-48.

MEMBER: British Association of Plastic Surgeons, North of England Surgical Society, Numismatic Literary Guild (life member), Hadrianic Society (Durham; chairman, 1975—).

AWARDS, HONORS: Premier Award, Doctors' Hobbies Exhibition, London, 1959, for manuscript of *Board and Table Games from Many Civilizations.*

WRITINGS:

Board and Table Games from Many Civilizations, Oxford University Press, Volume I, 1960, Volume II, 1969, 3rd edition published in one volume, Dover, 1979.
Commercial Coins, 1787-1804, Corbitt & Hunter, 1963.
Copper Commercial Coins, 1811-1819, Corbitt & Hunter, 1964.
Tangram Teasers, Corbitt & Hunter, 1965.
Tradesmen's Tickets and Private Tokens, 1785-1819, Corbitt & Hunter, 1966.
Specious Tokens and Those Struck for General Circulation, 1784-1804, Corbitt & Hunter, 1968.
Tyneside Pottery, Studio Vista, 1971.
(With M.R.Y. Gill) *The Potteries of Tyneside,* Graham, 1973.
The Use of Skin Grafts (monograph), Oxford University Press, 1973.
Discovering Old Board Games, Shire, 1973.
Diaries from the Days of Sail, Holt, 1974.
Discovering Backgammon, Shire, 1975.
(Consultant and author of introduction) *Games of the World,* Holt, 1975.
Unofficial Farthings, 1820-1870, B. A. Seaby, 1975, *Supplement,* Schwer, 1988.
Building Medalets of Kempson and Skidmore, Frank Graham, 1978.
The Board Game Book, Marshall Cavendish Ltd., 1979.
Discovering Dice and Dominoes, Shire, 1980.
Board and Table Game Antiques, Shire, 1981.
Maling and Other Tyneside Pottery, Shire, 1986.
Political Pieces Simulating Tradesmens' Tokens, 1770-1802, Schwer, 1987.
(With Michael Cornelius) *Board Games and Their Use in Teaching Mathematics,* Cambridge University Press, 1988.

Also author of five booklets on games, published by Shire. Contributor to *World Coins, Token Tales, Coin Monthly,* and *Gamer.*

WORK IN PROGRESS: A book on political tokens of the eighteenth century.

SIDELIGHTS: R. C. Bell told *CA:* "My three chief subjects are board games, Tyneside pottery, and tradesmen's tokens. All, I felt, were neglected subjects of considerable interest, and I wrote to try to 'put them on the map' and stimulate interest. I hope I have succeeded."

*   *   *

BELLAIRS, John   1938-

PERSONAL: Born January 17, 1938, in Marshall, Mich.; son of Frank Edward and Virginia (Monk) Bellairs; married Priscilla Braids, June 24, 1968; children: Frank. *Education:* University of Notre Dame, A.B., 1959; University of Chicago, M.A., 1960. *Politics:* Democrat. *Religion:* None.

ADDRESSES: Home—28 Hamilton Ave., Haverhill, Mass. 01830. *Agent*—Richard Curtis, 164 East 64th St., New York, N.Y. 10021.

CAREER: Free-lance writer. College of St. Teresa, Winona, Minn., instructor in English, 1963-65; Shimer College, Mount Carroll, Ill., member of humanities faculty, 1966-67; Emmanuel College, Boston, Mass., instructor in English, 1968-69; Merrimack College, North Andover, Mass., member of English faculty, 1969-71.

MEMBER: Authors League of America, Authors Guild.

AWARDS, HONORS: Woodrow Wilson fellowship; Utah Childrens Book Award, 1981; *New York Times* outstanding book citation, 1973, for *The House with a Clock in Its Walls.*

WRITINGS:

St. Fidgeta and Other Parodies, Macmillan, 1966.
The Pedant and the Shuffly, Macmillan, 1968.
The Face in the Frost, Macmillan, 1969.
The House with a Clock in Its Walls, Dial, 1973.
The Figure in the Shadows, Dial, 1975.
The Letter, the Witch, and the Ring, Dial, 1976.
The Treasure of Alpheus Winterborn, Harcourt, 1978.
The Curse of the Blue Figurine, Dial, 1983.
The Mummy, the Will, and the Crypt, Dial, 1983.
The Dark Secret of Weatherend, Dial, 1984.
The Spell of the Sorcerer's Skull, Dial, 1984.
The Revenge of the Wizard's Ghost, Dial, 1985.
The Eyes of the Killer Robot, Dial, 1986.
The Lamp from the Warlock's Tomb, Dial, 1987.

SIDELIGHTS: John Bellairs is a fantasy writer "of amazing brilliance and charm," writes Lin Carter in *Imaginary Worlds.* According to *A Reader's Guide to Fantasy,* his style "is light and funny, full of puns; his brand of magic is light-hearted." In Bellairs' world, continues the *Guide,* "a good magician has to have a good sense of humor."

"A sure sign of Bellairs' enormous potential," Darrell Schweitzer of *Science Fiction Review* believes, "is his ability to shift from . . . scenes of sheer horror to wacky humor and back again without ever ruining the other." For instance, *The Face in the Frost,* the story of a wizard's quest to save his homeland from an unspeakable evil, "is, in many places, a very scary book," according to *A Reader's Guide to Fantasy,* "[but] it is also a very funny book." Similarly, a contributor to *Fantasy Literature* describes the novel as being "genuinely frightening at times and quite serious about its magic, but a playfully humorous tone is rarely absent. Occasionally, in fact, one suspects the author of writing a parody of fantasy." Carter finds *The Face in the Frost* "rich, hilarious, inventive, filled with infectious good humor, grisly horrors, slithering Evil, bumbling monarchs, and . . . Various and Sundry Menaces of the supernatural variety." He continues, "Bellairs is a marvelous writer who has obviously read all the right books with enthusiasm, and his own venture into the genre [of fantasy] is one of the most exciting debuts in a long time."

Besides *The Face in the Frost,* Bellairs has written much popular children's horror and mystery fiction. A *Washington Post Book World* reviewer once described him as "one of the best writers of witty Gothic puzzlers, laced with supernatural elements," and *Fantasy Review* contributor Allene Stuart Phy remarks that he is "a master at creating mood and atmosphere." While avoiding "the sentimentalities that so perniciously pervade many juvenile books," comments Phy, Bellairs "honor[s] that inviolable convention of the [children's literature] genre, the happy ending." Many of his stories "are set in the early 1950s, when the author was a child," notes Craig Shaw Gardner in the *Washington Post Book World,* "and the books are filled with detailed and often very funny reminiscences of what it felt like to be young then." He adds, "It's this balance between the supernatural and the everyday, told with Bellairs' humor, that makes his books so special."

AVOCATIONAL INTERESTS: Archaeology, history, "trivia of all kinds."

BIOGRAPHICAL/CRITICAL SOURCES:

BOOKS

Carter, Lin, *Imaginary Worlds: The Art of Fantasy,* Ballantine, 1973.

Searles, Baird, Beth Meacham, and Michael Franklin, *A Reader's Guide to Fantasy,* Avon, 1982.

Tymn, Marshall B., Kenneth J. Zahorski, and Robert H. Boyer, *Fantasy Literature: A Core Collection and Reference Guide,* Bowker, 1979.

PERIODICALS

Booklist, July 1, 1969, May 15, 1975, October 1, 1976.
Changing Times, November, 1978.
Commonweal, November 18, 1966, November 23, 1973.
Fantasy Review, April, 1984, March, 1985, April, 1987.
Library Journal, September 1, 1966.
National Observer, December 25, 1976.
New York Times Book Review, June 10, 1973, July 8, 1973, May 4, 1975, April 30, 1978, September 25, 1983.
Science Fiction and Fantasy Book Review, November, 1983.
Science Fiction Review, March, 1979.
Thrust, summer, 1979.
Times Literary Supplement, March 28, 1980.
Voice of Youth Advocates, April, 1984, April, 1985.
Washington Post Book World, November 11, 1984, January 12, 1986.
West Coast Review of Books, July, 1979.

*　　*　　*

BENDER, Todd K.   1936-

PERSONAL: Born January 8, 1936, in Stark County, Ohio; son of Kenneth W. and Minnie (Hill) Bender; married Patricia Ann Minor, September 6, 1958; children: Kirsten Ann, Claire Elaine. *Education:* Kenyon College, B.A., 1958; University of Sheffield, graduate study, 1958-59; Stanford University, Ph.D., 1962.

ADDRESSES: Office—Department of English, University of Wisconsin, Madison, Wis. 53706.

CAREER: Instructor in English at Stanford University, Stanford, Calif., 1961-62, and Dartmouth College, Hanover, N.H., 1962-63; University of Virginia, Charlottesville, assistant professor of English, 1963-66; University of Wisconsin—Madison, associate professor, 1966-73, professor of English, 1973—. Visiting professor at University of Athens, Athens, Greece, 1978-79, Justus-Liebig-Universitaet, Giessen, West Germany, 1985, and Georg-August-Universitaet zu Goettingen, Goettingen, West Germany, 1986.

AWARDS, HONORS: Fulbright scholar at University of Sheffield, 1958-59; American Council of Learned Societies grant-in-aid for work at Oxford University, 1963, and fellowship at Bibliotheque Nationale, Paris, France, 1965-66; senior Fulbright scholar at University of Athens, 1978-79.

WRITINGS:

Gerard Manley Hopkins: The Classical Background and Critical Reception of His Work, Johns Hopkins Press, 1966.
(With Robert J. Dilligan) *A Concordance to the English Poetry of Gerard Manley Hopkins,* University of Wisconsin Press, 1970.
(With Sybyl C. Jackson) *Concordance to Joseph Conrad's "Heart of Darkness,"* Southern Illinois University Press, 1973.

(With James W. Parins and others) *A Concordance to Conrad's "Lord Jim,"* Garland Publishing, 1976.
Modernism in Literature, Holt, 1976.
(With Sue M. Briggum) *A Concordance to Conrad's "Almayer's Folly,"* Garland Publishing, 1978.
A Concordance to Conrad's "Heart of Darkness," Garland Publishing, 1979.
A Concordance to Conrad's "The Secret Agent," Garland Publishing, 1979.
(With Parins and others) *A Concordance to Conrad's "Victory,"* Garland Publishing, 1979.
Concordances to Conrad's "The Shadow Line" and "Youth," Garland Publishing, 1980.
(With Dilligan) *A Concordance to Ezra Pound's "Cantos,"* Garland Publishing, 1981.
(With C. Ruth Sabol) *A Concordance to Bronte's "Jane Eyre,"* Garland Publishing, 1981.
(With Paul L. Gaston) *A Concordance to Conrad's "The Arrow of Gold,"* Garland Publishing, 1981.
(With Parins) *A Concordance to Conrad's "The Nigger of the Narcissus,"* Garland Publishing, 1981.
(With Sabol) *A Concordance to Ford Madox Ford's "The Good Soldier,"* Garland Publishing, 1981.
A Concordance to Conrad's "A Set of Six," Garland Publishing, 1981.
(With Michael G. Becker) *A Concordance to the "Poems of John Keats,"* Garland Publishing, 1981.
Concordance to Conrad's "Tales of Unrest" and "Tales of Hearsay," Garland Publishing, 1982.
(With others) *Concordances to Conrad's "Typhoon and Other Stories" and "Within the Tides,"* Garland Publishing, 1982.
(With David Leon Higdon) *A Concordance to Conrad's "Under Western Eyes,"* Garland Publishing, 1983.
Concordances to Conrad's "The Mirror of the Sea" and "The Inheritors," Garland Publishing, 1983.
(With Sobol) *A Concordance to Bronte's "Wuthering Heights,"* Garland Publishing, 1984.
A Concordance to Conrad's "An Outcast of the Islands," Garland Publishing, 1984.
(With Parins) *A Concordance to Conrad's "Nostromo,"* Garland Publishing, 1984.
(With Higdon) *A Concordance to Conrad's "The Rover,"* Garland Publishing, 1985.
A Concordance to Conrad's "Romance," Garland Publishing, 1985.
A Concordance to Conrad's "The Rescue," Garland Publishing, 1985.
(With Higdon) *A Concordance to Henry James's "The American,"* Garland Publishing, 1985.
(With others) *A Concordance to James' "Daisy Miller" and the "American Reference Books on Literature,"* Garland Publishing, 1986.

Contributor to periodicals, including *Times Literary Supplement* and *Criticism.*

SIDELIGHTS: Todd K. Bender told *CA:* "I am particularly interested in placing the analysis of literary language on a sounder footing by examining closely the vocabulary, sentence structure, and textual transmission of the work. The emergence of the computer and peripheral equipment in the last twenty years has revolutionized the tasks of the lexicographer, the editor, and the critic.

"Many of my books are concordances or verbal indexes, which simply list in alphabetical order all words used in a work and direct the reader to their contexts while revealing the frequency of each word's occurrence and the relative frequency of each type and token in the author's lexicon. These tables are reference works which can be used to improve the reader's understanding of the range of meaning of a given word, or the verbal habits of an author, or the likelihood that a passage has been contaminated in the process of textual transmission.''

* * *

BENEDICTUS, David (Henry) 1938-

PERSONAL: Born September 16, 1938, in London, England; son of Henry Jules and Kathleen Constance (Ricardo) Benedictus; married Yvonne Antrobus (an actress). *Education:* Balliol College, Oxford, B.A., 1959; further study at University of Iowa.

ADDRESSES: Home—The Pelican, 20 Alexandra Rd., East Twickenham, Middlesex, England.

CAREER: British Broadcasting Corp. (BBC), London, England, assistant trainee, 1963-64, drama director, 1964-65, story editor, ''Wednesday Play,'' 1967; Thames Television, Bristol, England, trainee director, 1969-70; novelist, playwright, and author of short stories. Assistant director, Royal Shakespeare Company, 1970-71; visiting fellow, Churchill College, Cambridge, 1981-82; commissioning drama editor, Channel 4, 1984-86. Writer-in-residence at Sutton Public Library, Kibbutz Gezer, and the Eastern Library.

WRITINGS:

NOVELS

The Fourth of June, Blond, 1962, Dutton, 1963.
You're a Big Boy Now, Blond, 1963, Dutton, 1964.
This Animal Is Mischievous, New American Library, 1965.
Hump; or, Bone by Bone, Alive, Blond, 1967.
The Guru and the Golf Club, Blond, 1969.
The World of Windows, Weidenfeld & Nicolson, 1971.
The Rabbi's Wife, M. Evans, 1976.
A Twentieth Century Man, Blond, 1978.
Lloyd George, Weidenfeld & Nicolson, 1981.
Local Hero, Penguin, 1983.
Floating Down to Camelot, Macdonald, 1985.

Also author of *Who Killed the Prince Consort?*, Macmillan, and *Whose Life Is It Anyway?*, Severn.

PLAYS

''The Fourth of June,'' first produced in London, 1964.
''Angels (Over Your Grave) and Geese (Over Mine),'' first produced in Edinburgh at the Traverse Theatre, 1967.
''Dromedary,'' first produced in Newcastle upon Tyne, 1969.
''What a Way to Run a Revolution!,'' first produced in London, 1971.
''The Golden Key,'' first produced in Cambridge, 1982.
''Betjemania,'' first produced in London, 1977.
''Esprit de Corps,'' first produced in London, 1983.

NONFICTION

Junk: A Guide to Bargain Hunting, Macmillan, 1976.
The Antique Collectors' Guide, Macmillan, 1981.
The Essential Guide to London, Sphere, 1984, 2nd revised edition published as *The Absolutely Essential Guide to London*, Sphere, 1986.

Also author of *The Streets of London*, Thames.

OTHER

Contributor of short stories to periodicals, including *Seventeen, Pointer, Penthouse,* and *Men Only.*

SIDELIGHTS: David Benedictus favorably impressed many critics with his first novel, *The Fourth of June,* published in 1962. In it, he satirized life at Eton and Balliol, the exclusive British schools he had attended. ''The timing of Benedictus's first novel was admirable,'' writes *Dictionary of Literary Biography* essayist T. Winnifrith, ''as it coincided with a wave of satire directed against the Macmillan government, full of old Etonians and racked by sexual scandals.'' *The Fourth of June* was denounced by Eton's headmaster as false and pornographic, although Winnifrith states that ''it is difficult at first to see the justification for the . . . charge'' and calls the book ''comparatively tame by today's standards.''

''Like many satirists, from Juvenal onward, Benedictus can be accused of incoherence and of being so busy attacking everything that he ends up offering no positive values,'' admits Winnifrith. ''Nevertheless, *The Fourth of June* is full of promise and extraordinary verbal felicity. . . . The novel was an instant commercial success.'' Benedictus produced five more novels before turning to nonfiction with *Junk: A Guide to Bargain Hunting,* which Winnifrith describes as ''an excellent if slightly facetious account of the antique market.'' In more recent works of fiction, the author moves beyond the satire of his earliest novels. For example, *The Rabbi's Wife* follows a woman through her ordeal of kidnapping by Israeli terrorists, and ''shows far more compassion than earlier novels.''

AVOCATIONAL INTERESTS: Antiques.

BIOGRAPHICAL/CRITICAL SOURCES:

BOOKS

Dictionary of Literary Biography, Volume XIV: *British Novelists since 1960*, Gale, 1983.

PERIODICALS

New Yorker, February 16, 1963.
New York Herald Tribune, October 21, 1962.
Times (London), August 22, 1985.
Times Literary Supplement, January 23, 1981.

* * *

BEN-EZER, Ehud 1936-

PERSONAL: Born April 3, 1936, in Petah Tikva, Palestine (now Israel); son of Binyamin (an agriculturist) and Devora (Lipsky) Ben-Ezer; married Anat Fienberg, August 31, 1969 (divorced, 1972); married Yehudit Tomer (a nurse), September 24, 1974; children: (second marriage) Binyamin. *Education:* Hebrew University of Jerusalem, B.A., 1963. *Religion:* ''Jew, Secular.''

ADDRESSES: Home—20 Hakalir, P.O. Box 22135, Tel Aviv, Israel.

CAREER: Free-lance writer, lecturer, and editor. Member of Kibbutz Ein Gedi on shore of Dead Sea, Israel, 1956-58; teacher in night school for adults, near Jerusalem, Israel, 1959-66. *Military service:* Israeli Army, Nahal troops, 1955-56. Israeli Army Reserve, 1959—; served in first aid unit in Six Day War, 1967.

MEMBER: PEN, Hebrew Writers Association.

AWARDS, HONORS: Israeli Prime Minister Prize for creativity, 1975.

WRITINGS:

Hamahtzeva (novel; also see below; title means ''The Quarry''), Am Oved, 1963.

''Hamahtzeva'' (two-act play; based on his novel of the same title), first produced in Tel Aviv at Zuta Theatre, April, 1964.

Anshei Sedom (novel; title means ''The People of Sodom''), Am Oved, 1968.

Lo Lagiborim Hamilhama (novel; title means ''Nor the Battle to the Strong''), Levin-Epshtien, 1971.

Laila Beginat Hayerakot Hanirdamim (juvenile; title means ''Night in the Sleeping Vegetable Garden''), Massada, 1971.

(Editor) *Unease in Zion* (interviews), Quadrangle, 1974, Hebrew translation published as *Ein Sha'ananim Betsion*, Am Oved, 1986.

Hapri Ha'asur (short stories; title means ''The Forbidden Fruit''), Achiasef, 1977.

Oferit Blofferit (juvenile; title means ''Offerit the Bluffer''), Yavneh, 1977.

Efrat (short stories), Tarmil, 1978.

Hasheket Hanafshi (novel; title means ''Peace of Mind''), Zmora, Bitan, Modan, 1979.

Bein Holot Vekhol Shamaim (title means ''Sand Dunes and Blue Sky''), illustrations by Nachum Gutman, Yavneh, 1980.

Mi Mesaper Et Hasaparim? (juvenile; title means ''Who Barbers the Barbers?''), Yavneh, 1982.

Otzar Habe'er Harishona (juvenile; title means ''The Treasure of the First Well''), Schocken, 1982.

Be'eikvot Yehudei Hamidbar (juvenile; title means ''In Search of the Jews of the Desert''), Schocken, 1983.

(Editor) *Ester Raab: Gan Sheharav* (selected stories and poems of Ester Raab; title means ''A Ruined Garden''), Tarmil, 1983.

(Editor) *Nachum Gutman* (album), Massada, 1984.

Hane'ehavim Vehaneimim (novel; title means ''Lovely and Pleasant''), Bitan, 1985.

Lashut Beklipat Avatiach (novel; title means ''To Sail in a Watermelon Shell''), Rachgold-Sagiv, 1987.

Betset Yisrael Mimitsraim (juvenile; title means ''When Israel Went Out of Egypt''), illustrations by Nachum Gutman, Yavneh, 1987.

(Editor) *Haggadah* (juvenile; title means ''Order of the Home-Service on Passover Night''), illustrations by N. Gutman, Yavneh, 1987.

50 Shirei Mitbagrim (juvenile; title means ''50 Puberty Cracks''), illustrations by Dani Kerman, Rachgold-Sagiv, 1987.

Erga (short stories; title means ''Yearning''), Zmora-Bitan, 1987.

(Editor) Ester Raab, *Kol Shirei Ester Raab* (poems; title means ''The Verse of Ester Raab''), Zmora-Bitan, 1987.

(Editor) Yehuda Raab, *Hatelem Harishon* (title means ''The First Furrow''; contains *To the History of Eliezer Raab and His Son Yehuda Raab* and *To the History of the First Years of Petah Tikva*), Hasifria Hatsionit, 1987.

Contributor of weekly column to *Ha'aretz* (daily newspaper), 1970-78. Also contributor to periodicals.

WORK IN PROGRESS: Research on the image of the Arab in Hebrew literature since the 1880s; a book of poems; a saga about the life of a family in Palestine since the 1830s; a lexicon of articles about more than two hundred Hebrew books; biography of Shraga Netser; second volume of *Oferit Blofferit*.

SIDELIGHTS: Ehud Ben-Ezer once told *CA:* ''The Ben-Ezer (Raab) family has been living in Palestine since 1875. Yehuda Raab (Ben-Ezer), my grandfather, was one of the first settlers of Petah-Tikva in 1878, when that first Jewish colony in Palestine was founded.''

MEDIA ADAPTATIONS: Ben-Ezer's novel *Hamahtzeva* was adapted and broadcast on the Israel National Broadcasting Service, Kol Israel, in 1964, and again in six installments on the ''Popular Hebrew'' radio program in 1969.

*   *   *

BENFORD, Gregory (Albert) 1941-

PERSONAL: Born January 30, 1941, in Mobile, Ala.; son of James Alton (a colonel in the U.S. Army) and Mary Eloise (a teacher; maiden name, Nelson) Benford; married Joan Abbe (an artist), August 26, 1967; children: Alyson Rhandra, Mark Gregory. *Education:* University of Oklahoma, B.S., 1936; University of California, San Diego, M.S., 1965, Ph.D., 1967.

ADDRESSES: Home—1105 Skyline Dr., Laguna Beach, Calif. 92651. *Office*—Department of Physics, University of California, Irvine, Calif. 92717.

CAREER: Lawrence Radiation Laboratory, Livermore, Calif., fellow, 1967-69, research physicist, 1969-71; University of California, Irvine, assistant professor, 1971-73, associate professor, 1973-79, professor of physics, 1979—. Visiting fellow at Cambridge University, 1976 and 1979. Consultant to Physics International Co.

MEMBER: American Physical Society, Science Fiction Writers of America, Royal Astronomical Society.

AWARDS, HONORS: Woodrow Wilson fellowship, 1963-64; Nebula Award from Science Fiction Writers of America, 1975, for novella ''If the Stars Are Gods,'' and 1981, for novel *Timescape;* British Science Fiction Association award, John W. Campbell Award from World Science Fiction Convention, and Dilmar Award for International Novel, all 1981, for *Timescape*. Recipient of grants from Office of Naval Research, 1975—, and 1982—, National Science Foundation, 1972-76, Army Research Organization, 1977-82, Air Force Office of Scientific Research, 1982—, and California Space Office, 1984-85.

WRITINGS:

SCIENCE FICTION NOVELS

Deeper Than the Darkness, Ace Books, 1970, revised edition published as *The Stars in Shroud*, Putnam, 1979.

Jupiter Project, Thomas Nelson, 1975, 2nd edition, 1980.

(With Gordon Eklund) *If the Stars Are Gods* (based on the authors' novella of the same title), Putnam, 1977.

In the Ocean of Night: A Novel, Dial, 1977.

(With Eklund) *Find the Changeling*, Dell, 1980.

(With William Rotsler) *Shiva Descending*, Avon, 1980.

Timescape, Simon & Schuster, 1980.

Against Infinity, Simon & Schuster, 1983.

Across the Sea of Suns, Simon & Schuster, 1984, Ultramarine Publications, 1984.

Time's Rub, Cheap Street, 1984.

Artifact, Tor Books, 1985.

Of Space-Time and the River, Cheap Street, 1985.
In Alien Flesh, Tor Books, 1986.
(With David Brin) *Heart of the Comet*, Bantam, 1986.
Great Sky River, Bantam, 1987.
(With others) *Under the Wheel*, Baen Books, 1987.

Also author, with others, of *Threads of Time*, Amereon.

CONTRIBUTOR TO ANTHOLOGIES

Harlan Ellison, editor, *Again, Dangerous Visions*, Doubleday, 1972.
Terry Carr, editor, *Universe 4*, Random House, 1974.
Robert Silverberg, editor, *New Dimensions, 5*, Harper, 1975.
Carr, editor, *Universe 8*, Doubleday, 1978.
Carr, editor, *Universe 9*, Doubleday, 1979.

OTHER

(Editor with Martin H. Greenberg) *Hitler Victorious: Eleven Stories of the German Victory in World War II*, Berkley Publishing, 1987.

Also author of a number of research papers. Contributor of articles and stories to magazines, including *The Magazine of Fantasy and Science Fiction*, *Smithsonian*, *Natural History*, and *Omni*.

SIDELIGHTS: American astrophysicist and leading science fiction writer Gregory Benford "is one of the major talents to bring the science back into SF," says *Publishers Weekly* contributor Rosemary Herbert. In fact, Benford's achievements in the field of physics, writes Mark J. Lidman in the *Dictionary of Literary Biography*, may overshadow his literary accomplishments. Benford holds a Ph.D. in theoretical physics and has done research on solid state physics, plasma physics, and high energy astrophysics, as well as astronomical research on the dynamics of pulsars, violent extragalactic events, and quasars. At the same time, his science fiction novels have earned him the respect of critics, fans, and his fellow writers, and "he has made no small achievement in writing since he took it up as a 'hobby' to distract himself from the pressures of studying for his doctorate in physics," Herbert relates. As a scientist, Lidman feels, Benford is "acutely aware of modern society's fascination with technology, but his novels also stress the negative aspects of living in a technological age. His works about alien contact have an appeal that is widespread in the 1980s, and his works which deal with science show us that we must learn to live intelligently in a technological world." The essayist states that Benford's novels "are characterized by thoughtful composition and scientific expertise, and his work experience lends authenticity to his perspective on science."

In a piece on science fiction for the *Voice Literary Supplement*, Debra Rae Cohen lists Benford among the writers who "represent the idea of science as technology, of plot as problem solving. . . . SF has always been a forum for scientists to work out ideas that are unproven yet still right. . . . Gregory Benford [and others] . . . test interdisciplinary limits [between fiction and science], not the limits of technology." For example, *Fantasy Review* contributor Gary K. Wolfe notes that *Artifact*, a thriller involving an archaeological find that has the potential to destroy the earth, combines "enough non-stop action and international intrigue [as the artifact is shuttled, sometimes illegally, from country to country] to satisfy the most jaded Robert Ludlum fan" together with ". . . the familiar Benford elements—a very believable and at times satirical portrayal of academic politics, a fully-realized near-future world which is

kept discretely in the background . . . , and a lot of real physics, carefully worked out and meticulously confined to a few plausible speculations." Like other reviewers, Wolfe observes that this attempt to crossbreed the science fiction novel and the international thriller yields "mixed results." Even so, maintains Gregory Feeley in a *Los Angeles Times* review, "It is the scientific side of 'Artifact' that redeems the novel. . . . It is the subject matter and authority of the writer that intrigue, not the style of presentation." Writing in the *Washington Post Book World*, Feeley remarks, "As before, Benford effectively dramatizes the excitement and procedures of discovery, and his evocation of academic research, its protocols and rivalries, is impeccable."

Benford won the Nebula Award in 1981 and the praise of reviewers with the novel *Timescape*. "Its protagonists are physicists deeply and obsessively involved in the entangled arduous pursuit of (relatively) pure knowledge," John Clute reports in the *Times Literary Supplement*. Benford closes "the gap" between science and fiction in the novel by narrating the scientific activities of two groups of physicists; one group, living in 1998, is desperately trying to communicate to scientists in the 1960s the message that will prevent the destruction of the earth's ecosystem at the end of the century. The message consists of imaginary but plausible faster-than-light particles called tachyons sent in morse code to a California physicist who is working with a substance which is "sensitive to tachyon bombardment," explains Clute. *Washington Post Book World* reviewer George R. R. Martin comments that Benford "makes research fully as intense and gripping as the events of any thriller, without compromising a whit, and manages the extremely difficult feat of conveying not only the meaning of his speculations in physics and cosmology, but the excitement as well. . . . [*Timescape*] is not only splendid science fiction, it is a thoroughly splendid novel."

Benford once told *CA:* "I am a resolutely amateur writer, preferring to follow my own interests rather than try to produce fiction for a living. And anyway, I'm a scientist by first choice and shall remain so.

"I began writing from the simple desire to tell a story (a motivation sf writers seem to forget as they age, and thus turn into earnest moralizers). It's taken me a long time to learn how. I've been labeled a 'hard sf' writer from the first, but in fact I think the job of sf is to do it *all*—the scientific landscape, peopled with real persons, with 'style' and meaning ingrained, etc. I've slowly worked toward that goal, with many dead ends along the way. From this comes my habit of rewriting my older books and expanding early short stories into longer works (sometimes novels). Ideas come to me in a lapidary way, layering over the years. Yet, it's not the stirring moral message that moves me. I think writers are interesting when they juxtapose images or events, letting life come out of the stuff of the narrative. They get boring when they preach.

"To some extent, my novels reflect my learning various subcategories of sf. *Deeper than Darkness* (later revised into *The Stars in Shroud*) was the galactic empire motif; *Jupiter Project*, the juvenile; *If the Stars Are Gods* and *In the Ocean of Night*, both the cosmic space novel. *Timescape* is rather different; it reflects my using my own experiences as a scientist. Yet short stories, where I labored so long, seem to me just as interesting as novels. I learned to write there. Nowadays, my novels begin as relatively brisk plotlines and then gather philosophical moss as they roll. If all this sounds vague and intuitive, it is: That's the way I work. So I cannot say precisely why I undertake certain themes. I like Graham Greene's division of novels into 'serious' and 'entertainments,' though I suspect the author himself cannot say with certainty which of his own are which.

"It seems to me my major concerns are the vast landscape of science, and the philosophical implications of that landscape on mortal, sensual human beings. What genuinely interests me is the strange, the undiscovered. But in the end it is how people see this that matters most."

BIOGRAPHICAL/CRITICAL SOURCES:

BOOKS

Bridges to Science Fiction, Southern Illinois University Press, 1981.
Carr, Terry, editor, *Universe 6,* Popular Library, 1976.
Dictionary of Literary Biography Yearbook, 1982, Gale, 1983.
Platt, Charles, *Dream Makers: The Uncommon People Who Write Science Fiction; Interviews by Charles Platt,* Berkley Books, 1980.

PERIODICALS

Analog: Science Fiction/Science Fact, November, 1985, June, 1986.
Chicago Tribune Book World, March 23, 1986.
Christian Science Monitor, May 16, 1986.
Fantasy Review, September, 1985, February, 1986, July, 1986.
Foundation, winter, 1977-78.
Los Angeles Times, December 16, 1985, April 18, 1986.
New York Times Book Review, January 27, 1977, March 27, 1977, November 25, 1984.
Publishers Weekly, May 23, 1986.
Science Fiction and Fantasy Book Review, September, 1983.
Science Fiction Chronicle, October, 1985, June, 1986, July, 1986.
Science Fiction Review, August, 1984, August, 1985, November, 1985, February, 1986, May, 1986, June, 1986.
Times Literary Supplement, December 5, 1980.
Voice Literary Supplement, December, 1983.
Washington Post Book World, June 22, 1980, May 29, 1983, February 26, 1984, October 27, 1985, March 23, 1986.

*   *   *

BERARDO, Felix M(ario)   1934-

PERSONAL: Born February 7, 1934, in Waterbury, Conn.; son of Rocco and Maria (Gurrera) Berardo; married; wife's name, Donna H.; children: (previous marriage) Marcellino Antonio, Benito Antonio (sons). *Education:* University of Connecticut, B.A., 1961; Florida State University, Ph.D., 1965. *Religion:* Roman Catholic.

ADDRESSES: Home—2432 Northwest 14th Pl., Gainesville, Fla. 32605. *Office*—Department of Sociology, University of Florida, Gainesville, Fla. 32611.

CAREER: Washington State University, Pullman, assistant professor of sociology and assistant rural sociologist, 1965-69; University of Florida, Gainesville, associate professor, 1969-73, professor of sociology, 1973—, associate chairman, 1972-77; chairman of department, 1985—. *Military service:* U.S. Air Force, 1952-56.

MEMBER: American Sociological Association (secretary of family section, 1976-79; section organizer, 1979), Rural Sociological Society (member of membership committee, 1969-

72), National Council on Family Relations (section chairman, 1970; member of publications board, 1972-81, 1986-88; chairman of publications board, 1974-76), Gerontological Society of America (member of program committee, 1983), Southeastern Council on Family Relations (member of leadership roundtable, 1984), Southern Sociological Society (section chairman, 1971; chairman of Florida membership committee, 1972; member of program committee, 1973; chairman of program committee, 1975; member of committee on status of women, 1980-82), Foundation of Thanatology (member of professional advisory board, 1969—), Pacific Sociological Association (section chairman, 1968), Pacific Northwest Council on Family Relations, Florida Council on Family Relations, Phi Beta Kappa, Phi Kappa Phi, Alpha Kappa Delta.

WRITINGS:

(Editor and author of introduction with F. Ivan Nye, and contributor) *Emerging Conceptual Frameworks in Family Analysis,* Macmillan, 1966, reprinted, Praeger, 1981.
(With Nye) *The Family: Its Structure and Interaction,* Macmillan, 1973.
(Editor) *Decade Review: Family Research, 1970-1979,* National Council on Family Relations, 1980.
(Editor with H. Wass and R. Neimeyer) *Dying: Facing the Facts,* Hemisphere, 1988.

CONTRIBUTOR

Benjamin Schlessinger, editor, *The One-Parent Family,* University of Toronto Press, 1969.
Jeffrey K. Hadden and Marie L. Borgatta, editors, *Marriage and the Family: A Comprehensive Reader,* F. E. Peacock, 1969.
Raymond J. R. King, editor, *Family Relations: Concepts and Theories,* Glendessary Press, 1969.
Howard Bahr, editor, *Disaffiliated Man: Essays and Bibliography on Skid Row, Vagrancy, and Outsiders,* University of Toronto Press, 1970.
Jacquelin P. Wiseman, editor, *People as Partners: Individual and Family Relationships in Today's World,* Canfield Press, 1971.
Marcia E. Lassell and Thomas E. Lassell, editors, *Love-Marriage-Family: A Developmental Approach,* Scott, Foresman, 1973.
Daniel H. Carson, editor, *Man-Environment Interactions: Evaluations and Applications,* Volume VI: *Privacy,* Environmental Design Research Association, 1974.
Jack R. Delora and Joann D. Delora, editors, *Intimate Life Styles: Marriage and Its Alternatives,* 2nd edition, Goodyear Publishing, 1975.
Anthony H. Richmond and Daniel Kubat, editors, *International Migration: The New World and the Third World,* Sage Publications, 1976.
Thomas Burch, Luis Felipe Lira, and Valdecir F. Lopes, editors, *La familia como unidad de estudio demografico,* Centro Latino Americano de Demografia, 1976.
Robert Fulton, *Death and Identity,* revised edition, Wiley, 1976.
Edward A. Powers and Mary W. Lees, editors, *Encounter with Family Realities,* West Publishing, 1977.
Susan Thomas, editor, *Education for Family Living: Who Is Responsible?,* Department of Home and Family Life, Florida State University, 1978.
Donald Light, Jr. and Suzanne Keller, editors, *The Professional Resource Book for Sociology,* Knopf, 1979, 4th edition, 1985.

Martin L. Levin, editor, *Graduate Student Handbook,* Department of Sociology, Emory University, 1980.

Jill S. Quadagno, editor, *Aging in Modern Society: Readings in Social Gerontology,* St. Martin's, 1980.

Man Singh Das and Clinton J. Jesser, editors, *The Family in Latin America,* Vikas Publishing, 1980.

Bruce W. Brown, editor, *Readings in Family Sociology,* 2nd edition, Ginn Custom, 1982.

(With wife, Donna H. Berardo) Donald Light, Jr. and Suzanne Keller, *The Professional Resource Book for Sociology,* 3rd edition, Knopf, 1982.

(With Michael L. Radelet and Margaret Vandiver) Fred Fedler, editor, *Reporting for the Print Media,* 3rd edition, Harcourt, 1984.

Standard Education Almanac, Marquis Professional Publications, 1985.

OTHER

Also author of numerous professional papers presented at conferences and seminars. Contributor of articles and reviews to journals in United States and Brazil. Associate editor, *International Journal of Sociology of the Family,* 1970—, *Family Coordinator,* 1972-75, *Social Forces,* 1976-79, *Death Education,* 1979—, and *Journal of Aging Studies,* 1986—; *Journal of Marriage and the Family,* associate editor, 1972-75 and 1982-85, editor, 1976-81. Guest editor for special issues, *Journal of Marriage and the Family,* November, 1971, *Family Coordinator: Journal of Education, Counseling, and Service,* January, 1972, *The Annals of the American Academy of Political and Social Sciences,* November, 1982, and *Gerontiles,* fall, 1985. Member of editorial advisory board of *Population and Policy Review,* 1980—, and *Sage Family Studies Abstracts,* 1981—. Consulting editor, *Death Studies,* 1986—. Referee, *American Sociological Review, Human Organization, Journal of Comparative Family Studies, Journal of Gerontology, Psychology and Aging, Journal of Marriage and the Family, Family Relations, Death Education,* and *Social Forces.*

WORK IN PROGRESS: Research on "age-discrepant marriages, widowhood, and survivorship; social change and the family."

*   *   *

BERKSON, Bill 1939-

PERSONAL: Born August 30, 1939, in New York, N.Y.; son of Seymour (a journalist) and Eleanor (Lambert) Berkson; married; children: one son, one daughter. *Education:* Attended Brown University, 1957-59, Columbia University, 1959-60, and New School for Social Research, 1959-61.

ADDRESSES: Home—P.O. Box 389, Bolinas, Calif. 94924.

CAREER: Art News, New York City, editorial associate, 1960-63; free-lance art critic, 1962—; WNDT-TV, New York City, associate producer, "Art-New York" series, 1964-65; New School for Social Research, New York City, instructor in creative writing and literature, 1964-69; Yale University, New Haven, Conn., visiting fellow, 1969-70; Big Sky Books (publisher), Bolinas, Calif., editor, 1971-78; poet-teacher, Poets in the Schools, 1974-84; Southampton College of Long Island University, Long Island, N.Y., adjunct professor, 1980; California College of Arts and Crafts, Oakland, associate professor, 1983-84; San Francisco Art Institute, San Francisco, Calif., instructor and coordinator of public lectures, 1984—. Part-time writer, editor, and researcher, Museum of Modern Art, New York City, 1965-69; editor, Best & Co., 1969.

AWARDS, HONORS: Dylan Thomas Memorial Award for Poetry, New School for Social Research, 1959; grant from Poets Foundation, 1968; resident at Yaddo, 1968; National Endowment for the Arts fellowship for creative writing in poetry, 1979-80; Briarcombe fellowship, 1983; Marin Arts Council grant, 1987, for poetry.

WRITINGS:

Saturday Night: Poems 1960-61, Tibor de Nagy, 1961.

(Editor) Frank O'Hara, *In Memory of My Feelings,* illustrated by 30 American artists, Museum of Modern Art, 1967.

Shining Leaves, Angel Hair, 1969.

Recent Visitors, Angel Hair, 1974.

Ants, Arif, 1975.

100 Women, Simon & Schuster, 1975.

Enigma Variations, Big Sky, 1975.

Blue Is the Hero: Poems 1960-75, L Publications, 1976.

(Editor with Joe LeSueur) *Homage to Frank O'Hara,* Creative Arts, 1980.

Start Over, Tombouctou, 1983.

Lush Life, Z Press, 1984.

Serenade, BLT, 1987.

Also contributor to various anthologies. Contributor of poetry and articles to numerous periodicals, including *Poetry, Paris Review, Locus Solus, Art and Literature, Sun and Moon, Zzyzyva,* and *Art in America.*

BIOGRAPHICAL/CRITICAL SOURCES:

PERIODICALS

Poetry, August, 1962.

World, Number 29, 1974.

*   *   *

BERNS, Walter (Fred) 1919-

PERSONAL: Born May 3, 1919, in Chicago, Ill.; son of Walter Fred and Agnes (Westergard) Berns; married Irene Sibley Lyons, June 16, 1951; children: Elizabeth, Emily, Christopher. *Education:* University of Iowa, B.Sc., 1941; graduate study at Reed College, 1948-49, and at London School of Economics and Political Science, 1949-50; University of Chicago, M.A., 1951, Ph.D., 1963.

ADDRESSES: Home—4986 Sentinel Dr., No. 402, Bethesda, Md. 20816. *Office*—Department of Government, Georgetown University, 1400 37th St., N.W., Washington, D.C. 20057; and American Enterprise Institute, 1150 17th St. N.W., Washington, D.C. 20036.

CAREER: Louisiana State University, Baton Rouge, assistant professor of political science, 1953-56; Yale University, New Haven, Conn., assistant professor of political science, 1956-59; Cornell University, Ithaca, N.Y., associate professor, 1959-62, professor of government and chairman of department, 1963-68; University of Toronto, Toronto, Ontario, visiting professor, 1969, professor of political science, 1970-79; Georgetown University, Washington, D.C., John M. Olin University Professor, 1979—. Adjunct scholar, American Enterprise Institute in Washington, D.C. Lecturer at Salzburg Seminar in American Studies, 1959; Charles Evans Hughes Visiting Professor of Political Science at Colgate University, 1970. Member of advisory board of National Institute of Law Enforcement and Criminal Justice, 1974-76. Member, National Council on the Humanities, 1983—.

MEMBER: American Political Science Association.

AWARDS, HONORS: Carnegie teaching fellow, 1952-53; Rockefeller fellow, 1965-66; Fulbright fellow, 1965-66; Clark Distinguished Teaching Award from Cornell University, 1969; grants from Earhart Foundation, 1969 and 1972; grant from U.S. Department of Justice, 1975-76; Guggenheim fellowship, 1978-79.

WRITINGS:

Freedom, Virtue, and the First Amendment, Louisiana State University Press, 1957.
(Co-author) *Essays on the Scientific Study of Politics,* edited by Herbert J. Storing, Holt, 1962.
(Editor) *Constitutional Cases in American Government,* Crowell, 1963.
The First Amendment and the Future of American Democracy, Basic Books, 1976.
For Capital Punishment: Crime and the Morality of the Death Penalty, Basic Books, 1979.
(Editor) *After the People Vote: Steps in Choosing the President,* American Enterprise Institute for Public Policy Research, 1983.
In Defense of Liberal Democracy, Regnery Gateway, 1985.
Taking the Constitution Seriously, Simon & Schuster, 1985.

CONTRIBUTOR

Robert A. Goldwin, editor, *Readings in World Politics,* Oxford University Press, 1962.
Leo Strauss and Joseph Cropsey, editors, *History of Political Philosophy,* Rand McNally, 1963.
Goldwin, editor, *A Nation of States: Essays on the American Federal System,* Rand McNalley, 1963.
Hans W. Baade, editor, *Law and Contemporary Problems,* Basic Books, 1963.
Goldwin, editor, *Political Parties,* Rand McNally, 1964.
Goldwin, editor, *One Hundred Years of Emancipation,* Rand McNally, 1964.
Goldwin, editor, *How Democratic Is America?,* Rand McNally, 1971.
Harry Clor, editor, *Censorship and Freedom of Expression,* Rand McNally, 1971.
Morton J. Frisch and Richard G. Stevens, editors, *American Political Thought,* Scribner, 1971.
Clor, editor, *The Mass Media and Modern Democracy,* Rand McNally, 1974.
Robert Horwitz, editor, *The Moral Foundations of the American Republic,* University of Virginia Press, 1977.
Leonard J. Theberge, editor, *The Judiciary in a Democratic Society,* Lexington Books, 1979.

OTHER

Contributor of numerous articles to scholarly journals, including *Western Political Quarterly, Journal of Politics, American Political Science Review, Yale Law Journal,* and *Political Science Reviewer.*

SIDELIGHTS: When Walter Berns wrote *For Capital Punishment: Crime and the Morality of the Death Penalty,* he took up a debate that has been raging for centuries. The penal system of today, he maintains, puts its emphasis on rehabilitation or deterrence instead of where it rightfully belongs: on punishment. Francis Canavan of the *National Review* explains that "both rehabilitation and deterrence shift the focus of attention from the crime to the criminal: he is to be either reformed, or prevented by fear from committing crimes in the first place. But he is not to be punished. To inflict a penalty on him because the intrinsic character of his crime *merits* punishment

reveals a barbaric desire for revenge unworthy of this enlightened age." Berns, however, argues that society must have the moral dignity to "demand that criminals be paid back, and that the worst of them be made to pay back with their lives."

In his book Berns discusses the popular arguments against the death penalty—biblical, moral, constitutional—and determines them all to be lacking in significant areas. He then goes on to point out the need for the basic principle that the death penalty stands for: punishment of the criminal to fit the crime in order to retain the dignity and responsibility of the rest of society. According to Graham Hughes, such thinking can be likened to "going back to rubbing two sticks together because we are unhappy about nuclear power." He goes on to claim that "reading Berns's book powerfully evokes righteous anger and moral indignation. His retributivist theory turns out on inspection to consist of either disguised and unconvincing utilitarian propositions or mystical calls for death that deserve psychoanalytic rather than philosophical refutation." *New York Times* writer Christopher Lehmann-Haupt, however, declares that *For Capital Punishment* "should be attended to by anyone who takes its subject seriously." Canavan, moreover, commends the book, noting that Berns "offers a calm and reasoned case for inflicting the death penalty for certain crimes." Like the author himself, Canavan concludes that "we must come to believe again that punishment, regularly and predictably inflicted, will in fact deter, and, moreover, that crime deserves to be punished."

BIOGRAPHICAL/CRITICAL SOURCES:

BOOKS

Contemporary Issues Criticism, Volume I, Gale, 1982.

PERIODICALS

Commentary, August, 1979.
Nation, November 24, 1979.
National Review, August 17, 1979.
New York Review of Books, June 28, 1979.
New York Times, July 16, 1979.
New York Times Book Review, August 19, 1979.

*   *   *

BILLINGS, Charlene W(interer) 1941-

PERSONAL: Born January 11, 1941, in Manchester, N.H.; daughter of George E. (a power company employee) and Alice (a nurse; maiden name, Labbee) Winterer; married Barry A. Billings (an electrical engineer), December 16, 1961; children: Cheryl, Sharon. *Education:* University of New Hampshire, B.A. (cum laude), 1962; Rivier College, M.S., 1973.

ADDRESSES: Home—39 Coburn Ave., Nashua, N.H. 03063. *Agent*—Janet D. Chenery, Chenery Associates Literary Agency, 440 East 23rd St., New York, N.Y. 10010.

CAREER: Hopkinton High School, Hopkinton, N.H., science teacher, 1962-63; University of New Hampshire, Durham, research assistant in biochemistry, 1963-64; writer.

MEMBER: American Society of Journalists and Authors, Society of Children's Book Writers, Phi Beta Kappa, Sigma Xi (honorary associate member), Phi Kappa Phi, Phi Sigma.

AWARDS, HONORS: "Outstanding Science Trade Book for Children" designations from the National Association of Science Teachers, 1984, for *Microchip: Small Wonder,* and 1986, for *Space Station: Bold New Step beyond Earth,* for *Fiber*

Optics: Bright New Way to Communicate, and for *Christa McAuliffe: Pioneer Space Teacher; Fiber Optics* was also chosen one of Dodd's best four children's books of 1986 by the Cooperative Children's Book Center, University of Wisconsin.

WRITINGS:

CHILDREN'S BOOKS; NONFICTION

Spring Peepers Are Calling, illustrations by Susan Bonners, Dodd, 1978.
Salamanders, Dodd, 1981.
Scorpions, Dodd, 1983.
Microchip: Small Wonder, Dodd, 1984.
Space Station: Bold New Step beyond Earth, Dodd, 1986.
Fiber Optics: Bright New Way to Communicate, Dodd, 1986.
Christa McAuliffe: Pioneer Space Teacher, Enslow Publishers, 1986.
Loon: Voice of the Wilderness, Dodd, in press.

WORK IN PROGRESS: A biography of Rear Admiral Grace Murray Hopper for Enslow Publishers.

SIDELIGHTS: Charlene W. Billings once told *CA:* "Writing about science for children brings together my love for both. The boundless enthusiasms and curiosity of young people continues to motivate me. Well-written science books for children are of the utmost importance. They must be accurate and should convey the excitement of science. They provide the opportunity to discover, understand, and appreciate the natural and technical world we all share. Besides writing, I enjoy cooking, photography, camping, swimming, and walks in the country. Many of these activities include my family."

BIOGRAPHICAL/CRITICAL SOURCES:

PERIODICALS

Appraisal: Children's Science Books, spring, 1980.
Booklist, January 1, 1985, July 1, 1986, December 1, 1986.
Bulletin of the Center for Children's Books, September, 1986, November, 1986.
Instructor, May, 1979.
Journal of Reading, March, 1985.
School Library Journal, April, 1979, February, 1985, September, 1986, December, 1986.
Science and Children, January, 1980, May, 1985.
Science Books and Films, September-October, 1985, February, 1987.

*   *   *

BLAIR, Shannon
  See KAYE, Marilyn

*   *   *

BLAUER, Ettagale   1940-
  (Ettagale Laure)

PERSONAL: Born June 8, 1940, in New York, N.Y.; daughter of Samuel and Minnie (Canton) Blauer; married Jason Laure (a photojournalist), May 5, 1974 (divorced January 16, 1984). *Education:* Hunter College (now Herbert H. Lehman College of the City University of New York), B.A., 1961.

ADDRESSES: Home—8 West 13th St., New York, N.Y. 10011.

CAREER: Worked as a public relations writer for Chemstrand Co., Seligman & Latz, Walter Dorwin Teague Associates,

Clairol Inc., and Monsanto Co., 1961-71; Chilton Co., New York, N.Y., writer, 1971-83; free-lance writer, 1983—.

AWARDS, HONORS: National Book Award finalist, 1975, and Notable Book in the Field of Social Studies selection, joint committee of the National Council of Social Studies and the Children's Book Council, 1975, both for *Joi Bangla! The Children of Bangladesh;* Jesse Neal Editorial Achievement Award from American Business Press, 1977, for stories on women and discrimination, and 1979, for a series on gold; American Library Association notable book citation for *South Africa: Coming of Age under Apartheid;* New York Public Library Book for the Teen Age selections, 1980, 1981, and 1982, all for *Joi Bangla! The Children of Bangladesh,* and *Jovem Portugal: After the Revolution,* and 1981 and 1982, for *South Africa: Coming of Age under Apartheid.*

WRITINGS:

UNDER NAME ETTAGALE LAURE

(With Jason Laure) *Joi Bangla!: The Children of Bangladesh* (young adult), Farrar, Straus, 1974.
(With J. Laure) *Joven Portugal: After the Revolution* (young adult), Farrar, Straus, 1977.
(With J. Laure) *South Africa: Coming of Age under Apartheid* (young adult), Farrar, Straus, 1980.

OTHER

Contributor to magazines, including *Signature, Junior Scholastic, Ornament, The World and I,* and *Savvy.* Editor, *Jewelers' Circular Keystone,* 1972-83.

SIDELIGHTS: Ettagale Blauer told *CA:* "As a writer of nonfiction, I consider it both my task and my pleasure to learn about foreign subjects and people and bring that information to my readers who cannot make those same journeys except through my writings."

BIOGRAPHICAL/CRITICAL SOURCES:

PERIODICALS

Chicago Tribune Book World, November 9, 1980.
Los Angeles Times Book Review, August 3, 1980.

*   *   *

BLOCH, Barbara   1925-
  (Phoebe Edwards)

PERSONAL: Born May 26, 1925, in New York, N.Y.; daughter of Emil William (a stockbroker) and Dorothy (a bacteriologist and executive administrator; maiden name, Lowengrund) Bloch; married Joseph Bennet Sanders, August 3, 1944 (divorced January 4, 1961); married Theodore Simon Benjamin (a publisher), September 20, 1964; children: (first marriage) Elizabeth Sanders-Hines, Ellen; (stepchildren from second marriage) Phyllis, Jill. *Education:* Attended New York University and New School for Social Research; study with American Symphony Orchestra League. *Politics:* Democrat. *Religion:* "Jewish/Humanist by affiliation."

ADDRESSES: Home and office—International Cookbook Services, 21 Dupont Ave., White Plains, N.Y. 10605.

CAREER: Westchester Democratic County Committee, White Plains, N.Y., office manager, 1955-56; Westchester Symphony Orchestra, Scarsdale, N.Y., manager, 1957-62; P. K. Halstead Associates, Larchmont, N.Y., assistant to president, 1962-63; Active Employment Service, White Plains, office manager, 1963-65; International Cookbook Services, White Plains, president, 1978—.

WRITINGS:

(Under pseudonym Phoebe Edwards) *Anyone Can Quilt,* Benjamin Co., 1975.
The Meat Board Meat Book, introduction by Julia Child, McGraw, 1977.
If It Doesn't Pan Out: How to Cope with Cooking Disasters (Book-of-the-Month Cooking and Craft Club selection), Dembner, 1981.

AUTHOR OF "AMERICANIZED" EDITIONS

The Cuisine of Olympe, New Century, 1982.
Favorite Family Baking, Meredith Corp., 1982.
The Book of Baking, Meredith Corp., 1983.
Cakes and Pastries, Morrow, 1983.
Baking Easy and Elegant, H. P. Books, 1984.
Best of Cold Foods, H. P. Books, 1985.
The Art of Cooking (Better Homes & Gardens Book Club selection), H. P. Books, 1986.
The Art of Baking (Better Homes & Gardens Book Club selection), H. P. Books, 1987.

Also "Americanizer" of a cookbook series for Octopus, 1980, and for Marshall Cavendish, 1980, 1981, and 1982.

EDITOR

(And contributor) *The All Beef Cookbook,* Scribner, 1973.
(And contributor) Anne Borella, *In Glass Naturally,* Benjamin Co., 1974.
Microwave Miracles, Rutledge/Benjamin, 1974.
(And contributor) *Fresh Ideas with Mushrooms,* Benjamin Co., 1977.
Good Food Ideas Cheese Cookbook, Benjamin Co., 1977.
Polly-O Cooking with Cheese, Polly-O Cheese Co., 1977.
Cook's Choice, Benjamin Co., 1979.
Yesterday and Today: From the Kitchens of Stokely, Benjamin Co., 1980.
The Sun Maid Cookbook, Benjamin Co., 1980.
The Any Oven Cookbook, Benjamin Co., 1981.
Ovenware of the Future Cookbook, Benjamin Co., 1981.
Any Way You Make It, Benjamin Co., 1982.
The Complete Chicken Cookbook, Benjamin Co., 1984.
Guilden's Makes Good Food Taste Great, Benjamin Co., 1984.
The Convenience of Canned, the Flavor of Fresh, Benjamin Co., 1986.

OTHER

Author of microwave cooking column in *House Beautiful,* 1984—.

SIDELIGHTS: Barbara Bloch told *CA:* "Outside of my family and career, my main interests have been classical music, liberal politics, and young people. My interest in travel did not develop until I could afford it, and my interest in food did not develop until my second marriage, when I found I had a husband who enjoyed eating good food.

"I became a full-time writer, editor, and teacher about fifteen years ago when I decided I could not sit through another meeting, or listen to the reading of the minutes of the previous meeting. It was also the time at which I concluded my four daughters no longer needed a full-time mother, a concept from which very few of us had been liberated at that time.

"Although I have always specialized in cookbooks, in recent years I have added another specialty—that of Americanizing cookbooks. Both English and American publishers are finally coming to the realization that, although we speak the same language over the dinner table, we do not speak the same language in the kitchen. It is a specialty that has developed into a surprisingly successful business.

"I have been a guest on several radio and television programs, and I lecture periodically. I have also taught cooking classes and love teaching, although I no longer have the time to include it in my schedule.

"The number of poorly written cookbooks published every year distresses me. Too often, books are written by people who seem to be good cooks, but do not understand the demands of proper cookbook writing—and evidently there are not enough good cookbook editors around to make proper judgments. Cookbooks should be written carefully and clearly, and the recipes should be completely reliable—both food and time are too expensive to waste on improperly written recipes. However, in spite of the fact that I take the writing of a cookbook very seriously, my advice for most people who cook is 'relax.' People who make a fetish of food and cooking make me uncomfortable.

"I have always had an enormous urge to be creative. Having finally acknowledged that I could not act, paint, or make music, I have found a satisfying creative outlet in the combination of cooking and writing."

*   *   *

BLUTH, B(etty) J(ean) 1934-

PERSONAL: Born December 5, 1934, in Philadelphia, Pa.; daughter of Robert Thomas (a realtor) and Catherine (a model; maiden name, Boxman) Gowland; married Thomas Del Bluth, August 20, 1960 (deceased); children: Robert, Richard. *Education:* Bucknell University, B.A. (cum laude), 1957; Fordham University, M.A., 1960; University of California, Los Angeles, Ph.D., 1970.

ADDRESSES: Home—7116 Bedstraw Ct., Springfield, Va. 22152. *Office*—Code SSE, Space Station Program Office, NASA Headquarters, 600 Independence Ave., Washington, D.C. 20546.

CAREER: Reading Laboratory, Philadelphia, Pa., instructor, 1958-59; high school teacher of history, civics, and English in San Diego, Calif., 1959-60; Immaculate Heart College, Los Angeles, Calif., instructor, 1960-63, assistant professor of sociology, 1963-65; California State University, Northridge, assistant professor, 1965-75, associate professor, 1975-79, professor of sociology, 1979—, fellow at Institute for the Advancement of Teaching and Learning, 1974, grantee at NASA Space Station Office in Washington, D.C., 1983—. Member of United Nations team on the relevance of space activities to economic and social development; member of Citizens Advisory Council on National Space Policy; public speaker. Consultant to businesses and religious groups, including General Dynamics, Comworld Productions, Rico-Lion, Ltd., Daughters of Mary and Joseph, Dominican Sisters, and Immaculate Heart Community.

MEMBER: International Academy of Astronautics, American Sociological Association, American Institution of Aeronautics and Astronautics, American Astronautical Society, Institute for the Social Science Study of Space (member of academic advisory board), Space Studies Institute, Air Force Association, L-5 Society (member of board of directors), Institute for the Advancement of Engineering, British Interplanetary Society, Phi Beta Kappa.

AWARDS, HONORS: Teaching award from Alpha Omega, 1966, 1974; Distinguished Teaching Award, California State University, Northridge, 1968; certificate of appreciation from American Astronautical Society, 1978, for "The SMD III and Spacelab Simulation: A Critical Look"; grants from Rockwell International Corp., TRW, Inc., and Lockheed Corp., 1978-80; certificate of appreciation from Society of American Military Engineers, 1980, for presentation "Social and Psychological Aspects of Long Duration Space Flight"; special program award from Los Angeles section of American Institution of Aeronautics and Astronautics, 1980, for "An Evening with Krafft Ehricke"; Hypathia Cluster Award for excellence in furthering manned space flight, 1984.

WRITINGS:

(Editor with Robert Chianese, James Kellenberger, and others) *Search for Identity Reader,* Xerox College Publishing, 1973.
(With John Irving, Sherry May, and Dick Smith) *Search for Community Reader,* Xerox College Publishing, 1977.
(Editor with S. R. McNeal) *Update on Space,* Behavior Systems, Volume I, 1981, Volume II, 1982.
Parson's General Theory of Action: A Summary of the Basic Theory, National Behavior Systems, 1982.
Space Station Habitability Report, Boeing Aerospace Company, 1983.
Space Station/Nuclear Submarines Analog, Boeing Aerospace Company, 1983.
Soviet Space Stations as Analogs, Boeing Aerospace Company, 1983, 2nd edition, NASA, 1986.
Space Station/Antarctic Analogs, NASA, 1984.
Human Performance in Space, Robert E. Krieger, 1987.

CONTRIBUTOR

R. Van Patten and others, editors, *The Industrialization of Space: Advances in the Astronautical Sciences,* Volume XXXVI, Part II, Univelt, 1978.
Richard Johnson and others, editors, *The Future of the U.S. Space Program: Advances in the Astronautical Sciences,* Univelt, Volume XXXVI, Part II, 1979, Volume XXXVIII, Part II, 1979.
Stan Kent, editor, *Remember the Future: The Apollo Legacy,* Univelt, 1979.
Stephen Cheston, editor, *NASA Guide for Teaching and Student Research,* Georgetown University, 1981.
Cheston, editor, *Space Humanization Series,* Volume II, NASA, 1982.
James E. Katz, editor, *People in Space,* Transaction Books, 1985.
Manned Mars Mission, NASA, 1985.

OTHER

Contributor to scientific journals.

WORK IN PROGRESS: Research on Soviet and U.S. social and psychological aspects of long-duration space flight, techniques of stress reduction, and women in space.

SIDELIGHTS: B. J. Bluth told *CA:* "Being involved with mankind's evolution into space is a distinctly exciting and challenging enterprise—worth a life. Unlike those at the departure of Columbus, we are able to participate in the momentous changes to come as a result of the exploration and habitation of space, because we can anticipate their impor-

tance. By moving off-planet, humanity will probably grow and change far beyond our present imagination, and I hope to do all I can to be part of and help others be part of that change."

*   *   *

BOBROW, Edwin E.   1928-

PERSONAL: Born April 8, 1928; son of Abraham David and Emma (Goldstein) Bobrow; married Gloria Lefkowitz, May 3, 1954; children: Mark David. *Education:* Long Island University, B.Sc., 1949; New York University, advanced study at Graduate School of Business Administration.

ADDRESSES: Home—4465 Douglas Ave., Riverside, N.Y. 10471. *Office*—Bobrow Consulting Group, Inc., 175 Fifth Ave., New York, N.Y. 10010.

CAREER: Decro Wall Corp., Elmsford, N.Y., former director of marketing; Bobrow Sales Associates, Inc., New York, N.Y., chairman of the board, 1955—; president of Bobrow Consulting Group, Inc. President, Oded International Corp. and China Uninte Development Corp. Partner, Bobrow Realty Co. Adjunct associate professor at New York University and past program coordinator for marketing management program, Management Institute; guest lecturer at Fairleigh Dickinson University, Long Island University, and University of Wisconsin. Former member of board of directors of Business Games Group, Graduate School of Business Administration, Long Island University, and of Solidaridad Humana, Inc. Conductor of workshops; lecturer to business groups and at conferences. United Jewish Appeal of Greater New York, member of Leadership Council, past chairman of Hardware, Housewares, Paint, Garden and Outdoor Living Division; committee member of Israel Bond Drive; committee member, 1978 National United Nations Day; Arthritis Foundation, New York chapter, senior vice-president and member of board of governors. Member of Volunteer Urban Consulting Group, Inc.; consultant to firms, including Honeywell and other Fortune 500 companies.

MEMBER: American Arbitration Association (member of panel of arbitrators), American Management Association, American Marketing Association, Manufacturers' Agents National Association, National Council of Salesmen's Organizations (past vice-president), Institute of Management Consultants, Society of Professional Management Consultants (past member of board of directors), Authors Guild, Authors League of America, Hardware Boosters, Sales Executives Club of New York.

AWARDS, HONORS: State of Israel Leadership Award; United Jewish Appeal Scroll of Honor and Leadership Citation; Manufacturers' Agents Associations Special Award; Distinguished Alumnus Award, Long Island University; Certificate of Highest Achievement in Teaching, University of Wisconsin (twice); Distinguished Service Marketing Award, Sales Executives Club of New York; Hardware Retailing Magazine Industry Service Award; Appreciation Award, Automotive Affiliates Representatives Partners in Successful Marketing; Appreciation Award, Volunteer Urban Consulting Group, Inc.,; Wheel Award for contribution to new product development and marketing; numerous citations from the Institute for Mass Marketing.

WRITINGS:

How to Make Big Money as an Independent Sales Agent, Parker Publishing, 1967.
Selling the Volume Retailer: A Practical Plan for Success, Chain Store Publishing, 1975.

How to Sell Your Way into Your Own Business with Little or No Capital, Bill Communications, 1977.

Marketing through Manufacturers' Agents, Bill Communications, 1978.

(Editor with others) *Sales Manager's Handbook,* Dow Jones-Irwin, 1983.

(Co-editor) *Marketing Handbook,* Dow Jones-Irwin, 1985, Volume I: *Marketing Practices,* Volume II: *Marketing Management.*

(Co-author) *Pioneering New Products,* Dow Jones-Irwin, 1987.

Also author of a booklet, *Is the Independent Sales Agent for You?,* for the U.S. Government Small Business Administration; also co-author of two booklets, *Checklist for Marketing Hardlines through Mass Merchandisers* and *Checklist for Successfully Marketing New Products.*

Also contributor to *New Products Handbook* and to *AMA Marketing Handbook.* Columnist, *Housewares Review* for two years, *Income Opportunities,* and for a number of other business publications. Contributor of more than one hundred articles on marketing and sales to trade journals. Editor of *Selling through Reps* and *Sales and Marketing Management Newsletter;* contributing editor of *Income Opportunities Magazine;* member of editorial advisory board of *Journal of Applied Management.*

* * *

BOELL, Heinrich (Theodor) 1917-1985

PERSONAL: Born December 21, 1917, in Cologne, Germany (now West Germany); died July 16, 1985, at his home in Huertgen Forest in the Eifel Mountains, near Bonn, West Germany; son of Viktor (a master furniture maker) and Maria (Hermanns) Boell; married Annemarie Cech (a translator), 1942; children: Christoph (died, 1945), Raimund (died, 1982), Rene, Vincent. *Education:* Completed college preparatory school; attended the University of Cologne, 1939. *Religion:* Roman Catholic.

ADDRESSES: Home—An der Nuellheck 19, 5165 Huertgenwald-Grosshau, West Germany.

CAREER: Apprentice to a book dealer in Bonn, Germany, 1938; writer, 1947-85. Guest lecturer of poetics, University of Frankfurt, 1964. *Military service:* German Army, 1939-45; American prisoner of war, 1945.

AWARDS, HONORS: Prize from "Group 47," 1951, for short story "The Black Sheep"; Rene Schickele Prize, 1952; Cultural Prize of German Industry; Southern German Radio Prize and German Critics Prize, both 1953, both for radio play "Moench and Raeuber"; French Publishers Prize for best foreign novel, *Tribune de Paris,* 1954; Edward von der Heydt Prize from City of Wuppertal, 1958; Grand Art Prize of North Rhine-Westphalia, 1959; Charles Veillon Prize, 1960; Literature Prize of City of Cologne, 1960; Premio d'Isola d'Elba, 1965; Premio Calabria, 1966; George Buechner Prize, German Academy for Language and Poetry, 1967; Nobel Prize for Literature, 1972, for contributions to "a renewal of German literature in the postwar era"; honorary doctorates from Trinity College, University of Dublin, University of Aston, University of Birmingham, and Brunel University, all 1973; Carl von Ossietzky Medal, International League of Human Rights, 1974; first Neil Gunn fellow, Scottish Arts Council, 1974; named honorary member of American Academy of Arts and Letters, and of American National Institute of Art and Literature, both 1974; named honorary citizen of City of Cologne, 1983; hon-

orary title of professor conferred by North Rhine-Westphalia, 1983.

WRITINGS:

FICTION

Der Zug war puenktlich (also see below; novella), F. Middelhauve (Opladen), 1949, reprinted, Deutscher Taschenbuch (Munich), 1973, translation by Richard Graves published as *The Train Was on Time,* Criterion Books, 1956, new translation by Leila Vennewitz, Secker & Warburg, 1973.

Wanderer, kommst du nach Spa (also see below; short stories; includes "Damals in Odessa"), F. Middelhauve, 1950, reprinted, Deutscher Taschenbuch, 1971, translation by Mervyn Savill published as *Traveller, If You Come to Spa,* Arco, 1956, bilingual edition translated and edited by Savill and John Bednall, Max Hueber (Munich), 1956.

Wo warst du, Adam? (also see below; novel), F. Middlehauve, 1951, reprinted, Deutscher Taschenbuch, 1972, translation by Savill published as *Adam, Where Art Thou?,* Criterion Books, 1955, new translation by Vennewitz published as *And Where Were You, Adam?,* McGraw, 1970.

Nicht nur zur Weihnachtszeit (also see below; satire), Frankfurter Verlags-Anstalt (Frankfurt), 1952, expanded edition with other satires published as *Nichtnurzur Weihnachtszeit: Satiren,* Deutscher Taschenbuch, 1966, new edition, Kiepenheuer & Witsch, 1981.

Und sagte kein einziges Wort (also see below; novel), Kiepenheuer & Witsch, 1953, reprinted with epilogue by Gerhard Joop, Ullstein (Frankfurt), 1972, translation by Graves published as *Acquainted with the Night,* Holt, 1954, new translation by Vennewitz published as *And Never Said a Word,* McGraw, 1978.

Haus ohne Hueter (also see below; novel), Kiepenheuer & Witsch, 1954, reprinted, 1974, translation by Savill published as *Tomorrow and Yesterday,* Criterion Books, 1957 (published in England as *The Unguarded House,* Arco, 1957).

Das Brot der fruehen Jahre: Erzaehlung (also see below; novella), Kiepenheuer & Witsch, 1955, reprinted, 1980, translation by Savill published as *The Bread of Our Early Years,* Arco, 1957, new translation by Vennewitz published as *The Bread of Those Early Years,* McGraw, 1976.

So ward Abend und Morgen: Erzaehlungen (stories), Verlag der Arche (Zurich), 1955.

Unberechenbare Gaeste: Heitere Erzaehlungen (stories), Verlag der Arche, 1956.

Abenteuer eines Brotbeutels, und Andere Geschichten (stories), edited by Richard Plant, Norton, 1957.

Im Tal der donnernden Hufe: Erzaehlung (also see below; novella), Insel-Verlag (Wiesbaden), 1957.

Doktor Murkes gesammeltes Schweigen, und andere Satiren (also see below; satires; includes "Doktor Murkes gesammeltes Schweigen" and "Der Wegwerfer"), Kiepenheuer & Witsch, 1958, reprinted, 1977.

Erzaehlungen (contains *Der Zug war puenktlich* and *Wanderer kommst du nach Spa*), F. Middelhauve, 1958.

Billard um halbzehn (also see below; novel), Kiepenheuer & Witsch, 1959, translation by Patrick Bowles published as *Billiards at Half-Past Nine,* Weidenfeld & Nicolson, 1961, McGraw, 1962, new translation by Vennewitz, Avon, 1975.

Der Bahnhof von Zimpren: Erzaehlungen (stories), Peter List (Munich), 1959.

Die Waage der Baleks, und andere Erzaehlungen (stories), Union Verlag (Berlin), 1959.

Der Mann mit den Messern: Erzaehlungen; mit einem autobiographischen Nachwort (stories with an autobiographical epilogue), Reclam (Stuttgart), 1959, reprinted, 1972.

Nicht nur zur Weihnachtszeit [and] *Der Mann mit den Messern,* edited by Dorothea Berger, American Book Company, 1959.

Als der Krieg ausbrach; als der Krieg zu Ende war (also see below), Insel, 1962, published as *Als der Krieg ausbrach: Erzaehlungen,* Deutscher Taschenbuch, 1966.

Ansichten eines Clowns (also see below; novel), Kiepenheuer & Witsch, 1963, translation by Vennewitz published as *The Clown,* McGraw, 1965.

Heinrich Boell, 1947 bis 1951: Der Zug war puenktlich, Wo Warst du, Adam?, und sechsundzwanzig Erzaehlungen (also see below) F. Middlehauve, 1963.

Doktor Murkes gesammeltes Schweigen, and Other Stories, edited by Gertrude Seidmann, introduction by H. M. Waidson, Harrap, 1963.

Entfernung von der Truppe (also see below; novella), Kiepenheuer & Witsch, 1964.

Fuenf Erzaehlungen (also see below; stories), De Roos, 1964.

Absent without Leave: Two Novellas (translation by Vennewitz of *Entfernung von der Truppe* and *Als der Krieg ausbrach; als der Krieg zu Ende war* under the titles ''Absent without Leave'' and ''Enter and Exit''), McGraw, 1965.

Ende einer Dienstfahrt (also see below; novel), Kiepenheuer & Witsch, 1966, translation by Vennewitz published as *The End of a Mission,* McGraw, 1967.

Eighteen Stories (translations by Vennewitz; contains translation of *Im Tal der donnernden Hufe: Erzaehlung* published as ''In the Valley of the Thundering Hooves,'' of ''Doktor Murkes gesammeltes Schweigen'' published as ''Murke's Collected Silences,'' and of ''The Wegwerfer'' published as ''The Thrower Away''), McGraw, 1966.

Absent without Leave, and Other Stories (translations by Vennewitz), Weidenfeld & Nicholson, 1967.

Und sagte kein einziges Wort [and] *Haus ohne Hueter* [and] *Das Brot der fruehen Jahre,* Kiepenheuer & Witsch, 1969.

Children Are Civilians Too (story translations by Vennewitz; contains translation of *Wanderer, kommst du nach Spa,* which includes ''Damals in Odessa'' published as ''That Time We Were in Odessa,'' and selected stories from *Heinrich Boell, 1947 bis 1951*), McGraw, 1970.

Adam, and, The Train: Two Novels (translation by Vennewitz of *Wo warst du, Adam?* and *Der Zug war puenktlich*), McGraw, 1970.

Gruppenbild mit Dame (novel), Kiepenheuer & Witsch, 1971, translation by Vennewitz published as *Group Portrait with Lady,* McGraw, 1973.

Die Essenholer, und andere Erzaehlungen (stories), Hirschgraben-Verlag (Frankfurt), 1971.

Fuenf Erzaehlungen (stories), Hyperion-Verlag (Freiburg), 1971.

Billard um halb zehn [and] *Ansichten eines Clowns* [and] *Ende einer Dienstfahrt,* Kiepenheuer & Witsch, 1971.

Erzaehlungen, 1950-1970 (stories), Kiepenheuer & Witsch, 1972.

Erzaehlungen (shortened and simplified stories for schools and self-study), Grafisk Forlag (Copenhagen), 1973.

Die verlorene Ehre der Katharina Blum; oder, wie Gewalt enstehen und wohin sie fuehren kann (novel with epilogue), Kiepenheuer & Witsch, 1974, translation by Vennewitz published as *The Lost Honor of Katharina Blum:*

How Violence Develops and Where It Can Lead, McGraw, 1975.

Mein trauriges Gesicht: Humoresken und Satiren, Phillip Reclam (Leipzig), 1974.

Berichte zur Gesinnungslage der Nation (satire), Kiepenheuer & Witsch, 1975.

Fuersorgliche Belagerung (novel), Kiepenheuer & Witsch, 1979, translation by Vennewitz published as *The Safety Net,* Knopf, 1982.

Du Faehrst zu oft nach Heidelberg (stories), Lamuv (Bornheim-Merten), 1979, published as *Du faehrst zu oft nach Heidelberg und andere Erzaehlungen,* Deutscher Taschenbuch, 1982.

Gesammelte Erzaehlungen (stories), Kiepenheuer & Witsch, 1981.

Das Vermaechtnis (novel originally written in 1948), Lamuv, 1982, translation by Vennewitz published as *A Soldier's Legacy,* Knopf, 1985.

Die Verwundung und andere fruehe Erzaehlungen (stories from 1948-1952), Lamuv, 1983, translation by Vennewitz published as *The Casualty,* Farrar, Straus, 1986.

Der Angriff: Erzaehlungen, 1947-1949 (stories), Kiepenheuer & Witsch, 1983.

Die schwarzen Schafe: Erzaehlungen, 1950-1952 (stories), Kiepenheuer & Witsch, 1983.

Veraenderungen in Staech: Erzaehlungen, 1962-1980 (stories), Kiepenheuer & Witsch, 1984.

Frauen vor Flusslandschaft: Roman in Dialogen und Selbstgespraechen (novel; title means ''Women before a River Landscape''), Kiepenheuer & Witsch, 1985.

The Stories of Heinrich Boell (translations by Vennewitz), Random House, 1986.

Also author of *Meistererzaehlungen* (stories), R. Mohn.

PLAYS

Die Spurlosen (also see below; radio play), Hans Bredow-Institut (Hamburg), 1957.

Bilanz [and] *Klopfzeichen: Zwei Hoerspiele* (also see below; radio plays; *Bilanz* first produced, 1957; translation of *Klopfzeichen* produced as ''The Knocking,'' British Broadcasting Corp., September, 1967), Reclam, 1961.

Ein Schluck Erde (stage play), Kiepenheuer & Witsch, 1962.

Zum Tee bei Dr. Borsig: Hoerspiele (radio plays), Deutscher Taschenbuch, 1964.

Die Spurlosen: Drei Hoerspiele (radio plays), Insel-Verlag (Leipzig), 1966.

Vier Hoerspiele (radio plays), edited by G. P. Sonnex, Methuen, 1966.

Hausfriedensbruch: Hoerspiel [and] *Aussatz: Schauspiel* (radio play and theatre play, respectively; *Aussatz* first produced at Aachen's City Theatre, October 17, 1970), Kiepenheuer & Witsch, 1969.

(With Dorothee Soelle and Lucas Mariz Boehmer) *Politische Meditationen zu Glueck und Vergeblichkeit* (television plays), Luchterhand (Darmstadt), 1973.

Ein Tag wie sonst: Hoerspiele (radio plays), Deutscher Taschenbuch, 1980.

POETRY

Gedichte, Literarisches Colloquium (Berlin), 1972.

Gedichte mit Collagen von Klaus Staeck, Lamuv, 1975, revised edition with poems through 1980, Deutscher Taschenbuch, 1981.

NONFICTION

Irisches Tagebuch, Kiepenheuer & Witsch, 1957, reprinted, 1972, translation by Vennewitz published as *Irish Journal*, McGraw, 1967, reprinted, Secker & Warburg, 1983.

Brief an einen jungen Katholiken, Kiepenheuer & Witsch, 1961.

Frankfurter Vorlesungen (lectures), Kiepenheuer & Witsch, 1966.

Hierzulande: Aufsaetze (essays), Deutscher Taschenbuch, 1967.

Aufsaetze, Kritiken, Reden (essays, reviews, and speeches), Kiepenheuer & Witsch, 1967.

Neue politische und literarische Schriften (also see below; essays on politics and literature), Kiepenheuer & Witsch, 1973.

Schwierigkeiten mit der Bruederlichkeit: Politische Schriften (selections from *Neue politische und literarische Schriften*), Deutscher Taschenbuch, 1976.

Einmischung erwuenscht (selection of essays and speeches published 1971-1976), Kiepenheuer & Witsch, 1977.

Missing Persons and Other Essays (translations by Vennewitz of selected essays, reviews, and speeches from 1952-1976), McGraw, 1977.

Spuren der Zeitgenossenschaft: Literarische Schriften (selection of literary essays and speeches from 1971-1976), Deutscher Taschenbuch, 1980.

Gefahren von falschen Bruedern: Politische Schriften (selection of political essays and speeches from 1971-1976), Deutscher Taschenbuch, 1980.

Was soll aus dem Jungen bloss werden? Oder Irgendwas mit Buechern (autobiography), Lamuv, 1981, translation by Vennewitz published as *What's to Become of the Boy? Or Something to Do with Books*, Knopf, 1984.

Vermintes Gelaende: Essayistische Schriften 1977-1981 (essays), Kiepenheuer & Witsch, 1982.

Bild, Bonn, Boenisch (political analysis), Lamuv, 1984.

AUTHOR OF TEXT FOR PHOTOGRAPHY BOOKS

Karl Hargesheimer, *Im Ruhrgebiet*, Kiepenheuer & Witsch, 1958.

Chargesheimer (pseudonym for Hargesheimer), *Unter Krahnenbaeumen: Bilder aus einer Strasse*, Greven Verlag (Cologne), 1958.

Chargesheimer, *Menschen am Rhein*, Kiepenheuer & Witsch, 1960.

Karl Pawek, editor, *Weltausstellung der Photographie: 555 Photos von 264 Photographen aus 30 Laendern zu dem Thema, "Was ist der Mensch?,"* H. Nannen (Hamburg), 1964.

August Sander, die Zerstoerung Koelns: Photographien, 1945-46, Schirmer/Mosel, 1985.

"HEINRICH BOELL WERKE" SERIES; OMNIBUS EDITIONS

Heinrich Boell Werke: Romane und Erzaehlungen 1947-1977 (contains all novels, novellas, and stories from 1947-1977), five volumes, edited by Bernd Balzer, Kiepenheuer & Witsch, 1977.

. . . *Essayistische Schriften und Reden* (contains all essays, reviews, and speeches through 1978), three volumes, edited by Balzer, Kiepenheuer & Witsch, 1979.

. . . *Interviews* (contains all interviews and conversations through 1978), edited by Balzer, Kiepenheuer & Witsch, 1979.

. . . *Hoerpiele, Theaterstuecke, Drehbuecher, Gedichte* (contains all plays for radio, theater, and film through 1978, and poems through 1972), edited by Balzer, Kiepenheuer & Witsch, 1979.

TRANSLATOR OF NOVELS AND STORIES INTO GERMAN; WITH WIFE, ANNEMARIE BOELL

Kay Cicellis, *Kein Name bei den Leuten* (translation of *No Name in the Street*), Kiepenheuer & Witsch, 1953.

(And with G. Goyert and W. Baechler) Adriaan Morrieen, *Ein unordentlicher Mensch* (translation from the Dutch of *Een slordign mens*), Biedenstein (Munich), 1955.

Cicellis, *Tod einer Stadt* (translation of *Death of a Town*), Kiepenheuer & Witsch, 1956.

Paul Horgan, *Weihnachtsabend in San Cristobal* (translation of *The Saintmaker's Christmas Eve*), Walter (Freiburg), 1956.

Patrick White, *Zur Ruhe kam der Baum des Menschen nie* (translation of *The Tree of Man*), Kiepenheuer & Witsch, 1957.

Horgan, *Der Teufel in der Wueste* (translation of *The Devil in the Desert*), Walter, 1958.

Horgan, *Eine Rose zur Weihnachtszeit* (translation of *One Red Rose for Christmas*), Walter, 1960.

Bernard Malamud, *Der Gehilfe* (translation of *The Assistant*), Kiepenheuer & Witsch, 1960.

Tomas O'Crohan, *Die Boote fahren nicht mehr aus: Bericht eines irischen Fischers* (translation of *The Islandman*), Walter, 1960.

(And with Elisabeth Schnack) J. D. Salinger, *Kurz vor dem Krieg gegen die Eskimos und andere Kurzgeschichten* (translation of "Just before the War with the Eskimos" and other stories), Kiepenheuer & Witsch, 1961.

Salinger, *Der Faenger im Roggen* (translation of *The Catcher in the Rye*), revised translation, Kiepenheuer & Witsch, 1962.

Salinger, *Franny und Zooey* (translation of *Franny and Zooey*), Kiepenheuer & Witsch, 1963.

Eilis Dillon, *Die Insel der Pferde* (translation of *The Island of Horses*), Herder (Frieburg), 1964.

Salinger, *Hebt den Dachbalken hoch, Zimmerleute* [and] *Seymour wird vorgestellt* (translation of *Raise High the Roof Beam, Carpenters* and *Seymour: An Introduction*), Kiepenheuer & Witsch, 1965.

Brendan Behan, *Der Spanner* (translation of *The Scarperer*), Kiepenheuer & Witsch, 1966.

Flann O'Brien (pseudonym for Brian O'Nolan), *Das harte Leben* (translation of *The Hard Life*), Nannen (Hamburg), 1966.

(And with Schnack) Salinger, *Neun Erzaehlungen* (translation of *Nine Stories*), Kiepenheuer & Witsch, 1966.

Louise Fatio, *Das Geheimnis des gluecklicken Loewen* (translation of *The Happy Lion's Treasure*), Herder, 1971.

Malamud, *Schwarz ist meine Lieblingsfarbe, und andere Erzaehlungen* (translation of *Idiots First and Other Stories*), Kiepenheuer & Witsch, 1971.

George Bernard Shaw, *Handbuch des Revolutionaers* (translation of *John Tanner: The Revolutionist's Handbook*), Suhrkamp, 1972.

O. Henry, *Gesammelte Stories* (translation of *Collected Works*), three volumes, Walter, 1973-74.

TRANSLATOR OF PLAYS; WITH A. BOELL

Behan, *Die Geisel* (translation of *The Hostage*), Kiepenheuer & Witsch, 1958.

Behan, *Der Mann von morgen frueh* (translation of *The Quare Fellow*), Kiepenheuer & Witsch, 1959.

John Synge, *Ein wahrer Held* (translation of *The Playboy of the Western World*), Kiepenheuer & Witsch, 1960.

Behan, *Stuecke fuers Theater*, Luchterhand (Neuwied-Berlin), 1962.

Shaw, *Caesar und Cleopatra* (translation of *Caesar and Cleopatra*), Suhrkamp, 1965.

Behan, "Der Umzug" [and] "Eine Gartenparty" (translations of *The Move* and *A Gardenparty*), broadcast on North German Radio (Hamburg), 1968.

Shaw, *Candida* (translation of *Candida*), Suhrkamp, 1971.

Shaw, *Mensch und Uebermensch* (translation of *Man and Superman*), Suhrkamp, 1972.

Shaw, *Kaiser von Amerika* (translation of *The Applecart: A Political Extravaganza*), Suhrkamp, 1973.

Also translator of "Don Juan in der Hoelle," from Shaw's "Don Juan in Hell," for German television, 1975.

EDITOR

(With Erich Kock; also author of introduction) *Unfertig ist der Mensch*, Mensch und Arbeit, 1967.

(With Helmut Gollwitzer and Carlo Schmid) *Anstoss und Ermutigung: Gustav W. Heinemann Bundespraesident, 1969-1974*, Suhrkamp, 1974.

(With Freimut Duve and Klaus Staeck) *Briefe zur Verteidigung der Republik*, Rowohlt (Reinbeck bei Hamburg), 1977.

(With Duve and Staeck) *Briefe zur Verteidigung der buergerlichen Freiheit: Nachtraege 1978*, Rowohlt, 1978.

(With Duve and Staeck) *Ausblicke auf die achtziger Jahre*, Rowohlt, 1980.

(With Duve and Staeck) *Zuviel Pazifismus?*, Rowohlt, 1981.

(With Duve and Staeck) *Verantwortlich fuer Polen?*, Rowohlt, 1982.

(Also author of foreword) *Niemandsland*, Lamuv, 1985.

CONTRIBUTOR

H. M. Waidson, editor, *Modern German Stories*, Faber, 1961.

Albrecht Beckel, *Mensch, Gesellschaft, Kirche bei Heinrich Boell* (contains "Interview mit mir selbst"), Verlag A. Fromm (Osnabruech), 1966.

(Author of introductory comments) Christian Schmidt-Haeuer and Adolf Mueller, *Viva Dubcek: Reform und Okkupation in der CSSR*, Kiepenheuer & Witsch, 1968.

Tschechoslowakei 1968: Die Reden von Peter Bichsel, Friedrich Duerrenmatt, Max Frisch, Guenter Grass, Kurt Marti und ein Brief von Heinrich Boell, Verlag der Arche, 1968.

Janko Musulin, editor, *Offene Briefe an die Deutschen* (addresses, essays, and lectures), Molden, 1969.

Marjorie L. Hoover, Charles W. Hoffmann, and Richard Plant, editors, *Erzaehlungen von Franz Kafka, Bertolt Brecht, und Heinrich Boell*, Norton, 1970.

Manes Sperber, editor, *Wir und Dostojewskij: Eine Debatte mit Heinrich Boell, Siegfried Lenz, Andre Malraux, Hans Erich Nossack*, Hoffmann & Campe (Hamburg), 1972.

Wie kritisch darf engagierte Kunst sein: Der Fall Staeck als Sympton der "Tenderenzwerde"; eine Dokumentation, Presseausschuss Demokratische Initiative (Munich), 1976.

J. Davis, P. Broughton, and M. Wood, editors, *Literature, Fiction, Poetry, Drama* (contains translation by Denver Lindley of *Nicht nur zur Weihnachtszeit* published as "Christmas Every Day"), Scott Foresman, 1977.

Hans Maier, *Sprache und Politik: Essay Ueber aktuelle Tendenzen; brief dialog mit Heinrich Boell*, Edition Interfrom (Zurich), 1977.

Hilla and Max Jacoby, *Shalom: Impressionen aus dem Heiligen Land*, Hoffmann & Campe, 1978.

(Author of foreword) Edward Kocbeck, *Dichtungen*, C. Gauke, 1978.

Faelle fuer den Staatsanwalt: Vier Erzaehlungen, Residenz Verlag (Vienna), 1978.

Warum haben wir aufeinander geschossen?, Lamuv, 1981.

(With others) J. Albrecht Cropp, *Der Rhein: Won den Alpen bis zur Nordsee*, Umschau Verlag, 1982.

Das Ende: Kriegszerstoerungen im Rheinland, Rheinland Verlag (Cologne), 1983.

OTHER

Aus unseren Tagen, edited by Gisela Stein, Holt, 1960.

Erzaehlungen, Hoerspiele, Aufsaetze (short stories, radio plays, and essays), Kiepenheuer & Witsch, 1961.

(With others) *Der Rat der Welt-Unweisen*, S. Mohn (Guetersloh), 1965.

Die Spurlosen, by Heinrich Boell [and] *Philemon und Baukis, by Leopold Ahlsen*, Odyssey Press, 1967.

Gespraech mit dem Zauberer (conversation with Alexander Adrion), Olten, 1968.

Mein trauriges Gesicht: Erzaehlungen und Aufsaetze (stories and essays), Verlag Progress (Moscow), 1968.

Geschichten aus zwoelf Jahren, Suhrkamp, 1969.

Boell fuer Zeitgenossen: Ein kulturgeschichtliches Lesebuch, edited by Ralph Ley, Harper, 1970.

Edition Text [*und*] *Kritik* (conversation with Heinz Ludwig Arnold), Richard Boorberg (Munich), 1971.

Heinrich Boell: The Novel Prizewinner Reflects on His Career (sound recording; interview by Edwin Newman), Center for Cassette Studies (North Hollywood, Calif.), c. 1974.

Drei Tage im Maerz (conversations with Christian Linder), Kiepenheuer & Witsch, 1975.

Der Lorbeer ist immer noch bitter: Literarische Schriften, Deutscher Taschenbuch, 1976.

(With others) *Die Erschiessung des Georg von Rauch*, Wagenbuch (Berlin), 1976.

Querschnitte: Aus Interviews, Aufsaetzen und Reden, edited by Viktor Boell and Renate Matthaei, Kiepenheuer & Witsch, 1977.

Mein Lesebuch, Fischer-Taschenbuch (Frankfurt), 1978.

Eine deutsche Erinnerung (translation from the French by Annette Lallenmand of interview with Rene Wintzen), Kiepenheuer & Witsch, 1979.

Warum haben wir aufeinander gesehossen? (conversation with Lew Kopelew), Lamuv, 1981.

Antikommunismus in Ost und West (conversations with Kopelew and Heinrich Vormeg), Bund-Verlag (Cologne), 1982.

Ueber Phantasie: Siegfried Lenz, Gespraeche mit Heinrich Boell, Guenter Grass, Walter Kempowski, Pavel Kohout (interview), Hoffmann & Campe, 1982.

Das Heinrich Boell Lesebuch, edited by Viktor Boell, Deutscher Taschenbuch, 1982.

Ein- und Zusprueche: Schriften, Reden und Prosa 1981-1983 (essays, speeches, and prose), Kiepenheuer & Witsch, 1984.

Weil die Stadt so fremd geworden ist (conversation with Vormweg), Lamuv, 1985.

Die Faehigkeit zu trauern: Schriften und Reden, 1983-85, Lamuv, 1986.

Also author of collected work, entitled *Novellen; Erzaehlungen; Heiter-satirische Prosa; Irisches Tagebuch, Aufsaetze*, Buchclub Ex Libris.

SIDELIGHTS: When German writer Heinrich Boell died on July 16, 1985, the world press frequently repeated the summation that he represented the conscience of his nation. This definition of Boell as a moralist was not a new formulation; it had originated, in fact, with literary critics who derided him as nothing more than a moral trumpeter. But even as the expression took on more positive meaning, Boell particularly disliked the epithet because this purely ethical assessment of his work, he thought, hindered appreciation of his art. Furthermore, Boell believed that a nation whose conscience was found primarily in its writers instead of in its politicians, its religious leaders, or its people was already a lost land.

Nonetheless, since the end of World War II when Boell's writings first began to appear, critics and ordinary readers alike had sensed in his language a powerful moral imperative. Whatever the genre—novel, story, satire, play, poem, or essay—the dominant force of the work was always the author's Christian ethics. Boell became one of the most important literary phenomena of the postwar era because his writings, regardless of their subject matter, clearly revealed where he stood as author. He was against war, militarism, and all hypocrisy in politics, religion, and human relations. He excoriated the opportunism of Nazis who became overnight democrats after 1945, and he refused to let Germans forget their recent past. He railed against the Catholic church, of which he was a member, for its cooperation in German rearmament and its role in the restoration of German capitalism. He pointed out repeatedly in the 1950s and 1960s the dangers of the cold war. In the 1960s and 1970s he supported Willy Brandt's *Ostpolitik* (a program to come to terms with West Germany's Communist neighbors); Boell campaigned for Brandt in the 1972 election—as did other wirters like Guenter Grass and Siegfried Lenz. In the 1980s his practical idealism led him to support the newly formed Green party, a pro-environmental, anti-nuclear group critical of capitalist policies. He was consistently active in the peace movement throughout the postwar era and in the 1980s demonstrated against the deployment of Pershing II's and cruise missiles on German soil.

Boell stood for democratic socialism with its inherent respect for people, especially for those who were without spokesmen or advocates. His work, however, never failed to criticize the politics of the left when it showed disregard for the rights of ordinary people, dissidents, and writers, as in the Soviet Union, Poland, or Czechoslovakia. Still, he never disguised his social ideal: a utopian Christian-Marxism. Although he was no communist, he dreamed, as he once said to Heinz Ludwig Arnold in an *Edition Text* [*und*] *Kritik* interview, of a "profitless, classless society," and he argued persuasively through his characters for a gentle, natural, undogmatic socialism based on enduring religious-humanistic principles.

The Eastern bloc praised Boell for his anti-militarism and his anti-fascism and lauded him as a model proletarian writer. In all the Eastern European countries he was read and admired. He was a best-selling author in East Germany, Poland, Czechoslovakia, Hungary, and especially in the Soviet Union, where sales of his books totaled roughly three million copies during his lifetime. In the West, Boell's death was reported on the first page of most major newspapers. The *New York Times* quoted the words of his Nobel Prize citation, praising him for his contribution "to the renewal of German literature." In France, *Liberation* gave three full pages to Boell's death, and *Monde,* comparing him to Albert Camus and Jean-Paul Sartre, praised his morality as an artist, his respect for language, and his responsibility as a writer.

The ideals Boell advocated in public, on radio or TV, he put into his novels, stories, plays, and poetry, as well as practiced

in his private life. He said he preferred to write for his own age instead of for posterity, and he always insisted, as he stated most clearly in his 1983 acceptance speech of honorary citizenship to Cologne (collected in *Ein- und Zusprueche*), that "articles, reviews, and speeches are literature too." It is not surprising, therefore, that essays represent about half of his oeuvre. Boell lived what he wrote and wrote what he lived. As he stated in his University of Frankfurt lectures on aesthetics, collected in *Frankfurter Vorlesungen,* he intended to construct with his writing "an inhabitable language in an inhabitable land." Thus, to comprehend his importance as a writer, his life and his work must be taken as a whole.

Christian Linder argues correctly in his *Boersenblatt* article that to understand Boell one must understand his youth. Born in the middle of World War I, Boell claimed his earliest memory was of being held in his mother's arms and watching out the family's apartment window while Hindenburg's defeated army marched through Cologne in 1919. By 1923 the inflation caused by Germany's defeat had ravaged the German population worse than the war had done. Boell remembered his father, a master furniture maker, going to the bank to get money in a cart to pay the employees in the family workshop. The money had to be spent immediately because it would be without purchasing power the next day. Boell never forgot the misery brought to his family, friends, and neighbors by the inflation of the 1920s. The stock market crash of 1929 brought the depression and the unemployment of the 1930s, which caused even more suffering. The economic uncertainties of that period also helped fire the flames of hatred in the recently formed National Socialist Party, and Boell witnessed the first Nazi marches through the streets of Cologne and saw how Nazi terror made the once peaceful streets unsafe for ordinary citizens.

Boell's family, like everyone else he knew, lost what financial security they had and with it their faith in an economic-political system that had failed twice in a decade. The fear of social turmoil became part of the psyche of every German. Economic insecurity, the concern for the next meal and a place to stay became the daily worry of a generation. To survive these times when hard work and the occupational skills of Boell's father were not enough, the Boells relied on family solidarity, mutual help, and religious faith for survival.

Although the setting for Boell's stories became Germany after World War II, the formative experiences of these earlier times essentially determined his oeuvre. The security of love, the values of food and drink, the luxury of a cigarette (things often taken for granted in an affluent world, especially in prosperous, modern West Germany) pervade his work. Never far from the surface of Boell's stories is his distrust of prosperity because he knew that wealth could disappear over night and that it was often the enemy of familial cohesiveness and the foe of social unity when it began to divide people into haves and have-nots.

The Boells themselves survived the 1920s, 1930s, and the war of the 1940s by never loosening the bonds that held them together. This familial model, this strategy for survival, forms the essence of Boell's work. Whether his characters are the working poor not knowing where money for rent and food will come from, or whether they are the rich facing the troubles of affluence, the solution for their problems lies in the maintenance of family ties.

This solution may seem simplistic, naive, or sentimental, and all these objections have been raised against Boell's work; but the power of his prose, the realism of his situations, and the moral imperative in his writing triumph over these possible shortcomings. Trying to conserve traditional human values within the person, family, neighborhood, and society and remaining suspicious of progress, technology, prosperity, and all power over others that resulted from wealth and position, Boell the leftist can be called a conservative writer.

The author acknowledged a tendency in his work to maintain lost values. Speaking of his hope for Germany after 1945, he revealed, as Linder's article reports: "If I am conservative, and I tend to accept that judgement, not just as author, but also as a contemporary, then it is because I wish to conserve, if possible, that which held more or less all Germans together in 1945, the feeling of liberation, the hope for a new state with a new communality after the common suffering of the fascist period which was a terror system, an absolute twelve years of permanent terror—which, however, we don't like to admit. And 1945 was the liberation from this terror. And I conserve permanently within myself, if I can use this expression, the moment of this liberation. I live from it; my whole life, my family life, my work, all live from it. In this sense I am a conservative." This conservatism confers on Boell's work a utopian dimension that manifests itself in his use of multiple variations on simple symbols and elemental themes and in his treatment of contemporary political and moral problems.

In 1937, when Boell completed his secondary education, he went to Bonn to begin an apprenticeship to a book dealer. But his training was interrupted during the winter of 1938-1939 by induction into the labor service. After completion of this semi-military obligation, he enrolled briefly as a student at the University of Cologne where he intended to study philology. But before he could really call himself a student, three months before the Second World War started, he was drafted into the army. In the course of the next six years he served as an infantryman on the western front in France and on the eastern front in Russia and in other Eastern European countries as the German army retreated before the Russian forces. During these six years Boell was wounded four times and reached the rank of corporal. Although it was customary for soldiers with his education to be officers, his hatred of the war and army life prevented him from cooperating with the military. At the risk of court-martial and summary execution, he frequently forged papers to see his family or, after his marriage to Annemarie Cech in 1942, to visit his wife in the Rhineland. In April of 1945 Boell was taken prisoner by American troops and interned in Allied POW camps until September of 1945. After his release, he immediately returned to Cologne, which lay eighty percent in ruins, to begin his life as a writer. Having chosen his vocation at the age of seventeen, he had written novels and poems before the war; some of these early works remain in the Boell Archive in Cologne.

The conditions for Boell, as for many Germans, when he returned home were reminiscent of the struggles for food and shelter after World War I; now, however, the problems included not only earning money for rent but finding an apartment still standing, not only buying food but finding food at all, not only paying for heat but finding fuel of any kind. In these first years after the war Boell's wife earned most of the family income as a teacher of English while he took only random jobs; even his reenrollment in the university was merely a strategy to obtain a legal ration card without employment so that he could dedicate the majority of his time to writing.

In these early years, Boell, like other postwar German writers, had to struggle with finding a new German literary language. Under the Nazis German had become polluted by fascist ideology, and the German literary tradition that had served Boell's older contemporaries belonging to the generation of Thomas Mann no longer seemed valid in a post-Auschwitz age. Boell was fortunate in that he found his own style early, one appropriate for his ideas and suitable to the content of his stories. That style can be described as a kind of Hemingwayesque minimalism—simple words in simple sentences conveying a plainness appropriate to the Germany of 1945, a time when the expression of truth, to be believable again, had to possess the certainty and simplicity of a mathematical statement, like $2+2=4$. The opening lines of any of the stories written before 1950 illustrate the style. "Damals in Odessa" ("That Time We Were in Odessa") starts with seven words: "In Odessa it was very cold then." The story concludes: "It was cold in Odessa, the weather was beautifully clear, and we boarded the plane; and as it rose, we knew suddenly that we would never return, never...." Between the terse opening sentence and the final lines, the story tells of soldiers eating and drinking to forget their fears before going to die. In the history of German literature Boell's sober language has the place accorded a Shaker chair in the history of American furniture.

In 1947 these first stories began to appear in various periodicals. They were collected in 1950 as *Wanderer, kommst du nach Spa (Traveller, If You Come to Spa)*. In 1983 twenty-two more of these early stories were discovered in the Boell Archive in Cologne and published in the collection *Die Verwundung und andere fruehe Erzaehlungen (The Casualty)*. Of these early stories the twenty-five in *Traveller, If You Come to Spa* can be found in *Children Are Civilians Too*, while those in *Die Verwundung* have only recently been made available in English. The subject matter of these works is the war and the return of soldiers to a homeland morally impoverished and physically destroyed. Containing none of the heroism and gallantry of popular war literature written during the Weimar Republic, Boell's earliest narratives feature men who die without honor for an inhuman cause. Despite the stark realism of war Boell did not dwell on battle scenes; he more often depicted the boredom of military life and fear of death. In these tales the only haven from despair is love, discovered in momentary encounters between soldiers and women on the periphery of the war.

Two novellas, *Der Zug war puenktlich (The Train Was on Time)* and *Das Vermaechtnis (A Soldier's Legacy)*, and the episodic novel, *Wo warst du, Adam? (And Where Were You, Adam?)*, represent Boell's longer treatment of the war. While they differ from one another in structure, they, like the shorter works, share a fatalism that death is bigger than life and proclaim a Christian optimism that heavenly consolation is greater than suffering. Thus the war narratives acknowledge that God is still in his heaven, although all is not right with the world.

Boell's epigraph for *And Where Were You, Adam?* (which he took from Antoine de Saint-Exupéry's *Flight to Arras*) can stand as a motto for all his war stories from this period: "When I was younger, I took part in real adventures: establishing postal air routes across the Sahara and South America. But war is no true adventure; it is only a substitute for adventure. War is a disease just like typhus." In an essay collected in *The Second World War in Fiction*, Alan Bance claims that this apolitical perspective on the war was typical of German literature in the 1940s and 1950s. He even sees a kind of "realism" in this political vagueness because, as he says, "war is not conducive to clear thinking.'' In Boell's case the un-analytic response to the war (seeing international conflict as a natural illness) was compounded by his feeling of being a lucky survivor, for only one of four German men in his age group returned from battle. His sense of destiny forced Boell to deal subjectively rather than objectively with the suffering of the Hitler years.

This narrow perspective manifests itself in Boell's simplistic division of characters into two groups: victims and executioners, with the victims often being the Germans themselves. A dichotomous view of World War II is understandable and even accurate for someone who was himself an anti-fascist and a sufferer of twelve years of oppression. Still, the result of the dichotomy is that the war stories cannot reveal truly what the war was about because the limited categories of suffering innocents and brutal henchmen are too unrefined to do the job. This kind of dualism, as Walker Sokel calls it in his *In Sachen Boell* essay, is characteristic of Boell's work in this period but disappears from the later stories as they become more sophisticated in their characterizations. Guenter Wirth's indictment, in *Heinrich Boell*, of the early war stories as ''timeless irrationalism'' is to the point because certainly war is not like typhus or any other sickness that has biological causes. War is not nature's making; it is made by people who have political and economic interests.

But the novel *And Where Were You, Adam?* also has a second motto taken from the wartime diaries of the Catholic writer Theodor Haecker: ''A world catastrophe can serve many ends, one of which is to find an alibi before God. Where were you, Adam? 'I was in the World War.''' Of these two mottos the one from Haecker is clearly the more important, for Boell takes the title of his novel from it. Clear also is Haecker's irony, which equally informs Boell's novel: war is no excuse before God; ultimately people are responsible for what they do. This message goes far to undercut the metaphor that war is like typhus, especially since the main chapter of the novel is one in which a Nazi commandant of a concentration camp murders all his Jewish prisoners. This episode established Boell as one of the first German writers to acknowledge the Holocaust in literature. Moreover, the novel's presentation of the circumstances surrounding the episode reveals the guilt of all who cooperated with the Nazi system of extermination—from those who transported the victims to those who ordered and did the killing. The excuse that people did not intend what happened finds no support within the economy of the novel.

This bold, honest attitude resonates throughout Boell's writing. Though he may have viewed the world unhistorically in the 1940s and early 1950s under the influence of Christian existentialism, he learned quickly in the 1950s that without recognizing the forces of history he could not understand what was going on in the Europe around him. Boell's literary development from ahistoricity to historicity—from merely presenting the suffering of men and women to presenting and analyzing the causes of their suffering by giving the historical background of events—is a fundamental change in his work.

Written contemporaneously with these war stories were stories that recounted conditions in Germany immediately after the war. The narrators of these works are often weary veterans who refuse to work on Germany's restoration because they suffer physical and emotional delibitation from too much war and too many years of despotic command. Now that tyrannical authority has disappeared from their lives, they cannot on their own conjure up the energy to struggle with existence. Through these passive characters Boell began his criticism of postwar German society. His lethargic heroes stand in opposition to the robust, dynamic Germans eager to readjust, rebuild, and make money. These opportunists, men without a sense of guilt who have already forgotten Hitler's six years of war and twelve years of oppression and murder, dominate the political, social, and economic scene. These new democrats rush headlong into the economic race, leaving behind the slow starters burdened with a memory and a conscience.

In the stories treating conditions following the war, satire became Boell's main weapon in his chastisement of Germany. Certain of these works, such as *Nicht nur zur Weihnachtszeit* (''Christmas Every Day''), ''Dr. Murkes gesammeltes Schweigen'' (''Dr. Murke's Collected Silences''), and ''Der Wegwerfer'' (''The Thrower Away''), have become classics of postwar German literature. A humorous, bizarre fantasy characterizes these satires of developing West German society. In ''Christmas Every Day'' a tyrannical old aunt demands daily holidays to avoid confronting the guilt of the Hitler years. In ''Dr. Murke's Collected Silences'' a Ph.D. in psychology, working for a radio station, tries to preserve his sanity by collecting on tape snips of dead air cut from cultural programs. In ''The Thrower Away'' a fanatical time-study expert makes a place for himself in the business world by systematically destroying junk mail, the surplus production of the advertising industry. Boell's success in this genre, the satirical short story, has led critics such as Erhard Friedrichsmeyer, James Henderson Reid, and Walter Jens to conclude that Boell's acutest artistic sense was his eye for satire. These stories have garnered high critical acclaim because they take to task the shortcomings of all Western democracies even though they are grounded in West German economic and political reality. One recognizes, too, that Boell's satire hits the mark equally as well in the Eastern bloc, where culture is an industry, production often leads to waste, and people avoid confronting the unpleasant past.

Boell's sense of satire is also the high point of many of his novels and raises them in some cases to great literature and in others saves them from the doldrums. For example, in *Ansichten eines Clowns (The Clown)*, the scene of the penniless clown pantomiming his blindness during the visit of his millionaire industrialist father contains the essence of the novel's political content, and in *Entfernung von der Truppe* (''Absent without Leave''), the narrator's account of his latrine duty in World War II reveals his total alienation from society. In *Ende einer Dienstfahrt (End of a Mission)* Boell's choice of a pedantic, objective, understated tone confers on the novel the main feature of its readability; the dry reporting of the events of a trial of a father and son accused of burning an army jeep discloses how the courts and the press keep political protest under control. And Boell's last novel, *Frauen vor Flusslandschaft: Roman in Dialogen und Selbstgespraechen*, published just after his death in 1985, reaches its high point in a long interior monologue by a disenchanted intellectual whose job requires him to write speeches for a corrupt and stupid Christian Democratic minister. Here the monologue summarizes the novel's political intent by reavealing the politician's incompetence and moral emptiness as well as the intellectual's sellout of his ideals. This chapter confirms that Boell's satiric talent remained intact right up to his death, although this novel and the one preceding it, *Fuersorgliche Belagerung (The Safety Net)*, were in general received harshly by critics. Juergen Wallmann's talk of ''linguistic sloppiness and mistakes'' in his *Tagesspiegel* review of *The Safety Net* and Reinhard Baumgart's damning question, ''Where does art stop and kitsch begin?'' in his *Spiegel* review of *Frauen vor Flusslandschaft*, characterize the reception of these final novels.

For Boell the realization that West Germany had lost its chance to create a new society based on lessons learned from the Hitler period came as early as June 1948 with an important currency reform. In an interview with Margarette Limberg broadcast on North German Radio in June 1985 and published in *Ziet* in August 1985, Boell called this political-economic event ''the first shock which proved uneqivocally the reinstitution of total capitalism.'' With the 1948 currency reform and the establishment of the West German state the following year, Boell recognized that his hope for a radically democratic, Christian socialist Germany was lost forever. Throughout his oeuvre runs a sorrow and bitterness over this lost opportunity because it occurred without any form of public debate. Germany simply fell victim to the politics of the developing cold war and the division of Europe into two spheres of influence.

Beginning with the novel *Und sagte kein einziges Wort (And Never Said a Word)*, Boell developed a new method for dealing with contemporary reality. He began choosing themes, drawing characters, and selecting events tied directly to current developments in Germany. For this reason, his collected works provide a history of the Federal Republic and thereby justify Fritz J. Raddatz's *Zeit* description of the writer as ''the Balzac of the Second Republic.'' Read chronologically, the books treat every significant phase in West German history from the nation's establishment in 1949 to the mid-1980s, including the period of hunger after the war, the restoration of capitalism, the process of rearmament, the achievement of prosperity, the terrorist responses to social and political inequities produced by the economic recovery, and the soul-searching of the 1980s. Boell's writings deal also with the role of the Catholic church in West German politics, the problems of love and marriage amidst poverty and plenty, and the shortcomings of the press in a free and democratic society; moreover, the works imply a humane social alternative to ruthless competition, to the destructive militant forces of profit-taking, and to the demand for ever more production. Treating all these aspects of West German history not as isolated phenomena of the postwar era, but in light of the Hitler years and German history since the turn of the century, Boell's canon not only helped to establish West German literature after the war but also provides a political and social understanding of German development in this century.

Because *And Never Said a Word* develops a thematic method that Boell started in the early stories and continued throughout his work, this novel can serve as a paradigm of his fiction. In *Heinrich Boell* Robert Conard defines the method simply as ''setting a moral person in an immoral situation.'' In *And Never Said a Word* Fred Bogner, his wife, and their three children are forced to live in a single rented room and find that their lives are determined by the pressures of these harsh circumstances. The Bogners' poverty and the oppressive closeness of their living conditions produce the episodes of the novel, which in turn provides a strong criticism of institutional Catholicism's role in Germany's economic revival. The church proves indifferent to the needs of its members while it concerns itself with social and political power in a devleoping free-market economy that creates two classes of West German citizens: the privileged and the under-privileged. The Bishop of Cologne and the Bogners' Catholic landlady are the figures through which the novel reveals the church's disregard of social justice. The Catholic Bogners, on the other hand, dem-

onstrate how religion can be the source of Christian piety that enables them to practice a practical love of neighbor.

The novel is also paradigmatic in that it is Boell's first experiment with changing narrative perspective, a technique used in several later novels: *Haus ohne Hueter (Tomorrow and Yesterday)*, *Billard um halbzehn (Billiards at Half-Past Nine)*, *The Safety Net*, and *Frauen vor Flusslandschaft*. In *And Never Said a Word* the Bogners' story is told in alternating first-person narratives by husband and wife. The history of the family is revealed slowly and fragmentarily through flashbacks, interior monologues, and conversations.

In addition, the book demonstrates a third paradigm typical of Boell's later work. The duration of the novel's action is quite short, from Saturday morning to Monday morning, the weekend of St. Jerome's Day, September 30, 1951. Yet in its course the reader learns, through flashbacks and other narrative techniques, of fifteen years of the Bogners' married life during war and peace. The novel thus shows how the past affects the present.

Similarly, *Tomorrow and Yesterday* takes place during a single week in the summer of 1953 but treats events from the war years through the early 1950s. *Billiards at Half-Past Nine* focuses upon September 6, 1958, the eightieth birthday of the architect Heinrich Faehmel, but covers fifty years of German history from 1907 to 1958. *The Clown* tells the life story of the mime Hans Schnier through one evening of phone calls and reminiscences in his apartment. *The Safety Net* reflects West German economic development from 1945 to the advent of terrorism in the late 1970s, while confining its actual time to the twenty-four hours between the election of protagonist Fritz Tolm to the presidency of a National Association of Entrepreneurs and his resignation. And *Frauen vor Flusslandschaft* exposes the political development of West Germany from the chancellorship of Konrad Adenauer (1949-1963) to the mid-1980s by presenting the machinations of leading figures in the Christian Democratic party who, during a single twenty-four hour period, replace a minister and choose a new head of state.

Boell frequently referred to this kind of structure (reducing the narrative present while broadening the novel's historical horizon) as an ideal demonstrated by a story that lasted just one minute but laid bare the forces of history affecting a character's life and determining his or her decisions. This method permitted him to examine how actions and thoughts are actually conditioned by past political and economic events and to show why things are as they are and how people have become who and what they are; at the same time the method allowed him to reveal that persons in responsible positions are answerable to history.

In Boell's work ordinary people become objects of social forces, often victims of the decisions of others. In *Die verlorene Ehre der Katharina Blum; oder, wie Gewahlt enstehen und wohin sie fuehren kann (The Lost Honor of Katharina Blum: How Violence Develops and Where It Can Lead)*, which takes place during four days of carnival in Cologne, Boell showed how an unpolitical, law-abiding young woman could be turned into a vengeful murderer by society's toleration of social injustice. The protagonist, Katharina, becomes a ''dangerous'' person because she finds herself a victim of character assassination perpetrated by those institutions most responsible for a just democratic society: the press, the police, the law.

The philosophical position implied in Boell's assumption that a person is a product of social forces may be called Marxist, except that it is thoroughly religious, lacks Marxist optimism, and never suggests social change through political organization. Social solutions are not found in Boell's work. Implied, however, is the belief that if people in power practiced more compassion in the execution of their offices, society would be more just. In general, a certain sadness about the human condition prevails in Boell's work, even though a mild optimism flourishes within narrow limits. His protagonists always make important decisions regarding their own lives. They are not completely passive; they do not yield to or accept injustice. Their decisions affirm their individual human dignity and assert a militant humanism. Although their actions may not effect significant social change but merely permit them to live with their consciences, their decisiveness symbolically opposes an unjust world and thereby suggests that social awareness and conscious opposition are the way to a better future. The story of Katharina Blum's vengeance neither recommends nor condones murder, but merely illustrates the simple truth that injustice, when tolerated, is often the cause of social violence.

Decisiveness and action on the part of individuals is a prevailing pattern in Boell's work. At the conclusion of *And Never Said a Word,* Fred Bogner chooses to return to his wife and children despite the crowded conditions of their single room because he is determined to try to save his marriage and his family. In *Billiards at Half-Past Nine* Heinrich Faehmel accepts his son's destruction of the abbey of St. Anthony as a moral protest against the church's collusion with the Nazis. Heinrich's refusal to attend the dedication of his restored architectural masterpiece asserts that individual lives can be made happier through moral decisions even if these decisions cannot immediately change society. Moreover, Heinrich's reclusive son Robert chooses to reintegrate himself into society by adopting the orphan Hugo to give the boy a better life and to revitalize his own. In *Tomorrow and Yesterday* the father figure "Uncle" Albert decides to marry the widowed Mrs. Brielach because it means a better life for himself, for her, and for her young son. In *The Clown* Hans Schnier chooses to become a white-faced beggar in the Bonn train station because he believes that his desperate performances there may prick the consciences of at least some of his friends who see him. In *The Safety Net* Fritz Tolm rejects the prestigious presidency of a national organization to show solidarity with the anti-materialist values of his children. And in *Frauen vor Flusslandschaft,* after a day of political intrigue, the intellectual, proletarian speech writer Grobsch decides to change parties from the Christian Democrats to the Social Democrats, and the septuagenarian Count Heinrich von Kreyl chooses to reject the offer of the nation's presidency to retire to his ancestral home in the north. While such decisions do not alter the course of West German history, they show that individuals can be courageous and virtuous. Moreover, the choices made at the end of Boell's novels frequently involve groups, members of a family or a circle of friends. These small groups who decide to put their own moral lives in order represent Boell's model for a more humane society.

When the Swedish Academy awarded Boell the Nobel Prize in 1972, it singled out the novel *Gruppenbild mit Dame (Group Portrait with Lady)* for special praise, calling that work the summation of Boell's oeuvre. Although the writer continued to publish novels, stories, poems, plays, and essays regularly after 1971, *Group Portrait with Lady* is still regarded as the work that most fully represents the whole of Boell's canon.

The book recapitulates his major themes and provides their most masterful formulation.

Boell stated his intention for the novel in an *Akzente* interview with Dieter Wellershoff: "I tried to describe or to write the story of a German woman in her late forties who had taken upon herself the burden of history from 1922-1970." In this story of Leni Gruyten-Pfeiffer, her family, and friends, Boell challenged the norms of West German society with a model of radical socialism and religious humanism. The protagonist Leni synthesizes in her person seeming contradictions. Although she is a simple person, she confounds any attempt at simple explanation. She is a materialist who delights in the senses but also a mystic who penetrates the mystery of the virgin birth, an innocent in her heart and a tramp in the eyes of society, a communist by intuition and an embodiment of the fascist ideal of "the German girl." In her, her Russian lover Boris, and their son Lev, Boell created a holy family that proclaims an undogmatic Christian socialism as a gospel for modern times.

Around Leni are grouped more than 125 characters representing all classes of society and various nations: communists and capitalists, industrialists and proletarians, fascists and anti-fascists, Jews and Moslems, Turks and Germans, rich and poor, saints and sinners—the whole spectrum of German society from 1922-1970. To hold the various levels of the story together and to keep Leni in the center of the novel, the work employs two narrative techniques. In the first half of the novel an unnamed narrator scrupulously relates the events of Leni's life. This half of the book consists of the narrator's meticulous research on Leni and his comments on the accuracy and validity of his findings. Leni's story proceeds chronologically from her birth to March 2, 1945, the day in which a nine-hour Allied raid on Cologne effectively brought the war to an end for the people of that city. After this event, midway through the novel, the narrator relinquishes his role as narrator to assume a role as a member of Leni's circle of friends, and to become an actor in the events of the book. At this point various characters tell their life stories from the day of the terrible bombing to 1970. Since these people have contact with Leni, their stories also reveal from various perspectives Leni's own life during this twenty-five year period. Again Boell found a structure that allowed him to come to terms with recent German history and postwar developments.

Politically the novel condemns communism as strongly as it does capitalism, and because it criticizes actions of the Communist party in the period between the Russo-German non-aggression pact of 1939 and the Warsaw Pact invasion of Czechoslovakia in 1968, the novel has appeared in the Soviet Union only in abridged form, lacking all criticism of Communists and even omitting some sexual passages. Despite its political evenhandedness, the novel's criticism of the Western and Eastern systems differs. It shows a society based on production for profit instead of for human need to lack compassion and justice; the practice of capitalism as presented in the book becomes a philosophy of greed run amok. The work's criticism of communism, in contrast, is not of its ideals but of its failure to live up to them. From this point of view the novel's unfavorable assessment of established socialism parallels its criticism of the institutional church. Through Leni, and especially her son, Lev, the work demonstrates that socialist and religious principles go hand in hand as partners of a shared humanism.

Group Portait with Lady is, indeed, the summation of Boell's writing, for it crystalizes the radical message that runs through all of his work since *And Never Said a Word:* Christianity and capitalism are incompatible with each other; their long standing marriage survives only because organized religion continually surrenders its humanistic values to the demands of economics and politics.

MEDIA ADAPTATIONS: ''The Lost Honor of Katharina Blum,'' adapted from Boell's novel of the same title, was released by New World Pictures in 1975.

BIOGRAPHICAL/CRITICAL SOURCES:

BOOKS

Amery, Carl, *Die Kapitulation oder deutscher Katholizismus heute,* Rowohlt, 1963.

Balzer, Bernd, editor, *Werke: Romane und Erzaehlungen, 1947-1951,* Kiepenheuer & Witsch, 1977.

Beckel, Albrecht, *Mensch, Gesellschaft, Kirche bei Heinrich Boell,* Verlag A. Fromm (Osnabruech), 1966.

Bernhard, Hans Joachim, *Die Romane Heinrich Boells: Gesellschaftskritik und Gemeinschaftsutopie,* 2nd edition, Ruetten & Loening (Berlin), 1973.

Beth, Hanno, editor, *Heinrich Boell: Eine Einfuehrung in das Gesamtwek in Einzelinterpretationen,* Scriptor Verlag (Kronberg), 1975.

Bienek, Horst, *Werkstattgespraeche mit Schriftstellern,* Hanser (Munich), 1962.

Boell, Alfred, *Bilder einer deutschen Familie: Die Boells,* Gustav Luebbe Verlag (Bergisch Gladbach), 1981.

Boell, Heinrich, *Wo warst du, Adam?,* F. Middlehauve, 1951, reprinted Deutscher Taschenbuch, 1972, translation by Savill published as *Adam, Where Art Thou?,* Criterion Books, 1955, new translation by Vennewitz published as *And Where Were You, Adam?,* McGraw, 1970.

Boell, Heinrich, *Children Are Civilians Too* (story translations by Vennewitz), McGraw, 1970.

Boell, Heinrich, *Was soll aus dem Jungen bloss werden? Oder Irgendwas mit Buechern* (autobiography), Lamuv, 1981, translation by Vennewitz published as *What's to Become of the Boy? Or Something to Do with Books,* Knopf, 1984.

Boell, Rene, Viktor Boell, Reinhold Neven DuMont, Klaus Staeck, and Gerhard Steidl, editors, *Ein Autor schafft Wirklichkeit: Heinrich Boell zum 65,* Kiepenheuer & Witsch, 1983.

Bruhn, Peter and Henry Glade, *Heinrich Boell in der Sowjetunion 1952-1979: Einfuehrung in die sojetische Boell-Rezeption und Biographie der in der USSR in russischer Sprache erscheinen Schriften von und ueber Heinrich Boell,* Eric Schmidt (Berlin), 1980.

Conard, Robert C., *Heinrich Boell,* Twayne, 1981.

Contemporary Literary Criticism, Gale, Volume II, 1974, Volume III, 1975, Volume VI, 1976, Volume XI, 1979, Volume XV, 1980, Volume XXVII, 1984, Volume XXXIX, 1986.

Crampton, Patricia, translator, *Heinrich Boell, on His Death: Selected Obituaries and the Last Interview,* Inter Nationes (Bonn), 1985.

Daemmrich, Horst S., and Diether H. Haenicke, editors, *The Challenge of German Literature,* Wayne State University Press, 1971.

dell'Agli, Anna Maria, *Zu Heinrich Boell,* Klett, 1983.

Deschner, Karlheinz, *Talente, Dichter, Dilettanten: Ueberschaetzte und unterschaetzte Werke in der deutschen Literatur der Gegenwart,* Limes (Wiesbaden), 1964.

Dictionary of Literary Biography Yearbook: 1985, Gale, 1986.

Durzak, Manfred, editor, *Der deutsche Literatur der Gegenwart,* Reclam, 1971.

Durzak, Manfred, editor, *Der deutsche Roman der Gegenwart,* Kohlhammer (Stuttgart), 1971.

Durzak, Manfred, editor, *Gespraeche ueber den Roman,* Suhrkamp, 1976.

Edition Text [und] Kritik, Richard Boorberg, 1971.

Enright, D. J., *Conspirators and Poets,* Chatto & Windus, 1966.

Friedmann, Hermann and Otto Mann, editors, *Christliche Dichter der Gegenwart,* Rothe (Heidelberg), 1955.

Friedrichsmeyer, Erhard, *The Major Works of Heinrich Boell: A Critical Commentary,* Monarch Press, 1974.

Friedrichsmeyer, Erhard, *Die satirische Kurzprosa Heinrich Boells,* University of North Carolina Press, 1981.

Geissler, Rolf, editor, *Moeglichkeiten des deutschen Romans: Analysen und Interpretationsgrundlagen zu Romanen von Thomas Mann, Alfred Doeblin, Hermann Broch, Gerd Gaiser, Max Frisch, Alfred Andersch und Heinrich Boell,* Diesterweg (Frankfurt), 1962.

Grimm, Reinhold and Jost Hermand, editors, *Basis: Jahrbuch fuer deutsche Gegenwartsliteratur,* Volume III, Athenaeum Verlag (Frankfurt), 1972.

Gruetzbach, Frank, editor, *Heinrich Boell: Freies Geleit fuer Ulrike Meinhof; ein Artikel und seine Folgen,* Kiepenheuer & Witsch, 1972.

Hoffman, Leopold, *Heinrich Boell: Einfuehrung in Leben und Werk,* 2nd edition, Verlag Edi-Centre (Luxembourg), 1973.

Hoffmann, Gabriele, *Heinrich Boell,* Lamuv, 1986.

Jens, Walter, *Deutsch Literatur der Gegenwart: Themen, Stile, Tendenzen,* 4th edition, Piper (Munich), 1962.

Jeziorkowski, Klaus, *Rhythmus und Figur: Zur Technik der epischen Konstruktion in Heinrich Boells ''Der Wegwerfer'' und ''Billard um Halbzehn,''* Gehlen (Bad Homburg), 1968.

Jurgensen, Manfred, *Boell: Untersuchungen zum Werk,* Francke (Bern), 1975.

Klein, Holger, John Flower, and Eric Homberger, editors, *The Second World War in Fiction,* Macmillan, 1984.

Leiser, Peter, *Heinrich Boell: ''Das Brot der fruehen Jahre''/ ''Ansichten eines Clowns,''* Hollfeld, Beyer, 1974.

Lengning, Werner, editor, *Der Scrifsteller Heinrich Boell: Ein biographisch-bibliographischer Abriss,* Deutscher Taschenbuch, 5th edition, 1977 (previous editions each contain different essay on Boell).

Ley, Ralph, *Boell fuer Zeitgenossen: Ein kulturgeschichtliches Lesebuch,* Harper, 1970.

MacPherson, Enid, *A Student's Guide to Boell,* Heinemann, 1972.

Mann, Otto, editor, *Christliche Dichter im 20. Jahrhundert,* Francke Verlag (Bern), 1968.

Martin, Werner, compiler, *Heinrich Boell: Eine Bibliographie seiner Werke,* Georg Olms (Hildsheim), 1975.

Matthaei, Renate, *Die subversive Madonna: Ein Schluessel zum Werk Heinrich Boells,* Kiepenheuer & Witsch, 1975.

Mueller, Helmut L., *Die literarische Republik: Westdeutsche Schriftsteller und die Politik,* Beltz Verlag, 1982.

Naegele, Rainer, *Heinrich Boell: Einfuehrung in das Werk und in die Forschung,* Athenaeum Fischer Taschenbuch Verlag (Frankfurt), 1976.

Reich-Ranicki, Marcel, editor, *In Sachen Boell,* Kiepenheuer & Witsch, 1968, 3rd edition, 1970.

Reid, James Henderson, *Heinrich Boell: Withdrawal and Re-Emergence,* Wolff, 1973.

Schroeter, Klaus, *Heinrich Boell in Selbstzeugnissen und Bilddokumenten*, Rowohlt, 1982.

Schultz, Uwe, editor, *Das Tagebuch und der moderne Autor*, C. Hanser, 1965.

Schwarz, Wilhelm Johannes, *Der Erzaehler Heinrich Boell: Seine Werke und Gestalten*, 2nd edition, Francke Verlag, 1968.

Schwartz, Wilhelm Johannes, *Heinrich Boell, Teller of Tales: A Study of His Works and Characters*, Ungar, 1969.

Smith, Brian-Keith, editor, *Essays on Contemporary German Literature: German Men of Letters*, Wolff, 1966.

Stresau, Hermann, *Heinrich Boell*, Colloquium Verlag (Berlin), 1964.

Thomas, R. Hinton and Wilfred Van Der Will, *The German Novel and the Affluent Society*, University of Toronto Press, 1968.

Wagener, Hans, editor, *Zeitkritische Romane des 20. Jahrhunderts: Die Gesellschaft in der Kritik der deutschen literature*, Reclam, 1975.

Wirth, Guenter, *Heinrich Boell: Essayistische Studie ueber religioese und gesellschaftliche Motive im Prosawerk des Dichters*, Union Verlag, 1968.

Ziltner, Walter, *Heinrich Boell und Guenter Grass in den USA: Tendenzen der Rezeption*, Peter Lang (Bern), 1982.

PERIODICALS

Akzente, Volume XVIII, 1971.

America, February 6, 1965, September 18, 1965, April 20, 1968, May 12, 1973, May 17, 1975, March 12, 1977, February 25, 1978.

Antioch Review, fall, 1986.

Atlantic, April, 1965, July 1973, November, 1984, July, 1985.

Boersenblatt, July 23, 1985.

Books Abroad, summer, 1960, spring, 1967, summer, 1972, winter, 1973, spring, 1975.

Books and Bookmen, October, 1973.

Book World, May 19, 1968, February 8, 1970, November 22, 1970.

Boston University Journal, Volume XXII, number 2, 1973.

Buecherkommentare, Volume 1, 1974.

Chicago Tribune Book World, February 7, 1982, July 14, 1985, March 23, 1986.

Christian Science Monitor, February 11, 1965, September 30, 1965, April 19, 1968, May 16, 1973, December 16, 1977, July 12, 1978.

Commonweal, January 6, 1956, June 29, 1956, November 1, 1957, February 12, 1965.

Essays in Literature, Volume I, 1974.

Forum for Modern Language Studies, April, 1973.

Germanic Review, summer, 1978, summer, 1984.

German Life and Letters, July, 1959.

German Quarterly, March, 1960, Volume XLV, 1972, Volume L, 1977.

German Tribune, August 5, 1979.

Literatur in Wissenschaft und Unterricht, Volume VIII, number 1, 1975.

London Magazine, May, 1967.

London Review of Books, April 1, 1982, October 23, 1986.

Los Angeles Times, July 11, 1985.

Los Angeles Times Book Review, November 25, 1984, March 30, 1986, July 19, 1987.

Maclean's, April 22, 1986.

Manchester Guardian, June 2, 1961.

Massachusetts Review, summer, 1967.

Michigan Academician, Volume X, number 1, 1977, Volume XIV, number 1, 1981.

Modern Fiction Studies, autumn, 1975.

Modern Language Notes, Volume VII, 1962.

Modern Language Review, Volume LXIX, 1974.

Modern Languages, September, 1973.

Nation, May 3, 1965, October 2, 1967, June 22, 1970, July 30, 1973, February 19, 1977.

National Review, April 6, 1965, August 1, 1975, October 4, 1985.

New Republic, March 20, 1965, November 27, 1965, November 12, 1966, April 26, 1975, March 3, 1982, October 21, 1985, April 7, 1986.

New Statesman, June 2, 1961, June 25, 1965, March 3, 1967, January 26, 1973, May 11, 1973, October 17, 1975, February 25, 1977, December 9, 1977, September 29, 1978, March 26, 1982, July 29, 1983, March 1, 1985, October 11, 1985, November 21, 1986.

Newsweek, February 8, 1965, September 14, 1970, May 14, 1973, February 22, 1982, October 15, 1984, June 10, 1985.

New Yorker, June 16, 1956, November 20, 1965, October 7, 1967, February 28, 1970, May 19, 1975, August 7, 1978, June 14, 1982, November 12, 1984, April 7, 1986.

New York Review of Books, February 11, 1965, December 29, 1966, September 14, 1967, March 26, 1970, November 5, 1970, May 31, 1973, March 18, 1982.

New York Times, January 25, 1965, September 6, 1965, December 31, 1966, August 25, 1967, October 20, 1972, May 9, 1973, May 21, 1975, May 31, 1979, February 5, 1982, October 7, 1984.

New York Times Book Review, January 24, 1965, September 12, 1965, October 16, 1966, August 13, 1967, April 5, 1970, November 5, 1972, May 6, 1973, December 2, 1973, April 27, 1975, January 23, 1977, November 6, 1977, January 8, 1978, May 27, 1979, May 31, 1979, January 31, 1982, February 5, 1982, June 23, 1985, December 29, 1985, February 23, 1986, March 29, 1987, August 23, 1987.

Novel, Volume I, 1968.

Observer, July 4, 1965, March 5, 1967, July 28, 1968, April 29, 1973, August 5, 1973, January 30, 1976, February 20, 1977, January 15, 1978, September 17, 1978, April 18, 1982, February 17, 1985.

San Francisco Review of Books, summer, 1985.

Saturday Review, June 2, 1956, October 19, 1957, July 29, 1962, January 30, 1965, September 11, 1965, December 10, 1966, January 7, 1967, March 28, 1970, September 12, 1970, January, 1982, November, 1984.

Saturday Review of the Arts, November 11, 1972.

Saturday Review/World, July 31, 1973.

Seminar, Volume XIII, number 3, 1977.

Spectator, June 9, 1961, March 5, 1977, November 4, 1978.

Spiegel, September 2, 1985.

Stimmen der Zeit, Volume XCVI, 1971.

Sueddeutsche Zeitung, August 10-11, 1974.

Tagesspeigel, July 22, 1979.

Time, October 21, 1957, January 4, 1963, January 29, 1965, September 24, 1965, March 29, 1968, March 2, 1970, May 28, 1973, February 8, 1982.

Times (London), October 10, 1985, October 16, 1986.

Times Educational Supplement, October 2, 1981, July 26, 1985, February 28, 1986, January 16, 1987.

Times Literary Supplement July 8, 1965, September 8, 1966, November 10, 1966, March 9, 1967, January 4, 1968,

August 8, 1968, March 12, 1970, October 8, 1971, January 12, 1973, June 1, 1973, October 11, 1974, October 25, 1974, January 31, 1975, January 30, 1976, February 25, 1977, February 10, 1978, June 30, 1978, March 7, 1980, April 2, 1982, May 7, 1982, August 19, 1983, July 26, 1985, February 14, 1986, May 15, 1987.

University of Dayton Review, Volume X, number 2, 1973, Volume XI, number 2, 1974, Volume XII, number 2, 1976.

Unterrichtspraxis, Volume VII, number 2, 1975.

Virginia Quarterly Review, winter, 1967, summer, 1975, summer, 1978.

Washington Post, July 6, 1987.

Washington Post Book World, May 13, 1973, November 20, 1977, January 24, 1982, November 16, 1984, July 6, 1987.

Weimarer Beitraege, Volume X, 1964.

World Literature Today, summer, 1965, autumn, 1977, summer, 1979, spring, 1980, spring, 1985, spring, 1986.

Yale Review, winter, 1955.

Zeit, October 9, 1959, August 10, 1971, July 19, 1985, August 2, 1985.

OBITUARIES:

PERIODICALS

Boston Globe, July 17, 1985.
Chicago Tribune, July 17, 1985.
Los Angeles Times, July 17, 1985.
Monde (international edition), July 18-24, 1985.
New York Times, July 17, 1985.
Observer, July 21, 1985.
Time, July 29, 1985.
Times (London), July 17, 1985.
Toronto Star, July 17, 1985.
Washington Post, July 17, 1985, July 28, 1985.†

—*Sidelights by Robert C. Conard*

*   *   *

BOLL, Heinrich (Theodor)
See BOELL, Heinrich (Theodor)

*   *   *

BOND, (Thomas) Michael   1926-

PERSONAL: Born January 13, 1926, in Newbury, Berkshire, England; son of Norman Robert and Frances Mary (Offer) Bond; married Brenda Mary Johnson, June 29, 1950 (divorced, 1981); married Susan Marfrey Rogers, 1981; children (first marriage) Karen Mary Jankel, Anthony Thomas. *Education:* Attended Presentation College, 1934-40.

ADDRESSES: Office—c/o 94B Tachbrook St., London SWN 2NB, England. *Agent*—Harvey Unna & Stephen Durbridge Ltd., 24 Pottery Lane, Holland Park, London W11 4L2, England.

CAREER: Writer. British Broadcasting Corp., London, England, television cameraman, 1954-66. Director, Paddington Productions, Ltd. *Military service:* Royal Air Force, 1943-44, air crew; British Army, Middlesex Regiment, 1944-47.

AWARDS, HONORS: American Library Association Notable Book citation for *Tales of Olga Da Polga.*

WRITINGS:

(Editor) *Michael Bond's Book of Bears,* Purnell, 1971.
The Day the Animals Went on Strike (picture book), illustrations by Jim Hodgson, American Heritage, 1972.
(Editor) *Michael Bond's Book of Mice,* Purnell, 1972.
(Translator with Barbara von Johnson) *The Motormalgamation,* Studio-Vista, 1974.
Windmill, illustrations by Tony Cattaneo, Studio-Vista, 1975.
How to Make Flying Things (non-fiction), photographs by Peter Kibble, Studio-Vista, 1975.
Mr. Cram's Magic Bubbles, illustrations by Gioia Fiammenghi, Penguin, 1975.
Picnic on the River, Collins, 1980.
J. D. Polson and the Liberty Head Dime, illustrations by Roger Wade Walker, hand lettering by Leslie Lee, Mayflower, 1980.
J. D. Polson and the Dillogate Affair, illustrations by Walker, Hodder, 1981.
The Caravan Puppets, illustrations by Vanessa Julian-Ottie, Collins, 1983.
(With Paul Parnes) *Oliver the Greedy Elephant,* Methuen, 1985, Western Publishing, 1986.
The Pleasures of Paris (guidebook), photographs by the author, Pavilion, 1987.

Also author of radio and television plays for adults and children, including "Simon's Good Deed," "Napoleon's Day Out," "Open House," and "Paddington" (various short- and full-length animated films), which have been shown in Great Britain, the United States, France, Germany, Scandinavia, Canada, South Africa, the Netherlands, Hong Kong, Italy, Ceylon, and many other countries. Contributor to British periodicals.

"PADDINGTON" SERIES

A Bear Called Paddington (also see below), illustrations by Peggy Fortnum, Collins, 1958, Houghton, 1960.
More About Paddington (also see below), illustrations by Fortnum, Collins, 1959, Houghton, 1962.
Paddington Helps Out (also see below), illustrations by Fortnum, Collins, 1960, Houghton, 1961.
Paddington Abroad, illustrations by Fortnum, Collins, 1961, Houghton, 1972.
Paddington at Large (also see below), illustrations by Fortnum, Collins, 1962, Houghton, 1963.
Paddington Marches On, Collins, 1964, illustrations by Fortnum, Houghton, 1965, Fontana, 1986.
Adventures of Paddington (also see below), Collins, 1965.
Paddington at Work (also see below), illustrations by Fortnum, Collins, 1966, Houghton, 1967.
Paddington Goes to Town, illustrations by Fortnum, Collins, 1968, Houghton, 1969, Fontana, 1986.
Paddington Takes the Air, illustrations by Fortnum, Collins, 1970, Houghton, 1971.
Paddington's 'Blue Peter' Story Book, illustrations by Ivor Wood, Collins, 1973, published as *Paddington Takes to T.V.,* Houghton, 1974.
Paddington on Top, illustrations by Fortnum, Collins, 1974, Houghton, 1975.
(With Albert Bradley) *Paddington on Stage* (play; adapted from Bond's *Adventures of Paddington*), illustrations by Fortnum, Collins, 1974, Samuel French (acting edition), 1976, Houghton, 1977.
Paddington Takes the Test, illustrations by Fortnum, Collins, 1979, Houghton, 1980.

Paddington: A Disappearing Trick and Other Stories (anthology; also see below), Collins, 1979.

Paddington for Christmas (also see below), Collins, 1979.

Paddington on Screen: The Second 'Blue Peter' Story Book, illustrations by Barry Macey, Collins, 1981, Houghton, 1982.

The Hilarious Adventures of Paddington (contains *A Bear Called Paddington, More about Paddington, Paddington at Large, Paddington at Work,* and *Paddington Helps Out;* issued as a boxed set), Dell, 1986.

Author of fifty-six episodes of animated Paddington films and three half-hour Paddington specials for Home Box Office.

"PADDINGTON" PICTURE BOOKS

Paddington Bear, illustrations by Fred Banbery, Collins, 1972, Random House, 1973.

Paddington's Garden, illustrations by Banbery, Collins, 1972, Random House, 1973.

Paddington Goes Shopping, Collins, 1973.

Paddington at the Circus, illustrations by Banbery, Collins, 1973, Random House, 1974.

Paddington Goes Shopping, illustrations by Banbery, Collins, 1973, published as *Paddington's Lucky Day,* Random House, 1974.

Paddington at the Tower, illustrations by Banbery, Collins, 1975, Random House, 1978.

Paddington at the Seaside, illustrations by Banbery, Collins, 1975, Random House, 1976.

Paddington Takes a Bath, Collins, 1976.

Paddington Goes to the Sales, Collins, 1976.

Paddington's New Room, Collins, 1976.

Paddington at the Station, Collins, 1976.

Paddington Hits Out, Collins, 1977.

Paddington Does It Himself, Collins, 1977.

Paddington in the Kitchen, Collins, 1977.

Paddington Goes Out, Collins, 1980.

Paddington Weighs In, Collins, 1980.

Paddington at Home, Collins, 1980.

Paddington and Aunt Lucy, illustrations by Barry Wilkinson, Collins, 1980.

Paddington in Touch, illustrations by Wilkinson, Collins, 1980.

Paddington Has Fun, Collins, 1982.

Paddington Works Hard, Collins, 1982.

Paddington's Storybook, illustrations by Fortnum, Collins, 1983, Houghton, 1984.

Paddington on the River, illustrations by Wilkinson, Collins, 1983.

Paddington Weighs In, illustrations by Wilkinson, Collins, 1983.

Great Big Paddington Bear Picture Book, Pan, 1984.

Paddington at the Zoo, illustrations by McKee, Collins, 1984, Putnam, 1985.

Paddington and the Knickerbocker Rainbow, illustrations by McKee, Collins, 1984, Putnam, 1985.

Paddington's Art Exhibition, illustrations by McKee, Collins, 1985, published as *Paddington's Painting Exhibition,* Putnam, 1986.

Paddington at the Fair, illustrations by McKee, Collins, 1985, Putnam, 1986.

Paddington at the Palace, illustrations by David McKee, Putnam, 1986.

Paddington Minds the House, illustrations by McKee, Collins, 1986.

Paddington Spring Cleans, Collins, 1986.

Paddington Cleans Up, Putnam, 1986.

Paddington's Busy Day, illustrations by McKee, Collins, 1987.

Paddington and the Marmalade Maze, illustrations by McKee, Collins, 1987.

Paddington's Magical Christmas, illustrations by McKee, Collins, 1988.

"PADDINGTON" LEARNING AND ACTIVITY BOOKS

The Great Big Paddington Book, illustrations by Banbery, Collins & World, 1976.

Paddington's Loose-End Book: An ABC of Things to Do, illustrations by Wood, Collins, 1976.

Paddington's Party Book, illustrations by Wood, Collins, 1976.

Fun and Games with Paddington, Collins & World, 1977.

Paddington's Birthday Party, Collins, 1977.

Paddington Carpenter, Collins, 1977.

Paddington Conjurer, Collins, 1977.

Paddington Cook, Collins, 1977.

Paddington Golfer, Collins, 1977.

Paddington's First Book, Collins, 1978.

Paddington's Picture Book, Collins, 1978.

Paddington's Play Book, Collins, 1978.

Paddington's Counting Book, Collins, 1978.

Paddington's Cartoon Book, illustrations by Wood, Collins, 1979.

(With daughter, Karen Bond) *Paddington at the Airport,* illustrations by Toni Goffe, Hutchinson, 1986.

(With Karen Bond) *Paddington Mails a Letter,* illustrations by Goffe, Macmillan, 1986 (published in England as *Paddington Bear Posts a Letter,* Hutchinson, 1986).

(With Karen Bond) *Paddington's Clock Book,* Hutchinson, 1986.

(With Karen Bond) *Paddington's London,* Hutchinson, 1986.

"PADDINGTON" POP-UP BOOKS

Paddington's Pop-Up Book, Collins, 1977.

Paddington and the Snowbear, Collins, 1981.

Paddington at the Launderette, Collins, 1981.

Paddington's Shopping Adventure, Collins, 1981.

Paddington's Birthday Treat, Collins, 1981.

SOUND RECORDINGS

A Bear Called Paddington, Caedmon, 1978.

Paddington: A Disappearing Trick and Other Stories, Caedmon, 1979.

Paddington for Christmas, Caedmon, 1979.

Paddington Turns Detective, Caedmon, 1979.

Also author of an audio version of *Paddington's Storybook.*

"THURSDAY" SERIES

Here Comes Thursday!, illustrations by Daphne Rowles, Harrap, 1966, Lothrop, 1967.

Thursday Rides Again, illustrations by Beryl Sanders, Harrap, 1968, Lothrop, 1969.

Thursday Ahoy!, illustrations by Leslie Wood, Harrap, 1969, Lothrop, 1970.

Thursday in Paris, illustrations by Wood, Harrap, 1971, Penguin, 1974.

"OLGA DA POLGA" SERIES

Tales of Olga Da Polga (omnibus volume), illustrations by Hans Helweg, Penguin, 1971, Macmillan, 1973.

Olga Meets Her Match, illustrations by Helweg, Penguin, 1973, Hastings House, 1975.

Olga Carries On, illustrations by Helweg, Penguin, 1976, Hastings House, 1977.

Olga Takes Charge, illustrations by Helweg, Penguin, 1982, Dell, 1983.

The Complete Adventures of Olga da Polga (omnibus volume), illustrations by Helweg, Houghton, 1982.

First Big Olga da Polga Book, illustrations by Helweg, Longman, 1983.

Second Big Olga da Polga Book, illustrations by Helweg, Longman, 1983.

Also author of *Eight Olga Readers,* 1975.

"OLGA DA POLGA" PICTURE BOOKS

Olga Counts Her Blessings, E.M.C., 1977.
Olga Makes a Friend, E.M.C., 1977.
Olga Makes a Wish, E.M.C., 1977.
Olga Makes Her Mark, E.M.C., 1977.
Olga Takes a Bite, E.M.C., 1977.
Olga's New Home, E.M.C., 1977.
Olga's Second House, E.M.C., 1977.
Olga's Special Day, E.M.C., 1977.

"PARSLEY" SERIES

Parsley's Tail, illustrations by Esor, BBC Publications, 1969.
Parsley's Good Deed, illustrations by Esor, BBC Publications, 1969.
Parsley's Last Stand, BBC Publications, 1970.
Parsley's Problem Present, BBC Publications, 1970.
Parsley's Parade [and] *Parsley the Lion,* Collins, 1972.
Parsley and the Herbs, edited by Sheila M. Lane and Marion Kemp, Ward, Lock, 1976.

Also author of "The Herbs" (thirteen-episode puppet series) and "The Adventures of Parsley" (thirty-two episode puppet series).

ADULT MYSTERIES

Monsieur Pamplemousse, Hodder, 1983, Beaufort, 1985.
Monsieur Pamplemousse and the Secret Mission, Hodder, 1984, Beaufort, 1986.
Monsieur Pamplemousse on the Spot, Hodder, 1986, Beaufort, 1987.
Monsieur Pamplemousse Takes the Cure, Hodder, 1987.

WORK IN PROGRESS: "Olga da Polga" for television; *Monsieur Pamplemousse Aloft.*

SIDELIGHTS: On Christmas Eve in 1957, Michael Bond stopped in a London store to find a present for his wife. "On one of the shelves I came across a small bear looking, I thought, very sorry for himself as he was the only one who hadn't been sold," Bond recalls in *Something about the Author Autobiography Series.* He continues, "I bought him and because we were living near Paddington station at the time, we christened him Paddington. He sat on a shelf of our one-roomed apartment for a while, and then one day when I was sitting in front of my typewriter staring at a blank sheet of paper, wondering what to write, I idly tapped out the words 'Mr. and Mrs. Brown first met Paddington on a railway platform. In fact, that was how he came to have such an unusual name for a bear, for Paddington was the name of the station.' It was a simple act, and in terms of deathless prose, not exactly earth shattering, but it was to change my life considerably.... Without intending it, I had become a children's author."

Since then, Paddington has "become part of the folklore of childhood," writes Marcus Crouch in *The Nesbit Tradition: The Children's Novel in England 1945-70.* The now worldfamous bear is recognized, despite a variety of illustrators, by his unkempt appearance, Wellington boots, and raincoat. A foreigner from Peru, Paddington exhibits both innocence and a knack for trouble. "The humour of Paddington is largely visual; it is not what he is but what he does and how he does it that is funny," claims Crouch. In the *New York Times Book Review,* Ellen Lewis Buell cites the bear's "endearing combination of bearishness and boyishness" as one reason for his popularity. According to Pico Iyer in the *Village Voice,* "Paddington is a resolute little fellow of strong principles and few prejudices, full of resourcefulness and free of rancor: both the bear next door and something of a role model."

Despite the many accounts of Paddington's adventures, "One is immensely impressed by the way each collection of stories comes up so fresh and full of humorous and highly original situations," writes Eric Hudson in the *Children's Book Review.* Each additional book, praises a *Times Literary Supplement* contributor, gives "added substance and credibility ... instead of flogging a good idea to death." And reports Iyer, "Through all the blandishments of multimedia fame—grasping toy-makers, television makeup men, translations into 20 tongues, and imitators neither sincere nor flattering—the little bear manages, as ever, to land on his paws with good nature intact."

In 1972, Bond started a Paddington picture book series, working with new illustrators and moving away from the popular original drawings by Peggy Fortnum. The transition was not a smooth one. Some reviewers agree with Katherine Heylman, who declares in the *School Library Journal* that "this is no substitute for the original Paddington." Zena Sutherland concurs in a *Bulletin of the Center for Children's Books,* writing that for her, the simplified language and action strip away much of the original charm of the stories, leaving "no opportunity to develop the small Peruvian bear as a character." Still, in the *Wilson Library Bulletin,* Barbara Dill finds that while the more recent Banbery illustrations create a different image for the bear, she feels that "this one is just as beguiling with a character all his own."

Bond's other juvenile series also focus on very human animals. The "Thursday" series features mice as protagonists, with no supporting human characters. A *Times Literary Supplement* contributor praises them as "captivating creatures," and calls the books "far more ambitious" than the Paddington stories. Another creation, Olga da Polga the guinea-pig, contains "a touch of Bunter and Falstaff," comments a *Times Literary Supplement* reviewer. Olga is unlike the freewheeling Paddington, as she lives a sheltered life. Zena Sutherland writes in the *Bulletin of the Center for Children's Books,* "The humor is not so much in Olga's adventures, since she is hutchbound, but in her personality."

Bond enjoys his role as children's author. In *Something about the Author Autobiography Series,* he remarks: "One of the nice things about writing for children is their total acceptance of the fantastic. Give a child a stick and a patch of wet sand and it will draw the outline of a boat and accept it as such. I did learn though, that to make fantasy work you have to believe in it yourself. If an author doesn't believe in his inventions and his characters nobody else will. Paddington to me is, and always has been, very much alive."

In the early eighties, Bond moved to adult fiction with the tales of food inspector Monsieur Pamplemousse. While a human character, Pamplemousse does have canine assitance in his dog, Pommes Frites; the duo solve mysteries throughout France. Critics find the author's transition to adult fiction smooth and enjoyable. "Sympathetic characterisation, plenty of nice touches of verbal humour, and a delight in pursuing the absurd to the point where it merges in to the farcical, have all been translated intact and without incongruity into the adult sphere," says Reginald Hill in *Books and Bookmen*. Pamplemousse's adventures contain more humor than blood and mayhem. Writes Polly Morrice of *Pamplemousse on the Spot* in the *New York Times Book Review*, "Like a successful souffle, this is light, fluffy, skillfully made, with no aftertaste or afterthoughts to disturb the reader."

Reflecting on his characters and life as a writer, Bond muses in the *Something about the Author Autobiography Series*, "Writing is a lonely occupation, but it's also a selfish one. When things get bad, as they do for everyone from time to time, writers are able to shut themselves away from it, peopling the world with their characters, making them behave the way they want them to behave, saying the things they want to hear. Sometimes they take over and stubbornly refuse to do what you tell them to do, but usually they are very good. Sometimes I am Paddington walking down Windsor Gardens en route to the Portobello Road to buy his morning supply of buns, but if I don't fancy that I can always be Monsieur Pamplemousse, sitting outside a cafe enjoying the sunshine over a baguette split down the middle and filled with ham, and a glass of red wine. I wouldn't wish for anything nicer."

Paddington's adventures have been published in nearly twenty countries, including Japan, Israel, South Africa, Iceland, Poland, Russia, Portugal, Holland, and Greece. The bear has been reproduced as a stuffed animal; there is a Paddington corner in the London Toy Museum.

AVOCATIONAL INTERESTS: Motoring, wine, theatre, and gardening.

CA INTERVIEW

CA interviewed Michael Bond by telephone on April 13, 1987, at his home in London, England.

CA: Your Paddington Bear is now known and loved around the world as a toy, in book form, on television, and as the endorser of various products. This all started when you took a lonesome toy bear home one Christmas Eve in the mid-1950s. How have you kept Paddington fresh enough in your own mind to see him through the adventures and changes of thirty years?

BOND: It hasn't been difficult because he's very real to me. Also, I think he occupies the kind of strange world that characters in children's books often do. He lives in a very contemporary world, yet he goes back to the safe pre-war world. When Paddington goes back home, it's the world that I remember from my childhood. In England, if you try to make a telephone call now, you find that the telephone box has been vandalized. Paddington lives in a world where that hasn't happened yet. So he's always on two levels. If you have a character who's fairly clear in your mind, you just put him into a situation and things start to happen because he is that particular character.

CA: You've also done books about the guinea pig Olga da Polga, the armadillo J. D. Polson, and various other creatures. Is it sometimes a relief to get away from Paddington?

BOND: I know Paddington pretty well now. If I start writing a story about him, I know in the end I'll get there, so it isn't a tremendous challenge. The other thing about Paddington is that, over a long period of time, he's done most things; there have been thirteen novel-length books, each of which has seven complete stories in it, so he's been in nearly a hundred situations in those. Until I've got enough ideas that will work, I don't really want to do another one, although I still write Paddington stories for younger children, but that's different. It's nice in a way to get around to other characters and start afresh, as it were. I do like some kind of challenge.

Olga has been around for four novel-length books, and I'm about to start on a television series based on them, which will be fun. I think with series you build in problems right from the beginning. Paddington is a bear who lives in his own little environment in London. That works, but I don't ever see him going to the moon or doing anything like that. Olga has even more problems because she lives in a hutch, so she has to weave her own stories and exert her influence on the other animals in her life. I think I turned to J. D. Polson because he was a creature who could go anywhere and do anything. He can go to the moon; he can go travel to any part of the world that he wants to visit.

CA: I suppose there could be an entire field of study on the universal popularity of bears. What's your own theory about it?

BOND: It's a very interesting subject, but I'm not a great bear collector. Over the years, because I write about them, a lot of people have written to me. It's very clear that people will quite happily throw away their dolls when they get older and forget about them, but it's different with bears. I think that children, however happy their lives are at home, need some creature they can talk to and tell their secrets to. And bears have this strange kind of look about them: you feel you can tell them your secrets and they're not going to tell anybody else. If you look into their history, you find that in times past they were worshipped as gods, and real-life bears are really rather fearsome creatures. Until the teddy bear was made, this wasn't an animal you could actually relate to and love. If you go to the zoo, you'll always find people who make towards the bears and look at them and worship them in a way. And when it comes to writing stories, they have the advantage over other animals in that they do stand on their hind feet, so they're partly humanized already.

CA: Grown-ups like to tell their bears secrets too, not just children.

BOND: Oh, yes. I often get letters from adults who say, I haven't told anybody else this, but I still have my bear and I still talk to it. I know sixty percent of the sales of Paddington Bear in England are to adults. Certainly teenagers who've left home and are getting their first flat in London want some kind of father figure they can stand in the corner and relate to; everything feels safe once they've got something like that. And there's a Paddington fan club in Japan—I think the average age is twenty-one or twenty-two. So it's not just an Anglo-Saxon thing, though I think we relate to them more than, say, the French or Germans do. I get more letters from the States than anywhere else, about twenty letters from America for every one I get from England.

CA: The Paddington picture books began in 1972 and a Paddington learning series in 1976. What is the new series like, the "activity" books you started in 1986?

BOND: I've been working on them with my daughter, Karen Jankel. Karen was brought up with Paddington; she was born the year the first book came out. When she left college, she kind of moved away from Paddington and then came back a few years ago, and we joined forces. She has a talent for writing and comes up with ideas, one of which was creating activity books for small children, so we started doing this series together. One book, *Paddington at the Airport,* is about what happens when you're traveling by airplane and your suitcase disappears through the hole. Another one was about what happens to a letter when you mail it. Then we did a book which is a mock-up of a London bus—it has wheels and it goes on a tour of the city with Paddington. There's a clock book for very young children. Karen has a daugher who's about two years old now, so she's into what children that age want to read and do. We have some other books planned for that age group. Paddington was originally not written for children, or for any particular age group, so it's a new challenge.

CA: How else is your daughter involved in the Paddington industry?

BOND: I have an office which looks after the other side of Paddington, television and merchandising. It's very hard to say what any particular day will turn up, because we're always getting strange requests. We get involved with charities and all sorts of things. Karen runs that in addition to the books we do together.

CA: A large part of the Paddington business, obviously, is endorsements. How is it decided whether to let Paddington endorse a product or not?

BOND: In the beginning, when Paddington first went on television, it was a vicious circle here because the cost of making the first series was so horrendous that we needed help to pay for it, and the only way to do that was to license products. I think in the early days one just worked by instinct; there were some products that you felt wouldn't be right for Paddington, and others that were. It's strange: there were a number of things then that I let go through and wished I hadn't afterward; now ten years later suddenly they have a kind of curiosity value. There's a Paddington Corner in the London Toy Museum, and they have things in there that I regretted letting go through at the time, but now they have a certain charm.

Now, if there's something which I feel is at all offensive, I won't grant a license. Somebody wanted to have a Paddington toilet roll, for example. I said no to that because it didn't seem right. That's a fairly obvious thing. Somebody else made a waste-paper basket with a detachable top which was Paddington's head. I thought that was nasty. Other things are slightly more difficult. It's a very subjective thing, really. Just because I don't like it doesn't mean other people won't. It's really a matter of taste. Things have settled down from the early days, though. The level of requests now is more normal, and there's time to think about things. Also, I think I got much tougher. When it first started happening, people would come up and ask for product approval. When I said I didn't like something, often they'd say, "Oh, dear. It's already being made at this very moment. What are we going to do?" And I'd tell them to go ahead with it. Now I say, "Too bad. You shouldn't have let it happen."

CA: Has presenting Paddington in so many forms—books, television, products—created artistic problems?

BOND: It has in the sense that, to me, Paddington is epitomized in the original drawings done by Peggy Fortnum in the first books. She had the ability with just a few strokes of the pen to create a living, breathing creature. But if you want to use the Paddington that she drew in something more practical, it becomes very difficult. Looking at the original illustrations, you see that they vary in shape and size according to the story. When you come to something like film, or even a picture book, there's got to be continuity. It's very difficult to find an artist who can draw Paddington, humans, and backgrounds at the same time. So there have been a lot of different versions. In a way, I think Paddington has his own strength that is immediately recognizable. Though I did the first book very quickly and it was kind of fortuitous, I think dressing him in a duffel coat and a hat and Wellington boots gave him a signature. As long as he has at least one of those items, he's immediately recognizable.

CA: You were a television cameraman before you became Paddington's full-time father. Had writing been a conscious ambition earlier?

BOND: I always wanted to do something creative. I had a horror of being on this earth for so many years and then departing and not leaving anything behind. My first creative effort was to send a cartoon to *Punch* when I was about fourteen years old. They rejected it, but they did a very nice thing: they sent the rejection slip back with "Not quite right" written across it, so I wasn't totally discouraged. I was in Egypt with the army in 1947, living in a tent, and I was very bored, so I sat down and wrote a short story and sent it off to an English magazine and it sold. Then I thought, I want to be a writer. When I came out of the army, I learned the hard way that it wasn't so easy. There was a long period of time when, if I sold one story out of twenty, I thought I was having a good year.

The only thing to do if you want to write is sit down and do it. People often send me letters saying, "I want to be a writer. What do I do?" The only advice you can give someone is that nobody else is going to do it for you; you just have to put a piece of blank paper in the typewriter and sit down and write something—anything to get the brain working. I still get ideas that seem good at the time, but when I start work, the very first word I type is wrong, so I have to begin again. It's really quite hard work to keep starting things over and working at them until they're right.

CA: For adults, if we must make the distinction, you've been writing the wonderfully bizarre Monsieur Pamplemousse gastronomic mysteries. Can you tell me about the birth of the detective Pamplemousse and his doggy helper, Pommes Frites?

BOND: I was brought up in a house where books were part of the furniture. If I go into a house now where there aren't any books around, I feel there's something wrong with it. My mother was a great detective fan. She always read to me when I was small, and when I was old enough, I realized that she used to go to the library every week and come back with half-a-dozen books. When I first started to read them, I found they were usually English mystery stories. There's a great tradition of English detectives. She didn't approve of American crime books; she thought they were too bloodthirsty. So I was reading detective books at an early age.

For a long time after I left the BBC and was writing full-time, I had in the back of my mind writing a story about a French detective. I've always been very fond of France, and I go there quite often. In fact, I've just completed a guidebook called *The Pleasures of Paris*. It's coming out in the States next spring. I'm a great Georges Simenon fan; I like Maigret, and I wanted to write a book about a detective who was all that he wasn't. Maigret solved his cases by hard work and inspiration; I tend to write humorous books, and I wanted to write about a detective who usually solved his cases by accident.

For whatever reason—I don't quite know why—I had in mind a detective who was the last one in France to ride a bicycle. I even bought a bicycle to get the feel of it, but I decided that I was much too old and the hills were steeper than I remembered them, so that didn't seem like a good idea. Then I happened to be in a restaurant in France in a place called Valence, near Lyons, which specializes in cooking a chicken inside a pig's bladder. I had ordered one and when it arrived the waiter produced a knife and proceeded to cut it open with great ceremony, and the headwaiter came along and cut it open. As he did so, I thought, Supposing it isn't a chicken inside; supposing it's something else? And suddenly it all gelled in my mind. Monsieur Pamplemousse—I already had the name by then—wouldn't be a detective but an *ex*-detective who had become a food inspector. That would give him a reason for going outside Paris, and wherever he went, because of his background he would get involved in some kind of crime. And there was a dog at this hotel that I was rather fond of, so I thought Monsieur Pamplemousse ought to have a dog that he could relate to, and probably it would act as a food taster and help to solve the crimes. That how Pommes Frites came on the scene.

As soon as I got back to England, I set about writing. I started with the middle chapter, because I wanted to see if I could get down on paper the relationship between Monsieur Pamplemousse and Pommes Frites; I thought if that worked I'd go back to the beginning and start again. That's how the first book came about. The fourth one comes out over here later this year, and I'll be starting number five soon.

CA: They're wonderfully funny. I hope they'll go on forever.

BOND: I've just been to New York, and I must say it gave me great pleasure to see them in the bookshops. They're in paperback now. I actually enjoy writing them, and it's also a very good excuse to go to different parts of France. I pick out an area where I think the story is going to take place, and I go there and soak up the atmosphere. If you're writing fantasy, which all stories are in a way, to make it believable you've got to get certain basic facts right. If I know what time of year the story's going to be set in, I find out while I'm there what flowers are going to be out, for example.

The last one I wrote was set near Lake Geneva, and I realized at the start that I knew nothing about Lake Geneva. I didn't even know whether you could see across to the other side of it or not. So I stayed right there to get the feel of it. If you get those facts right, then I think you can do anything you like with the character. So I do quite a lot of research beforehand. The one I'm just coming up to doing is set in Brittany. It's going to involve an airship and a small traveling circus. I'm trying to research those two things at the moment before actually going there. I would like to carry on writing about Monsieur Pamplemousse as long as possible. It's quite nice to get back to writing adult stories after children's fiction; you've got a lot more freedom.

CA: It's hard to imagine who could play the part of Pommes Frites, but is there nevertheless a possibility that the gastronomic detective stories will appear in movie or television form?

BOND: You've hit on a problem. About a year ago I got enormous enthusiasm from a big American film company—so much so that they were talking about casting. I went to New York and we talked seriously about all these things, but as often happens with film, I came back to England and haven't heard from them since. I think it could well be done. Pommes Frites *would* be a problem, actually. You need a dog with acting experience, and if he's got a good agent, you could be in trouble. I can see various people in the part of Monsieur Pamplemousse, but Pommes Frites? Although it's been done before. There were the Thin Man films, with the detective couple Nick and Nora Charles and their dog Asta. I always build problems into the things I write. Paddington is a basic problem to film. There've also been various stage productions and the difficulties of working with someone dressed in a bear skin are sometimes unbelievable.

CA: Between the books, the television productions, the travel, and managing the Paddington industry, you must be incredibly busy. How do you do it all?

BOND: I'm pretty much a workaholic. I never sit around waiting for ideas. As far as my working day goes, my best time is early in the morning. If I'm doing something like a Monsieur Pamplemousse and it's going well, I may get up at four or five in the morning and work quite happily. There was a time when I had two desks in my office: one was for Paddington and one was for Olga, and I would go between the two. But life is much more organized now. I work every day. If I set myself a target of, say, a thousand words a day ready for the printer, that's quite a good day's work. It doesn't sound very much, but I tend to rewrite a lot. If I do three or four pages of finished product by the end of the day, in three or four months I find I've got a book. After writing in the mornings, I catch up on other things in the afternoon, the practical things.

CA: Will Paddington go on as he is indefinitely, so far as you can tell at this point?

BOND: I hope so. He's very much a part of my life, and I think the nice thing about children's characters is that they are fairly ageless. As long as ideas come and people want to read them, and as long as I'm doing them because I want to do them, I'll go on. If you do them for any other reason, you're selling yourself short to readers.

One thing that's nice about books anyway is finding a new author you like, and learning that he's written twenty or thirty books. I just recently discovered Rex Stout, who wrote the Nero Wolfe stories. I'm working my way through them and it's a lovely warm feeling to know he's written so many. I think people feel this with Paddington. You can put him in disastrous situations, and half of you says, No, don't do it, and the other half wants him to carry on in order to see how he gets out of them. I think the most important part of a story is the opening, so that people want to read on. The next most important thing is the ending, so that you leave them feeling happy and wanting to read another one.

CA: One of the greatest things about Paddington is that, no matter what a mess he makes of things, he never feels he can't keep going.

BOND: One of the big problems with Paddington is that, no matter how he wrecks the joint, as it were, you've got to find a reason, however tenuous, that justifies his doing it. Somebody has to benefit in some way. I think it would be wrong if he got away with things too much, but usually somebody benefits or somebody deserves to be punished. That's very important, particularly with children's books. That's the difficult part of the story. It's quite easy to put Paddington into a situation and think what would happen if he played tennis at Wimbledon or whatever comes to mind, but actually finding a story with a beginning, a middle, and an end and having him come out on top despite all the odds is the challenge. That's what children like, the fact that he does come out on top. I find that, though Paddington isn't intended this way, I quite often get letters from teachers of deprived children saying that they've latched on to Paddington. I think it's because they equate themselves with him. If he can do things, being an oddity in a strange world, and come out on top, they probably can too.

BIOGRAPHICAL/CRITICAL SOURCES:

BOOKS

Blount, Margaret, *Animal Land,* Hutchinson, 1974.
Children's Literature Review, Volume I, Gale, 1976.
Crouch, Marcus, *The Nesbit Tradition: The Children's Novel in England, 1945-70,* Benn, 1972.
Something about the Author Autobiography Series, Volume III, Gale, 1986.

PERIODICALS

Books and Bookmen, February, 1985.
Bulletin of the Center for Children's Books, November, 1973, February, 1974.
Children's Book Reviews, February, 1971.
Contemporary Review, November, 1971, January, 1984.
Los Angeles Times Book Review, June 9, 1985.
New Yorker, December 4, 1971, December 1, 1975.
New York Times Book Review, August 27, 1961, May 9, 1965, November 9, 1969, March 1, 1987.
Observer, March 10, 1985.
Saturday Review, November 9, 1968, April 17, 1971.
School Library Journal, December, 1973.
Times Literary Supplement, November 24, 1966, November 12, 1970, October 22, 1971, November 3, 1972, December 6, 1974, October 1, 1976, September 30, 1983.
Village Voice, July 16, 1985.
Wilson Library Bulletin, January, 1974.

—*Interview by Jean W. Ross*

*   *   *

BORCHARDT, D(ietrich) H(ans) 1916-

PERSONAL: Born April 14, 1916, in Hanover, Germany; son of Max Noah (a physician) and Mina (Lewinski) Borchardt; married Janet Duff Sinclair, December 20, 1944; children: Sandra Helen, Ann Sinclair (deceased), Max William. *Education:* Received early education in Germany and Italy; Victoria University of Wellington, M.A. (with honors), 1946; New Zealand Library School, Diploma, 1947.

ADDRESSES: Home—57 Aylmer St., North Balwyn, Victoria 3104, Australia.

CAREER: Farm worker in Germany, Italy, and Spain, 1934-36, and in New Zealand, 1939-43; book dealer in Florence,

Italy, 1936-39 and in Wellington, New Zealand, 1943-46. University of Otago, Dunedin, New Zealand, acquisitions librarian, 1947-50; University of Tasmania, Hobart, deputy librarian, 1950-53, librarian, 1953-64; La Trobe University, Bundoora, Victoria, Australia, chief librarian, 1965-81. UNESCO library expert in Turkey, 1964-65; lecturer in bibliography at Graduate Library School, George Peabody College for Teachers (now George Peabody College for Teachers of Vanderbilt University), Nashville, Tenn., summers, 1968 and 1973. Director of Mannings Library Services; director of Blackwell Pacific. Consultant in subject bibliography, National Library of Australia.

MEMBER: Library Association of Australia (fellow; past president of university and college libraries section; member of board of examiners, 1962-64, 1966-69), New Zealand Library Association, Bibliographical Society of Australia and New Zealand, Society of Indexers.

AWARDS, HONORS: Carnegie grant to visit Europe and United States, 1958; Queen Elizabeth II Jubilee medal, 1977; H. C. L. Anderson Award, Library Association of Australia, 1979; Order of Australia, 1982; D.Soc.Sc., Melbourne Institute of Technology, 1987.

WRITINGS:

(Compiler with B. Tilley, and author of introduction) *The Roy Bridges Collection in the University of Tasmania,* Cremorne, Stone, 1956.
Checklist of Royal Commissions, Select Committees of Parliament and Boards of Inquiry, Part 1: *Commonwealth of Australia, 1900-1950,* Cremorne, Stone, 1958, supplement published as *Commonwealth of Australia, 1950-1960,* Wentworth Books, 1973, Part 2: *Tasmania, 1956-1959,* Cremorne, Stone, 1960, Part 3: *Victoria, 1856-1960,* Wentworth Books, 1970, Part 4: *New South Wales,* 1856-1960, La Trobe University Library, 1975, Part 5: *Queensland, 1859-1960,* La Trobe University Library, 1978, Part 6: *Tasmania, Victoria, New South Wales, and Queensland, 1960-1980,* La Trobe University Library, 1986.
Australian Bibliography: A Guide to Printed Sources of Information, F. W. Cheshire, 1963, 3rd edition, Pergamon, 1976.
Senescence and Fertility (La Trobe University inaugural lectures), F. W. Cheshire, 1967.
How to Find Out in Philosophy and Psychology, Pergamon, 1968.
The Spread of Printing: Australia, Hertzberger, 1968, published as *Australia,* A. Schram, 1969.
(With J. I. Horacek) *Librarianship in Australia, New Zealand, and Oceania: A Brief Survey,* Pergamon, 1975, revised edition, 1986.
(Editor) *Seven Essays on Australian Subject Bibliography,* Australian Advisory Council on Bibliographical Services, 1977.
(Editor) *Australian Official Publications,* Longman Cheshire, 1979.
(Editor) *Twelve Essays on Australian Subject Bibliography,* National Library of Australia, 1980.
(Compiler with J. D. Thawley) *Guide to the Availability of Theses Compiled for the Section of University Libraries and Other General Research Libraries,* K. G. Saur, 1981.
(Editor) *The Literature Related to Commonwealth Studies: Access, Dissemination, and Use; Papers and Proceedings of a Conference of Commonwealth University Librarians*

(South Pacific Region), Mysore, 17-20 March 1980, La Trobe University Library, 1981.
A Bibliovision Splendid, La Trobe University, 1982.
(With Robert Stafford) *Devindex Australia: Index to Australian Literature on Social and Economic Development, 1975-1979*, Borchardt/La Trobe Library, 1983.
(With R. D. Francis) *How to Find Out in Psychology: A Guide to the Literature and Methods of Research*, Pergamon, 1984.
Australians: A Guide to Sources, Fairfax, Syme, Weldon and Associates, 1987.
Australia: Bibliographic Library Science, Academic Press, in press.

Contributor of more than sixty articles and reviews to library journals. Editor, *Australia Academic and Research Libraries*, 1970-84, and *Australian Historical Bibliography Bulletin*, 1982-86.

WORK IN PROGRESS: Checklist of collective bibliography.

SIDELIGHTS: D. H. Borchardt once told *CA:* "I have always believed that it is useless to try and remember everything. Better by far, as Samuel Johnson already stressed, to know where to find out. That is what bibliography is all about—it is the veritable and only key to knowledge, and those who hold it are the true powerbrokers of our age."

Borchardt more recently added: "Librarians must come to identify themselves with the notions of Universal Bibliographic Control and Universal Access to Publications—these are the foundations of our profession, are endorsed by IFLA, and represent the only safeguards for a true democracy."

AVOCATIONAL INTERESTS: Gardening.

* * *

BORGESE, Elisabeth Mann 1918-

PERSONAL: Born April 24, 1918, in Munich, Germany; daughter of Thomas (a writer) and Katia (Pringsheim) Mann; married G. A. Borgese (a writer), November 23, 1939 (deceased); children: Angelica, Dominica. *Education:* Conservatory of Music, Zurich, diploma, 1938; University of Chicago, further study, 1939-41. *Religion:* "I do not belong to any organized religion."

ADDRESSES: Office—Department of Political Science, Dalhousie University, Halifax, Nova Scotia, Canada. *Agent*—John Schaffner Literary Agency, 425 East 51st St., New York, N.Y. 10022.

CAREER: Writer; Dalhousie University, Halifax, Nova Scotia, professor of political science, 1979—. Senior fellow at Center for the Study of Democratic Institutions, 1964-76; chairman of planning council for International Ocean Institute at University of Malta, 1972—; adviser to Austrian delegation and the preparatory commission to the United Nations Conference on the Law of the Sea; chairman of International Centre for Ocean Development, Canada.

MEMBER: World Academy of Arts and Science, Third World Academy of Science, American Academy of Political Science, American Society of International Law, Club of Rome.

WRITINGS:

To Whom It May Concern (short stories), Braziller, 1962.
Ascent of Woman, Braziller, 1964.
The Language Barrier: Beasts and Men, Holt, 1965.

The White Snake, MacGibbon & Kee, 1966.
The Ocean Regime, Center for the Study of Democratic Institutions, 1968.
The Drama of the Oceans, Abrams, 1976.
(Editor with Norton Ginsburg) *Ocean Yearbook*, University of Chicago Press, No. 1, 1979, No. 2, 1981, No. 3, 1982, No. 4, 1984, No. 5, 1985, No. 6, 1986.
Seafarm, Abrams, 1981.
The Mines of Neptune: Minerals and Metals from the Sea, Abrams, 1985.
The Future of the Oceans: A Report to the Club of Rome, Harvest House, 1986.

Also author of plays. Contributor to journals. Editor of *Common Cause*, 1948-52; executive secretary of board of editors of *Encyclopaedia Britannica*, 1964-66.

WORK IN PROGRESS: Law of the Sea; The New International Economic Order; research on aquaculture, sea-farming, and international cooperation in technology development.

SIDELIGHTS: Elisabeth Borgese, daughter of German novelist Thomas Mann, has had books translated into sixteen languages. She writes: "I have a life-long commitment to socialism, developing countries, and world order."

BIOGRAPHICAL/CRITICAL SOURCES:

PERIODICALS

National Observer, March 11, 1968.
New York Times Book Review, May 19, 1968.

* * *

BOUCHER, Alan (Estcourt) 1918-

PERSONAL: Born January 3, 1918, in Frowlesworth, Leicestershire, England; son of Robin Estcourt (a civil servant) and Kathrine Veronica (Burns) Boucher; married Aslaug Thorarinsdottir, February 28, 1942; children: Alice Kristin, Robin Gunnar, Antony Leifur. *Education:* Attended Winchester College, England; Trinity College, Cambridge, B.A., 1939, M.A., 1942, Ph.D., 1951; University of Iceland, postgraduate study, 1948-50. *Religion:* Roman Catholic.

ADDRESSES: Home—Tjarnargata 41, Reykjavik, Iceland. *Office*—Department of English, University of Iceland, Reykjavik, Iceland.

CAREER: Ampleforth School, York, England, assistant master in English, 1946-48; British Broadcasting Corp., London, England, producer and program organizer in the schools broadcasting department, with special responsibilities in field of English literature and travel, 1951—; former supervisor in old Icelandic studies, Cambridge University, Cambridge, England; currently professor of English, University of Iceland, Reykjavik. *Military service:* British Army, Royal Artillery and Intelligence Corps, 1939-46; became captain.

AWARDS, HONORS: Dame Bertha Phillpots Award for northern research, 1950, 1951; M.B.E., 1980; Knight's Cross, Icelandic Order of the Falcon, 1983.

WRITINGS:

Iceland, Some Impressions, [Reykjavik], 1949.
The Runaways, Nelson, 1959.
The Path of the Raven, Constable, 1960.
Venturers North, Nelson, 1962.
The Greenland Farers, Constable, 1962.

The King's Men, Doubleday, 1962.
The Empty Land, Nelson, 1963.
The Wineland Venture, Constable, 1963.
The Cottage in the Woods, Nelson, 1963.
The Wild Ones, Nelson, 1964.
Sea-Kings and Dragon Ships, Walker, 1964.
The Land-Seekers, Deutsch, 1964.
The Raven's Flight, Constable, 1964.
The Hornstranders, Constable, 1966.
(Compiler and translator) *Mead Moondaughter, and Other Icelandic Folktales*, Hart-Davis, 1967.
Stories of the Norsemen, Burke, 1967.
The Sword of the Raven, Scribner, 1969.
Modern Nordic Plays, Universitets Forlag Oslo, 1973.
Northern Voices, Wilfion, 1984.

TRANSLATOR FROM THE ICELANDIC; PUBLISHED BY ICELAND REVIEW BOOKS

Poems of Today, 1972.
Short Stories of Today, 1973.
A Quire of Seven, 1974.
Iceland's Folktales, three volumes, 1977.
O. J. Sigurdsson, *The Changing Earth and Selected Poems*, 1979.
A Tale of Icelanders, 1980.
The Saga of Hallfred, 1981.
Tales from the Eastfirth, 1981.
The Saga of Gunnlaug, together with the Tale of Scald-Helgi, 1983.
The Saga of Hord and the Holm-Dwellers, 1983.
The Saga of Havard the Halt, together with the Saga of Hen-Thorir, 1986.
The Saga of Viga-Glum, 1986.

IN ICELANDIC

Enskur Ordafordi Fyris Islandinga, Prentfell, 1951.
Litil Synisbok Enskra Bokmennta, Isafold, 1952.
Vid Sagnabrunninn, Mal og Menning, 1971.
Vid Timans Fljot, Mal og Menning, 1985.

OTHER

Also translator of play, ''Delerium Bubonis,'' and of radio plays. Contributor to publications in Iceland.

WORK IN PROGRESS: Editing *Travellers in Iceland.*

BIOGRAPHICAL/CRITICAL SOURCES:

PERIODICALS

Books, February, 1970.
Washington Post Book World, February 9, 1969.
Young Readers Review, December, 1968.

*   *   *

BOULLE, Pierre (Francois Marie-Louis)   1912-

PERSONAL: Born February 20, 1912, in Avignon, France; son of Eugene and Therese (Seguin) Boulle. *Education:* Ecole superieure d'Electricite, license en sciences, engineering diploma. *Religion:* Catholic.

ADDRESSES: Home—18 rue Duret, 75116 Paris, France.

CAREER: Engineer in France, 1933-35; rubber planter in Malaya, 1936-48; full-time writer, 1949—. *Military service:* French Army, World War II; sent to Malaya, 1941, joined Free French forces there and became secret agent, using name Peter John

Rule, and posing as a Mauritius-born Englishman; fought in Burma, China, and Indochina; taken prisoner and subsequently escaped in 1944; returned to France; awarded French Legion d'Honeur, Croix de Guerre, Medaille de la Resistance.

AWARDS, HONORS: Prix Sainte-Beuve, 1952, for *Le Pont de la riviere Kwai;* Grand Prix de la Nouvelle, 1953, for *Contes de l'absurde;* Grand Prix de la Societe des Gens de Lettres de France, 1976, for body of work.

WRITINGS:

NOVELS

William Conrad, Julliard, 1950, translation by Xan Fielding published as *Not the Glory*, Vanguard, 1955 (published in England as *William Conrad*, Secker & Warburg, 1955, published as *Spy Converted*, Collins, 1960).
Le Sacrilege malais, Julliard, 1951, translation by Fielding published as *S.O.P.H.I.A.*, Vanguard, 1959 (published in England as *Sacrilege in Malaya*, Secker & Warburg, 1959).
Le Pont de la riviere Kwai (also see below), Julliard, 1952, translation by Fielding published as *The Bridge over the River Kwai*, Vanguard, 1954 (published in England as *The Bridge on the River Kwai*, Secker & Warburg, 1954), French language edition with foreword by Boulle, edited by Georges Joyaux, Scribner, 1963.
La Face, Julliard, 1953, translation by Fielding published as *Face of a Hero*, Vanguard, 1956 (published in England as *Saving Face*, Secker & Warburg, 1956).
Le Proces Chinois, Les Oeuvres Libres, 1954.
Le Bourreau, Julliard, 1954, translation by Fielding published as *The Executioner*, Vanguard, 1961 (published in England as *The Chinese Executioner*, Secker & Warburg, 1962).
L'Epreuve des hommes blancs, Julliard, 1955, translation by Fielding published as *Test*, Vanguard, 1957 (published in England as *White Man's Test*, Secker & Warburg, 1957).
Les Voies de salut, Julliard, 1958, translation by Richard Howard published as *The Other Side of the Coin*, Vanguard, 1968.
Un Metier de Seigneur, Julliard, 1960, translation by Fielding published as *A Noble Profession*, Vanguard, 1960 (published in England as *For a Noble Cause*, Secker & Warburg, 1961).
Le Planete de singes, Julliard, 1963, translation by Fielding published as *Planet of the Apes*, Vanguard, 1963 (published in England as *Monkey Planet*, Secker & Warburg, 1964).
Le Jardin de Kanashima, Julliard, 1964, translation published as *Garden on the Moon*, Vanguard, 1965.
Le Photographe, Julliard, 1967, translation by Fielding published as *The Photographer*, Vanguard, 1968 (published in England as *An Impartial Eye*, Secker & Warburg, 1968).
Les Jeux de l'esprit, Julliard, 1971, translation by Patricia Wolf published as *Desperate Games*, Vanguard, 1973.
Les Oreilles de jungle, Flammarion, 1972, translation by Michael Dobry and Linda Cole published as *Ears of the Jungle*, Vanguard, 1972.
Les Vertus de l'enfer, Flammarion, translation by Wolf published as *The Virtues of Hell*, Vanguard, 1974.
Le Bon Leviathan, Julliard, 1978, translation by Margaret Giovanelli published as *The Good Leviathan*, Vanguard, 1978.
Les Caulisses du ciel, Julliard, 1979, published as *Trouble in Paradise*, Vanguard, 1981.

Miroitements, Flammarion, 1982, translation published as *Mirrors of the Sun,* Vanguard, 1986.

La Baleine des Malouines, Julliard, 1983, translation published as *The Whale of the Victoria Cross,* Vanguard, 1983 (published in England as *The Falklands Whale,* W. H. Allen, 1984).

Pour l'amour de l'art, Julliard, 1985.

SHORT STORIES

Contes de l'absurde (also see below; contains "L'Hallucination," "Une Nuit interminable," "Le Poids d'un sonnet" [also see below], "Le Regne des sages," and "Le Parfait Robot"), Julliard, 1953, translation by Fielding and Elizabeth Abbott published as *Time out of Mind, and Other Stories,* Vanguard, 1966.

Le Cas du procureur Berthier (story), Les Oeuvres Libres, 1953.

Contes de l'absurde [and] *E=MC²,* Julliard, 1957.

Le Poids d'un sonnet, Les Oeuvres Libres, 1963.

Histoires charitables (contains "Le Saint enigmatique," "L'Homme qui ramassait les epingles," "Histoire du bon petit ecrivain," "L'Arme diabolique," "Le Compte a rebours," and "L'Homme qui haissait les machines"), Julliard, 1964.

Quia absurdum (sur la terre comme au ciel), Julliard, 1970, translation by Elizabeth Abbot published as *Because It Is Absurd (on Earth as in Heaven),* Vanguard, 1971.

Histoires perfides, Flammarion, 1976, translation by Giovanelli published as *The Marvelous Palace,* Vanguard, 1977.

OTHER

"The Bridge on the River Kwai" (screenplay based on his own novel), produced by Horizon Pictures, 1958.

Walt Disney's Siam (screenplay), Nouvelles Editions (Lausanne), 1958.

William Conrad (play), Les Oeuvres Libres, 1962.

Aux Sources de la riviere Kwai (autobiography), Julliard, 1966, translation by Fielding published as *My Own River Kwai,* Vanguard, 1967 (published in England as *The Source of the River Kwai,* Secker & Warburg, 1967).

L'Etrange Croisade de l'empereur Frederic II, Flammarion, 1968.

(Compiler) *Images d'heir et d'aujourd'hui,* A.C.A.M., 1976.

L'Energie du desespoir, Julliard, 1981.

L'Univers ondoyant (essay), Julliard, 1987.

SIDELIGHTS: French novelist and short story writer Pierre Boulle has combined suspenseful plots with accurate psychological portraits to produce such popular novels as *Le Pont de la riviere Kwai* and *La Planete des Singes*—published in English translations as *The Bridge over the River Kwai* and *Planet of the Apes.* Boulle's insight into his characters has a way of "turning his books on war and spies into real literature," believes *Saturday Review* contributor Ladislas Farago. The author's early life was filled with adventures that served as background for him when he turned to writing. He left France in 1936 in take a position on a rubber plantation in Malaya. When World War II broke out, he was called to serve in the French armed forces in Indochina. After the French surrender to Germany, Boulle fled his unit to join the Free French Forces in Singapore. As a resistance fighter, he returned to the jungles of Indochina on an intelligence mission. He was captured and spent two years as a prisoner, only to escape and rejoin the Free French Forces for the remainder of the war.

After his wartime adventures, Boulle returned to his job on the rubber plantation, but found he was no longer satisfied in that position. Although he had no education in literature and read little, it occurred to him one night that he should make his living as an author. That same night, he wrote a letter of resignation to his employer. Within days he was back in Paris for the first time in nine years, ready to begin his new career. Only a year later *William Conrad* was published. This story featuring British characters is praised in the *New York Herald Tribune Book Review* by Taliaferro Boatwright as "a penetrating, ironic, but deeply sympathetic study of the British national character." *Saturday Review* contributor Edmund Fuller describes the author of *William Conrad* as "an able and highly individualized artist."

Boulle's early novels often featured the Oriental locales with which he had become so familiar. He drew heavily on his own background in writing *Le Sacrilege malais,* the story of a young engineer working in Malaya. This novel, published in England as *Sacrilege in Malaya* and in the United States as *S.O.P.H.I.A.,* reveals the damage done when a powerful corporation expands its interests in the jungles of Indochina. John Lord reports in the *New York Herald Tribune Book Review* that *S.O.P.H.I.A.* "is actually a highly artful exposition of the character of a corporation in terms of the young man's initial infatuation with it, growing knowledge of its caprices, and final, grudgingly respectful disillusionments, as he comes to know himself better."

Le Pont de la riviere Kwai is one of Boulle's most widely known works, and it is the basis for the popular film "The Bridge on the River Kwai," for which Boulle wrote the screenplay. The story centers on "a situation that is simultaneously droll, pathetic, and appalling," reports J. Rolo in an *Atlantic* review of the book's American translation, *The Bridge over the River Kwai.* Colonel Nicholson, a stern British Army officer, is captured with his unit during World War II and is set to work building a strategically vital railway bridge for the Japanese. For a time, his men perform the worst work possible for their captors. Eventually, however, Colonel Nicholson begins to feel that his men should build the best bridge they can as a way of demonstrating British superiority to the Japanese. As Nicholson's troops labor to complete the bridge, British intelligence sends a commando team to destroy it before it can be used. Critics praise Boulle for skillfully combining fast-paced action with psychological tension in what Rolo calls "a thoroughly unusual novel." Boulle points out man's weakness and follies in a cool, ironic tone, yet he treats all of his characters—including the Japanese prison camp commander—with understanding. Robert Minton praises the French author for his insight into the British mind, writing in *Saturday Review* that the character of Colonel Nicholson is "superbly set down with great sympathy and respect." *The Bridge over the River Kwai* does away with "sentimental notions of what is right and proper," concludes Kingsley Amis in *Spectator.*

Boulle explored science fiction in later novels, including *Le Jardin de Kanashima* and *La Planete des singes.* The latter book, translated as *Planet of the Apes,* became famous as the basis of several films and a television series. Boulle's characteristic irony is evident in this story of a man caught in a world where apes rule and men are beasts. "The meaning of [this] cheerful parable is not a mocking warning but an observation: human dignity is both precarious and precious; too often it is based on pride in achievements that can be matched by clever mimics of what has been done before," notes a *Time* reviewer. "Like the Red Queen, Western man has to keep running if he is to keep his place as the lord of creation."

Boulle's novels are usually "ironic, onion-peeling dissections of the self-deluding folly of man," assesses Taliaferro Boatwright in the *New York Herald Tribune Book Review*. Boulle's memoir of his war days, *Aux Sources de la riviere Kwai*, poses fewer moral questions for the reader. Instead, it is a "humorous, personal recollection that illuminates some little-known areas of the war in Asia, when South Vietnam was still called Cochin-China and Ho Chi Minh was being supplied with guns by the forerunner of the Central Intelligence Agency . . . ," writes Robert Trumbull in his *New York Times Book Review* article on the book's translation, *My Own River Kwai*. "This is a pleasant, amusing book with moments of high excitement and much vivid description of a remote part of the world."

MEDIA ADAPTATIONS: Planet of the Apes, adapted by Rod Serling and Michael Wilson, was filmed by Twentieth Century-Fox, 1968; several sequels and a television series were later based on Boulle's characters.

BIOGRAPHICAL/CRITICAL SOURCES:

BOOKS

Boulle, Pierre, *Aux Sources de la riviere Kwai*, Julliard, 1966, translation by Fielding published as *My Own River Kwai*, Vanguard, 1967 (published in England as *The Source of the River Kwai*, Secker & Warburg, 1967).
Peyre, Henri, *French Novelists of Today*, Oxford University Press, 1967.

PERIODICALS

Atlantic, November, 1954, November, 1955, February, 1973.
Booklist, December 15, 1961.
Chicago Sunday Tribune, October 3, 1954, September 25, 1955.
Christian Science Monitor, March 4, 1965, December 9, 1967.
Critic, April, 1969.
Guardian, February 2, 1962.
Harper's, December, 1967.
L'Express, April 3-9, 1967.
Los Angeles Times Book Review, October 27, 1985.
Manchester Guardian, October 16, 1956.
National Review, November 19, 1968.
New Statesman & Nation, April 10, 1954.
New Yorker, October 20, 1956, November 23, 1968, December 18, 1971, September 16, 1985.
New York Herald Tribune Book Review, September 25, 1955, November 17, 1957, October 26, 1958, January 10, 1960, November 6, 1960.
New York Times, November 30, 1972.
New York Times Book Review, October 23, 1960, March 7, 1965, November 6, 1966, October 15, 1967, May 6, 1979.
Saturday Review, October 8, 1955, January 7, 1960, December 3, 1960, March 13, 1965, November 18, 1967, December 7, 1968.
Spectator, April 9, 1954, December 11, 1959.
Time, November 8, 1963.
Times (London), March 15, 1984.
Times Literary Supplement, October 12, 1956, February 9, 1962, October 21, 1965, June 8, 1967, June 4, 1971, June 2, 1972, October 11, 1985.

—*Sketch by Joan Goldsworthy*

BOWDEN, Roland Heywood 1916-

PERSONAL: Born December 19, 1916, in London, England; son of Reginald (an engineer) and Marjorie (Heywood) Bowden; married Riki Rainer (a clerical assistant), January 2, 1946; children: Katherine Bowden Bradley, Mark. *Education:* University of Liverpool, B.Arch., 1939. *Politics:* "Left-wing radical." *Religion:* Agnostic.

ADDRESSES: Home—2 Roughmere Cottage, Lavant, Chichester, Sussex, England.

CAREER: Teacher at grammar school in Harrow, England, 1948-49, and comprehensive school in Harrow (also head of department), 1949-55; Manhood High School, Selsey, England, art teacher and head of department, 1956-79; writer, 1979—. *Military service:* British Army, Royal Army Medical Corps, 1939-45.

MEMBER: National Poetry Secretariat.

AWARDS, HONORS: Arts Council grant, 1976; Cheltenham Poetry Prize, 1982; Downland Poetry Prize, 1983.

WRITINGS:

Poems from Italy, Chatto & Windus, 1970.
Every Season Is Another, Peterloo Poets, 1986.

PLAYS

"And" (one-act), first produced in London at Questors Theatre, October, 1971.
"The Last Analysis" (two-act), first produced in London at Questors Theatre, June 10, 1974.
"The Death of Pasolini" (three-act), first produced in Edinburgh, Scotland, at Heriot-Watt Theatre, August 15, 1980.
"After Neruda" (three-act), first produced in London at Riverside Studios, 1984.
"The Fence" (three-act; about Greenham Peace Women), first produced in Brighton, 1985.

OTHER

Also author of three-act play, "The Sea of Azov" (based on Takovsky's dilemma); also author of three-act play, "Voices in Exile" (about Russian dissident Osip Mandelstam); also author of three "Stories from Italy," broadcast on B.B.C. Radio 3. Contributor to *Arts Review*.

SIDELIGHTS: Roland Heywood Bowden wrote: "Drama should disturb and disrupt. At present the media are drowning us with opiates, brainwashing us with consumerist values. As Ernest Fischer commented, 'Art is the irreconcilable, the resistance of the human being to its vanishing in the established order and systems.'

"Drama is the ideal medium through which to expose the conflict between the artist's search for increased sensibility, greater individuation, and the destructive, dehumanizing forces of the society in which he lives. The artist is the ideal protagonist: so often in him is brought into focus the creative essence and potential of the period in which he lives. Hence my last three plays deal with the death of Pablo Neruda in Chile, of Pier Paolo Pasolini in Italy, and of Osip Mandelstam in Stalinist Russia.

"Poetry, on the other hand (and the short story, which is very much an extension of poetry), I regard as the most direct and concise mehtod of both expressing and continually reintegrating the flux of one's own personal awareness.

"In the drama my main influences have been Georg Buechner, Chekhov, Gorki, John Arden, Edward Albee, Samuel Beckett; in poetry, influences so numerous as to be beyond listing."

*   *   *

BOWERS, Edgar   1924-

PERSONAL: Born March 2, 1924, in Rome, Ga.; son of William Edgar (an agronomist) and Grace (Anderson) Bowers. *Education:* University of North Carolina, B.A., 1947; Stanford University, M.A., 1949, Ph.D., 1953.

ADDRESSES: Home—1502 Miramar Beach, Santa Barbara, Calif. 93106. *Office*—English Department, University of California, Santa Barbara, Calif. 93106.

CAREER: Duke University, Durham, N.C., instructor in English, 1952-55; Harpur College, Endicott, N.Y., assistant professor of English, 1955-58; University of California, Santa Barbara, assistant professor, 1958-61, associate professor, 1961-67, professor of English, 1967—. *Military service:* U.S. Army, 1943-46; became technical sergeant.

MEMBER: Sierra Club.

AWARDS, HONORS: Fulbright Fellow; Guggenheim Fellow; Edward F. Jones fellowship; *Sewanee Review* fellowship; University of California Creative Arts Institute grant; Ingram Merrill Award; Brandeis University creative arts award; Poetry Silver Medal, California Commonwealth Club, 1973, for *Living Together*.

WRITINGS:

POETRY

The Form of Loss, A. Swallow, 1956.
(Contributor to anthology) Thom Gunn and Ted Hughes, editors, *Five American Poets*, Faber, 1963.
The Astronomers, A. Swallow, 1965.
Living Together: New and Selected Poems, David Godine, 1973.
Witnesses, Symposium Press, 1981.

Poems anthologized *New Poets of England and America*.

OTHER

Contributor of poetry to periodicals, including *Paris Review*, *New Statesman, Poetry, Listen, New York Times*, and *Sewanee Review*.

SIDELIGHTS: Edgar Bowers's poems "demonstrate that quality of high seriousness which has faded from poetry" in the last half of the twentieth century, believes *New York Times Book Review* contributor Joseph Bennett. Bowers's work is also distinguished from that of many modern poets by its use of classic forms and what Anne Stevenson calls in the *Times Literary Supplement* "an intelligent control of language." The spare, compact style that is the poet's trademark is highly expressive, according to Bennett, who declares that "some of [Bowers's] compressed forms accomplish more in a single poem than many poets do in a lifetime."

Paul Ramsey concurs that Bowers is a powerful writer. In an essay appearing in the *Sewanee Review*, Ramsey states that the collection *Living Together* contains poems that "are in my judgment among the best American poems." Stevenson also generally praises *Living Together*, but questions whether Bowers's tightly controlled style leaves room for emotion: "It is perhaps ungenerous to suggest that Professor Bowers's book suffers from a too excellent, too self-conscious control of his ideas. Such control by and through language is admirable, but a reader does not want to read language alone. When a man can write so well without metrical props—as he does in a sequence called 'Autumn Shade' when he lets his iambics breathe—why depend on them so much?" Ramsey insists, however, that Bowers's technical excellence is applied to profound themes. "Value, knowledge, beauty, faith—and an epistemology that makes them impossible—are his recurrent subjects, unsolved but explored with subtlety, dignity and pain."

F. H. Griffin Taylor affirms the seriousness of Bowers's work. Reviewing *The Astronomer* for the *Sewanee Review,* Taylor compares reading the book to "spending a day with a hermit in a dark Himalayan cave furnished only with the top part of a skull from which one is offered glacier water for good cheer. The skill of the poet is that he makes of it an existentialist experience of death. The burden of these beautifully wrought verses, and of all the love and fire that went into their making, is in the relentless contemplation of the horror of being and not-being. . . . Pervading and unifying all of these poems is the poets' keen, raw-rubbed sensibility, tortured, fearful, and courageous."

Dictionary of Literary Biography essayist Leon V. Driskell concludes: "Tightness of control and refusal to join in the intensely subjective confessional poetry of the 1960s and 1970s perhaps account for Bowers's relative obscurity; his work has had neither the critical nor popular attention it deserves and might have enjoyed at an earlier time. The poems are chiseled and spare; they are artificial in the best sense of the word, but, unfortunately, many readers have come to suspect the product of artifice and to prefer the spontaneous. The poems' precision, once understood, demands admiration."

AVOCATIONAL INTERESTS: Travel, music, gardening, cooking.

BIOGRAPHICAL/CRITICAL SOURCES:

BOOKS

Contemporary Literary Criticism, Volume IX, Gale, 1978.
Dictionary of Literary Biography, Volume V: *American Poets since World War II*, Gale, 1980.
Howard, Richard, *Alone with America: Essays on the Art of Poetry in the United States since 1950*, Atheneum, 1969.
Winters, Yvor, *Forms of Discovery; Critical and Historical Essays on the Forms of the Short Poem in English*, A. Swallow, 1967.

PERIODICALS

Commonweal, September 24, 1965.
Hudson Review, autumn, 1974.
New York Times Book Review, November 14, 1965.
Sewanee Review, spring, 1964, spring, 1969.
Southern Review, summer, 1973, winter, 1977.
Times Literary Supplement, February 10, 1978.

*   *   *

BRAZOS, Waco
See JENNINGS, Michael Glenn

*   *   *

BREMER, Lisa
See JANAS, Frankie-Lee

BRIN, David 1950-

PERSONAL: Born October 6, 1950, in Glendale, Calif.; son of Herbert (an editor) and Selma (a teacher) Brin. *Education:* California Institute of Technology, B.S., 1972; University of California, San Diego, M.S., 1979, Ph.D., 1981.

ADDRESSES: Home—11625 Montana, Number 9, Los Angeles, Calif. 90049-4676. *Office*—Heritage Press, 2130 South Vermont Ave., Los Angeles, Calif. 90007. *Agent*—Richard Curtis Associates, Inc., 164 East 64th St., New York, N.Y. 10021.

CAREER: Hughes Aircraft Research Laboratories, Newport Beach and Carlsbad, Calif., electrical engineer in semiconductor device development, 1973-77; managing editor, *Journal of the Laboratory of Comparative Human Cognition,* 1979-80; Heritage Press, Los Angeles, Calif., book reviewer and science editor, 1980—. Post-doctoral research fellow, California Space Institute, La Jolla, Calif., 1982-84.

MEMBER: British Interplanetary Society.

AWARDS, HONORS: Locus Award, Locus Publications, 1984, for *Startide Rising,* and 1986, for *The Postman;* Nebula Award, Science Fiction Writers of America, 1984, for *Startide Rising;* Hugo Award, World Science Fiction Convention, 1984, for *Startide Rising,* and 1985, for the short story "The Crystal Spheres"; John W. Campbell Memorial Award, 1986, for *The Postman.*

WRITINGS:

Sundiver (novel), Bantam, 1980.
Startide Rising, Bantam, 1983, hardcover edition, Phantasia Press, 1985.
The Practice Effect, Bantam, 1984.
The Postman, Bantam, 1985.
(With Gregory Benford) *Heart of the Comet,* Bantam, 1986.
The River of Time (short stories), Dark Harvest, 1986.
The Uplift War, Phantasia Press, 1987.

CONTRIBUTOR

Jerry Pournelle, Jim Baen, and John F. Carr, editors, *Far Frontiers,* Baen, 1985.

OTHER

Contributor of articles and stories to scientific journals and popular magazines, including *Analog* and *Isaac Asimov's Science Fiction Magazine.*

WORK IN PROGRESS: More novels; a nonfiction academic book covering extraterrestrial intelligent life; continuing research on the nature and origins of the solar system.

SIDELIGHTS: When *Sundiver,* the first novel by American astrophysicist David Brin, was published, few if any science fiction fans were familiar with its author's name. But his second book, *Startide Rising,* quickly gained him fame as one of the genre's best young writers. Sweeping the field's major awards, this novel won the Hugo for its popularity among readers, and the Nebula for impressing the critics. Brin also won the John W. Campbell Memorial Award for Best Novel for *The Postman,* one of his contributions to mainstream fiction.

Though Brin's first two novels were most commended by the science fiction community, the ideas and ethical concerns they explore have earned them recognition from outside the genre, say reviewers Debra Rae Cohen of the *Voice Literary Supplement* and Donald M. Hassler of the *Science Fiction and Fantasy Book Review.* At home on both sides of that boundary, the novels also provide "space opera characteristics," notes Hassler. Both *Sundiver* and *Startide Rising* are set in the Progenitors universe, which teems with inhabited galaxies and their numerous races, complicated by conflicts and technological problems on an epic scale. The most intelligent races in its five galaxies believe they were "uplifted" to sapience through the efforts of an elder but now-missing species, and that it is their duty to use genetic engineering to raise other species to the status of participants in their culture. "Some of these 'Galactics' are moderates; other races appear fanatical to a beleaguered humanity," Brin told *CA.* Without the presumably necessary aid of patrons, humans had achieved the ability to travel in space and to "uplift" dolphins and chimpanzees. Such audacity must be checked, believe the "fanatics," who fight each other for the right to "adopt" the humans into a remedial retraining program.

Sundiver introduces this universe, notes *Analog* reviewer Tom Easton; *Startide Rising,* taking place 200 years later, shows the Earth ship *Streaker* pursued by aliens and grounded on the water-world planet of Kithrup for repairs. The few humans aboard are observers of the ship's crew, a team of uplifted dolphins who speak in a poetic language akin to haiku. "Each of Brin's dolphins is a distinct and unique individual, without ever losing an essential dolphinity," writes Stephen B. Brown in a *Washington Post Book World* review. In Brown's opinion, "the care and empathy with which Brin describes the relationships between his aquatic characters elevates this book into a substantial achievement." Brown commends the author for skillfully weaving "the byzantine intrigues of . . . various dolphin factions" while consistently developing "the idea that a viable human/dolphin collaboration can be something greater than each race on its own."

"Brin's toying with the vision of evolution is probably the strongest feature in both books," Hassler remarks. Brin's "notion of managed development" as opposed to natural selection, "which by contrast seems blind, [and] inefficient," says Hassler, allows the author to examine ethical problems that result from the subordination of uplifted species to their patrons, and the universal search for the Progenitors, the supposed first species, as well. Hassler comments, "Such tales of origins and the running debate between [Charles] Darwin and [Erich] Von Daniken are truly sublime." Whereas most reviewers praised *Startide Rising*'s fast-paced action and complex plot, *Minneapolis Tribune* contributor D. R. Martin expressed his wish that "someone—Brin or his editor—had tightened things up along the way." Brin revised the book extensively for its hardcover printing by Phantasia Press in 1985, a reissue *Publishers Weekly* dubbed "an SF event."

Because he feels that the creation of fictional worlds can foster egotistic and "self-indulgent" writing, Brin explained to *CA* interviewer Jean W. Ross that he limits himself to write no more than two books in a row about any given universe. Consequently, he interrupted the telling of the story of the search for the Progenitors with a third novel in a lighter vein. In *The Practice Effect,* he gives indulgence full play, venting "all the bad puns" that don't belong, as he told Ross, in the "more serious work." Accordingly, reviewers find *The Practice Effect* an enjoyable time-travel romance in the tradition of Mark Twain's *A Connecticut Yankee in King Arthur's Court.* Like Twain's "Yankee," Brin's Dennis Nuel enters a strange world, rescues a princess, defeats a formidable enemy and contributes to progress by virtue of skills that would be considered quite ordinary at home. This formula has been used often since Twain wrote the prototype, say reviewers, but Brin gives it a new twist: Nuel finds himself in a world where repeated use improves objects instead of wearing them out. Sequences showing what many simple objects become as the result of "practice" (flint knives become super-sabers; a zipper becomes a saw) are interlaced with Nuel's adventures "which can only be called rollicking," writes Baird Searles in *Isaac Asimov's Science Fiction Magazine*. Adding to the fun are sometimes slant references to "the great moments of SF history," notes the reviewer, who believes that "the high spirits and inventiveness of the [practice effect] idea more than compensate" for the plot's occasional "repetitiveness" and the author's somewhat "collegiate" humor.

Brin gives a new treatment to another branch of fiction with *The Postman*, his portrayal of life in America after nuclear world war. Unlike other post-apocalypse novels that bemoan total destruction, *The Postman* depicts what Brin told Ross is "the real horror of such a war"—the prospect of surviving in a holocaust-ravaged environment. "The world Brin draws is terrifying," says *Los Angeles Times Book Review* contributor Ronald Florence, referring to the power-hungry paramilitary bands that tyrannize people who live in small, unprotected settlements. Stripped by the bandits, protagonist Gordon Krantz finds a mail carrier's remains and borrows the dead postman's uniform. Thereafter, the villagers see him "as a symbol of civilization," relates *Washington Post Book World*'s Gregory Frost. Maintaining ever-larger lies about his identity, Krantz accepts the role of public servant and civil authority they ascribe to him. The story develops "Brin's premise that people need something bigger than survival to believe in," notes a *New York Times Book Review* contributor. *Analog*'s Tom Easton finds it a recommendable demonstration of "the value of myths." Like other reviewers, Frost notes several "weaknesses" he later deems "minor," and praises the "mythic dimension" Brin brings to almost every element of the novel.

If these books prove that Brin finds the science fiction category a bit too confining, his next book, *The Heart of the Comet*, say *Chicago Tribune Book World* reviewers James and Eugene Sloan, confirms his place among those writers "who are busy putting the hard science back into science fiction." Works in the genre drifted toward "softer" speculation and fantasy during the past decade, John R. Cramer reports in the *Los Angeles Times*. However, he notes with pleasure, the then NASA scientist Brin and co-author Gregory Benford present "accurate physics and biology" when narrating the conditions that threaten a crew of scientists as they ride Halley's Comet to the farthest point of its range and try to move it into an orbit closer to earth. Brin was not an established writer when the two astrophysicists began to work on the book, which was planned to come out near the time of the comet's visit in 1986. Applause from the critics included the Sloans's remark that *Heart of the Comet* "may well be the masterpiece of [the hard science revival]. . . . Light years ahead of [Carl] Sagan's rival effort, this book is what science fiction is."

In *The Uplift War*, Brin goes back to the universe of his first two novels for a closer look at uplifted chimpanzees as they relate to humans in the struggle to rebuild an ecologically damaged planet while trying to resist alien invaders. Brin's message, observes Easton, is the positive value of a sense of humor. "Humans and neochimps and Tymbrimi [a race of alien pranksters] together defeat [their attackers] and score massive points in the Uplift culture with the aid of one of the grandest jokes in galactic history," relates Easton, who finds Brin's handling of the Uplift concept enjoyable, his plots satisfying, and his ideas "beautifully" developed.

A quick rise to fame has adversely affected other writers, says *Science Fiction Review* critic Darrell Schweitzer. Brin, he notes, "is suddenly in the forefront of the field before his talents have fully developed. One can only hope that he will remain above the adulation and continue to grow." Brin aspires to the same hope, as he once revealed in a comment to *CA*: "People are often surprised to find that [Aldous] Huxley wrote nothing but science fiction, though sometimes he kept it a secret until the last five pages of a book. All of the best writers play with reality. They ask the questions that are normally asked, inefficiently, by college sophomores, and they do it in a manner that illuminates a self or a world. Maybe someday I will be able to do that."

MEDIA ADAPTATIONS: Warner Bros. has purchased the rights to make a film based on *The Postman*.

CA INTERVIEW

CA interviewed David Brin by telephone on January 12, 1987, in London, England, where he was spending a sabbatical year.

CA: You have an enviable dual career. As a scientist, you work with hard fact; as a writer, you can go beyond what's been proven to create whole new worlds. The two pursuits must enrich each other tremendously.

BRIN: I think that's true. Certainly there are many individuals who have had careers straddling both science and art. For example, there was no music department at Cal Tech, where I was an undergraduate, but it seemed everybody played musical instruments. My friend and collaborator Gregory Benford, with whom I wrote the novel *Heart of the Comet*, is a very skilled physicist and a wonderful writer. I have to confess that, while I may have my union card (that is, a Ph.D.), I really don't consider myself to be a first-rate scientist. I putter around the edges of subjects trying to point out things that I think some people have missed, for instance, in my paper dealing with the search for extraterrestrial intelligence, pointing out some inconsistencies in prior work in SETI [Search for Extraterrestrial Intelligence]. And my time at the California Space Institute mostly involved critiquing the U.S. space program. I would have liked very much to have been a better scientist, but at least I can take part in the adventure. And certainly my education has helped in my writing career.

CA: Contemporary Literary Criticism says that you became interested in writing while you were studying at Cal Tech. Is that accurate, or had you thought earlier of being a writer?

BRIN: I'd always dabbled in writing, for fun and relaxation. Perhaps one reason I tried so hard to become a scientist was because it was difficult, whereas I always figured I'd get around to writing sooner or later.

CA: In The Postman you paid tribute to Theodore Sturgeon by naming a building for him on the post-holocaust University of Oregon campus. Was he a special inspiration for you?

BRIN: There have been others who have had a greater influence on me, but I admired the man very much, and it happened I was rewriting that chapter set in Eugene, Oregon, on the day

I received word that Theodore Sturgeon had died in the very same city. It seemed a way to indicate how I felt. I think he was a fine writer and a very warm human being.

CA: What writers do you consider great influences on your work, either directly or indirectly?

BRIN: Of course many of the old masters: Aldous Huxley, James Joyce, and especially Mark Twain. *Huckleberry Finn* is widely acclaimed as the prototypical American novel, and it has everything—biting social irony, touching irony, fine characters and excellent craft in language. And yet, a twelve-year-old can ignore all that and read it as an adventure yarn. He proved that good literature doesn't have to be opaque or inaccessible.

Modern writers I admire are Alfred Bester, Greg Bear, Thomas Pynchon (when he's not opaque), Frederik Pohl, Kim Stanley Robinson. I also read a lot of nonfiction, and particularly admire Melvin Konner.

CA: You won both the Nebula and the Hugo awards for your second novel, Startide Rising, *which is set in a universe you created earlier for* Sundiver. *Can you tell me something about the genesis of that universe in your mind, and how it evolved?*

BRIN: Well, first of all, let me say this: I think the "universe" approach to writing is sometimes overused in science fiction. I think it sometimes leads to self-indulgence. I have promised myself that I will not write two books in a row in a "universe" per se, and that I will write limited universes. This one, the Progenitors universe, will contain at most six or seven novels. I have many other ideas that I want to work on. Given that, I'd say that many authors have used fictive universes to explore in depth and in detail a scenario, one possible way in which the world might work out.

The Progenitors universe combines several ideas that I wanted to explore. One is using genetic engineering to modify our fellow creatures on this planet. It has already begun with domesticated animals, such as cattle. I wanted to explore the ethical problems involved in changing more sophisticated creatures such as dolphins or apes, to give them the capabilities to become fellow-citizens in our culture. Do we have the right to meddle with species that have their own dignity? There are serious ethical questions about this whole matter of uplift, of being patrons of a client species. We'll face these questions in the real world in just a few years.

The other thing I wanted to explore was a problem that I've noticed in a great many science fiction stories, those with large galactic settings and containing many acrimonious alien races. That is an illogical situation: if there were a great many alien races filling the galaxy, copious traces of their visits or past colonizations would be apparent on earth and in the solar system. And yet, there are no creditable signs that the earth has ever been visited in the past. If our world had been colonized, *we* probably never would have come about. Look at it logically: if we have lots of species running around with faster-than-light starships, we get an unstable situation, probably leading to an ecological holocaust across the galaxy.

I wanted to come up with a scenario in which a civilization would be possible in the galaxy which would have conservation of so-called "nursery worlds" like the earth as a paramount objective. One way in which that could happen is if *everybody* performed this uplift of species that are on the edge

of intelligence. And if their status as galactic starfarers depended on how many of these upliftings they had performed, they would be very conservative about places where such presentient races might develop, and they would want to protect them.

It's basically a "gedanken-experiment" or thought experiment. One role of SF is to explore the limits of an idea. Fortunately, most people seem to find that this doesn't stand in the way of reading an entertaining story.

CA: In Startide Rising, *your dolphins speak in very poetic language and poetic forms. What sort of work went into devising that language?*

BRIN: I studied everything I could find about cetology, particularly the very good work done by Louis Herman at the University of Hawaii, which is starting to give us a good idea just how intelligent the high dolphins are. But when push comes to shove, it really comes down to my imagination, and I am not the boss there; my imagination tells me what to do. I know who brings home the bread and butter, so while, to an extent, I bring logic into my writing, where poetry is concerned it comes straight from the back of the skull. That's my way of saying, Don't give me the credit—or the blame!

CA: There was a sequel announced to Startide, The Uplift War. *What's the status of that book?*

BRIN: It's all finished. Phantasia Press will publish it in hard cover in April, and Bantam Books in paperback in July. It's a very large book—220,000 words—and not so much a sequel as a parallel volume. This one deals with simians, with chimpanzees and gorillas. As with *Startide,* I spent about a year as sort of a graduate student, being an amateur student of simian science. I had a good time with the book. It's more fun than *Startide,* less ethereal. The apes get a little gritty at times. There's a scene in which a riot breaks out in a blue-collar, working chimps' bar. I think readers might like that.

CA: Was it a hard decision to follow the prize-winning Startide Rising *with a very different kind of novel,* The Practice Effect?

BRIN: The Practice Effect was a light adventure-fantasy and romance which is accessible to bright children, I should think. When I wrote it, I had just finished a long period as a graduate student. Also, for a beginner, *Startide Rising* was a very exhausting work. So I decided to have some fun with a strict formula piece that was completely self-indulgent. Incidentally, it let me purge myself of all the bad puns that were threatening to spill over into more serious work.

Let me explain that last remark. I'm very much a believer that in the arts we suffer from self-indulgence much more often than in the sciences. One reason is that the sciences have a mutual system of criticism and validation, verification. Many scientists get very egotistical, but there are institutions that help them keep it under control. On the other hand many of my favorite artists, writers, and actors I have seen ruined by self-indulgence, believing their ego. I happen to have a very large ego, but one thing that I hope protects me from it is the fact that I very much believe the ego can be the death of an artist's energy. That's why I've tried to set up patterns to help me protect myself. One of these is to occasionally become self-indulgent and put that self-indulgence into a ghetto. That's one of the practical reasons I did *The Practice Effect.* It's a romp, it's fun, and once it was done I was ready to move on.

CA: To The Postman.

BRIN: Yes. After *The Practice Effect* I wrote *The Postman,* which had more of a mythical tone. Bantam published that not as a science-fiction novel, but as a literary mainstream novel. I'm off next week on a tour to promote the British publication of *The Postman.* Also, it has been optioned by Warner Brothers, and they've finished a screenplay. I still don't know what they're going to do. I'll believe it when I see it.

CA: Tell me how the collaboration between you and Gregory Benford came about on Heart of the Comet, *written for the year of the return of Halley's Comet, and how it worked in the actual process of writing.*

BRIN: For one thing, my doctoral dissertation dealt with comets and asteroids. That helped. At the time we decided to do this, Greg was a prominent writer and I was a young punk from nowhere. Subsequently I did considerably better in my career and we took on the project more as equals. We were inspired by Halley's Comet. Ironically, for commercial reasons we should have chosen almost any other year, because people said, "Oh, no, not another comet book!" It got wonderful reviews almost everywhere; it was very nicely treated. But in almost every rave review the critic would say, "In spite of the book's gimmicky aspect in coming out in the year of the comet, I thought it was. . . ."

It wasn't all that difficult collaborating. Every collaboration has a different style to it. Some collaborators just about live in each other's houses and don't know who wrote what after all is said and done. Benford and I lived 150 miles apart and had incompatible word processors. As a result, we carefully outlined the book, divided it up among three points of view represented by three characters whose scenes alternated through the book. Benford took one character and wrote all of that person's scenes; I took another character and all of his scenes. We took turns with the third. It resulted in a very different voice for each character. It was a most intriguing, interesting experiment, and, I feel, a successful one. We may do it again.

CA: The River of Time, *another 1986 book, contains your Hugo-winning story "The Crystal Spheres." Do you enjoy writing the short stories and novellas as much as doing novels?*

BRIN: I feel I get different things from the three different lengths. The short stories are attempts at epiphanies, at making a ringing note that will hang in the reader's ear, like the effect Joyce achieved in his smaller works. It's like a painting; you take it all in. My large novels, on the other hand, tend to be very complicated. They're explorations of many ideas, woven together trying to make a complex tapestry. In between is the length known as the novella, which happens to be my favorite. This length allows one to explore a mythic theme that one can't afford to muddy up with all sorts of complexities. This is the length that I believe is right for legend. And I think this helps explain why *The Postman,* of all of my novels, has more of a mythic feel to it; it actually is made up of three separate novellas.

CA: That book is very believable. Unlike many post-holocaust books, it seems the most possible, the most likely.

BRIN: In the case of *The Postman,* I felt no need for a science fictional setting. It brings the feeling much closer to home to have the people in recognizable, familiar settings. Another thing is that people who write post-holocaust novels—and I do not

exclude myself from this—very often have an ax to grind. Most of the stories we've seen in recent years, particularly in the mass media, have fallen into two categories: either doom-and-gloom, oh-gee-we're-all-going-to-die morality tales about war, in which case the author paints all the dying and suffering; or survival fantasies—hey, boys, look at all the fun we're going to have now that all the rules are off. Both have made me quite sick. The latter are essentially a bunch of adolescent male escapist trips, and the former, I think, *downplay* the real horror of nuclear war by saying we're all going to die. The real horror, to me, is not death and destruction. We've had that all our lives, and for thousands of years. If the curtain is all coming down, a la *On the Beach,* then it's all over; nobody suffers anymore. But it strikes me as more likely that some of our descendants would survive even the worst nuclear war, and they would probably go back to living like Michael Landon in "Little House on the Prairie." But they would not be as happy as our pioneer forebears. They would be fundamentally scarred forever because of one fact: they would know how close we came to a sane, decent, better world, and that might-have-been would haunt them. I happen to believe we're in a renaissance right now. If we muck it up, we'll have mucked up just on the threshold of a truly wonderful creation. That, I think, is the real horror of such a war.

CA: In science fiction now, there's talk about the hard science revival, of which Publishers Weekly *called you "one of the stars." There is also talk about so-called cyberpunk. Are there other new things happening in the field?*

BRIN: I just finished writing what might be labelled a cyberpunk story. I respect some of the cyberpunks, although when they say what they're doing is new it makes me smile. People always try to fit things into categories. The authors I most respect don't really fit the neat pigeonholes well because they're always exploring. Personally, I don't even like being categorized as strictly a science fiction author. I write what I want to write and what I think will both entertain the reader and get some ideas across. More often than not I find that, if I can set the story in the future a little ways, I can strike a great contrast with the world in which we now live. I don't mean to sound pretentious in saying that; it's just one of the values of the better end of science fiction. Gedanken-experiment, thought experiment, playing games and making warnings. I think that's the value of extrapolative or speculative fiction, whether you call it science fiction or not.

CA: Are you doing some specific scientific work now?

BRIN: Not much. I'm working on a book for Cambridge University Press on the SETI question, and I'm still doing some minor studies having to do with space stations and use of space resources. Mostly I'm enjoying a sabbatical year in Britain, doing a little bit of teaching, spending some time in the British Library and the British Museum, trying to write several long-delayed projects. It *is* an enviable life. I can sleep as late as I want and do pretty much as I please with my days. I'm not complaining in that respect. I consider writing to be an art, and I am very thankful that I can participate in the excitement of the English language. Still, I was just good enough in mathematics to squint myopically at its beauties, and there's no question in my mind that people such as Alan Guth at MIT [Massachusetts Institute of Technology], who are talking to God in the language He used to make the universe, are particularly blessed. I must admit I'm a bit envious of them.

Well, I've had so much luck in my life. I have a union card, at least, in my favorite profession, and I appear to be fairly good in my second favorite. How many people can say that? I'm not complaining.

BIOGRAPHICAL/CRITICAL SOURCES:

BOOKS

Contemporary Literary Criticism, Volume XXXIV, Gale, 1985.

PERIODICALS

Amazing, January, 1984.
Analog: Science Fiction/Science Fact, November, 1983, July, 1984, March, 1986, November, 1987.
Booklist, September 1, 1987.
Book World, October 19, 1986.
Chicago Tribune Book World, March 23, 1986.
Fantasy Review, September, 1985.
Isaac Asimov's Science Fiction Magazine, mid-December, 1983, July, 1984.
Los Angeles Times, December 16, 1985, April 1, 1986.
Los Angeles Times Book Review, December 15, 1985, January 12, 1986.
Minneapolis Tribune, December 25, 1983.
New York Times Book Review, November 24, 1985.
Publishers Weekly, August 12, 1983, September 6, 1985, January 10, 1986, June 13, 1986, October 11, 1985, March 27, 1987.
San Jose Mercury News, March 11, 1984.
Science Fiction and Fantasy Book Review, September, 1983, November, 1983.
Science Fiction Chronicle, December, 1985, March, 1987, June, 1987.
Science Fiction Review, August, 1984.
Voice Literary Supplement, December, 1983.
Washington Post Book World, April 22, 1984, December 22, 1985.

—*Sketch by Marilyn K. Basel*

—*Interview by Jean W. Ross*

*   *   *

BRIQUEBEC, John
   See ROWLAND-ENTWISTLE, (Arthur) Theodore
   (Henry)

*   *   *

BUCKLEY, William F(rank), Jr.   1925-

PERSONAL: Born November 24, 1925, in New York, N.Y.; son of William Frank (a lawyer and oilman) and Aloise (Steiner) Buckley; married Patricia Austin Taylor, July 6, 1950; children: Christopher. *Education:* Attended University of Mexico, 1943-44; Yale University, B.A. (with honors), 1950. *Politics:* Republican. *Religion:* Roman Catholic.

ADDRESSES: Office—National Review, 150 East 35th St., New York, N.Y. 10016.

CAREER: Yale University, New Haven, Conn., instructor in Spanish, 1947-51; affiliated with the Central Intelligence Agency (C.I.A.) in Mexico, 1951-52; *American Mercury* (magazine), New York City, associate editor, 1952; free-lance writer and editor, 1952-55; *National Review* (magazine), New York City, founder, president, and editor-in-chief, 1955—; syndicated columnist, 1962—; host of "Firing Line" weekly television

program, 1966—. Conservative Party candidate for mayor of New York City, 1965; member of National Advisory Commission on Information, U.S. Information Agency, 1969-72; public member of the U.S. delegation to the United Nations, 1973. Lecturer, New School for Social Research, 1967-68; Froman Distinguished Professor, Russell Sage College, 1973. Chairman of the board, Starr Broadcasting Group, Inc., 1969-78. *Military service:* U.S. Army, 1944-46; became second lieutenant.

MEMBER: Council on Foreign Relations, Century Association, Mont Pelerin Society, New York Yacht Club, Bohemian Club, Philadelphia Society.

AWARDS, HONORS: Freedom Award, Order of Lafayette, 1966; George Sokolsky Award, American Jewish League against Communism, 1966; Best Columnist of the Year Award, 1967; University of Southern California Distinguished Achievement Award in Journalism, 1968; Liberty Bell Award, New Haven County Bar Association, 1969; Emmy Award, National Academy of Television Arts and Sciences, 1969, for "Firing Line"; Man of the Decade Award, Young Americans for Freedom, 1970; Cleveland Amory Award, *TV Guide,* 1974, for best interviewer/interviewee on television; fellow, Sigma Delta Chi, 1976; Bellarmine Medal, 1977; Americanism Award, Young Republican National Federation, 1979, for contributons to the American principles of freedom, individual liberty , and free enterprise; Carmel Award, American Friends of Haifa University, 1980, for journalism excellence; American Book Award, 1980, for *Stained Glass;* New York University Creative Leadership Award, 1981. Honorary degrees: L.H.D. from Seton Hall University, 1966, Niagara University, 1967, Mount Saint Mary's College, 1969, and University of South Carolina, 1985; LL.D. from St. Peter's College, 1969, Syracuse University, 1969, Ursinus College, 1969, Lehigh University, 1970, Lafayette College, 1972, St. Anselm's College, 1973, St. Bonaventure University, 1974, University of Notre Dame, 1978, New York Law School, 1981, and Colby College, 1985; D.Sc.O. from Curry College, 1970; Litt.D. from St. Vincent College, 1971, Fairleigh Dickinson University, 1973, Alfred University, 1974; College of William and Mary, 1981, William Jewell College, 1982, Albertus Magnus College, 1987, College of St. Thomas, 1987, and Bowling Green State University, 1987.

WRITINGS:

God and Man at Yale: The Superstitions of "Academic Freedom," Regnery, 1951, reprinted, Gateway Editions, 1977.
(With L. Brent Bozell) *McCarthy and His Enemies: The Record and Its Meaning,* Regnery, 1954.
Up from Liberalism, Obolensky, 1959.
Rumbles Left and Right: A Book about Troublesome People and Ideas, Putnam, 1963.
The Unmaking of a Mayor, Viking, 1966.
(Author of introduction) Edgar Smith, *Brief against Death,* Knopf, 1968.
The Jeweler's Eye: A Book of Irresistible Political Reflections, Putnam, 1968.
(Author of introduction) *Will Mrs. Major Go to Hell?: The Collected Work of Aloise Buckley Heath,* Arlington House, 1969.
Quotations from Chairman Bill: The Best of William F. Buckley, Jr., compiled by David Franke, Arlington House, 1970.
The Governor Listeth: A Book of Inspired Political Revelations, Putnam, 1970.

Cruising Speed: A Documentary, Putnam, 1971.
Taiwan: The West Berlin of China, St. John's University Center of Asian Studies, 1971.
Inveighing We Will Go, Putnam, 1972.
Four Reforms: A Guide for the Seventies, Putnam, 1973.
United Nations Journal: A Delegate's Odyssey, Putnam, 1974.
The Assault on the Free Market (lecture), Kansas State University, 1974.
Execution Eve and Other Contemporary Ballads, Putnam, 1975.
Airborne: A Sentimental Journey, Macmillan, 1976.
A Hymnal: The Controversial Arts, Putnam, 1978.
Atlantic High: A Celebration, Doubleday, 1982.
Overdrive: A Personal Documentary, Doubleday, 1983.
Right Reason, Doubleday, 1985.
The Temptation of Wilfred Malachey (juvenile), Workman Publishing, 1985.
Racing through Paradise: A Pacific Passage, Random House, 1987.

EDITOR

(With others) *The Committee and Its Critics: A Calm Review of the House Committee on Un-American Activities*, Constructive Action, 1963.
Odyssey of a Friend: Whittaker Chambers' Letters to William F. Buckley, Jr., 1954-1961, Putnam, 1970.
Did You Ever See a Dream Walking?: American Conservative Thought in the Twentieth Century, Bobbs-Merrill, 1970.
(With Charles R. Kesler) *The Tablet Keepers: American Conservative Thought in the 20th Century*, Harper, 1987.

Also editor, with Stuart W. Little, of *The Buckley-Little Catalogue*, 1984-87.

ESPIONAGE NOVELS

Saving the Queen, Doubleday, 1976.
Stained Glass, Doubleday, 1978.
Who's On First, Doubleday, 1980.
Marco Polo, If You Can, Doubleday, 1982.
The Story of Henri Tod, Doubleday, 1984.
See You Later, Alligator, Doubleday, 1985.
High Jinx, Doubleday, 1986.
Mongoose, R.I.P., Random House, 1988.

CONTRIBUTOR

Ocean Racing, Van Nostrand, 1959.
The Intellectuals, Free Press, 1960.
F. S. Meyer, editor, *What Is Conservatism?*, Holt, 1964.
Dialogues in Americanism, Regnery, 1964.
Edward D. Davis, editor, *The Beatles Book*, Cowles, 1968.
S. Endleman, editor, *Violence in the Streets*, Quadrangle, 1968.
R. Campbell, editor, *Spectrum of Catholic Attitudes*, Bruce Publishing, 1969.
Great Ideas Today Annual, 1970, Encyclopaedia Britannica, 1970.
Fritz Machlup, editor, *Essays on Hayek*, New York University Press, 1976.

OTHER

Also author of "Celestial Navigation," a videocassette. Author of syndicated column "On the Right," 1962—. Contributor to *Esquire, Saturday Review, Harper's, Atlantic, Playboy, New Yorker, New York Times Magazine*, and other publications.

SIDELIGHTS: William F. Buckley, Jr., is one of the most recognized and articulate spokesmen for American conserva-

tives. On his television program "Firing Line," in the pages of *National Review*, the magazine he edits, and through the books and syndicated columns he writes, Buckley argues for individual liberty, the free market, and the traditional moral values of Western culture. His eloquence, wit, and appealing personal style have made him palatable even to many of his political opponents. "The Buckley substance," a writer for *Time* reports, "is forgiven for the Buckley style."

Buckley's writings have been instrumental to the phenomenal growth of the American conservative movement. In the 1950s, when Buckley first appeared on the scene, conservatism was a peripheral presence on the national political spectrum. But in 1980 the conservatives elected Ronald Reagan, a longtime reader of Buckley's *National Review*, as president of the United States. "When the tide of intellectual and political history seemed headed inexorably leftward . . . ," Morton Kondracke writes in the *New York Times Book Review*, "Mr. Buckley had the temerity to uphold the cause of Toryism. He and his magazine nurtured the movement . . . and gave it a rallying point and sounding board as it gradually gained the strength and respectability to win the Presidency. Conservatism is far from the dominant intellectual force in the country today, but neither is liberalism. There is now a balance between the movements, a permanent contest, and Mr. Buckley deserves credit for helping make it so."

Buckley first came to public attention in 1951 when he published *God and Man at Yale: The Superstitions of "Academic Freedom,"* an attack against his alma mater, Yale University. The book accuses Yale of fostering values—such as atheism and collectivism—which are anathema to the school's supporters. Further, Buckley claims that Yale stifled the political freedom of its more conservative students. Those students who spoke out against the liberal views of their professors were often ostracized. The book's charges stemmed from Buckley's own experiences while attending Yale, where his views on individualism, the free market, and communism found little support among the liberal academics.

God and Man at Yale raised a storm of controversy as Yale faculty members denounced the charges made against them. Some reviewers joined in the denunciation. McGeorge Bundy, writing in the *Atlantic*, called the book "dishonest in its use of facts, false in its theory, and a discredit to its author." Peter Viereck agreed with Buckley that "more conservatism and traditional morality" were needed at universities and wrote in the *New York Times* that "this important, symptomatic, and widely held book is a necessary counterbalance. However, its Old Guard antithesis to the outworn Marxist thesis is not the liberty security synthesis the future cries for." Frank D. Ashburn of the *Saturday Review of Literature* claimed that *God and Man at Yale* "has the glow and appeal of a fiery cross on a hillside at night. There will undoubtedly be robed figures who gather to it, but the hoods will not be academic. They will cover the face."

But other critics found *God and Man at Yale* to be a serious contribution to the political dialogue. Writing in the *American Mercury*, Max Eastman claimed that the book "is brilliant, sincere, well-informed, keenly reasoned, and exciting to read." Selden Rodman of the *Saturday Review of Literature* called it "an important book, perhaps the most thought-provoking that has appeared in the last decade on the subject of higher education in the United States. . . . That the author happens also to be a conservative, with whose specific religious and economic ideas I find myself not in sympathy, is less important than that he challenges forcefully that brand of 'liberal' materialism which, by making all values 'relative,' honors none.'' Because of the wide-spread controversy raised by *God and Man at Yale,* Buckley became well-known among the nation's conservatives.

This position as conservative spokesman was vastly strengthened in 1955 when Buckley founded *National Review,* a magazine of conservative opinion. In a statement of purpose published in the magazine's first issue, Buckley states: ''The profound crisis of our era is, in essence, the conflict between the Social Engineers, who seek to adjust mankind to conform with scientific utopias, and the disciples of Truth, who defend the organic moral order.'' At the time of its founding, Richard Brookhiser remarks in *National Review*'s thirtieth anniversary issue, ''the forces of conservatism in American thinking were insignificant.'' But Buckley used the magazine as a rallying point to consolidate the nation's conservatives. He formed a coalition, George H. Nash explains in his *The Conservative Intellectual Movement in America since 1945,* of ''New Conservatives, libertarians, and anti-communists.'' From this core of supporters the *National Review* reached out to a larger audience. Buckley hoped, Nash writes, ''to establish a journal which would reach intellectuals.'' Buckley has said on other occasions that ''what we are trying for is the maximum leverage that conservatives can exert.''

Although *National Review,* in common with most other magazines of political opinion, has never made a profit (it is subsidized by reader contributions and Buckley's own money), it has become one of the most influential political journals in the country. Nash credits it with a central role in the growth of American conservative thought. ''If *National Review* (or something like it) had not been founded,'' Nash writes, ''there would probably have been no interlocking intellectual force on the Right in the 1960's and 1970's. To a very substantial degree, the history of reflective conservatism in America after 1955 is the history of the individuals who collaborated in—or were discovered by—the magazine William F. Buckley, Jr. founded.'' Gene M. Moore points out in the *Dictionary of Literary Biography Yearbook: 1980* that over the years *National Review* has helped to ''launch the careers of such authors and columnists as Renata Adler, Joan Didion, John Leonard, and Garry Wills.''

With the growth of the conservative movement, *National Review* now enjoys a circulation of over one hundred thousand. And it can boast of some influential readers as well. President Ronald Reagan, for example, has declared that *National Review* is his favorite magazine. Speaking at the magazine's thirtieth anniversary celebration in 1985—a celebration attended by such notables as Charlton Heston, Tom Selleck, Jack Kemp, and Tom Wolfe—Reagan remarked: ''If any of you doubt the impact of *National Review*'s verve and attractiveness, take a look around you this evening. The man standing before you now was a Democrat when he picked up his first issue in a plain brown wrapper; and even now, as an occupant of public housing, he awaits as anxiously as ever his biweekly edition— without the wrapper.''

In addition to his writing and editing for the *National Review,* Buckley also writes a syndicated column, ''On the Right,'' which appears in 350 newspapers three times weekly, as well as articles of opinion for various national magazines. Many of these columns and articles have been published in book-length collections. These shorter pieces display Buckley's talent for political satire. John P. Roche of the *New York Times Book Review,* speaking of Buckley's articles in *Execution Eve and Other Contemporary Ballads,* claims that ''no commentator has a surer eye for the contradictions, the hypocrisies, the pretensions of liberal and radical pontiffs . . . even when you wince, reading Buckley is fun.'' A *Choice* critic, reviewing *A Hymnal: The Controversial Arts,* explains that ''Buckley excels in the use of language, the sparkling epigram, and biting sarcasm that penetrates to the heart of a matter.'' And Steven R. Weisman of the *New York Times Book Review* maintains that ''Bill Buckley certainly deserves his reputation as one of the wittiest political satirists writing today.''

In other books, Buckley turns from politics to his personal life. *Cruising Speed: A Documentary* is a diary-like account of a typical Buckley week. *Overdrive: A Personal Documentary* follows a similar format. Because of the many activities in which he is typically engaged, and the social opportunities afforded by his political connections and inherited wealth, Buckley's life makes fascinating reading. And he unabashedly shares it with his readers, moving some reviewers to criticize him. Nora Ephron of the *New York Times Book Review,* for example, calls *Overdrive* ''an astonishing glimpse of a life of privilege in America today.'' She complains that ''it never seems to cross [Buckley's] mind that any of his remarks might be in poor taste, or his charm finite.'' And yet Carolyn See of the *Los Angeles Times* believes that the Buckley found in *Overdrive* ''is a social butterfly, a gadabout, a mindless snob (or so he would have us believe). . . . Buckley shows us a brittle, acerbic, duty-bound, 'silly,' 'conservative' semi-fudd, with a heart as vast and varicolored and wonderful to watch as a 1930s jukebox.''

More universally appreciated are Buckley's sailing books. An avid yachtsman, he chronicles several of his sailing expeditions in *Airborne: A Sentimental Journey, Atlantic High: A Celebration,* and *Racing through Paradise: A Pacific Passage.* These books are as much celebrations of the sailing life as they are the records of particular voyages. Speaking of *Atlantic High,* the account of Buckley's month-long journey from the Virgin Islands to Spain, Morton Hunt of the *New York Times Book Review* calls it ''more than an account of that trip, this is a book about a special and precious kind of human experience—the camaraderie of people who join together in a physical enterprise that is, at times, brutally demanding and hazardous and, at other times, idyllically tranquil and beautiful. . . . The shared experience of the sea . . . produces an intimacy and openness that life on shore might need years to achieve. And it is this, more than the experience of the sea itself, that Mr. Buckley is writing about.''

When not writing about politics or sailing, Buckley has found time to pen a series of bestselling espionage novels featuring C.I.A. agent Blackford Oakes. The ''arch and politically sophisticated'' series, as Derrick Murdoch describes the books in the Toronto *Globe and Mail,* is set in the Cold War years of the 1950s and 1960s and takes readers behind the scenes of the major political crises of the time. In doing so, the novels provide Buckley with the opportunity to dramatize some of his ideas concerning East-West relations. As Christopher Lehmann-Haupt of the *New York Times* remarks, ''not only can Buckley execute the international thriller as well as nearly anyone working in the genre . . . he threatens to turn this form of fiction into effective propaganda for his ideas.''

Saving the Queen, the first of the Blackford Oakes novels, is based in part on Buckley's own experiences in the C.I.A. ''The training received by Blackford Oakes is, in exact detail, the training I received,'' Buckley explains. ''In that sense, it's autobiographical.'' Oakes, a thinly-disguised version of his creator, also shares Buckley's school years at an English public school and at Yale University. The story concerns a leak of classified information at the highest levels of the British government. Oakes is sent to locate the source of the leak and his investigation uncovers a treasonous cousin in the royal family. Robin W. Winks of the *New Republic* finds *Saving the Queen* to be ''replete with ambiguity, irony, suspense— all those qualities we associate with [Eric] Ambler, [Graham] Greene, [and John] le Carre.'' Amnon Kabatchnik of the *Armchair Detective* calls *Saving the Queen* ''an entertaining yarn, graced with a literate style, keen knowledge and a twinkling sense of humor [which] injected a touch of sophistication and a flavor of sly irony to the genre of political intrigue.''

Buckley's second novel, *Stained Glass,* is set in postwar Germany and revolves around the efforts of both East and West to prevent the reunification of Germany under the popular Count Axel Wintergrin. Both sides fear that a united Germany would be a military threat to the peace of Europe. Oakes penetrates Wintergrin's political organization disguised as an engineer hired to restore a local church. His restoring of broken church windows contrasts ironically with his efforts to keep Germany divided. ''This novel is a work of history,'' Winks maintains, ''for it parallels those options that might well have been open to the West [in the 1950s]. . . . *Stained Glass* is closer to the bone than le Carre has ever cut.'' Jane Larkin Crain of the *Saturday Review* calls it a ''first-rate spy story and . . . a disturbing lesson in the unsavory realities of international politics.'' *Stained Glass* won an American Book Award in 1980.

Later Blackford Oakes novels have concerned the Cuban missile showdown, the launching of Sputnik, and the construction of the Berlin Wall, among other Cold War crises. Buckley recounts these historical events faithfully. Anne Janette Johnson, speaking of *See You Later, Alligator,* which revolves around the Cuban missile crisis, asserts in the *Detroit Free Press* that ''history buffs and spy-thriller enthusiasts alike should enjoy this in-depth portrayal of a unique moment in the history of the Western hemisphere.'' Stefan Kanfer of *Time* acknowledges that ''it is to Buckley's credit that within his fiction, actual events are made as urgent and terrifying as they were.''

But actual history is only a part of the Blackford Oakes novels. Oakes's missions take place behind the scenes of history. As Michael Malone explains in the *New York Times Book Review,* ''Buckley slides his quite fascinatingly imagined, and appallingly conceivable, intrigues into the unknowns surrounding the secret skirmishes between *us* and *them*.'' In several novels Buckley presents the case for an alternative policy from that which was actually followed. ''He raises the sort of questions that only the most naive and the most sophisticated political observers would dare to ask,'' Anatole Broyard remarks in the *New York Times.* ''He says, 'What if—' and then proposes something that is as attractive as it is preposterous, something so nearly commonsensical that it throws the entire Western world into pandemonium.''

In building his novels around actual events Buckley is obliged to include historical figures in his cast of characters, something he does quite well. Speaking of *See You Later, Alligator,* Murdoch believes that ''the telling personal [details] are helping to make the Blackford Oakes series unique in spy fiction.'' In his review of *The Story of Henri Tod,* Broyard claims that ''the best part . . . is [Buckley's] portrait of former President John F. Kennedy. His rendering of Nikita Khrushchev is quite

good too, and this tempts me to suggest that Mr. Buckley seems most at home when he projects himself into the minds of heads of state.'' Similarly, Elaine Kendall of the *Los Angeles Times Book Review* speculates that Buckley may be evolving into ''a psychic historian who can project himself into the most convoluted political minds.''

Perhaps Buckley's most influential popular means of spreading the conservative message is his weekly television program, ''Firing Line,'' which reaches several million viewers over the Public Broadcasting System. It is now the thirteenth-longest-running program on either public or commercial television, having been broadcast since 1966, and was the winner of an Emmy Award in 1969. The hour-long show presents debates between Buckley and selected guests from politics or the arts. His guests have ranged from Jorge Luis Borges to Jimmy Carter. ''Whether the matter at hand is perfection of the soul or perfection of the state,'' Michiko Kakutani maintains in the *New York Times,* ''exchanges on 'Firing Line' have always been animated by a love of language and a delight in logic.''

An articulate and witty television host, Buckley nonetheless upsets some of his guests with his incisive questions. R. Z. Sheppard of *Time* calls him a ''TV Torquemada.'' Describing a typical ''Firing Line'' show, Phil Garner of the *Atlanta Journal & Constitution* observes that ''Buckley's first question, characteristically, sought out the most likely weaknesses in his guests' most cherished positions.'' Frederick C. Klein compares ''the spectacle of William F. Buckley, Jr. spearing a foe'' to ''the sight of a cat stalking a bird. If you sympathize with the bird, you can still find it possible to admire the grace and ferocity of its pursuer.'' Buckley explains to Kakutani that many people are anxious to appear on ''Firing Line,'' but that ''some people aren't so eager—people with positions not so easily defended in the face of rather relentless scrutiny.''

Despite his long involvement in the nation's political life, Buckley has only once sought public office. In 1965 he ran for mayor of New York City in a highly visible, perhaps not-quite-serious campaign. Or maybe, as Buckley explained, it was just that he couldn't work up the ''synthetic optimism'' his followers expected. When asked, for example, what he would do if elected, Buckley replied: ''Demand a recount.'' Although he lost the election, garnering 13.4% of the vote, Buckley managed to draw public attention to several issues he felt to be of importance, including welfare reform, the New York City traffic problem, and the treatment of criminals. Buckley now considers his political career over. ''The only thing that would convince me to run again,'' he states, ''would be a direct order from my Maker, signed in triplicate by each member of the Trinity.''

But in 1973 Buckley found himself in government office, this time as a public member of the U.S. delegation to the 28th General Assembly of the United Nations. He was appointed to the post by President Richard Nixon. Although a critic of the U.N. and skeptical of its effectiveness, Buckley took the job. ''I saw myself there,'' Buckley writes of his reasons for accepting the position, ''in the center of the great assembly at the U.N. . . . holding the delegates spellbound . . . I would cajole, wheedle, parry, thrust, mesmerize, dismay, seduce, intimidate. The press of the world would rivet its attention on the case the American delegate was making for human rights.'' But Buckley's dream was not to be. ''[If] the Gettysburg Address were to be delivered from the floor of the United Nations,'' Buckley later told an interviewer, ''it would go unnoticed. . . . I soon became aware that the role of oratory was purely ceremonial. No one takes any notice of what is actually said. One listens for the overtones.'' Buckley has also served as a presidential appointee to the National Advisory Commission on Information, charged with assessing the work of the United States Information Agency. His only other brush with government work came in 1980 when President Reagan, who had just been elected, asked Buckley what position he would like to have in the new administration. ''Ventriloquist,'' said Buckley.

As columnist, television host, novelist, and magazine editor, Buckley is known as ''one of the most articulate, provocative, and entertaining spokesmen for American conservatism,'' as Moore writes. For his role in the development of the modern conservative movement, Buckley ''is a man who richly deserves praise,'' Kondrake believes. ''He is generous, erudite, witty and courageous, and he has performed a service to the whole nation, even to those who disagree with him.'' Writing in the *Los Angeles Times Book Review,* John Haase calls Buckley ''witty, erudite, multifaceted, perhaps one of the few great exponents of the English language. He is politically contentious, a 'farceur,' I suspect, but we are willing to forgive all, because mostly Buckley is fun.'' Summing up Buckley's role in the nation's political life, Moore finds that his ''flickering tongue and flashing wit have challenged a generation to remember the old truths while searching for the new, to abhor hypocrisy and to value logic, and to join in the worldwide struggle for human rights and human freedom.''

CA INTERVIEW

CA interviewed William F. Buckley, Jr., by telephone on March 28, 1987, at his home in Sharon, Connecticut.

CA: In an interview in Playboy, *you said that the most conspicuous attribute of the twentieth-century American was his egocentricity. Do you still agree with that judgment?*

BUCKLEY: The part of that statement that gives me pause is the word *conspicuous.* A book that very much influenced me at the time I said that was *The Odyssey of the Self-Centered Self* by Robert Fitch. I don't think he would take back anything that he said then, though perhaps our survival of the especially trying challenges of the late '60s and early '70s would earn us a mitigating qualifier. So I would say yes, although it's probably the twentieth-century American's most conspicuous attribute, it's not as assertive as it was twenty years ago.

CA: Your father was a very successful oilman and lawyer. As busy as he must have been, was he able to devote much time to his children?

BUCKLEY: He devoted a tremendous amount of time to us. He was away a great deal—usually four or five days a week—but he totally supervised our education, was in constant correspondence with us by mail and by telephone, and was intimately aware of the problems of each of us. I would say it was about as close a relationship as one could have with a father, given that he was not physically on the scene for so much of the time.

CA: Did you spend some of your formative years in Camden, South Carolina?

BUCKLEY: Yes, I did. I was there every winter beginning in 1936—with the exception of the year I was in England, 1938-1939—up until I went to prep school in 1941. Kamschatka, the family house, was sold about two years ago. It is an antebellum house rebuilt by my father in 1936.

CA: In your reminiscences about your days at Millbrook School you said that the headmaster there gave his first A in 1942. That's very interesting in view of the drop in educational standards and the corresponding inflation in grades throughout the educational system in the last twenty years or so.

BUCKLEY: I think that's definitely true. It happened that I was the top scholar in my class, and I think I had two *A*s, two *B*s, and a *C*, where I can't imagine anybody being the top scholar in his class nowadays without having all *A*s. It used to be easier a generation ago to get into the college of your choice than it is now, but even so, as of when I graduated, Millbrook, with one exception, had never failed to place a graduate in the college of his choice, even though Millbrook was a young school (the first graduating class was 1936). I don't think any school comes near that standard now, in part because more people are crowding those same colleges, and in part also because I suspect the standards aren't quite as high as they were.

CA: You were terribly unhappy with the liberal bias at Yale when you were there. Do you think things have become less liberal since you wrote your first book, God and Man at Yale?

BUCKLEY: No. I think they've gotten worse. This is an impressionistic judgment, based on what I hear from people who are there and who were recently there. Paradoxically, even though conservative-oriented research has advanced enormously in the last thirty-five years in several disciplines, it seems not to have made much of a foothold at Yale or in several other major universities.

CA: Why do you think the conservative philosophy has been relatively unsuccessful in making inroads at these universities?

BUCKLEY: Universities tend to be peopled by those who consider themselves ''critics'' of accepted institutions. It is more natural to be a collectivist in a libertarian culture; agnostic in a Christian culture. There is, moreover, the special appeal of liberalism: it suggests that Ph.D.s are better at shaping social events than the marketplace. It is tempting to the ambitious instincts of the professor to conclude that he could do better than the marketplace to shape a desirable society.

CA: You indicated in Overdrive *that you are often very reluctant to be a commencement speaker because of the possibility of a lot of student reaction to your presence.*

BUCKLEY: Yes, although in fact that's only happened two or three times, and I guess I've given thirty-five or forty commencement addresses. But when I get such invitations, I tend to be reluctant to accept them, that being one reason. The other reason is that nobody pays any attention to commencement addresses. The students are preoccupied with other things.

CA: In the same Playboy *interview I mentioned earlier, you said that you were distressed over how few conservatives had any talent for writing a finished essay. Do you think that's still true?*

BUCKLEY: No. There's been a tremendous flowering of talent among young conservatives since I said that. I can think of eight or ten or twelve people at the age of thirty or under who are as talented as any of their contemporaries on the other side. Richard Brookhiser and Joe Sobran would be excellent examples.

CA: Do you feel, as many conservatives do, that there's a strong liberal bias in the media?

BUCKLEY: Yes. It is demonstrably so, and has been documented by scholarly studies. Something like eighty or eighty-five percent of those involved in the media voted Democratic at a time when the majority of the country went Republican. I should add that I am not particularly surprised, as media news analysts tend to think of themselves as critics, in the same way that college faculty do.

CA: Would you comment on why you ran for the office of Mayor of New York City in 1965?

BUCKLEY: I ran for office because in 1965 the Republican Party was dominated by men and women whose political attitudes were not noticeably different from those of Democrats. Their hero was John Lindsay—who a few years later formally joined the Democratic party, where he always belonged. I thought to give voice, by my candidacy, to genuine dissent.

CA: Why haven't you considered running for public office since?

BUCKLEY: One decides, somewhere along the line, whether to be a critic primarily, or an activist. I decided to continue as a critic. Moreover, if you dispose of the proper cockpits in influence-molding, as I did—through the editorship of a magazine, as a columnist, television host, and lecturer—you are exchanging the greater lever for the lesser lever on public affairs if you give all that up in order to achieve one vote in Congress.

CA: Your television show "Firing Line" has provided some very heated arguments, with the heat usually on your guest. Would you comment on some of the shows you consider most memorable?

BUCKLEY: No. There have been too many: over one thousand shows. No one or two or three or half-dozen stick out in my mind.

CA: You've been friends with President Reagan for a long time, and in Overdrive *you mentioned that you have an arrangement by which your letters are put on the President's personal pile of mail. Do you think you have exerted any important influence on his decision making in the White House?*

BUCKLEY: I have no reason to suppose so beyond the fact that he reads *National Review* very diligently and *National Review* is full of advice now, as it has been in the past. So every two weeks we give the best that we have. I would assume that he may have drawn some inspiration from that.

CA: In general, have you been happy with the Reagan administration?

BUCKLEY: I have in general, yes. I think there's an extremely important decision coming up now on which we may draw sharp differences with the President; that is the European zero-option decision. We stand to come out in favor of the denuclearization of Europe, which I think would be a great mistake.

CA: How would you assess the current administration overall? What do you think will likely go down in the history books about Reagan?

BUCKLEY: He will go down in history concretely as having drawn attention to the antisocial effects of high government overhead. Symbolically, he will go down in history as a figure whose wholesomeness challenged the great waves of skepticism and cynicism that threatened to engulf the whole American enterprise.

CA: Do you have someone in mind that you hope will be the next President of the United States?

BUCKLEY: No. Here I imitate John Kenneth Galbraith. He's in favor of the "leftward most viable candidate," and I'm in favor of the rightward most viable candidate. But I don't know who that is right now. Maybe Jack Kemp; under certain circumstances it could be George Bush or Robert Dole. I haven't made a commitment, nor has the magazine.

CA: Since you began National Review *in 1955, have your aims for the magazine changed in any way, or your ideas about what readership it should be directed to?*

BUCKLEY: No. We are a journal of opinion seeking to attract the attention of bright people oriented toward the traditional ideals of the republic.

CA: You've captivated perhaps another readership entirely— or at least enlarged your previous one—with the series of spy novels featuring your hero Blackford Oakes. What prompted you to add fiction-writing to your already long list of activities?

BUCKLEY: I found it interesting to respond to the challenge to tell a story. Rather, to discover *whether* I could tell a story. I have attempted in these stories (they number eight at this point) to frame some of the dilemmas of fighting in apocalyptic times, against such an enemy as we contend against.

CA: With all the praise and attention your spy novels have gotten, do you wish you had begun writing fiction earlier?

BUCKLEY: Fiction is another means of expression, and if you mean, do I wish I had discovered that particular skill earlier, the answer is yes. I'm not sure I can think of anything that I have in fact written that I wish a novel might have replaced. If it's a question of whether I could do more than one book a year, I would find that very hard to do.

CA: You've said on several occasions that you find it very difficult to write, that there's a certain amount of misery involved in it. Do you find fiction easier to write than nonfiction?

BUCKLEY: Only easier because research is less intensive. There are advantages to improvising our own facts, as politicians teach us. But of all the books that I do, those that take the most time are the anthologies, because they take so much reading and assembling and *this*ing and *that*ing. They have to have a sort of a narrative line that brings them together. I've just finished my eighth novel, and I've used up my writing time in Switzerland, which is about five weeks. That's never less than the time I give the nonfiction collections.

CA: You've recently done the videocassette "Celestial Navigation." Has that been commercially successful?

BUCKLEY: I think it's moderately successful. It happens to have coincided with almost a complete lack of interest in celestial navigation, now that electronic tools are so handy. Thirty years ago, ocean sailors of my age would simply make it a point to learn celestial navigation, if they wanted to do as much sailing as I did; but nowadays they just plain don't. They depend on electronics. But I think the "Celestial Navigation" tape has sold about seven thousand copies.

CA: Are you planning to do more videocassettes?

BUCKLEY: There are always proposals; there's nothing definitely scheduled for videocassettes.

CA: Since you are involved in so many different activities, do you have to set up some kind of schedule allotting time for each one?

BUCKLEY: Yes, but I do it more or less by feel. The only thing I'm absolutely rigid about is the writing time for my books in Switzerland.

CA: You even do a certain amount of work riding in your limousine, don't you?

BUCKLEY: It depends on whether I'm working on a deadline—which I usually am. If I need to write in the car, I do. But it's awkward, and I usually manage to avoid doing so.

CA: Lately the John Birch Society isn't much in the news. Is that organization about defunct?

BUCKLEY: I think it's about defunct. The death of Robert Welch took the steam out of it, and of course it was pretty well discredited after *National Review*'s analysis of Welch back in 1965.

CA: Your son Christopher is becoming a writer of some note. Did you have a good deal to do with nurturing his development in that direction?

BUCKLEY: I suppose indirectly. I never gave concrete advice, but he's interested in my work, though he's less ideological than I am.

CA: How would you assess the strength and viability of the Conservative movement in this country now, and its outlook for the future?

BUCKLEY: The Zeitgeist does not encourage anti-collectivist, traditionalist, Judeo-Christian principles. But it is a plainspoken fact that brainy work and a reaffirmation of enduring values are being done by "conservatives." These efforts are not likely to be vitiated by routine political oscillations.

BIOGRAPHICAL/CRITICAL SOURCES:

BOOKS

Buckley, William F., Jr., *The Unmaking of a Mayor*, Viking, 1966.

Buckley, William F., Jr., *Cruising Speed: A Documentary*, Putnam, 1971.

Buckley, William F., Jr., *United Nations Journal: A Delegate's Odyssey*, Putnam, 1974.

Buckley, William F., Jr., *Overdrive: A Personal Documentary*, Doubleday, 1983.

Cain, Edward R., *They'd Rather Be Right: Youth and the Conservative Movement*, Macmillan, 1963.

Contemporary Issues Criticism, Volume I, Gale, 1982.

Contemporary Literary Criticism, Gale, Volume VII, 1977, Volume XVIII, 1981, Volume XXXVII, 1986.

Dictionary of Literary Biography Yearbook: 1980, Gale, 1981.

Forster, Arnold and B. R. Epstein, *Danger on the Right*, Random House, 1964.

Judis, John, *William F. Buckley, Jr.: Patron Saint of the Conservatives*, Simon & Schuster, 1988.

Markmann, Charles L., *The Buckleys: A Family Examined*, Morrow, 1973.

Nash, George H., *The Conservative Intellectual Movement in America since 1945*, Basic Books, 1976.

Phelps, Donald, *Covering Ground: Essays for Now*, Croton Press, 1969.

Tuccille, J., *It Usually Begins with Ayn Rand: A Libertarian Odyssey*, Stein & Day, 1972.

PERIODICALS

American Mercury, December, 1951.

Armchair Detective, June, 1976.

Atlanta Journal & Constitution, March 3, 1974.

Atlantic, November, 1951, May, 1954, July, 1968.

Catholic World, November, 1959.

Chicago Tribune, November 8, 1959.

Choice, April, 1979.

Christian Century, July 3, 1968.

Christian Science Monitor, August 29, 1968, August 16, 1978, December 20, 1980, February 24, 1984.

Commentary, April, 1974, November, 1983.

Commonweal, February 15, 1952, May 3, 1963, December 23, 1966, March 1, 1974.

Detroit Free Press, February 24, 1985.

Detroit News, September 19, 1982, August 21, 1983.

Esquire, January, 1961, November, 1966, January, 1968, August, 1969, September, 1969, February, 1972, July, 1976.

Globe and Mail (Toronto), February 18, 1984, April 13, 1985.

Harper's, March, 1967, November, 1971, October, 1983.

Life, September 17, 1965.

Listener, July 3, 1975, March 11, 1976.

Los Angeles Times, August 11, 1983.

Los Angeles Times Book Review, February 7, 1982, September 12, 1982, January 22, 1984, April 7, 1985, March 23, 1986.

Mademoiselle, June, 1961.

Modern Age, summer, 1967, summer, 1974.

Nation, October 2, 1972, April 26, 1980.

National Observer, November 29, 1975.

National Review, May 7, 1963, November 15, 1966, July 30, 1968, September 13, 1974, October 24, 1975, December 5, 1975, February 20, 1976, May 13, 1977, June 9, 1978, November 24, 1978, April 4, 1980, January 22, 1982, October 15, 1982, September 2, 1983, February 24, 1984, December 31, 1985.

Negro Digest, April, 1969.

New Leader, January 19, 1976.

New Republic, October 19, 1959, June 10, 1978.

New Statesman, March 12, 1976.

Newsweek, October 17, 1966, March 25, 1968, August 2, 1971, September 30, 1974, January 5, 1976, February 19, 1979.
New Yorker, August 8, 1970, August 21, 1971, August 28, 1971.
New York Review of Books, July 18, 1974, October 13, 1983.
New York Times, November 4, 1951, April 4, 1954, October 6, 1971, April 5, 1978, February 6, 1980, February 25, 1981, December 28, 1981, August 18, 1983, December 21, 1983, February 4, 1985, March 27, 1986.
New York Times Book Review, March 25, 1962, April 28, 1963, October 30, 1966, September 15, 1968, August 2, 1970, September 26, 1971, October 8, 1972, January 13, 1974, September 28, 1975, December 26, 1976, January 11, 1978, May 14, 1978, November 19, 1978, February 17, 1980, March 30, 1980, January 24, 1982, March 7, 1982, September 5, 1982, August 7, 1983, February 5, 1984, March 3, 1985, January 5, 1986, February 9, 1986, April 6, 1986, May 31, 1987.
New York Times Magazine, September 5, 1965.
Observer, June 8, 1975.
Playboy, May, 1970.
Progressive, January, 1969.
Publishers Weekly, August 26, 1974.
Punch, July 12, 1978.
Reader's Digest, September, 1971.
Saturday Evening Post, April, 1977.
Saturday Review, April 3, 1954, October 10, 1959, April 27, 1963, August 8, 1970, May 13, 1978, January, 1982.
Saturday Review of Literature, December 15, 1951.
Spectator, June 21, 1975.
Time, October 31, 1960, November 4, 1966, November 3, 1967, August 2, 1971, November 18, 1974, January 5, 1976, December 6, 1976, June 19, 1978, February 19, 1979, February 25, 1980, January 18, 1982, October 25, 1982, December 9, 1985, February 4, 1986, March 31, 1986, June 15, 1987.
Times Literary Supplement, March 12, 1976, July 27, 1984.
Village Voice, February 21, 1974, December 8, 1975.
Wall Street Journal, November 15, 1966, January 31, 1967.
Washington Post, February 12, 1980.
Washington Post Book World, June 30, 1968, January 23, 1972, February 12, 1980, January 10, 1982, September 4, 1983, March 24, 1985, March 9, 1986, May 24, 1987.
Worldview, June, 1972.
Yale Review, December, 1959.

—*Sketch by Thomas Wiloch*

—*Interview by Walter W. Ross*

*   *   *

BUERO VALLEJO, Antonio 1916-

PERSONAL: Surname listed in some sources as Buero-Vallejo; born September 29, 1916, in Guadalajara, Spain; son of Francisco Buero (a military engineer) and Cruz Vallejo; married Victoria Rodriguez (an actress), 1959; children: Carlos, Enrique. *Education:* San Fernando School of Fine Arts, Madrid, Spain, 1934-36.

ADDRESSES: Home and office—Calle General Diaz Porlier 36, Madrid 28001, Spain.

CAREER: Playwright, 1949—. Lecturer at universities in the United States, 1966; speaker at Symposium on Spanish Theater, University of North Carolina at Chapel Hill, 1970.

MEMBER: International Committee of the Theatre of the Nations, Hispanic Society of America (corresponding member), American Association of Teachers of Spanish and Portuguese (honorary fellow), Society of Spanish and Spanish-American Studies (honorary fellow), Modern Language Association (honorary fellow), Deutscher Hispanistenverband (honorary fellow), Sociedad General de Autores de Espana, Real Academia Espanola, Ateneo de Madrid (honorary fellow), Circulo de Bellas Artes de Madrid (honorary fellow).

AWARDS, HONORS: Premio Lope de Vega, 1949, for "Historia de una escalera"; Premio Amigos de los Quintero, 1949, for "Las palabras en la arena"; Premio Maria Rolland, 1956, for "Hoy es fiesta," 1958, for "Un sonador para un pueblo," and, 1960, for "Las Meninas"; Premio Nacional de Teatro, 1957, for "Hoy es fiesta," 1958, for "Las cartas boca abajo," 1959, for "Un sonador para un pueblo," and 1980; Premio March de Teatro, 1959, for "Hoy es fiesta"; Premio de la critica de Barcelona, 1960, for "Un sonador para un pueblo"; Premio Larra, 1962, for "El concierto de San Ovidio"; Premio Leopoldo Cano, 1966, 1970, 1972, 1974, and 1976; Medalla de Oro del *Espectador y la critica,* 1967, 1970, 1974, 1976, 1977, 1981, 1984, and 1986; Premio Mayte and Premio Foro Teatral, both 1974; Medalla de Oro "Gaceta illustrada," 1976; Officier des Palmes Academiques de France, 1980; Premio Ercilla and Medalla "Valle-Inclan" de la Asociacion de Escritores y Artistas, both 1985; Premio Pablo Iglesias and Premio Miguel de Cervantes, both 1986; Medalla de Oro e Hijo Predilecto de Guadalajara, 1987.

WRITINGS:

IN ENGLISH TRANSLATION

En la ardiente oscuridad: Drama en tres actos (title means "In the Burning Darkness: Three-Act Drama"; first produced in Madrid at Teatro Nacional Maria Guerrero, December 1, 1950; also see below), Alfil (Madrid), 1951, reprinted, Escelicer (Madrid), 1970, critical Spanish edition edited by Samuel A. Wofsy, Scribner, 1954, translation by Marion Peter Holt of original Spanish version published as "In the Burning Darkness" in *Three Plays* (also see below), Trinity University Press (San Antonio, Tex.), 1985.
La tejedora de suenos: Drama en tres actos (title means "The Dream Weaver: Three-Act Drama"; first produced in Madrid at Teatro Espanol, January 11, 1952; also see below), Alfil, 1952, translation by William I. Oliver published as "The Dreamweaver" in *Masterpieces of the Modern Spanish Theatre,* edited by Robert W. Corrigan, Collier Books, 1967.
Las Meninas: Fantasia velazquena en dos partes (title means "The Ladies-in-Waiting: Velazquen Fantasy in Two Parts"; first produced in Madrid at Teatro Espanol, December 9, 1960; first published in *Primer Acto,* January, 1961; also see below), Alfil, 1961, critical Spanish edition edited by Juan Rodriguez Castellano, Scribner, 1963, translation by Holt published as *Las Meninas: A Fantasy,* Trinity University Press, 1987.
El concierto de San Ovidio: Parabola en tres actos (title means "The Concert at Saint Ovide: Three-Act Parable"; first produced in Madrid at Teatro Goya, November 16, 1962; first published in *Primer Acto,* December, 1962; also see below), Alfil, 1963, critical Spanish edition edited by Pedro N. Trakas, Scribner, 1965, translation by Farris Anderson of original Spanish version published as *The Concert at Saint Ovide,* Pennsylvania State University

Press, 1967, Anderson's translation also published in *The Modern Spanish Stage: Four Plays,* edited by Holt, Hill & Wang, 1970.

El tragaluz: Experimento en dos partes (title means "The Skylight: Two-Part Experiment"; first produced in Madrid at Teatro Bellas Artes, October 7, 1967; first published in *Primer Acto,* November, 1967; also see below), Alfil, 1968, critical Spanish edition edited by Anthony M. Pasquariello and Patricia W. O'Connor, Scribner, 1977, translation by O'Connor of original Spanish version published as "The Basement Window" in *Plays of Protest from the Franco Era,* Sociedad General Espanola de la Libreria (Madrid), 1981.

La doble historia del doctor Valmy: Relato escenico en dos partes (title means "The Double Case-History of Doctor Valmy: Story with Scenes, in Two Parts"; first produced in English translation in Chester, England, at Gateway Theatre, November 22, 1968; first produced in Spanish in Madrid at Teatro Benavente, January 29, 1976; first published in *Artes hispanicas/Hispanic Arts* [bilingual; English translation by Anderson], 1967), edited and annotated by Alfonso M. Gil, Center for Curriculum Development (Philadelphia), 1970, critical Spanish edition edited by William Giuliano, Scribner, 1986.

El sueno de la razon: Fantasia en dos actos (title means "The Sleep of Reason: Two-Act Fantasy"; first produced in Madrid at Teatro de la Reina Victoria, February 6, 1970), Escelicer, 1970, critical Spanish edition edited by John C. Dowling, Center for Curriculum Development, 1971, translation by Holt published as "The Sleep of Reason" in *Three Plays* (also see below), Trinity University Press, 1985.

"La fundacion" (two parts; also see below), first produced in Madrid at Teatro Figaro, January 15, 1974, English translation by Holt published as "The Foundation" in *Three Plays* (also see below), Trinity University Press, 1985.

Three Plays (contains "The Sleep of Reason," "The Foundation," and "In the Burning Darkness"), translation by Holt, Trinity University Press, 1985.

IN SPANISH; PLAYS

"Las palabras en la arena: Tragedia en un acto" (title means "Words in the Sand: Tragedy in One Act"; also see below), first produced in Madrid at Teatro Espanol, December 19, 1949.

Historia de una escalera: Drama en tres actos (title means "Story of a Stairway: Three-Act Drama"; first produced in Madrid, at Teatro Espanol, October 14, 1949; also see below), Jose Janes (Barcelona), 1950, critical Spanish edition edited by Jose Sanchez, Scribner, 1955, critical Spanish edition edited by H. Lester and J. A. Zabalbeascoa Bilbao, University of London Press, 1963.

La senal que se espera: Comedia dramatica en tres actos (title means "The Expected Sign: Three-Act Dramatic Comedy"; first produced in Madrid at Teatro de la Infanta Isabel, May 21, 1952), Alfil, 1952.

Casi uncuento de hadas: Una glosa de Perrault, en tres actos (title means "Almost a Fairy Tale: Three-Act Variation on Perrault"; first produced in Madrid at Teatro Alcazar, January 10, 1953), Alfil, 1953, reprinted, Narcea, 1981.

El terror inmovil: Fragmentos de una tragedia irrepresentable (title means "Motionless Terror: Fragments of An Unrepresentable Tragedy"), Alfil, 1954.

Madrugada: Episodio dramatico en dos actos (title means "Daybreak: Two-Act Dramatic Episode"; first produced

in Madrid at Teatro Alcazar, December 9, 1953; also see below), Alfil, 1954, critical Spanish edition edited by Donald W. Bleznick and Martha T. Halsey, Blaisdell (Waltham, Mass.), 1969.

Irene o el tesoro: Fabula en tres actos (title means "Irene; or, The Treasure: Three-Act Fable"; first produced in Madrid at Teatro Nacional Maria Guerrero, December 14, 1954; also see below), Alfil, 1955.

Aventura en lo gris: Drama en dos actos unidos por un sueno increible (title means "Adventure in Grayness: Drama with Two Acts United by An Incredible Dream"; first published as "Aventura en lo gris: Dos actos grises, unidos por un sueno increible [subtitle means "Two Gray Acts, United by an Incredible Dream"] in *Teatro: Revista internacional de la escena* [Madrid], January-March, 1954), Ediciones Puerta del Sol, 1955, revised version published as *Aventura en lo gris: Dos actos y un sueno* (subtitle means "Two Acts and A Dream"; first produced in Madrid at Teatro Recoletas, October 1, 1963), Alfil, 1964.

Hoy es fiesta: [Tragi]comedia en tres actos (title means "Today Is a Holiday: Three-Act [Tragi]comedy"; first produced in Madrid at Teatro Nacional Maria Guerrero, September 20, 1956; also see below), Alfil, 1957, reprinted, Alman, 1978, critical Spanish edition edited by J. E. Lyon, Harrap, 1964, Heath, 1966.

Las cartas boca abajo: Tragedia espanola en dos partes, y cuatro cuadros (title means "The Cards Face Down: Spanish Tragedy in Two Parts and Four Scenes"; first produced in Madrid at Teatro de la Reina Victoria, November 5, 1957; also see below), Alfil, 1958, critical Spanish edition edited by Felix G. Ilarraz, Prentice-Hall, 1967.

Un sonador para un pueblo: Version libre de un episodio historico, en dos partes (title means "A Dreamer for the People: A Version of a Historical Episode, in Two Parts"; first produced in Madrid at Teatro Espanol, December 18, 1958; also see below), Alfil, 1959, critical Spanish edition edited by Manuela Manzanares de Cirre, Norton, 1966.

Llegada de los dioses (title means "The Gods' Arrival"; first produced in Madrid at Teatro Lara, September 17, 1971; also see below), Aguilar, 1973.

"La detonacion" (two parts; title means "The Detonation"; also see below), first produced in Madrid at Teatro Bellas Artes, September 20, 1977.

"Jueces en la noche" (two parts; title means "Judges in the Night"; also see below), first produced in Madrid at Teatro Lara, October 2, 1979.

"Caiman" (two parts; title means "Alligator"; also see below), first produced in Madrid at Teatro de la Reina Victoria, September 10, 1981.

Dialogo secreto (two parts; title means "Secret Dialogue"; first produced in San Sebastian, Spain, at Teatro Victoria Eugenia, August 6, 1984), Espasa-Calpe, 1985.

Lazaro en el laberinto (two parts; title means "Lazarus in the Labyrinth," first produced at Teatro Maravillas, December 18, 1986), Espasa-Calpe, 1987.

Also author of unpublished plays "Historia despiada" and "Otro juicio de Salomon," both before 1949, and "Una extrana armonia," 1957.

OMNIBUS VOLUMES

Historia de una escalera [and] *Las palabras en la arena,* Alfil, 1952, reprinted, Escelicer, 1974.

Teatro, Losada (Buenos Aires), Volume I: *En la ardiente oscuridad, Madrugada, Hoy es fiesta, Las cartas boca abajo,*

1959, Volume II: *Historia de una escalera, La tejedora de suenos, Irene o el tesoro, Un sonador para un pueblo,* 1962.
Teatro selecto: Historia de una escalera, Las cartas boca abajo, Un sonador para un pueblo, Las Meninas, El concierto de San Ovidio, edited by Luce Moreau-Arrabal, Escelicer, 1966.
Buero Vallejo: Antologia teatral (contains fragments of "Historia de una escalera," "En la ardiente oscuridad," and "Irene o el tesoro"), Coculsa (Madrid), 1966.
Dos dramas de Buero Vallejo: Aventura en lo gris [and] *Las palabras en la arena,* edited by Isabel Magana Schevill, Appleton-Century-Crofts, 1967.
En la ardiente oscuridad [and] *Irene o el tesoro,* Magisterio Espanol (Madrid), 1967.
Teatro: Hoy es fiesta, Las Meninas, [and] *El tragaluz* (includes interviews and critical essays by others), Taurus (Madrid), 1968.
El tragaluz [and] *El sueno de la razon,* Espasa-Calpe, 1970.
El concierto de San Ovidio [and] *El tragaluz,* edited by Ricardo Domenech, Castalia, 1971.
En la ardiente oscuridad [and] *Un sonador para un pueblo,* Espasa-Calpe, 1972.
Historia de una escalera [and] *Llegada de los dioses,* Salvat, 1973.
Historia de una escalera [and] *Las Meninas,* prologue by Domenech, Espasa-Calpe, 1975.
La doble historia del Doctor Valmy [and] *Mito,* prologue by Francisco Garcia Pavon, Espasa-Calpe, 1976.
La tejedora de suenos [and] *Llegada de los dioses,* edited by Luis Iglesias Feijoo, Catedra, 1976.
La detonacion [and] *Las palabras en la arena,* Espasa-Calpe, 1979.
Jueces en la noche [and] *Hoy es fiesta,* prologue by Feijoo, Espasa-Calpe, 1981.
Caiman [and] *Las cartas boca abajo,* Espasa-Calpe, 1981.

CONTRIBUTOR

Charles Davillier, *Viaje por Espana,* Castilla (Madrid), 1949.
Don Juan y el teatro en Espana: Fotografias de Juan Gyenes, Mundo Hispanico (Madrid), 1955.
Informaciones: Extraordinario teatral del sabado de gloria, [Madrid], 1956.
Guillermo Diaz-Plaja, editor, *El teatro: Enciclopedia del arte escenico,* Noguer (Barcelona), 1958.
Homenaje a Vicente Aleixandre, El Bardo (Barcelona), 1964.

CONTRIBUTOR TO "TEATRO ESPANOL" SERIES; EDITED BY F. C. SAINZ DE ROBLES

Teatro espanol, 1949-1950 (includes "Historia de una escalera"), Aguilar, 1951.
. . ., *1950-1951* (includes "En la ardiente oscuridad"), Aguilar, 1952.
. . ., *1951-1952* (includes "La tejedora de suenos"), Aguilar, 1953.
. . ., *1953-1954* (includes "Madrugada"), Aguilar, 1955.
. . ., *1954-1955* (includes "Irene o el tesoro"), Aguilar, 1956.
. . ., *1957-1958* (includes "Las cartas boca abajo"), Aguilar, 1959.
. . ., *1958-1959* (includes "Un sonador para un pueblo"), Aguilar, 1960.
. . ., *1960-1961* (includes "Las Meninas"), Aguilar, 1962.
. . ., *1962-1963* (includes "El concierto de San Ovidio"), Aguilar, 1964.
. . ., *1967-1968* (includes "El tragaluz"), Aguilar, 1969.

. . ., *1969-1970* (includes "El sueno de la razon"), Aguilar, 1971.
. . ., *1971-1972* (includes "Llegada de los dioses"), Aguilar, 1973.
. . ., *1973-1974* (includes "La fundacion"), Aguilar, 1975.

CONTRIBUTOR TO ANTHOLOGIES

Fernando Diaz-Plaja, editor, *Teatro espanol de hoy: Antologia (1939-1958),* Alfil, 1958, 2nd edition published as *Teatro espanol de hoy: Antologia (1939-1966),* Alfil, 1967.
Antonio Espina, editor, *Las mejores escenas del teatro espanol e hispano-americano,* Aguilar, 1959.
Festival de la literatura espanola contemporanea, Volume IV: *Teatro,* Ediciones Tawantinsuyu (Lima, Peru), 1960.
Teatro: Buero Vallejo, Delgado Benavente y Alfonso Sastre, Ediciones Tawantinsuyu, 1960.
Richard E. Chandler and Kessel Schwartz, editors, *A New Anthology of Spanish Literature,* Louisiana State University Press, 1967.
Robert W. Corrigan, editor, *Masterpieces of the Modern Spanish Theatre,* Collier, 1967.
Diego Marin, editor, *Literatura espanola,* Holt, 1968.
Walter T. Pattison and Donald W. Bleznick, editors, *Representative Spanish Authors,* 3rd edition, Volume II, Oxford University Press, 1971.
Spanische Stucke, Henschelverlag (Berlin), 1976.
Anos dificiles, Bruguera, 1977.

TRANSLATOR OF PLAYS

William Shakespeare, *Hamlet: Principe de Dinamarca* (first produced in Madrid at Teatro Espanol, December 15, 1961), Alfil, 1962.
Bertolt Brecht, *Madre Coraje y sus hijos: Una cronica de la Guerra de los Treinta Anos* (first produced in Madrid at Teatro Bellas Artes, October 6, 1966), Alfil, 1967.

Also translator of "Vildanden" by Henrik Ibsen, first produced as "El pato silvestre" in Madrid at Teatro Nacional Maria Guerrero.

OTHER

(Author of prologue) Juan B. Devoto and Alberto Sabato, *Un responso para Lazaro,* Almafuerte (Buenos Aires), 1956.
Mito: Libro para una opera (title means "Myth: Book for an Opera"; first published in *Primer Acto,* November-December, 1968), Alfil, 1968.
Tres maestros ante el publico (biographical essays; title means "Three Masters before the Public"), Alianza, 1973.

Also author of screenplays and of sound recording *Me llamo Antonio Buero Vallejo* (title means "My Name is Buero Vallejo"), Discos Aguilar (Madrid), 1964. Contributor to periodicals, including *Correo Literario, Primer Acto, Revista de Occidente, Pipirijaina, Cuadernos de Agora,* and *Estreno.*

SIDELIGHTS: "The 1949-1950 theatrical season represents a turning point in Spanish drama," writes Martha T. Halsey in *Antonio Buero Vallejo,* "because of the new direction represented by" Buero Vallejo's play "Historia de una escalera" ("Story of a Stairway"). Although this was the Spanish playwright's first produced play, its impact, according to Marion Peter Holt in *The Contemporary Spanish Theater (1949-1972),* was comparable to that of Arthur Miller's "Death of a Salesman," which triumphed on the American stage during the same season. Not only were both plays popular and critical successes during their first theater runs, but they were also tragic portrayals of everyday existence in their respective societies.

The effect of Buero Vallejo's play on Spanish drama is described in an Arturo del Hoyo essay which Holt translates (it first appeared in the Spanish literary review *Insula* shortly after "Historia de una escalera" opened). "From the first moments of the performance," del Hoyo notes, "the spectator was aware that *Story of a Stairway,* with its sense of dramatic values, was what had been needed in our theater to help free itself from paralysis, from mediocrity. For since 1939 the Spanish theater had been living among the ruins of the past."

Spanish theater had been living "among the ruins" caused by the bloody Spanish civil war, which devastated the country from 1936 to 1939. Joelyn Ruple's *Antonio Buero Vallejo: The First Fifteen Years* gives a picture of the bleak state of postwar Spanish theater: "During the years immediately following the war the government used the theater and movies for propaganda. There were translations of works from other countries, presentations of the Spanish classics, and some works by contemporary writers, but works censored and in general of limited value."

Strict censorship caused many writers to produce light, inoffensive works rather than risk government reprisals. "The early postwar years," Halsey explains, "had been characterized by a new type of escape theater, termed 'theater of evasion,' which renounced any purposeful interpretation of reality in favor of adventures of a strictly imaginative nature."

However, when Buero Vallejo (who had been studying painting) decided to become a playwright after the war, government censorship and the general evasiveness of Spanish plays of the period were not his most important concerns. He was an ex-prisoner, having been sentenced to death—later commuted to six years imprisonment—for his activities with the Republican (Loyalist) army during the war. But, whereas many writers chose to flee Fascist rule, Buero Vallejo decided instead to remain in Spain and produce plays. While he chose not to overtly attack Spanish authorities in his works, his plays nevertheless subtly protest Spain's repressive society.

Because of Buero Vallejo's technique of veiled criticism, Francis Donahue lists the playwright in *Books Abroad* as the leader of the Spanish "Theater of Commitment." "Spain's Theater of Commitment," Donahue remarks, "is a non-political, political theater, for it makes its impact by indirect means. . . . The antagonist in the Theater of Commitment is the Establishment. To point out specifically the nature of that antagonist . . . would mean the play would remain unstaged. . . . The cause of the evil conditions remains unspecified, but implied: The Spanish Establishment."

Buero Vallejo's first play, "En la ardiente oscuridad" ("In the Burning Darkness"), is a good example of his theater in general and shows how a playwright of the Theater of Commitment voices criticism in his or her work. According to Halsey the play "contains much of the thematics and symbolism . . . more fully developed in [Buero Vallejo's] later works." Holt concurs, noting, "A consideration of *In the Burning Darkness* . . . is fundamental to an understanding of the playwright's ideas and dramatic techniques."

Although Buero Vallejo may seem to avoid the issue of government oppression in, for example, "In the Burning Darkness" because he writes about a school for the blind, his meaning is subtly revealed. The play tells the story of Ignacio's arrival at the school and how his anger at being blind disrupts

the formerly tranquil life of the students. Ruple explains the social protest inherent in the play: "In ['In the Burning Darkness'] we find a philosophical or religious struggle within the protagonist as he pleads to society to look about and see the conditions under which it actually exists, to stop pretending that all is right with the world. . . . He . . . protests a lethargic society which refuses to recognize and reject a dictator." In *The Tragic Stages of Antonio Buero Vallejo,* Robert L. Nicholas agrees that this play, and many of Buero Vallejo's other works, can be viewed in terms of two levels: the surface story and its underlying philosophical truth. "As the play develops," he notes, "it becomes clear that physical blindness is symbolic of spiritual blindness and that a longing for truth, and not physical sight, is the real source of Ignacio's torment."

Many of Buero Vallejo's plays deal with a quest for the truth and the fate of those who look for it in a society blind to its own tragic reality. The seekers of truth in his plays are often "visionaries," according to Holt in his introduction to *Three Plays,* who look "beyond the present reality to a more enlightened future." Ignacio, the blind "trouble-maker" of "In the Burning Darkness," is such a visionary. In three later plays, Buero Vallejo chooses as protagonists figures from Spanish history—the painters Diego de Silva Velazquez and Francisco Jose de Goya, and the writer Mariano Jose de Larra. The three plays in which these historical characters appear—"Las Meninas" ("The Ladies-in-Waiting"), "El sueno de la razon" ("The Sleep of Reason"), and "La detonacion" ("The Detonation"), respectively—deal with, as Halsey comments in *Hispanic Journal,* "the role of the intellectual in a repressive society."

"Las Meninas" takes its name from Velazquez's masterpiece, a 10' x 9' painting of five-year-old Princess Margarita and other members of Philip IV's royal household. The painting has fascinated art critics for centuries because the wonderful portrait of the princess also includes the shadowy images of Spain's king and queen in a background mirror. Buero Vallejo's play explores the political and social implications of the painting, and "the painter . . . ," observes Nicholas, "is portrayed as the lonely intellectual who attacks all that is false and unjust in seventeenth-century Spanish society." According to Nicholas, "Las Meninas" "is a . . . plea for justice. More than that, it is a call to responsibility for the intelligentsia. Buero [Vallejo] has pictorially revived a moment in history in order to address and indict his contemporaries. . . . *Las Meninas* is a direct yet subtly conceived attack against censorship."

Nicholas, Halsey, and Ruple comment on the importance of a scene in the play in which Pedro, a half-blind beggar, reacts to Velasquez's preliminary sketch for *Las Meninas.* Ruple translates Pedro's words: "Yes, I think I understand. A serene picture, but containing all the sadness of Spain. Anyone who sees these creatures will understand how irredeemably condemned they are to suffer. They're living ghosts whose truth is death. Whoever sees them in the future will notice it with terror." By implication, Buero Vallejo suggests that under Franco repression Spaniards of the twentieth century are also "irredeemably condemned . . . to suffer."

"El sueno de la razon" takes its name from a late eighteenth-century etching by Goya entitled *El sueno de la razon produce monstruos* ("The Sleep of Reason Produces Monsters"). The etching carries the caption: "Imagination abandoned by reason produces impossible monsters: united with her, she is the mother of the arts and the source of their wonders.'' The etching is a self-portrait of the artist asleep at his desk while evil-looking winged creatures hover about his head and a large cat-like animal watches him with glowing eyes. The terror depicted in the etching is masterfully portrayed in Buero Vallejo's play, according to critics. Through a variety of techniques he captures the misery of the great artist left totally deaf by illness and under constant threat of harrassment or death from the authorities. The playwright uses projections of the ''Black Paintings''—strange dark scenes with which Goya covered the interior walls of his country house—to express his emotional turmoil.

Holt refers to a characteristic Buero Vallejo dramatic device introduced in ''In the Burning Darkness'' and later refined in ''The Sleep of Reason.'' This technique, which the playwright calls ''interiorizacion'' (''interiorization''), appears in the earlier play in a scene that makes Ignacio's blindness startlingly real to the audience. While Ignacio speaks of his horror at being blind, the stage lights begin to dim until the entire theater is completely dark. The darkness lasts through four or five lines of dialogue before the lights are turned on again.

In ''The Sleep of Reason'' Buero Vallejo forces the audience to experience Goya's deafness: in the latter's presence the actors mouth their lines of dialogue but make no sound. To simulate the artist's inner anguish, amplified heartbeats and the noise of flapping wings fill the theater, but only Goya reacts to them—they are not heard by the other characters. To heighten the drama, the projections of Goya's ''Black Paintings'' flash across the stage in an ever increasing tempo.

Holt comments: ''The momentary dimming of the stage and houselights to a point of absolute darkness in one crucial scene of *In the Burning Darkness* is a far cry from the frequent scenes of silently mouthed dialogue or the visual and aural bombardment of the audience with projections and amplified sounds in *The Sleep of Reason*. . . . The audience is drawn into the mind of a character or into a crucial dramatic situation with intensified personal identification, as the proscenium barrier is bridged and momentarily ceases to exist.''

Halsey refers to the techniques of interiorization as ''psychic participation.'' She concludes that through interiorization in both ''In the Burning Darkness'' and in ''The Sleep of Reason,'' Buero Vallejo produces ''a more authentic participation in the reality of the tragedy.'' According to Halsey the reality in both of these plays ''is symbolic, for the blindness portrayed represents . . . man's lack of spiritual vision and the deafness, his alienation or estrangement from his fellow human beings.''

The protagonist of Buero Vallejo's ''La detonacion'' (''The Detonation''), Mariano Jose de Larra, is a visionary similar to the playwright's Ignacio, Velazquez, and Goya. Larra lived during the early 1800s, another period of political struggle in Spain characterized by strict censorship. Just as during Buero Vallejo's time, writers of Larra's era tried to avoid direct confrontation with the authorities by writing comedies. Larra refused to do so, writing instead satirical essays in which he attacked almost every facet of society. In *Hispanic Journal* Halsey calls Larra an ''author surrogate.'' She notes: ''Larra stated that to write in Madrid was to weep. Buero [Vallejo] no doubt experienced the same sentiment during the Franco era and initial transition period'' after the dictator's death.

In spite of tremendous obstacles, Buero Vallejo achieved success as a playwright from the very beginning of his career. ''The Sleep of Reason'' is probably his most notable play;

after being acclaimed in Madrid it was subsequently produced in a number of European countries. In 1974, it became the first Buero Vallejo play to be produced professionally in the United States. In *The Contemporary Spanish Theater* Holt calls ''The Sleep of Reason'' ''one of the most impressive achievements of [Buero Vallejo's] career'' and later adds: ''With this play Buero [Vallejo] . . . sustained his right to be included among the major international writers of his day.''

In a *Hispania* essay Patricia W. O'Connor comments that because of Buero Vallejo's position as a highly respected playwright, Spanish censors have given him ''relatively few problems'' during his long career. But, almost all of his plays underwent at least a few *tachaduras,* or cuts, before they were allowed to be produced. ''Aventura en lo gris'' (''Adventure in Gray''), for example, although written in 1953, was not performed in Spain until 1963 and then only after extensive revision. The playwright's 1964 work ''La doble historia del doctor Valmy'' (''The Double Case-History of Doctor Valmy''), which deals with the torture of political prisoners, was not performed in Spain until 1976, after the death of Franco.

Even with the lifting of censorship in the post-Franco era, Buero Vallejo continues to deal with social issues in his plays. He writes about the tragic nature of man in order to hope for a better society. Nicholas observes: ''Buero [Vallejo] is no genius—he is not a Goya; he is just an honest, courageous playwright who tries to expose social injustice, and a good, humble man who seeks to understand human suffering. Each is an endless task.''

Buero Vallejo told *CA:* ''After three years of war and six long years in prison, I had fallen so far behind in my painting studies that I gave them up, and I set out to write for the theatre since, naturally, I had also loved the theatre since I was a child. Under Franco's strict censorship this undertaking proved even more difficult, but a set of favorable circumstances permitted me to continue onward. For me and for others, this censorship was a challenge, not just an obstacle, and I wasn't the only one to accept it. Poets, novelists, essayists, and other dramatists tried to convince the Spanish people (and themselves) that, although frequently very painful, a critical and reformative literature was possible in spite of all the environmental and administrative obstacles.

''In regards to the theatre, the official, unwritten watchwords were patriotism, escapism, moralism, and as much laughter as possible. Therefore, one had to do the opposite: tragedy which revealed instead of concealed the fact that one's destiny is a result of human and social factors instead of fate; a denunciation of injustices and frauds, a defense of liberty. And one had, at the same time, to produce serious experiences. Others will say to what extent each of us has attained these goals; perhaps they'll explain it tomorrow when the biases against this literature, which remain very strong, have been dismantled sociologically. I believe undeniably that, between all of us, something, and perhaps even a lot, has been gained. And because of this, our nation also had more support for resistance, hope and clear thinking.

''The Greek tragedians, Shakespeare, Cervantes, Calderon, Unamuno, Ibsen, Pirandello, Brecht have been, among others, my teachers, and their imprint can be observed in my theatre. Although less frequently noted, but perhaps even more important in some of my works, is the presence of Wells and Kafka. As a poet-friend of mind says about himself, I am also a 'child of well-known parents.' My originality, if I have any, is not based on denying them.''

MEDIA ADAPTATIONS: "Madrugada" was made into a film.

AVOCATIONAL INTERESTS: Painting.

BIOGRAPHICAL/CRITICAL SOURCES:

BOOKS

Bejel, Emilio F., *Lo moral, lo social y lo metafisico en el teatro de Buero Vallejo,* Florida State University, 1970.

Buero Vallejo, Antonio, *Teatro: Hoy es fiesta, Las Meninas* [and] *El tragaluz,* Taurus, 1968.

Buero Vallejo, Antonio, *Three Plays,* edited and translated by Marion Peter Holt, Trinity University Press, 1985.

Contemporary Literary Criticism, Gale, Volume XV, 1980, Volume XLVI, 1988.

Corrigan, Robert W., *Masterpieces of the Modern Spanish Theatre,* Collier, 1967.

Domenech, Ricardo, *El teatro de Buero Vallejo,* Gredos, 1973.

Feijoo, Luis Iglesias, *La trayectoria dramatica de Antonio Buero Vallejo,* University of Santiago, 1982.

Halsey, Martha T., *Antonio Buero Vallejo,* Twayne, 1973.

Holt, Marion Peter, *The Modern Spanish Stage: Four Plays,* Hill & Wang, 1970.

Holt, Marion Peter, *The Contemporary Spanish Theater (1949-1972),* Twayne, 1975.

Nicholas, Robert L., *The Tragic Stages of Antonio Buero Vallejo,* Estudios de Hispanofila, 1972.

Ruple, Joelyn, *Antonio Buero Vallejo: The First Fifteen Years,* Eliseo Torres & Sons, 1971.

PERIODICALS

Books Abroad, summer, 1969.

Hispania, March, 1968, September, 1968, December, 1968, May, 1969, September, 1969, December, 1969, September, 1971, December, 1972, May, 1973, September, 1974, September, 1978.

Hispanic Journal, spring, 1984, fall, 1986.

Hispanofila, May, 1970.

Modern Drama, September, 1977.

Modern Language Journal, February, 1972, January, 1973, December, 1978, spring, 1984, fall, 1986.

Revista de estudios hispanicos, November, 1969, May, 1978.

—*Sketch by Marian Gonsior*

*   *   *

BULL, Angela (Mary)   1936-

PERSONAL: Born September 28, 1936, in Halifax, Yorkshire, England; daughter of Eric Alexander (a company director) and Joyce (Benson) Leach; married Martin Wells Bull (a Church of England clergyman), September 15, 1962; children: Timothy Martin, Priscilla Emily. *Education:* University of Edinburgh, M.A., (with honors), 1959; St. Hugh's College, Oxford, graduate study, 1959-61. *Religion:* Church of England.

ADDRESSES: Home—The Vicarage, Hall Bank Dr., Bingley, West Yorkshire BD16 4BZ, England.

CAREER: Writer. Casterton School, Kirkby Lonsdale, Westmorland, England, teacher of English, 1961-62; Bodleian Library, Oxford University, Oxford, England, assistant to keeper of western manuscripts, 1963.

AWARDS, HONORS: Other Award, 1980, for *The Machine Breakers: The Story of the Luddites.*

WRITINGS:

The Friend with a Secret, Collins, 1965, Holt, 1966.

(With Gillian Avery) *Nineteenth Century Children,* Hodder & Stoughton, 1965.

Wayland's Keep, Collins, 1966, Holt, 1967.

Child of Ebenezer, Collins, 1974.

Treasure in the Fog, Collins, 1976.

Griselda, Collins, 1977.

The Doll in the Wall, Collins, 1978.

The Machine Breakers: The Story of the Luddites, Collins, 1980.

The Bicycle Parcel, Hamish Hamilton, 1981.

The Accidental Twins, Faber, 1982.

Noel Streatfeild, Collins, 1984.

Anne Frank, Hamish Hamilton, 1984.

Florence Nightingale, Hamish Hamilton, 1985.

Marie Curie, Hamish Hamilton, 1986.

A Hat for Emily, Collins, 1986.

The Visitors, Hamish Hamilton, 1987.

Green Gloves, Blackie, 1987.

Elizabeth Fry, Hamish Hamilton, 1987.

WORK IN PROGRESS: Martyrs and Heroines, for Virago Press.

*   *   *

BULLINS, Ed   1935-
(Kingsley B. Bass, Jr.)

PERSONAL: Born July 2, 1935, in Philadelphia, Pa.; son of Edward and Bertha Marie (Queen) Bullins; married; wife's name, Trixie. *Education:* Attended Los Angeles City College and San Francisco State College (now University).

ADDRESSES: Home—2128A Fifth St., Berkeley, Calif. 94710. *Agent*—Helen Merrill, 435 West 23rd St., No. 1A, New York, N.Y. 10011.

CAREER: Left Philadelphia, Pa. for Los Angeles, Calif. in 1958, moved to San Francisco, Calif. in 1964; co-founder, Black Arts/West; co-founder of the Black Arts Alliance, Black House (Black Panther Party headquarters in San Francisco), cultural director until 1967, also serving briefly as Minister of Culture of the Party; joined The New Lafayette Theatre, New York, N.Y., in 1967, becoming playwright in residence, 1968, associate director, 1971-73; writers unit coordinator, New York Shakespeare Festival, 1975-82; People's School of Dramatic Arts, San Francisco, playwriting teacher, 1983; City College of San Francisco, instructor in dramatic performance, play directing, and playwriting, 1984—. Playwright in residence, American Place Theatre, beginning 1973; producing director, The Surviving Theatre, beginning 1974; public relations director, Berkeley Black Repertory, 1982; promotion director, Magic Theatre, 1982-83; group sales coordinator, Julian Theatre, 1983; playwriting teacher, Bay Area Playwrights Festival, summer, 1983. Also instructor in playwriting at numerous colleges and universities, including Hofstra University, New York University, Fordham University, Columbia University, Amherst College, Dartmouth College, Antioch University, and Sonoma State University. *Military service:* U.S. Navy, 1952-55.

MEMBER: Dramatists Guild.

AWARDS, HONORS: American Place Theatre grant, 1967; Vernon Rice Drama Desk Award, 1968, for plays performed at American Place Theatre; four Rockefeller Foundation grants, including 1968, 1970, and 1973; National Endowment for the Arts playwriting grant; Obie Award for distinguished playwriting, and Black Arts Alliance award, both 1971, for "The

Fabulous Miss Marie'' and ''In New England Winter''; Guggenheim fellowship for playwriting, 1971 and 1976; grant from Creative Artists Public Service Program, 1973, in support of playwriting; Obie Award for distinguished playwriting and New York Drama Critics Circle Award, both 1975, for ''The Taking of Miss Janie''; Litt.D., Columbia College, Chicago, 1976.

WRITINGS:

The Hungered One (collected short fiction), Morrow, 1971.
The Reluctant Rapist (novel), Harper, 1973.

PUBLISHED PLAYS

How Do You Do?: A Nonsense Drama (one-act; first produced as ''How Do You Do'' in San Francisco at Firehouse Repertory Theatre, August 5, 1965; produced Off-Broadway at La Mama Experimental Theatre Club, February, 1972), Illuminations Press, 1967.
(Editor and contributor) *New Plays from the Black Theatre* (includes ''In New England Winter'' [one-act; first produced Off-Broadway at New Federal Theatre of Henry Street Playhouse, January 26, 1971]), Bantam, 1969.
Five Plays (includes: ''Goin' a Buffalo'' [three-act; first produced in New York City at American Place Theatre, June 6, 1968], ''In the Wine Time'' [three-act; first produced at New Lafeyette Theatre, December 10, 1968], ''A Son Come Home'' [one-act; first produced Off-Broadway at American Place Theatre, Feburary 21, 1968; originally published in *Negro Digest*, April, 1968], ''The Electronic Nigger'' [one-act; first produced at American Place Theatre, February 21, 1968], and ''Clara's Ole Man'' [one-act; first produced in San Francisco, August 5, 1965; produced at American Place Theatre, February 21, 1968]), Bobbs-Merrill, 1969 (published in England as *The Electronic Nigger, and Other Plays*, Faber, 1970).
''Ya Gonna Let Me Take You Out Tonight, Baby?'' (first produced Off-Broadway at Public Theatre, May 17, 1972), published in *Black Arts*, Black Arts Publishing (Detroit), 1969.
''The Gentleman Caller'' (one-act; first produced in Brooklyn, N.Y., with other plays as ''A Black Quartet'' by Chelsea Theatre Center at Brooklyn Academy of Music, April 25, 1969), published in *A Black Quartet*, New American Library, 1970.
The Duplex: A Black Love Fable in Four Movements (one-act; first produced at New Lafeyette Theatre, May 22, 1970; produced at Forum Theatre of Lincoln Center, New York, N.Y., March 9, 1972), Morrow, 1971.
The Theme Is Blackness: The Corner, and Other Plays (includes: ''The Theme Is Blackness'' [first produced in San Francisco by San Francisco State College, 1966], ''The Corner'' [one-act; first produced in Boston by Theatre Company of Boston, 1968, produced Off-Broadway at Public Theatre, June 22, 1972], ''Dialect Determinism'' [one-act; first produced in San Francisco, August 5, 1965; produced at La Mama Experimental Theatre Club, February 25, 1972], ''It Has No Choice'' [one-act; first produced in San Francisco by Black Arts/West, spring, 1966, produced at La Mama Experimental Theatre Club, February 25, 1972], ''The Helper'' [first produced in New York by New Dramatists Workshop,'' June 1, 1970], ''A Minor Scene'' [first produced in San Francisco by Black Arts/West, spring, 1966; produced at La Mama Experimental Theatre Club, February 25, 1972], ''The Man Who Dug Fish'' [first produced by Theatre Company of Boston, June 1, 1970], ''Black Commercial #2,'' ''The American Flag Ritual,'' ''State Office Bldg. Curse,'' ''One Minute Commercial,'' ''A Street Play,'' ''Street Sounds'' [first produced at La Mama Experimental Theatre Club, October 14, 1970], ''A Short Play for a Small Theatre,'' and ''The Play of the Play''), Morrow, 1972.
Four Dynamite Plays (includes: ''It Bees Dat Way'' [one-act; first produced in London, September 21, 1970; produced in New York at ICA, October, 1970], ''Death List'' [one-act; first produced in New York by Theatre Black at University of the Streets, October 3, 1970], ''The Pig Pen'' [one-act; first produced at American Place Theatre, May 20, 1970], and ''Night of the Beast'' [screenplay]), Morrow, 1972.
(Editor and contributor) *The New Lafayette Theatre Presents; Plays with Aesthetic Comments by Six Black Playwrights: Ed Bullins, J. E. Gaines, Clay Gross, Oyamo, Sonia Sanchez, Richard Wesley*, Anchor Press, 1974.
''The Taking of Miss Janie'' (first produced in New York at New Federal Theatre, May 4, 1975) published in *Famous American Plays of the 1970s*, edited by Ted Hoffman, Dell, 1981.

Plays represented in anthologies, including *New American Plays*, Volume III, edited by William M. Hoffman, Hill & Wang, 1970. Also author of ''Malcolm: '71 or Publishing Blackness,'' published in *Black Scholar*, June, 1975.

UNPUBLISHED PLAYS

(With Shirley Tarbell) ''The Game of Adam and Eve,'' first produced in Los Angeles at Playwrights' Theatre, spring, 1966.
(Under pseudonym Kingsley B. Bass, Jr.) ''We Righteous Brothers'' (adapted from Albert Camus's *The Just Assassins*), first produced in New York at New Lafayette Theatre, April 1969.
''A Ritual to Raise the Dead and Foretell the Future,'' first produced in New York at New Lafayette Theatre, 1970.
''The Devil Catchers,'' first produced at New Lafayette Theatre, November 27, 1970.
''The Fabulous Miss Marie,'' first produced at New Lafayette Theatre, March 5, 1971; produced at Mitzi E. Newhouse Theatre of Lincoln Center, May, 1979.
''Next Time . . . ,'' first produced in Bronx, N.Y. at Bronx Community College, May 8, 1972.
''The Psychic Pretenders (A Black Magic Show),'' first produced at New Lafayette Theatre, December, 1972.
''House Party, a Soul Happening,'' first produced at American Place Theatre, fall 1973.
''The Mystery of Phillis Wheatley,'' first produced at New Federal Theatre, February 4, 1976.
''I Am Lucy Terry,'' first produced at American Place Theatre, February 11, 1976.
''Home Boy,'' first produced in New York at Perry Street Theatre, September 26, 1976.
''JoAnne!,'' first produced in New York at Theatre of the Riverside Church, October 7, 1976.
''Storyville,'' first produced in LaJolla at the Mandeville Theatre, University of California, May 1977.
''DADDY!,'' first produced at the New Federal Theatre, June 9, 1977.
''Sepia Star,'' first produced in New York at Stage 73, August 20, 1977.
''Michael,'' first produced in New York at New Heritage Repertory Theatre, May, 1978.
''C'mon Back to Heavenly House,'' first produced in Amherst, Mass. at Amherst College Theatre, 1978.

"Leavings," first produced in New York at Syncopation, August, 1980.

"Steve and Velma," first produced in Boston by New African Company, August, 1980.

OTHER

Editor of *Black Theatre*, 1968-73; editor of special black issue of *Drama Review*, summer, 1968. Contributor to *Negro Digest, New York Times,* and other periodicals.

SIDELIGHTS: Ed Bullins is one of the most powerful black voices in contemporary American theater. He began writing plays as a political activist in the mid-1960s and soon emerged as a principal figure in the black arts movement that surfaced in that decade. First as Minister of Culture for California's Black Panther Party and then as associate director of Harlem's New Lafayette Theatre, Bullins helped shape a revolutionary "theater of black experience" that took drama to the streets. In over fifty dramatic works, written expressly for and about blacks, Bullins probed the disillusionment and frustration of ghetto life. At the height of his militancy, he advocated cultural separatism between races and outspokenly dismissed white aesthetic standards. Asked by *Race Relations Reporter* contributor Bernard Garnett how he felt about white critics' evaluations of his work, Bullins replied: "It doesn't matter whether they appreciate it. It's not for them." Despite his disinterest, by the late 1960s establishment critics were tracking his work, more often than not praising its lyricism and depth and commending the playwright's ability to transcend narrow politics. As C. W. E. Bigsby points out in *The Second Black Renaissance: Essays in Black Literature,* Bullins "was one of the few black writers of the 1960s who kept a cautious distance from a black drama which defined itself solely in political terms." In the 1970s, Bullins won three Obie Awards for disinguished playwriting, a Drama Critics Circle Award, and several prestigious Guggenheim and Rockefeller playwriting grants.

Bullins's acceptance into the theatrical mainstream, which accelerated as the black arts movement lost momentum, presents some difficulty for critics trying to assess the current state of his art. The prolific output of his early years has been replaced by a curious silence. One possible explanation, according to *Black American Literature Forum* contributor Richard G. Scharine, is that Bullins is facing the same artistic dilemma that confronts Steve Benson, his most autobiographical protagonist: "As an artist he requires recognition. As a revolutionary he dare not be accepted. But Bullins has been accepted. . . . The real question is whether, severed from his roots and his hate, Bullins can continue to create effectively." In a written response published with the article, Bullins answered the charge: "I was a conscious artist before I was a conscious artist-revolutionary, which has been my salvation and disguise. . . . I do not feel that I am severed from my roots."

Whatever the reasons, productions of Bullins's work have been absent from the New York stage for a number of years. There is no indication, however, that the author has stopped writing. Bullins remains at work on his "Twentieth Century Cycle"— a projected series of twenty plays, six of which have been produced. This dramatic cycle, which features several recurring characters at different times and in different places, will portray various facets of black life. Bullins's hope, as he explained to Jervis Anderson in a 1973 *New Yorker* interview, is "that the stories will touch the audience in an individual way, with some fresh impressions and some fresh insights into

their own lives [and] help them to consider the weight of their experience."

Bullins's desire to express the reality of ordinary black experience reflects the philosophy he developed during his six-year association with the New Lafayette Theatre, a community-based playhouse that was a showpiece of the black arts movement until it closed for lack of funds in 1973. During its halcyon days, the New Lafayette provided a sanctuary wherein the black identity could be assuaged and nurtured, a crucial goal of Bullins and all the members of that theatrical family. "Our job," former New Lafayette director Robert Macbeth told Anderson, "has always been to show black people who they are, where they are, and what condition they are in. . . . Our function, the healing function of theatre and art, is absolutely vital."

In order to reach his black audience, Bullins has consistently ignored many accepted playwrighting conventions. "Bullins has never paid much attention to the niceties of formal structure, choosing instead to concentrate on black life as it very likely really is—a continuing succession of encounters and dialogues, major events and non-events, small joys and ever-present sorrows," Catharine Hughes comments in *Plays and Players.* New York theatre critic Clive Barnes calls him "a playwright with his hand on the jugular vein of people. He writes with a conviction and sensitivity, and a wonderful awareness of the way the human animal behaves in his human jungle. . . . Bullins writes so easily and naturally that you watch his plays and you get the impression of overhearing them rather than seeing them."

Part of the authenticity Bullins brings to his dramas may stem from his use of characters drawn from real life. Steve Benson, Cliff Dawson, and Art Garrison are but three of the recurring protagonists who have been closely identified with the author himself. In the early 1970s Steve Benson, who appears in Bullins's novel *The Reluctant Rapist* as well as in "It Has No Choice," "In New England Winter" and other plays, became so closely associated with his creator that Bullins threatened to eliminate him. "Everybody's got him tagged as me," he told *New York Times* contributor Mel Gussow. "I'm going to kill him off." To a large extent, Steve Benson has disappeared from Bullins's recent dramas, but the link between his art and his life experiences remains a strong one. *Dictionary of Literary Biography* contributor Leslie Sanders explains: "While Bullins frequently warns against turning to his writing for factual details of his life and against identifying him with any single one of his characters, he has never denied the autobiographical quality of his writing. Thus, the tenor, if not the exact substance, of his early years emerges from several of his plays."

Bullins was born and raised in a North Philadelphia ghetto, but was given a middle-class orientation by his mother, a civil servant. He attended a largely white elementary school, where he was an excellent student, and spent his summers vacationing in Maryland farming country. As a junior high student, he was transferred to an inner-city school and joined a gang, the Jet Cobras. During a street fight, he was stabbed in the heart and momentarily lost his life (as does his fictional alter-ego Steve Benson in *The Reluctant Rapist*). The experience, as Bullins explained to *New York Times* contributor Charles M. Young, changed his attitude: "See, when I was young, I was stabbed in a fight. I died. My heart stopped. But I was brought back for a reason. I was gifted with these abilities and I was sent into the world to do what I do because that is the only thing I can do. I write.''

Bullins did not immediately recognize his vocation, but spent several years at various jobs. After dropping out of high school, he served in the Navy from 1952-55, where he won a shipboard lightweight boxing championship and started a program of self-education through reading. Not much is known about the years he spent in North Philadelphia after his discharge, but Sanders says ''his 1958 departure for Los Angeles quite literally saved his life. When he left Philadelphia, he left behind an unsuccessful marriage and several children.'' In California, Bullins earned a GED high school equivalency degree and started writing. He turned to plays when he realized that the black audience he was trying to reach did not read much fiction and also that he was naturally suited to the dramatic form. But even after moving to San Francisco in 1964, Bullins found little encouragement for his talent. ''Nobody would produce my work,'' he recalled of his early days in the *New Yorker*. ''Some people said my language was too obscene, and others said the stuff I was writing was not theatre in the traditional sense.'' Bullins might have been discouraged had he not chanced upon a production of two plays by LeRoi Jones, ''Dutchman'' and ''The Slave,'' that reminded him of his own. ''I could see that an experienced playwright like Jones was dealing with the same qualities and conditions of black life that moved me,'' Bullins explained.

Inspired by Jones's example, Bullins and a group of black revolutionaries joined forces to create a militant cultural-political organization called Black House. Among those participating were Huey Newton and Bobby Seale, two young radicals whose politics of revolution would soon coalesce into the Black Panther Party. But the alliance between the violent ''revolutionary nationalists,'' such as Seale and Newton, and the more moderate ''cultural nationalists,'' such as Bullins, would be short-lived. As Anderson explains in the *New Yorker:* ''The artists were interested solely in the idea of a cultural awakening while the revolutionaries thought, in Bullins' words, that 'culture was a gun.''' Disheartened by the experience, Bullins resigned the post he had been assigned as Black Panther Minister of Culture, severed his ties with the ill-fated Black House, and accepted Robert Macbeth's invitation to work at the New Lafayette Theater in New York.

To date, Bullins's six-year association with the New Lafayette Theatre has been one of the most productive creative periods in his life. Between 1967 and 1973 Bullins created and/or produced almost a dozen plays, some of which are still considered his finest work. He also edited the theatre magazine, *Black Theatre,* and compiled and edited an anthology of six New Lafayette plays. During this time, Bullins was active as a playwriting teacher and director as well. Despite Bullins's close ties to the New Lafayette, his plays were also produced Off-Broadway and at other community theaters, notably the American Place Theatre where he became playwright in residence after the New Lafayette's demise.

Bullins's plays of this period share common themes. ''Clara's Ole Man,'' an early drama that established the playwright's reputation in New York during its 1968 production, introduces his concerns. Set in the mid-fifties, it tells the story of 20-year-old Jack, an upwardly mobile black who goes to the ghetto to visit Clara one afternoon when her ''ole man'' is at work. Not realizing that Clara's lover is actually Big Girl, a lesbian bully who is home when Jack calls, he gets brutally beaten as a result of his ignorance. Leslie Sanders believes that ''in

Clara's Ole Man, Bullins's greatest work is foreshadowed. Its characters, like those in many of his later plays, emerge from brutal life experiences with tenacity and grace. While their language is often crude, it eloquently expresses their pain and anger, as well as the humor that sustains them.'' C. W. E. Bigsby believes that ''Clara's Ole Man,'' as well as ''Goin' A Buffalo,'' ''In the Wine Time,'' ''In New England Winter,'' and other plays that Bullins wrote in the mid-to-late 1960s project the ''sense of a brutalized world.... Love devolves into a violent sexuality in which communion becomes simple possession, a struggle for mental and physical dominance. Money is a dominating reality, and alcohol and drugs, like sexuality, the only relief. The tone of the plays is one of desperation and frustration. Individuals are locked together by need, trapped by their own material and biological necessities. Race is only one, and perhaps not even the dominant, reality.''

By and large, Bullins's plays of this period have fared well artistically while being criticized, by both black and white critics, for their ideology. Some blacks have objected to what Bigsby calls the ''reductive view of human nature'' presented in these dramas, along with ''their sense of the black ghetto as lacking in any redeeming sense of community or moral values.'' Other blacks, particularly those who have achieved material success, resent their exclusion from this art form. ''I am a young black from a middle-class family and well-educated,'' reads a letter printed in the *New York Times Magazine* in response to a black arts article. ''What sense of self will I ever have if I continue to go to the theatre and movies and never see blacks such as myself in performance?'' For the white theater-going community, Bullins's exclusively black drama has raised questions of cultural elitism that seems ''to reserve for black art an exclusive and, in some senses, a sacrosanct critical territory,'' Anderson believes.

Bullins some time ago distanced himself from the critical fray, saying that if he'd listened to what critics have told him, he would have stopped writing long ago. ''I don't bother too much what anyone thinks,'' he told Anderson. ''When I sit down in that room by myself, bringing in all that I ever saw, smelled, learned, or checked out, I am the chief determiner of the quality of my work. The only critic that I really trust is me.''

BIOGRAPHICAL/CRITICAL SOURCES:

BOOKS

Bigsby, C. W. E., *The Second Black Renaissance: Essays in Black Literature,* Greenwood Press, 1980.
Contemporary Literary Criticism, Gale, Volume I, 1973, Volume V, 1976, Volume VII, 1977.
Dictionary of Literary Biography, Volume VII: *Twentieth Century American Dramatists,* Gale, 1981.
Dictionary of Literary Biography, Volume XXXVIII: *Afro-American Writers after 1955—Dramatists and Prose Writers,* Gale, 1985.
Gayle, Addison, editor, *The Black Aesthetic,* Doubleday, 1971.

PERIODICALS

Black American Literature Forum, fall, 1979.
Black Creation, winter, 1973.
Black World, April, 1974.
CLA Journal, June, 1976.
Nation, November 12, 1973, April 5, 1975.
Negro Digest, April, 1969.
Newsweek, May 20, 1968.
New Yorker, June 16, 1973.

New York Times, September 22, 1971, May 18, 1975, June 17, 1977, May 31, 1979.
New York Times Book Review, June 20, 1971, September 30, 1973.
New York Times Magazine, September 10, 1972.
Plays and Players, May, 1972, March, 1973.
Race Relations Reporter, February 7, 1972.

—*Sketch by Donna Olendorf*

*   *   *

BURSK, Christopher 1943-

PERSONAL: Born April 23, 1943, in Cambridge, Mass.; son of Edward C. (a professor and editor) and Catherine (Irwin) Bursk; married Mary Ann Adzarito, June 19, 1967; children: Christian, Norabeth, Justin. *Education:* Tufts University, B.A., 1965; Boston University, Ph.D., 1975. *Politics:* Democrat. *Religion:* Episcopalian.

ADDRESSES: Home—704 Hulmeville Ave., Langhorne Manor, Pa. 19047. *Office*—Department of Language and Literature, Bucks County Community College, Swamp Rd., Newtown, Pa. 18940.

CAREER: Shaw University, Raleigh, N.C., assistant professor of English, 1968-69; Bucks County Community College, Newtown, Pa., associate professor of language and literature, 1970—. Volunteer counselor for local prison-probation program.

MEMBER: Amnesty International.

AWARDS, HONORS: Guggenheim fellowship, 1984.

WRITINGS:

POETRY

(With Paul Hannigan and William Corbett) *Three New Poets,* Pym-Randall Press, 1968.
Standing Watch, Houghton, 1978.
Little Harbor, Quarterly Review of Literature Poetry Series, 1982.
Places of Residence, Sparrow Press, 1983.
Making Wings, State Street, 1983.

Contributor of poetry to literary magazines, including *Sun, Xanadu, Images,* and *Poetry Now.*

*   *   *

BUSBY, F. M. 1921-

PERSONAL: Born March 11, 1921, in Indianapolis, Ind.; son of F. M., Sr. (a teacher) and Clara (a teacher; maiden name, Nye) Busby; married Elinor Doub, April 28, 1954; children: Michele B., Rowley. *Education:* Washington State University, B.Sc., 1946, B.Sc.E.E., 1947. *Politics:* "Eclectic; consider issues individually." *Religion:* "Much the same. . . ."

ADDRESSES: Home and office—2852 14th Ave. W., Seattle, Wash. 98119.

CAREER: Alaska Communication System Headquarters, Seattle, Wash., "trick chief" and project supervisor, 1947-53, telegraph engineer, 1953-70; writer, 1970—. *Military service:* National Guard, active duty, 1940-41. U.S. Army, 1943-45.

MEMBER: Science Fiction Writers of America (vice-president, 1974-76), Authors Guild, Authors League of America, Mystery Writers of America, Seattle Freelances.

WRITINGS:

SCIENCE FICTION

Cage a Man (Science Fiction Book Club selection; also see below), New American Library, 1974.
The Proud Enemy (also see below), Berkley Publishing, 1975.
Rissa Kerguelen (also see below), Putnam, 1976.
The Long View (also see below), Putnam, 1976.
All These Earths, Berkley Publishing, 1976.
Rissa Kerguelen (contains *Rissa Kerguelen* and *The Long View*), Berkley Publishing, 1977, published as *Young Rissa, Rissa and Tregare,* [and] *The Long View,* Berkley Publishing, 1984.
Zelde M'tana, Dell, 1980.
The Demu Trilogy (includes *Cage a Man, The Proud Enemy,* and *End of the Line*), Pocket Books, 1980.
Star Rebel, Bantam, 1984.
The Alien Debt, Bantam, 1984.
Rebel's Quest, Bantam, 1985.
Rebel's Seed, Bantam, 1986.
Getting Home (story collection), Ace Books, 1987.
The Breeds of Man, Bantam, 1988.

CONTRIBUTOR TO ANTHOLOGIES

New Dimensions 3, edited by Robert Silverberg, New American Library, 1973.
Best Science Fiction of the Year, edited by Terry Carr, Ballantine, 1974.
Universe 5, edited by Carr, Random House, 1974.
Golden Age, second series, edited by Brian Aldiss, Futura (London), 1975.
Best Science Fiction of the Year, edited by Lester del Rey, Dutton, 1976.
1979 Annual World's Best Science Fiction, edited by Donald A. Wollheim, DAW Books, 1979.
Best of New Dimensions, edited by Silverberg, Pocket Books, 1979.
Universe 10, edited by Carr, Doubleday, 1980.
Dream's Edge, edited by Carr, Sierra Club Books, 1980.
Amazons II, edited by Jessica Amanda Salmonson, DAW Books, 1982.
Heroic Visions, edited by Salmonson, Ace Books, 1983.

OTHER

Contributor of about forty stories to science fiction magazines.

WORK IN PROGRESS: Slow Freight to Forever, a science fiction novel; short stories.

SIDELIGHTS: F. M. Busby writes: "I 'played' with writing off-and-on for years before the chance came to take early retirement and try it in earnest. I like to deal with characters who are pushed hard by necessity and who generally manage to cope, more than not. Science fiction allows me to put characters into predicaments that could not exist in our own past and present; I like the challenge and enjoy working with it."

*   *   *

BUSH, Patricia (Jahns) 1932-

PERSONAL: Born June 13, 1932, in Saginaw, Mich.; daughter of Edwin Earl (a teacher) and Marcia (a teacher; maiden name, Rozell) Jahns; married James Ter Bush (a Naval officer and defense analyst), June 27, 1954; children: Sunley Hamilton, James Ter, Jr. *Education:* University of Michigan, B.S.,

1954; University of London, M.Sc., 1972; University of Minnesota, Ph.D., 1978.

ADDRESSES: Home—1325 21st St. N.W., Washington, D.C. 20036. *Office*—Department of Community and Family Medicine, School of Medicine, Georgetown University, Washington, D.C. 20007. *Agent*—The Peter Miller Agency, Inc., Box 764, Midtown Station, New York, N.Y. 10018.

CAREER: Medical University of South Carolina, Charleston, instructor in pharmacy, 1965-69; Georgetown University, Washington, D.C., assistant professor of community and family medicine, 1972-77; University of Southern California, Los Angeles, assistant professor of pharmacy, 1978; Georgetown University, assistant professor of community and family medicine, 1978—. Assistant professor at Howard University, 1980-81. Member of advisory council, National Center for Maternal and Child Health, 1987—. Member of planning committee, National Women's Conference on Preventing Nuclear War, 1984; member, Women's Agenda Center for Defense Information, and Lombardi Cancer Center Cancer Control Task Force, 1985—. Principal or co-principal investigator for nine federally-funded research grants; member of National Institute for the Humanities review sections and study groups, 1979, 1982-86.

MEMBER: American Public Health Association (chairperson of drug policy and pharmacy services committee, 1980-92; member of governing council, 1983-85; chairperson of medical care section nominations committee, 1986—), Association for Social Sciences in Health (member of executive council, 1987-88), Sigma Xi, Rho Chi, Phi Kappa Phi.

AWARDS, HONORS: Bush Foundation fellowship, 1976-77; also recipient of two other awards from private foundations.

WRITINGS:

(Editor with A. I. Wertheimer) *Perspectives on Medicines in Society*, Drug Intelligence Publications, 1977.
Drugs, Alcohol, and Sex, Richard Marek, 1981.
(With Bob Goldman) *Death in the Locker Room*, Icarus, 1984.
Evaluation of a Pharmacy and Formulary at an HMO, National Technical Information Service, 1984.

Also editor of *The Pharmacist Role in Public Health*, American Society of Hospital Pharmacists. Also contributor to books. Editor of column, "CAPSULE," in *Medical Care*, 1985—. Contributor of about fifty articles and reviews to professional journals.

WORK IN PROGRESS: "Know Your Body" evaluation project (research); *Development of a Pediatric Health Risk Appraisal System; Black Children's Substance Abuse: Longitudinal Influences; Risk Reduction Intervention for Pregnant Adolescents.*

SIDELIGHTS: Patricia Bush wrote *CA:* "I particularly want to take scientific material on medicines and the results of research and transform them into useful information to help people with their everyday lives.

"People can be helped in two ways. Physicians can learn how to be better prescribers, and other people can learn how to take more responsibility for the medicines they take. This means that people need to have information, and they need to learn how to use it, whether they are physicians or patients."

She adds: "Children can take far more responsibility for their medicine use than most adults believe. If physicians would

talk to children and place them in charge, instead of their parents, it is likely that compliance with medical use directives would improve."

Bush continues: "Some people take medicines too lightly and some abusable substances too seriously. In terms of the harm done to individuals and society, alcohol and tobacco are clearly way out in front. We need to recognize that many of society's views and laws on drugs are morally based and do not reflect their potential for physical or psychological damage.

"Although my writing has been mainly for the academic press to date, *Drugs, Alcohol, and Sex* has convinced me that it is possible to translate academic gobbledespeak into stuff that ordinary people can use."

*   *   *

BUTLER, Octavia E(stelle)   1947-

PERSONAL: Born June 22, 1947, in Pasadena, Calif.; daughter of Laurice and Octavia M. (Guy) Butler. *Education:* Pasadena City College, A.A., 1968; attended California State University, Los Angeles, 1969.

ADDRESSES: Home—P.O. Box 6604, Los Angeles, Calif. 90055.

CAREER: Free-lance writer, 1970—.

MEMBER: Science Fiction Writers of America.

AWARDS, HONORS: Hugo Award, World Science Fiction Convention, 1984, for short story "Speech Sounds"; Hugo Award, World Science Fiction Convention, Nebula Award, Science Fiction Writers of America, and Locus Award, *Locus* magazine, all 1985, all for novelette "Bloodchild."

WRITINGS:

SCIENCE FICTION NOVELS

Patternmaster, Doubleday, 1976.
Mind of My Mind, Doubleday, 1977.
Survivor, Doubleday, 1978.
Kindred, Doubleday, 1979.
Wild Seed, Doubleday, 1980.
Clay's Ark, St. Martin's, 1984.
Dawn: Xenogenesis, Warner Books, 1987.

CONTRIBUTOR

Robin Scott Wilson, editor, *Clarion*, New American Library, 1970.
Roy Torgeson, editor, *Chrysalis 4*, Zebra Books, 1979.

Contributor to *Isaac Asimov's Science Fiction Magazine, Future Life, Transmission*, and other publications.

SIDELIGHTS: Concerned with genetic engineering, psionic powers, advanced alien beings, and the nature and proper use of power, Octavia E. Butler's science fiction presents these themes in terms of racial and sexual awareness. "Butler consciously explores the impact of race and sex upon future society," as Frances Smith Foster explains in *Extrapolation*. As one of the few black writers in the science fiction field, and the only black woman, Butler's racial and sexual perspective is unique. This perspective, however, does not limit her fiction or turn it into mere propaganda. "Her stories," Sherley Anne Williams writes in *Ms.*, "aren't overwhelmed by politics, nor are her characters overwhelmed by racism or sexism." Speaking of how Butler's early novels deal with racial questions in particular, John R. Pfeiffer of *Fantasy Review* maintains that "nevertheless, and therefore more remarkably, these are the novels of character that critics so much want to find in science fiction—and which remain so rare. Finally, they are love stories that are mythic, bizarre, exotic and heroic and full of doom and transcendence."

After attending the Clarion Science Fiction Writers' Workshop in 1970, where she studied under some of the field's top writers, Butler began to sell her short stories to science fiction magazines. But she had been writing for many years before Clarion. "I began writing," she comments, "when I was about ten years old for the same reason many people begin reading—to escape loneliness and boredom. I didn't realize then that writing was supposed to be work. It was too much fun. It still is."

Butler's stories have been well received by science fiction fans. In 1985 she won three of the field's top honors—the Nebula Award, the Hugo Award, and the Locus Award—for her novella "Bloodchild," the story of human males on another planet who bear the children of an alien race. "Bloodchild," Williams maintains, "explores the paradoxes of power and inequality, and starkly portrays the experience of a class who, like women throughout most of history, are valued chiefly for their reproductive capacities."

It is through her novels, especially those set in the world of the "Patternists," that Butler reaches her largest audience. These novels tell of a society dominated by an elite, specially-bred group of telepaths who are mentally linked together into a heirarchical pattern. Led by a four thousand-year-old alien who survives by killing and then taking over younger bodies, these telepaths seek to create a race of superhumans. The Patternist society is also wracked by an alien plague which genetically alters human beings. The novels range over vast reaches of time and space, tracing many hundreds of years of human history from the remote past to the space-faring future.

Among Butler's strengths as a writer is her creation of believable, independent female characters. "Her major characters are black women," Foster explains, and through these characters Butler explores the possibilities for a society open to true sexual equality. In such a society Butler's female characters, "powerful and purposeful in their own right, need not rely upon eroticism to gain their ends," Foster writes. Williams finds that Butler posits "a multiracial society featuring strong women characters."

Critics also praise Butler's controlled, economical prose style. Writing in the *Washington Post Book World,* Elizabeth A. Lynn calls Butler's prose "spare and sure, and even in moments of great tension she never loses control over her pacing or over her sense of story." "Butler," writes Dean R. Lambe of the *Science Fiction Review,* "has a fine hand with lean, well-paced prose."

Butler's only novel not set in the Patternist society is *Kindred,* a novel her publisher marketed as mainstream fiction despite its time-travel theme. It concerns Dana, a contemporary black woman who is pulled back in time by her great-great-grandfather, a white plantation owner in the antebellum American South. To insure that he will live to father her great-grand-

mother, and thus insure her own birth in the twentieth century, Dana is called upon to save the slaveowner's life on several occasions. "Butler makes new and eloquent use of a familiar science-fiction idea, protecting one's own past, to express the tangled interdependency of black and white in the United States," Joanna Russ writes in the *Magazine of Fantasy and Science Fiction.* Williams calls *Kindred* "a startling and engrossing commentary on the complex actuality and continuing heritage of American slavery."

"I began writing science fiction and fantasy," Butler explains, "because both inspire a high level of creativity and offer a great deal of freedom." But she soon found that few science fiction writers exercised this creative freedom. "I remember that when I began reading science fiction," she continues, "I was disappointed at how little this creativity and freedom was used to portray the many racial, ethnic, and class variations. Also, I could not help noticing how few significant women characters there were in science fiction. Fortunately, all of this has been changing over the past few years. I intend my writing to contribute to the change."

Butler enjoys a solid reputation among both readers and critics of science fiction. Although Williams notes that Butler has a "cult status among many black women readers," she also notes that "Butler's work has a scope that commands a wide audience." Speaking of *Kindred* and *Wild Seed,* Pfeiffer argues that with these books Butler "produced two novels of such special excellence that critical appreciation of them will take several years to assemble. To miss them will be to miss unique novels in modern fiction." Margaret Anne O'Connor of the *Dictionary of Literary Biography* simply calls Butler "one of the most promising new writers in America today."

BIOGRAPHICAL/CRITICAL SOURCES:

BOOKS

Contemporary Literary Criticism, XXXVIII, Gale, 1986.
Dictionary of Literary Biography, Volume XXXIII: *Afro-American Fiction Writers after 1955,* Gale, 1984.

PERIODICALS

Analog: Science Fiction/Science Fact, January 5, 1981, November, 1984.
Black American Literature Forum, summer, 1984.
Black Scholar, March/April, 1986.
Equal Opportunity Forum Magazine, Number 8, 1980.
Essence, April, 1979.
Extrapolation, spring, 1982.
Fantasy Review, July, 1984.
Janus, winter, 1978-79.
Los Angeles Times, January 30, 1981.
Magazine of Fantasy and Science Fiction, February, 1980, August, 1984.
Ms., March, 1986, June, 1987.
Salaga, 1981.
Science Fiction Review, May, 1984.
Thrust: Science Fiction in Review, summer, 1979.
Washington Post Book World, September 28, 1980, June 28, 1987.

—*Sketch by Thomas Wiloch*

C

CADE, Toni
See BAMBARA, Toni Cade

*   *   *

CALDER, Lyn
See CALMENSON, Stephanie

*   *   *

CALLWOOD, June   1924-

PERSONAL: Born June 2, 1924, in Chatham, Ontario, Canada; daughter of Harold (a manufacturer) and Gladys (an office manager; maiden name, Lavoie) Callwood; married Trent Gardiner Frayne (a writer and columnist), May 13, 1944; children: Jill Callwood, Brant Homer, Jennifer Ann, Casey Robert (deceased, 1982). *Education:* Educated in Canada. *Politics:* Socialist democrat. *Religion:* "Don't know."

ADDRESSES: Home and office—21 Hillcroft Dr., Islington, Ontario, Canada M9B 4X4.

CAREER: Brantford Expositor, Brantford, Ontario, reporter, 1941-42; *Globe and Mail,* Toronto, Ontario, reporter, 1942-45; free-lance writer, 1946—; *Globe and Mail,* columnist, 1975-78, 1983—. Founding affiliate, Yorkville Digger House, 1966-71; Nellie's Hostel for Women, co-founding president, 1974-78, director, 1986—; Jessie's Center for Teenagers, founding president, 1982-83, director, 1983-85, 1986—, president, 1987—; Davenport-Perth Neighborhood Center, founding director, 1985-86, member of Family Services Resource Group, 1986—; founding president, Casey House Hospice, 1987—.

Member, National Advisory Committee on the Battered Child, 1973; founding member of executive committee, Community Resources Consultants, 1975-78; co-chair, First National Conference on Human Rights, 1978; chair, Task Force on Teenaged Mothers, 1979-82; Ontario Ministry of Health, member of Assistive Devices Advisory Committee, 1981—, chair of ADP Incontinence and Ostomy Sub-Committee, 1983—; member, Metro Toronto Child Care Project Steering Committee, 1985-86; founder and chair, Hospice Steering Committee for AIDS Committee of Toronto, 1985-87. Canadian Broadcasting Corp. (CBC), panel member of "Court of Opin-

ions," CBC-Radio, 1959-67, host of "Human Sexuality," CBC-Radio, 1966, host of "Generations," 1966, and of "In Touch," 1975-78, both for CBC-TV. Judge for numerous awards, including National Newspaper Awards, 1976-83, National Magazine Awards, 1977, and Governor-General's Literary Award, 1984-86; founding director, Toronto Arts Awards, 1984—. Gordon Fairweather Lecturer on Human Rights, University of Ottawa, 1984. Founding director, Ontario Film Development Corp., 1986.

MEMBER: Writers Union of Canada (founding member, 1973; chairman, 1979-80; chair of Rights and Freedom Committee, 1986-87), PEN Canada (founding member, 1984; secretary, 1985-87; vice-president, 1987—), Periodical Writers Association of Canada (founding member, 1976; vice-president, 1977-78), Writers Development Trust (founding member, 1977; vice-president, 1978; director, 1987—), Canadian Civil Liberties Association (founding vice-president, 1965—), Amnesty International—Canada (council member, 1978—), Canadian Institute for the Administration of Justice (director, 1983-84), Canadian Council of Christians and Jews (director, 1978—), Law Society of Upper Canada (bencher, 1987-91), Canadian Association for the Repeal of Abortion Laws (founding member, 1972; honorary director, 1982—), Coalition against Return of the Death Penalty, Learnxs Foundation (founding member, 1974; president, 1977-79), Justice for Children (founding member, 1978; president, 1980), Bereaved Families of Ontario (honorary chairman, 1983—), Women for Political Action (founding member, 1972), Feminists against Censorship (founding member, 1984—), Maggie's: Canadian Organization for the Rights of Prostitutes (founding member; director, 1986—), Ian Adams Defense Fund (chair, 1980-81), Polish Journalists Aid Committee, Canadian Environmental Defence Fund (honorary director, 1985—), Canadian Native Arts Foundation (honorary director, 1985—), Canadian Magazines Awards Foundation (director, 1981-83), City of Toronto Children's Network, Toronto Arts Council (director, 1985—; chair of Literary Committee, 1985—), Toronto Memorial Society.

AWARDS, HONORS: "Woman of the Year," B'nai B'rith, 1969; award of merit from city of Toronto, 1974; member, Order of Canada, 1978; humanitarian award, 1978, and Ida Nudel Humanitarian Award, 1983, both from Canadian Council of Christians and Jews; named to Canadian News Hall of

Fame, 1984; Order of the Buffalo Hunt, Manitoba, 1984; Ontario Bicentennial Medal, 1984; award from Family Services Association, 1985; award from Planned Parenthood Federation of Canada, 1985; "Toronto Woman of Distinction," YWCA, 1986; officer, Order of Canada, 1986; certificate of appreciation from Metropolitan Community Church of Toronto, 1987; Quill Award, Windsor Press Club, 1987; humanitarian award, Ontario Psychological Association, 1987; Doctor of the University, University of Ottawa, 1987.

WRITINGS:

(With Marian Hillard) *A Woman Doctor Looks at Life and Love,* Doubleday, 1957.
Love, Hate, Fear, and Anger, Doubleday, 1964, revised edition published as *Emotions: What They Are and How They Affect Us,* 1986.
(With Charles W. Mayo) *Mayo: The Story of My Family and Career,* Doubleday, 1968.
(With Marvin Zuker) *Canadian Woman and the Law,* Copp Clark, 1971.
(With Barbara Walters) *How to Talk to Practically Anybody About Practically Anything,* Doubleday, 1973.
(With Judianne Densen-Gerber) *We Mainline Dreams,* Doubleday, 1974.
(With Zuker) *The Law Is Not for Women,* Pitman, 1976.
(With Otto Preminger) *Otto Preminger Remembers,* Doubleday, 1977.
The Naughty Nineties: Canada's Illustrated Heritage, McClelland & Stewart, 1978.
Portrait of Canada, Doubleday, 1981.
Emma: The True Story of Canada's Unlikely Spy, Stoddart, 1984.
Twelve Weeks in Spring, Lester & Orpen Dennys, 1986.
(With Bob White) *Hard Bargains: My Life on the Line,* McClelland & Stewart, 1987.

Also author of television and radio scripts. Author of "The Informal . . . ," a column in *Globe and Mail,* 1975-78. Contributor of nearly 300 articles to magazines, including *Maclean's* and *Chatelaine.*

SIDELIGHTS: In *Emma: The True Story of Canada's Unlikely Spy,* Canadian writer and reformer June Callwood chronicles the life of Emma (Woikin) Sawula, a young Doukhobor woman from Saskatchewan convicted of spying for the Soviet Union and imprisoned in the late 1940s. Callwood's account details the controversial nature of Sawula's conviction, in particular the civil rights infractions that occurred at the time of her arrest and questioning. "More important than the circumstances of Emma's wrongdoing was the method of convicting her," observes William French in the Toronto *Globe and Mail,* "and . . . here Callwood, the noted civil libertarian, is at her best. Emma and . . . 12 [other] 'spies' . . . were scooped up, detained, interrogated and charged under conditions that, as Callwood notes, prevailed before King John signed the Magna Carta." French adds that Emma emerges in the book as "one of those tragic characters unwittingly caught up in the whirlpool of history, a victim perhaps of her naivete."

Twelve Weeks in Spring is the true story of Margaret Frazer, a terminally-ill retired school teacher whose wish to die at home was honored by friends and acquaintances—under Callwood's direction—who banded together to care for her. The book is both a detailed account of the group's coordinated response to Frazer's needs and, as Mary Lassance Parthun comments in the *Globe and Mail,* "a memorial to the dead Margaret Frazer and a tribute to friendship and the heights to

which people can rise in a crisis." More importantly though, the book is a statement of the group's commitment "to help Frazer . . . retain control over her life and death, in spite of the encroachments of society's definition of dying as a medical problem rather than an individual crisis or rite of passage." Parthun further states: "[Callwood] has been on the cutting edge of many attempts to adapt services to current needs. It is not surprising, then, that she has turned her energies to this particular problem of modern society—the sterile institutional death among strangers."

BIOGRAPHICAL/CRITICAL SOURCES:

PERIODICALS

Globe and Mail (Toronto), October 13, 1984, July 5, 1986, November 1, 1986, October 24, 1987.

*   *   *

CALMENSON, Stephanie   1952- (Lyn Calder)

PERSONAL: Born November 28, 1952, in Brooklyn, N.Y.; daughter of Kermit (a podiatrist and educator) and Edith (a medical secretary; maiden name, Goldberg) Calmenson. *Education:* Brooklyn College of the City University of New York, B.A. (magna cum laude), 1973; New York University, M.A., 1976.

ADDRESSES: Home—150 East 18th St., Apt. 2P, New York, N.Y. 10003.

CAREER: Teacher of early childhood grades at public schools in Brooklyn, N.Y., 1974-75; Doubleday & Co., New York City, editor, 1976-80; Parents Magazine Press, New York City, editorial director, 1980-84; author of children's books, 1982—.

MEMBER: Society of Children's Book Writers, Mystery Writers of America.

WRITINGS:

JUVENILES

Never Take a Pig to Lunch and Other Funny Poems about Animals, illustrated by Hilary Knight, Doubleday, 1982.
My Book of the Seasons, Western Publishing, 1982.
One Little Monkey, illustrated by Ellen Appleby, Parents Magazine Press, 1982.
Barney's Sand Castle, illustrated by Sheila Becker, Western Publishing, 1983.
Bambi and the Butterfly, Western Publishing, 1983.
The Thee Bears, Western Publishing, 1983.
It's Not Fair!, Grosset & Dunlap, 1983.
The Kindergarten Book, illustrated by Beth L. Weiner, Grosset & Dunlap, 1983.
Where Will the Animals Stay?, Parents Magazine Press, 1983.
The Birthday Hat: A Grandma Potamus Story, illustrated by Susan Gantner, Grosset & Dunlap, 1983.
Where Is Grandma Potamus?, illustrated by Gantner, Grosset & Dunlap, 1983.
The Afternoon Book, illustrated by Weiner, Grosset & Dunlap, 1984.
Ten Furry Monsters, illustrated by Maxie Chambliss, Parents Magazine Press, 1984.
All Aboard the Goodnight Train, illustrated by Normand Chartier, Grosset & Dunlap, 1984.
Waggleby of Fraggle Rock, illustrated by Barbara McClintock, Holt, 1985.

Ten Items or Less, Western Publishing, 1985.

Rainy Day Walk, Parachute Press, 1985.

(Compiled with Joanna Cole) *The Laugh Book: A New Treasury of Humor for Children,* illustrated by Marylin Hafner, Doubleday, 1986.

The Toy Book, Western Publishing, 1986.

What Babies Do, Western Publishing, 1986.

The Shaggy Bunny, the Shaggy Little Monster, the Little Chick, illustrated by Chambliss, Simon & Schuster, 1986.

The Sesame Street ABC Book, Western Publishing, 1986.

The Sesame Street Book of First Times, Western Publishing, 1986.

Little Duck's Moving Day, Western Publishing, 1986.

(Compiled with Cole) *The Read-Aloud Treasury for Young Children,* illustrated by Ann Schweninger, Doubleday, 1987.

Fido, illustrated by Chambliss, Scholastic Inc., 1987.

Tiger's Bedtime, Western Publishing, 1987.

The Bambi Book, Western Publishing, 1987.

The Giggle Book, illustrated by Chambliss, Parents Magazine Press, 1987.

Where's Rufus?, illustrated by Chambliss, Parents Magazine Press, 1987.

One Red Shoe (The Other One's Blue!), Western Publishing, 1987.

Spaghetti Manners, Western Publishing, 1987.

"The Busy Garage," "Who Said Moo?," "A Visit to the Firehouse," Parachute Press, 1987.

What Am I?, illustrated by Karen Gundersheimer, Harper, 1988.

The Children's Aesop: Selected Fables, illustrated by Robert Byrd, Doubleday, 1988.

Little Duck and the New Baby, Western Publishing, 1988.

Wanted: Warm, Furry Friend, illustrated by Amy Schwartz, Macmillan, in press.

UNDER PSEUDONYM LYN CALDER; JUVENILES

Happy Birthday, Buddy Blue, Western Publishing, 1984.

Blast Off, Barefoot Bear!, Cloverdale Press, 1985.

Gobo and the Prize from Outer Space, Holt, 1986.

The Gloworm Bedtime Book, Random House, 1986.

Also author, as Lyn Calder, of *The Little Red Hen* and *Little Red Riding Hood,* both by Western Publishing.

OTHER

Contributor of educational stories and fiction to books and magazines, including *Humpty Dumpty's Magazine.*

WORK IN PROGRESS: Several picture books and anthologies.

SIDELIGHTS: Stephanie Calmenson wrote to *CA:* "I am often asked how I came to be a children's book writer. Some might imagine that I spent my childhood furiously filling up notebooks with wild and wonderful stories. I didn't. I never even considered the possibility that I might someday earn my living as a writer. For me, having found work I enjoy so much is a happy surprise.

"There are two things I remember that might have been clues. The first was that from the day I learned to read, I never missed reading a word on a copyright page. No matter how tiny the notice, or how long the roman numeral copyright date, I read it. It was not that I dreamed of seeing my name there someday. It was just that I wanted to know every inch of this amazing thing called a book.

"The second clue, which came somewhat later and has lasted to this day, was that as soon as I learned to write, I wrote letters. I wrote to a pen pal on the other side of the world; I wrote to friends and family when I went away to summer camp; I wrote to companies and to magazines, letting them know what I thought of their product or point of view. I see now that this was a good way to begin writing because letters are not scrutinized the way school compositions are. (And I would do anything to avoid writing school compositions!)

"The one thing I have always been sure of is that I wanted to work with children in some way. So I pursued a degree in elementary education. In the end, I taught only briefly, being a casualty of a city-wide budget crisis, but I turned to something related, finding a job as a editorial secretary, and eventually becoming an editorial director, for a children's book publisher. In the evenings I went to graduate school and it was there that I took a course called, 'Writing for Children.' The first story I wrote was called 'Buffy's Wink.' It needed work, but everyone seemed to like it and the story was eventually published in a children's magazine. Over the next few years several professors and editors, to whom I will always be grateful, encouraged me to keep on writing. And I have never stopped.

"I assume that many of the people reading this article have been flirting with the idea of writing professionally. To those people I would say, try looking for clues of your own. Do you write lots of letters, as I did? Do you leave more notes than necessary on the refrigerator door? When the bathroom gets steamy, do you find yourself writing poems on the mirror? Don't stop there. Take the next step. Give yourself a writing assignment with a specific market in mind. Or take a writing course to get some feedback on your work. You may be in for a happy surprise."

Calmenson's book *Ten Items or Less* has been translated into French.

MEDIA ADAPTATIONS: One Little Monkey was given a BBC television reading, 1984.

*   *   *

CAMERON, Ian
See PAYNE, Donald Gordon

*   *   *

CAMERON, Kenneth Walter   1908-

PERSONAL: Born October 12, 1908, in Martins Ferry, Ohio; son of Albert Ernest (an executive) and Zoe Shockley (Barker) Cameron. *Education:* West Virginia University, A.B., 1930, A.M., 1931; General Theology Seminary, S.T.B., 1935; Yale University, Ph.D., 1940. *Politics:* Republican.

ADDRESSES: Home—23 Wolcott St., Hartford, Conn. 06106. *Office*—Transcendental Books, Box A, Station A, Hartford, Conn. 06106.

CAREER: Ordained Episcopal priest, 1935. North Carolina College of Agriculture and Mechanic Arts (now North Carolina State University), Raleigh, instructor in English, 1938-43; Temple University, Philadelphia, assistant professor of English, 1945-46; Trinity College, Hartford, Conn., assistant professor, 1946-58, associate professor of English, 1958—. Manager of Transcendental Books, Hartford. Archivist and historiographer of Diocese of Connecticut.

MEMBER: Modern Language Association of America. Modern Humanities Research Association of America, Modern Humanities Research Association, Melville Society, Thoreau Society, Emerson Society (executive secretary, 1955—).

WRITINGS:

(Editor and author of introduction) Ralph Waldo Emerson, *Nature* (1836 reprint), Scholar's Facsimiles Reprints, 1940.

(Editor) John Heywood, *Gentleness and Nobility,* Thistle Press, 1941.

Authorship and Sources of "Gentleness and Nobility," Thistle Press, 1941.

Background of John Heywood's "Witty and Wittless," Thistle Press, 1941.

John Heywood's "Play of the Wether," Thistle Press, 1941.

Ralph Waldo Emerson's Reading, Thistle Press, 1941, reprinted, Haskell, 1973, revised edition, Transcendental Books, 1962.

Emerson the Essayist: An Outline of His Philosophical Development through 1836, two volumes, Thistle Press, 1945.

(Editor) Emerson, *Indian Superstition,* Friends of the Dartmouth College Library, 1954, 2nd edition, 1963.

Genesis of Hawthorne's "The Ambitious Guest," Thistle Press, 1955.

The Genesis of Christ Church, Stratford, Connecticut, Christ Church, 1957.

Index of the Pamphlet Collection of the Diocese of Connecticut, The Historiographer, 1958.

Centennial History of Trinity Episcopal Church, Bridgeport, Connecticut, Trinity Episcopal Church, 1963.

The Catholic Revival in Episcopal Connecticut, 1850-1925. Trinity Episcopal Church, 1963.

PUBLISHED BY TRANSCENDENTAL BOOKS

The Presbury Family of Maryland and the Ohio Valley, 1950.

The Transcendental Workbook, 1957.

An Emerson Index; or, Names, Exempla, Sententiae, Symbols, Words, and Motifs on Selected Notebooks of Ralph Waldo Emerson, 1958.

The Transcendentalists and Minerva (also see below), three volumes, 1958.

Emerson and Thoreau as Readers (contains selected chapters from *The Transcendentalists and Minerva*), 1958, 2nd edition, 1972.

A Commentary on Emerson's Early Lectures, 1833-1836, with Index-Concordance, 1961.

Companion to Thoreau's Correspondence, 1964.

Emerson's Workshop: An Analysis of His Reading in Periodicals through 1836, 1964.

The Pardoner and His Pardons: Indulgences Circulating in England on the Eve of Reformation, 1965.

Transcendental Epilogue, 1965.

Thoreau's Harvard Years, 1966.

Transcendental Climate, 1967.

Hawthorne Index, 1968.

Transcendental Reading Patterns: Library Charging Lists, 1970.

Young Emerson's Transcendental Vision: An Exposition of His World View with an Analysis of the Structure, Backgrounds, and Meaning of Nature, 1971.

Emerson the Essayist: An Outline of His Philosophical Development through 1836 with Special Emphasis on the Sources and Interpretation of Nature, also Bibliographical Appendices, 1972.

Letter-book of the Reverend Henry Caner, S.P.G. Missionary in Colonial Connecticut and Massachusetts until the Revolution, 1972.

Longfellow's Reading in Libraries: The Charging Records of a Learned Poet Interpreted, 1973.

Response to Transcendental Concord, 1974.

Young Thoreau and the Classics, 1975.

Transcendental Apprenticeship, 1976.

Anglicanism in Early Connecticut and New England, 1977.

Young Reporter of Concord: A Checklist of F. B. Sanborn's Letters, 1978.

The Papers of Loyalist Samuel Peters, 1978.

Strictly Personal: A Teacher's Reminiscences, 1980.

Transcendentalists in Transition, 1980.

An Anglican Library in Colonial New England, 1980.

The Younger Doctor William Smith (1754-1820), 1980.

Samuel Seabury among His Contemporaries, 1981.

Parameters of American Romanticism and Transcendentalism, 1981.

The Episcopal Church in Connecticut and New England, 1981.

Correspondence of Franklin Benjamin Sanborn the Transcendentalist, 1982.

Abraham Jarvis: Connecticut's Second Anglican Bishop, 1982.

Seabury Traditions: The Reconstructed Journals of Connecticut's First Diocesan, two volumes, 1983.

Emerson's Transcendentalism and British Swedenborgism, 1984.

Transcendental Curriculum; or, Bronson Alcott's Library: To Which Is Added a Sheaf of Ungathered Letters, 1984.

Colonial Anglicanism in New England: A Guide, 1984.

Connecticut's First Diocesan: A Supplement to Seabury Traditions, 1985.

Hawthorne among Connecticut Congregationalists: The Odyssey of a Letter, 1985.

Studies in Emerson, Thoreau and the American Renaissance, 1987.

EDITOR; PUBLISHED BY TRANSCENDENTAL BOOKS

Emerson, Thoreau, and Concord in Early Newspapers, 1957.

Thoreau's Literary Notebook in the Library of Congress, 1964.

Over Thoreau's Desk: New Correspondence 1838-1861, 1965.

Thoreau and His Harvard Classmates with Henry William's Memorials of the Class of 1837, 1965.

Poems of Jones Very, 1965.

Thoreau's Fact Book in the Harry Elkins Widener Collection in the Harvard College Library, three volumes, 1966.

The Works of Samuel Peters of Hebron, Connecticut, New England Historian, Satirist, Folklorist, Anti-patriot, and Anglican Clergyman, 1735-1826, with Historical Indexes, 1967.

Facsimiles of Early Episcopal Church Documents (1759-1789), 1970.

Phiothea or Plato against Epicurus: A Novel of the Transcendental Movement, 1975.

Whitman, Bryant, Melville and Holmes among Their Contemporaries, 1976.

The Church of England in Pre-Revolutionary Connecticut, 1976.

Samuel Hart, *Old Connecticut: Historical Papers,* 1976.

Romanticism and the American Renaissance, 1977.

The Episcopal Church of the American Renaissance, 1977.

Literary Comment in American Renaissance Newspapers, 1977.

Scholars' Companion to the American Renaissance, 1977.

Lowell, Whittier, Very and the Alcotts among Their Contemporaries, 1978.

Longfellow among His Contemporaries, 1978.

American Renaissance and Transcendentalism: Historical, Cultural, and Bibliographical Dimensions, 1978.

Samuel Seabury's Ungathered Imprints: Historical Perspectives, 1978.
Samuel Seabury (1729-1796): His Election, Consecration and Reception, 1978.
The New England Writers and the Press, 1980.
Ethos of Anglicanism in Colonial New England and New York 1981.
Further Response to Transcendental Concord, 1982.
Anglican Church Music in America, 1763-1830, 1982.
The Vestry Lectures and a Rare Sermon by Ralph Waldo Emerson, 1983.
The Correspondence of Samuel Parker: Colonial Anglican Clergyman at Boston, 1984.
Anglican Apologetic in Colonial New England: Rare Tracts Defending the Polity, Theology and Liturgy of the Church of England before and during the Revolution, 1984.
The Correspondence of Loyalist Samuel Peters: An Inventory of Additions, 1985.

EDITOR OF BOOKS BY FRANKLIN BENJAMIN SANBORN; PUBLISHED BY TRANSCENDENTAL BOOKS

Lectures on Literature and Philosophy, 1975.
Transcendental and Literary New England, 1975.
Sixty Years of Concord: 1855-1915, 1976.
The Transcendental Eye, 1981.
Ungathered Poems and Transcendental Papers, 1981.
Table Talk, 1981.
Transcendental Horizons: Essays and Poetry by Franklin Benjamin Sanborn, 1984.

COMPILER; PUBLISHED BY TRANSCENDENTAL BOOKS

Early Anglicanism in Connecticut, 1962.
Index-Concordance to Emerson's Sermons, 1963.
Emerson among His Contemporaries: A Harvest of Estimates, Insights, and Anecdotes from the Victorian Literary World and an Index, 1967.
Research Keys to the American Renaissance: Scarce Indexes of "The Christian Examiner," "The North American Review," and "The New Jerusalem Magazine," for Students of American Literature, Culture, History, and New England Transcendentalism, 1967.
Connecticut Churchmanship: Records and Historical Papers Concerning the Anglican Church in Connecticut in the Eighteenth and Early Nineteenth Centuries, 1969.
The Massachusetts Lyceum during the American Renaissance: Materials for the Study of the Oral Tradition in American Letters, 1969.
Concord Harvest: Publications of the Concord School of Philosophy and Literature, 1970.
Contemporary Dimension—An American Renaissance Literary Notebook of Newspaper Clippings, [and] *Victorian Notebook: Literary Clippings from Nineteenth-Century American Newspapers,* 1970.
The Anglican Episcopate in Connecticut: A Sheaf of Biographical and Institutional Studies for Churchmen and Historians (1784-1899), 1970.
American Episcopal Clergy: Registers of Ordinations in the Episcopal Church in the United States, 1970.
Transcendental Log, 1973.
Anglican Climate in Connecticut: Historical Perspectives from Imprints of the Late Colonial and Early National Years, 1974.
Ammi Rogers and the Episcopal Church in Connecticut, 1790-1832: His Memoirs and Documents Illuminating Historical, Religious, and Personal Backgrounds, 1974.

Episcopal Connecticut in Our Day: An Index to Illustrations in the "Connecticut Churchman," 1983.
American Authors in Pictures: The Major Nineteenth Century Writers and Their Backgrounds, 1983.
Vanished and Vanishing Episcopal Churches of Early Connecticut: A Pictorial Record, 1984.
An Index to the "Connecticut Churchman," 1906-1970, 1985.
The Emerson Tertiary Bibliography with Researcher's Index, 1986.

OTHER

Also author of *The Anglican Experience in Revolutionary Connecticut, New York and Areas Adjacent.* Editor of *Emerson Society Quarterly, Historiographer of the Episcopal Diocese of Connecticut, American Transcendental Quarterly,* and *American Renaissance Literary Report: An Annual.*

WORK IN PROGRESS: Concord and the Media: Early Reports of Thoreau, Emerson, Hawthorne, the Alcotts and Others.

SIDELIGHTS: Kenneth Walter Cameron wrote *CA:* "My Scottish background and love of books from childhood have encouraged me ever to break through the parameters of my ignorance, especially in the areas of history and literature. Five great teachers, during my formative years, gave indispensable direction. As I look back on a long career as professor and scholar, four 'blessings' stand out in my mind: the privilege of entering into the lives and works of a few authors, the sense of arriving at special competence in a few areas, the delight from association with a few productive and humane scholars and critics, and the hope (since so much has been passed on to me by others) that I may, perhaps, have been able to communicate some of my enthusiasm for ideas to my students."

*   *   *

CAMPBELL, R(obert) Wright   1927-
(Robert Campbell; F. G. Clinton, a pseudonym)

PERSONAL: Born June 9, 1927, in Newark, N.J.; son of William James (a city water department employee) and Florence Gladys (a housewife; maiden name, Clinton) Campbell. *Education:* Pratt Institute, Brooklyn, N.Y., certificate in illustration, 1947.

ADDRESSES: Home—Box 412, Carmel, Calif. 93921. *Agent*—JET Associates, 124 East 84th St., New York, N.Y. 10028.

CAREER: Artist, novelist, screenwriter. Free-lance illustrator, 1947-50. *Military service:* U.S. Army, 1950-52.

MEMBER: Writers Guild of America.

AWARDS, HONORS: Academy Award nomination, 1957, for "Man of a Thousand Faces"; National Book Award nomination, 1976, for *The Spy Who Sat and Waited;* Edgar Allan Poe Award, Mystery Writers of America, 1987, for *The Junkyard Dog;* PEN Award nomination, 1988, for *Alice in La-La Land.*

WRITINGS:

NOVELS

The Spy Who Sat and Waited, Putnam, 1975.
Circus Couronne (Book-of-the-Month Club alternate selection), Putnam, 1977.
Killer of Kings, Bobbs-Merrill, 1979.
Malloy's Subway, Atheneum, 1981.

Fat Tuesday, Ticknor & Fields, 1983.
Honor, Tor Books, 1987.

SCREENPLAYS

"Five Guns West," American Releasing, 1955.
"Naked Paradise," American-International, 1957.
"Gun for a Coward," Universal, 1957.
"Quantez," Universal, 1957.
"Man of a Thousand Faces," Universal, 1957.
"Machine Gun Kelly," American-International, 1958.
"A New World," Azteca, 1958.
"Teenage Caveman," American-International, 1958 (released in England as "Out of the Darkness").
"The Night Fighters," United Artists, 1960.
"The Young Racers," American-International, 1963.
"The Masque of the Red Death," American-International, 1964.
"The Secret Invasion," United Artists, 1964.
"Hells Angels on Wheels," U.S. Films, 1967.
"Captain Nemo and the Underwater City," Metro-Goldwyn-Mayer, 1969.

UNDER NAME ROBERT CAMPBELL; NOVELS

The Junkyard Dog, New American Library, 1986.
In La-La Land We Trust, Mysterious Press, 1986.
The Six Hundred Pound Gorilla, New American Library, 1987.
Hip-Deep in Alligators, New American Library, 1987.
Alice in La-La Land, Poseidon, 1987.
Plugged Nickle, Pocket Books, 1988.
Thinning the Turkey Herd, New American Library, 1988.
Juice, Poseidon, 1989.
Sweet La-La Land, Poseidon, in press.
The Cat's Meow, New American Library, in press.
Red Cent, Pocket Books, in press.

UNDER PSEUDONYM F. G. CLINTON; NOVELS

The Tin Cop, Pinnacle, 1983.

OTHER

Also author of play, "Wondersmith," 1977, and of filmscripts for television programs, including "Medic," "Maverick," "Cheyenne," "Mr. Garland," "Twelve O'Clock High," "The Loretta Young Show," "The Star and the Story," "Marcus Welby, M.D.," "Born Free," and "Harry-O."

WORK IN PROGRESS: A new novel; a play, "Grotius"; novels *The Beasts of Benin, The Wizard of La-La Land, The Lion's Share,* and *Thin Dime.*

SIDELIGHTS: R. Wright Campbell told *CA:* "To build a loyal readership a writer must usually offer the same kind of book each time. That works against my desire for variety. But I think I've learned enough about the marketplace to satisfy the requirements of consistency while giving myself new challenges. I've concentrated the last year or so on what is roughly called the mystery field. That seems to include novels of suspense, books about espionage, and crime novels, as well as the standard puzzle exercises, English cozies and police procedurals. Having declared myself such a writer, I'm receiving more attention than during the ten years I labored in the vineyards of the so-called mainstream novel.

"I've discovered that the crime novel is the most accommodating matrix available for the kinds of novels I view as Dickensian. That is to say, large canvases upon which bold figures and events can be painted, entertaining but sociologically significant as well. In a preface to *Oliver Twist,* Dickens wrote: 'Once upon a time it was held to be coarse and shocking circumstance, that some of the characters in these pages are chosen from the most criminal and degraded of London's population. It appeared to me that to draw a knot of such associates in crime as really did exist; to paint them in all their deformity, in all their wretchedness, in all the squalid misery of their lives; to show them as they really were, forever skulking uneasily through the dirtiest paths of life . . . would be to attempt something which was needed, and which would be of service to society.' I have a different view of such criminals and villains. Some too often are fluctuating themselves and their plunder in the finest theaters and restaurants, seemingly immune from the law and destiny alike. In my books, I take the view that there is a compensatory fate for such people if my hero just gives it a little nudge."

AVOCATIONAL INTERESTS: Gardening.

BIOGRAPHICAL/CRITICAL SOURCES:

PERIODICALS

Los Angeles Times, December 23, 1986.
New Republic, April 7, 1979, October 21, 1981.
New York Times Book Review, January 15, 1978, May 13, 1979, November 29, 1981, March 6, 1983, September 14, 1986, December 28, 1986, May 3, 1987.
Spectator, March 6, 1976.
Times Literary Supplement, May 28, 1976, July 18, 1980.
Tribune Books (Chicago), October 12, 1986, October 19, 1986, January 4, 1987.
Washington Post Book World, November 16, 1986.

*   *   *

CAMPBELL, Robert
    See CAMPBELL, R(obert) Wright

*   *   *

CANTWELL, Aston
    See PLATT, Charles

*   *   *

CAREW, Jocelyn
    See AEBY, Jacquelyn

*   *   *

CARLSEN, G(eorge) Robert   1917-

PERSONAL: Born April 15, 1917, in Bozeman, Mont.; son of Charles E. (an attorney) and Carolyn (Mason) Carlsen; married Ruth Christoffer (a writer), April 5, 1941; children: Christopher, Kristin, Peter, Jane. *Education:* University of Minnesota, B.A., 1939, B.S., 1940, M.A., 1943, Ph.D., 1948.

ADDRESSES: Home—817 North Gilbert, Iowa City, Iowa 52240.

CAREER: University of Minnesota, Minneapolis, instructor in English and education, 1942-47; University of Colorado, Boulder, associate professor of English and education, 1947-52; University of Texas at Austin, associate professor of curriculum and instruction, 1952-58; University of Iowa, Iowa City, professor of English and education, 1958-82, professor emeritus, 1982—. Faculty member at University of Colorado, summers, 1953, 1955, 1958, and University of Hawaii, 1957, 1970.

MEMBER: National Council of Teachers of English (second vice-president, 1959; first vice-president, 1961; president, 1962), Phi Beta Kappa, Phi Delta Kappa.

AWARDS, HONORS: Award for distinguished contributions in secondary school teaching, 1957, and Distinguished Service Award, 1970, both National Council of Teachers of English; Distinguished Service Award, Assembly of Literature for Adolescents, 1974; Distinguished Service Award, Iowa Council of English Teachers, 1975.

WRITINGS:

Brown-Carlsen Test of Listening Comprehension, World Publishing, 1952.

(With Richard S. Alm) *Social Understanding through Literature: A Bibliography for Secondary Schools,* National Council for Social Studies, 1954.

(Editor with wife, Ruth C. Carlsen) *The Great Auto Race, and Other Stories of Men and Cars,* Scholastic Book Services, 1965.

(Editor with R. C. Carlsen) *Fifty-two Miles to Terror* (collection), Scholastic Book Services, 1966.

Books and the Teenage Reader: A Guide for Teachers, Librarians, and Parents, Harper, 1967, 2nd revised edition, 1980.

(Editor with R. C. Carlsen and others) *Encounters: Themes in Literature,* McGraw, 1967, 4th edition, 1985.

(Editor with R. C. Carlsen and others) *Western Literature: Themes and Writers,* McGraw, 1967, 3rd edition published as *British and Western Literature,* 1979, 4th edition published as *British and Western Literature: A Thematic Approach,* 1985.

(With others) *Teacher's Resource Guide for Western Literature: Themes and Writers,* McGraw, 1967, 2nd edition, 1975.

(With Edgar H. Schuster and Anthony Tovatt) *American Literature: Themes and Writers,* McGraw, 1967, 4th edition published as *American Literature: A Thematic Approach,* 1985.

(With A. Tovatt and others) *Insights: Themes in Literature,* McGraw, 1967, 4th edition, 1985.

(Editor with R. C. Carlsen and others) *Perception: Themes in Literature,* McGraw, 1969, 4th edition, 1985.

(With A. Tovatt and Patricia O. Tovatt) *Focus: Themes in Literature,* McGraw, 1969, 4th edition, 1985.

(Editor with R. C. Carlsen and others) *English Literature: A Chronological Approach,* McGraw, 1984.

(With others) *American Literature: A Chronological Approach,* McGraw, 1985.

Also author with R. C. Carlsen of teacher's manual for each text in each edition of "Themes and Writers" literature series, for which Carlsen has served as general editor and which includes Volume I: *Focus* (grade seven), Volume II: *Perception* (grade eight), Volume III: *Insights* (grade nine), Volume IV: *Encounters* (grade ten), Volume V: *American Literature* (grade eleven), and Volume VI: *British and Western Literature* (grade twelve). The series became known as the McGraw-Hill literature series in 1984.

WORK IN PROGRESS: Fifth edition of McGraw-Hill literature series; *Voices of Readers* with Anne Sherrill for the National Council of Teachers of English.

SIDELIGHTS: G. Robert Carlsen once told *CA:* "I had a delightful time with books in the elementary schools: *Heidi, Hans Brinker, Tom Swift.* But in adolescence I was forced to read classics which I hated: *Ivanhoe, As You Like It, Evangeline, Silas Marner.* As I taught high school English classes, I became more and more conscious of the gap between children's books and the mature classics. So I constantly strove to map out a path leading from one to the other that would be less painful than my passage had been.

"Later as a college teacher in my course called 'Literature for the Adolescent,' I always asked my students, who usually intended being either English teachers or librarians, to write a reading autobiography detailing only their reading experiences. I urged them to try and remember what incidents and people made them like or dislike books. As time moved on, I became impressed with the predictability of the pattern these hundreds of individuals followed in becoming avid readers. To put this material into a format that would be useful for parents as well as those professionally interested in helping today's youngsters become readers, I wrote *Books and the Teenage Reader.*"

Carlsen more recently added: "With the help of one of my former graduate students, Anne Sherrill, I have culled from thousands of reading autobiographies significant quotations about the experiences of people with books. These range from listening to stories read aloud, to dreading book reports demanded in English classes, to inventing ploys to escape librarians' censorship of their reading. Such experiences are organized into thirteen chapters in *Voices of Readers.*"

BIOGRAPHICAL/CRITICAL SOURCES:

PERIODICALS

Los Angeles Times, March 26, 1980.

*   *   *

CARLSEN, Ruth C(hristoffer)   1918-

PERSONAL: Born February 21, 1918, in Milwaukee, Wis.; daughter of Carl Severin (a railroad official) and Lydia (Diefenthaeler) Christoffer; married George Robert Carlsen (a professor at University of Iowa), April 5, 1941; children: Christopher, Kristin, Peter, Jane. *Education:* University of Minnesota, B.A. (cum laude), 1939. *Religion:* Unitarian.

ADDRESSES: Home—817 North Gilbert, Iowa City, Iowa 52240.

CAREER: Writer.

MEMBER: Authors Guild, Authors League of America, National PEN Women's League, Athens Historical Circle, P.E.O. Sisterhood, Theta Sigma Phi.

WRITINGS:

CHILDREN'S FICTION

Mr. Pudgins, Houghton, 1953.
Henrietta Goes West, Houghton, 1966.
Hildy and the Cuckoo Clock, Houghton, 1966.
Monty and the Tree House, Houghton, 1967.
Sam Bottleby, Houghton, 1968.
Ride A Wild Horse, Houghton, 1970.
Sometimes It's Up, Houghton, 1971.
Half Past Tomorrow, Houghton, 1973.

EDITOR WITH HUSBAND, G. ROBERT CARLSEN

The Great Auto Race, and Other Stories of Men and Cars, Scholastic Book Services, 1965.

Fifty-two Miles to Terror (collection), Scholastic Book Services, 1966.
(And others) *Encounters: Themes in Literature*, McGraw, 1967, 4th edition, 1985.
(And others) *Western Literature: Themes and Writers*, McGraw, 1967, 3rd edition published as *British and Western Literature*, 1979, 4th edition published as *British and Western Literature: A Thematic Approach*, 1985.
(And others) *Perception: Themes in Literature*, McGraw, 1969, 4th edition, 1985.
(And others) *English Literature: A Chronological Approach*, McGraw, 1984.

OTHER

Also author, with G. R. Carlsen, of teacher's manual for each text in each edition of "Themes and Writers" literature series, which became the McGraw-Hill literature series in 1984.

WORK IN PROGRESS: Fifth edition of four volumes, with G. R. Carlsen, in the McGraw-Hill literature series; an epistolary recounting of thirty years of *Life at the Carlsens'*, as revealed in hundreds of letters written during that period with only a limited publication in mind.

SIDELIGHTS: Ruth C. Carlsen told *CA:* "I have always felt that laughter is a very precious and a much too scarce experience in children's lives. And so, I have written my stories hoping to catch my audience unaware and surprise them into giggles and snorts. To hear children laughing out loud when one of my stories is read to them is one of the delights of my life.

"My first book, *Mr. Pudgins,* was immediately accepted on first reading by Houghton Mifflin which gave me super-confidence that my next books would cause as few birth pangs. How wrong I was proved. My next attempts were either aborted or stillborn. I had no other books published until fifteen years after Mr. Pudgin's appearance and then I was doubly blessed when *Hildy and the Cuckoo Clock* and *Henrietta Goes West* both came out in 1966.

"I have always tried to have real children living in a real world experience fantastic incidents which can almost but not quite be explained by the knowledge of the real world. It gives me the sensation of walking a tightrope, and keeping my balance is not easy.

"Now I have reached another plateau. My mind is filled with stories, but I never seem to have the time to type them down on paper. Instead I work away at my husband's literary series which keeps me writing, but not in the old way."

More recently, Carlsen added: "Now I have been converted to using a word processor and often find myself at war with a machine. Since I'm self-taught, I often get into situations where my personal computer delights in proving how superior is the mind of a machine over that of a lowly human. After nine months of humiliation at its keyboard, I discovered that the seller had neglected to install a conductor to make the computer and the drive compatible. It is no wonder that I seriously thought of having a nervous breakdown during the stress of the conflict. Now it is not all delight. But at least I have moved into a more tranquil period and I relish the ease with which one can change a bit of writing here and a bit more there without retyping page after page of manuscript."

AVOCATIONAL INTERESTS: Travel, quilt making, needlepoint, speeches.

CESAIRE, Aime (Fernand) 1913-

PERSONAL: Born June 25, 1913, in Basse-Pointe, Martinique, West Indies; son of Fernand (a comptroller with the revenue service) and Marie (Hermine) Cesaire; married Suzanne Roussi (a teacher), July 10, 1937; children: Jacques, Jean-Paul, Francis, Ina, Marc, Michelle. *Education:* Attended Ecole Normale Superieure, Paris; Sorbonne, University of Paris, licencie es lettres.

ADDRESSES: Office—Assemblee Nationale, 75007 Paris, France; and La Mairie, 97200 Fort-de-France, Martinique, West Indies.

CAREER: Lycee of Fort-de-France, Martinique, teacher, 1940-45; member of the two French constituent assemblies, 1945-46; mayor of Fort-de-France, 1945—; deputy for Martinique in the French National Assembly, 1946—. Conseiller general for the fourth canton (district) of Fort-de-France; president of the Parti Progressiste Martiniquais.

AWARDS, HONORS: Aime Cesaire: The Collected Poetry was nominated for *Los Angeles Times* Book Award, 1984.

WRITINGS:

(With Gaston Monnerville and Leopold Sedar-Senghor) *Commemoration du centenaire de l'abolition de l'esclavage: Discours pronounces a la Sorbonne le 27 avril 1948* (title means "Commemoration of the Centenary of the Abolition of Slavery: Speeches Given at the Sorbonne on April 27, 1948"), Presses Universitaires de France, 1948.
Discours sur le colonialisme, Reclame, 1950, 5th edition, Presence Africaine (Paris), 1970, translation by Joan Pinkham published as *Discourse on Colonialism*, Monthly Review Press, 1972.
Lettre a Maurice Thorez, 3rd edition, Presence Africaine, 1956, translation published as *Letter to Maurice Thorez*, Presence Africaine, 1957.
Toussaint L'Ouverture: la revolution francaise et le probleme coloniale (title means "Toussaint L'Ouverture: The French Revolution and the Colonial Problem"), Club Francais du Livre, 1960, revised edition, Presence Africaine, 1962.
Ouvres completes (title means "Complete Works"), three volumes, Editions Desormeaux, 1976.
(Contributor) *Studies in French*, William Marsh Rice University, 1977.
Culture and Colonization, University of Yaounde, 1978.

POEMS

Les armes miraculeuses (title means "The Miracle Weapons"; also see below), Gallimard, 1946, reprinted, 1970.
Soleil Cou-Coupe (title means "Solar Throat Slashed"), K (Paris), 1948, reprinted (bound with *Antilles a main armee* by Charles Calixte), Kraus, 1970.
Cahier d'un retour au pays natal, Presence Africaine, 1956, 2nd edition, 1960, translation by Emil Snyders published as *Return to My Native Land*, Presence Africaine, 1968, translation by John Berger and Anna Bostock published under same title, Penguin Books, 1969.
Ferrements (title means "Shackles"; also see below), Editions du Seuil, 1960.
Cadastre (also see below), Editions de Seuil, 1961, translation by Gregson Davis published as *Cadastre*, Third Press, 1972, translation by Snyders and Sanford Upson published under same title, Third Press, 1973.

State of the Union, translation by Clayton Eshleman and Dennis Kelly of selections from *Les armes miraculeuses, Ferrements,* and *Cadastre,* [Bloomington, Ill.], 1966.

Aime Cesaire: The Collected Poetry, translation and with an introduction by Eshleman and Annette Smith, University of California Press, 1983.

Non-Vicious Circle: Twenty Poems, translation by Davis, Stanford University Press, 1985.

Also author of *Corps perdu* (title means "Lost Body"), illustrations by Pablo Picasso, 1949, and of *Moi, laminaire.*

PLAYS

Et les chiens se taisaient: Tragedie (title means "And the Dogs Were Silent: A Tragedy"), Presence Africaine, 1956.

La tragedie du roi Christophe, Presence Africaine, 1963, revised edition, 1973, translation by Ralph Manheim published as *The Tragedy of King Christophe,* Grove, 1970.

Une saison au Congo, Editions du Seuil, 1966, translation by Manheim published as *A Season in the Congo* (produced in New York at the Paperback Studio Theatre, July, 1970), Grove, 1969.

Une tempete: d'apres "le tempete" de Shakespeare. Adaptation pour un theatre negre (title means "A Tempest: After 'The Tempest' by Shakespeare. Adaptation for the Negro Theatre"), Editions du Seuil, 1969.

OTHER

Editor of *Tropiques,* 1941-45, and of *L'Afrique.*

SIDELIGHTS: Because of his role in creating and promoting negritude, a cultural movement which calls for black people to renounce Western society and adopt the traditional values of black civilization, Aime Cesaire is a prominent figure among blacks in the Third World. A native of the Caribbean island of Martinique, where he has served as mayor of the city of Fort-de-France since 1945, Cesaire also enjoys an international literary reputation for his poems and plays. His 1,000-line poem *Return to My Native Land,* a powerful piece written in extravagant, surreal language and dealing with the reawakening of black racial awareness, is a major work in contemporary French-language literature. Cesaire is, Serge Gavronsky states in the *New York Times Book Review,* "one of the most powerful French poets of this century."

At the age of 18 Cesaire left his native Martinique, at that time a colony of France, to attend school in Paris. The city was the center for a number of political and cultural movements during the 1930s, several of which especially influenced the young Cesaire and his fellow black students. Marxism gave them a revolutionary perspective, while surrealism provided them with a modernist esthetic by which to express themselves. Together with Leon-Goutran Damas and Leopold Sedar Senghor, who later became president of Senegal, Cesaire founded the magazine *L'Etudiant Noir,* in which the ideology of negritude was first developed and explained. "Negritude . . . proclaimed a pride in black culture and, in turning their contemporaries' gaze away from the fascination of things French, these young students began a revolution in attitudes which was to make a profound impact after the war," Clive Wake explains in the *Times Literary Supplement.* The influence of the movement on black writers in Africa and the Caribbean was so pervasive that the term negritude has come to refer to "large areas of black African and Caribbean literature in French, roughly from the 1930s to the 1960s," Christopher Miller writes in the *Washington Post Book World.*

The first use of the word negritude occurred in Cesaire's poem *Return to My Native Land (Cahier d'un retour au pays natal),* first published in the magazine *Volontes* in 1939. In this poem, Cesaire combines an exuberant wordplay, an encyclopedic vocabulary, and daring surreal metaphors with bits of African and Caribbean black history to create an "exorcism . . . of the poet's 'civilized' instincts, his lingering shame at belonging to a country and a race so abject, servile, petty and repressed as is his," Marjorie Perloff writes in the *American Poetry Review.* Gavronsky explains that the poem "is a concerted effort to affirm [Cesaire's] stature in French letters by a sort of poetic one-upmanship but also a determination to create a new language capable of expressing his African heritage." *Return to My Native Land,* Perloff maintains, is "a paratactic catalogue poem that piles up phrase upon phrase, image upon image, in a complex network of repetitions, its thrust is to define the threshold between sleep and waking—the sleep of oppression, the blind acceptance of the status quo, that gives way to rebirth, to a new awareness of what is and may be."

Written as Cesaire himself was leaving Paris to return to Martinique, *Return to My Native Land* reverberates with both personal and racial significance. The poet's definition of his own negritude comes to symbolize the growing self-awareness of all blacks of their cultural heritage. Judith Gleason, writing in the *Negro Digest,* believes that Cesaire's poetry is "grounded in the historical sufferings of a chosen people" and so "his is an angry, authentic vision of the promised land." Jean Paul Sartre, in an article for *The Black American Writer: Poetry and Drama,* writes that "Cesaire's words do not describe negritude, they do not designate it, they do not copy it from the outside like a painter with a model: they *create* it; they compose it under our very eyes."

Several critics see Cesaire as a writer who embodies the larger struggles of his people in all of his poetry. Hilary Okam of *Yale French Studies,* for example, argues that "Cesaire's poetic idiosyncracies, especially his search for and use of uncommon vocabulary, are symptomatic of his own mental agony in the search for an exact definition of himself and, by extension, of his people and their common situation and destiny." Okam concludes that "it is clear from [Cesaire's] use of symbols and imagery, that despite years of alienation and acculturation he has continued to live in the concrete reality of his Negro-subjectivity." Writing in the *CLA Journal,* Ruth J. S. Simmons notes that although Cesaire's poetry is personal, he speaks from a perspective shared by many other blacks. "Poetry has been for him," Simmons explains, "an important vehicle of personal growth and self-revelation, [but] it has also been an important expression of the will and personality of a people. . . . It is . . . impossible to consider the work of Cesaire outside of the context of the poet's personal vision and definition of his art. He defines his past as African, his present as Antillean and his condition as one of having been exploited. . . . To remove Cesaire from this context is to ignore what he was and still is as a man and as a poet."

The concerns found in *Return to My Native Land* ultimately transcend the personal or racial, addressing liberation and self-awareness in universal terms. Gleason calls *Return to My Native Land* "a masterpiece of cultural relevance, every bit as 'important' as 'The Wasteland,' its remarkable virtuosity will ensure its eloquence long after the struggle for human dignity has ceased to be viewed in racial terms." Andre Breton, writing in *What Is Surrealism?: Selected Writings,* also sees larger issues at stake in the poem. "What, in my eyes, renders this protest invaluable," Breton states, "is that it continually transcends the anguish which for a black man is inseparable from the lot of blacks in modern society, and unites with the protest of every poet, artist and thinker worthy of the name . . . to embrace the entire intolerable though amendable condition created for *man* by this society.''

Cesaire's poetic language was strongly influenced by the French surrealists of the 1930s, but he uses familiar surrealist poetic techniques in a distinctive manner. Breton claims that Cesaire ''is a black man who handles the French language as no white man can handle it today.'' Alfred Cismaru states in *Renascence* that Cesaire's ''separation from Europe makes it possible for him to break with clarity and description, and to become intimate with the fundamental essence of things. Under his powerful, poetic eye, perception knows no limits and pierces appearances without pity. Words emerge and explode like firecrackers, catching the eye and the imagination of the reader. He makes use of the entire dictionary, of artificial and vulgar words, of elegant and forgotten ones, of technical and invented vocabulary, marrying it to Antillean and African syllables, and allowing it to play freely in a sort of flaming folly that is both a challenge and a tenacious attempt at mystification.''

The energy of Cesaire's poetic language is seen by some critics as a form of literary violence, with the jarring images and forceful rhythms of the poetry assaulting the reader. Perloff finds that Cesaire's ''is a language so violently charged with meaning that each word falls on the ear (or hits the eye) with resounding force.'' Gleason explains this violence as the expression of an entire race, not just of one man: ''Cesaire's is the turbulent poetry of the spiritually dislocated, of the damned. His images strike through the net. . . . Cesaire's is the Black Power of the imagination.''

This violent energy is what first drew Cesaire to surrealism. The surrealist artists and writers of the 1930s saw themselves as rebels against a stale and outmoded culture. Their works were meant to revive and express unconscious, suppressed, and forbidden desires. Politically, they aligned themselves with the revolutionary left. As Gavronsky explains, ''Cesaire's efforts to forge a verbal medium that would identify him with the opposition to existing political conditions and literary conventions [led him to] the same camp as the Surrealists, who had combined a new poetics that liberated the image from classical restraints with revolutionary politics influenced by Marx and his followers.'' Cesaire was to remain a surrealist for many years, but he eventually decided that his political concerns would best be served by more realistic forms of writing. ''For decades,'' Karl Keller notes in the *Los Angeles Times Book Review*, ''[Cesaire] found the surreal aesthetically revolutionary, but in the face of the torture and the suffering, he has pretty well abandoned it as a luxury.''

In the late 1950s Cesaire began to write realistic plays for the theatre, hoping in this way to attract a larger audience to his work. These plays are more explicitly political than his poetry and focus on historical black nationalist leaders of the Third World. *The Tragedy of King Christophe (La tragedie du roi Christophe)* is a biographical drama about King Henri Christophe of Haiti, a black leader of that island nation in the early nineteenth century. After fighting in a successful revolution against the French colonists, Christophe assumed power and made himself king. But his cruelty and arbitrary use of power led to a rebellion in turn against his own rule, and Christophe committed suicide. Writing in *Studies in Black Literature*, Henry Cohen calls *The Tragedy of King Christophe* ''one of French

America's finest literary expressions.'' *A Season in the Congo (Une saison au Congo)* follows the political career of Patrice Lumumba, first president of the Republic of the Congo in Africa. Lumumba's career was also tragic. With the independence of the Congo in 1960, Lumumba became president of the new nation. But the resulting power struggles among black leaders led in 1961 to Lumumba's assassination by his political opponents. The reviewer for *Prairie Schooner* calls *A Season in the Congo* ''a passionate and poetic drama.'' Wake remarks that Cesaire's plays have ''greatly widened [his] audience and perhaps tempted them to read the poetry.'' Gavronsky claims that ''in the [1960s, Cesaire] was . . . the leading black dramatist writing in French.''

Despite the international acclaim he has received for his poetry and plays, Cesaire is still best known on Martinique for his political career. Since 1945 he has served as mayor of Fort-de-France and as a member of the French National Assembly. For the first decade of his career Cesaire was affiliated with the Communist bloc of the assembly, then moved to the Parti du Regroupement Africain et des Federalistes for a short time, and is now president of the Parti Progressiste Martiniquais, a leftist political organization. Cesaire's often revolutionary rhetoric is in sharp contrast to his usually moderate political actions. He opposes independence for Martinique, for example, and was instrumental in having the island declared an oversea department of France—a status similar to that of Puerto Rico to the United States. And as a chief proponent of negritude, which calls for blacks to reject Western culture, Cesaire nonetheless writes his works in French, not in his native black language of creole.

But what may seem contradictory in Cesaire's life and work is usually seen by critics as the essential tension that makes his voice uniquely important. A. James Arnold, in his *Modernism and Negritude: The Poetry and Poetics of Aime Cesaire*, examines and accepts the tension between Cesaire's European literary sources and his black subject matter and between his modernist sensibility and his black nationalist concerns. Miller explains that ''Arnold poses the riddle of Cesaire with admirable clarity'' and ''effectively defuses . . . either a wholly African or a wholly European Cesaire.'' This uniting of the European and African is also noted by Clayton Eshleman and Annette Smith in their introduction to *Aime Cesaire: The Collected Poetry*. They describe Cesaire as ''a bridge between the twain that, in principle, should never meet, Europe and Africa. . . . It was by borrowing European techniques that he succeeded in expressing his Africanism in its purest form.'' Similarly, Sartre argues that ''in Cesaire, the great surrealist tradition is realized, it takes on its definitive meaning and is destroyed: surrealism—that European movement—is taken from the Europeans by a Black man who turns it against them and gives it vigorously defined function.''

It is because of his poetry that Cesaire is primarily known worldwide, while in the Third World he is usually seen as an important black nationalist theoretician. Speaking of his poetry, Gavronsky explains that Cesaire is ''among the major French poets of this century.'' Cismaru believes that Cesaire ''is a poet's poet when he stays clear of political questions, a tenacious and violent propagandist when the theme requires it. His place in contemporary French letters . . . is assured in spite of the fact that not many agree with his views on Whites in general, nor with his opinions on Europe, in particular.'' *Return to My Native Land* has been his most influential work, particularly in the Third World where, Wake notes, ''by the 1960s it was widely known and quoted because of its ideological and political significance." To European and American critics, *Return to My Native Land* is seen as a masterpiece of surrealist literature. Cesaire's coining of the term negritude and his continued promotion of a distinctly black culture separate from Western culture has made him especially respected in the emerging black nations. Eshleman and Smith report that "although Cesaire was by no means the sole exponent of negritude, the word is now inseparable from his name, and largely responsible for his prominent position in the Third World."

BIOGRAPHICAL/CRITICAL SOURCES:

BOOKS

Aime Cesaire: Ecrivain Martiniquais, Fernand Nathan, 1967.
Arnold, A. James, *Modernism and Negritude: The Poetry and Poetics of Aime Cesaire,* Harvard University Press, 1981.
Bigsby, C. W. E., editor, *The Black American Writer: Poetry and Drama,* Volume II, Penguin Books, 1971.
Breton, Andre, *What Is Surrealism?: Selected Writings,* edited by Franklin Rosemont, Monad Press, 1978.
Contemporary Literary Criticism, Gale, Volume XIX, 1981, Volume XXXII, 1985.
Kesteloot, Lilyan, *Aime Cesaire,* P. Seghers, 1962, new edition, 1970.
Leiner, Jacqueline, *Soleil eclate: Melanges offerts a Aime Cesaire a l'occasion de son soixante-dixieme anniversaire par une equipe internationale d'artiste et de chercheurs,* Gunter Narr Verlag (Tubingen), 1985.

PERIODICALS

American Poetry Review, January-February, 1984.
CLA Journal, March, 1976.
Comparative Literature Studies, summer, 1978.
Le Monde, December, 1981.
Los Angeles Times Book Review, December 4, 1983.
Negro Digest, January, 1970.
New York Times Book Review, February 19, 1984.
Prairie Schooner, spring, 1972.
Renascence, winter, 1974.
Studies in Black Literature, winter, 1974.
Times Literary Supplement, July 19, 1985.
Twentieth Century Literature, July, 1972.
Washington Post Book World, February 5, 1984.
Yale French Studies, Number 53, 1976.†

—*Sketch by Thomas Wiloch*

*   *   *

CHARLES, Donald
See MEIGHAN, Donald Charles

*   *   *

CHASE, Alice
See McHARGUE, Georgess

*   *   *

CHEVALIER, Christa   1937-

PERSONAL: Born March 25, 1937, in Limbach, Germany (now Limboch-Oberfrohna, East Germany); came to the United States in 1957, naturalized citizen, 1959; daughter of Heinz (in business) and Hilde (Kassubeck) Huebler; married David Chevalier (in business), July 23, 1956; children: Diana, Denise. *Education:* Attended art schools in Braunschweig, West Germany, 1953, and Wiesbaden, West Germany, 1969.

ADDRESSES: Home—29 Dewey St., Richford, Vt. 05476.

CAREER: Richford High School, Richford, Vt., teacher, 1974-79; full-time writer and illustrator, 1980—. Member of faculty at Johnson State College, 1977-78.

WRITINGS:

JUVENILES

Little Green Pumpkins, Albert Whitman, 1981.
Spence Makes Circles, Albert Whitman, 1982.
Spence and the Sleepytime Monster, Albert Whitman, 1984.
The Little Bear Who Forgot, Albert Whitman, 1984.
Spence Isn't Spence Anymore, Albert Whitman, 1985.
Spence and the Mean Old Bear, Albert Whitman, 1986.
Spence Is Small, Albert Whitman, 1987.

SIDELIGHTS: Christa Chevalier told *CA:* "At my present stage as an author, I am too exhausted from the struggle to utter words of wisdom. I am overwhelmed that I made it."

AVOCATIONAL INTERESTS: Gardening, cooking, reading, skiing, collecting "old-time stuff."

*   *   *

CHILCOTE, Ronald H.   1935-

PERSONAL: Born February 20, 1935, in Cleveland, Ohio; son of Lee A. (a businessman) and Katherine (Hodell) Chilcote; married Frances Tubby, January 6, 1961; children: Stephen, Edward. *Education:* Dartmouth College, B.A., 1957; Stanford University, M.B.A., 1959, M.A., 1963, Ph.D., 1965; University of Lisbon, Diploma Superior, 1960; University of Madrid, Diploma Estudios Hispanicos, 1961.

ADDRESSES: Home—1940 San Remo Dr., Laguna Beach, Calif. 92651. *Office*—Department of Political Science, University of California, Riverside, Calif. 92502.

CAREER: Stanford University, Stanford, Calif., assistant director of Institute of Hispanic American and Luso-Brazilian Studies, 1961-63; University of California, Riverside, 1963—, began as assistant professor, currently professor of political science, coordinator of Latin American research program, 1964-70.

MEMBER: International Political Science Association, Latin American Studies Association, African Studies Association, American Political Science Association.

AWARDS, HONORS: University of California faculty fellowship, 1965; Haynes Foundation fellowship, 1966; Organization of American States grant, 1971; Social Science Research Council grants, 1971 and 1974-75; Fulbright senior lectureship and grant (Brazil), 1983 and 1984.

WRITINGS:

The Press in Spain, Portugal, and Latin America: A Summary of Recent Developments, Institute of Hispanic American and Luso-Brazilian Studies, Stanford University, 1963.
Portuguese Africa, Prentice-Hall, 1967.
Spain's Iron and Steel Industry (monograph), Bureau of Business Research, University of Texas, 1968.
Emerging Nationalism in Portuguese Africa: A Bibliography of Documentary Ephemera through 1965, Hoover Institution on War, Revolution, and Peace, 1969, new edition, 1972.
(Compiler) *Protest and Resistance in Angola and Brazil,* University of California Press, 1972.

The Brazilian Communist Party: Conflict and Integration, 1922-1972, Oxford University Press, 1974.

(Editor with Joel C. Edelstein) *Latin America: The Struggle with Dependency and Beyond*, Schenkman, 1974.

(Compiler) *Brazil and Its Radical Left: An Annotated Bibliography, 1922-1972*, Kraus International, 1981.

Theories of Comparative Politics: The Search for a Paradigm, Westview, 1981.

(Editor) *Dependency and Marxism: Toward a Resolution of the Debate*, Westview, 1982.

O Partido Comunista Brasileiro, Edicoes Graal, 1982.

(Editor with Dale Johnson) *Theories of Development: Mode of Production or Dependency?*, Sage Publications, 1983.

Theories of Development and Underdevelopment, Westview, 1984.

(Compiler with Sherry C. Lutjens) *Cuba, 1953-1978: A Bibliographical Guide to the Literature*, two volumes, Kraus International, 1986.

(With Joel C. Edelstein) *Latin America: Capitalist and Socialist Perspectives of Development and Underdevelopment*, Westview, 1986.

Also editor of volume on "The Americas," *Worldmark Encyclopedia of Nations*, 1963; also contributor to encyclopedias and yearbooks. Contributor of about one hundred fifty articles and reviews to journals and newspapers, including *Latin American Research Review*, *Comparative Political Studies*, *Nation*, *New Republic*, *Journal of Modern African Studies*, *International Journal of Comparative Sociology*, and *Los Angeles Times*. Assistant editor of *Hispanic American Report*, 1961-63; managing editor of *Latin American Perspectives*, 1974—.

WORK IN PROGRESS: Power and Ruling Classes in Two Communities of Backlands Brazil.

* * *

CLARK, Christopher (Anthony) Stuart
 See STUART-CLARK, Christopher (Anthony)

* * *

CLARKE, Brenda (Margaret Lilian) 1926-
 (Brenda Honeyman)

PERSONAL: Born July 30, 1926, in Bristol, England; daughter of Edward (an insurance agent) and Lilian Rose (Brown) Honeyman; married Ronald John Clarke (a civil servant), March 5, 1955; children: Roger Stephen, Gwithian Margaret. *Education:* Cambridge University, school certificate, 1942. *Politics:* Socialist. *Religion:* Methodist.

ADDRESSES: Home—25 Torridge Rd., Keynsham, Bristol, Avon BS18 1QQ, England. *Agent*—David Grossman Literary Agency Ltd., 110/114 Clerkenwell Rd., London EC1M 5SA, England.

CAREER: British Civil Service, Ministry of Labour, Bristol, England, clerical officer, 1942-55; writer, 1968—. Section leader for British Red Cross, 1941-45.

MEMBER: Society of Authors, Wessex Writers' Association.

WRITINGS:

The Glass Island, Collins, 1978.
The Lofty Banners, Fawcett, 1979.
The Far Morning, Fawcett, 1982.
All through the Day, Hamlyn Paperbacks, 1983.

UNDER NAME BRENDA HONEYMAN

Richard by Grace of God, R. Hale, 1968.
The Kingmaker, R. Hale, 1969.
Richmond and Elizabeth, R. Hale, 1970, Pinnacle, 1973.
Harry the King, R. Hale, 1971, published as *The Warrior King*, Pinnacle, 1972.
Brother Bedford, R. Hale, 1972.
Good Duke Humphrey, R. Hale, 1973.
The King's Minions, R. Hale, 1974.
The Queen and Mortimer, R. Hale, 1974.
Edward the Warrior, R. Hale, 1975.
All the King's Sons, R. Hale, 1976.
The Golden Griffin, R. Hale, 1976.
At the King's Court, R. Hale, 1977.
A King's Tale, R. Hale, 1977.
Macbeth, King of Scots, R. Hale, 1977.
Emma, the Queen, R. Hale, 1978.
Harold of the English, R. Hale, 1979.
A Rose in May, Hutchinson, 1985.
Three Women, Hutchinson, 1985.
Winter Landscape, Century Hutchinson, 1986.
Under Heaven, Bantam, 1988.

SIDELIGHTS: Brenda Clarke told *CA:* "Acquiring an agent changed the course of my writing career. Instead of 'factional' novels about the Middle Ages and Saxon England, [my agent] persuaded me to turn my attention to romantic fiction."

AVOCATIONAL INTERESTS: Theatre, reading, history, music.

* * *

CLARKE, James Hall
 See ROWLAND-ENTWISTLE, (Arthur) Theodore (Henry)

* * *

CLARKE, John Henrik 1915-

PERSONAL: Born January 1, 1915, in Union Springs, Ala.; son of John (a farmer) and Willella (Mays) Clarke; married Eugenia Evans (a teacher), December 24, 1961; children: Nzingha Marie, Sonni Kojo. *Education:* Attended New York University, 1948-52, New School for Social Research, 1956-58, University of Ibadan (Nigeria), University of Ghana. *Politics:* Socialism. *Religion:* Nondenominational.

ADDRESSES: Home—223 West 137th St., New York, N.Y. 10030. *Agent*—Ronald Hobbs Literary Agency, 516 Fifth Ave., Suite 507, New York, N.Y. 10036.

CAREER: Pittsburgh Courier, Pittsburgh, Pa., feature writer, 1957-58; *Ghana Evening News*, Accra, Ghana, feature writer, 1958; New School for Social Research, New York City, occasional teacher of African and Afro-American history, 1956-58, developer of African Study Center, 1957-59, assistant to director, 1958-60; Hunter College of the City University of New York, New York City, associate professor of Black and Puerto Rican studies, 1970—. Director, Haryou-Act (teaching program), 1964-69; director of training program in Black history, Columbia University, summer, 1969; Carter G. Woodson distinguished visiting professor in African history, Cornell University, 1969—; visiting lecturer, New York University; teacher (by special license) at Malverne High School (People's College), Malverne, N.Y. Research director for African Heritage Exposition in New York City, 1959; coordinator and special consultant to Columbia Broadcasting System, Inc. (CBS-TV) television series, "Black Heritage," 1968; consultant to American Heritage Press and John Wiley & Sons (publishers). Member of board of directors of Langston Hughes Center for Child Development, 1967—; member of advisory board of Martin Luther King Library Center, 1969. *Military service:* U.S. Army Air Forces, 1941-45; became master sergeant.

MEMBER: International Society of African Culture, African Studies Association, American Society of African Culture, Black Academy of Arts and Letters (founding member), Association for Study of Negro Life and History (vice-president, 1949-55), American Historical Society, American Academy of Political and Social Science, African Heritage Studies Association (president, 1969-73), African Scholars Council (member of board of directors), Harlem Writers Guild (founding member).

AWARDS, HONORS: Carter G. Woodson Award, 1968, for creative contribution in editing, and 1971, for excellence in teaching; National Association for Television and Radio Announcers citation for meritorious achievement in educational television, 1969; L.H.D. from University of Denver, 1970.

WRITINGS:

Rebellion in Rhyme (poems), Dicker Press, 1948.
(Editor) *Harlem U.S.A.: The Story of a City within a City,* Seven Seas Books (Berlin), 1964, revised edition, Collier, 1970.
(Editor) *Harlem: A Community in Transition,* Citadel, 1965, 3rd edition, 1970.
(Editor) *American Negro Short Stories,* Hill & Wang, 1966.
(Editor) *William Styron's Nat Turner: Ten Black Writers Respond,* Beacon Press, 1968, reprinted, Greenwood Press, 1987.
Black Soldier, illustrated by Harold James, Doubleday, 1968.
(Editor and author of introduction) *Malcolm X: The Man and His Times,* Macmillan, 1969.
(Editor with Vincent Harding) *Slave Trade and Slavery,* Holt, 1970.
(Editor) *Harlem* (short stories), New American Library, 1970.
(Editor with others) *Black Titan: W. E. B. Du Bois,* Beacon Press, 1970.
(Editor) J. A. Rogers, *World's Great Men of Color,* two volumes, Macmillan, 1972.
(Editor with Amy Jacques Garvey, and author of introduction and commentaries) *Marcus Garvey and the Vision of Africa,* Random House, 1974.
(Guest editor) *Black Families in the American Economy,* Education-Community Counselors Association (Washington, D.C.), 1975.
(Editor) *Dimensions of the Struggle against Apartheid: A Tribute to Paul Robeson,* African Heritage Studies Association in cooperation with United Nations Centre against Apartheid, 1979.

Also author of "The Lives of Great African Chiefs" published serially in *Pittsburgh Courier,* 1957-58, and of syndicated column, "African World Bookshelf." Author of numerous papers on African studies presented at international conferences. Contributor to *Negro History Bulletin, Chicago Defender, Journal of Negro Education, Phylon, Presence Africaine,* and others. Book review editor, *Negro History Bulletin,* 1947-49; co-founder and associate editor, *Harlem Quarterly,* 1949-51; editor, *African Heritage,* 1959; associate editor, *Freedomways,* 1962—.

WORK IN PROGRESS: The Black Woman in History; an African curriculum for elementary school teachers.

SIDELIGHTS: As an editor, essayist, and educator, John Henrik Clarke has written and lectured extensively about African and Afro-American history both in the United States and West Africa. *Malcolm X: The Man and His Times,* a collection of essays about and writings by Malcolm X edited by Clarke, is described by the *New York Times*'s Christopher Lehmann-Haupt: "Malcolm is seen through different eyes at various stages of his career as Muslim, ex-Muslim, and founder of the Organization of Afro-American Unity. He is defined and redefined by friends and followers." And although Lehmann-Haupt considers the collection "overwhelmingly sympathetic," he thinks that Clarke has produced a "multifaceted picture that . . . traces his development from drifter to prophet, spells out his aims (and thereby dispels his distorted image as apostle of violent separatism) and explains why his stature among so many blacks today is heroic." Similarly, in the *New York Review of Books,* Charles V. Hamilton finds that "Clarke has done an excellent job of pulling together various stimulating sources to give the reader what the title promises, a look at the man and his time—a look at a genuine folk hero of black Americans and a master of the Politics of Sportsmanship."

BIOGRAPHICAL/CRITICAL SOURCES:

BOOKS

Authors in the News, Volume I, Gale, 1976.

PERIODICALS

Atlanta Journal, April 8, 1973.
Black World, February, 1971.
New York Review of Books, September 12, 1968.
New York Times, May 10, 1967, August 1-2, 1968, September 29, 1969.
New York Times Book Review, March 5, 1967, August 11, 1968, September 28, 1969.
Saturday Review, January 14, 1967, August 12, 1968.†

*　　*　　*

CLARKE, Lea
　See ROWLAND-ENTWISTLE, (Arthur) Theodore (Henry)

*　　*　　*

CLARKE, Robert
　See PLATT, Charles

*　　*　　*

CLIFTON, (Thelma) Lucille　1936-

PERSONAL: Born June 27, 1936, in Depew, N.Y.; daughter of Samuel Louis, Sr. (a laborer) and Thelma (a laborer; maiden name, Moore) Sayles; married Fred James Clifton (an educator, writer, and artist), May 10, 1958 (died November 10, 1984); children: Sidney, Fredrica, Channing, Gillian, Graham, Alexia. *Education:* Attended Howard University, 1953-55, and Fredonia State Teachers College (now State University of New York College at Fredonia), 1955.

ADDRESSES: Agent—Marilyn Marlow, Curtis Brown Ltd., 10 Astor Pl., New York, N.Y. 10003.

CAREER: New York State Division of Employment, Buffalo, claims clerk, 1958-60; U.S. Office of Education, Washington,

D.C., literature assistant for CAREL (Central Atlantic Regional Educational Laboratory), 1969-71; Coppin State College, Baltimore, Md., poet in residence, 1971-74; writer. Visiting writer, Columbia University School of the Arts; Jerry Moore Visiting Writer, George Washington University, 1982-83; University of California, Santa Cruz, professor of literature and creative writing, 1985—. Trustee, Enoch Pratt Free Library, Baltimore.

MEMBER: International PEN, Authors Guild, Authors League of America.

AWARDS, HONORS: Discovery Award, New York YW-YMHA Poetry Center, 1969; *Good Times: Poems* cited as one of the year's ten best books by the *New York Times*, 1969; National Endowment for the Arts awards, 1970 and 1972; Poet Laureate of the State of Maryland, 1979-82; Juniper Prize, 1980; Coretta Scott King Award, 1984, for *Everett Anderson's Goodbye*. Honorary degrees from University of Maryland and Towson State University.

WRITINGS:

ADULTS

Good Times: Poems, Random House, 1969.
Good News about the Earth: New Poems, Random House, 1972.
An Ordinary Woman (poetry), Random House, 1974.
Generations: A Memoir (prose), Random House, 1976.
Two-Headed Woman (poetry), University of Massachusetts Press, 1980.
Good Woman: Poems and a Memoir, 1969-1980, Boa Editions, 1987.
Next: New Poems, Boa Editions, 1987.

JUVENILES

The Black BCs (alphabet poems), Dutton, 1970.
Good, Says Jerome, illustrations by Stephanie Douglas, Dutton, 1973.
All Us Come Cross the Water, pictures by John Steptoe, Holt, 1973.
Don't You Remember?, illustrations by Evaline Ness, Dutton, 1973.
The Boy Who Didn't Believe in Spring, pictures by Brinton Turkle, Dutton, 1973.
The Times They Used to Be, illustrations by Susan Jeschke, Holt, 1974.
My Brother Fine with Me, illustrations by Moneta Barnett, Holt, 1975.
Three Wishes, illustrations by Douglas, Viking, 1976.
Amifika, illustrations by Thomas DiGrazia, Dutton, 1977.
The Lucky Stone, illustrations by Dale Payson, Delacorte, 1979.
My Friend Jacob, illustrations by DiGrazia, Dutton, 1980.
Sonora Beautiful, illustrations by Michael Garland, Dutton, 1981.

"EVERETT ANDERSON" SERIES; JUVENILE

Some of the Days of Everett Anderson, Holt, 1970.
Everett Anderson's Christmas Coming, illustrations by Ness, Holt, 1971.
Everett Anderson's Year, illustrations by Ann Grifalconi, Holt, 1974.
Everett Anderson's Friend, illustrations by Grifalconi, Holt, 1976.
Everett Anderson's 1 2 3, illustrations by Grifalconi, Holt, 1977.

Everett Anderson's Nine Month Long, illustrations by Grifalconi, Holt, 1978.
Everett Anderson's Goodbye, illustrations by Grifalconi, Holt, 1983.

OTHER

(Contributor) Marlo Thomas and others, *Free to Be . . . You and Me,* McGraw-Hill, 1974.
(Contributor) Langston Hughes and Arna Bontemps, *Poetry of the Negro, 1746-1970,* Doubleday, 1970.

Also contributor to *Free to Be a Family,* 1987, *Norton Anthology of Literature by Women, Coming into the Light,* and *Stealing the Language.* Contributor of fiction to *Negro Digest, Redbook, House and Garden,* and *Atlantic.* Contributor of nonfiction to *Ms.* and *Essence.*

SIDELIGHTS: Lucille Clifton "began composing and writing stories at an early age and has been much encouraged by an ever-growing reading audience and a fine critical reputation," writes Wallace R. Peppers in a *Dictionary of Literary Biography* essay. "In many ways her themes are traditional: she writes of her family because she is greatly interested in making sense of their lives and relationships; she writes of adversity and success in the ghetto community; and she writes of her role as a poet." Clifton's work emphasizes endurance and strength through adversity. Ronald Baughman suggests in his *Dictionary of Literary Biography* essay that "Clifton's pride in being black and in being a woman helps her transform difficult circumstances into a qualified affirmation about the black urban world she portrays." Writing in Mari Evans's *Black Women Writers (1950-1980): A Critical Evaluation,* Haki Madhubuti (formerly Don L. Lee) states: "She is a writer of complexity, and she makes her readers work and think. Her poetry has a quiet force without being pushy or alien. Whether she is cutting through family relationships, surviving American racial attitudes, or just simply renewing love ties, she puts something heavy on your mind. The great majority of her published poetry is significant. At the base of her work is concern for the Black family, especially the destruction of its youth. Her eye is for the uniqueness of our people, always concentrating on the small strengths that have allowed us to survive the horrors of Western life."

Clifton's first volume of poetry, *Good Times: Poems,* which was cited by the *New York Times* as one of 1969's ten best books, is described by Peppers as a "varied collection of character sketches written with third person narrative voices." Baughman notes that "these poems attain power not only through their subject matter but also through their careful techniques; among Clifton's most successful poetic devices . . . are the precise evocative images that give substance to her rhetorical statements and a frequent duality of vision that lends complexity to her portraits of place and character." Calling the book's title "ironic," Baughman indicates, "Although the urban ghetto can, through its many hardships, create figures who are tough enough to survive and triumph, the overriding concern of this book is with the horrors of the location, with the human carnage that results from such problems as poverty, unemployment, substandard housing, and inadequate education." Baughman recognizes that although "these portraits of human devastation reflect the trying circumstances of life in the ghetto . . . the writer also records some joy in her world, however strained and limited that joy might be." Madhubuti thinks that although this is her first book of poetry, it "cannot be looked upon as simply a 'first effort.' The work is unusually compacted and memory-evoking." As Johari Amini (formerly

Jewel C. Latimore) suggests in *Black World*, "The poetry is filled with the sensations of coming up black with the kind of love that keeps you from dying in desperation."

In Clifton's second volume of poetry, *Good News about the Earth: New Poems*, "the elusive good times seem more attainable," remarks Baughman, who summarizes the three sections into which the book is divided: the first section "focuses on the sterility and destruction of 'white ways,' newly perceived through the social unheavals of the early 1970s"; the second section "presents a series of homages to black leaders of the late 1960s and early 1970s"; and the third section "deals with biblical characters powerfully rendered in terms of the black experience." Harriet Jackson Scarupa notes in *Ms.* that after having read what Clifton says about blackness and black pride, some critics "have concluded that Clifton hates whites. [Clifton] considers this a misreading. When she equates whiteness with death, blackness with life, she says: 'What I'm talking about is a certain kind of white arrogance—and not all white people have it—that is not good. I think airs of superiority are very dangerous. I believe in justice. I try not to be about hatred.'" Writing in *Poetry*, Ralph J. Mills, Jr. says that Clifton's poetic scope transcends the black experience "to embrace the entire world, human and non-human, in the deep affirmation she makes in the teeth of negative evidence. She is a master of her style, with its spare, elliptical, idiomatic, rhythmical speech, and of prophetic warning in the same language." Angela Jackson, who thinks that it "is a book written in wisdom," concludes in *Black World* that "Clifton and *Good News about the Earth* will make you shake yo head. Ain't nothing else to say."

An Ordinary Woman, Clifton's third collection of poems, "abandons many of the broad racial issues examined in the two preceding books and focuses instead on the narrower but equally complex issues of the writer's roles as woman and poet," says Baughman. Peppers notes that "the poems take as their theme a historical, social, and spiritual assessment of the current generation in the genealogical line" of Clifton's great great-grandmother who had been taken from her home in Dahomey, West Africa, and brought to America in slavery in 1830. Peppers notes that by taking an ordinary experience and personalizing it, "Clifton has elevated the experience into a public confession" which may be shared, and "it is this shared sense of situation, an easy identification between speaker and reader, that heightens the notion of ordinariness and gives... the collection an added dimension." Helen Vendler writes in the *New York Times Book Review* that "Clifton recalls for us those bare places we have all waited as 'ordinary women,' with no choices but yes or no, no art, no grace, no words, no reprieve." "Written in the same ironic, yet cautiously optimistic spirit as her earlier published work," observes Peppers, the book is "lively, full of vigor, passion, and an all-consuming honesty."

In *Generations: A Memoir*, "it is as if [Clifton] were showing us a cherished family album and telling us the story about each person which seemed to sum him or her up best," says a *New Yorker* contributor. Calling the book an "eloquent eulogy of [Clifton's] parents," Reynolds Price writes in the *New York Times Book Review* that "as with most elegists, her purpose is perpetuation and celebration, not judgment. There is no attempt to see either parent whole; no attempt at the recovery of history not witnessed by or told to the author. There is no sustained chronological narrative. Instead, clusters of brief anecdote gather round two poles, the deaths of father and mother." Price, however, believes that *Generations* stands "worthily"

among the other modern elegies which assert that "we may survive, some lively few, if we've troubled to *be* alive and loved." However, a contributor to *Virginia Quarterly Review* thinks that the book is "more than an elegy or a personal memoir. It is an attempt on the part of one woman to retrieve, and lyrically to celebrate, her Afro-American heritage."

"Clifton is a poet of a literary tradition which includes such varied poets as Walt Whitman, Emily Dickinson, and Gwendolyn Brooks, who have inspired and informed her work," writes Audrey T. McCluskey in Evans's *Black Women Writers (1950-1980)*. McCluskey finds that "Clifton's belief in her ability (and ours) to make things better and her belief in the concept of personal responsibility pervade her work. These views are especially pronounced in her books for children." Clifton's books for children are characterized by a positive view of black heritage and an urban setting peopled by non-traditional families. Critics recognize that although her works speak directly to a specific audience, they reveal the concerns of all children. In a *Language Arts* interview with Rudine Sims, Clifton was asked where she gets her ideas for stories: "Well, I had six kids in seven years, and when you have a lot of children, you tend to attract children, and you see so many kids, you get ideas from that. And I have such a good memory from my own childhood, my own time. I have great respect for young people; I like them enormously."

Clifton's books for children are designed to help them understand their world. *My Friend Jacob*, for instance, is a story "in which a black child speaks with affection and patience of his friendship with a white adolescent neighbor... who is retarded," writes Zena Sutherland in *Bulletin of the Center for Children's Books*. "Jacob is Sam's 'very very best friend' and all of his best qualities are appreciated by Sam, just as all of his limitations are accepted... it is strong in the simplicity and warmth with which a handicapped person is loved rather than pitied, enjoyed rather than tolerated." Critics find that Clifton's characters and their relationships are accurately and positively drawn. Ismat Abdal-Haqq notes in *Interracial Books for Children Bulletin* that "the two boys have a strong relationship filled with trust and affection. The author depicts this relationship and their everyday adventures in a way that is unmarred by the mawkish sentimentality that often characterizes tales of the mentally disabled." And a contributor to *Reading Teacher* states that "in a matter-of-fact, low-keyed style, we discover how [Sam and Jacob] help one another grow and understand the world."

Clifton's children's books also facilitate an understanding of black heritage specifically, which in turn fosters an important link with the past generally. Her *All Us Come Cross the Water*, for example, "in a very straight-forward way... shows the relationship of Africa to Blacks in the U.S. without getting into a heavy rap about 'Pan-Africanism,'" states Judy Richardson in the *Journal of Negro Education*, adding that Clifton "seems able to get inside a little boy's head, and knows how to represent that on paper." An awareness of one's origins figures also in *The Times They Used to Be*. Called a "short and impeccable vignette—laced with idiom and humor of rural Black folk," by Rosalind K. Goddard in *School Library Journal*, it is further described by Lee A. Daniels in the *Washington Post* as a "story in which a young girl catches her first glimpse of the new technological era in a hardware store window, and learns of death and life." "Most books that awaken adult nostalgia are not as appealing to young readers," says Sutherland in *Bulletin of the Center for Children's Books*, "but this brief story has enough warmth and vitality and humor for any reader.''

In addition to quickening an awareness of black heritage, Clifton's books for children frequently include an element of fantasy as well. Writing about *Three Wishes,* in which a young girl finds a lucky penny on New Year's Day and makes three wishes upon it, Christopher Lehmann-Haupt in the *New York Times Book Review* calls it ''an urbanized version of the traditional tale in which the first wish reveals the power of the magic object . . . the second wish is a mistake, and the third undoes the second.'' Lehmann-Haupt adds that ''too few children's books for blacks justify their ethnicity, but this one is a winning blend of black English and bright illustration.'' And *The Lucky Stone,* in which a lucky stone provides good fortune for all of its owners, is decribed by Ruth K. MacDonald in *School Library Journal* as: ''Four short stories about four generations of Black women and their dealings with a lucky stone. . . . Clifton uses as a frame device a grandmother telling the history of the stone to her granddaughter; by the end, the granddaughter has inherited the stone herself.'' A contributor to *Interracial Books for Children Bulletin* states that ''the concept of past and present is usually hard for children to grasp but this book puts the passing of time in a perspective that children can understand. . . . This book contains information on various aspects of Black culture—slavery, religion and extended family—all conveyed in a way that is both positive and accurate.'' Michele Slung writes in the *Washington Post Book World* that the book ''is at once talisman and anthology: over the years it has gathered unto it story after story, episodes indicating its power, both as a charm and as a unit of oral tradition. Clifton has a knack for projecting strong positive values without seeming too goody-goody; her poet's ear is one fact in this, her sense of humor another.''

While Clifton's books for children emphasize an understanding of the past, they also focus on the present. Her series of books about Everett Anderson, for instance, explore the experiences of a young child's world in flux. Writing in *Language Arts* about *Everett Anderson's 1 2 3,* in which a young boy's mother considers remarriage, Ruth M. Stein notes that ''previous books contained wistful references to Everett Anderson's absent daddy; the latest one tells how the worried little boy gradually became reconciled to the idea of a new father joining the family.'' And writing about *Everett Anderson's Nine Month Long,* which concerns the anticipated birth of the family's newest member, a contributor to *Interracial Books for Children Bulletin* considers that ''this book, written in wonderful poetic style . . . projects a warm, loving, understanding and supportive family.'' Joan W. Blos, who feels that ''the establishment of an active, effective, and supportive male figure is an important part of this story,'' adds in *School Library Journal,* ''So is its tacit acknowledgement that, for the younger child, a mother's pregnancy means disturbing changes now as well as a sibling later.'' However, just as the birth of a sibling can cause upheaval in a child's world, so, too, can death. In *Everett Anderson's Goodbye,* Everett has difficulty coping with the death of his father; he ''misses his Daddy, as he moves through the five stages of grief: denial, anger, bargaining, depression and acceptance,'' writes a *Washington Post Book World* contributor.

Barbara Walker writes in *Interracial Books for Children Bulletin* that ''Clifton is a gifted poet with the greater gift of being able to write poetry for children.'' Clifton indicates to Sims that she doesn't think of it as poetry especially for children, though. ''It seems to me that if you write poetry for children,

you have to keep too many things in mind other than the poem. So I'm just writing a poem.'' *Some of the Days of Everett Anderson* is a book of nine poems, about which Marjorie Lewis observes in *School Library Journal,* ''Some of the days of six-year-old 'ebony Everett Anderson' are happy; some lonely—but all of them are special, reflecting the author's own pride in being black.'' In the *New York Times Book Review,* Hoyt W. Fuller thinks that Clifton has ''a profoundly simple way of saying all that is important to say, and we know that the struggle is worth it, that the all-important battle of image is being won, and that the future of all those beautiful black children out there need not be twisted and broken.'' *Everett Anderson's Christmas Coming* concerns Christmas preparations in which ''each of the five days before Everett's Christmas is decribed by a verse,'' says Anita Silvey in the *Horn Book,* observing that ''the overall richness of Everett's experiences dominates the text.'' Jane O'Reilly suggests in the *New York Times Book Review* that ''Everett Anderson, black and boyish, is glimpsed, rather than explained through poems about him.'' *Everett Anderson's Year* celebrates ''a year in the life of a city child . . . in appealing verses,'' says Beryl Robinson in *Horn Book,* adding that ''mischief, fun, gaiety, and poignancy are a part of his days as the year progresses. The portrayals of child and mother are lively and solid, executed with both strength and tenderness.''

Language is important in Clifton's writing. In answer to Sim's question about the presence of both black and white children in her work, Clifton responds specifically about *Sonora Beautiful,* which is about the insecurities and dissatisfaction of an adolescent girl and which has only white characters: ''In this book, I *heard* the characters as white. I have a tendency to *hear* the language of the characters, and then I know something about who the people are.'' However, regarding objections to the black vernacular she often uses, Clifton tells Sims: ''I do not write out of weakness. That is to say, I do not write the language I write because I don't know any other. . . . But I have a certain integrity about my art, and in *my* art you have to be honest and you have to have people talking the way they really talk. So all of my books are not in the same language.'' Asked by Sims whether or not she feels any special pressures or special opportunities as a black author, Clifton responds: ''I do feel a responsibility. . . . First, I'm going to write books that tend to celebrate life. I'm about that. And I wish to have children see people like themselves in books. . . . I also take seriously the responsibility of not lying. . . . I'm not going to say that life is wretched if circumstance is wretched, because that's not true. So I take that responsibility, but it's a responsibility to the truth, and to my art as much as anything. I owe everybody that. . . . It's the truth as I see it, and that's what my responsibility is.''

''Browsing through a volume of Lucille Clifton's poems or reading one of her children's books to my son,'' says Scarupa, ''always makes me feel good: good to be black, good to be a woman, good to be alive.'' ''I am excited about her work because she reflects me; she tells my story in a way and with an eloquence that is beyond my ability,'' concurs Madhubuti, who concludes: ''To be original, relevant, and revolutionary in the mouth of fire is the mark of a dangerous person. Lucille Clifton is a poet of *mean* talent who has not let her gifts separate her from the work at hand. She is a teacher and an example. To read her is to give birth to bright seasons.'' Clifton, herself, has commented on her role as a poet in *Black Women Writers (1950-1980):* ''I am interested in trying to render big ideas in a simple way . . . in being understood not admired. I wish to celebrate and not be celebrated (though a little celebration is a lot of fun). I am a woman and I write from that experience. I am a Black woman and I write from that experience. I do not feel inhibited or bound by what I am.'' She adds: ''Sometimes I think that the most anger comes from ones who were late in discovering that when the world said nigger it meant them too. I grew up knowing that the world meant me too but that was the world's insanity and not mine. I have been treated in publishing very much like other poets are treated, that is, not really very well. I continue to write since my life as a human only includes my life as a poet, it doesn't depend on it.''

BIOGRAPHICAL/CRITICAL SOURCES:

BOOKS

Beckles, Frances N., *20 Black Women*, Gateway Press, 1978.
Children's Literature Review, Volume V, Gale, 1983.
Contemporary Literary Criticism, Volume IX, Gale, 1981.
Dictionary of Literary Biography, Gale, Volume V: *American Poets since World War II*, 1980, Volume XLI: *Afro-American Poets since 1955*, 1985.
Dreyer, Sharon Spredemann, *The Bookfinder: A Guide to Children's Literature about the Needs and Problems of Youth Aged 2-15*, Volume I, American Guidance Service, 1977.
Evans, Mari, editor, *Black Women Writers (1950-1980): A Critical Evaluation*, Doubleday-Anchor, 1984.

PERIODICALS

America, May 1, 1976.
Black Scholar, March, 1981.
Black World, July, 1970, February, 1973.
Book World, March 8, 1970, November 8, 1970, November 11, 1973, November 10, 1974, December 8, 1974, December 11, 1977, September 14, 1980, July 20, 1986, May 10, 1987.
Bulletin of the Center for Children's Books, March, 1971, November, 1974, March, 1976, September, 1980.
Horn Book, December, 1971, August, 1973, February, 1975, December, 1975, October, 1977.
Interracial Books for Children Bulletin, Volume V, numbers 7 and 8, 1975, Volume VII, number 1, 1976, Volume VIII, number 1, 1977, Volume X, number 5, 1979, Volume XI, numbers 1 and 2, 1980, Volume XII, number 2, 1981.
Journal of Negro Education, summer, 1974.
Journal of Reading, February, 1977, December, 1986.
Kirkus Reviews, April 15, 1970, October 1, 1970, December 15, 1974, April 15, 1976, February 15, 1982.
Language Arts, January, 1978, February 2, 1982.
Ms., October, 1976.
New Yorker, April 5, 1976.
New York Times, December 20, 1976.
New York Times Book Review, September 6, 1970, December 6, 1970, December 5, 1971, November 4, 1973, April 6, 1975, March 14, 1976, May 15, 1977.
Poetry, May, 1973.
Reading Teacher, October, 1978, March, 1981.
Redbook, November, 1969.
Saturday Review, December 11, 1971, August 12, 1972, December 4, 1973.
School Library Journal, May, 1970, December, 1970, September, 1974, December, 1977, February, 1979, March, 1980.
Tribune Books, August 30, 1987.

Virginia Quarterly Review, fall, 1976.
Voice of Youth Advocates, April, 1982.
Washington Post, November 10, 1974, August 9, 1979.
Washington Post Book World, February 10, 1980.
Western Humanities Review, summer, 1970.†

—*Sketch by Sharon Malinowski*

*   *   *

CLIMO, Shirley 1928-
(Shirley Beistle)

PERSONAL: Born November 25, 1928, in Cleveland, Ohio; daughter of Morton J. (a paving contractor) and Aldarilla (a writer; maiden name, Shipley) Beistle; married George F. Climo (a corporate historian), June 17, 1950; children: Robert, Susan, Lisa. *Education:* Attended DePauw University, 1946-49. *Politics:* ''Variable.'' *Religion:* Protestant.

ADDRESSES: Home—24821 Prospect Ave., Los Altos, Calif. 94022.

CAREER: WGAR-Radio, Cleveland, Ohio, scriptwriter for weekly juvenile series, ''Fairytale Theatre,'' 1949-53; free-lance writer, 1976—. President of Morning Forum of Los Altos, 1971-73.

MEMBER: California Writers, Society of Children's Book Writers.

WRITINGS:

Piskies, Spriggans, and Other Magical Beings: Tales From the Droll-Teller, Retold by Shirley Climo (juvenile), illustrations by Joyce Audy dos Santos, Crowell, 1981.
The Cobweb Christmas (picture book), illustrations by Joe Lasker, Crowell, 1982.
(Contributor) Sylvia K. Burack, *Writing and Selling Fillers, Light Verse, and Short Humor*, Writer, Inc., 1982.
Gopher, Tanker, and the Admiral (juvenile), illustrations by Eileen McKeating, Crowell, 1984.
Someone Saw a Spider (juvenile), illustrations by Dirk Zimmer, Crowell, 1985.
A Month of Seven Days (juvenile historical novel), Crowell, 1987.
King of the Birds (picture book), illustrations by Ruth Heller, Harper, 1988.
T. J.'s Ghost (juvenile), Crowell, 1988.
The Egyptian Cinderella (picture book), illustrations by Heller, Crowell, in press.

Also contributor to magazines, including *Family Weekly, Writer, Cricket, Ranger Rick*, and *Seventeen*, and to newspapers. Member of advisory board for *Children's Album*.

WORK IN PROGRESS: Great Beginnings (tentative title), a children's writing workbook; *The Korean Cinderella*, a picture book.

SIDELIGHTS: Shirley Climo told *CA:* ''To be a children's book writer always seemed the most wonderful aspiration in the world to me—and the most natural. My earliest memory is of being rocked in a creaky wicker carriage while my mother, a children's author, recited her stories. Long before I could read, I'd begun telling my own tales to myself and to anyone else willing to listen.

''I grew up, raised three children, a half dozen dogs, a clutch of cats, a horse, and a straggle of chickens. Each new addition provided additional story-telling material, and many two-legged and four-legged household members have found their way into print. Most important, I have found that writing books for youngsters is, indeed, quite wonderful.

"Lately, I'm spending a considerable part of each school year visiting classrooms and talking with children about *their* writing. I have fun, and there's no better way to keep in touch with your readers. But I always manage to save time for my own writing. The urge to tell stories remains a persistent itch, relieved only by a thick, soft pencil and a yellow, ruled legal pad. It proves the quotation from Somerset Maugham that's pasted on my desk lamp: "Until you're fifty, writing is hard work. Then it becomes just another bad habit.""

BIOGRAPHICAL/CRITICAL SOURCES:

PERIODICALS

Booklist, November, 1980.
Chicago Tribune Book World, December 12, 1982.
New York Times Book Review, July 5, 1981.
Writer, June, 1978, December, 1979.

*   *   *

CLINTON, F. G.
See CAMPBELL, R(obert) Wright

*   *   *

COLLINS, Pat(ricia) Lowery   1932-

PERSONAL: Born October 6, 1932, in Los Angeles, Calif.; daughter of Joseph Michael (an accountant) and Margaret (a radio scriptwriter; maiden name, Meyer) Lowery; married Wallace Collins (an engineering manager), April 18, 1953; children: Christopher, Kimberly (Mrs. David Jermain), Colleen, Cathlin, Mathias. *Education:* Attended the University of California, Los Angeles, 1949, and Immaculate Heart College, 1950; University of Southern California, A.B., 1953; further study at Choinard Art Institute (Los Angeles, Calif.), De Cordova Museum (Lincoln, Mass.), and Brandeis University. *Politics:* Republican. *Religion:* Roman Catholic.

ADDRESSES: Home and office—15 Reservoir St., Nashua, N.H. 03060; 3 Wauketa Rd. W., Gloucester, Mass. 01930 (summer).

CAREER: Writer, artist. Somerset Art Association, Far Hills, N.J., teacher of pastels, 1981—. Currently associated with art galleries in Gloucester, Mass., Boston, Mass., Nashua, N.H., and Manchester, N.H.; has had artwork exhibited throughout New England, New Jersey, and in New York City.

MEMBER: Society of Children's Book Writers, New Hampshire Art Association, Boston Visual Artists Union, Nashua Symphony and Choral Society.

WRITINGS:

(Contributor) *Anthology of Writing by Women,* University of Chicago Press, 1980.
My Friend Andrew (juvenile), illustrated by Howard Berelson, Prentice-Hall, 1981.
The River Shares Its Secret (textbook), Houghton, 1981.
Tumble Tumble Tumbleweed (juvenile), illustrated by Charles Robinson, Albert Whitman, 1982.
(Contributor) *Ten Times Round,* Ginn & Company, 1987.
(Contributor) *Mystery Sneaker,* Ginn & Company, 1987.
Taking Care of Tucker, Putnam, in press.

Contributor to periodicals and journals, including *Northshore, Primavera, Sackbut Review, Small Pond Review, WIND/Literary Journal,* and *Snippits: Pin Prick Press.* Contributing editor, *My Own Magazine,* July-August, 1987.

WORK IN PROGRESS: Poetry and short stories; author-illustrated picture book; middle grade novel; book on childbirth.

SIDELIGHTS: Pat Lowery Collins wrote to *CA:* "As a writer, I'm a poet first and believe that the best children's books at the level I prefer to address, preschool and picture book, are in themselves poems, having a simple, singular vision. They are [as] concise and powerful as the best poetry for any age, and writing them hones my skills for all levels of poetry.

"My work takes other directions as well, into older juvenile and adult fiction and some nonfiction, and though not related by content, all are related somewhat by style and approach.

"I'm also a visual artist and consider my drawings and paintings, which more and more have taken a narrative voice, extensions of the same need for expression fostered early in a very creative family environment.

"Today, judging from the excellence of the small press offerings and the popularity of short story collections published by major trade book publishers, there are a number of talented writers emerging to an appreciative audience. However, it appears to me that the children's field still relies heavily on formula and action-dominated fiction. Unfortunately, there is much more acceptance of experimentation in illustration than there is in the written text. I look forward to the day when children's books are more universally children's literature."

*   *   *

COMPTON-HALL, (Patrick) Richard   1929-

PERSONAL: Born July 12, 1929, in Reigate, England; son of Richard William (a surveyor) and Gwynedd (Goode) Compton-Hall; married Gillian Slade-Baker, March 29, 1952 (deceased); married Eve Kilpatrick, December 27, 1962; children: Richard Mark, Simon Cunynghame (deceased). *Education:* Attended Naval Staff College, 1961-62, and Joint Services Staff College, 1966-67. *Politics:* "Old-fashioned socialist." *Religion:* Church of England.

ADDRESSES: Home—Upper Ffynnon Fair, Rhayader, Powys LD6 5LA, Wales. *Office*—Royal Navy Submarine Museum, H.M.S. *Dolphin,* Gosport, Hampshire PO12 2AB, England.

CAREER: Royal Navy, career officer and submarine specialist, 1943-68, loaned to U.S. Navy as operations analysis officer for the submarine development group, 1958-60, retired as commander; John Lewis Partnership (department store and supermarket chain), London, England, director of services, 1968-71; full-time writer in France, 1971-75; Royal Navy Submarine Museum, Gosport, England, director and curator, 1975—. Part-time technical translator for French government, 1977—.

MEMBER: Royal Society of Arts (fellow), Royal United Service Institute, Writers Guild of Great Britain, Society of Authors, Translators Association.

AWARDS, HONORS: Member of Order of the British Empire, 1964.

WRITINGS:

"Below Us Bootle" (cassette recording of humorous submarine short stories), Royal Navy Submarine Museum, 1980.

Submarines, Wayland, 1982.
The Underwater War, 1939-1945, Sterling, 1982.
Submarine Boats, Conway Maritime Press, 1983.
The Submariner's World, Kenneth Mason Publications, 1983.
(Translator) *Naval Warfare Today and Tomorrow,* Basil Blackwell, 1983.
(With John Moore) *Submarine Warfare Today and Tomorrow,* Adler & Adler, 1987.
"Bootle Is Back" (cassette recording of humorous submarine short stories), Royal Naval Submarine Museum, 1987.
Submarine versus Submarine, David & Charles, 1988.
Submarines and the 1914-18 War, Macmillan, in press.

Radio and television writer. Frequent contributor to history and military journals.

SIDELIGHTS: Richard Compton-Hall reported: "My writing career arose from my having taken the first *conventional* submarine, H.M.S. *Grampus,* deep under the polar ice pack with some difficulty, damage, and a good deal of pleasurable excitement. The Navy required articles for journals and newspapers. The discovery that serious, even dangerous, operations and events can be treated as light comedy, and make a far greater impression than when treated heavily, led to a style that has since (apparently) become popular and much in demand.

"In particular I find a light approach evokes an important point to be made (one only!) in each book, article, or broadcast; and that one point is usually accepted, with this light treatment, by the people I am aiming at—politicians, senior naval officers, and the public alike. The most significant success in this direction is my plea in *The Underwater War* for much more effort and money to be spent on truly proving weapon systems in peacetime because otherwise they simply will not work in war, whatever highly prejudiced claims manufacturers and over-optimistic officers in all navies may make. In other words, my campaign in this respect is against 'wishful thinking,' particularly evident in the United States and Royal navies.

"My continuing campaign is against arrogance—in the church, business, trade unions, politics, and wherever; comedy, or at least light humor, is a splendid weapon."

*   *   *

CONGDON, William Grosvenor 1912-

PERSONAL: Born April 15, 1912, in Providence, R.I.; son of Gilbert Maurice (an industrialist) and Caroline (Grosvenor) Congdon. *Education:* Yale University, B.A., 1934; attended Demetrious School of Sculpture, 1935, 1939, and Pennsylvania Academy of Fine Arts, 1935. *Religion:* Roman Catholic.

ADDRESSES: Home—Via Marconi 33, 20090 Buccinasco (Mi), Italy.

CAREER: Painter, living and working in Italy, with occasional periods of residence in other countries. Held one-man shows in New York, Washington, D.C., Santa Barbara, Chicago, Boston, Venice, Italy, and other locations, 1949-64, and at Palazzo Diamanti in Ferrara, Italy, 1981; also participated in shows at Carnegie Institute, Whitney Museum of American Art, Museum of Modern Art, Rhode Island Museum, and other museums and galleries in America, Italy, England, and Japan. Works owned by private collectors and by Metropolitan Museum of Art, Whitney Museum of American Art, Detroit Institute of Arts, New York Museum of Modern Art, and a number of other museums, galleries, and universities. *Wartime*

service: American Field Service, attached to British 8th Army in Middle East and Europe, 1942-45.

AWARDS, HONORS: Temple Gold Medal, Pennsylvania Academy of Fine Arts, 1951; purchase award, University of Illinois, 1952; W. A. Clark Award, Corcoran Gallery of Art, 1953; first International Sacred Art Award, Trieste, Italy, 1961.

WRITINGS:

In My Disc of Gold, Reynal, 1962.
Esistenza Viaggio: Di pittore americano diario, Jaca Book, 1975.
America Addio: Letters to Belle, Jaca Book, 1980.
How an Artist Creates, Jaca Book, 1982.
Cantiere dell'Artista, Jaca Book, 1983.
Ikon, Image, Vision: Notes on the Art of William Congdon, Jaca Book, 1987.

Contributor to *Atlantic Monthly, Botteghe Oscure, Critic,* and *America.*

SIDELIGHTS: William Grosvenor Congdon told *CA:* "I write as a prolongation of my painting. The catapult to hurtle me into creativity dates from infant rebellion against the puritan, moralistic ambience of my New England origin. My association with the Action Painters in New York from 1948 to 1952 favored this. The problem of my life has been to spiritually grow to a contemplative equilibrium between an exasperated subjectivity and the objectivity of things as they essentially (not apparently) are. The two shores of my life are departure from New York (the "City" series of 1949-50) and arrival at the Po Valley lowlands in Italy in 1980-81."

He cites his "conversion to Catholic faith" as an influential factor in his painting and states he sees "only the spiritual desolation of the contemporary scene." Congdon advises aspiring writers/painters to "recognize as God-given, and obey your creative 'gift' (if you have it)."

BIOGRAPHICAL/CRITICAL SOURCES:

BOOKS

Congdon, William Grosvenor, *Ikon, Image, Vision: Notes on the Art of William Congdon,* Jaca Book, 1987.

*   *   *

CONROY, Pat 1945-

PERSONAL: Born October 26, 1945, in Atlanta, Ga.; son of Don (a military officer) and Peg (Peek) Conroy; married Barbara Bolling, 1969 (divorced, 1977); married Lenore Gurewitz, March 21, 1981; children: (first marriage) Megan; Jessica, Melissa (stepdaughters); (second marriage) Susannah; Gregory, Emily (stepchildren). *Education:* Citadel, B.A., 1967.

ADDRESSES: Office—1069 Juniper St. N.E., Atlanta, Ga. 30309. *Agent*—Julian Bach Literary Agency, 747 Third Ave., New York, N.Y. 10017.

CAREER: Writer. Worked as schoolteacher in Daufuski, S.C., 1969.

AWARDS, HONORS: Anisfield-Wolf Award, Cleveland Foundation, 1972, for *The Water Is Wide; The Lords of Discipline* was nominated for the Robert Kennedy Book Award, Robert F. Kennedy Memorial, 1981.

WRITINGS:

The Boo, McClure, 1970.

The Water Is Wide, Houghton, 1972.
The Great Santini, Houghton, 1976.
The Lords of Discipline, Houghton, 1980.
The Prince of Tides, Houghton, 1986.

SIDELIGHTS: Best-selling novelist Pat Conroy has worked some of his bitterest experiences into stories that present ironic, often jarring, yet humorous views of life and relationships in the contemporary South. Garry Abrams in the *Los Angeles Times* reports that "Misfortune has been good to novelist Pat Conroy. It gave him a family of disciplinarians, misfits, eccentrics, liars and loudmouths. It gave him a Southern childhood in which the bizarre competed with the merely strange. It gave him a military school education apparently imported from Sparta by way of Prussia. It gave him a divorce and a breakdown followed by intensive therapy. It gave him everything he needed to write best sellers, make millions and live in Rome." Brigitte Weeks touches on Conroy's appeal in the *Washington Post.* "With his feet set firmly on his native earth, Conroy is, above all, a storyteller. His tales are full of the exaggeration and wild humor of stories told around a camp fire."

While his most recent works are fictional, critics frequently consider Conroy's novels autobiographical. Conroy's father was a Marine Corps pilot from Chicago who believed in strong discipline; his mother was an outwardly yielding Southerner who actually ran the household. "When he [Conroy's father] returned home from work my sister would yell, 'Godzilla's home' and the seven children would melt into whatever house we happened to be living in at the time. He was no match for my mother's byzantine and remarkable powers of intrigue. Neither were her children. It took me 30 years to realize that I had grown up in my mother's house and not my father's," Conroy is quoted in the *Book-of-the-Month Club News.* Still, critics frequently mention the ambivalent father-son relationships that appear in his novels. Gail Godwin in the *New York Times Book Review* describes Conroy's work: "The Southern-boy protagonists of Pat Conroy's fiction have twin obsessions—oppressive fathers or father figures, and the South. Against both they fight furiously for selfhood and independence, yet they never manage to secede from their seductive entrappers. Some fatal combination of nostalgia and loyalty holds them back; they remain ambivalent sons of their families and their region, alternately railing against, then shamelessly romanticizing, the myths and strictures that imprison them."

Conroy's first work to receive national attention was openly autobiographical. After graduation, Conroy taught English in public high schools, but unsatisfied, he looked for a new challenge. When a desired position in the Peace Corps did not surface, he took a job teaching nearly illiterate black children on Daufuskie Island, a small, isolated area off the South Carolina coast. But he was not prepared for his new students. They did not know the name of their country, that they lived on the Atlantic Ocean, or that the world was round. On the other hand, Conroy found his pupils expected him to know how to set a trap, skin a muskrat, and plant okra. Conroy came to enjoy his unusual class, but eventually his unorthodox teaching methods and disregard for the authorities turned numerous school officials against him and cost him his job. As a way of coping with his fury at the dismissal, Conroy wrote *The Water Is Wide*, an account of his experiences. As he told Ted Mahar for the *Oregonian*, "When you get fired like that, you have to do something. I couldn't get a job with the charges the school board leveled against me." The process of writing did more than cool him down however; he also gained a new

perspective on his reasons for choosing Daufuskie (Yamacraw Island in the book) and on his own responses to racism. Anatole Broyard describes Conroy in the *New York Times Book Review* as "a former redneck and self-proclaimed racist, [who] brought to Yamacraw the supererogatory fervor of the recently converted." In *The Water Is Wide*, Conroy agrees: "At this time of my life a black man could probably have handed me a bucket of cow p—, commanded me to drink it in order that I might rid my soul of the stench of racism, and I would only have asked for a straw. . . . It dawned on me that I came to Yamacraw for a fallacious reason: I needed to be cleansed, born again, resurrected by good works and suffering, purified of the dark cankers that grew like toadstools in my past."

After the successful publication of *The Water Is Wide*, Conroy began writing full-time. Although his following book, *The Great Santini*, was a novel, many critics think it represents his adolescence. An article in the *Virginia Quarterly Review* states that "The dialogue, anecdotes, and family atmosphere are pure Marine and probably autobiographical." Conroy did draw heavily on his family background to write the story of a tough Marine, Bull Meecham, his long-suffering wife, Lillian, and the eldest son Ben, who is striving for independence outside his father's control. Robert E. Burkholder writes in *Critique: Studies in Modern Fiction*, that *The Great Santini* "is a curious blend of lurid reality and fantastic comedy, which deals with approximately one year in the life of Ben Meecham and his family. It is primarily a novel of initiation, but central to the concept of Ben's initiation into manhood and to the meaning of the whole novel is the idea that individual myths must be stripped away from Ben and the other major characters before Ben can approach reality with objectivity and maturity." Part of Ben's growing up involves rejecting the image of his father's infallibility. In one scene, Ben finally beats his father at a game of basketball. As the game ends, he tells him: "Do you know, Dad, that not one of us here has ever beaten you in a single game? Not checkers, not dominoes, not softball, nothing."

According to Robert M. Willingham in the *Dictionary of Literary Biography*, after his defeat, "Bull does not outwardly change. He still blusters, curses, flashes toughness and resoluteness, but his family has become more to him than before. When Colonel Meecham's plane crashes and he is killed, one learns that the crash was unavoidable, but Bull's death was not: 'Am commencing starbord turn to avoid populated area. Will attempt to punch out when wings are level. Wish me luck. Over.' The priority was to avoid populated areas, 'where people lived and slept, where families slept. Families like my family, wives like my wife, sons like my sons, daughters like my daughters.' He never punched out."

Bull Meecham is modeled on Conroy's father, Colonel Donald Conroy, who "would make John Wayne look like a pansy," as Conroy told Bill McDonald for the South Carolina *State*. Conroy reports that his father initially disliked *The Great Santini*. The author said to *Chicago Tribune* contributor Peer Gorner that "Dad could only read the book halfway through before throwing it across the room. Then people started telling him he actually was lovable. Now, he signs Christmas cards 'The Great Santini,' and goes around talking about childrearing and how we need to have more discipline in the home—a sort of Nazi Dr. Spock." The movie created from the novel helped to change the Colonel's attitude. "The Great Santini" starred Robert Duvall, and the Colonel liked the way "his" character came across. In a *Washington Post* interview, Conroy related an incident of one-upmanship that seems borrowed from the book. "He (the Colonel) came to the opening of 'The Great Santini' movie here in Washington. I introduced the film to the audience, and in the course of my remarks I pointed out why he had chosen the military as a career. It was, of course, something that occurred to him on the day when he discovered that his body temperature and his IQ were the same number. Then, when it was his turn to talk, all he said was, 'I want to say that my body temperature has always been 160 degrees.' People laughed harder. So you see, I still can't beat him." Conroy's father, however, says it is important to remember that *The Great Santini* is fiction. Willingham adds, "Colonel Conroy offers these comments: 'Pat embellished everything. Where's the truth in all these incidents? There is a moment of truth. Where it is, I suspect only Pat and I recognize.'"

Another period of Conroy's life appeared in his next book, *The Lords of Discipline*. According to his father's wishes, Conroy attended the Citadel, South Carolina's venerable military academy. "Quirky, eccentric, and unforgettable," Conroy describes the academy in the preface to *The Boo*, his first book, which gave a nostalgic look at the Citadel and its Commander of Cadets during the 1960s. But Willingham describes the Citadel in another way: "It is also an anachronism of the 1960s with a general disregard for the existence of the outside world." *The Lords of Discipline* paints an even bleaker picture of its fictionalized institution, the Carolina Military Institute. This school, says Frank Rose in the *Washington Post Book World*, "combines some of the more quaint and murderous aspects of the Citadel, West Point, and Virginia Military Institute."

The Lords of Discipline concerns Will, the narrator, and his three roommates. Will is a senior cadet assigned to watch over the Institute's first black student. The novel's tension lies in the conflict between group loyalty and personal responsibility. Will eventually discovers the Ten, "a secret mafia whose existence has long been rumored but never proven, a silent and malevolent force dedicated . . . to maintain the purity of the Institute—racial purity included," comments Rose. He continues, "What Conroy has achieved is twofold; his book is at once a suspense-ridden duel between conflicting ideals of manhood and a paen to brother love that ends in betrayal and death. Out of the shards of broken friendship a blunted triumph emerges, and it is here, when the duel is won, that the reader finally comprehends the terrible price that any form of manhood can exact."

According to its author, *The Lords of Discipline* describes the love between men. "I wrote it because I wanted to tell about how little women understand about men," he said in a *Washington Post* article. "The one cultural fact of life about military schools is that they are men living with men. And they love each other. The love between these men is shown only in obscure ways, which have to be learned by them. The four roommates who go through this book are very different from each other, but they have a powerful code. They have ways to prove their love to each other, and they're part of the rites of passage." And contradicting an old myth, Conroy adds, "There is no homosexuality under these conditions. If you smile, they'll kill you. You can imagine what would happen to a homosexual."

While *The Lords of Discipline* portrays deep friendships, it also contains a theme common to many of Conroy's books: the coexistence of love and brutality. "This book . . . makes 'The Lord of the Flies' sound like 'The Sound of Music,'" writes Christian Williams in the *Washington Post*. A *Chicago*

Tribune Book World reviewer warns, "Conroy's chilling depictions of hazing are for strong stomachs only." And George Cohen in a later Chicago *Tribune Books* article describes the novel's pull for readers: "It is our attraction to violence—observed from the safest of places—together with our admiration for the rebel who beats the system, and Conroy's imposing ability as a storyteller that make the novel engrossing."

Conroy's wildest tale is *The Prince of Tides,* which follows Tom Wingo, an unemployed high school English teacher and football coach on a journey from coastal South Carolina to New York City to help his twin sister Savannah. Savannah, a well-known poet, is recovering from a nervous breakdown and suicide attempt. In an attempt to help Savannah's psychiatrist understand her patient, Tom relates the Wingo family's bizarre history. Despite the horrors the Wingos have suffered, including several rapes and the death of their brother, a sense of optimism prevails. Writes Judy Bass in Chicago *Tribune Books,* "Pat Conroy has fashioned a brilliant novel that ultimately affirms life, hope and the belief that one's future need not be contaminated by a monstrous past. In addition, Conroy . . . deals with the most prostrating crises in human experience—death of a loved one, parental brutality, injustice, insanity—without lapsing into pedantry or oppressive gloom."

The Price of Tide's style drew more attention than that of Conroy's other books. Some critics felt the novel was overblown: Richard Eder in the *Los Angeles Times Book Review* claims that "Inflation is the order of the day. The characters do too much, feel too much, suffer too much, eat too much, signify too much, and above all, talk too much. And, as with the classical American tomato, quantity is at the expense of quality." Godwin says that while "the ambition, invention and sheer irony in this book are admirable . . . many readers will be put off by the turgid, high-flown rhetoric that the author must have decided would best match his grandiose designs. And as the bizarre, hyperbolic episodes of Wingo family life mount up, other readers are likely to feel they are being bombarded by whoppers told by an overwrought boy eager to impress or shock." But more critics have appreciated what *Detroit News* contributor Ruth Pollack Coughlin calls "spectacular, lyrical prose with a bitter sense of humor." The novel is long, says Weeks, "monstrously long, yet a pleasure to read, flawed yet stuffed to the endpapers with lyricism, melodrama, anguish and plain old suspense. Given all that, one can brush aside its lapses like troublesome flies."

Conroy's family judged the novel more harshly than did the reviewers. Although his mother is the inspiration for shrimper's wife Lila Wingo, she died before he finished the novel and never saw it. Conroy's sister, who did see the book, was offended. As Conroy told Rick Groen for the Toronto *Globe and Mail,* "Yes, my sister is also a poet in New York who has also had serious breakdowns. We were very close, but she has not spoken to me . . . since the book. I'm saddened, but when you write autobiography, this is one of the consequences. They're allowed to be mad at you. They have the right." This, however, was not the first time a family member reacted negatively to one of Conroy's books. *The Great Santini* infuriated his Chicago relatives: "My grandmother and grandfather told me they never wanted to see me or my children again," Conroy told Sam Staggs for *Publishers Weekly.* Conroy's Southern relatives have also responded to the sex scenes and "immodest" language in his books. Staggs relates, "After *The Lords of Discipline* was published, Conroy's Aunt Helen telephoned him and said, 'Pat, I hope someday you'll write a book a Christian can read.' 'How far did you get?' her nephew asked. 'Page four, and I declare, I've never been so embarrassed.'"

But Hollywood has given Conroy's novels a warm reception. *The Great Santini* wasn't his only book to become a movie. *The Water Is Wide* was made into "Conrack," starring Jon Voight, and later became a musical also entitled "Conrack." *The Lords of Discipline* kept the same title as a film and featured David Keith. Conroy himself wrote a screenplay for *The Prince of Tides*, learning a lesson about Hollywood in the process. When producers offered him $100,000 to write the screenplay, he took it happily. They liked his work, but then decided to send it to an experienced Hollywood rewrite man—who received $500,000 for the job.

When Staggs asked why Conroy's books "make such entertaining movies," the author replied, "I always figure it's because I'm incredibly shallow. I write a straight story line, and I guess that's what they need. The dialogue also seems to be serviceable in a Hollywood way. But most important, I do the thing that Southerners do naturally—I tell stories. I always try to make sure there's a good story going on in my books." Conroy further explained his method of writing to Gorner: "When I'm writing, I have no idea where I'm going. People get married, and I didn't realize they were engaged. People die in these novels and I'm surprised. They take on this little subterranean life of their own. They reveal secrets to me even as I'm doing it. Maybe this is a dangerous way to work, but for me it becomes the pleasure of writing. . . . Critics call me a popular novelist, but writing popular novels isn't what urges me on. If I could write like Faulkner or Thomas Wolfe, I surely would. I'd much rather write like them than like me. Each book has been more ambitious. I'm trying to be more courageous."

MEDIA ADAPTATIONS: The film "Conrack," based on *The Water Is Wide*, was produced by Twentieth-Century Fox in 1974; the musical "Conrack" was adapted for the stage by Granville Burgess, and was first produced off-off Broadway at AMAS Repertory Theater, November, 1987; "The Great Santini" was produced by Warner Brothers in 1979; "The Lords of Discipline" was produced by Paramount in 1983.

BIOGRAPHICAL/CRITICAL SOURCES:

BOOKS

Authors in the News, Volume I, Gale, 1976.
Contemporary Literary Criticism, Volume XXX, Gale, 1984.
Dictionary of Literary Biography, Volume VI: *American Novelists since World War II, Second Series*, Gale, 1980.

PERIODICALS

Book-of-the-Month Club News, December, 1986.
Chicago Tribune, November 25, 1986.
Chicago Tribune Book World, October 19, 1980, September 14, 1986, October 19, 1986.
Cincinnati Enquirer, March 25, 1974.
Critique: Studies in Modern Fiction, Vol. XXI, no. 1, 1979.
Detroit News, October 12, 1986, December 20, 1987.
Globe and Mail (Toronto), February 28, 1987, November 28, 1987.
Los Angeles Times, February 19, 1983, October 12, 1986, October 19, 1986, December 12, 1986.
Los Angeles Times Book Review, October 19, 1986.
New York Times, January 10, 1987.
New York Times Book Review, July 13, 1972, September 24, 1972, December 7, 1980, October 12, 1986.

Oregonian, April 28, 1974.
Publishers Weekly, May 15, 1972, September 5, 1986.
State (Columbia, South Carolina), March 31, 1974.
Time, October 13, 1986.
Tribune Books (Chicago), September 14, 1986, October 19, 1986.
Virginia Quarterly Review, autumn, 1976.
Washington Post, October 23, 1980.
Washington Post Book World, October 19, 1980, October 12, 1986.

—*Sketch by Jani Prescott*

*   *   *

CONSTANTELOS, Demetrios J.   1927-
(Dimitris Stachys)

PERSONAL: Born July 27, 1927, in Spilia, Messenia, Greece; became U.S. citizen in 1958; son of John B. (a farmer) and Christine (Psilopoulos) Constantelos; married Stella Croussouloudis, August 15, 1954; children: Christine, John, Helen, Maria. *Education:* Holy Cross Greek Orthodox Theological School, Diploma in Theology, 1951, B.A. in Th., 1958; Princeton Theological Seminary, Th.M., 1959; Rutgers University, M.A., 1963, Ph.D., 1965.

ADDRESSES: Home—304 Forest Dr., Linwood, N.J. 08221. *Office*—Arts and Humanities, Stockton State College, Pomona, N.J. 08240.

CAREER: St. Demetrios Greek Orthodox Church, Perth Amboy, N.J., pastor, 1955-64; Dumbarton Oaks Research Library, Washington, D.C., junior fellow, 1964-65; Holy Cross Greek Orthodox Theological School, Brookline, Mass., assistant professor, 1965-67, associate professor of history, 1967-71; Stockton State College, Pomona, N.J., professor of history and religious studies, 1971-86, Charles Cooper Townsend Distinguished Professor of History and Religious Studies, 1986—. Visiting lecturer in history, Boston College, 1967-68. Representative of Greek Orthodox Archdiocese of North and South America at national and international congresses.

MEMBER: American Historical Association, American Society of Church History, Mediaeval Academy of America, American Academy of Religion, Orthodox Theological Society of America (president, 1968-71), U.S. National Committee for Byzantine Studies.

WRITINGS:

An Old Faith for Modern Man, Greek Orthodox Archdiocese (New York), 1964.
The Greek Orthodox Church: History, Faith and Practice, Seabury, 1967.
Byzantine Philanthropy and Social Welfare, Rutgers University Press, 1968, 2nd edition, 1987.
Marriage, Sexuality, and Celibacy: A Greek Orthodox Perspective, Light & Life Press, 1975.
Understanding the Greek Orthodox Church, Seabury, 1982.
Poverty, Society and Philanthropy in the Late Medieval Greek World, Caratzas, 1987.

EDITOR

Encyclicals and Documents of the Greek Orthodox Archdiocese, Institute for Patristic Studies, 1975.
(With C. J. Efthymiou) *Greece: Today and Tomorrow*, Krikos, 1979.

Orthodox Theology and Diakonia: Trends and Prospects, Hellenic College Press, 1981.
Understanding the Greek Orthodox Church, Seabury, 1982.

CONTRIBUTOR

Bruce M. Metzger, editor, *The Oxford Annotated Apocrypha*, Oxford University Press, 1977.
A. E. Laiou-Thomadakis, editor, *Charanis Studies*, Rutgers University Press, 1980.
G. H. Anderson and T. F. Stransky, editors, *Christ's Lordship and Religious Pluralism*, Orbis, 1981.
J. J. Allen, editor, *Orthodox Synthesis: The Unity of Theological Thought*, St. Vladimir's Seminary Press, 1981.
Joseph R. Strayer, *Dictionary of the Middle Ages*, Scribner, 1982—.
Mircea Eliade, editor, *The Encyclopedia of Religion*, Macmillan, 1987.

OTHER

Also contributor of more than forty studies, essays, articles, and reviews to theology and history journals, and numerous articles and reviews of a more popular nature to U.S. and Greek publications, some under pseudonym Dimitris Stachys.

*   *   *

CORK, Richard (Graham)   1947-

PERSONAL: Born March 25, 1947, in Eastbourne, England; son of Hubert Henry and Beatrice Hester (Smale) Cork; married Vena Jackson, March 21, 1970; children: Adam, Polly, Katy, Joe. *Education:* Trinity Hall College, Cambridge, received degree (with first class honors), 1969, Ph.D., 1978.

ADDRESSES: Home—24 Milman Rd., London NW6, England.

CAREER: Evening Standard, London, England, art critic, 1969-77; *Studio International*, London, editor, 1975-79; *Standard*, London, art critic, 1980-83; currently art critic for *Listener*, London. Member of art panel of Arts Council of Great Britain, 1971-74.

AWARDS, HONORS: Llewelyn Rhys Prize from National Book League, 1977, for *Vorticism and Abstract Art in the First Machine Age*; Sir Banister Fletcher Prize, 1985, for *Art beyond the Gallery in Early Twentieth-Century England*.

WRITINGS:

Vorticism and Abstract Art in the First Machine Age, Volume I: *Origins and Development*, Volume II: *Synthesis and Decline*, University of California, 1976.
The Social Role of Art: Essays in Criticism for a Newspaper Public, Gordon Fraser, 1980, State Mutual Book, 1981.
Art beyond the Gallery in Early Twentieth-Century England, Yale University Press, 1985.
David Bomberg, Yale University Press, 1987.

Contributor to magazines and newspapers, including *Art in America* and *New Statesman*.

WORK IN PROGRESS: A history of art made for hospitals, from Della Robbia to Naum Gabo; a study of art in World War I.

SIDELIGHTS: As an art critic and art historian, Richard Cork's scholarly studies have been instrumental in recreating several modernist movements in England. In his two-volume *Vorticism and Abstract Art in the First Machine Age* Cork chron-

icles the rise and fall of the early twentieth-century English movement known as Vorticism. "Cork in about 200,000 words on nearly 600 large and very well illustrated and well documented pages has provided us with . . . a view of Vorticism as a group effort of a dozen young men and women . . . which was to provide this country with an equivalent of Italian Futurism, French Cubism and German Expressionism. . . . Cork keeps to a fairly strict chronology, and moves from one artist to another, taking us month by month through that exciting time,'' writes Alan Bowness in the *Times Literary Supplement*. Though he respects Cork's "skillful'' achievement, Bowness remarks on a few of the book's shortcomings. According to Bowness, Cork downplays the role of Wyndham Lewis in the whole Vorticist movement: "Cork's treatment of the lesser figures is generally first rate, but I am tempted to say that he simply does not understand what Lewis was about.'' In another sense, Bowness feels that "it is . . . Cork's determination to pursue abstraction as the aim and end of Vorticism that mars his otherwise magnificent study.''

In two separate reviews of Cork's two-volume work, *Spectator* contributor Bryan Robertson finds that Cork "has written an elaborately detailed survey of Vorticism. He is scrupulously fair to all the protagonists.'' In contrast with Bowness, Robertson believes Cork has emphasized the special role Lewis played in this movement. Regarding volume one of Cork's study, *Origins and Development*, Robertson feels the book is "an important contribution to art history, and with it Cork occupies a position of honour among those younger art historians who are busily setting the record straight'' concerning the evolution of art in England. As for the second volume, *Synthesis and Decline*, Robertson says "Cork has brought the whole period back to life. The intellectual clarity with which he illuminates a factually and analytically dense narrative is sustained to the last page.''

Cork wrote to *CA*: "I like to perform a dual role, as art historian and art critic. Both roles are equally important to me, and I see them as complementary activities. *Art beyond the Gallery in Early Twentieth-Century England* links up directly with my interest (as a critic) in contemporary art, which attempts to operate in a whole variety of ways outside the gallery system.''

BIOGRAPHICAL/CRITICAL SOURCES:

PERIODICALS

Art Line, January-February, 1985.
Artscribe, July, 1977.
Arts Review, September 16, 1977.
Observer (London), February 8, 1987.
Spectator, May 8, 1976, January 8, 1977, June 22, 1985.
Times Literary Supplement, March 18, 1977, June 13, 1980, February 6, 1987.

*   *   *

CORNISH, Sam(uel James)   1935-

PERSONAL: Born December 22, 1935, in Baltimore, Md.; son of Herman and Sarah Cornish; married Jean Faxon, September, 1967. *Education:* Attended schools in Baltimore, Md., Goddard College, Vt., and Northwestern University.

ADDRESSES: Home—50 Monastery Rd., Brighton, Mass. 02135. *Office*—Department of English, Emerson College, 100 Beacon St., Boston, Mass. 02116.

CAREER: Enoch Pratt Library, Baltimore, Md., writing specialist, 1965-66, 1968-69; bookseller, 1966-67; Central Atlantic Regional Educational Laboratories (CAREL), Washington, D.C., editorial consultant, 1967-68; Highland Park Free School, Roxbury, Mass., teacher of creative writing, 1969—; currently instructor in Afro-American Survey, Emerson College, Boston, Mass.; poet. Former editor of *Chicory* (magazine), for the Enoch Pratt Library, and of *Mimeo,* a poetry magazine. Education Development Center, Open Education Follow Through Project, Newton, Mass., staff adviser and consultant on children's writing, 1973-78; consultant in elementary school teaching, CAREL. *Military service:* U.S. Army Medical Corps, 1958-60.

AWARDS, HONORS: National Endowment for the Arts grant, 1968; poetry prize, Humanities Institute of Coppin State College, 1968.

WRITINGS:

JUVENILES

Your Hand in Mind, illustrated by Carl Owens, Harcourt, 1970.
Grandmother's Pictures, illustrated by Jeanne Johns, Bookstore Press, 1974.
My Daddy's People Were Very Black, illustrated by Johns, Open Education Follow Through Project, Education Development Center, 1976.
Walking the Streets with Mississippi John Hurt, Bradbury, 1978.

Also author of *Harriet Tubman,* published by Third World Press.

VERSE

In This Corner: Sam Cornish and Verses, Fleming-McCallister Press, 1964.
People beneath the Window, Sacco Publishers, 1962, reprinted, 1987.
Generations, and Other Poems, edited by Jean Faxon, Beanbag Press, 1964, enlarged edition with preface by Ruth Whitman published as *Generations: Poems,* Beacon Press, 1971.
Angles, Beanbag Press, 1965.
Winters, Sans Souci Press, 1968.
Short Beers, Beanbag Press, 1969.
A Reason for Intrusion: An Omnibus of Musings from the Files of Sam Cornish, Pamela Williams [and] *Paul D. McAllister,* Fleming-McAllister Publishers, 1969, reprinted, 1987.
Streets, Third World Press, 1973.
Sometimes: Ten Poems, Pym-Randall Press, 1973.
Sam's World: Poems, Decatur House, 1978.
Songs of Jubilee: New and Selected Poems, 1969-1983, Unicorn Press, 1986.

WORK REPRESENTED IN ANTHOLOGIES

LeRoi Jones and Larry Neal, editors, *Black Fire: An Anthology of Afro-American Writing,* Morrow, 1968.
Harry Smith, editor, *Smith Poets,* Horizon Press, 1969.
Clarence Major, editor, *New Black Poetry,* International Publishers, 1969.
George Plimpton and Peter Ardery, editors, *American Literary Anthology 3,* Viking, 1970.
Ted Wilentz and Tom Weatherly, editors, *Natural Process,* Hill & Wang, 1972.
Arnold Adoff, editor, *One Hundred Years of Black Poetry,* Harper, 1972.

A Penguin Anthology of Indian, African, and Afro-American Poetry, Penguin, 1973.
David Alan Evans, editor, *New Voices in American Poetry,* Winthrop, 1973.
Adoff, editor, *Celebrations: A New Anthology of Black American Poetry,* Follett, 1977.

OTHER

(Editor with Lucian W. Dixon) *Chicory: Young Voices from the Black Ghetto* (poetry and prose collection), Association Press, 1969.
(Editor with Hugh Fox, and contributor) *The Living Underground: An Anthology of Contemporary American Poetry,* Ghost Dance Press, 1969.

Contributor of poems and reviews to *Ann Arbor Review, Poetry Review, Journal of Black Poetry, Essence, Boston Review of the Arts,* and Boston newspapers.

SIDELIGHTS: "Sam Cornish emerged as one of the numerous Afro-American poets who gained an audience during the revolution in the arts that took place in the late 1960s," writes Jon Woodson in a *Dictionary of Literary Biography* essay. Calling his poems simple, direct, and honest, Woodson suggests that although he is "not as public a figure as several of the writers in the black arts movement, Cornish produced some of the most profound work to come out of that group. Though his work reflects the dictates of the black aesthetic, with its emphasis on popular speech, social protest, and the celebration of black culture, it is never at the expense of craft, insight, and individuality. Because of the intelligence and clarity of his poems, Cornish has won the interest of a wide reading audience and the admiration of poets of differing schools."

Cornish comments that he has been influenced by Robert Lowell, T. S. Eliot, and LeRoi Jones. He said: "Most of my major themes are of urban life, the Negro predicament here in the cities, and my own family. I try to use a minimum of words to express the intended thought or feeling, with the effect of being starkly frank at times. Main verse form is unrhymed, free."

BIOGRAPHICAL/CRITICAL SOURCES:

BOOKS

Dictionary of Literary Biography, Volume XLI: *Afro-American Poets since 1955,* Gale, 1985.

PERIODICALS

Black World, July, 1970.
Choice, September, 1978, October, 1986.
Commonweal, May 22, 1970.†

*   *   *

CORWIN, Norman   1910-

PERSONAL: Born May 3, 1910, in Boston, Mass.; son of Samuel Haskell and Rose (Ober) Corwin; married Katherine Locke, March 17, 1947; children: Anthony, Diane. *Education:* Attended public schools in Boston and Winthrop, Mass.

ADDRESSES: Home—1840 Fairburn Ave., Los Angeles, Calif. 90025. *Agent*—William Morris Agency, 151 El Camino, Beverly Hills, Calif. 90212.

CAREER: Greenfield Daily Recorder, Greenfield, Mass., sports editor, 1927-29; *Springfield Daily Republican* and *Springfield Sunday Republican,* Springfield, Mass., reporter and radio editor, 1929-36; Columbia Broadcasting System, Inc. (CBS), New York City, writer, director, performer, and producer, 1938-47; screenwriter for various production companies, including Metro-Goldwyn-Mayer, RKO General, Twentieth Century-Fox, and CBS, 1945—; United Nations Radio, New York City, chief of special projects, 1949-52; writer, director, and producer of radio and television programs. University of California, Los Angeles, member of board of directors for theatre group, 1960-64, teacher, 1967-69; University of Southern California, teacher of telecommunications, 1970, and creative radio, 1979-80; director of creative writing, University of Southern California, Idyllwild, 1971—; lecturer, University of North Carolina, 1972; distinguished visiting lecturer, San Diego State University, 1977-78; Patten Memorial Lecturer, Indiana University, 1981; Stasheff Lecturer, University of Michigan, 1984. Writers Branch Executive Commission, board of governors, 1980—, chairman, 1981—.

MEMBER: Academy of Motion Pictures Foundation (secretary, 1983—), Academy of Motion Picture Arts and Sciences (chairman of documentary awards committee, 1963-81; co-chairman of scholarship committee, 1970-76), Authors League of America, Directors Guild of America, Screen Writers Guild (West), Dramatists League, American Society of Composers, Authors and Publishers.

AWARDS, HONORS: Has received numerous awards for individual radio programs and for general contributions to broadcasting, including Institute for Education by Radio Award, 1939, for "Words without Music" and "They Fly through the Air with the Greatest of Ease," and 1940, for "Pursuit of Happiness"; Bok Medal, 1942; American Academy of Arts and Letters Award, 1942; Peabody Medal, 1942, for "We Hold These Truths"; American Newspaper Guild Page One Award, 1944; National Council of Teachers of English Citation, 1945, Page One Award, 1945, and Institute for Education by Radio Award, 1946, all for "On a Note of Triumph!"; Wendell Wilkie One World Award, 1946; Freedom Foundation Honor Medal, 1950, for "Between Americans"; National Conference of Christians and Jews Award, 1951, for "Document A/777"; Foreign Language Press Film Critics Award and Academy of Motion Picture Arts and Sciences Academy Award nomination, both 1957, both for "Lust for Life"; Women's ORT Award, 1960, for "The Story of Ruth"; admitted to Radio Hall of Fame, 1962; Litt.D., Columbia College, 1967; Emmy Award, Academy of Television Arts and Sciences, 1970, for "The Plot to Overthrow Christmas"; Writers Guild of America Valentine Davies Award, 1972; Pacific Pioneer Broadcasters Carbon Mike Award, 1974; Broadcasters Promotion Association Award, 1984; PEN Body of Work Award, 1986; American College of Radio Arts, Crafts and Sciences fellow.

WRITINGS:

On a Note of Triumph!, Simon & Schuster, 1945.
Prayer for the Seventies, Doubleday, 1969.
Holes in a Stained Glass Window, Lyle Stuart, 1978.
Network at Fifty, Ritchie, 1979.
Greater Than the Bomb, Santa Susana Press, 1981.
A Date with Sandburg, Santa Susana Press, 1981.
Trivializing America, Lyle Stuart, 1984.

RADIO SCRIPTS

They Fly through the Air with the Greatest of Ease, Vrest Orton, 1939.
Thirteen by Corwin, Holt, 1942.

We Hold These Truths, Soskin Howell, 1942.
More by Corwin, Holt, 1944.
"Untitled" and Other Radio Dramas, Holt, 1947.
The Plot to Overthrow Christmas (first produced on Columbia Broadcasting System [CBS Radio], December 25, 1938), Holt, 1952.

Also author of scripts for numerous other radio series and special broadcasts, including "Words without Music," "Pursuit of Happiness," "Between Americans," and "Document A/777."

PLAYS

The Warrior (opera; first produced on Broadway at Metropolitan Opera House, November, 1947), Rullman, 1946.
Dog in the Sky: The Authentic and Unexpurgated Odyssey of Runyon Jones (first produced as "The Odyssey of Runyon Jones" in Los Angeles at Valley Music Theater, December 16, 1972), Simon & Schuster, 1952.
The Rivalry (first produced in Vancouver at Georgia Auditorium, September 23, 1957; produced on Broadway at Bijou Theater, February 7, 1959), Dramatists' Play Service, 1960.
The World of Carl Sandburg (first produced in Portland, Me., at State Theater, October 12, 1959; produced on Broadway at Henry Miller's Theater, September 14, 1960), Harcourt, 1961, acting edition, Samuel French, 1961.
Overkill and Megalove (first produced in Hollywood at Desilu Theater, July 24, 1964), World Publishing, 1963.
"Cervantes," first produced in Washington, D.C. at American Theater, September 6, 1973.
Jerusalem Printout (first produced in Los Angeles at Convention Center Auditorium, November 22, 1972), Raintree Press, 1978.

Also author of "Together Tonight: Jefferson, Hamilton, Burr," first produced in Bloomington, Ind., 1976.

CONTRIBUTOR

This Is War, Dodd, 1942.
Radio in Wartime, Greenberg, 1942.
The Three Readers, Readers Club, 1943.
Off Mike, Duell, Slown & Pearce, 1944.
While You Were Gone, Simon & Schuster, 1946.
Literature for Our Time, Henry Holt, 1947.
The American System of Government, McGraw, 1959.
War Poems of the United Nations, Dial, 1961.
Lincoln: A Contemporary Portrait, Doubleday, 1962.

OTHER

"The Golden Door" (cantata), first produced in Cleveland, Ohio at Music Hall, March 23, 1955.
(And host) "Academy Leaders" (television series), Public Broadcasting Service (PBS-TV), 1979.

Also author of screenplays, "The Blue Veil," 1951, "Scandal at Scourie," 1953, "Lust for Life," 1956, "The Story of Ruth," 1959, and "Winds of Change." Author of television scripts, including "The Plot to Overthrow Christmas," "F.D.R.," "Inside the Movie Kingdom," "The Court Martial of the Tiger of Malaya," "Norman Corwin Presents," "The Last GIs," and "The Trial of Yamashita." Author of column, "Corwin on Media," *Westways*, 1973-80.

SIDELIGHTS: Since the 1920s, Norman Corwin has written, directed, and produced programs for television, radio, film, and theatre. His motion picture script "Lust for Life" earned an Academy Award nomination, and his television adaptation of his radio play "The Plot to Overthrow Christmas" received an Emmy Award. But "more than anything else these days, Corwin is an outspoken essayist, a heavyweight gadfly, examining the way we are," writes Charles Champlin in the *Los Angeles Times*. In *Trivializing America*, Corwin expresses concern over the changes in American society since World War II. "The fabric of the society is loosening . . . ," he told Champlin. "We're better off in some ways. . . . But the quality of life has diminished." Corwin sees the breakdown in a national attitude that strives for momentary pleasure and is "amenable to getting-along-by-going-along, comfortable with mediocrity."

Richard G. Lillard praises *Trivializing America*, mentioning its suggestions for improving public institutions, private commercial enterprises, and personal lives. He declares in the *Los Angeles Times* that Corwin "chooses his topics and shapes his ideas in the high tradition of analysts who take on the whole scope of life in America . . . all of them writers sufficiently optimistic at heart to become stern critics of deficiencies in Americans and their institutions." But Robert B. Tucker, also writing for the *Los Angeles Times*, believes that Corwin is overly pessimistic: "In leaving out of his book any signs of a detrivialization process at work, Corwin ignores a growing number of writers who find cause for optimism and relief from just the sort of conditions about which he is concerned." Corwin, however, insists he believes in the resiliency of the American public. He told Champlin that "the American people have miraculously preserved their sanity, their decency and their integrity. They're slow sometimes to catch on, as about Vietnam, but they're catching on fast now, and that's heartening."

Corwin added to *CA*: "A writer should start worrying about his work not when it comes hard, but when it seems easy."

MEDIA ADAPTATIONS: Corwin's radio play "My Client Curley" was made into a movie entitled "Once upon a Time," starring Cary Grant.

BIOGRAPHICAL/CRITICAL SOURCES:

BOOKS

Authors in the News, Volume II, Gale, 1976.
Bannerman, R. LeRoy, *The Golden Age of Norman Corwin and Radio*, University of Alabama Press, 1985.
Barnouw, Erik, *The Golden Web*, Oxford University Press, 1968.
Bradbury, Ray, *About Norman Corwin*, Santa Susana Press, 1980.
Cousins, Norman, Studs Terkel, Charles Kuralt, Norman Lear and others, *Thirteen for Corwin*, Perpetua Press, 1985.
Julian, Joseph, *This Was Radio*, Viking, 1975.

PERIODICALS

Coronet, December, 1945.
Courier Journal and Times (Louisville, Ky.), February 1, 1976.
Liberty, February 10, 1945.
Los Angeles Times, May 16, 1984, April 27, 1985, March 1, 1987.
Los Angeles Times Book Review, October 30, 1983, June 8, 1986.
Newsweek, July 31, 1939.
New York Times Magazine, August 2, 1942.
Readers Theatre News, fall/winter, 1978.
San Diego Union, February 4, 1979.
Theatre Arts Monthly, September, 1942.

Time, November 20, 1939, April 15, 1940.
Variety, July 26, 1939.
Washington Star, February 5, 1979.

*   *   *

COULSON, Robert S(tratton) 1928-
(Thomas Stratton, a joint pseudonym)

PERSONAL: Surname is pronounced *Col*-son; born May 12, 1928, in Sullivan, Ind.; son of Springer (a house painter) and Mary (Stratton) Coulson; married Juanita Wellons (a writer and artist), August 21, 1954; children: Bruce Edward. *Education:* International Correspondence Schools, completed course in electrical engineering, 1960. *Politics:* "Political liberal, economic conservative." *Religion:* Agnostic.

ADDRESSES: Home—Route 3, Hartford City, Ind. 47348.

CAREER: Writer; text editor of *Yandro* (science fiction magazine), beginning 1953. Factory hand, Heckman's Bookbindery, North Manchester, Ind., 1947-57; Honeywell, Inc., Wabash, Ind., draftsman, 1957-59, technical writer, 1959-65; Overhead Door Co., Hartford City, Ind., lead draftsman, 1965-68, head draftsman, 1968-86. President of Filk Foundation, Inc., 1978—.

AWARDS, HONORS: Joint nominee with wife, Juanita Coulson, for Hugo Award, 1960-64, 1966-67, for best amateur science fiction magazine, *Yandro*, joint winner with J. Coulson, Hugo award, 1965, for *Yandro*, and co-Fan Guest of Honor, with J. Coulson, 30th World Science Fiction Convention, 1972, all from World Science Fiction Society.

WRITINGS:

(With Gene DeWeese) *Gates of the Universe*, Laser Books, 1975.
(With DeWeese) *Now You See Him/It/Them*, Doubleday, 1975.
To Renew the Ages, Laser Books, 1976.
(With Piers Anthony) *But What of Earth?*, Laser Books, 1976.
(Contributor) Sandra Ley, editor, *Beyond Time*, Pocket Books, 1976.
(With DeWeese) *Charles Fort Never Mentioned Wombats*, Doubleday, 1977.
(With DeWeese) *Nightmare Universe* (interactive science fiction novel; based on *Gates of the Universe*), TSR, 1985.
High Spy, TSR, 1987.
(Contributor) *Science Fiction Encyclopedia*, Viking, 1988.

WITH GENE DeWEESE, UNDER JOINT PSEUDONYM THOMAS STRATTON

The Invisibility Affair: Man from U.N.C.L.E., No. 11, Ace Books, 1967.
The Mindtwisters Affair: Man from U.N.C.L.E., No. 12, Ace Books, 1967.
(Contributor) L. Sprague DeCamp and George Scithers, editors, *The Conan Grimoire: Essays in Swordplay and Sorcery*, Mirage Press, 1972.

OTHER

Contributor to *Dictionary of Literary Biography*. Book reviewer for *Amazing Stories*, 1983-86, and *Comic Buyer's Guide*, 1983-86. Regular contributor to *Empire Fantasy*, 1981-84; also contributor, with DeWeese, of short stories to magazines, including *Amazing Stories* and *Magazine of Fantasy and Science Fiction*. Text editor of Science Fiction Writers of America's *Forum*, 1971-72.

SIDELIGHTS: Robert S. Coulson told *CA:* "I write primarily for the money and for the fun of it; mostly the latter. I still do columns for a couple of science fiction magazines (amateur, non-paying publications), because I like the people involved and enjoy giving opinions in the only publishing field completely free of market considerations and mostly free of status considerations. I write primarily science fiction because I enjoy the field and the people in it. I met my wife at a science fiction fan club meeting, and almost our entire social life is with science fiction people. I don't believe in conforming to anyone else's ideas, whether those ideas are middle-class, artistic, or revolutionary; I make up my own mind, and the science fiction community doesn't care what ideas I hold, as long as I'm willing to grant the same tolerance to others. I have, so far, had a hell of a good time in my life, made a lot of friends, and expect to keep on doing both for quite a few years yet."

*   *   *

COURT, Wesli
See TURCO, Lewis (Putnam)

*   *   *

COWAN, Ian Borthwick   1932-

PERSONAL: Born April 16, 1932, in Dumfries, Scotland; son of William McAuley (a banker) and Annie (Borthwick) Cowan; married Anna Little Telford, July 16, 1954; children: Gillian Alexandra, Susan Jane, Ingrid Kirsten. *Education:* University of Edinburgh, M.A. (with honors), 1954, Ph.D., 1961.

ADDRESSES: Home—119 Balshagray Ave., Glasgow G11 7EG, Scotland. *Office*—Department of Scottish History, University of Glasgow, 9 University Gardens, Glasgow G12 8QH, Scotland.

CAREER: University of Edinburgh, Edinburgh, Scotland, assistant lecturer in Scottish history, 1956-59; Newbattle Abbey College, Dalkeith, Scotland, lecturer in Scottish history, 1959-62; University of Glasgow, Glasgow, Scotland, lecturer, 1962-70, senior lecturer, 1970-77, reader, 1977-83, professor of Scottish history, 1983—. *Military service:* Royal Air Force, 1954-56; became flying officer.

MEMBER: Historical Association (vice-president, 1981—), Scottish History Society, Scottish Church History Society (president, 1971-74).

WRITINGS:

Blast and Counterblast: Contemporary Writings on the Scottish Reformation, Saltire Society, 1960.
The Parishes of Medieval Scotland, Scottish Record Society, 1967.
(Editor with A. I. Dunlop) *Calendar of Scottish Supplications to Rome,* Scottish History Society, 1970.
The Enigma of Mary Stuart, St. Martin's, 1971.
The Scottish Covenanters: 1660-1689, Gollancz, 1976.
(Reviser) D. E. Easson, *Medieval Religious Houses in Scotland* (1st edition, 1957), Longmans, 1976.
Regional Aspects of the Scottish Reformation, Historical Association, 1978.
The Scottish Reformation: Church and Society, Weidenfeld & Nicolson, 1982.
(Editor with D. Shaw) *The Renaissance and Reformation in Scotland: Essays in Honour of Gordon Donaldson,* Scottish Academic Press, 1982.

(Editor with H. McKay and A. Macquarrie) *The Knights of St. John,* Scottish History Society, 1983.
Ayrshire Abbeys: Crossroguel and Kilwinning, Ayrshire Archaeological Society, 1986.
Mary Queen of Scots, Saltire Society, 1987.

Contributor to history journals.

WORK IN PROGRESS: Heads of Medieval Religious Houses in Scotland, for Scottish Record Society.

SIDELIGHTS: Ian Borthwick Cowan told *CA:* "I feel it most desirable that the history of Scotland should be given universal prominence. My main interest is in medieval ecclesiastical history and to this end I have spent at least four weeks each year for the past decade travelling in Italy and studying in the Vatican archives."

Times Literary Supplement contributor Edward Playfair describes Gordon Donaldson as "one of the most learned of Scottish historians; also among the most generally useful ones, thanks to his ability and willingness to write for the ordinary reader as well as for the student." Of the book Cowan and D. Shaw edited, *The Renaissance and Reformation in Scotland: Essays in Honour of Gordon Donaldson,* Playfair writes: "The aim of the editors has been, very reasonably, to concentrate their contributors on Professor Donaldson's sixteenth century. By stressing the Renaissance in their title, they have acted as Procrustes to those of their contributors who have accepted both parts of the remit. . . . They have produced a mixed bag of readable matter."

BIOGRAPHICAL/CRITICAL SOURCES:

PERIODICALS

Times Literary Supplement, August 26, 1982.

*   *   *

COWLES, Fleur

PERSONAL: Born in New York, N.Y.; married third husband, Tom Montague Meyer (owner of a timber company), November 18, 1955. *Education:* Attended Pratt Institute.

ADDRESSES: Home and office—A5 Albany, Piccadilly, London W.1, England. *Agent*—Michael Shaw, Director, Curtis Brown, 162-168 Regent St., London W1R 5TA, England.

CAREER: Look, New York City, assistant editor, 1946-55, foreign agency correspondent, 1955-58; *Flair,* New York City, founder and editor, 1950-53; *Quick,* New York City, assistant editor, 1951-53. Special consultant to Famine Emergency Commission, 1946; personal representative of President Eisenhower, with rank of ambassador, at coronation of Queen Elizabeth II, 1952; member of advisory committee on women's participation, Civil Defense Administration, 1953-55. Trustee of Social Rehabilitation of the Facially Disfigured, and of Elmira College; member of council, American Museum, Bath, England.

MEMBER: Ordre les Compagnons de Rabelais, Women's National Press Club, Overseas Press Club, Theta Sigma Phi.

AWARDS, HONORS: Chevalier of the Legion of Honor (France), 1951; Queen's Medal (England), 1952; Order of the Southern Cross, Cavalier Class (Brazil), 1953, commander, 1973; La Dama de Isobel Catolica (Brazil); Order of Bienfascene (Greece), 1955; LL.D., Elmira College, 1955.

WRITINGS:

Bloody Precedent: The Peron Story, Random House, 1951.
The Case of Salvador Dali, Little, Brown, 1960.
The Hidden World of the Hadramoutt, Stevens, 1962.
Flair Book, Random House, 1963.
Friends and Memories, Morrow, 1974.
All Too True, Quartet Books, 1981.
The Flower Game, Morrow, 1983.
Flower Decorations, Random House, 1985.
People as Animals, Quartet Books, 1985, Morrow, 1986.

ILLUSTRATOR; ALL WITH TEXT BY ROBERT VAVRA

Tiger Flower, introduction by Yehudi Menuhin, Collins, 1968,
    Reynal, 1969.
Lion and Blue, introduction by Prince Bernhard of the Neth-
    erlands, Reynal, 1974.
Romany Free, Reynal, 1977.
The Love of Tiger Flower, introduction by Princess Grace of
    Monaco, Morrow, 1980.
To Be a Unicorn, Morrow, 1985.

OTHER

Contributor to *Atlantic Monthly, Daily Telegraph* (London),
Vogue (London), and to other newspapers and magazines.

WORK IN PROGRESS: A book on flowers.

SIDELIGHTS: "Fleur Cowles . . . has been awarded highest
honors by four governments—France, England, Greece and
Brazil," writes *Detroit News* art critic Joy Hakanson. "Major
museums have exhibited her paintings. The publishing world
regards her as a legend for her trail-blazing use of magazine
graphic arts." In the course of her career as an artist, author,
and publisher, Cowles has become acquainted with "kings,
queens, ambassadors and assorted celebrities from many walks
of life," notes Hakanson.

Moving in such exalted circles has given Cowles a solid base
of experience from which to write. Her books *Bloody Precedent: The Peron Story* and *The Case of Salvador Dali*, though
criticized for their careless, disorganized approach, have been
praised for the new information only personal experience can
bring to light. As V. L. Warren writes in his *New York Times*
review of *Bloody Precedent*, "Here is perhaps the most perceptive and accurate picture of Evita [Peron] published to date,
with illuminating details only . . . Cowles could provide."
Similarly, *The Case of Salvadore Dali* has been called "highly
readable and comprehensive" by *Springfield Republican*'s
Richard McLaughlin. Millie Robbins of the *San Francisco
Chronicle* adds that "the author has sifted and distilled into
intelligible and logical form most of the welter of printed Da-
liana, has unearthed some important hitherto unpublished data,
and spiked all the ingredients with her personal observations."
Cowles's *Friends and Memories* again draws heavily from this
fund of experience and anecdote. Although frequent writing
about influential people in Cowles's voluble style has brought
upon her occasional charges of sounding like a gossip columnist, her written works give readers a glimpse of the fascinating life she has led.

The *Detroit News*'s Cyndi Meagher emphasizes that the style
of Cowles's work as an artist is greatly removed from such a
celebrity existence, however. The paintings are characterized
by "otherworldliness," gentle simplicity, and a "friendly
quality" in which the tigers and lions that populate them wear
neither ferocious expressions nor claws. These animals, along
with birds and an occasional human being, also act as the basis

for Cowles's fantasy books *Tiger Flower, Lion and Blue, Romany Free*, and *The Love of Tiger Flower*. "Her paintings fit
none of the usual art classifications, although they have been
called naive, surreal, realistic, literary and illustrative," observes Hakanson. "The truth is that Fleur Cowles is an original, who creates her own world on canvas."

BIOGRAPHICAL/CRITICAL SOURCES:

BOOKS

Authors in the News, Volume I, Gale, 1976.

PERIODICALS

Detroit News, September 22, 1974, October 10, 1974.
New York Times, January 13, 1952.
San Francisco Chronicle, May 15, 1960.
Springfield Republican, May 15, 1960.
Washington Post, October 14, 1983.

*   *   *

COX, Constance   1915-

PERSONAL: Born October 25, 1915, in Sutton, Surrey, England; daughter of J. Frederick (an educator) and Anne E.
(Vince) Shaw; married Norman C. Cox (a Royal Air Force
pilot), June 7, 1933 (deceased). *Education:* Attended schools
in England.

ADDRESSES: Home—2 Princes Ave., Hove, Sussex, England. *Agent*—Eric Glass Ltd., 28 Berkeley Sq., London W1X
6HD, England.

CAREER: Playwright and adapter of classics for stage, 1942—;
writer and adapter for television, 1955—. Former racing and
competition driver; amateur actress and producer at Brighton
Little Theatre Co. and New Venture Theatre, both Brighton,
England.

MEMBER: Sussex Playwrights' Club (honorary treasurer), West
Sussex Writer's Club.

AWARDS, HONORS: News Chronicles award for best televi-
sion play of the year, 1956; Television and Screenwriters'
Guild Special Award for adaptations of the classics, 1964; Prix
Jeunesse International (second place) for thirteen-part televi-
sion serial, "The Old Curiosity Shop," 1964; Television and
Screenwriters' Guild Award, 1967, for television serial "The
Forsyte Saga."

WRITINGS:

PUBLISHED PLAYS

Vanity Fair (adapted from the novel by William Makepeace
    Thackeray), Samuel French, 1947.
The Picture of Dorian Gray (adapted from the novel by Oscar
    Wilde), Fortune Press, 1948.
Madame Bovary (adapted from the novel by Gustave Flau-
    bert), Fortune Press, 1948.
Northanger Abbey (adapted from the novel by Jane Austen),
    Fortune Press, 1950.
Mansfield Park (adapted from the novel by Jane Austen), Ev-
    ans Brothers, 1950, reprinted, Hub Publications, 1977.
The Count of Monte Cristo (adapted from the novel by Alex-
    ander Dumas), Fortune Press, 1950.
Spring at Marino (adapted from Ivan Turgenev's novel *Fa-
    thers and Sons*), Samuel French, 1951.
The Desert Air, English Theatre Guild, 1951.
Because of the Lockwoods, Evans Brothers, 1953.

Three Knaves of Normandy (adapted from the medieval comedy "The Farce of the Worthy Master Pierre Patelin"), Evans Brothers, 1958.

Jane Eyre (adapted from the novel by Charlotte Bronte), J. Garnet Miller, 1959.

Pride and Prejudice (adapted from the novel by Jane Austen), J. Garnet Miller, 1960, reprinted, 1972.

The Caliph's Minstrel, Evans Brothers, 1961.

Lord Arthur Saville's Crime (adapted from the short story by Oscar Wilde), Samuel French, 1963.

A Miniature 'Beggar's Opera' (adapted from the play by John Gay), Evans Brothers, 1964.

The Three-Cornered Hat (adapted from the play by Juan Ruiz Alarcon y Mendoza), Evans Brothers, 1966.

Trilby (adapted from the novel by George duMaurier), Evans Brothers, 1967.

The Woman in White (adapted from the novel by Wilkie Collins), Evans Brothers, 1967.

Everyman (adapted from the anonymous medieval morality play), Samuel French, 1967.

Maria Marten; or, Murder in the Red Barn, Samuel French, 1969.

Miss Letitia, Samuel French, 1970.

Wuthering Heights (adapted from the novel by Emily Bronte), English Theatre Guild, 1974.

The Murder Game, Samuel French, 1976.

Lady Audley's Secret, Samuel French, 1976.

A Time for Loving, Samuel French, 1986.

UNPUBLISHED, PRODUCED PLAYS

"The Romance of David Garrick," 1942.
"The Nine Days' Wonder," 1944.
"Remembering Dick Sheridan," 1944.
"The Hunchback of Notre Dame," 1944.
"Elizabeth and Darcy," 1945.
"Sleeping Dogs," 1947.
"Georgia Story," 1949.
"The Enemy in the House," 1951.
"The Woman in White," 1953.
"Heathcliff," 1959.
"Nightmare," 1963.

Also author of plays produced on television, "The Trial of Admiral Byng," "Trilby," "Heathcliff," "Lord Arthur Saville's Crime," "Georgia Story," "The Nine Days' Wonder," "Spring at Marino," and "Miss Letitia."

OTHER

Author of television serials, "Jane Eyre," "Vanity Fair," "Precious Bane," "The History of Mr. Polly," "The Lost King," "Champion Road," "Thunder in the West," "The Golden Spur," "Pride and Prejudice," "Little Women," "Good Wives," "Jo's Boys," "Bleak House," "Angel Pavement," "Oliver Twist," "The Old Curiosity Shop," "Lorna Doone," "Martin Chuzzlewit," "Rogue Herries," "Silas Marner," "Judith Paris," "A Tale of Two Cities," "John Halifax, Gentleman," "Jane Eyre" (new version), "The Master of Ballantrae," "The Franchise Affair," "The House under the Water," "Katy, and What Katy Did at School," "The Forsyte Saga," parts four, five, and seven, and "Rebecca of Sunnybrook Farm."

Author of radio series, "The Herries Chronicle," 1969, "War and Peace," 1971, "The Barchester Chronicles," 1974, "The Pickwick Papers," 1980, and "Christmas at Dingley Dell."

Also author of librettos for musical plays, "Vanity Fair," with Julian Slade, "Two Cities," 1969, and "Smiling Through," with John Hanson, 1974.

*   *   *

COX, William (Robert)   1901-
(Willard d'Arcy, Mike Frederic, John Parkhill, Joel Reeve, Wayne Robbins, Roger G. Spellman, Jonas Ward)

PERSONAL: Born April 14, 1901, in Peapack, N.J.; son of William and Marion Grace (Wenz) Cox; married second wife Casey Collins.

ADDRESSES: Home—Sherman Oaks, Calif. *Agent*—Don Congdon Associates, 177 East 70th St., New York, N.Y. 10021.

CAREER: Professional writer.

MEMBER: Writers Guild of America, Western Writers of America (past president).

WRITINGS:

NOVELS

Make My Coffin Strong, Fawcett, 1954.
The Lusty Men, Pyramid, 1957.
The Tycoon and the Tigress, Fawcett, 1958.
Hell to Pay, New American Library, 1958.
Comanche Moon: A Novel of the West, McGraw, 1959.
Murder in Vegas, New American Library, 1960.
Death Comes Early, Dell, 1961.
Death on Location, New American Library, 1962.
The Duke, New American Library, 1962.
The Outlawed, New American Library, 1963, published as *Navajo Blood*, 1973.
Bigger than Texas, Fawcett, 1963.
(Under pseudonym Roger G. Spellman) *Tall for a Texan*, Fawcett, 1965.
The Gunsharp, Fawcett, 1965.
Way to Go, Doll Baby!, Avon, 1966.
Black Silver, Profit Press, 1967.
Day of the Gun, Belmont, 1967.
Firecreek (based on screenplay by Calvin Clements), Bantam, 1968.
Moon of Cobre, Bantam, 1969.
Law Comes to Razor Edge, Popular Library, 1970.
The Sixth Horseman, Ballantine, 1972.
Jack o'Diamonds, Dell, 1972.
Chicano Cruz, Bantam, 1972.
Hot Times, Fawcett, 1973.
The Fourth-of-July Kid, Tower, 1981.
Cemetery Jones, Fawcett, 1985.
Cemetery Jones and the Maverick Kid, Fawcett, 1986.

NOVELS UNDER PSEUDONYM JONAS WARD; PUBLISHED BY FAWCETT

Buchanan's War, 1970.
Trap for Buchanan, 1971.
Buchanan's Gamble, 1972.
Buchanan's Siege, 1973.
Buchanan on the Run, 1973.
Get Buchanan!, 1974.
Buchanan Takes Over, 1975.
Buchanan Calls the Shots, 1975.
Buchanan's Big Showdown, 1976.
Buchanan's Texas Treasure, 1977.

Buchanan's Stolen Railway, 1978.
Buchanan's Manhunt, 1979.
Buchanan's Range War, 1979.
Buchanan's Big Fight, 1980.
Buchanan's Black Sheep, 1985.
Buchanan's Stage Line, 1986.

YOUNG ADULT NOVELS

Five Were Chosen: A Basketball Story, Dodd, 1956.
Gridiron Duel, Dodd, 1959.
The Wild Path, Dodd, 1963.
Tall on the Court, Dodd, 1964.
Third and Eight to Go, Dodd, 1964.
(Under pseudonym Mike Frederic) *Frank Merriwell, Freshman Quarterback*, Award, 1965.
(Under pseudonym Mike Frederic) *Frank Merriwell, Freshman Pitcher*, Award, 1965.
(Under pseudonym Mike Frederic) *Frank Merriwell, Sports Car Racer*, Award, 1965.
Big League Rookie, Dodd, 1965.
Trouble at Second Base, Dodd, 1966.
(Under pseudonym Joel Reeve) *Goal Ahead*, S. G. Phillips, 1967.
The Valley Eleven, Dodd, 1967.
Jump Shot Joe, Dodd, 1968.
Rookie in the Backcourt, Dodd, 1970.
Big League Sandlotters, Dodd, 1971.
Third and Goal, Dodd, 1971.
Gunner on the Court, Dodd, 1972.
Playoff, Bantam, 1972.
The Backyard Five, Dodd, 1973.
The Running Back, Bantam, 1974.
The Unbeatable Five, Dodd, 1974.
Game, Set, and Match, Dodd, 1977.
Battery Mates, Dodd, 1978.
Home Court Is Where You Find It, Dodd, 1980.

OTHER

Luke Short and His Era, Doubleday, 1961 (published in England as *Luke Short, Famous Gambler of the Old West: A Biography*, Foulsham for Fireside Press, 1962).
The Mets Will Win the Pennant (nonfiction), Putnam, 1964.
(Editor) *Rivers to Cross* (collection of stories by members of Western Writers of America), Dodd, 1966.

Author of several screenplays, including "The Veils of Bagdad," 1953, and "Tanganyika" with William Sackheim and Alan Simmons, 1954. Also author of more than one hundred television scripts for "Fireside Theater," "Broken Arrow," "Zane Grey Theatre," "Wells Fargo," "Bonanza," "The Grey Ghost," "Route 66," "Alcoa Theatre," "The Virginian," and other programs. Contributor of more than one thousand stories, including many under the pseudonyms Willard d'Arcy, John Parkhill, Joel Reeve, and Wayne Robbins, to crime and western publications and to such magazines as *Saturday Evening Post, Collier's, This Week, Argosy, American, Pic, Blue Book,* and *Cosmopolitan.*

WORK IN PROGRESS: A novel.

SIDELIGHTS: William Cox's career as a writer spans more than sixty years and includes as many novels, several screenplays, more than one hundred television scripts, and more than one thousand short stories. Cox's manuscripts are collected at the University of Oregon and the University of Wyoming.

CRAWFORD, Charles P.   1945-

PERSONAL: Born January 23, 1945, in Wayne, Pa.; son of Fronefield (an attorney) and Nancy Lee (Parker) Crawford; married Nancy Miller (a management training consultant), June 17, 1967 (divorced); children: Chad Wayne. *Education:* Williams College, B.A., 1966; Johns Hopkins University, M.A.T., 1967.

ADDRESSES: Home—360 Croton Rd., Wayne, Pa. 19087.

CAREER: Radnor Township School District, Wayne, Pa., 1967—, began as humanities teacher and coordinator, currently English teacher.

MEMBER: Philadelphia Children's Reading Roundtable.

WRITINGS:

JUVENILE NOVELS

Bad Fall, Harper, 1972.
Three-legged Race, Harper, 1974.
Letter Perfect, Dutton, 1977.
Split Time, Harper, 1987.

WORK IN PROGRESS: Additional juvenile novels.

SIDELIGHTS: Charles P. Crawford wrote *CA:* "I grew up in the town in which I now reside and teach, having attended the school at which I am employed. The setting of each of the juvenile novels is this town, thinly fictionalized. The inspiration for the stories comes from both my past and the current scene. I tend to use my own fading emotional feelings about my own adolescence in Wayne, Pennsylvania with whatever current trends, language and interests seem to be part of the contemporary scene. It helps, certainly, to be teaching the age group for which I write—I get a constant stimulus five days a week. And although my characters—despite what my students may think, having recognized the locations—are completely fictional, they gain, I hope, a veneer of reality thanks to my familiarization with the middle school scene.

"The town, the school, and, I suppose, the youth have all changed to a fair degree over the last twenty years. The territory bounded by my novels lies somewhere in between today and two decades ago—and because of that, I do try constantly to avoid any material which is 'dated' and would tend to place the stories in any particular year or time."

*　　*　　*

CREWS, Judson (Campbell)   1917-

PERSONAL: Born June 30, 1917, in Waco, Tex.; son of Noah George (a nurseryman) and Tommie (Farmer) Crews; married Mildred Tolbert (a photographer and writer), October 19, 1947 (divorced January, 1980); children: Anna Bush, Carole Judith. *Education:* Baylor University, A.B., 1941, M.A. (with honors), 1944, study in fine arts, 1946-47; University of Texas at El Paso, graduate study, 1967. *Politics:* None. *Religion:* None.

ADDRESSES: Home—P.O. Box 4435, Albuquerque, N.M. 87196.

CAREER: Landscape architect in Waco, Tex., 1936-39; publisher of Motive Press, Waco, Tex., and Este Es Press, Taos, N.M., 1946-66; El Paso County Child Welfare Unit, caseworker, 1966-67; Taos *Star, El Crepusculo,* and Taos News Publishing Co., printer, 1948-66; Wharton Junior College, Wharton, Tex., instructor in sociology and psychology, 1967-70; Community Mental Health Service, Gallup, N.M., psychological counsellor and community services coordinator, 1970-71; University of New Mexico Branch College, Gallup, lecturer in sociology, 1971-72; State School for Girls, Chillicothe, Mo., director of intensive care unit, 1973; University of Zambia, Lusaka, lecturer in social development studies, 1974-78. *Military service:* U.S. Army Medical Corps, 1942-44.

MEMBER: Yale Library Associates, Rio Grande Writers Association.

WRITINGS:

POETRY

Psalms for a Late Season, Iconograph Press, 1942.
No Is the Night, privately printed, 1949.
A Poet's Breath, privately printed, 1950.
Come Curse the Moon, privately printed, 1952.
The Anatomy of Proserpine, privately printed, 1955.
The Wrath Wrenched Splendor of Love, privately printed, 1956.
The Heart in Naked Hunger, Motive Book Shop, 1958.
To Wed beneath the Sun, privately printed, 1958.
The Ogres Who Were His Henchmen, Hearse Press, 1958.
Inwade to Briney Garth, Este Es Press (Taos, N.M.), 1960.
(Contributor) Fred Baver, compiler, *River,* River Spring, 1960.
The Feel of the Sun and Air upon Her Body, Hearse Press, 1960.
A Unicorn When Needs Be, Este Es Press, 1963.
Hermes Past the Hour, Este Es Press, 1963.
(Contributor) Louis Untermeyer, editor, *An Uninhibited Treasury of Erotic Poetry,* Dial, 1963.
Selected Poems, Renegade Press, 1964.
You, Mark Antony, Navigator upon the Nile, privately printed, 1964.
Angels Fall, They Are Towers, Este Es Press, 1965.
(With Wendell B. Anderson; under real name and under pseudonym Cerise Farallon) *Three on a Match,* privately printed, 1966.
The Stones of Konarak, American Poets Press, 1966.
(Contributor) A. W. Stevens, editor, *Poems Southwest,* Prescott College Press, 1968.
(Contributor) Robert L. Williams, compiler, *Mehy in His Carriage,* Summit Press, 1968.
(Contributor) Lawrence Ferlinghetti, editor, *City Lights Anthology,* City Lights, 1974.
(Contributor) Paul Foreman and Joanie Whitebird, editors, *Travois: An Anthology of Texas Poetry,* Thorp Springs Press, 1976.
Notions to Nations, Cherry Valley, 1976.
Nolo Contendere, edited by Joanie Whitebird, preface by Robert Creeley, Wings Press, 1978.
Modern Onions and Sociology, St. Valentine's Press, 1978.
Roma a Fat At, Instantaneous Centipede Publications, 1979.
Gluons, Q, Namaste Press, 1979.
The Noose, a Retrospective: Four Decades, edited by Larry Goodell and John Brandi, Duende Press, 1980.
The Clock of Moss, edited by Carol Berge and Dale Boyer, Ahsahta, 1983.

Also author of *A Sheaf of Christmas Verse,* published by Three Hands (Washington, D.C.).

OTHER

The Southern Temper, Motive Book Shop, 1946.
(With Wendell B. Anderson and Mildred Crews) *Patocinio Barela: Taos Wood Carver,* privately printed, 1955, revised edition, Taos Recordings and Publications, 1962.

Contributor to approximately 350 periodicals, including *Beloit Poetry Journal, Poetry Now, Wormwood Review, Puerto del Sol,* and *Southwestern American Literature.*

WORK IN PROGRESS: Three new collections of poetry.

SIDELIGHTS: Judson Crews told *CA* that during "an earlier phase [of my career], I was involved in editing and publishing several avant-garde magazines of the thirties, forties, and fifties. They ranged from *Vers Libre,* which lasted over two years, to *Taos,* a deluxe magazine of the arts which was a one-shot deal. In addition to the two above, *Motive, The Flying Fish, Suck-Egg Mule, The Deer and Dachshund, Poetry Taos,* and *The Naked Ear* were my sole responsibility. I was more than slightly involved with *Crescendo,* edited by Scott Greer, and *Gale,* edited by Jay Waite."

Crews later wrote *CA:* "I studied English and classical versification for two years, but in my own practice I have never regretted that I have chosen contemporary models for closest study. Any perceptive reviewer of my books will readily note two or three obvious influences on my work (William Carlos Williams, Wallace Stevens), but often enough two or three which simply do not apply (Sylvia Plath, Charles Olson); all seem to have missed the deep and lasting influence, quite early, of some of Delmore Schwartz's earliest and best work, or for that matter, James Agee.

"I disavow all formalist aspects of 'the [surrealistic] movement'—yet it is clear that the essential effect of my best and most characteristic work achieves an interface with the borderline of exceptional feelings and experiencings that may be most usefully thought of as the surreal.

"Thematically, my subjects extend to the entire range of human verities. But the one ever-recurring motif is the erotic, often explicit, in 'the naming of parts.' This work does not fit so very easily in the 'poetry of love' genre with much of the work of E. E. Cummings or Robert Graves, or for that matter Kenneth Rexroth and Kenneth Patchen.

"The over-riding project of most of my sixties has been a personal memoir begun in Africa in 1976. I worked regularly through most of the small hours of the morning on this project for seven years. I gave up the writing of poetry during this period. I worked exclusively from memory completing some 9,500 pages of narrative, bringing the story up to my midthirties.

"However, as I continued writing about the 1950s, I began to feel a greater and greater need for literal accuracy concerning my impressions of peoples and events in such a recent time. Earlier, I had been willing to rely on 'symbolic' accuracy, feeling-tones—the way it was to me. This change of approach was not total—I had no wish and no intention to 'research' my own life. But I did require access to my archives for the late fifties and early sixties housed in the Harry Ransom Humanities Research Center at the University of Texas. Here I ran into an impregnable wall in the form of several Catch 22s—conditions which I could not meet without grant money, a research assistant, and secretarial help. I have been stalled by a bureaucracy.

"I returned to the writing of poetry in 1982, and in the first three months produced a hundred poems from which Carol Berge culled *The Clock of Moss* collection."

Extensive archives of Crew's materials, including manuscripts and letters, are at University of Texas, Austin, University of

California, Los Angeles, Yale University, University of Zambia, and University of New Mexico.

BIOGRAPHICAL/CRITICAL SOURCES:

PERIODICALS

Poetry Now, Volume VI, number 6, 1982.

* * *

CRONIN, James E(mmet) 1908-

PERSONAL: Born November 10, 1908, in New York, N.Y.; son of James B. (a superintendent) and Anna (Scully) Cronin; married Elizabeth Goodwin (a voice teacher), July 6, 1940; children: Phoebe Cronin Solomon, Timothy. *Education:* Wesleyan University, B.A., 1930, M.A., 1934; Yale University, Ph.D., 1946. *Religion:* Roman Catholic.

ADDRESSES: Home—Townshend, Vt. 05353; and 3511 20th Ave. S.W., Largo, Fla. 33540.

CAREER: St. Joseph College, West Hartford, Conn., assistant professor of English, 1935-38; College of New Rochelle, New Rochelle, N.Y., assistant professor of English, 1938-42; *Time* (magazine), New York, N.Y., circulation promotion director of international editions, 1945-47; St. Louis University, St. Louis, Mo., director of Writer's Institute, 1948-62; Wesleyan University, Middletown, Conn., adjunct professor of English and director of Graduate Summer School, 1962-73. *Military service:* U.S. Naval Reserve, 1942-45; became lieutenant commander.

AWARDS, HONORS: M.A., Wesleyan University, 1973.

WRITINGS:

Hermann von Schrenk, Kuehn, 1959.
(Editor with Joseph Rogers and Maurice McNamee) *Literary Types and Themes,* Holt, 1960.
(Editor) *The Diary of Elihu Hubbard Smith,* American Philosophical Society, 1973.
Industrial Conflict in Modern Britain, Rowman & Littlefield, 1979.
(Editor with Jonathan Schneer) *Social Conflict and the Political Order in Modern Britain,* Rutgers University Press, 1982.
(Editor with Carmen Sirianni) *Work, Community, and Power: The Experience of Labor in Europe and America, 1900-1925,* Temple University Press, 1983.

* * *

CUNLIFFE, Barrington Windsor 1939-
(Barry Cunliffe)

PERSONAL: Born December 10, 1939, in Portsmouth, England; son of George (a naval officer) and Beatrice (Mersh) Cunliffe. *Education:* St. John's College, Cambridge, B.A., 1961, M.A., 1963, Ph.D., 1966, Litt.D., 1976.

ADDRESSES: Home—Oxford, England. *Office*—Institute of Archaeology, Oxford University, 36 Beaumont St., Oxford, England. *Agent*—Curtis Brown Ltd., 1 Craven Hill, London W2 3EW, England.

CAREER: University of Bristol, Bristol, England, lecturer in classics, 1963-66; University of Southampton, Southampton, England, professor of archaeology, 1966-72; Oxford University, Institute of Archaeology, Oxford, England, professor of

European archaeology and fellow of Keble College, 1972—. Commissioner, Historic Buildings and Monuments Commission.

MEMBER: British Academy (fellow), Society of Antiquaries (fellow), Royal Archaeological Institute, Prehistoric Society, Medieval Society, Society for the Promotion of Roman Studies, *Antiquity* Trust, *Vindolanda* Trust.

WRITINGS:

UNDER NAME BARRY CUNLIFFE

Excavations at Richborough, Volume V, Society of Antiquaries, 1968.
(Editor and contributor) *Roman Bath,* Society of Antiquaries, 1969.
Excavations at Fishbourne: 1961-1969, two volumes, Society of Antiquaries, 1971.
Fishbourne: A Roman Palace and Its Gardens, Johns Hopkins Press, 1971.
Roman Bath Discovered, Routledge & Kegan Paul, 1971, 2nd edition, 1984.
Guide to the Roman Remains of Bath, Gerrard, 1971, published as *Roman Baths: A Guide to the Baths and Roman Museum,* Bath Archaeological Trust, 1980.
The Cradle of England, British Broadcasting Corp., 1972.
The Making of the English, British Broadcasting Corp., 1973.
The Regni, Duckworth, 1974.
Iron Age Communities in Britain, Routledge & Kegan Paul, 1974, 2nd edition, 1978.
Excavations at Porchester Castle, Hants, Society of Antiquaries, Volume I: *1961-71: Roman,* 1975, Volume II: *1961-71: Saxon,* 1976, Volume III: *1961-71: Mediaeval—The Outer Bailey and Its Defenses,* 1977, Volume IV: *1973-79: Mediaeval—The Inner Bailey,* 1985.
Rome and the Barbarians, Walck, 1975.
(With Trevor Rowley) *Oppida: The Beginnings of Urbanisation in Barbarian Europe,* State Mutual Book and Periodical Service, 1976.
Iron Age Communities in Britain, Routledge & Kegan Paul, 1978.
Hengistbury Head, Merrimack Book Service, 1978.
Rome and Her Empire, McGraw, 1978.
The Celtic World, McGraw, 1979.
(Editor) *Excavations in Bath, 1950-75,* Committee for Rescue Archaeology in Avon, Gloucestershire and Somerset, 1979.
(Editor) *Coinage and Society in Britain and Gaul: Some Current Problems,* Council for British Archaeology, 1981.
(Editor) *Antiquity and Man,* Thames & Hudson, 1982.
Danebury: Anatomy of an Iron Age Hillfort, Batsford, 1983, published as *Danebury: An Iron Age Hillfort in Hampshire,* two volumes, Council for British Archaeology, 1984.
(Editor with David Miles) *Aspects of the Iron Age in Central Southern Britain,* Committee for Archaeology, Oxford University, 1984.
Heywood Sumner's Wessex, Gasson, 1985.
(With Peter Davenport) *Temple of Sulis Minerva at Bath,* Volume I: *The Site,* Committee for Archaeology, Oxford University, 1985.
The City of Bath, Sutton, 1986.
(Editor) *Origins: The Roots of European Civilization,* BBC Publications, 1987.

Also author of television scripts for British Broadcasting Corp., "Cradle of England" (six episodes), 1972, "Making of the English" (six episodes), 1973, "Pompeii," 1974, and "Throne of Kings" (six episodes), 1975; author of scripts for BBC radio program, "Origins." Contributor to archaeological journals, and contributor of reviews to *Times Literary Supplement, Nature,* and *New Scientist.* Executive editor of *World Archaeology.*

WORK IN PROGRESS: Results of archaeological excavations in Great Britain; research on Europe during the thousand years before the Romans invaded it.

AVOCATIONAL INTERESTS: Travel (East Europe, Mediterranean, "especially France and Iberia"), food, Chinese pottery.

BIOGRAPHICAL/CRITICAL SOURCES:

PERIODICALS

Times Literary Supplement, February 17, 1984.

*   *   *

CUNLIFFE, Barry
  See CUNLIFFE, Barrington Windsor

*   *   *

CURRY, Jane L(ouise) 1932-

PERSONAL: Born September 24, 1932, in East Liverpool, Ohio; daughter of William Jack, Jr., and Helen Margaret (Willis) Curry. *Education:* Attended Pennsylvania State University, 1950-51; Indiana State College (now Indiana University of Pennsylvania), B.S., 1954; attended University of California, Los Angeles, 1957-59; University of London, graduate study, 1961-62, 1965-66; Stanford University, M.A., 1962, Ph.D., 1969.

ADDRESSES: Home—Palo Alto, Calif.

CAREER: Writer and artist. Art teacher in Los Angeles, Calif., city schools, 1955-59; Stanford University, Stanford, Calif., teaching assistant, 1959-61 and 1964-65, acting instructor in English literature, 1967-68 and 1983-84, lecturer, 1987. Paintings shown in London at group exhibitions, including Royal Society of British Artists.

MEMBER: International Arthurian Society, Authors Guild, Authors League of America, Children's Literature Association, Society of Children's Book Writers, Modern Language Association of America, Philological Association of the Pacific Coast, Southern California Council on Literature for Children and Young People.

AWARDS, HONORS: Fulbright grant, 1961-62, and Stanford-Leverhulme fellowship, 1965-66, both for study in London;

Honor Book Award, *Book World* Spring Children's Book Festival, and Outstanding Book by a Southern California Author Award, Southern California Council on Literature for Children and Young People, 1970, both for *The Daybreakers;* "Book of the Month" citation from Deutsche Akademie fuer Kinder-und Jugenliteratur in Volkach, 1971; Ohioana Book Award, Martha Kinney Cooper Ohioana Library Association, 1977, for *Poor Tom's Ghost;* Edgar Allan Poe Special Award ("Edgar"), Mystery Writers of America, 1978, for *Poor Tom's Ghost,* and 1979, for *The Bassumtyte Treasure;* Distinguished Contribution to the Field of Children's Literature Award, Southern California Council on Literature for Children and Young People, 1979, for body of work.

WRITINGS:

JUVENILES

Down from the Lonely Mountain, 1965, self-illustrated edition, Dobson, 1967.
Beneath the Hill, Harcourt, 1967.
The Sleepers, Harcourt, 1968.
The Change-Child, Harcourt, 1969.
The Daybreakers, Harcourt, 1970.
Mindy's Mysterious Miniature, Harcourt, 1970.
Over the Sea's Edge, Harcourt, 1971.

PUBLISHED BY ATHENEUM

The Ice Ghosts Mystery, 1972.
Parsley, Sage, Rosemary, and Time, 1975.
The Watchers, 1975.
The Magical Cupboard, 1976.
Poor Tom's Ghost, 1977.
The Birdstones, 1977.
The Bassumtyte Treasure, 1978.
Ghost Lane, 1979.
The Wolves of Aam, 1981.
Shadow Dancers, 1983.
The Great Flood Mystery, 1985.
The Lotus Cup, 1986.
Back in the Beforetime, 1987.
Me, Myself, and I, 1987.

WORK IN PROGRESS: Little Eyases.

SIDELIGHTS: Some of Jane L. Curry's works have been translated into German.

AVOCATIONAL INTERESTS: Cooking, gardening, painting, travel, reading mysteries.

D

DALES, Richard C(lark) 1926-

PERSONAL: Born April 17, 1926, in Akron, Ohio; son of Gerald Lee (a jeweler) and Lucile (Miller) Dales; married Nancy Gene Vogeler (a teacher), July 7, 1950; children: Susan Zoe, David Richard. *Education:* University of Rochester, B.A., 1949; University of Colorado, M.A., 1952, Ph.D., 1955.

ADDRESSES: Home—616 Chatham Pl., Flintridge, Calif. 91011. *Office*—Department of History, University of Southern California, Los Angeles, Calif. 90007.

CAREER: North Dakota Agricultural College (now North Dakota State University), Fargo, instructor in history, 1954-55; Lewis and Clark College, Portland, Ore., instructor, 1955-56, assistant professor, 1956-59, associate professor of history, 1959-63; University of Southern California, Los Angeles, associate professor, 1964-66, professor of history, 1966—, chairman of department, 1969-72, acting chairman of department of classics, 1975-76. Visiting associate professor at University of Southern California, 1962-63, and University of California, Santa Barbara, 1963-64. Member of Institute for Advanced Study, Princeton, N.J., 1966-67. *Military service:* U.S. Army, Corps of Engineers, 1946-47.

AWARDS, HONORS: Danforth fellowship, 1957; American Council of Learned Societies fellowship, 1960-61, grant, 1973; American Philosophical Society travel grant, 1967; University of Southern California Associates' Award, 1975, for creative scholarship and research.

WRITINGS:

(Editor) *Roberti Grosseteste Commentarius on VIII Libros Physicorum Aristotelis,* University of Colorado Press, 1963.
The Scientific Achievement of the Middle Ages, University of Pennsylvania Press, 1973.
Marius on the Elements: An Edition with English Translation, University of California Press, 1976.
The Intellectual Life of Western Europe in the Middle Ages, University Press of America, 1979.
(Editor with Servus Gieben) Grosseteste, *Hexaemeron,* Oxford University Press, 1982.
(Editor with Edward King) Grosseteste, *British Academy-Auctores Britannici Medii Aevi VII: De Cessatione Legalirum,* Oxford University Press, 1986.

Contributor of about twenty articles to *Viator, Isis, Mediaeval Studies, Journal of the History of Ideas,* and other journals.

*   *   *

DALEY, Robert 1930-

PERSONAL: Born May 10, 1930; son of Arthur (a newspaper columnist) and Betty Daley; married Peggy Ernest, 1954; children: Theresa, Suzanne, Leslie Anne. *Education:* Fordham University, B.A.,1951.

ADDRESSES: Agent—Morton Janklow Associates, 598 Madison Ave., New York, N.Y. 10022.

CAREER: New York Giants football team, New York City, publicity director, 1953-58; *New York Times,* New York City, foreign correspondent in Europe and North Africa, 1959-64; deputy police commissioner, New York City Police Department, 1971-72; writer and free-lance photographer. Has exhibited work in Baltimore Museum, Art Institute of Chicago, and New York Gallery of Modern Art. *Military service:* U.S. Air Force, 1951-52.

MEMBER: Authors Guild.

WRITINGS:

The World Beneath the City, Lippincott, 1960.
Cars at Speed: The Grand Prix Circuit, Lippincott, 1961.
Sports in Europe, Morrow, 1962.
The Bizarre World of European Sports, Morrow, 1963.
The Cruel Sport, illustrated with photographs by Daley, Prentice-Hall, 1963.
The Swords of Spain, illustrated with photographs by Daley, Dial, 1966.
The Whole Truth, New American Library, 1967.
Only a Game, New American Library, 1968.
A Priest and a Girl, World Publishing, 1969.
(Editor) James McCracken and Sandra Warfield, *A Star in the Family: An Autobiography in Diary Form,* Coward, 1971.
Target Blue: An Insider's View of the N.Y.P.D., Delacorte, 1973.
Strong Wine, Red as Blood (novel), Harper Magazine Press, 1975.
To Kill a Cop, Crown, 1976.
The Fast One, Crown, 1977.

Treasure (Book-of-the-Month Club alternate selection), Random House, 1977.

Prince of the City: The Story of a Cop Who Knew Too Much (Book-of-the-Month Club selection and *Reader's Digest* Condensed Book Club selection), Houghton, 1978.

An American Saga: Juan Trippe and His Pan Am Empire, Random House, 1980.

Year of the Dragon (novel; Literary Guild alternate selection), Simon & Schuster, 1981.

The Dangerous Edge (novel; Book-of-the-Month Club alternate selection), Simon & Schuster, 1983.

Hands of a Stranger (Literary Guild alternate selection), Simon & Schuster, 1985.

Man with a Gun (novel; Literary Guild selection and Reader's Digest Condensed Book Club selection), Simon & Schuster, 1988.

Contributor of fiction, articles, and photographs to *American Heritage, Saturday Evening Post, Reader's Digest, Cosmopolitan, Esquire, New York Times Magazine, Playboy, Vogue, New York, Life, Newsweek,* and other periodicals.

WORK IN PROGRESS: Portraits of France.

SIDELIGHTS: A prolific writer of both fiction and nonfiction, Robert Daley has published books covering a wide variety of topics, such as bullfighting in *The Swords of Spain,* celibacy and the priesthood in *A Priest and a Girl,* wine production in *Strong Wine, Red as Blood,* and police corruption in *Prince of the City: The Story of a Cop Who Knew Too Much.* Because of his talent and versatility, Anne Chamberlin describes him in the *Saturday Review* as a writer who "could make good copy out of the Omaha, Nebraska telephone book." While most of his work has been well received by readers and reviewers alike, it is his stories of police corruption, politics, and intrigue that have made him a best-selling author and attracted national attention. A former deputy police commissioner for the city of New York, Daley brings first-hand experience to his police books and effectively recreates the inner working of a large metropolitan police bureau.

Target Blue: An Insider's View of the N.Y.P.D. is Daley's account of his year as deputy police commissioner. Mary Perot Nichols explains in the *New York Times Book Review* that this book "is a compendium of episodes leading up to Robert Daley's appointment by Patrick Murphy to his police public-relations post and his one-year career thereafter." A reviewer for *Publishers Weekly* believes that *Target Blue* is "overwhelming in its total depiction of the cop's lot on every level—patrolman, detective, precinct chief, top brass. It is compulsive reading from first to last. If it is flawed by lurid moments, so is a cop's life. Daley's narrative sums up a year of anxiety, humiliation, terror." L. W. Lindsay remarks in the *Christian Science Monitor* that "while *Target Blue* confirms a lot of the worst charges made against the police, its total effect is to create appreciation for—even admiration of—the lowly patrolmen. And the 'insider's view of the N.Y.P.D.' promised on the jacket—the Knapp commission hearings, the aftermath of 'French Connection,' the enigmatic commissioner Murphy and his handpicked lieutenants—is just fascinating."

Daley's *Prince of the City: The Story of a Cop Who Knew Too Much* is the engrossing and true story of undercover police officer Robert Leuci and his special assignment to the Knapp Commission. The Knapp Commission was established to investigate charges of corruption within the New York Police Department. Daley became familiar with Leuci's undercover investigations during the year he served as deputy police com-

missioner. When Leuci asked him to help tell the story of his work for the Knapp Commission, Daley became interested in Leuci's view of it and agreed to write *Prince of the City.* Although Daley initially experienced difficulty finding a publisher for the book, *Prince of the City* quickly achieved best-seller status, and shortly thereafter a movie deal was made.

Most critics found *Prince of the City* to be a gripping account of big city police corruption and politics and one man's struggle to do the right thing when faced with formidable obstacles. For example, J. A. Leonard remarks in *Library Journal* that *Prince of the City* is a "compelling drama of a man torn between loyalty to the police fraternity and the need to seek redemption for past indiscretions. . . . His efforts as an undercover agent led to the indictment of dishonest cops, crooked lawyers, and organized crime figures."

"Right from the start, this fascinating true-life tale catches an unusually complicated hero in crisis," writes Tony Schwartz in *Newsweek.* "By beginning with Leuci's most heroic gesture—the decision to go undercover—and showing his extraordinary skill in that role, Daley . . . builds enormous sympathy for the detective. In the second half of the book he intersperses details of Leuci's highly checkered past with the trials in which he begins to testify. All along, Leuci feels caught between two powerful standards of morality: one set by the law, the other developed by cops themselves to get by in a lawless world." Finally, Ted Morgan of the *New York Times Book Review* states that "the policeman as flawed hero, a recurrent and enormously popular figure in contemporary writing . . . has never been done better than in *Prince of the City.* . . . Daley . . . has coaxed his sources into providing material that is guaranteed to raise the hair on the back of the neck of every reader."

In addition to his nonfiction police stories, Daley has written five novels involving police intrigue, mystery, and department politics: *To Kill a Cop, Year of the Dragon, The Dangerous Edge, Hands of a Stranger,* and *A Man with a Gun.* Most of these books have been made into either feature-length films or television movies, with *To Kill a Cop* serving as the basis for the NBC television series "Eischied." Richard R. Lingeman believes that Robert Daley's police novels are "a cut above the usual police story" and states in a *New York Times* review that "the most pleasure in . . . Daley's [*To Kill a Cop*] derives from his rather cynical insights into the bureaucratic intrigues of the [Police] Department. . . . When it comes to police procedure, . . . Daley could have written the manual."

"Mr. Daley seems to be thoroughly at home in the roomy house of fiction," remarks Anatole Broyard in the *New York Times.* In his review of Daley's *The Dangerous Edge* Broyard writes that there is "none of the awkwardness, forcing or stilted invention that spoils some suspense novels. . . . Mr. Daley also disturbs our complacency, but he does it without breaking any laws—even the laws, if such a conception still survives, of novel writing." "[*The Dangerous Edge*] by Robert Daley is not only a non-stop thriller but also a story of surprising depth," comments Stanley Ellin in the *New York Times Book Review.* "This is engrossing and rewarding reading to the last word." Gerry Clark writes in a *Best Sellers* review, that *The Dangerous Edge* is "a psychological novel that peers into the soul of both criminal and policeman with equal, brutal honesty." And a reviewer for *Publishers Weekly* concludes that "Daley's knowledge of police procedure, his compassionate insight into human nature and his talent as a storyteller add up here to a gripping detective novel that is also a romantic, moving love story."

Aside from his books on police corruption and mystery thrillers, Daley has written a number of works of nonfiction that have also been very well received. One such publication is *The Swords of Spain*, a book about bullfighting that includes nearly 200 photographs taken by Daley at bullfights in Spain. Robert Lipsyte remarks in the *New York Times* that "this book is probably the finest general introduction to the art-sport, and, as an emotional, educational and esthetic experience, the next thing to a good afternoon in the plaza." Barnaby Conrad comments in the *New York Times Book Review:* "Robert Daley has created a fine, accurate, informative and, incidentally, beautiful book.... This volume will gladden many a heart, for besides his many superb photographs, Daley's word portraits ... are incisive and informative—unromantic looks at the leaders of a much romanticized profession. They give the best idea of what a bullfighter's life is really like that I have read anywhere."

Another one of his many nonfiction works to draw favorable reviews is Daley's biography of Juan Trippe and the history of Pan Am Airways. For example, a critic comments in *Booklist* that Daley's *An American Saga: Juan Trippe and His Pan Am Experience* is "another excellent account of the aviation and corporate pioneers who built air empires. [This] neat combination of biography and history also ... discusses the advantages [Pan Am] helped to make in long-distance flights, aerial navigation, and the introduction of jumbo jets."

Anne Chamberlin writes in *Saturday Review* that *An American Saga* "is a mesmerizing account of the early buccaneering days of American commercial aviation that will keep you gasping for breath, clutching for your seatbelt, and once in a while ... wiping away a tear. By the time the story winds down ... you find you've rolled through five pages of financial tables and all the chapter source notes without thinking to put on the brakes."

CA INTERVIEW

CA interviewed Robert Daley by telephone on April 27, 1987, at his home.

CA: Your father, Arthur Daley, was a sports columnist for the New York Times. *Was it partly through his example that you became a writer?*

DALEY: I suppose so. There are two things. I remember once, early on, going to La Guardia Field, as it was called then, standing at the foot of the steps and watching him come off a plane in the night carrying a typewriter. I thought that was really neat. I have no idea how old I was. The other thing is that I started to read in the summers, and I'd read all day long. My father would get very irritated with me and tell me to go out and play, not just sit around. I started then wanting to write stories and books like the ones that had been delighting me. I wrote my first novel at twelve! My father told me I could use his typewriter if I would learn to type with all ten fingers, so I did. I got constant encouragement from him as I grew up, writing for the high school paper and then the college paper. I never wanted to be anything else other than a writer, and I always wanted to be a novelist. I got enthused at some point with becoming the greatest writer who ever lived, which I think is common to nearly everybody. Then, in order to get married and have a job and bring home some money, I got into journalism.

CA: How did you happen, meantime, to go to work as publicity director for the New York Giants, from 1953 to 1958?

DALEY: I was twenty-three years old and fresh out of the air force, and my father's best friend was Jack Mara, who owned the Giants. He offered me this job at $65 a week with a nice title. The principal function for the person in this job was to go buy liquor for the coaches after practice; it was called "The 5:30 Club." Nobody was much interested in pro football at that time. Even when the Giants won the so-called world championship, exactly thirty years before they won it again last January, there were 8,000 to 10,000 empty seats. There was a crowd of only 56,000 people that year, 1956, when the Giants beat the Chicago Bears.

I kept that job for six seasons. I was able to leave during the off-season if I had enough money, because they didn't need me. So every year we didn't have babies, we took what we had and went to Europe for six months. And I tried to write all the time, but especially during those six-month periods, I wrote articles, I wrote stories, I wrote another novel. I had written the one when I was twelve that I mentioned earlier, which I tore up the next year. I wrote another when I was twenty-two, which is still in a drawer, and a third one when I was twenty-five, which is also still in a drawer. And God knows how many short stories that are still in drawers. After six years with the Giants, I made an arrangement with the *New York Times* to be a roving, part-time sports correspondent in Europe, so we spent all our money on first-class tickets on a ship, and we left.

CA: It was through research for an article that you became deputy police commissioner for the New York Police Department in 1971-1972. Target Blue *is your account of that experience. What prompted your interest in the NYPD originally?*

DALEY: Life magazine asked me to write an article about Sergeant David Durk. It was Durk who instigated the famous Knapp Commission in 1970. He was a friend of Patrolman Serpico. A gambler gave Serpico $300. Serpico didn't know what to do with it, so he went straight to Sergeant Durk. Durk then began to take Serpico around to all the agencies to try to get an investigation into police corruption going. Nobody would give either one of them the time of day. Serpico had the evidence, but Durk had the drive to try to get it going.

Life magazine asked me to write an article about Durk, which I did, and through Durk I met Serpico. I found Serpico charming and wrote a cover article about him for *New York* magazine. Then the editor of *New York* magazine at the time, Clay Felker, sent me to do an article on the new police commissioner, Patrick V. Murphy, who had new ideas, who believed Durk and Serpico, and who had promised to end corruption, update the department, and so forth. The first day I was with Murphy, he asked me if I wanted to go to work for him. I had no interest whatever in going into the police department; I had no use for cops, no respect for cops. But he kept after me.

It all came about through the magazine articles, and really it was almost an accident. Murphy caught me at a weak moment: I was sick of sitting home in a little room every day. I could see that it might be interesting, and certainly it was a chance to do public service. If you think you're one of the good guys and yet you don't accept such an offer, then you're *not* one of the good guys. So I walked in there not knowing what I was going to find. The second or third day I went to the chief of detectives and asked for some information about the case of two cops who had been assassinated by the Black Liberation Army. He refused to give it to me. So I went back to the police commissioner and said, "He won't tell me." Murphy said, "You're to know everything I know." At that moment I thought, I may have lucked out here.

CA: How do you feel about that part of your life now, looking back on it?

DALEY: I'm very grateful I had it.

CA: A lot of books have come out of that experience.

DALEY: A lot of books by me, and also a lot of books by other people. At the time I went in there, nobody was looking at the police department, and cops were not allowed to say boo to anybody without permission. Certainly they were not allowed to write anything without permission. The first thing I did was say, "Look. Anybody can talk to anybody he wants, and anybody can write anything he wants. Let's let the people see what they have here. The cops will behave better as a result, and so will the public." At least I accomplished that, and maybe one or two other things.

As far as I personally was concerned, it fitted in with my New York City, Irish-Catholic, good-and-evil, black-and-white, right-and-wrong type of background. Every time I got involved in a major investigation, I would run into some detective that I had been in grade school with. I really was *home* in the New York City Police Department. I had the right name, the right everything to fit in, to get close, to see what was happening, and then afterward to try to put it into perspective and do something with it.

What's important, for instance, is not what caliber gun cops are issued when they take the oath of office, but the fact that that gun weighs on their lives and their consciousnesses. It's more badge than their badges. It's their badge of honor. They must never be without it; they're always looking around for where they put it. There are other things I came to understand by being in there that you don't ever learn any other way. And those are the important things.

CA: Another of your nonfiction police books was Prince of the City, *about NYPD undercover agent Robert Leuci. How did Leuci feel about having his story written, and how did the two of you work together on it?*

DALEY: Murphy thought I should know everything that was going on, but he never told me about Leuci, who was under cover all this time. Murphy used to come into these executive conference meetings and say, "What have you heard? What investigations don't I know about?" He was plainly worried about something, but nobody knew what; he kept it strictly to himself. Then the story broke and Leuci came to light. My reaction was, Well, I certainly don't want anything to do with any crooked cop.

I had heard along the way that somebody was going to write his life story. That was fine; I didn't particularly care one way or the other. That arrangement fell through and he called me up. I didn't much want to talk to him, but he was a policeman, and by this time I had a deep feeling for cops, who are really the most despised minority on the face of the earth. I thought I owed him at least the courtesy of talking to him. So he came around to my house and started to tell me his story, and it

turned out that that week was the final trial, the trial of his partner, which is the climax of the book and also of the movie. In fact, he was up there testifying against himself.

I thought there was a news peg here: I could write an article for *New York* about this, and maybe then we could get a book contract. I wouldn't lose anything by it because at least I would have the fee for the magazine article. By this time, of course, I was intrigued. It is a dazzling story, and terribly sad. It had a lot of elements in it to which I respond. I didn't know how I responded to Leuci at the time—I still don't—but I knew exactly how I responded to everybody else in the story and to the police department temptations, traumas, and so on.

Once the article came out in *New York* magazine, we tried to get a book contract, and nobody wanted it. Finally Houghton Mifflin agreed to take it for $25,000, which wasn't enough to pay for the time it would take to write it. I brooded about that for such a long time, and finally I thought, Well, I can knock this off fast. I have most of the information already. It's my material and I know what to do with it, and I don't have anything else going for me right now.

Leuci came to my house every day; we virtually lived together. He had wonderful recall, and it was also possible to get all the documents to back him up—the eavesdropping tapes on people he entrapped, the trial minutes, the police reports. I interviewed all the prosecutors involved. When I began trying to write it, it was agony. It was impossible to tell who was the good guy and the bad guy in each of the scenes. Ultimately, after a very long time—maybe a year and a half—it was finished. I started another book the next day; I was in debt by then and never expected *Prince of the City* to make a nickel. Lo and behold, it sold to the movies for half a million dollars, it was a $650,000 paperback sale, and it was a full selection of the Book-of-the-Month Club and the Reader's Digest Condensed Book Club. It was the biggest financial success of my life to that time.

I remember I went on tour with Leuci afterwards, when the book came out, and I was carrying with me the manuscript of the book I'd written next, the one I started the day afer I finished *Prince of the City,* and editing it in odd moments. Leuci and I toured sixteen cities in six weeks. We did ninety-six interviews. The one line from the interviews that I remember best was when one of these talk-show guys who really considered himself a sharp questioner said to Leuci, "I want to know just one thing, Detective. Who's your psychiatrist?" I said, "I am. What's the next question?" That was the first time I realized that I really *had* been.

CA: Some of your police books show how fuzzy the line can be between right and wrong, how ever-present the temptations are, and how easy the choices can be to rationalize.

DALEY: That was part of what was so exciting about being in the department. The whole Irish-Catholic ethos of my boyhood was that everybody can tell what's black and what's white, and black is a sin and white is not. The police department is imbued with that. I don't know what the percentage of Irish-Catholic cops on the force is at this point, but even the Jewish cops obey the Irish-Catholic rules, in which the worst sin is adultery or fornication, but being a drunk is okay. That's oversimplifying, but not by much.

CA: To Kill a Cop and Prince of the City *were filmed, and* To Kill a Cop *became the television series "Eischied." Were you pleased with the transformations of those books to film and television?*

DALEY: Yes. I've now had five books that have been filmed. Of the five, I'm very happy with three. "Prince of the City" is one. It was as noble and honorable an attempt at something brilliant as has ever happened. I had nothing whatever to do with the film; that was all Sidney Lumet. I think he made a few mistakes; he came up against the same problems I did here and there, and I think I solved them and he didn't. He should have just done it the way I did, or something like. "To Kill a Cop" was more or less the book word-for-word. The only thing I might say is that it's a pity they didn't have three or four times as much money to really make it perfect. Every film, not just films made from my books, is a compromise. "Hands of a Stranger" played on NBC, with a screenplay by Arthur Kopit. It's just about as good as you can hope for. I have reservations about it too, but you have to say to yourself, Look: they only have so much money to shoot it, they only have so much time to shoot it, you can't have such and such a scene because they would have to pay a new actor to do this scene, and they can't do that. When you make allowances for all the restrictions the form imposes, then you ask yourself what was possible and how close they came to what was possible. They came pretty close to a hundred percent on all three of those films.

Then you have "Year of the Dragon" by Michael Cimino, and he didn't reach ten percent. It's a disgrace. He kept nothing from the book except a few violent incidents, to which he added a hundred even more violent incidents plus a good deal of sexism and racism, and he made a stupid film. But I'm very lucky to have three good movies out of five.

CA: How well generally do you think police work is portrayed on television?

DALEY: I watch relatively few of the police shows, but on the whole they are ridiculous. These writers all copy each other, and none of them know anything about it. They get a couple of nice words of jargon and use them, and think they have authenticity. Then they misuse other things. For instance, "Cagney and Lacey," which is a show I love whenever it sticks to the relationship between those two women, at one point had them supposedly doing surveillance in broad daylight in front of somebody's house, sitting in the front seat of the car, which is ridiculous to start with. Secondly, the guy they're watching calls the police. The police car pulls up, and Cagney explains to the patrolman that she's now about to reach into her pocket for her shield. That's the kind of thing cops do in certain desperate situations, when everybody is so terrified that their hands are trembling on the trigger. You don't have to do that in broad daylight. So this reduces something that is potentially an important detail to silliness. That's just a simple example of the kind of thing I'm talking about.

I wrote an article for the *New York Times Magazine* in the early '70s about these shows. Later there was an incident in "Hill Street Blues," a show everybody raves about, where a cop takes a bribe from an undercover cop. Then he apologizes for it, tells how broken-hearted he is, and they let him stay. That isn't the way it is. You're cheapening the whole world we live in when you portray something like that. Any such cop would be indicted instantly, and certainly fired from his job. He might not go to jail, or he might; but he certainly couldn't be forgiven. One of the terrible things about law enforcement is that there's no confession; there's no absolution.

You're stuck with it, buddy, and they can get you many years later—as the Leuci story proves.

CA: You've had your photographs exhibited at the Art Institute of Chicago, among other galleries. How did photography come into your career?

DALEY: When I went to Europe for the *New York Times*, I was not on the staff. I'd had the idea that I could go to famous sporting events and report them. I would do this for $50 a story and I'd pay my own expenses. The sports editor, James Roach, was an absolutely lovely man. First I had gone to the managing editor, who said no. Then I dropped down to another editor, who said no. And finally I went to James Roach, who said yes. He went to the top editors and argued it through and then he and I made the final arrangements.

I was to do two stories a week, so I'd get $100 a week. This was in 1958, '59. As I was leaving, Roach said, "Oh, get a camera. If we use any of your pictures, you get $15 extra." So I got a camera, and the first week, which was the world bobsled championship at St. Moritz, I took about fourteen pictures, at which point the camera froze. I sent the roll of film to the *Times,* and the next Sunday four of those pictures were published, which meant $60. But even more than that, they were pretty good pictures. They thrilled me. I began to get fascinated by it and to take more and more pictures and buy better and better cameras. At one point I loved it so much that I thought, Maybe I'll stop being a writer and become a photographer.

I did a picture book on Grand Prix car racing called *The Cruel Sport* and one on bullfighting called *The Swords of Spain.* The first book had 165 of my photos, and the second about 200. Of course I took many other photos of all kinds, and many of them were published in the *Times.* I used to average about seventy-five a year in the *Times* and in the *Times Magazine.* I had a cover of *Newsweek* once. I really loved it. Then there was an exhibition being planned called "Man in Sport," which made a major museum tour. I had about twenty photos in the exhibition. Some very big names in photography were in it.

When I left the *New York Times* and came back to America, I suddenly realized that I couldn't bear to take just snapshots. They had to be great photos or nothing, so I gave it up completely. But now I've started on a book to be called *Portraits of France,* which will be part memoir, part old-fashioned travel book, and inevitably part history of France. I'm going to try to get a hundred pictures in that, too, so I've started to take pictures again, and I'm getting all excited about it again.

CA: Your wife, I know, is French, and your 1983 novel The Dangerous Edge *was set in France. Do you spend a lot of time there?*

DALEY: We keep an apartment in Nice, so we've been going back at least twice a year for the last twenty-some-odd years, and sometimes more often. At one point our youngest daughter, who was born there, was the only one who didn't speak French fluently, so we went back for four months and put her in a French school. Whenever we would go back, I'd usually get some magazine assignments to pay for the trip. Or I've gone back because I was writing books about the country. We've already done two or three trips to get material for *Portraits of France.*

As far as *The Dangerous Edge* was concerned, I needed to get some information about the French police, among other things.

I knew about smuggling cigarettes in France, but I didn't know many of the details, which I needed to know in order to find dramatic scenes for my story. The first cop that I talked to was a man whose name somebody gave me. We went out to dinner with him, and we weren't with him ten minutes before I said to myself: This man is a New York City detective. He doesn't have a word of English, but he's a New York City detective anyway. I understood an enormous amount about him going in. They even have the same jargon, though I'm sure there's been no intercommunication between the two departments. Nobody in France ever told the cops there that the American cops call the bad guys animals, and yet the French cop suddenly started talking about *les animaux.*

CA: You do an almost incredible amount of research. For Year of the Dragon *you went all the way to Hong Kong. For* Treasure, *the story of Mel Fisher's search for the sunken galleon* Atocha, *you joined Fisher and his family and crew in the actual diving and went to Madrid to study the archives that Fisher's historian, Eugene Lyon, had worked with. Your research for* An American Saga: Juan Trippe and His Pan American Empire *involved extensive interviews. Obviously research is a part of the process that you enjoy very much.*

DALEY: Yes. Sometimes something happens that's very special. For instance, the week I spent in Seville going through those archives was one of the most delightful weeks of my life. Interviewing people, hanging around people—yes, that's fun. For *Hands of a Stranger* I interviewed rape victims, including one who was still trembling, her rape was so recent. That's a tremendous experience. I don't know many people who've had it. I've had that and many others.

CA: Your work with the New York Giants and the New York Police Department involved heavy public contact, as some of the research for the books has done. When it comes to the lonely work of sitting down to put words on paper, do you miss being with people?

DALEY: It is two different things, and sometimes I think it's two different talents. Sometimes it works out well. With *An American Saga* I would do all the research on one chapter and then come back and write it, then go back and research another. That's not always possible, but when it is, you get a nice break right at the point where you're bloody sick of waiting in an anteroom until somebody will see you, or sick of having looked forward all week to an interview that turns out to be a bust. I did I don't know how many interviews with Juan Trippe for *An American Saga;* I spent I don't know how many hours with him. He was getting paid—he got something like fifteen percent of the royalties on that book—and he didn't give me one good line the whole time. It was terribly frustrating. It was almost dishonest. He'd been avoiding answering questions for so many years, he probably didn't know how to answer questions.

CA: Your fiction and nonfiction have dovetailed very nicely. Do you feel equally at home in both forms?

DALEY: I think so. At a certain point I get tired of one and I'm happy to go to the other. I've done four novels in a row, and now I'm doing a nonfiction book. I looked forward to it, thinking, Oh, this is going to be so much easier. No longer do I have to figure out still another way to describe a sunset. And yet I sit down trying to write this material, and I think,

If only I could make it up and not have to adhere to facts that don't quite fit together!

MEDIA ADAPTATIONS: The Cruel Sport was adapted as a film and released under the title "Grand Prix" by Metro-Goldwyn-Mayer in 1966; *To Kill a Cop* was adapted for television and produced as a four-hour miniseries by the National Broadcasting Co. in 1978, and was the basis of the television series "Eischied," produced by NBC, 1979-80; *Prince of the City* was adapted as a film and released by Warner Brothers in 1981; *Year of the Dragon* was adapted as a film and released by Metro-Goldwyn-Mayer in 1985; *Hands of a Stranger* was adapted for television and produced as a four-hour miniseries by NBC in 1987.

BIOGRAPHICAL/CRITICAL SOURCES:

PERIODICALS

Best Sellers, November 15, 1969, July, 1980, October, 1983.
Booklist, May 1, 1980.
Book Week, May 7, 1967.
Christian Science Monitor, July 5, 1973, July 6, 1977.
Library Journal, December 15, 1963, November 1, 1969, March 15, 1973, November 15, 1978.
Listener, August 10, 1967.
Newsweek, April 17, 1967, June 11, 1973, January 29, 1979.
New York Times, May 13, 1966, April 14, 1967, April 17, 1972, May 21, 1975, November 12, 1976, April 28, 1977, April 28, 1978, June 21, 1979, August 13, 1983, October 3, 1983.
New York Times Book Review, April 3, 1966, November 2, 1969, May 27, 1973, Februrary 10, 1974, November 14, 1976, May 1, 1977, May 14, 1978, January 7, 1979, November 29, 1981, August 13, 1983, September 25, 1983, August 25, 1985.
Observer, October 16, 1983.
Publishers Weekly, April 2, 1973, December 10, 1973, July 18, 1977, November 13, 1978, September 4, 1981, June 10, 1983, June 29, 1984, June 28, 1985.
Saturday Review, December 16, 1967, April 5, 1975, May, 1980.
Time, April 21, 1967.
Virginia Quarterly Review, winter, 1976.
Washington Post Book World, October 19, 1969, January 21, 1979, July 10, 1980, August 19, 1983.

—*Sketch by Margaret Mazurkiewicz*

—*Interview by Jean W. Ross*

*   *   *

DANIELS, Les(lie Noel III) 1943-

PERSONAL: Born October 27, 1943, in Danbury, Conn.; son of Leslie Noel, Jr. (a copywriter) and Eva (Ruppaner) Daniels. *Education:* Brown University, B.A., 1965, M.A., 1968.

ADDRESSES: Home—Box 814, Providence, R.I. 02901. *Agent*—Merrilee Heifetz, Writer's House, 21 West 26th St., New York, N.Y. 10010.

CAREER: Musician, composer, and writer. Formerly associated with the musical group "Soop."

WRITINGS:

Comix: A History of Comic Books in America, Outerbridge & Dienstfrey, 1971.
Living in Fear: A History of Horror in the Mass Media, Scribner, 1975.

(Editor) *Dying of Fright: Masterpieces of the Macabre*, Scribner, 1976.

(Editor) *Thirteen Tales of Terror* (textbook), Scribner, 1976.

The Black Castle (novel), Scribner, 1978.

The Silver Skull (novel), Scribner, 1979.

Citizen Vampire (novel), Scribner, 1981.

Yellow Fog, Donald Grant, 1986, expanded edition, Tor Books, 1988.

(Contributor) Dennis Etheison, editor, *Cutting Edge*, Doubleday, 1986.

No Blood Spilled (novel), Tor Books, 1988.

*　　*　　*

DANIELS, Shouri
See RAMANUJAN, Molly

*　　*　　*

d'ARCY, Willard
See COX, William (Robert)

*　　*　　*

DAVIDSON, Roger H(arry) 1936-

PERSONAL: Born July 31, 1936, in Washington, D.C.; son of Ross Wallace (a botanist) and Mildred (Younger) Davidson; married Nancy Dixon (an editorial assistant at Brookings Institution), September 29, 1961; children: Douglas Ross, Christopher Reed. *Education:* University of Colorado, B.A. (magna cum laude), 1958; Columbia University, Ph.D., 1963.

ADDRESSES: Office—2144 Le Frak Hall, University of Maryland, College Park, Md. 20742.

CAREER: Fort Collins Coloradoan, Fort Collins, Colo., municipal reporter, summers, 1957-59; Brookings Institution, Washington, D.C., research assistant, 1960; Dartmouth College, Hanover, N.H., assistant professor of government, 1962-68; University of California, Santa Barbara, associate professor, 1968-71, professor of political science, 1971-82; U.S. Library of Congress, Congressional Research Service, Washington, D.C., senior specialist on American government, 1980-87; University of Maryland, College Park, professor of government and politics, 1987—. Staff associate, W. E. Upjohn Institute for Employment Research, Washington, D.C., 1965-66; chairman, Upper Valley Human Rights Council, Hanover, N.H., 1967-68; scholar-in-residence, National Manpower Policy Task Force, 1970-71; professional staff member, Select Committee on Committees of U.S. House of Representatives, 1973-74, and of U.S. Senate, 1976-77. Member of Gioleta Valley Citizens Planning Group, Santa Barbara, Calif., 1974-75.

MEMBER: National Academy of Public Administration, American Political Science Association, American Association of University Professors, Western Political Science Association, Phi Beta Kappa, Delta Sigma Rho.

AWARDS, HONORS: Faculty fellowship, Dartmouth College, 1965-66.

WRITINGS:

(With D. M. Kovenock and M. K. O'Leary) *Congress in Crisis: Politics and Congressional Reform*, Wadsworth, 1966.

(With J. F. Bibby) *On Capitol Hill: Studies in Legislative Politics*, Holt, 1967, 2nd edition, 1972.

(With Sar A. Levitan) *Antipoverty Housekeeping: The Administration of the Economic Opportunity Act*, Institute of Labor and Industrial Relations, University of Michigan/Wayne State University, 1968.

The Role of the Congressman, Pegasus, 1969.

The Politics of Comprehensive Manpower Legislation, Johns Hopkins University Press, 1972.

(With Samuel Charles Patterson and Randall B. Ripley) *A More Perfect Union: Introduction to American Government*, Dorsey, 1972, 3rd edition, 1985.

(With W. V. Oleszek) *Congress against Itself*, Indiana University Press, 1977.

(With Oleszek) *Congress and Its Members*, Congressional Quarterly Press, 1981, 2nd edition, 1985.

(With Oleszek) *Governing*, Congressional Quarterly Press, 1987.

Contributor to *American Behavioral Scientist, American Journal of Political Science, Western Political Quarterly,* and other journals.

WORK IN PROGRESS: Continuing research into public opinion and attitudes of the public toward legislative bodies.

*　　*　　*

DAYTON, Donald W(ilber) 1942-

PERSONAL: Born July 25, 1942, in Chicago, Ill.; son of Wilber Thomas (a professor and college president) and Donna (a librarian and college teacher; maiden name, Fisher) Dayton; married Lucille Sider, June 9, 1969; children: Charles Soren. *Education:* Houghton College, B.A. (magna cum laude), 1963; Columbia University, graduate study, 1963-64; Yale University, B.D., 1969; University of Kentucky, M.S. in L.S., 1969; University of Chicago, Ph.D., 1978; also attended American Institute in Jerusalem and Asbury Theological Seminary. *Politics:* Independent Democrat. *Religion:* Wesleyan Church of America.

ADDRESSES: Home—5104 North Christiana Ave., Chicago, Ill. 60625. *Office*—Department of Theology, Northern Baptist Theological Seminary, 660 East Butterfield Rd., Lombard, Ill. 60148.

CAREER: Asbury Theological Seminary, Wilmore, Ky., instructor, 1970-71, assistant professor of bibliography, 1971-72, acquisitions librarian at B. L. Fisher Library, 1969-72; North Park Theological Seminary, Chicago, Ill., assistant professor, 1972-77, associate professor of theology, 1977-80, director of Mellander Library, 1972-80; Northern Baptist Theological Seminary, Lombard, Ill., professor of theology, 1980—. Staley lecturer, Anderson College, 1977; member of faculty, Seminary Consortium on Urban Pastoral Education, 1977—. Member of board of directors of Chicago Urban Life Center, 1972—.

MEMBER: World Methodist Historical Society, Karl Barth Society of North America (member of board of directors, 1972—), American Society of Church History, Wesleyan Theological Society (member of executive committee, 1974—), American Academy of Religion, Society of Biblical Literature, Conference on Faith and History, Society for Pentecostal Studies, American Theological Library Association (member-at-large of board of directors, 1976-79), Christian Holiness Association (member of board of administration, 1973—), Chicago Area Theological Library Association (chairman, 1975-76), Theta Phi.

AWARDS, HONORS: Woodrow Wilson fellowship, 1964-65.

WRITINGS:

Theological Bibliography and Reference Resources, Asbury Theological Seminary, 1970, revised edition, 1972.

The American Holiness Movement: A Bibliographic Introduction, Asbury Theological Seminary, 1971, 2nd edition, in press.

(With David Faupel and Susan Schultz) *Resources for Research,* Asbury Theological Seminary, 1972.

(Editor and author of introduction) *Five Sermons and a Tract by Luther Lee,* Holrad House, 1975.

(Editor) *Contemporary Perspectives on Pietism,* Covenant Press, 1976.

Discovering an Evangelical Heritage, Harper, 1976.

(Compiler) Charles G. Finney, *Reflections on Revival,* Bethany Fellowship, 1979.

(Editor with M. Darrol Bryant) *Coming Kingdom: Essays in American Millennialism and Eschatology,* Paragon House, 1984.

EDITOR; "HIGHER CHRISTIAN LIFE" SERIES; PUBLISHED BY GARLAND PUBLISHING

Account of the Union Meeting for the Promotion of Scriptural Holiness: Held at Oxford, August 29, to September 7, 1874, 1985.

The Devotional Writings of Robert Pearsall Smith and Hannah Whitall Smith, 1985.

Holiness Tracts Defending the Ministry of Women, 1985.

Late Nineteenth-Century Revivalist Teachings of the Holy Spirit, 1985.

The Sermons of Charles F. Parham, 1985.

(And author of preface) *Seven "Jesus Only" Tracts,* 1985.

Three Early Pentecostal Tracts, 1985.

The Work of T. B. Baratt, 1985.

(With Cecil M. Robeck) *Witness to Pentecost: The Life of Frank Bartleman,* 1985.

W. E. Boardman, *The Higher Christian Life,* 1985.

John P. Brooks, *The Divine Church,* 1985.

Russell K. Carter, *Russell Kelso Carter on "Faith Healing": The Atonement for Sin and Sickness, "Faith Healing" Reviewed after Twenty Years,* 1985.

W. H. Daniels, *Dr. Cullis and His Work,* 1985.

James H. Fairchild, *Oberlin: The Colony and the College,* 1985.

John B. Figgis, *Keswick from Within,* 1985.

Paul Fleisch, *Die Moderne Gemeinschaftsbewegung in Deutschland,* 1985.

Earnest B. Gordon, *Adoniram Judson Gordon,* 1985.

A. M. Hills, *Holiness and Power for the Church and the Ministry,* 1985.

Ralph C. Horner, *From the Altar to the Upper Room,* 1985.

Agnes N. LaBerge, *What God Hath Wrought,* 1985.

Luther Lee, *Autobiography of the Rev. Luther Lee,* 1985.

Asa Mahan, *Out of Darkness into Light,* 1985.

William McDonald and John E. Searless, *The Life of the Rev. John S. Inskip,* 1985.

A. McLean and J. W. Easton, *Penual; or Face to Face with God,* 1985.

Aimee S. McPherson, *This Is That: Personal Experiences, Sermons and Writings,* 1985.

Carrie J. Montgomery, *The Life and Teaching of Carrie Judd Montgomery,* 1985.

Phoebe Palmer, *The Devotional Writings of Phoebe Palmer,* 1985.

Palmer, *The Promise of the Father,* 1985.

(With Palmer) *Pioneer Experiences,* 1985.

G. P. Pardington, *Twenty-Five Wonderful Years, Eighteen Eighty-Nine to Nineteen Fourteen: A Popular Sketch of the Christian and Missionary Alliance,* 1985.

Also editor of *Phineas F. Bresse: A Prince in Israel,* by E. A. Girvin.

CONTRIBUTOR

Paul Hostetler, editor, *Perfect Love and War,* Evangel Press (Nappanee, Ind.), 1974.

Craig Ellison, editor, *The Urban Mission,* Eerdmans, 1974.

H. Vinson Synan, editor, *Aspects of Pentecostal and Charismatic Origins,* Logos International, 1975.

Robert Welsh, editor, *Ecumenical Exercise IV,* World Council of Churches, 1976.

(Contributor of bibliography) Richard and Joyce Boldrey, *Chauvinist Or Feminist?: Paul's View of Women,* Baker Book, 1976.

OTHER

Also author of a booklet, *Evangelical Roots of Feminism.* Contributor to *Baker's Dictionary of Christian Ethics, The New International Dictionary of the Christian Church,* and to theology journals. Book editor of *Sojourners,* 1975— . Contributing editor of *Post-American,* 1974— , and *Epworth Pulpit,* 1977— ; *Covenant Quarterly,* member of editorial committee, 1974— , acting editor, 1975; editorial associate of *Other Side,* 1975— ; member of editorial network of ethics section of *Religious Studies Review,* 1975— .

WORK IN PROGRESS: Karl Barth in English: An Annotated Bibliography of Primary and Secondary Literature, for Scarecrow; editing *Women Called and Chosen: Historical Sources for a Distinctively Christian Feminism,* with wife, Lucille Sider Dayton, and Nancy Hardesty, for John Knox; editing *The Wesleyans,* with Howard Snyder; editing an anthology of essays showing the signficance of Karl Barth for American life and theology, with Walt Lowe; "Women in the Holiness Movement: Feminism in the Evangelical Tradition," to be included in *Women of Spirit: Female Leadership in Religion, Past and Future,* edited by Rosemary Reuther and Eleanor McLaughlin, for Simon & Schuster; research for a book on the theological roots of Pentecostalism.

SIDELIGHTS: Donald W. Dayton once told *CA:* "*Discovering an Evangelical Heritage* was an effort to get my head together with regard to relating to my own roots in 'evangelicalism.' By reaching back behind recent fundamentalist experience I was able to recover a tradition of social activism rooted in evangelical religion that supported commitments I had made in the 1960s to civil rights movements and other currents for social justice. . . . One of the most formative experiences in my life was to spend most of 1967 in Israel, living through the Six-Day War in Jerusalem and then living five months on a kibbutz near Haifa."

AVOCATIONAL INTERESTS: Modern drama, book collecting.

BIOGRAPHICAL/CRITICAL SOURCES:

PERIODICALS

Christian Century, October 20, 1976.†

*   *   *

DEAKIN, James   1929-

PERSONAL: Born December 3, 1929, in St. Louis, Mo.; son

of Rogers (a surgeon) and Dorothy (Jeffrey) Deakin; married Doris Kanter (a free-lance writer), April 14, 1956; children: David Andrew. *Education:* Washington University, St. Louis, Mo., B.A., 1951, graduate study, 1951-52. *Politics:* Independent.

ADDRESSES: Home—815 Cape Harbor Dr., Southport, N.C. 28461.

CAREER: St. Louis Post-Dispatch, 1951-81, member of staff of Washington Bureau, Washington, D.C., 1954-81, White House correspondent, 1955-81; George Washington University, Washington, D.C., adjunct associate professor of journalism and faculty associate for political communications, 1981-87.

MEMBER: White House Correspondents' Association (president, 1974-75).

AWARDS, HONORS: Distinguished Alumnus Citation, Washington University, 1973; Merriman Smith Award for White House reporting, 1977; Woodrow Wilson International Center for Scholars fellow, 1980-81; Markle Foundation grant, 1981.

WRITINGS:

The Lobbyists, Public Affairs Press, 1966.
Lyndon Johnson's Credibility Gap, Public Affairs Press, 1968.
(Co-author) *Smiling through the Apocalypse,* Esquire Press, 1971.
The Presidency and the Press, L.B.J. School of Public Affairs, University of Texas at Austin, 1977.
The White House Press on the Presidency, University Press of Virginia, 1983.
The American Presidency: Principles and Problems, Volume II, University Press of Virginia, 1983.
Straight Stuff: The Reporters, the White House and the Truth, Morrow, 1984.

Contributor to periodicals, including *New Republic, Esquire,* and *Progressive.*

SIDELIGHTS: Straight Stuff: The Reporters, the White House and the Truth is James Deakin's "impertinent, laconic and very entertaining account of his 25 years in the White House press corps," offers Gene Lyons in *Newsweek.* According to *Washington Post Book World* critic Charles B. Seib, *Straight Stuff,* which looks as far back as the Eisenhower administration, is "partly an anecdotal history of the press relations of presidents . . . , partly an old-timer-remembers-when account and partly a serious exploration of the issues and problems besetting national news coverage. . . . Deakin deals thoughtfully with the subtleties of the relationships between the press and president. He sees one relationship as symbiotic; the press needs the president and [the president] needs the press." For *New York Times Book Review* critic Steven R. Weisman, Deakin has a "romantic view of the White House press corps as essentially a group of truth seekers, and he tells endless stories about the deceitfulness of Presidents. . . . At his best, he captures some of the silliness of the world of White House correspondents."

BIOGRAPHICAL/CRITICAL SOURCES:

PERIODICALS

Nation, June 16, 1984.
Newsweek, March 5, 1984.
New York Times Book Review, May 13, 1984.
Times Literary Supplement, December 7, 1984.
Washington Post Book World, February 12, 1984.

DELPHOS, Omar
   See ALD, Roy A(llison)

*   *   *

DeMARCO, Donald   1937-

PERSONAL: Born April 20, 1937, in Fall River, Mass.; married Mary Arendt; children: Jocelyn, Donald, Jr., Paul, Peter, Elizabeth. *Education:* Stonehill College, B.S., 1959, A.B., 1961; graduate study at State College at Bridgewater (now Bridgewater State College) and at Gregorian University, 1961-62; St. John's University, Jamaica, N.Y., M.A., 1965, Ph.D., 1969. *Religion:* Roman Catholic.

ADDRESSES: Home—101 Silverspring Cr., Kitchener, Ontario, Canada N2M 4P3. *Office*—St. Jerome's College, University of Waterloo, Waterloo, Ontario, Canada N2L 3G3.

CAREER: Stonehill College, North Easton, Mass., lecturer in music aesthetics, 1960-61; junior high school teacher of mathematics in Fall River, Mass., 1962; high school teacher of mathematics and science in Dartmouth, Mass., 1962-63; teacher of mathematics and sciences in private school in Fairhaven, Mass., 1963-64; St. John's University, Jamaica, N.Y., 1965-70, began as instructor, became assistant professor of philosophy; University of Waterloo, St. Jerome's College, Waterloo, Ontario, assistant professor, 1970-75, associate professor of philosophy, 1975—. Scholar-in-residence, Holy Apostles' College, Cromwell, Conn.; visiting professor, St. Joseph's University College, Edmonton, Alberta, and Catholic Bible College of Canada, Canmore, Alberta; teacher of medical ethics at St. Joseph's School of Nursing, Guelph, Ontario, 1972, and at St. Mary's School of Nursing, Kitchener, Ontario, 1972-75. Piano teacher in Fall River, 1962-64; has directed choirs and given piano recitals. Birthright of Kitchener-Waterloo, president of board of directors, 1971—, currently member of international board; member of board of Federated Appeal of Kitchener-Waterloo, 1975—.

MEMBER: Fellowship of Catholic Scholars.

WRITINGS:

The Peace Movement without Peer (booklet), Carmelite Nuns of Fort Worth, Tex., 1973.
Abortion in Perspective: The Rose Palace or the Fiery Dragon?, Hiltz, 1974.
(Contributor) Mykola Kolankiwsky, editor, *The Passion of Christ,* Niagara Falls Art Gallery and Museum, 1974.
(Contributor) E. J. Kremer and E. A. Synon, editors, *Death before Life,* Griffin House, 1974.
Sex and the Illusion of Freedom, Mission Press, 1981.
(Contributor) Hilgers, Horan, and Mall, editors, *New Perspectives on Human Abortion,* Altheia Books, 1981.
Today's Family in Crisis, Marian Press, 1982.
The Anaesthetic Society, Christendom College Press, 1982.
The Shape of Love, Fidelity House, 1983.
(Contributor) James Bopp, Jr., editor, *Human Life and Health Care Ethics* (anthology), University Publications of America, 1985.
Life Issues and the Catholic Church, Trinity Communications, 1987.
The Incarnation in a Divided World, Christendom College Press, 1987.

Also contributor to anthologies. Columnist and feature writer, *Toronto Catholic Register*, 1972—. Contributor of hundreds of articles and reviews to more than sixty professional journals, magazines, and newspapers, including *American Ecclesiastical Review, New Oxford Review, Communio, Human Life Review, Social Justice Review, National Catholic Register,* and *Theologisches*. Associate editor, *Child and Family Quarterly*.

SIDELIGHTS: Donald DeMarco told *CA:* "There are two elementary forces at work in the universe and in the human heart: grace and gravity. Writing is the stubborn and heroic refusal to allow gravity to be victorious. It is a way of providing both light and lightness, but at the same time the art of curing pain wth pain."

*   *   *

DESSAU, Joanna 1921-

PERSONAL: Surname is pronounced Dess-so; born June 11, 1921, in London, England; daughter of George William Darling (an educator) and Hilda (Ledward-Wallers) Thomsett; married Walter Saloman, June 3, 1949 (divorced, 1959); married Henry Montague Dessau-Greene (an accountant), August 27, 1971; children: (first marriage) Nicholas. *Education:* Studied at Royal Academy of Music, 1927-37; Rachel McMillan Training College, qualified teacher, 1938-41, nursery school diploma, 1941. *Religion:* Church of England.

ADDRESSES: Home—12 Wavertree Rd., South Woodford, London E18 1BL, England.

CAREER: Teacher at nursery school at Glyndebourne Opera House, Sussex, England, 1941-45; nursery school teacher in London, England, 1946-49; headmistress of nursery school in London, 1949-53; teacher of general subjects at infant school in London, 1958-66; Avondale Park School, London, teacher of remedial subjects, 1966-70, music specialist, 1970-77; full-time writer, 1977—. Guest on radio programs.

AWARDS, HONORS: First prize in a national poetry competition, 1965, for "Neptune."

WRITINGS:

NOVELS

The Red-Haired Brat (first volume of a trilogy), R. Hale, 1978, St. Martin's, 1979.
Absolute Elizabeth (second volume of trilogy), R. Hale, 1978, St. Martin's, 1979.
Fantastic Marvellous Queen (third volume of trilogy), R. Hale, 1979.
The Grey Goose, R. Hale, 1979.
Cock Robin, R. Hale, 1980.
Amazing Grace, R. Hale, 1980.
Lord of the Ladies, R. Hale, 1981.
The Constant Lover, R. Hale, 1982.
The Blacksmith's Daughter, R. Hale, 1983.
Crown of Sorrows, R. Hale, 1983.
No Way Out, R. Hale, 1984.

OTHER

Also author of children's plays, including "Long Ago on Christmas Eve," published in *Child Education*, 1952, "Virtue Victorious," "Virus Victrix," "The Misadventures of Miss," "Never Say Die," and "Press on Regardless."

SIDELIGHTS: Joanna Dessau told *CA:* "I have written all my life, but not for publication. In 1959 my marriage broke down and my husband and I divorced. The next ten years were very difficult indeed and I had a great struggle with tough circumstances and declining health, but I never stopped writing. I wrote plays, stories, and music for children, all of which were used and/or performed in the schools in which I taught.

"One of my pupils was the pop music star Adam Ant, with whom I never lost touch, for he was one of my son's greatest friends; he still writes to me and telephones me.

"In 1971 I remarried and at once my life became less pressured. I found myself able to relax enough to collect my thoughts, to have time to sit and work on a project that had been dear to my heart for a very long time—a historical novel on the subject of my favorite lady, Queen Elizabeth I. History is a passion with me and was one of the subjects I taught.

"I did not hurry over this project, for my new husband owned a large-ish Victorian house on the edge of Essex which was in dire and urgent need of decoration and restoration. Regretfully, I gave up my beloved flat in St. John's Wood, and turned many of my energies to the herculean task of the house. We did it all ourselves and, in the main, it was great, for I love interior decorating. I made enormous curtains, covered furniture, brought the garden back to life, and discovered a talent for wallpapering and plastering!

"During this time I was working in a deprived area in West London, driving myself right across London every day. I had also become a music specialist, working in the mornings only, on doctor's orders.

"In 1976 my book was ready to send to a publisher. Six weeks later the manuscript was accepted, with an option for two more novels. I have not stopped writing since then, and all my work has been published.

"My mother was descended from Sir John Dowdall, a courtier at the court of Queen Elizabeth I. His daughter, Elizabeth, married the Cromwellian general Sir Hardress Waller, the Wolf of Cornwall. He was Oliver Cromwell's aide-de-camp and cousin to Edmund Waller, the Restoration poet-laureate under King Charles II. My mother was also descended from Sir Josiah Wedgwood of pottery fame, and from Charles Darwin, the naturalist.

"My father is descended from a farming family in Scotland, a son of which left for England in the eighteenth century and became a lighthouse keeper at Bamburgh, a remote village on the coast of Northumberland. His name was Robert Darling. His son, William, succeeded him as lighthouse keeper and William's youngest daughter was the famous Grace Darling. William's elder brother, Robert, left for London in 1797, and my father is descended from this branch of the family.

"*Amazing Grace* is the story of the life and death of Grace Darling, England's first national heroine, who, with her father, rowed out in a terrible storm to rescue shipwrecked survivors stranded on a rock far out to sea. She lived with her parents in the lonely lighthouse and was very shy; her resultant fame was really the cause of her death.

Dessau later wrote *CA* about her more recent books: "*The Blacksmith's Daughter* is about the life and death of the notorious Lady Hamilton, who became wife to Sir William Hamilton, the British Ambassador to the Court of the Kingdom of the Two Sicilies and mistress to the great naval hero, Admiral Lord Nelson, whose daughter she bore.

"*Crown of Sorrows* is about the tragic King Richard II, who came to the throne of England in 1377 at the age of ten years. He was centuries ahead of his time; an anti-war, peace-loving humanitarian, who could read and write—which was considered effeminate! He saved England from a revolution by his personal bravery at the age of fourteen, but despite all this, was deposed and murdered by his jealous cousin who took the crown for himself.

"*No Way Out* tells of Elisabeth, Empress of Austria, a wild, affectionate, freedom-loving young girl, who was forced into a dynastic marriage with her cousin, the Emperor Franz Joseph, at the age of sixteen. He loved her, but never attempted to understand her, and, because of the restrictions of Court protocol and the unkind attitude of her aunt-mother-in-law, became a neurotic anorexic. She was assassinated on the 10th of September, 1898, in Geneva, whilst on holiday.''

AVOCATIONAL INTERESTS: "I draw and paint, knit and sew, play the piano and write music, and am a very keen photographer. I am greatly interested in architecture and archaeology and social history. I am a voracious reader with an extremely catholic taste. I model in clay and sing to professional standard. I have, in addition, a great attraction to psychology and psychiatry, finding people and their motivations utterly fascinating. I am an astrologer and draw up birth charts; although I was not trained to do this, I come from a very psychic family.''

*   *   *

DeWEESE, Gene
See DeWEESE, Thomas Eugene

*   *   *

DeWEESE, Jean
See DeWEESE, Thomas Eugene

*   *   *

DeWEESE, Thomas Eugene   1934-
(Gene DeWeese; Jean DeWeese, a pseudonym; Thomas Stratton, Victoria Thomas, joint pseudonyms)

PERSONAL: Born January 31, 1934, in Rochester, Ind.; son of Thomas Jacob and Alfreda (a print shop worker; maiden name, Henning) DeWeese; married Beverly Joanne Amers (a librarian), May, 1955. *Education:* Valparaiso Technical Institute, associate degree in electronics, 1953; also attended University of Wisconsin—Milwaukee, Indiana University, and Marquette University. *Politics:* Independent. *Religion:* None.

ADDRESSES: Home and office—2718 North Prospect, Milwaukee, Wis. 53211. *Agent*—Sharon Jarvis & Co., Inc., 260 Willard Ave., Staten Island, N.Y. 10314.

CAREER: Delco Radio, Kokomo, Ind., technician, 1954-59; Delco Electronics, Milwaukee, Wis., technical writer, 1959-74; free-lance writer, 1974—.

MEMBER: Science Fiction Writers of America, Mystery Writers of America.

AWARDS, HONORS: Awards for best novel, 1976, for *Jeremy Case,* 1982, for *A Different Darkness,* and award for best juvenile book, 1979, for *Major Corby and the Unidentified Flapping Object,* all from Council for Wisconsin Writers; *Computers in Entertainment and the Arts* was selected as a

Notable Science Book of the Year by the National Science Teachers of America, 1984.

WRITINGS:

UNDER NAME GENE DeWEESE

Fundamentals of Space Navigation (four-volume programmed text), NASA, 1968.
Fundamentals of Digital Computers, GM, 1972.
Fundamentals of Integrated Circuits (two-volume programmed text), GM, 1972.
(With Gini Rogowski) *Making American Folk Art Dolls,* Chilton, 1975.
(With Robert Coulson) *Gates of the Universe* (science fiction), Laser Books, 1975.
(With Coulson) *Now You See It/Him/Them . . .* (science fiction), Doubleday, 1975, large print edition, G. K. Hall, 1976.
Jeremy Case (science fiction), Laser Books, 1976.
(With Coulson) *Charles Fort Never Mentioned Wombats* (science fiction), Doubleday, 1977.
Major Corby and the Unidentified Flapping Object (juvenile science fiction), Doubleday, 1979.
The Wanting Factor (horror), Playboy Press, 1980.
Nightmares from Space (juvenile science fiction; illustrated with photographs by Susan Kuklin), F. Watts, 1981.
A Different Darkness (horror), PBJ Books, 1982.
Something Answered (horror), Dell, 1983.
Adventures of a Two-Minute Werewolf (juvenile science fiction; illustrations by Ronald Fritz), Doubleday, 1983.
Computers in Entertainment and the Arts (juvenile), F. Watts, 1984.
(With Coulson) *Nightmare Universe* (interactive science fiction novel; based on *Gates of the Universe*), TSR, 1985.
Black Suits from Outer Space (juvenile science fiction), Putnam, 1985.
Dandelion Caper (juvenile science fiction; sequel to *Black Suits from Outer Space*), Putnam, 1986.
The Calvin Nullifier (juvenile science fiction), Putnam, 1987.
Chain of Attack ("Star Trek" novel), Pocket Books, 1987.

UNDER PSEUDONYM JEAN DeWEESE

The Reimann Curse (Gothic fantasy), Ballantine, 1975.
The Moonstone Spirit (Gothic fantasy), Ballantine, 1975.
The Carnelian Cat (Gothic fantasy), Ballantine, 1975.
Web of Guilt (Gothic novel), Ballantine, 1976.
Cave of the Moaning Wind (Gothic fantasy), Ballantine, 1976.
The Doll with Opal Eyes (romantic suspense), Doubleday, 1976.
Nightmare in Pewter (Gothic fantasy), Doubleday, 1978.
Hour of the Cat (mystery), Doubleday, 1980.
The Backhoe Gothic (Gothic mystery), Doubleday, 1981.

SCIENCE FICTION, WITH ROBERT COULSON, UNDER JOINT PSEUDONYM THOMAS STRATTON

The Invisibility Affair: Man from U.N.C.L.E., No. 11, Ace Books, 1967.
The Mindtwisters Affair: Man from U.N.C.L.E., No. 12, Ace Books, 1967.
(Contributor) L. Sprague de Camp and George Scithers, editors, *The Conan Grimoire: Essays in Swordplay and Sorcery,* Mirage Press, 1972.

WITH CONNIE KUGI, UNDER JOINT PSEUDONYM VICTORIA THOMAS

Ginger's Wish, Doubleday, 1987.

OTHER

Contributor of short stories and articles to periodicals, including *Amazing Stories, Magazine of Fantasy and Science Fiction, Mike Shayne's Mystery Magazine,* and *Woman's World.* Science fiction and mystery reviewer for *Comics Buyer's Guide, Milwaukee Shepherd Express,* and *Midwest Book Review.*

WORK IN PROGRESS: "Two more 'Star Trek' novels and a fourth juvenile science fiction title for Putnam, a sequel to the first three."

SIDELIGHTS: "The first thing I remember writing was in grade school, something about Mickey Mouse, I think, inspired by one of his science fictional adventures in Walt Disney comics," Gene DeWeese told *CA.* "The first thing actually printed was probably an account of an ice storm in the high school paper, which was printed as an insert in the *Rochester News Sentinel.* The first money I ever got for anything I wrote was for a series of articles on local people and businesses and a science fiction column for the same *News Sentinel.* I was still in high school, and I got the magnificent sum of a nickel per column inch. Between that and my first 'professional fiction' sale were lots of 'payment-in-contributor's-copies' contributions to science fiction amateur magazines (fanzines) such as *Yandro, Indiana Fantasy, Fan-Fare,* and the *Chigger Patch of Fandom.*

"That first professional sale was a 'Man from U.N.C.L.E.' novel, a collaboration with Robert Coulson under the name Thomas Stratton. It was made primarily because the editor of the series happened to subscribe to a fanzine Coulson and his wife published and because she (Juanita Coulson, who had already sold a couple of sf novels) didn't really want to do an 'U.N.C.L.E.' novel when said editor offered her the chance. All of which partially explains why the dedication page reads, 'To Serendipity.'

"Incidentally, that book, *The Invisibility Affair,* may have the distinction of being the only book for which the text was accepted but the title, author's names and dedication were all rejected. The original title, *The Invisible Dirigible Affair,* was too long for their cover format (though it was restored in the French translation). Using two names was considered too confusing, no explanation given. Then, with only one author's name appearing on the cover, the original dedication, 'To my wives and child,' was considered too racy for the intended pre-teen audience, which I suppose shows how things have changed in the last couple of decades.

"Since then I've plowed through approximately thirty books of various sorts and varying quality, with *Jeremy Case, The Wanting Factor, Two-Minute Werewolf,* and *Black Suits* at the top of my own personal list of favorites. As you can tell from the books listed above, I've written in a number of fields, but one book, *The Doll with Opal Eyes,* may have established a record of sorts on its own, having been published in the U.S. as 'romantic suspense,' in England as a straight crime novel, in France and Argentina as a romance, and as an occult in a U.S. paperback edition.

"The only 'advice' I've ever gotten that has been consistently helpful (and consistently difficult to follow) is simply, 'If you want to be a writer, sit down and *write!*' Don't dream about it or talk about it or read about it—do it. (Having a spouse with a steady job doesn't hurt, either.)"

MEDIA ADAPTATIONS: "The Adventures of a Two-Minute Werewolf" (two-part "ABC Weekend Special"), ABC-TV, February-March, 1985.

DIAL, Joan 1937-
(Katherine Kent, Amanda York)

PERSONAL: Born November 9, 1937, in Liverpool, England; came to the United States in 1956, naturalized citizen, 1973; daughter of Edwin (a police officer) and Sarah G. Rogers; married Paul E. Dial (a supervisor), February 10, 1956; children: Criag Edwin, Gary William, Sharon Lisa. *Education:* Attended public schools in Liverpool, England. *Politics:* Democrat.

CAREER: Writer, 1975—. Also worked as secretary and editorial assistant.

WRITINGS:

NOVELS

Susanna, Fawcett, 1978.
Lovers and Warriors, Fawcett, 1978.
Deadly Lady, Fawcett, 1979.
Roses in Winter, Pocket Books, 1982.
Echoes of War, St. Martin's, 1984.

NOVELS; UNDER PSEUDONYM KATHERINE KENT

Druid's Retreat, Pinnacle Books, 1979.
Tawny Rose, Walker & Co., 1984.

NOVELS; UNDER PSEUDONYM AMANDA YORK

Beloved Enemy, Pocket Books, 1978.
Somewhere in the Whirlwind, Pocket Books, 1979.

SIDELIGHTS: Joan Dial writes: "I spent my childhood surrounded by colorful characters—from aristocrats to gypsies—growing up in England. An early and precocious reader, I was frequently disappointed that storytellers often tossed aside a potentially exciting thread of their plots without fully exploring all of the possibilities. I wanted to do better—I still do. As a child I would study my parents' rather exotic friends and ask myself: 'What if that man had met this woman (instead of that one) earlier in his life—how would their lives have been different?' 'What if that woman had been born into the upper class instead of the working class?' 'What if . . .?' *'What if . . .?'* My mind reeled with the endless possibilities for drama in even the most mundane of lives.

"I knew I'd be a writer when I read my first book. I didn't know I would marry, travel extensively, and have three children first.

"The most mystical metamorphosis of my life was when I married an American, came to live here, and—slowly—fell in love with a country."

When asked her opinion on other contemporary writers, Dial responded: "This country has a tremendous pool of writing talent and a steadily growing number of readers. In my opinion, American writers now lead the world in sheer innovative genius. (Since I am only an American by adoption, I feel objective enough to arrive at this conclusion.)"

Dial advises aspiring writers to "write, don't talk about it. Remember that your readers want to be entertained (and try not to bore them!)." She herself writes for a minimum of eight hours a day, Monday through Friday, and "more when I'm researching as well as writing. Weekends are for outdoor activities."

Reviewing *Beloved Enemy* for the *Santa Ana Register,* Diane Hoyle calls it a "heart pounding love story." "Its suspense," she added, "is a literary bribe that hastens one to the last stirring page." *Lovers and Warriors* is a "neat blending of fact and fiction . . . bound to hold the interest of devotees to the genre," writes a *Publishers Weekly* critic.

BIOGRAPHICAL/CRITICAL SOURCES:

PERIODICALS

Publishers Weekly, July 3, 1978.
Santa Ana Register, May 7, 1978, October 1, 1978.†

*   *   *

DICKEY, William 1928-

PERSONAL: Born December 15, 1928, in Bellingham, Wash.; son of Paul Condit (a contracting officer) and Anne Marie (Hobart) Dickey; married Shirley Anne Marn (a psychiatric nurse), January 7, 1959 (divorced January 22, 1973). *Education:* Reed College, B.A., 1951; Harvard University, M.A., 1955; State University of Iowa, M.F.A., 1956; postgraduate study at Jesus College, Oxford University, 1959-60. *Politics:* Democrat. *Religion:* None.

ADDRESSES: Home—121 Liberty St., San Francisco, Calif. 94110. *Office*—Department of English, San Francisco State University, San Francisco, Calif. 94132.

CAREER: Cornell University, Ithaca, N.Y., instructor in English, 1956-59; Denison University, Granville, Ohio, assistant professor of English, 1960-62; San Francisco State University, San Francisco, Calif., assistant professor, 1962-65, associate professor, 1965-70, professor of English and creative writing, 1970—, chairman of creative writing sequence, 1974-1977. Visiting professor, University of Hawaii, 1972. Former poetry reviewer for the *Hudson Review.*

MEMBER: Modern Language Association of America (member of delegate assembly, 1974-77), American Federation of Teachers, American Society for Eighteenth Century Studies, Phi Beta Kappa.

AWARDS, HONORS: Yale Series of Younger Poets prize, 1959, for *Of the Festivity;* Fulbright award, Jesus College, Oxford, 1959-60; Union League Foundation prize, *Poetry* magazine, 1962; Commonwealth Club of California silver medal, 1972, for *More under Saturn;* Jupiter Prize, University of Massachusetts Press, 1978, for *The Rainbow Grocery;* National Endowment for the Arts creative writing fellowship, 1978; creative writing award, American Institute of Arts and Letters, 1980; best volume of poetry in 1986 citation, Bay Area Book Reviewers, for *The King of the Golden River.*

WRITINGS:

Of the Festivity (poems), foreword by W. H. Auden, Yale University Press, 1959, reprinted, AMS Press, 1971.
(Contributor) Paul Engle and Joseph Langland, editors, *Poet's Choice* (anthology), Dial, 1962.
(Contributor) William Cole, editor, *Erotic Poetry* (anthology), Random House, 1963.
Interpreter's House (poems), Ohio State University Press, 1963.
(Contributor) Anthony Ostroff, editor, *The Contemporary Poet as Artist and Critic: Eight Symposia,* Little, Brown, 1964.
Rivers of the Pacific Northwest (long poem), Twowindows Press, 1969.
More under Saturn (poems), Wesleyan University Press, 1971.

Sheena, designed and illustrated by Paul Funge, Funge Art Centre (Gorey, Ireland), 1975.
The Rainbow Grocery (poems), University of Masachusetts Press, 1978.
(With Adrianne Marcus and Wayne Johnson) *Carrion House: World of Gifts* (satire on mail-order catalogues), St. Martin's Press, 1980.
The Sacrifice Consenting (poems), Pterodactyl Press, 1981.
Six Philosophical Songs, Pterodactyl Press, 1983.
Joy, Pterodactyl Press, 1983.
Brief Lives (poems), Heyeck Press, 1985.
The Fish Upstairs (audiocassette), The Watershed Foundation, 1985.
The King of the Golden River, Pterodactyl Press, 1985.

Contributor of several hundred poems to *New Yorker, Harper's, Saturday Review, Atlantic,* and other periodicals. Former managing editor of *Western Review* and editorial assistant for *Civil War History.*

WORK IN PROGRESS: The Pruned Roses, poems; *Dear Miss Bradbury,* fiction, with Adrianne Marcus.

SIDELIGHTS: American poet William Dickey, says Brown Miller in the *San Francisco Review of Books,* "is a national treasure" who remains largely unknown even to dedicated followers of contemporary poetry for a number of reasons. Namely, as Miller notes, the poet "works harder on the writing of his work than the promoting of it, does only three or four readings a year, and often prefers to publish his poetry with small, independent presses whose books are lovingly crafted works of art in their own right." Dickey's talent, however, is not unknown to critics; it "was recognized early when his first collection, *Of the Festivity,* was chosen to be published as part of the Yale Series of Younger Poets in 1959," Thomas Goldstein writes in the *Dictionary of Literary Biography.* Dickey's "balanced observations and parables captured the imagination of no less a judge than W. H. Auden," Goldstein relates. The British poet says in the book's introduction that great poetry contains a personal vision conveyed in lines that have "the power to *speak*" as they record keen observations, and that Dickey's poems satisfy these criteria. "The critical consensus about the volume supports Auden's judgment . . . [that] many of the poems are great," Goldstein reports. He feels that Dickey's humor and seriousness achieve an "equilibrium" in *Of the Festivity.*

In later books, say some reviewers, the balance tips toward the darker, sometimes nightmarish elements of Dickey's personal vision. Humor becomes sardonic in the poet's fourth collection, observes Goldstein, who notes that the jokes made in *More under Saturn* are made "at someone's expense." *Hudson Review* contributor Vernon Young believes Dickey is "best when firmly confronting the public condition with serene loathing . . . or, alternatively, treasuring the private hour, reverent, but skeptical." Writing in *Parnassus,* Paul Zweig acknowledges this distance, but praises the poet's "willingness to entertain difficult ideas" in comparison "to the overly simple . . . bent of so much contemporary poetry." Abstract ideas often function successfully as theme in the poems, and for this reason, readers "may tend to miss the earth in them," comments John R. Reed in a *Poetry* magazine review. Dickey received a silver medal from the Commonwealth Club of California for *More under Saturn* in 1972.

The Rainbow Grocery, winner of the 1978 Juniper Prize from the University of Massachusetts Press, and *The Sacrifice Consenting* have also been generally well-received. Poems in *The*

Rainbow Grocery "are more loosely constructed, more sexual, and more frenzied" than poems in *Of the Festivity;* "cynicism has overcome the humor," and "the terrors of the subconscious have overcome the rational mind" in these poems, Goldstein believes. For others such as Robert B. Shaw, however, the jesting and despair maintain a precarious balance. When so poised, comments Shaw in *Poetry,* "Dickey writes a rare and enviable sort of poem, truly humorous and truly serious at once." Miller concurs, "In his work generally and in *The King of the Golden River* and *Brief Lives* [both published in 1985] specifically, [Dickey] integrates insight and feeling to an outstanding degree," achieving gracefulness of phrase without ". . . sacrificing a raw, gutsy contact with reality."

BIOGRAPHICAL/CRITICAL SOURCES:

BOOKS

Contemporary Literary Criticism, Gale, Volume III, 1975, Volume XXVIII, 1984.
Dickey, William, *Of the Festivity,* foreword by W. H. Auden, Yale University Press, 1959, reprinted, AMS Press, 1971.
Dictionary of Literary Biography, Volume V: *American Poets since World War II,* Gale, 1980.
Ostroff, Anthony, editor, *The Contemporary Poet as Artist and Critic: Eight Symposia,* Little, Brown, 1964.

PERIODICALS

Antioch Review, spring, 1963.
Hudson Review, spring, 1970, winter, 1971-72.
New England Review, autumn, 1979.
New York Times Book Review, September 6, 1959, July 5, 1964.
Parnassus, fall/winter, 1972.
Poetry, January, 1960, May, 1964, April, 1973, December, 1982.
San Francisco Review of Books, August, 1987.
Saturday Review, July 25, 1959.
Sewanee Review, winter, 1965.
Times Literary Supplement, May 7, 1964.
World Literature Today, spring, 1965.
Yale Review, December, 1959.†

*   *   *

DINNERSTEIN, Leonard 1934-

PERSONAL: Born May 5, 1934, in New York, N.Y.; son of Abraham and Lillian (Kubrik) Dinnerstein; married Myra Rosenberg, August 20, 1961; children: Andrew, Julie. *Education:* City College (now City College of the City University of New York), B.S.S., 1955; Columbia University, M.A., 1960, Ph.D., 1966. *Politics:* Democrat. *Religion:* Jewish.

ADDRESSES: Home—5821 East 7th St., Tucson, Ariz. 85711. *Office*—Department of History, University of Arizona, Tucson, Ariz. 85721.

CAREER: New York Institute of Technology, New York City, instructor in American history, 1960-65; Brooklyn College of the City University of New York, Brooklyn, N.Y., lecturer, 1965; City College of the City University of New York, New York City, instructor in American history, 1966-67; Fairleigh Dickinson University, Teaneck, N.J., assistant professor of American history, 1967-70; University of Arizona, Tucson, professor of history, 1970—. Adjunct assistant professor at Columbia University, summers, 1969, 1972, 1974, 1981, 1987, and at New York University, 1969-70, 1982, 1986; visiting

professor, University of Colorado, summer, 1985. Lecturer at Hunter College in the Bronx (now Herbert H. Lehman College of the City University of New York), 1966. Scholar-in-residence, Temple Beth-Israel, 1987. National Endowment for the Humanities, director of summer seminar, 1980, 1983, referee, division of fellowships, 1982, 1983. Judge, Kenneth B. Smilen *Present Tense* Literary Awards, 1984. Panelist and commentator for various historical association conferences.

MEMBER: American Historical Association, Organization of American Historians.

AWARDS, HONORS: Anisfield-Wolf Award from *Saturday Review,* 1969, for *The Leo Frank Case;* National Endowment for the Humanities summer fellowships, 1970, 1977 and 1987, research fellowship, 1978, travel grant, 1985; research grants from the University of Arizona, 1971-72, 1979-81, 1983-85, Immigration History Research Center, 1975, Harry S Truman Library, 1976, Eleanor Roosevelt Institute, 1977, University of Arizona Foundation, 1979, Herbert Hoover Library, 1979, and American Philosophical Society, 1979, 1982.

WRITINGS:

The Leo Frank Case, Columbia University Press, 1968, reprinted, University of Georgia Press, 1987.
(With David M. Reimers) *Ethnic Americans: A History of Immigration and Assimilation,* Dodd, 1975, 3rd edition, Harper, 1988.
(With Roger L. Nichols and Reimers) *Natives and Strangers: Ethnic Groups and the Building of Modern America,* Oxford University Press, 1979.
America and the Survivors of the Holocaust, Columbia University Press, 1982.
Uneasy at Home: Antisemitism and the American Jewish Experience, Columbia University Press, 1987.

EDITOR

(With Fred Cople Jaher) *The Aliens: A History of Ethnic Minorities in America,* Appleton, 1970, 2nd edition published as *Uncertain Americans,* Oxford University Press, 1977.
(With Kenneth T. Jackson) *American Vistas,* Oxford University Press, 1971, 5th edition, 1987.
Antisemitism in the United States, Holt, 1971.
(With Mary Dale Palsson) *Jews in the South,* Louisiana State University Press, 1973.
(With Jean Christie) *Decisions and Revisions: Interpretations of Twentieth-Century American History,* Praeger, 1975.
(With Christie) *America since World War II: Historical Interpretation,* Praeger, 1976.

CONTRIBUTOR

Jaher, editor, *The Age of Industrialism in America,* Free Press, 1968.
Leon Friedman and Fred L. Israel, editors, *The Justices of the United States Supreme Court, 1789-1969: Their Lives and Major Decisions,* four volumes, Bowker, 1969.
A. M. Schlesinger, editor, *History of American Presidential Elections,* four volumes, McGraw, 1971.
Schlesinger, editor, *History of the United States Political Parties,* four volumes, Chelsea House, 1973.
(With George Lankevich) *The Study of American History,* two volumes, Dushkin, 1974.
Hans L. Trefousse, editor, *Germany and America: Essays on Problems of International Relations and Immigration,* Brooklyn College Press, 1980.

Bernard J. Weiss, editor, *American Education and the European Immigrant: 1840-1940*, University of Illinois Press, 1982.

Jack P. Greene, editor, *Encyclopedia of American Political History: Studies of the Principle Movements and Ideas*, Scribner, 1984.

Wilbur J. Cohen, editor, *The Roosevelt New Deal: A Program Assessment Fifty Years After*, Lyndon B. Johnson School of Public Affairs, 1986.

William F. Levantrosser, editor, *Harry S. Truman: The Man from Independence*, Greenwood Press, 1986.

Michael Curtis, editor, *Antisemitism in the Contemporary World*, Westview, 1986.

David A. Gerber, editor, *Anti-Semitism in American History*, University of Illinois Press, 1986.

OTHER

Also author of papers presented at historical association conferences in the United States, Canada, and Israel. Contributor of articles to *American Jewish Historical Quarterly, Jewish Social Studies, American Jewish Archives, Diplomatic History, Humanities, Alabama Review, Virginia Magazine of History and Biography, New York History*, and other periodicals. Contributor of book reviews to *American Jewish Historical Quarterly, Arizona and the West, American Journal of Sociology, International Migration Review, Jewish Social Studies, Journal of American History, New Jersey History, New York History, The Historian, Western Historical Quarterly, Congressional Studies*, and other periodicals.

BIOGRAPHICAL/CRITICAL SOURCES:

PERIODICALS

Chicago Tribune Book World, September 26, 1982.
Spectator, July 5, 1968.

*　　*　　*

DiPALMA, Ray(mond) 1943-

PERSONAL: Born September 27, 1943, in New Kensington, Pa. *Education:* Duquesne University, B.A., 1966; University of Iowa, M.F.A., 1968.

ADDRESSES: Home—226 West 21st St., Apt. 4-R, New York, N.Y. 10011.

CAREER: Bowling Green University, Bowling Green, Ohio, instructor in English and creative writing, 1968-75; adjunct professor, Union Graduate School, 1976-77. Founder and editor, Doones Press and *Doones Magazine*, 1969.

WRITINGS:

Max, Body Press, 1969.
(With Stephen Shrader) *Macaroons*, Doones Press, 1969.
Between the Shapes, Zeitgeist, 1970.
Clinches, Abraxas Press, 1970.
The Gallery Goers, Ithaca House, 1971.
All Bowed Down, Burning Deck Press, 1972.
Works in a Drawer, Blue Chair Press, 1972.
Borgia Circles, Sand Project Press, 1972.
(With Asa Benveniste and Tom Raworth) *Time Being*, Trigram Press, 1972.
(Editor) Merrill Gilfillan and others, *Shirt*, Doones Press, 1973.
Five Surfaces, Tottel's no. 12, 1974.
The Sargasso Transcries, 'X' Editions, 1974.
Max, a Sequel, Burning Deck Press, 1974.

Soli, Ithaca House, 1974.
Accidental Interludes, Turkey Press, 1975.
Marquee, 'X' Editions, 1976.
10 Faces, Doones Press, 1976.
Outrageous Modesty, Doones Press, 1976.
The Black Notebook, Doones Press, 1977.
Genesis, 'X' Editions, 1977.
Matak, Doones Press, 1977.
Tzuuka, Doones Press, 1977.
Marquee: A Score, Asylum's Press, 1977.
Cuiva Sails, Sun & Moon Press, 1978.
Observatory Gardens, Tuumba Press, 1979.
Planh, Casement Books, 1979.
January Zero, Coffee House Press, 1984.

*　　*　　*

DODSON, Fitzhugh (James) 1923-

PERSONAL: Born October 28, 1923, in Baltimore, Md.; son of Fitzhugh James (a stockbroker) and Lillian (Northam) Dodson; married former wife, Grace Goheen (a preschool director), August 1, 1958; married second wife, Cecilia Kovacs, January 26, 1974; children: (first marriage) Robin Ellyn, Randall James, Rustin Fitzhugh. *Education:* Johns Hopkins University, A.B. (cum laude), 1944; Yale University, B.D. (magna cum laude), 1948; University of Southern California, Ph.D., 1957. *Politics:* Democrat. *Religion:* Presbyterian.

ADDRESSES: Agent—Sterling Lord, 660 Madison Ave., New York, N.Y. 10021.

CAREER: Ordained to Presbyterian ministry, 1948; minister in Portland, Ore., 1949-51. Lewis and Clark College, Portland, Ore., lecturer, 1949-52; director of counseling centers in Los Angeles, Calif., and Portland, Ore., 1957-58; private practice in clinical psychology, Redondo Beach, Calif., 1959—; La Primera Schools, Torrance, Calif., owner and administrator, 1963-70. Lecturer, Claremont College, 1959; instructor, El Camino College, 1959-60; assistant professor, Long Beach State College, 1962-63; lecturer, Chadwick School, 1964-1970. Consultant, Project Head Start, Long Beach, Calif., 1966-67.

MEMBER: American Psychological Association, American Group Therapy Association, American Anthropological Association, American Sociological Association, American Association for the Advancement of Science, Academy of Religion and Mental Health, Society for the Study of Religion, Western Psychological Association, California Psychological Association, Los Angeles Psychological Association, Los Angeles Society of Clinical Psychologists, Phi Beta Kappa.

WRITINGS:

How to Parent, Nash Publishing, 1970.
Dr. Dodson's Whiz-Bang, Super-Economy Parent's Survival Kit, New American Library, 1971.
How to Father, edited by Jeanne Harris, Nash Publishing, 1974.
The You That Could Be, Follett, 1976.
How to Discipline, with Love: From Crib to College, Rawson Associates, 1977.
I Wish I Had a Computer That Makes Waffles: Teaching Your Child with Modern Nursery Rhymes, illustrated by Al Lowenheim, Oak Tree Publications, 1978.
(With Paula Reuben) *The Carnival Kidnap Caper*, Oak Tree Publications, 1979.
Give Your Child a Head Start in Reading, illustrated by A. Lowenheim, Simon & Schuster, 1981.

(With P. Reuben) *How to Grandparent*, Harper, 1981.

(With Ann Alexander) *Your Child: Pregnancy through Preschool*, Simon & Schuster, 1986.

Also contributor to *Life and Health*, 1971.

WORK IN PROGRESS: Sex Education for Parents and *How to Cope with Your Teen-ager*.

AVOCATIONAL INTERESTS: Camping, backpacking, painting, papier-mache, sculpture, and travel.†

*   *   *

DODSON, Owen (Vincent)   1914-1983

PERSONAL: Born November 28, 1914, in Brooklyn, N.Y.; died June 21, 1983, of a heart attack in New York, N.Y.; son of Nathaniel (a journalist) and Sarah Elizabeth (Goode) Dodson. *Education:* Bates College, B.A., 1936; Yale University, M.F.A., 1939.

ADDRESSES: Home—New York, N.Y.

CAREER: Spelman College, Atlanta, Ga., drama director, 1938-41; Atlanta University, Atlanta, instructor and director of drama, 1938-42; Hampton Institute, Hampton, Va., instructor and director of drama, 1942-43; Howard University, Washington, D.C., faculty member, 1947-69, professor of drama and department chairman, 1960-69. Lecturer at Vassar College, Kenyon College, and Cornell University; poet in residence, Ruth Stephen Poetry Center, University of Arizona, 1969-70. Consultant to Community Theatre, Harlem School of Arts, 1970-71; director of Summer Theatre, Theatre Lobby, Washington, D.C.; director of theatre at Lincoln University. Conducted seminars in theatre and playwriting. *Military service:* U.S. Navy, 1942-43.

MEMBER: American Film Center (executive secretary; member of executive committee for mass education in race relations), American Negro Theatre (member of board of directors), Phi Beta Kappa.

AWARDS, HONORS: General Education Board fellowship, 1937; winner of Tuskegee Institute Playwriting Contest, 1939; winner of Maxwell Anderson Verse Play Contest, Stanford University, 1940; Rosenwald fellowship, 1945; Guggenheim fellowship, 1953; *Paris Review* short story prize, 1956; D.Litt. from Bates College, 1967; Rockefeller Foundation fellowship, 1968; Outstanding Pioneer Award from Audience Development Committee, 1975.

WRITINGS:

Powerful Long Ladder (poems), Farrar, Straus, 1946, reprinted, 1970.

Boy at the Window (novel), Farrar, Straus, 1951, reprinted, 1977, paperback edition published as *When Trees Were Green*, Popular Library, 1951.

The Confession Stone: A Song Cycle Sung by Mary about Jesus (poems), [Washington, D.C.], published as *The Confession Stone*, Broadside Press, 1970 (published in England as *The Confession Stone: Song Cycles*, P. Bremen, 1970, 2nd edition, 1971).

Come Home Early, Child (novel), Popular Library, 1977.

(With James Van Der Zee and Camille Billops) *The Harlem Book of the Dead* (foreword by Toni Morrison), Morgan & Morgan, 1978.

Also author of *Cages* (poems), 1953.

PLAYS

"Divine Comedy," 1938, produced in New York City at New Federal Theatre, January, 1977.

"New World A-Coming: An Original Pageant of Hope," first produced in New York City at Madison Square Garden, 1944.

Also author of "The Shining Town," 1937; "With This Darkness" (revised as "Garden of Time"), 1939; "Amistad," 1939; "Doomsday Tale," 1941; "Gonna Tear Them Pillars Down," 1942; "Heroes on Parade" (collection of short plays), 1943; (with Countee Cullen) "The Third Fourth of July," 1946; "Bayou Legend," 1946; "The Decision" [and] "For the Riesers," 1947; (with Cullen) "Medea in Africa," 1963.

OTHER

"Long Look: Owen Dodson" (sound recording), Pacifica Tape Library, 1975.

Also author of operas, "A Christmas Miracle," 1955, and "Till Victory Is Won," 1967, both with music by Marx Fax; also author, with Gary Keyes, of *Sound of Soul*, 1978. Also contributor to anthologies. Contributor to periodicals.

WORK IN PROGRESS: A libretto entitled "The Morning Duke Ellington Praised the Lord and Seven Little Black Davids Tap Danced Unto."

SIDELIGHTS: In his twenty-three years in the drama department of Howard University, Owen Dodson was an important influence on black theater. Jeff Newman, chairman of the drama department at Howard, states in the *New York Times* that "there were not many professionals in the business who did not come through him." A diverse group of artists can be listed as former students of Dodson, including Debbie Allen, Roxie Roker, Amiri Baraka, Earle Hyman, and Ossie Davis. Dodson was especially noted for attracting leading drama professionals to speak to his classes, such as Sir John Gielgud, Sidney Poitier, and Vivien Leigh. In 1949, Dodson led the Howard Unviersity Players on a fourteen-city European tour—the first U.S. State Department-sponsored European tour by a black theater group—in which they presented over fifty performances of plays by Henrik Ibsen and DuBose Heyward.

In 1974, a collection of Dodson's writing was adapted by the Black Repertory Theatre of Washington, D.C., as a tribute in dramatic collage entitled "Owen's Song."

BIOGRAPHICAL/CRITICAL SOURCES:

PERIODICALS

Black World, October, 1971, May, 1972.
New York Times Book Review, February 13, 1977.

OBITUARIES:

PERIODICALS

Los Angeles Times, June 24, 1983.
New York Times, June 22, 1983.

*   *   *

DOIG, Ivan   1939-

PERSONAL: Born June 27, 1939, in White Sulphur Springs, Mont.; son of Charles Campbell (a ranch worker) and Berneta (Ringer) Doig; married Carol Muller (a professor), April 17, 1965. *Education:* Northwestern University, B.S., 1961, M.S., 1962; University of Washington, Seattle, Ph.D., 1969.

ADDRESSES: Home—17021 10th Ave. N.W., Seattle, Wash. 98177.

CAREER: Writer. Lindsay-Schaub Newspapers, Decatur, Ill., editorial writer, 1963-64; *Rotarian*, Evanston, Ill., assistant editor, 1964-66; free-lance writer, 1969-78. *Military service:* U.S. Air Force Reserve, 1962-68; became sergeant.

MEMBER: Authors Guild, Authors League of America, PEN.

AWARDS, HONORS: National Book Award nomination and Christopher Award, both 1979, both for *This House of Sky: Landscapes of a Western Mind;* Pacific Northwest Booksellers Award for Literary Excellence, 1979, 1980, 1982, and 1984; National Endowment for the Arts fellowship, 1985; D.Lit., Montana State University, 1984, and Lewis and Clark College, 1987.

WRITINGS:

(With wife, Carol M. Doig) *News: A Consumer's Guide*, Prentice-Hall, 1972.
The Streets We Have Come Down (textbook), Hayden, 1975.
Utopian America: Dreams and Realities, Hayden, 1976.
Early Forestry Research, U.S. Forestry Service, 1976.
This House of Sky: Landscapes of a Western Mind (memoir), Harcourt, 1978.
Winter Brothers: A Season at the Edge of America (nonfiction), Harcourt, 1980.
The Sea Runners (novel), Atheneum, 1982.
(With Duncan Kelso) *Inside This House of Sky,* Atheneum, 1983.
English Creek (first novel in McCaskill family trilogy), Atheneum, 1984.
Dancing at the Rascal Fair (second novel in McCaskill family trilogy), Atheneum, 1987.

Contributor to periodicals, including *Modern Maturity, New York Times, Editor and Publisher,* and *Writer's Digest.*

WORK IN PROGRESS: The final novel in the McCaskill family trilogy.

SIDELIGHTS: "Ivan Doig doesn't exactly own the Pacific Northwest," notes James Kaufmann in the *Los Angeles Times Book Review,* "but the loving and lively ways he describes it mark him as a regional writer in the absolute best sense of the word." Indeed, Doig has integrated his knowledge of this area of the United States into a number of well-known nonfiction books and novels, including *This House of Sky: Landscapes of a Western Mind, Winter Brothers: A Season on the Edge of America,* and *English Creek* and *Dancing at the Rascal Fair,* the first two books of a fictional trilogy.

Of *This House of Sky*—a memoir that describes the harsh but rewarding life of the author's forebears, who settled in the mining towns of western Montana—*Washington Post* critic Curt Suplee says, "This is no country for tennis-shoe ecologists or Snail Darter evangels—in the uneasy lee of the great mountains, amid the heartless rocky sprawl, nature is not a friend, but an omnipotent and endlessly inventive adversary, and a daily measure of courage is needful as water." Remarking that the memoir format in general "is notorious for snaring even gifted writers in thickets of anecdotage and sentiment," *Time's* Frank Trippet finds that Doig "avoids such traps. Exercising a talent at once robust and sensitive, he redeems the promise of [his] first fetching sentences." The author, Trippet concludes, "lifts what might have been marginally engaging reminiscence into an engrossing and moving recovery of an obscure human struggle. There is defeat and triumph here, grief and joy, nobility and meanness, all arising from commonplace events, episodes and locales."

Winter Brothers is a nonfiction work with an unusual premise: Doig recreated the journey of a nineteenth-century traveller named James Gilchrist Swan, who left a wife and children in antebellum Boston to explore the Pacific Northwest. Doig, who studied Swan's extensive diaries, intersperses passages of Swan's writing with his own comments on the trip he took with his wife. "Sometimes the exercise is forced; sometimes it pushes [the author] into overwriting," states Raymond A. Sokolov in the *New York Times Book Review*. "But the occasional patches of dullness or lushness should deter no one from devouring this gorgeous tribute to a man and a region unjustly neglected heretofore. The reader has the pleasure of encountering two contrasting styles and two angles of view, both infused with the fresh air and spirit of the Northwest."

Internal conflict among members of the McCaskill family and the coming-of-age of its younger son in 1939 form the basis for *English Creek,* a novel that "achieves a flawless weld of fact and fiction," according to Carol Van Strum in a *USA Today* article. As in his previous nonfiction, Doig describes the Pacific region of years past, evoking, as Van Strum says, "the sturdy, generous spirit of an era when survival—of child and adult—demanded quick wits, hard work and humor enough to fuel both." *English Creek* "is old-fashioned in the best sense of the word," notes *Christian Science Monitor* critic James Kaufmann. "Doig is concerned with telling a story that entertains, and he is also concerned with the novel's moral and ethical implications. He mounts no soapbox, however."

To *Newsday* reviewer Wendy Smith, Doig's novel "is neither nostalgic nor simple: It's too concrete and detailed in its evocation of the past, too tough-minded in its evaluation of human behavior for that. There are no truly evil characters, but there are weak ones, and Doig makes it clear that the West is cruel to those who can't stand up to its demands." Concluding that *English Creek* is "firmly anchored in the American West," Smith adds that the book "nonetheless resembles a 19th Century European novel in its leisurely pace, measured tone and focus on understanding rather than action. In supple, muscular prose as terse and yet redolent with meaning as the speech of Montana, [Doig] grapples with universal issues of character and morality."

"I am Montana-born and now live within half a mile of Puget Sound," the author told *CA.* "Inevitably, or so it seems to me, my books are the result of those popular pulls of the Rocky Mountains and the Pacific. But whichever the setting, and fiction or non-, in every book I try to work two stubborn substances, research and craft, into becoming the hardest alloy of all—a good story."

AVOCATIONAL INTERESTS: Reading, hiking.

BIOGRAPHICAL/CRITICAL SOURCES:

BOOKS

Doig, Ivan, *This House of Sky: Landscapes of a Western Mind,* Harcourt, 1978.
Doig, Ivan, *Winter Brothers: A Season at the Edge of America,* Harcourt, 1980.

PERIODICALS

Boston Globe, October 10, 1982.
Chicago Tribune, September 17, 1978, December 10, 1987.
Christian Science Monitor, December 24, 1984.

Los Angeles Times, September 13, 1978, October 20, 1980.
Los Angeles Times Book Review, December 9, 1984, October 18, 1987.
Montana: The Magazine of Western History, winter, 1985.
Newsday (Long Island, N.Y.), November 11, 1984.
New Yorker, January 21, 1985.
New York Times Book Review, January 11, 1981, October 3, 1982, November 1, 1987.
Time, September 11, 1978.
Tribune Books (Chicago), August 30, 1987.
USA Today, October 26, 1984.
Washington Post, December 11, 1978, January 6, 1981, November 28, 1987.
Washington Post Book World, October 17, 1982, October 18, 1987.

*   *   *

DOMJAN, Joseph (Spiri)   1907-

PERSONAL: Born March 15, 1907, in Budapest, Hungary; naturalized U.S. citizen; married March 13, 1944; wife's name, Evelyn (a graphic artist); children: Alma, Michael Paul, Daniel George. *Education:* Attended Royal Academy of Fine Arts, Budapest, Hungary, 1935-42.

ADDRESSES: Home—Tuxedo Park, N.Y. 10987.

CAREER: Hungarian Royal Academy of Fine Arts, Budapest, assistant professor of fine arts, 1941-42; self-employed woodcut artist in Budapest, 1942-56, Switzerland, 1956-57, and the United States, 1957—. Work exhibited at 425 one-man shows on four continents and contained in permanent collections of more than 175 museums, including Victoria and Albert Museum, Metropolitan Museum of Art, Bibliotheque National, Smithsonian Institution, and Library of Congress. Lecturer and author.

MEMBER: Metropolitan Museum of Art (life fellow), Print Council of America, American Color Print Society, Silvermine Guild of Artists, Goetheanum (Switzerland), Society of Illustrators, Society of American Graphic Artists, Societe d'encouragement au progres, National Academy of Design.

AWARDS, HONORS: National Salon prize, 1936; Fine Arts Hall prize, 1941; Nemes Marcell prize, 1942; Purchase Awards, Johansen Abstract Collection, 1948, International Color Woodcut Exhibition, Victoria and Albert Museum, 1950, and International Exhibition of Graphic Arts, 1952; Mihaly Zichy Prize for graphic arts, 1952; Munkacsy Prize of fine arts and "Master of the Color Woodcut" (China), both 1955; Kossuth Prize of fine arts, 1956; Rockefeller Foundation grant, 1957; named "printmaker of 1961," Print Club of Albany, 1961; book awards from National Educational Society and American Institute of Graphic Arts, both 1964; award of faithfulness, Washington-Kossuth Historical Society, 1966; Sonia Watter Award, American Color Print Society and award of merit, Society of Illustrators, both 1967; award of excellence, Society of Illustrators, 1968; silver medal and diploma, Societe d'encouragement au progres, 1969; medal of honor, Hungarian Helicon Society, George Washington Award, American Hungarian Studies Foundation, and silver medal and diploma, International Academy of Literature, Arts and Science, all 1970; Chapelbrook Foundation grant, 1972; Rakoczi award (Hungary), 1976; Rakoczi Foundation award (Toronto), 1980.

WRITINGS:

(Fine arts editor) *Hunyadi* (album), [Budapest], 1956.

(Illustrator) Ruth Laurene, *Bellringer* (poems), Opus, 1975.
(Illustrator) Evelyn A. Domjan, *The Edge of Paradise,* Domjan Studio, 1980.
(Illustrator) E. A. Domjan, *Eternal Wool,* Domjan Studio, 1980.

SELF-ILLUSTRATED AND DESIGNED

Wildflowers, Medimpex (Budapest), 1954.
Thirty-two Color Woodcuts, Corvina (Budapest), 1956.
Ungarische Legende, Atlantis Verlag (Zurich), 1957.
Henry Hudson of the River, Art Edge, 1959.
Janos Hunyadi: Ten Woodcuts, Art Edge, 1960.
Hungarian Heroes and Legends, Van Nostrand, 1963.
Peacock Festival, Art Edge, 1964.
The Proud Peacock, Holt, 1965.
The Little Princess Goodnight, Holt, 1966.
Domjan the Woodcutter (monograph), Art Edge, 1966.
The Fifteen Decisive Battles of the World, Limited Editions Club, 1969.
The Little Cock, Lippincott, 1969.
Hungarian Song, American-Hungarian Literary Guild, 1969.
Domjan Portfolio, Art Edge, 1970.
I Went to the Market, Holt, 1970.
The Joy of Living, Holt, 1971.
Faraway Folk Tales, Holt, 1972.
Domjan, in the Forest of the Golden Dragon, Pierre Mornnand, 1973.
Domjan, Arte, Ancona, 1973.
The Artist and the Legend: A Visit to China Is Remembered and the Legends Unfold, Opus Publications, 1975.
Wing Beat (collection of eagle woodcuts) introduction by G. E. Pogany, Domjan Studio, 1976.
Pacatus: A Trademark from Antiquity, Domjan Studio, 1979.
Sungates, Domjan Studio, 1980.
Toldi, Helicon (Budapest), 1981.

SIDELIGHTS: Joseph Domjan told *CA:* "I live in nature. True, you can't see me carrying an easel into the woods or painting outdoors, but I look and preserve an impression. I may walk out into the garden in the middle of the night. I look at the summer stars, the deep velvet-blue sky, the silver moon. [At dawn there is] the sunrise, pale pink-orange in the far distance over the lake and hills, trees and flowers brushed lightly with morning glow.

"Nothing happens just by chance in my life, although it seems that I came to make woodcuts by chance. The first series was born as a result of a misunderstanding: I was told to fill the rooms of an exhibition hall with woodcuts, which I did. As I look back and compare these early works (keyblocks in red with underprintings of red) to my present works (all color), I can say that it was a miracle. I am a painter, but I am very happy that I have the woodcut as my tool. I love black-and-white woodcuts, but when the time comes to make them into color it will be a holiday; for such holidays it is worthwhile to live."

BIOGRAPHICAL/CRITICAL SOURCES:

BOOKS

John R. Biggs, *Woodcuts,* Bradford Press, 1958.

*   *   *

DONLEAVY, J(ames) P(atrick)   1926-

PERSONAL: Born April 23, 1926, in Brooklyn, N.Y.; became Irish citizen, 1967; married Valerie Heron (divorced); married

Mary Wilson Price, 1970; children: (first marriage) Philip, Karen; (second marriage) Rebecca Wallis, Rory. *Education:* Attended Trinity College, Dublin.

ADDRESSES: Home and office—Levington Park, Mullingar, County Westmeath, Ireland.

CAREER: Writer and playwright. Founder with son Philip Donleavy and producer Robert Mitchell of De Alfonce Tennis Association for the Promotion of the Superlative Game of Eccentric Champions. *Military service:* U.S. Navy, served in World War II.

AWARDS, HONORS: Most Promising Playwright Award, *Evening Standard,* 1960, for *Fairy Tales of New York;* Brandeis University Creative Arts Award, 1961-62, for two plays, *The Ginger Man* and *Fairy Tales of New York;* citation from National Institute and American Academy of Arts and Letters, 1975.

WRITINGS:

FICTION

The Ginger Man (novel; also see below), Olympia Press (Paris), 1955, published with introduction by Arland Ussher, Spearman (London), 1956, Obolensky, 1958, complete and unexpurgated edition, Delacorte, 1965, published with illustrations by Graham McCallum, Edito-Service, 1973, published as limited edition with illustrations by Skip Liepke, Franklin Library, 1978.

A Singular Man (novel), Little, Brown, 1963.

Meet My Maker the Mad Molecule (short stories; also see below), Little, Brown, 1964, reprinted, Penguin, 1981.

The Saddest Summer of Samuel S (novel; also see below), Delacorte/Seymour Lawrence, 1966.

The Beastly Beatitudes of Balthazar B (novel), Delacorte/Seymour Lawrence, 1968.

The Onion Eaters (novel), Delacorte, 1971, reprinted, Penguin in association with Eyre and Spottiswoode, 1986.

A Fairy Tale of New York (novel; also see below), Delacorte/Seymour Lawrence, 1973.

The Destinies of Darcy Dancer, Gentleman (novel), illustrations by Jim Campbell, Delacorte/Seymour Lawrence, 1977, published as limited edition, Franklin Library, 1977.

Schultz (novel), Delacorte/Seymour Lawrence, 1979.

Meet My Maker the Mad Molecule and The Saddest Summer of Samuel S, Dell, 1979.

Leila: Further in the Destinies of Darcy Dancer, Gentleman (novel; sequel to *The Destinies of Darcy Dancer, Gentleman*), Delacorte/Seymour Lawrence, 1983, published as limited edition with "A Special Message for the First Edition from J. P. Donleavy," Franklin Library, 1983 (published in England as *Leila: Further in the Life and Destinies of Darcy Dancer, Gentleman,* Allen Lane, 1983).

Are You Listening Rabbi Loew? (novel; sequel to *Schultz*), Viking, 1987.

PLAYS

The Ginger Man (adaptation of his novel of same title; first produced at Fortune Theatre, London, September 15, 1959; produced at Gaiety Theatre, Dublin, October 26, 1959; produced on Broadway at Orpheum Theatre, November 21, 1963; contains introduction "What They Did in Dublin"; also see below), Random House, 1961 (published in England as *What They Did in Dublin with The Ginger Man,* MacGibbon and Kee, 1961; also see below).

Fairy Tales of New York (based upon his novel *A Fairy Tale of New York;* first produced at Comedy Theatre, London, January 24, 1961; also see below), Random House, 1961.

A Singular Man (first produced at Comedy Theatre, October 21, 1964; produced at Westport County Playhouse, Connecticut, September 4, 1967; also see below), Bodley Head, 1964.

The Plays of J. P. Donleavy; with a Preface by the Author (contains *What They Did in Dublin with The Ginger Man, The Ginger Man, Fairy Tales of New York, A Singular Man, The Saddest Summer of Samuel S*), photographs of productions by Lewis Morley, Delacorte/Seymour Lawrence, 1973.

"The Beastly Beatitudes of Balthazar B" (adaptation of his novel of same title; first produced in London, 1981).

Also author of radio play, *Helen,* 1956.

OTHER

The Unexpurgated Code: A Complete Manual of Survival and Manners, illustrations by the author, Delacorte/Seymour Lawrence, 1975.

De Alfonce Tennis: The Superlative Game of Eccentric Champions, Its History, Accoutrements, Rules, Conduct, and Regimen, Dutton/Seymour Lawrence, 1984.

J. P. Donleavy's Ireland: In All Her Sins and in Some of Her Graces, Viking, 1986 (published in England as *Ireland: In All Her Sins and in Some of Her Graces,* M. Joseph, 1986).

Contributor of short fiction and essays to *Atlantic, Playboy, Queen* (London), *Saturday Evening Post,* and *Saturday Review.*

WORK IN PROGRESS: The History of The Ginger Man; The Unexpurgated Code of Foxhunting; the third volume of *The Destinies of Darcy Dancer, Gentleman;* screenplay for film adaptation of *The Ginger Man.*

SIDELIGHTS: "If there is an archetypal post-World War II American writer-in-exile it may well be James Patrick Donleavy," writes William E. Grant in a *Dictionary of Literary Biography* essay. The son of Irish immigrant parents, Donleavy renounced the America of their dreams for an Ireland of his own, and became a citizen when Ireland granted tax-free status to its authors. Although literary success came several years after the publication of his stylistically innovative first novel, *The Ginger Man,* Donleavy is now internationally recognized for having written what many consider a modern classic. Referring to the "sense of exile and alienation that seems to haunt his life as well as his work," Grant observes that "even achieving the literary success he thought America would deny him has not lessened his alienation from his country, though it has enhanced the style in which he expresses his exile status." Donleavy now writes at his expansive two-hundred-year-old manor situated on nearly two hundred acres in County Westmeath. "He's a sort of born-again Irishman who enthusiastically embraces the life of a man of letters and leisure, adopting not only an Irish country estate but also the appropriate deportment and brogue," says Peter Ross in the *Detroit News.* "He also happens to be one of the funniest and most audacious writers around."

Donleavy's decision to emigrate, although precipitated by difficulty finding a publisher for his first novel, appears to have been the result of a slowly evolving dissatisfaction with what he refers to in his *Atlantic* essay, "An Expatriate Looks at America," as "a country corrosive of the spirit." Donleavy explains: "Each time I go to these United States I start anew trying to figure them out. After two weeks I decide that like anywhere, greed, lust and envy make them work. But in America it is big greed, big lust, big envy." Although Donleavy remembers his childhood in the Bronx as peaceful, New York City became an increasingly threatening presence, and the omnipresent violence made him fearful of death there. He recalls in the *Atlantic* that "something in one's bowels was saying no to this land. Where my childhood friends were growing up, just as their parents did, to be trapped trembling and terrified in a nightmare." Skeptical of America's treatment of its artists as well, Donleavy felt at the outset of his career that he stood little chance of achieving literary success in a land he describes in the *Atlantic* as a place "where your media mesmerized brain shuts off when the media does." He adds, "And if I stayed they would, without even trying, or knowing, kill me."

Donleavy was resolved to achieve recognition and relates in a *Paris Review* interview with Molly McKaughan: "I realized that the only way you could ever tackle the world was to write something that no one could hold off, a book that would go everywhere, into everyone's hands. And I decided then to write a novel which would shake the world. I shook my fist and said I would do it." That novel, *The Ginger Man,* is set in post-World War II Dublin and details the hedonistic existence of Sebastian Dangerfield who, according to Alfred Rushton in the Toronto *Globe and Mail,* gave "moral turpitude a new lease on life." Donleavy began crafting the novel while still a student in Dublin but returned to New York to complete and publish it. He indicates in the *Paris Review* that Scribners, to whom he first took the manuscript, thought it was one of the best ever brought to them; its content, however, prevented them from publishing it. Forty-five publishers rejected the novel because they "thought it was a dirty book—scatological, unreadable, obscene," Donleavy tells David Remnick in the *Washington Post.* "My life literally depended on getting this book into print, and when I couldn't, it just drove me out of America."

In the *Paris Review,* Donleavy recalls his reluctance to edit *The Ginger Man* into acceptability: "I had a sense that the book held itself together on the basis of these scatological parts. That its life was in these parts. And I was quite aware that cutting them would be severely damaging to it." Brendan Behan, the legendary Irish playwright and patriot with whom Donleavy became friends during his Dublin days, suggested sending the manuscript to the Olympia Press in Paris, where it eventually was accepted. Following its publication as part of an overtly pornographic series, however, a lengthy legal battle ensued in which Donleavy emerged as the owner of the publishing house. Despite "the potential for literary damage, publication by Olympia Press had the generally salutary effect of establishing the unexpurgated edition of *The Ginger Man* as an underground classic before complete editions became available," notes Grant. In order to ensure the novel's publication in England, though, and to get it recognized and reviewed, Donleavy agreed to certain cuts, stating in the *Paris Review:* "It was an act of pure practicality. If someone wanted to read the unexpurgated edition, they could buy it in Paris. I had published it as I had written it, so it wasn't wrong, then, to publish it to establish my reputation."

Although Donleavy's reputation had to endure both court battles and censors, his experience as a litigant proved invaluable in negotiating subsequent contracts with publishers. "He's very courtly, but he's a very sharp businessman," comments Donleavy's longtime publisher Seymour Lawrence, according to

Samuel Allis in the *Washington Post.* "He does all of his negotiating and, unlike most authors, he understands copyrights. He drives a hard bargain, but he's the most professional author I've ever known."

Critics were unsure at first how to categorize Donleavy and his *The Ginger Man.* Grant observes that the critical establishment "debated whether Donleavy belonged with Britain's Angry Young Men, America's black humorists, or France's existentialists." In his *Doings and Undoings,* Norman Podhoretz calls *The Ginger Man* "fundamentally a book without hope." Similarly, in his *Radical Innocence: Studies in the Contemporary American Novel,* Ihab Hassan considers the novel to be "full of gusto, seething with life, but its energy may be the energy of negation, and its vitality has a nasty edge." The nihilism in *The Ginger Man* "refers us to the postwar, existential era," states Hassan. "Traditional values are not in the process of dying, they have ceased entirely to operate, and their stark absence leaves men to shift for themselves as best they can." The "freshness" of the characterization of Sebastian Dangerfield was one of the most critically acclaimed aspects of the novel, notes Grant, who adds that some critics recognized that the character "existed almost totally outside any system of ideas."

Despite the commercial success of Donleavy's subsequent work, the critics generally consider his reputation to rest solely on *The Ginger Man.* "So far as most critics and reviewers are concerned, the later works have been but pale shadows of the first brilliant success, and the publication of each succeeding novel has seen a decline in critical attention," writes Grant. Some critics believe that Donleavy has run out of ideas, that he is refurbishing old material, reworking or resurrecting earlier work. For instance, in a *Harper's* review of *The Destinies of Darcy Dancer, Gentleman,* Michael Malone compares a Donleavy book to Guinness stout: "It's distinctive, it's carbonated, it's brimmed with what Hazlitt called 'gusto,' and those who like it can drink it forever. The ingredients never change." Donleavy pays attention to the critics only in a "fairly superficial way" because, as he says in the *Paris Review,* "A writer must always be aware that he has to be a supreme critic. . . . And only his judgement matters." Allis indicates, however, that Donleavy "displays something close to hostility toward academics and the people who review his books and plays," and that he discourages academic interest in his work because he says, "I never want [to] get that self-conscious of my literary position." Grant suggests that "though none individually rivals the first masterpiece, several of these later works deserve wider attention than they have had from the American reading public and critical establishment alike."

Critics point to several characteristics of the bleak but bawdy *The Ginger Man* that surface in Donleavy's later work: Beneath the bawdy humor lies an inherent despondency, with licentiousness masking the more profound search for love; and bizarre, eccentric characters, around whom his books revolve, tend to be alienated, victimized by life, and weakened by impending death. "The novels range from variations of the humorous—slapstick, scatological, sardonic—to the sentimental in an idiosyncratic style that conveys the pressure of time on language," writes Thomas LeClair in *Contemporary Literature.* "But such features of Donleavy's work are finally extensions of and returns to death, the test of man's mettle in landscapes made pale by death's presence."

An awareness of death figures significantly in Donleavy's work, and the question Donleavy's heroes "answer in their own, progressively inefficacious ways," writes LeClair in *Twentieth Century Literature,* is, "How does a man weakened by an awareness of death survive in a world experienced as magical with malevolence?" LeClair observes that "to evade his consciousness of mortality, Sebastian Dangerfield . . . lives a hedonistic life in the present and dreams of relaxed ease for the future"; and the rich and reclusive George Smith of Donleavy's *A Singular Man,* who is absorbed with the idea of death and even builds his own mausoleum, "separates himself from the world in a parody of Howard Hughes' and John Paul Getty's attempts to avoid the disease of life." LeClair notes in *Critique: Studies in Modern Fiction* that "the heroes of *The Saddest Summer of Samuel S, The Beastly Beatitudes of Balthazar B,* and *The Onion Eaters* all attempt to overcome their fear of their own death or their sadness about the death of others through love."

According to Grant, the theme of love and loss is also important in much of Donleavy's work. Concerning *The Saddest Summer of Samuel S,* about an eminent literary figure in the United States who undergoes psychoanalysis in Vienna in order to live a more conventional life, Grant writes: "Longing for a love he has never had and cannot find because in spite of his need he cannot give, Samuel S is the victim of a life that cannot be lived over and a destiny that cannot be changed." The character, observes Grant, is withdrawn and "trapped in a life-in-death state of mind with neither belief nor passion to motivate him." Similarly, in *The Beastly Beatitudes of Balthazar B,* a novel that details the lonely life of a wealthy young man whose marriage collapses, the hero is "separated from those he loves . . . and seeks completion by loving others, a simple but impossible quest," says Shaun O'Connell in the *Nation.* Robert Scholes observes in the *Saturday Review* that although this "shy and gentle" character seeks love, "it proves elusive, even harder to keep than to find." And O'Connell sees in Donleavy "the joy of the artist who can embody his vision, however bleak, the self-certainty of the writer who can so eloquently move his hero to name his pain."

However, writing in *Book World* about Donleavy's *The Destinies of Darcy Dancer, Gentleman,* a novel in which a young aristocrat is thwarted in several of his attempts at love, Curt Suplee suggests that "Donleavy does not write novels so much as Oedipal fairy tales: semirealistic fables in which the same patterns are obsessively reenacted. Invariably, a young man finds himself trapped in a society dominated by hostile father-figures and devoid of the uncritical comfort afforded by mothers. . . . Every time the young man attempts to assert his ego in this world, he fails or is beaten, and flees to succour—either to the manic medium of alcohol or the overt mother-surrogates who provide sex and self-esteem, for a while." O'Connell finds, though, that Donleavy's characters "press the possibilities of life with high style and win many tactical victories of great hilarity . . . before they are defeated," and he believes that "Donleavy's vision of sadness seems earned, won by a search of all the possible routes toward happiness."

Focusing on the bawdiness in Donleavy's work, critics sometimes fault it for what they consider to be gratuitously lewd language and a reliance upon sexual slapstick. A *Times Literary Supplement* reviewer of *The Onion Eaters,* for instance, states that "the scenes of violence and the sexual encounters suggest an attitude to the human body and its functions, weaknesses and pleasures, which is anything but tender, compassionate, or celebratory." The novel is about a young and handsome character named Clayton Claw Clever Clementine, who in addition to being somewhat freakishly over-endowed sex-

ually, has inherited an Irish manor and must confront what a *New Statesman* contributor refers to as a "bizarre collection of servants and . . . an ever-growing crew of sex-obsessed weirdies." Guy Davenport finds in the *National Review* that "Donleavy is uninterruptedly bawdy, yet his obscenity is so grand and so open, that it rises above giving offense into a realm of its own, unchallenged and wild." Critics also recognize, however, that Donleavy's humor belies an inherent sadness. "Donleavy writes sad and lonely books," says R. Z. Sheppard in a *Time* review of *The Onion Eaters.* Sheppard finds that Donleavy's fictional worlds are "closed worlds, their boundaries no more distant than the most prominent erectile tissue. Alone, without context or meaning, the flesh is all." Sheppard suggests that the absence of meaning in the novel as well as its "animal warmth, at once grotesque and touching," is perhaps Donleavy's way of asserting that "this warmth is the only thing about which we can be certain."

Writing in *Newsweek* about Donleavy's nonfictional *The Unexpurgated Code: A Complete Manual of Survival and Manners,* Arthur Cooper describes Donleavy's humor: "Like Mel Brooks, he knows that bad taste is merely a joke that doesn't get a laugh. And like Brooks, Donleavy's demonic humor is utterly democratic, thrusting the needle into everyone regardless of race, creed, color, or ability to control one's bowels." Referring to the book as "a collection of bilious and often funny rules for living," Melvin Maddocks observes in *Time* that "between the lines, Donleavy's diatribes manage to say more." Maddocks believes that Donleavy's "visions of grace, chivalry and order" reveal the author as "an inverted romantic, profoundly sad beneath his disguise because he and the world are no better than they happen to be." Similarly, in a *Midwest Quarterly* assessment of *The Unexpurgated Code,* Charles G. Masinton suggests that "Donleavy normally proceeds by means of instinct, inspiration, and intuition—the tools of a romantic artist. He aims to produce belly laughs and . . . a sympathetic response to his chief characters; he does not set out to impose order and rationality on experience. And instead of elevated language (which he often parodies quite effectively), he records with great skill an earthy vernacular full of both comic and lyric possibilities." While Grant believes that Donleavy's "characteristic tone of pessimism, melancholia, alienation, and human failure . . . suggest Jonathan Swift's misanthropic humor," he also finds it reminiscent of Mark Twain's later work, "which combines pessimism and humor in an elegiac, melancholic, and misanthropic voice."

In assessing Donleavy's fiction, notes Lask, "critics keep citing his first book . . . some saying that nothing after it has equaled that first effort, and objecting to his language, which has a syntax of its own, without connectives or prepositions, shifting tense at will." Stylistically innovative, *The Ginger Man* employs not only a shifting point of view (from first to third person) so that Dangerfield becomes both observer and observed but, according to Grant, it "relies on rapidly moving, nearly staccato sentence fragments which capture brilliantly the chaotic and fragmented qualities of Dangerfield's world." Donleavy explains that the language is "designed to reflect the way the mind works," says Lask in a *New York Times* review of *Schultz,* a novel about the exploits of an American producer of vulgar plays in London. In the *Paris Review,* Donleavy offers a more detailed explanation: "You're trying to get what you've written on your page into a reader's mind as quickly as possible, and to keep them seeing it. That is why I use the short, truncated telegraphic sentences. They are the most efficient use of language, and I think the brain puts words together the way I do.''

Some critics think Donleavy has become a ''prisoner of style,'' says Paul Abelman in the *Spectator,* that ''he has never escaped from the prose techniques which he invented for his fine first novel.'' Abelman believes that ''the style of the later books is not really that of *The Ginger Man* at all but simply one that employs superficial aspects of it and neglects the lyrical essence.'' Unlike *The Ginger Man,* says Abelman, the other books are ''monster prose poems founded on the most plodding, leaden metrical foot known to the English language [the spondee—two stressed syllables regularly repeated].'' Abelman, though, considers Donleavy ''possibly the greatest lyrical humorist to emerge since the war,'' and adds that he ''has that to his credit which few living writers can claim: a modern classic.'' Although Donleavy indicates to Thomas Lask in the *New York Times* that he's as ''delighted'' with *The Ginger Man* as when he first worte it, he feels that his subsequent books keep *The Ginger Man* alive. Commenting to Remnick that he does not feel *The Ginger Man* represents his ''best work,'' Donleavy states, ''When I pick it up and read it now critically as a piece of writing, in technical terms, it doesn't compare to later books.'' Acknowledging in the *Paris Review* that his subsequent writing has not provided the pleasure that *The Ginger Man* did, Donleavy says: ''I don't think you ever have that again. When an author's recognized, all that leaves him, because that's what he's needed to force himself to go through the terrible agony of being unknown and being able to face the world and the fact that it's a giant, vast place where nearly every man is saying: Dear God, hear my tiny voice.''

Grant believes that ''Donleavy remains essentially the exile who once wrote of America, 'there it goes, a runaway horse, with no one in control.''' Donleavy recalls in his *Atlantic* essay, that ''each time you arrive anew in America, you find how small you are and how dismally you impress against the giantness and power of this country where you are so obviously, and with millions like yourself, so totally fatally expendable.'' Grant notes that this vision is often expressed in Donleavy's portrayal of the United States as a nightmare. In *A Fairy Tale of New York,* for instance, the wife of the Brooklyn-born, Bronx-raised, and Europe-educated Cornelius Christian dies on their way to New York; and without money or friends, Christian is taken advantage of by everyone. ''Affection, loathing, nostalgia and fear are the main components of the attitude he brings to bear upon his native place,'' writes Julian Moynahan in the *Washington Post Book World,* adding that ''hidden away in the book for those who can find it is a good deal of personal revelation, a good deal of alembicated and metamorphosed autobiography.'' As D. Keith Mano states in the *New York Times Book Review,* the book is ''about social impotence and despair. Valleys of humiliation, sloughs of despond.'' The story focuses on the brutality of New York City; and Christian, who lacks the funds to move, sees emigration as the only answer to his liberation. ''Yet Donleavy's thunderous, superb humor has the efficacy of grace,'' says Mano. ''It heals and conquers and ratifies.'' And a *Times Literary Supplement* contributor, who remarks that ''few writers know how to enjoy verbal promiscuity like . . . Donleavy,'' considers that ''it is largely because of the confidence of the style, too, that you come out of the welter of failure and misery feeling good—nastiness is inevitably laced with hilarity and sentiment in his telling it.''

Moving to Ireland changed his life ''utterly,'' he says in the *Paris Review.* ''It also romanticized the United States for me so that it became a subject for me as a writer.'' However, in the *Atlantic,* Donleavy speaks about the indelibility of his American beginnings: ''As far away as you may go, or as foreign as your life can ever become, there is something that always stays stained American in you.' About living among the Irish, however, Donleavy remarks in a *Publishers Weekly* interview: ''Literally, everywhere you go here, they're half nuts. It's very tough to discover real insanity, because the whole race is like that, and, indeed, this is the place to come if you're not right in the head.'' John Kelly writes in the *Times Literary Supplement* that ''during a disconsolate return to his native America,'' Donleavy discovered that ''Ireland is a state of mind'' and his recent *J. P. Donleavy's Ireland: In All Her Sins and Some of Her Graces* ''attempts a description of that state of mind.'' Donleavy recreates autobiographically his first exposure to the postwar Dublin that, says Kelly, provided the ''raw material'' for ''Donleavy's myth-making imagination.'' In a Toronto *Globe and Mail* review of the book, Rushton thinks that ''Donleavy belongs to the people he describes, and acknowledges their kinship by giving them their full due.'' As Kevin E. Gallagher comments in the *Los Angeles Times Book Review,* it is ''a love story that, I think never ends for anyone who cares, like this, about a place.''

Although Donleavy's *The Ginger Man* remains the standard by which the entirety of his work is measured, his writing has generated the full spectrum of critical response. Ken Lawless in an *Antioch Review* of *The Destinies of Darcy Dancer, Gentleman,* for example, writes that ''no literary artist working in English today is better than J. P. Donleavy, and few merit comparison with him.'' On the other hand, in the *New York Times Book Review,* Geoffrey Wolff reacts to similar critical assessments of Donleavy's work with: ''Nonsense. He is an Irish tenor who sets his blarney to short songs that are sometimes as soft as velvet or good stout, sometimes plangent, elliptical and coarse.'' However, Grant suggests that ''at the very least, he represents the example of a writer who goes very much his own way, eschewing both the popular success of the best-sellers and the literary acclaim of the academic establishment. At best, a case can be made for a few of his novels as primary expressions within the black humorist tradition of modern literature. Certainly he is a foremost American exponent of the Kafkaesque vision of the modern world, and his better works strongly express that sense of universal absurdity at which we can only laugh.''

''After all my years of struggle, it makes me realize that in my own way I have conquered America, totally silently, totally from underground and from within and that television or being interviewed doesn't matter,'' Donleavy relates in the *Paris Review.* In his *Saturday Review* essay, ''The Author and His Image,'' Donleavy ponders the complexities of an author's image in its various aspects from obscurity through success, and concludes: ''But you know no matter what you do the world will always finally turn its face away. Back into all its own troubled lives. . . . Forgetting what you wanted them to see. Silent with what you wanted them to say. And empty with what you wanted them to feel. Except somewhere you know there will be a voice. At least once asking. Hey what happened to that guy, did he die, you know the one, who wrote that book, can't remember his name but he was famous as hell. That was the author. And that was his image.''

CA INTERVIEW

CA interviewed J. P. Donleavy by telephone on April 20, 1987, at his home in Mullingar, Ireland.

CA: Since your experience with trying to get The Ginger Man *published in the United States in the mid-1950s, you've found this country a bad place to be a writer in, and in 1967 you changed your citizenship to make Ireland your official home. Do you still find the Irish countryside, and your estate in Mullingar, compatible with writing?*

DONLEAVY: Yes, very much so. I suppose it's the way I live in Ireland, where I am slightly isolated, so in effect it doesn't make that much difference being here.

CA: In your 1986 book, J. P. Donleavy's Ireland, *the chapters on your first discovering Dublin when you went there to attend Trinity College read like a love affair with the city. Now, you say at the end of the book, you see "destitute, ragged" scholars, and buildings tumbling down. Does any of your first feeling about Dublin remain?*

DONLEAVY: It does, in spite of today's conditions in Ireland. This is mostly regarding the architecture and the fabric of the city, which is undergoing tremendous changes of development but in most cases simply doesn't get developed.

CA: Do you see much of the spirit of the city that you saw at first?

DONLEAVY: There are traces of it still. It has changed dramatically simply because Ireland has now become a modern state in terms of the rest of the world's visiting here. There's a great deal more foreign presence in Ireland now. In those early days of my time here, it was very much isolated from the world.

CA: You've said in the past that the countryside, though providing the quiet you need for your writing, didn't really fuel the work. Does it need a combination of country and city?

DONLEAVY: The stimulation of the city is something that one misses in the country; the countryside isn't exactly in itself a stimulating atmosphere in which to write. But if you reside in a city, it's equally isolating, or even more so.

CA: Do you come to New York anymore?

DONLEAVY: Yes. I travel to New York on average once or twice a year, usually.

CA: You studied zoology at Trinity but seemed more intent on your painting than on any sort of career your studies might lead to. Was it what you envisioned as a life's work in those pre-writing days?

DONLEAVY: It's possible that painting was something I intended to do. Writing became a more sympathetic thing for me to do, or at least a more satisfying thing to do—cerebrally if not physically. Writing more or less involved one seven days a week, but I continued to paint at odd times and accumulated a great deal of work over the years. I hadn't done much about it until recently, when I did have an exhibition of paintings in Dublin and sold a great deal of work. So it appears I will be having more exhibitions, probably doing more painting than I have for some years.

CA: Sebastian Dangerfield hit the world at a time when a lot of young people were ripe for such an anti-hero figure. How do you think he has weathered through the three decades since The Ginger Man *was first published?*

DONLEAVY: He appears to have weathered very well. I'm never certain, because he's changed people's attitudes and influenced people enough that the awareness of him comes back to me now through other people. I'm stopped and told by some people that the reading of the book at a very young age changed their lives a great deal, and it seems to be the case still. I presume that, without my knowing it, the influence of Dangerfield seems to have made itself felt and may somehow have even changed something in the world, if not externally then internally in people's lives. But there's no real telling.

CA: William E. Grant, writing for Dictionary of Literary Biography, *called Sebastian Dangerfield "a failed conformist rather than a romantic rebel." How do you think of your character?*

DONLEAVY: I think that's a good description. Contrary to what most people felt about Dangerfield, he more or less was attempting to take his own place in society. But he was in fact missing what he thought was the most important thing, which was a private income.

CA: Your lawsuit against Olympia Press for the way they published The Ginger Man *came to an end when you actually acquired the press through a bankruptcy auction. Is Olympia Press now active only in terms of copyright holdings?*

DONLEAVY: Yes. It doesn't actually publish; it's simply a repository of an enormous number of pornographic books written by various authors at the time it was active. But the Olympia Press was suing me over all those years, not I them.

CA: So you've never had any plans to use it as an active press?

DONLEAVY: Not really, although I have sometimes toyed with the idea of using it as a publishing medium—not to publish my work, but simply to make it active again.

CA: Are there out-of-print books in the press's holdings that might deserve to be reprinted?

DONLEAVY: It's possible. I haven't researched the actual status of many of the books, although there exists a handbook by Patrick J. Kearney who has done—not perhaps to the extent of establishing the position of copyright as regards the Olympia Press, but more or less historically establishing what books the press had in fact published, and when. I think there are about 285 titles altogether.

CA: In a 1975 Paris Review *interview you said that "being a good novelist really comes down to being a good newspaper reporter . . . trying to get what you've written on your page into a reader's mind as quickly as possible, and to keep them seeing it. That's why I use the short, truncated, telegraphic sentences." Was it a technique that came naturally in the first writing, or something you had to work at developing?*

DONLEAVY: I think I had to work at developing it, as in rewriting the first draft of *The Ginger Man* I began to formulate the style. It did come in that sense. I also found it present in letters that one wrote at the time. It more or less found its way into developing from both my letter-writing and just as a basis of communication.

CA: Your sentences seem to have become more staccato since that first book. Is that due to a natural evolution?

DONLEAVY: I don't think that's absolutely accurate. The style I use to write does in fact change with various novels, such as *The Destinies of Darcy Dancer, Gentleman*. The style of writing changes practically with the place, pace and time and characters one is writing about. I don't think it's the same all the way through my various books.

CA: What about the business of going back and forth between first and third person in the same book? How did you hit on that?

DONLEAVY: I think I was merely adapting a three-dimensional manner of using the language. It was just a practical way of seeing things in another dimension.

CA: A means of stepping back and looking from another point of view?

DONLEAVY: Yes, and from that viewpoint making it objectivized, and for the reader as well, I suppose.

CA: Your humor has sometimes been called aimless and irresponsible. Would you comment on your ideas about humor and whether you feel it has some implied responsibility to the reader?

DONLEAVY: I don't feel it has any implied responsibility to the reader, but the one thing people do pay attention to is something that they clearly think is funny. It's not that one writes in that way because one thinks someone will read it for that reason, but I think in storytelling basically in Ireland, that is one of the reasons a story is generally told—because it's amusing and funny.

CA: Pieces of some of your books have appeared first in magazines. Have any of the books been written in a fragmentary way, or have they all been conceived and done straight through from start to finish?

DONLEAVY: I think at times some books have been written in a fragmentary way, only in the sense that I might have stopped at a certain point in working on the book and gone back to it again, and perhaps in the interim refined part of it. It might then have turned into some other form than a novel. My first play, called *Helen*, was part of *A Fairy Tale of New York*. This was in fact broadcast as a radio play. And in the case of *Fairy Tales of New York*, the stageplay, it was fragmented and taken from the novel *A Fairy Tale of New York*, which remained unpublished at the point at which the play was produced. I don't think this was the case with anything else. I wrote my short stories with the intention of their being short stories.

CA: You told Samuel Allis for the Washington Post *that you discourage academic interest in your work. What are your concerns about the academic critics?*

DONLEAVY: I think it was merely the observation that a book like *The Ginger Man* was criticized at the time of its first publication and I noticed that because the book persisted over

the years these same critics were now pointing to its importance, and were using it as a critical weapon against me, while attempting to ignore subsequent persisting works such as *The Beastly Beatitudes of Balthazar B, A Fairy Tale of New York* and *The Destinies of Darcy Dancer, Gentleman*, read by a younger generation who often had never heard of *The Ginger Man*. This has made me realize that, with rare exceptions, critical opinion was a political stance taken for the benefit of the critic and had little to do with the merit of an author's actual work.

CA: One thing that's often mentioned in writing about your work is the combination of influences—American, English, and Irish. Can you separate them and say how the writing has benefited from each, or are they too intertwined?

DONLEAVY: I think all three became influences: the American because I have probably absorbed it, having been raised there; a British one from one's background and education, and also from living in England; and then an Irish one, from both educational and residential bases. And in a particular venue, as it were, or in the place where a book is set, I tend to write in the vernacular of that setting.

*CA: For some time—perhaps still—*The Ginger Man *was officially banned in Ireland, and yet it could be bought in book stores there. Is it something peculiarly Irish to invite writers and artists by offering them very liberal tax laws, but on the other hand impose state sanctions on what they produce?*

DONLEAVY: I think this was always a characteristic. I'm sure the status of the tax laws will probably change; they have threatened to change it, and I think the change would be in the long tradition of how the artist is treated in Ireland in the modern day. This existing tax benefit certainly became an example of how the artist *ought* to be treated, but one still never knows when they may revert to kind.

CA: There seems to be some good writers coming along in Ireland. Do you keep up with current writing there?

DONLEAVY: No, I've not really followed the literary world in either Ireland, England, or America. I don't suppose I've deliberately stayed out of it, but I don't write book reviews, and this has possibly made me unaware of what is happening.

CA: What does the working farm at Mullingar consist of?

DONLEAVY: It's just under two hundred acres, and it consists of cattle which are bred for market and some fox-hunting horses. There are no crops, mostly because of the weather here, which is quite difficult to harvest crops in.

CA: How do you actually divide your time between tending the farm and doing your writing?

DONLEAVY: I mostly deal with farming matters at the end of the day. I have to treat it as exercise and distraction. It can be an unfortunate distraction at times, and at other times a pleasant one.

CA: It was announced in the New York Times *that* The Ginger Man *is finally to be filmed by a newly formed independent company coheaded by your son Philip. How are the plans progressing?*

DONLEAVY: They are progressing quite well. The film industry is a highly unpredictable one. However, you can provide a certain stronghold over the progress of a property, you can to some degree predict matters, and so far one appears to be making headway. I've already done the screenplay for the film. The problem often in a case of a book like *The Ginger Man* comes with casting. It's very difficult to find what would now be a contemporary Sebastian Dangerfield.

CA: Will you be very involved in making the film?

DONLEAVY: Only to the degree that one knows what's happening at every stage. I don't myself exert influences other than the fact that I'm aware of who's chosen to do certain things. Mostly I try to remain a reference point.

CA: What's in progress besides the movie? Are you indeed writing a legal history of The Ginger Man, *as has been reported?*

DONLEAVY: Yes. But it's more autobiography with the legal part mostly a background. One did have this legal battle with the Olympia Press. It was mostly a case of the Olympia Press's suing me in various countries, and it existed from practically 1956 for the twenty-two years following. At the end of it, when I acquired the Olympia Press itself, I was in the strange situation at one latter stage when I was in fact in a French court suing myself, since I owned the other side of the litigation.

CA: Do you have plans beyond that book and the movie version of The Ginger Man?

DONLEAVY: I'm writing the third volume of *The Destinies of Darcy Dancer, Gentleman*—the second being *Leila,* which has already been published.

BIOGRAPHICAL/CRITICAL SOURCES:

BOOKS

Authors in the News, Volume II, Gale, 1976.
Contemporary Fiction in America and England, 1950-1970, Gale, 1976.
Contemporary Literary Criticism, Gale, Volume I, 1973, Volume IV, 1975, Volume VI, 1976, Volume X, 1979, Volume XLV, 1987.
Dictionary of Literary Biography, Volume VI: *American Novelists since World War II,* Gale, 1980.
Donleavy, J. P., *The Ginger Man,* Olympia Press, 1955, published with introduction by Arland Ussher, Spearman, 1956, Obolensky, 1958, complete and unexpurgated edition, Delacorte, 1965, published with illustrations by Graham McCallum, Edito-Service, 1973, published as limited edition with illustrations by Skip Liepke, Franklin Library, 1978.
Donleavy, J. P., *J. P. Donleavy's Ireland: In All Her Sins and in Some of Her Graces,* Viking, 1986.
Hassan, Ihab, *Radical Innocence: Studies in the Contemporary American Novel,* Princeton University Press, 1961.
Masinton, Charles G., *J. P. Donleavy: The Style of His Sadness and Humor,* Popular Press, 1975.
Podhoretz, Norman, *Doings and Undoings,* Farrar, Straus, 1964.
Sharma, R. K., *Isolation and Protest: A Case Study of J. P. Donleavy's Fiction,* Ajanta (New Delhi), 1983.

PERIODICALS

America, May 3, 1969, May 10, 1980.

Antioch Review, winter, 1978, winter, 1980.
Architectural Digest, November, 1986.
Atlantic, December, 1968, December, 1976, December, 1977, June, 1979.
Books, November, 1987.
Chicago Tribune, May 25, 1958, May 19, 1985.
Chicago Tribune Book World, October 28, 1979.
Commonweal, August 15, 1958, December 2, 1966, March 7, 1969.
Contemporary Literature, Volume XII, number 3, 1971.
Critique: Studies in Modern Fiction, Volume IX, number 2, 1976, Volume XII, number 3, 1971, Volume XVII, number 1, 1975.
Detroit News, October 2, 1983, June 9, 1985.
Economist, November 10, 1973.
Globe and Mail (Toronto), October 13, 1984, January 17, 1987, April 18, 1987.
Harper's, December, 1977.
Listener, May 11, 1978, October 29, 1987.
Los Angeles Times, October 28, 1983.
Los Angeles Times Book Review, October 7, 1979, May 5, 1985, November 16, 1986.
Michigan Academician, winter, 1974, summer, 1976.
Midcontinent American Studies Journal, spring, 1967.
Midwest Quarterly, winter, 1977.
Nation, May 24, 1958, December 14, 1963, January 20, 1969.
National Review, October 18, 1971.
New Leader, December 19, 1977.
New Republic, December 14, 1963, March 1, 1969, July 24, 1971, December 15, 1979.
New Statesman, April 17, 1964, February 7, 1969, July 16, 1971, May 12, 1978, March 28, 1980, October 14, 1983.
Newsweek, November 11, 1963, March 21, 1966, November 18, 1968, September 15, 1975.
New Yorker, October 25, 1958, May 16, 1964, October 15, 1966, October 8, 1973, December 19, 1977.
New York Herald Tribune Book Review, May 11, 1958.
New York Review of Books, January 2, 1969.
New York Times, May 11, 1958, November 16, 1979, April 17, 1987.
New York Times Book Review, November 24, 1963, November 7, 1965, December 5, 1965, March 20, 1966, December 29, 1968, September 5, 1971, September 23, 1973, November 6, 1977, October 7, 1979, October 26, 1980, October 11, 1983, October 30, 1983, April 28, 1985.
Observer (London), November 8, 1987.
Paris Review, fall, 1975.
Publishers Weekly, October 31, 1986.
Punch, October 21, 1987.
Saturday Review, May 10, 1958, November 23, 1963, November 23, 1968, November 12, 1977, January 20, 1979.
Spectator, September 22, 1973, May 13, 1978, April 12, 1980, December 8, 1984, July 19, 1986.
Studies in Contemporary Satire, number 1, 1975.
Time, March 18, 1966, December 6, 1968, July 5, 1971, October 29, 1973, September 22, 1975, November 14, 1977, October 15, 1979.
Times (London), October 13, 1983, July 17, 1986, October 29, 1987.
Times Literary Supplement, April 30, 1964, May 6, 1965, May 5, 1967, March 20, 1969, July 23, 1971, September 7, 1973, May 12, 1978, April 4, 1980, October 28, 1983, November 16, 1984, December 19, 1986.
Tribune Books, January 25, 1987.
Twentieth Century Literature, January, 1968, July, 1972.

Village Voice, September 17, 1979.
Washington Post, October 30, 1979, February 24, 1985.
Washington Post Book World, September 30, 1973, November 13, 1977.
World Literature Today, summer, 1978, summer, 1980, spring, 1984.
Yale Review, October, 1966.

—Sketch by Sharon Malinowski
—Interview by Jean W. Ross

*   *   *

DONOVAN, Josephine (Campbell)   1941-

PERSONAL: Born March 10, 1941, in Manila, Philippines; American citizen born abroad; daughter of William N. (a physician) and Josephine (Devigne) Donovan. *Education:* Bryn Mawr College, A.B. (cum laude), 1962; University of Wisconsin (now University of Wisconsin—Madison), M.A., 1967, Ph.D, 1971.

ADDRESSES: Home—294 Dennett St., Portsmouth, N.H. 03801.

CAREER: University of Kentucky, Lexington, assistant professor in honors program, 1971-76; University of New Hampshire, Durham, coordinator of women's studies program, 1977-80; University of Tulsa, Tulsa, Okla., visiting scholar, 1982; George Washington University, Washington, D.C., visiting assistant professor, 1983-84; University of Maine, Orono, associate professor of English, 1984—. Consultant to National Endowment for the Humanities.

MEMBER: Modern Language Association of America, Women's Caucus for the Modern Languages, National Women's Studies Association.

AWARDS, HONORS: Outstanding academic book, *Choice* magazine, 1986, for *The Intellectual Traditions of American Feminism.*

WRITINGS:

(Contributor) Susan Koppelman-Cornillon, editor, *Images of Women in Fiction,* Bowling Green Popular Press, 1972.
(Editor and contributor) *Feminist Literary Criticism: Explorations in Theory,* University Press of Kentucky, 1975.
(Contributor) Lina Mainiero, editor, *American Women Writers: A Critical Reference Guide From Colonial Times to the Present,* Ungar, 1979.
(Contributor) Ruth Borker, Nelly Furman, and Sally McConnell-Ginet, editors, *Women and Language in Literature and Society,* Praeger, 1980.
Sarah Orne Jewett, Ungar, 1980.
(Contributor) *Feminist Literary Criticism,* National Humanities Center, 1981.
New England Local Color Literature: A Women's Tradition, Ungar, 1983.
(Contributor) Gwen L. Nagel, editor, *Critical Essays on Sarah Orne Jewett,* G. K. Hall, 1984.
The Intellectual Traditions of American Feminism, Ungar, 1985.
(Contributor) Shari Benstock, editor, *Feminist Issues in Literary Scholarship,* Indiana University Press, 1987.

Contributor of articles and reviews to literature journals, including *Minnesota Review, Critical Inquiry,* and *Massachusetts Review.*

WORK IN PROGRESS: After the Fall: The Writings of Edith Warton, Willa Cather, and Ellen Glasgow.

SIDELIGHTS: Josephine Donovan told *CA:* "Feminist literary criticism assumes that there is a moral dimension to literature, that literature functions as part of the cultural propaganda of society, that it does affect people's lives, their ways of thinking, their behavior. In much of Western literature the moral being of women has been denied or repressed. Feminist literary criticism points this out and looks for works (often by women) in which women characters seek to achieve fullness of being.

"In this feminist critical process numerous lost and important works by women have been (and are being) recovered. Feminist literary historians are now beginning to chart the traditions of this lost women's literature. I hope to continue to participate in this work of retrieval and revision: recovering and reanalyzing women's works and rewriting literary history."

*   *   *

DORN, Frank   1901-1981

PERSONAL: Born June 25, 1901, in San Francisco, Calif.; died July 26, 1981, in Washington, D.C., of cancer; son of Walter E. (a lawyer) and Ellen J. (O'Reilly) Dorn; married Phyllis Moore Gallagher (a writer), February 24, 1964. *Education:* San Francisco Institute of Art, student, 1915-18; U.S. Military Academy at West Point, B.S., 1923; College of Chinese Studies, Peking, further study, 1934-35. *Religion:* Roman Catholic.

CAREER: U.S. Army, cadet, 1919-23, commissioned officer, 1923-53, retiring as brigadier general, 1953; General Logging Co., Santa Rosa, Calif., president, 1954-57. Painter, with one-man shows in Paris, Madrid, Majorca, Mexico City, Washington, D.C., and five shows in California.

MEMBER: Various officers associations and clubs; Georgetown Club (Washington, D.C.), Old Capital Club (Monterey, Calif.)

AWARDS, HONORS—Military: Distinguished Service Medal, Silver Star, Bronze Star, Army Commendation Medal, Legion of Merit, two decorations from China, and eight other awards and campaign ribbons.

WRITINGS:

Forest Twilight (novel of the Philippines), Harrap, 1935.
(Self-illustrated) *The Dorn Cookbook: A Treasury of Fine Recipes from All Around the World,* Regnery, 1953.
Good Cooking with Herbs and Spices, Harvey House, 1958.
The Forbidden City: The Biography of a Palace, Scribner, 1970.
Walkout, Crowell, 1971.
The Sino-Japanese War, 1937-41, Macmillan, 1974.
Appointment with Yesterday, Woodhill, 1978.
When Next I Wake, Woodhill, 1978.
Safari, Woodhill, 1979.
The Silent Whisper, Woodhill, 1979.
Sunwatch, Woodhill, 1980.

Contributor to magazines and military publications.

SIDELIGHTS: Frank Dorn spent more than seven years in China, and traveled throughout the Far East, western Europe, and in Mexico. He was consultant and assistant to the director of three motion pictures.†

DRAKE, Joan H(oward)

PERSONAL: Born in Wallasey, Cheshire, England; daughter of Sidney James (a bank manager) and Marjorie (Howard) Drake; married John Emry Davies (a veterinary surgeon), January 2, 1954. *Education:* Attended high schools and private schools in Wallasey and Liverpool, England.

ADDRESSES: Home—Castle Rock, 46 Marine Dr., Barry, South Glamorganshire, South Wales.

CAREER: Writer of books and short stories for children, with first book published when she was sixteen. Lectures occasionally on writing for children. Justice of the Peace, 1970-85.

WRITINGS:

The Story of Wimpy a Wump, Harrap, 1940.
More About Wimpy, Harrap, 1941.
Wimpy Goes on Holiday, Harrap, 1946.
Wimpy Goes Abroad, illustrations by Marjorie Ann Watts, Harrap, 1954.
Jiggle Woggle Bus, illustrations by Eileen Bradpiece, Brockhampton Press, 1957.
Mr. Grimpwinkle, illustrations by Irwin, Brockhampton Press, 1958.
Mr. Grimpwinkle's Marrow, illustrations by Irwin, Brockhampton Press, 1959, Hodder & Stoughton, 1976.
Mr. Grimpwinkle, Pirate Cook, Brockhampton Press, 1960.
Mr. Grimpwinkle Buys a Bus, illustrations by Gordon Burrell, Brockhampton Press, 1961, Hodder & Stoughton, 1977.
Mr. Grimpwinkle's Holiday, illustrations by Burrell, Brockhampton Press, 1963.
Mr. Grimpwinkle's Visitor, illustrations by Burrell, Brockhampton Press, 1964.
Jiggle Woggle Saves the Day, illustrations by Burrell, Brockhampton Press, 1966.
Sally Seal's Summer, Hutchinson, 1967.
James and Sally Again, illustrations by Val Biro, Hutchinson, 1970.
Mr. Bubbus and the Apple-Green Engine, illustrations by Biro, Brockhampton Press, 1971.
Miss Hendy's House, illustrations by Shirley Hughes, Brockhampton Press, 1974.
Mr. Bubbus and the Railway Smugglers, illustrations by Biro, Hodder & Stoughton, 1976.
Mr. Bubbus and the Railway Rescue, illustrations by Biro, Hodder & Stoughton, 1978.
Fire!, Hamlyn, 1978.

Contributor of stories to British Broadcasting Corp. "Children's Hour" and to youth magazines.

AVOCATIONAL INTERESTS: Animals (dogs in particular), ballet, traditional jazz, serious music, cooking and entertaining, flowers and gardening, interior decorating, talking to children.

*   *   *

DRAPER, Hal   1914-

PERSONAL: Born September 19, 1914, in Brooklyn, N.Y.; married Anne Kracik, July 7, 1939 (died March 25, 1973). *Education:* Brooklyn College (now Brooklyn College of the City University of New York), B.A., 1934; University of California, Berkeley, M.L.S., 1960. *Politics:* Marxist, Independent Socialist. *Religion:* None.

ADDRESSES: Home—2450 Warring St., Berkeley, Calif. 94704.

CAREER: High school teacher in New York City, 1936-42; Los Angeles Shipyard, San Pedro, Calif., sheet metal mechanic, 1942-44; Western P&S, San Pedro, shipyard engineer, 1944-45; editor, *The New International,* New York City, 1948-49, and *Labor Action,* 1949-57; University of California, Berkeley, librarian/bibliographer, 1960-70; full-time writer, 1970—; Center for Socialist History, Berkeley, director, 1981—. National secretary, Young People's Socialist League (4th International; youth group of Socialist Workers Party), New York City, 1938-39; chairman, Independent Socialist Committee, Berkeley, 1963-70.

WRITINGS:

Introduction to Independent Socialism, Independent Socialist Press, 1963, 2nd edition, 1970.
Berkeley: The New Student Revolt, Grove, 1965.
(Contributor) R. J. Simons, editor, *As We Saw the Thirties,* University of Illinois Press, 1967.
(With wife, Anne Draper) *The Dirt on California: Agribusiness and the University,* Independent Socialist Press, 1968.
(Contributor) W. Laqueur, editor, *The Israel/Arab Reader,* Citadel, 1969.
(Editor) *Karl Marx and Frederick Engels: Articles in the New American Encyclopaedia,* Independent Socialist Press, 1969.
(Editor) *Marx and Engels: Writings on the Paris Commune,* Monthly Review Press, 1971.
Karl Marx's Theory of Revolution, Monthly Review Press, Volume I: *The State and Bureaucracy,* 1977, Volume II: *The Politics of Social Classes,* 1978, 2nd edition, 1981, Volume III: *The "Dictatorship of the Proletariat,"* 1986.
(Translator) *The Complete Poems of Heinrich Heine: A Modern English Version,* Suhrkamp/Insel, 1982.
(Editor with Center for Socialist History) *The Marx-Engels Cyclopedia Series,* Schocken, Volume I: *The Marx-Engels Chronicle: A Day-by-Day Chronology of Marx and Engels' Life and Activity,* 1985, Volume II: *The Marx-Engels Register: A Complete Bibliography of Marx and Engels' Individual Writings,* 1985, Volume III: *The Marx-Engels Glossary: Glossary to the Chronicle and Register, and Index to the Glossary,* 1986.
The Dictatorship of the Proletariat from Marx to Lenin, Monthly Review Press, 1987.

Also author and editor of articles, brochures, and pamphlets on socialist theory and history; also author of science-fiction stories and articles on librarianship. Member of editorial board, *New Politics,* 1960-74.

WORK IN PROGRESS: Additional volumes of *Karl Marx's Theory of Revolution;* an encyclopedia of socialist history.

SIDELIGHTS: Hal Draper told *CA:* "After quitting the financial shelter of the University of California library staff in 1970 and undertaking to write full-time without starving, I went through a revulsion against spending time on journalistic writing of any sort, no matter on what level, and swore to confine my efforts to producing (only) a number of books which I had to get out of my system. This still goes; periodical stuff is ephemeral. . . Increasingly my work will be focused on the new project, the Center for Socialist History. Founded in 1981, . . . it fills a great lacuna; its major task is the production of an encyclopedia of socialist history. Why is there an encyclopedia or 'dictionary'-type handbook on every subject and field under the sun, from Antiques to Zoos, but none on socialism and its related isms? In fact, there *never* has been one worth mentioning in English."

*   *   *

DREYFACK, Raymond

PERSONAL: Born in New York, N.Y.; son of Marcus (a manufacturer) and Frances (Wagner) Dreyfack; married Tess Karlitz (a special assistant to a psychiatrist); children: Kenneth, Madeleine. *Education:* Attended City College (now City College of the City University of New York), Columbia University, and New York University, 1945-55.

ADDRESSES: Home—3 Clubhouse Ln., Marlboro, N.J. 07746.

CAREER: Henry Kelly Importing and Distributing Co., New York, N.Y., data processing manager, 1947-52; Faberge Perfumes, Inc., Ridgefield, N.J., systems director, 1953-63; freelance writer and public relations consultant, 1963—. Former lecturer at New York University.

MEMBER: American Society of Journalists and Authors.

WRITINGS:

Twelve Psychic Selling Strategies That Will Multiply Your Income, Parker Publishing, 1975.
Sure Fail: The Art of Mismanagement, Morrow, 1976.
How to Boost Company Productivity and Profits, Dartnell, 1976.
The Image Makers (novel), Major, 1976.
Zero-Base Budgeting: Pros and Cons, Dartnell, 1977.
The Complete Book of Walking, Farnsworth Publishing, 1979.
Profitable Salesmanship in the Eighties, Chilton, 1980.
Making It in Management the Japanese Way, Farnsworth Publishing, 1982.
Customers: How to Get Them, How to Serve Them, How to Keep Them, Dartnell, 1983.
Business Perks and Benefits, Dartnell, 1985.

Also ghostwriter of books and articles. Contributor of chapters of books and articles to business and management journals. Special projects editor, *Plant Engineering;* contributing editor, *Supervision* and *American Salesman;* former editor and copublisher, *Profit Improvement News.*

WORK IN PROGRESS: A book on management; a book on paranormal phenomena.

*   *   *

DUBALL, Michael
See ALD, Roy A(llison)

*   *   *

DUNLOP, Ian G(eoffrey) D(avid)   1925-

PERSONAL: Born August 19, 1925, in Rajkot, Kathiawar (now Gujarat), India; son of Walter N. U. (in Indian civil service) and Marguerite Irene (Shakerley) Dunlop; married Deirdre Marcia Jamieson, November 2, 1957. *Education:* Attended Winchester College, 1938-43; New College, Oxford, B.A., 1948, M.A., 1956; Strasbourg University, diplome, 1953; additional study at Lincoln Theological College, 1954-56.

ADDRESSES: Home—24 The Close, Salisbury, Wiltshire SP1 2EH, England.

CAREER: Church of England, curate in Hertfordshire, 1956-59, chaplain at Westminster School, London, 1959-62; vicar at Bures, Suffolk, 1962-72; canon and chancellor at Salisbury Cathedral, Salisbury, Wiltshire, England, 1972—. Teacher of English at schools in Strasbourg, France, 1952-53, and Versailles, France, 1953-54. Trustee, Historic Churches Preservation Trust, 1970. Member, General Synod, 1975-85, and Cathedral's Advisory Commission, 1981-86. *Military service:* Irish Guards, 1943-45; became lieutenant.

MEMBER: National Book League, Society of Antiquaries (fellow), Guards Boat Club, Army and Navy Club.

WRITINGS:

Versailles, Batsford, 1956, revised edition, Taplinger, 1970.
Palaces and Progresses of Elizabeth I, J. Cape, 1962, Taplinger, 1970.
Chateaux of the Loire, Taplinger, 1969.
Collins Companion Guide to the Ile de France, Collins, 1979.
French Cathedrals, 1150-1250, Taplinger, 1981.
The Cathedrals' Crusade: The Rise of the Gothic Style in France, Taplinger, 1982.
Royal Palaces of France, W. W. Norton, 1985.

Contributor to *Country Life, Connoisseur* and *Church Times.*

SIDELIGHTS: Ian G. D. Dunlop comments: "I write in order to share with as many others as possible the pleasure and interest I derive from architecture, especially that of France. Too much architectural writing is confined to the study of style; nobody puts up buildings as an essay in style. What makes buildings so fascinating to me is that they express the ideas that their 'authors' set out to express—Versailles tells us all we need to know about Louis the XIV's ideas on the monarchy—and they enshrine historical memories of those most closely associated with them."

Dunlop's passion for architecture is reflected in his book *The Cathedrals' Crusade: The Rise of the Gothic Style in France.* London *Times* reviewer George Hill says of it, "[Dunlop's] book is not an exhaustive history or guide, but a civilized and learned account of the dozen buildings which best summarize [the twelfth and thirteenth centuries'] work. His judgement is sound and sensitive . . ." Jonathan Sumption, writing for the *Times Literary Supplement,* is moved to similar sentiments: "Ian Dunlop does something to fill this [historiographical] gap with an account, building by building, of the twelve greatest Gothic cathedrals of France. . . . In no sense is this a work of original scholarship, but what it does achieve is an observant description of the building and a good summary of modern scholarship about it, together with some interesting anecdotal background." He concludes, "The result is a useful book for serious travellers in France. There is nothing better of its kind."

AVOCATIONAL INTERESTS: Birdwatching, painting, the countryside (especially the Scottish Highlands).

BIOGRAPHICAL/CRITICAL SOURCES:

PERIODICALS

Times (London), March 11, 1982.
Times Literary Supplement, March 26, 1982.

*   *   *

DURBRIDGE, Francis (Henry)   1912-
(Paul Temple, a joint pseudonym)

PERSONAL: Born November 25, 1912, in Hull, England; son

of Francis and Gertrude Durbridge; married Norah Elizabeth Lawly, 1940; children: two sons. *Education:* Attended Birmingham University.

ADDRESSES: Home—4 Fairacres, Roehampton Lane SW15 5LX, England. *Agent*—Harvey Unna and Stephen Durbridge Ltd., 24 Pottery Ln., Holland Park, London W11 4LZ, England.

CAREER: Playwright and novelist. Writer and executive producer of television series, 1952—.

WRITINGS:

NOVELS

Send for Paul Temple, John Long, 1938.
(With Charles Hatton) *Paul Temple and the Front Page Men,* John Long, 1939.
News of Paul Temple, John Long, 1940.
Paul Temple Intervenes, John Long, 1944.
Send for Paul Temple Again!, John Long, 1948.
Back Room Girl, John Long, 1950.
Design for Murder, John Long, 1951.
Beware of Johnny Washington, John Long, 1951.
The Other Man, Hodder & Stoughton, 1958, reprinted, White Lion, 1973.
A Time of Day, Hodder & Stoughton, 1959.
The Scarf, Hodder & Stoughton, 1960, published as *The Case of the Twisted Scarf,* Dodd, 1961.
Portrait of Alison, Dodd, Mead, 1962, reprinted, Henry Publications, 1980.
The World of Tim Frazer, Dodd, Mead, 1962.
My Friend Charles, Hodder & Stoughton, 1963.
Tim Frazer Again, Hodder & Stoughton, 1964.
Another Woman's Shoes, Hodder & Stoughton, 1965.
The Desperate People, Hodder & Stoughton, 1966.
Dead to the World, Hodder & Stoughton, 1967.
My Wife Melissa, Hodder & Stoughton, 1967.
The Geneva Mystery: A Paul Temple Novel, Hodder Paperbacks, 1971.
The Curzon Case: A Paul Temple Novel, Coronet, 1972.
Paul Temple and the Kelby Affair, White Lion, 1973.
Paul Temple and the Harkdale Robbery, White Lion, 1976.
The Doll, Hodder & Stoughton, 1982.

WITH JAMES DOUGLAS RUTHERFORD McCONNELL; PUBLISHED BY HODDER & STOUGHTON

(Under joint pseudonym Paul Temple) *The Tyler Mystery,* 1957, reprinted, White Lion, 1973.
(Under joint pseudonym Paul Temple) *East of Algiers,* 1959, reprinted, White Lion, 1975.
The Pig-Tail Murder, 1969.
A Man Called Harry Brent, 1970.
Bat out of Hell, 1972.
A Game of Murder, 1975.
The Passenger, 1977.
Tim Frazer Gets the Message, 1978.
Breakaway, 1981.

PLAYS; PUBLISHED BY SAMUEL FRENCH

Suddenly at Home, 1973.
The Gentle Hook, 1975.
Murder with Love, 1977.
House Guest, 1982.
Deadly Nightcap, 1986.

OTHER

Author of screenplays with John Argyle "Send for Paul Temple," 1946, with A. R. Rawlinson "Calling Paul Temple," 1948, "Paul Temple Returns," 1952, with James Matthews "The Teckman Mystery," 1954, "The Vicious Circle," 1957.

Author of numerous television serials, 1952—, including "The Broken Horseshoe," "Portrait of Alison," "My Friend Charles," "The Scarf," "The Desperate People," "A Game of Murder," "The World of Tim Frazer," "A Man Called Harry Brent," "The Other Man," "Melissa," "Bat out of Hell," "Stupid Like a Fox," and "The Doll." Also author of radio plays, including "Promotion," and contributor of articles to periodicals, including *London Daily Mail, Birmingham Post, London Evening News,* and *Radio Times.*

SIDELIGHTS: Francis Durbridge is recognized as a successful writer of television serials, many of which he has turned into novels. His serials, which have one of the largest television audiences in Europe, have been broadcast in over sixteen countries, including Germany, France, Italy, and the United States. In the German-speaking countries alone, they regularly reach an audience of over twenty-five million viewers.

Apart from his work for television, Durbridge is also well known for his BBC radio plays featuring Paul Temple, a character who also appears in some of his novels. In collaboration with James Douglas Rutherford McConnell, Durbridge gave life to this character by writing two books "by Paul Temple."

Durbridge once told *CA:* "I believe in the Arnold Bennett and Anthony Trollope approach to writing: regular hours, nose to the grindstone technique. I like traveling, getting local colour for my stories, and attending rehearsals of my plays."

AVOCATIONAL INTERESTS: Reading and travel (has visited most countries in Europe and has traveled extensively in the United States).

*   *   *

DYE, Harold E(ldon)   1907-

PERSONAL: Born April 5, 1907, in Tulsa, Okla; son of Harvey Smith and Pearl Belle (Upton) Dye; married Ina Pearl Hollaway, December 21, 1927; children: Lila Belle (Mrs. Richard Hopkins), Joyce (Mrs. Robert Lowry), Jeanne (Mrs. Charles Hightower), Leland Eldon. *Education:* Attended Montezuma Baptist College, 1925-27. *Politics:* Democrat.

ADDRESSES: Home—1193 East Fewtrell Dr., Campbell, Calif. 95008.

CAREER: Pastor of Baptist churches in Las Cruces, N.M., 1934-44, Clovis, N.M., 1946-49, and Bakersfield, Calif., 1949-52; Baptist Temple, San Jose, Calif., pastor, 1952-74. Trustee of Golden Gate Baptist Theological Seminary, 1950—, and California Southern Baptist Board of Christian Higher Education, 1959—.

MEMBER: California Writers Club.

WRITINGS:

Robes of Splendor, Broadman, 1944.
Shining Like the Stars, Baptist Home Mission Board, 1947.
Through God's Eyes, Broadman, 1947.

The Prophet of Little Cane Creek, Baptist Home Mission Board,
    1949.
The Weaver, Broadman, 1952.
Under the North Star, Baptist Home Mission Board, 1954.
This Gold Is Mine, Broadman, 1958.
His to Command, Baptist Home Mission Board, 1960.
Stories to Remember, Broadman, 1962.
Pablo and the Magi, Broadman, 1967.
The Weaver, Broadman, 1974.
No Rocking Chair for Me!, Broadman, 1976.
The Touch of Friendship, Broadman, 1979.
A Daily Miracle, Broadman, 1986.

Also author of *The World in Her Hands.* Contributor to Southern Baptist Sunday School Board publications for more than
twenty-five years and to other Baptist publications. Editor,
Baptist New Mexican, 1944-46.

E

EAST, Michael
See WEST, Morris L(anglo)

* * *

EBB, Fred 1935-

PERSONAL: Born April 8, 1935, in New York, N.Y.; son of Harry and Anna (Gritz) Ebb. *Education:* Attended New York University and Columbia University.

ADDRESSES: Agent—International Creative Management, 40 West 57th St., New York, N.Y. 10019.

CAREER: Lyricist and librettist.

AWARDS, HONORS: Emmy Awards from National Academy of Television Arts and Sciences, 1973, for "Liza with a Z," and 1975, for "Gypsy in My Soul"; Academy Awards (Oscars) from American Academy of Motion Picture Arts and Sciences, 1974, for "Norman Rockwell," and 1976, for "How Lucky Can You Get"; "Chicago" received Antoinette Perry (Tony) Award from League of New York Theatres and Producers for book and lyrics, Grammy Award from National Academy of Recording Arts and Sciences for the album, and Golden Globe Award from Hollywood Foreign Press Association, all 1976.

WRITINGS:

LYRICIST; MUSICALS

"Flora, the Red Menace," first produced on Broadway at Alvin Theatre, May, 1965; revival with new songs produced in New York at Vineyard Theater, December, 1987.
Cabaret (also see below; score by John Kander; produced on Broadway at Broadhurst Theatre, November 20, 1966), Random House, 1967.
"The Happy Time," produced on Broadway at Imperial Theatre, January 18, 1968.
Zorba (score by Kander; produced on Broadway at Imperial Theatre, November 17, 1968), Random House, 1969.
(And author of book) "70, Girls, 70," produced on Broadway at Broadhurst Theatre, April 15, 1971.
(And librettist with Bob Fosse) "Chicago," produced, 1975.
"In Person," produced in Chicago, July 4, 1977; produced as "The Act" in New York City, October, 1977.

"Woman of the Year," score by Kander, produced on Broadway at Palace Theatre, March 29, 1981.
"The Rink," produced on Broadway at Martin Beck Theatre, February 9, 1983.

SCREENPLAYS

(Lyricist) "Cabaret," Allied Artists, 1972.
"Norman Rockwell," produced, 1974.
(Lyricist) "Funny Lady," Columbia, 1975.
(Lyricist) "Lucky Lady," Twentieth Century-Fox, 1975.
(Lyricist) "A Matter of Time," American International Pictures, 1976.
(Lyricist) "New York, New York," United Artists, 1977.

TELEVISION SPECIALS

"Liza," produced June, 1970.
"Liza with a Z," produced, 1972.
"Ole Blue Eyes Is Back," produced, 1974.
"Gypsy in My Soul," produced, 1976.
"Baryshnikov on Broadway," produced, 1980.

OTHER

Writer and director, "Liza in Concert at Carnegie Hall," produced in New York, September, 1979.

SIDELIGHTS: For two decades, lyricist Fred Ebb and composer John Kander have been creating some of Broadway's most famous musicals, including "Cabaret," "Zorba," and "Woman of the Year." The team's success on stage, in movies and on television underscores the irony that their names are not as famous as those of such contemporaries as Stephen Sondheim or the late Michael Bennett. The relative anonymity, however, suits them fine. As Kander tells Larry Kart in a *Chicago Tribune* interview with the partners, "Neither one of us lives what you might call a show business life. We work in the theater and we love that, but the things we find personally entertaining have nothing to do with that world."

"For me," Ebb says in the same interview, "a show consists of moments, and what you do is write those moments. You try to remain aware of the form of the piece, and then you just go. . . . I think that if you can walk away from a show and be proud of it, if you feel that you've satisfied your own intentions, then theoretically at least you have had a success. But I have to admit that's a very hard feeling to hang onto if they're taking the marquee down.''

AVOCATIONAL INTERESTS: Collecting musical show albums.

BIOGRAPHICAL/CRITICAL SOURCES:

PERIODICALS

Chicago Tribune, February 12, 1984.
New York Times, December 31, 1987.

*   *   *

EDWARDS, George Charles III   1947-

PERSONAL: Born January 3, 1947, in Rochester, N.Y.; son of George Charles, Jr., and Mary Elizabeth Laing Edwards; married May 22, 1981; wife's name Carmella P.; children: Jeffrey Allen. *Education:* Stetson University, B.A. (magna cum laude), 1969; University of Wisconsin—Madison, M.A., 1970, Ph.D., 1973.

ADDRESSES: Home—2317 Bristol, Bryan, Tex. 77801. *Office*—Department of Political Science, Texas A & M University, College Station, Tex. 77843.

CAREER: Tulane University, New Orleans, La., assistant professor of political science, 1973-78; Texas A & M University, College Station, associate professor, 1978-81, professor of political science, 1981—. Visiting assistant professor at University of Wisconsin—Madison, summer, 1976.; visiting professor of social sciences, United States Military Academy, 1985-88.

MEMBER: American Political Science Association (president of presidency research section, 1984-85), Policy Studies Organization, Center for the Study of the Presidency, Midwest Political Science Association, Southern Political Science Association, Phi Beta Kappa, Pi Sigma Alpha, Phi Alpha Theta. Phi Kappa Phi, Pi Alpha Alpha.

AWARDS, HONORS: Woodrow Wilson fellow, 1969-70.

WRITINGS:

(Editor with William Gwyn, and contributor) *Perspectives on Public Policy-Making,* Tulane Studies in Political Science, 1975.
(With Ira Sharkansky) *The Policy Predicament,* W. H. Freeman, 1978.
Presidential Influence in Congress, W. H. Freeman, 1980.
Implementing Public Policy, Congressional Quarterly Press, 1980.
The Public Presidency, St. Martin's, 1983.
(Editor with Stephen Wayne, and contributor) *Studying the Presidency,* University of Tennessee Press, 1983.
(Editor) *Public Policy Implementation,* Jai Press, 1984.
(With Stephen Wayne) *Presidential Leadership,* St. Martin's, 1985.
(Editor with Steven A. Shull and Norman Thomas) *The Presidency and Public Policy Making,* University of Pittsburgh Press, 1985.
(Editor with Earl Walker) *National Security and the Constitution,* Johns Hopkins University Press, 1988.
At the Margins, Yale University Press, 1988.

(With Alec Gallup) *Presidential Performance and Public Approval,* Johns Hopkins University Press, in press.

CONTRIBUTOR

Steven A. Shull and Lance T. LeLoup, editors, *The Presidency: Studies in Policy-Making,* King's Court, 1979.
Thomas R. Dye and Virginia Gray, editors, *The Determinants of Public Policy,* Lexington Books, 1980.
Norman R. Luttberg, editor, *Public Opinion and Public Policy,* F. E. Peacock, 1981.
Thomas E. Cronin, editor, *Rethinking the Presidency,* Little, Brown, 1982.
Michael Nelson, editor, *The Presidency and the Political System,* Congressional Quarterly Press, 1983.
Robert Harmel, editor, *Presidents and Their Parties,* Praeger, 1984.
David Kozack and Kenneth Ciboski, editors, *The American Presidency,* Nelson-Hall, 1984.
Frank Rourke, editor, *Bureaucratic Power in National Politics,* 4th edition, Little, Brown, 1986.
Bryan Jones, editor, *Political Leadership from Political Science Perspectives,* University of Kansas Press, 1988.

OTHER

Contributor of articles and reviews to political science journals. Editor of newsletter of Presidency Research Group; member of editorial board of *American Journal of Political Science, American Politics Quarterly, Policy Studies Journal, Presidential Studies Quarterly,* and *Congress and the President.*

SIDELIGHTS: George Charles Edwards III told *CA:* "Our libraries contain countless volumes that describe the life and times of presidents and the various roles they have played in the establishment of public policies. There is an equally large number of polemics reputing to place presidential administrations in the proper perspective. Despite all these contributions, we face a striking paradox; the single most important institution in American politics is the one we understand the least.

"My writings are concerned with bridging the gap between facts and polemics about the American presidency, on the one hand, and understanding of it, on the other. They focus on explaining why the public, Congress, the White House staff, and the bureaucracy behave in the ways they do toward the president and what difference the president's behavior makes. In other words, I am less interested in what a president did than in why he did it and what the consequences of his actions were. Why were certain decisions made? Why did the president succeed or fail to obtain the support of Congress or the public? Why were policies implemented as they were?

"Writing nonfiction that is both original and intellectually sound and at the same time appeals to an audience larger than a few dozen scholars poses a formidable challenge to an author. This is especially the case if one believes, as I do, that we should bring as much scientific rigor as possible to the examination of our topics. Anything smacking of statistics has a tendency to discourage many potential readers. Yet it is just this challenge, plus that of trying to understand the complex world of policymaking in America, that keeps me writing."

*   *   *

EDWARDS, Phoebe
See BLOCH, Barbara

EISENHOWER, Dwight D(avid)   1890-1969

PERSONAL: Born October 14, 1890, in Denison, Tex.; died March 28, 1969; son of David and Ida Elizabeth (Stover) Eisenhower; married Mamie Geneva Doud, July 1, 1916 (deceased); children: Doud Dwight (deceased), John Sheldon Doud. *Education:* West Point Military Academy, graduate, 1915; Command and General Staff College, graduate, 1926; attended Army War College and Army Industrial College. *Politics:* Republican. *Religion:* Presbyterian.

CAREER: Thirty-fourth president of the United States. U.S. Army, commissioned 2nd lieutenant, 1915, executive officer at Camp Gaillard, Canal Zone, 1922-24, member of American Battle Monuments Commission, 1927-29, assistant executive to assistant secretary of war, 1929-33; American Military Mission to Philippine Islands, assistant to General Douglas MacArthur, 1935-39; chief of staff of U.S. Third Army, 1941, appointed commanding general of European theater of operations, 1942, commander in chief of Allied forces, North Africa, 1942-43, supreme commander of Allied Expeditionary Force, 1943-45, Army chief of staff, 1945-48; Columbia University, New York, N.Y., president, 1948-52, on leave, 1950-51; Joint Chiefs of Staff, Washington, D.C., chairman ex-officio, 1950-51; NATO commander of Allied powers in Europe, 1951-52; elected president of the United States as Republican party candidate, 1952, reelected, 1956, retired, 1961.

WRITINGS:

Eisenhower's Own Story of the War: The Complete Report by the Supreme Commander, General Dwight D. Eisenhower, on the War in Europe from the Day of Invasion to the Day of Victory, Arco, 1946, published as *Report by the Supreme Commander to the Combined Chiefs of Staff on the Operations in Europe of the Allied Expeditionary Force, 6 June 1944 to 8 May 1945,* U.S. Government Printing Office, 1946.

Crusade in Europe (Book-of-the-Month Club selection), Doubleday, 1948, reprinted, Da Capo Press, 1977.

The White House Years, Doubleday, Volume I: *Mandate for Change, 1953-56,* 1963, Volume II: *Waging Peace, 1956-61,* 1965.

Sir Winston Churchill: Champion of Freedom, Marble Hill Press, 1965.

At Ease: Stories I Tell to Friends, Doubleday, 1967.

In Review, Pictures I've Kept: A Concise Pictorial Autobiography, Doubleday, 1969.

Letters to Mamie, edited by son John S. D. Eisenhower, Doubleday, 1978.

The Eisenhower Diaries, edited by Robert H. Ferrell, Norton, 1981.

COLLECTIONS

Eisenhower Speaks, Excerpts from the General's Speeches, with a Biographical Sketch, edited by H. S. Bagger, Interallied, 1946.

Eisenhower Speaks: Dwight D. Eisenhower in His Messages and Speeches, edited by Rudolph Treuenfels, Farrar, Straus, 1948.

Peace with Justice: Selected Addresses, Columbia University Press, 1961.

The Quotable Dwight D. Eisenhower, edited by Elsie Gollagher and others, Droke, 1967.

The Papers of Dwight D. Eisenhower: The War Years, edited by Alfred D. Chandler, Jr. and others, five volumes, Johns Hopkins Press, 1970.

Selected Speeches of Dwight David Eisenhower, Thirty-fourth President of the United States, Selected from Three Principal Periods of His Life: As Supreme Allied Commander in Europe during the War Years, as Supreme NATO Commander, and as President, U.S. Government Printing Office, 1970.

Dear General: Eisenhower's Wartime Letters to Marshall, edited by Joseph Patrick Hobbs, Johns Hopkins Press, 1971.

Ike: A Great American, edited by Don Ramsey, with an introduction by Mamie Doud Eisenhower, Hallmark, 1972.

Eisenhower Declassified, edited by V. Pinkley and J. F. Scheer, Revell, 1979.

The Declassified Eisenhower, edited by Blanche Wiesen Cook, Doubleday, 1981.

OTHER

Also author of speeches, addresses, government papers, and military reports published by the U.S. Government Printing Office and other government and public organizations. Contributor of articles to *Reader's Digest, Saturday Evening Post,* and other magazines.

AVOCATIONAL INTERESTS: Golf, swimming, fishing, painting, playing bridge, watching western films, Civil War literature.

SIDELIGHTS: Following a distinguished military career which culminated in his appointment as commander in chief of the Allied forces in Europe during the Second World War, Dwight D. Eisenhower was elected the thirty-fourth President of the United States. In both his military and political roles, Eisenhower was known as a superb administrator. He was, Ronald Steel commented in *Saturday Review,* "a man whose genius lay not in strategy . . . but in an ability to organize, delegate authority, and mediate." Townsend Hoopes of the *Washington Post Book World* called Eisenhower "tough, yet wise; decisive, yet careful; not intellectual, but smart. A natural leader. He understood and used power with considerable finesse, but with an innate appreciation of its limited efficacy. . . . He was, above all, a man of proportion who exerted himself to neutralize the extremes of his time." The eight years of the Eisenhower Administration were a time of economic prosperity, peace, and domestic tranquility.

Eisenhower first came to public attention in 1942 when General George C. Marshall chose him to be commander in chief of the Allied forces fighting Nazi Germany. Until that assignment, Eisenhower had served as a career army officer, rising to the rank of lieutenant colonel in the army's War Plans Division. "There he won the admiration of George Marshall," Steel explained. Marshall, impressed with Eisenhower's ability to moderate differences among subordinates, promoted him over 366 more senior army officers to the important post of overseeing Allied military efforts in Europe.

As commander in chief, Eisenhower was in charge of the joint military operations of the United States, Britain, and France in their fight against Nazi Germany. Running such a massive effort required the ability to satisfy the varied needs and expectations of foreign allies, domestic politicians, and the military leaders of three countries. Eisenhower, Hoopes remarked, "had a natural gift, unequalled by any of his contemporaries, for diplomatic persuasion." A writer for the *Times Literary Supplement* maintained that Eisenhower was "a superlative manager of men and an excellent chairman of committees." Gerald Clarke of *Time* called him "the ideal choice to lead contentious allies." By war's end, Eisenhower had become one of the best known and most popular figures in the United States.

This popularity led the Republican party in 1952 to nominate Eisenhower as its presidential candidate. He won election that year and reelection in 1956, serving a total of eight years as president. Cabell Phillips of the *New York Times Book Review* reported that Eisenhower was a popular president: "No President of recent times has enjoyed such sustained and uncritical affection." As Stephen E. Ambrose commented in the *New Republic*, "The 1950s saw peace and prosperity, no riots, relatively high employment, a growing GNP, virtually no inflation, no arms race, no great reforms, no great changes, low taxes, little government regulation of industry and commerce, and a president who was trusted and admired." "Dwight Eisenhower," Steel wrote, "was first in war, peace, and the hearts of his countrymen. . . . His reputation both as General and as President has become nearly as sacrosanct as the flag."

But at the time of his presidency, Eisenhower was often depicted in the press as a lazy and unsophisticated leader who did little because he was unaware of what to do. His casual and unassuming style, along with his reluctance to use governmental power except in extreme cases, also won Eisenhower severe criticism. "Most impartial students of public affairs today," Phillips remarked in 1967, "rate the Eisenhower Presidency rather low on the scale of vigor and accomplishment."

In later years, however, after access to Eisenhower's private papers and diaries had become available, critical evaluation of Eisenhower took a dramatic turn for the better. Eisenhower's casual leadership style, which had made him seem unconcerned about the nation's affairs to some observers, was reevaluated as a shrewd pose designed to keep his adversaries off balance. He was "as shrewd and calculating a mind as has ever won a war or run a country," Clarke observed. "What emerges from the recent studies of Eisenhower," Steel wrote, "is a man of extreme self-assurance, at ease with himself and his convictions. . . . A man who was skillful to the point of cunning."

When compared to the presidents who followed him, Eisenhower also fared well. Ambrose maintained that the initial hostility to Eisenhower came from comparing him to his immediate predecessors, Franklin D. Roosevelt and Harry S Truman. But when compared to "his successors rather than his predecessors," wrote Ambrose, Eisenhower would be placed "in the top 10, if not the top five, of all our presidents." Eisenhower, "to judge from what followed rather than what preceded him, seems a man of decent instincts, incorruptible and unimpressed by titles, . . . and not noticeably afflicted with insecurities," Steel wrote.

Even Eisenhower's critics spoke kindly of him. Writing in the *Saturday Review*, Ernest R. May explained that "admirers and critics of President Eisenhower have held remarkably similar views of him. Both have thought of him as a kindly, good-natured fellow with sound instincts." Charles Burton Marshall of the *New Republic* found that "it is impossible not to like him. He is thorough, comprehensible, forthright, desirous of everyone's benefit, and mild rather than spiteful. . . . One wonders whether any President ever better epitomized his nation." Ambrose noted that Presidents Roosevelt and Eisenhower held the unique distinction of having "a higher reputation and broader popularity when they left office than when they entered." And Hoopes maintained that "as an enduringly

popular and trusted American political leader, through thick and thin, [Eisenhower] was without peer in this century."

BIOGRAPHICAL/CRITICAL SOURCES:

BOOKS

Ambrose, Stephen E., *The Supreme Commander: The War Years of General Dwight D. Eisenhower*, Doubleday, 1971.
Ambrose, Stephen E., *Ike's Spies: Eisenhower and the Espionage Establishment*, Doubleday, 1981.
Benson, Ezra, *Cross-Fire: The Eight Years with Eisenhower*, Doubleday, 1962.
Childs, Marquis W., *Eisenhower, Captive Hero: A Critical Study of the General and the President*, Harcourt, 1958.
Collection of Manuscripts and Archives in the Dwight D. Eisenhower Library, Abilene, Kansas, U.S. National Archives and Records Service, 1970.
Davis, Kenneth, *Soldier of Democracy*, Doubleday, 1945.
Divine, Robert A., *Eisenhower and the Cold War*, Oxford University Press, 1981.
Donovan, Robert, *Eisenhower: The Inside Story*, Harper, 1956.
Durham, J. C., *A Moderate among Extremists*, Nelson-Hall, 1981.
Eisenhower, Dwight D., *Crusade in Europe*, Doubleday, 1948, reprinted, Da Capo Press, 1977.
Eisenhower, Dwight D., *The White House Years*, Doubleday, Volume I: *Mandate for Change, 1953-56*, 1963, Volume II: *Waging Peace, 1956-61*, 1965.
Eisenhower, Dwight D., *The Eisenhower Diaries*, edited by Robert H. Ferrell, Norton, 1981.
Eisenhower, John S. D., *Strictly Personal*, Doubleday, 1974.
Ewald, William Bragg, Jr., *Eisenhower the President: Crucial Days, 1951-1960*, Prentice-Hall, 1981.
Gunther, John, *Eisenhower: The Man and the Symbol*, Harper, 1952.
Hatch, Alden, *General Ike*, Holt, 1952.
Hatch, Alden, *Young Ike*, Messner, 1953.
Hicks, Wilson, *This Is Ike*, Holt, 1952.
Historical Materials in the Dwight D. Eisenhower Library, U.S. National Archives and Records Service, 1972.
Lee, R. A., *Eisenhower*, Nelson-Hall, 1981.
Lovelace, D. W., *Ike Eisenhower: Statesman and Soldier of Peace*, Crowell, 1956.
Pusey, Merlo, *Eisenhower, the President*, Macmillan, 1956.
Rovere, Richard, *The Eisenhower Years: Affairs of State*, Farrar, Straus, 1956.
Smith, Walter, *Eisenhower's Six Great Decisions: Europe, 1944-45*, Longmans, Green, 1956.
Taylor, Allan, editor, *What Eisenhower Thinks*, Crowell, 1952.
Vexler, Robert, editor, *Dwight D. Eisenhower, 1890-1969: Chronology, Documents, Bibliographical Aids*, Oceana, 1970.
Weigley, Russell F., *Eisenhower's Lieutenants*, Indiana University Press, 1981.

PERIODICALS

Contemporary Review, March, 1983.
New Republic, November 6, 1965, April 10, 1971, May 9, 1981.
New Yorker, December 11, 1965.
New York Review of Books, January 6, 1966, May 6, 1971, September 24, 1981.
New York Times, October 22, 1965.
New York Times Book Review, October 31, 1965, June 18, 1967, May 10, 1970, March 5, 1978, June 28, 1981.
Saturday Review, October 16, 1965, June 20, 1970.

Spectator, April 16, 1983.
Time, August 3, 1981.
Times Literary Supplement, April 14, 1966, January 25, 1968, May 21, 1970.
Washington Post Book World, May 17, 1981.

OBITUARIES:

PERIODICALS

Life, April 4, 1969.
National Review, April 22, 1969.
Newsweek, April 7, 1969.
New Yorker, April 5, 1969.
New York Times, March 29, 1969.
Time, April 4, 1969.
U.S. News & World Report, April 7, 1969.†

—*Sketch by Thomas Wiloch*

*   *   *

EKLUND, Gordon (Stewart) 1945-

PERSONAL: Born July 24, 1945, in Seattle, Wash.; son of Alfred James (a dental technician) and DeLois (Stewart) Eklund; married Dianna Jean Mylarski, March 12, 1969 (separated); children: Jeremy Clark. *Education:* Attended Contra Costa College, San Pablo, Calif., 1973-75.

ADDRESSES: Home—6305 East D. St., Tacoma, Wash. 98403. *Agent*—Kirby McCauley, 220 East 26th St., New York, N.Y. 10010.

CAREER: Worked at numerous odd jobs in the San Francisco area, 1967-71; writer, principally of science fiction, 1968—. *Military service:* U.S. Air Force; became sergeant.

MEMBER: Science Fiction Writers of America, Lilapa.

AWARDS, HONORS: Nebula Award nomination, Science Fiction Writers of America, 1971, for first published short story, "Dear Aunt Annie"; Nebula Award for best science fiction novelette, 1975, for *If the Stars Are Gods*.

WRITINGS:

The Eclipse of Dawn, Ace Books, 1971.
A Trace of Dreams, Ace Books, 1972.
Beyond the Resurrection, Doubleday, 1973.
(Contributor) Robert Silverberg, editor, *Chains of the Sea: Three Original Novellas of Science Fiction*, T. Nelson, 1973.
(Contributor) Terry Carr, editor, *Universe 3*, Random House, 1973.
(Contributor) Lester Del Ray, editor, *Best Science Fiction Stories of the Year*, Ace Books, 1973.
All Times Possible, DAW Books, 1974.
(With Poul Anderson) *The Inheritors of Earth*, Chilton, 1974.
(Contributor) Donald A. Wollheim, editor, *The 1974 Annual World's Best Science Fiction*, DAW Books, 1974.
Serving in Time, Laser Books, 1975.
Falling Toward Forever, Laser Books, 1975.
The Grayspace Beast, Doubleday, 1976.
(Contributor with Gregory Benford) Carr, editor, *Universe 6*, Popular Library, 1976.
Dance of the Apocalypse, Laser Books, 1976.
(With Benford) *If the Stars Are Gods*, Putnam, 1977.
(Contributor) Carr, editor, *Universe 8*, Popular Library, 1978.
The Starless World, Bantam, 1978.
Devil World, Bantam, 1979.

(With Benford) *Find the Changeling*, Dell, 1980.
The Garden of Winter, Berkley Publishing, 1980.
Lord Tedric: Space Pirates #2, Ace Books, 1980.
(With Smith) *Lord Tedric III: Black Knight of the Iron Sphere*, Ace Books, 1981.

Contributor to science fiction magazines, including *Galaxy, Fantasy and Science Fiction, Analog Science Fiction/Science Fact, Amazing Stories*, and *Fantastic*.

WORK IN PROGRESS: A Thunder on Neptune, a novel for Arbor House; *World's Chronicle*, a novel.

SIDELIGHTS: The Science Fiction Writers of America nominated Gordon Eklund for the Nebula award in 1971 on the strength of his first published story. In "Dear Aunt Annie," which appeared in a 1970 issue of *Fantastic* magazine, a robot columnist advises unlucky lovers of the future. American life in the future is the most frequent subject of Eklund's work of the seventies, notes *Dictionary of Literary Biography Yearbook* contributor Mark Lidman. The 1971 novel *The Eclipse of Dawn* portrays presidential election politics in a 1988 nuclear-war-damaged America; *All Times Possible* follows leftist revolutionary hero Tommy Bloom as he creates a New America in an alternate time-line that runs parallel to that of actual history, which remains unchanged; and *Beyond the Resurrection*, "set in a future complete with automated cars and mindless professional soldiers, . . . looks at the frightening aspects of genetic engineering and the moral issues involved, [having at] the center of attention an outsider alienated from the mainstream of humanity," Lidman reports.

These books brought their author more acclaim than later books, says the essayist, who identifies the zenith of Eklund's literary popularity as the novelette *If the Stars Are Gods*. Co-authored with astrophysicist Gregory Benford, the Nebula Prize winner compares the glory-seeking aspirations behind human space travel to those of wisdom-seeking aliens who hope to find guidance from a benevolent Sun. By the end of the story, hero Bradley Reynolds, who is an ambassador of sorts to the aliens, identifies with the alien view. Together they meet disappointment when it is learned, after "communing" with the Sun, that its core is cold, and its benevolence not equal to their hopes.

Eklund's later projects—two Star Trek adventures (*The Starless World* and *Devil World*) "seem to be commercial rather than artistic efforts," writes Lidman, who concludes by saying, "it is hoped that Eklund can recover the enthusiasm and involvement with his work that made him one of science fiction's most promising figures in the 1970s."

BIOGRAPHICAL/CRITICAL SOURCES:

BOOKS

Carr, Terry, editor, *Universe 6*, Popular Library, 1976.
Dictionary of Literary Biography Yearbook: 1983, Gale, 1984.

PERIODICALS

Analog Science Fiction/Science Fact, June, 1976.
Magazine of Fantasy and Science Fiction, June, 1972, August, 1973, October, 1975.
New York Times Book Review, March 27, 1977.
Publishers Weekly, December 4, 1972, April 8, 1974, September 23, 1974, June 28, 1976.
Times Literary Supplement, June 16, 1978.

ELLER, Vernard (Marion) 1927-

PERSONAL: Born July 11, 1927, in Everett, Wash.; son of Jay Vernard (a professor) and Geraldine (Crill) Eller; married Phyllis Kulp, July 9, 1955; children: Sander Mack, Enten Vernard, Rosanna Kathryn. *Education:* La Verne College (now University of La Verne), B.A., 1949; Bethany Theological Seminary, B.D., 1955; Northwestern University, M.A., 1958; Pacific School of Religion, Th.D., 1964. *Politics:* Democratic.

ADDRESSES: Home—2448 Third St., La Verne, Calif. 91750. *Office*—Department of Religion, University of La Verne, La Verne, Calif. 91750.

CAREER: Clergyman, Church of the Brethren. Church of the Brethren, Elgin, Ill., editor of youth publications, 1950-56; University of La Verne, La Verne, Calif., assistant professor, 1958-63, associate professor, 1963-68, professor of religion, 1968—. Adjunct professor, Fuller Theological Seminary; member of faculty, Pacific School of Religion, summer, 1971.

MEMBER: American Academy of Religion, American Society of Christian Ethics, American Society of Church History, Brethren Journal Association, Swenson-Kierkegaard Foundation (fellow).

AWARDS, HONORS: Named Alumnus of the Year, La Verne College, 1970.

WRITINGS:

Kierkegaard and Radical Discipleship: A New Perspective, Princeton University Press, 1968.
His End Up, Abingdon, 1969.
The Promise: Ethics in the Kingdom of God, Doubleday, 1970.
The MAD Morality or the Ten Commandments Revisited, Abingdon, 1970.
The Sex Manual for Puritans, Abingdon, 1971.
In Place of Sacraments: A Study of Baptism and the Lord's Supper, Eerdmans, 1972.
King Jesus' Manual of Arms for the Armless: War and Peace from Genesis to Revelation, Abingdon, 1973, enlarged edition, Herald Press, 1981.
The Simple Life: The Christian Stance toward Possessions, Eerdmans, 1973.
The Most Revealing Book of the Bible: Making Sense out of Revelation, Eerdmans, 1974.
Cleaning up the Christian Vocabulary, Brethren Press, 1976.
A Study Guide to the Most Revealing Book of the Bible, La Verne College Press, 1977.
The Outward Bound: Caravaning as the Style of the Church, Eerdmans, 1980.
Thy Kingdom Come: A Blumhardt Reader, Eerdmans, 1981.
The Language of Canaan and the Grammar of Feminism, Eerdmans, 1982.
A Pearl of Christian Counsel for the Brokenhearted, University Press of America, 1982.
Towering Babble: God's People without God's Word, Brethren Press, 1983.
Proclaim Good Tidings: Evangelism for the Faith Community, Brethren Press, 1987.
Christian Anarchy: Jesus' Primacy over the Powers, Eerdmans, 1987.
The Beloved Disciple: His Name, His Story, His Thought, Eerdmans, 1987.

CONTRIBUTOR

Donald Durnbaugh, editor, *The Church of the Brethren, Past and Present,* Brethren Press, 1971.

Paul M. Robinson, editor, *Call the Witnesses,* Brethren Press, 1974.
Christians and Van Hook, editors, *Jacques Ellul: Interpretive Essays,* University of Illinois Press, 1981.

OTHER

Regular contributor to *Christian Century* and periodicals of Church of the Brethren; occasional contributor to other religion journals.

SIDELIGHTS: Vernard Eller told *CA:* "Undoubtedly there will be more books (there always are), but at this point I am rejecting rather than accepting ideas. It is not that I mind writing books; but I would like to find some way of being successful without being so slam-bang controversial."

*   *   *

ELLERBECK, Rosemary (Anne L'Estrange) (Anna L'Estrange, Nicola Thorne, Katherine Yorke)

PERSONAL: Born in Cape Town, South Africa.

ADDRESSES: Home—96 Townshend Court, Mackennal St., London NW8 6LD, England.

CAREER: Editor, until 1976; writer, 1976—.

WRITINGS:

NOVELS

Inclination to Murder, Hodder & Stoughton, 1965, reprinted, 1985.
Hammersleigh, McKay, 1976.
Rose, Rose, Where Are You?, Coward, 1978.

NOVELS; UNDER PSEUDONYM ANNA L'ESTRANGE

Return to Wuthering Heights (historical novel), Pinnacle Books, 1977.

NOVELS; UNDER PSEUDONYM NICOLA THORNE

The Girls, Random House, 1967.
Bridie Climbing, Ace Books, 1974.
In Love, Quartet, 1974.
A Woman Like Us, St. Martin's, 1979.
The Perfect Wife and Mother, St. Martin's, 1981.
Sisters and Lovers (historical novel), Doubleday, 1982 (published in England as *The Daughters of the House,* Mayflower Books, 1982).
Cashmere (historical novel), Doubleday, 1982 (published in England as *Where the Rivers Meet,* Granada, 1982).
Affairs of Love (historical novel), Doubleday, 1983.
The Enchantress Saga (based on *The Enchantress, Lady of the Lakes,* and *Falcon Gold;* also see below), Grafton Books, 1985.
Never Such Innocence, Grafton Books, 1985.
Yesterday's Promises, Grafton Books, 1986.
Bright Morning, Grafton Books, 1986.
A Place in the Sun, Grafton Books, 1987.

NOVELS; UNDER PSEUDONYM KATHERINE YORKE

The Enchantress, Pocket Books, 1979.
Lady of the Lakes, Futura, 1982.
The Pair Bond, Macdonald, 1984.

Also author of *Falcon Gold,* Pinnacle Books, and *A Woman's Place.*

SIDELIGHTS: Rosemary Ellerbeck wrote *CA:* "My first novel was published in 1965. It was a thriller and apart from two 'gothics' was never followed by another, though I am listed in *Romance and Gothic Writers.* I do enjoy an element of mystery and suspense in most things I write, I must say—the idea that things are never as they seem.

"For a short time I abandoned novel writing and went into business as a small-time publisher. This was largely a fiasco because of insufficient backing. I discovered I was a better novelist than a businesswoman, though I did have some very good ideas, also a great sympathy for and interest in writers which made them want to keep in touch with me long after the business folded. I began to write full time in 1976. At first I did editorial jobs to eke out a living. Happily in the eighties I have started to be very successful. My first real success was *Where the Rivers Meet,* which was published in the United States as *Cashmere.* That was on the best-seller list in Great Britain for quite a long time.

"In 1983 I started on an epic work which I completed in the summer of 1986. It didn't start off as an epic, just as a novel; but at the end, it was four volumes long and the time span was from 1898 to 1967. I could have gone on and on, but I was becoming obsessed by the main family, the Askhams, who dominate the series of novels that I call the 'Askham Chronicles: 1898-1967' [which includes *Never Such Innocence, Yesterday's Promises, Bright Morning,* and *A Place in the Sun*]. Luckily, I just happened to be free, and wondering what to do next, when my agent was approached by the Booker conglomerate. They wanted to link a book with a television series that was then being hatched on the other side of the Channel simply called 'Champagne.' I had been suggested to them as the best person to do it, which was very flattering—also very fortunate for me as I am both a Francophile and I love champagne! That's what I'm working on now. As for the future, I hope that after the publication of over twenty novels, I can have a little time in the sun myself—maybe from the results of 'Champagne'! Who knows?"

BIOGRAPHICAL/CRITICAL SOURCES:

PERIODICALS

Times Literary Supplement, January 2, 1981.
Washington Post Book World, December 5, 1982.

*   *   *

ELLIOT, Jeffrey M. 1947-

PERSONAL: Born June 14, 1947, in Los Angeles, Calif.; son of Gene (a corporation executive) and Harriet (an interior decorator; maiden name, Sobsey) Elliot. *Education:* University of Southern California, B.A. (with high honors), 1969, M.A., 1970; graduate study, Carnegie-Mellon University, 1973-74, California State University, Long Beach, 1975, and Old Dominion University, 1979; Claremont Graduate School, D.A., 1978.

ADDRESSES: Home—1419 Barliff Place, Durham, N.C. 27712. *Office*—Department of Political Science, North Carolina Central University, Durham, N.C. 27707. *Agent*—The Young Agency, 14 Maiden Lane, Suite 9, New York, N.Y. 10038.

CAREER: Glendale College, Glendale, Calif., instructor in political science, 1969-72; Cerritos College, Norwalk, Calif., instructor in political science, 1970-72; University of Alaska-

Anchorage Community College, Anchorage, assistant professor of history and political science, 1972-74; Miami-Dade Community College, Miami, Fla., assistant dean of academic affairs and assistant professor of social science, 1974-76; freelance newspaper and magazine journalist, 1976-78; Virginia Wesleyan College, Norfolk, assistant professor of political science, 1978-79; Education Development Center, Newton, Mass., senior curriculum specialist in political science and history, 1979-81; North Carolina Central University, Durham, professor of political science, 1981—.

Political speechwriter and campaign strategist for U.S. Senator Howard W. Cannon, 1969—; co-founder and historian of the People's Lobby, 1970-72; host of "Commentary," a weekly program on KPFK-Radio, 1971-72; associate editor of *Community College Social Science Journal,* 1972-75; member of Dade County Social Studies Instructional Materials Council and Miami Community Services Advisory Council, both 1975; member of national advisory board of *Community College Frontiers,* 1975—; vice-chairman of Florida Committee for Educational Stability, 1976; contributing editor of *Negro History Bulletin,* 1976-79; election commentator for WGH-Radio, 1978; contributing editor, *West Coast Writer's Conspiracy,* 1978-79; chairman of board of directors of Crispus Attucks Theater for the Arts Foundation, 1978-79; contributing editor of *Questar* magazine, 1979-80; assistant editor of Borgo Press, 1978—, contributing editor of *American Fantasy,* 1982—; assistant editor of *The Year's Scholarship in Science Fiction, Fantasy, and Horror Literature,* 1982-84; member of national editorial board of Caribbean-American Research Institute, 1984—; editor, *Journal of Caribbean-American Studies* and *Journal of Congressional Studies,* both 1985—; distinguished advisor on foreign affairs to U.S. Congressman Mervyn M. Dymally, 1985—; member of Durham County Community-Based Alternatives Task Force, 1986—.

MEMBER: International Visual Literacy Association, American Association of University Professors, American Historical Association, American Political Science Association, National Council for the Social Studies, Association for the Study of Afro-American Life and History, Association for Supervision and Curriculum Development, Community College Social Science Association (member of board of directors, 1973-77; president, 1975-77), Southern Political Science Association, Western Political Science Association,Western College Reading Association, Phi Delta Kappa, Pi Sigma Alpha.

AWARDS, HONORS: Excellence in Teaching Citation from Cerritos College, 1971; Outstanding Educator Citation from U.S. Senator Mike Gravel, 1973; Distinguished Service through Community Effort award from Florida Association of Community Colleges, 1976; Outstanding Educator of Florida award from Florida Committee for Educational Stability, 1976; Balrog Award finalist for outstanding science fiction and fantasy author, 1981; Distinguished Literary Achievement award for books, articles and interviews from American Biographical Institute, 1981; Small Press Writers and Artists Organization finalist for best writer in nonfiction, 1982; Balrog Award finalist, 1984, for best nonfiction writer, and 1985, for best science fiction anthology; Outstanding Academic Achievement award, North Carolina Central University, 1984; Best Book in Black Studies award, Congress of Racial Equality, 1985; citation for Outstanding Literary Contributions to the Study of Black Politics and History and Personal Achievements in Civil Rights and Civil Liberties from U.S. Congress, 1986; Commemorative Medal of Honor from American Biographical Institute, 1986; proclamation for Distinguished Literary Achievements from the City of Newark, N.J., 1986. Litt.D., Shaw University, 1985; LL.D., City University of Los Angeles, 1986.

WRITINGS:

Oglethorpe, The Hip Hippopotamus, Wonder Books, 1966.
(With Francis Shieh) *Keys to Economic Understanding*, Kendall/Hunt, 1976.
The Middle East: A Confederative Solution?, Society for Middle East Confederation, 1977.
Science Fiction Voices: Number Two, Borgo, 1979.
Science Fiction Voices: Number Three, Borgo, 1980.
Science Fiction Voices, Number Four: Interviews with Science-Fiction Authors, Borgo, 1980.
Literary Voices, Number One, Borgo, 1980.
Fantasy Voices, Number One: Interviews with Fantasy Authors, Borgo, 1980.
The Future of the U.S. Space Program—Large Corporations and Society: Discussions with Twenty-two Science Fiction Authors, Borgo, 1980.
(With Steven E. Miller and Lawrence H. Fuchs) *Political Ideals, Policy Dilemmas*, Education Development Center, 1981.
(With Miller and Fuchs) *Treaty Rights and Dual Status: Who Owes What to Native Americans*, Education Development Center, 1981.
(With Miller and Fuchs) *Making a Living: Equal Opportunity and Affirmative Action*, Education Development Center, 1981.
(With Miller and Fuchs) *Educational Opportunity: Equal for Everyone?*, Education Development Center, 1981.
(With Miller and Fuchs) *Immigration and Public Policy: Who Can Become an American?*, Education Development Center, 1981.
(With Miller and Fuchs) *Getting and Using Power: Political Access without Discrimination*, Education Development Center, 1981.
(With Catherine Cob Morocco and Marilyn Clayton Felt) *The American Experiment: E Pluribus Unum*, Education Development Center, 1981.
(With Robert Reginald) *The Analytical Congressional Directory*, Borgo, 1981.
(With Reginald) *If J. F. K. Had Lived: A Political Scenario*, Borgo, 1981.
Political Voices, Number One: Interviews with Prominent American Politicians, Borgo, 1982.
Pulp Voices: Interviews with Pulp Magazine Writers and Editors, Borgo, 1982.
Urban Society: Annual Editions, Dushkin, 1982, 3rd edition, 1986.
Masters of "Hard" Science Fiction: A Primary and Secondary Bibliography, G. K. Hall, 1983.
Great Issues: The Battle for Congressional Reform, Borgo, 1983.
(With Joseph R. Aicher, Jr.) *American Government: One Hundred Classroom Games*, Borgo, 1983.
A. E. van Vogt, Borgo, 1983, published as *Reader's Guide to A. E. van Vogt*, edited by Roger C. Schlobin, Starmont House, 1984.
Black Voices, Number One: Interviews with Prominent Afro-Americans, Borgo, 1983.
Pulp Voices or Science Fiction Voices Number Six: Interviews with Pulp Magazine Writers and Editors, Borgo, 1983.
(With Philip Brasfield) *Deathman Pass Me By: Two Years on Death Row*, Borgo, 1983.

(With Reginald) *Tempest in a Teapot: The Falkland Islands War*, Borgo, 1983.
Literary Masters: An Exercise In Autobiography, Borgo, 1984.
Kindred Spirits: An Anthology of Gay and Lesbian Science Fiction Stories, Alyson, 1984.
(With Shiekh R. Ali) *The Presidential-Congressional Political Dictionary*, ABC-Clio, 1984.
(With Aicher) *Brown v. Board of Education: Problems and Prospects*, North Carolina State University, 1984.
(With Ali) *The State and Local Government Political Dictionary*, ABC-Clio, 1985.
The Work of Robert Reginald: An Annotated Bibliography and Guide, Borgo, 1985.
Black Voices in American Politics, Harcourt, 1985.
(With Mervyn M. Dymally) *The Cancellation of the Debt or the Political Death of Democratic Processes in Latin America*, Editora Politica, 1985.
(Author of introduction) *Sieg Heil!: The 1940 Book Catalogue of the Publishing House of the Nazi Party*, Borgo, 1985.
(With Dymally) *Fidel Castro: The Future of the International Olympics Movement*, Editora Politica, 1985.
(With Dymally) *Fidel Castro: The Debt Crisis and Social Upheaval*, Editora Politica, 1985.
(With Dymally) *Fidel Castro: The Inevitability of History*, Editora Politica, 1985.
Afro-American Voices: Interviews with Prominent Black Americans, Borgo, 1986.
(With George Zebrowski) *Perfecting Visions, Slaying Cynics: The Life and Work of George Zebrowski*, Borgo, 1986.
(With Reginald) *The Work of George Zebrowski: An Annotated Bibliography and Guide*, Borgo, 1986.
(Editor) *Discrimination in America: An Annotated Resource Guide*, Pierian, 1986.
(With Dymally) *Fidel Castro: Nothing Can Stop the Course of History*, Pathfinder, 1986.
The Third World: Annual Editions, Dushkin, 1987.
American Political Voices, Harcourt, 1987.
(With Ali) *The Trilemma of World Oil Politics*, Borgo, 1987.
Orchids for Doc: An Interview with Robert A. W. Lowndes, Borgo, 1987.
Skyclimber: The Autobiography of Raymond Z. Gallum, Borgo, 1987.
Adventures of a Freelancer: The Autobiography of Stanton A. Coblentz, Borgo, 1987.
(With Dymally) *Fidel by Fidel*, Borgo, 1987.
The Work of Pamela Sargent: An Annotated Bibliography and Guide, Borgo, 1987.
(With Reginald) *The Dictionary of Arms Control, Disarmament and Military Security*, ABC-Clio, 1987.
(With Dymally) *Michael Manley: Peace with Justice*, Curbstone, 1987.
(With Dymally) *Fidel Castro: Resources on Contemporary Persons*, Pierian, 1987.
(With Aicher) *Political Science Journals and Serials: An Analytical Guide*, Greenwood Press, 1987.
The Work of Jack Dann: An Annotated Bibliography and Guide, Borgo, 1987.
Mervyn M. Dymally: The Making of a U.S. Congressman, Borgo, 1987.
(With Dymally) *The Black Politician: The New Struggle for Power*, Borgo, 1987.
(With Dymally) *Cuba in Transition: A New Force in the Western Hemisphere*, Borgo, 1987.
(With Robert Nathan) *Portrait of Nathan: Robert Nathan at Ninety-one*, Borgo, 1987.

(With John Weeks) *A Superman of Letters: R. Reginald and the Borgo Press,* Borgo, 1987.
The Scortia Factor, Borgo, 1988.
The Gernsback Days, Starmont House, 1988.
John Norman: The Gor Series, Ungar, 1988.
Glenn Burke: Coming to Terms, Alyson, 1988.
(With Richard Neely) *Who Runs America?: Policy, Process, and Institutions,* Harcourt, 1988.
(With Aicher) *Political Science Newsletters: An Analytical Guide,* Greenwood Press, 1988.

Contributor of nearly five hundred and fifty articles to magazines and newspapers.

SIDELIGHTS: Jeffrey M. Elliot told *CA:* "I view myself as a multigenre writer, having authored academic treatises, empirical research, reference works, textbooks, anthologies, interviews, essays, book reviews, biographies, novels, film reviews, bibliographies, editorials, popular articles, etc. In recent years, however, I have concentrated on 'celebrity' interviews, writing more than forty such pieces a year. My subjects include political leaders, authors, sports figures, entertainers, business leaders, poets, scientists, philosophers, newsmakers, artists, and countless others.

"Before I interview a person—let's say, a writer—I invest heavily in preparation: an investment of time and energy. I scour myriad bookshops and libraries to find everything I can by the author. I read not only that person's works, but everything I can find that has been written *about* the author. I also try to track down people who know the author and who are willing to share their perceptions of the writer and his work.

"Before I ever make my call on the author, I think through the direction, the *shape* of the interview, and prepare anywhere from fifty to one hundred questions. Once the session begins, I ask these questions and others as the interview develops, often departing significantly from my original list of questions. Usually, I tape anywhere from several hours to several days of conversation with the person.

"Typically, I arrive at the author's home early in the morning—just after breakfast—armed with a tape recorder, a pad of ammunition, and an arsenal of tapes. We work all through the morning—and it is work, although by no means unpleasant. We break for lunch, often in the company of my photographer, but although the tape recorder is left behind, the questioning will not cease. And after dessert and coffee, it is back to the person's home and back to work until very nearly dinner time.

"Now, with the interview completed, my work really begins. First, I transcribe all of the tapes, leaving me with anywhere from forty to two hundred pages of text. From there I edit the interview to the required length, usually about thirty-five typed pages. This is a herculean undertaking, as I must pare down the transcript to the specified length. This is no simple feat. At this point, I take my cut-down version and begin the process of editing it for consistency, flow, lucidity, and language. This phase will often require three to five separate edits, until I reach the point where I am satisfied with the finished product. Now, I am ready to write my introduction, the aim of which is to put the interview into proper perspective, providing the reader with a behind-the-scenes account of what it was like to interview the person. The introduction will run anywhere from two to ten pages, depending on the length of the article.

"At this point, I think up an appropriate title, which is often more difficult than one might surmise. And finally, I select anywhere from five to ten photographs to accompany the piece. At the end, I am left with the least pleasant task—namely, typing up the finished article, during which time I also make some slight editorial changes. Then, it is off to the publisher, not to be seen again until the galleys are sent or the piece is published."

In 1986, California State College, San Bernardino established the Jeffrey M. Elliot Collection, a permanent archive of the author's published manuscripts, including books, articles, reviews, interviews, and letters.

*　*　*

ELLIOTT, Mark Rowe 1947-

PERSONAL: Born July 21, 1947, in Stearns, Ky.; son of Carmon W. (a bookkeeper) and Mildred (a teacher; maiden name, Trammell) Elliott; married Darlene Montgomery (a teacher), June 20, 1970; children: (adopted) Fernando, Pablo, Heather, Roberto. *Education:* Asbury College, B.A. (cum laude), 1969; University of Kentucky, M.A., 1971, Ph.D., 1974. *Religion:* Methodist.

ADDRESSES: Home—221 South Williston St., Wheaton, Ill. 60187. *Office*—Institute for the Study of Christianity and Marxism, Wheaton College, Wheaton, Ill. 60187.

CAREER: Asbury College, Wilmore, Ky, assistant professor, 1974-80, associate professor, 1980-84, professor of history, 1984-86; Wheaton College, Wheaton, Ill., associate professor of history, 1986—, director, Institute for the Study of Christianity and Marxism, 1986—.

MEMBER: American Historical Association, American Association for the Advancement of Slavic Studies, Conference on Faith and History, Association for the Study of Nationalities.

AWARDS, HONORS: Grants from Kennan Institute for Advanced Russian Studies, Woodrow Wilson International Center for Scholars, 1977, 1984, from Southern Regional Education Board, 1980, 1986, from Earhart Foundation, 1982, 1987, and from National Endowment for the Humanities, 1984, 1985.

WRITINGS:

Pawns of Yalta: Soviet Refugees and America's Role in Their Repatriation, University of Illinois Press, 1982.
(Editor with David Fletcher) *Christianity and Marxism,* Wheaton College, 1987.

Contributor to *Modern Encyclopedia of Russian and Soviet History.* Contributor to history and political science journals.

WORK IN PROGRESS: The Relationship between Soviet Christians and Western Churches and Para-Church Organizations; Christianity and Marxism Worldwide: An Annotated Bibliography.

SIDELIGHTS: Mark Rowe Elliott told *CA* he wrote *Pawns of Yalta* because "no scholarly study existed detailing America's part in the repatriation of Soviet nationals after World War II. In addition, Washington declassified literally tons of wartime records in the seventies making it possible to examine thoroughly all aspects of this nightmarish saga. Beyond my purpose of writing a serious historical study, I came to see the publication of an objective book on repatriation as something of a mission. Millions of innocent victims of a shameful Soviet-American agreement deserved to have their story told.

And I hope Americans of conscience will listen so that citizens of the United States can say along with the victims of a better-known holocaust, 'Never again.'"

BIOGRAPHICAL/CRITICAL SOURCES:

PERIODICALS

Chicago Sun-Times, January 31, 1982.
Inquiry, March 29, 1982.
Sunday Independent (Ashland, Ky.), April 18, 1982.

*   *   *

ELLIS, Anyon
   See ROWLAND-ENTWISTLE, (Arthur) Theodore (Henry)

*   *   *

ELLIS, Marc H.   1952-

PERSONAL: Born August 27, 1952, in Miami, Fla.; son of Herbert Moore (in sales) and June (a teacher and executive; maiden name, Goldwin) Ellis; married Ann M. McDonald (a lawyer), August 3, 1980; children: Aaron Moore. *Education:* Florida State University, B.A. (magna cum laude), 1974, M.A., 1976; Marquette University, Ph.D, 1980. *Religion:* Jewish.

ADDRESSES: Home—25 Montgomery St., Ossining, N.Y. 10562. *Office*—Institute for Justice and Peace, Maryknoll School of Theology, Maryknoll, N.Y. 10545.

CAREER: Catholic Worker Movement, New York City, staff member, 1974-75; substitute teacher at public schools in New York City, 1975; Hope House, Inc., New Orleans, La., instructor, 1976-77; Our Lady of the Holy Cross College, New Orleans, instructor, 1977; Maryknoll School of Theology, Maryknoll, N.Y., assistant professor, 1980-83, associate professor of twentieth-century religious history and social theory, 1984—, founder and director of Institute for Justice and Peace, 1981. Visiting lecturer and sabbatical scholar, Heythrop College, University of London, 1987. Speaker and lecturer at numerous universities and seminars in many countries, including England, Israel, West Germany, Japan, and China. Administrator, International Peace and Justice Studies Program, Molloy College, 1982-85, and the Summer School for Peace and Reconciliation, Fellowship of Reconciliation/Pax Christi/Maryknoll Institute for Justice and Peace, London, 1987—. Consultant, Glenmary Commission on Justice, Neon, Kentucky, 1981-85, and Institute for Evangelization and Justice, Holy Ghost Missioners, Dublin, Ireland, 1982-86.

MEMBER: American Academy of Religion, American Catholic Historical Association, Catholic Theological Society, Association of Catholic Colleges and Universities (advisory council, 1983—), College Theology Society, Phi Beta Kappa, Phi Alpha Theta, Alpha Sigma Nu.

WRITINGS:

A Year at the Catholic Worker, Paulist Press, 1978.
Peter Maurin: Prophet in the Twentieth Century, Paulist Press, 1981.
Faithfulness in an Age of Holocaust, Amity House, 1986.
Toward a Jewish Theology of Liberation, Orbis Books, 1987.
The Future of Religious Resistance: Jews and Christians in the Struggle for Liberation, Orbis Books, 1988.

CONTRIBUTOR

American Spirituality and Liberation Theology, Mission Institute, 1981.
William Tabb, editor, *Churches in Struggle: Liberation Theologies and Social Change in North America,* Monthly Review Press, 1986.
Regina Bechtle and John Rathschmidt, editors, *Mission and Mysticism: Evangelization and the Experience of God,* Maryknoll School of Theology, 1987.
(And editor) *Theology and Struggle: Essays in Honor of Gustavo Gutierrez,* Orbis Books, 1988.
Patrick Coy, editor, *The Catholic Worker Movement: Past and Present,* Temple University Press, 1988.
Maura Peter-Raoul, editor, *Liberation Struggles in a Global Context,* Orbis Books, 1988.
John K. Roth, editor, *Liberation Theology and Public Policy,* Washington Institute for Values in Public Policy, 1988.
Yehuda Bauer, editor, *Remembering for the Future: The Impact of the Holocaust and Genocide on Jews and Christians,* Pergamon, 1988.

OTHER

Also editor of *Abraham Joshua Heschel Studies in Progressive Jewish Theology,* ten volumes, beginning 1988. Contributor to numerous periodicals, including *Christian-Jewish Relations, Fellowship, New Catholic World, Heythrop Journal,* and *Cross Currents.* Orbis Books, editorial consultant, 1981-86, advisory editor, 1986—.

WORK IN PROGRESS: Editing *Abraham Joshua Heschel Studies in Progressive Jewish Theology,* a ten-volume series.

SIDELIGHTS: Marc H. Ellis once told *CA* that "a major theme" of works he completed in the early 1980s "is that the twentieth century has bequeathed a variety of legacies, one of them being a new understanding of solitude. This new form of solitude is not that of the monk searching out God in the silence but rather the silence found in the suffering of the victims of our time, the poor and the innocent who have died in war and holocaust. The solitude of the suffering points as well to the silence in which the 'victims' dwell—what I call the solitude of modernity. This is a world of energetic economies, global militarism—hence, a powerful world—but one distanced from the symbols and structures which give meaning and depth to the world. The essential question I seek to ask is: How does one move from solitude to solidarity?"

His writing in the second half of the decade "explores the understanding of fidelity as it is lived out within the confines of our history," he said in 1987. "As Jews and Christians struggle to be faithful in an age of triage and holocaust, a new understanding of our faith comes into view. The question of belief shifts to activity on behalf of those who struggle for justice. This is precisely where the new ecumenical dialogue is taking place: in the arena of the struggle for liberation."

Books by Ellis have been translated into Spanish, Portuguese, Hebrew, and Arabic.

*   *   *

ELLISON, Ralph (Waldo)   1914-

PERSONAL: Born March 1, 1914, in Oklahoma City, Okla.; son of Lewis Alfred (a construction worker and tradesman) and Ida (Millsap) Ellison; married Fanny McConnell, July, 1946. *Education:* Attended Tuskegee Institute, 1933-36.

ADDRESSES: Home and office—730 Riverside Dr., New York, N.Y. 10031, and Plainfield, Mass. *Agent*—Owen Laster, William Morris Agency, 1350 Ave. of the Americas, New York, N.Y. 10019.

CAREER: Writer, 1937—; worked as a researcher and writer on Federal Writers' Project in New York City, 1938-42; edited *Negro Quarterly*, 1942; lecture tour in Germany, 1954; lecturer at Salzburg Seminar, Austria, fall, 1954; U.S. Information Agency, tour of Italian cities, 1956; Bard College, Annandale-on-Hudson, N.Y., instructor in Russian and American literature, 1958-61; New York University, New York City, Albert Schweitzer Professor in Humanities, 1970-79, professor emeritus, 1979—. Alexander White Visiting Professor, University of Chicago, 1961; visiting professor of writing, Rutgers University, 1962-64; visiting fellow in American studies, Yale University, 1966. Gertrude Whittall Lecturer, Library of Congress, January, 1964; delivered Ewing Lectures at University of California, Los Angeles, April, 1964. Lecturer in American Negro culture, folklore, and creative writing at other colleges and universities throughout the United States, including Columbia University, Fisk University, Princeton University, Antioch University, and Bennington College.

Member of Carnegie Commission on Educational Television, 1966-67; honorary consultant in American letters, Library of Congress, 1966-72. Trustee, Colonial Williamsburg Foundation, John F. Kennedy Center for the Performing Arts, 1967-77, Educational Broadcasting Corp., 1968-69, New School for Social Research, 1969-83, Bennington College, 1970-75, and Museum of the City of New York, 1970-86. Charter member of National Council of the Arts, 1965-67, and of National Advisory Council, Hampshire College. *Military service:* U.S. Merchant Marine, World War II.

MEMBER: PEN (vice-president, 1964), Authors Guild, Authors League of America, American Academy and Institute of Arts and Letters, Institute of Jazz Studies (member of board of advisors), Century Association (resident member).

AWARDS, HONORS: Rosenwald grant, 1945; National Book Award and National Newspaper Publishers' Russwurm Award, both 1953, both for *Invisible Man;* Certificate of Award, *Chicago Defender*, 1953; Rockefeller Foundation award, 1954; Prix de Rome fellowships, American Academy of Arts and Letters, 1955 and 1956; *Invisible Man* selected as the most distinguished postwar American novel and Ellison as the sixth most influential novelist by *New York Herald Tribune Book Week* poll of two hundred authors, editors, and critics, 1965; recipient of award honoring well-known Oklahomans in the arts from governor of Oklahoma, 1966; Medal of Freedom, 1969; Chevalier de l'Ordre des Arts et Lettres (France), 1970; Ralph Ellison Public Library, Oklahoma City, named in his honor, 1975; National Medal of Arts, 1985, for *Invisible Man* and for his teaching at numerous universities. Honorary doctorates from Tuskegee Institute, 1963, Rutgers University, 1966, Grinnell College, 1967, University of Michigan, 1967, Williams College, 1970, Long Island University, 1971, Adelphi University, 1971, College of William and Mary, 1972, Harvard University, 1974, Wake Forest College, 1974, University of Maryland, 1974, Bard College, 1978, Wesleyan University, 1980, and Brown University, 1980.

WRITINGS:

Invisible Man (novel), Random House, 1952, published as a limited edition with illustrations by Steven H. Stroud, Franklin Library, 1980, original edition reprinted with new introduction by author as special thirtieth-anniversary edition, Random House, 1982.

(Contributor) Granville Hicks, editor, *The Living Novel: A Symposium*, Macmillan, 1957.

(Author of introduction) Stephen Crane, *The Red Badge of Courage and Four Great Stories*, Dell, 1960.

Shadow and Act (essays), Random House, 1964.

(With Karl Shapiro) *The Writer's Experience* (lectures; includes "Hidden Names and Complex Fate: A Writer's Experience in the U.S.," by Ellison, and "American Poet?," by Shapiro), Gertrude Clarke Whittall Poetry and Literature Fund for Library of Congress, 1964.

(Contributor) *Education of the Deprived and Segregated* (report of seminar on education for culturally-different youth, Dedham, Mass., September 3-15, 1963), Bank Street College of Education, 1965.

(Contributor) Robert Penn Warren, *Who Speaks for the Negro?*, Random House, 1965.

(With Whitney M. Young and Herbert Gnas) *The City in Crisis*, introduction by Bayard Rustin, A. Philip Randolph Educational Fund, 1968.

(Author of introduction) Romare Bearden, *Paintings and Projections* (catalogue of exhibition, November 25-December 22, 1968), State University of New York at Albany, 1968.

(Contributor) James MacGregor Burns, editor, *To Heal and to Build: The Programs of Lyndon B. Johnson*, prologue by Howard K. Smith, epilogue by Eric Hoffer, McGraw, 1968.

(Author of foreword) Leon Forrest, *There Is a Tree More Ancient than Eden*, Random House, 1973.

(Contributor) Bernard Schwartz, editor, *American Law: The Third Century, the Law Bicentennial Volume*, F. B. Rothman for New York University School of Law, 1976.

Going to the Territory (essays), Random House, 1986.

WORK REPRESENTED IN ANTHOLOGIES

Hans Otto Storm and others, editors, *American Writing*, J. A. Decker, 1940.

Edwin J. O'Brien, editor, *The Best Short Stories, 1941*, Houghton, 1941.

Edwin Seaver, editor, *Cross Section: A Collection of New American Writing, 1944*, L. B. Fischer, 1944.

New World Writing, 5, New American Library, 1954.

New World Writing, 9, New American Library, 1956.

Charles A. Fenton, editor, *Best Short Stories of World War II*, Viking, 1957.

Robert Penn Warren and Albert Erskine, editors, *A New Southern Harvest: An Anthology*, Bantam, 1957.

Langston Hughes and Arna Bontemps, editors, *The Book of Negro Folklore*, Dodd, 1958.

Dorothy Sterling, editor, *I Have Seen War: Twenty-five Stories from World War II*, Hill & Wang, 1960.

Herbert Gold and David L. Stevenson, editors, *Stories of Modern America*, St. Martin's, 1961.

John Alfred Williams, editor, *The Angry Black*, Lancer Books, 1962, 2nd edition published as *Beyond the Angry Black*, Cooper Square, 1966.

Herbert Hill, editor, *Soon, One Morning: New Writing by American Negroes, 1940-1962* (includes previously unpublished section from original manuscript of *Invisible Man*), Knopf, 1963 (published in England as *Black Voices*, Elek Books, 1964).

L. Hughes, editor, *The Best Short Stories by Negro Writers: An Anthology from 1899 to the Present*, Little, Brown, 1967.

Douglas Angus and Sylvia Angus, editors, *Contemporary American Short Stories,* Fawcett, 1967.

Don Gold, editor, *The Human Commitment: An Anthology of Contemporary Short Fiction,* Chilton, 1967.

Marcus Klein and Robert Pack, editors, *Short Stories: Classic, Modern, Contemporary,* Little, Brown, 1967.

James A. Emanuel and Theodore L. Gross, editors, *Dark Symphony: Negro American Literature in America,* Free Press, 1968.

Arnold Adoff, editor, *Brothers and Sisters: Modern Stories by Black Americans,* Macmillan, 1970.

Theodore Solotaroff, editor, *American Review 16: The Magazine of New Writing,* Bantam, 1973.

James H. Pickering, editor, *Fiction 100: An Anthology of Short Stories,* Macmillan, 1974.

Michael Timko, *Twenty-nine Short Stories: An Introductory Anthology,* Knopf, 1975.

John L. Kimmey, editor, *Experience and Expression: Reading and Responding to Short Fiction,* Scott, Foresman, 1976.

Joseph Maiolo and Jill N. Brantley, editors, *From Three Sides: Reading for Writers,* Prentice-Hall, 1976.

David Thorburn, editor, *Initiation: Stories and Short Novels on Three Themes,* 2nd edition, Harcourt, 1976.

Max Apple, editor, *Southwest Fiction,* Bantam, 1980.

Nancy Sullivan, compiler, *The Treasury of American Short Stories,* Doubleday, 1981.

OTHER

"Ralph Ellison: An Interview with the Author of Invisible Man" (sound recording), Center for Cassette Studies, 1974.

(With William Styron and James Baldwin) "Is the Novel Dead?: Ellison, Styron and Baldwin on Contemporary Fiction" (sound recording), Center for Cassette Studies, 1974.

Contributor to *Proceedings, American Academy of Arts and Letters and the National Institute of Arts and Letters,* second series, 1965 and 1967. Also contributor of short fiction, critical essays, articles, and reviews to numerous journals and periodicals, including *American Scholar, Contemporary Literature, Iowa Review, New York Review of Books, New York Times Book Review, Noble Savage, Partisan Review, Quarterly Review of Literature, Reporter, Time,* and *Washington Post Book World.* Contributing editor, *Noble Savage,* 1960, and member of editorial board of *American Scholar,* 1966-69.

WORK IN PROGRESS: A second novel, as yet untitled, to be published by Random House, portions of which have been published under various titles, including "And Hickman Arrives" in *Noble Savage,* March, 1960, "The Roof, the Steeple, and the People" in *Quarterly Review of Literature,* Number 3, 1960, "It Always Breaks Out" in *Partisan Review,* spring, 1963, "Juneteenth" in *Quarterly Review of Literature,* Volume 13, numbers 3-4, 1969, "Song of Innocence" in *Iowa Review,* spring, 1970, and "Cadillac Flambe" in *American Review 16: The Magazine of New Writing,* edited by Theodore Solotaroff, Bantam, 1973.

SIDELIGHTS: Growing up in Oklahoma, a "frontier" state that "had no tradition of slavery" and where "relationships between the races were more fluid and thus more human than in the old slave states," Ralph Ellison became conscious of his obligation "to explore the full range of American Negro humanity and to affirm those qualities which are of value beyond any question of segregation, economics or previous condition of servitude." This sense of obligation, articulated in his 1964 collection of critical and biographical essays, *Shadow and Act,* led to his staunch refusal to limit his artistic vision

to the "uneasy sanctuary of race" and committed him instead to a literature that explores and affirms the complex, often contradictory frontier of an identity at once black and American and universally human. For Ellison, whom John F. Callahan in a *Chant of Saints: A Gathering of Afro-American Literature, Art, and Scholarship* essay calls a "moral historian," the act of writing is fraught with both great possibility and grave responsibility; as Ellison asserts, writing "offers me the possibility of contributing not only to the growth of the literature but to the shaping of the culture as I should like it to be. The American novel is in this sense a conquest of the frontier; as it describes our experience, it creates it."

For Ellison, then, the task of the novelist is a moral and political one. In his preface to the thirtieth anniversary edition of *Invisible Man,* Ellison argues that the serious novel, like the best politics, "is a thrust toward a human ideal." Even when the ideal is not realized in the actual, he declares, "there is still available that fictional *vision* of an ideal democracy in which the actual combines with the ideal and gives us representations of a state of things in which the highly placed and the lowly, the black and the white, the Northerner and the Southerner, the native-born and the immigrant are combined to tell us of transcendent truths and possibilities such as those discovered when Mark Twain set Huck and Jim afloat on the raft." Ellison sees the novel as a "raft of hope" that may help readers stay above water as they try "to negotiate the snags and whirlpools that mark our nation's vacillating course toward and away from the democratic ideal."

This vision of pluralism and possibility as the basic definition of self and serious fiction has its roots in Ellison's personal history, a history marked by vacillations between the ideal and the real. He recalls in *Shadow and Act* that, as teenagers, he and his friends saw themselves as "Renaissance Men" unlimited by any sense of racial inferiority and determined to be recipients of the American Dream, to witness the ideal become the real. Ellison recounts two "accidents" that contributed to his sense of self as something beyond the external definition of race. The first occurred while he lived in a white, middle-class neighborhood where his mother worked as a building custodian. He became friends with a young white boy, a friendship based not on the "race question as such" but rather on their mutual loneliness and interest in radios. The other contact with "that world beyond the Negro community" came as his mother brought home discarded copies of magazines such as *Vanity Fair* and *Literary Digest* and old recordings of operas. Ellison remembers that these books and music "spoke to me of a life which was broader" and which "I could some day make my own."

This sense of a world beyond his but to which he would ultimately belong translated itself into his sense of the world that *was* his and to which he *did* belong. He was profoundly aware of the richness, vitality, and variety in his black community; he was aware, also, that the affirmative reality of black life was something he never found in the books he read, was never taught in the schools he attended. Ellison had experienced the nonverbal articulation of these qualities in the jazz and blues that were so much a part of his upbringing. In particular he recalls, in *Shadow and Act,* Jimmy Rushing, the blues singer who "represented, gave voice to, something which was very affirming of Negro life, feelings which you couldn't really put into words." But recording and preserving the value of black life only in this medium did not satisfy Ellison; he was haunted, he admits, by a need "for other forms of transcendence and identification which I could only associate with classical music." As he explains, "I was taken very early with a passion to link together all I loved within the Negro community and all those things I felt in the world which lay beyond." This passion to join separate worlds and disparate selves into a unity of being infuses the content and style of *Invisible Man* and lies at the heart of Ellison's theory of fiction.

Early in his career, however, Ellison conceived of his vocation as a musician, as a composer of symphonies. When he entered Alabama's Tuskegee Institute in 1933 he enrolled as a music major; he wonders in *Shadow and Act* if he did so because, given his background, it was the only art "that seemed to offer some possibility for self-definition." The act of writing soon presented itself as an art through which he could link the disparate worlds he cherished, could verbally record and create the "affirmation of Negro life" he knew was so intrinsic a part of the universally human. To move beyond the old definitions that separated jazz from classical music, vernacular from literary language, the folk from the mythic, he would have to discover a prose style that could equal the integrative imagination of the "Renaissance Man."

Shadow and Act records that during 1935, his second year at Tuskegee, Ellison began his "conscious education in literature." Reading Emily Bronte's *Wuthering Heights* and Thomas Hardy's *Jude the Obscure* produced in him "an agony of unexpressible emotion," but T. S. Eliot's *The Waste Land* absolutely seized his imagination. He admits: "I was intrigued by its power to move me while eluding my understanding. Somehow its rhythms were often closer to those of jazz than were those of the Negro poets, and even though I could not understand then, its range of allusion was as mixed and varied as that of Louis Armstrong." Determined to understand the "hidden system of organization" that eluded him, Ellison began to explore the sources that Eliot had identified in the footnotes to the poem. This reading in ancient mythology, history, literature, and folklore led, in turn, to his reading of such twentieth-century writers as Ezra Pound, Ernest Hemingway, and Gertrude Stein, who led him back to the nineteenth-century authors Herman Melville and Mark Twain. The more Ellison read in literature and the sources of literature, the more he found that the details of his own history were "transformed." Local customs took on a "more universal meaning"; he became aware of the universal in the specific. His experience with *The Waste Land*, which forced him to wonder why he "had never read anything of equal intensity and sensibility by an American Negro writer," was his introduction to the universal power of the folk tradition as the foundation of literature.

During this same year, Ellison took a sociology course, an experience he describes in *Shadow and Act* as "humiliating." Presenting a reductive, unrealistic portrait of the American black as the "lady of the races," this sociological view denied the complex richness of black life that Ellison had so often experienced. In *The Craft of Ralph Ellison* Robert G. O'Meally argues that this encounter with a limited and limiting definition of blacks created in Ellison "an accelerated sense of urgency" to learn more about black culture and to find an artistic form to capture the vital reality of the black community that he had heard in the blues sessions, in the barbershops, and in the stories and jokes he had heard from some classmates as they returned from seasonal work in the cotton fields. Ironically, an accident intervened that propelled him on this course. Because of a mix-up about his scholarship, Ellison found himself without the money to return to Tuskegee. He went instead to New York, enacting the prototypical journey North, confident

that he would return to Tuskegee after he had earned enough money.

Because Ellison did not get a job that paid him enough to save money for tuition, he stayed in New York, working and studying composition until his mother died in Dayton, Ohio. After his return to Dayton, he and his brother supported themselves by hunting. Though Ellison had hunted for years, he did not know how to wing-shoot; it was from Hemingway's fiction that he learned this process. Ellison studied Hemingway to learn writing techniques; from the older writer he also learned a lesson in descriptive accuracy and power, in the close relationship between fiction and reality. Like his narrator in *Invisible Man*, Ellison did not return to college; instead he began his long apprenticeship as a writer, his long and often difficult journey toward self-definition.

Ellison's early days in New York, before his return to Dayton, provided him with experiences that would later translate themselves into his theory of fiction. Two days after his arrival in "deceptively 'free' Harlem," he met black poet Langston Hughes who introduced him to the works of Andre Malraux, a French writer defined as Marxist. Though attracted to Marxism, Ellison sensed in Malraux something beyond a simplistic political sense of the human condition. Says Ellison: Malraux "was the artist-revolutionary rather than a politician when he wrote *Man's Fate,* and the book lives not because of a political position embraced at the time, but because of its larger concern with the tragic struggle of humanity." Ellison began to form his definition of the artist as a revolutionary concerned less with local injustice than with the timelessly tragic.

Ellison's view of art was furthered after he met black novelist Richard Wright. Wright urged him to read Joseph Conrad, Henry James, James Joyce, and Feodor Dostoevsky and invited Ellison to contribute a review essay and then a short story to the magazine he was editing. Wright was then in the process of writing *Native Son,* much of which Ellison read, he declares in *Shadow and Act,* "as it came out of the typewriter." Though awed by the process of writing and aware of the achievement of the novel, Ellison, who had just read Malraux, began to form his objections to the "sociological," deterministic ideology which informed the portrait of the work's protagonist, Bigger Thomas. In *Shadow and Act,* which Arthur P. Davis in *From the Dark Tower: Afro-American Writers, 1900 to 1960* accurately describes as partly an *apologia pro vita sua* (a defense of his life), Ellison articulates the basis of his objection: "I, for instance, found it disturbing that Bigger Thomas had none of the finer qualities of Richard Wright, none of the imagination, none of the sense of poetry, none of the gaiety." Ellison thus refutes the depiction of the black individual as an inarticulate victim whose life is one only of despair, anger, and pain. He insists that art must capture instead the complex reality, the pain and the pleasure of black existence, thereby challenging the definition of the black person as something less than fully human. Such a vision of art, which is at the heart of *Invisible Man,* became the focal point of an extended debate between Ellison and Irving Howe, who in a 1963 *Dissent* article accused Ellison of disloyalty to Wright in particular and to "protest fiction" in general.

From 1938 to 1944, Ellison published a number of short stories and contributed essays to journals such as *New Masses.* As with most of Ellison's work, these stories have provoked disparate readings. In an essay in *Black World,* Ernest Kaiser calls the earliest stories and the essays in *New Masses* "the healthiest" of Ellison's career. The critic praises the economic theories that inform the early fiction, and he finds Ellison's language pure, emotional, and effective. Lamenting a change he attributes to Ellison's concern with literary technique, Kaiser charges the later stories, essays, and novel with being no longer concerned with people's problems and with being "unemotional."

Other critics, like Marcus Klein in *After Alienation: American Novels in Mid-Century,* see the early work as a progressive preparation for Ellison's mature fiction and theory. In the earliest of these stories, "Slick Gonna Learn," Ellison draws a character shaped largely by an ideological, naturalistic conception of existence, the very type of character he later repudiated. From this imitation of proletarian fiction, Ellison's work moves towards psychological and finally metaphysical explorations of the human condition. His characters thus are freed from restrictive definitions as Ellison develops a voice that is his own, Klein maintains.

In the two latest stories of the 1938-1944 period, "Flying Home" and "King of the Bingo Game," Ellison creates characters congruent with his sense of pluralism and possibility and does so in a narrative style that begins to approach the complexity of *Invisible Man.* As Arthur P. Davis notes, in "Flying Home" Ellison combines realism, folk story, symbolism, and a touch of surrealism to present his protagonist, Todd. In a fictional world composed of myriad levels of the mythic and the folk, the classical and the modern, Todd fights to free himself of imposed definitions. However, it is in "King of the Bingo Game," published just before he began *Invisible Man,* that Ellison's growth is most evident.

As in "Flying Home," the writer experiments in "King of the Bingo Game" with integrating sources and techniques. As in all of Ellison's early stories, the protagonist is a young black man fighting for his freedom against forces and people that attempt to deny it. In "King of the Bingo Game," O'Meally argues, "the struggle is seen in its most abstracted form." This abstraction results from the "dreamlike shifts of time and levels of consciousness" that dominate the surrealistic story and also from the fact that "the King is Ellison's first character to sense the frightening absurdity of everyday American life." In an epiphany which frees him from illusion and which places him, even if for only a moment, in control, the King realizes "that his battle for freedom and identity must be waged not against individuals or even groups, but against no less than history and fate," O'Meally declares. The parameters of the fight for freedom and identity have been broadened. Ellison sees his black hero as one who wages the oldest and most universal battle in human history: the fight for freedom to be timelessly human, to engage in the "tragic struggle of humanity," as the writer asserts in *Shadow and Act.* The King achieves awareness for a moment; the Invisible Man not only becomes aware but is able to articulate fully the struggle. As Ellison notes in his preface to the anniversary edition of the novel, too often characters have been "figures caught up in the most intense forms of social struggle, subject to the most extreme forms of the human predicament but yet seldom able to articulate the issues which tortured them." The Invisible Man is endowed with eloquence; he is Ellison's radical experiment with a fiction that insists upon the full range and humanity of the black character.

Ellison began *Invisible Man* in 1945. Although he was at work on a never-completed war novel at the time, Ellison recalls in his 1982 preface that he could not ignore the "taunting, disembodied voice" he heard beckoning him to write *Invisible*

Man. Published in 1952 after a seven-year creative struggle, and awarded the National Book Award in 1953, *Invisible Man* received critical acclaim. Although some early reviewers were puzzled or disappointed by the experimental narrative techniques, most now agree that these techniques give the work its lasting force and account for Ellison's influence on later fiction. The novel is a veritable fugue of cultural fragments, blended and counterpointed in a uniquely Ellisonian composition. Echoes of Homer, Joyce, Eliot, and Hemingway join forces with the sounds of spirituals, blues, jazz, and nursery rhymes. The Invisible Man is as haunted by Louis Armstrong's "What did I do / To be so black / And blue?" as he is by Hemingway's bullfight scenes and his matadors' grace under pressure. The linking together of these disparate cultural elements is what allows the Invisible Man to draw the portrait of his inner face that is the way out of his wasteland.

In the work, Ellison clearly employs the traditional motif of the *Bildungsroman,* or novel of education: the Invisible Man moves from innocence to experience, from darkness to light, from blindness to sight. Complicating this linear journey, however, is the narrative frame provided by the Prologue and Epilogue which the narrator composes after the completion of his above-ground educational journey. Yet readers begin with the Prologue, written in his underground chamber on the "border area" of Harlem where he is waging a guerrilla war against the Monopolated Light & Power Company by invisibly draining their power. At first denied the story of his discovery, readers must be initiated through the act of re-experiencing the events that led them and the narrator to this hole. Armed with some suggestive hints and symbols, readers then start the journey toward a revisioning of the Invisible Man, America, and themselves.

The journey is a deliberate baptism by fire. From the Battle Royal where the Invisible Man swallows his own blood in the name of opportunity; to the madness of The Golden Day; to the protagonist's anguished expulsion from the College; to the horror of his lobotomy; to his dehumanization by the Brotherhood; to his jubilant discovery of the unseen people of Harlem; to the nightmare that is Ras and the riots; and finally to the descent underground and the ritualistic burning of the contents of his briefcase, readers are made to participate in the plot because they, finally, are a part of it. The novel is about plots: the plots against the Invisible Man by Bledsoe and the Brotherhood; the conspiracy against himself that is the inevitable result of his illusions; the plot of the American ideal that keeps him dodging the forces of the actual; the plot of the reader against the writer; and the plot, ultimately, against every human being by life itself. The multiplicity of plot is part of the brilliance of the novel. Like the Invisible Man, readers are duped, time and time again, resisting the reality before them. And like him, they undergo a series of deaths and rebirths in their narrative journey. They are cast out of the realism of the college scenes into the surrealistic void of the riots, wondering what they did to be, if not always black, at least so blue. They are made to feel, in the words of the novel, every "itch, taunt, laugh, cry, scar, ache, rage or pain of it." And readers come to know that they—and the Invisible Man— share the responsibility for all of it.

In the Prologue and Epilogue the Invisible Man is the conscious, reflexive artist, recording his perceptions of self and other as he articulates the meaning of the journey and the descent. In the Epilogue he lets readers understand more clearly the preparatory hints and symbols he offered in the Prologue. He articulates his understanding of the old woman's words when she told him that freedom lay not in hating but in loving and in "knowing how to say" what is in one's head. Here too he unveils his insight into his grandfather, an ex-slave who "never had any doubts about his humanity" and who accepted the principle of America "in all its human and absurd diversity." As the Invisible Man records his journey through the underground America, he asserts a vision of America as it should be. He becomes the nation's moral conscience, embodying its greatest failure and its highest possibility. He reclaims his full humanity and freedom by accepting the world as a "concrete, ornery, vile and sublimely wonderful" reflection of the perceptive self.

The act of writing, of ordering and defining the self, is what gives the Invisible Man freedom and what allows him to manage the absurdity and chaos of everyday life. Writing frees the self from imposed definitions, from the straitjacket of all that would limit the productive possibilities of the self. Echoing the pluralism of the novel's form, the Invisible Man insists on the freedom to be ambivalent, to love and to hate, to denounce and to defend the America he inherits. Ellison himself is well-acquainted with the ambivalence of his American heritage; nowhere is it more evident than in his name. Named after the nineteenth-century essayist and poet Ralph Waldo Emerson, whom Ellison's father admired, the name has created for Ellison embarrassment, confusion, and a desire to be the American writer his namesake called for. And Ellison places such emphasis on his unnamed yet self-named narrator's breaking the shackles of restrictive definitions, of what others call reality or right, he also frees himself, as Robert B. Stepto in *From Behind the Veil: A Study of Afro-American Narrative* argues, from the strictures of the traditional slave narratives of Frederick Douglas and W. E. B. DuBois. By consciously invoking this form but then not bringing the motif of "ascent and immersion" to its traditional completion, Ellison revoices the form, makes it his own, and steps outside it.

This stepping outside of traditional form, however, can be a dangerous act. In *Invisible Man,* Tod Clifton steps outside the historically powerful Brotherhood and is shot for "resisting reality." At the other extreme, Rinehart steps outside all definitions and becomes the embodiment of chaos. In *City of Words: American Fiction, 1950-1970* Tony Tanner notes that Ellison presents an overriding preoccupation of postmodern fiction: the fear of a rigid pattern that would limit all freedom of self, coupled with the fear of no pattern, of a chaotic void that would render illusory all sense of self. The Invisible Man is well aware of form and formlessness. As he says, "Without light I am not only invisible but formless as well; and to be unaware of one's form is to live a death." But step outside, or underneath, the Invisible Man does, although he would be the first to admit that he has had to be hit over the head to do it. Ellison, too, steps outside in his creation of the form of *Invisible Man;* he also steps inside the history of great literature that refuses to diminish the complexity of human identity and the search for the self.

The search for identity, which Ellison says in *Shadow and Act* is "*the* American theme," is the heart of the novel and the center of many critical debates over it. At novel's end, the journey is not complete; the Invisible Man must emerge from his hole and test the sense of self formed in hibernation. As he journeys toward this goal, toward the emergence of a sense of self that is at once black and American and universally human, questions recur: In his quest for pluralism, does he sacrifice his blackness? In his devotion to an imaginative rendering of self, does he lose his socially active self?

In her 1979 *PMLA* essay, Susan Blake argues that Ellison's insistence that black experience be ritualized as part of the larger human experience results in a denial of the unique social reality of black life. Because Ellison so thoroughly adapts black folklore into the Western tradition, Blake finds that the definition of black life becomes "not black but white"; it "exchanges the self-definition of the folk for the definition of the masters." Thorpe Butler, in a 1984 *College Language Association Journal* essay, defends Ellison against Blake's criticism. He declares that Ellison's depiction of specific black experience as part of the universal does not "diminish the unique richness and anguish" of that experience and does not "diminish the force of Ellison's protest against the blind, cruel dehumanization of black Americans by white society." This debate extends arguments that have appeared since the publication of the novel. Underlying these controversies is the old, uneasy argument about the relationship of art and politics, of literary practice and social commitment.

Ellison's sensitivity to this issue is painfully clear. He repeatedly defends his view, here voiced in *Shadow and Act,* that "protest is an element of all art, though it does not necessarily take the form of speaking for a political or social program." In a 1970 *Time* essay, Ellison defines further his particular definition of protest, of the "soul" of his art and his people: "An expression of American diversity within unity, of blackness with whiteness, soul announces the presence of a creative struggle against the realities of existence." Insisting in *Shadow and Act* that the novelist is a "manipulator and depictor of moral problems," Ellison claims that as novelist he does not try to escape the reality of black pain. He frequently reminds readers that he knows well the pain and anger that come with being black; his mother was arrested for violating Jim Crow housing laws, and in Alabama he was subjected daily to the outrageous policies of segregation. But for Ellison there needs to be more than even an eloquent depiction of this part of reality; he needs, as he says in *Shadow and Act,* "to transform these elements into art . . . to transcend, as the blues transcend the painful conditions with which they deal." In *Invisible Man* he declares that Louis Armstrong "made poetry out of being invisible." Social reality may place the creator in the underground, render him invisible, but his art leads him out of the hole, eloquent, visible, and empowered by the very people who put him there.

Although the search for identity is the major theme of *Invisible Man,* other aspects of the novel receive a great deal of critical attention. Among them, as Joanne Giza notes in her essay in *Black American Writers: Bibliographical Essays,* are literary debts and analogies; comic elements; the metaphor of vision; use of the blues; and folkloric elements. Although all of these concerns are part of the larger issue of identity, Ellison's use of blues and folklore has been singled out as a major contribution to contemporary literature and culture. Since the publication of *Invisible Man,* scores of articles have appeared on these two topics, a fact which in turn has led to a rediscovery, a revisioning of the importance of blues and folklore to American literature and culture in general.

Much of Ellison's groundbreaking work is presented in *Shadow and Act.* Published in 1964, this collection of essays, says Ellison, is "concerned with three general themes: with literature and folklore, with Negro musical expression—especially jazz and the blues—and with the complex relationship between the Negro American subculture and North American culture as a whole." This volume has been hailed as one of the most profound pieces of cultural criticism of the century. Writing in *Commentary*, Robert Penn Warren praises the astuteness of Ellison's perceptions; in *New Leader*, Stanley Edgar Hyman proclaims Ellison "the profoundest cultural critic we have." In the *New York Review of Books*, R. W. B. Lewis explores Ellison's study of black music as a form of power and finds that "Ellison is not only a self-identifier but the source of self-definition in others."

Published in 1986, *Going to the Territory* is a second collection of essays reprising many of the subjects and concerns treated in *Shadow and Act*—literature, art, music, the relationships of black and white cultures, fragments of autobiography, tributes to such noted black Americans as Richard Wright, Duke Ellington, and painter Romare Beardon. With the exception of "An Extravagance of Laughter," a lengthy examination of Ellison's response to Jack Kirkland's dramatization of Erskine Caldwell's novel *Tobacco Road*, the essays in *Going to the Territory* are reprints of previously published articles or speeches, most of them dating from the 1960s. While it conveniently gathers this material, the volume provides few new insights into the direction Ellison's work may take.

Ellison's influence as both novelist and critic, as artist and cultural historian, is enormous. Whether in agreement with or reaction against, writers respond passionately to his work. In special issues of *Black World* and *College Language Association Journal* devoted to Ellison, strident attacks appear alongside equally spirited accolades. Perhaps another measure of Ellison's stature and achievement is his readers' vigil for his long-awaited second novel. Although Ellison often refuses to answer questions about the work-in-progress, there is enough evidence to suggest that the manuscript is very large, that all or part of it was destroyed in a fire and is being rewritten, and that its creation has been a long and painful task. Most readers wait expectantly, believing that Ellison, who has said in *Shadow and Act* that he "failed of eloquence" in *Invisible Man,* is waiting until his second novel equals his imaginative vision of the American novel as conquerer of the frontier, equals the Emersonian call for a literature to release all people from the bonds of oppression.

Eight excerpts from this novel-in-progress have been published in journals such as *Quarterly Review of Literature, Massachusetts Review,* and *Noble Savage.* Set in the South in the years spanning the Jazz Age to the Civil Rights movement, these fragments seem an attempt to recreate modern American history and identity. The major characters are the Reverend Hickman, a one-time jazz musician, and Bliss, the light-skinned boy whom he adopts and who later passes into white society and becomes Senator Sunraider, an advocate of white supremacy. As O'Meally notes in *The Craft of Ralph Ellison,* the major difference between Bliss and Ellison's earlier young protagonists is that despite some harsh collisions with reality, Bliss refuses to divest himself of his illusions and accept his personal history. Says O'Meally: "Moreover, it is a renunciation of the blackness of American experience and culture, a refusal to accept the American past in all its complexity."

Like *Invisible Man,* this novel promises to be a broad and searching inquiry into identity, ideologies, culture, and history. The narrative form is similar as well; here, too, is the blending of popular and classical myth, of contradictory cultural memories, of an intricate pattern of images of birth, death, and rebirth. In *Shadow and Act* Ellison describes the novel's form as "a realism extended beyond realism" in which he explores again the multifaceted meanings of the folk as the basis of all literature and culture. What the ultimate form of

the novel will be—if, indeed, these excerpts are to be part of one novel—remains hidden. But the pieces seize the reader's imagination even if they deny systematic analysis.

One thing does seem certain about these stories. In them Bliss becomes a traitor to his own race, loses his hold on those things of transforming, affirmative value. Hickman, on the other hand, accepts and celebrates his heritage, his belief in the timeless value of his history. As O'Meally writes in his book-length study of Ellison, Hickman "holds fast to personal and political goals and values." Ellison, too, holds fast to his values in the often chaotic and chameleon world of art and politics. The tone of these excerpts is primarily tragicomic, a mode well-suited to Ellison's definition of life. As he says in *Shadow and Act,* "I think that the mixture of the marvelous and the terrible is a basic condition of human life and that the persistence of human ideals represents the marvelous pulling itself up out of the chaos of the universe." Elsewhere in the book, Ellison argues that "true novels, even when most pessimistic and bitter, arise out of an impulse to celebrate human life." As *Invisible Man* before and the Hickman novel yet to come, they celebrate the "human and absurd" commixture of American life.

AVOCATIONAL INTERESTS: Jazz and classical music, photography, electronics, furniture-making, bird-watching, gardening.

BIOGRAPHICAL/CRITICAL SOURCES:

BOOKS

Allen, Walter Ernest, *The Modern Novel in Britain and the United States,* Dutton, 1964.

Alvarez, A., editor, *Under Pressure: The Writer in Society; Eastern Europe and the U.S.A.,* Penguin, 1965.

Baker, Houston, A., Jr., *Long Black Song: Essays in Black American Literature and Culture,* University Press of Virginia, 1972.

Baumbach, Jonathan, *The Landscape of Nightmare: Studies in the Contemporary American Novel,* New York University Press, 1965.

Benston, Kimberly W., editor, *Speaking for You: The Vision of Ralph Ellison,* Howard University Press, 1987.

Bigsby, C. W. E., editor, *The Black American Writer,* Volume I, Everett Edwards, 1969.

Bloom, Harold, editor, *Ralph Ellison: Modern Critical Views,* Chelsea Publishing, 1986.

Bone, Robert, *The Negro Novel in America,* Yale University Press, revised edition, 1965.

Breit, Harvey, *The Writer Observed,* World Publishing, 1956.

Callahan, John F., *In the African-American Grain: The Pursuit of Voice in Twentieth-Century Black Fiction,* University of Illinois Press, 1988.

Concise Dictionary of American Literary Biography: The New Consciousness, 1941-1948, Gale, 1987.

Contemporary Fiction in America and England, 1950-1970, Gale, 1976.

Contemporary Literary Criticism, Gale, Volume 1, 1973, Volume 3, 1975, Volume 11, 1979.

Cooke, Michael, *Afro-American Literature in the Twentieth Century: The Achievement of Intimacy,* Yale University Press, 1984.

Covo, Jacqueline, *The Blinking Eye: Ralph Waldo Ellison and His American, French, German, and Italian Critics, 1952-1971: Bibliographic Essays and a Checklist,* Scarecrow, 1974.

Davis, Arthur P., *From the Dark Tower: Afro-American Writers (1900 to 1960)*, Howard University Press, 1974.

Davis, Charles T., *Black Is the Color of the Cosmos: Essays on Afro-American Literature and Culture, 1942-1981*, edited by Henry Louis Gates, Jr., Garland, 1982.

Dictionary of Literary Biography, Volume 2: American Novelists since World War II, Gale, 1978.

Dietze, Rudolf F., *Ralph Ellison: The Genius of an Artist*, Carl (Nuremburg), 1982.

Ellison, Ralph, *Shadow and Act*, Random House, 1964.

Fabre, Michael, editor, *Delta Number 18: Ralph Ellison*, University Paul Valery (Paris), 1984.

Fischer-Hornung, Dorothea, *Folklore and Myth in Ralph Ellison's Early Works*, Hochschul (Stuttgart), 1979.

Fisher, Dexter, and Robert B. Stepto, editors, *Afro-American Literature: The Reconstruction of Instruction*, Modern Language Association of America, 1979.

Gayle, Addison, Jr., editor, *Black Expression: Essays by and about Americans in the Creative Arts*, Weybright & Talley, 1969.

Gayle, Addison, Jr., compiler, *The Black Aesthetic*, Doubleday, 1971.

Gayle, Addison, Jr., *The Way of the New World: The Black Novel in America*, Anchor Press, 1975.

Gibson, Donald B., compiler, *Five Black Writers: Essays on Wright, Ellison, Baldwin, Hughes, and Le Roi Jones*, New York University Press, 1970.

Gottesman, Ronald, editor, *Studies in Invisible Man*, Merrill, 1971.

Graham, John, *The Writer's Voice: Conversations with Contemporary Writers*, edited by George Garrett, Morrow, 1973.

Gross, Seymour L., and John Edward Hardy, editors, *Images of the Negro in American Literature*, University of Chicago Press, 1966.

Harper, Michael S., and R. B. Stepto, editors, *Chant of Saints: A Gathering of Afro-American Literature, Art, and Scholarship*, University of Illinois Press, 1979.

Henderson, Bill, editor, *The Pushcart Prize, III: Best of the Small Presses*, Avon, 1979.

Hersey, John, editor, *Ralph Ellison: A Collection of Critical Essays*, Prentice-Hall, 1974.

Hill, Herbert, editor, *Anger and Beyond: The Negro Writer in the United States*, Harper, 1966.

Inge, M. Thomas, and others, editors, *Black American Writers: Bibliographical Essays, Volume II: Richard Wright, Ralph Ellison, James Baldwin, and Amiri Baraka*, St. Martin's, 1978.

Kazin, Alfred, *Bright Book of Life: American Novelists and Storytellers from Hemingway to Mailer*, Atlantic-Little, Brown, 1973.

Klein, Marcus, *After Alienation: American Novels in Mid-Century*, World Publishing, 1964.

Kostelanetz, R., *On Contemporary Literature: An Anthology of Critical Essays on the Major Movements and Writers of Contemporary Literature*, Avon, 1964.

Margolies, Edward, *Native Sons: A Critical Study of Twentieth-Century Negro American Authors*, Lippincott, 1968.

O'Brien, John, *Interviews with Black Writers*, Liveright, 1973.

O'Meally, Robert G., *The Craft of Ralph Ellison*, Harvard University Press, 1980.

Ottley, Roi, William J. Weatherby, and others, editors, *The Negro in New York: An Informal Social History*, New York Public Library, 1967.

Plimpton, George, editor, *Writers at Work: The Paris Review Interviews*, second series, Viking, 1963.

Reilly, John M., editor, *Twentieth-Century Interpretations of Invisible Man: A Collection of Critical Essays*, Prentice-Hall, 1970.

Stepto, R. B., *From Behind the Veil: A Study of Afro-American Narrative*, University of Illinois Press, 1979.

Tanner, Tony, *City of Words: American Fiction, 1950-1970*, Harper, 1971.

Trimmer, Joseph F., editor, *A Casebook on Ralph Ellison's Invisible Man*, Crowell, 1972.

Waldmeir, Joseph J., editor, *Recent American Fiction: Some Critical Views*, Houghton, 1963.

Warren, Robert Penn, *Who Speaks for the Negro?*, Random House, 1965.

The Writer as Independent Spirit, [New York], 1968.

PERIODICALS

American Quarterly, March, 1972.

American Scholar, autumn, 1955.

Atlantic, July, 1952, December, 1970, August, 1986.

Barat Review, January, 1968.

Black Academy Review, winter, 1970.

Black American Literature Forum, summer, 1978.

Black Books Bulletin, winter, 1972.

Black Creation, summer, 1970.

Black World, December, 1970 (special Ellison issue).

Book Week, October 25, 1964.

Boundary 2, winter, 1978.

Brown Alumni Monthly, November, 1979.

Carleton Miscellany, winter, 1980 (special Ellison issue).

Chicago Review, Volume 19, number 2, 1967.

Chicago Tribune Book World, August 10, 1986.

College Language Association Journal, December, 1963, June, 1967, March, 1970 (special Ellison issue), September, 1971, December, 1971, December, 1972, June, 1973, March, 1974, September, 1976, September, 1977, Number 25, 1982, Number 27, 1984.

Commentary, November, 1953, Number 39, 1965.

Commonweal, May 2, 1952.

Crisis, March, 1953, March, 1970.

Critique, Number 2, 1968.

Daedalus, winter, 1968.

Daily Oklahoman, August 23, 1953.

December, winter, 1961.

English Journal, September, 1969, May, 1973, November, 1984.

'48 Magazine of the Year, May, 1948.

Grackle, Volume 4, 1977-78.

Harper's, October, 1959, March, 1967, July, 1967.

Journal of Black Studies, Number 7, 1976.

Los Angeles Times, August 8, 1986.

Massachusetts Review, autumn, 1967, autumn, 1977.

Modern Fiction Studies, winter, 1969-70.

Motive, April, 1966.

Muhammad Speaks, September, 1972, December, 1972.

Nation, May 10, 1952, September 9, 1964, November 9, 1964, September 20, 1965.

Negro American Literature Forum, July, 1970, summer, 1973, Number 9, 1975, spring, 1977.

Negro Digest, May, 1964, August, 1967.

Negro History Bulletin, May, 1953, October, 1953.

New Criterion, September, 1983.

New Leader, October 26, 1964.

New Republic, November 14, 1964, August 4, 1986.

Newsday, October, 1967.
Newsweek, August 12, 1963, October 26, 1964.
New Yorker, May 31, 1952, November 22, 1976.
New York Herald Tribune Book Review, April 13, 1952.
New York Review of Books, January 28, 1964, January 28, 1965.
New York Times, April 13, 1952, April 24, 1985.
New York Times Book Review, April 13, 1952, May 4, 1952, October 25, 1964, January 24, 1982, August 3, 1986.
New York Times Magazine, November 20, 1966.
Paris Review, spring, 1955, spring/summer, 1957.
Partisan Review, Number 25, 1958.
Phoenix, fall, 1961.
Phylon, winter, 1960, spring, 1970, spring, 1973, summer, 1973, summer, 1977.
PMLA, January, 1979.
Renascence, spring, 1974, winter, 1978.
Saturday Review, April 12, 1952, March 14, 1953, December 11, 1954, January 1, 1955, April 26, 1958, May 17, 1958, July 12, 1958, September 27, 1958, July 28, 1962, October 24, 1964.
Shenandoah, summer, 1969.
Smith Alumni Quarterly, July, 1964.
Southern Humanities Review, winter, 1970.
Southern Literary Journal, spring, 1969.
Southern Review, fall, 1974, summer, 1985.
Studies in American Fiction, spring, 1973.
Studies in Black Literature, autumn, 1971, autumn, 1972, spring, 1973, spring, 1975, spring, 1976, winter, 1976.
Tamarack Review, October, 1963, summer, 1964.
Time, April 14, 1952, February 9, 1959, February 1, 1963, April 6, 1970.
Times Literary Supplement, January 18, 1968.
Village Voice, November 19, 1964.
Washington Post, August 19-21, 1973, April 21, 1982, February 9, 1983, March 30, 1983, July 23, 1986.
Washington Post Book World, May 17, 1987.
Wisconsin Studies in Literature, winter, 1960, summer, 1966.
Y-Bird Reader, autumn, 1977.

—*Sidelights by Judy R. Smith*

*   *   *

ELY, Virginia (Shackelford) 1899-

PERSONAL: Born July 16, 1899, in Denton, Tex.; daughter of Franklin Pierce and Susan (Coleman) Ely. *Education:* Bowie Commercial College, diploma, 1920; Texas Wesleyan College, B.A., 1937; Southwestern Baptist Theological Seminary, M.R.E., 1937; Texas State College for Women (now Texas Woman's University), M.S., 1950. *Religion:* Baptist.

CAREER: Clay County, Tex., public school teacher, 1918; legal stenographer and court reporter, 1920-22; Wichita Falls Building and Loan Association, Wichita Falls, Tex., head of correspondence, sales department, 1925-27; First Baptist Church, Wichita Falls, business and education secretary, 1927-34; Mary Hardin-Baylor College (now University of Mary Hardin-Baylor), Belton, Tex., member of public relations staff, 1938-40; 97th District Court, Henrietta, Tex., clerk, 1943-46; United States Public Health Hospital, Fort Worth, Tex., medical librarian, 1950-66. Worked as a teacher in church secretarial education, Southwestern Baptist Theological Seminary, Fort Worth, in religious education, First Baptist Church, Henderson, Tex., and in nursing education, Baptist Hospital, Columbia, S.C.

WRITINGS:

(Editor) *I Quote: A Collection of Ancient and Modern Wisdom and Inspiration*, G. W. Stewart, 1947, Lutterworth Press (London), 1964.
Adoration: Devotions for Personal and Group Worship, Fleming Revell, 1951.
A Book of Installation Services, Fleming Revell, 1955.
Drugs Destroy: A Warning to Youth, Broadman, 1955.
Come, Let Us Adore Him: A Book of Worship Services, Fleming Revell, 1956.
The Church Secretary, Moody Press, 1956.
(Editor) *A Time Apart: Daily Devotions for Young People*, Fleming Revell, 1957.
Devotion: For Personal and Group Worship, Fleming Revell, 1960.
Stewardship: Witnessing for Christ, Fleming Revell, 1962.
Dedication Services for All Occasions, Fleming Revell, 1964.
Your Hand in His, Fleming Revell, 1966.
Some of My Best Friends Were Addicts, Fleming Revell, 1968.†

*   *   *

ENTWISTLE, (Arthur) Theodore (Henry) Rowland
  See ROWLAND-ENTWISTLE, (Arthur) Theodore (Henry)

*   *   *

EPAFRODITO
  See WAGNER, C(harles) Peter

*   *   *

ETTER, Dave 1928-

PERSONAL: Born March 18, 1928, in Huntington Park, Calif.; son of Harold Pearson and Judith (Goodenow) Etter; married Margaret Cochran, August 8, 1959; children: Emily Louise, George Goodenow. *Education:* University of Iowa, B.A., 1953. *Politics:* Democrat.

ADDRESSES: Home and office—414 Gates St., P.O. Box 413, Elburn, Ill. 60119.

CAREER: Before 1961, did odd jobs in Iowa, Indiana, Illinois, Massachusetts, and California; Northwestern University Press, Evanston, Ill., editor, 1961-63; *Encyclopaedia Britannica*, Chicago, Ill., editor and writer, 1964-73; Northern Illinois University Press, De Kalb, Ill., editor, 1974-80; free-lance writer and editor, 1980—. *Military service:* U.S. Army, 1953-55.

AWARDS, HONORS: Bread Loaf Writers Conference fellow in poetry, 1967; Midland Poetry Award and Friends of Literature poetry award, both 1967, both for *Go Read the River*; Illinois Sesquicentennial Poetry Prize, 1968, for *The Last Train to Prophetstown*; Theodore Roethke Poetry Prize, 1971; Carl Sandburg Award, 1981.

WRITINGS:

POETRY

Go Read the River, University of Nebraska Press, 1966.
The Last Train to Prophetstown, University of Nebraska Press, 1968.
Strawberries, Juniper Press, 1970.
Voyages to the Inland Sea (also includes prose), University of Wisconsin, 1971.

Crabtree's Woman, BkMk Press, 1972.
Well You Needn't, Raindust Press, 1975.
Bright Mississippi, Juniper Press, 1975.
Central Standard Time: New and Selected Poems, BkMk Press, 1978.
Alliance, Illinois, Kylix Press, 1978, 2nd edition, Spoon River Poetry Press, 1983.
Open to the Wind, Uzzano, 1978.
Riding the Rock Island through Kansas, Wolfsong Press, 1979.
Cornfields, Spoon River Poetry Press, 1980.
West of Chicago, Spoon River Poetry Press, 1981.
Boondocks, Uzzano, 1982.
Home State, Spoon River Poetry Press, 1985.
Live at the Silver Dollar, Spoon River Poetry Press, 1986.
Selected Poems, Spoon River Poetry Press, 1987.

CONTRIBUTOR

Lucien Stryk, editor, *Heartland: Poets of the Midwest*, Northern Illinois University Press, 1967.
R. Schreiber, editor, *31 New American Poets*, Hill & Wang, 1969.
M. Williams, compiler, *Contemporary Poetry in America*, Random House, 1973.
Robert Killoren, editor, *Late Harvest: Plains and Prairie Poets*, BkMk Press, 1977.
Dan Jaffe and John Knoepfle, editors, *Frontier Literature: Images of the American West*, McGraw, 1979.
David R. Pichaske, editor, *Beowulf to Beatles and Beyond: The Variations of Poetry*, Macmillan, 1981.

Also contributor to more than sixty anthologies and textbooks.

OTHER

Contributor to more than 175 literary magazines, including *Prairie Schooner, Massachusetts Review, Midwest, Choice, Poetry Northwest, Beloit Poetry Journal, Saturday Review, Poetry, Nation,* and *North American Review.*

WORK IN PROGRESS: Three books of poems.

SIDELIGHTS: "If there is a poet anywhere in the Midwest who picks up where [Carl] Sandburg, [Vachel] Lindsay and [Edgar Lee] Masters left off, it is Dave Etter," comments Norbert Blei in the *Chicago Tribune Book World*, adding that "Etter is to Midwestern poetry what Garrison Keillor is to 'A Prairie Home Companion.'" Blei notes in the *Milwaukee Journal:* "Whatever it is that characterized the Midwest—cows, crows, cicadas, hollyhocks, the back screen door banging real good—Etter has made a poem of it. . . . He knows the lay of the land and the junctions, loves the sleepy, small-town life, and records it all as carefully as the village clerk."

Approximately two hundred monologues spoken by townspeople comprise Etter's *Alliance, Illinois*, which Joel A. Lipman calls a "brilliant, sustained work" in *Old Northwest.* Reviewing this collection for *Chicago,* G. E. Murray finds Etter's vision "indelible and immediate . . . one that names the names that truly know and echo the secrets of the heartland." Moreover, Murray believes that the work "displays a huge appetite

for the life it creates and then generates into an unusual energy." Lipman suspects, however, that the "apparent simplicity of Etter's subject matter and language disguises his talent and commitment to craft." Etter's poems "establish an instant unassuming, offhand bond" between the reader and the poet, says Lipman, who also considers the poetry "alive, humorous, and honest—excellent art that can be returned to for insight and pleasure." In recording the "speech, presence, and circumstance" of the Midwest, writes Murray, Etter has created an art that "renders an exceptional spirit of place, one imbued with supremely ordinary people, their interconnectedness, their ruins, and abundances, their fertile but perilous land." And for this, Murray adds, "Etter deserves praise and attention." Recently, Etter indicated to *CA* that "*Alliance, Illinois* has been adapted for the stage by three different drama groups and has been seen by large and enthusiastic audiences throughout Illinois."

"I have always written about the small town and rural Midwest because that is all I know well, all I have a real feel for, all I really care about deeply," Etter once told *CA.* "There is an endless wealth of poem material right in my hometown; I will never be forced to look elsewhere. It is not easy to say for sure what authors have influenced me the most but I would surely have to list Walt Whitman, Sherwood Anderson, Carl Sandburg, Mark Twain, George Ade, Thomas Hardy, William Faulkner, and Richard Bissell. Recently, I have been considerably influenced by some of America's jazz greats, particularly Thelonious Monk, Dizzy Gillespie, and Miles Davis—they have shown me new rhythms, new ways to break the line, new structures."

BIOGRAPHICAL/CRITICAL SOURCES:

BOOKS

Blei, Norbert, *Door to Door*, Ellis Press, 1985.
Bray, Robert C., *Rediscoveries: Literature and Place in Illinois*, University of Illinois Press, 1982.
Killoren, Robert, editor, *Late Harvest: Plains and Prairie Poets*, BkMk Press, 1977.

PERIODICALS

Chicago, December, 1980, January, 1984.
Chicagoland, November, 1968, March, 1969.
Chicago Tribune Book World, October 3, 1982.
Indiana Review, fall, 1985.
Midwest Quarterly, spring, 1987.
Milwaukee Journal, October 7, 1979.
New Letters, fall, 1984.
Old Northwest, fall, 1983.
Panorama (Chicago Daily News), July 16, 1966.
Poetry, February, 1967, February, 1971, July, 1984.
San Francisco Review of Books, winter, 1983/84.

*   *   *

EVANS, Alan
  See STOKER, Alan

F

FAIRLEY, Peter 1930-

PERSONAL: Born November 2, 1930, in Kuala Lumpur, Malaya; son of Frank and Ethel (Griggs) Fairley; married Vivienne Richards, June 4, 1954; children: Josephine, Alastair, Duncan, Simon. *Education:* Sidney Sussex College, Cambridge, B.A. (honors), 1953. *Politics:* None. *Religion:* Church of England.

ADDRESSES: Home—Pacific, 149 Hayes Lane, Bromley, Kent, England. *Office:* Independent Television Network, ITN House, 48 Wells St., London W1, England.

CAREER: Science editor, *Evening Standard,* London, England, Independent Television Network News, London, and *TV Times.* Appears regularly on several television programs and produces the British Broadcasting Corp. science program, "Tomorrow's World." *Military service:* British Army, 1949-51; became captain.

MEMBER: Association of British Science Writers, Medical Journalists Association, Sportsman Club (London).

AWARDS, HONORS: Glaxo traveling fellowship, 1967, for best science writing of the year.

WRITINGS:

This Is Cambridge: An Informal Account of University Life, illustrations by Barrington Brown, Metcalfe, 1959.
Man on the Moon, Arthur Barker, 1969.
The ABC of Space, Independent TV Books, 1969.
Project X: The Exciting Story of British Invention, Mayflower Books, 1970, revised edition published as *British Inventions of the 20th Century,* Hart-Davis, 1972.
Peter Fairley's Space Annual, Independent TV Books, 1970.
Peter Fairley's World of Wonders Annual, Independent TV Books, 1970.
The A-Z of Space, Hart-Davis, 1974, revised edition, 1976.
Is There Life in Outer Space?, illustrations by David Jefferis, Independent TV Books, 1976.
Television behind the Screen, Independent TV Books, 1976.
North Sea Bonanza, Hart-Davis, 1977.
Space: A Collection of Documents, Jackdaw for Thames Television, 1977.
The Conquest of Pain, Joseph, 1978, Scribner, 1980.

Also author of television scripts and contributor to magazines.

WORK IN PROGRESS: Two books, *Behind the Ballyhoo* and *The Name on the Bullett.*

AVOCATIONAL INTERESTS: Swimming, tennis, cricket, woodworking.

BIOGRAPHICAL/CRITICAL SOURCES:

PERIODICALS

Times Literary Supplement, October 16, 1969†

* * *

FELD, Werner (Joachim) 1910-

PERSONAL: Born April 10, 1910, in Dusseldorf, Germany; son of Bruno and Irma (Loebl) Feld; married Betty Tandy, October 1, 1957. *Education:* University of Berlin, LL.B., 1933; Tulane University of Louisiana, Ph.D., 1962. *Religion:* Episcopalian.

ADDRESSES: Home—3743 Blue Merion Court, Colorado Springs, Colo. 80906. *Office*—Department of Political Science, University of Colorado Springs, P.O. Box 7150, Colorado Springs, Colo. 80933-7150.

CAREER: Dixie Specialty Co., Inc., Mobile, Ala., president, 1947-61; North Georgia College, Dahlonega, assistant professor of political science, 1961-62; Moorhead State College, Moorhead, Minn., 1962-65, began as assistant professor, became professor of political science; University of New Orleans, New Orleans, La., professor of political science, 1965-86; University of Colorado, Colorado Springs, adjunct professor, 1986—. Civil Defense director, Mobile, Ala., 1956-57; consultant to U.S. Department of State, 1965-70. *Military service:* U.S. Army Reserve, 1943-63, with active duty in World War II and Korean War; became lieutenant colonel.

MEMBER: American Political Science Association, International Studies Association (executive committee, 1966-67), Southern Political Science Association (secretary, 1966-67).

WRITINGS:

Reunification and West German-Soviet Relations, Nijhoff, 1963.
The Court of the European Communities: New Dimension in International Adjudication, Nijhoff, 1964.
The European Common Market and the World, Prentice-Hall, 1967.

(Editor with others) *The Enduring Questions of Politics,* Prentice-Hall, 1969, revised edition, 1974.
Transnational Business Collaboration among Common Market Countries, Praeger, 1970.
Non-governmental Forces and World Politics, Praeger, 1972.
(With John K. Wildgen) *Domestic Political Realities and European Integration,* Westview, 1976.
The European Community in World Affairs, Alfred Publishing, 1976.
International Relations: A Transnational Approach, Alfred Publishing, 1976.
Multinational Corporations and U.N. Politics, Pergamon, 1980.
(With Gavin Boyd) *Comparative Regional Systems,* Pergamon, 1980.
West Germany and the European Community, Praeger, 1981.
(With Wildgen) *NATO and the Atlantic Defense,* Praeger, 1982.
(With Robert S. Jordan) *International Organization: A Comparative Approach,* Praeger, 1983, 2nd revised edition, 1987.
American Foreign Policy: Aspirations and Reality, Wiley, 1984.
(Contributor) Robert J. Jackson, editor, *Continuity of Discord,* Praeger, 1985.
(Contributor) Walter Goldstein, *Fighting Allies,* Brassey's Defence Publishers, 1986.
Arms Control and the Atlantic Community, Praeger, 1987.

Contributor to political science, law, and other journals.

*　　*　　*

FINCH, Robert (Duer Claydon) 1900-

PERSONAL: Born May 14, 1900, in Freeport, Long Island, N.Y.; son of Edward and Ada Finch. *Education:* University of Toronto, B.A., 1925; attended University of Paris, 1928.

ADDRESSES: Home—University of Toronto, Massey College, 4 Devonshire Place, Toronto, Ontario, Canada M5S 2E1.

CAREER: University of Toronto, University College, Toronto, Ontario, lecturer, 1928-30, assistant professor, 1931-42, associate professor, 1942-51, professor of French, 1952-68, professor emeritus, 1970—, writer-in-residence, 1970-71. Poet, literary critic, painter. Member of board of trustees, Massey College, University of Toronto, and Leonard Foundation.

MEMBER: Societe Internationale d'Etudes Francaises, Royal Society of Canada (fellow).

AWARDS, HONORS: Jardine Memorial Prize, 1924, for poetry; Governor General's Awards, 1946, for *Poems,* and 1961, for *Acis in Oxford;* Lorne Pierce Gold Medal, 1968; LL.D., University of Toronto, 1973, York University, Toronto, 1976, University of Winnipeg, 1984.

WRITINGS:

(Contributor) *New Provinces: Poems of Several Authors,* Macmillan (Toronto), 1936.
Poems, Oxford University Press, 1946.
The Strength of the Hills (poems), McClelland & Stewart, 1948.
A Century Has Roots (masque), University of Toronto Press, 1953.
(Editor with C. R. Parsons) Chateaubriand, *Rene,* University of Toronto Press, 1957.
Acis in Oxford and Other Poems, privately printed, 1959, University of Toronto Press, 1961.

Dover Beach Revisited and Other Poems, Macmillan, 1961.
Silverthorn Bush and Other Poems, Macmillan, 1966.
The Sixth Sense: Individualism in French Poetry, 1686-1760, University of Toronto Press, 1966.
(Editor with Eugene Joliat) *French Individualist Poetry, 1686-1760: An Anthology,* University of Toronto Press, 1971.
(Contributor) Alan Jarvis, editor, *Douglas Duncan: A Memorial Portrait,* University of Toronto Press, 1974.
(Contributor) Arnold Edinborough, editor, *The Enduring Word: A Centennial History of Wycliffe College,* University of Toronto Press, 1978.
(Editor with Joliat) Saint-Evremond, *Sir Politick Would-Be,* Droz, 1978.
(Editor with Joliat) Saint-Evremond, *Les Opera,* Droz, 1979.
Variations and Theme (poems), Porcupine's Quill, 1980.
Has and Is (poems), Porcupine's Quill, 1981.
Twelve for Christmas, Porcupine's Quill, 1982.
The Grand Duke of Moscow's Favorite Solo (poems), Porcupine's Quill, 1983.
Double Tuning (poems), Porcupine's Quill, 1984.
For the Back of a Likeness (poems), Porcupine's Quill, 1986.

Contributor to *University of Toronto Quarterly, Contemporary Verse* (Chicago), *Saturday Review,* and other periodicals. Work is represented in Canadian and international anthologies.

SIDELIGHTS: Robert Finch is a poet, essayist, musician, painter, and literary critic who writes elegant, controlled verse. "At its best," writes L. A. MacKay in *Saturday Night,* his poetry "has a mannered dexterity, an ornate lucidity, and a studiously restrained tone that is capable alike of light grace and poignant though delicately phrased emotion." Writing in *Canadian Literature,* George Woodcock observes that Finch "writes with poise and self-consciousness. The Dionysic fury never leads him where his reason would not have him go, and his craftsmanship is controlled and accurate. Thus, one imagines, Flaubert might write if another incarnation made him a Canadian poet instead of a French novelist."

BIOGRAPHICAL/CRITICAL SOURCES:

BOOKS

Contemporary Literary Criticism, Volume XVIII, Gale, 1981.

PERIODICALS

Canadian Forum, December, 1967.
Canadian Literature, summer, 1962.
Comparative Literature, winter, 1968.
Saturday Night, May, 1949.

*　　*　　*

FINK, Stevanne Auerbach
See AUERBACH, Stevanne

*　　*　　*

FLYNN, George L. 1931-

PERSONAL: Born November 2, 1931, in Chicago, Ill.; son of Clifford Joseph (a traffic manager) and Louise (Maloney) Flynn; married Jill Gilbert, October 12, 1957; children: Kathleen, George Thomas, William Clifford. *Education:* University of Detroit, B.S., 1953. *Politics:* Independent. *Religion:* Roman Catholic.

ADDRESSES: Home—97 Minnehaha Blvd., Oakland, N.J. 07436.

CAREER: Prentice-Hall, Inc., Englewood Cliffs, N.J., 1957-67, began as field representative, became editor; Simon & Flynn, Inc., New York, N.Y., vice-president, 1967-71; freelance writer, editor, and film producer, 1971—. *Military service:* U.S. Air Force, 1954-56; became first lieutenant.

AWARDS, HONORS: Award from Council on International Nontheatrical Events and Ohio State award, both 1971, for television documentary "A Man Named Lombardi."

WRITINGS:

Vince Lombardi on Football, two volumes, New York Graphic Society, 1973, revised edition, distributed by Van Nostrand, 1981.

The Vince Lombardi Scrapbook, Grosset, 1976.

Commitment to Excellence (also see below), American Telephone & Telegraph, 1978.

(With Ernest M. Vandeweghe) *Growing with Sports: A Parent's Guide to the Young Athlete,* Prentice-Hall, 1979.

Great Moments in Baseball (also see below), Bison Books, 1987.

Great Moments in Football (also see below), Bison Books, 1987.

TELEVISION AND VIDEO PRODUCTIONS

"Vince Lombardi's The Art and Science of Football" (a series of twelve half-hour films), CBS-TV, 1969-70.

"A Man Named Lombardi," NBC-TV, 1971.

"What Price Winning?" (one-hour documentary), Landsberg Productions, Inc., 1985.

"Vince Lombardi on Football" (one-hour video), BSI, International with Alpert Productions, 1987.

"Great Moments in Football (one-hour video), BSI, International with Alpert Productions, 1988.

"The Flight of the Pacific Clipper" (television mini-series), Landsberg Productions, Inc., 1988.

OTHER

Also author of *The Expert's Sports Quiz Book* and *The Schenley Football Annuals,* 1977, 1978, 1979; also scriptwriter of "The Rivals" (television pilot), 1972, "This Was Boxing," 1974, "Commitment to Excellence" (sales motivational film), 1976, "Boxing's Biggest Showdown," 1981, and "The Equitable Life Sportsmedicine Series" (sixteen half-hour video tapes), 1981-82.

WORK IN PROGRESS: The Flight of the Pacific Clipper.

SIDELIGHTS: George L. Flynn played varsity basketball in college and has worked with many well-known sports figures, including Vince Lombardi, Red Smith, and Howard Cosell, in the production of his films and books.

*　　　*　　　*

FORD, D(ouglas) W(illiam) Cleverley　1914-

PERSONAL: Born March 4, 1914, in Sheringham, England; son of Arthur James (a clerk) and Mildred (Cleverley) Ford; married Olga Mary Gilbart-Smith, June 28, 1939. *Education:* University of London, A.L.C.D. (with first class honors) and B.D., 1936, M.Th., 1941.

ADDRESSES: Home—Rostrevor, Lingfield, Surrey RH7 6BZ, England.

CAREER: Ordained Anglican priest, 1937; curate in Bridlington, England, 1939-42; vicar in Hampstead, London, 1942-

55, and in Kensington Gore, England, 1955-74; senior chaplain to Archbishop of Canterbury, England, 1975-80. Director of College of Preachers, 1960-73; chairman, Queen Alexandra's House Association, 1965-74; governor, Westminster City School, 1965-74; rural dean of Westminster, 1965-74; prebendary of St. Paul's Cathedral, London, 1968; canon of York, 1969; chaplain to Queen Elizabeth II, 1973-84; tutor, Southwark Ordination course, 1980-85; lecturer, Wey Institute of Religious Studies, 1980-85; Six Preacher of Canterbury Cathedral, 1982—.

MEMBER: Athenaeum Club (London).

WRITINGS:

Why Men Believe in Jesus Christ, Lutterworth, 1950.

An Expository Preacher's Notebook, Hodder & Stoughton, 1960, Harper, 1961.

A Theological Preacher's Notebook, Hodder & Stoughton, 1962.

A Pastoral Preacher's Notebook, Hodder & Stoughton, 1965.

A Reading of Saint Luke's Gospel, Lippincott, 1967.

Preaching at the Parish Communion, Mowbray, Volume I, 1967, Volume II, 1968, Volume III, 1969, Volume VII, 1975.

Preaching Today, Epworth, 1969.

Preaching through the Christian Year, Mowbray, 1971.

Praying through the Christian Year, Mowbray, 1973.

Have you Anything to Declare?, Mowbray, 1973.

Preaching on Special Occasions, Mowbray, Volume I, 1975, Volume II, 1982.

New Preaching from the Old Testament, Mowbray, Volume I, 1976, Volume II, 1983.

New Preaching from the New Testament, Mowbray, Volume I, 1977, Volume II, 1982.

The Ministry of the Word, Hodder & Stoughton, 1979, Eerdmans, 1980.

Preaching through the Acts of the Apostles, Mowbray, 1980.

More Preaching from the New Testament, Mowbray, 1982.

More Preaching from the Old Testament, Mowbray, 1983.

Preaching through the Psalms, Mowbray, 1984.

Preaching through the Life of Christ, Mowbray, 1985.

Preaching on Devotional Occasions, Mowbray, 1986.

From Strength to Strength, Mowbray, 1987.

Preaching the Risen Christ, Mowbray, 1988.

Contributor to *Expository Times.*

SIDELIGHTS: D. W. Cleverley Ford told *CA* that he began his writing career as a result of people wishing to read what he had said in lectures and sermons. "Since my spoken word had always been carefully prepared, having been written and rewritten, this was not difficult. Writing for speaking is different from writing for reading, but it is good training in the art of clarity. I believe that a writer's work will be flat if it pays attention only to conveying information couched in a good literary style; it also needs to move the reader. This implies a sense of drama. I suppose a person either has or has not this sense. A rough and ready test of a good piece of writing is whether or not the reader is sorry when he has come to the end."

AVOCATIONAL INTERESTS: Languages, music, gardening.

*　　　*　　　*

FOWLER, Charles B(runer)　1931-

PERSONAL: Born May 12, 1931, in Peekskill, N.Y.; son of Charles B. (a conductor) and Mabel (Ackerman) Fowler. *Ed-*

ucation: State University Teachers College (now State University of New York College at Potsdam), B.S.Mus.Ed., 1952; Northwestern University, M.M., 1957; Boston University, D.M.A., 1964.

ADDRESSES: Home and office—320 Second St. S.E., Washington, D.C. 20003.

CAREER: Vocal music supervisor in elementary schools in Rochester, N.Y., 1952-56; Mansfield State College, Mansfield, Pa., assistant professor of music, 1957-62; Northern Illinois University, DeKalb, associate professor of music, 1964-65; Music Educators National Conference, Washington, D.C., editor of *Music Educators Journal,* 1965-71; director of publications, 1970-71; writer and consultant in the arts, 1971—. Manager of publications and editor-in-chief of *Parks and Recreation,* National Recreation and Parks Association, Washington, D.C., 1973-75. Writer and consultient for opening of Walt Disney World, 1971; writer and creative consultant to the executive producer, Radio City Music Hall Productions, Inc., 1979-82; communications designer for opening events of Epcot Center, Walt Disney World, October, 1982.

MEMBER: Music Educators National Conference (life member), Music Critics Association, American Council for the Arts, Educational Press Association of America (member of board of directors of District of Columbia chapter, 1969-71), Kappa Delta Pi, Pi Kappa Lambda, Phi Mu Alpha Sinfonia (honorary life member).

AWARDS, HONORS: Danforth grants, 1962-63, 1963-64; certificate of excellence in educational journalism, Educational Press Association of America, 1970; William G. Anderson Award, 1985, for contributions to dance; Minerva Award (highest alumni award), State University of New York at Potsdam, College of Arts and Sciences.

WRITINGS:

(With Robert W. Buggert) *The Search for Musical Understanding,* Wadsworth, 1973.
The Arts Process, Pennsylvania State Department of Education, 1973.
Dance Is (booklet and slide/tape presentation), National Dance Association, 1978.
"Careers in Entertainment" (videotape), Walt Disney Productions, 1979.
(Editor and contributor) *An Arts in Education Source Book,* John D. Rockefeller III Fund, 1980.
"Arts Education: A Promise" (slide/tape presentation), John F. Kennedy Center, 1980.
"Carmen Opera Box" (multi-media teaching tool), Metropolitan Opera, 1980.
"Porgy and Bess Opera Box" (multi-media teaching tool), Metropolitan Opera, 1981.
"First Flights: The Kennedy Center's Programs for Children and Youth" (slide/tape presentation), John F. Kennedy Center, 1981.
"Alaska 1984" (live and televised production), Radio City Music Hall Productions, 1981.
(Author of narration) "The Glory of Christmas: A Living Nativity," Crystal Cathedral, 1981.
(Author of narration) "Encore: The Fiftieth Anniversary Show," Radio City Music Hall, 1982.
Arts in Education/Education in Arts, National Endowment for the Arts, 1985.
A Mets Fan at the Met (story for children), Metropolitan Opera Guild, 1986.

Symposium '85 Report: Music Is Essential to Quality Education, Texas Music Educators Association, 1986.
(Editor) *Sing!* (secondary school textbook), Hinshaw, 1987.
"An Evening at the Kennedy Center" (script), United Way, 1987.
(Editor) *The Crane Symposium: Toward an Understanding of the Teaching and Learning of Musical Performance,* State University of New York at Potsdam, in press.

Also author of two series for National Public Radio, "Alleluia!," 26 weeks, 1984, and "The 1984 Santa Fe Chamber Music Festival," 13 weeks, 1985. Also contributor to *Encyclopedia of Education.*

Author of education column in *Musical America,* 1974—. Contributor of more than two hundred articles to music and education journals. Consulting editor, *Design for Arts Education,* 1980-85, and *Journal of Arts Management and Law,* 1986—.

SIDELIGHTS: Charles Fowler told *CA:* "While I probably would be categorized as a technical writer because much of my work is focused on arts education and music, I bring as much artfulness and craft to the task as my wits permit. Like most writers, I study writing by reading, and I enjoy giving life and veracity to an idea by casting it in the right clothes. I've found that making a living as an independent writer in the arts requires versatility. I've written books, articles, reports, pamphlets, and flyers, scripts for radio, theatre, and multi-media presentations, treatments for film and television—almost anything that comes along. The trick is to turn what could be mundane into something vibrant. To me, the challenge is to touch the reader's mind and heart—to find the essence and make it indelible."

AVOCATIONAL INTERESTS: Painting, theatre, gardening, exercise, travel.

* * *

FRANCIS, Dorothy Brenner 1926-
(Sue Alden, Ellen Goforth, Pat Louis)

PERSONAL: Born November 30, 1926, in Lawrence, Kan.; daughter of Clayton (a district judge) and Cecile (Goforth) Brenner; married Richard M. Francis (a professional musician), August 30, 1950; children: Lynn Ann Francis Tank, Patricia Louise Francis Pocius. *Education:* University of Kansas, Mus.B., 1948. *Politics:* Republican. *Religion:* Methodist.

ADDRESSES: Home—1505 Brentwood Ter., Marshalltown, Iowa 50158.

CAREER: Band and vocal instructor in Orange, Calif., 1948-50, Pleasant Hill, Mo., 1950-51, Cache, Okla., 1951-52, and Gilman, Iowa, 1961-62; former teacher of piano and trumpet and director of a Methodist junior high choir; correspondence teacher for Institute of Children's Literature, Redding Ridge, Conn. Member of board of community Chamber Orchestra, Marshalltown, 1967.

MEMBER: P.E.O. Sisterhood, Marshalltown Tuesday Music Club (former president), Mu Phi Epsilon.

WRITINGS:

Adventure at Riverton Zoo, Abingdon, 1966.
Mystery of the Forgotten Map, Follett, 1968.
(With Daphne Dixon) *Diets for Sick Children,* 2nd edition (Francis was not associated with 1st edition), Blackwell Scientific Publications, 1969, 3rd edition, 1975.

Laugh at the Evil Eye, Messner, 1970.
Another Kind of Beauty, Criterion, 1970.
Hawaiian Interlude, Avalon, 1970.
Studio Affair, Avalon, 1972.
Nurse on Assignment, Avalon, 1972.
A Blue Ribbon for Marni, Avalon, 1973.
Nurse under Fire, Avalon, 1973.
Nurse in the Caribbean, Avalon, 1973.
Murder in Hawaii, Scholastic Book Services, 1973.
Nurse of the Keys, Avalon, 1974.
Golden Girl, Scholastic Book Services, 1974.
Nurse of Spirit Lake, Avalon, 1975.
Keys to Love, Avalon, 1975.
The Flint Hills Foal, Abingdon, 1976.
Nurse at Playland Park, Avalon, 1976.
The Legacy of Merton Manor, Avalon, 1976.
Murder in the Balance, Avalon, 1976.
(Under pseudonym Sue Alden) *The Magnificent Challenge,* Avalon, 1976.
(Under pseudonym Sue Alden) *Nurse at St. John,* Avalon, 1977.
Two against the Arctic, Pyramid, 1977.
Piggy Bank Minds and Other Object Lessons for Children, Abingdon, 1977.
Run of the Sea Witch, Abingdon, 1978.
The Boy with the Blue Ears and Forty-nine Other Object Lessons for Children, Abingdon, 1979.
Shoplifting: The Crime Everybody Pays For, Lodestar, 1980, 3rd edition, 1982.
(Under pseudonym Ellen Goforth) *Path of Desire,* Silhouette, 1980.
New Boy in Town, Silhouette, 1981.
Special Girl, Silhouette, 1981.
(Under pseudonym Pat Louis) *Treasure of the Heart,* Silhouette, 1982.
A New Dawn, Silhouette, 1982.
Say Please, Silhouette, 1982.
Secret Place, Silhouette, 1982.
Captain Morgana Mason, Lodestar, 1982.
A Blink of the Mind, Dell, 1982.
The Ghost of Graydon Place, Scholastic Book Services, 1982.
Just Friends, Silhouette, 1983.
Vandalism: The Crime of Immaturity, Lodestar, 1983.
Promises and Turtle Shells, Abingdon, 1984.
Kiss Me Kit, Silhouette, 1984.
The Magic Circle, Silhouette, 1984.
The Warning, Scholastic Book Services, 1984.
Bid for Romance, Silhouette, 1985.
Follow Your Heart, Silhouette, 1986.
The Tomorrow Star, Weekly Reader Books, 1986.
Write On, Silhouette, 1986.
Stop Thief, Silhouette, 1986.
Computer Crime, Lodestar, 1987.
The Right Kind of Girl, Lodestar, 1987.
Vonnie and Monique, Silhouette, 1987.

Contributor of short stories to Augsburg publications; contributor of light verse to magazines.

WORK IN PROGRESS: A book on teen suicide, for Lodestar.

SIDELIGHTS: Dorothy Brenner Francis told *CA,* "In all my books for children, I've tried to show different lifestyles which I hope will make the reader wonder and think and continue to read." Several of Francis's books have been translated into foreign languages.

FRANCIS, Richard (H.)   1945-

PERSONAL: Born May 14, 1945, in Shawford, England; son of Leslie (a civil servant) and Marian (Rennie) Francis; married Jo Watson (a teacher), January 14, 1967; children: William Rennie, Helen Elizabeth. *Education:* Magdalene College, Cambridge, B.A. (with honors), 1967; attended Harvard University, 1970-72; University of Exeter, Ph.D., 1976. *Politics:* None. *Religion:* None.

ADDRESSES: Home—9 Glenfield Road, Heaton Chapel, Stockport SK4 2QP, England. *Agent*—A. D. Peters & Co. Ltd., 10 Buckingham St., London WC2N 6BU, England. *Office*—Department of American Studies, Victoria University of Manchester, Manchester, England.

CAREER: Victoria University of Manchester, Manchester, England, lecturer in American literature, 1972—. Lecturer at Al-Fateh University, 1976-77; visiting professor, University of Missouri—Columbia, 1987-88.

WRITINGS:

Blackpool Vanishes (novel with poems), Faber & Faber, 1979.
Daggerman (novel with poems), Faber & Faber, 1980.
The Enormous Dwarf (novel), Granada, 1982.
The Whispering Gallery (novel), Deutsch, 1984.
Swansong (novel), Atheneum, 1986.

Contributor to *American Quarterly, Critical Quarterly,* and *Studies in the American Renaissance.* Member of editorial board of Peterloo Poets.

WORK IN PROGRESS: A novel, as yet untitled.

SIDELIGHTS: Richard Francis told *CA:* "In all my published works, the central issue is the same—an attempt to reveal the implications of an alien perspective in the 'normal' world, in effect to explore the possibilities of transcendentalism. In *Blackpool Vanishes* the perspective is provided by the presence of what might be called interterrestrial life, beings who come not from other worlds but from interstices in what we complacently think of as the continuum of reality. In *Daggerman,* the alien vision belongs to the deranged consciousness of a mass-murderer and is formulated into a religion of the 'third alternative.' In *The Enormous Dwarf* the problem is seen as one of accommodating in the present an event which took place in the past, an event which was so horrific that it challenges imaginative reconstruction. In my two most recent novels, the emphasis has shifted slightly. I am now interested in exploring the effectiveness of human accounts of reality (the theme of news in *The Whispering Gallery,* and of strategies for changing the world [politics] in *Swansong*). Nevertheless, the contrast between 'normality' and the essentially intractable and mysterious nature of the universe is maintained.

"I think that my doctoral research into New England transcendentalism has a bearing on my concerns as a novelist. What interested me about the transcendentalists was the peculiarly practical manner with which they undertook a task that is usually regarded as an essentially mystical one. They searched for a formula—I eventually decided to call it the 'Law of Series'—which would unite the one and the many, the relative perspective of the individual and the total viewpoint that we traditionally consign to God. The fact that my own cast of mind is not transcendentalist in either the philosophical or the popular sense does not diminish my admiration for this sort of enterprise. Even though the required synthesis proves unavailable in my own novels (so far, at least!) my belief in the importance of the theme continues unabated; after all, the very word fiction implies that one says 'This is not so' while doing one's utmost to convince the reader that in fact it is.''

AVOCATIONAL INTERESTS: "My other interests include twentieth-century American poetry, music (especially Mozart's operas), travel, and collecting the works of such contemporary painters as Bevis Sale and Gaylord Treat Meech. I brew my own beer, but this should perhaps be regarded not so much as a hobby as a financial necessity."

BIOGRAPHICAL/CRITICAL SOURCES:

PERIODICALS

New York Times Book Review, December 2, 1984.
Times Literary Supplement, March 21, 1980, July 27, 1984.

*   *   *

FRANKLIN, Eugene
  See BANDY, (Eugene) Franklin

*   *   *

FREDERIC, Mike
  See COX, William (Robert)

*   *   *

FREDRICKSON, George M(arsh) 1934-

PERSONAL: Born July 16, 1934, in Bristol, Conn.; son of George (a merchant) and Gertrude (Marsh) Fredrickson; married Helene Osouf, October 16, 1956; children: Anne Hope, Laurel, Thomas, Caroline. *Education:* Harvard University, B.A., 1956, Ph.D., 1964; University of Oslo, graduate study, 1956-57.

ADDRESSES: Home—741 Esplanada Way, Stanford, Calif. 94305. *Office*—Department of History, Stanford University, Stanford, Calif. 94305.

CAREER: Harvard University, Cambridge, Mass., instructor in history, 1963-66; Northwestern University, Evanston, Ill., associate professor, 1966-71, professor of history, 1971-84, William Smith Mason Professor of American History, 1979-84; Stanford University, Stanford, Calif., Edgar E. Robinson Professor of United States History, 1984—. *Military service:* U.S. Navy, 1957-60; became lieutenant junior grade.

MEMBER: American Academy of Arts and Sciences, American Antiquarian Association, American Historical Association, Organization of American Historians, Southern Historical Society.

AWARDS, HONORS: Anisfield-Wolf Award in race relations, 1972, for *The Black Image in the White Mind: The Debate on Afro-American Character and Destiny;* Ralph Waldo Emerson Award from Phi Beta Kappa, 1981, and Avery Craven prize from Organization of American Historians, 1982, both for *White Supremacy: A Comparative Study in American and South African History.*

WRITINGS:

The Inner Civil War: Northern Intellectuals and the Crisis of the Union, Harper, 1965.

(Editor) Albion Tourgee, *A Fool's Errand,* Torchbooks, 1966.
(Editor) Hinton R. Halper, *The Impending Crisis of the South,* Harvard University Press, 1968.
(Editor) *William Lloyd Garrison,* Prentice-Hall, 1968.
The Black Image in the White Mind: The Debate on Afro-American Character and Destiny, Harper, 1971, reprinted, Wesleyan University Press, 1987.
(Contributor) Huggins, Kilson, and Fox, editors, *Key Issues in the Afro-American Experience,* Harcourt, 1971.
(Editor) *A Nation Divided: Problems and Issues of the Civil War and Reconstruction,* Burgess, 1975.
White Supremacy: A Comparative Study in American and South African History, Oxford University Press, 1981.
(With Robert A. Divine and others) *America: Past and Present,* Scott, Foresman, 1984.

Contributor to *American Historical Review, Journal of Southern History, Civil War History, New York Review of Books,* and other periodicals.

WORK IN PROGRESS: A book on the transformation of American society, 1865-1900; a comparative study of black movements and ideologies in the United States and South Africa.

SIDELIGHTS: In *White Supremacy: A Comparative Study in American and South African History,* his history of race relations in the United States and South Africa, George M. Fredrickson systematically analyzes the similarities and differences between the two countries. Although *New York Times Book Review* critic David Brion Davis believes that such a comparison "evokes resistance," Robert Dawidoff of the *Los Angeles Times Book Review* suggests that "*White Supremacy* illustrates how clarifying and absorbing and how challenging comparative history can be. [Fredrickson] has written about white European domination of native and imported, slave and otherwise, unfree nonwhite people in South Africa and the United States." And, in doing so, says *Washington Post Book World* writer Jim Hoagland, Fredrickson "deftly picks apart the tangled threads of two brands of white power and traces them back to their sources."

In both countries, white supremacy began in the 1600s with the subjugation of natives who were not black and, in both cases, reactions to these native groups were preceded by "rehearsals" elsewhere on the part of the parent nations. "In England," explains C. Vann Woodward in the *New York Review of Books,* "the brutal subjugation of the 'Wild Irish' . . . was such a rehearsal. At the same time the Dutch commercially exploited the East Indies with the milder motives of trade, without the need for expropriation of the land or extermination of the natives. The English repeated their experience in colonizing America, treating the Indians as they had the 'Wild Irish.' The Dutch repeated theirs at the Cape of Good Hope." Neither the English nor the Dutch considered the indigenous populations their social or intellectual equals, and both groups found the natives unsuitable as sources of cheap labor or slaves.

Both societies solved their labor problems by importing slaves: Americans from West Africa, Cape colonists from East Africa, Madagascar, and the East Indies. Kathryn Marshall in *Commonweal* says, "Fredrickson points out that the institution of racial slavery was intimately linked to tensions within the white social order, with the dehumanization of blacks creating a basis for inter-class unity among whites," an important consideration when dealing with the chaos of a frontier society. Eventually both slave societies developed an ideology of what

Fredrickson calls "*Herrenvolk* democracy"—or as Woodward explains it, "the equality of all white males—to justify white supremacy, and each developed its own style of patriarchalism."

Despite these and other similarities, there were also important differences in the way the countries developed. The descendants of the Dutch settlers, for instance, were primarily herdsmen, while the white Americans were farmers who wanted to clear, cultivate and claim title to the land. Responsive to the demands of its citizens, the American government committed itself to the spread of "civilization" and did little to protect helpless minorities. According to *New York Times Book Review* critic Davis, "these distinctive conditions of American settlement and expansion, when compared with those of South Africa, led at first to a more ruthless dispossession of the indigenes, to a more thoroughgoing commitment to Negro slavery and to a much earlier insistence on a rigid and impermeable color line." On the other hand, writes *Washington Post Book World* reviewer Hoagland, "South Africans will also have to register Fredrickson's conclusions that for all its imperfections and fitful halts, the United States has since the

Civil War worked hard at eliminating the legalized 'dominative racism' while a new central government in South Africa has moved in exactly the opposite direction, with disastrous results."

Despite the temptation to moralize, Fredrickson restrains himself "and thereby fuels the reader's thinking on the issues he raises," *Los Angeles Times Book Review* critic Dawidoff says. "Without saying what should or will happen, he does show what can happen here, because it did. He also suggests . . . that it might all have been different and therefore may yet be."

BIOGRAPHICAL/CRITICAL SOURCES:

PERIODICALS

Chicago Tribune Book World, April 5, 1981.
Commonweal, June 5, 1981.
Los Angeles Times Book Review, March 29, 1981.
New York Review of Books, March 5, 1981.
New York Times Book Review, January 25, 1981.
Washington Post Book World, March 1, 1981.

G

GAEDEKE, Ralph M(ortimer)   1941-

PERSONAL: Born May 25, 1941, in East Prussia; son of Horst F. and Margot (Boltz) Gaedeke; married Johanna V. House (an administrative assistant), June 19, 1965; children: Jolene R., Michael C. *Education:* University of Washington, Seattle, B.A., 1964, M.A., 1965, Ph.D., 1969.

ADDRESSES: Home—237 Hartnell Pl., Sacramento, Calif. 95825; and P.O. Box 46, Anchor Point, Alaska 99556 (summer address). *Office*—School of Business and Public Administration, California State University at Sacramento, 6000 J St., Sacramento, Calif. 95819.

CAREER: University of Saskatchewan, Saskatoon, Canada, instructor in business administration, 1965-66; University of Washington, Seattle, instructor, 1967-69; California State University, Sacramento, associate professor of marketing and international business, 1969-71; University of Alaska, Anchorage, associate professor of business administration, 1971-73; California State University, Sacramento, associate professor, 1973-74, professor of marketing and international business, 1974—. Summer professor at University of Alaska, 1974. Consultant to Small Business Administration and private corporations in Anchorage, 1971-72 and 1974-75, and Sacramento, 1974—; consultant to Community Economic Development Corp., Anchorage, 1974-75. Also consultant to various savings and loan associations, Campbell-Hausfeld, and Detwiler Corporation.

MEMBER: Academy of International Business, American Marketing Association (president, Sacramento Valley Chapter, 1974-75), Beta Gamma Sigma, Delta Sigma Pi.

WRITINGS:

(With Guy Gordon, John Wheatley, John Hallag, and D. McNabb) *The Impact of a Consumer Credit Limitation Law—Washington State: Initiative 245* (monograph), University of Washington Press, 1970.
(With Warren W. Etcheson) *Consumerism: Viewpoints from Business, Government and the Consumer Interest,* Canfield Press, 1972.
(With Dean F. Olson and Jack W. Peterson) *A Study of the Impact of Ten Rural Consumer Cooperative Stores* (monograph), Office of Economic Opportunity, 1973.

(With Eugene Eaton) *Dimensions of Relevant Markets: The Case of Urethane Building Insulation in Alaska* (monograph), Upjohn, 1975.
Village Development Alternatives for Old Chitina (monograph), AHTNA Regional Corp., 1975.
(Editor) *Marketing in Private and Public Nonprofit Organizations: Perspectives and Illustrations,* Goodyear Publishing, 1977.
(With Dennis H. Tootelian) *Small Business Management: Operations and Profiles,* Goodyear Publishing, 1978, 2nd edition, Scott, Foresman, 1984.
(Editor, with Tootelian) *Marketing Management,* Scott, Foresman, 1979.
(With Tootelian) *Small Business Management,* Goodyear Publishing, 1980, 2nd edition, Scott, Foresman, 1984.
(With Tootelian and Leete A. Thompson) *Marketing Management: Cases and Readings,* Goodyear Publishing, 1980, 2nd edition, Scott, Foresman, 1984.
(With Tootelian) *Marketing: Principles and Applications,* West Publishing, 1983.
U.S. Trade with the People's Republic of China with Special Emphasis on Trade Flowing through the San Francisco Customs District, CSUS, 1985.
(With Tootelian) *Cases and Classics in Marketing,* Harcourt, 1986.
(Contributor) Hale N. Tongren and Richard Hise, editors, *Business Research: Marketing,* Research Publishing, 1986.

Also contributor to *Encyclopedia of Professional Management,* 1979, and American Institute for Decision Sciences *Proceedings and Abstracts,* 1979, 1980. Contributor of book reviews and articles to professional journals.

*   *   *

GAINES, Ernest J(ames)   1933-

PERSONAL: Born January 15, 1933, in Oscar, La. (some sources cite River Lake Plantation, near New Roads, Pointe Coupee Parish, La.); son of Manuel (a laborer) and Adrienne J. (Colar) Gaines. *Education:* Attended Vallejo Junior College; San Francisco State College (now University), B.A., 1957; graduate study at Stanford University, 1958-59.

ADDRESSES: Office—Department of English, University of Southwestern Louisiana, East University Ave., Lafayette, La.

70504. *Agent*—JCA Literary Agency, Inc., 242 West 27th St., New York, N.Y. 10001.

CAREER: "Writing, five hours a day, five days a week." Denison University, Granville, Ohio, writer in residence, 1971; Stanford University, Stanford, Calif., writer in residence, 1981; University of Southwestern Louisiana, Lafayette, professor of English and writer in residence, 1983—. Whittier College, visiting professor, 1983, and writer in residence, 1986. *Military service:* U.S. Army, 1953-55.

AWARDS, HONORS: Wallace Stegner Fellow, Stanford University, 1957; Joseph Henry Jackson Award, San Francisco Foundation, 1959, for "Comeback" (short story); award from National Endowment for the Arts, 1967; Rockefeller grant, 1970; Guggenheim fellowship, 1971; award from Black Academy of Arts and Letters, 1972; fiction gold medal, Commonwealth Club of California, 1972, for *The Autobiography of Miss Jane Pittman*, and 1984, for *A Gathering of Old Men;* award from Louisiana Library Association, 1972; honorary doctorate of letters, Denison University, 1980, Brown University, 1985, Bard College, 1985, and Louisiana State University, 1987; award for excellence of achievement in literature, San Francisco Arts Commission, 1983; D.H.L., Whittier College, 1986; literary award from American Academy and Institute of Arts and Letters, 1987.

WRITINGS:

FICTION

Catherine Carmier (novel), Atheneum, 1964.
Of Love and Dust (novel), Dial, 1967.
Bloodline (short stories; also see below), Dial, 1968.
A Long Day in November (story originally published in *Bloodline*), Dial, 1971.
The Autobiography of Miss Jane Pittman (novel), Dial, 1971.
In My Father's House (novel), Knopf, 1978.
A Gathering of Old Men (novel), Knopf, 1983.

Contributor of stories to anthologies and periodicals.

SIDELIGHTS: The fiction of Ernest J. Gaines, including his 1971 novel *The Autobiography of Miss Jane Pittman*, is deeply rooted in the black culture and storytelling traditions of rural Louisiana where the author was born and raised. His stories have been noted for their convincing characters and powerful themes presented within authentic—often folk-like—narratives that tap into the complex world of Southern rural life. Gaines depicts the strength and dignity of his black characters in the face of numerous struggles: the dehumanizing and destructive effects of racism; the breakdown in personal relationships as a result of social pressures; the choice between secured traditions and the sometimes radical measures necessary to bring about social change. Although the issues presented in Gaines's fiction are serious and often disturbing, "this is not hot-and-breathless, burn-baby-burn writing," Melvin Maddocks points out in *Time;* rather, it is the work of "a patient artist, a patient man." Expounding on Gaines's rural heritage, Maddocks continues: "[Gaines] sets down a story as if he were planting, spreading the roots deep, wide and firm. His stories grow organically, at their own rhythm. When they ripen at last, they do so inevitably, arriving at a climax with the absolute rightness of a folk tale." Larry McMurtry in the *New York Times Book Review* adds that as "a swimmer cannot influence the flow of a river, . . . the characters of Ernest Gaines . . . are propelled by a prose that is serene, considered and unexcited." Jerry H. Bryant in the *Iowa Review* writes that Gaines's fiction "contains the austere dignity and sim-

plicity of ancient epic, a concern with man's most powerful emotions and the actions that arise from those emotions, and an artistic intuition that carefully keeps such passions and behavior under fictive control. Gaines may be one of our most naturally gifted story-tellers."

Gaines's boyhood experiences growing up on a Louisiana plantation provide many of the impressions upon which his stories are based. Particularly important, he told Paul Disruisseaux in the *New York Times Book Review*, were "working in the fields, going fishing in the swamps with the older people, and, especially, listening to the people who came to my aunt's house, the aunt who raised me." Although Gaines moved to California at the age of fifteen and subsequently went to college there, his fiction has been based in an imaginary Louisiana plantation region named Bayonne, which a number of critics have compared to William Faulkner's Yoknapatawpha County. Gaines has acknowledged looking to Faulkner, in addition to Ernest Hemingway, for language and to French writers such as Gustave Flaubert and Guy de Maupassant for style. A perhaps greater influence, however, has been 19th-century Russian authors. In a profile by Beverly Beyette for the *Los Angeles Times*, Gaines explains that reading the works of authors such as Nikolai Gogol, Ivan Turgenev, and Anton Chekhov helped unlock the significance of his rural past. "I found something that I had not truly found in American writers," he told Beyette. "They [the Russian writers] dealt with peasantry differently. . . . I did not particularly find what I was looking for in the Southern writers. When they came to describing my own people, they did not do it the way that I knew my people to be. The Russians were not talking about my people, but about a peasantry for which they seemed to show such feeling. Reading them, I could find a way to write about my own people." That Gaines knew a different South from the one he read about in books also provided an incentive to write. "If the book you want doesn't exist, you try to make it exist," he told Joseph McLellan in the *Washington Post*. Gaines later told Beyette: "That's the book that influenced me most. . . . I tried to put it there on that shelf, and I'm still trying to do that."

Gaines's first novel, *Catherine Carmier,* is "an apprentice work more interesting for what it anticipates than for its accomplishments," notes William E. Grant in the *Dictionary of Literary Biography*. The novel chronicles the story of a young black man, Jackson Bradley, who returns to Bayonne after completing his education in California. Jackson falls in love with Catherine, the daughter of a Creole sharecropper who refuses to let members of his family associate with anyone darker than themselves, believing Creoles racially and socially superior. The novel portrays numerous clashes of loyalty: Catherine torn between her love for Jackson and love for her father; Jackson caught between a bond to the community he grew up in and the experience and knowledge he has gained in the outside world. "Both Catherine and Jackson are immobilized by the pressures of [the] rural community," writes Keith E. Byermann in the *Dictionary of Literary Biography*, which produces "twin themes of isolation and paralysis [that] give the novel an existential quality. Characters must face an unfriendly world without guidance and must make crucial choices about their lives." The characters in *Catherine Carmier*—as in much of Gaines's fiction—are faced with struggles that test the conviction of personal beliefs. Winifred L. Stoelting in *CLA Journal* explains that Gaines is concerned more "with how they [his characters] handle their decisions than with the rightness of their decisions—more often than not predetermined by social changes over which the single individual has little control.''

Gaines sets *Catherine Carmier* in the time of the Civil Rights movement, yet avoids making it a primary force in the novel. Grant comments on this aspect: ''In divorcing his tale from contemporary events, Gaines declares his independence from the political and social purposes of much contemporary black writing. Instead, he elects to concentrate upon those fundamental human passions and conflicts which transcend the merely social level of human existence.'' Grant finds Gaines ''admirable'' for doing this, yet also believes Jackson's credibility marred because he remains aloof from contemporary events. For Grant, the novel ''seems to float outside time and place rather than being solidly anchored in the real world of the modern South.'' Byerman concurs, stating that the novel ''is not entirely successful in presenting its major characters and their motivations.'' Nonetheless, he points out that in *Catherine Carmier*, ''Gaines does begin to create a sense of the black community and its perceptions of the world around it. Shared ways of speaking, thinking, and relating to the dominant white society are shown through a number of minor characters.''

Gaines's next novel, *Of Love and Dust,* is also a story of forbidden romance, and, as in *Catherine Carmier,* a ''new world of expanding human relationships erodes the old world of love for the land and the acceptance of social and economic stratification,'' writes Stoelting. *Of Love and Dust* is the story of Marcus Payne, a young black man bonded out of prison by a white landowner and placed under the supervision of a Cajun overseer, Sidney Bonbon. Possessed of a rebellious and hostile nature, Marcus is a threat to Bonbon, who in turn does all that he can to break the young man's spirit. In an effort to strike back, Marcus pays special attention to the overseer's wife; the two fall in love and plot to run away. The novel ends with a violent confrontation between the two men, in which Marcus is killed. After the killing, Bonbon claims that to spare Marcus would have meant his own death at the hands of other Cajuns. Grant notes a similarity between *Of Love and Dust* and *Catherine Carmier* in that the characters are ''caught up in a decadent social and economic system that determines their every action and limits their possibilities.'' Similarly, the two novels are marked by a ''social determinism [which] shapes the lives of all the characters, making them pawns in a mechanistic world order rather than free agents.''

Of Love and Dust demonstrates Gaines's development as a novelist, offering a clearer view of the themes and characters that dominate his later work. Stoelting writes that ''in a more contemporary setting, the novel . . . continues Gaines's search for human dignity, and when that is lacking, acknowledges the salvation of pride,'' adding that ''the characters themselves grow into a deeper awareness than those of [his] first novel. More sharply drawn . . . [they] are more decisive in their actions.'' Byerman writes that the novel ''more clearly condemns the economic, social, and racial system of the South for the problems faced by its characters.'' Likewise, the first-person narrator in the novel—a co-worker of Marcus—''both speaks in the idiom of the place and time and instinctively asserts the values of the black community.''

Gaines turns to a first-person narrator again in his next novel *The Autobiography of Miss Jane Pittman,* which many consider to be his masterwork. Miss Jane Pittman—well over one hundred years old—relates a personal history that spans the time from the Civil War and slavery up through the Civil

Rights movement of the 1960s. ''To travel with Miss Pittman from adolescence to old age is to embark upon a historic journey, one staked out in the format of the novel,'' writes Addison Gayle, Jr., in *The Way of the World: The Black Novel in America.* ''Never mind that Miss Jane Pittman is fictitious, and that her 'autobiography,' offered up in the form of taped reminiscences, is artifice,'' adds Josh Greenfield in *Life,* ''the effect is stunning.'' Gaines's gift for drawing convincing characters reaches a peak in *The Autobiography of Miss Jane Pittman.* ''His is not . . . an 'art' narrative, but an authentic narrative by an authentic ex-slave, authentic even though both are Gaines's inventions,'' Bryant comments. ''So successful is he in *becoming* Miss Jane Pittman, that when we talk about her story, we do not think of Gaines as her creator, but as her recording editor.''

The character of Jane Pittman could be called an embodiment of the black experience in America. ''Though Jane is the dominant personality of the narrative—observer and commentator upon history, as well as participant—in her odyssey is symbolized the odyssey of a race of people; through her eyes is revealed the grandeur of a people's journey through history,'' writes Gayle. ''The central metaphor of the novel concerns this journey: Jane and her people, as they come together in the historic march toward dignity and freedom in Sampson, symbolize a people's march through history, breaking old patterns, though sometimes slowly, as they do.'' The important historical backdrop to Jane's narrative—slavery, Reconstruction, the Civil Rights movement, segregation—does not compromise, however, the detailed account of an individual. ''Jane captures the experiences of those millions of illiterate blacks who never had a chance to tell their own stories,'' Byerman explains. ''By focusing on the particular yet typical events of a small part of Louisiana, those lives are given a concreteness and specificity not possible in more general histories.''

In his fourth novel, *In My Father's House,* Gaines focuses on a theme which appears in varying degrees throughout his fiction: the alienation between fathers and sons. As the author told Desruisseaux: ''In my books there always seems to be fathers and sons searching for each other. That's a theme I've worked with since I started writing. Even when the father was not in the story. I've dealt with his absence and its effects on his children. And that is the theme of this book.'' *In My Father's House* tells of a prominent civil rights leader and reverend (Phillip Martin) who, at the peak of his career, is confronted with a troubled young man named Robert X. Although Robert's identity is initially a mystery, eventually he is revealed to be one of three offspring from a love affair the reverend had in an earlier, wilder life. Martin hasn't seen or attempted to locate his family for more than twenty years. Robert arrives to confront and kill the father whose neglect he sees as responsible for the family's disintegration: his sister has been raped, his brother imprisoned for the murder of her attacker, and his mother reduced to poverty, living alone. Although the son's intent to kill his father is never carried out, the reverend is forced ''to undergo a long and painful odyssey through his own past and the labyrinthine streets of Baton Rouge to learn what really happened to his first family,'' writes William Burke in the *Dictionary of Literary Biography Yearbook.* McMurtry notes that as the book traces the lost family, ''we have revealed to us an individual, a marriage, a community and a region, but with such an unobtrusive marshaling of detail that we never lose sight of the book's central thematic concern: the profoundly destructive consequences of the breakdown of parentage, of a father's abandonment of his children and the terrible and irrevocable consequences of such an abandonment.''

Burke writes that *In My Father's House* presents the particular problem of manhood for the black male, which he notes as a recurring theme in Gaines's fiction: ''Phillip Martin's failure to keep his first family whole, to honor his and [his companion's] love by marriage, and the dissipation of the first half of his adult life—these unfortunate events are clearly a consequence of Martin's fear of accepting the responsibilities of black manhood.'' Burke highlights the accumulated effects of racism on black males, and cites Gaines's comments to Desruisseaux: ''You must understand that the blacks who were brought here as slaves were prevented from becoming the men that they could be. . . . A *man* can speak up, he can do things to protect himself, his home and his family, but the slaves could never do that. If the white said the slave was wrong, he was wrong. . . . So eventually the blacks started stepping over the line, [saying] 'Damn what *you* think I'm supposed to be— I will be what I ought to be. And if I must die to do it, I'll die'. . . . Quite a few of my characters step over that line.''

A Gathering of Old Men, Gaines's most recent novel, presents a cast of aging Southern black men who, after a life of subordination and intimidation, make a defiant stand against injustice. Seventeen of them, together with the 30-year-old white heiress of a deteriorating Louisiana plantation, plead guilty to murdering a hostile member (Beau Boutan) of a violent Cajun clan. While a confounded sheriff and vengeful family wait to lynch the black they've decided is guilty, the group members—toting recently fired shotguns—surround the dead man and ''confess'' their motives. ''Each man tells of the accumulated frustrations of his life—raped daughters, jailed sons, public insults, economic exploitation—that serve as sufficient motive for murder,'' writes Byerman. ''Though Beau Boutan is seldom the immediate cause of their anger, he clearly represents the entire white world that has deprived them of their dignity and manhood. The confessions serve as ritual purgings of all the hostility and self-hatred built up over the years.'' Fifteen or so characters—white, black, and Cajun—advance the story through individual narrations, creating ''thereby a range of social values as well as different perspectives on the action,'' notes Byerman. Reynolds Price writes in the *New York Times Book Review* that the black narrators ''are nicely distinguished from one another in rhythm and idiom, in the nature of what they see and report, especially in their specific laments for past passivity in the face of suffering.'' The accumulated effect, observes Elaine Kendall in the *Los Angeles Times Book Review,* is that the ''individual stories coalesce into a single powerful tale of subjugation, exploitation and humiliation at the hands of landowners.'' Price comments that although ''some of them, especially at the beginning, are a little long-winded and repetitive, in the manner of country preachers[,] . . . a patient reader will sense the power of their stories through their dead-level voices, which speak not from the heart of a present fear but from lifetimes of humiliation and social impotence. They are choosing now to take a stand, on ground where they've yielded for centuries—ground that is valuable chiefly through their incessant labor.''

Another theme of *A Gathering of Old Men,* according to Ben Forkner in *America,* is ''the simple, natural dispossession of old age, of the traditional and well-loved values of the past, the old trades and the old manners, forced to give way to modern times.'' Sam Cornish writes in the *Christian Science Monitor* that the novel's ''characters—both black and white— understand that, before the close of the novel, the new South

must confront the old, and all will be irrevocably changed. Gaines portrays a society that will be altered by the deaths of its 'old men,' and so presents an allegory about the passing of the old and birth of the new.''

Alice Walker writes in the *New York Times Book Review* that Gaines ''claims and revels in the rich heritage of Southern Black people and their customs; the community he feels with them is unmistakable and goes deeper even than pride. . . . Gaines is mellow with historical reflection, supple with wit, relaxed and expansive because he does not equate his people with failure.'' Gaines has been criticized by some, however, who feel his writing does not more directly focus on problems facing blacks. Gaines responds to Desruissaux that he feels ''too many blacks have been writing to tell whites all about 'the problems,' instead of writing something that all people, including their own, could find interesting, could enjoy.'' Gaines has also remarked that more can be achieved than strictly writing novels of protest. In an interview for *San Francisco,* the author states: ''So many of our writers have not read any farther back than [Richard Wright's] *Native Son.* So many of our novels deal only with the great city ghettos; that's all we write about, as if there's nothing else.'' Gaines continues: ''We've only been living in these ghettos for 75 years or so, but the other 300 years—I think this is worth writing about.''

MEDIA ADAPTATIONS: ''The Autobiography of Miss Jane Pittman,'' adapted from Gaines's novel, aired on the Columbia Broadcasting System (CBS-TV), January 31, 1974, starring Cicely Tyson in the title role; the special won nine Emmy Awards. ''The Sky is Gray,'' a short story originally published in *Bloodline,* was adapted for public television in 1980. ''A Gathering of Old Men,'' adapted from Gaines's novel, aired on CBS-TV, May 10, 1987, starring Lou Gossett, Jr., and Richard Widmark.

BIOGRAPHICAL/CRITICAL SOURCES:

BOOKS

Authors in the News, Volume I, Gale, 1976.
Bruck, Peter, editor, *The Black American Short Story in the Twentieth Century: A Collection of Critical Essays,* B. R. Gruner (Amsterdam), 1977.
Contemporary Literary Criticism, Gale, Volume 3, 1975, Volume 11, 1979, Volume 18, 1981.
Dictionary of Literary Biography, Gale, Volume 2: *American Novelists since World War II,* 1978, Volume 33: *Afro-American Fiction Writers after 1955,* 1984.
Dictionary of Literary Biography Yearbook: 1980, Gale, 1981.
Gayle, Addison, Jr., *The Way of the New World: The Black Novel in America,* Doubleday, 1975.
Hicks, Jack, *In the Singer's Temple: Prose Fictions of Barthelme, Gaines, Brautigan, Piercy, Kesey, and Kosinski,* University of North Carolina Press, 1981.
O'Brien, John, editor, *Interview with Black Writers,* Liveright, 1973.

PERIODICALS

America, June 2, 1984.
Black American Literature Forum, Volume XI, 1977
Chicago Tribune Book World, October 30, 1983.
Christian Science Monitor, December 2, 1983.
CLA Journal, March, 1971, December, 1975.
Iowa Review, winter, 1972.
Life, April 30, 1971.
Los Angeles Times, March 2, 1983.
Los Angeles Times Book Review, January 1, 1984.

Nation, February 5, 1968, April 5, 1971, January 14, 1984.
Negro Digest, November, 1967, January, 1968, January, 1969.
New Orleans Review, Volume I, 1969, Volume III, 1972.
New Republic, December 26, 1983.
New Statesman, September 2, 1973, February 10, 1984.
Newsweek, June 16, 1969, May 3, 1971.
New Yorker, October 24, 1983.
New York Times, July 20, 1978.
New York Times Book Review, November 19, 1967, May 23, 1971, June 11, 1978, October 30, 1983.
Observer, February 5, 1984.
San Francisco, July, 1974.
Southern Review, Volume X, 1974.
Studies in Short Fiction, summer, 1975.
Time, May 10, 1971, December 27, 1971.
Times Literary Supplement, February 10, 1966, March 16, 1973, April 6, 1984.
Voice Literary Supplement, October, 1983.
Washington Post, January 13, 1976.
Washington Post Book World, June 18, 1978, September 21, 1983.

—*Sketch by Michael E. Mueller*

*   *   *

GALAND, Rene 1923-
(Reun ar C'halan)

PERSONAL: Born January 27, 1923, in Chateauneuf-du-Faou, France; came to United States in 1947, naturalized citizen, 1953; son of Pierre and Anna (Nedelec) Galand; married France Texier, December 23, 1959; children: Joel, Caroline. *Education:* Universite de Rennes, Licence es Lettres, 1944; Yale University, Ph.D., 1952.

ADDRESSES: Home—8 Leighton Rd., Wellesley, Mass. 02181. *Office*—Department of French, Wellesley College, Wellesley, Mass. 02181.

CAREER: Yale University, New Haven, Conn., instructor in French, 1949-51; Wellesley College, Wellesley, Mass., assistant professor, 1951-57, associate professor, 1958-63, professor of French, 1964—, head of department, 1969-72. *Military service:* French Army, 1944-46; became first lieutenant.

MEMBER: Modern Language Association of America, American Association of Teachers of French, Societe des Professeurs francais en Amerique.

AWARDS, HONORS: Decorated Chevalier Ordre des Palmes Academiques by the Republic of France, 1971; Xavier de Langlais Prize, 1979.

WRITINGS:

L'Ame celtique de Renan, Yale University Press, 1959.
Baudelaire: Poetiques et poesie, Nizet, 1969.
(Contributor) Lois Boe Hyslop, editor, *Baudelaire as a Love Poet and Other Essays*, Pennsylvania State University Press, 1969.
Saint-John Perse, Twayne, 1972.
(Contributor) George Stambolian and Elaine Marks, editors, *Homosexualities and French Literature*, Cornell University Press, 1979.
(Contributor) *The Binding of Proteus: Perspectives on Myth and the Literary Process*, Bucknell University Press, 1980.
(Contributor) *Critical Bibliography of French Literature*, Syracuse University Press, 1980.

UNDER NAME REUN AR C'HALAN; IN BRETON

Levr ar Blanedenn (poetry), Al Liamm, 1981.
(Contributor) *Du a Gwyn*, Lolfa Press, 1982.
(Contributor) *Danevellou*, Hor Yezh, 1985.
Klemmgan Breizh (poetry), Al Liamm, 1985.

OTHER

Contributor of reviews to *World Literature Today*, 1979—; also contributor to *Bulletin baudelairien, Collier's Year Book, French Review, PMLA, Romanic Review, Symposium*, and *Yale French Studies*. Contributor of articles, poems, and short stories under name Reun ar C'halan to numerous Breton language periodicals. Assistant editor of *French Review*, 1967-74.

WORK IN PROGRESS: Strategie de la lecture; contributions to *Princeton Encyclopedia of Poetry and Poetics.*

*   *   *

GALVIN, Brendan 1938-

PERSONAL: Born October 20, 1938, in Everett, Mass.; son of James Russell (a letter carrier) and Rose (McLaughlin) Galvin; married Ellen Baer, August 1, 1968; children: Kim, Peter, Anne Maura. *Education:* Boston College, B.S., 1961; Northwestern University, M.A., 1964; University of Massachusetts at Amherst, M.F.A., 1967, Ph.D., 1970.

ADDRESSES: Home—P.O. Box 54, Durham, Conn. 06422. *Office*—Department of English, Central Connecticut State University, Stanley St., New Britain, Conn. 06050.

CAREER: Northeastern University, Boston, Mass., instructor in English, 1963-65; Slippery Rock State College, Slippery Rock, Pa., assistant professor of English, 1968-69; Central Connecticut State University, New Britain, assistant professor, 1969-74, associate professor, 1974-80, professor of English, 1980—. Founder and director of Connecticut Writers Conference; visiting writer, Connecticut College, 1975-76; affiliated with Wesleyan-Suffield Writer-Reader Conference, 1977-1978, and Martha's Vineyard Poetry Seminar, 1986.

AWARDS, HONORS: Fine Arts Work Center fellowship, 1971; National Endowment for the Arts creative writing fellowship 1974; Artist Foundation fellowship, 1978; Connecticut Commission on the Arts fellowship, 1981, 1984.

WRITINGS:

POETRY

The Narrow Land, Northeastern University Press, 1971.
The Salt Farm, Fiddlehead, 1972.
No Time for Good Reasons, University of Pittsburgh Press, 1974.
The Minutes No One Owns, University of Pittsburgh Press, 1977.
Atlantic Flyway, University of Georgia Press, 1980.
Winter Oysters, University of Georgia Press, 1983.
A Birder's Dozen, Ampersand Press, 1984.
Seals in the Inner Harbor, Carnegie-Mellon University Press, 1985.

OTHER

"Massachusetts Story" (documentary filmscript), produced by Gordon Massingham, 1978.

Contributor to numerous periodicals, including *American Review, Atlantic, Connecticut English Journal, Harper's, Hud-*

son Review, Massachusetts Studies in English, New Yorker, Ploughshares, Poetry, and Sewanee Review. Editor with George Garrett of *Poultry: A Magazine of Voice*, 1981—.

WORK IN PROGRESS: New and Selected Poems; Senjekontucket Traveler.

SIDELIGHTS: Brendan Galvin once wrote: "I grew up on Cape Cod and in a suburb of Boston, and these two poles have affected my work strongly, in that my poems are full of imagery from the sea, the land, austere and muted, of the outer Cape, and the urban blight that infects humans who come in contact with it, especially through their work, most of which is unfulfilling and worthless." George Garrett remarks in the *Dictionary of Literary Biography* that "whether he is being serious or funny, or, as is usual, a combination of both, it appears that Galvin is facing up to the desperate elements in nature as well as in social and private situations; he is working out crucial events with strokes both bold and delicate."

BIOGRAPHICAL/CRITICAL SOURCES:

BOOKS

Critical Survey of Poetry, Salem Press, 1982.
Dictionary of Literary Biography, Volume V: *American Poets since World War II*, Gale, 1980.

PERIODICALS

American Book Review, January-February, 1982.
American Poetry Review, January-February, 1979.
Hudson Review, spring, 1981.
Pembroke Magazine, spring, 1988.
Ploughshares, Volume IV, 1978.
Poetry, June, 1977.
Tar River Poetry, fall, 1987.
Texas Review, spring, 1988.
Three Rivers Poetry Journal, Volumes 19-20, 1982.

*   *   *

GIBLIN, James Cross   1933-

PERSONAL: Surname is pronounced with a hard "g"; born July 8, 1933, in Cleveland, Ohio; son of Edward Kelley (a lawyer) and Anna (a teacher; maiden name, Cross) Giblin. *Education:* Western Reserve University (now Case Western Reserve University), B.A., 1954; Columbia University, M.F.A., 1955.

ADDRESSES: Home—200 East 24th St., Apt. 1410, New York, N.Y. 10010. *Office*—Clarion Books, 52 Vanderbilt Ave., New York, N.Y. 10017.

CAREER: Criterion Books, Inc. New York City, assistant editor, 1959-62; Lothrop, Lee & Shepard Co., New York City, associate editor, 1962-65, editor, 1965-67; Seabury Press, Inc., New York City, editor-in-chief of Clarion Books (for children), 1967-79, vice-president, 1975-79; Ticknor & Fields, New York City, editor and publisher of Clarion Books, 1979—.

MEMBER: Society of Children's Book Writers (member of board of directors), Authors Guild, Authors League of America, Children's Book Council (president, 1976), Children's Reading Round Table of Chicago.

AWARDS, HONORS: Golden Kite Award for nonfiction, 1982, and American Book Award for children's nonfiction, 1983, both for *Chimney Sweeps: Yesterday and Today;* Golden Kite Award for nonfiction, 1984, for *Walls: Defenses throughout*

History; Boston Globe-Horn Book Award Nonfiction Honor Book, 1986, for *The Truth about Santa Claus;* American Library Association notable children's books include *The Scarecrow Book*, 1980, *The Skyscraper Book*, 1981, *Chimney Sweeps: Yesterday and Today*, 1982, *The Truth about Santa Claus*, 1985, and *Milk: The Fight for Purity*, 1986.

WRITINGS:

CHILDREN'S BOOKS

(With Dale Ferguson) *The Scarecrow Book*, Crown, 1980.
The Skyscraper Book, illustrated by Anthony Kramer, photographs by David Anderson, Crowell, 1981.
Chimney Sweeps: Yesterday and Today (nonfiction), illustrated by Margot Tomes, Crowell, 1982.
Fireworks, Picnics, and Flags: The Story of the Fourth of July Symbols (Junior Literary Guild Selection), illustrated by Ursula Arndt, Clarion Books, 1983.
Walls: Defenses throughout History (nonfiction), Little, Brown, 1984.
The Truth about Santa Claus (nonfiction), Crowell, 1985.
Milk: The Fight for Purity (nonfiction), Crowell, 1986.
From Hand to Mouth; or, How We Invented Knives, Forks, Spoons, and Chopsticks and the Table Manners to Go with Them (nonfiction), Crowell, 1987.
Let There Be Light: A Book about Windows (nonfiction), Crowell, 1988.
The Truth about Unicorns, Crowell, in press.

OTHER

My Bus Is Always Late (adult; one-act play; first produced in Cleveland, Ohio, at Western Reserve University, December 14, 1953), Dramatic Publishing, 1955.

Contributor to magazines, including *Writer's Digest, Cricket, School Library Journal, Horn Book, Writer, Highlights for Children*, and *Publishers Weekly*. Member of editorial board of *Children's Literature in Education*.

SIDELIGHTS: A noted editor and author of children's books, James Cross Giblin has spent nearly thirty years working in a field that he believes, as Wendy Smith quotes him in *Publishers Weekly*, has "a special responsibility to offer the best [it] can to a child." Since 1967 Giblin has worked as editor-in-chief of Clarion Books, where he has edited many respected children's authors, including Paul Galdone, Lila Perl, and Dick Gachenback. One of the main reasons Giblin works with children's books is that "they make a special impact on readers," he explains to Smith. "Kids don't have that much to remember yet; if a book does make an impression, it can be a lasting one."

As the author of children's books, Giblin has been praised for his interesting factual-based accounts, including the award-winning *Chimney Sweeps: Yesterday and Today*, which Ann Sperber in the *New York Times Book Review* calls a "compactly entertaining little history." Regarding his writing, Giblin told *CA:* "When I speak before an audience of librarians, teachers, or young readers, I'm invariably asked where I get the ideas for my books, and I reply, 'From anywhere and everywhere,' because that's the way it seems to happen. The trick is to recognize a good idea when it comes along. For example, I got the idea for *Chimney Sweeps* when I was flying to Oklahoma City to give a lecture and sat next to a long-haired young man who turned out to be a chimney sweep. I thought his work sounded fascinating, and decided to research the history of chimney sweeps when I returned to New York."

Giblin added: "Researching a new book is great fun for me. I love going to libraries in New York and Washington, making up bibliographies, and searching for unusual anecdotes, complete with authentic dialogue, that will bring a person or event to life. I keep my eye out especially for actual happenings that will move a reader, or even better, make him laugh. For too long, children's nonfiction had a reputation of being dull and boring; I want to dispel that impression if I can."

BIOGRAPHICAL/CRITICAL SOURCES:

PERIODICALS

New York Times Book Review, November 21, 1982.
Publishers Weekly, July 26, 1985.
Washington Post Book World, February 14, 1988.

*   *   *

GIDLEY, Charles
    See WHEELER, (Charles) Gidley

*   *   *

GIFFORD, Griselda   1931-
    (Mary Macdonald)

PERSONAL: Born May 26, 1931, in Monte Carlo, Monaco; daughter of James A. and Jill (Denton) Willoughby; married Paul Julian David Gifford (a sales executive), March 18, 1955 (divorced, 1987); children: Mark Richard, Nicola Jane. *Education:* Attended schools in England. *Politics:* Conservative. *Religion:* Anglican.

ADDRESSES: Home—3 Edwin Close, Bow Brickhill, Milton Keynes MK17 9JX, England. *Agent*—Watson, Little Ltd., Suite 8, 26 Charing Cross Rd., London WC2H 0DG, England.

CAREER: Writer. Has worked as a secretary for various British businesses and organizations, including the Foreign Office, London, 1950-53, the Festival of Britain, 1951, A. M. Heath & Co. Ltd., London, 1955, and Constable & Co. Adult education teacher of writing for children, 1980—.

MEMBER: Amnesty International, International PEN.

WRITINGS:

FOR CHILDREN

The Youngest Taylor, illustrations by Victor Ambrus, Bodley Head, 1963.
Ben's Expedition, illustrations by Robert Micklewright, Bodley Head, 1964.
The Story of Ranald (historical novel), illustrations by Edward Gage, Bodley Head, 1968, paperback edition, Canongate Publishing, 1985.
Jenny and the Sheep Thieves, illustrations by Carol Lawson, Gollancz, 1975.
(With Helen Clare) *Mystery of the Wooden Legs*, Bodley Head, 1975.
Mirabelle's Secret, illustrations by Jael Jordon, Gollancz, 1976.
Because of Blunder, illustrations by Mary Rayner, Gollancz, 1977.
Cass the Brave, illustrations by Rayner, Gollancz, 1978.
The Rescue, Longman, 1980.
Silver's Day, illustrations by Rayner, Gollancz, 1980.
Earwig and Beetle, Gollancz, 1981.
The Magic Mitre, Hamish Hamilton, 1982.
Pete and the Doodle-Bug, Macmillan, 1983.

Too Many Grains, Macmillan, 1987.
Miranda's Monster (picture book), illustrations by Alicia Garcia de Lynam, Hodder & Stoughton, 1987.

OTHER

Contributor of adult fiction to magazines under pseudonym Mary Macdonald.

WORK IN PROGRESS: An adult novel.

SIDELIGHTS: Griselda Gifford explained the elements which have influenced her children's books: "I had always wanted to write, and when the British Broadcasting Corporation aired my short stories seventeen years ago, I was encouraged to write my first book for children. This was based on my mother's family, but I brought it up-to-date. Many of my ideas have come from experience; from meeting an old lady, for instance, who kept a herd of sheep and knew them all by name or from the legends about a fig tree that grew against a small Cornish church.

"I suppose being an only child is often a little lonely, so most of my stories are about families, except for one in which a mother and daughter live in a basement flat, just as I once did, and my novel *Earwig and Beetle*, about a boy whose parents divorce. I am more interested in my characters than in the plot, although, of course, this is obviously important. In *Cass the Brave* I wondered what it would be like to be an identical twin and yet want to assert oneself as an individual.

"I think girls can be leaders just as well as boys, so several of my stories have girl heroines. I am a struggling Christian, and I feel that right and wrong and the joy of life should be shown in books, but without any kind of preaching. And children can be shown how to be sympathetic towards people with problems. I also think children's books should have plenty of humor, because I like laughing!

"What I find most difficult is disciplining myself to work. There are so many distractions—runnng the house, looking after the family, friends, going for walks, reading, church and other meetings—that I do admire those writers who settle down, come what may, and do a specified number of hours each day."

Gifford reports that currently she is becoming interested in writing plays.

AVOCATIONAL INTERESTS: Community activities, animals, jazz and classical music, reading modern children's books and adult fiction.

BIOGRAPHICAL/CRITICAL SOURCES:

PERIODICALS

Times Educational Supplement, March 12, 1982.
Times Literary Supplement, September 19, 1975, July 16, 1976, March 25, 1977.

*   *   *

GIFFORD, Terry   1946-

PERSONAL: Born June 28, 1946, in Cambridge, England; son of Dennis (a gardener) and Edna (White) Gifford; married Judith Hickling (a teacher), August, 1968; children: Tom, Ruth. *Education:* Sheffield City College of Education, Certificate of Education, 1967; University of Lancaster, B.Ed. (with honors), 1973; University of Sheffield, M.A., 1978. *Politics:* Labour.

ADDRESSES: Home—56 Conduit Rd., Sheffield S10 1EW, Yorkshire, England.

CAREER: Teacher in grammar school in Sheffield, England, 1967; British Broadcasting Corporation (BBC-Radio), Sheffield, seconded teacher, 1970-71; Yewlands Comprehensive School, Sheffield, head of English department, 1979-85; Bretton Hall College of Higher Education, Wakefield, England, currently senior lecturer in English.

WRITINGS:

(Contributor) John Macbeath, editor, *A Question of Schooling*, Hodder & Stoughton, 1976.
(With Neil Roberts) *Ted Hughes: A Critical Study*, Faber, 1981.
(Contributor) Keith Sagar, editor, *The Achievement of Ted Hughes*, Manchester University Press, 1983.
(Contributor with John Brown) Bernard Harrison, editor, *English Studies 11-18: An Arts Based Approach*, Hodder & Stoughton, 1983.
(Contributor) Robert Prougherough, editor, *Teaching Literature for Examinations*, Open University Press, 1986.
(Contributor) V. J. Lee, editor, *English Literature in Schools*, Open University Press, 1987.
The Stone Spiral, Giant Steps, 1987.

Contributor of poems and articles on Brecht, teenage literature, social education, and Thomas Hardy to journals. Contributor of rock-climbing articles to magazines.

WORK IN PROGRESS: A second collection of poetry; a book on notions of nature in contemporary British poetry.

BIOGRAPHICAL/CRITICAL SOURCES:

PERIODICALS

Times Literary Supplement, July 24, 1981.

*   *   *

GILFOND, Henry

PERSONAL: Son of Louis and Vera Gilfond; married; wife's name, Edythe; children: Michael, Pamela.

ADDRESSES: Home and office—P.O. Box 357, Hampton Bays, N.Y. 11946. *Agent*—Bertha Case, 345 West 58th St., New York, N.Y. 10019.

CAREER: Writer. Teacher in New York (N.Y.) schools for a number of years.

MEMBER: American National Theatre and Academy, Dramatists Guild of the Authors League of America.

WRITINGS:

Journey without End, Philosophical Library, 1958.
How to Run for School Office, Hawthorn, 1969.
Heroines of America, Fleet Press, 1971.
The Reichstag Fire, February, 1933: Hitler Utilizes Arson to Extend His Dictatorship, F. Watts, 1973.
Black Hand at Sarajevo, Bobbs-Merrill, 1975.
Voodoo, F. Watts, 1976.
The New Ice Age, F. Watts, 1977.
Genealogy: How to Find Your Roots, F. Watts, 1978.
Syria, F. Watts, 1978.
Water: A Scarce Resource, F. Watts, 1978.
How to Give a Speech, F. Watts, 1980.
Afghanistan, F. Watts, 1980.

Gambia, Ghana, Liberia, Sierra Leone, F. Watts, 1981.
Countries of the Sahara, F. Watts, 1981.
The Executive Branch, F. Watts, 1981.
Disastrous Earthquakes, F. Watts, 1981.
The Northeastern States, F. Watts, 1983.

WITH GENE SCHOOR; JUVENILES; PUBLISHED BY MESSNER

The Jim Thorpe Story, 1952.
The Story of Ty Cobb, 1952.
Red Grange, 1952.
Christy Mathewson, 1953.
Casey Stengel, 1953.
The Jack Dempsey Story, 1954.
The Ted Williams Story, 1954.
The Stan Musial Story, 1955.

EDITOR; PUBLISHED BY WALKER & CO.

Plays for Reading, 1966.
American Plays for Reading, 1966.
Holiday Plays for Reading, 1967.
Plays for Today, 1967.
Mythology Plays, 1967.
African Plays for Reading, 1967.
Latin American Plays for Reading, 1967.
Favorite Short Stories, 1967.
Asian Plays for Reading, 1968.

OTHER

A Light in the Window, Bowmar/Noble, 1978.

Ghostwriter on subjects ranging from pediatrics to politics. Author of radio and television scripts and full-length plays, "The Wick and the Tallow," recorded by Folkways, 1967, and "Region of the Cross," a workshop production at Circle-in-the-Square. Contributor to *Reader's Digest* compendiums, 1972-80, and to *New York Times Book Review*. Former editor, *New World Monthly* (literary magazine) and *Dance Observer*.

WORK IN PROGRESS: Poems: 1962-1982; Poems: 1983-1987; free-lance editing.

SIDELIGHTS: Henry Gilfond told *CA:* "Ask me to write anything from a letter to an introduction to *Hamlet* (which in fact I have done) and much more than likely I'll do it, for money or, as often as not, for the love of writing. I've written everything from a fifty-year history of a small church to brochures for artists, for love and for the gratification that comes with a work appreciated. Actually there is little I enjoy more than hitting the keys of a typewriter, and with good reason. After all, it is the act of creating that may well be equated with the art of living."

*   *   *

GLAZE, Andrew (Louis III) 1920-

PERSONAL: Born April 21, 1920, in Nashville, Tenn.; son of Andrew Louis, Jr. (a physician) and Mildred (Ezell) Glaze; married Dorothy Elliott; married second wife, Adriana Keathley (a dancer), August 12, 1962; children: (first marriage) Betsy, Peter. *Education:* Harvard College, A.B. (cum laude), 1942; Stanford University, additional study, 1946-47. *Politics:* Independent. *Religion:* None.

ADDRESSES: Home—803 Ninth Ave., New York, N.Y. 10019.

CAREER: Birmingham Post-Herald, Birmingham, Ala., staff-writer, 1949-56; British Tourist Authority, New York, N.Y., press officer, beginning 1958; free-lance writer, 1982—. Member of faculty, Breadloaf Writer's Conference, 1969. Participant in workshops held at Brown University, Martha Washington College, University of Alabama in Birmingham, and New York University. Has given poetry readings at numerous universities, organizations, and institutions. *Military service:* U.S. Army Air Forces, ground communications, 1942-46; became first lieutenant.

MEMBER: Dramatist's Guild.

AWARDS, HONORS: Eunice Tietjens Award, *Poetry* magazine, 1951; American Library Association Notable Books List, 1966, for *Damned Ugly Children;* Hackney Literary Award, 1968 and 1975.

WRITINGS:

POETRY

Lines, Editions Heraclita, 1964.
Damned Ugly Children, Trident, 1966.
Masque of Surgery, Menard Press, 1974.
The Trash Dragon of Shensi, Copper Beech Press, 1978.
I Am the Jefferson County Courthouse, Thunder City, 1981.
Someone Will Go On Owing: New and Selected Poems, Ford-Brown, 1988.

Also author of *Reality Street,* in press.

PLAYS

"Who Stole the Lollipop," performed by the Tullio Garzone Company, 1962.
"Miss Pete," first produced Off-Broadway at the American Place Theatre, 1966.
"Kleinhoff Demonstrates Tonight," first produced at the Texas Summer Drama Festival, 1971.
"The Man-Tree," first produced at the New York Shakespeare Festival, 1975.
"Uneasy Lies," first produced in New York City at Gene Frankel Theatre, 1983.

Also author of seven nonproduced plays.

CONTRIBUTOR TO ANTHOLOGIES

New Yorker Book of Poems, Viking, 1969.
New Directions 26, New Directions, 1973.
Western Wind, Random House, 1974.
The Doctor Generosity Poets, Damascus, 1975.
Contemporary Southern Poetry, Louisiana State University Press, 1979.
Best Loved Poems, Merit Publications, 1980.

OTHER

Also author of two unpublished novels, *Spectacular Travelers* and *Decisions,* and an operetta. Contributor to many periodicals, including *New Yorker, Saturday Review, Audience, Tri-Quarterly, Folio, Open Places, Pivot, Negative Capability, New York Quarterly, Pulpsmith,* and *Home Planet News.*

SIDELIGHTS: Andrew Glaze wrote *CA:* "I speak, write, read, and translate French, I study ballet, my major interests are in anthropology, philosophy, psychology and music. [Since I retired I have devoted] myself entirely to writing, speculative investment, readings, and teaching."

BIOGRAPHICAL/CRITICAL SOURCES:

BOOKS

Doreski, William, editor, *Earth That Sings: On the Poetry of Andrew Glaze,* Ford-Brown, 1985.

PERIODICALS

Star-Ledger, March 18, 1983.

* * *

GODMAN, Arthur 1916-

PERSONAL: Born October 10, 1916, in Hereford, England; son of Arthur Andrew (a schoolmaster) and Mary (Newman) Godman; married Jean Barr Morton, June 24, 1950; children: Ian Barr, Diana Barr Godman Allan, Brian Barr. *Education:* University of London, B.Sc. (with honors), 1937, B.Sc. (with honors), 1938; Institute of Education, London, Diploma in Education, 1939. *Politics:* None. *Religion:* "Nominally Church of England."

ADDRESSES: Home—Sondes House, Patrixbourne, Canterbury, Kent, England.

CAREER: Overseas Civil Service, London, England, assistant director of education in Federation of Malaya, 1946-58; Cambridge University, Local Examinations Syndicate, Cambridge, England, examiner, 1952-70, chief examiner, 1970-84. Member of staff, Overseas Civil Service in Hong Kong, 1958-63. Honorary fellow of Eliot College, University of Kent at Canterbury; member of board of directors of Educational Publishing Services, Singapore. *Military service:* British Army, Royal Artillery, 1939-46; became captain.

MEMBER: Royal Chemical Society, Royal Asiatic Society, Society of Authors, Royal Overseas League, Association for Science Education.

WRITINGS:

(Editor) *The Attainment and Ability of Hong Kong Primary IV Pupils,* Oxford University Press, 1964.
The Colour Coded Guide to Microcomputers, Macdonald & Co., 1983.
Thesaurus of Computer Science, Cambridge University Press, 1984.
Thesaurus of Science and Technology, Cambridge University Press, 1985.
(With Tim Tregear) *Cambridge Illustrated Dictionary for Young Computer Users,* Cambridge University Press, 1986.

PUBLISHED BY LONGMANS, GREEN

(With Walter Vivian Hobson) *Everyday Science for the Tropics,* Book I, 1956, Book II, 1957, Book III, 1959, Book IV, 1962, Book V, 1964.
Health Science for the Tropics, 1962, revised edition, 1967, new edition with Anne C. Gutteridge published as *A New Health Science for Africa,* 1979.
(With J. Copeland) *Upper Primary Arithmetic,* 1964.
(With Hobson) *Everyday Science for Malaysia,* 1965.
(With J. F. Talbert) *Malaysian General Mathematics,* 1965.
(With H. Lau) *Remove Mathematics,* 1967.
(With A. Johnson and D. Chua) *General Science Certificate Course,* 1968.
(With N. Muraguri) *Practical Certificate Chemistry,* 1969.
(With Sam 'Tunde Bajah) *Chemistry: A New Certificate Approach,* 1969, revised edition, 1978.
(With Johnson) *Junior Tropical Biology,* 1970.
Health Science, 1970.

PUBLISHED BY LONGMAN

(With Talbert) *Additional Mathematics: Pure and Applied,* 1971, revised edition, 1976.

Physical Science, Book I, 1973, revised edition, 1976, Book II, 1973, revised edition, 1978.
(With C. J. Webb) *Certificate Human and Social Biology,* 1974.
(With Louis Ekue Folivi) *New Certificate Physics,* 1974, new edition, 1977.
Human and Social Biology, 1978.
(With E. M. F. Payne) *Longman Dictionary of Scientific Usage,* 1979.
(Editor) *Longman Illustrated Science Dictionary,* 1981.
(With Gutteridge) *Objective Tests,* 1981.
(With Gutteridge) *Certificate Notes,* 1981.
Longman Illustrated Dictionary of Chemistry, 1981.

WORK IN PROGRESS: English Usage in Science; revising a chemistry book.

SIDELIGHTS: Arthur Godman told *CA:* "My army service in the Far East led to an interest in Oriental languages, and it increased when I was in government service in Malaya. Teaching and examining science in both English and Malaya showed me cross-cultural difficulties in translating scientific and technical books. This led to my present research on problems of nonnative speakers of English when they read technical literature.

"Research is aimed at a thesaurus-type of approach to the listing of verbs. Groups of verbs, which are usually described as synonyms, or near synonyms, require individual members of a group to be distinguished clearly, so that a nonnative speaker of English can understand and use each member correctly. This topic was started in the *Dictionary of Scientific Usage* and is being extended to academic English generally."

*   *   *

GOFORTH, Ellen
   See FRANCIS, Dorothy Brenner

*   *   *

GOLDBERG, Maxwell Henry   1907-

PERSONAL: Born October 22, 1907, in Malden, Mass.; son of Felix and Zelda (Kushlansky) Goldberg; married July 29, 1962; wife's name, Ethel Stella; three children from previous marriage. *Education:* University of Massachusetts, B.S., 1928; Yale University, A.M., 1932, Ph.D., 1933.

ADDRESSES: Home—1865 Fernwood-Glendale Rd., Spartanburg, S.C. 29302.

CAREER: University of Massachusetts, Amherst, instructor in English,1928-30, 1933-34, assistant professor, 1934-47, associate professor, 1947-48,professor, 1948-62, Commonwealth Professor of Humanities and university professor-at-large, 1960-62, professor emeritus, 1962—, head of department, 1955-60; Pennsylvania State University, State College, professor of humanities and English, 1962-72, professor emeritus, 1972—, associate director of Center for Continuing Liberal Education, 1962-72; Converse College, Spartanburg, S.C., Andrew J. R. Helmus Distinguished Professor of Humanities and Literature and director of continuing liberal studies at Center for Humanities, 1972-76, professor emeritus, 1976—. Director of division of Humanities, University of South Florida, Tampa, 1959-60; president of Humanities Center for Liberal Education, Inc., 1962-71. Lecturer for U.S.D.A. graduate seminar at Oak Ridge Associated Universities, 1965; Danforth

visiting lecturer, 1968-72. Member of National Council of Churches advisory committee on technological change and society, 1965-67; education director of Wildacres Retreat, 1978; member of educational committee, South Carolina Appalachian Council of Governments, 1985—. Editor for College English Association, 1950-59. Chief consultant, National Endowment for the Humanities project, Morehouse College, 1970-83; consultant to Public Broadcasting Corp., National Endowment for the Humanities, and U.S. Department of Health, Education and Welfare. Participant in many symposiums and seminars.

MEMBER: Modern Language Association of America (life member), College English Association (executive director, 1950-59; president-elect, 1967; honorary life member), American Association of Retired Persons, Nature Conservancy, Audubon Society, Phi Beta Kappa, Alpha Epsilon Pi.

AWARDS, HONORS: Fund for Adult Education fellowship, 1956-57; associate alumni distinguished alumnus, University of Massachusetts, 1963; Debate Society distinguished alumnus, University of Massachusetts, 1967; citation, College English Association, 1976; South Carolina Governor's Citation, for directing bicentennial community forums, 1976; Spartanburg Sesquicentennial Medallion, 1981; distinguished service award, Shepherd's Center of Spartanburg, 1985; distinguished service citation, Friends of the Spartanburg County Library, 1985.

WRITINGS:

Amherst as Poetry, Newell Press, 1941.
(With Patricia Kochanek) *Technological Change and Human Dignity: A Study in Human Values,* Center for Continuing Liberal Education, Pennsylvania State University, 1966.
(Editor with John R. Swinton) *Blindness Research: The Expanding Frontiers—A Liberal Studies Perspective,* Pennsylvania State University Press, 1969.
(Editor) *Needles, Burrs, and Bibliographies: Study Resources in Technological Change, Human Values, and the Humanities,* Center for Continuing Liberal Education, Pennsylvania State University, 1969.
Design in Liberal Learning, Jossey-Bass, 1971.
Cybernation, Systems, and the Teaching of English: The Dilemma of Control, National Council of Teachers of English, 1972.
(Editor with Frederick F. Ritsch, Jr.) *Probes and Projections: Papers from the CCH-SCCH Humanities Project on Greater Spartanburg in Transition,* Center for Humanities, Converse College, 1974.
(Editor) *Community Self-Renewal and Telec Imaging: Humanisitic Perspectives,* Center for Humanities, Converse College, 1976.
Robert Frost: A Personal Recollection, Metro Press, 1980.
Tocqueville's Futurism, University of South Carolina at Spartanburg, 1981.
(Editor and contributor) *The Church's Ministry with the Aging: The Growing Fronts,* Shepherd's Center of Spartanburg, 1983.

CONTRIBUTOR

Holmes and Towle, editors, *The Complete College Reader,* Houghton, 1950.
(Author of introduction) R. D. Blackmore, *Lorna Doone,* Pocket Books, 1956.
(Author of introduction) George Eliot, *Adam Bede,* Pocket Books, 1956.

(Author of introduction) Eliot, *The Mill on the Floss,* Pocket Books, 1956.

Bernad Ducret and Rafe-Uz Zamen, editors, *The University Today: Its Role and Place in Society,* [Geneva, Switzerland], 1960.

Samuel Baskin, editor, *Higher Education: Some Newer Developments,* McGraw, 1965.

Meaning and Metaphor, Center for the Study of Liberal Education for Adults, 1965.

The Impact of Science on Society, Oak Ridge Institute of Nuclear Studies, 1965.

The Evolving Society, Institute for Cybercultural Research Press, 1966.

William W. Bruckman and Stanley Lehrer, editors, *Automation, Education and Human Values,* School and Society Books, 1966.

Magnanimity in Motley, College English Association, 1966.

C. Conrad Cherry and John Y. Fenton, editors, *Religion in the Public Domain,* Center for Continuing Liberal Education, 1966.

The American University and the World of Scholars, Rutgers University, 1967.

Peter Strulka, editor, *Yearbook of Comparative Criticism,* Pennsylvania State University Press, 1971.

Henry B. Maloney, editor, *Goal Making for English Teaching,* National Council of Teachers of English, 1973.

G. Lester Anderson, editor, *Land-Grant Universities and Their Continuing Challenge,* Michigan State University Press, 1976.

Frederick F. Ritsch, Jr., editor, *Issues and Commitment,* Converse College Center for the Humanities, 1976.

Ernestine P. Swell and Billi M. Rogers, editors, *Confronting Crisis,* University of Texas at Arlington Press, 1979.

Malinda R. Maxfield, editor, *Images and Innovations: Update '70s,* Converse College Center for the Humanities, 1979.

Ritsch, editor, *Ways of Knowing: Further Considerations,* Converse College, 1979.

Ritsch, editor, *Concept of Power,* Converse College, 1980.

AUDIO CASSETTES

Continuing Liberal Studies and Self-Emergence, Sound Seminars, 1970.

Humanism Goals and Behavioral Objectives, Spring Institute, 1972.

Conversations with Senior Citizens, South Carolina Commission on Aging, 1976.

OTHER

Contributor to *Yearbook of Comparative Criticism.* Contributor to educational journals; member of editorial board of *Educational Forum,* 1972-75; associate literary editor of *Intellect,* 1974-75.

SIDELIGHTS: Maxwell Henry Goldberg told *CA:* "A number of factors and circumstances have been important to the shaping of my career. Among these have been my being born into a bookish culture, a bookish people, a bookish family, and a bookish personal predilection. I was early reminded that we Jews have been called—and rightly—'the People of the Book,' and my father, professionally an engraver, was himself a writer of poems, short stories in the vein of Shalom Aleichem, and a big romantic novel covering two continents and parts of two centuries. In addition to my own love of reading and writing, I must add another motivation important for my career. This was to make my parents proud of me, and to give them justification for all the risks they had undergone, and the sacri-

fices they had made in coming to this new land, in trying to make a living in this strange place, and to give us, their children, the American social and cultural advantages they lacked. Through a successful career, through making a name for myself, I would be showing my gratitude; I would be giving them a new pride.

"What I have hoped to achieve specifically through my writings has varied with the assignment at hand. Intellectually, I have wanted to help people see clearly and understand. In the words of one of the steelworkers I had as student in a course on human values, I have wanted to help people 'think with their own brains.' Morally, I have wanted to help people to think and feel and act with the understanding heart. I have wanted to help them toward esthetic, intellectual, ethical and cultural enrichment. Ideally, I have wanted them to hold life steady and see it whole.

"I have been influenced by other writers, and differently at different periods. Those that stand out are: George Roy Elliott (Amherst College), Tucker Brooke and Karl Young (Yale), and poets David Morton and Robert Frost, of Amherst College. Among the 'greats' of literature, I would list also John Milton, Goethe, Thomas Carlyle, and John Henry Newman. All in all, the influence of those cited has been in terms of craftsmanship, intellectual enlargement and illumination, esthetic and imaginative stimulation, ethos—stamina, morale, values, purposes, will, consolation and courage; and as exemplary or emulative models. A master influence has been to keep my mind, and hence my writing, open to modes of experiencing, knowing, and communicating outside the limits set by customary criteria—such as those of 'reason and common sense,' positivism, and empiric rationalism. Most of the writers I have named have helped me to strengthen my grasp on the distinction between comprehension alone and as augmented by apprehension of that which lies outside the field of comprehension.

"I would refer aspiring writers to observations made by Sir Herbert Grierson. Himself a copious writer of scholarly and critical works, Sir Herbert spoke of two major crises that an aspiring writer has to face: the crisis of *virtuosity,* and the crisis of *vision.* The first of these has to do with mastery of the craft, developing one's own distinctive 'voice', one's own way of working. The second has to do with apprehending and expressing the vision to which one is to apply his virtuosity. Sir Herbert was of the opinion that more writers successfully come through the first crisis than through the second. According to this view, the Isaiahan 'Where the vision fails, the people perish,' should be revised to say: 'Where the vision fails, the writer perishes.' I would add that the writer cannot wait until he has successfully weathered the crisis of virtuosity before he faces the challenge of vision. I believe that, from the start, the aspiring writer needs to work on identifying and clarifying his *vision,* and of making it the central motivation for his serious work, and his ultimate goal."

Maxwell Henry Goldberg's work formed part of the "Native Son's Bicentennial Exhibit of Writings" at the Lucius Beebe Memorial Library, Wakefield, Mass., in 1976. Parts of Joe D. Thomas's *History of the College English Association* are also devoted to him, and the University of Massachusetts Archives established the Maxwell H. Goldberg Collection in 1976.

MEDIA ADAPTATIONS: Goldberg's essay "Freedom, Dignity, and the Telic Intent" was recorded on audio cassette by the National Council of Teachers of English.

AVOCATIONAL INTERESTS: Gardening, hiking, photography and dramatics.

* * *

GOLDMAN, Peter (Louis) 1933-

PERSONAL: Born February 8, 1933, in Philadelphia, Pa.; son of Walter S. (a sales representative) and Dorothy (Semple) Goldman; married Helen Dudar (a writer), July 16, 1961. *Education:* Williams College, B.A., 1954; Columbia University, M.S.J., 1955. *Religion:* Jewish.

ADDRESSES: Home—36 Gramercy Pk., New York, N.Y. 10003. *Office*—*Newsweek*, 444 Madison Ave., New York, N.Y. 10022. *Agent*—Robbins Office Inc., 2 Dag Hammarskjold Plaza, 866 Second Ave., 12th Floor, New York, N.Y. 10017.

CAREER: St. Louis Globe-Democrat, St. Louis, Mo., reporter, 1955-62; *Newsweek*, New York, N.Y., associate editor, 1962-64, general editor, 1965-68, senior editor, 1969—.

MEMBER: Phi Beta Kappa.

AWARDS, HONORS: Nieman fellow, Harvard University, 1960-61; Sigma Delta Chi award for magazine reporting, 1963; National Headliners Award, 1963, for coverage of riot at University of Mississippi, 1962; Robert F. Kennedy Journalism Award, 1972; American Bar Association Silver Gavel Award, 1972, for a report on criminal justice in America; National Magazine Award, 1982, for *Newsweek* issue on Vietnam veterans; has also received Women in Communication Clarion Award, New York Newspaper Guild's Page One Award, American Legion's Fourth Estate Award, and an Overseas Press Club citation for excellence.

WRITINGS:

Civil Rights: The Challenge of the Fourteenth Amendment, Coward, 1965, revised edition, 1967.
Report from Black America, Simon & Schuster, 1970.
The Death and Life of Malcolm X, Harper, 1973, revised edition, University of Illinois Press, 1979.
(Contributor) John Hope Franklin and August Meier, editors, *Black Leadership of the Twentieth Century*, University of Illinois, 1982.
(With Tony Fuller, Richard Manning, Stryker McGuire, Wally McNamee, and Vern E. Smith) *Charlie Company: What Vietnam Did to Us*, Morrow, 1983.
(With Fuller) *The Quest for the Presidency 1984*, Bantam, 1985.
The End of the World That Was: Six Lives in the Atomic Age, Dutton, 1986.
(With Sylvester Monroe and others) *Brothers*, Morrow, 1988.

Also author of *The Quest for the Presidency 1988* and of *Newsweek*'s fiftieth anniversary commemorative issue, "American Dream," 1983.

SIDELIGHTS: Peter Goldman told *CA:* "I am a career journalist, fulfilling an early boyhood ambition. I write about U.S. affairs, with subspecialties in national politics and the black American situation; and, as an avocation, about sports—particularly basketball.

Goldman's biography of political and religious leader Malcolm X, *The Death and Life of Malcolm X*, "owes its interest chiefly to the fact that it was written by a white man—which is surely a remarkable achievement in itself, since Malcolm X was vehemently anti-white," offers *Spectator* critic Dillibe Onyeama. Goldman and Malcolm X met often between 1962 and 1964 when Goldman was a reporter for the *St. Louis Globe-Democrat*. According to Orde Coombs in the *New York Times Book Review*, Goldman "does not pretend to have had Malcolm's ear or friendship, but he shows how Malcolm's vision of America altered [Goldman's] perception of the world and forced him to abandon the blinders he had worn when confronting the enormity of this country's racial antagonism." Coombs further finds *The Death and Life of Malcolm X* "a rich biography that pays little attention to Malcolm's early life, but elucidates in minute detail his last years, his death and subsequent sainthood.... In the final section of his book ... Goldman, shiningly eloquent, accurately gauges the impact of Malcolm's life on a whole generation of black people." With a somewhat varied viewpoint, the *New York Times*'s Christopher Lehmann-Haupt finds that Goldman's biography "is not an exciting book to read, but it is an eminently serviceable one.... By dealing with Malcolm X's life in its public, ideological aspect, Mr. Goldman goes a long way toward setting the record straight—or at least toward trimming the mythology to more manageable dimensions.... For a good deal of what Mr. Goldman reveals tends to soften Malcolm's image as a man of violence.... By reading Mr. Goldman on the hopeful 1960's ... we can begin to see more clearly what Malcolm meant to all of us, both black and white."

Turning to the subject of the Vietnam war, Goldman, with the aid of Tony Fuller and others, updated and expanded a 1981 *Newsweek* report based on several interviews with Vietnam veterans who had been members of the same army company. The resultant book, *Charlie Company: What Vietnam Did to Us*, answers the question "What in hell happened in Vietnam?" writes *Los Angeles Times Book Review* critic Malcolm Boyd. "This book answers the question graphically, with soul-searching, vivid description and a needed sense of dimension." *Washington Post* reviewer Jonathan Yardley maintains that "none of the points [the book] makes about the horrors of the war or the callousness of our treatment of those who fought it will come as a surprise to anyone who has paid reasonably close attention to the subject; but by addressing that subject in terms of the individual stories of ordinary soldiers, it gives an intimacy to Vietnam and its legacy that makes much of the rest of the literature on that war seem trivial and evasive by comparison." Though Anatole Broyard in the *New York Times* suspects some exaggeration or distortion from those interviewed, he claims "a careful reader will find more truth in [*Charlie Company*] than most of us may care to take on. In fact, the story the book tells is so sad and so ugly that it might almost pass for a prize-winning piece of serious fiction."

BIOGRAPHICAL/CRITICAL SOURCES:

PERIODICALS

Atlantic, October, 1985.
Los Angeles Times Book Review, April 10, 1983.
New York Times, January 8, 1973, April 2, 1983.
New York Times Book Review, January 28, 1973, May 1, 1983, August 18, 1985.
Spectator, July 13, 1974.
Times Literary Supplement, August 16, 1974.
Washington Post, March 9, 1983.
Washington Post Book World, July 21, 1985.

GOLDSTEIN, Milton 1915-

PERSONAL: Surname pronounced *Gold*-stine; born May 30, 1915, in New York, N.Y.; son of Samuel and Sarah (Sobel) Goldstein; married Lillian Friedman, February 23, 1936 (died March 31, 1972); married Martha Ann Greaves, June 10, 1973; children: (first marriage) Jalona. *Education:* City College (now City College of the City University of New York), B.S.S., 1937, M.B.A., 1948; La Salle Extension University, LL.B., 1957. *Politics:* Republican. *Religion:* "Universal."

CAREER: New York City Department of Welfare, New York City, statistician, 1939-43; New York City Office of Comptroller, New York City, assistant division chief, 1943-49; Frazer & Torbet, Los Angeles, Calif., manager of tax department, 1949-51, resident manager, 1952; certified public accountant in Beverly Hills, Calif., 1952-62; attorney in private practice, Beverly Hills, 1959-81, Bishop, Calif., 1981—; photographer, 1969—. Artist, Smithsonian Institution Photography Exhibitions, 1973-77. Religion in Media, Los Angeles, executive vice-president and director. Has appeared on television to discuss his writings and photographs.

MEMBER: American Bar Association, California Society of C.P.A.s, Los Angeles Bar Association, Phi Beta Kappa, Beta Gamma Sigma.

AWARDS, HONORS: TV Angel Award, Religion in Media, 1980, 1981.

WRITINGS:

The Magnificent West: Yosemite, Doubleday, 1973.
The Magnificent West: Grand Canyon, Doubleday, 1977.

WORK IN PROGRESS: Several volumes for "The Magnificent West" series; *Biblical Heritage: Visions and Reflections; A Companion of Universal Prayers; A Newer Testament.*

*   *   *

GONZALEZ, Gloria 1940-

PERSONAL: Born January 10, 1940, in New York, N.Y.; daughter of Angel and Mary (Cabrera) Gonzalez; children: Arleen, Kelly, Troy. *Education:* Studied playwrighting at the New School with Harold Callen and Jean-Claude van Itallie, playwrighting and directing with Lee Strasberg, and acting with Anthony Mannino.

ADDRESSES: Home—5907 Boulevard East, Apt. A7, West New York, N.J. 07093. *Agent*—Selma Luttinger, Brandt & Brandt, 1501 Broadway, New York, N.Y. 10030.

CAREER: Investigative reporter for various New Jersey daily newspapers; free-lance writer; now full-time playwright.

MEMBER: Dramatists Guild, Authors League of America, Women in Film, Inc., Drama Desk.

AWARDS, HONORS: First prize in Jacksonville University College of Fine Arts national playwrighting contest, 1975, for "Curtains"; finalist for Stanley Drama Award, 1975; Webster Groves Russell B. Sharp Annual Playwrighting Award, 1976, for "Lights."

WRITINGS:

PUBLISHED PLAYS

Chicken Little's Ass Is Falling (produced in New York City at Playbox Theatre, December, 1970), Studio Duplicating Service, 1970.

Moving On! (all one-acts; includes "Moving On!," first produced in New York City at Playbox Theatre, October, 1972; "Cuba: Economy Class!"; and "The New America"), Samuel French, 1971.
(Contributor) Frances Griffith and others, editors, *One-Act Plays for Our Times,* Popular Library, 1973.
Shadow of a Sovereign (one-act), Performance Publishing, 1973.
Curtains (produced in New York City at Hudson Guild Theatre, October, 1975), Dramatists Play Service, 1976.
(Contributor) Stanley Richards, editor, *Best Short Plays of 1976,* Dodd, 1976.

Also author of *Checkmate of a Queen,* Performance Publishing.

UNPUBLISHED PLAYS

(With Edna Schappert) "Celebrate Me," first produced in New York City at Playbox Theatre, April, 1971.
"Love Is a Tuna Casserole," produced by New York Theatre Ensemble, September, 1971.
(With Schappert and Joseph Gath) "Tidings, Comfort and Joy," produced in New York City at Playbox Theatre, November, 1971.
"Waiting Room," produced in New York City at Theatre at Noon, January, 1974.
"A Sanctuary in the City," produced in Altadena, Calif., at Theatre Americana, March, 1975.
"Let's Hear It for Miss America," produced in St. Petersburg, Fla., at Country Dinner Playhouse, August, 1976.
"Lights," produced in St. Louis, Mo., August, 1976.
"A Former Gotham Gal," produced in Washington, D.C., at New Playwrights Theatre, February, 1980.

Also author of "A Day in the Port Authority," "Woola-Boola," "Cafe con Leche," "Revolutionaries Don't Sit in the Orchestra," "Black Thoughts on a Bright Monday," "Double Play," and "The Puppet Trip."

TELEVISION DRAMAS

"Gaucho" (also see below), first broadcast on Columbia Broadcasting System, Inc. (CBS-TV), June 2, 1970.

Also author of "The Day the Women Got Even."

JUVENILE NOVELS

The Glad Man, Knopf, 1975.
Gaucho (based on her television drama), Knopf, 1977.
A Deadly Rhyme, Dell, 1986.

OTHER

Developer of situation comedies for network television. Contributor of articles to *New York Times* and *New York Daily News;* regular contributor to *Dramatists Quarterly.*

SIDELIGHTS: Gloria Gonzalez once told *CA:* "Despite the inherent pain, frustrations and anguish—the theatre, for me, remains the only arena worth writing for. I require the excitement and challenges of an instant reaction from a friendly or hostile audience as opposed to book reviews months, even a year after the book is written."

BIOGRAPHICAL/CRITICAL SOURCES:

PERIODICALS

Horn Book, April, 1978.
Washington Post, February 13, 1980.†

GORDON, Donald
See PAYNE, Donald Gordon

*   *   *

GOULD, Jay R(eid) 1906-

PERSONAL: Born March 15, 1906, in Aylesford, Nova Scotia, Canada; son of L. B. and Eleanor (West) Gould; married Rebecca Ritter (a librarian), 1941; children: Lee P., Emilie W. *Education:* Acadia University, B.A., 1926; Harvard University, M.A., 1929.

ADDRESSES: Home—Box 227, R.R. 5, Wynantskill, N.Y. 12198. *Office*—Department of Languages and Literature, Rensselaer Polytechnic Institute, Troy, N.Y. 12181.

CAREER: East Greenwich Academy, East Greenwich, R.I., teacher of English, 1928; Rensselaer Polytechnic Institute, Troy, N.Y., 1929-72, began as assistant professor, became professor of English, professor emeritus, 1972—, director of Technical Writers Institute, 1953-72, associate director of Medical Writers Institute, 1960-72, chairman of department of language and literature, 1968-72. Visiting professor, New South Wales Institute of Technology, 1974. Consultant, New York State Department of Health, IBM Corp., and other firms; consultant in communication, American Chemical Society, 1972—.

MEMBER: Society of Technical Communication (fellow), American Business Communication Association (fellow), Society of Technical Writers and Publishers (fellow), American Business Writing Association, National Council of Teachers of English, American Medical Writers Association.

AWARDS, HONORS: Drama League scholar in England, 1933-34; Rensselaer Polytechnic Institute and Baywood Publishing Co. established the annual Jay R. Gould Awards for Excellence in Technical Communication.

WRITINGS:

Opportunities in Technical Writing, Vocational Guidance Manuals, 1946, revised edition (with Wayne A. Losano) published as *Opportunties in Technical Writing Today,* 1975.
(Editor with S. P. Olmsted) *Exposition: Technical and Popular,* Longmans, Green, 1947.
(With J. N. Ulman, Jr.) *Technical Reporting,* Holt, 1957, 3rd edition, 1972.
Practical Technical Writing, American Chemical Society, 1975.
(Editor) *Directions in Technical Writing and Communications,* Baywood, 1978.
(With Losano) *Opportunities in Technical Communications,* Vocational Guidance Manuals, 1980, revised edition, 1984.
(Editor) *New Essays in Technical and Scientific Communication,* Baywood, 1983.

PLAYS

The Running Tide, Dramatic Publishing, 1952.
The Death of the Hired Man (one-act), Dramatic Publishing, 1956.
The Long Silence (one-act), Dramatic Publishing, 1960.
Steps from Beyond, Baker's Plays, 1963.
The Necklace, Dramatic Publishing, 1968.

OTHER

General editor of "Communication Series," Baywood, 1987—. Contributor of about fifty articles to professional journals. Editor, *Journal of Technical Writing and Communication,* 1970-83.

*   *   *

GRAEBNER, Norman A. 1915-

PERSONAL: Born October 19, 1915, in Kingman, Kan.; son of Rudolph W. (a minister) and Helen (Brauer) Graebner; married Laura Baum, August 30, 1941; children: Harriet, Norman Brooks, Emily. *Education:* Milwaukee State Teachers College (now University of Wisconsin—Milwaukee), B.S., 1939; University of Oklahoma, M.A., 1940; University of Chicago, Ph.D., 1949. *Religion:* Lutheran.

ADDRESSES: Home—542 Worthington Dr., Charlottesville, Va. 22901. *Office*—Department of History, University of Virginia, Charlottesville, Va. 22904.

CAREER: Taught high school in Oklahoma; Oklahoma College for Women (now University of Science and Arts of Oklahoma), Chickasha, assistant professor, 1942-43, 1946-47; Iowa State University, Ames, 1948-56, began as assistant professor, became professor of history; University of Illinois at Urbana-Champaign, professor of history, 1956-67, chairman of department, 1961-63; University of Virginia, Charlottesville, Edward R. Stettinius Professor of Modern American History, 1967-82, Randolph P. Compton Professor of History and Public Affairs Emeritus, 1982—. Visiting associate professor, Stanford University, 1952-53; Commonwealth Fund lecturer, University of London, 1958; visiting professor, Stanford University, 1959 and 1972; Walter Lynwood Fleming Lecturer, Louisiana State University, 1962; Fulbright lecturer, University of Queensland, 1963, University of Sydney, 1983; Distinguished Visiting Professor, Pennsylvania State University, 1975-76; Harold Vyvyan Harmsworth Professor, Oxford University, 1978-79; Pettyjohn Distinguished Lecturer, Washington State University, 1980; visiting professor, U.S. Military Academy, West Point, 1981-82; Phi Beta Kappa Visiting Scholar, 1981-82; Thomas Jefferson Visiting Scholar, Downing College, Cambridge University, 1985. Radio broadcaster from classroom, WILL, Champaign, 1958-59 and 1966, and of weekly program, "Background of the News," WBBM, Chicago, Ill., 1958-60. Has represented historical organizations on Joint Committee on Historians and Archivists and National Archives Advisory Council; former member of Advisory Committee for American Studies Abroad. *Military service:* U.S. Army, Ordnance Corps, 1943-46; became first lieutenant; received Commendation Ribbon for establishing first school for American soldiers in Japan, 1946.

MEMBER: Society for Historians of American Foreign Relations (vice-president, 1970-71; president, 1971-72), Society of American Historians, American Historical Association, American Association of University Professors, Organization of American Historians (member of executive board), Southern Historical Association, Massachusetts Historical Society, Illinois State Historical Society, Phi Beta Kappa (honorary member), Phi Alpha Theta.

AWARDS, HONORS: Outstanding teacher award, University of Illinois, 1962; D.Litt., Albright College, 1976; M.A., Oxford University, 1978; D.H.L., University of Pittsburgh, 1981; D.H.L., Valparaiso University, 1981; honorary degree from Eastern Illinois University; Alumni Association Distinguished Professor Award, University of Virginia; Thomas Jefferson Award, University of Virginia, 1985; Outstanding Service

Medal, West Point; awards from the Z Society, the IMP Society, and the Raven Society.

WRITINGS:

Empire on the Pacific, Ronald, 1955, 2nd edition, 1983.
The New Isolationism: A Study in Politics and Foreign Policy since 1950, Ronald, 1956.
Cold War Diplomacy: American Foreign Policy, 1945-1960, Van Nostrand, 1962, 2nd edition, 1977.
Ideas and Diplomacy, Oxford University Press, 1964.
(With Gilbert C. Fite and Philip L. White) *A History of the United States*, two volumes, McGraw, 1970.
(With Fite and White) *A History of the American People*, McGraw, 1970, 2nd edition, 1975.
(With Fite) *Recent United States History*, Ronald, 1972.
The Age of Global Power: The United States since 1939, Wiley, 1979.
America as a World Power: A Realist Appraisal from Wilson to Reagan, Scholarly Resources, 1984.
Foundations of American Foreign Policy: A Realist Appraisal from Franklin to McKinley, Scholarly Resources, 1985.

EDITOR

The Enduring Lincoln, University of Illinois Press, 1959.
Politics and the Crisis of 1860, University of Illinois Press, 1961.
An Uncertain Tradition: American Secretaries of State in the Twentieth Century, McGraw, 1961.
The Cold War: Ideological Conflict or Power Struggle?, Heath, 1963, 2nd edition, 1976.
Ideas and Diplomacy: Readings in the Intellectual Tradition of American Foreign Policy, Oxford University Press, 1964.
Manifest Destiny, Bobbs-Merrill, 1968.
Nationalism and Communism in Asia: The American Response, Heath, 1977.
Freedom in America: A 200-Year Perspective, Pennsylvania State University Press, 1977.
American Diplomatic History before 1900, Harlan Davidson, 1978.
(With Kenneth W. Thompson) *Traditions and Values: American Diplomacy, 1790-1865*, University Press of America, 1985.
(With Thompson) *Traditions and Values: American Diplomacy, 1865-1945*, University Press of America, 1985.
The National Security: Its Theory and Practice in the United States, 1945-1960, Oxford University Press, 1986.

CONTRIBUTOR

Lincoln for the Ages, Doubleday, 1960.
Lincoln Images, Augustana College Library, 1960.
Why the North Won the Civil War, Louisiana State University Press, 1960.
America's Ten Greatest Presidents, Rand McNally, 1961.
Contemporary Civilization, Scott, Foresman, 1961.
The Unity of Western Europe, Washington State University Press, 1964.

Contributor to *Collier's Encyclopedia Yearbook*, 1959-75.

OTHER

Also author of essays, chapters, and over 120 articles for periodicals. Contributing editor, *Current History*.

WORK IN PROGRESS: A general history of America's foreign relations; a brief history of the Cold War.

SIDELIGHTS: Norman A. Graebner writes to *CA:* "My writings on U.S. foreign relations since the eighteenth century cover a wide variety of topics, but all advocate, as did the writings of the Founding Fathers, that national interests be precisely defined and never permitted to exceed the true intentions of government."

*   *   *

GRAY, Dulcie

PERSONAL: Born in Kuala Lumpur, Malaysia; daughter of Arnold Savage (a lawyer) and Kate Edith Clulow (Gray) Bailey; married Michael Denison (an actor), April 29, 1939. *Education:* Educated in England and Malaya. *Religion:* Anglican.

ADDRESSES: Home—Shardeloes, Amersham, Buckinghamshire, England. *Agent*—Douglas Rae Management, Ltd., 28 Charing Cross Rd., London WC2H 0DB, England.

CAREER: Actress, 1939—; writer. Has starred in forty-one London plays, including Shaw's "Candida" and "Heartbreak House," and played on tour in South Africa, Australia, Hong Kong, Berlin; most recent London roles were in Sir Ronald Mallar's "A Coat of Varnish," at the Haymarket Theatre, 1982, and Richard Sheridan's "A School for Scandal," at the Haymarket Theatre, 1983, and at the Duke of York Theatre, 1984. Films include "They Were Sisters," with James Mason, and "The Glass Mountain," with her husband as co-star. Also has made more than five hundred radio and television appearances; most recent television role was in "Howards' Way," 1985-86.

MEMBER: Crime Writers Association, Mystery Writers of America, British Actors Equity.

AWARDS, HONORS: Queen's Silver Jubilee Medal, 1977; Times Educational Supplement Senior Information Award, 1979, for *Butterflies on My Mind*.

WRITINGS:

Love Affair (play; first produced in London at the Lyric Theatre Hammersmith, 1956), Samuel French, 1957.
Murder on the Stairs, Arthur Barker, 1957.
Murder in Melbourne, Arthur Barker, 1958.
Baby Face, Arthur Barker, 1959.
Epitaph for a Dead Actor, Arthur Barker, 1960.
Murder on a Saturday, Arthur Barker, 1961.
Murder in Mind, Macdonald & Co., 1963.
The Devil Wore Scarlet, Macdonald & Co., 1964.
Quartet for a Star, Macdonald & Co., 1964.
(With husband, Michael Denison) *The Actor and His World*, Gollancz, 1964.
(Contributor) *The Girl on the Bus* (anthology of love stories), Pan Books, 1966.
The Murder of Love, Macdonald & Co., 1967.
Died in the Red, Macdonald & Co., 1967.
Murder on Honeymoon, Macdonald & Co., 1969.
For Richer, for Richer, Macdonald & Co., 1970.
Deadly Lampshade, Macdonald & Co., 1971.
Understudy to Murder, Macdonald & Co., 1972.
Dead Give-Away, Macdonald & Co., 1974.
Ride on a Tiger, Macdonald & Co., 1975.
Stage Door Fright (short stories), Macdonald & Co., 1977.
Death in Denims (juvenile), Everest Books, 1977.
Butterflies on My Mind, Angus & Robertson, 1978.
Dark Calypso, Macdonald & Co., 1979.
The Glanville Women, M. Joseph, 1982.

Anna Starr, M. Joseph, 1984.

Also author of seven radio plays for British Broadcasting Corp., of musical play, "Love a la Carte." Contributor to eleven anthologies of horror stories published by Pan Books. Contributor of articles to *Sunday Express, Daily Sketch*, and *Tatler*, and of short stories to *Evening Standard* and *Evening News*.

WORK IN PROGRESS: A novel about obsession.

SIDELIGHTS: Dulcie Gray wrote *CA:* "I began my writing career when I was in my teens, working as a school mistress in the Malaysian jungle, at Fraser's Hill. The play was so bad that I felt I must augment my income. There were three gossip columns then running in 'The Straits Tribune'—a Singapore-based newspaper—'Our Singapore Notes,' 'Our Penang Notes,' and 'Our Kuala Lumpur Notes.' I published a fourth, 'Our Fraser's Hill Notes,' which ran weekly until I left Malaysia for England. A long time later, when I had been an actress for about fifteen years, I became ill, and was told I would never act again (happily untrue). So I began writing again. I first wrote a play, 'Love Affair'—then my first novel, *Murder on the Stairs*."

*   *   *

GRAY, Ralph D(ale)   1933-

PERSONAL: Born October 13, 1933, in Otwell, Ind.; son of Lee M. (a grocer) and Voris R. (Gray) Gray; married Janice R. Everett, September 2, 1956; children: Karen, David, Sarah. *Education:* Hanover College, B.A., 1955; University of Durham, 1955-56; University of Delaware, M.A., 1958; University of Illinois, Ph.D., 1962.

ADDRESSES: Home—1724 West 73rd Pl., Indianapolis, Ind. 46260. *Office*—Department of History, Indiana University-Purdue University at Indianapolis, 425 Agnes St., Indianapolis, Ind. 46202.

CAREER: Ohio State University, Columbus, instructor in history, 1961-64; Indiana University, Kokomo Center, Kokomo (now Indiana University at Kokomo), assistant professor, 1964-67, associate professor of history, 1967-68; Indiana University-Purdue University at Indianapolis, associate professor, 1968-72, professor of history, 1972—. Special consultant to Monon Railroad, 1966, and Cabot Corp., 1971.

MEMBER: Society for Historians of the Early American Republic, American Historical Association, Organization of American Historians, Business History Conference, Indiana Historical Society, Indiana Oral History Roundtable (president, 1975-76), Marion County/Indianapolis Historical Society (director, 1981—).

AWARDS, HONORS: Fulbright scholar in England, 1955-56; Dickerson Award, University of Illinois, 1966, for *The National Waterway;* distinguished faculty service award, Indiana University-Purdue University at Indianapolis, 1978; McKean Cup, Antique Automobile Club of America, 1980, for *Alloys and Automobiles: The Life of Elwood Haynes*.

WRITINGS:

The National Waterway: A History of the Chesapeake and Delaware Canal, 1769-1965, University of Illinois Press, 1967, 2nd edition, Army Corps of Engineers, 1988.

(Editor) *Gentlemen from Indiana: National Party Candidates, 1836-1940*, Indiana Historical Bureau, 1977.

Alloys and Automobiles: The Life of Elwood Haynes, Indiana Historical Society, 1979.

(Editor and author of introductions to sections) *The Hoosier State: Readings in Indiana History*, Eerdmans, 1981.

(Editor and author of foreword) *Indianapolis: The First Century*, Indianapolis Historical Society, 1987.

Also author of *Stellite: A History of the Stellite Company, 1912-1972*, 1974. Contributor to *Encyclopedia of World Biography*, McGraw, 1973, *Dictionary of American Biography*, Supplement V, 1977, *Encyclopedia of Southern History*, 1979, and *Biographical Directory of the Governors of the U.S.*, Meckler, 1985. Contributor of articles and reviews to business history and regional history journals. Founder and editor, *Journal of the Early Republic*, 1981—.

WORK IN PROGRESS: Coediting a Civil War diary tentatively titled, *Soldier Boy from Indiana: The Civil War Diary of Samuel P. Herrington;* a study of the life and career of Meredith Nicholson, a Hoosier writer and diplomat.

SIDELIGHTS: Ralph D. Gray told *CA:* "My current work, in addition to editing the *Journal of the Early Republic . . .*, focuses largely upon Indiana and its remarkable group of both politicians and writers, particularly those active around the turn of the century. Studying the life of Meredith Nicholson, both a best-selling author and a politician-diplomat later in life, as well as an informal historian of his beloved home state, has offered additional insight into all of the above topics. Perhaps I came to this study naturally, having lived for a time in the home of still another author-editor-historian, my maternal grandmother, Beulah B. Gray, who then was editing a small-town newspaper (*The Otwell Star*) and filling its columns with reams of historical, genealogical, and human interest stories."

AVOCATIONAL INTERESTS: All sports, woodworking, photography.

*   *   *

GRAY, Vanessa
See AEBY, Jacquelyn

*   *   *

GREEN, Roger C(urtis)   1932-

PERSONAL: Born March 15, 1932, in Ridgewood, N.J.; son of Robert Jefferson (a chain store manager) and Eleanor (Richards) Green; married Kaye Chandler Smith, December 20, 1958 (separated, 1969); children: Ian Rotui, Nai Vivian (both adopted). *Education:* University of New Mexico, B.A., 1954, B.Sc., 1955; Harvard University, Ph.D., 1964.

ADDRESSES: Office—Department of Anthropology, University of Auckland, Private Bag, Auckland, New Zealand.

CAREER: American Museum of Natural History, New York, N.Y., research associate in anthropology and leader of expeditions into Mangareva and Moorea, 1959-61; University of Auckland, Auckland, New Zealand, senior lecturer in anthropology and deputy dean of Faculty of Arts, 1961-67; B. P. Bishop Museum, Honolulu, Hawaii, visiting associate anthropologist, 1965, anthropologist, 1967-73, associate chairman of department of anthropology, 1969-70; University of Auckland, professor of pre-history, 1973—, head of department, 1980-82. Visiting associate professor, University of Hawaii, 1965, 1967-70. Has conducted field research in Southwest

United States, New Zealand, French Polynesia, Fiji, Samoa, Tonga, Hawaii, and the Solomon Islands.

MEMBER: American Anthropological Association (fellow), Society for American Archaeology, Royal Society of New Zealand, Polynesian Society, New Zealand Archaeological Association (honorary member; president, 1964; member of editorial board), Phi Kappa Phi, Sigma Gamma Epsilon.

AWARDS, HONORS: Peabody Museum research grant, 1949-55; National Science Foundation grant, 1963-67; Captain James Cook fellowship, New Zealand, 1970-73; Fulbright grant and Wenner-Gren Foundation grant.

WRITINGS:

A Review of the Prehistoric Sequence in the Auckland Province, University Bookstore (Dunedin, New Zealand), 1963, revised edition, 1970.
(Contributor) Nicholas Tarling, editor, *China and Its Place in the World,* Paul's Book Arcade, 1967.
(Contributor) Genevieve A. Highland and others, editors, *Polynesian Culture History,* Bishop Museum Press, 1967.
(Editor and contributor with J. M. Davidson) *Archaeology in Western Samoa,* Auckland Institute and Museum, Volume I, 1969, Volume II, 1974.
(Editor with Marion Kelly, and contributor) *Studies in Oceanic Culture History,* Bishop Museum Press, Volume I, 1970, Volume II, 1971, Volume III, 1972.
(Contributor) G. Kuschel, editor, *Biogeography and Ecology in New Zealand,* W. Junk, 1972.
(Contributor) Noel Barnard, editor, *Early Chinese Art and Its Possible Influence in the Pacific Islands,* Volume III, Intercultural Arts Press, 1972.
(Editor with M. M. Cresswell) *Southeast Solomon Islands Cultural History: A Preliminary Survey,* Royal Society of New Zealand, 1976.
Makaha before 1880 A.D., edited by Bonnie T. Clause and D. E. Yen, Department of Anthropology, Bernice P. Bishop Museum, 1980.
(Editor with Wilmot Bennitt) *Canonbury Tower* (based on Richard Oakley's "Brief History of Canonbury Tower"), Tavistock Repertory Company, 1981.
Battle for the Franklin: Conversations with the Combatants in the Struggle for South West Tasmania, photographs by Geoffrey Lea, Fontana/Australia Conservation Foundation, 1981.
(Compiler) *The Train,* Oxford University Press, 1982.

Author of research reports. Contributor to symposia and encyclopedias. Contributor of more than one hundred articles and reviews to anthropology journals, including *American Antiquity, Asian Perspectives, Man, Asian and Pacific Archaeology,* and *Current Anthropology,* and New Zealand Archaeological Association *Newsletter.* Member of editorial board, *Asian Perspectives.*

SIDELIGHTS: Roger C. Green once told *CA:* "If one is in research, one writes to communicate one's results and to enter into a kind of formally structured dialogue with one's colleagues on the subject in question. I write for these reasons and because I think there is something worth contributing to our growing history of man's past. Writing is the hardest part of my research programme and its only logical conclusion— so I keep at it despite the many other demands of a university and museum career."

GREENE, Janice Presser
See PRESSER, Janice

*   *   *

GREENFIELD, Jeff   1943-

PERSONAL: Born June 10, 1943, in New York, N.Y.; son of Benjamin (a lawyer) and Helen (a teacher; maiden name, Greenwald) Greenfield; married Harriet Carmichael (an actress), May 11, 1968; children: Casey Carmichael (daughter). *Education:* University of Wisconsin, B.A. (with honors), 1964; Yale University, LL.B. (with honors), 1967.

ADDRESSES: Home—322 West 72nd St., New York, N.Y. 10023. *Agent*—Sterling Lord Agency, 660 Madison Ave., New York, N.Y. 10021.

CAREER: Legislative aide to late Senator Robert Kennedy, Washington, D.C., 1967-68; assistant to Mayor John Lindsay, New York City, 1968-70; Garth Associates, New York City, consultant, 1970-76; writer; political and media critic for Columbia Broadcasting System (CBS) and American Broadcasting Companies (ABC).

WRITINGS:

(With Jerry Bruno) *The Advance Man,* Morrow, 1971.
(With Jack Newfield) *A Populist Manifesto: The Making of a New Majority,* Praeger, 1972.
No Peace, No Place, Doubleday, 1973.
Tiny Giant (juvenile), Raintree, 1975.
The World's Greatest Team: A Portrait of the Boston Celtics, 1957-1969, Random House, 1976.
Television: The First Fifty Years, Abrams, 1977.
(With Gerry Sussman) *Jeff Greenfield's Book of Books* (satire), Simon & Schuster, 1979.
Playing to Win: An Insider's Guide to Politics, Simon & Schuster, 1980.
The Real Campaign: The Media and the Battle for the White House, Summit, 1982.

Contributor to national magazines.

SIDELIGHTS: In his book *The Real Campaign: The Media and the Battle for the White House* Jeff Greenfield challenges one longstanding assumption: that the media is influential in the outcome of a presidential election. "The thesis of this book," says Greenfield in its pages, "is that television and the media made almost no difference in the outcome of the 1980 presidential campaign." According to the author, as *Nation* critic Dean Valentine notes, the Republicans won "because [the party was] better organized, more unified and richer than the Democrats, and put forth ideas that the American public found relevant and 'coherent.' Above all, [Ronald] Reagan was running against a President [Jimmy Carter] regarded even by many in his own party as an amiable nobody."

While underplaying the power of the media "is not exactly hot off the wires," remarks Valentine, until Greenfield's book, the thesis had "never been presented either with such clarity or in such exhaustive detail." Similarly mixed reviews come from Larry Sabato in a *New York Times Book Review* piece. The author, he says, "has a trained eye for appealing anecdotes and revealing illustrations of important concepts. But his style tends to be too breezy, and his writing has been infected with an irritating tendency toward excessive italicization." Beyond stylistic shortcomings, Sabato feels that Greenfield's assertions are not valid for the case of every modern Presidential campaign, although "as far as the 1980 election goes, [the author] is convincing and perceptive. If past practice is any indication, most of the press, particularly television, will not react kindly to the sort of charges Greenfield levels at it."

MEDIA ADAPTATIONS: Greenfield was featured on a sound recording of *Television: The First Fifty Years,* released by the Center for Cassette Studies.

BIOGRAPHICAL/CRITICAL SOURCES:

BOOKS

Greenfield, Jeff, *The Real Campaign: The Media and the Battle for the White House,* Summit, 1982.

PERIODICALS

Nation, July 24, 1982.
New York Review of Books, April 6, 1978.
New York Times Book Review, January 1, 1978, June 22, 1980, June 20, 1982.
Washington Post Book World, June 20, 1982.

*   *   *

GREENFIELD, Patricia Marks   1940-

PERSONAL: Born July 18, 1940, in Newark, N.J.; daughter of David Marks, Jr. (a life insurance agent) and Doris (Pollard) Marks; married Sheldon Greenfield (a physician), March 13, 1965; children: Lauren, Matthew. *Education:* Radcliffe College, A.B. (summa cum laude), 1962; attended University of Dakar, 1963-64; Harvard University, Ph.D., 1966.

ADDRESSES: Office—Department of Psychology, University of California, Los Angeles, Calif. 90024.

CAREER: Syracuse University, Syracuse, N.Y., investigator at Research and Development Center in Early Childhood Education, 1967, research associate, 1967-68; Harvard University, Cambridge, Mass., research fellow in psychology, Center for Cognitive Studies, 1968-72, lecturer on social relations, 1970; Stanford University, Stanford, Calif., acting assistant professor of psychology, 1972-73; University of California, Santa Cruz, assistant professor, 1973-74; University of California, Los Angeles, associate professor, 1974-78, professor of psychology, 1978—. Science scholar, Bunting Institute, Radcliffe College, 1986-87. Visiting lecturer, Clark University, 1971; external examiner in psychology, University of Lagos, 1977-79; visiting researcher, Laboratoire de Psychologie Experimentale, Universite Rene Descartes, Paris, 1979-80; collaborating scientist, Yerkes Regional Primate Center, Emory University, 1979-83; visiting professor, University of Rome, 1987. Program advisor, Bromley-Heath Infant Daycare Center, 1969-70; National Institute of Education, member of literacy grant review panel, 1978, member of unsolicited grant review panel, 1979; affiliate member, Teaching English as a Second Language/Applied Linguistics Program, University of California, Los Angeles, 1984-85. Speaker at numerous seminars, conferences, and symposiums. Consultant to numerous institutions, including Education Development Center, Cambridge, 1972, University of California, Los Angeles, School of Medicine, 1972-73, and Health Services Research Center, 1976—, and to Northwest Regional Educational Laboratory, 1978-80; member of international advisory board, International Congress on Early Childhood Education, Israel, 1978-80.

MEMBER: International Association for Cross-Cultural Psychology (member of executive committee, 1972-74), Ameri-

can Psychological Association (fellow), Association of Academic Women (member of board of directors, 1984—), American Association for the Advancement of Science (fellow), Phi Beta Kappa.

AWARDS, HONORS: First Award of Sixth Annual Creative Talent Awards Program of American Institute for Research, 1967, for dissertation, "Culture, Concepts, and Conservation: A Comparative Study of Cognitive Development in Senegal"; grants from Spencer Foundation, 1975-81, Society for the Psychological Study of Social Issues, 1978, and National Institute of Education, 1979-81; U.C.L.A. Distinguished Teaching Award, 1985; honorable mention, Division 2 Teaching Award, American Psychological Association, 1985; College Institute Award, university research grant, and Center for the Study of Women grant, all from University of California, Los Angeles; Bunting Science fellow.

WRITINGS:

(Editor with Jerome S. Bruner, R. R. Olver, and others) *Studies in Cognitive Growth,* Wiley, 1966.
(With F. Tronick) *Infant Curriculum: The Bromley-Heath Guide to the Care of Infants in Groups,* Media Projects, 1973, 2nd edition, Goodyear Books, 1980.
(With J. Smith) *The Structure of Communication in Early Language Development,* Academic Press, 1976.
Mind and Media: The Effects of Television, Video Games, and Computers, Harvard University Press, 1984.

CONTRIBUTOR

D. Goslin, editor, *Handbook of Socialization Theory,* Rand McNally, 1963.
D. Price-Williams, editor, *Cross-Cultural Studies: Selected Readings,* Penguin, 1969.
R. Cancro, editor, *Intelligence: Genetic and Environmental Influences,* Grune, 1971.
Bruner, editor, *The Relevance of Education,* Norton, 1971.
P. Adams, editor, *Language in Thinking,* Penguin, 1972.
V. P. Clark, P. A. Escholz, and A. F. Rosa, editors, *Language: Introductory Readings,* St. Martin's, 1972.
Bruner, editor, *Beyond the Information Given,* Norton, 1973.
M. Haehr and W. M. Stallings, editors, *Culture, Child, and School: Socio-Cultural Influences on Learning,* Brooks/Cole Publishing, 1975.
H. C. Lindgren, editor, *Child Behavior,* National Press Books, 1975.
J. L. M. Dawson and W. J. Lonner, editors, *Proceedings of the Inaugural Meeting of the International Association for Crosscultural Psychology,* Hong Kong University Press, 1975.
K. F. Reigel and J. A. Meacham, editors, *The Developing Individual in a Changing World,* Volume I: *Historical and Cultural Issues,* Mouton, 1976.
D. O. Walter, L. Rogers, and J. M. Finzi-Fried, editors, *Human Brain Function,* UCLA Brain Information Service/Brain Research Institute, 1976.
G. Steiner, editor, *Piaget and Beyond: The Psychology of the 20th Century,* Volume VII, Kindler Verlag (Zurich), 1977.
P. Dasen, editor, *Cross-Cultural Contributions,* Gardner Press, 1977.
A. Lock, editor, *Action, Symbol, and Gesture: The Emergence of Language,* Academic Press, 1978.
N. Waterson and C. Snow, editors, *Development of Communication: Social and Pragmatic Factors in Language Acquisition,* Wiley, 1978.

E. O. Keenan, editor, *Studies in Developmental Pragmatics,* Academic Press, 1978.

K. Nelson, editor, *Children's Language,* Gardner Press, Volume I, 1978, Volume II, 1980, Volume III, 1982.

P. French, editor, *The Development of Meaning,* Bunka Hyoron Press (Japan), 1979.

D. Olson, editor, *The Social Foundations of Language and Thought: Essays in Honor of J. S. Bruner,* Norton, 1980.

N. Warren, editor, *Studies in Cross-Cultural Psychology,* Volume II, Academic Press, 1980.

G. Forman, editor, *Action and Thought: From Sensorimotor Schemes to Symbolic Operations,* Academic Press, 1981.

D. Wagner and H. Stevenson, editors, *Cultural Perspectives on Child Development,* W. H. Freeman, 1982.

B. Bain, editor, *The Sociogenesis of Language and Human Conduct,* Plenum, 1983.

Video Games and Human Development: Research Agenda for the '80s, Monroe C. Gutman Library, Graduate School of Education, 1983.

B. Rofgoff and J. Lave, editors, *Everyday Cognition: Its Development in Social Context,* Harvard University Press, 1984.

M. Barrett, editor, *Children's Single-Word Speech,* Wiley, 1985.

D. E. Berger, K. Pezdek, and W. P. Banks, editors, *Applications of Cognitive Psychology,* Lawrence Erlbaum, 1987.

Also contributor to *Readings in Developmental Psychology Today,* 2nd edition, 1977, and to *Papers and Reports on Child Language Development,* 1978 and 1979.

OTHER

Also author, with Bruner and Allegra M. May, of filmscript "Early Words: Language and Action in the Life of a Child," and of cassette tape, "What Can We Learn from Cultural Variation in Child Care?" Contributor of articles and reviews to professional journals, including *Journal of Child Language, Recherche Pedagogie et Culture, Journal of Cross-Cultural Psychology, Journal of Psycholinguistic Research, Contemporary Psychology,* and *Child Behavior.* Member of editorial board, *Child Development,* 1969-71, *Journal of Applied Developmental Psychology* and *Journal of Mental Imagery;* corresponding associate commentator, *The Behavioral and Brain Sciences,* 1979—.

WORK IN PROGRESS: Building Tree Structures at Three Levels of Hierarchical Complexity: A Developmental Study, with J. Hubner; *Hierarchical Organization in Language and Action: Neural and Behavioral Aspects;* several journal articles.

SIDELIGHTS: In *Mind and Media: The Effects of Television, Video Games, and Computers,* Patricia Greenfield argues that if properly used, "these media hold the promise of revolutionizing education," writes Diane Dowling in *Psychology Today.* Greenfield suggests, for example, that television be used to teach children to become sophisticated viewers, and that video games be used to help develop their inductive reasoning abilities and spatial skills. Toronto *Globe and Mail* contributor Chris Dickman concludes: "Greenfield may be thanked for providing a well-meaning, if limited, introduction to the field. She raises more issues than she can find answers to, but her contribution is one of the first, tentative attempts to assess just what the impending automation of the classroom has in store for our children."

Mind and Media: The Effects of Television, Video Games, and Computers has been translated into five languages. Greenfield

is competent in French and in Wolof, a major Senegalese language.

AVOCATIONAL INTERESTS: Travel, skiing, "social action."

BIOGRAPHICAL/CRITICAL SOURCES:

PERIODICALS

Globe and Mail (Toronto), July 21, 1984.
Los Angeles Times Book Review, June 3, 1984.
Psychology Today, June, 1984.

*   *   *

GREENHAW, H(arold) Wayne   1940-

PERSONAL: Born February 17, 1940, in Colbert County, Ala.; son of Harold Reed (a salesman) and Lee (Able) Greenhaw; married Faye Berry, September, 1965 (divorced August, 1967); married Sarah Virginia Maddox, August, 1972. *Education:* Attended Instituto Allende, San Miguel, Mexico, summer, 1959; University of Alabama, B.S. in Ed., 1966.

ADDRESSES: Home—Montgomery, Ala. *Office*—3239 Lexington Rd, Montgomery, Ala. 36106; and 25 Washington Ave., Montgomery, Ala. 36104. *Agent*—Charles D. Taylor, Books and Production East, 24 Elm St., Manchester, Mass. 02144.

CAREER: Tuscaloosa News, Tuscaloosa, Ala., part-time sports reporter, 1958-62; Tuscaloosa Country Club, Tuscaloosa, assistant manager, 1960-63; *Graphic Weekly,* Tuscaloosa, sports columnist, 1963-64; Draper Correctional Center, Elmore, Ala., writer for experimental educational project, 1964-65; *Alabama Journal,* Montgomery, general assignment reporter, 1965-76; Maxwell Federal Prison Camp, Montgomery, Ala., director of creative writing program; instructor in journalism at Alabama State University, Montgomery, and at Troy State University, Troy, Ala.; editor and publisher, *Alabama Magazine,* 1984—.

AWARDS, HONORS: First place in investigative reporting and second place in feature writing, Alabama Associated Press Awards, 1966; Nieman fellow, Harvard University, 1972-73.

WRITINGS:

The Golfer, Lippincott, 1967.
The Making of a Hero: Lt. William Calley and the My Lai Massacre, Touchstone Publishing, 1971.
Watch Out for George Wallace, Prentice-Hall, 1976.
Elephant in the Cottonfields: Ronald Reagan and the New Republican South, Macmillan, 1982.
Flying High: Inside Big-Time Drug Smuggling, Dodd, 1985.
Alabama on My Mind: People, Politics, History and Ghost Stories, Sycamore Press, 1987.

Writer of two six-part series for Alabama Educational Television. Contributor of more than 200 articles to magazines.

WORK IN PROGRESS: A novel about childhood in the South; a film on the early history of Alabama.

SIDELIGHTS: H. Wayne Greenhaw recently told *CA:* "While editing and publishing *Alabama Magazine,* I have developed a new perspective on this land where I live and have lived most of my life. It is a new daily growth which helps me with my other writing. During this time, I have also written a novel, set in central Alabama, which is making the rounds of New York publishers."

GREER, Francesca
See JANAS, Frankie-Lee

*   *   *

GREGORIAN, Joyce Ballou   1946-
(Joyce Gregorian Hampshire)

PERSONAL: Born July 5, 1946, in Boston, Mass.; daughter of Arthur T. (an Oriental rug importer) and Phebe (Ballou) Gregorian; married John Benjamin Hampshire (architect), July 4, 1986. *Education:* Attended Edinburgh University, 1963-64; Radcliffe College, B.A. (wth honors), 1968. *Politics:* "Minimal." *Religion:* Protestant.

ADDRESSES: Home—Upland Farm, Highland St., Holliston, Mass. 01746. *Office*—Arthur T. Gregorian, Inc., 2284 Washington St., Newton Lower Falls, Mass. 02162.

CAREER: Iran Bethel School, Tehran, Iran, teacher, 1968-69; Arthur T. Gregorian, Inc. (import and retail business), Newton Lower Falls, Mass., officer, 1969—. Lecturer and teacher on subject of Oriental rugs to museums, schools, and private organizations, 1969—; owner and operator of Upland Farm, Inc. President, Armenian Library and Museum of America, Inc. Trustee, Beaver Country Day School.

MEMBER: Arabian Horse Club Registry of America, New England Dressage Association, American Horse Shows Association.

WRITINGS:

JUVENILES; SELF-ILLUSTRATED

The Broken Citadel (first book in trilogy), Atheneum, 1975.
Castledown (second book in trilogy), Atheneum, 1977.
The Great Wheel, (third book in trilogy), Ace Books, 1987.

OTHER

(With father, Arthur T. Gregorian) *Armenian Rugs from the Gregorian Collection,* Consolidated Graphics, 1987.

Contributor of book reviews to *Boston Globe.*

SIDELIGHTS: "For the past twenty years," Joyce Ballou Gregorian told *CA,* "I have traveled extensively. I breed and train Arabian horses and operate a small boarding stable as well. When I published *The Broken Citadel* in 1975 and *Castledown* in 1977, I expected the third to follow in short order. However, I spent some of my royalties on an Arabian broodmare and in 1978 sold my suburban farmhouse to buy a rural farm. A few hundred horses later, in 1987, *The Great Wheel* finally saw print. It is a paperback original since the other two books achieved their greatest sales in that format.

"Now that I am married I travel less; with more time at home and with the horse population kept strictly under forty head, I once more have time to read and write. I have just finished work on the first book devoted to inscribed Armenian rugs. Other technical articles and monographs are in my immediate future. Another novel is also waiting, a relation possibly to my trilogy."

AVOCATIONAL INTERESTS: Arabian horses, dressage, combined training, voice, opera, early music.

*   *   *

GREY, Brenda
See MACKINLAY, Leila Antoinette Sterling

GROSS, Alan   1947-

PERSONAL: Born June 29, 1947, in Chicago, Ill.; son of Melvin (a retailer) and Shirlee (Marks) Gross; married second wife, Norma Topa (an artist), June 26, 1978. *Education:* Attended University of Missouri, 1965-69.

ADDRESSES: Home and office—Writer's Group, Inc., 1730 North Wells, Chicago, Ill. 60614.

CAREER: Writer, teacher, director, and actor. Worked as writer and creative director in advertising in Chicago, Ill., 1969-77. Teacher for Chicago Public Library, Roosevelt University, and Northwestern University; adjunct professor, Columbia College. Actor with "Second City" and theaters and workshops.

MEMBER: Dramatists Guild, Authors League of America.

AWARDS, HONORS: Two Chicago Emmys from the Academy of Television Arts and Sciences; three Joseph Jefferson Awards; Midland Writers Award; finalist in O'Neill Festival National Playwrights Conference, 1978.

WRITINGS:

JUVENILE

Sometimes I Worry, Children's Press, 1978.
What If the Teacher Calls On Me?, Children's Press, 1979.
The I Don't Want to Go to School Book, Children's Press, 1981.

PLAYS

"Lunching" (two-act), first produced in Chicago, Ill., at The Body Politic, December, 1977, produced on Broadway, October, 1979.
"The Phone Room" (two-act), first produced in Chicago at Theatre Building, February, 1978.
"The Man in 605" (two-act), first produced in Chicago at Theatre Building, June, 1979, produced Off-Broadway at Theater DeLys, April, 1980.
"Morning Call" (one-act), first produced in Louisville, Ky. at Actor's Theater, May, 1980.
"La Brea Tarpits" (two-act), first produced in Chicago at Victory Gardens Theater, May, 1981, produced on Broadway at WPA Theatre, May, 1984.
"The Houseguest" (two-act), first produced in Chicago at Theater Building, May, 1981.
"A Recipe for Petcha" (one-act), first produced in Chicago at N.A.B. Gallery, November, 1984.
"The Secret Life of American Poets" (one-act), first produced in Chicago at Gare St. Lazare Theater, March, 1985.
(Contributor) "The Seed Show: untitled #1," produced in Chicago at Organic Lab Theater, February, 1986.

OTHER

Contributor to periodicals, including *Chicago Tribune, Leisure, Chicagoland Monthly,* and *Tables.*

SIDELIGHTS: Chicago playwright Alan Gross gave up a secure career in advertising for the satisfactions of becoming "a real writer," he told *Chicago Tribune* interviewer Richard Christiansen. His decision has resulted in such favorably reviewed plays as "The Man in 605," and "La Brea Tarpits." In a review of the latter play, Christiansen suggests that Gross's greatest strength is "his ability to create dramatic truth and clever dialog out of the flotsam and jetsam of modern middlebrow urban living . . . suffused with a sharp knowledge of and deep affection for the people who must try to make a life for themselves in this environment.'' Of his career change, the author remarked to Christiansen, ''I love to write, and I love to be a playwright. Everybody should be a playwright! They are the spoiled brats of the American literary scene.''

BIOGRAPHICAL/CRITICAL SOURCES:

PERIODICALS

Chicago Tribune, July 26, 1978, March 13, 1980, March 26, 1980, June 5, 1981.†

*   *   *

GROVELANDS, Sarah
See SCHNEIDER, Myra

*   *   *

GRUBER, Gary R.   1940-

PERSONAL: Born November 19, 1940, in New York, N.Y.; married; two children. *Education:* City College of the City University of New York, B.S. (with honors), 1962; Columbia University, M.A., 1964; Yeshiva University, Ph.D., 1969.

ADDRESSES: P.O. Box 657, Mill Valley, Calif. 94941.

CAREER: Author; developer and producer of research, learning, and testing programs. Cambridge University Press, New York, N.Y., chief editor in physics and mathematics, 1969; Hofstra University, Hempstead, Long Island, N.Y., assistant professor of physics and astronomy and director of astronomy and mathematical physics, 1969-73, senior research scientist, 1973-74. Director of public affairs and the public understanding of science, New York Academy of Sciences, 1973-74. Senior projects director, Center for the Study of Instruction, Harcourt, Brace, Jovanovich, Inc., 1976-77. Consultant to Prentice-Hall, John Wiley & Sons, and Oxford University Press, 1969—. Has developed and conducted Scholastic Aptitude Test preparation courses and critical thinking programs. Lecturer on education and science to seminars, universities, and research institutes. Has appeared on numerous radio and television programs.

MEMBER: American Physical Society, American Association for the Advancement of Science, American Mathematical Society, American Astronomical Society, American Association of Physics Teachers, American Association of University Professors, National Association of Science Writers.

AWARDS, HONORS: Research fellowship, University of Glasgow, 1966-68; National Science Foundation grant, 1971-72.

WRITINGS:

Physics, Monarch, 1971.
High School Equivalency Examination Test, Simon & Schuster, 1971, 3rd updated edition, 1976.
General Mathematical Ability, Simon & Schuster, 1971.
Correctness and Effectiveness of Expression, Simon & Schuster, 1971.
Reading Interpretation in the Natural Sciences and Literature, Simon & Schuster, 1971.
(With Edward C. Gruber) *Graduate Record Examination Aptitude Test: A Complete Review for the Verbal and Math Parts of the Test,* Simon & Schuster, 1971, 3rd updated edition, 1976.

(With E. C. Gruber) *Test of English as a Foreign Language,* Monarch, 1973, 6th updated edition, 1982.
College-Level Examination Program, Monarch, 1973, 2nd updated edition, 1979.
Standard Written English Test, Simon & Schuster, 1974.
American College Testing Programs for College Entrance, Simon & Schuster, 1974.
Graduate Management Admissions Test, Simon & Schuster, 1975.
Professional and Administrative Career Program for the Federal Government, Simon & Schuster, 1976.
New Medical College Admission Test, Contemporary Books, 1977.
(With E. C. Gruber and Barry S. Willdorf) *Law School Admission Test,* Monarch, 1977, 2nd updated edition, 1979.
Scholastic Aptitude Test, Contemporary Books, 1978.
Math Review for the Graduate Management Admission Test, Monarch, 1982.
Shortcuts and Strategies for the Graduate Management Admission Test, Monarch, 1982.
Shortcuts and Strategies for the Graduate Record Examination, Monarch, 1982.
Inside Strategies for the SAT, Educational Design, 1982.
Dr. Gruber's Essential Test-Taking Guide for Kids Grades 3-5 and 6-9, Morrow, 1986.
Gruber's Complete Preparation for SAT, Harper, 1987.

Also author of a tape recording, ''Add Up to 300 Points to Your SAT,'' Great American Audio, 1986. Contributor of articles to journals.

WORK IN PROGRESS: ''A critical thinking test which will not only accurately diagnose thinking but provide an immediate mechanism for improvement of thinking and restructuring school curriculums.''

SIDELIGHTS: Recognized as an expert in the field of educational testing, Gary R. Gruber is the author of over twenty-five examination preparation manuals and of special examination review courses. Arville Finacom, writing in the *Daly City Record,* explains that ''Gruber's activities today involve preparing high school and college students to confront and conquer the battery of aptitude tests challenging them on successive steps of the academic ladder.''

In his book *Inside Strategies for the SAT* Gruber writes that the Scholastic Aptitude Test, ''which is supposed to measure verbal and math aptitude, is perhaps the most important exam anyone can take: This one test can determine a person's future career and his or her goals for a lifetime. The SAT is supposed to be an indicator of the intelligence and aptitude of the nation's young people, just as the Dow Jones Average is an indicator of the nation's economic health. . . . With colleges now increasing their standards, it is extremely important for a student to do well on this exam.''

According to *Independent Journal's* Mark Whittington, ''Gruber gives the students an overview of the tests and teaches them strategies and shortcuts. But the key is practicing those techniques. The kids who improve the most are those who practice at home.'' However, Finacom believes that Gruber's strategies do more than just prepare students for a single test. He points out that ''the skills Gruber teaches are those of critical thinking, analytical methods applicable easily to any number of problem solving situations in home or business as well as school. In effect, students who master Gruber's modes find themselves well prepared for the conditions and transactions they must approach objectively as they move through academic, career and personal futures.''

Noting that average SAT scores have declined steadily over the past two decades, Gruber believes that the average scores would be even lower if the Educational Testing Service had not revised the exam over the years to make it simpler. As Gruber told the *Pacific Sun:* ''Actually, I'll bet if you took a ten-year-old exam and used it instead of today's exam, the average score would be 300 instead of 400. . . . The verbal scores are low because kids don't read that much anymore. The math scores are declining because kids have been memorizing the math; then when they take the SAT and haven't had algebra or geometry for two years they're in trouble.'' Gruber continues: ''The ironic thing is I think today's kids are as bright if not brighter than [their parents]. They're more alert, more aware of politics. The kids today seem to want to be entertained more than ever. . . . What kids don't realize—and here is the tragedy—is that work isn't necessarily tedious . . . that the process can be enjoyable. The kids are missing out on the enjoyment of working.''

Gruber told *CA:* ''I am out to bring out the potential of every student in this country. When I was in fifth grade I scored a 90 on an IQ test. I was so upset and my self-esteem became so low that [I] needed to prove that I could show myself that I was not what the IQ test indicated. I became so fascinated with test-taking and thinking that I developed my own strategies and thinking skills enough to increase my IQ to 150. This taught me a lesson. There are so many kids who have potential, and this potential does not come out unless a student is exposed to particular thinking skills. The tests can destroy a kid's self-image if the student doesn't learn how to think critically. I want to show all these kids how smart they really can be.

'' 'Many a flower is born to blush unseen / and waste its sweetness on the desert air'—let's not let this happen to America's kids!''

BIOGRAPHICAL/CRITICAL SOURCES:

BOOKS

Gruber, Gary R., *Inside Strategies for the SAT*, Educational Design, 1982.

PERIODICALS

Chicago Tribune, September 29, 1981.
Daly City Record, July 23, 1980.
Detroit News, October 3, 1982.
Houston Chronicle, October 3, 1982.
Independent Journal, March 21-22, 1981.
Los Angeles Times, November 29, 1981.
Oregonian, February 17, 1987.
Pacific Sun, August 21-27, 1981.
San Francisco Chronicle, February 21, 1981.

*   *   *

GUTHRIE, A(lfred) B(ertram), Jr.   1901-

PERSONAL: Born January 13, 1901, in Bedford, Ind.; son of Alfred Bertram (an educator) and June (Thomas) Guthrie; married Harriet Larson, June 25, 1931 (divorced, 1963); married Carol Bischman, April 3, 1969; children: Alfred Bertram III, Helen Guthrie Atwood. *Education:* Attended University of Washington, Seattle, 1919-20; University of Montana, A.B., 1923; Harvard University, graduate study, 1944-45.

ADDRESSES: Home—The Barn, Choteau, Mont. 59422. *Agent*—Brandt & Brandt, 1501 Broadway, New York, N.Y. 10036.

CAREER: Lexington Leader, Lexington, Ky., reporter, 1926-29, city editor and editorial writer, 1929-45, executive editor, 1945-47; University of Kentucky, Lexington, teacher of creative writing, 1947-52; writer.

AWARDS, HONORS: Litt.D., University of Montana, 1949; Pulitzer Prize for fiction, 1950, for *The Way West;* Western Heritage Wrangler Award, 1970, for *Arfive;* Distinguished Achievement Award of the Western Literature Association, 1972; Dr. of Humane Letters, Indiana State University, 1975; Montana Governor's Award for distinguished achievement in the arts; Kentucky Governor's Award; Indiana Governor's Award.

WRITINGS:

NOVELS

Murders at Moon Dance, Dutton, 1943.
The Big Sky, Sloane, 1947.
The Way West, Sloane, 1949.
These Thousand Hills, Houghton, 1956, published with a new introduction by Fred Erisman, Gregg, 1979.
Arfive, Houghton, 1970.
Wild Pitch, Houghton, 1973.
The Last Valley, Houghton, 1975.
The Genuine Article, Houghton, 1977.
No Second Wind, Houghton, 1980.
Fair Land, Fair Land, Houghton, 1982.
Playing Catch-Up, Houghton, 1985.

OTHER

''Shane'' (screenplay), produced by Paramount, 1953.
''The Kentuckian'' (screenplay), produced by United Artists, 1955.
The Big It and Other Stories, Houghton, 1960, published as *Mountain Medicine*, Pocket Books, 1961.
The Blue Hen's Chick (autobiography), McGraw, 1965.
Once upon a Pond (juvenile), Mountain Press, 1973.

Contributor to periodicals, including *Esquire* and *Holiday*.

SIDELIGHTS: A. B. Guthrie, Jr., is considered one of the foremost writers on the American West. His best-known novels, *The Big Sky, The Way West,* and *These Thousand Hills,* realistically depict the taming of the frontier from 1830 to the beginning of the twentieth century. His keen insight into the people who accomplished that task has earned high praise from many critics, including Richard Bradford, who asserts in the *New York Times Book Review:* ''Guthrie himself is a marrow-deep American writer, one of the best our country has produced. No one has ever written better of the fibrous men who wrestled a giant land.'' Born in Indiana, Guthrie moved with his parents to Choteau, Montana when he was only six months old, at a time when Montana was still a frontier. He developed a deep love for the rugged country at an early age, a love that remained strong even during Guthrie's twenty-year stint as a newspaper editor in Lexington, Kentucky. His feelings for his home state and his adopted state merged in his first major novel: *The Big Sky* relates the story of a young Kentuckian's powerful encounter with the Rocky Mountain frontier.

The Big Sky begins as seventeen-year-old Boone Caudill flees his Kentucky home, mistakenly believing he has killed his oppressive father. For the next thirteen years, Boone lives the solitary life of a mountain man, travelling the Mississippi from St. Louis to its headwaters in the Rockies. His experiences as an explorer, guide, trapper, and trader provide an informative account of early frontier life. Far from romanticizing Boone, however, Guthrie presents him as a deeply flawed individual, one in flight from the responsibilities inherent in human relationships. *Dictionary of Literary Biography* contributor Ben Merchant Vorpahl believes that Boone's colorful adventures therefore "ultimately serve to state the novel's larger and deeper design—a compelling study of displacement, orphanhood, and loss."

The Big Sky was immediately popular. Its success enabled its author to leave his position as executive editor of the *Lexington Leader* and devote himself exclusively to writing. He began working on a sequel to *The Big Sky*, and in just six months he had completed his story of a wagon train's 1846 journey from Missouri to Oregon. Published as *The Way West*, the novel possesses the "same imaginative conviction" as *The Big Sky* but is "a humanly richer and wiser book," according to *New York Times Book Review* critic Robert Gorham Davis. "Its pattern of character is more various, more human, and warmer," concurs Elrick B. Davis in the *New York Herald Tribune Book Review*. *The Way West*'s depiction of group dynamics is as surely handled as Boone Caudill's solitary life, and allows Guthrie to make a statement that is "intelligently humanistic in the best and largest sense," reports Vorpahl. "Although the terrain and climate of the frontier put serious obstacles in the way of emigration, obstacles that are even more serious originate with the emigrants themselves. Once greed, lust, jealousy, and aggression are tamed, Guthrie seems to argue, then the mountains and rivers can be crossed—not easily, but with sanity and courage." On the strength of *The Way West*, Guthrie won the Pulitzer Prize for fiction in 1950.

Guthrie's next novel, *These Thousand Hills*, marks the closing of the frontier and the climax of what Walter Van Tilburg Clark calls in the *New York Times Book Review* Guthrie's "spiritual epic of the Northeast." Westward movement ceases when Lat Evans, a descendant of the Oregon settlers featured in *The Way West*, moves east to Montana. For a time he lives a free, wild life similar to Boone Caudill's in *The Big Sky*, but unlike Boone, Lat eventually accepts a "civilized" life, having successfully reconciled the conflicting sides of his nature. Guthrie continued to sketch the evolution of the West in his later novels, with *The Last Valley* concluding in time shortly after World War II.

Guthrie has consistently won praise for his awareness of both the dream and the reality of the American West. His novels celebrate the grandeur of the wilderness, but at the same time, "the brutality and the plain squalor of life in the early West come through," finds *Nation* contributor Margaret Marshall. Stylistically, he "shuns romanticism, preferring a kind of dramatic reportage told in language which is clean, informal, and direct," says John R. Milton in *The Novel of the American West*. J. M. Lalley describes Guthrie's prose in less favorable terms in a *New Yorker* review, calling it "a sort of sturdy buckskin dialect lavishly embellished with poetical fofaraw." But *New York Herald Tribune Weekly Book Review* writer Dorothy Canfield Fisher finds Guthrie's style perfectly suited to his subject; in her opinion, it is "sober, simple American, natural and unselfconscious. . . . The author looks at the reader out of clear, honest, truth-telling eyes and says what he has to say, without uneasiness, without heroics."

Guthrie's work is "grounded on his respect for research and facts, a virtue which even his harshest critics seem to grant," notes Thomas W. Ford, author of *A. B. Guthrie, Jr.* "Along with regard for the facts [is] his equally important desire to suggest the spiritual qualities of the [Western] movement, and his use of landscape, sky, and space [become] the primary implement for suggesting these qualities. In these ways, Guthrie is the Western realist who treats the physical and historical West plus the idea of the West and moves between fact and dream."

A *New York Times* interviewer notes that while Guthrie pays tribute to the courage and ingenuity of the pioneers, his "work is also marked by a strong [negative] thematic statement; namely, that the conquest of the West by the American settlers was in many ways destructive, and led to the spoiling of the land." Guthrie agreed with the interviewer's interpretation, remarking of the settlers, "They destroyed the bison, cut the forest and dug gaping holes to extract precious metals and coal and then moved on to another valley." The author moved back to Montana shortly after the success of *The Big Sky* and now lives in a house he built near his childhood home. He told the *New York Times* interviewer, "I've always thought of Montana as my center of the universe."

MEDIA ADAPTATIONS: RKO produced a film based on Guthrie's novel *The Big Sky* in 1952, Twentieth Century-Fox produced one on *These Thousand Hills* in 1959, and United Artists produced one on *The Way West* in 1967.

BIOGRAPHICAL/CRITICAL SOURCES:

BOOKS

Contemporary Literary Criticism, Volume XXIII, Gale, 1983.
Dictionary of Literary Biography, Volume VI: *American Novelists since World War II*, Gale, 1980.
Folsom, James K., *The American Western Novel*, College & University Press, 1966.
Ford, Thomas W., *A. B. Guthrie, Jr.*, Steck-Vaughn, 1968.
Milton, John R., *The Novel of the American West*, University of Nebraska Press, 1980.

PERIODICALS

Christian Science Monitor, December 3, 1975.
College English, February, 1951.
Nation, May 24, 1947.
National Observer, September 13, 1975.
New Yorker, May 3, 1947.
New York Herald Tribune Book Review, October 9, 1949.
New York Herald Tribune Weekly Book Review, May 4, 1947.
New York Times, March 3, 1983.
New York Times Book Review, May 4, 1947, October 9, 1949, November 18, 1956, January 17, 1971.
Saturday Review, November 17, 1956, February 20, 1960.
Western American Literature, fall, 1971, winter, 1972.†

—*Sketch by Joan Goldsworthy*

*   *   *

GUYER, Paul 1948-

PERSONAL: Born January 13, 1948, in New York, N.Y.; son of Irving Henry (an artist) and Betty (an administrator; maiden name, Rubenstein) Guyer; married Pamela Foa (an attorney), May 21, 1978; children: Nora Francesca Foa Guyer. *Education:* Harvard University, A.B. (summa cum laude), 1969, A.M., 1971, Ph.D., 1974.

ADDRESSES: Home—2417 Delancy Pl., Philadelphia, Pa. 19103. *Office*—Department of Philosophy, University of Pennsylvania, Philadelphia, Pa. 19104.

CAREER: University of Pittsburgh, Pittsburgh, Pa., assistant professor of philosophy, 1973-78, director of Graduate Studies and Graduate Admissions, undergraduate advisor; University of Illinois at Chicago Circle, Chicago, associate professor of philosophy, 1978-83, director of Graduate Studies, Graduate Admissions, and Graduate Placement; University of Pennsylvania, Philadelphia, professor of philosophy, 1983—, acting chair of department, 1984-85, chair, 1985-88. Visiting assistant professor, University of Michigan, winter, 1975; lecturer at Ohio University and Tufts University, 1975-76, McGill University, 1976-77, University of Edinburgh and University of London, 1978-79, and Northwestern University, University of Chicago, and University of California, San Diego, all 1979-80; visiting associate professor, University of Pennsylvania, fall, 1982; lecturer and session chair at Moscow Colloquium on Hegel's Logic. Member of advisory board, North American Kant Society, 1985—.

MEMBER: American Philosophical Association, American Society for Aesthetics.

AWARDS, HONORS: University of Pittsburgh faculty of arts and sciences summer grant, 1975; National Endowment for the Humanities fellowship for independent study and research, 1978-79; Franklin J. Matchette Prize, American Philosophical Organization, 1982, for *Kant and the Claim of Knowledge;* Guggenheim memorial fellowship, 1982-83.

WRITINGS:

(Contributor) Rolf-Peter Horstmann, editor, *Seminar: Dialektik in der Philosophie Hegels,* Suhrkamp Verlag, 1978.
Kant and the Claims of Taste, Harvard University Press, 1979.
(Editor with Ted Cohen, and contributor) *Essays in Kant's Aesthetics,* University of Chicago Press, 1982.
Kant and the Claims of Knowledge, Cambridge University Press, 1987.
(Contributor) Eva Schaper and Wilhelm Vossenkuhl, editors, *Transcendental Turnings,* Cambridge University Press, in press.

General editor with Allen Wood, *Cambridge Edition of the Works of Immanuel Kant in English,* 1985—. Contributor of articles and reviews to philosophy and aesthetics journals, including *Journal of Philosophy, American Philosophical Quarterly, Review of Metaphysics,* and *Journal of Aesthetics and Art Criticism.*

WORK IN PROGRESS: A book on Kant's moral and political philosophy; a new translation of Kant's *Critique of Pure Reason,* for the *Cambridge Edition of the Works of Immanuel Kant in English;* a book on eighteenth-century aesthetics; a book on the impact of Kant on subsequent philosophy.

H

HAINES, Pamela Mary   1929-

PERSONAL: Born November 4, 1929, in Harrogate, England; daughter of Harry Beeley (a lawyer) and Muriel (Armstrong) Burrows; married Anthony Haines (a physician), June 24, 1955; children: Charlotte Haines Brignall, Lucy, Nicholas, Hal, Emily. *Education:* Newnham College, Cambridge, M.A., 1952.

ADDRESSES: Home—57 Middle Lane, London N.8, England. *Agent*—A. D. Peters & Co. Ltd., 10 Buckingham St., London WC2N 6BU, England.

CAREER: Writer, 1971—.

MEMBER: International PEN, Society of Authors.

AWARDS, HONORS: New writing prize from *Spectator,* 1971, for story, "Foxy's Not at Home"; young writers award from Yorkshire Arts Society, 1975, for *Tea at Gunter's.*

WRITINGS:

NOVELS

Tea at Gunter's, Heinemann, 1974.
A Kind of War, Heinemann, 1976.
Men on White Horses, Collins, 1978.
The Kissing Gate (Book-of-the-Month Club alternate selection), Doubleday, 1981.
The Diamond Waterfall, Doubleday, 1984.
The Golden Lion, Scribners, 1986.
Daughter of the Northern Fields, Collins, 1987.

WORK IN PROGRESS: The Delectable Mountains, a novel set in Yorkshire and Canada.

BIOGRAPHICAL/CRITICAL SOURCES:

PERIODICALS

Washington Post, May 16, 1981.

*   *   *

HALL, Peter (Geoffrey)   1932-

PERSONAL: Born March 19, 1932, in London, England; son of Arthur Vickers (a civil servant) and Bertha (a housewife; maiden name, Keefe) Hall; married Carla Maria Wartenberg, 1962 (marriage dissolved, 1967); married Magdalena Mroz (a researcher), February 13, 1967. *Education:* St. Catherine's

College, Cambridge, M.A., 1957, Ph.D., 1959. *Politics:* Social Democrat.

ADDRESSES: Home—5 Bedford Rd., London W4 1JD, England. *Office*—Department of City and Regional Planning, University of California, Berkeley, Calif. 94720. *Agent*—Literistic Ltd., 264 Fifth Ave., New York, N.Y. 10001.

CAREER: University of London, London, England, Birkbeck College, assistant lecturer, 1957-60, lecturer in geography, 1960-65, London School of Economics and Political Science, reader in geography with special reference to regional planning, 1966-67; University of Reading, Reading, England, professor of geography, 1968—, head of department, 1968-80; University of California, Berkeley, professor of city and regional planning, 1980—, director of Institute of Urban and Regional Development, 1980—. Member, South East Economic Planning Council, 1966-79, Environmental Board, 1975-79, European Economic Community Expert Group on New Tendencies of Social and Economic Development, 1975-79. Chairman of planning committee, Social Science Research Council, 1975-80. Governor, Centre for Environmental Studies, 1975-80. Member, Transport and Road Research Laboratory Advisory Committee on Transport, 1973—, Standing Advisory Committee on Trunk Road Assessment, 1978-80. Consultant to British Government on many occasions; has served on numerous government committees.

MEMBER: British Academy (fellow), Royal Geographic Society, Association of American Geographers, American Institute of Planners, Regional Studies Association (executive committee, 1967—; honorary journal editor, 1967-78), Royal Town Planning Institute (honorary member).

AWARDS, HONORS: Gill Memorial Prize, Royal Geographic Society, 1968; Adolphe Bentinck Prize, 1979.

WRITINGS:

The Industries of London since 1861, Hillary House, 1962.
London 2000, Faber, 1963, 2nd edition, Praeger, 1969.
(Editor) *Labour's New Frontiers,* London House & Maxwell, 1964.
(Editor) *Land Values: The Report of the Proceedings of a Colloquium Held in London on March 13 and 14, 1965, under the Auspices of the Acton Society Trust,* Sweet & Maxwell, 1965.

The World Cities, McGraw, 1966, 3rd edition, St. Martin's, 1984.
(Editor) J. H. von Thuenen, *Isolated State*, Pergamon, 1966.
(With others) *An Advanced Geography of North-West Europe*, Hulten, 1967.
(With others) *Acton Essays*, Acton Society Trust, 1968.
Theory and Practice of Regional Planning, Pemberton Publishing, 1970.
(With others) *The Containment of Urban England*, Sage Publications, 1973, Volume I: *Urban and Metropolitan Growth Processes*, Volume II: *The Planning System: Objectives, Operations, Impacts*.
(With Marion Clawson) *Planning and Urban Growth: An Anglo-American Comparison*, Johns Hopkins University Press, 1973.
Law and Population Growth in Singapore, Fletcher School of Law and Diplomacy, Tufts University, 1973.
Urban and Regional Planning: An Introduction, Wiley, 1974, 2nd edition, Penguin, 1982.
(Editor) *The Penguin World Atlas*, Penguin, 1974.
(With Roger Sammons) *Urban Activity Patterns and Modal Split in the Journey to Work*, Department of Geography, University of Reading, 1974.
(With Edward Smith) *Better Use of Railways*, Department of Geography, University of Reading, 2nd edition, 1976.
(Editor) *Europe 2000*, Columbia University Press, 1977.
(Editor with Ross Davies) *Issues in Urban Society*, Penguin, 1978.
(Editor) *The New Penguin World Atlas*, Penguin, 1979.
(With Dennis Hay) *Growth Centres in the European Urban System*, University of California Press, 1980.
(Editor) *Radical Agenda for London*, Fabian Society, 1980.
Great Planning Disasters, Weidenfeld & Nicolson, 1980, University of California Press, 1982.
(Editor) *The Inner City in Context: The Final Report of the Social Science Research Council Inner Cities Working Party*, Heinemann, 1981.
(Editor with Ann Markusen) *Silicon Landscapes*, Allen & Unwin, 1985.
(With Carmen Hass-Klau) *Can Rail Save the Cities?: The Impact of Rail Rapid Transit and Pedestrianisation on British and German Cities*, Gower, 1985.
(With Markusen and Amy Glasmeier) *High Tech America: The What, How, Where, and Why of the Sunrise Industries*, Allen & Unwin, 1986.
(With Michael Brehery and others) *Western Sunrise: The Genesis and Growth of Britain's Major High Tech Corridor*, Allen & Unwin, 1987.

Regular contributor to *New Society*. Also author of papers on city and regional planning, and on the computer industry. Editor of *Built Environment*, 1977—, and of *Regional Studies*.

WORK IN PROGRESS: The Fifth Kondratieff: Technical Innovation and Economic Development; a history of town planning in the twentieth century.

SIDELIGHTS: Peter Hall told *CA:* "I aim to work at the fringes of academia and higher journalism. That is to say, I want everything I write to be readable by the informed general reader, however specialized and academic the content may be. I like to write books that will have some influence on the development of public policy."

London 2000 has been translated into Italian. *The World Cities* has been translated into Dutch, French, and Italian.

AVOCATIONAL INTERESTS: Writing, reading, and talking.

BIOGRAPHICAL/CRITICAL SOURCES:

PERIODICALS

Economist, March 4, 1978, April 5, 1980.
Listener, February 9, 1978.
Observer, March 30, 1980.
Times Literary Supplement, September 3, 1974, July 4, 1980.

*   *   *

HALL, (Patrick) Richard Compton
    See COMPTON-HALL, (Patrick) Richard

*   *   *

HALL-CLARKE, James
    See ROWLAND-ENTWISTLE, (Arthur) Theodore (Henry)

*   *   *

HALLIBURTON, Warren J.   1924-

PERSONAL: Born August 2, 1924, in New York, N.Y.; son of Richard H. (a book shipping manager) and Blanche (Watson) Halliburton; married Marion Jones, December 20, 1947; married second wife, Frances Fletcher (a teacher), February 11, 1971; children: (first marriage) Cheryl, Stephanie, Warren, Jr., Jena. *Education:* New York University, B.S., 1949; Columbia University, M.Ed., 1975, D.Ed., 1977.

ADDRESSES: Home—22 Scribner Hill Rd., Wilton, Conn. 06897.

CAREER: Prairie View Agricultural and Mechanical College (now Prairie View A & M University), Prairie View, Tex., instructor in English, 1949; Bishop College, Dallas, Tex., instructor in English, 1951; associate, Institute of International Education, 1952; *Recorder* (newspaper), New York City, reporter and columnist, 1953; teacher and dean in Brooklyn, N.Y. high school, 1958-60; coordinator for New York City Board of Education, and associate of New York State Department of Education, 1960-65; McGraw Hill, Inc., New York City, editor, 1967; Hamilton-Kirkland Colleges, Clinton, N.Y., visiting professor of English, 1971-72; Columbia University, Teachers College, New York City, editor, research associate, and director of scholarly journal, government program, and Ethnic Studies Center, 1972-77; currently editor and writer, *Reader's Digest*, New York City. Free-lance editor and writer. *Military service:* U.S. Army Air Forces, 1943-46.

WRITINGS:

(Editor with Mauri E. Pelkonen) *New Worlds of Literature*, Harcourt, 1966.
The Heist (novel), McGraw, 1969.
Cry, Baby! (novel), McGraw, 1969.
Some Things that Glitter (novel), illustrated by Elzia Moon, McGraw, 1969.
(With William L. Katz) *American Majorities and Minorities: A Syllabus of United States History for Secondary Schools*, Arno, 1970.
(With Laurence Swinburne and Steve Broudy) *They Had a Dream*, Pyramid Publications, 1970.
(Editor and contributor) *America's Color Caravan*, four volumes, Singer Graflex, 1971.
The Picture Life of Jesse Jackson, F. Watts, 1972, 2nd edition, 1984.

(Editor) *Short Story Scene*, Globe, 1973.
The History of Black Americans, Harcourt, 1973.
(With Agnes A. Postva) *Composing with Sentences*, Cambridge Books, 1974.
(With Ernest Kaiser) *Harlem: A History of Broken Dreams*, Doubleday, 1974.
Pathways to the World of English, Globe, 1974.
The Fighting Redtails: America's First Black Airmen, illustrated by John Gampert, Contemporary Perspectives, 1978.
Flight to the Stars: The Life of Daniel James, Jr., Contemporary Perspectives, 1979.
The People of Connecticut: A History Textbook on Connecticut, Connecticut Yankee, 1984.
The Picture Life of Michael Jackson, F. Watts, 1984.

Also adapter of text editions of Jack London's *Call of the Wild*, Douglas Wallop's *The Year the Yankees Lost the Pennant*, and Paddy Chayefsky's *Marty* and *Printer's Measure*, all McGraw, 1968.

Contributor of about one hundred short stories, adaptations, and articles to periodicals; writer of fifteen filmstrips and a motion picture, "Dig!"

SIDELIGHTS: Warren J. Halliburton comments: "Writing is a sanctuary of self-realization, affording me the opportunity for adventure and discovery of my relation with the world. This is a rare if not unique privilege in today's pigeon-holing society."

AVOCATIONAL INTERESTS: Jogging, a follow-through of his days in track and field competition.

BIOGRAPHICAL/CRITICAL SOURCES:

PERIODICALS

New Republic, March 1, 1985.†

* * *

HAMILTON, Mollie
    See KAYE, M(ary) M(argaret)

* * *

HAMPSHIRE, Joyce Gregorian
    See GREGORIAN, Joyce Ballou

* * *

HANDLEY, Graham Roderick   1926-

PERSONAL: Born January 8, 1926, in Hampstead, England; son of Vernon Douglas (a paper maker) and Claudia Lillian (George) Handley; married Ruth Barbara Tunnicliffe, September 26, 1951; children: Roland John, Rosamund Kathleen (deceased), Elaine Melissa. *Education:* Received B.A. (with honors) and M.A. from University of Sheffield; Bedford College, London, Ph.D., 1962.

ADDRESSES: Home—Glasgow Stud Farmhouse, Crews Hill, Enfield, Middlesex EN2 9DY, England.

CAREER: Assistant master at school in London, England, 1953-57; English teacher and department head at grammar schools in Borehamwood, England, 1957-62, and Hatfield, England, 1962-67; College of All Saints, London, senior lecturer, 1967-76, principal lecturer in English, 1976-80; writer, 1980—. Extramural lecturer at University of London, 1973—. *Military*

service: British Army, Intelligence Corps, 1945-48; served in the Far East; became sergeant.

WRITINGS:

PUBLISHED BY PAN BOOKS

Brodie's Notes on William Golding's "Lord of the Flies," 1965.
Brodie's Notes on D. H. Lawrence's "Sons and Lovers," 1967.
Notes on This Day and Age, 1968.
Brodie's Notes on Aldous Huxley's "Brave New World," 1977.
Steinbeck's "The Grapes of Wrath" and "Of Mice and Men" and "The Pearl," 1977.
Brodie's Notes on Ernest Hemingway's "For Whom the Bell Tolls," 1977.
Greene's "The Power and the Glory," 1977.
Brodie's Notes on Joseph Heller's "Catch-22," 1977.
Brodie's Notes on Barry Hines's "A Kestrel for a Knave," 1977.
Brodie's Notes on James Joyce's "A Portrait of the Artist as a Young Man," 1977.
(With Stanley King) *Brodie's Notes on Ken Kesey's "One Flew Over the Cuckoo's Nest,"* 1977.
Brodie's Notes on Keith Waterhouse's "Billy Liar," 1977.
Brodie's Notes on Charles Dickens's "Oliver Twist," 1977.
George Eliot's "The Mill on the Floss," 1978.
Brodie's Notes on F. Scott Fitzgerald's "The Great Gatsby," 1978.
Brodie's Notes on Selected Poems and Letters of John Keats, 1978.
Brodie's Notes on "Selected Poems" by W. H. Auden, 1978.
Brodie's Notes on "Chosen Poems of Thomas Hardy," 1978.
Brodie's Notes on Thomas Mann's "Death in Venice" and "Tonio Kroger," 1978.
(With King) *Brodie's Notes on Charles Dickens's "Bleak House,"* 1978.
(With Paul Harris) *Selected Tales of D. H. Lawrence*, 1978.
Brodie's Notes on William Blake's "Songs of Innocence and Experience," 1978.
Brodie's Notes on Oscar Wilde's "The Importance of Being Earnest," 1978.
Brodie's Notes on William Congreve's "The Way of the World," 1978.
(With W. T. Currie) *Brodie's Notes on W. B. Yeats Selected Poetry*, 1978.
Shakespeare's "Sonnets," 1978.
Brodie's Notes on Ten Twentieth-Century Poets, 1978.
Dickens's "Dombey and Son," 1978.
Brodie's Notes on Charles Dickens's "Our Mutual Friend," 1979.
Brodie's Notes on Charles Dickens's "Little Dorrit," 1980.
Brodie's Notes on Graham Greene's "Brighton Rock," 1980.
(With King) *Brodie's Notes on Sean O'Casey's "Shadow of a Gunman" and "The Plough and the Stars,"* 1980.
(With wife, Barbara Handley) *Brodie's Notes on Wilkie Collins's "The Woman in White,"* 1980.
Brodie's Notes on Evelyn Waugh's "Scoop," 1980.
(With King) *Brodie's Notes on Graham Greene's "The Quiet American,"* 1981.
The Metaphysical Poets, 1981.
Brodie's Notes on "Macbeth," 1984.
Brodie's Notes on "As You Like It," 1985.
Brodie's Notes on Jane Austen's "Pride and Prejudice," 1985.
Brodie's Notes on Shakespeare's "Twelfth Night," 1985.
Brodie's Notes on "Much Ado about Nothing," 1986.

Brodie's Notes on "The Winter's Tale," 1986.
Brodie's Notes on Jane Austen's "Emma," 1986.
Brodie's Notes on Hardy's "Tess of the D'Urbervilles," 1986.
Brodie's Notes on William Wycherley's "The Country Wife," 1986.

PUBLISHED BY PENGUIN BOOKS

Harper Lee's "To Kill a Mockingbird," 1985.
Thackeray's "Vanity Fair," 1985.
Chaucer's "The Pardoner's Tale," 1986.
L. P. Hartley's "The Go-Between," 1987.
Trollope's "Barchester Towers," 1987.

OTHER

Mrs. Gaskell's "Sylvia's Lovers," Basil Blackwell, 1967.
Dickens's "Hard Times," Basil Blackwell, 1968.
Self-Test English, Seymour Press, 1970.
(With Eric Newton) *A Guide to Teaching Poetry,* University of London Press, 1971.
The College of All Saints, 1964-1978: An Informal History of One Hundred Years, 1878-1978, John Roberts Press, 1978.
(Editor) *Sport* (stories), J. Murray, 1980.
(Editor) Emily Bronte, *Wuthering Heights,* Macmillan, 1982.
(Editor) George Eliot, *Daniel Deronda,* Oxford University Press, 1984.
(Editor) George Eliot, *The Mill on the Floss,* Macmillan, 1985.
Middlemarch (study), Macmillan, 1985.
Silas Marner (study), Macmillan, 1986.

WORK IN PROGRESS: Studies of Hardy's *Far from the Madding Crowd,* Hardy's *The Return of the Native,* John Christopher's *The Death of Grass,* Mrs. Gaskell's *North and South,* Defoe's *Journal of the Plague Year,* Dickens's *David Copperfield,* and George Eliot's *Daniel Deronda* (for World's Classics).

*   *   *

HANNA, J. Marshall   1907-

PERSONAL: Born October 7, 1907, in Oregon, Mo.; son of William A. and Lettie Hanna; married Mary Webber, 1937; children: Mary Jane, Anne Elizabeth. *Education:* University of Nebraska, B.Sc., 1932; Columbia University, M.A., 1935; New York University, Ed.D., 1939.

ADDRESSES: Home—101 Trinity Lakes Drive, Box 268, Sun City Center, Fla. 33570.

CAREER: University of Virginia, Mary Washington College, Charlottesville, professor of business education, 1939-40; Western Michigan University, Kalamazoo, head of business department, 1940-47; Ohio State University, Columbus, professor of education, 1947-74, professor emeritus, 1974—. Dean, Territorial College of Guam, 1955-57; education consultant to Ministry of Education, Government of India, 1962-64. *Military service:* U.S. Navy, 1943-45; became lieutenant.

MEMBER: National Business Teachers Association (national president, 1959), Policies Commission for Business and Economic Education (member of national commission, 1958-61), Delta Pi Epsilon (national president, 1953).

AWARDS, HONORS: Delta Pi Epsilon Research Award, 1940; John Robert Gregg Award, 1972.

WRITINGS:

(With Max Herbert Freeman and Gilbert Kahn) *Bookkeeping and Accounting Simplified,* McGraw, 1958, published as *Accounting 10/12,* four volumes, 1968, 3rd edition, 1976.
(With Vernon A. Musselman) *Methods of Teaching Accounting,* McGraw, 1960, 3rd edition, 1978.
(With Beamer and Estelle A. Popham) *Effective Secretarial Practices,* South-Western, 1962, 6th edition (with Popham and Rita Sloan Tilton) published as *Secretarial Procedures and Administration,* 1973, 7th edition, 1978.
College Business Mathematics, H. M. Rowe, 1964, 2nd edition, 1981.
(With David H. Weaver and others) *Sun-n-Ski: An Accounting Simulation* (with cassette), McGraw, 1977.
(With Arthur Lee Walker) *How to Use Adding and Calculating Machines,* 4th edition, McGraw, 1979.

Editor, *National Business Education Quarterly,* 1955-57.

*   *   *

HANSON, Anthony Tyrrell   1916-

PERSONAL: Born November 24, 1916, in London, England; son of Philip Herbert (a civil servant) and Deena (Tyrrell) Hanson; married Miriam Joselin, September 25, 1945; children: Philip, Andrew. *Education:* Attended Cheltenham College; Trinity College, University of Dublin, B.D., 1942, D.D., 1953.

ADDRESSES: Home—Orchard Villa, Melbourne Place, Topcliffe Rd., Sowerby Y07 1QY, England. *Office*—Department of Theology, University of Hull, Hull, Humberside, England.

CAREER: Clergyman of Anglican Church. Curate in County Down, Ireland, 1941-43; Student Christian Movement, London, England, secretary, 1943-46; Andhra United Theological College, Dornakal, Andhra Pradesh, India, tutor, 1947-55; United Theological College, Bangalore, India, tutor, 1955-59; St. Anne's Cathedral, Belfast, Northern Ireland, canon theologian, 1959-62; University of Hull, Hull, England, professor of theology, 1963-82. Helped to organize interdenominational theology department (Roman Catholic, Reformed, Anglican) at Lesotho, South Africa; also helped to obtain affiliation of Irish School of Ecumenics, Dublin, to the University of Hull.

WRITINGS:

(With R. H. Preston) *Revelation of St. John the Divine,* S.C.M. Press, 1949.
(With wife, Miriam Hanson) *The Book of Job,* S.C.M. Press, 1953, revised edition, 1970.
Jonah and Daniel, Madras, 1955.
The Wrath of the Lamb, S.P.C.K., 1957.
The Pioneer Ministry, S.C.M. Press, 1961.
The Church of the Servant, S.C.M. Press, 1962.
St. Paul's Understanding of Jesus, University of Hull Press, 1963.
Beyond Anglicanism, Longman & Todd, 1965.
Jesus Christ in the Old Testament, S.P.C.K., 1965.
(Editor) *The Pastoral Letters,* Cambridge University Press, 1966.
(Editor) *Vindications,* S.C.M. Press, 1966.
Studies in the Pastoral Epistles, S.P.C.K., 1968.
(Editor) *Teilhard Reassessed,* Longman & Todd, 1970.
Studies in Paul's Technique and Theology, Eerdmans, 1974.
Grace and Truth, S.P.C.K., 1975.
Church, Sacraments, and Ministry, Mowbrays, 1975.

The New Testament Interpretation of Scripture, S.P.C.K., 1980.
(With Richard P. C. Hanson) *Reasonable Belief: A Survey of the Christian Faith,* Oxford University Press, 1980.
The Pastoral Epistles: Based on the Revised Standard Version, Eerdmans, 1982.
The Image of the Invisible God, S.C.M. Press, 1982.
(With Hanson) *The Identity of the Church,* S.C.M. Press, 1987.
The Paradox of the Cross in the Thought of St. Paul, Sheffield Academic Press, 1987.

*   *   *

HARE, Nathan 1934-

PERSONAL: Born April 9, 1934, in Slick, Okla.; son of Seddie Henry (a farmer) and Tishia (Davis) Hare; married Julie Reed (a public relations specialist), December 27, 1956. *Education:* Langston University, A.B., 1954; University of Chicago, M.A., 1957, Ph.D. (sociology), 1962; California School of Professional Psychology, Ph.D., 1975; also studied at Northwestern University, 1959.

ADDRESSES: Office—1801 Bush St., San Francisco, Calif. 94109.

CAREER: Briefly, a professional boxer; Virginia State College, Petersburg, instructor in sociology, 1957-58; National Opinion Research Center, Chicago, Ill., interviewer, 1959-61; Howard University, Washington, D.C., instructor, 1961-63, assistant professor of sociology, 1964-67; San Francisco State College (now University), director of Black Studies Curriculum, 1968, chairman of department of Black Studies, 1968-69; director, Center for Educational Innovation, summer, 1968; *Black Scholar,* Sausalito, Calif., founding publisher, 1969-75; Child Development Services, Oakland, Calif., clinical psychologist, 1975-76; psychologist in private practice, 1977—; San Francisco State University, lecturer, 1984—. Part-time visiting professor, Lone Mountain College, 1972-73; chairman of task force on demographic and communal characteristics, Teachers College, Columbia University, 1966-67. Chairman of workshop on education, National Conference on Black Power, 1968; founding president, Black World Foundation, 1970. Member of board of advisors, San Francisco Black Exposition, 1972; member of board of directors, North American Committee, Second World Black and African Festival of Arts and Culture, Lagos, Nigeria, 1974, and San Francisco Local Development Corporation; affiliated with Complete Help and Assistance Necessary for College Education (CHANCE) project, 1976. President and chairman of the board, Black Think Tank, 1982—. *Military service:* U.S. Army Reserve, 1958-64, active duty, 1958.

MEMBER: American Sociological Association, Association of Behavioral and Social Sciences, American Psychological Association, Association of Orthopsychiatry, American Association of University Professors, Eastern Sociological Association, New York Academy of Sciences, Sigma Gamma Rho.

AWARDS, HONORS: Danforth fellow, 1954-57; "Black Is Beautiful" citation from United Black Artists, 1968; Distinguished Alumni Award, Langston University, 1975; community-clinical psychology award, Southern Regional Education Board, Atlanta, 1978; Professional Person of the Year, San Francisco chapter of the National Association of Negro Business and Professional Women's Clubs, 1980; presidential citation, National Association for Equal Opportunity in Higher Education, 1982; national award, National Council on Black Studies, 1983.

WRITINGS:

The Black Anglo-Saxons, Marzani & Munsell, 1965.
(Author of introduction) W. E. B. DuBois, *The Souls of Black Folk,* Signet, 1969.
(Author of introduction) Lenneal Henderson, editor, *Black Political Life in the United States,* Chandler Publishing, 1972.
(Editor with Robert Chrisman) *Contemporary Black Thought: The Best from the Black Scholar,* Bobbs-Merrill, 1973.
(Editor with Chrisman) *Pan-Africanism,* Bobbs-Merrill, 1974.
(Contributor) David W. Swift, editor, *American Education: A Sociological View,* Houghton, 1976.
(With wife, Julia Hare) *The Endangered Black Family: Coping with the Unisexualization and Coming Extinction of the Black Race,* Black Think Tank, 1984.

Contributor of about sixty articles to sociology and black studies journals and to national periodicals, including *Newsweek, Ramparts, Saturday Review,* and *U.S. News and World Report.* Contributing editor, *Journal of Black Studies, Ebony, Black Scholar, Journal of Black Education,* and *Black Law Journal.*

SIDELIGHTS: Nathan Hare is "a major leader of the Black Studies movement," write Richard Barksdale and Keneth Kinnamon in *Black Writers of America: A Comprehensive Anthology.* Characterized by them as "an unorthodox academician," Hare sparked controversy while serving on the faculty of Howard University in the 1960s through his opposition to the war in Vietnam and the draft, his advocacy of Black power, his stint as a professional boxer, and his criticism of the university administration. In 1968 he launched a Black Studies program at San Francisco State College, and in 1969 began publication of the *Black Scholar,* in Barksdale's and Kinnamon's words, an "important 'Journal of Black Studies and Research.'"

Hare's work centers on the necessity for blacks everywhere to recognize the power of traditional black mores and ideas. For instance, in Hare's opinion, the mission of the black scholar is to rethink European modes of thought, replacing them with new insights and solutions to old problems. In an article published in Barksdale's and Kinnamon's *Black Writers of America,* he states, "[The black scholar must] de-colonize his mind so that he may effectively guide other intellectuals and students in their search for liberation." Because of the legacy of miseducation and abuse of learning, he continues, white society is "increasingly corrupt and bloody with no clear future. The air is filled with pollution and the land and forests are being destroyed as human alienation and conflict remain on the rise." The cure for this problem, according to Hare, lies in the removal of "icons of objectivity, amoral knowledge and its methodology, and the total demolition of the anti-social attitudes of Ivory-Towerism."

Similar views are expressed in Hare's book *The Black Anglo-Saxons* and the volume which he co-edited with Robert Chrisman called *Pan-Africanism. The Black Anglo-Saxons* is a critique of the black middle class, a group which Hare perceives as having shed black values and mores in favor of assimilated ethics and standards from a white culture. *Pan-Africanism* is a collection of essays by both Africans and Afro-Americans which promotes traditional black political concepts of communalism, as opposed to European socialism, in an attempt to chart Africa's future. Both works encourage a return to pre-colonial black ideals as a solution to problems in modern life.

Hare continues to advance ideals and mores drawn from black tradition. He says, in an article in *Ebony* magazine, "The

Black middle class could begin now to solve the problems of juvenile delinquency, of in-group violence, school drop-outs, low academic performance, and many another ailment—maybe even racism—if we could come together, return to our own people, live with them, love them, learn from the wisdom of a long-suffering and creative race. But it will first be necessary to abandon the unbridled pursuit of materialism and the all-engulfing frenzy for White approval and acceptance.''

BIOGRAPHICAL/CRITICAL SOURCES:

BOOKS

Barksdale, Richard, and Kenneth Kinnamon, editors, *Black Writers of America: A Comprehensive Anthology*, Macmillan, 1972.

PERIODICALS

American Sociological Review, December, 1965.
Annals of the American Academy, November, 1965.
Choice, June, 1974.
Ebony, August, 1987.
New York Times Book Review, February 21, 1971.

*   *   *

HARPER, Michael S(teven) 1938-

PERSONAL: Born March 18, 1938, in Brooklyn, N.Y.; son of Walter Warren and Katherine (Johnson) Harper; married Shirley Ann Buffington, December 24, 1965; children: Roland Warren, Patrice Cuchulain, Rachel Maria. *Education:* Los Angeles City College, A.A., 1959; Los Angeles State College of Applied Arts and Sciences (now California State University, Los Angeles), B.A., 1961, M.A., 1963; University of Iowa, M.F.A., 1963; additional study, University of Illinois, 1970-71.

ADDRESSES: Home—26 First St., Barrington, R.I. 02806. *Office*—Department of English, Box 1852, Brown University, Providence, R.I. 02912.

CAREER: Contra Costa College, San Pablo, Calif., instructor in English, 1964-68; Lewis and Clark College, Portland, Ore., poet in residence, 1968-69; California State College (now University), Hayward, associate professor of English, 1970; Brown University, Providence, R.I., associate professor, 1971-73, professor, 1973—, I. J. Kapstein Professor of English, 1983—, director of writing program. Visiting professor at Reed College, 1968-69; Harvard University, 1974, and Yale University, 1977; Benedict Distinguished Professor of English, Carleton College, 1979; Elliston poet, University of Cincinnati, 1979; National Humanities Distinguished Professor, Colgate University, 1985. Bicentennial poet, Bicentennary Exchange: Britain/USA, 1976. American specialist, International Congress of Africanists (ICA) State Department tour of Africa, 1977; lecturer, German University ICA tour of nine universities, 1978. Council member, Massachusetts Council on the Arts and Humanities, 1977-80; board member, Yaddo Artists Colony, Sarasota Springs, N.Y.; original founding member, African Continuum, St. Louis, Mo. Judge, National Book Awards in poetry, 1978.

MEMBER: American Academy of Arts and Letters.

AWARDS, HONORS: Fellow, Center for Advanced Study, University of Illinois, 1970-71; Black Academy of Arts and Letters award, 1972, for *History Is Your Own Heartbeat;* National Institute of Arts and Letters award and American Acad-

emy award in literature, both 1972; Guggenheim fellowship, 1976; National Endowment for the Arts creative writing award, 1977; nomination for National Book Award for poetry and Melville-Cane Award, both 1978, both for *Images of Kin: New and Selected Poems.*

WRITINGS:

POEMS

Dear John, Dear Coltrane, University of Pittsburgh Press, 1970.
History Is Your Own Hearbeat, University of Illinois Press, 1971.
Photographs, Negatives: History as Apple Tree (also see below), Scarab Press, 1972.
Song: I Want a Witness (includes *Photographs, Negatives: History as Apple Tree*), University of Pittsburgh Press, 1972.
Debridement, Doubleday, 1973.
Nightmare Begins Responsibility, University of Illinois Press, 1974.
Images of Kin: New and Selected Poems, University of Illinois Press, 1977.
Rhode Island: Eight Poems, Pym-Randall, 1981.
Healing Song for the Inner Ear, University of Illinois Press, 1985.

OTHER

(Compiler) Ralph Dickey, *Leaving Eden: Poems,* Bonewhistle Press, 1974.
(Editor with Robert B. Stepto, and contributor) *Chant of Saints: A Gathering of Afro-American Literature, Art, and Scholarship,* University of Illinois Press, 1979.
(Compiler) Sterling Allen Brown, *The Collected Poems of Sterling A. Brown,* Harper, 1980.
(Contributor) R. Baxter Miller, editor, *Black American Literature and Humanism,* University Press of Kentucky, 1981.

Also contributor to poetry anthologies, including *The Poetry of Black America, To Gwen with Love, Starting with Poetry, Understanding the New Black Poetry, The Black Poets,* and *Natural Process.* Contributor to periodicals, including *Black Scholar, Black World, Chicago Review, Negro American Literature Forum, Negro Digest,* and *Poetry.* Guest editor, *Iowa Review, Massachusetts Review,* and *American Poetry Review.* Editor with John Wright of special issue of *Carleton Miscellany* on Ralph Ellison, winter, 1980. Member of editorial boards of *TriQuarterly,* the *Georgia Review,* and *Obsidian.*

SIDELIGHTS: "Michael Harper is a deeply complex poet whose mission is to unite the fractured, inhumane technologies of our time with the abiding deep well of Negro folk traditions,'' says John Callahan in the *New Republic.* Harper does this, notes *Poetry* reviewer Paul Breslin, by drawing "upon black history, literature, and myth,'' as do many other black writers. However, "what distinguishes Harper as a unique poet,'' states Norris B. Clark in the *Dictionary of Literary Biography,* "is a distinctive voice that captures the colors, mood, and realities of the personal, the racial, and the historical past, and a philosophy that bridges the traditional schism between black America and white America.''

Harper himself supports Clark's statements, telling *CA* that his voice evolved from travels made in the late 1960s "to Mexico and Europe where those landscapes broadened my scope and interest in poetry and culture of other countries while I searched my own family and racial history for folklore, history and myth for themes that would give my writing the tradition and context where I could find my own voice. My travels made me look closely at the wealth of human materials in my own life, its ethnic richness, complexity of language and stylization, the tension between stated moral idealism and brutal historical realities, and I investigated the inner reality of those struggles to find the lyrical expression of their secrets in my own voice.''

Harper's interest in history pervades his poetry, and his thesis in much of his work is directly related to this interest; in the words of David Lehman in *Poetry* magazine, his efforts are "attempts of a more historical nature to illuminate the black experience in America." He uses stories from both his family's past and from events in black history in general to illustrate his points: Harper's grandfather facing a mob threatening to burn his home; John Henry Louis, a Vietnam veteran and Congressional Medal of Honor winner, shot in the streets of Detroit by a shopkeeper who owed him money; a slave who, told to saw a limb off a tree, sat on the limb itself while working. Harper's poems also incorporate jazz and blues rhythms to "revive the past through the readers' inner feelings, by creating a new sense of time and by arranging a historical awareness," says Clark. His success in this is marked by a sense of "history automatically yielding up its metaphor, as the facts are salvaged by the careful eye and ear informed by a remarkable imagination which balances the American present and past," according to Laurence Lieberman in the *Yale Review*.

However, Harper's concentration on the past is not what makes his work unique. Robert B. Stepto, writing in the *Hollins Critic*, relates Harper's work to a primary tradition in Afro-American letters: "the honoring of kin," a tradition that Harper shares with writers such as Ralph Ellison and Robert Hayden. Although Harper's earlier work included many poems about his wife's family, his wife, and their children, it was not until the publication of *Nightmare Begins Responsibility* that Harper began to write about his own past. In that collection, Harper wrote poems for both his grandfathers and his mother's mother, poems whose "matter-of-fact, stoic lines," in Callahan's opinion, "enlarge the scale" of their lives. Callahan calls these poems "masterful and unforgettable"; he notes that "in [his work] Harper evokes for his children the lives of people whose legacy is a strength and integrity that crossed over the turf of survival.''

Besides personal family figures Harper also uses, in Lieberman's words, the lives of key figures "in the black man's struggle to achieve an American identity" in collections such as *Debridement* and *Dear John, Dear Coltrane*. Figures such as the baseball player Jackie Robinson, the novelist Richard Wright, the poet Sterling Brown, and the jazz musician John Coltrane are akin to Harper; they are "kin who share the goal of artistic excellence in whatever may be their craft or endeavor," says Stepto. Michael G. Cooke points out in *Afro-American Literature in the Twentieth Century: The Achievement of Intimacy* that Harper's honoring is not limited to ties of blood or race; he says, "*kinship* means social bonding, a recognition of likeness in context, concern, need, liability value. It is humanistic, a cross between consanguinity and technical organization." "While [Harper] invokes blood relations in several inspired cases," he continues, "his approach to kinship is a radiant one, reaching out across time, across space, even across race" to include white men such as the Puritan

dissident and founder of Rhode Island, Roger Williams, and the farmer-turned-abolitionist, John Brown.

Harper's acceptance of both black and white historical figures as kin is recognized by critics as an original factor in his poetry. Clark indicates that Harper "is neither a black poet nor a white poet; as he freely acknowledges, he uses both traditions and heritages rightfully his and America's to create images of power and beauty." He points out that Harper has stated that he reads white authors "to see how they make use of form, as well as to evaluate black character and motivation." Yet, although Harper criticizes white poets who, in his opinion, use the black idiom inconsistently, he does not reject them. Clark concludes, "[Harper] is comfortable in not denying a dual tradition as many white American writers and black American writers have done. [He] continues to be a poet of harmony—accepting unity and diversity—rather than discord.''

BIOGRAPHICAL/CRITICAL SOURCES:

BOOKS

Contemporary Literary Criticism, Gale, Volume VII, 1977, Volume XXII, 1982.
Cooke, Michael G., *Afro-American Literature in the Twentieth Century: The Achievement of Intimacy*, Yale University Press, 1984.
Dictionary of Literary Biography, Volume XLI: *Afro-American Poets since 1955*, Gale, 1985.
Harper, Michael S., and Robert B. Stepto, editors, *Chant of Saints: A Gathering of Afro-American Literature, Art, and Scholarship*, University of Illinois Press, 1979.
O'Brian, John, editor, *Interviews with Black Writers*, Liveright, 1973.

PERIODICALS

Hollins Critic, June, 1976.
Los Angeles Times, January 21, 1987.
Nation, June 21, 1980.
New Republic, May 17, 1985.
New York Times Book Review, March 5, 1978, October 13, 1985.
Parnassus: Poetry in Review, fall/winter, 1975.
Poetry, December, 1973.
Saturday Review, August 8, 1970.
Times Literary Supplement, May 30, 1980.
Virginia Quarterly Review, autumn, 1970.
World Literature Today, winter, 1981, winter, 1986.
Yale Review, October, 1973.†

—*Sketch by Kenneth R. Shepherd*

*   *   *

HARTMAN, Patience
   See ZAWADSKY, Patience

*   *   *

HASTINGS, Paul G(uiler)   1914-

PERSONAL: Born February 6, 1914, in Upland, Ind.; son of Howard Guiler (a missionary) and Alice (Cooper) Hastings; married Elsa C. Belford, September 28, 1947 (divorced, 1978); children: Margery Rita Christina, David Jonathan Craig. *Education:* Oberlin College, A.B., 1937; University of Pennsylvania, M.B.A., 1939, Ph.D., 1950. *Politics:* "Mostly Democratic, occasionally Republican." *Religion:* Protestant.

ADDRESSES: Home—7426 Gallant Cir., Citrus Heights, Calif. 95610. *Office*—Department of Management, California State University, 6000 J St., Sacramento, Calif. 95819.

CAREER: Accountant, university teacher and lecturer, 1939-50; Texas Christian University, Fort Worth, professor, director of Bureau of Business Research, 1950-59; California State University, Sacramento, professor, 1959-64, head of department of finance, 1964—. President, Sacramento NSU Wankel Sales & Service, Inc. (auto dealership), beginning 1965. *Military service:* U.S. Army Air Forces, 1942-46; became sergeant.

MEMBER: American Finance Association, American Economic Association, American Association of University Professors, Western Finance Association.

AWARDS, HONORS: Fellowships from Forum in Finance, 1957, and Ford Foundation, 1961.

WRITINGS:

A Canada-United States Customs Union, Rochester University Press, 1954.
(Co-author) *Public Finance,* Pitman, 1957.
Consumer Credit in Texas, Bureau of Business Research, Texas Christian University, 1958.
Fundamentals of Business Enterprise, Van Nostrand, 1961.
The Management of Business Finance, Van Nostrand, 1966.
Introduction to Business, McGraw, 1968, 2nd edition, 1974.
(With Norbert J. Mietus) *Personal Finance,* McGraw, 1972, 2nd edition, 1977.

*   *   *

HAVLIK, John F(ranklin)   1917-1984

PERSONAL: Born March 22, 1917, in Milwaukee, Wis.; died December 10, 1984, of a heart attack; son of Joseph (a machinist) and Maude (Schwab) Havlik; married Anna Mae Erwin, December 27, 1938; children: Brenda Rachel (Mrs. Thomas E. Ferrill). *Education:* Baylor University, B.A., 1946; Southern Baptist Theological Seminary, B.D., 1949; Central Baptist Theological Seminary, Th.M., 1953; Luther Rice Seminary, Th.D., 1969. *Politics:* Independent.

ADDRESSES: Home—1284 Oakcrest Dr. S.W., Atlanta, Ga. 30311. *Office*—1350 Spring St. N.W., Atlanta, Ga. 30309.

CAREER: Ordained minister of Southern Baptist Convention, 1938; pastor, Center Baptist Church, Green County, Mo., 1938-39, Fair Park Baptist Church, Dallas, Tex., 1940-41, Baden Baptist Church, St. Louis, Mo., 1942-43, East Baptist Church, Louisville, Ky., 1946-49, and Beaumont Baptist Church, Kansas City, Mo., 1950-56; state secretary of evangelism, Kansas Convention of Southern Baptists, Wichita, 1956-61, and Louisiana Baptist Convention, Alexandria, 1961-64; Home Mission Board, Southern Baptist Convention, Atlanta, Ga., director of department of evangelism development, 1965-78, director of evangelism education and writing, 1978-82. Adjunct professor of evangelism, Midwestern Baptist Theological Seminary, Kansas City, 1971-82. Trustee, Southwest Baptist College, Bolivar, Mo., 1951-55; member of board of Radio and Television Commission, SBC, Fort Worth, Tex., 1960; director of Trans-Pacific Crusade, Wellington, New Zealand, 1965; member of executive committee, Key '73 National Interdenominational Evangelism Campaign; chairman of Mayor's Committee "Affirmation Atlanta," 1974; member of anti-discrimination committee, Atlanta School Board, 1975.

AWARDS, HONORS: Named honorable citizen, New Orleans, Louisiana, 1964, and Shreveport, Louisiana, 1964; recipient of public service accolade, Georgia Conference of Social Workers, 1974.

WRITINGS:

(With Robert G. Witty) *Pastor's Guide for Revival,* Convention Press, 1968.
(Contributor) Joseph A. Green and Wayne Ward, editors, *Is the Bible a Human Book?,* Broadman, 1970.
People-Centered Evangelism, Broadman, 1971.
Old Wine in New Bottles, Broadman, 1972.
The Evangelistic Church, Convention Press, 1976.
You Can Be Born Again, Pinnacle Books, 1978.
Where in the World Is Jesus Christ?, Broadman, 1980.
How to Enjoy Reading the Bible, Broadman, 1981.

Contributor to *Southern Baptist Encyclopedia.* Writer and narrator of four cassette tapes issued by Broadman. Editor of four manuals for lay evangelism. Contributor to religious periodicals.

[Date of death provided by wife, Anna Mae Havlik]

*   *   *

HAYDEN, Robert C(arter), Jr.   1937-

PERSONAL: Born August 21, 1937, in New Bedford, Mass.; son of Robert C. (deceased) and Josephine (Hughes) Hayden; children: Deborah, Kevin, Karen. *Education:* Boston University, B.A., 1959, Ed.M., 1961, doctoral candidate, 1973—; Harvard University, certificate, 1966.

ADDRESSES: Home—P.O. Box 5453, Boston, Mass. 02102. *Office*—MassPEP, 553 Huntington Ave., Boston, Mass. 02115.

CAREER: Junior high school teacher of science in Newton, Mass.,1961-65; American Education Publications, Xerox Education Division, Middletown, Conn., editor and writer, 1966-68; Ginn & Co., Xerox Education Division, Boston, Mass., editor, 1968-69; Metropolitan Council for Educational Opportunity, Boston, Mass., executive director, 1970-73; Education Development Center, Newton, Mass., director of ethnic studies for Career Opportunities Program, 1973-74, managing director of Project Torque, 1974-76; Northeastern University, Boston, lecturer in African-American studies, 1978—; Boston Public Schools, Boston, special assistant and executive assistant to superintendent, 1982-85; director of project development, 1985-86; executive director of Massachusetts Pre-Engineering Program, 1987—. Instructor at State University of New York at Buffalo, summers, 1964, 1966, and Boston College, 1974-75; guest lecturer at Boston University, Harvard University, Boston State College, Tufts University, Simmons College, and University of Suffolk. Massachusetts Institute of Technology, community fellow, 1976—, director of secondary technical education project, 1980-82. Member of corporation of Museum of Afro-American History; member of board of directors of Roxbury Federation of Neighborhood Centers; member of advisory board of Child's World Day Care Centers, Inc.

MEMBER: Association for the Study of Afro-American Life and History (executive council member), National Alliance of Black School Educators, National Association of Science Writers, National Association for the Advancement of Colored People, Kappa Alpha Psi.

AWARDS, HONORS: All-American Award from Educational Press Association of America, 1968; local National Association for the Advancement of Colored People award, 1972; outstanding book award from National Science Teachers-Association and Children's Book Council, 1976, for *Nine Black American Doctors.*

WRITINGS:

Why You Are You: The Science of Heredity, Sex, and Development, American Education Publications, 1968.
Black in America: Episodes in U.S. History, Xerox Education Publications, 1969.
Seven Black American Scientists, Addison-Wesley, 1970.
Eight Black American Inventors, Addison-Wesley, 1972.
(With Jacqueline Harris) *Nine Black American Doctors,* Addison-Wesley, 1976.
Faith, Culture, and Leadership: A History of the Black Church in Boston (booklet), National Association for the Advancement of Colored People (Boston), 1983.

Contributor to *Dictionary of American Negro Biography, Boston's NAACP History: 1910-82,* and *A History of the Metropolitan Council for Educational Opportunity.* Author of "Boston's Black History," a weekly column in *Bay State Banner,* 1974-82. Book review editor of *Science Activities,* 1969-73; regional editor, *Western Journal of Black Studies,* 1976-83.

WORK IN PROGRESS: A biography of Roland Hayes.

SIDELIGHTS: Robert C. Hayden, Jr. comments that he "writes to provide youth of all ethnic and racial groups with accurate, useful information on the work of black Americans in science, invention, and medicine." In his work Hayden makes extensive use of oral history.

BIOGRAPHICAL/CRITICAL SOURCES:

BOOKS

Selected Black American Authors: An Illustrated Bio-Bibliography, G. K. Hall, 1977.

PERIODICALS

Horn Book, March, 1985.
New York Amsterdam News, April 9, 1977.

*	*	*

## HAYDEN, Robert E(arl)	1913-1980

PERSONAL: Name originally Asa Bundy Sheffey; name legally changed by foster parents; born August 4, 1913, in Detroit, Mich.; died February 25, 1980, in Ann Arbor, Mich.; son of Asa and Gladys Ruth (Finn) Sheffey; foster son of William and Sue Ellen (Westerfield) Hayden; married Erma I. Morris, June 15, 1940; children: Maia. *Education:* Detroit City College (now Wayne State University), B.A., 1936; University of Michigan, M.A., 1944. *Religion:* Baha'i.

CAREER: Federal Writers' Project, Detroit, Mich., researcher, 1936-40; University of Michigan, Ann Arbor, teaching fellow, 1944-46; Fisk University, Nashville, Tenn., 1946-69, began as assistant professor, became professor of English; University of Michigan, professor of English, 1969-80. Bingham Professor, University of Louisville, 1969; visiting poet, University of Washington, 1969, University of Connecticut, 1971, and Denison University, 1972. Member, Michigan Arts Council, 1975-76; Consultant in Poetry, Library of Congress, 1976-78.

MEMBER: American Academy and Institute of Arts and Letters, Academy of American Poets, PEN, American Poetry Society, Authors Guild, Authors League of America, Phi Kappa Phi.

AWARDS, HONORS: Jules and Avery Hopwood Poetry Award, University of Michigan, 1938 and 1942; Julius Rosenwald fellow, 1947; Ford Foundation fellow in Mexico, 1954-55; World Festival of Negro Arts grand prize, 1966, for *A Ballad of Remembrance;* Russell Loines Award, National Institute of Arts and Letters, 1970; National Book Award nomination, 1971, for *Words in the Mourning Time;* Litt.D., Brown University, 1976, Grand Valley State College, 1976, Fisk University, 1976, Wayne State University, 1977, and Benedict College, 1977; Academy of American Poets fellow, 1977; Michigan Arts Foundation Award, 1977; National Book Award nomination, 1979, for *American Journal.*

WRITINGS:

(Editor and author of introduction) *Kaleidoscope: Poems by American Negro Poets* (juvenile), Harcourt, 1967.
(Author of preface) Alain LeRoy Locke, editor, *The New Negro,* Atheneum, 1968.
(Editor with David J. Burrows and Frederick R. Lapides) *Afro-American Literature: An Introduction,* Harcourt, 1971.
(Editor with James Edwin Miller and Robert O'Neal) *The United States in Literature,* Scott, Foresman, 1973, abridged edition published as *The American Literary Tradition, 1607-1899,* 1973.
Collected Prose, edited by Frederick Glaysher, University of Michigan Press, 1984.

POEMS

Heart-Shape in the Dust, Falcon Press (Detroit), 1940.
(With Myron O'Higgins) *The Lion and the Archer,* Hemphill Press (Nashville), 1948.
Figure of Time: Poems, Hemphill Press, 1955.
A Ballad of Remembrance, Paul Breman (London), 1962.
Selected Poems, October House, 1966.
Words in the Mourning Time, October House, 1970.
The Night-Blooming Cereus, Paul Breman, 1972.
Angle of Ascent: New and Selected Poems, Liveright, 1975.
American Journal, limited edition, Effendi Press, 1978, enlarged edition, Liveright, 1982.
Robert Hayden: Collected Poems, edited by Glaysher, Liveright, 1985.

RECORDINGS

(With others) "Today's Poets," Folkways, 1967.

CONTRIBUTOR

The Legend of John Brown, Detroit Institute of Arts, 1978.

Contributor to periodicals, including *Atlantic, Negro Digest,* and *Midwest Journal.* Drama and music critic, *Michigan Chronicle,* late 1930s.

SIDELIGHTS: Robert E. Hayden was the first black poet to be chosen as Consultant in Poetry to the Library of Congress, a position described by Thomas W. Ennis of the *New York Times* as "the American equivalent of the British poet laureate designation." Hayden's formal, elegant poems about the black historical experience earned him a number of other major awards as well. "Robert Hayden is now generally accepted," Frederick Glaysher stated in Hayden's *Collected Prose,* "as the most outstanding craftsman of Afro-American poetry."

The historical basis for much of Hayden's poetry stemmed from his extensive study of American and black history. Beginning in the 1930s, when he researched black history for the Federal Writers' Project in his native Detroit, Hayden studied the story of his people from their roots in Africa to their present condition in the United States. "History," Charles T. Davis wrote in *Modern Black Poets: A Collection of Critical Essays*, "has haunted Robert Hayden from the beginning of his career as a poet." As he once explained to Glenford E. Mitchell of *World Order*, Hayden saw history "as a long, tortuous, and often bloody process of becoming, of psychic evolution."

Other early influences on Hayden's development as a poet were W. H. Auden, under whom Hayden studied at the University of Michigan, and Stephen Vincent Benet, particularly Benet's poem "John Brown's Body." That poem describes the black reaction to General Sherman's march through Georgia during the Civil War and inspired Hayden to also write of that period of history, creating a series of poems on black slavery and the Civil War that won him a Hopwood Award in 1942.

After graduating from college in 1944, Hayden embarked on an academic career. He spent some twenty-three years at Fisk University, where he rose to become a professor of English, and ended his career with an eleven-year stint at the University of Michigan. Hayden told Mitchell that he considered himself to be "a poet who teaches in order to earn a living so that he can write a poem or two now and then."

Although history plays a large role in Hayden's poetry, many of his works are also inspired by the poet's adherence to the Baha'i faith, an Eastern religion which believes in a coming world civilization. Hayden served for many years as the poetry editor of the group's *World Order* magazine. The universal outlook of the Baha'is also moved Hayden to reject any narrow racial classification for his work. James Mann of the *Dictionary of Literary Biography* claimed that Hayden "stands out among poets of his race for his staunch avowal that the work of black writers must be judged wholly in the context of the literary tradition in English, rather than within the confines of the ethnocentrism that is common in contemporary literature written by blacks." As Lewis Turco explained in the *Michigan Quarterly Review*, "Hayden has always wished to be judged as a poet among poets, not one to whom special rules of criticism ought to be applied in order to make his work acceptable in more than a sociological sense."

This stance earned Hayden harsh criticism from other blacks during the polarized 1960s. He was accused of abandoning his racial heritage to conform to the standards of a white, European literary establishment. "In the 1960s," William Meredith wrote in his foreword to *Collected Prose*, "Hayden declared himself, at considerable cost in popularity, an American poet rather than a black poet, when for a time there was posited an unreconcilable difference between the two roles. . . . He would not relinquish the title of American writer for any narrower identity."

Ironically, much of Hayden's best poetry is concerned with black history and the black experience. "The gift of Robert Hayden's poetry," Vilma Raskin Potter remarked in *MELUS*, "is his coherent vision of the black experience in this country as a continuing journey both communal and private." Hayden wrote of such black historical figures as Nat Turner, Frederick Douglass, Malcolm X, Harriet Tubman, and Cinquez. He also wrote of the Underground Railroad, the Civil War, and the American slave trade. Edward Hirsch, writing in the *Nation*,

called Hayden "an American poet, deeply engaged by the topography of American myth in his efforts to illuminate the American black experience."

Though Hayden wrote in formal poetic forms, his range of voices and techniques gave his work a rich variety. "Hayden," Robert G. O'Meally wrote in the *Washington Post Book World*, "is a poet of many voices, using varieties of ironic black folk speech, and a spare, ebullient poetic diction, to grip and chill his readers. He draws characters of stark vividness as he transmutes cardinal points and commonplaces of history into dramatic action and symbol." "His work," Turco wrote, "is unfettered in many ways, not the least of which is in the range of techniques available to him. It gives his imagination wings, allows him to travel throughout human nature." Speaking of Hayden's use of formal verse forms, Mann explained that Hayden's poems were "formal in a nontraditional, original way, strict but not straight-jacketed" and found that they also possessed "a hard-edged precision of line that molds what the imagination wants to release in visually fine-chiseled fragmental stanzas that fit flush together with the rightness of a picture puzzle."

It wasn't until 1966, with the publication of *Selected Poems*, that Hayden first enjoyed widespread attention from the nation's literary critics. As the *Choice* critic remarked at the time, *Selected Poems* showed Hayden to be "the surest poetic talent of any Negro poet in America; more importantly, it demonstrated a major talent and poetic coming-of-age without regard to race or creed." With each succeeding volume of poems his reputation was further enhanced until, in 1976 and his appointment as Consultant in Poetry to the Library of Congress, Hayden was generally recognized as one of the country's leading black poets.

Critics often point to Hayden's unique ability to combine the historical and the personal when speaking of his own life and the lives of his people. Writing in *Obsidian: Black Literature in Review*, Gary Zebrun argued that "the voice of the speaker in Hayden's best work twists and squirms its way out of anguish in order to tell, or sing, stories of American history— in particular the courageous and plaintive record of Afro-American history—and to chart the thoughts and feelings of the poet's own private space. . . . Hayden is ceaselessly trying to achieve . . . transcendence, which must not be an escape from the horror of history or from the loneliness of individual mortality, but an ascent that somehow transforms the horror and creates a blessed permanence."

BIOGRAPHICAL/CRITICAL SOURCES:

BOOKS

Concise Dictionary of Literary Biography, Volume I: *The New Consciousness, 1941-1968*, Gale, 1987.
Contemporary Authors Bibliographical Series, Volume II, Gale, 1986.
Contemporary Literary Criticism, Gale, Volume V, 1976, Volume IX, 1978, Volume XIV, 1980, Volume XXXVII, 1986.
Conversations with Writers, Volume I, Gale, 1977.
Davis, Arthur P., editor, *From the Dark Tower: Afro-American Writers, 1900-1960*, Howard University Press, 1974.
Dictionary of Literary Biography, Volume V: *American Poets since World War II*, Gale, 1980.
Fetrow, Fred M., *Robert Hayden*, Twayne, 1984.
Gayle, Addison, Jr., editor, *The Black Aesthetic*, Doubleday, 1971.

Gibson, Donald B., editor, *Modern Black Poets: A Collection of Critical Essays,* Prentice-Hall, 1973.

Harper, Michael S. and Robert B. Stepto, editors, *Chant of Saints: A Gathering of Afro-American Literature, Art, and Scholarship,* University of Illinois Press, 1979.

Hatcher, John, *From the Auroral Darkness: The Life and Poetry of Robert Hayden,* George Ronald, 1984.

How I Write/1, Harcourt, 1972.

Jackson, Blyden and Louis D. Rubin, Jr., *Black Poetry in America: Two Essays in Historical Interpretation,* Louisiana State University Press, 1974.

Littlejohn, David, *Black on White: A Critical Survey of Writing by American Negroes,* Grossman, 1966.

Litz, Walton, editor, *American Writers: A Collection of Literary Biographies,* Scribner, 1981.

O'Brien, John, *Interviews with Black Writers,* Liveright, 1973.

Rush, Theresa Gunnels, Carol Fairbanks Myers, and Esther Spring Arata, editors, *Black American Writers Past and Present,* Scarecrow, 1975.

Whitlow, Roger, *Black American Literature,* Nelson Hall, 1973.

Young, James O., *Black Writers of the Thirties,* Louisiana State University Press, 1973.

PERIODICALS

America, February 7, 1975.
Booklist, July, 1985.
Bulletin of Bibliography, September, 1985.
Carleton Miscellany, winter, 1980.
Choice, May, 1967, December, 1984.
College Language Association Journal, number 17, 1973, number 20, 1976, number 21, 1978, number 22, 1979.
Commentary, September, 1980.
Georgia Review, winter, 1984.
Hudson Review, spring, 1986.
Massachusetts Review, winter, 1977.
MELUS, spring, 1980, spring, 1982.
Michigan Quarterly Review, spring, 1977, winter, 1982, fall, 1983.
Midwest Quarterly, spring, 1974.
Nation, December 21, 1985.
Negro American Literature Forum, spring, 1975.
Negro Digest, June, 1966, January, 1968.
New York Times Book Review, January 17, 1971, February 22, 1976, October 21, 1979.
Obsidian: Black Literature in Review, spring, 1981.
Ontario Review, spring-summer, 1979.
Poetry, July, 1967, July, 1977.
Research Studies, September, 1979.
Virginia Quarterly Review, autumn, 1982.
Washington Post Book World, June 25, 1978.
World Order, spring, 1971, summer, 1975, winter, 1976, fall, 1981.

OBITUARIES:

PERIODICALS

AB Bookman's Weekly, April 21, 1980.
Black Scholar, March/April, 1980.
Chicago Tribune, February 27, 1980.
Encore, April, 1980.
Los Angeles Times, March 3, 1980.
New York Times, February 27, 1980.
Time, March 10, 1980.
Washington Post, February 27, 1980.†

—Sketch by Thomas Wiloch

HELLMANN, John 1948-

PERSONAL: Born February 14, 1948, in Louisville, Ky.; son of John Michael (a production manager) and Louise (Stickel) Hellmann; married Marilyn McKinley (an arts council director), September 14, 1968. *Education:* University of Louisville, B.A., 1970, M.A., 1973; Kent State University, Ph.D., 1977.

ADDRESSES: Office—Department of English, Ohio State University, Lima, Ohio 45804.

CAREER: Ohio State University—Lima Campus, assistant professor, 1977-83, associate professor of English, 1983—.

MEMBER: Modern Language Association of America, American Studies Association.

AWARDS, HONORS: American Council of Learned Societies fellowship, 1982-83; Senior Fulbright Lectureship, Belgium, 1985.

WRITINGS:

Fables of Fact: The New Journalism as New Fiction, University of Illinois Press, 1981.
American Myth and the Legacy of Vietnam, Columbia University Press, 1986.

Contributor to literature journals and literary magazines, including *South Atlantic Quarterly, Genre, Critique, Centennial Review,* and *Journal of American Folklore.*

WORK IN PROGRESS: Studies of American myth and history and of the relation of Alfred Hitchcock's films to American culture.

SIDELIGHTS: John Hellman attempts "to provide a satisfying mythic explanation of Vietnam" in the book *American Myth and the Legacy of Vietnam,* notes Thomas Myers in a *Modern Fiction Studies* review. Hellman suggests that the war damaged America's view of itself as a nation of frontiersmen with a mission to bring order to the wilderness in the manner of James Fenimore Cooper's *Deerslayer* hero, Natty Bumppo. Critics question this thesis and generally concur with Philip French's view, published in the *Times Literary Supplement,* that the study "does not range far enough." Myers, for instance, notes that Hellman mentions only those "texts that fit conveniently, or sometimes uncomfortably, into [his] formulaic landscape." Myers qualifies his criticisms with the concession that "Overall, Hellmann is partially correct that the 'memoirs, novels, and films of the Vietnam experience explore the war as a symbolic landscape inverting America's frontier mythos,' but one may note that deep within another symbolic Vietnam John Rambo carries a traditional long rifle nicknamed American Victimization." *American Literature* contributor Stanley Trachtenberg concludes, "Despite its limitations, this complex and subtle discussion of a pivotal era in our history sharply illumines many of the current confusions in our national psyche and, even more, reveals something of the process by which Vietnam has shaped no less than reflected our dreams. . . . It makes a useful, even necessary part of the ongoing discussion."

BIOGRAPHICAL/CRITICAL SOURCES:

BOOKS

Hellmann, John, *American Myth and the Legacy of Vietnam,* Columbia University Press, 1986.

PERIODICALS

American Literature, March, 1987.
Christian Science Monitor, April 8, 1986.
Journal of American History, December, 1986.
Modern Fiction Studies, summer, 1986.
Times Literary Supplement, January 15, 1982, June 6, 1986.

* * *

HENRY, T. E.
See ROWLAND-ENTWISTLE, (Arthur) Theodore (Henry)

* * *

HESS, Beth B(owman)

PERSONAL: Born in Buffalo, N.Y.; daughter of Albert A. (an advertising executive) and Yetta (a social worker; maiden name, Lurie) Bowman; married Richard C. Hess (a businessman), April 26, 1953; children: Laurence Albert, Emily Frances. *Education:* Radcliffe College, B.A. (magna cum laude), 1950; Rutgers University, M.A., 1966, Ph.D., 1970. *Politics:* Democrat. *Religion:* Jewish.

ADDRESSES: Home—2 Hampshire Dr., Mendham, N.J. 07945. *Office*—Department of Social Sciences, County College of Morris, Dover, N.J. 07801.

CAREER: County College of Morris, Dover, N.J., assistant professor, 1969-73, associate professor, 1973-79, professor of social sciences, 1979—. Adjunct professor at Graduate Center, City University of New York, 1979; visiting professor at Gerontology Center, Boston University, 1980-81; lecturer at Douglass College, 1981.

MEMBER: American Sociological Association, Sociologists for Women in Society (president, 1987-89), Association for Humanist Sociology (president, 1987), Society for the Study of Social Problems (director, 1981-83), Gerontological Society (fellow), Eastern Sociological Society (executive secretary, 1978-81; president, 1988-89).

AWARDS, HONORS: Peter I. Gellman Distinguished Service Award from Eastern Sociological Society, 1982.

WRITINGS:

(With Matilda White Riley and Anne Foner) *Aging and Society,* Volume I, Russell Sage Foundation, 1968.
(Editor) *Growing Old in America,* Transaction Books, 1976, 3rd edition (with Elizabeth W. Markson), 1985.
(With Markson) *Aging and Old Age: An Introduction to Social Gerontology,* Macmillan, 1980.
(Editor with Kathleen Bond) *Leading Edges: Recent Research on Psychosocial Aging,* U.S. Government Printing Office, 1981.
(With Markson and Peter J. Stein) *Sociology,* Macmillan, 1982, 3rd edition, 1988.
(Editor with Marvin B. Sussman) *Women and the Family: Two Decades of Change,* Haworth Press, 1984.
(With Myra Marx Ferree) *Controversy and Coalition: The New Feminist Movement,* G. K. Hall, 1985.
(With Ferree) *Analysing Gender,* Sage Publications, 1987.

CONTRIBUTOR

(With Riley, Toby, and Foner) D. Goslin, editor, *Handbook of Socialization Theory and Research,* Rand McNally, 1969.

Riley, Foner, and Marilyn Johnson, editors, *Aging and Society,* Volume III, Russell Sage Foundation, 1971.
(With Joan Waring) Richard Lerner and Graham Spanier, editors, *Child Influences on Marital and Family Interaction,* Academic Press, 1978.
Older Women in the City, Arno, 1979.
Markson and G. R. Batra, editors, *Public Policies for an Aging Population,* Lexington Books, 1980.
M. Haug, editor, *Communications Technology and the Elderly: Issues and Forecasts,* Springer Publishing Co., 1982.
(With Waring) Markson, editor, *The World of Older Women,* Lexington Books, 1982.
R. Genovese, editor, *Families and Change: Social Needs and Public Policies,* J. F. Bergin, 1982.
(With Paula Dressel) E. Macklin and R. Rubin, editors, *Contemporary Family and Alternative Life Styles: Handbook on Research and Theory,* Sage Publications, 1982.
(With Ben Soldo) W. J. Sauer and R. T. Coward, editors, *Social Support Networks and the Care of the Elderly,* Springer Publishing Co., 1983.

OTHER

Contributor to *Proceedings of Association for Gerontology in Higher Education,* 1975, and to *New Encyclopedia,* 1983. Contributor of reviews and articles to scholarly journals, including *Contemporary Sociology, The Gerontologist,* and *Social Policy.* Associate editor of *Society, Research on Aging, Contemporary Sociology,* and *Teaching Sociology.*

WORK IN PROGRESS: A book with Matilda White Riley and Bettina Huber for Sage Publications entitled *Social Structures and Human Lives.*

SIDELIGHTS: Beth B. Hess told *CA:* "It seems that the theme which best describes my adulthood, as for so many older women today, is 'balance'; that is, managing the demands of scholarship, teaching, parenthood and marriage. This has been a richly rewarding mix, one which I hope will increasingly characterize the lives of both men and women.

"I have also sought to balance my commitment to sociology with an obligation to social activism. My biography in this respect is no doubt similar to that of most academics my age: active involvement at the community level in the major movements of the last two decades: civil liberties, civil rights, antiwar, and, most significantly, the feminist movement.

"Admittedly, this balancing act can strain one's abilities and energies; to achieve all one wishes in all these roles is perhaps impossible. So, while there is much that I regret not doing better, there is little to which I would not commit myself again."

* * *

HICKS, Clifford B. 1920-

PERSONAL: Born August 10, 1920, in Marshalltown, Iowa; son of Nathan LeRoy and Kathryn Marie (Carson) Hicks; married Rachel G. Reimer, May 12, 1945; children: David, Douglas, Gary. *Education:* Northwestern University, B.A. (cum laude), 1942.

CAREER: Popular Mechanics, Lombard, Ill., member of editorial staff, 1945-60, editor, 1960-63, special projects editor, 1963—. *Military service:* U.S. Marine Corps Reserve, 1942-45, became major; received Silver Star.

MEMBER: Sigma Delta Chi.

AWARDS, HONORS: First Boy on the Moon was named Best Juvenile Book of the Year by Friends of American Writers, 1960.

WRITINGS:

Do-It-Yourself Materials Guide, Popular Mechanics Press, 1955.
First Boy on the Moon, Winston, 1959.
Marvelous Inventions of Alvin Fernald, Holt, 1960.
Alvin's Secret Code, Holt, 1963.
The World Above, Holt, 1965.
Alvin Fernald, Foreign Trader, Holt, 1966.
Alvin Fernald, Mayor for a Day, Holt, 1970.
Peter Potts, Dutton, 1971.
Alvin Fernald, Superweasel, Holt, 1974.
Alvin's Swap Shop, Holt, 1976.
Alvin Fernald, TV Anchorman, Holt, 1980.
The Wacky World of Alvin Fernald, Holt, 1981.
Pop and Peter Potts, Holt, 1984.
Alvin Fernald, Master of a Thousand Disguises, Holt, 1986.
Peter Potts Book of World Records, Holt, 1987.

Editor of *Popular Mechanics Do-It-Yourself Encyclopedia.* Contributor of fiction and nonfiction to magazines.

*   *   *

HOBBS, Robert C(arleton)   1946-

PERSONAL: Born December 6, 1946, in Brookings, S.D.; son of Charles Seright (a college professor) and Corinne (a teacher; maiden name, Clay) Hobbs. *Education:* University of Tennessee, B.A., 1969; University of North Carolina, Ph.D., 1975.

ADDRESSES: Home—2701 Revere St., Apt. 237, Houston, Tex. 77098.

CAREER: Yale University, New Haven, Conn., instructor in art history, 1975-76; Cornell University, Ithaca, N.Y., associate professor of art history and curator, 1976-83; University of Iowa Museum of Art, director, 1983-86. Chief curator at Tehran Museum of Contemporary Art, 1978. *Military service:* U.S. Army Reserve, 1968-74.

MEMBER: International Association of Art Critics, College Art Association of America Contemporary Curator's Group.

AWARDS, HONORS: Kress fellowship from University of North Carolina at Chapel Hill, 1974; Helena Rubenstein fellowship from Whitney Museum of American Art, 1975.

WRITINGS:

(With Gail Levin) *Abstract Expressionism: The Formative Years,* Cornell University Press, 1981.
Robert Smithson: Sculpture, Cornell University Press, 1981.
(Co-author) *Artistic Collaboration in the Twentieth Century,* Smithsonian Institution Press, 1984.
(Co-editor with Fredrick Woodard) *Human Rights/Human Wrongs: Art and Social Change,* University of Washington Press, 1986.
The University of Iowa Museum of Art: 101 Masterworks, University of Iowa Museum of Art, 1986.
Edward Hopper, Abrams, 1987.
(Co-author) *Art of the Red Earth People: The Mesquakie of Iowa,* University of Iowa Musem of Art, 1988.

Guest editor of *College Art Journal,* autumn, 1982.

WORK IN PROGRESS: Co-author of *Richard Pousette-Dart,* for the Indianapolis Museum of Art.

HODGES, Donald Clark   1923-

PERSONAL: Born October 22, 1923, in Fort Worth, Tex.; son of Count Hal and Elinor (Clark) Hodges; married Gabrielle Baptiste, November 14, 1949 (divorced, 1963); married Margaret Helen Deutsch, January 3, 1963 (divorced, 1980); married Deborah Elizabeth Hepburn, June 21, 1980; children: (first marriage) Justin Blake, Peter Robin; (second marriage) MacIntyre Hardy, John Oliver, Ernest Van Every; (third marriage) Sojourner Truth. *Education:* Attended Swarthmore College, 1942-43; New York University, B.A. (summa cum laude), 1947; Columbia University, M.A., 1948, Ph.D., 1954.

ADDRESSES: Home—Route 7, MLC 50, Tallahassee, Fla. 32308. *Office*—Department of Philosophy, Florida State University, Tallahassee, Fla. 32306.

CAREER: Hobart and William Smith Colleges, Geneva, N.Y., instructor in philosophy, 1949-52; University of Missouri—Columbia, instructor, 1952-54, assistant professor, 1954-57, associate professor of philosophy, 1957-63, chairman of humanities department; University of South Florida, Tampa, professor of philosophy, 1963-64; Florida State University, Tallahassee, professor of philosophy, 1964—, head of department, 1964-69, director of Center for Graduate and Postgraduate Studies in Social Philosophy, 1967-71, director of Latin American and Caribbean studies, 1987—. Visiting professor at University of Nebraska, 1963, University of Hawaii, 1965-66, and National Autonomous University of Mexico, 1982. Associate member, Institute for Social Philosophy, Pennsylvania State University.

MEMBER: American Philosophical Association, Society for the Philosophical Study of Dialectical Materialism (secretary-treasurer, 1963-73), Society for the Philosophical Study of Marxism (secretary-treasurer, 1973-87).

WRITINGS:

(Editor with Kuang T. Fann) *Readings in U.S. Imperialism,* Sargent, 1971.
(Editor with Abu Shanab) *National Liberation Fronts,* Morrow, 1973.
(Editor and translator) *Philosophy of the Urban Guerilla: The Revolutionary Writings of Abraham Guillen,* Morrow, 1973.
Socialist Humanism: The Outcome of Classical European Morality, Warren Green, 1974.
The Latin American Revolution, Morrow, 1974.
Argentina 1941-1976: The National Revolution and Resistance, University of New Mexico Press, 1976.
The Legacy of Che Guevara, Thames & Hudson, 1977.
(With Abraham Guillen) *Revaloracion de la guerrilla urbana,* El Caballito, 1977.
(With Ross Gandy) *El destino de la revolucion Mexicana,* El Caballito, 1977, 3rd edition, enlarged and updated, 1987.
Marxismo y revolucion en el siglo XX, El Caballito, 1978.
(With Gandy) *Mexico 1910-1976: Reform or Revolution?,* Zed Press, 1979.
The Bureaucratization of Socialism, University of Massachusetts, 1981, 2nd edition, enlarged and updated, published as *Mexico 1910-1982: Reform or Revolution?,* 1983.
(With Gandy) *Todos los revolucionarios van al infierno,* Costa-Amic, 1983, 2nd edition, 1987.
Intellectual Foundations of the Nicaraguan Revolution, University of Texas, 1987.

Work represented in numerous anthologies. Contributor of articles to many periodicals, including *Journal of Philosophy, Modern Schoolman, Archives of Criminal Psychodynamics, Science and Society, Inquiry,* and *Il Politico.* Consulting editor, *Indian Sociological Bulletin,* 1963—; member of editorial board, *Philosophy and Phenomenological Research,* 1969—; co-editor, *Social Theory and Practice,* 1971—, and *Latin American Perspectives,* 1978—.

SIDELIGHTS: Although Donald Hodges was born in Texas, he grew up in Argentina. He returned to the United States to attend college. His works have been published in West Germany and Mexico.

* * *

HOFSOMMER, Don(ovan) L(owell)   1938-

PERSONAL: Born April 10, 1938, in Fort Dodge, Iowa; son of Vernie G. and Helma J. (Schager) Hofsommer; married Sandra L. Rusch (a high school teacher), June 13, 1964; children: Kathryn Anne, Kristine Beret, Knute Lars. *Education:* University of Northern Iowa, B.A., 1960, M.A., 1966; Oklahoma State University, Ph.D., 1973. *Religion:* Presbyterian.

ADDRESSES: Home—1100 East 38th St., Sioux Falls, S.D. 57105. *Office*—Center for Western Studies, Augustana College, Sioux Falls, S.D. 57197.

CAREER: High school history teacher in Fairfield, Iowa, 1961-65; Lea College, Albert Lea, Minn., instructor in history, 1966-70; Wayland College, Plainview, Tex., associate professor of history and head of department, 1973-81; Southern Pacific Transportation Co., San Francisco, Calif., special representative and historian, 1981-85; Burlington Northern, Inc., Seattle, Wash., historical consultant, 1985-87; Augustana College, Center for Western Studies, Sioux Falls, S.D., executive director, 1987—. Guest professor in history, University of Montana, 1986-87. *Military service:* Iowa National Guard, 1960-66.

MEMBER: Organization of American Historians, Western History Association, Railway and Locomotive Historical Association, National Railway Historical Association, Lexington Group, State Historical Society of Iowa, Texas Historical Society, Phi Alphta Theta, Phi Delta Kappa.

AWARDS, HONORS: Award from American Association for State and Local History, 1976, for *Prairie Oasis;* Muriel H. Wright Heritage Endowment Award from Oklahoma Historical Society, 1979.

WRITINGS:

Prairie Oasis: The Railroads, Steamboats, and Resorts of Iowa's Spirit Lake Country, Waukon & Mississippi Press, 1975.
(Compiler) *Railroads of the Trans-Mississippi West: A Selected Bibliography of Books,* Llano Estacado Musuem, 1976.
Katy Northwest: The Story of a Branch Line Railroad, Pruett, 1976.
(Editor) *Railroads in Oklahoma,* Oklahoma Historical Society, 1977.
(Editor) *Railroads in the West,* Sunflower University Press, 1978.
The Southern Pacific, 1901-1985, Texas A & M University Press, 1986.

(With R. W. Hidy, M. E. Hidy, and R. V. Scott) *The Great Northern Railway: A History,* Harvard Business School, 1988.

Contributor of more than thirty articles to history and transportation journals and to newspapers. Editor of *Lexington Newsletter;* member of editorial board of *Railroad History, Journals of the West,* and *Annals of Iowa.*

WORK IN PROGRESS: The Quanah Route: A History of the Quanah, Acme & Pacific Railway and *The "Louie": A History of the Minneapolis & St. Louis Railway.*

* * *

HOLMES, Jack D(avid) L(azarus)   1930-

PERSONAL: Surname originally Lazarus; born July 4, 1930, in Long Branch, N.J.; son of John Daniel (a realtor) and Waltrude (Hendrickson) Lazarus; married Anne Elizabeth Anthony, 1952 (divorced, 1965); married Martha Austin Reid, 1966 (divorced, 1967); married Gayle Carlson Pannell, 1967 (divorced, 1970); married Stephanie Pasneker (an elementary teacher), April 10, 1971; children: (first marriage) David H. Jack Forrest, Ann M.; (third marriage) Daniel J. *Education:* Florida State University, B.A. (cum laude), 1952, graduate study, 1953-54; University of Florida, M.A., 1953; National University of Mexico, graduate study, 1954; University of Texas, Ph.D., 1959; University of Alabama in Birmingham, postdoctoral study, 1963-64.

ADDRESSES: Home and office—520 South 22nd Ave., Birmingham, Ala. 35205.

CAREER: Memphis State University, Memphis, Tenn., instructor in history, 1956-58; *Memphis Press-Scimitar,* Memphis, staff writer, 1957-58; McNeese State University, Lake Charles, La., assistant professor of history, 1959-61; University of Maryland Overseas Division, Constantina, Spain, lecturer in history, 1962; University of Alabama in Birmingham, associate professor, 1963-68, professor of history and political science, 1968-79. Writer and lecturer. Director, Louisiana Collection Series of Books and Documents on Colonial Louisiana. Reading clerk, Florida House of Representatives, 1955. Historical consultant to U.S. Parks Service, 1962, Historic Pensacola Preservation Board, Pensacola, Fla., 1968-70, Mississippi Department of Archives and History, 1978, State of Alabama, 1978, Livingston University, Livingston, Ala., 1980, and the U.S. Post Office, 1980. Evaluator, National Endowment for the Humanities, 1974—. Off-shore oil rig dispatcher in the Gulf of Mexico for Chevron and ODECO corporations, 1982. *Military service:* U.S. Army, 1951.

MEMBER: Southern Historical Association (life member), Society for the History of Discoveries, Jean Laffitte Study Group (president, 1980-84), Louisiana Historical Association (life member), Florida Historical Society, Mississippi Historical Society, Tennessee Squire, Phi Beta Kappa, Phi Kappa Phi, Phi Alpha Theta, Sigma Delta Pi, Pi Kappa Phi.

AWARDS, HONORS: American Philosophical Society and Fulbright grants for research in Spain, 1961-62; McClung Award for best articles appearing in the *Publications of the East Tennessee Historical Society,* 1962, 1964; Louisiana Library Association Award for best book published on Louisiana in 1965, for *Gayoso: The Life of a Spanish Governor in the Mississippi Valley, 1789-1799;* Alabama Writers' Conclave Award in biography and history, 1965, 1966, and 1967; American Association for the Study of State and Local History grant, 1966;

American Philosophical Society grant, 1966; faculty research committee grants-in-aid, University of Alabama, 1968, 1970, 1971-79, and University of Alabama in Birmingham, 1964, 1966; Louisiana Historical Association Award for best article in *Louisiana History*, 1970; Hackney Literary Award for History, second place, 1974; award of merit, American Association for State and Local History, 1978; knighted Caballero in the Order of Isabel la Catolica by Juan Carlos I of Spain, 1979; first prize essay, *Tampa Bay History*, 1982.

WRITINGS:

The Planned Suburban Shopping Center: An Annotated Bibliography, Bureau of Business Research, University of Texas, 1957, revised edition published as *Selected and Annotated Bibliography of the Planned Suburban Shopping Center*, 1960.

(Editor) *Documentos ineditos para la historia de la Luisiana, 1792-1810*, Ediciones Turanzas (Madrid), 1963.

(Editor) *Louisiana Collection Series of Books and Documents on Colonial Louisiana*, Jack D. L. Holmes, Volume I: *Honor and Fidelity: The Louisiana Infantry Regiment and the Louisiana Militia Companies, 1766-1821*, 1965, Volume II: *A Guide to Spanish Louisiana, 1762-1806*, 1970, Volume III: *Louisiana in 1776: A Memoria of Francisco Bouligney*, 1977.

Gayoso: The Life of a Spanish Governor in the Mississippi Valley, 1789-1799, Louisiana State University Press, for Louisiana Historical Association, 1965.

(Editor) *Jose de Evia y sus reconocimientos del Golfo de Mexico, 1783-1796*, Ediciones Turanzas, 1968.

(Editor) Francis Baily, *Journal of a Tour in Unsettled Parts of North America in 1796 and 1797*, abridged edition, Southern Illinois University Press, 1969.

(With Raymond J. Martinez) *New Orleans: Facts and Legends*, Hope Publications (New Orleans), 1970, 3rd edition, 1982.

New Orleans Drinks and How To Mix Them, Hope Publications, 1973.

A History of the University of Alabama Hospitals, University Hospital Auxiliary, 1974.

The 1779 "Marcha de Galvez": Louisiana's Giant Step Forward in the American Revolution, Baton Rouge Bicentennial Corp., 1974.

Stephen Minor, Louisiana Collection Series, 1983.

CONTRIBUTOR

John F. McDermott, editor, *The French in the Mississippi Valley*, University of Illinois Press, 1965.

Raymond J. Martinez, *The Story of Spanish Moss: What It Is and How It Grows*, Hope Publications, 1968.

McDermott, editor, *Frenchmen and French Ways in the Mississippi Valley*, University of Illinois Press, 1969.

(Author of introduction) Luis de Onis, *Memoria sobre las negociaciones entre Espana y los Estados Unidos de America*, Ediciones Turanzas, 1969.

Ernest W. Dibble and Earle W. Newton, editors, *In Search of Gulf Coast Colonial History*, Historic Pensacola Preservation Board, 1970.

(With William S. Coker) Dibble and Newton, editors, *Spain and Her Rivals on the Gulf Coast*, Historic Pensacola Preservation Board, 1971.

Minnie Mae Davis, *Confederate Patriots of Jones County*, privately printed, 1971.

Mary H. Kitchens and Theresa Blackledge, editors, *A Mini-Confederacy: The Free State of Jones, 1862-186-, a Source Book*, privately printed, 1971.

James R. McGovern, editor, *Colonial Pensacola*, Pensacola-Escambia County Development Commission, 1972, revised edition, 1974.

(Author of foreword) John Walton Caughey, *Bernardo de Galvez in Louisiana, 1776-1783*, Pelican Publishing, 1972.

R. A. McLemore, editor, *History of Mississippi*, two volumes, University Press of Mississippi, 1973.

McDermott, editor, *The Spanish in the Mississippi Valley, 1762-1804*, University of Illinois Press, 1974.

Charles M. Hudson, editor, *Four Centuries of Southern Indians*, University of Georgia Press, 1975.

(Author of foreword) Martinez, *Rousseau—The Last Days of Spanish New Orleans*, 2nd edition, Hope Publications, 1975.

Handbook of Texas, supplement, Texas State Historical Association, 1976.

Encyclopedia of Southern History, Louisiana State University Press, 1978.

Glenn R. Conrad, editor, *Readings in Louisiana History*, Louisiana Historical Association, 1978.

Beatriz Ruiz Gaytan, Samuel Proctor, and others, editors, *Cardinales de dos independencias (Noreste de Mexico Sureste de los Estados Unidos)*, Fomento Cultural Banamex, 1978.

Proceedings of the Fourth Meeting of the French Colonial Historical Society, University Press of America, 1979.

Enrique Ruiz-Fornells and Cynthia Ruiz-Fornells, editors, *The United States and the Spanish World*, Sociedad Generale Espanola de Libreria (Madrid), 1979.

Sal J. Foderano, editor, *Academic American Encyclopedia*, Arete Publishing, 1980.

James B. Lloyd, editor, *Lives of Mississippi Authors, 1817-1966*, University Press of Mississippi, 1981.

Patricia K. Galloway, editor, *La Salle and His Legacy: Frenchmen and Indians in the Lower Mississippi Valley*, University Press of Mississippi, 1982.

Coker and Robert R. Rea, editors, *Anglo-Spanish Confrontation on the Gulf Coast during the American Revolution*, Gulf Coast History and Humanities Conference, 1982.

Edward F. Haas, editor, *Encyclopedia of American Forest and Conservation History*, two volumes, Macmillan, 1983.

Samuel S. Hill, editor, *Encyclopedia of Religion in the South*, Mercer University Press, 1984.

OTHER

Contributor of many articles in English and Spanish to historical, educational, and business journals.

WORK IN PROGRESS: Biographies of Philip Nolan, early frontiersman, Alexander O'Reilly, governor of Louisiana, 1769-1770, and Bernardo de Galvez, captain-general and governor of Louisiana, 1777-1782; editing correspondence between Stephen Minor and Manuel Gayoso de Lemos, 1792-1799, and the works of Joseph, Baron de Pontalba; also writing on the status of blacks in Spanish Louisiana and West Florida, on Alabama settlers, 1780-1813, and on Pensacola settlers, 1781-1821; a Choctaw history; Jose Gabriel y Estenoz's "Description of Louisiana"; sketches of Louisiana governors Iberville, Blenville, O'Reilly, Galvez, and Gayoso.

SIDELIGHTS: Jack D. L. Holmes draws his book materials from a collection of 50,000 pages of eighteenth-century documents, mostly microfilmed in archives of Mexico, Spain, France, and England.

HONEYMAN, Brenda
See CLARKE, Brenda (Margaret Lilian)

*   *   *

HONIG, Donald 1931-

PERSONAL: Born August 17, 1931, in Maspeth, Long Island, N.Y.; son of George and Mildred (Elson) Honig; divorced; children: Catherine Rose.

ADDRESSES: Home—Cromwell, Conn.

CAREER: Professional writer.

MEMBER: Dramatists Guild, Authors League of America.

AWARDS, HONORS: New York State Council of the Arts grant, 1972; Connecticut Commission on the Arts Grant, 1974, 1981.

WRITINGS:

Sidewalk Caesar (novel), Pyramid Books, 1958.
Walk Like a Man (novel), Morrow, 1961.
Divide the Night (novel), Regency Books, 1961.
(Editor) *Blue and Gray: Great Writings of the Civil War,* Avon, 1961.
No Song to Sing (novel), Morrow, 1962.
(Editor) *Short Stories of Stephen Crane,* Avon, 1962, McGraw, 1967.
The Adventures of Jed McLane, McGraw, 1967.
Jed McLane and the Stranger, McGraw, 1969.
In the Days of the Cowboy, Random House, 1970.
Up from the Minor Leagues, Cowles, 1970.
Dynamite, Putnam, 1971.
Johnny Lee, McCall Publishing, 1971.
Judgment Night, Belmont Books, 1971.
The Journal of One Davey Wyatt, F. Watts, 1972.
The Love Thief, Belmont Books, 1972.
An End of Innocence, Putnam, 1972.
The Severith Style, Scribner, 1972.
Way to Go Teddy, F. Watts, 1973.
Illusions, Doubleday, 1974.
Playing for Keeps, F. Watts, 1974.
Breaking In, F. Watts, 1974.
The Professional, F. Watts, 1974.
Coming Back, F. Watts, 1974.
Fury on Skates, Four Winds Press, 1974.
With the Consent of the Governed: Conversations with Eight U.S. Senators, Dell, 1975.
Baseball: When the Grass Was Real, Coward, 1975.
Running Harder, F. Watts, 1976.
Going the Distance, F. Watts, 1976.
Baseball between the Lines, Coward, 1976.
The Man in the Dugout, Follett, 1977.
I Should Have Sold Petunias, Jove, 1977.
The Last Great Season, Simon & Schuster, 1979.
The October Heroes, Simon & Schuster, 1979.
The Image of Their Greatness, Crown, 1979.
Marching Home, St. Martin's, 1980.
The 100 Greatest Baseball Players of All Time, Crown, 1981.
The Brooklyn Dodgers: An Illustrated Tribute, St. Martin's, 1981.
The New York Yankees: An Illustrated History, Crown, 1981.
Baseball's 10 Greatest Teams, Macmillan, 1982.
The Los Angeles Dodgers: An Illustrated Tribute, St. Martin's, 1983.
The National League: An Illustrated History, Crown, 1983.

The American League: An Illustrated History, Crown, 1983.
The Boston Red Sox: An Illustrated Tribute, St. Martin's, 1984.
Baseball America, Macmillan, 1985.
The New York Mets: The First Quarter Century, Crown, 1986.
The World Series: An Illustrated History, Crown, 1986.
Mantle, Mays, Snider: A Celebration, Macmillan, 1987.
The All-Star Game: An Illustrated History, Sporting News, 1987.
Baseball in the Fifties: An Illustrated History, Crown, 1987.
Baseball's Great Pitchers, Crown, 1988.
Baseball's Great First Basemen, Crown, 1988.
The Donald Honig Reader, Simon & Schuster, 1988.

Author with Leon Arden of play "The Midnight Ride of Alvin Blumm," first produced in 1966. Contributor of 200 stories and articles to various trade publications.

*   *   *

HOSFORD, Bowen I. 1916-

PERSONAL: Born December 1, 1916, in Atlanta, Ga.; son of James I. and Anne (Bowen) Hosford; married Virginia Dunn, January, 1946 (divorced September, 1947); married Frances Moore (a registered nurse), June 18, 1949; children: Christopher Francis, Bowen I., Jr., Kenneth J., Susan Hosford Andrews, Janet. *Education:* Emory University, A.B., 1939; American University, M.A., 1956; George Washington University, J.D., 1967. *Religion:* Protestant.

ADDRESSES: Home and office—8817 Higdon Dr., Vienna, Va. 22180.

CAREER: WMAZ-Radio, Macon, Ga., newswriter, 1947-49; editor and publisher of a weekly newspaper in Warner Robins, Ga., 1949-51; U.S. Air Force, career officer, 1951-63, retiring as major. National Institutes of Health, Bethesda, Md., branch chief and freedom of information officer, 1965-86, faculty member at graduate school, 1987—. Lawyer and freelance writer, 1987—; admitted to the bars of Virginia, Washington, D.C., and Supreme Court. Member of Fairfax (Va.) Hospital ethics committee; member of N.I.H. Clinical Center liason group to bioethics chief. *Military service:* U.S. Army Air Forces, 1942-45.

MEMBER: American Medical Writers Association, Washington Independent Writers, Coif.

WRITINGS:

The Grave of the Twin Hills (novel), Norton, 1961.
Making Your Medical Decisions: Your Rights and Harsh Choices Today, Ungar, 1982.
Bioethics Committees: The Health Care Provider's Guide, Aspen Publishers, 1986.

Author of "Hosford's Law," a weekly newspaper column, 1971-78.

WORK IN PROGRESS: The Nurse's Plain-Language Guide to Law and Bioethics, for Aspen Publishers.

SIDELIGHTS: Bowen I. Hosford told *CA:* "My early novel *The Grave of the Twin Hills* was concerned with compassion by members of formerly enemy races towards each other. In the book, an American flier, who has previously seen Japan only as bombs fell from his plane onto it, and whose twin brother has been murdered by the Japanese, returns to that country after World War II and learns to forgive and be forgiven. Today, I am examining compassion in the application by medical people of their new capabilities and in the attitudes of patients and families in making harsh medical decisions.

"The book *Bioethics Committees: The Health Care Provider's Guide* describes groups that affect such decisions in hospitals, hospices and nursing homes. The committee members advise doctors and others and may write guidelines for the institutions. Their existence, unfortunately, is usually unknown to patients and their families. Many of the dilemmas that the members examine concern withdrawing treatment from patients who are in vegetative state or terminal condition. Other subjects include patients' confidentiality, informed consent, and patients' and families' right to refuse treatment.

"I am also interested in the attitudes of people who are accused of crimes or of burdening others. I find that they often submit, dropping out of life or begging for punishment that is disproportionate to their offenses. That is particularly likely when they lack family or legal support. Such people may include, for example, a teen-ager who fails to meet educational expectations, a father who fist-fights with a son or breaks a law, or an old, ill person who could ease a burden on others by dying. Although every human is guilty of something, only a few are evil. I want to give courage to some of them through a small law practice and to a larger number through my writing."

*   *   *

HOSTETLER, Marian 1932-

PERSONAL: Born February 9, 1932, in Ohio; daughter of M. Harry (a grocer; in insurance) and Esther (Hostetler) Hostetler. *Education:* Goshen College, B.A., 1954; Goshen Biblical Seminary, graduate study, 1957-58; Indiana University, M.S., 1973. *Religion:* Mennonite.

ADDRESSES: Home—1910 Morton, Elkhart, Ind. 46516.

CAREER: Mennonite Board of Missions, Elkhart, Ind., editorial assistant, 1958-60, teacher in Algeria, 1960-70; Concord Community Schools, Elkhart, Ind., elementary teacher, 1971—.

MEMBER: National Education Association, Indiana State Teachers Association.

WRITINGS—All published by Herald Press:

African Adventure, 1976.
Foundation Series Curriculum, Grade 3, Quarter 2, 1977.
Journey to Jerusalem, 1978.
Fear in Algeria, 1979.
Secret in the City, 1980.
(Translator) Pierre Widmer, *Some People Are Throwing You into Confusion*, 1984.
Mystery at the Mall, 1985.
They Loved Their Enemies, 1988.

SIDELIGHTS: Marian Hostetler writes: "The years I spent in North Africa were important in giving me the occasion to begin writing as well as giving me background useful in most of what I've written. Travels in Chad, Nepal, Egypt, and Cyprus have been helpful as well. On a 1985-86 sabbatical from teaching, I had a nine-month writing assignment in West Africa (Cote d'Ivoire, Benin, and Burkina Faso) with the Mennonite Board of Missions, Centre de Publications Evangeliques, and Africa Inter-Mennonite Mission."

AVOCATIONAL INTERESTS: Painting, reading, archaeology.

HOWATCH, Susan 1940-

PERSONAL: Born July 14, 1940, in Leatherhead, Surrey, England; daughter of George (a stockbroker) and Ann (Watney) Sturt; married Joseph Howatch (a sculptor and writer), August 15, 1964 (legally separated); children: Antonia. *Education:* Kings College, London, bachelor of laws, 1961.

ADDRESSES: Home—Cambridge, England. *Agent*—Harold Ober Associates, Inc., 40 East 49th St., New York, N.Y. 10017; Aitken & Stone, 29 Fernshaw Rd., London SW10 0TG, England.

CAREER: Writer. Masons of London, London, England, law clerk, 1961-62; R.C.A. Victor Record Corp., secretary, 1964-65.

MEMBER: Authors Guild, Authors League of America, Society of Authors.

WRITINGS:

MYSTERY NOVELS

The Dark Shore (also see below), Ace Books, 1965, hardcover edition, Stein & Day, 1972.
The Waiting Sands (also see below), Ace Books, 1966, hardcover edition, Stein & Day, 1972.
Call in the Night (also see below), Ace Books, 1967, hardcover edition, Stein & Day, 1973.
The Shrouded Walls (also see below), Ace Books, 1968, hardcover edition, Stein & Day, 1971.
April's Grave (also see below), Ace Books, 1969.
The Devil on Lammas Night (also see below), Ace Books, 1971, hardcover edition, Stein & Day, 1972.
A Susan Howatch Treasury (two volumes; contains *The Dark Shore, The Waiting Sands, Call in the Night, The Shrouded Walls, April's Grave,* and *The Devil on Lammas Night*), Stein & Day, 1978.

SAGA NOVELS

Penmarric, Simon & Schuster, 1971.
Cashelmara, Simon & Schuster, 1974.
The Rich Are Different, Simon & Schuster, 1977.
Sins of the Fathers, Simon & Schuster, 1980.
The Wheel of Fortune, Simon & Schuster, 1984.

OTHER

Glittering Images (novel), Knopf, 1987.
Glamorous Powers (novel), Knopf, 1988.
Ultimate Prizes (novel), Knopf, in press.

Contributor to *The Writer*.

SIDELIGHTS: Susan Howatch told *CA* that her writing "has so far had three phases, all quite distinct from one another." Her first six books were mystery novels written during the 1960s. During the next phase, Howatch specialized in complex family sagas. These long novels involved considerable research, for although they are set in modern times, the author bases her characters on historical personages and events. She explained to Philippa Toomey in a London *Times* interview: "*Penmarric* is the story of Henry II, *Cashelmara* the three Edwards, *The Rich Are Different* is Julius Caesar, Cleopatra and Mark Antony, and *The Sins of the Fathers* is about Julia, daughter of the Emperor Augustus."

Howatch elaborated on her reasons for updating these classic stories in 1980: "My prime interest is in the people, the historical thing is really a background, something that has to be researched. I start with the general research, reading a lot of books about both periods, the original one, and the one I'm resetting it in. I do feel that the historical detail can get in the way, and if you can strip away the trappings the people are revealed. You do tend to get tangled up in togas.'' The historical saga *The Wheel of Fortune*, published in 1984, marks the end of the second phase of Howatch's writing interests.

The third phase opens with the novels *Glittering Images* and *Glamorous Powers*, indicated Howatch, who describes her new emphasis for *Publishers Weekly* interviewer Sybil Steinberg. Together with *Ultimate Prizes*, these two novels form ''a trilogy of what might be called 'serious fiction': books based on events concerning the Church of England in the 20th century,'' Steinberg notes. Howatch underwent ''a constructive mid-life crisis'' in the early 1980s, she told Steinberg. Some ''go mad and marry a platinum blonde of 19,'' but Howatch chose ''to go back to writing, but write completely differently.'' She also changed publishers, she said, ''to make a statement that [*Glittering Images* is] very different . . . [in] characterization, spiritual depth, and philosophical resonances'' from the earlier *Penmarric* saga. The plot touches on historical, theological, and philosophical sources as a young minister investigates an apparent menage a trois involving a prominent Anglican bishop, the interviewer explains. ''Previously, my books were marketed for the popular reader. I hope this book will also be popular, but it's more intellectually demanding,'' related Howatch, who said she still believes ''it's an author's primary duty to entertain.'' *Glittering Images* favorably impressed Steinberg, who calls it ''an immensely readable book.''

Howatch's novels are sometimes dismissed by critics, but they are unfailingly popular with the reading public. Reviewer Sandy Rovner defends the author's talent in the *Washington Post*: ''That Susan Howatch is considered something less than belles-lettres seems somehow unjust. She tells a mean story with a remarkably keen, often amusing, ear for dialogue and her literary set decorations are transporting. Literarily, she might be placed somewhere between Barbara Cartland and Joyce Carol Oates, but a bit closer to Oates. She can be as suspenseful as Stephen King.''

AVOCATIONAL INTERESTS: Reading, theology.

MEDIA ADAPTATIONS: Penmarric was produced as a television mini-series by the British Broadcasting Corp.

BIOGRAPHICAL/CRITICAL SOURCES:

BOOKS

Authors in the News, Volume I, Gale, 1976.

PERIODICALS

Los Angeles Times Book Review, June 1, 1980, November 15, 1987.
New York Times Book Review, June 29, 1980, November 18, 1987.
Publishers Weekly, October 16, 1987.
Star-Ledger (Newark, N.J.), June 13, 1974.
Times (London), November 1, 1980.
Washington Post, June 7, 1980, June 2, 1984, October 6, 1987.†

*   *   *

HOWELL, Joseph T(oy III)   1942-

PERSONAL: Born April 1, 1942, in Nashville, Tenn.; son of Joseph T., Jr. (a banker) and Carroll (Cole) Howell; married Embry Martin (a health planner and statistician), December 28, 1965; children: Andrew Martin, Jessica Ramsey. *Education:* Davidson College, B.A., 1964; Union Theological Seminary, New York, N.Y., M.Div., 1968; University of North Carolina, M.R.P., 1970. *Politics:* Democrat. *Religion:* Episcopalian.

ADDRESSES: Home—2923 Macomb St. N.W., Washington, D.C. 20008. *Office*—National Corporation for Housing Partnerships, 1133 15th St. N.W., Washington, D.C. 20005.

CAREER: University of North Carolina, Chapel Hill, research associate at Center for Urban and Regional Studies, 1970-72; Gladstone Associates (economic consultants), Washington, D.C., associate, 1972-74; Episcopal Diocese of Washington, Washington, D.C., director of housing, 1974-78; National Corporation for Housing Partnerships, Washington, D.C., director of development, 1978—.

MEMBER: Omicron Delta Kappa.

AWARDS, HONORS: Rockefeller Foundation fellowship, 1965; Mellon fellowship, 1969; U.S. Department of Health, Education, and Welfare social policy fellowship, 1970.

WRITINGS:

Hard Living on Clay Street: Portraits of Blue Collar Families, Doubleday, 1973.
(With Robert B. Zehner, and F. Stuart Chapin, Jr.) *Across the City Line: A White Community in Transition*, Heath, 1974.
Real Estate Development Syndication, Praeger, 1983.

SIDELIGHTS: Joseph T. Howell told *CA*: ''*Hard Living on Clay Street* is written about blue collar families in Washington, D.C., whom I got to know when I was 'participant observer' in their neighborhood, 1970-1971. This particular study is part of a larger study undertaken by the Center for Urban and Regional Studies and funded by the National Institute of Mental Health.'' *Ms.* contributor Frances Fox Piven describes the study as ''an intensely immediate, even gripping, account of daily life among the white urban poor.'' Gordon Burnside concludes in the *New York Times Book Review*: ''Joseph Howell's sober little book should be *the* chapter on the working class at home.''

BIOGRAPHICAL/CRITICAL SOURCES:

PERIODICALS

Ms. May, 1974.
New York Times Book Review, September 30, 1973.

*   *   *

HOWELLS, John G(wilym)   1918-

PERSONAL: Born June 24, 1918, in Amlwch, Wales; son of Richard David and Mary (Hughes) Howells; married Ola Harrison, December 11, 1943; children: David John Barry, Richard Keith, Cheryll Mary, Roger Bruce. *Education:* University of London, B.S. and M.B., 1943, M.D., 1951; University of Goettingen, graduate study, 1947.

ADDRESSES: Office—*International Journal of Family Psychiatry*, Hill House, Higham, Colchester CO7 6LD, United Kingdom.

CAREER: Licentiate of Royal College of Physicians of London, London, England, 1943; Charing Cross Hospital, London, house physician and senior house surgeon, 1943; diploma in psychological medicine, 1947; University of London, Institute of Psychiatry and Institute of Neurology, London, registrar, 1947-49; consulting psychiatrist, 1949-83; Institute of Family Psychiatry, Ipswich, England, director, 1949-83. Member of the Royal College of Surgeons of England, 1943; fellow of the Royal College of Psychiatrists, 1971. World Health Organization, fellow in United States, 1961, and consultant. Visiting professor, University of Nebraska, 1962. Originator of family psychiatry system of practice and organizer of first hospital department of family psychiatry.

MEMBER: World Psychiatric Association, Royal Society of Medicine, British Medical Association, American Psychiatric Association (distinguished fellow).

WRITINGS:

Family Psychiatry, Oliver & Boyd, 1963.
Theory and Practice of Family Psychiatry, Oliver & Boyd, 1968.
Remember Maria, Butterworth, 1974.
(Editor) *World History of Psychiatry,* Brunner/Mazel, 1974.
Contemporary Issues in Psychiatry, Butterworth, 1974.
Principles of Family Psychiatry, Brunner/Mazel, 1975.
(Editor) *Advances in Family Psychiatry,* two volumes, International Universities Press, 1980-81.
Integral Clinical Investigation, Macmillan, 1982.
(With W. Guirguis) *Family and Schizophrenia,* International Universities Press, 1983.
(With M. L. Osborn) *A Reference Companion to the History of Abnormal Psychology,* Greenwood Press, 1984.
(With W. Brown) *Family Diagnosis,* International Universities Press, 1986.

Editor of ''Modern Perspectives in Psychiatry'' series, nine volumes, 1965-81; editor of ''Clinical Psychiatry'' series, Brunner, 1987—. Deviser, with J. R. Lickorish, of psychological test, ''Family Relations Indicator.'' Contributor of about 150 articles to medical journals. Editor of *International Journal of Family Psychiatry,* 1980—.

WORK IN PROGRESS: Continued work on ''Modern Perspectives in Psychiatry'' series and volumes; research in family psychiatry.

AVOCATIONAL INTERESTS: Growing clematis; music, art, poetry, ''rumination.''

*   *   *

HUGHES, Shirley 1927-

PERSONAL: Born July 16, 1927, in Hoylake, near Liverpool, England; married; children: two sons, one daughter. *Education:* Attended Liverpool Art School and Ruskin School of Drawing and Fine Arts.

ADDRESSES: Home—63 Lansdowne Rd., London W.11, England.

CAREER: Author and illustrator of books for children.

AWARDS, HONORS: Other Award, Children's Rights Workshop, 1976, for *Helpers;* Kate Greenaway Medal, British Librarians Association, 1978, for *Dogger;* Eleanor Farjeon Award, Children's Book Circle, 1984; Horn Book Honor List, 1986, for *Bathwater's Hot.*

WRITINGS:

JUVENILES; SELF-ILLUSTRATED

The Trouble with Jack, Bodley Head, 1970.

Sally's Secret, Bodley Head, 1973, Merrimack Book Service, 1980.
Helpers, Bodley Head, 1975, published as *George the Babysitter,* Prentice-Hall, 1977.
Dogger, Bodley Head, 1977, published as *David and Dog,* Prentice-Hall, 1978.
It's Too Frightening for Me!, Hodder & Stoughton, 1977, published as *Haunted House,* Prentice-Hall, 1978.
Moving Molly, Bodley Head, 1978, Prentice-Hall, 1979.
Clothes, Merrimack Book Service, 1979.
Up and Up, Prentice-Hall, 1979.
(Editor) *Over the Moon: A Book of Sayings,* Merrimack Book Service, 1980.
Here Comes Charlie Moon, Bodley Head, 1980, Lothrop, 1986.
Charlie Moon and the Big Bonanza Bust Up, Bodley Head, 1982, Merrimack Book Service, 1984.
Chips and Jessie, Lothrop, 1983.
When We Went to the Park, Lothrop, 1985.
Noisy, Lothrop, 1985.
Bathwater's Hot, Lothrop, 1985.
All Shapes and Sizes (nursery collection), Lothrop, 1986.
Colors (nursery collection), Lothrop, 1986.
Two Shoes, New Shoes (nursery collection), Lothrop, 1986.
Another Helping of Chips, Bodley Head, 1986, Lothrop, 1987.

''LUCY AND TOM'' SERIES; JUVENILES; SELF-ILLUSTRATED

Lucy and Tom's Day, David & Charles, 1960.
Lucy and Tom Go to School, Gollancz, 1973.
Lucy and Tom at the Seaside, Gollancz, 1976.
Lucy and Tom's Christmas, Gollancz, 1981.
Lucy and Tom's a.b.c., Gollancz, 1984.
Lucy and Tom's 1-2-3, Gollancz, 1987.

''ALFIE'' SERIES; JUVENILES; SELF-ILLUSTRATED

Alfie Gets in First, Bodley Head, 1981, Lothrop, 1982.
Alfie's Feet, Bodley Head, 1982, Lothrop, 1984.
Alfie Gives a Hand, Bodley Head, 1983, Lothrop, 1984.
An Evening at Alfie's, Lothrop, 1984.

JUVENILES; ILLUSTRATOR

Louisa May Alcott, *Little Women,* Puffin Books, 1953, reprinted, 1982.
Doris Rust, *Story a Day,* Faber, 1954.
Rust, *All Sorts of Days,* Faber, 1955.
Diana Ross, *Willam and the Lorry,* Faber, 1956.
Edward H. Lang, *Curious Adventures of Tabby,* Faber, 1956.
Rust, *Animals at Number Eleven,* Faber, 1956.
Rust, *Animals at Rose Cottage,* Faber, 1957.
Edward H. Lang, *Storm over Skye,* Harcourt, 1957.
Rust, *Mixed-Muddly Island,* Faber, 1958.
Dorothy Clewes, *The Singing Strings,* Collins, 1961.
Hans Christian Andersen, *Fairy Tales,* Blackie, 1961.
Barbara Softly, *Place Mill,* Collins, 1962.
Margaret McPherson, *The Shinty Boys,* Harcourt, 1963.
Ruth Sawyer, *Roller Skates,* Bodley Head, 1964.
Mabel Esther Allan, *Mystery on the Fourteenth Floor,* Abelard, 1965.
Helen Morgan, *A Dream of Dragons, and Other Tales,* Faber, 1965.
Margaret Storey, *Kate and the Family Tree,* Faber, 1965.
Storey, *The Smallest Doll,* Faber, 1966.
Nina Bawden, *The Witch's Daughter,* Puffin Books, 1966.
Donald Bisset, *Little Bear's Pony,* Benn, 1966.
Angela Bull, *Wayland's Keep,* Collins, 1966.

Barbara Ireson, editor, *The Faber Book of Nursery Stories,* Faber, 1966, reprinted, 1984.

Margaret J. Baker, *Porterhouse Major,* Prentice-Hall, 1967.

Morgan, *Mary Kate and the Jumble Bear, and Other Stories,* Prentice-Hall, 1967.

McPherson, *The New Tenants,* Harcourt, 1968.

John Randle, *Grandpa's Balloon,* Benn, 1968.

Helen Cresswell, *A Day on Big O,* Follet, 1968.

Ursula M. Williams, *A Crown for a Queen,* Meredith Press, 1968.

Elizabeth Cheatham Walton, *Voices in the Fog,* Abelard-Schuman, 1968.

Leonard Clar, compiler, *Flutes and Cymbals,* Crowell, 1969.

Ann Thwaite, *The Holiday Map,* Follett, 1969.

Williams, *The Toymaker's Daughter,* Meredith Press, 1969.

Sara Corrin, editor, *Stories for Seven-Year-Olds and Other Young Readers,* F. Watts, 1969, revised edition with Stephen Corrin, Faber, 1982.

Ainsworth, *The Bicycle Wheel,* Hamilton, 1969.

Irma Chilton, *Goldie,* Hamilton, 1969.

Morgan, *Mrs. Pinny and the Sudden Snow,* Faber, 1969.

Septima, *Something to Do,* with diagrams by W. D. Bland, Collins, 1969.

Helen Griffiths, *Moshie Cat: The Adventures of a Mallorquin Kitten,* Hutchinson, 1970.

Ainsworth, *The Ruth Ainsworth Book,* Heinemann, 1970.

Morgan, *Satchkin Patchkin,* M. Smith, 1970.

Cresswell, *Rainbow Pavement,* Benn, 1970.

Williams, *The Three Toymakers,* revised edition, Hamilton, 1970.

Clewes, *Adventure on Rainbow Island,* Howard Baker, 1970.

Sheena Porter, *The Bronze Chrysanthemum,* Oxford University Press, 1970.

Charles Perrault, *Cinderella; or, The Little Glass Slipper,* translated by Robert Samber, Bodley Head, 1970.

Geraldine Kaye, *Eight Days to Christmas,* Macmillan, 1970.

Clewes, *The Jade Green Cadillac,* Howard Baker, 1970.

Clewes, *The Lost Tower Treasure,* Howard Baker, 1970.

Williams, *Malkin's Mountain,* revised edition, Hamilton, 1970.

Morgan, *Mary Kate and the School Bus, and Other Stories,* Faber, 1970.

Elizabeth Jean Roberton, reteller, *Fairy Tales by Hans Andersen,* from the original English version by Caroline Peachey, Blackie, 1970, expanded edition published as *Hans Andersen's Fairy Tales,* Blackie, 1970, Schocken, 1979.

Roberton, reteller, *More Fairy Tales by Hans Andersen,* from the original English version by Peachey, Blackie, 1970.

Jo Rice, *Robbie's Mob,* World's Work, 1971.

Griffiths, *Federico,* Hutchinson Junior Books, 1971.

Sara Corrin and Stephen Corrin, editors, *Stories for Eight-Year-Olds and Other Young Readers,* Faber, 1971.

Morgan, *Mother Farthing's Luck,* Faber, 1971.

Barbara Sleigh, *The Sell of Privet,* Hutchinson, 1971.

Bawden, *Squib,* Gollancz, 1971.

Elizabeth Goudge, *The Lost Angel: Stories,* Hodder & Stoughton, 1971.

Julia Cunningham, *Burnish Me Bright,* Heinemann, 1971.

Robina Beckles Wilson, *Dancing Day,* Benn, 1971.

Mary Stewart, *The Little Broomstick,* Brockhampton Press, 1971, Morrow, 1972.

Frances Margaret Fox, *The Little Cat That Could Not Sleep,* Faber, 1971, Scroll Press, 1972.

Morgan, *Mary Kate,* Thomas Nelson, 1972.

Margaret Mahy, *The First Margaret Mahy Story Book,* Dent, 1972.

Cresswell, *L'Arc-en-ciel,* translated by Ralph Sage, Benn, 1972.

Kaye, *Ginger,* Macmillan, 1972.

Leila Berg, *Hospital Day,* Macmillan, 1972.

Joan G. Robinson, *The House in the Square,* Collins, 1972.

Cresswell, *Les Jeunes Corsaires,* translated by Sage, Benn, 1972.

Susan Dickinson, editor, *Mother's Help: For Busy Mothers and Playgroup Leaders,* diagrams by Maureen Verity, Collins, 1972.

Jenny Overton, *The Thirteen Days of Christmas,* Faber, 1972.

Morgan, *Mrs. Pinny and the Salty Sea Day,* Faber, 1972.

Mary Crockett, *Rolling On,* Methuen, 1972.

Margaret Kornitzer, *The Hollywell Family,* Bodley Head, 1973, Merrimack Book Service, 1980.

Storey, *The Family Tree,* Thomas Nelson, 1973.

Mahy, *The Second Margaret Mahy Story Book,* Dent, 1973.

Ainsworth, *Another Lucky Dip,* Penguin, 1973.

Sara Corrin and Stephen Corrin, editors, *Stories for Five-Year-Olds and Other Young Readers,* Faber, 1973.

Ainsworth, *The Phantom Fisherboy: Tales of Mystery and Magic,* Deutsch, 1974.

Jean Sutcliffe, *Jacko, and Other Stories,* Puffin Books, 1974.

Sara Corrin and Stephen Corrin, editors, *Stories for Under Fives,* Faber, 1974.

Alison Farthing, *The Gauntlet Fair,* Chatto & Windus, 1974.

Joan Drake, *Miss Hendy's House,* Brockhampton Press, 1974.

Bisset, *Hazy Mountain,* Puffin Books, 1975.

Marjorie Lloyd, *Fell Farm Campers,* Puffin Books, 1975.

Mahy, *The Third Margaret Mahy Story Book,* Dent, 1975.

Allan, *The Sign of the Unicorn: A Thriller for Young People,* White Lion Publishers, 1975.

Morgan, *Mrs. Pinny and the Blowing Day,* Puffin Books, 1976.

Noel Streatfeild, *New Town: A Story about the Bell Family,* White Lion Publishers, 1976.

Streatfeild, *The Pained Garden: A Story of a Holiday in Hollywood,* revised edition, Puffin Books, 1976.

Ruth Tomalin, *The Snake Crook,* Faber, 1976.

Sara Corrin and Stephen Corrin, editors, *Stories for Six-Year-Olds and Other Young Readers,* Puffin Books, 1976.

Allan, *Fiona on the Fourteenth Floor,* Dent, 1976.

May Byron, *J. M. Barrie's "Peter Pan and Wendy,"* Hodder and Stoughton, 1976.

Winifred Finlay, *Tattercoats, and Other Folk Tales,* Kaye & Ward, 1976, Harvey House, 1977.

Alison M. Abel, editor, *Make Hay while the Sun Shines: A Book of Proverbs,* Faber, 1977.

Ainsworth, *Phantom Roundabout,* Deutsch, 1977.

Young, *A Throne for Sesame,* Deutsch, 1977.

Cresswell, *Donkey Days,* Benn, 1977.

Alison Uttley, *From Spring to Spring: Stories of the Four Seasons,* edited by Kathleen Lines, Faber, 1978.

Williams, *Bogwoppit,* Hamilton, 1978.

Brenda Sivers, *The Snailman,* Little, Brown, 1978, published as *Timothy and the Snailman,* Abelard-Schuman, 1979.

Oliver Selfridge, *Trouble with Dragons,* Addison-Wesley, 1978.

Sara Corrin and Stephen Corrin, editors, *More Stories for Seven-Year-Olds and Other Young Readers,* Puffin Books in association with Faber, 1978.

Ainsworth, *The Phantom Carousel, and Other Ghostly Tales,* Follet, 1978.

Nancy Northcote, *Pottle Pig,* Kaye & Ward, 1978.

Sara Corrin and Stephen Corrin, editors, *Stories for Nine-Year-Olds and Other Young Readers,* Puffin Books in association with Faber, 1979.

Ainsworth, *The Pirate Ship, and Other Stories*, Heinemann, 1980.
Mary Welfare, *Witchdust*, John Murray, 1980.
Rikki Cate, *A Cat's Tale*, Harcourt, 1982.
Honore de Balzac, *Cousin Pons*, Folio Society, 1984.

"NAUGHTY LITTLE SISTER" SERIES; JUVENILES; ILLUSTRATOR

Dorothy Edwards, *My Naughty Little Sister*, Methuen, 1962, reprinted, 1982.
Edwards, *My Naughty Little Sister's Friends*, Methuen, 1962.
Edwards, *When My Naughty Little Sister Was Good*, Methuen, 1968, reprinted, 1983.
Edwards, *All about My Naughty Little Sister*, Methuen, 1969.
Edwards, *More Naughty Little Sister Stories*, Methuen, 1970.
Edwards, *My Naughty Little Sister and Bad Harry*, Methuen, 1974.
Edwards, *My Naughty Little Sister Goes Fishing*, Methuen, 1976.
Edwards, *My Naughty Little Sister and Bad Harry's Rabbit*, Methuen, 1977, Prentice-Hall, 1981.
Edwards, *My Naughty Little Sister at the Fair*, Methuen, 1979.

"WOOD STREET" SERIES; JUVENILES; ILLUSTRATOR

Mabel Esther Allan, *The Wood Street Group*, Methuen, 1970.
Allan, *The Wood Street Secret*, Abelard-Schuman, 1970.
Allan, *The Wood Street Rivals*, Methuen, 1971.
Allan, *The Wood Street Helpers*, Methuen, 1973.
Allan, *Away from Wood Street*, Methuen, 1975.

SIDELIGHTS: Shirley Hughes told *CA:* "I think that I was lucky to have the experience of illustrating a lot of other people's stories before somebody suggested that I should do a book of my own. This was when my own children were very young, at an age of being read to, so I knew how important the text in a picture book is however sparse the words. But, of course, the pictures aren't just the icing on the cake, they are crucial to the way the reader perceives the story, a first introduction to fiction. The characterisation, the setting of the scene and a lot of the humour goes into the pictures. It is a shared entertainment, with two people pointing things out to one another and enhancing their responses; a particularly rewarding audience to work for.

"I draw all my characters out of my head (I rarely use models) although for story ideas I do rely on real experiences. Whenever possible I lurk about in children's playgrounds with a sketchbook, to get the right feeling of movement. Now my own family are grown-up, but fortunately I'm invited to meet lots of children in schools and libraries up and down the country, and find their reactions endlessly refreshing and a great spur to invention."

As the illustrator and author of over 150 books for children, Shirley Hughes has received numerous awards and honors, including the Eleanor Farjeon Award for distinguished service to children's literature. Kicki Moxon Browne in the *Times Literary Supplement* remarks that "Hughes's books [are] . . . totally irresistible, with her crumpled, lived-in people and relaxed prose," while Julia Eccleshare, also in the *Times Literary Supplement*, adds that "underneath the pleasant appearance of her illustrations she has always shown a remarkable ability to see things from a child's perspective."

BIOGRAPHICAL/CRITICAL SOURCES:

PERIODICALS

Times Literary Supplement, December 2, 1977, November 21, 1980, November 20, 1981, September 17, 1982, June 15, 1984, September 27, 1985, October 25, 1985.

HULL, William E(dward) 1930-

PERSONAL: Born May 28, 1930, in Birmingham, Ala.; son of William E. and Margaret J. King Hull; married Julia Wylodine Hester, July 26, 1952; children: David William, Susan Virginia. *Education:* Attended University of Alabama, 1948-50; Howard College (now Samford University), B.A., 1951; Southern Baptist Theological Seminary, M.Div., 1954, Ph.D., 1960; postdoctoral study at University of Goettingen, 1962-63, and Harvard University, 1971.

ADDRESSES: Office—Samford University, Birmingham, Ala. 35229.

CAREER: Ordained Baptist minister, 1950; pastor in Wetumpka, Ala., 1950-51, Owenton, Ky., 1952-53, and New Castle, Ky., 1953-58; Southern Baptist Theological Seminary, Louisville, Ky., instructor, 1955-58, assistant professor, 1958-61, associate professor, 1961-67, professor of New Testament interpretation, 1967-75, chairman of department of New Testament, 1958-60, 1963-68, director of graduate studies in School of Theology, 1968-70, dean of School of Theology, 1969-75, provost, 1972-75; First Baptist Church, Shreveport, La., pastor, 1975-87; Samford University, Birmingham, Ala., professor and provost, 1987—. Interim pastor, Highland Baptist Church, Louisville, 1966-67; visiting preaching associate, Metropolitan Baptist Church, Cambridge, Mass., 1971; minister of preaching, Crescent Hill Baptist Church, Louisville, 1972.

Guest professor, Baptist Theological Seminary, Ruschlikon-Zurich, Switzerland, 1963; visiting lecturer, Southwestern Baptist Theological Seminary, 1965, and Louisiana State University School of Medicine, 1975-78; Throgmorton Lecturer, Southern Illinois University, 1972; Staley Distinguished Christian Scholar Lecturer, Mobile College, 1973; Baptist College at Charleston, 1978, Samford University, 1978, 1982, and Louisiana College, 1986; Harwell Lecturer, Auburn University and University of Alabama, both 1973; Spell Lecturer, Mississippi College, 1977; visiting professor, Southern Baptist Theological Seminary, 1979, and Nigerian Baptist Theological Seminary, 1982; Deere Lecturer, Golden Gate Baptist Theological Seminary, 1983; speaker at Baptist conventions and conferences, missions in Europe, Middle East, and Southeast Asia, radio programs, and U.S. Air Force preaching missions in Turkey.

Louisiana Baptist Convention, committee on order of business, member, 1976-79, chairman, 1978-79; representative to North American Baptist Fellowship, Southern Baptist Convention, 1980-85. Louisiana College, member of board of trustees, 1978-82, chairman of board of trustees, 1980-82, member of board of development, 1985-87. Member of board of directors, Metropolitan YMCA, Louisville, 1972-75; City of Shreveport, member of Census Correct Committee and of Mayor's Capital Evaluation Committee, both 1980; member of chancellor's advisory board, Louisiana State University, 1982-84.

MEMBER: Baptist World Alliance (chairman of commission on Baptist doctrine, 1970-75, and of commission on pastoral leadership, 1980-85), American Academy of Religion, National Association of Baptist Professors of Religion (president, 1967-68), Society of Biblical Literature, Northwest Louisiana Baptist Association (member of executive board, 1975-87; chairman of public affairs committee, 1979-81), Rotary International, University Club (Shreveport), Phi Eta Sigma, Omicron Delta Kappa, Phi Kappa Phi.

AWARDS, HONORS: Theological fellow, Southwestern Baptist Theological Seminary, 1965; Denominational Service Award, Samford University, 1974; Liberty Bell Award, Shreveport Bar Association, 1984; Brotherhood and Humanitarian Award, National Conference of Christians and Jews, Shreveport and Bossier City Chapter, 1987.

WRITINGS:

The Bible, Covenant Press, 1974.
Beyond the Barriers, Broadman, 1981.
Shreveport Sermons, First Baptist Church (Shreveport), Volume I, 1981, Volume II, 1982.
Love in Four Dimensions, Broadman, 1982.
The Christian Experience of Salvation, Broadman, 1987.

CONTRIBUTOR

Professor in the Pulpit, Broadman, 1963.
I Dedicate Myself, Women's Missionary Union, 1964.
Messages on Evangelism, Golden Rule Press, 1964.
Joseph Nordenhaug, editor, *The Truth That Makes Men Free,* Broadman, 1966.
Clifton J. Allen, general editor, *Broadman Bible Commentary,* Volume IX, Broadman, 1970.
Salvation in Our Time, Broadman, 1978.
Set Apart for Service, Broadman, 1980.
Celebrating Christ's Presence through the Spirit, Broadman, 1981.
The Twentieth Century Pulpit, Volume II, Abingdon, 1981.
James W. Cox, editor, *Biblical Preaching: An Expositor's Treasury,* Westminster, 1983.
Cox, editor, *Minister's Manual (Doran's),* Harper & Row, 1983-1985.
James C. Barry, compiler, *Preaching in Today's World,* Broadman, 1984.
(Author of foreword) *Why the Church Must Teach,* Broadman, 1984.

OTHER

Also author of pamphlets *The Gospel of John,* Broadman, 1964, and *Christ and the Modern Mood,* Druid Hills Baptist Church, 1960. Author of curriculum materials, "Life and Work Curriculum" series and "Uniform Lesson" series, for Baptist Sunday School Board. Contributing editor, *Best Sermons,* Harper & Row, 1986—, and *Minister's Personal Library,* Word, 1987—. Contributor to *Messages on Evangelism Delivered at Georgia Baptist Evangelistic Conference,* 1970, 1971, and to proceedings of the Eastern Baptist Religious Education Association, Southwestern Baptist Religious Education Association, and Southern Baptist Religious Education Association. Contributor of articles to theological journals and to religious and denominational publications, including *Journal of Biblical Literature, Review and Expositor, Theological Education, Covenant Champion, Christian Century, Christianity Today, Baptist Faculty Paper, Beam International,* and *Window.* Member of editorial board of *Survey,* 1960-63, and *Review and Expositor,* 1964-68; contributing editor of *Baptist Message,* 1977-78.

*   *   *

HUMPHREYS, Emyr Owen   1919-

PERSONAL: Born April 15, 1919, in Prestatyn, Wales; son of William and Sarah (Owen) Humphreys; married Elinor My-fanwy Jones, April 25, 1946; children: Dewi, Mair, Sion, Robyn. *Education:* University College of Wales, University of Wales, B.A.; additional study at University College of North Wales.

ADDRESSES: Home—Llinon Penyberth Llanfairpwll, Gwynedd LL61 CYT, Wales. *Agent*—Richard Scott Simon Ltd., 32 College Cross, London N1 1PR, England.

CAREER: Junior Technical College at Wimbledon, London, England, teacher, 1948-51; grammar school teacher in Pwllheli, Wales, 1951-55; British Broadcasting Corp. in Wales, radio and television drama producer, 1955-65; University College of North Wales, Bangor, drama lecturer, 1965-72; full-time writer, 1972—. Made a series of films in Pennsylvania on the Welsh experience in the United States, 1975. *Wartime service:* Conscientious objector working as a farm laborer and war relief worker, 1940-46.

AWARDS, HONORS: Somerset Maugham Award for *Hear and Forgive,* 1953; Hawthornden Prize for *A Toy Epic,* 1959; Welsh Arts Council Prize, 1972 and 1975; Gregynog Arts fellow, 1975; Society of Authors Prize, 1979.

WRITINGS:

The Little Kingdom, Eyre & Spottiswoode, 1947.
The Voice of a Stranger, Eyre & Spottiswoode, 1949.
A Change of Heart, Eyre & Spottiswoode, 1951.
Hear and Forgive, Gollancz, 1953.
A Man's Estate, Eyre & Spottiswoode, 1955.
The Italian Wife, Eyre & Spottiswoode, 1957.
Y Tri Llais, Llyfrau'r Dryw, 1958.
A Toy Epic, Eyre & Spottiswoode, 1959.
The Gift, Eyre & Spottiswoode, 1963.
Outside the House of Baal, Eyre & Spottiswoode, 1965.
Natives (stories), Secker & Warburg, 1968.
Ancestor Worship (poetry), Gee, 1970.
(With W. S. Jones) *Dinas,* Llyfrau'r Dryw, 1970.
National Winner (novel), Macdonald & Co., 1971.
Cymod Cadarn, Lwyfan, 1973.
Flesh and Blood (novel), Hodder & Stoughton, 1974.
Landscapes (poetry), Oxford University Press, 1976.
The Best of Friends (novel), Hodder & Stoughton, 1978.
The Kingdom of Bran (poetry), Ragged Robin Press, 1979.
The Anchor Tree, Hodder & Stoughton, 1980.
Miscellany Two, Poetry Wales Press, 1981.
The Taliesin Tradition, Black Raven Press, 1983.
Jones (novel), Dent, 1984.
Salt of the Earth, Dent, 1985.
An Absolute Hero, Dent, 1986.

SIDELIGHTS: Emyr Owen Humphreys "may be the most distinguished novelist at present writing in and about Wales," according to *Dictionary of Literary Biography* essayist Roland Mathias. "In an affluent and irreligious modern society, Emyr Humphreys is both a Christian and a Welsh nationalist, a combination which separates him from other modern novelists. He is concerned largely, if not constantly, with issues raised by an ongoing Christianity and a concern for the future of Wales."

Humphreys was raised in an anglicized area of Wales and spoke no Welsh as a child, although at grammar school he did meet and become friendly with Welsh-speaking children from rural districts. It was only after becoming involved with student politics during his university days that he became an ardent Welsh nationalist and learned the ancient language. He also embraced a pacifist philosophy. While his first published novel, *The Little Kingdom,* makes a strong case for Welsh nationalism, it is also a condemnation of the use of violence to achieve political ends.

Themes of Christian duty dominate much of Humphreys's work. Romantic love is usually depicted as an unpredictable and destructive phenomenon—one which often works against the idealism of Christian charity. *Hear and Forgive* charts the spiritual journey of David Flint, a novelist who eventually leaves his rich mistress to return to his provincial wife. According to Mathias, Flint's decision leaves him "joyless but determined to do what is right." In *Jones,* a man's irresponsible handling of his relationships torments him at the end of his life even more painfully than does his rejection of his Welsh heritage. *Times Literary Supplement* contributor J. K. L. Walker praises Humphreys for his "skill in creating a likeable and amusing protagonist" in this serious novel.

While Humphreys's themes may seem deeply traditional, he often uses experimental techniques in his fiction, including cinematic cutting, interweaving of contracting time sequences, and abandonment of quotation marks. Mathias notes that the author "has never altered his fundamental position: life is serious." However, Mathias adds, "To infer from this basic seriousness that Humphreys's novels are boringly earnest would be a grave error: their surface is remarkably cool and their plots are complex; comedy of incident often embellishes themes that have tragic overtones."

BIOGRAPHICAL/CRITICAL SOURCES:

BOOKS

Dictionary of Literary Biography, Volume XV: *British Novelists, 1930-1959,* Gale, 1983.
Williams, Ioan, *Emyr Humphreys,* University of Wales Press, 1980.

PERIODICALS

Anglo-Welsh Review, Number 70, 1982.
Planet, Number 39, 1977.
Times (London), August 2, 1984.
Times Literary Supplement, August 1, 1980, August 10, 1984.

*   *   *

HUNTER, J(ames) Paul   1934-

PERSONAL: Born June 29, 1934, in Jamestown, N.Y.; son of Paul Wesley (a clergyman) and Florence (Walmer) Hunter; married Kathryn Montgomery, July 1, 1971; children: Debra, Lisa, Paul III, Anne. *Education:* Indiana Central College, A.B., 1955; Miami University, Oxford, Ohio, M.A., 1957; Rice University, Ph.D., 1963.

ADDRESSES: Home—1218 East Madison Pk., Chicago, Ill. 60615. *Office*—406 Wieboldt Hall, University of Chicago, Chicago, Ill. 60637.

CAREER: Instructor in English at University of Florida, Gainesville, 1957-59, and Williams College, Williamstown, Mass., 1962-64; University of California, Riverside, assistant professor of English, 1964-66; Emory University, Atlanta, Ga., associate professor, 1966-68, professor of English, 1968-80, department chairman, 1973-79; University of Rochester, Rochester, N.Y., dean of arts and science, 1981-86; University of Chicago, Chicago, Ill., professor of English, 1987—.

MEMBER: Modern Language Association of America, American Society of Eighteenth Century Studies.

AWARDS, HONORS: Guggenheim fellow, 1976-77; National Endowment for the Humanities fellow, 1986; National Humanities Center fellow, 1986.

WRITINGS:

The Reluctant Pilgrim: Defoe's Emblematic Method and Quest for Form in "Robinson Crusoe," Johns Hopkins Press, 1966.
(Editor) Daniel Defoe, *Moll Flanders* (critical edition), Crowell, 1970.
(Editor) *Norton Introduction to Literature,* Norton, 1973, 4th edition, 1986.
Norton Introduction to Poetry, Norton, 1973, 3rd edition, 1986.
Occasional Form: Henry Fielding and the Chains of Circumstance, Johns Hopkins University Press, 1975.
Before Novels: The Cultural Contexts of Eighteenth-Century English Fiction, Norton, in press.

Contributor to *Philological Quarterly, Review of English Studies, Journal of English and Germanic Philology, Novel,* and *Scriblerian.*

WORK IN PROGRESS: A book on poetic careers.

*   *   *

HURD, Clement (G.)   1908-1988

PERSONAL: Born January 12, 1908, in New York, N.Y.; died February 5, 1988, of Alzheimer's disease in San Francisco, Calif.; son of Richard M. (a mortgage banker) and Lucy (Gazzam) Hurd; married Edith Thacher (a writer), June 24, 1939; children: John Thacher. *Education:* Yale University, Ph.B., 1930; studied painting in Paris with Fernand Leger, 1931-33.

ADDRESSES: Home—1635 Green St., San Francisco, Calif. 94123. *Agent*—Curtis Brown Ltd., 10 Astor Pl., New York, N.Y. 10003.

CAREER: Illustrator and writer. *Military service:* U.S. Army, 1942-46.

WRITINGS:

Town, W. R. Scott, 1939.
Country, W. R. Scott, 1939.
The Race (self-illustrated), Random House, 1940, published as *The Race between the Monkey and the Duck,* Wonder Books, 1946.
The Merry Chase (self-illustrated), Random House, 1941.
Run, Run, Run, Harper, 1951.

ILLUSTRATOR

Margaret Wise Brown, *Bumble Bugs and Elephants,* W. R. Scott, 1938, revised edition, 1941.
Gertrude Stein, *The World Is Round* (also see below), limited autographed edition, W. R. Scott, 1939, 2nd edition, 1967, round edition, Arion, 1986.
Brown, *Runaway Bunny,* Harper, 1942.
Brown, *Goodnight Moon,* Harper, 1947.
Brown, *The Bad Little Duckhunter,* W. R. Scott, 1947.
Morrell Gipson, *Hello Peter,* Doubleday, 1948.
Brown, *My World,* Harper, 1949.
Brown, *The Peppermint Family,* Harper, 1950.
Jane Siepmann, *Lion on Scott Street,* Oxford University Press, 1952.
Brown, *Little Brass Band,* Harper, 1955.
Brown, *Diggers,* Harper, 1960.
May Garelick, *Winter's Birds,* W. R. Scott, 1965.

Edna Mitchell Preston, *Monkey in the Jungle,* Viking, 1968.
G. Cowles, *Nicholas,* Seabury, 1975.
The Goodnight Moon Room (pop-up book; based on Margaret Wise Brown's *Goodnight Moon*), Harper, 1984.

ILLUSTRATOR; WRITTEN BY WIFE, EDITH HURD

Hurry, Hurry (also see below), W. R. Scott, 1938, published as *Hurry Hurry: A Story of What Happened to a Hurrier,* 1947.
Engine, Engine, No. 9, Lothrop, 1940.
Sky High, Lothrop, 1941.
The Annie Moran, Lothrop, 1942.
Speedy, the Hook and Ladder Truck, Lothrop, 1942.
Benny the Bulldozer, Lothrop, 1947.
Toughy and His Trailer Truck, Lothrop, 1948.
Willy's Farm, Lothrop, 1949.
Caboose, Lothrop, 1950.
Old Silversides, Lothrop, 1951.
St. George's Day in Williamsburg, Va., Colonial Williamsburg, 1952.
Somebody's House, Lothrop, 1953.
Nino and His Fish, Lothrop, 1954.
The Devil's Tail: Adventures of a Printer's Apprentice in Early Williamsburg, Doubleday, 1954.
The Cat from Telegraph Hill, Lothrop, 1955.
Mr. Charlie's Chicken House, Lippincott, 1955.
Mr. Charlie's Gas Station, Lippincott, 1956.
Windy and the Willow Whistle, Sterling, 1956.
Mary's Scary House, Sterling, 1956.
It's Snowing, Sterling, 1957.
Mr. Charlie's Camping Trip, Lippincott, 1957.
Johnny Littlejohn, Lothrop, 1957.
Fox in a Box, Doubleday, 1957.
Mr. Charlie, the Fireman's Friend, Lippincott, 1958.
The Faraway Christmas: A Story of the Farallon Islands, Lothrop, 1958.
Mr. Charlie's Pet Shop, Lippincott, 1959.
Last One Home Is a Green Pig, Harper, 1959.
Hurry Hurry (based on a story of same title first published in 1938), Harper, 1960.
Mr. Charlie's Farm, Lippincott, 1960.
Stop, Stop, Harper, 1961.
Come and Have Fun, Harper, 1962.
Christmas Eve, Harper, 1962.
No Funny Business, Harper, 1962.
Follow Tomas, Dial, 1963.
The Day the Sun Danced, Harper, 1965.
Johnny Lion's Book, Harper, 1965, reprinted, 1985.
The So-So Cat, Harper, 1965.
What Whale? Where?, Harper, 1966.
Little Dog Dreaming, Harper, 1967.
The Blue Heron Tree, Viking, 1968.
Rain and the Valley, Coward, 1968.
This Is the Forest, Coward, 1969.
Johnny Lion's Bad Day, Harper, 1970.
Catfish, Viking, 1970.
The Mother Beaver, Little, Brown, 1971.
Wilson's World, Harper, 1971, published in England as *Wilkie's World,* Faber, 1973.
The Mother Deer, Little, Brown, 1972.
Johnny Lion's Rubber Boots, Harper, 1972.
The Mother Whale, Little, Brown, 1973.
Catfish and the Kidnapped Cat, Harper, 1974.
The Mother Owl, Little, Brown, 1974.
The Mother Kangaroo, Little, Brown, 1976.

Look for a Bird, Harper, 1977.
The Mother Chimpanzee, Little, Brown, 1977.
Dinosaur My Darling, Harper, 1978.
The Black Dog Who Went into the Woods, Harper, 1980.
Under the Lemon Tree, Harper, 1980.
The World Is Not Flat (a square companion volume to the round edition of *The World Is Round* by Gertrude Stein, as related by Edith Hurd), Arion, 1986.

SIDELIGHTS: Since 1939, Clement Hurd has illustrated over seventy-five children's books. Some of his best known illustrations are found in Margaret Wise Brown's 1947 classic, *Goodnight Moon,* on which Hurd based his 1984 pop-up book, *The Goodnight Moon Room.* Another of Hurd's more enduring projects is his illustration of three editions of Gertrude Stein's children's book *The World Is Round. Los Angeles Times Book Review* contributor Myra Cohn Livingston comments: "It is perhaps unprecedented in publishing history that in slightly less than half a century, Stein's book should be issued in three varying formats, all interpreted by the same illustrator, Clement Hurd. To view these three editions together is to marvel how Hurd's illustrations remain vital and fresh, yet how significantly changes in the world have affected the pictorialization and attitude toward children's responses."

Hurd's description of his approach to illustrating in a 1966 *Publishers Weekly* article explains the vitality and timelessness of his work. "Having illustrated more than 50 books in 28 years, . . ." Hurd stated, "I don't feel any more sure now of creating pictures that speak directly to children than I did the first time I approached a manuscript. When your audience is so fresh and full of wonder, it seems to me that a book for them must share some of this freshness."

BIOGRAPHICAL/CRITICAL SOURCES:

BOOKS

The Children's Bookshelf, Bantam, 1965.
Huck, Charlotte S., and D. A. Young, *Children's Literature in the Elementary School,* Holt, 1961.

PERIODICALS

Los Angeles Times Book Review, March 9, 1986.
Publishers Weekly, February 7, 1966.

OBITUARIES:

PERIODICALS

New York Times, February 10, 1988.
Publishers Weekly, February 26, 1988.

*   *   *

HURD, Edith (Thacher)   1910-
(Juniper Sage, a joint pseudonym)

PERSONAL: Born September 14, 1910, in Kansas City, Mo.; daughter of Hamilton John and Edith (Gilman) Thacher; married Clement Hurd (an artist and illustrator), June 24, 1939; children: John Thacher. *Education:* Radcliffe College, A.B., 1933; attended Bank Street College of Education, 1934. *Politics:* Democrat.

ADDRESSES: Home—1635 Green St., San Francisco, Calif. 94123. *Agent*—Marilyn Marlow, Curtis Brown Ltd., 10 Astor Pl., New York, N.Y. 10003.

CAREER: Writer. Taught four years at the Dalton School, New York, N.Y.; U.S. Office of War Information, San Francisco, Calif., news analyst, 1942-45.

WRITINGS:

The Wreck of the Wild Wave, Oxford University Press, 1942.
Jerry, the Jeep, Lothrop, 1945.
The Galleon from Manila, Oxford University Press, 1949.
Mr. Shortsleeves' Great Big Store, Simon & Schuster, 1952.
The Golden Hind, Crowell, 1960.
Sandpipers, Crowell, 1961.
Starfish, Crowell, 1962.
Sailors, Whalers and Steamers, Lane, 1964.
Who Will Be Mine?, Golden Gate, 1966.
Come with Me to Nursery School, Coward, 1970.
The White Horse, Harper, 1970.
I Dance in My Red Pajamas, pictures by Emily Arnold McCully, 1982.
Song of the Sea Otter, illustrated by Jennifer Dewey, Pantheon, 1983.

WITH MARGARET WISE BROWN

(Under joint pseudonym Juniper Sage) *The Man in the Manhole and the Fix-it Men*, W. R. Scott, 1946.
Five Little Firemen, Simon & Schuster, 1948.
Two Little Miners, Simon & Schuster, 1949.
The Little Fat Policeman, Simon & Schuster, 1950.

ILLUSTRATED BY HUSBAND, CLEMENT HURD

Hurry, Hurry (also see below), W. R. Scott, 1938, published as *Hurry Hurry: A Story of What Happened to a Hurrier*, 1947.
Engine, Engine, No. 9, Lothrop, 1940.
Sky High, Lothrop, 1941.
The Annie Moran, Lothrop, 1942.
Speedy, the Hook and Ladder Truck, Lothrop, 1942.
Benny the Bulldozer, Lothrop, 1947.
Toughy and His Trailer Truck, Lothrop, 1948.
Willy's Farm, Lothrop, 1949.
Caboose, Lothrop, 1950.
Old Silversides, Lothrop, 1951.
St. George's Day in Williamsburg, Va., Colonial Williamsburg, 1952.
Somebody's House, Lothrop, 1953.
Nino and His Fish, Lothrop, 1954.
The Devil's Tail: Adventures of a Printer's Apprentice in Early Williamsburg, Doubleday, 1954.
The Cat from Telegraph Hill, Lothrop, 1955.
Mr. Charlie's Chicken House, Lippincott, 1955.
Mr. Charlie's Gas Station, Lippincott, 1956.
Windy and the Willow Whistle, Sterling, 1956.
Mary's Scary House, Sterling, 1956.
It's Snowing, Sterling, 1957.
Mr. Charlie's Camping Trip, Lippincott, 1957.
Johnny Littlejohn, Lothrop, 1957.
Fox in a Box, Doubleday, 1957.
Mr. Charlie, the Fireman's Friend, Lippincott, 1958.
The Faraway Christmas: A Story of the Farallon Islands, Lothrop, 1958.
Mr. Charlie's Pet Shop, Lippincott, 1959.
Last One Home Is a Green Pig, Harper, 1959.
Hurry Hurry (based on a story of same title first published in 1938), Harper, 1960.
Mr. Charlie's Farm, Lippincott, 1960.
Stop, Stop, Harper, 1961.
Come and Have Fun, Harper, 1962.
Christmas Eve, Harper, 1962.
No Funny Business, Harper, 1962.
Follow Tomas, Dial, 1963.

The Day the Sun Danced, Harper, 1965.
Johnny Lion's Book, Harper, 1965, reprinted, 1985.
The So-So Cat, Harper, 1965.
What Whale? Where?, Harper, 1966.
Little Dog Dreaming, Harper, 1967.
The Blue Heron Tree, Viking, 1968.
Rain and the Valley, Coward, 1968.
This Is the Forest, Coward, 1969.
Johnny Lion's Bad Day, Harper, 1970.
Catfish, Viking, 1970.
The Mother Beaver, Little, Brown, 1971.
Wilson's World, Harper, 1971, published in England as *Wilkie's World*, Faber, 1973.
The Mother Deer, Little, Brown, 1972.
Johnny Lion's Rubber Boots, Harper, 1972.
The Mother Whale, Little, Brown, 1973.
Catfish and the Kidnapped Cat, Harper, 1974.
The Mother Owl, Little, Brown, 1974.
The Mother Kangaroo, Little, Brown, 1976.
Look for a Bird, Harper, 1977.
The Mother Chimpanzee, Little, Brown, 1977.
Dinosaur My Darling, Harper, 1978.
The Black Dog Who Went into the Woods, Harper, 1980.
Under the Lemon Tree, Harper, 1980.
The World Is Not Flat (a square companion volume to the round edition of *The World Is Round* by Gertrude Stein, as related by Edith Hurd), Arion, 1986.

OTHER

Contributor of poetry to *Grade Teacher*.

BIOGRAPHICAL/CRITICAL SOURCES:

BOOKS

Books for Children, 1960-1965, American Library Association, 1966.
The Children's Bookshelf, Bantam, 1965.
Huck, Charlotte S., and D. A. Young, *Children's Literature in the Elementary School*, Holt, 1961.
Larrick, Nancy, *A Parent's Guide to Children's Reading*, 3rd edition, Doubleday, 1969.

PERIODICALS

Los Angeles Times Book Review, March 9, 1986.
New York Times Book Review, July 27, 1980.

*   *   *

HURD, (John) Thacher 1949-

PERSONAL: Born March 6, 1949, in Burlington, Vt.; son of Clement G. (an illustrator of children's books) and Edith (an author of children's books; maiden name, Thacher) Hurd; married Olivia Scott (a counselor), June 12, 1976; children: Manton, Nicholas. *Education:* Attended University of California, Berkeley, 1967-68; California College of Arts and Crafts, B.F.A., 1972.

ADDRESSES: Home—2954 Hillegass Ave., Berkeley, Calif. 94705. *Agent*—Marilyn Marlow, Curtis Brown Ltd., 10 Astor Pl., New York, N.Y. 10003.

CAREER: Writer and illustrator of children's books. Grabhorn-Hoyem Press (now Arion Press), San Francisco, Calif., apprentice printer, 1967 and 1969; self-employed builder, designer, and cabinetmaker, 1972-78; California College of Arts and Crafts, Oakland, and Dominican College, San Rafael,

Calif., teacher of writing and illustrating children's books, 1981—; co-owner with wife, Olivia Hurd, of Peaceable Kingdom Press (a children's book poster publishing company), 1983—. Artist with group show at California College of Arts and Crafts, 1972; one-man show in Monkton, Vt., 1973. Lecturer and guest speaker at seminars, conferences, and schools.

MEMBER: Society of Children's Book Writers.

AWARDS, HONORS: Boston Globe-Horn Book Award for illustration, 1985, for *Mama Don't Allow.*

WRITINGS:

(With mother, Edith Hurd) *Little Dog Dreaming* (juvenile), illustrated by father, Clement G. Hurd, Harper, 1965.

SELF-ILLUSTRATED JUVENILE BOOKS

The Old Chair, Greenwillow, 1978.
The Quiet Evening, Greenwillow, 1978.
Hobo Dog, Scholastic Book Services, 1980.
Axle the Freeway Cat, Harper, 1981.
Mystery on the Docks, Harper, 1983.
Hobo Dog's Christmas Tree, Scholastic Inc., 1983.
Mama Don't Allow, Harper, 1984.
Hobo Dog in the Ghost Town, Scholastic Inc., 1985.
Pea Patch Jig, Crown, 1986.
A Night in the Swamp (pop-up book), Harper, 1987.

WORK IN PROGRESS: A sequel to *Pea Patch Jig;* illustrating *Wheel Away,* by Dayle Ann Dodds, for Harper.

SIDELIGHTS: Children's author and illustrator Thacher Hurd was trained in the fine arts, but several years after graduating from California College of Arts and Crafts he "became fascinated with the idea of telling a story in pictures, of making pictures in a series that were bound together by a common thread," as he once explained to *CA.* Commenting on the transition from artist to storyteller and illustrator, Hurd told *Publishers Weekly* editor Diane Roback: "All of a sudden, I felt like I could relax and let my hair down. I would write a very simple text, and as soon as I started drawing the pictures, I found that the text sparked a whole new way of working for me. I could do things in books that I'd been trying to do for years in my art, that I'd been frustrated with and couldn't get at. . . . Suddenly, in children's books, there was this story, a whole reason for the pictures I hadn't had before."

Describing his initial efforts at storytelling, Hurd told *CA:* "I'm not particularly proud of my first book efforts, which were rejected by a number of publishers. My first attempts at children's books were stiff, pale fairy tales with watery morals and dangling plots. Slowly, though, I began to think 'closer to home,' so to speak. I became aware of my own childhood memories and childlike feelings within myself. I began to realize that stories could come out of the feelings that were closest to me. My book *The Old Chair* came in this way, very simply and directly out of my own childhood feelings for the comfortable chair we had in our house when I was growing up."

Hurd's book *Pea Patch Jig,* which he calls one of his favorites, is likewise drawn from childhood experiences. The story relates the adventures of Baby, a mischievous mouse who lives with her family in Farmer Clem's garden. Hurd told Roback: "I feel very close to that book. . . . I have tried a number of times to write about our family home in Vermont, but each

time the story became maudlin, heavy, overweight with a message. Somehow, discovering this light, mischievous mouse bouncing around our garden freed me to write about something I have deep feelings about." Reviewers responded with equal enthusiasm for *Pea Patch Jig.* A *Booklist* reviewer observes, "The artwork is some of Hurd's best, featuring bright watercolors in summertime hues and strong, energetic line work." A *Horn Book* reviewer calls *Pea Patch Jig* "a festive salad of a book, filled with snap, crackle, and crunch," and a *Publishers Weekly* critic similarly concludes, "[Hurd's] kaleidoscopic colors and mischievous sense of humor make this book ripe for the picking."

Describing the process of creating and developing ideas for his storybooks, Hurd told *CA:* "I find that lots of ideas come and go, and I say to myself as they come: 'Oh, I must write that down, that would be a terrific story,' but then they have gone again almost as quickly as they came, and I can't for the life of me remember what they were. Or if I do write them down, I will look at them a few months later and wonder what could have possessed me to write down such an idea. Perhaps this is because all too often they have that quality of being ideas rather than something more. These ideas have a surface quality, a contrived quality, a quality of being forced or of being too obvious. Often they are simply not true to one's feelings.

"Then there are the other kinds of ideas, the ones that spring from real feelings, that rise up as intuitions, without plot, characters, or action. Just a feeling, welling up, bubbling into consciousness from some broader field than one's limited ordinary consciousness. These are the feelings that hang around, that cling to one and won't go away. Slowly they gestate in one's mind, until they are ready to be born. Then they cry out: 'Write me! Draw me!' Six months or a year may go by before they start to come out, but when the book is ready, it seems to come of itself."

MEDIA ADAPTATIONS: Adaptations of *Mystery on the Docks* and *Mama Don't Allow* were broadcast on "Reading Rainbow," Public Broadcasting Service (PBS-TV), 1984 and 1986 respectively; *Mama Don't Allow* was adapted into a filmstrip produced by Random House and broadcast on "CBS Storybreak," Columbia Broadcasting System, Inc. (CBS-TV), 1986.

BIOGRAPHICAL/CRITICAL SOURCES:

PERIODICALS

Booklist, September 15, 1986.
Horn Book, June, 1983, November/December, 1986.
Oakland Tribune, November 26, 1981.
Publishers Weekly, June 27, 1986, January 23, 1987.
School Library Journal, October, 1984, November, 1986.

*   *   *

HUTTON, Malcolm 1921-

PERSONAL: Born November 23, 1921, in London, England; son of Bert (a customs officer) and Gladys (Daniels) Hutton; married Patricia Milbourn, September 26, 1943 (divorced, 1956); married Diana Atkins (an artist), May 14, 1957; children: Beverley Hutton Randolph, Anne Hutton Baker, Graham, Stephen, Susan Hutton Mackintosh, Kim. *Education:* University of London, B.Commerce, 1943.

ADDRESSES: Home and office—55 Broomsleigh St., London NW6 1QQ, England.

CAREER: Worked for British Government, 1946-81, Department of Civil Defence, London, England, assistant director of London region, 1960-63, Joint Computer Organisation of the Home Office and the Metropolitan Police, London, head of unit, 1970-81. Freeman of the City of London. *Military service:* Royal Air Force, 1941-46; became flight lieutenant.

MEMBER: British Computer Society, Society of Authors.

WRITINGS:

NOVELS

Jenny Nobody, R. Hale, 1979.
Address Unknown, St. Martin's, 1981.
Mark Peterson's Daughter, R. Hale, 1982.
Georgina and Georgette, St. Martin's, 1984.
Tara, R. Hale, 1984.

The Chinese Girl, R. Hale, 1985.
Child of Malice, R. Hale, 1987.

OTHER

Contributor of stories to magazines and newspapers.

SIDELIGHTS: Malcolm Hutton told *CA:* "I write about the unlikely things that happen to ordinary people and how, therefore, they can happen to any of us. Although I try to entertain people, I hope my novels make them think a little too."

Hutton's *Address Unknown* has been translated into German and Danish.

BIOGRAPHICAL/CRITICAL SOURCES:

PERIODICALS

New York Times Book Review, February 7, 1982, June 6, 1982.

I-J

IVASK, Ivar Vidrik 1927-

PERSONAL: Born December 17, 1927, in Latvia (annexed by Soviet Union, 1940); naturalized U.S. citizen; son of Vidrik and Ilze (Guters) Ivask; married Astrid Harmanis (a writer), February 26, 1949. *Education:* Attended University of Marburg, 1946-49; University of Minnesota, M.A., 1950, Ph.D., 1953. *Politics:* Democrat. *Religion:* Protestant.

ADDRESSES: Home—Norman, Okla. *Office—World Literature Today,* 630 Parrington Oval, Norman, Okla. 73019.

CAREER: St. Olaf College, Northfield, Minn., assistant professor, 1952-57, associate professor, 1958-63, professor of German, 1964-67, acting head, 1956-57, head of department, 1964-67; University of Oklahoma, Norman, professor of modern languages and editor of *World Literature Today* (formerly *Books Abroad;* international literary quarterly), 1967—. Has had one-man exhibitions of his drawings and collages at University of Oklahoma, 1979 and 1984; has illustrated several books. *Military service:* U.S. Army, Medical Corps, 1954-56.

MEMBER: Modern Language Association of America, South Central Modern Language Association, Estonian Learned Society, Institute of Estonian Language (University of Stockholm), Estonian PEN in Exile, PEN American Center, Association for the Advancement of Baltic Studies, Finnish Literature Society, Phi Beta Kappa.

AWARDS, HONORS: Named Commander of the Lion of Finland; distinguished service citation, University of Oklahoma.

WRITINGS:

Taehtede taehendus (title means "The Meaning of Stars"), Eesti Kirjanike Kooperatiiv (Lund, Sweden), 1964.
Paev astub kukesammul (title means "The Day Arrives with a Rooster's Step"), Eesti Kirjanike Kooperatiiv, 1966.
Gespiegelte Erde, Ungar, 1967.
Ajaloo aiad (title means "The Garden of History"), Eesti Kirjanike Kooperatiiv, 1970.
Oktoober Oklahomas (title means "October in Oklahoma"), Eesti Kirjanike Kooperatiiv, 1973.
Verikivi (title means "Bloodstone"), Eesti Kirjanike Kooperatiiv, 1976.
Elukogu (title means "Life Collection"), Eesti Kirjanike Kooperatiiv, 1978.

Verandaraamat (title means "The Veranda Book"), Eesti Kirjanike Kooperatiiv, 1981.

EDITOR

(With Juan Marichal) *Luminous Reality: The Poetry of Jorge Guillen,* University of Oklahoma Press, 1969.
(With Lowell Dunham) *The Cardinal Points of Borges,* University of Oklahoma Press, 1971.
(With Gero von Wilpert) *Moderne Weltliteratur,* Alfred Kroener (Stuttgart), 1972.
(With von Wilpert) *World Literataure since 1945,* Ungar, 1973.
The Perpetual Present: The Poetry and Prose of Octavio Paz, University of Oklahoma Press, 1973.
(With Jaime Alazraki) *The Final Island: The Fiction of Julio Cortazar,* University of Oklahoma Press, 1978.
Odysseus Elytis: Analogies of Light, University of Oklahoma Press, 1981.

SIDELIGHTS: Ivar Vidrik Ivask was already highly respected for his "scholarly and incisive criticism" when his first book of poetry, *Taehtede taehendus,* revealed him as "a poet of remarkable talent and unusual depth," writes Alexander Aspel in *Books Abroad.* Most of Ivask's poetry can be classified as nature poetry. It is far from simplistic, however, according to Valev Uibopuu. In an article in *World Literature Today,* he states that Ivask's poetry proves that "a fundamentally nature-worshipping, pantheistic world view is but a step away from the cosmic experience of reality."

Ivask is competent in German, Finnish, French, and Spanish, as well as Latvian and Estonian.

BIOGRAPHICAL/CRITICAL SOURCES:

BOOKS

Contemporary Literary Criticism, Volume XIV, Gale, 1983.

PERIODICALS

Books Abroad, summer, 1965, winter, 1970, autumn, 1973.
World Literature Today, summer, 1977, spring, 1979, winter, 1984.

*   *   *

JAFFE, Rona 1932-

PERSONAL: Born June 12, 1932, in New York, N.Y.; daughter of Samuel (an elementary school teacher and principal) and Diana (a teacher; maiden name, Ginsberg) Jaffe. *Education:* Radcliffe College, B.A., 1951.

ADDRESSES: Home—201 East 62nd St., New York, N.Y. 10021. *Agent*—Morton Janklow Associates, 598 Madison Ave., New York, N.Y. 10022.

CAREER: File clerk and secretary, New York City, 1952; Fawcett Publications, New York City, associate editor, 1952-56; writer, 1956—.

WRITINGS:

The Last of the Wizards (juvenile), Simon & Schuster, 1961.
Mr. Right Is Dead (novella and five short stories), Simon & Schuster, 1965.

NOVELS

The Best of Everything, Simon & Schuster, 1958.
Away from Home, Simon & Schuster, 1960, published as *Carnival in Rio* in Europe, South America, and Scandinavia.
The Cherry in the Martini, Simon & Schuster, 1966.
The Fame Game, Random House, 1969.
The Other Woman, Morrow, 1972.
Family Secrets, Simon & Schuster, 1974.
The Last Chance, Simon & Schuster, 1976.
Class Reunion: A Novel, Delacorte, 1979.
Mazes and Monsters: A Novel, Delacorte, 1981.
After the Reunion: A Novel, Delacorte, 1985.

SIDELIGHTS: "In Rona Jaffe," notes Elaine Dundy in the *Times Literary Supplement,* "we have a good storyteller who is a good storywriter as well." Jaffe has written six bestsellers, including her first novel, *The Best of Everything.* The book, described by Judy Klemesrud in the *Chicago Tribune* as a "novel about New York career girls trying to sleep and claw their way out of the steno pool," brought the author both fame and fortune while still in her twenties.

In several ways *The Best of Everything* is like many of Jaffe's later novels. The book deals with life in New York City, focuses on conflicts in male/female relationships, and follows the stories of several main characters—three characteristics often found in her work. In one of Jaffe's most ambitious novels, *Family Secrets,* for example, some thirty-two characters appear over the course of the story.

Reviewers commenting on Jaffe's later books almost always compare the work being reviewed to Jaffe's first novel, thereby continuing interest in it. Written in the late fifties, the book has a distinctly pre-women's liberation movement slant which places it firmly in that decade. Although the women in *The Best of Everything* have jobs, they are not career women; men and the possibility of marrying one of them are far more important to these women than their work. At one point in the story one of the women characters thinks to herself: "It's hell to be a woman . . . ; to want so much love, to feel like only half a person, to need so much. What was it Plato had said? A man and a woman are each only half a person until they unite. Why hadn't he made that clearer to the men?"

Some critics, such as Judith Christ, objected to Jaffe's depiction of women in *The Best of Everything,* but the author asserts that the work gives an accurate picture of life in the fifties. According to Jaffe, the characters have much in common with people she knew or interviewed while doing research for the book. Jaffe explained to Klemesrud: In the fifties "girls were brought up to fulfill the image of what boys wanted. They

feigned great interest in things they hated because they were only supposed to talk about the boys' interest. . . . They always tried to look their best. . . . It was all part of the fifties ratrace toward the altar."

The fifties also play an important role in Jaffe's *Class Reunion,* a novel that has been described as an updated version of Mary McCarthy's story about coming of age in the 1930s, *The Group.* Alluding to McCarthy's title, a *Time* reviewer observes, "Change Vassar to Radcliffe, the '30s to the '50s, take away the wry tone, and you have Rona Jaffe's readable reworking, *Class Reunion.*" In her *Washington Post* review of the book, Lynn Darling notes that in the novel Jaffe "follows the trials and tribulations of eight members of the Class of '57 . . . as they try to crawl out from under the mind-numbing conformity of the '50s." Darling sees Jaffe's novels as a sort of exorcism of unpleasant memories. "Her observations," Darling comments, "are edged in irony, but like any veteran of a vicious war, past skirmishes are with her still, and she is still in the trenches."

In *Class Reunion* and other novels written since *The Best of Everything,* Jaffe deals with married as well as single women and how they cope with more significant dilemmas than how to catch a man. Divorce, cocaine addiction, teenage suicide, and other contemporary problems are dealt with in detail. But, while Jaffe's recent novels are praised for their readability as well as her skill in capturing the essence of life in New York City, reviews are often mixed.

In the *New York Times Book Review* Katha Pollitt, for example, calls *Class Reunion* "a wry and very readable tale," while in Eve Zibert's *Washington Post* review of the same book, the critic finds the novel "like a soap opera, . . . absorbing and embarrassing at the same time." And, while Nora Johnson in her essay on *The Last Chance* in the *New York Times Book Review* comments, "You have to keep reading Jaffe, she's competent and dependable, and she piles on the delicious details," in Nora Peck's review of *After the Reunion* appearing in the same journal, the critic notes, "Though the soul-searching in this novel may be on the level of [the television programs] 'Dynasty' or 'Dallas,' it proves equally entertaining."

While Leslie Garis does not propose a completely positive view of Jaffe's work, her *Ms.* review of *Family Secrets* does offer a brief summary of the qualities in Jaffe's writing that critics and readers alike find most appealing: "Breezy, immediate, conversational, elliptical—Rona Jaffe writes like [French novelist] Francoise Sagan's American cousin. She's more clean-cut, and less arrogant than Sagan, but their detachment, their simple statements that reduce complex emotional development to one measurable moment, their readiness to describe a childhood in a paragraph, are similar in spirit, if not in content. And when their subjects match their style, both writers carry it off brilliantly."

MEDIA ADAPTATIONS: The Best of Everything was made into a 1959 movie produced by Jerry Wald; *Mazes and Monsters* was made into a 1982 CBS-TV movie.

CA INTERVIEW

CA interviewed Rona Jaffe by telephone on February 10, 1987, at her home in New York, New York.

CA: According to Tom Bent in People *magazine, you were submitting stories to the* New Yorker *at the age of nine. And once, when you got a rejection slip from them, you "stormed over to the magazine's office to find out why." How did you come to such an early certainty that you wanted to be a writer?*

JAFFE: I knew that even before. When I was about four I decided I wanted to be a writer.

CA: And there was a lot of encouragement from your parents?

JAFFE: Yes. Apparently I dictated my first poem to my mother at the age of two and a half. She wrote it down on a paper bag in the kitchen, and that's how my literary career started. I'm sure she must have said to me, "That's a good poem," or "You'll be a writer" or something.

CA: Is the wonderful story about your storming over to the New Yorker *really true?*

JAFFE: Yes. I stormed over because the story came back by return mail, so I didn't think anybody had even read it. So I asked somebody there, who I guess was the mailroom boy— I didn't know who he was, but I knew he was older than I was—"Why did they send the story back? Didn't anybody read it?" He didn't seem to know.

CA: When The Best of Everything *was published in 1958, you became a sudden bestselling writer. Was the success hard to deal with at that age?*

JAFFE: It was very unreal. By the time I got used to the idea that I really was that well known, all the fuss was over and I could get on with my real life before I even understood what was happening to me. What I did immediately was write a second book, because I didn't want to be a one-book author.

CA: Did you quit the office job when The Best of Everything *did so well?*

JAFFE: I quit before, so I could write. I had started to sell to magazines, and I realized that I could make as much money selling two stories to magazines as I could working a whole year in my job. So I decided to take a chance on supporting myself as a writer. I spent about a year writing an eighty-seven-page novella which I sent to every publisher in New York, and nobody knew what to do with it. I had an agent at that time who was sending it out. Then it got to Simon & Schuster, and the editor in chief said to me, "I think you could write a hell of a novel. Why don't you write a novel?" He didn't mean a novel expanding this little thing I'd written, but just another novel. I'd spent all this time on the novella, and I didn't know. But I decided I did want to write a novel, and it became *The Best of Everything*. He told me if I would give him fifty pages, he would give me a contract. I think I gave him a hundred pages, because I wanted to introduce all the characters.

CA: I think your characters, and their hopes and dreams, are a large part of what holds your readers. Even when they seem very much New York City types, they're easy to identify with. Are you living with them intimately during that long thinking-out process that precedes the writing of each book?

JAFFE: Yes. I have to know them. They have to take on a life of their own, because my plot always comes from character.

CA: In The Best of Everything *and* The Cherry in the Martini *at least, characters are modeled on yourself and your friends. Does this ever endanger a friendship?*

JAFFE: There was one person from another book who wouldn't talk to me anymore. I suppose if I saw her now, after all these years, she would. And of course you don't take everything from one person. The characters are usually bits and pieces.

CA: In After the Reunion, *your characters who came of age in the fifties are coming to terms with a very changed set of circumstances and opportunities. Do you hear from a lot of readers from the same generation who've faced similar problems?*

JAFFE: Yes, I get letters from people who say that. And a lot of times, to refer back to what you said before, they're not from New York. They might be from New York or they might be from across the country, but they've had the same experience.

CA: And do you also have a readership that comes to the books with less than a nodding acquaintance with the fifties?

JAFFE: Sure. I have my *Best of Everything* girls, as I think of the people who grew up with me, and I have their daughters. Lots of people of all ages read my books, including twenty-year-olds. They read them because they enjoy them. You don't have to have lived through that period to enjoy what's going on in the story.

CA: Do you hear from a lot of readers who've gotten the books in other languages?

JAFFE: Strangely enough, I do. All the books are in translations. But I get letters from people in Scandinavian countries and they write to me in English, so I don't know whether they've read the books in English or in their own language.

CA: You have a very deft way with your young characters. There seems to be a tremendous amount of sympathy there. Do you have a special feeling for children and young adults?

JAFFE: I think it's because of the child in me that's still there. I am a child at heart, and I really identify with them. For example, when people ask me which character is me in *After the Reunion*, I say Teddy, really, the kid with the journal. Even though I didn't have his life, I feel very close to him. In *Family Secrets*, I show each generation as it grows up, so there are loads of kids.

CA: Does the interest in kids maybe also have to do partly with an interest in the family as an entity?

JAFFE: I've never really thought about it that way. But there was a point in the seventies when people were saying the family was falling apart. I guess they're still saying it now. I wanted to look at why. In the particular instance of *Family Secrets*, I felt that it was good that those people all left. But I just seem to be reporting on people and what they are living with. Most of us are living with family and friends. We all have some kind of extended family; if we don't have a family, we certainly have friends who mean family to us.

CA: You did a juvenile, The Last of the Wizards, *which was published in 1961. How did that come about?*

JAFFE: When I was a kid, I used to write children's books and send them to publishers and they would get rejected, though I never said I was a kid. When I was an adult, I had always wanted to write a children's book, so I had an idea and I wrote it. And since I was an adult, I was able to have it published. But it was like fulfilling a childhood dream. It wasn't something I wanted to do after that. My mind doesn't really work that way.

CA: You did a lot of planning and research for Family Secrets, *and you said some years ago that it was your favorite among your books. Is that still true?*

JAFFE: It's one of my favorites, certainly, because it took me fifteen years to get it put together. In between I was writing other books, but it was an idea that finally came to fruition when it should have.

CA: The writing process seems to run very smoothly for you. You said once, "If I waited for 'inspiration,' I'd get too scared to write at all." Do you never have a problem with writer's block?

JAFFE: Oh sure I do. Between books I always think I'll never get another idea.

CA: Are there always long periods between books when you're not writing every day?

JAFFE: I don't write every day until I have my whole book planned in my head. I don't sit down and say, Let's see what today will bring. I sit down knowing exactly what I'm going to do. It means that I spend a year and a half planning a book, but I probably spend less than six months writing it.

CA: You studied acting and playwriting at Lee Strasberg's Actors' Studio. How do you feel that has helped in the writing?

JAFFE: It's helped more in the sense of writing for actors than in the sense of writing a novel. What I used to do for acting scenes was a piece of one of my books instead of taking a scene from a play, as people usually did—although sometimes people would take a scene from a short story. I would take a scene from one of my books and see how it played. You know, it's greatly condensed when you do it as an actor. It's much less dialogue, because you're doing things physically that people can see that carry through. It was interesting to see that difference. Some people really don't understand. They think you can just take a book and turn it into a play with people saying the lines.

CA: Has that experience helped in your work in television?

JAFFE: Yes. I was fortunate in that I was able to be with *Mazes and Monsters* all the way through the television production, through the script rewriting (most of which I did myself) and through the shooting of the film. I was allowed to sit in and watch them edit it. I was allowed to sit in while they dubbed the sound and mixed it. I realized that a lot of people who write scripts don't have that opportunity. They write the script and then they go away. When you see what can be done with all the other things that are not the writing, like the editing and the acting and the filming, it makes it easier. The final product is like doing a novel, except that a novelist is the one in charge of all those things. In a movie,

it's all different people—basically the director, but also the others who are doing different things with it.

CA: You enjoy the television work, don't you?

JAFFE: Yes. I enjoy it as a break from novel writing because it's less lonely.

CA: Several accounts say you work without an agent. Is that true?

JAFFE: I don't know why people think I have no agent. I did have an agent for years, and then I got my lawyer who then became my agent, and recently I signed with Mort Janklow. I think it's very hard to do it without an agent.

CA: You seem to be very much a city person. Is it important to the writing for you to be in New York?

JAFFE: No. I've written in the country and different places. I live in New York, so obviously I do quite a bit of my work in New York, but I have written in other cities. I'm *not* one of those people who can go on a book tour with a typewriter. I don't know how they do that. When I go on a book tour, I'm lucky to get enough sleep even.

CA: Do you do a tour for every book?

JAFFE: With the last several books I have. But there were books when I didn't.

CA: The format of multiple main characters with interwoven stories has worked very well for you. How do you feel about doing a big book with one main character or set of characters?

JAFFE: I don't know. I did one book with one person, *The Other Woman,* but there were a lot of other people in the book. I generally use several characters because I want to show several points of view. I think it would be interesting to do a book with one main character. It would depend on what I wanted to say in that book.

CA: What's in the future? Is there work you can talk about?

JAFFE: I'm planning another book, but I never talk about work in progress.

BIOGRAPHICAL/CRITICAL SOURCES:

PERIODICALS

Book World, November 9, 1969.
Chicago Tribune, May 27, 1968.
Listener, January 25, 1968.
Los Angeles Times Book Review, November 10, 1985, July 27, 1986.
Ms., November, 1974.
New Leader, November 7, 1966.
New Yorker, August 30, 1976.
New York Times, October 2, 1969.
New York Times Book Review, May 2, 1965, October 2, 1966, September 28, 1969, October 29, 1972, October 27, 1974, September 5, 1976, July 31, 1977, July 8, 1979, July 22, 1979, November 8, 1981, September 22, 1985.
Observer, March 8, 1970, June 8, 1975, October 17, 1976.
People, October 19, 1981.
Saturday Review, September 6, 1958, May 8, 1965.
Spectator, February 6, 1982.

Time, May 21, 1965, October 7, 1966, July 2, 1979.
Times Literary Supplement, February 1, 1968, August 8, 1975.
Virginia Quarterly Review, winter, 1977.
Wall Street Journal, November 29, 1985.
Washington Post, June 23, 1979.
Washington Post Book World, June 24, 1973, September 13, 1981, August 25, 1985, July 13, 1986.

—*Sketch by Marian Gonsior*

—*Interview by Jean W. Ross*

*   *   *

JANAS, Frankie-Lee   1908-
(Lisa Bremer, Francesca Greer, Saliee O'Brien; Zachary Ball, a joint pseudonym)

PERSONAL: Born November 19, 1908, in Appleton City, Mo.; daughter of Benjamin Franklin (a rural mail carrier) and Lillian (Bremer) Griggs; married third husband, Eugene Janas, January 22, 1950; children: (from previous marriage) Thurlow Benjamin Weed. *Education:* Attended Iola Junior College (now Allen County Community College) and University of Texas. *Religion:* Protestant.

ADDRESSES: Home—Hollywood, Fla. *Agent*—Jay Garon, Jay Garon-Brooke Associates, Inc., 415 Central Park W., New York, N.Y. 10025.

CAREER: Proofreader and writer. Active in amateur dramatics and radio work.

WRITINGS:

WITH KELLY R. MASTERS, UNDER JOINT PSEUDONYM ZACHARY BALL

Pull Down to New Orleans, Crown, 1946.
Keelboat Journey, Dutton, 1958.

UNDER PSEUDONYM SALIEE O'BRIEN

Farewell the Stranger, Morrow, 1956.
Too Swift the Tide, Morrow, 1960.
Beelfontaine, Berkley Publishing, 1974.
Heiress to Evil, Ballantine, 1974.
Shadow of the Caravan, Berkley Publishing, 1974.
Night of the Scorpion, Bantam, 1976.
The Bride of Gaylord Hall, Pocket Books, 1978.
Bayou, Bantam, 1979.
So Wild the Woman, Bantam, 1979.
Captain's Woman, Pocket Books, 1979.
Black Ivory, Bantam, 1980.
Blood West, Pocket Books, 1980.
Cajun, Bantam, 1982.
Cayo, Bantam, 1983.
Creole, Bantam, 1983.

UNDER PSEUDONYM FRANCESCA GREER

First Fire, Warner Books, 1979.
Second Sunrise, Warner Books, 1981.
Bright Dawn, Warner Books, 1983.

OTHER

(Under pseudonym Lisa Bremer) *Isle of Strangers,* Blue Heron Press, 1984.

Contributor of hundreds of short stories to magazines.

WORK IN PROGRESS: A long novel under pseudonym Saliee O'Brien, tentatively titled *Born.*

JEFFREY, David Lyle   1941-

PERSONAL: Born June 28, 1941, in Ottawa, Ontario, Canada; son of Lyle Elmo (a farmer) and Florence (Brown) Jeffrey; married Wilberta Johnson, June 17, 1961 (divorced, 1984); married Katherine Beth Brown, July 28, 1984; children: (first marriage) Bruce, Kirstin, Adrienne. *Education:* Wheaton College, Wheaton, Ill., B.A., 1965; Princeton University, M.A., 1967, Ph.D., 1968.

ADDRESSES: Home—Box 1015, Morrisburg, Ontario, Canada. *Office*—Department of English, University of Ottawa, Ottawa, Ontario, Canada K1N 6N5.

CAREER: Jef-flite of Canada (luggage manufacturers), Arnprior, Ontario, sales manager, 1960-61, general manager, 1961-63; University of Victoria, Victoria, British Columbia, assistant professor of English, 1968-69; University of Rochester, Rochester, N.Y., assistant professor, 1969-72, associate professor of Medieval English, 1972-73; University of Victoria, associate professor of Medieval English and chairman of department of English, 1973-78; University of Ottawa, Ottawa, Ontario, professor of English, 1978—, chairman of department, 1978-81. Visiting professor at University of British Columbia, Regent College, summers, 1970, 1973, and University of Hull, 1971-72.

MEMBER: International Society for Arthurian Literature, Modern Language Association of America, Early English Text Society, Mediaeval Academy of America, Conference on Christianity and Literature, American Academy of Religion, Anglo-Norman Text Society, Association of Canadian University Teachers of English, Canadian Society of Biblical Studies, Institute for Advanced Christian Studies, Lambda Iota Tau.

AWARDS, HONORS: Awards from *Atlantic,* 1964, for short story "The Transfer," and 1965, for short stories "In Common Bond" and "New Hay," and for poems "To Marcel Proust" and "Nomad"; Woodrow Wilson fellowships, 1965, 1967-68; Canada Council humanities award, 1969, for research in Florence, Italy; Conference on Christianity and Literature annual book award, 1975, for *Franciscan Spirituality and the Early English Lyric;* Canadian Merit Award, 1978; Social Sciences and Humanities Research Council of Canada grant, 1983-86, for *A Dictionary of Biblical Tradition in English Literature.*

WRITINGS:

Modern Fictions and the Rebirth of Theology (monograph), State University of New York Press, 1973.
Franciscan Spirituality and the Early English Lyric, University of Nebraska Press, 1975.
(Editor) *By Things Seen: Reference and Recognition in Medieval Thought,* University of Ottawa Press, 1979.
(Editor and co-author) *Chaucer and Scriptural Tradition,* University of Ottawa Press, 1984.
Toward a Perfect Love: The Spiritual Counsel of Walter Hilton (study and translation), Multnomah, 1985.
Jack Hodgins: The Writer and His Work (monograph), ECW Press, 1987.
A Burning and a Shining Light: English Spirituality in the Age of Wesley, Eerdmans, 1987.
The Law of Love: English Spirituality in the Age of Wyclif, Eerdmans, 1987.

(Co-author and editor with Brian Levy) *The Anglo-Norman Lyric,* Pontifical Institute of Medieval Studies, 1988.

CONTRIBUTOR

C. A. Huttar, editor, *Imagination and the Spirit,* Eerdmans, 1971.

Neville Denny, editor, *Medieval English Drama,* Edward Arnold, 1973.

R. G. Collins and J. Wortley, editors, *The Rise of Vernacular Literatures in the Middle Ages,* University of Manitoba Press, 1975.

M. Halpin and M. Ames, editors, *Manlike Monsters: Early Records and Modern Evidence,* University of British Columbia Press, 1980.

W. J. Keith, editor, *A Voice in the Land: Essays by and about Rudy Wiebe,* Northwest Press, 1981.

R. Zimbardo and Neil Issacs, editors, *Tolkien and the Critics II,* Kentucky State University Press, 1981.

R. F. Yaeger, editor, *Fifteenth Century English Literature,* Archon Press, 1982.

David A. Kent, editor, *Lighting up the Terrain: Essays in Honour of Margaret Avison,* ECW Press, 1987.

OTHER

Contributor of articles and stories to professional journals, including *Journal of the American Academy of Religion, English Quarterly, Dalhousie Review, Shakespeare Studies, Journal of English and Germanic Philology, American Benedictine Review,* and *English Studies in Canada;* contributor of poetry to *Lit, Crux, Insignia, Green River Review, Wascana Review, Whetstone,* and *Northward Journal.*

WORK IN PROGRESS: Editing *A Dictionary of Biblical Tradition in English Literature* for Eerdmans; *Christianity and Literature: Philosophical Foundations of Literary Modernism;* a volume of short stories.

SIDELIGHTS: "For me," David Lyle Jeffrey told *CA,* "writing is just another way of reading the book of the world, and remembering. There is an old European proverb which gives me comfort; it says: 'One can write straight with crooked lines.' Brother Antoninus (William Everson) quotes a Portuguese version which has it that even God writes in this way, suggesting, I suppose, that indirection is a signature of creative intention. The optative quality of the first version, however, is less than comforting by itself. It hints that one's prayer or ambition to 'write straight' may also be rather easily seduced—probably by too much 'sincerity' respecting these intimate personal frailties to which each of our 'readings' bears its crooked witness. Sometimes in the shelves of my books I seem to hear faintly hushed laughter, a rustling of leaves; their outlaw whisper is *caveat lector! non est auctor!*

"In the volume of this book I thus confess myself a bastard. Much of my own writing has been in scholarship and criticism, principally concerning the history of interpretation—reading of 'readings.' When a few years ago I was asked to participate in a writers' conference, addressing the subject of 'Scholarly Writing as Creative Writing,' the teasing prospect made me smile. The writers who asked me were no doubt indulging the tribal conviction that interpreters and all their works compose but orgies of plagiarism. In some respects, of course, I am bound to concede, and not only for my own sins. Yet I do so (almost) insincerely, for what seems to be true of interpretation—that none can quite pretend to be original—seems no less to hold true when one commits an act of poetry, or of story. It is always an old tale that creeps out, however much

we try to tell it otherwise. But in admitting this too, I find a kind of comfort. In the telling again, even if to the wind and rain, old may become new, something transformed; or, as with that stony lady in *A Winter's Tale,* dead art may yet come back to life. They form an irresistable itinerary, these crooked lines, and one whose affection is for comfortable words can scarcely leave unconfessed that he gathers up their scattered analogues everywhere, tracing their image in crooked minims of his own execrable hand—writing—there, on the blotted page.

"'Scrivened' isn't the same thing as 'shriven,' of course. But, recently, I find myself turning more and more to the crooked intricacies of poem and story, just when I want to be straight about where it is my guilty conscience—and gratitude—are really taking me. It's the optative in the old proverb—its intrigue of possibility—which make me laugh, and cheers me. *Caveat, editor!*"

*   *   *

JENNINGS, Michael Glenn   1931-
(Waco Brazos, Wyatt E. Kinkaid)

PERSONAL: Born April 17, 1931, in Buena Vista, Va.; son of Glen Edward (a compositor and printer) and Vaughnye Mae (Bays) Jennings; married Patricia Motter, August 22, 1953 (divorced, August, 1975); married Susan Berger (a marketing director of children's books), October 25, 1975; children: Marc Emery, Jason Glenn, Dana Michael. *Education:* Attended high school in Little Falls, N.J. *Politics:* "Anti-Bella Abzug and ilk." *Religion:* "Unaffiliated Christian."

CAREER: Hicks & Greist, Inc. (advertising agency), New York City, began as mailboy, became copywriter, 1948-51; *Louisville Courier Journal,* Louisville, Ky., writer, 1955-56; Home Life Insurance Co., New York City, assistant advertising manager, 1956-58; Burke, Charles & Guignon (advertising agency), Long Island, N.Y., vice-president and creative director, 1958-61; Michael Jennings & Colleagues (advertising agency), Long Island, N.Y., president, 1961-65; Aeolian Piano Corp., advertising manager, 1966-68; G. P. Putnam's Sons/Coward McCann (publishers), New York City, promotion director, 1968-69; free-lance writer, 1969—. Douglas Samuel Advertising, Inc., West Caldwell, N.J., vice-president and creative director, beginning 1983. Disc jockey for WKLO-Radio, 1955-56; host of talk show for WLIR, 1956-66; narrator, Island Lyric Opera, Garden City, N.Y., 1978-79; theatre reviewer for WRKL, 1980-81. Advertising and publicity chairman for Antrim Players, Inc. (community theater group), 1977; liaison representative to Rockland County Council on the Arts. *Military service:* U.S. Air Force, newspaper reporter and editor, and writer-announcer for radio programs, 1951-55.

MEMBER: Authors Guild, Authors League of America, Dramatists Guild.

WRITINGS:

(Under pseudonym Waco Brazos) *There Was a Young Lady from Windmere* (erotic fiction), Venice Publishing, 1972.

JUVENILE FICTION

(Self-illustrated) *Mattie Fritts and the Flying Mushroom,* Windmill Books, 1973.

(Self-illustrated) *Mattie Fritts and the Cuckoo Caper,* Bobbs-Merrill, 1976.

The Bears Who Came to Breakfix, illustrations by Tom Dunnington, Children's Press, 1977.

Robin Goodfellow and the Giant Dwarf, illustrations by Tomie de Paola, McGraw, 1981.

JUVENILE NONFICTION

Tape Recorder Fun: Be Your Own Favorite Disc Jockey, McKay, 1978.

OTHER

Also co-author of "The Briar Patch" (play), 1982, and author of "No Halos in Hell" (screenplay), 1983. Contributor to horror comic magazines, *Metropolitan Review,* and *National Star-Chronicle;* contributor of erotic fiction to magazines, under pseudonyms Waco Brazos and Wyatt E. Kinkaid.

WORK IN PROGRESS: Tapdancing on Quicksand, for McKay; *Be-Bop, the Musical Cat,* juvenile; *Cold Wind from Nowhere,* a novel for young adults; *The Thirty-ninth Consecutive Season,* a novel about a community theater group.

SIDELIGHTS: When asked how he switched from writing erotic fiction to writing for children, Michael Glenn Jennings responded: "There has been none; I'm still doing both. That I am doing either is due to the way fate has cut the cards.

"In 1965, before I ever contemplated becoming a full-time writer, I wrote a porno-comedic novel, pretty much as a lark. It amused an influential friend and, to my astonishment, was accepted by an orthodox publisher. Alas, due to a merger, that house eventually defaulted on the contract. Nobody else was interested.

"By 1972 things had changed. For one thing, the porno boom was upon us. For another, I was broke, jobless, and forced to attempt to write for a living. The dusty manuscript was retrieved from a bottom drawer, 'dirtied-up' some more, and sent on the rounds of the paperback specialty houses. By then—among other forms—I was flailing away at a children's novel inspired by fanciful correspondence with my young sons, who no longer lived with me. Coincidentally, both works—seven years apart in the writing, several million light-years apart in content—were published within months of each other.

"Continuing endeavors along both lines have followed as logically as if I had first achieved some success with, say, a cookbook and a travel guide, and thereafter produced successive volumes of recipes and itineraries. One produces what one can sell, in order to support efforts that are perchance loftier or more ambitious, and are surely chancier.

"If at first you don't succeed, you probably never will."

AVOCATIONAL INTERESTS: Acting and directing with Antrim Players.†

*   *   *

JOHNPOLL, Bernard K(eith)   1918-

PERSONAL: Born June 3, 1918, in New York, N.Y.; son of I. Joseph and Rachel (Elkin) Johnpoll; married Lillian Kirtzman, 1944; children: two daughters. *Education:* Boston University, A.B. (magna cum laude), 1959; Rutgers University, A.M., 1963; State University of New York, Ph.D., 1966. *Politics:* Independent. *Religion:* None.

ADDRESSES: Home—10987 Lake Front Pl., Boca Raton, Fla. 33498.

CAREER: Boston Record-American, Boston, Mass., news editor, 1950-60; Rutgers University, New Brunswick, N.J., lecturer in political science, 1962-63; Hartwick College, Oneonta, N.Y., assistant professor of political science, 1963-65; University of Saskatchewan, Regina, visiting assistant professor, 1965-66; State University of New York at Albany, associate professor, 1966-71, professor of political science, 1971-82, professor emeritus, 1982—.

WRITINGS:

Canadian News Index, University of Saskatchewan Press, 1966.
The Politics of Futility: The General Jewish Workers Bund of Poland, 1917-1943, Cornell University Press, 1967.
Pacifist's Progress: Norman Thomas and the Decline of Socialism, Quadrangle, 1970, 2nd edition, Greenwood Press, 1987.
(Editor and author of introduction) Norman Thomas, *Norman Thomas on War: An Anthology,* Garland Publishing, 1974.
(Editor with Mark Yerburgh) *The League for Industrial Democracy: A Documentary History,* three volumes, Greenwood Press, 1980.
The Impossible Dream: Rise and Demise of the American Left, Greenwood Press, 1981.
(Editor with Harvey Klehr) *Biographical Dictionary of the American Left,* Greenwood Press, 1987.

Also author of "The American Diary," a thirteen-part television series for American National Enterprises, 1982, and "Years to Remember," a television series for Public Broadcasting System, 1983.

SIDELIGHTS: Bernard K. Johnpoll has a good knowledge of Yiddish and German. He can read Russian, Swedish, Norwegian, Danish, Spanish, and Portuguese.

K

KAGAN, Jerome 1929-

PERSONAL: Born February 25, 1929, in Newark, N.J.; son of Joseph (a businessman) and Myrtle (Liebermann) Kagan; married Cele Katzman, June 20, 1951; children: Janet. *Education:* Rutgers University, B.S., 1950; Yale University, Ph.D., 1954.

ADDRESSES: Home—210 Clifton St., Belmont, Mass. *Office*—William James Hall, Harvard University, Cambridge, Mass. 02138.

CAREER: Fels Institute, Yellow Springs, Ohio, researcher in developmental psychology, 1957-64; Harvard University, Cambridge, Mass., professor of human development, 1964—. Member of Committee on Learning and the Educational Process, Social Science Research Council, 1966-70, Advisory Committee on Training, National Institute of Child Health and Development, 1966-68, Committee on Fellowship Evaluation, National Academy of Sciences, 1967 and 1974, Panel on Educational Research, President's Science Advisory Committee, 1969-72, Panel on Development, National Institute of Education, 1970-74, and Committee on Brain Sciences, National Academy of Sciences, 1971-78. Member of board of directors, Foundation to Improve Television (Boston), 1969—, and of Foundations Fund for Research in Psychiatry, 1970-74. Consultant to Department of Pediatrics, Massachusetts General Hospital, 1965—. Consulting editor, Harcourt, Brace & World, Inc., 1965—. *Military service:* U.S. Army, 1955-57.

MEMBER: American Association for Advancement of Science, Society for Research in Child Development, American Psychological Association (member, Board of Scientific Affairs, 1965-66; president, Division of Developmental Psychology, 1966-67), American Academy of Arts and Sciences (fellow), Eastern Psychological Association (member, board of directors, 1973-75; president, 1974-75).

AWARDS, HONORS: Hofheimer Prize of American Psychiatric Association, 1963; Wilbur Lucius Cross Medal and honorary M.A., both from Yale University, both 1964.

WRITINGS:

(With H. Moss) *Birth to Maturity,* Wiley, 1962.

(With J. J. Conger and P. H. Mussen) *Child Development and Personality,* Harper, 1963, 5th edition, 1979.
(Editor with John C. Wright) *Basic Cognitive Processes in Children,* Child Development Publications, 1963, published with new introduction, University of Chicago Press, 1973.
(Editor with Mussen) *Readings in Child Development and Personality,* Harper, 1965, 2nd edition, 1970.
(Contributor) L. S. Shulman and E. R. Keisler, editors, *Learning by Discovery,* Rand McNally, 1966.
(Contributor) H. J. Klausmeier and C. W. Harris, editors, *Analyses of Concept Learning,* Academic Press, 1966.
(Editor) *Creativity and Learning,* Houghton, 1967.
(With Ernest Havemann) *Psychology: An Introduction,* Harcourt, 1968, 4th edition, 1980.
(Contributor) *Proceedings of Conference on Biology and Behavior,* Rockefeller University Press, 1968.
(Contributor) I. Janis, editor, *Personality Dynamics,* Harcourt, 1969.
(With others) *Change and Continuity in Infancy,* Wiley, 1971.
Personality Development, edited by Irving L. Janis, Harcourt, 1971.
(Editor with Marshall Haith and Catherine Caldwell) *Psychology: Adapted Readings,* Harcourt, 1971.
Understanding Children: Behavior, Motives, and Thought, Harcourt, 1971.
(Editor with Nathan Bill Talbot and L. E. Eisenberg) *Behavioral Science in Pediatric Medicine,* Saunders, 1971.
(Editor with Robert Coles) *Twelve to Sixteen: Early Adolescence,* Norton, 1972.
(Contributor) M. Lewis and L. Rosenblum, editors, *Origins of Behavior,* Wiley, Volume II: *Fear,* 1974, Volume III: *Social Interaction,* 1975.
(Editor with Mussen) *Basic Contemporary Issues in Developmental Psychology,* Harper, 1975.
(With R. Kearsley and P. Zelazo) *Infancy: Its Place in Human Development,* Harvard University Press, 1978.
Growth of the Child, Norton, 1978.
(With Cynthia Lang) *Psychology and Education: An Introduction,* Harcourt, 1978.
The Family, Norton, 1978.
(With O. S. Brim) *Constancy and Change in Human Development,* Harvard University Press, 1980.
The Second Year: The Emergence of Self-Awareness, Harvard University Press, 1981.

(Contributor with S. Hans, A. Markowitz, D. Lopez, and H. Sigal) B. A. Maher, editor, *Progress in Experimental Personality Research,* Academic Press, 1982.

(Contributor) R. Lerner, editor, *Developmental Psychology: Historical and Philosophical Perspectives,* Academic Press, 1983.

The Nature of the Child, Basic Books, 1984.

Contributor to P. H. Mussen, editor, *Manual of Child Psychology,* and to C. E. Izard, editor, *The Measurement of Emotion.* Editorial consultant to *Child Development, Journal of Experimental Child Psychology, Journal of Consulting Psychology, Merrill-Palmer Quarterly, Psychological Bulletin,* and *Journal of Educational Psychology.*

SIDELIGHTS: Jerome Kagan, "one of today's most eminent child experts, enunciates the developing edge of consensus in his field," observes Daniel Goleman in the *New York Times Book Review.* According to Mark Caldwell in the *Voice Literary Supplement,* Kagan "has contributed mightily to the literature of child development, but never so originally as in *The Nature of the Child.*" Challenging the widely held theory that an individual's personality is determined entirely by experiences during infancy, "the book begins and ends with [Kagan's] assertion that currently influential accounts of childhood—whether Freudian, Eriksonian, or Piagetian—are too rigid," says Caldwell. "They all see growing up as an inviolable, continuous, ultimately mechanical process that builds an adult personality the way drops of water doggedly amass a stalagmite."

Caldwell finds that Kagan's "view of the child, while informed by a thorough knowledge of research, is refreshingly hesitant. He offers biology as a promising guideline, but warns that since we haven't found a fully workable theoretical construct for growth and development of the child, we shouldn't burden the models we have with too much emotion." Noting that the prevalent conception of parental influence upon child development is "sentimental rather than scientific," Anatole Broyard indicates in his *New York Times* review of *The Nature of the Child,* "We are in the paradoxical position of trying to create our children while regarding them at the same time as self-determining." Considering it "inappropriate" to ask whether heredity or environment is more important in child development, Maya Pines suggests in the *Washington Post* that "they work together to create a human being." As Caldwell summarizes, "You can't take all the credit if your child grows up to be Eleanor Roosevelt, then again you don't have to take all the blame if she ends up in a Cheech and Chong movie." Broyard concludes that "while it's not for a layman to say whether . . . Kagan is right or wrong, he certainly stirs up interesting issues and brings a lot of experimental evidence to bear on them."

BIOGRAPHICAL/CRITICAL SOURCES:

PERIODICALS

American Sociological Review, October, 1963.
New York Times, September 14, 1984.
New York Times Book Review, December 12, 1978, November 18, 1984.
Science, April 19, 1963.
Voice Literary Supplement, November, 1984.
Washington Post, January 11, 1981.

KALS, W(illiam) S(teven)   1910-

PERSONAL: Born December 19, 1910, in Vienna, Austria; son of Otto (a bank manager) and Irma (Taussig) Kals; married Gertrude Ann Olwin (a teacher), March 28, 1963. *Education:* University of Vienna, U.S. (master's degree).

ADDRESSES: Home—8112 Ambach Way, Hypoluxo, Fla. 33462. *Agent*—Donald MacCampbell Inc., 12 East 41st St., New York, N.Y. 10017.

CAREER: Free-lance writer and teacher of adult education courses at Palm Beach Junior College. Has worked as photographer, advertising manager, inventor, and director of planetarium.

MEMBER: Authors Guild, Authors League of America, Institute of Navigation.

WRITINGS:

Practical Boating Inland and Offshore Power and Sail, Doubleday, 1969.
Practical Navigation: A Simplified Handbook of Chart-and-Compass, Electronic, and Celestial Navigation for Boatmen, Doubleday, 1972.
How to Read the Night Sky: A New and Easy Way to Know the Stars, Planets, and Constellations, Doubleday, 1974.
The Riddle of the Winds: A Comprehensive Book about Winds, Doubleday, 1977.
(And illustrator) *The Stargazer's Bible,* Doubleday, 1980.
Your Health, Your Moods, and the Weather: Better Control over Your Life by Knowing How Weather Affects You and Others, Doubleday, 1982.
Land Navigation Handbook: The Sierra Club Guide to Map and Compass, Sierra Books, 1983.

Contributor of articles, illustrations, and photographs to boating and science journals, including *Popular Science, Popular Mechanics, Photography, Boating, Yachting, Today's Health,* and *Sky and Telescope.*

WORK IN PROGRESS: A book about the science of chronobiology, the study of the influence of time of day and season on living matter; a book on coping with sleep disorders, night work, and jet lag; a study of the benefits of scientific scheduling.

SIDELIGHTS: W. S. Kals wrote that his strength is making hard subjects easy to read. "The recipe: An apparently casual style (the result of several revisions), simple graphics, and an occasional chuckle. My weakness: Over-researching. Most of the material for my boating book came from a single-handed cruise that lasted six years. Ashore now, I still overdo: I collect three mud-streaked icebergs for every tip that shows."

*   *   *

KAMINSKY, Marc   1943-

PERSONAL: Born October 8, 1943, in Bronx, N.Y.; son of Peretz (a poet and graphic designer) and Mintzie (a vocational counselor; maiden name, Schwartzman) Kaminsky; married. *Education:* Columbia University, B.A. (summa cum laude), 1964, M.A., 1967; Hunter College of the City University of New York, M.S.W., 1978.

ADDRESSES: Home—317 Sixth Ave., Brooklyn, N.Y. 11215. *Office*—Associated YM-YWHAs of Greater New York, 130 East 59th St., New York, N.Y. 10022. *Agent*—Geri Thoma,

Elaine Markson Agency, 44 Greenwich Ave., New York, N.Y. 10010.

CAREER: Hunter College of the City University of New York, New York City, lecturer in composition and dramatic literature, 1967-69; East Harlem Youth Employment Service, New York City, teacher, 1969-71; City University of New York, New York City, teacher in English as a second language program, 1971-72; Jewish Association for Services for the Aged, New York City, group worker, 1972-74, project director at West Side Senior Center, 1972-77; project director, Artists and Elders Project of the Teachers and Writers Collaborative, 1978-81; Hunter College of the City University of New York, Brookdale Institute for the Humanities, Arts, and Aging, New York City, co-director, 1981-85; currently director of program at Associated YM-YWHAs of Greater New York, New York City. Editor of Inwood Press, 1972-80. Conductor of workshops and seminars for Poets and Writers, Teachers and Writers, Jewish Association for Services of the Aged, and Association for Poetry Therapy, beginning 1972; writer-in-residence, Open Theatre, 1969, Talking Band, 1977-78, and Ballad Theatre, 1981-84. Gives poetry readings on radio, and at colleges, galleries, and senior citizen centers. Member of board of directors, Jewish Heritage Writing Project, and Teachers and Writers, Inc. Artist consultant, Post Masters Program on Social Work and the Arts, Hunter College School of Social Work.

MEMBER: Poets and Writers, Academy of American Poets, Gerontological Society of America (chair of committee on humanities and the arts, 1985), Phi Beta Kappa.

AWARDS, HONORS: Grants from New York Council on the Humanities, for Living History Project, Performing Artists for Nuclear Disarmament, and Santvoord Foundation; New York Public Library Award, and Art of Peace Award, both in 1984 for *The Road from Hiroshima.*

WRITINGS:

What's Inside You It Shines Out of You, Horizon Press, 1974.

POETRY

The Rime of Patch McFinn (chapbook), illustrated by Susan Lembeck, Jester of Columbia Publication, 1963.
Birthday Poems, Horizon Press, 1972.
A New House, Inwood/Horizon Press, 1974.
A Table with People, Sun Press, 1982.
Daily Bread, photographs by Leon Supraner, introduction by Robert Butler, University of Illinois Press, 1982.
The Road from Hiroshima, Simon & Schuster, 1984.

EDITOR

The Journal Project: Pages from the Lives of Old People, Teachers and Writers Press, 1980.
The Book of Autobiographies, Teachers and Writers Press, 1982.
(And contributor) *The Uses of Reminiscence; New Ways of Working with Older Adults,* introduction by Rose Dobrof, Haworth Press, 1984.

PLAYS

"Marriage of Masks," first produced at Minor Latham Playhouse, 1963.
"Two Yolkless Eggs," first produced at Minor Latham Playhouse, 1963.
"Casualties," first produced in New York at Judson Poets Theatre, 1967.

(With Talking Band) "Worksong," first produced in New York at the Theatre for the New City, February, 1978.
"In the Traffic of a Targeted City," first produced at Theatre for the New City, 1986.

Contributor to "Terminal," first produced at Open Theatre, 1969.

CONTRIBUTOR TO ANTHOLOGIES

Donald Gross, Beatrice Gross, and Sylvia Seidman, editors, *The New Old: Struggling for Decent Aging,* Anchor Press, 1978.
Howard Schwartz and Anthony Rudolph, editors, *Voices within the Ark: The Modern Jewish Poets,* Avon, 1981.
I. E. Mozeson, editor, *Ten Jewish American Poets,* The Downtown Poets, 1981.
Rosilyn Wilder and Naida Weissberg, editors, *Creative Arts with Older Adults,* Human Sciences Press, 1984.
George Getzel and Joanna Mellor, editors, *Gerontological Social Work in the Community,* Haworth Press, 1984.
Charles Fishman, editor, *Blood to Remember: American Poets on the Holocaust,* Avon, 1986.

OTHER

Translator of works of Yiddish poets, including Zisha Landau and Chaim Grade. Contributor of poetry, essays, and fiction to magazines and journals, including *Performing Arts Quarterly, American Scholar, Columbia Review, New York Quarterly,* and *Journal of Gerontological Social Work.*

BIOGRAPHICAL/CRITICAL SOURCES:

PERIODICALS

American Book Review, January, 1985.
Columbia Magazine, June, 1983.
Gerontologist, December, 1983.
International Journal of Aging and Human Development, November, 1983.
New York Times, February 9, 1975, March 2, 1981.
Soho News, November 27, 1975, February 9, 1983.
Washington Post, October 23, 1984.

*   *   *

KANE, Basil G(odfrey)   1931-

PERSONAL: Born December 12, 1931, in London, England; came to the United States in 1949, naturalized citizen, 1951; son of Harry (a cabinet maker) and Raychel (Spector) Kane; married Nancy Kunst, October 6, 1961; children: Jeffrey, Elisabeth, Brian. *Education:* University of Illinois, B.S., 1958; John Marshall Law School, graduate study.

ADDRESSES: Home—Evanston, Ill. *Office*—Menomonee Club for Boys and Girls, 244 West Willow, Chicago, Ill. 60614. *Agent*—John Boswell, International Literary Management, Inc., 767 Fifth Ave., Suite 601, New York, N.Y. 10022.

CAREER: Department of Public Aid, Chicago, Ill., social worker, 1959-64; Menomonee Club for Boys and Girls, Chicago, director, 1964—. Founding member of North Shore Soccer League and Young Sportsmen's Soccer League. *Military service:* U.S. Air Force, 1952-55; became staff sergeant.

WRITINGS:

Soccer for American Spectators, A. S. Barnes, 1970.
How to Play Soccer (juvenile), Grosset, 1973.
How to Play Soccer (for adults), Grosset, 1975.

Kyle Rote, Jr.'s Complete Book of Soccer, Simon & Schuster, 1978.
(With Giorgio Chinaglia) *Chinaglia!,* Simon & Schuster, 1980.
The Official Chicago Sting Book, foreword by Willy Roy, introduction by Lee Stern, Contemporary Books, 1983.

Contributor to soccer magazines.

WORK IN PROGRESS: Two novels, *Irving and the Sheik* and *The Beercan Murders.*

SIDELIGHTS: Basil G. Kane told *CA:* "Writing is a great source of enjoyment for me and has been so since I was twelve years old. It is only in the last ten years that I have realized others might want to read that which I have written, thus enabling me to derive financial benefits as well as joy from what I had always considered merely a hobby."†

*   *   *

KATES, Robert W.   1929-

PERSONAL: Born January 31, 1929, in Brooklyn, N.Y.; son of Simon Jack and Helen Gordon (Brener) Kates; married Eleanor Clare Hackman, February 9, 1948; children: Kathy Ann, Jonathan Simon, Barbara Ellen. *Education:* Attended New York University, 1946-48, Indiana University, Gary (now Indiana University Northwest), 1957; University of Chicago, M.A., 1960, Ph.D., 1962.

ADDRESSES: Office—Graduate School of Geography, Clark University, Worcester, Mass. 01610; and Brown University, Providence, R.I. 02912.

CAREER: Clark University, Graduate School of Geography, Worcester, Mass., assistant professor, 1962-65, associate professor, 1965-67, professor of geography, 1968—, university professor, 1974-81, Center for Technology, Environment and Development, research professor, 1981—; Brown University, Providence, R.I., university professor and director of Alan Shawn Feinstein World Hunger Program, 1986—. Staff member of Association of American Geographers summer geography institute for small southern colleges, 1966; lecturer, National Science Foundation summer institute in introductory college geography, 1966; University of Dar es Salaam, Tanzania, lecturer, 1967-68, honorary research professor, 1970-71; visiting scholar, University of Oklahoma, 1976; Phi Beta Kappa visiting lecturer, 1984-85. Director, Bureau of Resources Assessment and Land Use Planning, University College, Dar Es Salaam, 1967-69; Elm Park Center for Early Childhood Education, Inc., treasurer, 1972-78, clerk, 1979—.

U.S. National Committee on the Man and Biosphere Program, vice-chairman of directorate on perception of environmental quality, 1973, chairman of directorate and member of U.S. National Committee on the Man and Biosphere Program, 1974-76, member of directorate, 1977—; review coordinator, Project on Improving the Science of Climate Impact Assessment, Scientific Committee on Problems of the Environment, International Council of Scientific Unions, 1980—. Member of task group on human dimensions of the atmosphere, National Center for Atmospheric Research, 1966-67, study group on the societal consequences of weather modification, Southern Methodist University, 1971-73, human resources task force of Executive Office of Environmental Affairs, State of Massachusetts, 1972-73, energy task force, City of Worcester, 1974-75, and expert group on Climate Impact Studies, United Na-

tions Environmental Program, 1980. Member of board of directors committee on problems and policy, Social Science Research Council, 1982—; member of governing council, Perception and Management of Pests and Pesticides Research and Development Network, 1985—; member of board of science and technology in development, National Research Council, 1986—.

Has conducted and supervised research on the impact of floods, droughts, climate fluctuation, and other environmental or technological hazards on human populations and on other climate-related topics, in the United States and Africa. Consultant to C. W. Thornwaite Associates, 1963-64, UNESCO Interdisciplinary Symposium on Man's Role in Changing the Environment: Architecture and Urbanism for Growth and Change, 1970, and Natural Hazard Research Assessment, Institute of Behavioral Science, 1972-74; member of technical advisory committee, Natural Disaster Studies, U.S. Home and Housing Finance Agency, 1966, and science advisory group, Connecticut River Basin Program, New England River Basin Commission, 1973; senior consultant to Scientific Committee on Problems of the Environment, 1974-77.

MEMBER: Academy of Independent Scholars, American Academy of Arts and Sciences, National Academy of Sciences, American Association for the Advancement of Science (fellow), Association of American Geographers, Federation of American Scientists (member of national council, 1986—), American Association of University Professors (Clark University Chapter, vice-president, 1965-66, president, 1966-67), Tanzania Society, Phi Beta Kappa (honorary member).

AWARDS, HONORS: Woodrow Wilson International Center for Scholars fellow, 1979; Honors Award, Association of American Geographers, 1979; MacArthur Prize fellowship, 1981.

WRITINGS:

(Editor with Ian Burton) *Readings in Resource Management and Conservation,* University of Chicago Press, 1965.
(Author of introduction with R. J. Chorley) *Water, Earth, and Man,* Methuen, 1969.
(With Clifford S. Russell and David Arney) *Drought and Water Supply: Implications of the Massachusetts Experience for Municipal Planning,* Johns Hopkins Press, 1970.
(With Burton and Gilbert F. White) *The Environment as Hazard,* Oxford University Press, 1975.
(Editor with J. Eugene Haas and Martyn J. Bowden) *Reconstruction Following Disaster,* MIT Press, 1977.
Risk Assessment of Environmental Hazard, Wiley, 1978.
(With Roger Kasperson, Paul Slovic, Baruch Fischoff, Sarah Lichtenstein, and William Clark) *Managing Technological Hazard: Research Needs and Opportunities,* University of Colorado, 1978.
(Editor and contributor with Leonard Berry) *Making the Most of the Least: Alternative Ways to Development,* Holmes & Meier, 1980.
(Editor with Jesse H. Ausubel and Mimi Berberian) *Climate Impact Assessment: Studies of the Interaction of Climate and Society,* Wiley, 1985.
(Editor with Christoph Hohenemser and Jeanne X. Kasperson) *Perilous Progress: Managing the Hazards of Technology,* Westview, 1985.
(Editor with Burton) *Geography, Resources, and Environment,* Volume I: *Selected Writings of Gilbert F. White,*

Volume II: *Themes from the Work of Gilbert F. White*, University of Chicago Press, 1986.

CONTRIBUTOR

J. G. Jenson, editor, *Spatial Organization of Land Uses: The Willamette Valley*, Oregon State University, 1964.

Research and Education for Regional and Area Development, Iowa State University Press, 1966.

M. E. Garnsey and J. R. Hibbs, editors, *Social Science and the Environment*, University of Colorado Press, 1967.

(With W. R. D. Sewell and with W. J. Maunder) *Human Dimensions of the Atmosphere*, National Science Foundation, 1968.

Regional Planning: Challenge and Prospects, Praeger, 1969.

Student Resources: Geography in an Urban Age—Habitat and Resources, Macmillan, 1970.

T. R. Detwyler and M. G. Marcus, editors, *Urbanization and Environment: The Physical Geography of a City*, Duxbury, 1972.

W. P. Adams and F. N. Helleiner, editors, *International Geography, 1972*, Volume I, University of Toronto Press, 1972.

Patterns and Perspectives in Environmental Science, National Science Foundation, 1972.

G. F. White, editor, *Natural Hazards: Local, National, Global*, Oxford University Press, 1974.

A. E. Utton and D. H. Henning, editors, *Interdisciplinary Environmental Approaches*, Educational Media Press, 1974.

Science Year, 1976, Field Educational Publications, 1975.

Seymour Wapner, Saul Cohen, and Bernard Kaplan, editors, *Experiencing the Environment*, Plenum, 1976.

The Golden Jubilee Volume, 1976, Indian Geographical Society (Madras), 1976.

Desertification: Its Causes and Consequences, Pergamon, 1977.

Gerald J. Karaska and Judith B. Gertler, editors, *Transportation, Technology and Society: Future Options*, Clark University Press, 1978.

G. T. Goodman and W. D. Rowe, editors, *Energy Risk Management*, Academic Press (London), 1979.

R. L. Heathcote and B. G. Thom, editors, *Natural Hazards in Australia: Proceedings of a Symposium*, Australian Academy of Sciences (Canberra), 1979.

OTHER

Also author of numerous scientific monographs and research papers, including ones published by Department of Geography, University of Chicago, Bureau of Resource Assessment and Land Use Planning, University College, National Academy of Sciences and National Research Council, and Center for Technology, Environment, and Development, Clark University. Contributor to *World Book Encyclopedia*, 1974. Contributor to *Papers and Proceedings of the Regional Science Association*, Volume II, 1963, *Trends in Economics: Papers of the Fifth Conference of Pennsylvania Economists*, edited by W. E. Everett, 1963, *Proceedings of the University of East Africa Social Science Conference, 1968-69*, 1970, *Proceedings of the Conference on Rural Water Supply in East Africa*, 1971, and *Proceedings of the World Climate Conference*, 1979. Also contributor to scientific and professional journals, including *Bulletin of Atomic Scientists, Geographical Review, Ambio, Science, Environment, Economic Geography, Professional Geographer*, and *International Social Sciences Journal*. Assistant editor of *Economic Geography*, 1963-64; member of editorial board of *Geographical Review*, 1976-78.

KAUFMAN, William I(rving)   1922-

PERSONAL: Born June 8, 1922, in New York, N.Y.; married Rosamond Van Poznak (a writer), December 15, 1946 (divorced); married second wife, Jacqueline (an artist); children: (first marriage) Iva Anne, Lazarus Seley. *Education:* Attended Wake Forest College, 1940-41, and Leland Powers School of Radio and Theatre Technique, 1946-47. *Religion:* Hebrew.

ADDRESSES: Home and office—69645 Antonia Way, Ranchero Mirage, Calif. 92270.

CAREER: Affiliated with National Broadcasting Co. Television, New York, N.Y., 1947-63; free-lance writer, editor, photographer, and consultant, 1963—. Producer and director of UNICEF tours, 1971 and 1972; lecturer on the subject of international entertaining; conductor of more than twenty one-man shows and exhibitions of his photographs. *Military service:* U.S. Army, 1941-46.

MEMBER: Authors League of America, Authors Guild, Society of Photographers in Communication, Screen Actors Guild, Overseas Press Club, Chaine des Rotisseurs.

AWARDS, HONORS: Chevalier du Tastevin; Chevalier, Order des Coteaux; Officier, Order des Coteaux; Christopher Award, 1971; Gold Vine Award, 1981, for *William I. Kaufman's Pocket Encyclopedia of California Wine*.

WRITINGS:

(With Robert Colodzini) *Your Career in Television*, Merlin Press, 1950.

How to Write and Direct for Television, Hastings House, 1951.

(Editor) *How to Direct for Television*, Hastings House, 1955.

(Editor) *Cooking with the Experts: Over 400 Simple, Easy to Follow, Taste-Tempting Recipes Selected by Television's Best Cooks*, Random House, 1955.

(Editor) *How to Write for Television*, Hastings House, 1955.

(Editor) *How to Announce for Radio and Television*, Hastings House, 1956.

(With Sheridan Garth) *Cook's Pocket Travel Guide to Europe*, Pocket Books, 1963.

Cook's Pocket Travel Guide to the West Indies, Pocket Books, 1963.

The Better Carving Cookbook, Western Publishing, 1964.

The Wonderful World of Cooking, Dell, 1964-69, Volume I: *Recipes from the Far East and Near East*, Volume II: *Recipes from Italy, France, and Spain*, Volume III: *Recipes from Northern Europe and the British Isles*, Volume IV: *Recipes from the Caribbean and Latin America*.

1001 Top Jobs for High School Graduates, Bantam, 1965.

Cooking in a Castle: La Cuisine dans un Chateau, with translations by Rosamond Kaufman, Bonanza Books, 1965.

The Catholic Cookbook: Traditional Feast and Fast Day Recipes, Citadel, 1965.

Guide to the French Hotels of Character, with translations by R. Kaufman, Traversac, 1968.

The Hibachi Cookbook, Centaur, 1969.

Cooking with Bread, Corinthian Editions, 1969.

Desserts Flambe, Centaur, 1969.

The Easy Can Opener Cookbook, Hewitt House, 1969.

Eggs Exotique, Centaur, 1969.

(With Austen H. Schoen) *The Executive Diet Book*, Corinthian Editions, 1969.

Fish Cookery, Centaur, 1969.

Great Television Plays, Dell, 1969.

Oriental Cookery, Centaur, 1969.

Potages, Centaur, 1969.

Tear off a Pound: The No-Counting Calories, No-Keeping Score Diet, Corinthian Editions, 1969.

The New Blender Cookbook, Pyramid, 1969, published as *The Gourmet Blender Cookbook*, Galahad, 1976.

(Compiler and illustrator) *UNICEF Book of Children's Songs*, Stackpole, 1970.

(Compiler and illustrator) *UNICEF Book of Children's Legends*, adapted by R. Kaufman, Stackpole, 1970.

(Compiler and illustrator) *UNICEF Book of Children's Poems*, adapted by Joan Gilbert Van Poznak, Stackpole, 1970.

(Compiler and illustrator) *UNICEF Book of Children's Prayers*, adapted by R. Kaufman and Van Poznak, Stackpole, 1970.

Champagne, Viking, 1973.

Perfume, Dutton, 1974.

Cigars, Dutton, 1975.

The Peanut Butter Cookbook, Simon & Schuster, 1977.

The Mail-Order Food Book, Grosset, 1977.

The Whole-World Wine Catalog, Penguin, 1978.

Guide to Carbohydrates, Baronet, 1978.

Guide to Cholesterol, Baronet, 1978.

Guide to Protein, Baronet, 1978.

Help!, Baronet, 1978.

The Traveler's Guide to the Vineyards of North America, Penguin, 1980.

Mormon Tabernacle Choir, Harper, 1980.

Mormon Pioneer Songbook, Pressor, 1980.

William I. Kaufman's Pocket Encyclopedia of California Wine, edited by Ken Hoop and Maurice Sullivan, Wine Appreciation Guild, 1980, 7th edition, 1987.

The Diet Diary, Jove, 1981.

California Wine Drink Book, Wine Appreciation Guild, 1982.

Dictionary of American Wine, Wine Appreciation Guild, 1982.

(With Jeremy Tarcher) *Encyclopedia of American Wine*, Wine Appreciation Guild, 1984.

Pocket Encyclopedia of American Regional Wines East of the Rockies, Wine Appreciation Guild, 1986.

Pocket Encyclopedia of Pacific Northwest Wines, Wine Appreciation Guild, 1987.

PUBLISHED BY DOUBLEDAY

(With Sister Mary Ursula Cooper) *The Art of Creole Cookery*, edited by R. Kaufman, 1962.

(With Sarawathi Lakshaman) *The Art of India's Cookery*, 1964.

The Coffee Cookbook, 1964.

The Nut Cookbook, 1964 (published in England as *The Nut Cookery Book*, Faber, 1966).

The Sugar-Free Cookbook, 1964.

The "I Love Peanut Butter" Cookbook, 1965.

The Sugar-Free Cookbook of Family Favorites, 1965.

The Tea Cookbook, 1966.

The Hot Dog Cookbook, edited by R. Kaufman, 1966.

The "I Love Garlic" Cookbook, 1967.

The Apple Cookbook, edited by R. Kaufman, 1967.

The Cottage Cheese Cookbook, 1967.

The Art of Casserole Cookery, 1967.

Appetizers and Canapes, 1968.

The Fish and Shellfish Cookbook, 1968.

The Chocolate Cookbook, edited by R. Kaufman, 1968.

Three Hundred Sixty-five Meatless Main Dish Meals, 1974.

PUBLISHED BY PYRAMID

Casserole Cookery, 1965.

Budget Company Dinners, 1968.

Quick and Easy Desserts, 1968.

The Left-Over Cookbook, 1968.

(With Sybil Leek) *The Astrological Cookbook*, 1968.

Plain and Fancy Cookie Cookbook, 1969.

Plain and Fancy Chicken Cookbook, 1969.

Plain and Fancy Hamburger Cookbook, 1969.

(With Carmel Berman Reingold) *The Gourmet Fondue Cookbook*, 1970.

(With Reingold) *The Gourmet Chafing Dish Cookbook*, 1970.

The Fondue and Chafing Dish Cookbook, 1970.

Free for Women, 1971.

Pancakes, Crepes, and Waffles, 1972.

Brand Name Guide to Calories and Carbohydrates, 1973.

Calorie Counter for Six Quick-Weight-Loss Diets, 1973.

Calorie Guide to Brand Names, 1973.

Natural Foods and Health Foods Calorie Counter, 1973.

The New Low Carbohydrate Diet, 1973.

"INTERNATIONAL PARTY" SERIES; PUBLISHED BY BUZZA CARDOZO, 1971

South American Dinner Party.
French Flambe Party.
British Isles Dinner Party.
Scandinavian Dinner Party.
German Dinner Party.
Swiss Dinner Party.
Russian Dinner Party.
French Dinner Party.
Italian Dinner Party.
Spanish Dinner Party.
Greek Dinner Party.
Chinese Dinner Party.
Japanese Dinner Party.
India Dinner Party.
Hawaiian Dinner Party.
West Indies Dinner Party.
Mexican Dinner Party.
Japanese Hibachi Party.
Creole Mardi Gras Party.
Swiss Fondue Party.
Caribbean Punches for Parties.
Wine and Cheese Tasting Party.
Coffee Party.
Chocolate Fondue Party.

OTHER

Also author of *America's Guide to Best Buys*, Zebra Books, and "Watch Your Weight" series, Jove. Editor of *Best Television Plays*, Harcourt, 1950—.

*   *   *

KAY, Ernest 1915-
(George Ludlow, Alan Random)

PERSONAL: Born June 21, 1915, in Darwen, Lancashire, England; son of Harold (a mill manager) and Florence (Woodall) Kay; married Marjorie Peover (a journalist), August 11, 1942; children: John Michael, Richard Andrew, Belinda Jean. *Politics:* Labour. *Religion:* Quaker.

ADDRESSES: Home—418 Milton Rd., Cambridge CB4 1ST, England. *Agent*—David Higham Associates Ltd., 5-8 Lower John St., London W1R 4HA, England. *Office*—International Biographical Center, Cambridge CB2 3QP, England.

CAREER: Journalist, 1933-66; *Evening News*, London, England, managing editor, 1955-58; *John O'London's* (weekly),

London, editor, 1959-62; *Time and Tide* (news magazine), London, managing editor, 1962-66; International Biographical Center, Cambridge, England, and New York, N.Y., founder and director general, 1967—.

MEMBER: Royal Society of Arts, Royal Geographical Society, Community of European Writers.

WRITINGS:

Great Men of Yorkshire, Bodley Head, 1956.
Isles of Flowers: The Story of the Isles of Scilly, Redman, 1956, 2nd edition, 1963.
Pragmatic Premier: An Intimate Portrait of Harold Wilson, Frewin, 1967.
(Compiler) *The Wit of Harold Wilson,* Frewin, 1967, reprinted, 1984.
(Editor) *Two Thousand Women of Achievement,* Kay, Sons & Daughter (London), 1969, 2nd edition (honorary general editor) published as *Two Thousand Women of Achievement: A Biographical Record of Most Distinguished Achievement, Circulating throughout the World,* Melrose, 1970, Volume III, 1971, Volume IV, 1972.
(Editor) *Two Thousand Men of Achievement,* Kay, Sons & Daughter (Dartmouth), 1969, 2nd edition (honorary general editor) published as *Two Thousand Men of Achievement: A Biographical Record of Most Distinguished Achievement, Circulating throughout the World,* Melrose, 1970, 4th edition, 1972.
(Editor) *International Who's Who in Poetry,* 2nd edition, International Who's Who in Poetry, 1970, 5th edition, International Biographical Centre, 1977.
(Compiler) *Dictionary of International Biography: A Biographical Record of Contemporary Achievement Together with a Key to the Location of the Original Bibliographic Notes,* 6th edition, Dictionary of International Biography, 1970, 7th edition, Melrose, 1970, Volumes VIII-XII (honorary general editor), 1972-76, Volumes XIII and XIV, International Biographical Centre, 1977-78.
(Honorary general editor) *Dictionary of Latin American and Caribbean Biography,* 2nd edition, Melrose, 1971.
(Honorary general editor) *Dictionary of Scandinavian Biography,* Melrose, 1972, 2nd edition, 1976.
(Honorary general editor) *International Who's Who in Art and Antiques,* Melrose, 1972, 2nd edition (editorial director), 1976.
(Honorary general editor) *The World Who's Who of Women,* Melrose, Volume I, 1973, Volume II, 1975.
(Honorary general editor) *Men of Achievement,* Melrose, Volume I, 1974, Volume II (general editor), 1975, Volume III (editorial director), 1976, Volume IV, International Biographical Centre, 1977.
(Editor) *International Who's Who in Music and Musicians' Directory,* International Who's Who in Music, 7th edition, 1975.
(Editor) *The International Authors and Writers Who's Who,* Melrose, 7th edition, 1976, 10th edition, 1986.
(Editorial director) *International Who's Who in Education,* 2nd edition, International Who's Who in Education, 1981.
(General editor) *Who's Who in the Commonwealth,* International Biographical Centre, 1982, 2nd edition, 1984.

Also editor of other biographical reference books. Contributor of children's book reviews under the pseudonym George Ludlow, general book reviews under the pseudonym Alan Random, and articles to newspapers and magazines throughout Great Britain.

KAYE, M(ary) M(argaret)   1909-
(Mollie Hamilton, Mollie Kaye)

PERSONAL: Born in 1909, in Simla, India; married Godfrey John Hamilton (an army officer); children: Carolyn. *Education:* Educated in England.

ADDRESSES: c/o Allen Lane, Kingsgate House, 536 King's Rd., London SW10, England.

CAREER: Writer; painter.

WRITINGS:

HISTORICAL NOVELS

Shadow of the Moon, Messner, 1956, enlarged edition, St. Martin's, 1979.
Trade Wind, Coward, 1963, revised edition, St. Martin's, 1981.
The Far Pavilions, St. Martin's, 1978.

MYSTERIES

Death Walked in Kashmir, Staples Press, 1953, republished as *Death in Kashmir,* St. Martin's, 1984.
Death Walked in Berlin, Staples Press, 1955, republished as *Death in Berlin,* St. Martin's, 1985.
Death Walked in Cypress, Staples Press, 1956, republished as *Death in Cyprus,* St. Martin's, 1984.
(Under name Mollie Hamilton) *Later Than You Think,* Coward, 1958, republished as *Death in Kenya,* St. Martin's, 1983.
House of Shade, Coward, 1959, republished as *Death in Zanzibar,* St. Martin's, 1983.
Night on the Island, Longmans, Green, 1960, republished as *Death in the Andaman,* St. Martin's, 1984.

Also author of *Six Bars at Seven,* Hutchinson, and *Strange Island,* Thacker.

JUVENILES

(Under name Mollie Kaye) *Potter Pinner Meadow,* illustrations by Margaret Tempest, Collins, 1937.
(Self-illustrated) *The Animals' Vacation,* New York Graphic Society, 1964.
Thistledown, Quartet, 1982.
The Ordinary Princess, Doubleday, 1984.

Also author of *Black Bramble Wood, Willow Witches Brook;* and *Gold Gorse Common,* Collins.

OTHER

The Far Pavilions Picture Book, Bantam, 1979.
(Editor) Emily Bayley, *The Golden Calm: An English Lady's Life in Moghul Delhi,* Viking, 1980.

SIDELIGHTS: Previously a successful author of children's books and mysteries, M. M. Kaye set these genres aside to concentrate on the historical novel *The Far Pavilions.* After fourteen years and a grueling battle against cancer, Kaye finished the work that has been compared to *Gone with the Wind* and other classics of the genre.

The Far Pavilions gives readers a detailed look at life in colonial India. It is a subject on which she is well qualified to write, for she was born in Simla, India, into a British family that had already lived in that country for two generations. Although she was educated in England, Kaye returned to India after her schooling and married a British army officer. While she was thus a part of the ruling class in colonial India, Kaye's writing has been especially praised for its even-handed portrayal of both the native Indians and the English colonists. Brigitte Weeks writes in the *Washington Post Book World* that *The Far Pavilions* is so powerful, its "readers . . . cannot ever feel quite the same about either the Indian subcontinent or the decrepit history of the British Empire."

The Far Pavilions has been compared to Rudyard Kipling's *Kim*. Like Kipling's novel, Kaye's book features a young British boy who is orphaned, then raised as an Indian and a Hindu. Kaye's protagonist, Ash, is sent to live with aristocratic relatives in England when his parentage is finally revealed. Later, he returns to India as a soldier and finds himself torn between his two heritages. While some critics dismiss Kaye's plot as standard romantic-adventure fare, others praise her for skillfully combining Ash's adventures with an accurate historical account of the events between the Indian Mutiny and the Second Afghan War. Furthermore, emphasizes *Spectator* contributor Francis King, Kaye possesses a "gift for narrative"; he finds *The Far Pavilions* "absorbing" in spite of its over nine hundred pages. A *New Yorker* writer concurs that Kaye is "a topnotch storyteller and historian; . . . she holds the reader in thrall."

But critics most often point to Kaye's comprehensive vision of nineteenth-century India as the key to her novel's success. *Times Literary Supplement* reviewer Theon Wilkinson explains: "[Kaye] writes with the conviction that events must be told in their fullness or not at all, that ever[y] facet of information touching the characters must be embraced; and *The Far Pavilions* is a great oriental pot-pourri from which nothing is left out: Indian lullabys; regimental bawdy songs; regimental history, wars and campaigns; weddings; funerals; poisonous plants—a tribute to much painstaking research, some drawn from original diaries and journals. . . . The length of the book is a challenge but the effort is rewarded." And Rahul Singh writes in *Punch*, "There is none of the romantic sentimentality that saw India as a country of snake charmers and bejewelled princes, with the faithful Gunga Din thrown in. Nor the view of it as one vast, multiplying, putrefying sewer for which there was no possible hope. Ms Kaye sees India as many Indians do, and for this one must applaud her."

Before publishing *The Far Pavilions*, Kaye had written two other books similar to it. *Shadow of the Moon* dramatizes the events of the Indian Mutiny through the story of an orphaned Anglo-Spanish girl. *Trade Wind* is set in Zanzibar instead of India, but like *Shadow of the Moon* and *The Far Pavilions*, it examines two cultures in conflict while telling the exciting story of a young abolitionist from Massachusetts who is kidnapped by a handsome slave trader when she travels to Zanzibar. Neither book was particularly successful when first published, but when reissued after the publication of *The Far Pavilions*, both *Shadow of the Moon* and *Trade Wind* became best-sellers. Like *The Far Pavilions*, they have been praised for their fine descriptions of their exotic settings. Walter Shapiro, writing in the *Washington Post Book World*, notes that while its storyline might seem conventional, *Trade Wind* "transcends such easy labels as romance or exotic historical novel. It is a sophisticated treat for those traditional readers who favor good writing, subtle character development, clever plotting and a slightly ironic narrative tone."

MEDIA ADAPTATIONS: The Far Pavilions was produced as a mini-series by Home Box Office in 1984.

BIOGRAPHICAL/CRITICAL SOURCES:

BOOKS

Contemporary Literary Criticism, Volume XXVIII, Gale, 1984.

PERIODICALS

Chapter One, May-June, 1979.
Christian Science Monitor, November 13, 1978.
Detroit News, October 7, 1979.
Los Angeles Times, November 2, 1980, October 9, 1984, May 23, 1986.
Maclean's, September 24, 1979.
New Statesman, October 12, 1979.
Newsweek, September 11, 1978.
New Yorker, October 9, 1978, September 24, 1979, July 27, 1981.
New York Herald Tribune Book Review, September 1, 1957, September 20, 1959.
New York Times, October 26, 1958, December 3, 1978, March 25, 1979.
New York Times Book Review, November 18, 1979.
People, November 20, 1978.
Publishers Weekly, June 25, 1979.
Punch, November 14, 1979.
Sewanee Review, summer, 1980.
Spectator, April 12, 1957, September 9, 1978.
Times Literary Supplement, April 19, 1957, Augsut 22, 1958, September 22, 1978, November 21, 1980, March 26, 1982.
Washington Post, September 11, 1979, April 21, 1984.
Washington Post Book World, September 10, 1978, July 12, 1981, November 11, 1984.†

*   *   *

KAYE, Marilyn 1949-
(Shannon Blair)

PERSONAL: Born July 19, 1949, in New Britain, Conn.; daughter of Harold Stanley (a microbiologist) and Annette (Rudman) Kaye. *Education:* Emory University, B.A., 1967, M.L.S., 1974; University of Chicago, Ph.D., 1983. *Politics:* Liberal Democrat. *Religion:* Jewish.

ADDRESSES: Home—Brooklyn, N.Y. *Office*—Division of Library and Information Science, St. John's University, Grand Central and Utopia Parkways, Jamaica, N.Y. 11439. *Agent*—Amy Berkower, Writer's House, Inc., 21 West 26th St., New York, N.Y. 10010.

CAREER: Library Quarterly, Chicago, Ill., editorial assistant, 1977-79; University of South Carolina, Columbia, instructor in library science, 1980-82; St. John's University, Jamaica, N.Y., 1982—, began as instructor, professor of library and information science, 1986—. Editor, *Top of the News* (journal of the Association of Library Service to Children and Young Adult Sevices), 1982-85.

MEMBER: American Library Association (chairman of Notable Children's Books committee, 1981-82), Beta Phi Mu.

WRITINGS:

JUVENILES

Will You Cross Me?, Harper, 1985.
Max on Earth, Simon & Schuster, 1986.
Max in Love, Simon & Schuster, 1986.
Max on Fire, Simon & Schuster, 1986.
Max Flips Out, Simon & Schuster, 1986.
The Best Baby-Sitter in the World, Scholastic, Inc., 1987.
Phoebe, Harcourt, 1987.
Daphne, Harcourt, 1987.
Cassie, Harcourt, 1987.

Lydia, Harcourt, 1987.

UNDER PSEUDONYM SHANNON BLAIR; TEEN ROMANCES

Call Me Beautiful, Bantam, 1984.
Starstruck, Bantam, 1985.
Wrong Kind of Boy, Bantam, 1985.
Kiss and Tell, Bantam, 1985.

OTHER

(Editor with Betsy Hearne) *Celebrating Children's Books: Essays on Children's Literature in Honor of Zena Sutherland*, Lothrop, 1981.

Contributor of articles and reviews to library journals and newspapers.

WORK IN PROGRESS: A picture book for young children, and more stories about the "Sisters": Phoebe, Daphne, Cassie, and Lydia.

SIDELIGHTS: Marilyn Kaye told *CA:* "I began my writing career cautiously, unsure of what I was capable of doing. As a teacher of children's literature, I had read widely enough to believe I could possibly write an adequate teen romance. After four of these romances, however, I was curious as to the extent of my own abilities, and began to explore the possibilities of writing beyond the romance structure.

"Writing is enormously difficult for me. Each type of book I've attempted—comedy/fantasy, books for beginning readers, middle-grade fiction—has presented its own uniquely agonizing problems and challenges which I'm never quite sure I can meet. For me, writing is not a means of baring my soul or articulating personal angst. I want to tell stories, and as I write, I envision readers, and what they might want to hear. . . . Whenever I'm asked why I write children's books, I say that the child in me is close to surface, and she knows all the best stories."

*　　*　　*

KAYE, Mollie
See KAYE, M(ary) M(argaret)

*　　*　　*

KELLEY, Leo P(atrick) 1928-

PERSONAL: Born September 10, 1928, in Wilkes-Barre, Pa.; son of Leo A. and Regina (Caffrey) Kelley. *Education:* New School for Social Research, B.A., 1957.

ADDRESSES: 702 Lincoln Blvd., Long Beach, N.Y. 11561.

CAREER: McGraw-Hill Book Co., New York, N.Y., 1959-69, began as copywriter, became advertising and promotion manager; free-lance writer, 1969—.

MEMBER: Western Writers of America.

WRITINGS:

SCIENCE FICTION

The Counterfeits, Belmont Books, 1967.
Odyssey to Earthdeath, Belmont Books, 1968.
The Accidental Earth, Belmont Books, 1970.
Time Rogue, Lancer, 1970.
Brother John (based on a screenplay by Ernest Kinoy), Avon, 1971.
The Coins of Murph, Berkley Publishing, 1971.

(Contributor) Robert Hoskins, editor, *Infinity 3*, Lancer, 1972.
Mindmix, Fawcett, 1972.
Time: 110100, Walker & Co., 1972 (published in England as *The Man from Maybe*, Coronet, 1974).
Deadlocked, Fawcett, 1973.
The Earth Tripper, Fawcett, 1973.
Mythmaster, Dell, 1973.

JUVENILE SCIENCE FICTION

(Editor) *Themes in Science Fiction: A Journey into Wonder*, McGraw-Hill, 1972.
(Editor) *Fantasy: The Literature of the Marvelous*, McGraw-Hill, 1973.
(Editor) *The Supernatural in Fiction*, McGraw-Hill, 1973.
The Time Trap: Pacesetters, Children's Press, 1978.
Night of Fire and Blood, illustrated by Ed Diffenderfer, Fearon-Pitman, 1979.
Star Gold, Children's Press, 1979.

"GALAXY 5" SERIES

Dead Moon (also see below), Fearon-Pitman, 1979.
Goodbye to Earth (also see below), Fearon-Pitman, 1979.
King of the Stars (also see below), Fearon-Pitman, 1979.
On the Red World (also see below), Fearon-Pitman, 1979.
Vacation in Space (also see below), Fearon-Pitman, 1979.
Where No Sun Shines (also see below), Fearon-Pitman, 1979.
Galaxy 5 Science Fiction Series (contains *Dead Moon*, *Goodbye to Earth*, *King of the Stars*, *On the Red World*, *Vacation in Space*, and *Where No Sun Shines*), with teacher's guide, Fearon-Pitman, 1979.

"SPACE POLICE" SERIES

Backward in Time (also see below), Fearon-Pitman, 1979.
Death Sentence (also see below), Fearon-Pitman, 1979.
Earth Two (also see below), Fearon-Pitman, 1979.
Prison Satellite (also see below), Fearon-Pitman, 1979.
Sunworld (also see below), Fearon-Pitman, 1979.
Worlds Apart (also see below), Fearon-Pitman, 1979.
Space Police (contains *Backward in Time*, *Death Sentence*, *Earth Two*, *Prison Satellite*, *Sunworld*, and *Worlds Apart*), with teacher's guide, Fearon-Pitman, 1979.

WESTERN NOVELS

Luke Sutton: Outlaw, Doubleday, 1981.
Johnny Tall Dog, Pitman Learning, 1981.
Luke Sutton: Gunfighter, Doubleday, 1982.
Luke Sutton: Indian Fighter, Doubleday, 1982.
Luke Sutton: Avenger, Doubleday, 1983.
Luke Sutton: Outrider, Doubleday, 1984.
Luke Sutton: Bounty Hunter, Doubleday, 1985.
Morgan, Doubleday, 1986.
Luke Sutton: Hired Gun, Doubleday, 1987.
The Last Cowboy, David S. Lake Publishers, 1988.

"CIMARRON" SERIES; PUBLISHED BY NEW AMERICAN LIBRARY

Cimarron in the Cherokee Strip, 1983.
. . . and the Border Bandits, 1983.
. . . and the Bounty Hunters, 1983.
. . . and the Elk Soldiers, 1983.
. . . and the Hanging Judge, 1983.
. . . Rides the Outlaw Trail, 1983.
. . . in the No Man's Land, 1984.
. . . on Hell's Highway, 1984.
. . . and the High Rider, 1984.
. . . and the Medicine Wolves, 1984.

. . . and the Vigilantes, 1984.
. . . and the War Women, 1984.
. . . and the Bootleggers, 1984.
. . . and the Gun Hawks' Gold, 1985.
. . . and the Prophet's People, 1985.
. . . and the Scalp Hunters, 1985.
. . . and the Hired Guns, 1986.
. . . and the Red Earth People, 1986.

OTHER

Contributor of stories and poetry to numerous periodicals, including *Alfred Hitchcock's Mystery Magazine, Gallery, Magazine of Fantasy and Science Fiction, Saint Mystery Magazine, Swank,* and *Worlds of If.*

WORK IN PROGRESS: Luke Sutton: Lawman, Luke Sutton: Mustanger, and *A Man Named Dundee,* all for Doubleday.

*   *   *

KENDRIS, Christopher   1923-

PERSONAL: Original surname, Katsigiannis, legally changed to Kendris; born April 5, 1923, in Albany, N.Y.; son of Themistocles and Iphigenia (Anagnostopoulos) Katsigiannis; married Yolanda Fenyo, June 21, 1957; children: Alexander Dimitri, Theodore Nicholas. *Education:* Columbia University, B.S., 1948; Universite de Paris, two certificates, 1950; Northwestern University, M.A., 1954, Ph.D., 1955; Columbia University, additional study, 1962-63, M.S., 1967; Ecole Pedagogique, Alliance Francaise de Paris, certificate, 1986. *Religion:* Greek Orthodox.

ADDRESSES: Home—27 Par Cir., Albany, N.Y. 12208. *Office*—Department of Foreign Languages, Mont Pleasant Public High School, Schenectady, N.Y. 12303.

CAREER: Duke University, Durham, N.C., instructor in French, 1955-56; Rutgers University, New Brunswick, N.J., instructor in French and Spanish, 1957-59; Farmingdale High School, Farmingdale, Long Island, N.Y., chairman of foreign language department, 1959-64; State University of New York at Albany, assistant professor of French, 1964-69; Schenectady County Community College, Schenectady, N.Y., member of faculty, 1969-72; St. Mary's College of Maryland, St. Mary's City, member of faculty, 1972-75; Library of Congress, Washington, D.C., member of staff, 1975-77; Albany Academy, Albany, N.Y., teacher of French and Spanish, 1978-84; Mont Pleasant Public High School, Schenectady, member of faculty, 1985—. Visiting summer lecturer in French, University of Chicago, 1953. Foreign language consultant for Barron's Educational Series, Inc. (publishers). *Military service:* U.S. Army, 1942-43.

MEMBER: American Association of Teachers of French, American Association of Teachers of Spanish and Portuguese, New York State Teachers Association, New York State Association of Foreign Language Teachers, Alliance Francaise de Schenectady (secretary-treasurer).

AWARDS, HONORS: Rockefeller Foundation fellow; national winner, Rockefeller Foundation Fellowship for Teachers of Foreign Languages in American High Schools, 1986.

WRITINGS:

Lectures Variees (reader), Harper, 1959.

PUBLISHED BY BARRON'S

201 French Verbs Fully Conjugated in All the Tenses, 1963.

201 Spanish Verbs Fully Conjugated in All the Tenses, 1963.
Beginning to Write in French (workbook), 1966, revised edition, 1982.
Beginning to Write in Spanish (workbook), 1966, revised edition, 1982.
Fundamentals of Spanish Grammar, 1966.
Dictionnaire de 201 verbes espagnols, 1969.
Diccionario de 201 verbos franceses, 1969.
Dictionary of 501 French Verbs: Fully Conjugated in All the Tenses, 1970, 2nd edition published as *501 French Verbs Fully Conjugated in All the Tenses: In a New Easy to Learn Format, Alphabetically Arranged,* 1982.
Dictionary of 501 Spanish Verbs: Fully Conjugated in All The Tenses, 1971, 2nd edition published as *501 Spanish Verbs Fully Conjugated in All the Tenses: In a New Easy to Learn Format, Alphabetically Arranged,* 1982.
French Now: Level 1, 1980.
How to Prepare for the College Board Achievement Test in French, 1981, 4th edition, 1986.
301 French Verbs Fully Conjugated in All the Tenses, 1981.
How to Prepare for the College Board Achievement Test in Spanish, 1982, 5th edition, 1986.
French the Easy Way, Books I and II, 1982.
Spanish the Easy Way, Book II, 1982.
301 Spanish Verbs Fully Conjugated in All the Tenses, 1982.
(Translator) Maurice Grevisse, *Correct French,* 1982.
Master the Basics: French, 1987.
Master the Basics: Spanish, 1987.

OTHER

Also author of annual publications, *Barron's Regents Exams and Answers: French Level 3* and *Barron's Regents Exams and Answers: Spanish Level 3.*

WORK IN PROGRESS: French Now, Book II; *Spanish Now,* Book II; *101 Creative Ways to Remember French Forever; 101 Creative Ways to Remember Spanish Forever.*

SIDELIGHTS: Christopher Kendris told *CA:* "I like writing school books and language aids because I like to help people who are studying French and Spanish. It makes me feel good inside to know that my writings have helped students. I also like to help people through my church by tutoring (for no fee) any member, young or old, who wants to learn or who needs extra help in French or Spanish. I began my writing career while teaching; I saw the need for French and Spanish school books written simply and clearly.

"What advice do I have for aspiring writers? Write about what you know best and be honest and sincere. My favorite writers are Gustave Flaubert and Guy de Maupassant because their works are written simply, clearly, beautifully, and they have something to say. My favorite movie director is Francois Truffaut because he makes me think while I am watching a story unfold on the screen."

*   *   *

KENNEDY, Adam
(John Redgate)

PERSONAL: Born near Lafayette, Ind.; married wife, Susan (an actress); children: Regan (son), Jack. *Education:* Received B.A. (cum laude) from De Pauw University; also studied at Chicago Professional School of Art, Academie de la Grande Chaumiere, Alliance Francaise, and Neighborhood Playhouse.

CAREER: Actor, writer, and artist. Account executive with Grant Advertising, Inc., Chicago, Ill.; art director and illustrator for *Esquire* and *Coronet.*

AWARDS, HONORS: Oil painting prize from John Herron Museum; named outstanding American painter in Paris by Society for American Art in Paris, 1951; D.Litt. from De Pauw University, 1974.

WRITINGS:

NOVELS

The Scaffold, Trident, 1971.
Maggie D.: A Sexual History, Trident, 1973.
Somebody Else's Wife, Simon & Schuster, 1974.
The Domino Principle, Viking, 1975.
Love Song, Viking, 1976.
Just Like Humphrey Bogart, Viking, 1978.
Debt of Honor, Delacorte, 1981.
The Domino Vendetta, W. H. Allen, 1982.
In a Far Country, Delacorte, 1983.
No Place to Cry, W. H. Allen, 1986.
The Fires of Summer, W. H. Allen, 1987.
All Dreams Denied, W. H. Allen, 1988.

NOVELS UNDER PSEUDONYM JOHN REDGATE

The Killing Season, Trident, 1967.
Barlow's Kingdom, J. Cape, 1968, Trident, 1969.
The Last Decathlon, Delacorte, 1979.

SCREENPLAYS

"The Dove," Paramount Pictures, 1974.
"The Domino Principle" (adapted from his novel of the same title), Avco-Embassy, 1977.
"Raise the Titanic," Independent Television Corp., 1980.

Also author of "The Killing Season" and "Barlow's Kingdom," Paramount Pictures.

SIDELIGHTS: Adam Kennedy was born in the middle of winter, in a farmhouse without central heating or electricity. Two-and-one-half months premature and weighing less than three pounds, Kennedy was kept in a peach box incubator heated by water-filled fruit jars, where he thrived. He began working as a small boy, with such jobs as butcher, mortician's assistant, teacher, sign painter, singer, commercial artist, farm and construction worker, photographer's model, and radio announcer.

A professional actor, Kennedy appeared on stage in Europe and on Broadway and performed in more than three hundred television programs (starring in the series "The Doctors" and "The Californians") and a dozen feature films, including "Act of Love," "Men in War," "Until They Sail," and "The Court Martial of Billy Mitchell."

He studied painting and has had group and solo shows in the United States and Paris, where he is considered one of the more significant abstract painters of recent years.

Reviewing Kennedy's 1975 thriller, *The Domino Principle,* in the *New York Times Book Review,* Newgate Callendar writes, "Kennedy is a fine writer who maintains suspense that becomes all but excruciating after a while." "Kennedy is a most sensitive writer," lauds a *West Coast Review of Books* critic. Commenting on Kennedy's 1976 novel, *Love Song,* which is about a young small-town girl in love, the critic continues, "There's movement and tenderness, violence and grief here

and all of the people are fullblooded in the desperate aridity of Kennedy's setting." Callendar also praises the author's 1979 thriller set at the Moscow Olympics, *The Last Decathlon,* calling it "fast-paced, expertly written, with a good deal of information about the body and mind of a top athlete."

Duffy Odin, the main character in Kennedy's eighth novel, *Just Like Humphrey Bogart,* is a twenty-eight-year-old painter living in Paris who looks and acts like the late film star. "Duffy is small, not handsome, not conspicuously talented and has virtually no conversation," writes Anatole Broyard in the *New York Times Book Review.* Broyard adds that "Duffy is monotonously successful with beautiful women." John Leonard of the *New York Times* describes the character as "a self-made failure, a combination of Jean-Paul Sartre and Lenny Bruce and Gunga Din. . . . I like Duffy a lot." Praising Kennedy's style, Leonard continues, "Mr. Kennedy's very energy is winning. People . . . places . . . and rackets are hit smackdab; the paint and the wounds are fresh; all the motion is headlong."

AVOCATIONAL INTERESTS: Travel (including Europe, South America, New Zealand, Barbados, and Trinidad).

BIOGRAPHICAL/CRITICAL SOURCES:

BOOKS

Authors in the News, Volume I, Gale, 1976.

PERIODICALS

Louisville Courier Journal & Times, December 22, 1974.
New York Times, January 10, 1978.
New York Times Book Review, December 21, 1975, January 8, 1978, October 14, 1979.
West Coast Review of Books, January, 1977.

*   *   *

KENT, Katherine
    See DIAL, Joan

*   *   *

KEYES, Kenneth S(cofield), Jr.   1921-

PERSONAL: Surname rhymes with "eyes"; born January 19, 1921, in Atlanta, Ga.; son of Kenneth S. (in real estate) and Lucille (Thomas) Keyes; children: Kenneth S. III, Clara Lucille. *Education:* Attended Duke University, 1938-40; University of Miami, Coral Gables, Fla., A.B., 1953.

ADDRESSES: Home—Coos Bay, Ore. 97420.

CAREER: In real estate business, 1953-64; Keyes Realty International, Inc., Miami, Fla., vice-president, 1964-68; Keyes National Investors, Miami, president, 1968-71; Living Love Center, Berkeley, Calif., founder, 1973-77; founder of Cornucopia Institute, 1977—; founder of Ken Keyes College, 1985. *Military service:* U.S. Navy, 1941-45; became chief petty officer.

WRITINGS:

How to Develop Your Thinking Ability, McGraw, 1951.
How to Live Longer-Stronger-Slimmer, Fell, 1966, published as *Loving Your Body,* Living Love, 1974.
(With Jacque Fresco) *Looking Forward,* A. S. Barnes, 1969.
Handbook to Higher Consciousness, Living Love, 1973, 5th edition, 1975.
Taming Your Mind, Living Love, 1975.

(With Tolly Burkan) *How to Make Your Life Work; or, Why Aren't You Happy?*, Living Love, 1976.
A Conscious Person's Guide to Relationships, Living Love, 1979, 2nd edition, 1984.
How to Enjoy Your Life in Spite of It All, Living Love, 1980.
Prescriptions for Happiness, Living Love, 1981.
The Hundredth Monkey, Living Love, 1982, 2nd edition, 1984.
Your Heart's Desire, Living Love, 1983.
Your Life Is a Gift, Living Love, 1987.
(With Penny Keyes) *Gathering Power through Insight and Love*, Living Love, 1987.

AVOCATIONAL INTERESTS: Yachting, general semantics, classical music.

*   *   *

KIHL, Armand
See ALD, Roy A(llison)

*   *   *

KIMREY, Grace (Evelyn) Saunders   1910-

PERSONAL: Born December 3, 1910, in Candor, N.C.; daughter of Aaron Thomas (a saw-mill and textile plant employee) and Willie L. (Coble) Saunders; married Sam Clyde Kimrey (a roof contractor), February 22, 1930; children: Gary, Bernard. *Education:* Attended Randolph Technical Institute, 1964 and 1972; various college courses, 1963-67; attended Alamance Technical Institute, 1968-73. *Politics:* Nonpartisan. *Religion:* Southern Baptist.

ADDRESSES: Home and office—727 Liberty St., Ramseur, N.C. 27316.

CAREER: Bookkeeper for husband's roofing company, 1945-71; co-owner, with husband, and bookkeeper of home furnishings store, beginning 1963. Former training union leader, news correspondent, and church treasurer. Teacher of adult Sunday School classes.

MEMBER: United Amateur Press Association, Burlington Writers, Eastern Star, North Carolina Poetry Society, North Carolina Historical Society, Ramseur Book Club.

AWARDS, HONORS: Charlotte Writers award, 1959, for "Tinker and Wally-Waddle"; Burlington Writers awards, 1958-72, for poetry, short stories, and articles.

WRITINGS:

Songs of Sunny Valley (poetry), Banner Press, 1954.
Glimpses of Beauty (poetry), Banner Press, 1955.
Star of Hope (poetry), Banner Press, 1957.
Spent Wrath (illustrated booklet), Lore Press, 1971.
(Contributor) *Grains of Sand* (poetry anthology), C. D. Stephens, 1971.
(Contributor) *The Golden Hours* (poetry anthology), Edmond, 1972.
The Morning Star: A History of Ramseur, Gaus, 1977.
Of Heaven and of Earth (poetry), Gaus, 1979.

Also author of an unpublished novel, *Hallowed Be Thy Name*. Contributor to poetry anthologies *Year Book of Modern Poetry*, Young Publications, and *Towers by the Sea*, Laurel Publishers. Contributor of column, "Grace Notes," to *Randolph Guide*. Contributor to *Raleigh News*, *Biblical Recorder*, *Ideals*, *North Carolina Prison Paper*, *Greensboro Record*, and *Asheville Citizen Times*.

WORK IN PROGRESS: Memoirs.

SIDELIGHTS: Grace Saunders Kimrey once told *CA:* "Since I could remember, father eked out a meager living as a saw mill employee, then later, in a textile plant. Those were lean and impoverished years. [At fourteen] I was put to work in the mill, too, to help support our ever growing family. The day school opened that year, I cried all day because I wanted to continue my education so very much. . . . Abraham Lincoln became my guiding star; if he could educate himself and then go on to become the president of these Untied States, I, at least, could improve myself intellectually by reading. . . . Reading what? Our town had no library. Neither did our elementary school. Father possessed two books and our Bible. I had my Sunday School quarterlies. These I read over and over." Years later, in high school, Kimrey said she "was introduced to good literature for the first time in my life. I'll never forget my experience in reading *Tom Sawyer* the first time! Wow!!"

Kimrey more recently added: "The book upon which I'm now working is an effort to preserve a bit of Americana that will [otherwise] be lost. It is about life as I lived it and [my remembrances of] the lives of people who touched my life.

"Dr. Archibald Rutledge, poet laureate of South Carolina, was my mentor for many years. I now am helping others by telling them many things that Dr. Rutledge told me to help me find direction. One poet has two books now and wins state awards almost every year. I'm helping [another] one who has great promise!"

*   *   *

KING, Larry L.   1929-

PERSONAL: Born January 1, 1929, in Putnam, Tex.; son of Clyde Clayton (a farmer and blacksmith) and Cora Lee (Clark) King; married second wife, Rosemarie Coumarias (a photographer), February 20, 1965 (deceased, 1972); married Barbara S. Blaine (an attorney), May 6, 1979; children: (first marriage) Cheryl Ann, Kerri Lee, Bradley Clayton; (third marriage) Lindsay, Blaine. *Education:* Attended Texas Technological College (now Texas Tech University), 1949-50. *Politics:* Liberal-Internationalist-Democrat.

ADDRESSES: Agent—Barbara S. Blaine, Suite 1000, 1015 15th St., N.W., Washington, D.C. 20005.

CAREER: Oil field worker in Texas, 1944-46; newspaper reporter in Hobbs, N.M., 1949, Midland, Tex., 1950-51, and Odessa, Tex., 1952-54; radio station KCRS, Midland, Tex., news director, 1951-52; administrative assistant to U.S. Congressman J. T. Rutherford, Washington, D.C., 1955-62, and James C. Wright, Jr., 1962-64; *Capitol Hill* (magazine), Washington, D.C., editor, 1965; free-lance writer, 1964—. Member of Kennedy-Johnson campaign team, traveling in Southwest, 1960. Ferris Professor of Journalism, Princeton University, 1973-75. *Military service:* U.S. Army, Signal Corps, writer, 1946-48; became staff sergeant.

MEMBER: PEN International, National Writers Union, National Academy of Television Arts and Sciences, Authors Guild, Authors League of America, Dramatists Guild, Screenwriters Guild East, Actors' Equity.

AWARDS, HONORS: Neiman fellow at Harvard University, 1969-70; National Book Award nomination, 1971, for *Confessions of a White Racist*; Stanley Walker Journalism Award, Texas Institute of Letters, 1973, for "The Lost Frontier";

Duke Fellow of Communications at Duke University, 1976; Tony Award nomination for best book of a musical, 1979, for "The Best Little Whorehouse in Texas"; Emmy award, 1981, for "CBS Reports" (documentary on statehouse politics); elected to Texas Institute of Letters, 1970, and Texas Walk of Stars, 1987.

WRITINGS:

The One-Eyed Man (novel; Literary Guild selection), New American Library, 1966.
. . . And Other Dirty Stories (collected articles), World, 1968.
Confessions of a White Racist (nonfiction), Viking, 1971.
The Old Man and Lesser Mortals (collected articles), Viking, 1974.
(With Peter Masterson) "The Best Little Whorehouse in Texas" (musical; also see below), first produced in New York at Actors Studio, October, 1977, produced on Broadway at 46th Street Theater, June 19, 1978.
(With Bobby Baker) *Wheeling and Dealing*, Norton, 1978.
(With Ben Z. Grant) "The Kingfish" (play), first produced in Washington, D.C. at New Playwrights' Theater, August 9, 1979.
Of Outlaws, Con Men, Whores, Politicians and Other Artists (collected articles), Viking, 1980.
That Terrible Night Santa Got Lost in the Woods (also see below), with drawings by Pat Oliphant, Encino Press, 1981.
(With Masterson and Colin Higgins) "The Best Little Whorehouse in Texas" (screenplay; based on his musical of the same title), Universal Pictures, 1982.
The Whorehouse Papers (nonfiction), Viking, 1982.
"The Night Hank Williams Died" (play), first produced at Memphis State University, 1985, new version produced in Washington, D.C., at New Playwrights' Theater, February 3, 1988.
None but a Blockhead: On Being a Writer (nonfiction), Viking, 1986.
Warning: Writer at Work (nonfiction), TCU Press, 1986.
Christmas: 1933 (play based on the book *That Terrible Night Santa Got Lost in the Woods;* first produced in Memphis, Tenn., at Circuit Playhouse, 1986), Samuel French, 1987.

Contributing editor, *Texas Observer*, 1964-76, *Harper's*, 1967-71, *New Times*, 1974-77, *Texas Monthly*, beginning 1973, and *Parade* magazine, beginning 1983.

SIDELIGHTS: "Make no mistake about it—Larry L. King knows how to *write*," states Norman J. Ornstein in the *Washington Post Book World*. "Whether his subject is politics or country music, his locale New York, Texas, Washington or Las Vegas, King can weave together words, phrases and ideas to engross, touch, titillate or outrage the reader." King has applied his writing skills to diverse projects, from a serious look at racial prejudice in *Confessions of a White Racist* to his bawdy musical-comedy "The Best Little Whorehouse in Texas." Although the author has made his home in Washington, D.C., for many years, his Texan background influences all his writing; as *New York Times Book Review* contributor Richard Lingeman comments, King's work "is mostly about Texas, even when it is about such lesser places as Washington and New York City."

King had worked in the nation's capitol as an administrative assistant for several years when, in 1964, he impulsively left his position to return to Texas and write a novel. *The One-Eyed Man* examines the struggle for integration in a Southern university, a timely subject in the early 1960s. Critics dealt

harshly with King's first novel, however. He turned his attention to magazine writing and soon found success in that field. In the *New Republic*, Foster Hirsch characterized King's magazine work as that of a man who "is flagrantly a new journalist" with a highly personal style. Several collections of his articles have been published, including . . . *And Other Dirty Stories, The Old Man and Lesser Mortals*, and *Of Outlaws, Con Men, Whores, Politicians and Other Artists;* all have been very favorably reviewed.

Despite *The One-Eyed Man's* failure, reviewer Jonathan Yardley finds that King has many of the finer qualities of a novelist. Discussing *The Old Man and Lesser Mortals* in the *Washington Post Book World*, Yardley notes that most collections of a journalist's work only serve to point out the ephemeral nature of much magazine writing. He believes, however, "the pieces that Larry King has brought together in *The Old Man* do not merely weather the transition, they thrive on it. That is because King's work is notable for the persistence and consistency with which it explores certain themes. King is a novelist masquerading in journalist's clothing . . . and he has the novelist's sense of thematic unity. . . . He returns over and again to the same preoccupations. Chief among them, perhaps, are a reverence for the American past and a fierce dislike for the shabby commercialism with which it is being replaced. . . . King succeeds, however, in revering the past without sentimentalizing it."

Foster Hirsch also finds *The Old Man and Lesser Mortals* to be a remarkably unified collection. He suggests that the articles are bound together by King's "continuing wrestling match with his heritage. Smalltown folksiness underlies the slick magazine writer's polish." Whether writing about a trip to the Alamo, a visit to a small-town diner, or a football game, "King 'works' his material for larger purposes than local color portraiture. His trips home afford glimpses of the national state of mind. . . . Skillfully King builds his miniature subjects into capacious essays on the American character. . . . With these circumscribed, personally accented pieces drawn from the American heartland, King is unfailingly vivid."

Confessions of a White Racist is as intensely personal as any of King's magazine pieces, and it is widely regarded as his most serious work. It begins with the author's youth in west Texas, where intolerance toward blacks was the unquestioned norm. King relates how he assimilated those local attitudes, then grew beyond them and left his homeland. He found, however, that prejudice was as deeply rooted, if better concealed, in Washington and Cambridge as it was in Texas. Eventually he began to question the authenticity of his own tolerance. Christopher Lehmann-Haupt writes in the *New York Times* that "King is saying that . . . since the end of World War II, when President Truman ordered the desegregation of America's armed forces, we have scarcely lifted a finger to remove the stain of racism from our national fabric—all Supreme Court decisions, court orders, and benign neglect to the contrary notwithstanding. . . . He has reached the conclusion that those of us who are not white racists are simply not white."

Geoffrey Wolff praises King's emotional honesty in his *Newsweek* review of *Confessions of a White Racist*, stating, "Its twisting, backtracking course through the author's racial prejudice bespeaks an authentic complication of values." Other critics feel that for all its honesty, *Confessions* has little new to say on its subject. Walker Percy comments in the *New York Times Book Review:* "One would have wanted from King, an astute and sensitive political observer, a book which started where this one ended.'' But Hodding Carter III, writing in *Book World,* calls *Confessions* ''a gut-rending, excruciatingly honest account of one white man's attempt to confront and overcome within himself the sickness which afflicts us all. There is little that is loving or tender about *Confessions of a White Racist.* King hides nothing, obscures nothing, fuzzes nothing over—and thereby helps the more timid of us do the same for ourselves.''

King's best-known project is far removed from the pessimistic tone of *Confessions.* ''The Best Little Whorehouse in Texas'' is a rowdy musical-comedy based loosely on an article King sold to *Playboy* magazine in 1974 concerning the closing of a famous country brothel in Texas. Judith Martin of the *Washington Post* calls the show, which pits hypocritical do-gooders against the essentially decent women of the ''Chicken Ranch,'' ''a spirited celebration of an old-fashioned concept of naughtiness.'' ''The Best Little Whorehouse in Texas'' became one of Broadway's longest-running plays; a film version was also produced, starring Dolly Parton and Burt Reynolds. The play took King from the uncertain life of a free-lance journalist to the 1979 Tony Awards ceremony.

But success was not without problems, as King ''hilariously and venomously chronicles . . . with country-boy cunning'' in what *Time* reviewer J. D. Reed considers his ''best book,'' *The Whorehouse Papers.* Disagreements with collaborators, personality clashes, and a feeling of powerlessness as his original work was changed by others all contributed to King's worsening alcoholism as work on the musical progressed. Therefore, finds Reed, ''beyond the ribaldry and self-promotion lies a melancholy, intriguing tale of a writer in trouble.'' King emerges from his first Broadway venture ''brutalized, agonized and hospitalized, although 'about two-thirds rich.' '' Robert M. Kaus also finds much to admire in *The Whorehouse Papers,* which he calls in the *New York Times Book Review* ''a sharply written, funny, even moving book. . . . This is a book about making it, about how—for money, fame, or the sheer joy of it—people get things done. Such books are usually enlightening, often inspirational. This one is both. They could make a musical out of it.''

BIOGRAPHICAL/CRITICAL SOURCES:

BOOKS

King, Larry L., *. . . And Other Dirty Stories,* World, 1968.
King, Larry L., *Confessions of a White Racist,* Viking, 1971.
King, Larry L., *The Old Man and Lesser Mortals,* Viking, 1974.
King, Larry L., *The Whorehouse Papers,* Viking, 1982.
King, Larry L., *None but a Blockhead: On Being a Writer,* Viking, 1986.

PERIODICALS

Book World, July 4, 1971.
Chicago Tribune, May 23, 1980, July 26, 1982.
Detroit News, May 16, 1982.
Life, June 11, 1971.
New Republic, March 16, 1974.
Newsweek, June 7, 1971.
New York Review of Books, September 2, 1971.
New York Times, August 27, 1968, May 24, 1971, January 31, 1974, July 21, 1982, February 6, 1986.
New York Times Book Review, November 3, 1968, June 27, 1971, April 29, 1980, April 25, 1982, February 23, 1986.
Time, May 24, 1982.

Washington Post, June 8, 1979, August 11, 1979, January 25, 1980, April 28, 1982.
Washington Post Book World, February 17, 1974, April 7, 1980, February 12, 1986.

—*Sketch by Joan Goldsworthy*

*   *   *

KINKAID, Wyatt E.
See JENNINGS, Michael Glenn

*   *   *

KIRST, Michael W(eile) 1939-

PERSONAL: Born August 1, 1939, in West Reading, Pa.; son of Russell John and Marian Rick (Weile) Kirst; married Janet Lee Elliott, September 16, 1961; children: Michael E., Anne M. *Education:* Dartmouth College, A.B. (summa cum laude), 1961; Harvard University, M.P.A., 1963, Ph.D., 1964.

ADDRESSES: Home—131 Mimosa Way, Portola Valley, Calif. 94025. *Office*—School of Education, Stanford University, Stanford, Calif. 94305.

CAREER: U.S. Bureau of the Budget, Washington, D.C., budget examiner, 1964; U.S. Office of Education, Washington, D.C., program assistant to director of Division of Compensatory Education, 1965; National Advisory Council on Education of Disadvantaged Children, Washington, D.C., associate director of President's Commission on White House Fellows, 1966; U.S. Office of Education, Bureau of Elementary and Secondary Education, director of program planning and evaluation, 1967; U.S. Senate, Washington, D.C., staff director of subcommittee on manpower, employment, and poverty, 1968; Stanford University, School of Education, Stanford, Calif., 1969—, currently professor of education and business administration, director of Joint Program in Educational Administration, 1969-72, member of board of directors of Stanford Center on Research in Teaching, 1971-72. Academy professor, National Academy of School Executives; director of Teacher Leadership Institute for Educational Policy Formulation, 1972; commissioner on California State Commission on Management and Evaluation of Education, 1972-75; vice-president of California State Board of Education. Has testified before U.S. Congress. Director, McCutchan Publishing Corp. Consultant to Merrill Palmer Institute, White House Domestic Policy Council, Ford Foundation, Education Commission of the States, State of Florida, U.S. Senate, and National Institute for Education.

MEMBER: American Educational Research Association (chairman of special interest group in politics, 1972-74), American Political Science Association, Phi Beta Kappa, Phi Delta Kappa, Dartmouth Club (San Francisco).

AWARDS, HONORS: Alfred P. Sloan Foundation fellow; Ford Foundation research grant, 1972, to study response of local districts to state school finance in California and to state finance reform; U.S. Office of Education grant for comparative political study of states that have approved substantial school finance reforms; formal citation from Governor Reubin Askew.

WRITINGS:

Government without Passing Laws, University of North Carolina Press, 1969.

(Editor) *The Politics of Education at the Local, State, and Federal Level,* McCutchan, 1970.
(With Joel Berke and others) *Federal Aid to Education: Who Governs, Who Benefits,* Heath, 1972.
(With Frederick Wirt) *The Political Web of American Schools,* Little, Brown, 1972, published as *Political and Social Foundations of Education,* McCutchan, 1975.
(Editor) *State, School, and Politics,* Heath, 1972.
(With W. I. Garms) *Revising School Finance in Florida,* Office of the Governor of Florida, 1973.
(Contributor) Benjamin Rosner, editor, *The Power of Competency Based Teachers,* Allyn & Bacon, 1973.
Curriculum: A Key to Improving Academic Standards, College Entrance Examination Board, 1981.
(With Wirt) *Schools in Conflict: The Politics of Education,* McCutchan, 1982.
Who Controls Our Schools?: American Values in Conflict, Stanford Alumni Association, 1984.

Also author, with others, of *State School Finance Alternatives,* 1975. Contributor to yearbooks. Also contributor to *Review of Educational Research, Education and Urban Society, Education Digest,* and *Georgetown Law Review.* Member of editorial board of *Education and Urban Society,* 1973.

WORK IN PROGRESS: Guidelines for the Administration of Educational Television Projects in Developing Countries.

BIOGRAPHICAL/CRITICAL SOURCES:

PERIODICALS

American Political Science Review, March, 1970.
Educational Leadership, November, 1985.

*   *   *

KIZER, Carolyn (Ashley)   1925-

PERSONAL: Born December 10, 1925, in Spokane, Wash.; daughter of Benjamin Hamilton (a lawyer and planner) and M. (a biologist and professor; maiden name, Ashley) Kizer; married Charles Stimson Bullitt, January 16, 1948 (divorced, 1954); married John Marshall Woodbridge (an architect and planner), April 11, 1975; children: (first marriage) Ashley Ann, Scott, Jill Hamilton. *Education:* Sarah Lawrence College, B.A., 1945; graduate study at Columbia University, 1945-46, and University of Washington, 1946-47. *Politics:* Independent. *Religion:* Episcopalian.

ADDRESSES: Home—19772 8th St. E., Sonoma, Calif. 95476.

CAREER: Poet, educator, and critic. Studied poetry with Theodore Roethke, University of Washington, Seattle, 1953-54; *Poetry Northwest,* Seattle, founder and editor, 1959-65; National Endowment for the Arts, Washington, D.C., first director of literary programs, 1966-70; University of North Carolina at Chapel Hill, poet-in-residence, 1970-74; Ohio University, Athens, McGuffey Lecturer and poet-in-residence, 1975; Iowa Writer's Workshop, University of Iowa, Iowa City, professor of poetry, 1976; University of Maryland, College Park, professor, 1976-77; Stanford University, Stanford, Calif., professor of poetry, spring, 1986; Princeton University, Princeton, N.J., senior fellow in the humanities, fall, 1986. Hurst Professor of Literature at Washington University, St. Louis, Mo., 1971; lecturer at Barnard College, spring, 1972; acting director of graduate writing program at Columbia Uni-

versity, 1972. Participant in International Poetry Festivals, London, England, 1960, 1970, Yugoslavia, 1969, 1970, Pakistan, 1969, Rotterdam, Netherlands, 1970, and Knokke-le-Zut, Belgium, 1970. Volunteer worker for American Friends Service Committee, 1960; specialist in literature for U.S. State Department in Pakistan, 1964-65. Member of founding board of directors of Seattle Community Psychiatric Clinic.

MEMBER: International P.E.N., Amnesty International, Association of Literary Magazines of America (founding member), Poetry Society of America, Poets and Writers, Academy of American Poets, American Civil Liberties Union.

AWARDS, HONORS: Masefield Prize, Poetry Society of America, 1983; award in literature, American Academy and Institute of Arts and Letters, 1985; Pulitzer Prize in poetry, 1985, for *Yin: New Poems;* Governors Award from the state of Washington and an award from San Francisco Arts Commission, both for *Mermaids in the Basement: Poems for Women.*

WRITINGS:

POETRY

Poems, Portland Art Museum, 1959.
The Ungrateful Garden, Indiana University Press, 1961.
Knock upon Silence, Doubleday, 1965.
Midnight Was My Cry: New and Selected Poems, Doubleday, 1971.
Mermaids in the Basement: Poems for Women (also see below), Copper Canyon Press, 1984.
Yin: New Poems (contains some poems from *Mermaids in the Basement: Poems for Women*), Boa Editions, 1984.
The Nearness of You, Copper Canyon Press, 1986.

EDITOR

Woman Poet—The West, Women-in-Literature, 1980.
Robertson Peterson, *Leaving Taos,* Harper, 1981.
Muriel Weston, *Primitive Places,* Owl Creek Press, 1987.

CONTRIBUTOR

New Poems by American Poets, Ballantine, 1957.
New Poets of England and America, Meridian Publishing, 1962.
Anthology of Modern Poetry, Hutchinson, 1963.
Erotic Poetry, Random House, 1963.
New Modern Poetry, Macmillan, 1967.

OTHER

(Translator) *Carrying Over* (poetry), Copper Canyon Press, 1987.

Translator of *Sept Versants Sept Syllables* (title means "Seven Sides, Seven Syllables"). Contributor to periodicals, including *Poetry, New Yorker, Kenyon Review, Spectator, Paris Review, Shenandoah, Antaeus, Grand Street,* and *Poetry East.*

SIDELIGHTS: Although Carolyn Kizer's poetry collections are not vast in number, they bear witness to her much-praised meticulousness and versatility. Critics find that Kizer's subject matter has changed over the years, but not the calibre of her art; in 1985 her collection *Yin: New Poems*—twelve years in the making—won the Pulitzer Prize in poetry.

"Like some people, Carolyn Kizer is many people," notes *Washington Post* reviewer Meryle Secrest. Kizer received her

B.A. degree from Sarah Lawrence College in 1945 and then went on to do graduate work at both Columbia University and the University of Washington. During the mid-1950s, she studied poetry at the University of Washington under the tutelage of Theodore Roethke. She eventually co-founded the prestigious Seattle-based *Poetry Northwest,* a journal she edited from its inception in 1959 until 1965. In 1964, Kizer went to Pakistan as a U.S. State Department specialist and taught at various institutions, including the distinguished Kinnaird College for Women. Among her other activities, Kizer was the first director of literary programs for the newly created National Endowment for the Arts in 1966, a position she held until 1970. As literary director, she promoted programs to aid struggling writers and literary journals, and she worked to have poetry read aloud in inner city schools. In addition to teaching and lecturing nationwide, Kizer has translated Urdu, Chinese, and Japanese poetry, and, though hardly warranting last place on her list of accomplishments, she has been a wife and the mother of three children. According to Kizer, "what is so marvelous about living today is that it is possible to extend, like a flower, spreading petals in all directions," records Secrest.

Elizabeth B. House claims in the *Dictionary of Literary Biography: American Poets since World War II* that as a poet, "Kizer deals equally well with subjects that have often been treated by women and those that have not. Tensions between nature and humans or between civilization and chaos are topics no more and no less congenial to her than are love affairs, children, and women's rights." According to House, in Kizer's first two poetry collections, *The Ungrateful Garden* and *Knock upon Silence,* Kizer employs grotesque imagery, "lice cozily snuggling in a captured bat's wings, carrion birds devouring the last pulp of hell-bound bodies," and other unsettling topics, but neither is Kizer fearful of femininity and sentimentality. Sometime in the past, Roethke composed a list of common complaints made against women poets that included such things as lack of sense of humor, narrow range of subject matter, lamenting the lot of women, and refusing to face up to existence. In *Alone with America: Essays on the Art of Poetry in the United States since 1950,* Richard Howard believes Kizer has incurred and therefore overcome these complaints. "She does not fear—indeed she *wants*—to do all the things Roethke says women are blamed for, and indeed I think she does do them. . . . But doing them or not, being *determined* to do them makes her a different kind of poet from the one who manages to avoid the traps of his condition, and gives her a different kind of success."

The Ungrateful Garden, Kizer's first major collection, appeared in 1961. Devoted in large part to the examination of people's relationships to nature, it is a candid work, observes *Saturday Review* critic Robert D. Spector, and, "because candor is hardly ever gentle, her shocking images are brutal. She abuses adult vanity by setting it alongside a child's ability to endure the removal of an eye. Pretensions to immortality are reduced to rubbish by 'Beer cans on headstones, eggshells in the [cemetery] grass.'" In the title poem and in one of her better-known pieces, "The Great Blue Heron," Kizer presents her belief that nature has no malevolence toward man, that the two simply exist side by side. In "The Great Blue Heron," according to House, "the heron is a harbinger of death, but [Kizer] never suggests that the bird is evil. As a part of nature, he merely reflects the cycle of life and death that time imposes on all living creatures." In *The Ungrateful Garden,* House also sees Kizer emphasizing the distance between humans and nature, and also the perils of modern governments quashing

individual identity. Kizer demonstrates that a reprieve from the terrors of nature and government can be found in human relationships and especially in poetry. In the poem "From an Artist's House," for example, Kizer celebrates the unchanging nature of poetry. On the whole, D. J. Enright of the *New Statesman* feels there are "some remarkably good things in this strong-tasting collection, thick with catastrophes and fortitude."

Whereas *Poetry* critic William Dickey considers Kizer in *The Ungrateful Garden* to be "more concerned with the manner of [her poems'] expression than with the material to be expressed," *Saturday Review* contributor Richard Moore comments that Kizer's second poetry collection, *Knock upon Silence,* contains relaxed meters and simple diction: "There are no verbal fireworks, no fancy displays." As with much of Kizer's poetry, an Eastern influence is present in *Knock upon Silence* with its calm, cool, sensitive verse. *Knock upon Silence* consists of two long poems, "A Month in Summer" and "Pro Femina," a section called "Chinese Imitations," and several translations of the eighth-century Chinese poet Tu Fu. "She's at the top of her form, which is to say, devastating in her observations of the human animal," writes Gene Baro in the *New York Times Book Review.* "How true, one thinks, when this poet writes about feminine sensibility or about love."

Of *Knock upon Silence*'s two lengthier poems, "A Month in Summer" received mixed reviews. This diary of love gone sour, which contains both prose segments and occasional haiku, is viewed by Moore as the "weakest part of [Kizer's] book. . . . It is moving in places, witty in others; but there is also a tendency to be straggling and repetitive." In contrast, Bewley cites this piece as "the heart and triumph" of *Knock upon Silence:* "It manages to compress within a very few pages[,] alive with self-irony and submerged humor[,] more than most good novelists can encompass in a volume."

The other long selection in *Knock upon Silence* is "Pro Femina," a series of three conversational poems that discuss the role of the liberated woman in the modern world, particularly the woman writer. "Pro Femina" is a satiric piece keenly aware of the fact that women still confront obstacles related to their gender: "Keeping our heads and our pride while remaining unmarried; / And if wedded, kill guilt in its tracks when we stack up the dishes / And defect to the typewriter."

Kizer turns, in part, to different matters in her collection *Midnight Was My Cry: New and Selected Poems,* which contains several previously published poems and sixteen new ones. Though Kizer remains dedicated to meter and Eastern restraint—"the poet's mind continually judges, restrains, makes passion control itself," writes Eric Mottram in *Parnassus: Poetry in Review*—her newer poems express an interest in the social and political problems of the contemporary world, especially those of the 1960s. These poems center on anti-segregation sit-ins, Vietnam, and the loss of Robert Kennedy. For *Poetry* contributor Richard Howard, Kizer has "reinforced her canon by some dozen first-rate poems, observant, solicitous, lithe."

Catching the literary world a little by surprise, Kizer published two poetry volumes in 1984, *Mermaids in the Basement: Poems for Women* and *Yin: New Poems. Mermaids in the Basement* received minor critical attention, perhaps because it contains several poems from her previous collections, including "A Month in Summer" and "Pro Femina." According to Patricia

Hampl in the *New York Times Book Review,* "the craft for which . . . Kizer is known serves her well in [the poem] 'Thrall'; a remarkable compression allows her to review the entire disappointing history of her relationship with her father. . . . There is a great effort toward humor in these poems. But the tone is uneven; the humor, as well as the outrage, seems arch at times." *Yin,* in contrast, received a favorable critical reception from the outset, winning the Pulitzer Prize for poetry in 1985. "One could never say with certainty what 'a Carolyn Kizer poem' was—until now. . . . Now we know a Kizer poem is brave, witty, passionate, and not easily forgotten," proclaims *Poetry* critic Robert Phillips.

The word "yin" is Chinese for the feminine principle, and many of the poems in this award-winning collection focus on feminine perceptions and creativity. In her joint review of *Mermaids in the Basement* and *Yin,* Hampl considers the prose memoir in *Yin* entitled "A Muse" to be "a real find. . . . This piece, about . . . Kizer's extraordinary mother, is not only a fascinating portrait, but a model of detachment and self-revelation." "A Muse" examines Kizer's childhood feelings about the ambitions her mother had for her: "The poet describes a . . . mama smothering her precocious offspring with encouragement. . . . Only with the woman's death does the speaker's serious life as an artist begin," assessed Joel Conarroe in the *Washington Post Book World.* In addition, "Semele Recycled" is considered an imaginative treat with its description of a modern-day Semele symbolically torn apart at the sight of her lover and then made whole again.

Probably the most admired piece in the *Yin* collection is "Fanny." Written in Roman hexameter, this 224-line poem is the proposed diary of Robert Louis Stevenson's wife, Frances (Fanny), as she nurses her husband during the last years of his life. Remarks Kizer in Penelope Moffet's *Los Angeles Times* review: "'Fanny' is about what happens to women who are the surrogate of gifted men. Women who look after the great writers, whether mothers, sisters, wives or daughters. What they do with their creativity, because they can't engage in open or active competition. I think 'Fanny' [is] a political poem, if you consider feminism a political issue, as I do." In addition, Conarroe claims "Fanny" is "Keatsian in the sensuousness of its imagery, the laughing of its odors and textures. Kizer gives a shattering sense of a woman's sacrifice and isolation while communicating vividly the terrible beauty of the woman's obsession with her husband's health." Whereas Suzanne Juhasz in *Library Journal* considers *Yin* a "mixed bag, or blessing" and *New York Times Book Review* critic Anthony Libby writes that "despite many local triumphs, [*Yin*] is in many ways less striking, [and] technically and psychologically more self-conscious [than *Mermaids in the Basement*]," most reviewers agree with Phillips that *Yin* "is a marvelous book."

Although it is not common for her to write an overtly political poem, Kizer considers herself a political poet. Pleased by the fact that her second husband finds all of her poetry political, Kizer remarked to Moffet: "Because I do not feel that [it] is a steady undercurrent, just as feminism is, there are these parallel streams that I hope infuse everything that I do. And I find that stream getting more and more strong in my work. But I don't ever want to be hortatory or propagandistic." Moffet also quotes Kizer in regard to productivity: "I think a lot of younger poets get terrible anxiety that they'll be forgotten if they don't have a book all the time. Well, maybe they will be forgotten, but if they're any good they'll come back."

BIOGRAPHICAL/CRITICAL SOURCES:

BOOKS

Contemporary Authors Autobiography Series, Volume V, Gale, 1987.
Contemporary Literary Criticism, Gale, Volume XV, 1980, Volume XXXIX, 1986.
Dictionary of Literary Biography, Volume V: *American Poets since World War II,* Gale, 1980.
Howard, Richard, *Alone with America: Essays on the Art of Poetry in the United States since 1950,* Atheneum, 1969.
Kizer, Carolyn, *The Ungrateful Garden,* Indiana University Press, 1961.
Kizer, Carolyn, *Knock upon Silence,* Doubleday, 1965.

PERIODICALS

Library Journal, July, 1984.
Los Angeles Times, January 13, 1985.
New Statesman, August 31, 1962.
New York Review of Books, March 31, 1966.
New York Times Book Review, March 26, 1967, November 25, 1984, March 22, 1987.
Parnassus: Poetry in Review, fall-winter, 1972.
Poetry, November, 1961, August, 1972, March, 1985, November, 1985.
Saturday Review, July 22, 1961, December 25, 1965.
Tri-Quarterly, fall, 1966.
Washington Post, February 6, 1968.
Washington Post Book World, August 5, 1984.

—*Sketch by Cheryl Gottler*

*   *   *

KLUG, Ron(ald) 1939-

PERSONAL: Surname is pronounced "Kloog"; born June 26, 1939, in Milwaukee, Wis.; son of Harold A. (a factory worker) and Linda (Kavemeier) Klug; married Lynda Rae Hosler (an author), February 20, 1971; children: Rebecca, Paul, Hans. *Education:* Dr. Martin Luther College, B.S., 1962; graduate study at University of Wisconsin, Milwaukee, 1965-68. *Religion:* Lutheran.

ADDRESSES: Home—1115 South Division St., Northfield, Minn. 55057.

CAREER: St. Matthew Lutheran School, Oconomowoc, Wis., teacher, 1962-65; Concordia Publishing House, St. Louis, Mo., copywriter, 1968-69; Augsburg Publishing House, Minneapolis, Minn., book editor, 1970-76; American School, Fort Dauphin, Madagascar, missionary teacher, 1976-80; free-lance writer and editor, 1980—.

MEMBER: Society of Children's Book Writers.

WRITINGS:

Strange Young Man in the Desert: John the Baptist (juvenile), illustrated by Betty Wind, Concordia, 1971.
Lord, I've Been Thinking: Prayer Thoughts for High School Boys, Augsburg, 1978.
Psalms: A Guide to Prayer and Praise, Harold Shaw, 1979.
Following Christ: Prayers from the "Imitation of Christ" in the Language of Today, Concordia, 1981.
Philippians: God's Guide to Joy (adult), Harold Shaw, 1981.

How to Keep a Spiritual Journal, Thomas Nelson, 1982.
My Prayer Journal, Concordia, 1982.
Growing in Joy, Augsburg, 1983.
Job: God's Answer to Suffering, Harold Shaw, 1983.
You Promised, Lord, Augsburg, 1983.
Philippians: Living Joyfully (juvenile), Harold Shaw, 1983, published as *Philippians: Be Glad!,* 1986.
Psalms: Folk Songs of Faith, Harold Shaw, 1984.
Mark: A Daily Dialogue with God, Harold Shaw, 1984.
(With Joe Vaughn) *New Life for Men,* Augsburg, 1984.
Bible Readings on Prayer, Augsburg, 1986.

WITH WIFE, LYN KLUG

Family Prayers, Augsburg, 1979.
Please, God (juvenile), illustrated by Sally Mathews, Augsburg, 1980.
Thank You, God (juvenile), illustrated by Mathews, Augsburg, 1980.

I'm a Good Helper (juvenile), illustrated by Mathews, Augsburg, 1981.
My Christmas ABC Book (juvenile), illustrated by Jim Roberts, Augsburg, 1981.
Bible Readings for Parents, Augsburg, 1982.
(Editor) *Christian Family Bedtime Reading Book* (juvenile anthology), Augsburg, 1982.
Jesus Lives (juvenile), illustrated by Paul Konsterlie, Augsburg, 1983.
Jesus Comes (juvenile), illustrated by Konsterlie, Augsburg, 1986.
Jesus Loves (juvenile), illustrated by Konsterlie, Augsburg, 1986.
Christian Family Christmas Book (juvenile anthology), Augsburg, 1987.

OTHER

Editor of *Lutheran Libraries* (magazine).

L

LAMPLUGH, Lois 1921-

PERSONAL: Surname is pronounced "Lamploo"; born June 9, 1921, in Barnstaple, Devonshire, England; daughter of Aubrey Penfound and Ruth (Lister) Lamplugh; married Lawrence Carlile Davis (a sales representative), September 24, 1955; children: Susan Ruth, Hugh Lawrence. *Education:* B.A. (with honors), Open University, 1978.

ADDRESSES: Home—Springside, Bydown, Swimbridge, Devonshire EX32 0QB, England. *Agent*—A. P. Watt Ltd., 26/28 Bedford Row, London WC1R 4HL, England.

CAREER: Writer. Jonathan Cape Ltd., London, England, member of editorial staff, 1946-57; former part-time teacher at school for maladjusted boys. *Wartime service:* Served in Auxiliary Territorial Service, World War II.

MEMBER: Society of Authors, West Country Writers Association.

WRITINGS:

The Stream Way, Golden Galley Press, 1948.
Barnstaple: Town on the Taw, Phillimore, 1983.
A History of Ilfracombe, Phillimore, 1984.
Minehead and Dunster, Phillimore, 1987.

JUVENILES

Nine Bright Shiners, J. Cape, 1955.
The Pigeongram Puzzle, J. Cape, 1955, Verry, 1960.
Vagabonds' Castle, J. Cape, 1957, Verry, 1965.
Rockets in the Dunes, J. Cape, 1958.
The Sixpenny Runner, J. Cape, 1960.
Midsummer Mountains, J. Cape, 1961.
The Rifle House Friends, Deutsch, 1965.
The Linhay on Hunter's Hill, Deutsch, 1966.
The Fur Princess and Fir Prince, Dent, 1969.
(With Peter Dickinson) *Mandog,* BBC Publications, 1972.
Sean's Leap, Deutsch, 1979.
The Winter Donkey, Deutsch, 1980.
Falcon's Tor, Deutsch, 1984.

OTHER

Author of half-hour documentary "Coleridge," Harlech Television, 1966, and of over 300 five-minute stories for televi-sion, including "Honeyhill" series, Harlech Television, 1967-70.

WORK IN PROGRESS: A Shadowed Man, a biography of Henry Williamson.

SIDELIGHTS: Lois Lamplugh told *CA:* "It is possible that I became a writer simply because I happened to spend the first eighteen years of my life in or near the village of Georgeham [where] in the 1920s Henry Williamson was living—for part of the time in a cottage he rented from my grandmother. (He wrote most, if not all, of *Tarka the Otter* in that cottage.)"

A country child, Lamplugh still prefers country living, adding "for all that, I wrote my first children's books when I was living and working in London—perhaps a form of escape, since they were set in North Devon." She wrote a great deal of unpublished work, mainly novels and verse, in her teens and had a book accepted for publication by Faber in 1942. It was an account of her experiences in the Auxiliary Territorial Service, and the War Office withheld approval of publication on the grounds that it would discourage recruiting. The manuscript remains unpublished.

Sean's Leap arose from Lamplugh's experience of teaching at a school for maladjusted boys and was written "at intervals between courses [she was taking at the Open University] on 'Renaissance and Reformation,' 'The Nineteenth Century Novel,' and 'Twentieth Century Poetry.'" Lamplugh believes "the outlook for children's books in England is poor at present, with the cuts in spending affecting the buying of books for schools and children's libraries, and this is why I've been at work on books on the local history of places in southwest England in recent years," in addition to a "first attempt" at biography with a book on the life of children's author Henry Williamson. "Williamson," Lamplugh related, is "an obvious choice of subject, as he was a friend of my parents from 1923, and I possess a collection of letters from him written to them and, later, to myself."

AVOCATIONAL INTERESTS: Listening to music (especially Italian opera), gardening, walking.

BIOGRAPHICAL/CRITICAL SOURCES:

PERIODICALS

Times Literary Supplement, March 30, 1984.

LAN, David 1952-

PERSONAL: Born June 1, 1952, in Cape Town, South Africa; son of Chaim Joseph and Lois Lan. *Education:* University of Cape Town, B.A., 1972; London School of Economics and Political Science, B.Sc., 1976, Ph.D., 1983. *Politics:* Socialist.

ADDRESSES: Agent—Margaret Ramsay Ltd., 14-A Goodwin's Court, London WC2N 4LL, England.

CAREER: Playwright, 1974—. Worked as magician and puppeteer, 1966-69. Research associate, University of Zimbabwe, 1980-82.

MEMBER: Theatre Writers Union, Joint Stock Theatre Group.

AWARDS, HONORS: John Whiting Award from Arts Council of Great Britain, 1977, for "The Winter Dancers"; George Orwell Memorial Award, 1983; Raymond Firth Prize from London School of Economics, 1983.

WRITINGS:

Painting a Wall (one-act play; first produced in London, England, at Almost Free Theatre, April, 1974), Pluto Press, 1979.

Sergeant Ola and His Followers (play; first produced in London at Royal Court Theatre, October, 1979), Methuen, 1980.

Guns and Rain: Guerrillas and Spirit Mediums in Zimbabwe, University of California Press, 1985.

"The Sunday Judge" (teleplay), produced by the British Broadcasting Corp., 1985.

(With Caryl Churchill) *A Mouthful of Birds* (first produced in London at the Royal Court Theatre, November, 1986), Methuen, 1986.

Flight (first produced by the Royal Shakespeare Company in Stratford, England at The Other Place, April, 1986; produced in London, July, 1987), Methuen, 1987.

UNPUBLISHED PLAYS

"Bird Child," first produced in London at Royal Court Theatre Upstairs, May, 1974.

"Paradise," first produced in London at Royal Court Theatre Upstairs, May, 1975.

"Homage to Been Soup" (one-act), first produced in London at Royal Court Theatre Upstairs, June, 1975.

"The Winter Dancers," first produced in London at Royal Court Theatre Upstairs, 1977; produced Off-Broadway at the Phoenix Theatre, 1979.

"Not in Norwich," first produced in London at Royal Court Theatre Upstairs, 1977.

"Red Earth" (one-act), first produced in London at Institute of Contemporary Arts, October, 1978.

WORK IN PROGRESS: Projects for the National Theatre of Great Britain, Manchester Royal Exchange Theatre, and British Broadcasting Corporation.

BIOGRAPHICAL/CRITICAL SOURCES:

PERIODICALS

New York Times, February 3, 1987.
Times (London), April 9, 1986, November 29, 1986.
Times Literary Supplement, January 3, 1986.

LANDAU, Jacob M. 1924-

PERSONAL: Born March 20, 1924, in Chisinau, Romania; taken to Palestine in 1935; son of Michael (a civil servant) and Maria (a teacher; maiden name, Abeles) Landau; married Zipora Marcus (a teacher), July 29, 1947; children: Ronnit (daughter), Iddo (son). *Education:* Hebrew University of Jerusalem, M.A., 1946; School of Oriental and African Studies, Ph.D., 1949. *Religion:* Jewish.

ADDRESSES: Home—5 Mishael St., Jerusalem, Israel. *Office*—Department of Political Science, Hebrew University of Jerusalem, Jerusalem, Israel.

CAREER: Hebrew University of Jerusalem, Jerusalem, Israel, high school teacher, 1949-58, teaching fellow, 1958-62, senior lecturer, 1962-68, associate professor, 1968-74, professor of political science, 1974—. Visiting lecturer, Brandeis University, 1955-56; lecturer, University of Tel Aviv, 1956-59; visiting associate professor, University of California, Los Angeles, 1963-64; visiting professor, Wayne State University, 1968-69, Columbia University, 1969, University of Ankara, 1974, University of Texas at Austin, 1975, Candido Mendes University, Rio de Janeiro, 1975, and University of Utah, 1979. Fellow, Netherlands Institute for Advanced Study, 1983-84; senior research fellow, St. Antony's College, Oxford, 1987.

MEMBER: Israel Oriental Society, American Oriental Society, Middle East Studies Association of North America, Israel Association for Political Science (president, 1985-87), Academy of Political Science (New York).

AWARDS, HONORS: Fulbright travel grant, 1963; President Ben Zvi Memorial Award, 1968, for *Jews in Nineteenth-Century Egypt;* Itzhak Grunbaum Award, 1974, for *The Arabs in Israel: A Political Study;* Bosphorus University (Istanbul), Medal, 1981, for writings on modern Turkey.

WRITINGS:

Parliaments and Parties in Egypt, Praeger, 1954, reprinted, University Microfilm International, 1977.

Studies in the Arab Theater and Cinema, University of Pennsylvania Press, 1958.

A Word Count of Modern Arabic Prose, American Council of Learned Societies, 1958.

(Editor) *Teaching of Arabic as a Foreign Language* (in Hebrew), School of Education, Hebrew University, 1961.

(Editor) *Der Staat Israel,* Glock & Lutz (Nuernberg), 1964, 2nd edition, 1970.

(With M. M. Czudnowski) *The Israel Communist Party and the Elections for the Fifth Knesset, 1961,* Hoover Institution, 1965.

ha-Yehudim be-Mitsrayim ba-me'ah hatesha'-'esreh, Ben Zvi Institute, Hebrew University, 1967, revised edition translated and published as *Jews in Nineteenth-Century Egypt,* New York University Press, 1969.

(With H. A. R. Gibb) *Arabische Literaturgeschichte,* Artemis (Zurich), 1968.

The Arabs in Israel: A Political Study, Oxford University Press, for the Royal Institute of International Affairs, 1969.

The Hejaf Railway and the Muslim Pilgrimage: A Case of Ottoman Political Propaganda, Wayne State University Press, 1971.

(Editor) *Man, State and Society in the Contemporary Middle East,* Praeger, 1972.

Middle Eastern Themes: Papers in History and Politics, Cass, 1973.

Radical Politics in Modern Turkey, E. J. Brill, 1974.

The Arabs and the Histradut, Department of Higher Education (Tel Aviv), 1976.
Politics and Islam: The National Salvation Party in Turkey, University of Utah Press, 1976.
Abdul Hamid's Palestine, Deutsch, 1979.
Pan-Turkism in Turkey: A Study of Irredentism, Christopher Hurst, 1981.
Tekinalp, Turkish Patriot, Netherlands Historical Institute, 1984.
(Editor) *Ataturk and the Modernization of Turkey,* E. J. Brill, 1984.

Also contributor to several scholarly encyclopedias in Israel, Turkey, Holland, Greece, England, and the United States. Contributor to specialized journals, including *International Journal of the Sociology of Language, Middle Eastern Studies, Oriente Moderno, Western Political Quarterly, Bamah, Journal of Contemporary History,* and *Conscience et Liberte.*

SIDELIGHTS: Jacob M. Landau reads ten languages fluently: Hebrew, Arabic, Turkish, English, French, German, Italian, Spanish, Romanian, and Russian. *Studies in the Arab Theater and Cinema* has been translated into French and Arabic, *Arabische Literaturgeschichte* has been translated into Hebrew, and *Radical Politics in Modern Turkey* has been translated into Turkish.

BIOGRAPHICAL/CRITICAL SOURCES:

PERIODICALS

Times Literary Supplement, August 20, 1982.

*   *   *

LANGAN, Ruth Ryan   1937-

PERSONAL: Born December 12, 1937, in Detroit, Mich.; daughter of John Edward (a roofer and carpenter) and Beatrice (Curly) Ryan; married Thomas Joseph Langan (a bowling proprietor and developer), July 19, 1958; children: Thomas, Carol, Mary Margaret, Patrick, Michael. *Education:* Attended high school in Livonia, Mich. *Religion:* Roman Catholic.

ADDRESSES: Home—Southfield, Mich.

CAREER: General Cable Corp., Oak Park, Mich., secretary to the vice-president, 1955-59; writer. Participant in writing workshops throughout the United States. Guest on several television programs, including "Good Morning, America" and "Donahue."

MEMBER: Romance Writers of America (co-founder of Detroit chapter), Detroit Women Writers.

AWARDS, HONORS: Hidden Island, Beloved Gambler, Star Crossed, and *Nevada Nights* have all been finalists for Golden Medallion Award, Romance Writers of America.

WRITINGS:

ROMANCE AND ADVENTURE NOVELS

Just Like Yesterday, Simon & Schuster, 1981.
Hidden Island, Simon & Schuster, 1983.
Cross His Heart, Bantam, 1983.
Beloved Gambler, Silhouette Books, 1983.
No Gentle Love, Silhouette Books, 1984.
Eden of Temptation, Silhouette Books, 1984.
This Time Forever, Silhouette Books, 1985.
To Love a Dreamer, Silhouette Books, 1985.
Star Crossed, Silhouette Books, 1985.
Nevada Nights, Pocket Books, 1985.

Mysteries of the Heart, Silhouette Books, 1986.
Whims of Fate, Silhouette Books, 1986.
September's Dream, Pocket Books, 1986.
The Proper Miss Porter, Silhouette Books, 1987.
Destiny's Daughter, Pocket Books, 1987.
Passage West, Pocket Books, 1988.
The Heart's Secrets, Pocket Books, in press.

WORK IN PROGRESS: A romantic thriller set in Hollywood, Cannes, and the South Pacific; a contemporary romance set in Greece; a historical adventure/romance set in 1625 in England and France; a screenplay in collaboration with two other authors.

SIDELIGHTS: Ruth Ryan Langan told *CA:* "A lifelong interest in reading led to a decision to try writing. With the successful publication of my first novel, I knew that I would spend the rest of my life writing. I don't feel confined to any particular genre."

AVOCATIONAL INTERESTS: "Travel, nature, photography, and of course, reading everything and anything."

BIOGRAPHICAL/CRITICAL SOURCES:

PERIODICALS

Cosmopolitan, October, 1984.
Dayton Daily News, November 6, 1983.
Detroit Free Press, June 6, 1982.
Detroit News, July 1, 1984.
Michigan Woman, May, 1987.
Romance Writers Report, March/April, 1986.
Wall Street Journal, February 17, 1984.

*   *   *

LARKIN, Philip (Arthur)   1922-1985

PERSONAL: Born August 9, 1922, in Coventry, Warwickshire, England; died following surgery for throat cancer, December 2, 1985, in Hull, England; son of Sydney (a city treasurer) and Eva Emily (Day) Larkin. *Education:* St. John's College, Oxford, B.A. (with first class honors), 1943, M.A., 1947.

ADDRESSES: Office—Library, University of Hull, Yorkshire, England.

CAREER: Wellington Public Library, Wellington, England, librarian, 1943-46; University College Library, Leicester, England, librarian, 1946-50; Queen's University Library, Belfast, Ireland, sublibrarian, 1950-55; University of Hull, Hull, England, librarian, 1955-85. Visiting fellow at All Souls College, Oxford University, 1970-71; chairman of judges for Booker Prize, 1977; caretaker of National Manuscript Collection of Contemporary Writers for Arts Council of Great Britain; member of standing conference of national and university libraries.

MEMBER: Arts Council of Great Britain (member of literature panel), Poetry Book Society (former chairman), American Academy of Arts and Sciences (honorary member).

AWARDS, HONORS: Queen's Gold medal for Poetry, 1965; Loines Award from National Institute and American Academy of Arts and Letters, 1974; Commander, Order of the British Empire, 1975; Shakespeare prize from FVS Foundation (Hamburg, West Germany), 1976; Commander of Literature, 1978; W. H. Smith & Son Literary Award, 1985, for *Required Writing: Miscellaneous Pieces, 1955-82.*

WRITINGS:

The North Ship (poems), Fortune Press, 1946, new edition, Faber, 1966.

Jill (novel), Fortune Press, 1946, revised edition, St. Martin's, 1964, reprinted, Overlook Press, 1984.

A Girl in Winter (novel), Faber, 1947, St. Martin's, 1957.

XX Poems, [Belfast], 1951.

The Less Deceived (poems), Marvell Press, 1955, 4th edition, St. Martin's, 1958.

The Whitsun Weddings (poems), Random House, 1964.

All What Jazz: A Record Diary 1961-1968 (essays), St. Martin's, 1970, updated edition published as *All What Jazz: A Record Diary 1961-1971*, Farrar, Straus, 1985.

(Editor and contributor) *The Oxford Book of Twentieth-Century English Verse*, Oxford University Press, 1973.

High Windows (poems), Farrar, Straus, 1974.

Required Writing: Miscellaneous Pieces 1955-1982 (essays), Faber, 1983, Farrar, Straus, 1984.

RECORDINGS

Listen Presents Philip Larkin Reading "The Less Deceived," Marvell Press, 1959.

Philip Larkin Reads and Comments on "The Whitsun Weddings," Marvell Press, ca. 1966.

British Poets of Our Time, Philip Larkin: "High Windows," Poems Read by the Author, Arts Council of Great Britian, ca. 1975.

OTHER

Also editor, with Louis MacNeice and Bonamy Dobree, of *New Poets 1958*. Contributor to numerous anthologies; contributor of poetry and essays to periodicals. Jazz critic for *Daily Telegraph* (London), 1961-71.

SIDELIGHTS: Philip Larkin, a preeminent writer in postwar Great Britain, was commonly referred to as "England's *other* Poet Laureate" until his death in 1985. Indeed, when the position of Laureate became vacant in 1984, many poets and critics favored Larkin's appointment, but the shy, provincial author preferred to avoid the limelight. An "artist of the first rank" in the words of *Southern Review* contributor John Press, Larkin achieved acclaim on the strength of an extremely small body of work—just over one hundred pages of poetry in four slender volumes that appeared at almost decade-long intervals. These collections, especially *The Less Deceived, The Whitsun Weddings*, and *High Windows*, present "a poetry from which even people who distrust poetry, most people, can take comfort and delight," according to X. J. Kennedy in the *New Criterion*. Larkin employed the traditional tools of poetry—rhyme, stanza, and meter—to explore the often uncomfortable or terrifying experiences thrust upon common people in the modern age. As Alan Brownjohn notes in *Philip Larkin*, the poet produced without fanfare "the most technically brilliant and resonantly beautiful, profoundly disturbing yet appealing and approachable, body of verse of any English poet in the last twenty-five years."

Despite his wide popularity, Larkin refused to make poetry his sole means of support by teaching or giving readings. Instead he worked as a professional librarian for more than forty years and wrote in his spare time. In that manner he authored two novels, *Jill* and *A Girl in Winter*, two collections of criticism, *All What Jazz: A Record Diary 1961-1968* and *Required Writing: Miscellaneous Pieces 1955-1982*, and all of his verse. *Phoenix* contributor Alun R. Jones suggests that, as a wage earner at the remote University of Hull, Larkin "avoided the literary, the metropolitan, the group label, and embraced the nonliterary, the provincial, and the purely personal." In *Nine Contemporary Poets: A Critical Introduction*, Peter R. King likewise commends "the scrupulous awareness of a man who refuses to be taken in by inflated notions of either art or life." From his base in Hull, Larkin composed poetry that both reflects the dreariness of postwar provincial England and voices "most articulately and poignantly the spiritual desolation of a world in which men have shed the last rags of religious faith that once lent meaning and hope to human lives," according to Press. Critics feel that this localization of focus and the colloquial language used to describe settings and emotions endear Larkin to his readers. *Agenda* reviewer George Dekker notes that no living poet "can equal Larkin on his own ground of the familiar English lyric, drastically and poignantly limited in its sense of any life beyond, before or after, life today in England."

Throughout his life, England was Larkin's emotional territory to an eccentric degree. The poet distrusted travel abroad and professed ignorance of foreign literature, including most modern American poetry. He also tried to avoid the cliches of his own culture, such as the tendency to read portent into an artist's childhood. In his poetry and essays, Larkin remembered his early years as "unspent" and "boring," as he grew up the son of a city treasurer in Coventry. Poor eyesight and stuttering plagued Larkin as a youth; he retreated into solitude, read widely, and began to write poetry as a nightly routine. In 1940 he enrolled at Oxford, beginning "a vital stage in his personal and literary development," according to Bruce K. Martin in the *Dictionary of Literary Biography*. At Oxford Larkin studied English literature and cultivated the friendship of those who shared his special interests, including Kingsley Amis and John Wain. He graduated with first class honors in 1943, and, having to account for himself with the wartime Ministry of Labor, he took a position as librarian in the small Shropshire town of Wellington. While there he wrote both of his novels as well as *The North Ship*, his first volume of poetry. After working at several other university libraries, Larkin moved to Hull in 1955 and began a thirty-year association with the library at the University of Hull. He is still admired for his expansion and modernization of that facility.

In a *Paris Review* interview, Larkin dismissed the notion that he studied the techniques of poets that he admired in order to perfect his craft. Most critics feel, however, that the poems of both William Butler Yeats and Thomas Hardy exerted an influence on Larkin as he sought his own voice. Martin suggests that the pieces in *The North Ship* "reflect an infatuation with Yeatsian models, a desire to emulate the Irishman's music without having undergone the experience upon which it had been based." Hardy's work provided the main impetus to Larkin's mature poetry, according to critics. King contends that a close reading of Hardy taught Larkin "that a modern poet could write about the life around him in the language of the society around him. He encouraged [Larkin] to use his poetry to examine the reality of his own life.... As a result Larkin abandoned the highly romantic style of *The North Ship*, which had been heavily influenced by the poetry of Yeats, and set out to write from the tensions that underlay his own everyday experiences. Hardy also supported his employment of traditional forms and technique, which Larkin [went] on to use with subtlety and variety." In his work *Philip Larkin*, Martin also claims that Larkin learned from Hardy "that his own life, with its often casual discoveries, could become poems, and that he could legitimately share such experience with his readers. From this lesson [came Larkin's] belief that a poem is better based on something from 'unsorted' experience than on another poem or other art.''

Not surprisingly, this viewpoint allied Larkin with the poets of The Movement, a loose association of British writers who "called, implicitly in their poetry and fiction and explicitly in critical essays, for some sort of commonsense return to more traditional techniques," according to Martin in *Philip Larkin*. Martin adds that the rationale for this "antimodernist, antiexperimental stance is their stated concern with clarity: with writing distinguished by precision rather than obscurity. . . . [The Movement urged] not an abandonment of emotion, but a mixture of rationality with feeling, of objective control with subjective abandon. Their notion of what they felt the earlier generation of writers, particularly poets, lacked, centered around the ideas of honesty and realism about self and about the outside world." King observes that Larkin "had sympathy with many of the attitudes to poetry represented by The Movement," but this view of the poet's task antedated the beginnings of that group's influence. Nonetheless, in the opinion of *Washington Post Book World* contributor Chad Walsh, Larkin "seemed to fulfill the credo of the Movement better than anyone else, and he was often singled out, as much for damnation as for praise, by those looking for the ultimate Movement poet." Brownjohn concludes that in the company of The Movement, Larkin's own "distinctive technical skills, the special subtlety in his adaptation of a very personal colloquial mode to the demands of tight forms, were not immediately seen to be outstanding; but his strengths as a craftsman have increasingly come to be regarded as one of the hallmarks of his talent."

Those strengths of craftsmanship and technical skill in Larkin's mature works receive almost universal approval from literary critics. *Sunday Times* correspondent Ian Hamilton writes: "Supremely among recent poets, [Larkin] was able to accommodate a talking voice to the requirements of strict metres and tight rhymes, and he had a faultless ear for the possibilities of the iambic line." David Timms expresses a similar view in his book entitled *Philip Larkin*. Technically, notes Timms, Larkin was "an extraordinarily various and accomplished poet, a poet who [used] the devices of metre and rhyme for specific effects. . . . His language is never flat, unless he intends it to be so for a particular reason, and his diction is never stereotyped. He [was] always ready . . . to reach across accepted literary boundaries for a word that will precisely express what he intends." As King explains, Larkin's best poems "are rooted in actual experiences and convey a sense of place and situation, people and events, which gives an authenticity to the thoughts that are then usually raised by the poet's observation of the scene. . . . Joined with this strength of careful social observation is a control over tone changes and the expression of developing feelings even within a single poem . . . which is the product of great craftsmanship. To these virtues must be added the fact that in all the poems there is a lucidity of language which invites understanding even when the ideas expressed are paradoxical or complex." *New Leader* contributor Pearl K. Bell concludes that Larkin's poetry "fits with unresisting precision into traditional structures, . . . filling them with the melancholy truth of things in the shrunken, vulgarized and parochial England of the 1970s."

If Larkin's style is traditional, the subject matter of his poetry is derived exclusively from modern life. Press contends that Larkin's artistic work "delineates with considerable force and delicacy the pattern of contemporary sensibility, tracing the

way in which we respond to our environment, plotting the ebb and flow of the emotional flux within us, embodying in his poetry attitudes of heart and mind that seem peculiarly characteristic of our time: doubt, insecurity, boredom, aimlessness and malaise." A sense that life is a finite prelude to oblivion underlies many of Larkin's poems. King suggests that the work is "a poetry of disappointment, of the destruction of romantic illusions, of man's defeat by time and his own inadequacies," as well as a study of how dreams, hopes and ideals "are relentlessly diminished by the realities of life." To Larkin, Brownjohn notes, life was never "a matter of blinding revelations, mystical insights, expectations glitteringly fulfilled. Life, for Larkin, and, implicitly, for all of us, is something lived mundanely, with a gradually accumulating certainty that its golden prizes are sheer illusion." Love is one of the supreme deceptions of humankind in Larkin's world view, as King observes: "Although man clutches at his instinctive belief that only love will comfort, console and sustain him, such a hope is doomed to be denied. A lover's promise is an empty promise and the power to cure suffering through love is a tragic illusion." Stanley Poss in *Western Humanities Review* maintains that Larkin's poems demonstrate "desperate clarity and restraint and besieged common sense. And what they mostly say is, be beginning to despair, despair, despair."

Larkin arrived at his conclusions candidly, concerned to expose evasions so that the reader might stand "naked but honest, 'less deceived' . . . before the realities of life and death," to quote King. Many critics find Larkin withdrawn from his poems, a phenomenon Martin describes in the *Dictionary of Literary Biography* thusly: "The unmarried observer, a staple in Larkin's poetic world, . . . enjoys only a curious and highly limited kind of communion with those he observes." Jones likewise declares that Larkin's "ironic detachment is comprehensive. Even the intense beauty that his poetry creates is created by balancing on a keen ironic edge." King writes: "A desire not to be fooled by time leads to a concern to maintain vigilance against a whole range of possible evasions of reality. It is partly this which makes Larkin's typical stance one of being to one side of life, watching himself and others with a detached eye." Although *Harvard Advocate* contributor Andrew Sullivan states that the whole tenor of Larkin's work is that of an "irrelevant and impotent spectator," John Reibetanz offers the counter suggestion in *Contemporary Literature* that the poetry records and reflects "the imperfect, transitory experiences of the mundane reality that the poet shares with his readers." Larkin himself offered a rather wry description of his accomplishments—an assessment that, despite its levity, links him emotionally to his work. In 1979, he told the *Observer*: "I think writing about unhappiness is probably the source of my popularity, if I have any. . . . Deprivation is for me what daffodils were for Wordsworth."

Critics such as *Dalhousie Review* contributor Roger Bowen find moments of affirmation in Larkin's poetry, notwithstanding its pessimistic and cynical bent. According to Bowen, an overview of Larkin's oeuvre makes evident "that the definition of the poet as a modern anti-hero governed by a sense of his own mortality seems . . . justified. But . . . a sense of vision and a quiet voice of celebration seem to be asserting themselves" in at least some of the poems. Brownjohn admits that Larkin's works take a bleak view of human existence; at the same time, however, they contain "the recurrent reflection that others, particularly the young, might still find happiness in expectation." *Contemporary Literature* essayist James Naremore expands on Larkin's tendency to detach himself from the action in his poems: "From the beginning, Larkin's work has manifested a certain coolness and lack of self-esteem, a need to withdraw from experience; but at the same time it has continued to show his desire for a purely secular type of romance. . . . Larkin is trying to assert his humanity, not deny it. . . . The greatest virtue in Larkin's poetry is not so much his suppression of large poetic gestures as his ability to recover an honest sense of joy and beauty." The *New York Times* quotes Larkin as having said that a poem "represents the mastering, even if just for a moment, of the pessimism and the melancholy, and enables you—you the poet, and you, the reader—to go on." King senses this quiet catharsis when he concludes: "Although one's final impression of the poetry is certainly that the chief emphasis is placed on a life 'unspent' in the shadow of 'untruth,' moments of beauty and affirmation are not entirely denied. It is the difficulty of experiencing such moments after one has become so aware of the numerous self-deceptions that man practices on himself to avoid the uncomfortable reality which lies at the heart of Larkin's poetic identity."

Timms claims that Larkin "consistently maintained that a poet should write about those things in life that move him most deeply: if he does not feel deeply about anything, he should not write." Dedicated to reaching out for his readers, the poet was a staunch opponent of modernism in all artistic media. Larkin felt that such cerebral experimentation ultimately creates a barrier between an artist and the audience and provides unnecessary thematic complications. Larkin's "demand for fidelity to experience is supported by his insistence that poetry should both communicate and give pleasure to the reader," King notes, adding: ". . . It would be a mistake to dismiss this attitude as a form of simple literary conservatism. Larkin is not so much expressing an anti-intellectualism as attacking a particular form of artistic snobbery." In *Philip Larkin*, Martin comments that the poet saw the need for poetry to move toward the "paying customer." Therefore, his writings concretize "many of the questions which have perplexed man almost since his beginning but which in modern times have become the province principally of academicians. . . . [Larkin's poetry reflects] his faith in the common reader to recognize and respond to traditional philosophical concerns when stripped of undue abstractions and pretentious labels." Brownjohn finds Larkin eminently successful in his aims: "It is indeed true that many of his readers find pleasure and interest in Larkin's poetry for its apparent accessibility and its cultivation of verse forms that seem reassuringly traditional rather than 'modernist' in respect of rhyme and metre." As Timms succinctly notes, originality for Larkin consisted "not in modifying the medium of communication, but in communicating something different."

Larkin's output of fiction and essays is hardly more extensive than his poetry. His two novels, *Jill* and *A Girl in Winter*, were both published before his twenty-fifth birthday. *New Statesman* correspondent Clive James feels that both novels "seem to point forward to the poetry. Taken in their chronology, they are impressively mature and self-sufficient." James adds that the fiction is so strong that "if Larkin had never written a line of verse, his place as a writer would still have been secure." Although the novels received little critical attention when they first appeared, they have since been judged highly successful. Brownjohn calls *Jill* "one of the better novels written about England during the Second World War, not so much for any conscious documentary effort put into it as for Larkin's characteristic scrupulousness in getting all the

background details right." In the *New York Review of Books*, John Bayley notes that *A Girl in Winter* is "a real masterpiece, a quietly gripping novel, dense with the humor that is Larkin's trademark, and also an extended prose poem." Larkin's essay collections, *Required Writing* and *All What Jazz*, are compilations of critical pieces he wrote for periodicals over a thirty year period, including the jazz record reviews he penned as a music critic for the London *Daily Telegraph*. "Everything Larkin writes is concise, elegant and wholly original," Bayley claims in the *Listener*, "and this is as true of his essays and reviews as it is of his poetry." Elsewhere in the *New York Review of Books*, Bayley comments that *Required Writing* "reveals wide sympathies, deep and trenchant perceptions, a subterranean grasp of the whole of European culture." And in an essay on *All What Jazz* for Anthony Thwaite's *Larkin at Sixty*, James concludes that "no wittier book of criticism has ever been written."

Larkin stopped writing poetry shortly after his collection *High Windows* was published in 1974. In an *Observer* obituary, Kingsley Amis characterized the poet as "a man much driven in upon himself, with increasing deafness from early middle age cruelly emphasizing his seclusion." Small though it is, Larkin's body of work has "altered our awareness of poetry's capacity to reflect the contemporary world," according to *London Magazine* correspondent Roger Garfitt. A. N. Wilson draws a similar conclusion in the *Spectator*: "Perhaps the reason Larkin made such a great name from so small an *oeuvre* was that he so exactly caught the mood of so many of us. . . . Larkin found the perfect voice for expressing our worst fears." That voice was "stubbornly indigenous," according to Robert B. Shaw in *Poetry Nation*. Larkin appealed primarily to the British sensibility; he remained unencumbered by any compunction to universalize his poems by adopting a less regional idiom. Perhaps as a consequence, his poetry sells remarkably well in Great Britain, his readers come from all walks of life, and his untimely cancer-related death in 1985 has not diminished his popularity. Andrew Sullivan feels that Larkin "has spoken to the English in a language they can readily understand of the profound self-doubt that this century has given them. He was, of all English poets, a laureate too obvious to need official recognition."

BIOGRAPHICAL/CRITICAL SOURCES:

BOOKS

Alvarez, A., *All This Fiddle: Essays 1955-1967*, Random House, 1969.
Bayley, John, *The Uses of Division*, Viking, 1976.
Bedient, Calvin, *Eight Contemporary Poets*, Oxford University Press, 1974.
Bloomfield, B. C., *Philip Larkin: A Bibliography*, Faber, 1979.
Brownjohn, Alan, *Philip Larkin*, Longman, 1975.
Contemporary Literary Criticism, Gale, Volume III, 1975, Volume V, 1976, Volume VIII, 1978, Volume IX, 1978, Volume XIII, 1980, Volume XVIII, 1981, Volume XXXIII, 1985, Volume XXXIX, 1986.
Davie, Donald, *Thomas Hardy and British Poetry*, Oxford University Press, 1972.
Dictionary of Literary Biography, Volume XXVII: *Poets of Great Britain and Ireland, 1945-1960*, Gale, 1984.
Dodsworth, Martin, editor, *The Survival of Poetry: A Contemporary Survey*, Faber, 1970.
Enright, D. J., *Conspirators and Poets: Reviews and Essays*, Dufour, 1966.

Jones, Peter and Michael Schmidt, editors, *British Poetry since 1970: A Critical Survey,* Carcanet, 1980.

King, Peter R., *Nine Contemporary Poets: A Critical Introduction,* Methuen, 1979.

Kuby, Lolette, *An Uncommon Poet for the Common Man: A Study of Philip Larkin's Poetry,* Mouton, 1974.

Martin, Bruce K., *Philip Larkin,* Twayne, 1978.

Motion, Andrew, *Philip Larkin,* Methuen, 1982.

O'Connor, William Van, *The New University Wits and the End of Modernism,* Southern Illinois University Press, 1963.

Petch, Simon, *The Art of Philip Larkin,* Sydney University Press, 1981.

Rosenthal M. L., *The Modern Poets: A Critical Introduction,* Oxford University Press, 1960.

Rosenthal, M. L., *The New Poets: American and British Poetry since World War II,* Oxford University Press, 1967.

Schmidt, Michael, *A Reader's Guide to Fifty Modern British Poets,* Barnes & Noble, 1979.

Thwaite, Anthony, editor, *Larkin at Sixty,* Faber, 1982.

Timms, David, *Philip Larkin,* Barnes & Noble, 1973.

PERIODICALS

Agenda, autumn, 1974, summer, 1976.
American Scholar, summer, 1965.
Atlantic, January, 1966.
Bucknell Review, December, 1965.
Chicago Review, Volume XVIII, number 2, 1965.
Contemporary Literature, summer, 1974, autumn, 1976.
Critical Inquiry, Number 3, 1976-1977.
Critical Quarterly, summer, 1964, summer, 1981.
Dalhousie Review, spring, 1968, spring, 1978.
ELH, December, 1971.
Encounter, June, 1974, February, 1984.
Harvard Advocate, May, 1968.
Iowa Review, fall, 1977.
Journal of English Literary History, December, 1971.
Listener, January 26, 1967, March 26, 1970, December 22, 1983.
London Magazine, May, 1964, November, 1964, June, 1970, October-November, 1974, April-May, 1980.
Los Angeles Times, June 13, 1984.
Los Angeles Times Book Review, December 1, 1985.
Michigan Quarterly Review, fall, 1976.
New Criterion, February, 1986.
New Leader, May 26, 1975.
New Republic, March 6, 1965, November 20, 1976.
New Review, June, 1974.
New Statesman, June 14, 1974, July 26, 1974, March 21, 1975.
Newsweek, June 25, 1984.
New Yorker, December 6, 1976.
New York Review of Books, January 28, 1965, May 15, 1975.
New York Times, June 23, 1984, August 11, 1984.
New York Times Book Review, December 20, 1964, January 12, 1975, May 16, 1976, December 26, 1976, August 12, 1984, November 10, 1985.
Observer, February 8, 1970, December 16, 1979, November 20, 1983.
Paris Review, summer, 1982.
Phoenix, autumn and winter, 1973-74, spring, 1975.
PN Review, Volume IV, number 2, 1977.
Poetry Nation, Number 6, 1976.
Poetry Review, Volume LXXII, number 2, 1982.
Prairie Schooner, fall, 1975.

Review, June-July, 1962, December, 1964.
Southern Review, winter, 1977.
Stand, Volume XVI, number 2, 1975.
Time, July 23, 1984.
Times (London), December 8, 1983, June 20, 1985.
Times Literary Supplement, January 6, 1984.
Virginia Quarterly Review, spring, 1976.
Washington Post Book World, January 12, 1975.
Western Humanities Review, spring, 1962, autumn, 1975.

OBITUARIES:

PERIODICALS

Globe and Mail (Toronto), December 14, 1985.
Listener, December 12, 1985.
Los Angeles Times, December 3, 1985.
New Criterion, February, 1986.
New Republic, January 6 and 13, 1986.
New York Review of Books, January 16, 1986.
New York Times, December 3, 1985.
Observer, December 8, 1985.
Spectator, December 7, 1985.
Sunday Times (London), December 8, 1985.
Times (London), December 3, 1985, December 14, 1985.
Times Literary Supplement, January 24, 1986.
Washington Post, December 3, 1985.†

—*Sketch by Anne Janette Johnson*

*   *   *

LARSON, Muriel   1924-

PERSONAL: Born February 9, 1924, in Orange, N.J.; daughter of Eugene Louis and Helen (Fretz) Koller; children: Gay Maloney, Lori Rennie. *Education:* South River Bible Institute, diploma, 1957; Bob Jones University, additional study, 1967-69. *Politics:* Republican. *Religion:* Baptist.

ADDRESSES: Home—10 Vanderbilt Cir., Greenville, S.C. 29609.

CAREER: Stenographer with printing company in Dunellen, N.J., 1955-57, and with Tennessee Valley Authority, Chattanooga, 1962-63; Bob Jones University, Greenville, S.C., public relations writer, 1967-69; full-time writer, 1969—. Lecturer on creative writing. Has also served as a piano teacher, choir director, substitute teacher, home missionary, children's evangelist, church organist, and instructor at writers' conferences.

WRITINGS:

Devotions for Women's Groups, Baker Book, 1967.
How to Give a Devotion, Baker Book, 1967.
(Contributor) James R. Adair, editor, *God's Power to Triumph,* Moody, 1968.
Devotionals for Children's Groups, Baker Book, 1969.
(Contributor) Adair, editor, *Unhooked,* Baker Book, 1971.
Living Miracles, Warner Press, 1973.
It Took a Miracle, Warner Press, 1974.
You Are What You Think, Bible Voice, 1974.
God's Fantastic Creation, Moody, 1975.
The Bible Says Quiz Book, Moody, 1976.
Are You Real, God?, Bible Voice, 1976.
(Contributor) Grace Fox, editor, *The Hairy Brown Angel,* Victor Books, 1977.

I Give Up, God, Bible Voice, 1978.
Joy Every Morning, Moody, 1979.
What Happens When Women Believe, Bible Voice, 1979.
(Contributor) Ted Miller and Adair, editors, *Escape from Darkness,* Victor Books, 1982.
Living by Faith, Aglow, 1984.
Praise Every Day, Huntington House, 1984.
Ways Women Can Witness (Round Table Book Club book-of-the-month selection), Broadman, 1984.
Me and My Pet Peeves, Broadman, 1988.

Also author of play, "Miracles," and of gospel hymns and choruses. Contributor of numerous articles, stories, devotionals, and poems to *Moody Monthly, Home Life, Grit, Discipleship Journal, Reader's Digest,* and many other periodicals. Also prepares crossword puzzles for several publishers. Editor, *Reinhearter* (monthly church paper), Dallas, Tex., 1966-67.

WORK IN PROGRESS: Answers for Abused Wives; Morning Glories; Escape from Sodom.

SIDELIGHTS: Muriel Larson wrote *CA:* "I have always been interested in writing and started while in high school by writing for the school paper and preparing the social column for my town for a weekly paper.

"I began my career as a writer while a minister's wife. When I attended a national conference with my husband, a woman writer addressed us women and inspired me to start writing. The two stories I wrote on the way home from that conference were accepted eventually by two periodicals, and I was in business. Since then I have had more than forty-five hundred first and reprint right writings accepted for publication by over two hundred periodicals, as well as my sixteen books, seventeen gospel songs, and one play for radio.

"My main purpose in writing is to glorify God and point other people to Him, for I have found a wonderful life in serving and trusting the Lord. The purpose behind all my writings is to help others find the truth of God that leads to the abundant life He promised those who commit their way unto Him.

"The most important advice I give to aspiring writers at the conferences at which I teach is to keep trying. Persistence, perseverance, and self-discipline are necessary for success. Also, when you start submitting your work to editors, send two to four articles out to several places. Then if one is accepted, it encourages you to continue on. If you just send one out and it is rejected, you tend to lose heart and fall by the wayside."

AVOCATIONAL INTERESTS: Music (plays piano, organ, accordian, electronic keyboard, clarinet, and sings), gardening, camping.

*   *   *

LAUBER, Patricia (Grace)   1924-

PERSONAL: Born February 5, 1924, in New York, N.Y.; daughter of Hubert Crow (an engineer) and Florence (Walker) Lauber; married Russell Frost III, 1981. *Education:* Wellesley College, B.A., 1945.

ADDRESSES: Agent—McIntosh & Otis, Inc., 475 Fifth Ave., New York, N.Y. 10017.

CAREER: Writer of children's books, 1954—. *Look,* New York City, writer, 1945-46; Scholastic Magazines, New York City, writer and editor, 1946-55; Street & Smith, New York City, editor-in-chief of *Science World,* 1956-59; Grolier, Inc., New York City, chief editor, science and mathematics, *The New Book of Knowledge,* 1961-66.

AWARDS, HONORS: American Book Award nomination for children's nonfiction, 1982, for *Seeds Pop, Stick, Glide,* and 1983, for *Journey to the Planets; Washington Post*/Children's Book Guild Award, 1983, for her overall contribution to children's nonfiction literature; *Tales Mummies Tell* was named New York Academy of Sciences Honor Book, 1986; *Volcano: The Eruption and Healing of Mount St. Helen's* was named Newbery Honor Book, 1987.

WRITINGS:

JUVENILE NONFICTION

Magic up Your Sleeve, Teen-Age Book Club, 1954.
Battle against the Sea: How the Dutch Made Holland, Coward, 1956 (published in England as *Battle against the Sea: The Challenge of the Dutch and the Dikes,* Chatto & Windus, 1963), revised edition, 1971.
Highway to Adventure: The River Rhone of France, Coward, 1956.
Valiant Scots: People of the Highlands Today, Coward, 1957.
Penguins on Parade, Coward, 1958.
Dust Bowl: The Story of Man on the Great Plains, Coward, 1958.
Rufus: the Red-Necked Hornbill, Coward, 1958.
The Quest of Galileo, Doubleday, 1959.
Our Friend the Forest: A Conservation Story, Doubleday, 1959.
Changing the Face of North America: The Challenge of the St. Lawrence Seaway, Coward, 1959, revised edition, 1968.
All about the Ice Age, Random House, 1959.
Getting to Know Switzerland, Coward, 1960.
The Quest of Louis Pasteur, Doubleday, 1960.
All about the Planets, Random House, 1960.
The Story of Numbers, Random House, 1961.
Junior Science Book of Icebergs and Glaciers, Garrard, 1961.
The Mississippi: Giant at Work, Garrard, 1961.
Famous Mysteries of the Sea, Thomas Nelson, 1962.
All about the Planet Earth, Random House, 1962.
Your Body and How It Works, Random House, 1962.
The Friendly Dolphins, Random House, 1963.
Junior Science Book of Penguins, Garrard, 1963.
The Congo: River into Central Africa, Garrard, 1964.
Big Dreams and Small Rockets: A Short History of Space Travel, Crowell, 1965.
The Surprising Kangaroos and Other Pouched Mammals, Random House, 1965.
Junior Science Book of Volcanoes, Garrard, 1965.
The Story of Dogs, Random House, 1966.
The Look-It-Up Book of Mammals, Random House, 1967.
The Look-It-Up Book of Stars and Planets, Random House, 1967.
The Look-It-Up Book of the Fifty States, Random House, 1967.
Bats: Wings in the Night, Random House, 1968.
The Planets, Random House, 1968.
This Restless Earth, Random House, 1970.
Who Discovered America?: Settlers and Explorers of the New World before the Time of Columbus, Random House, 1970.
Of Man and Mouse: How House Mice Became Laboratory Mice, Viking, 1971.

Earthquakes: New Scientific Ideas about Why the Earth Shakes, Random House, 1973.
Everglades: A Question of Life or Death, Viking, 1973.
Cowboys and Cattle Ranching, Crowell, 1973.
Who Needs Alligators?, Garrard, 1974.
Life on a Giant Cactus, Garrard, 1974.
Too Much Garbage, Garrard, 1974.
Great Whales, Garrard, 1975.
Earthworms: Underground Farmers, Garrard, 1976.
Sea Otters and Seaweed, Garrard, 1976.
Mystery Monsters of Loch Ness, Garrard, 1978.
Tapping Earth's Heat, Garrard, 1978.
What's Hatching Out of That Egg?, Crown, 1979.
Seeds Pop, Stick, Glide, Crown, 1981.
Journey to the Planets, Crown, 1982, revised edition, 1987.
Tales Mummies Tell, Crowell, 1985.
What Big Teeth You Have!, Crowell, 1986.
Get Ready for Robots, Crowell, 1986.
Volcano: The Eruption and Healing of Mount St. Helens, Bradbury, 1986.
Dinosaurs Walked Here and Other Stories Fossils Tell, Bradbury, 1986.
From Flower to Flower: Animals and Pollination, Crown, 1986.
Snakes Are Hunters, Crowell, 1987.
Asteroids and Comets: Voyagers from Space, Crowell, 1987.

JUVENILE FICTION

Clarence, the TV Dog, Coward, 1955.
Clarence Goes to Town, Coward, 1957.
Found: One Orange-Brown Horse, Random House, 1957.
The Runaway Flea Circus, Random House, 1958.
Clarence Turns Sea Dog, Coward, 1959.
Adventure at Black Rock Cave, Random House, 1959.
Champ, Gallant Collie, Random House, 1960.
Curious Critters, Garrard, 1969.
Clarence and the Burglar, illustrations by Paul Galdone, Coward, 1973.
Clarence and the Cat (Junior Literary Guild selection), illustrations by P. Galdone, Coward, 1977.
Home at Last: A Young Cat's Tale, illustrations by Mary Chalmers, Coward, 1980.

OTHER

Contributor of adult short stories and light essays to magazines. Former editor of Coward's "Challenge Books" and Garrard's "Good Earth" series; free-lance editor, *Scientific American Illustrated Library.*

WORK IN PROGRESS: Two books of light fiction.

SIDELIGHTS: Patricia Lauber's *Tales Mummies Tell* makes "science accessible by illustrating how it can answer questions any normal youngster would find interesting," writes Michael Guillen in the *Washington Post Book World.* Named a New York Academy of Sciences Honor Book, *Tales Mummies Tell* "acquaints the young reader with paleontology, biology, archaeology, physics and anthropology by showing how these subjects are used to solve wide-ranging mysteries about our past," says Guillen, adding that "with her simple and engaging explanations of the lavish inferences scientists are able to make from such studies, Lauber makes science more attractive and not, thank goodness, merely more respectworthy."

AVOCATIONAL INTERESTS: The theatre, music, animals, sailing, and travel.

BIOGRAPHICAL/CRITICAL SOURCES:

PERIODICALS

New York Times, November 30, 1982.
New York Times Book Review, August 1, 1982.
Washington Post Book World, May 12, 1985.

*   *   *

LAURE, Ettagale
    See BLAUER, Ettagale

*   *   *

LAWRENCE, J. T.
    See ROWLAND-ENTWISTLE, (Arthur) Theodore (Henry)

*   *   *

LAWRENCE, John   1933-

PERSONAL: Born September 15, 1933, in Hastings, Sussex, England; son of Wilfred (a company representative) and Audrey (a pianist; maiden name, Thomas) Lawrence; married Myra Bell (an art teacher), 1957; children: two daughters. *Education:* Attended Hastings School of Art, 1951-53, and Central School of Arts and Crafts, London, 1955-57.

ADDRESSES: Home—6 Hartington Rd., London W4 3UA, England.

CAREER: Author and illustrator. Hamish Hamilton Ltd., London, England, illustrator, 1958—. Teacher of illustration at several art schools, including Maidstone, 1958-60, Brighton, 1960-68, and Camberwell School of Arts and Crafts, 1960—. *Military service:* British Army, 1953-55; served in West Africa.

AWARDS, HONORS: Francis Williams Book Illustration Award from the Victoria and Albert Museum, 1972 and 1977; *Rabbit and Pork* was selected for inclusion in the Children's Book Showcase by the Children's Book Council, 1976.

WRITINGS:

JUVENILES; SELF-ILLUSTRATED

The Giant of Grabbist, Hamish Hamilton, 1968, David White, 1969.
Pope Leo's Elephant, Hamish Hamilton, 1969, World Publishing, 1970.
(Adapter) *The King of the Peacocks,* Hamish Hamilton, 1970, Crowell, 1971.
Rabbit and Pork Rhyming Talk, Crowell, 1975.
Tongue Twisters, Hamish Hamilton, 1976.
(With Allan Ahlberg) *A Pair of Sinners,* Granada, 1980.
George, His Elephant and Castle, Hardy Books, 1983.
Good Babies, Bad Babies, MacRae Books, 1987.

ILLUSTRATOR

Alice P. Miller, *The Little Store on the Corner,* Abelard, 1961.
Daniel Defoe, *The History and Remarkable Life of the Truly Honourable Colonel Jack,* Folio, 1967.
Robert E. Rogerson and C. M. Smith, editors, *Enjoy Reading!,* W. & R. Chambers, Book II, 1968, Book III, 1969.
Margaret J. Miller, *Gunpowder Treason,* Macdonald & Co., 1968.
Daniel Roberts, *Histoires comme ci, comme ca,* J. Murray, 1968.

Frank Knight, *Rebel Admiral*, Macdonald & Co., 1968.
George Grossmith and Weedon Grossmith, *The Diary of a Nobody*, Folio, 1969.
Janet McNeill, *Dragons Come Home!, and Other Stories*, Hamish Hamilton, 1969.
Knight, *The Hero*, Macdonald & Co., 1969.
M. Miller, *Plot for the Queen*, Macdonald & Co., 1969.
Howard Jones, *The Spur and the Lily*, Macdonald & Co., 1969.
John Onslow, *Stumpf and the Cornish Witches*, J. Cape, 1969.
Alice Dalgliesh, *The Courage of Sarah Noble*, Hamish Hamilton, 1970.
Nicolas Freeling, *Kitchen Book*, Hamish Hamilton, 1970.
Knight, *That Rare Captain—Sir Francis Drake*, Macdonald & Co., 1970.
Laurence Sterne, *The Life and Opinions of Tristram Shandy, Gentleman*, edited by Graham Petrie, Folio, 1970.
Forbes Stuart, *The Boy on the Ox's Back, and Other African Legends*, Hamish Hamilton, 1971.
Edith Nesbit, *The Magician's Heart*, Hamish Hamilton, 1971.
James Reeves, *Maildun the Voyager*, Hamish Hamilton, 1971.
Jacynth Hope-Simpson, editor, *Tales in School: An Anthology of Boarding-School Life*, Hamish Hamilton, 1971.
J. B. Simpson, *To and Fro the Small Green Bottle*, Hamish Hamilton, 1971.
Freeling, *Cook Book*, Hamish Hamilton, 1972.
Gillian Avery, *Jemima and the Welsh Rabbit*, Hamish Hamilton, 1972.
Defoe, *The Life and Strange, Surprising Adventures of Robinson Crusoe of York, Mariner*, Folio, 1972.
Alphonse Daudet, *The Mule of Avignon*, translated from the French by Sybil Brown, Hamish Hamilton, 1972, Crowell, 1973.
Shirley Guiton, *No Magic Eden*, Hamish Hamilton, 1972.
McNeill, *A Fairy Called Andy Perks*, Hamish Hamilton, 1973.
Iris Macfarlane, adapter, *The Mouth of the Night: Gaelic Stories*, Chatto & Windus, 1973, Macmillan, 1976.
Leon Garfield, *The Sound of Coaches*, Kestrel Books, 1974.
Andrew Lang, compiler, *Blue Fairy Book*, revised edition edited by Brian Alderson, Kestrel Books, 1975, Viking, 1978 (Lawrence was not associated with earlier editions).
Mildred Davidson, *Dragons and More: Dark Fables with Some Light Patches*, Chatto & Windus, 1976, Merrimack Book Service, 1978.
Richard Adams, *Watership Down*, Kestrel Books, 1976.
Paul Theroux, *A Christmas Card*, Houghton, 1978.
Thomas Hardy, *Our Exploits at West Poley*, edited by Richard L. Purdy, Oxford University Press, 1978.
Sheila Lavelle, *Too Many Husbands*, Hamish Hamilton, 1978.
Theroux, *London Snow*, Hamish Hamilton, 1980.
Sybil Marshall, *The Everyman Book of English Folk Tales*, Dent, 1981.
Michael Berthoud, *Precisely Pig*, Collins, 1982.
Susan Hill, *The Magic Apple Tree*, Hamish Hamilton, 1982.
David and Kay Canter, *The Crank's Recipe Book*, Dent, 1982.
Penelope Lively, *Fanny and the Monsters*, Heinemann, 1983.
Jenny Koralek, *Mabel's Story*, Hardy Books, 1984.
Adrian Mitchell, *Nothingmas Day*, Allison & Busby, 1984.
Lively, *Uninvited Ghosts and Other Stories*, Heinemann, 1985.
K. Canter and Daphne Swann, *Entertaining with Cranks*, Dent, 1985.
Richard Edwards, *The Word Party*, Lutterworth, 1986.
Philippa Pearce, *Emily's Own Elephant*, MacRae Books, 1987.
Edwards, *Whispers from a Wardrobe*, Lutterworth, 1987.

WORK IN PROGRESS: Three books to be privately printed; one picture book.

SIDELIGHTS: John Lawrence told *CA:* "I regard myself as a general illustrator who needs good texts and pictorial situations in order to flourish most successfully. I try to get the feel of each new book and approach every job freshly. I like to have as wide a range of opportunity as possible so that I don't get stale, and although I worry a lot, I don't want this to show in the work itself. Humor is important to me."

AVOCATIONAL INTERESTS: Wood engraving, landscape drawing.

　　　　　*　　*　　*

LEE, Don L.
　　See MADHUBUTI, Haki R.

　　　　　*　　*　　*

LEE, Mary Price　1934-

PERSONAL: Born July 10, 1934, in Philadelphia, Pa.; daughter of Llewellyn and Elise (Mirkil) Price; married Richard Lee (a copywriter), May 12, 1956; children: Richard, Barbara, Monica. *Education:* University of Pennsylvania, B.A., 1956, M.S. in Ed., 1967.

ADDRESSES: Home—Flourtown, Pa.

CAREER: Author of young people's books. Teacher for short period; employed in public relations department at Westminster Press, Philadelphia, Pa., 1973-74. Has tutored foreign students in English.

MEMBER: Children's Reading Roundtable, Phi Beta Kappa, Philadelphia Athenaeum.

WRITINGS:

JUVENILES

Money and Kids: How to Earn It, Save It, and Spend It, Westminster, 1973.
Ms. Veterinarian, Westminster, 1976.
The Team That Runs Your Hospital, Westminster, 1980.
Your Name: All about It, Westminster, 1980.
A Future in Pediatrics: Medical and Non-medical Careers in Child Health Care, Messner, 1982.
Your Future in Research and Development in Industry, Rosen Publishing, 1983.
(With husband, Richard Lee) *Opportunities in Animal and Pet Care*, VGM Career Horizons, 1984.
(With R. Lee) *Exploring Careers in Robotics*, Rosen Publishing, 1984, revised edition, 1986.
(With R. Lee) *Last Names First*, Rosen Publishing, 1985.
(With R. Lee) *Exploring Careers in the Restaurant Industry*, Rosen Publishing, 1988.

OTHER

Columnist, *Chestnut Hill Local*, 1970-72. Contributor to *Philadelphia Magazine* and *Philadelphia Inquirer*. Contributing editor, *Today's Girl*, 1972-73.

WORK IN PROGRESS: A book for teen-agers on coping with money problems and revisions to *Your Future in Research and Development in Industry*, both with her husband, both for Rosen Publishing.

SIDELIGHTS: Mary Price Lee once told *CA*, "My children provide great incentive to write for their teenage group and serve both as guinea pigs and critics.'' She now explains that her original incentive has changed and that thorough research is the key to her work: ''With the world changing so rapidly, young peoples' career books serve their purpose best if they're as up-to-date as the publishing process allows. So I will cite references from daily newspapers as readily as from dusty historical tomes.''

She adds that her work is moving more from the entertainment approach of her two books on the origins and meanings of names to assistance and guidance for youth. ''Young pepole are much more on their own than they used to be,'' she asserts, ''and they don't necessarily welcome it. Changes in family structure, such as the growth of single-parent households, make teen-agers more dependent than ever on outside resources for help with career choices and personal problems. That's where I'd like to think my recent and current work fills a genuine need. If this sounds awfully dry, I make every effort to be just the opposite in my work. There's no reason why you cannot entertain as you inform.''

About her book-writing process, she states that her last four books (and her work in progress) have been written and edited in collaboration with her husband, Richard. In this working arrangement, Mary Lee outlines each book, does all the research, and then drafts some chapters, with Richard Lee drafting others. Then each edits the other's material ''with sometimes painful honesty,'' writes Lee, adding, ''but the results are worth it.''

*　　*　　*

LEES, Gene 1928-

PERSONAL: Born February 8, 1928, in Hamilton, Ontario, Canada; son of Harold (a musician, later a construction engineer) and Dorothy (Flatman) Lees; married former wife Carmen Lister, 1951; married former wife Micheline A. Ducreux, July, 1955; married Janet Suttle, 1971; children: (second marriage) Philippe. *Education:* Attended Ontario College of Art, Toronto, for one year.

ADDRESSES: Home and office—P.O. Box 1305, Oak View, Calif. 93022.

CAREER: Reporter for Canadian newspapers, 1948-55, first for *Hamilton Spectator,* later for *Toronto Telegram* and *Montreal Star; Louisville Times,* Louisville, Ky., classical music critic, and film and drama editor, 1955-58; studied the performing arts in Europe under Reid fellowship, 1958-59; *Down Beat* (jazz magazine), Chicago, Ill., editor, 1959-61; *Hi Fi/ Stereo Review,* New York, N.Y., contributing editor, 1962-65; columnist for *High Fidelity,* 1965-79; *Jazzletter,* Ojai, Calif., founder and principal writer, 1981—. Lyricist, composer, and collaborator with other composers on songs; toured Latin America under the auspices of U.S. Department of State as manager of jazz sextet, 1962; thirty songs with his lyrics, among them ''Waltz for Debby,'' ''Song of the Jet,'' ''Paris Is at Her Best in May,'' and ''Someone to Light Up My Life,'' were released in a Richmond Organization portfolio, 1968. Radio and television writer and singer for the Canadian Broadcasting Corp. and various independent Canadian radio stations.

MEMBER: Composers, Authors, and Publishers Association of Canada.

AWARDS, HONORS: ASCAP-Deems Taylor Award, American Society of Composers, Authors, and Publishers, 1978, for articles in *High Fidelity.*

WRITINGS:

And Sleep until Noon (novel), Simon & Schuster, 1966.
The Modern Rhyming Dictionary: How to Write Lyrics, Cherry Lane, 1981.
Singers and the Song (essays from the *Jazzletter*), Oxford University Press, 1987.
Meet Me at Jim and Andy's (essays from the *Jazzletter*), Oxford University Press, 1988.
Oscar Peterson: A Biography, Lester and Orpen Dennys, 1988.

Contributor of articles and short stories to the *New York Times, Los Angeles Times, Saturday Review, American Film,* and other periodicals in the United States, Canada, and Europe.

WORK IN PROGRESS: Henry Mancini: A Biography.

SIDELIGHTS: A distinguished lyricist known for his words to ''Quiet Nights'' and other bossa nova songs, Gene Lees helped introduce the bossa nova in America and has translated the Portuguese lyrics of many Brazilian songs into English. His songs have been recorded by Frank Sinatra, Tony Bennett, and others, and he has collaborated with such composers as Charles Aznavour of France, Antonio Carlos Jobim of Brazil, and Lalo Schifrin of Argentina. In 1976, Lees collaborated with Roger Kellaway on the musical score for the film ''The Mouse and His Child.''

In 1983, Lees adapted to music the English version of a group of poems by Pope John Paul II which Sarah Vaughan recorded in concert the following year. The resulting album—a suite of songs pleading for world peace—was released internationally under the title *The Planet Is Alive: Let It Live* and was critically well-received. In 1984, Choice Records released an album of Lees singing his own songs, and in 1985, Stash Records released *Gene Lees Sings the Gene Lees Song Book,* a performance with orchestra of songs that Lees wrote with Jobim and other composers.

Lees told *CA* that he used to consider himself primarily a lyricist and composer but now that perception has changed. ''Increasingly,'' he writes, ''I see jazz not only as a unique American contribution to the arts, but as profoundly significant, and since I have been deeply involved in it, both as observer and participant, a responsibility as chronicler seems to have devolved on me. I'm taking it very seriously. Some of the great masters, such as Arte Shaw and Benny Carter, are still with us, and I carry a lot of the music's unwritten history in my head. I think it matters to get as much of it as possible on paper for the sake of future generations; hence, the *Jazzletter.* Together with writing my own songs, that's what I intend to do in the next few years. I have finally come to accept nonfiction as art. Increasingly I see that what the sea was to Conrad, the world of jazz is to me.''

BIOGRAPHICAL/CRITICAL SOURCES:

PERIODICALS

BMI (publication of Broadcast Music, Inc.), November, 1967.
Calendar, April 15, 1984.
Jazztimes, August 24, 1986.
Los Angeles Times Book Review, January 17, 1982.

*　　*　　*

LEHMAN, David 1948-

PERSONAL: Born June 11, 1948, in New York, N.Y.; son of Joseph and Anne (Lusthaus) Lehman; married second wife,

Stefanie Green (a graphic designer), December 2, 1978. *Education:* Columbia University, B.A. (magna cum laude), 1970, Ph.D., 1978; Cambridge University, B.A., M.A., 1972. *Religion:* Jewish.

ADDRESSES: Home—159 Ludlowville Rd., Lansing, N.Y. 14882. *Office*—c/o *Newsweek,* 444 Madison Ave., New York, N.Y. 10022.

CAREER: Columbia University, New York City, preceptor in English, 1974-75; Brooklyn College of the City University of New York, Brooklyn, N.Y., instructor in English, 1975-76; Hamilton College, Clinton, N.Y., assistant professor of English, 1976-80; Cornell University, Ithaca, N.Y., fellow of Society for the Humanities, 1980-81; Wells College, Aurora, N.Y., lecturer in English, 1981-82; *Newsweek,* New York City, book critic, 1983—; free-lance writer, 1983—. Karolyi Memorial Foundation poet-in-residence, Vence, France, summer, 1977. Co-producer and host of "The Only Poetry Show" on WKCR-FM Radio, 1972-73.

MEMBER: National Book Critics Circle (member of board of directors), Phi Beta Kappa.

AWARDS, HONORS: Van Rennselaer Award, 1967 and 1970; Kellett fellow, 1970; Woodrow Wilson fellow, 1970; Book-of-the-Month Club creative writing fellow, 1970; Bennett A. Cerf Prize for Poetry, Columbia University, 1973, for "Baby Burning"; Academy of American Poets Prize, 1974, for "Threatening Weather"; Ingram Merrill Foundation grant, 1976, 1982, and 1984; National Endowment for the Humanities grant, summer, 1979; finalist, National Book Critics Circle Citation for Excellence in Reviewing, 1986; National Endowment for the Arts fellowship in poetry, 1987.

WRITINGS:

Some Nerve (poems), Columbia Review Press, 1973.
Day One (poems), Nobadaddy Press, 1979.
(Editor) *Beyond Amazement: New Essays on John Ashbery,* Cornell University Press, 1980.
(Contributor) Lloyd Schwartz and Sybil P. Estess, editors, *Elizabeth Bishop and Her Art,* University of Michigan Press, 1983.
(Editor with Charles Berger) *James Merrill: Essays in Criticism,* Cornell University Press, 1983.
An Alternative to Speech (poems), Princeton University Press, 1986.
(Editor) *Ecstatic Occasions, Expedient Forms: 65 Leading Contemporary Poets Select and Comment on Their Poems,* Macmillan, 1987.

CONTRIBUTOR TO ANTHOLOGIES

The Uses of Poetry, Holt, 1975.
Ardis Anthology of New American Poetry, Ardis, 1977.
The "Poetry" Anthology, 1912-1977, Houghton, 1978.
Anthology of Magazine Verse and Yearbook of American Poetry, Monitor, 1981.
Songs from Unsung Worlds: Science in Poetry, Birkhauser Boston, 1985.
Light Year '87, Bits Press, 1986.

OTHER

Contributor of poems, essays, articles, and reviews to periodicals, including *Poetry, Paris Review, Partisan Review, Times Literary Supplement, Newsday, Epoch, Shenandoah, Prairie Schooner, Parnassus: Poetry in Review,* and *Washington Post.* Editor of *Columbia Review,* 1969-70, and *Poetry in Motion,*

1976-80; contributing editor, *Columbia Today,* 1975, *Columbia College Today,* 1983—, and *Partisan Review,* 1987; poetry editor, *New York Arts Journal,* 1976-80.

WORK IN PROGRESS: A collection of poems with the tentative title *Operation Memory.*

AVOCATIONAL INTERESTS: Baseball.

BIOGRAPHICAL/CRITICAL SOURCES:

PERIODICALS

New York Times Book Review, March 1, 1987.
Times Literary Supplement, June 5, 1981.
Washington Post Book World, August 23, 1987.

*   *   *

LEIBENGUTH, Charla Ann
    See BANNER, Charla Ann Leibenguth

*   *   *

LEMAY, J(oseph) A(lberic) Leo   1935-

PERSONAL: Born January 7, 1935, in Bristow, Va.; son of Joseph Albert (a steelworker) and Valencia L. (Winslow) Lemay; married Muriel Ann Clarke (a real estate broker), August 11, 1965; children: John, Lee, Kate. *Education:* University of Maryland, A.B., 1957, A.M., 1962; University of Pennsylvania, Ph.D., 1964. *Politics:* Republican. *Religion:* Unitarian Universalist.

ADDRESSES: Home—4828 Kennett Pike, Greenville, Del. 19807. *Office*—Department of English, University of Delaware, Newark, Del. 19716.

CAREER: George Washington University, Washington, D.C., assistant professor of English, 1963-65; University of California, Los Angeles, assistant professor, 1965-70, associate professor, 1970-75, professor of English, 1975-77; University of Delaware, Newark, H. F. du Pont Winterthur Professor of English, 1977—. *Military service:* U.S. Army, 1957-59.

MEMBER: Modern Language Association of America, American Humor Studies Association (president, 1981), American Antiquarian Society, Institute for Early American History and Culture (council member, 1978-81), Society for the Study of Southern Literature, Maryland Historical Society, Pennsylvania Historical Society, Virginia Historical Society.

AWARDS, HONORS: Grants from American Philosophical Society and Colonial Williamsburg; Guggenheim fellow; Institute for Advanced Research fellow, University of Delaware, 1980-81; senior fellowship, National Endowment for the Humanities, 1983-84.

WRITINGS:

Ebenezer Kinnersley: Franklin's Friend, University of Pennsylvania Press, 1964.
Men of Letters in Colonial Maryland, University of Tennessee Press, 1972.
A Calendar of American Poetry in Colonial Newspapers and Magazines through 1765, American Antiquarian Society, 1972.
(Editor) *The Oldest Revolutionary: Essays on Benjamin Franklin,* University of Pennsylvania Press, 1976.
(Editor) *Essays in Early Virginia Literature Honoring Richard Beale Davis,* Burt Franklin, 1977.

(Editor) *The Autobiography of Benjamin Franklin: A Genetic Text*, University of Tennessee Press, 1981.

"New England's Annoyances": America's First Folk Song, University of Delaware Press, 1985.

(Editor with P. M. Zall) *Benjamin Franklin's Autobiography: A Norton Critical Edition*, Norton, 1986.

The Canon of Benjamin Franklin, 1722-1776: New Additions and Reconsiderations, University of Delaware Press, 1986.

(Editor) *Benjamin Franklin: Writings*, Library of America, 1987.

Contributor to periodicals, including *American Literature, New England Quarterly,* and *Virginia Magazine of History and Biography.*

WORK IN PROGRESS: The Ideology of Early American Humor; The Art of Poe's "Murders in the Rue Morgue"; The American Dream of Captain John Smith.

*   *   *

LENGYEL, Cornel Adam   1915-
(Cornel Adam)

PERSONAL: Surname pronounced Len-jell; born January 1, 1915, in Fairfield, Conn.; son of Elmer Alexander and Mary Elizabeth (Bismarck) Lengyel; married Teresa M. Delaney, July 10, 1933; children: Jerome Benedict, Paul Joel, Cornelia (Mrs. Charles Burke), Michael Sebastian.

ADDRESSES: Home—El Dorado National Forest, 7700 Wentworth Springs Rd., Georgetown, Calif. 95634.

CAREER: Poet, historian, and translator. Federal Writers' Project, editor, 1936-37; *Coast,* San Francisco, Calif., music critic, 1938-41; Office of Censorship, San Francisco, censor, 1942; Kaiser Shipyards, Richmond, Calif., shipwright, personnel interviewer, 1943-44; Forty-Niner Theatre, Georgetown, Calif., manager, 1946-49; W. H. Freeman Co., San Francisco, editor, 1952-54; Dragon's Teeth Press, Georgetown, founder and executive editor, beginning 1970. Visiting professor and lecturer, Sacramento State College (now California State University, Sacramento), 1962-63; writer-in-residence, Hamline University, 1968-69; guest lecturer, Massachusetts Institute of Technology, 1969. Editorial consultant, U.S. Department of Health, Education, and Welfare. Educational director, International Ladies Garment Workers Union, Local 22. *Wartime service:* U.S. Merchant Marine, 1944-45.

MEMBER: World Poetry Society Intercontinental, Authors Guild, Authors League of America, Modern Language Association of America, Poetry Society of America, American Historical Society, American Association of University Professors, P.E.N. American Center.

AWARDS, HONORS: Albert M. Bender award in literature, 1945; first prize, Maxwell Anderson Awards for poetic drama, 1950, for the play "The Atom Clock"; Huntington Hartford fellowship in literature, 1951, 1963; first prize, Poetry Society of Virginia, 1951; MacDowell Colony fellowship, 1967; Ossabaw Island Foundation fellowship, 1968; Alice Fay di Castagnola Award, Poetry Society of America, 1971; International Who's Who in Poetry Award, 1972-73; National Endowment for the Arts award in drama, 1976.

WRITINGS:

HISTORY

(With Noah Ben-Tovim) *American Testament: The Story of a Promised Land* (juvenile), Grace Books, 1956.

Four Days in July: The Story behind the Declaration of Independence, Doubleday, 1958, reprinted, Queen's House, 1976.

I, Benedict Arnold: The Anatomy of Treason, Doubleday, 1960.

Ethan Allen and the Green Mountain Boys (juvenile), Doubleday, 1961.

Presidents of the U.S.A.: Profiles and Pictures (juvenile), Bantam, 1966, revised edition published as *Presidents of the United States,* Golden Press, 1977.

The Declaration of Independence (juvenile), illustrated by Lyn Sweat, Grosset, 1969.

The Creative Self: Aspects of Man's Quest for Self-Knowledge and the Springs of Creativity (essay), Mouton, 1971.

POETRY

Thirty Pieces, Hoffman, 1933.

First Poems, Pacifica Press, 1940.

(Under name Cornel Adam) *Fifty Poems,* Acre Press, 1965.

Four Dozen Songs, Dragon's Teeth Press, 1970, revised edition, 1973.

The Lookout's Letter and Other Poems (sonnet sequence), foreword by George Santayana, Dragon's Teeth Press, 1971.

Late News from Adam's Acres, Dragon's Teeth Press, 1983.

El Dorado Forest: Selected Poems, Hillside Press (Vista, Calif.), 1986.

Also author of an unfinished poetry collection entitled "Latter Day Psalms."

PLAYS

"The World's My Village," first produced by the Berkeley Playcrafters, 1935.

The Atom Clock (first produced in Dubuque, Iowa, at the University of Dubuque, 1953), Fantasy, 1951.

(Under name Cornel Adams) *Omega: A Drama in Two Acts* (first produced under title, "Eden, Inc.," in Coral Gables, Fla., at Ring Theatre, 1954), Literary Discoveries (San Francisco), 1963.

(Under name Cornel Adams) *Will of Stratford* (first produced in Ohio, 1964), Literary Discoveries, 1964.

Three Plays, Chandler Publishing, 1964.

The Master Plan, Dragon's Teeth Press, 1978.

Also author of unpublished plays "Jonah Fugitive," 1936, "The Giant's Trap," 1938, "The Case of Benedict Arnold," 1975, "Doctor Franklin," 1976, "The Shadow Trap," 1977, "The Second Coming," 1985, and "The Case of Doktor Mengele," 1987.

CONTRIBUTOR TO ANTHOLOGIES

The Golden Year, Poetry Society of America, 1960.

Leo W. Schwarz, editor, *The Menorah Treasury,* Junior Poetry Society of America, 1964.

(Under name Cornel Adam) *A Treasury of Jewish Sea Stories,* J. David, 1965.

Baxter Geeting, editor, *Interpretation for Our Time,* W. C. Brown, 1966.

The Diamond Anthology, Poetry Society of America, 1971.

High Stakes and Desperate Men, Reader's Digest Press, 1974.

Contributor to additional anthologies, including *The Britannica Library of Great American Writing,* edited by Louis Untermeyer, 1961.

OTHER

Editor of *History of Music in San Francisco,* seven volumes,

1942, reprinted, AMS Press, 1970. Contributor of poems, stories, and articles to magazines, including *California Quarterly, Coast, Kayak, Blue Unicorn,* and *Saturday Review.* Columnist, *Argonaut.*

WORK IN PROGRESS: A Book of 150 Fables; a book of memoirs titled *A Clockmaker's Boy.*

SIDELIGHTS: Cornel Adam Lengyel told *CA:* "To realize an enduring work of the mind, the creative man must practice more than ordinary virtues. The strength and dedication and discipline required, and the energy expended to accomplish his work, rivals the legendary labors of Hercules. The practice of a creative art is a private rite which starts with the taming of the ancestral ape in any man. Whatever the morality of the artist, a work of art represents virtue in action. In an age of mass values the practice of an art is one of the few ways left in which the individual may test his highest capacities, draw on all his inner resources, and expend himself freely in his full humanity."

Four Days in July: The Story behind the Declaration of Independence has been translated into over thirty languages.

MEDIA ADAPTATIONS: "Selected Poems" (recording), Library of Congress, 1961.

BIOGRAPHICAL/CRITICAL SOURCES:

PERIODICALS

Los Angeles Times, February 13, 1974.

*   *   *

L'ESTRANGE, Anna
See ELLERBECK, Rosemary (Anne L'Estrange)

*   *   *

LEVI, Anthony H(erbert) T(igar)   1929-

PERSONAL: Born May 30, 1929, in Ruislip, England; son of Herbert Simon (a merchant) and Edith Mary (Tigar) Levi. *Education:* Studied philosophy for three years in Munich, modern languages for three years at Oxford University, and theology for four years; Oxford University, B.A., 1958, D.Phil., 1963; Heythrop College, S.T.L., 1963.

ADDRESSES: Home and office—East Castlemount, North Castle St., St. Andrews, Fife, Scotland.

CAREER: Engaged in business in England, 1946-49; member of Society of Jesus (Jesuits), 1949-71; Oxford University, Christ Church, Oxford, England, lecturer in French, 1966-71; University of St. Andrews, St. Andrews, Fife, Scotland, Buchanan Professor of French Language and Literature, 1971-87. University of Warwick, reader in French, 1966, personal chair in French, 1970. Company director, Fife Heritage Co. Ltd., 1984—.

WRITINGS:

French Moralists: The Theory of the Passions, 1585-1649, Oxford University Press, 1964.
Religion in Practice, Harper, 1966.
(Editor and contributor) *Humanism in France at the End of the Middle Ages and in the Early Renaissance,* Manchester University Press, 1970.
(Author of introduction and notes) Desiderius Erasmus, *The Praise of Folly,* Penguin, 1971.

(Editor with Francis Haskell and Robert Shackleton) *The Artist and the Writer in France: Essays in Honour of Jean Seznec,* Oxford University Press, 1974.
The Satires of Erasmus, Toronto University Press, 1986.
The Intellectual History of the Northern Renaissance, Yale University Press, 1988.
Antiquity and Modernity in 17th-Century France, Oxford University Press, in press.

CONTRIBUTOR

James Walsh, editor, *Spirituality through the Centuries,* Burns & Oates, 1964.
G. Richard-Molard, editor, *L'homme devant Dieu,* Droguet Ardant, 1964.
Terence C. Cave, editor, *Ronsard the Poet,* Methuen, 1973.
N. Hepp Strasbourg, editor, *Heroisme et creation litteraire,* Klincksieck, 1973.
R. R. Bolgar, editor, *Classical Influences on European Culture, A.D. 1500-1700,* Cambridge University Press, 1976.
Peter Sharratt, editor, *French Renaissance Studies, 1540-70: Humanism and the Encyclopedia,* Edinburgh University Press, 1976.

Also contributor to G. Hughes, *The Philosophical Assessment of Theology.*

OTHER

Contributor to periodicals, including *Heydrop Journal, Dublin Review,* and *Month.*

WORK IN PROGRESS: The History of Jansenism.

BIOGRAPHICAL/CRITICAL SOURCES:

PERIODICALS

Times Literary Supplement, August 14, 1987.

*   *   *

LISTER, Raymond (George)   1919-

PERSONAL: Born March 28, 1919, in Cambridge, England; son of Horace (an engineer) and Ellen (Arnold) Lister; married Pamela Brutnell, June 6, 1947; children: Rory Brian George, Delia Fionnuala. *Education:* Attended Cambridge schools until fifteen.

ADDRESSES: Home—Windmill House, Linton, Cambridgeshire CB1 6NS, England. *Office*—George Lister & Sons Ltd., 120 Church End, Cherry Hinton, Cambridge, England. *Agent*—A. S. Knight, Wildacre, The Warren, Ashtead, Surrey, England.

CAREER: George Lister & Sons Ltd. (architectural metalworkers), Cambridge, England, director, 1939—; Golden Head Press Ltd., Cambridge, managing director and editor, 1952-72. Wolfson College, Cambridge University, honorary senior member, 1971-75, fellow, 1975—, and syndic of Fitzwilliam Museum, 1980—. Miniature painter, with work exhibited occasionally at one-man shows in Federation of British Artists Galleries, London.

MEMBER: Royal Society of Arts, Royal Society of Miniature Painters, Sculptors and Engravers (treasurer, beginning 1958; president, 1970-80), Federation of British Artists (governor, 1972-80), Private Libraries Association (president, 1971-72), Liveryman of Worshipful Company of Blacksmiths, Sette of Odd Volumes (president, 1960), Atheneum Club, City Livery Club.

WRITINGS:

Decorative Wrought Ironwork in Great Britain, G. Bell, 1957,
    Tuttle, 1970, 2nd edition, David & Charles, 1970.
(Translator from the French) V. I. Stepanov, *Alphabet of
    Movements of the Human Body*, Golden Head Press, 1958.
Decorative Cast Ironwork in Great Britain, G. Bell, 1960.
The Craftsman Engineer, G. Bell, 1960.
*Private Telegraph Companies of Great Britain and Their
    Stamps*, Golden Head Press, 1961.
Great Craftsmen, G. Bell, 1962.
Edward Calvert, G. Bell, 1962.
The Miniature Defined (booklet), Golden Head Press, 1963.
How to Identify Old Maps and Globes, Archon Books, 1965.
*Beulah to Byzantium: A Study of Parallels in the Works of
    W. B. Yeats, William Blake, Samuel Palmer and Edward
    Calvert*, Dolmen Press, 1965.
College Stamps of Oxford and Cambridge, Golden Head Press,
    1966.
The Craftsman in Metal, G. Bell, 1966, A. S. Barnes, 1968.
Victorian Narrative Paintings, C. N. Potter, 1966.
Great Works of Craftsmanship, G. Bell, 1967, A. S. Barnes,
    1968.
William Blake: An Introduction to the Man and to His Work,
    G. Bell, 1968, Ungar, 1970.
Samuel Palmer and His Etchings, Watson-Guptill, 1969.
Hammer and Hand: An Essay on the Ironwork of Cambridge
    (booklet), privately printed, 1969.
Antique Maps and Their Cartographers, Archon Books, 1970.
British Romantic Art, G. Bell, 1973.
Samuel Palmer: A Biography, Faber, 1975.
(Editor) *The Letters of Samuel Palmer*, two volumes, Oxford
    University Press, 1975.
Infernal Methods: A Study of William Blake's Art Techniques,
    G. Bell, 1975.
Samuel Palmer: A Vision Recaptured, Victoria and Albert Mu-
    seum, 1978.
George Richmond: A Biography, R. V. Garton, 1981.
Prints and Printmaking, Methuen, 1984.
The Paintings of Samuel Palmer, Cambridge University Press,
    1985.
The Paintings of William Blake, Cambridge University Press,
    1986.
Samuel Palmer, His Life and Art, Cambridge University Press,
    1987.
A Catalogue Raisonne of the Works of Samuel Palmer, Cam-
    bridge University Press, 1987.

Also author of *Apollo's Bird*, 1975, *For Love of Leda*, 1977,
and *Great Images of British Printmaking*, 1978. Author of
numerous pamphlets. Contributor to *Connoisseur*, *Apollo*,
Journal of Royal Society of Arts, *Irish Book*, *Blake Studies*,
and *Blake Newsletter*.

AVOCATIONAL INTERESTS: Book collecting, mountaineer-
ing in the fens.

BIOGRAPHICAL/CRITICAL SOURCES:

BOOKS

Cammell, C. R., and others, *Raymond Lister: Five Essays*,
    Golden Head Press, 1963.
Lissim, Simon, *The Art of Raymond Lister*, Gray, 1958.

*   *   *

LIVINGSTONE, Marco (Eduardo)   1952-

PERSONAL: Born March 17, 1952, in Detroit, Mich.; son of

Leon (a professor) and Alicia (Arce) Livingstone. *Education:*
Attended State University of New York at Buffalo, 1969-70;
University of Toronto, B.A., 1974; Courtauld Institute of Art,
London, M.A., 1976.

ADDRESSES: Home—London, England. *Office*—The Dictio-
nary of Art, Macmillan Publishers Ltd., 4 Little Essex St.,
London WC2R 3LF, England.

CAREER: Free-lance journalist for Canadian and British popular music magazines and weekly newspapers, 1970-74; Walker
Art Gallery, Liverpool, England, assistant keeper of British
art, 1976-82; Museum of Modern Art, Oxford, England, deputy director, 1982-86; Macmillan Publishers, London, England, twentieth-century art editor of *The Dictionary of Art*,
1986-87, deputy editor, 1987—.

MEMBER: Society of Authors.

AWARDS, HONORS: Award from Arts Council of Great Britain, 1979.

WRITINGS:

Allen Jones: Retrospective of Paintings, 1957-1978, Walker
    Art Gallery, 1979.
Sheer Magic by Allen Jones, Congreve, 1979.
David Hockney, Holt, 1981.
Patrick Caulfield: Paintings, 1963-1981, Walker Art Gallery,
    1981.
Peter Phillips retroVISION: Paintings, 1960-1982, Walker Art
    Gallery, 1982.
Derek Boshier: Drawings 1960-1982, Bluecoat Gallery, 1983.
Anish Kapoor: Feeling into Form, Walker Art Gallery, 1983.
Graham Crowley: Home Comforts, Museum of Modern Art
    [London], 1983.
Duane Michals: Photographs/sequences/texts 1958-1984, Mu-
    seum of Modern Art, 1984.
Stephen Buckley: Many Angles, Museum of Modern Art, 1985.
David Mach: Toward a Landscape, Museum of Modern Art,
    1985.
R. B. Kitaj, Rizzoli International, 1985.
Arthur Tress: Talisman, Thames & Hudson, 1986.
David Hockney Faces, Thames & Hudson, 1987.
Pop Art U.S.A./U.K., Brain Trust [Tokyo], 1987.
Stephen Farthing, Museum of Modern Art, 1987.

Contributor to art journals.

SIDELIGHTS: Marco Livingstone commented: "Writing about
art provides an opportunity to explore the nature of the creative
process by recourse to specific example. My starting point,
therefore, is not in theory or dogma, but in the work itself. I
have chosen to write about contemporary British artists not
only because I am in sympathy with their work, but also because close personal contact and exhaustive interviews make
possible a fruitful collaboration.

"Though it would be presumptuous of me to claim a resemblance in methodology with that of art historians under whom
I have studied, such as John Golding and Lee Johnson, their
research methods in quite different fields have nevertheless
served as an inspiring model for the close analysis of works
on which I seek to base my own conclusions. My hope is that
careful documentation, together with the insights derived from
my identification with the artist, will help establish a foundation for subsequent understanding of each artist's work."

LONDON, Mel 1923-

PERSONAL: Born August 21, 1923, in New York, N.Y.; son of Harry and Faye (Feldman) London; married Sheryl Adams (a writer and filmmaker), June 2, 1946. *Education:* Attended City College (now of the City University of New York), 1941-42, and Columbia University, 1942-43.

ADDRESSES: Home—170 Second Ave., New York, N.Y. 10003.

CAREER: Worked at American Forces Network in Germany (now West Germany), 1944-47; radio and television director, producer, and writer, 1948-56; worked at On Film, Inc., 1956-60; Wilding International, New York City, president, 1960-65; David Wolper Associates, Hollywood, Calif., vice-president, 1965-66; Vision Associates, New York City, partner and filmmaker, 1966-79; Symbiosis, Inc., New York City, owner and filmmaker, 1979—; New York University, New York City, adjunct assistant professor of film, 1987—. Seminar leader; visiting scholar, Dalton School, New York City; lecturer at New York University, Northwestern University, and Memphis State University. *Military service:* U.S. Army, Signal Corps, 1943-47; became second lieutenant.

MEMBER: Directors Guild of America, American Film Institute.

AWARDS, HONORS: About two hundred fifty awards, including Academy Award nomination from Motion Picture Academy of Arts and Sciences, 1963, for documentary film "To Live Again"; eighteen Golden Eagle awards from Council on International Nontheatrical Events, for various films; four blue ribbons from American Film Festival.

WRITINGS:

Getting into Film, Ballantine, 1977, 2nd edition, 1986.
Bread Winners, Rodale Press, 1979.
(With wife, Sheryl London) *The Fish-Lovers' Cookbook: A Guide to Keeping, Preparing and Cooking Fresh, Whole Fish—Featuring Hundreds of Imaginative Recipes for Good Health and Good Eating,* Rodale Press, 1980.
Easy Going (travel), Rodale Press, 1981.
Second Spring (nonfiction), Rodale Press, 1982.
(With S. London) *Sheryl and Mel London's Creative Cooking with Grains and Pasta,* Rodale Press, 1982.
Bread Winners Too: Second Rising, edited by Charles Gerras, Rodale Press, 1983.
The Bread Winners' Cookbook, Simon & Schuster, 1983.
Making It in Film, Simon & Schuster, 1985.
(With S. London) *The Herb and Spice Cookbook: A Seasoning Celebration,* Rodale Press, 1986.

Also author of movie and television scripts.

SIDELIGHTS: Mel London told *CA:* "Though I had written television scripts, radio shows, and, eventually, motion picture documentary scripts, the idea of a book was frightening, even one that dealt with my primary profession, that of a filmmaker. Where television scripts were a 'sprint,' the book form represented the 'long distance run,' and even if I had one in me, did I have more?

"The first book, then, was the 'one book that everyone has in him.' I found that I like the long distance run—so *Getting into Film* was followed by a bestseller on bread baking. And now, only ten years after starting the first book, the eighth book was published last year.

"Through it all, I have wanted, and managed, to stay with film. The two as a double effort make a full, and sometimes difficult, life. My best advice to a young writer would be not to write the complete book before trying to sell it to a publisher. An outline, chapter details, and a sample chapter are really all that anyone is going to go through.

"Now, two publishers have suggested that I try a novel. After a book on film, a book on bread, one on fish, a travel book, and a book on middle age, that really frightens me. If writing a book is a long distance run, then writing a novel must certainly be a marathon event. We shall see.''

BIOGRAPHICAL/CRITICAL SOURCES:

BOOKS

Kranz, Stewart, *Science and Technology in the Arts,* Van Nostrand, 1974.

PERIODICALS

New York Times, September 28, 1980.

*   *   *

LONG, Richard A(lexander) 1927- (Ric Alexander)

PERSONAL: Born February 9, 1927, in Philadelphia, Pa.; son of Thaddeus B. and Lela (Washington) Long. *Education:* Temple University, A.B., 1947, M.A., 1948; further study at University of Pennsylvania and University of Paris; University of Poitiers, D.es L., 1965.

ADDRESSES: Office—Graduate Institute of the Liberal Arts, Emory University, Atlanta, Ga. 30322.

CAREER: West Virginia State College, Institute, instructor in English, 1949-50; Morgan State College (now University), Baltimore, Md., assistant professor, 1951-64, associate professor of English, 1964-66; Hampton Institute, Hampton, Va., professor of English and French, 1966-68; Atlanta University, Atlanta, Ga., professor of English and Afro-American studies, 1968-87; currently faculty member of Graduate Institute of the Liberal Arts, Emory University, Atlanta. Visiting lecturer in Afro-American Studies, Harvard University, 1970-72. *Military service:* U.S. Army, 1944-45.

MEMBER: American Dialect Society, American Studies Association, South Atlantic Modern Language Association, Modern Language Association of America, College Language Association (president, 1971-72), Modern Humanities Research Association, Linguistics Society of America, Southeastern Conference on Linguistics.

AWARDS, HONORS: Fulbright scholar, University of Paris, 1957-58.

WRITINGS:

(Editor with Albert H. Berrian) *Negritude: Essays and Studies,* Hampton Institute Press, 1967, revised edition, 1987.
(Editor with Eugenia W. Collier) *Afro-American Writing: An Anthology of Prose and Poetry,* two volumes, New York University Press, 1972, 2nd and enlarged edition, Pennsylvania State University Press, 1985.
Ascending and Other Poems, Du Sable Museum, 1975.
Black America, Chartwell, 1985.
Black Writers and the American Civil War, Blue and Gray Press, 1988.

DRAMATIC WORKS UNDER NAME RIC ALEXANDER

"The Pilgrim's Pride" (sketches), 1963.
"Stairway to Heaven" (gospel opera), 1964.
"Joan of Arc" (folk opera), 1964.
"Reasons of State" (play), 1966.
"Black Is Many Hues" (play), 1969.

OTHER

Member of editorial boards, *Phylon* and *Bulletin of Research in the Humanities.* Former member of editorial board of *Black Books Bulletin.*

BIOGRAPHICAL/CRITICAL SOURCES:

PERIODICALS

Journal of American Studies, April, 1987.
Library Journal, February 1, 1973.

*   *   *

LONGINO, Charles F(reeman), Jr.   1938-

PERSONAL: Born March 3, 1938, in Brookhaven, Miss.; son of Charles F. (a businessman) and Alma (Harris) Longino; married Loyce White, July 11, 1964; children: Laura Elizabeth, Charles F. III. *Education:* Mississippi College, B.A., 1960; University of Colorado, M.A., 1962; University of North Carolina, Ph.D., 1967; postdoctoral study, 1974-76. *Politics:* Democrat. *Religion:* Roman Catholic.

ADDRESSES: Home—15720 Southwest 84th Ct., Miami, Fla. 33157. *Office*—Department of Sociology, University of Miami, Coral Gables, Fla. 33124.

CAREER: University of North Carolina at Chapel Hill, assistant professor of sociology, 1967-68; University of Virginia, Charlottesville, assistant professor of sociology, 1968-74; research associate at Center for Program Effectiveness Studies, 1971-74; University of Kansas, Lawrence, associate professor of sociology, 1974-77, research associate at Institute for Social and Environmental Studies, 1975-77; University of Miami, Coral Gables, Fla., associate professor, 1977-83, professor of sociology, 1983—, director of Center for Social Research in Aging, 1983—, associate director of Center for Aging and Adult Development, 1986—. Chairman of board of directors, Overseas Medical Fund, 1972-74, and Human Development and Aging Initial Review Group for the National Institutes of Health, 1983-87; member of board of directors, American Federation for Aging Research, 1986—; member of advisory board, International Exchange Center on Gerontology, 1983—. Consultant to National Center for Health Services Research and Development, 1971-72, State of Kansas Department of Aging, 1975-76, Florida House of Representatives subcommittee on aging, 1978-79, American Chemical Society, 1979-82, and ABC News, NBC News, CNN, and *USA Today,* all 1983—.

MEMBER: American Sociological Association (member of council and section on aging, 1983-86), Gerontological Society (fellow, 1981; chairperson of membership committee, 1986-87), Association for Gerontology in Higher Education, Society for the Scientific Study of Religion, Southern Gerontological Society, Southern Regional Demographic Group, Southern Sociological Society.

WRITINGS:

(Editor with David G. Bromley) *White Racism and Black Americans,* Schenkman, 1972.

(With others) *The Medical Experience and Attitudes of Faculty and Staff Households at the University of Virginia,* Center for Program Effectiveness Studies, 1972.
(With others) *The Availability of Health Care in a Rural Virginia County,* Center for Delivery of Health Care, 1972.
(With C. S. Green) *Evaluation of the Effects of Coupled OJT Programs Conducted during 1971-72,* Environmental Protection Agency, 1973.
(With Jeffrey K. Hadden) *Gideon's Gang: A Case Study of the Church in Social Action,* Pilgrim, 1974.
(With others) *John Knox Village Residents: The Tangibles and Intangibles of Retirement Living,* Institute for Community Studies, 1976.
(With others) *Aged Migration in the United States, 1965-70,* Center for Public Affairs, 1979.
(With others) *A Study of Security, Health and Social Support Systems and Adjustment of Residents in Selected Congregate Living and Retirement Settings,* Institute for Community Studies, 1979.
A Statistical Profile of Older Floridians, Center for Social Research in Aging, 1983.
State-to-State Migration Patterns of Older Americans for Two Census Decades, Center for Social Research in Aging, 1986.
The Oldest Americans: State Profiles for Data-Based Planning, Center for Social Research in Aging, 1986.

CONTRIBUTOR

J. M. Pietrofesa, editor, *Student Personnel,* APGA Press, 1975.
F. Berghorn and D. Schafer, editors, *The Dynamics of Aging: Original Essays on the Experience and Process of Growing Old,* Westview Press, 1980.
Charles B. Nam, editor, *Florida's Migration Patterns: Planning and Policy,* Center for the Study of Population, 1980.
A. M. Warnes, editor, *Geographical Perspectives on the Elderly,* Wiley, 1981.
C. S. Kart and B. Manard, editors, *Aging in America: Readings in Social Gerontology,* 2nd edition, Alfred Publications, 1981.
J. S. Reed, editor, *Social Science Perspectives on the South: An Interdisciplinary Annual,* Gordon & Breach, 1981.

OTHER

Contributor to numerous journals, including *International Journal of Aging and Human Development, American Demographics, Journal of Applied Gerontology, Journal of Marriage and the Family, Social Forces, Sociological Analysis,* and *Journal of Social Psychology.* Associate editor, *Social Forces,* 1967-68; special issue editor, *Research on Aging,* June, 1980; member of editorial board, *Journal of Gerontology,* 1981—, and *Research on Aging,* 1983—.

SIDELIGHTS: Charles F. Longino, Jr., told *CA:* "There is a handful of writers who are engaged in a secret warfare against the scientific literary establishment, if it can be properly called literary. Although this foils my cover, I am a member. We believe in and subversively attempt to foster the notion that science can be fun to read—even for scientists. For decades the establishment has maintained that the duller the prose the more legitimate the science. In attempting to undermine the equation that formal means dull and dull means legitimate, we insist on engaging the reader's intellect, making him or her chuckle from time to time and even sprinkling scientific writing with literary references from philosophy, religion, fiction, classics, and folklore. The outcome of our effort is to create cognitive dissonance among the readers, scorn from some colleagues who think we aren't 'serious' enough, and gratitude from students, who have maintained all along that science should be fun.''

*   *   *

LOUIS, Pat
See FRANCIS, Dorothy Brenner

*   *   *

LOWE, Roberta (Justine) 1940-

PERSONAL: Born June 2, 1940, in Portland, Ore.; daughter of Robert Stuart and Noni (Ellingson) Long; married Donald Clark Lowe (a photographer), December 2, 1966. *Education:* Attended Reed College, 1958-60; Portland State University, B.A., 1969.

ADDRESSES: Home and office—P.O. Box 217, Sandy, Ore. 97055.

CAREER: Full-time writer. Professional dancer, 1961-63.

WRITINGS:

WITH PHOTOGRAPHS BY HUSBAND, DONALD LOWE

One Hundred Oregon Hiking Trails, Touchstone, 1969.
One Hundred Northern California Hiking Trails, Touchstone, 1970.
One Hundred Southern California Hiking Trails, Touchstone, 1972.
Eighty Northern Colorado Hiking Trails, Touchstone, 1973.
Seventy Hiking Trails: Northern Oregon Cascades, Touchstone, 1974.
Mount Hood, Caxton, 1975.
Fifty West Central Colorado Hiking Trails, Touchstone, 1976.
Sixty Hiking Trails: Central Oregon Cascades, Touchstone, 1978.
Sixty-two Hiking Trails: Northern Oregon Cascades, Touchstone, 1979.
Thirty-five Hiking Trails: Columbia George, Touchstone, 1980.
Forty-one Hiking Trails: Northwestern California, Touchstone, 1981.
The John Muir Trail, Caxton, 1982.
Thirty-three Hiking Trails: Southern Washington Cascades, Touchstone, 1985.
Fifty Hiking Trails: Portland and Northwest Oregon, Touchstone, 1986.
Fifty Hiking Trails: Lassen-Tahoe-Carson Pass, Touchstone, 1987.

OTHER

Monthly columnist on outdoors for *Oregon Times,* 1975-77, and *Willamette Week,* 1978-80; monthly columnist on hiking, cross-country skiing, and bicycling for *Northwest* (Sunday magazine of the *Oregonian*), 1982—. Weekly columnist on hiking and cross-country skiing for *Oregon Journal,* 1978-82; dance writer for *Willamette Week,* 1986—.

WORK IN PROGRESS: Fifty Hiking Trails: Ebbetts Pass to Yosemite.

AVOCATIONAL INTERESTS: Bicycling, dance, music.

*   *   *

LUCAS, Celia 1938-

PERSONAL: Born October 23, 1938, in Bristol, England; daughter of Joseph Vaughan (a physician) and Joan (a service club director; maiden name, Kirchner) Lucas; married Ian Skidmore (a writer and broadcaster), October 20, 1971. *Education:* St. Hilda's College, Oxford, B.A. (with honors), 1961. *Religion:* Roman Catholic.

ADDRESSES: Home and office—Virgin and Child Cottage, Brynsiencyn, Anglesey, North Wales.

CAREER: George Rainbird Ltd. (publisher), London, England, editorial assistant, 1962-65; W. H. Allen Ltd. (publisher), London, art editor, 1965-66; *Daily Mail,* London, researcher, 1966-68, reporter in Manchester, England, 1968-71; Welsh Border News Agency, Chester, England, partner, 1971-74, director, 1974-80; Lucas News Agency, Anglesey, North Wales, director, 1980—; Two's Company (public relations consultancy), Anglesey, director, 1986—.

WRITINGS:

The Prisoners of Santo Tomas (biography), Leo Cooper, 1974.
Steel Town Cats (juvenile), Tabb House, 1987.

Contributor to British newspapers and magazines.

WORK IN PROGRESS: Two children's books, *The Adventures of Marmaduke Purr Cat* and *Cat among the Penguins;* a biography of the pianist Moura Lympany, with husband Ian Skidmore.

SIDELIGHTS: Celia Lucas told *CA:* ''I wrote *The Prisoners of Santo Tomas* because I was moved by the subject—Mrs. Isla Corfield's account of life in a Japanese internment camp in the Philippines during World War II. The children's books are for my nephews and grandchildren.

''I enjoy the excitement, involvement, and precision of newspaper work, but writing children's fiction takes me into another world. There's a tremendous sense of freedom in drawing almost wholly on the imagination. The inspiration for my stories comes from our ginger cat, Marmaduke, and our greyhound/whippet, Miss Kip. Besides my own work, I get heavily involved in my husband's projects, helping to research his radio programs and translating documents from Latin, French, and Welsh for use in his books.

''The public relations consultancy, which is exceptionally busy, is an extension of my journalistic work. In 1986 I was appointed press officer to the Beaumaris Festival [in] Anglesey.''

AVOCATIONAL INTERESTS: Golf, European travel.

*   *   *

LUDLOW, George
See KAY, Ernest

*   *   *

LUTZ, John (Thomas) 1939-

PERSONAL: Born September 11, 1939, in Dallas, Tex.; son of John Peter and Jane (Gundelfinger) Lutz; married Barbara Jean Bradley, March 25, 1958; children: Steven, Jennifer, Wendy. *Education:* Attended Meramec Community College, 1965. *Politics:* ''Reasonable.''

ADDRESSES: Home and office—880 Providence Ave., Webster Groves, Mo. 63119. *Agent*—Dominick Abel Literary Agency Inc., 498 West End Ave., New York, N.Y. 10024.

CAREER: Writer. Has worked in construction and as a truck driver.

MEMBER: Mystery Writers of America, Private Eye Writers of America.

AWARDS, HONORS: Mystery Writers of America scroll, 1981, for short story "Until You Are Dead"; Shamus Award, Private Eye Writers of America, 1982; Edgar Allan Poe Award, Mystery Writers of America, 1986, for short story "Ride the Lightning."

WRITINGS:

MYSTERY NOVELS

The Truth of the Matter, Pocket Books, 1971.
Buyer Beware, Putnam, 1976.
Bonegrinder, Putnam, 1976.
Lazarus Man, Morrow, 1979.
Jericho Man, Morrow, 1980.
The Shadow Man, Morrow, 1981.
(With Bill Pronzini) *The Eye*, Mysterious Press, 1984.
Nightlines, St. Martin's, 1985.
The Right to Sing the Blues, St. Martin's, 1986.
Tropical Heat, Holt, 1986.
Ride the Lightning, St. Martin's, 1987.
Scorcher, Holt, 1987.

CONTRIBUTOR TO ANTHOLOGIES

Ellery Queen, editor, *Ellery Queen's Mystery Bay*, World Publishing, 1972.
Queen, editor, *Ellery Queen's Murdercade*, Random House, 1975.
E. Hoch, editor, *Best Detective Stories*, Dutton, 1976.
J. Gores and Pronzini, editors, *Tricks and Treats*, Doubleday, 1976.
Eleanor Sullivan, editor, *Tales to Take Your Breath Away*, Dial, 1977.
Sullivan, editor, *Alfred Hitchcock's Tales to Make Your Blood Run Cold*, Dial, 1978.
Sullivan, editor, *Tales to Scare You Stiff*, Dial, 1978.
Barry Malzberg and Pronzini, editors, *Dark Sins, Dark Dreams*, Doubleday, 1978.
Pronzini, editor, *Midnight Specials*, Bobbs-Merrill, 1978.
Sullivan, editor, *Tales to Be Read with Caution*, Dial, 1979.
Sullivan, editor, *Tales to Make Your Teeth Chatter*, Dial, 1980.
Queen, editor, *Ellery Queen's Circumstantial Evidence*, Dial, 1980.
Sullivan, editor, *Tales to Make You Weak in the Knees*, Dial, 1981.
Martin Greenberg, Malzberg, and Pronzini, editors, *Arbor House Treasury of Mystery and Suspense*, Arbor House, 1981.
Arbor House Treasury of Horror and the Supernatural, Arbor House, 1981.
Pronzini, editor, *Creature*, Arbor House, 1981.

OTHER

Contributor of about 150 stories to magazines.

WORK IN PROGRESS: Short stories; a novel.

SIDELIGHTS: John Lutz told *CA:* "It would be difficult for me to say exactly what motivated me to begin writing; it's possible that the original motivation is gone, much as a match that starts a forest fire is consumed in the early moments of the fire. I continue writing for selfish reasons. I thoroughly enjoy it."

LUZA, Radomir 1922-

PERSONAL: Born October 17, 1922, in Prague, Czechoslovakia; came to United States, 1953, naturalized U.S. citizen, 1959; son of Vojtech (a five-star army general) and Milada (Vecera) Luza; married Libuse Podhrazska, February 5, 1949; children: Radomir V., Sabrina. *Education:* Masaryk University, Ju.Dr., 1948; New York University, M.A., 1958, Ph.D., 1959.

ADDRESSES: Home—839 Roseland Pkwy., New Orleans, La. 70123. *Office*—Department of History, Tulane University, New Orleans, La. 70118.

CAREER: A member of the Czechoslovakia Resistance, Luza was jailed by the Gestapo in 1941 and lived underground during the rest of World War II; became deputy commanding officer of the Partisan Brigade and later headed the Social Democratic Youth in Czechoslovakia; escaped to France after the Communist takeover in 1948 and remained in Paris until 1953, when he came to the United States; M. L. Annenberg Foundation, Philadelphia, Pa., research associate, 1960-62; Educational Fund, Inc., Detroit, Mich., European representative, 1963-66; Louisiana State University, New Orleans, associate professor of modern European history, 1966-67; Tulane University, New Orleans, professor of history, 1967—. Visiting professor, University of Hamburg, 1969-70. Member of Council of Free Czechoslovakia, Washington, D.C., 1960—.

MEMBER: American Historical Association, Association for the Advancement of Slavic Studies, Authors Guild, Authors League of America, and numerous American historical associations.

AWARDS, HONORS: Received award from Theodor Koerner Foundation, 1965; grants from Social Research Council, 1969, American Philosophical Society, 1971, 1975, 1978, 1986, and American Council on Learned Societies, 1972, 1977, 1985; residency, Rockefeller Bellagio Study Center, 1987.

WRITINGS:

Odsun: Prispevek k historii ceskonemeckych vztahu v letech 1918-1952, Nase Cesta, 1952.
The Transfer of the Sudeten Germans: A Study of Czech-German Relations, 1933-62, New York University Press, 1964.
History of the International Socialist Youth Movement, Sijthoff, 1970.
(Editor with Victor S. Mamatey) *A History of the Czechoslovak Republic, 1918-1948*, Princeton University Press, 1973.
Austro-German Relations in the Auschluss Era, Princeton University Press, 1975.
Oesterreich in der NS-Zeit, Boehlau, 1977.
Geschichte der Tschechoslowakischen Republik, 1918-1948, Boehlau, 1980.
A History of the Resistance in Austria, 1938-1945, University of Minnesota Press, 1984.
Der Widerstand in Oesterreich, 1938-1945, Bundesverlag, 1985.

Member of editorial board of *Svedectvi*, an exile Czechoslovak political review, and of *East European Quarterly*.

*   *   *

LYNNE, Becky
See ZAWADSKY, Patience

LYONS, Dorothy M(arawee) 1907-

PERSONAL: Born December 4, 1907, in Fenton, Mich.; daughter of Daniel Franklin and Mary Louise (Adams) Lyons. *Education:* University of Michigan, A.B., 1929.

ADDRESSES: Home and office—900 Calle de Los Amigos, Santa Barbara, Calif. 93105.

CAREER: National Association of Book Publishers, New York, N.Y., secretary, 1931-36; *Honolulu Star-Bulletin,* Honolulu, Hawaii, stenographer, 1937; American Red Cross, secretary in Honolulu, 1937-42, district secretary in Los Angeles, Calif., 1943; executive secretary in Santa Barbara, Calif., 1943-48; California Department of Industrial Relations, Santa Barbara, secretary, 1960-70; Dorothy Lyons Horsemanship School (correspondence course in basic horsemanship), Santa Barbara, president, 1970-85.

MEMBER: American Connemara Pony Society, Goleta Valley Art Association, Santa Barbara Artists Association, Delta Zeta, Santa Barbara Sage Hens.

WRITINGS:

The Devil Made the Small Town (autobiography), Kilkerrin House, 1983.

JUVENILE

Silver Birch, Harcourt, 1939.
Midnight Moon, Harcourt, 1941.
Golden Sovereign, Harcourt, 1946.
Red Embers, Harcourt, 1948.
Harlequin Hullabaloo, Harcourt, 1949.
Copper Khan, Harcourt, 1950.
Dark Sunshine, Harcourt, 1951.
Blue Smoke, Harcourt, 1953.
Java Jive, Harcourt, 1955.
Bright Wampum, Harcourt, 1958.
Smoke Rings, Harcourt, 1960.
Pedigree Unknown, Harcourt, 1973.

SIDELIGHTS: Dorothy M. Lyons told *CA:* "To a woman who asked what moral precept I had included in a book, I replied, 'I write books to be enjoyed, books I hope the young ones will read and hate to put down, books they will want to reread over and over.' I do try to include 'growing things' such as warning a girl never to sign a paper she has not read, or a big word here and there to stretch the vocabulary, and, I suppose, moral (ugh!) precepts by implication.

"Much of my writing is by intuition. I will use an incident without knowing until later just how right it is. Basically, writing is *feeling,* and unless the author lives, suffers and enjoys with the characters, the result may very well be one-dimensional. Recently, I have been expanding the creative process by painting in oils, which I thoroughly enjoy, for unlike writing, painting is a sociable activity that permits the presence of other like-minded souls."

AVOCATIONAL INTERESTS: Bridge, reading, oil painting, Connemara ponies.

M

MACDONALD, Mary
See GIFFORD, Griselda

* * *

MacKAY, D(onald) I(ain) 1937-

PERSONAL: Born February 27, 1937, in Kobe, Japan; son of William and Rhona (Cooper) MacKay; married Diana Marjory Raffan, July 31, 1961; children: Deborah Jane, Paula Claire, Gregor Donald Raffan. *Education:* University of Aberdeen, M.A. (first class honors), 1959.

ADDRESSES: Home—145 Gamekeeper's Rd., Edinburgh EH4 6LU, Scotland.

CAREER: Systems analyst for an electric company in England, 1959-62; University of Aberdeen, Aberdeen, Scotland, lecturer, 1962-66; University of Glasgow, Glasgow, Scotland, lecturer, 1966-68, senior lecturer in applied economics, 1968-71; University of Aberdeen, professor of political economy, 1971-76; Heriot-Watt University, Edinburgh, Scotland, professor of economics, 1976-82; chairman of Pieda (planning and economic consultants), 1982—. Economic consultant to secretary of state for Scotland, 1971—.

WRITINGS:

Geographical Mobility and the Brain Drain: A Case Study of Aberdeen University Graduates, G. Allen, 1969.
(Contributor) Derek Robinson, editor, *Local Labor Markets and Wage Structures,* Gower Press, 1970.
Labor Markets under Different Employment Conditions, Allen & Unwin, 1971.
(With N. K. Buxton) *British Employment Statistics: A Guide to Sources and Methods,* Basil Blackwell, 1977.
(Editor) *Scotland 1980: The Economics of Self-Government,* Q. Press, 1977.
(With others) *The Economic Impact of North Sea Oil on Scotland,* H.M.S.O., 1978.
(Editor) *Scotland: The Framework for Change,* P. Harris, 1979.

Also editor, *Scottish Journal of Political Economy,* 1971-82.

AVOCATIONAL INTERESTS: Chess, bridge, all ball games, reading history and historical novels.

MACKINLAY, Leila Antoinette Sterling 1910-
(Brenda Grey)

PERSONAL: Born September 5, 1910, in London, England; daughter of Malcolm Sterling (a singing teacher and author) and Dagny (Hansen) Mackinlay. *Education:* Attended private schools. *Politics:* Conservative. *Religion:* Church of England.

ADDRESSES: Home—4N Portman Mansions, Chiltern St., London W1M 1LF, England.

CAREER: Trained as a singer and actress, but turned to writing as a career, 1930—. Regent Street Polytechnic, London, England, teacher of English to foreigners, 1938-39, and for a period after the war; London County Council, panel lecturer on writing at Regent Street Polytechnic, 1938-39, teacher at various evening institutes, 1946—. Amateur musical critic for *Dancing Times,* 1935-39, *Amateur Stage,* 1946-87. Publishers' reader.

MEMBER: Romantic Novelists' Association, National Book League (life), National Operatic and Dramatic Association (life), Royal Society of Literature.

WRITINGS:

Little Mountebank, Mills & Boon, 1930.
Fame's Fetters, Mills & Boon, 1931.
Madame Juno, Mills & Boon, 1931.
An Exotic Young Lady, Mills & Boon, 1932.
Willed to Wed, Mills & Boon, 1933.
Musical Productions (nonfiction), Jenkins, 1955.
Farewell to Sadness, R. Hale, 1970.
The Silken Purse, R. Hale, 1970.
Bridal Wreath, R. Hale, 1971.
Birds of Silence, R. Hale, 1975.
Fortune's Slave, R. Hale, 1975.
Twilight Moment, R. Hale, 1976.
The Uphill Path, R. Hale, 1979.

Also author of *Mixed Singles,* Gresham, *Strange Involvement,* 1973, and *Husband in Name.*

PUBLISHED BY WARD, LOCK

The Pro's Daughter, 1934.
Shadow Lawn, 1934.
Love Goes South, 1935.
Into the Net, 1935.

Night Bell, 1936.
Young Man's Slave, 1936.
Doubting Heart, 1937.
Apron-Strings, 1937.
Caretaker Within, 1938.
Theme Song, 1938.
Only Her Husband, 1939.
Reluctant Bride, 1939.
Man Always Pays, 1940.
Woman at the Wheel, 1940.
Ridin' High, 1941.
None Better Loved, 1941.
Time on Her Hands, 1942.
Brave Live On, 1942.
Green Limelight, 1943.
Lady of the Torch, 1944.
Two Walk Together, 1945.
Piper's Pool, 1946.
Piccadilly Inn, 1946.
Blue Shutters, 1947.
Echo of Applause, 1948.
Peacock Hill, 1948.
Restless Dream, 1949.
Pilot's Point, 1949.
Six Wax Candles, 1950.
Spider Dance, 1950.
Guilt's Pavilions, 1951.
Five Houses, 1952.
Unwise Wanderer, 1952.
Cuckoo Cottage, 1953.
Midnight Is Mine, 1954.
Fiddler's Green, 1954.
Riddle of a Lady, 1955.
Vagabond Daughter, 1955.
She Married Another, 1956.
Man of the Moment, 1956.
She Moved to Music, 1956.
Divided Duty, 1957.
Mantle of Innocence, 1957.
Love on a Shoestring, 1958.
The Secret in Her Life, 1958.
Seven Red Roses, 1959.
Uneasy Conquest, 1959.
Food of Love, 1960.
Spotlight on Susan, 1960.
Beauty's Tears, 1961.
Spring Rainbow, 1961.
Vain Delights, 1962.
Broken Armour, 1963.
False Relations, 1963.
Fool of Virtue, 1964.
Practice for Sale, 1964.
Ring of Hope, 1965.
No Room for Loneliness, 1965.
An Outside Chance, 1966.
The Third Boat, 1967.
Mists of the Moor, 1967.
Frost at Dawn, 1968.
Homesick for a Dream, 1968.
Wanted—Girl Friday, 1968.

UNDER PSEUDONYM BRENDA GREY

Modern Micawbers, Eldon Press, 1933.
Stardust in Her Eyes, Gresham, 1964.
Girl of His Choice, Gresham, 1965.

How High the Moon, Gresham, 1966.
Throw Your Bouquet, Gresham, 1967.
A Very Special Person, Gresham, 1967.
Shadow of a Smile, Gresham, 1968.
Tread Softly on Dreams, Gresham, 1970.
Son of Summer, Gresham, 1970.

AVOCATIONAL INTERESTS: Riding, driving, theatre, and reading.

*   *   *

MacPHERSON, Malcolm C(ook)   1943-

PERSONAL: Born August 23, 1943, in Blackrock, Conn.; son of Andrew Claudot and Gladys (Cook) MacPherson. *Education:* Trinity College, Hartford, Conn., B.A., 1965.

ADDRESSES: Home and office—32 Ifield Rd., London SW10 9AA, England. *Agent*—Knox Burger Associates Ltd., 39½ Washington Sq. S., New York, N.Y. 10012.

CAREER: Time, Inc., New York City, trainee, 1966-67; Fairchild Publications, New York City, reporter, 1967; *Seattle* (magazine), Seattle, Wash., associate editor, 1967-68; *Newsweek*, correspondent, 1968-78; free-lance writer, 1978—. *Military service:* U.S. Marine Corps Reserve, 1965-71.

MEMBER: Muthiaga Country Club (Kenya), Mount Kenya Safari Club, Annabel's (London).

WRITINGS:

Protege (novel), Dutton, 1980.
The Lucifer Key (novel), Dutton, 1981.
The Blood of His Servants: The True Story of One Man's Search for His Family's Friend and Executioner (history), Times Books, 1984.
(Editor) *The Black Box* (nonfiction), Quill, 1984.
Time Bomb: Fermi, Heisenberg, and the Race for the Atomic Bomb, Dutton, 1986.

WORK IN PROGRESS: The Resurrection of King Kong, an autobiographical novel; *The Tunnel*, a historical novel based on the battle of Messines Ridge in Belgium, 1917, with consequences in the present.

SIDELIGHTS: Malcolm C. MacPherson's nonfiction work entitled *The Blood of His Servants: The True Story of One Man's Search for His Family's Friend and Executioner* is "a bona fide thriller," remarks Rinna Samuel in the *New York Times Book Review*. "It is the real-life, detailed drama of the obsessive pursuit of one man by another, quite literally . . . a book that cannot be put aside until its 300-odd pages are read." In the Nazi onslaught of Poland in 1941, Pieter Menten, a Dutch art collector, forced several Jews in the Polish village of Podhorodse to walk the plank to a mass grave. Among those killed were the relatives of the established Israeli journalist Lieber "Bibi" Krumholtz. "[Krumholtz] had to contend with the fact that he knew the identity of the man who had killed his family," notes Michiko Kakutani in the *New York Times*. "The man . . . had once been a kind of father figure to him, and for years Mr. Krumholz agonized over how to bring him to justice. It is his story that . . . MacPherson attempts to tell in 'The Blood of His Servants.' On the surface, the story seems reminiscent of 'Eleni,' Nicholas Gage's account of his investigation of his mother's death. . . . Unfortunately, 'The Blood of His Servants' lacks the viceral appeal to the emotions of 'Eleni' and its finely observed sense of people and place. . . . As it is, the volume is a sort of hodgepodge of investigative reporting . . . that tends to stereotype the suffering of its characters.'' But for Samuel, MacPherson's account is ''one of the rarities'' in the growing collection of books concentrating on the Holocaust tragedy.

According to *Los Angeles Times Book Review* critic Chris Goodrich, *The Blood of His Servants* is ''more about politics than pursuit.'' Although Menten was not difficult to track down, he was difficult to prosecute because of his relationship with members of Dutch royalty. ''Instead of emphasizing the deeper questions aroused by Menten's near escape from punishment— why the reluctance to prosecute? How much did the Dutch and Polish governments know?—MacPherson attempts a more literary history. The writing is frequently overwrought . . . but given the power of the story, that is a minor quibble: The bringing to justice of Pieter Menten is enough to make the book worthwhile.''

BIOGRAPHICAL/CRITICAL SOURCES:

PERIODICALS

Los Angeles Times Book Review, September 2, 1984, August 10, 1986.
New York Times, July 5, 1984.
New York Times Book Review, April 29, 1984.
Publishers Weekly, December 9, 1983.
Washington Post, June 5, 1984.
Washington Post Book Review, June 22, 1986.

*   *   *

MADGWICK, P(eter) J(ames) 1925-

PERSONAL: Born August 15, 1925, in London, England; son of Frederick Martin (manager of printing firm) and Ellen (Miller) Madgwick; married Olive Hoskins (a research assistant), August 16, 1947; children: Rupert, Julia, Clare. *Education:* Magdalen College, Oxford, B.A. and M.A., 1950, Diploma in Education, 1951.

ADDRESSES: Home—60 Danycoed, Aberystwyth, Wales. *Office*—University College of Wales, University of Wales, Aberystwyth, Wales.

CAREER: University of Nottingham, Nottingham, England, lecturer in political science, 1952-65; University of Wales, University College of Wales, Aberystwyth, senior lecturer, 1965-74, reader in political science, 1974—. *Military service:* Royal Air Force, 1944-47; became sergeant.

WRITINGS:

(With Jonathan D. Chambers) *Conflict and Community: Europe since 1750,* George Philip & Son, 1968.
American City Politics, Humanities, 1970.
Introduction to British Politics, Hutchinson, 1970, 3rd edition, 1984.
The Politics of Rural Wales, Hutchinson, 1973.
(Contributor) M. Beloff and V. Vale, editors, *American Political Institutions in the 1970's,* Macmillan, 1975.
The Territorial Dimension in United Kingdom Politics, Macmillan, 1982.
(With Denis Balsom and Denis Van Mechelen) *The Political Consequences of Welsh Identity,* Centre for the Study of Public Policy, University of Strathclyde, 1982.
(With others) *Britain since 1945,* Longwood, 1982.

WORK IN PROGRESS: Contributing to *Linguistic Conflict as a Problem in Government,* for Routledge & Kegan Paul and *Leadership in Local Government,* for Charles Knight.†

MADHUBUTI, Haki R. 1942-
(Don L. Lee)

PERSONAL: Born February 23, 1942, in Little Rock, Ark.; son of Jimmy L. and Maxine (Graves) Lee; married Johari Amini; children: two. *Education:* Attended Wilson Junior College, Roosevelt University, and University of Illinois, Chicago Circle; University of Iowa, M.F.A., 1984.

ADDRESSES: Office—Third World Press, 7524 South Cottage Grove Ave., Chicago, Ill. 60619; Department of English, Speech, and Theatre, Chicago State University, 95th St. at King Dr., Chicago, Ill. 60628.

CAREER: DuSable Museum of African American History, Chicago, Ill., apprentice curator, 1963-67; Montgomery Ward, Chicago, stock department clerk, 1963-64; post office clerk in Chicago, 1964-65; Spiegels, Chicago, junior executive, 1965-66; Cornell University, Ithaca, N.Y., writer-in-residence, 1968-69; Northeastern Illinois State College, Chicago, poet-in-residence, 1969-70; University of Illinois, Chicago, lecturer, 1969-71; Howard University, Washington, D.C., writer-in-residence, 1970-78; Morgan State College, Baltimore, Md., 1972-73; Chicago State University, Chicago, Ill., associate professor of English, 1984—. Publisher and editor, Third World Press, 1967—. Director of Institute of Positive Education, Chicago, 1969—. *Military service:* U.S. Army, 1960-63.

MEMBER: African Liberation Day Support Committee (vice-chairperson), Congress of African People (past member of executive council), Organization of Black American Culture, Writers Workshop (founding member, 1967-75).

WRITINGS:

UNDER NAME DON L. LEE

Think Black, Broadside Press, 1967, revised edition, 1968, enlarged edition, 1969.
Black Pride, Broadside Press, 1967.
For Black People (and Negroes Too), Third World Press, 1968.
Don't Cry, Scream (poems), Broadside Press, 1969.
We Walk the Way of the New World (poems), Broadside Press, 1970.
(Author of introduction) *To Blackness: A Definition in Thought,* Kansas City Black Writers Workshop, 1970.
Dynamite Voices I: Black Poets of the 1960s (essays), Broadside Press, 1971.
(Editor with P. L. Brown and F. Ward) *To Gwen with Love,* Johnson Publishing, 1971.
Directionscore: Selected and New Poems, Broadside Press, 1971.
(Author of introduction) Marion Nicholas, *Life Styles,* Broadside Press, 1971.
The Need for an African Education (pamphlet), Institute of Positive Education, 1972.

UNDER NAME HAKI R. MADHUBUTI

Book of Life (poems), Broadside Press, 1973.
From Plan to Planet—Life Studies: The Need for Afrikan Minds and Institutions, Broadside Press, 1973.
(With Jawanza Kunjufu) *Black People and the Coming Depression* (pamphlet), Institute of Positive Education, 1975.
(Contributor) *A Capsule Course in Black Poetry Writing,* Broadside Press, 1975.

Enemies: The Clash of Races (essays), Third World Press, 1978.

Earthquakes and Sunrise Missions: Poetry and Essays of Black Renewal, 1973-1983 (poems), Third World Press, 1984.

Killing Memory, Seeking Ancestors (poems), Lotus, 1987.

Say That the River Turns: The Impact of Gwendolyn Brooks (poetry and prose), Third World Press, 1987.

OTHER

Also author of *Back Again, Home*, 1968, and *One Sided Shootout*, 1968. Contributor to more than one hundred anthologies. Contributor to numerous magazines and literary journals, including *Black World, Negro Digest, Journal of Black Poetry, Essence, Journal of Black History,* and *Chicago Defender.* Founder and editor of *Black Books Bulletin*, 1972—; contributing editor, *Black Scholar* and *First World.*

WORK IN PROGRESS: *Black Men: Obsolete, Single, Dangerous?*, essays; *Gifted Genius: African-American Political Poets*, criticism; *Collected Poetry (1966-1989)*; and *Collected Essays (1969-1989)*.

SIDELIGHTS: "Poetry in my home was almost as strange as money," Don L. Lee, also known by his Swahili name Haki R. Madhubuti, relates in *Dynamite Voices I: Black Poets of the 1960s.* Abandoned by his father, then bereaved of his mother at the age of sixteen, Madhubuti made his living by maintaining two paper routes and cleaning a nearby bar. Poetry was scarce in his early life, he explains in the same source, because "what wasn't taught, but was consciously learned, in our early educational experience was that writing of any kind was something that Black people just didn't do." Nonetheless, he has become one of the best known poets of the black arts movement of the 1960s, a respected and influential critic of Black poetry, and an activist dedicated to the cultural unity of his people. "In many ways," writes Catherine Daniels Hurst in the *Dictionary of Literary Biography*, Madhubuti "is one of the most representative voices of his time. Although most significant as a poet, his work as an essayist, critic, publisher, social activist, and educator has enabled him to go beyond the confines of poetry to the establishment of a black press and a school for black children."

The literature of the Harlem Renaissance—a literary movement of the 1920s and 1930s in which the works of many black artists became popular—was not deeply felt by the majority of America's black population, he writes. "In the Sixties, however, Black Art in all its various forms began to flourish as never before: music, theater, art (painting, sculpture), films, prose (novel[s], essays), and poetry. The new and powerful voices of the Sixties came to light mainly because of the temper of the times." The writers of this turbulent generation who worked to preserve a cultural heritage distinct from white culture did not look to previous literary traditions—black or white—for inspiration. Says Madhubuti, "The major influences on the new Black poets were/are Black music, Black life style, Black churches, and their own Black contemporaries."

An *Ebony* article on the poet by David Llorens hails him as "a lion of a poet who splits syllables, invents phrases, makes letters work as words, and gives rhythmic quality to verse that is never savage but often vicious and always reflecting a revolutionary black consciousness." As a result, his "lines rumble like a street gang on the page," remarks Liz Gant in a *Black World* review. Though Madhubuti believes, as he declares in *Don't Cry, Scream*, that "most, if not all blackpoetry

will be *political*," he explains in *Dynamite Voices I* that it must do more than protest, since "mere 'protest' writing is generally a weak reaction to persons or events and often lacks the substance necessary to motivate and move people." Black poetry will be powerful, he says, if it is "a genuine reflection of [the poet] and his people," presenting "the beauty and joy" of the black experience as well as outrage against social and economic oppression.

However, some critics hear only the voice of protest in Madhubuti's work. Paul Breman's piece in C. W. E. Bigsby's *The Black American Writer, Volume I: Poetry and Drama*, calls him a poet whose "all-out ranting ... has become outdated more rapidly than one could have hoped." And Jascha Kessler, writing in a *Poetry* review, sees no poetry in Madhubuti's books. "Anger, bombast, raw hatred, strident, aggrieved, perhaps charismatically crude religious and political canting, propaganda and racist nonsense, yes.... [Madhubuti] is outside poetry somewhere, exhorting, hectoring, cursing, making a lot of noise." But the same elements that grate against the sensibilities of such critics stem from the poet's cultural objectives and are much better received by the poet's intended audience, say others. "He is not interested in modes of writing that aspire to elegance," writes Gwendolyn Brooks in the introduction of *Don't Cry, Scream*. Madhubuti writes for and to Blacks, and "the last thing these people crave is elegance. It is very hard to enchant, with elegant song, the ears of a fellow whose stomach is growling," she notes. Explains Hurst, "often he uses street language and the dialect of the uneducated Black community.... He uses unconventional abbreviations and strung-together words ... in a visually rendered dialect designed to convey the stress, pitch, volume, texture, resonance, and the intensity of the black speaking voice. By these and other means, Madhubuti intends to engage the active participation of a black audience accustomed to the oral tradition of storytelling and song."

Poems in *Don't Cry, Scream* and *We Walk the Way of the New World* show the activist-poet's "increasing concern for incorporating jazz rhythms"; more and more, the poet styled the poems "for performance, the text lapsing into exultant screams and jazz scats," writes C. W. E. Bigsby in *The Second Black Renaissance.* The title poem of *Don't Cry, Scream*, believes Hurst, "should be dedicated to that consummate musician, John Coltrane, whose untimely death left many of his admirers in deep mourning. In this poem (which begs to be read out loud as only the poet himself can do it), Madhubuti strains to duplicate the virtuoso high notes of Coltrane's instrumental sound." Critic Sherley Anne Williams, speaking to interviewer Claudia Tate in *Black Women Writers at Work*, explains why this link to music is significant for the black writer. Whereas white Americans preserve themselves or their legacy through literature, black Americans have done so in music, in the blues form: "The blues records of each decade explain something about the philosophical basis of historical continuity for black people. It is a ritualized way of talking about ourselves and passing it on. This was true until the late sixties." Madhubuti elaborates in *Dynamite Voices I:* "Black music is our most advanced form of Black art. In spite of the debilitating conditions of slavery and its aftermath, Black music endured and grew as a communicative language, as a sustaining spiritual force, as entertainment, and as a creative extension of our African selves. It was one of the few mediums of expression open to Black people that was virtually free of interferences.... To understand ... art ... which is uniquely Black, we must start with the art form that has been least distorted, a form that has so far resisted being molded into a *pure* product of European-American culture.'' Numerous references to Black musicians and lines that imitate the sounds of Black music connect Madhubuti's poetry to that tradition and extend its life as well.

Hurst claims that the poet's "unique delivery has given him a popular appeal which is tantamount to stardom." In 1969, the poet averaged three appearances a week, reading his poetry and carrying on dialogs at institutions across the country. Phenomenal sales in excess of 100,000 by then alerted Helen Vendler that "something [was] happening." Writing in the *New York Times Book Review,* she attributed the sales to Madhubuti's "nerve, stamina, and satire. In him the sardonic and savage turn-of-phrase long present in black speech as a survival tactic finds its best poet." Daniel Greene suggested in the *National Observer* that a general concern about black militance and possible urban rioting accounted for sales, but went on to say that "people in the publishing industry are convinced that untold numbers of older and ill-educated Negroes, whose reading up till now might have been limited to comic and pulp fiction, are being lured to book shops and paperback stands by volumes exploring the 'black experience' in language they can understand."

Madhubuti's poetic voice softened somewhat during the 1970s, during which time he directed his energies to the writing of political essays (*From Plan to Planet—Life Studies: The Need for Afrikan Minds and Institutions* and *Enemies: The Clash of Races*). In addition, he contributed to the establishment of a black aesthetic for new writers through critical essays and reviews. *Dynamite Voices I,* for instance, "has become one of the major contemporary scholarly resources for black poetry," notes Hurst. Fulfilling the role of "cultural stabilizer," he also gave himself to the construction of institutions that promote the cultural independence and education of his people. In a fight against "brain mismanagement" in America, he founded the Third World Press in 1967 to encourage literacy and the Institute of Positive Education in 1969 "to provide educational and communication services to a community struggling to assert its identity amidst powerful, negative forces," he told Donnarae MacCann for an interview published in *Interracial Books for Children Bulletin.*

Students at the Institute in Chicago are schooled in the works of black writers because he feels black children need a better education than the one he received: "My education was . . . acculturation, that process in which one is brought into another's culture, regardless of the damage. For the most part, my generation did not question this acculturation process. . . . In school I read Hawthorne, Twain, Hemingway, Fitzgerald— the major Western writers. My generation learned from that Western tradition, but we were not given the tradition that spoke best to our insides." Black authors such as Langston Hughes, Margaret Walker, Gwendolyn Brooks and Richard Wright (discovered "by accident" when he was thirteen), helped him to become "complete."

In the same interview, he defines the publishing goals of the Third World Press: "We look for writers who continue to critically assess the ambivalence of being Black in America. . . . What we are trying to do is to service the great majority of Black people, those who do not have a voice, who have not made it. Black themes over the past years have moved from reaction and rage to contemplative assessments of today's problems to a kind of visionary look at the world," a vision that includes not only blacks, but all people. But the devel-

opment of the black community remains its main focus, he told David Streitfield for a *Washington Post* article. "There's just so much negative material out there, and so little that helps. That's not to say we don't publish material that is critical, but it has to be constructive." As Streitfield reports, "Third World's greatest succes has been with . . . Chancellor Williams' *Destruction of Black Civilization,* which has gone through 16 printings." Other articles as well commended the press for breaking even for the first time in nineteen years in 1987.

Summing up Madhubuti's accomplishment as a writer, Williams comments in *Give Birth to Brightness: A Thematic Study in Neo-Black Literature* that as one of "the vocal exponents of Neo-Black literature," he has "come to symbolize most of what is strong and beautiful and vital in Black Experience and Black Art." Hurst's summary states, "His books have sold more than a million copies, without benefit of a national distributor. Perhaps Madhubuti will even succeed in helping to establish some lasting institutions in education and in the publishing world. Whether he does or not, he has already secured a place for himself in American literature. He is among the foremost anthologized contemporary revolutionary poets, and he has played a significant role in stimulating other young black talent. As Stephen Henderson has observed, he is 'more widely imitated than any other Black poet with the exception of Imamu Baraka (LeRoi Jones). . . . His influence is enormous, and is still growing.'"

BIOGRAPHICAL/CRITICAL SOURCES:

BOOKS

Bigsby, C. W. E., *The Black American Writer, Volume I: Poetry & Drama,* Penguin, 1969.

Bigsby, C. W. E., *The Second Black Renaissance: Essays in Black Literature,* Greenwood Press, 1980.

Contemporary Literary Criticism, Gale, Volume II, 1974, Volume VI, 1976.

Dictionary of Literary Biography, Gale, Volume V: *American Poets since World War II,* 1980, Volume XLI: *Afro-American Poets since 1955,* 1985.

Gibson, Donald B., editor, *Modern Black Poets: A Collection of Critical Essays,* Prentice-Hall, 1973.

Henderson, Stephen, *Understanding the New Black Poetry: Black Speech and Black Music as Poetic References,* Morrow, 1973.

Lee, Don L., *Don't Cry, Scream,* Broadside Press, 1969.

Lee, Don L., *Dynamite Voices, I: Black Poets of the 1960s,* Broadside Press, 1971.

Mosher, Marlene, *New Directions from Don L. Lee,* Exposition, 1975.

Tate, Claudia, editor, *Black Women Writers at Work,* Continuum, 1983.

Vendler, Helen, *Part of Nature, Part of Us,* Howard University Press, 1980.

Williams, John A., and Charles F. Harris, editors, *Amistad 2,* Random House, 1971.

Williams, Sherley Anne, *Give Birth to Brightness: A Thematic Study in Neo-Black Literature,* Dial, 1972.

PERIODICALS

Black Collegian, February/March, 1971, September/October, 1974.

Black World, April, 1971, June, 1972, January, 1974.

Chicago Sun Times, December 11, 1987.

Chicago Sun Times Showcase, July 18, 1971.

Chicago Tribune, December 23, 1987.
College Literature Association Journal, September, 1971.
Ebony, March, 1969.
Interracial Books for Children Bulletin, Volume 17, number 2, 1986.
Jet, June 27, 1974.
Journal of Negro History, April, 1971.
National Observer, July 14, 1969.
Negro Digest, December, 1969.
New Lady, July/August, 1971.
New York Times, December 13, 1987.
New York Times Book Review, September 29, 1974.
Poetry, February, 1973.
Washington Post, June 6, 1971, January 17, 1988.

—*Sketch by Marilyn K. Basel*

*   *   *

MAEHLQVIST, (Karl) Stefan   1943-

PERSONAL: Born August 7, 1943, in Nykoeping, Sweden; son of Alexis (a bath attendant) and Asta (a clerk; maiden name, Persson) Maehlqvist; married Karin Johannisson (a university lecturer), July 26, 1967; children: Andreas Sergej, Aksel Sebastian. *Education:* University of Uppsala, B.A., 1967, Ph.D., 1977.

ADDRESSES: Home—Celsiusgatan 8, S-752 31, Uppsala, Sweden. *Office*—Bredmansgatan 4A, S-75224, Uppsala, Sweden. *Agent*—Foreign Rights' Manager, Raben & Sjoegren, Box 45022, S-1403, Stockholm 45, Sweden.

CAREER: Early in career worked as an actor; University of Uppsala, Uppsala, Sweden, assistant, 1969-73, research assistant, 1974-76, lecturer in comparative literature, 1978—; Swedish Institute for Children's Books, Stockholm, information secretary, 1976-78; author of books for children.

MEMBER: Swedish Union of Authors (secretary of children's literature section, 1978-85; board member, 1983—).

WRITINGS:

Buecker foer Svenska barn 1870-1950, Gidlunds, 1977.
Biggles i sverige (a study of the writings of W. E. Johns; title means "Biggles in Sweden"), Gidlunds, 1983.
Den andra roesten (title means "The Second Voice"), Faber, 1984.

JUVENILES

Inte farligt pappa, krokodilerna klarar jag, illustrations by Tord Nygren, Raben & Sjoegren, 1977, translation by author and Margaret McElderry published as *I'll Take Care of the Crocodiles,* Atheneum, 1978.
Kom in i min natt, kom in i min droem, illustrations by Nygren, Raben & Sjoegren, 1978, translation by Anthea Bell published as *Come into My Night, Come into My Dream,* Pepper Press, 1981.
Drakberget (title means "Dragon's Mountain"), illustrations by Nygren, Raben & Sjoegren, 1981.
Apan i arken (title means "The Ape in the Ark"), illustrations by Pia Forsberg, Raben & Sjoegren, 1982.
Ett hart paket (title means "A Hard Parcel"), Raben et Sjoegren, 1983.
Nattens svarta flagga (title means "The Black Flag of Night"), AWE/Gebers, 1985.
Ga pa stenar (title means "Walk on Stones"), AWE/Gebers, 1986.

OTHER

Author of teleplays for Swedish television, including "Ram tam tagger," a series of four pantomimes, aired in 1970-71, and "Circus tagger," a series of three programs, aired in 1972. Author of more than one hundred "Boktipset," short book promotions for television, aired beginning in 1976. Children's book critic and translator, *Dagens Nyheter* (newspaper), 1973—. Contributor of essays on children's literature and children's authors to periodicals, including *Barn och Kultur* and *Forfattaren.*

SIDELIGHTS: Stefan Maehlqvist once told *CA:* "I came into children's books through criticism and research. My theoretical background was well grounded before I suddenly, rather unintentionally, found myself in practice. A story came upon me while I was trying to keep awake for a nighttime work session, waiting for my boy to fall asleep. It came out in two hours, and I revised it by changing one word.

"My first three children's books, in collaboration with artist Tord Nygren, now form a thematic trilogy, 'excursions from a room.' The first is a daydream at bedtime, with a humorous slice of wish fulfillment; the second is a nightmare with streams of dark fantasy; the third contains a historical setting, and it enters into a pair of parallel fairy tales. I hope that my stories leave the door open to a wider social context.

"In general, the text for many picture books is, for my taste, much too simple, pedagogical, and idyllic. Picture books are usually read by a grownup to a preschool child. They are in a unique situation of direct communication—I try to make use of that, working with text and pictures on many levels. As a boy, I wrote and directed films, and later I went into acting. So dialogue and visual sensuality are of great importance to my writing. Some layers of meaning may be hidden from the child but engage the adult reader. My books are meant to reach these two readers at the same time. Unfortunately, these textual overtones are lost in the English translations, where I have found a very conservative and anxious attitude still very much alive.

"Nygren makes the same congenial references in his pictures that I make in my text, although the relationship between the two is different in each of the three parts of the trilogy. In *I'll Take Care of the Crocodiles,* the scenes take an active part in the telling of the story; things left out of the text are acted out visually. In *Come into My Night, Come into My Dream,* every scene tries to give a new emotional response by the use of a different dominant color. In *Dragon's Mountain,* the pictures differ according to the historical setting of the story. A tale about a medieval knight is illustrated with imitations of woodcuts, and the next tale about early industrial mining is illustrated with xylographs.

"Creative work for me means a lot of brooding about, collecting little pieces here and there, until it finally bursts out in fairly rapid writing sessions. But never again have I been so lucky as with my first story!"

More recently, Maehlqvist wrote: "Every new book is a new adventure for me, not only in the sense that I produce a new story—I try to find a new scheme for the story as such. My latest achievement 'Walk on Stones' is a novel for young adults where narration collapses in broken images. It had to be done that way in the eye of a new world picture as drawn by quantum mechanics. It's a meeting of stones (experiences) picked up by the I (subjective filter). The centre of the book contains a fictional discussion between Albert Einstein and Niels Bohr in front of the dead Victor Frankenstein. I don't like to lead the reader by the hand, I like to open up a conversation."

AVOCATIONAL INTERESTS: "I went through a whole lot of avocational interests in my youth and suppose I left them there."

BIOGRAPHICAL/CRITICAL SOURCES:

PERIODICALS

Bonniers Litterara Magasin, Number 4, 1980.
Dagens Nyheter, November 11, 1982.
Opsis Kalopsis, Number 2, 1986.

*   *   *

MAGOON, Robert A(rnold)   1922-

PERSONAL: Born January 30, 1922, in Salem, N.H.; son of William A. and Marion Magoon; married wife, Ronnie (a business education teacher); children: Robert Arnold, Jr., Brian Alan. *Education:* University of the Philippines, A.B., 1958; University of Virginia, M.Ed., 1960, Ed.D., 1967.

ADDRESSES: Home—P.O. Box 66781, St. Petersburg Beach, Fla. 33736. *Office*—College of Education, Old Dominion University, Norfolk, Va. 23129.

CAREER: University of Virginia, Charlottesville, associate professor of air science, 1958-62, director of Hampton Roads Center, 1962-64; Old Dominion University, Norfolk, Va., 1964-87, began as assistant professor, became associate professor, then professor of foundations of education and chairman of department, professor emeritus, 1987—. Member of summer faculty at University of Vermont, 1969-70. *Military service:* U.S. Air Force; became lieutenant colonel.

MEMBER: American Psychological Association, American Personnel and Guidance Association, American Association of University Professors, Southeastern Psychological Association, Virginia Psychological Association, Phi Delta Kappa, Kappa Delta Pi, Pi Kappa Phi.

WRITINGS:

(With K. C. Garrison) *Educational Psychology: An Integration of Psychology and Educational Practices,* with student workbook, C. E. Merrill, 1972, revised edition published as *Educational Psychology: An Integrated View,* 1976.
(Editor and contributor) *Education and Psychology: Past, Present, and Future,* C. E. Merrill, 1973.
(With H. G. Jellen) *Capitalizing on Student Interest and Motivation,* Human Development, 1980.
(With Jellen) *Leadership Development: Democracy in Action,* Human Development, 1980.
(With R. S. Cofer) *A Psychology for Living: Run for Your Lives the Existentialists Are Coming,* Ram Associates, 1982.
(Editor) *Learning and Living: Right Brain, Right Style,* Ginn, 1983.

SIDELIGHTS: Robert A. Magoon told *CA:* "I commenced writing because like the mountain it was there and to have failed to achieve the objective would have left me incomplete. I continue my writing because I want to help others to sharpen their perceptions, become more satisfied, self-accepting, and hopefully happier with their lives. With regard to major publishers, if they reject your manuscript(s), don't give up, consider self-publishing. [Of *A Psychology for Living: Run for Your Lives the Existentialists are Coming,*] Abraham Maslow

wrote Dick Cofer, 'This is a book which must be published!' However, editors thought otherwise, so we published it—to the continuing joy and appreciation of our readers."

AVOCATIONAL INTERESTS: Sailing, photography, golf.

*   *   *

MAHLQVIST, (Karl) Stefan
See MAEHLQVIST, (Karl) Stefan

*   *   *

MAINE, David
See AVICE, Claude (Pierre Marie)

*   *   *

MANIFOLD, J(ohn) S(treeter)   1915-

PERSONAL: Born April 21, 1915, in Melbourne, Victoria, Australia; son of John (a grazier) and Barbara Grey (Smith) Manifold; married Katharine Hopwood (a teacher, linguist, and singer), March 9, 1940 (died, 1969); children: Miranda (Mrs. Philip Howard Barton Macqueen), Nicholas. *Education:* Jesus College, Cambridge, B.A. (with honors), 1937.

ADDRESSES: Office—c/o University of Queensland Press, P.O. Box 42, Saint Lucia, Queensland 4067, Australia. *Agent*—David Higham Associates Ltd., 5-8 Lower John St., Golden Square, London W1R 4HA, England.

CAREER: Free-lance writer, 1946—, and musicologist. Has delivered Commonwealth Literary Fund lectures at the universities of New England, Queensland, and South Australia. Toured China as a guest of the Association for Cultural Relations with Foreign Countries, 1963; toured the U.S.S.R. as a guest of the Union of Soviet Writers, 1963; delegate, International Writers' Meeting, Berlin, 1965. *Military service:* British Army, Intelligence Corps, 1940-46; served in West Africa and Europe; became captain.

MEMBER: National Council of Realist Writers' Groups (vice-president), Fellowship of Australian Writers (president of Queensland branch, 1959), Brisbane Realist Writers' Group (president, 1956-66).

WRITINGS:

POETRY

Death of Ned Kelly and Other Ballads, Favil Press, 1941.
(With David Martin and Hubert Nicholson) *Trident,* Fore, 1944.
Selected Verse, John Day, 1947.
Nightmares and Sunhorses, Edwards & Shaw (Sydney, Australia), 1961.
Op. 8: Poems, 1961-69, University of Queensland Press, 1971.
Broadsheets, privately printed, 1973.
Six Sonnets on Human Ecology, privately printed, 1974.
Collected Verse, University of Queensland Press, 1978.
On My Selection: Poems, preface by A. D. Hope, drawings by daughter, Miranda Manifold Macqueen, Bibliophile Books (Adelaide), 1983.

MUSIC

The Amorous Flute: An Unprofessional Handbook for Recorder Players and All Amateurs of Music, Workers Music Association, 1948.
(Editor) Thomas Morley, *Three Pieces from the Plaine and Easie Introduction to Musick 1597,* Schott, 1948.

(Editor with Walter Bergmann) *Petite Suite for Two Descant Recorders and Piano*, Schott, 1948.

The Music in English Drama from Shakespeare to Purcell, Barrie & Rockliff, 1956, reprinted by Scholarly Press.

The Violin, the Banjo and the Bones: An Essay on the Instruments of Bush Music, Ram's Skull Press (Victoria, Australia), 1957.

(Editor) *The Queensland Centenary Pocket Songbook*, Edwards & Shaw, 1959.

(Editor) *The Penguin Australian Songbook*, Penguin (Melbourne), 1964.

Who Wrote the Ballads? Notes on Australian Folksong, Australasian Book Society (Sydney), 1964.

CONTRIBUTOR

Keidrych Rhys, editor, *Poems from the Forces*, Routledge & Kegan Paul, 1942.

More Poems from the Forces, Routledge & Kegan Paul, 1943.

War Poets, John Day, 1945.

A Little Treasury of Modern Poetry, Scribner, 1952.

A Book of Australian Verse, Oxford University Press, 1956.

Penguin Book of Australian Verse, Penguin, 1958.

Penguin Book of Australian Ballads, Penguin, 1965.

OTHER

The Changing Face of Realism, Communist Arts Group, 1971.

Contributor to music journals and other magazines, including *Eastern Horizon*, *Realist*, *Australian*, *Keynote*, *Canon*, and *Australian Musical Times*. Poetry editor of *Realist*. Editor of "Bandicoot Ballads" series in the 1950s.

SIDELIGHTS: J. S. Manifold has been performing Australian folk music for many years; he plays the recorder, guitar, and bassoon, and other regional folk instruments, but is interested as well in chamber music, organizing an amateur group and writing music for it. Some of Manifold's work has been translated into German, French, and Polish.

AVOCATIONAL INTERESTS: Cats, wine, cheese, and the Marx Brothers.

BIOGRAPHICAL/CRITICAL SOURCES:

BOOKS

Hall, Rodney, *J. S. Manifold: An Introduction to the Man and His Work*, University of Queensland Press, 1978.†

*   *   *

MANN, A. Philo
See ALD, Roy A(llison)

*   *   *

MANN, Jessica

PERSONAL: Born in London, England; daughter of Francis (a lawyer) and Eleonore (a lawyer; maiden name, Ehrlich) Mann; married A. Charles Thomas (a professor and archaeologist); children: Richard, Martin, Susanna, Lavinia. *Education:* Cambridge University, M.A.; University of Leicester, L.L.B.

ADDRESSES: Home—Lambessow, St. Clement, Cornwall, England. *Agent*—Bolt & Watson, Suite 8, 26 Charing Cross Rd., London W.C.2, England.

CAREER: Writer.

WRITINGS:

Deadlier than the Male: An Investigation into Feminine Crime Writing (literary criticism), David & Charles, 1981.

NOVELS

Charitable End, McKay, 1971.

Mrs. Knox's Profession, McKay, 1972.

Troublecross, McKay, 1973 (published in England as *The Only Security*, Macmillan, 1973).

The Sticking Place, McKay, 1974.

Captive Audience, Macmillan, 1975.

The Eighth Deadly Sin, Macmillan, 1976.

The Sting of Death, Doubleday, 1978.

Funeral Sites, Doubleday, 1981.

No Man's Land, Doubleday, 1983.

Grave Goods, Doubleday, 1984.

A Kind of Healthy Grave, Gage, 1987.

SIDELIGHTS: Jessica Mann "can't be pigeonholed conveniently into a genre slot," believes *Washington Post Book World* reviewer Jean M. White. Although Mann's plots usually involve mystery, critics often point to her subtle characterizations and elegant style as the strongest elements in her writing.

BIOGRAPHICAL/CRITICAL SOURCES:

PERIODICALS

Globe and Mail (Toronto), January 31, 1987.

New York Times Book Review, January 15, 1984.

Times Literary Supplement, June 5, 1981.

Washington Post Book World, March 18, 1984.

*   *   *

MARSHALL, James Vance
See PAYNE, Donald Gordon

*   *   *

MARTIN, David   1915-
(Spinifex)

PERSONAL: Born December 22, 1915, in Budapest, Hungary; came to Australia, 1949; son of Leo and Hedwig (Rosner) Detsinyi; married Elizabeth Richenda Powell, 1941; children: one son. *Education:* Educated in Germany. *Politics:* "I call myself an 'international nationalist.'"

ADDRESSES: Home—28 Wood St., Beechworth, Victoria 3747, Australia. *Agent*—c/o Curtis Brown Pty. Ltd., 86 Williams St., Sydney, New South Wales 2021, Australia.

CAREER: Worked in European service for British Broadcasting Corp. (BBC), as foreign correspondent for *London Daily Express*, and literary editor for *Reynolds News*, all in London, England, 1938-47; foreign correspondent in India, 1948-49; writer, 1949—. *Military service:* International Brigade, 1937-38; served in Spain.

MEMBER: Australian Society of Authors (council member, 1973—), Australian Literature Board.

AWARDS, HONORS: Australia Council senior fellowship, 1973-76.

WRITINGS:

NOVELS

Tiger Bay, Martin & Reid, 1946.

The Stones of Bombay, Wingate, 1950.
The Young Wife (also see below), Macmillan (London), 1962.
The Hero of the Town, Morrow, 1965 (published in England as *The Hero of Too,* Cassell, 1965).
The Littlest Neutral, Crown, 1966 (published in England as *The King Between,* Cassell, 1966).
Where a Man Belongs, Cassell, 1969.

JUVENILE FICTION

Hughie, St. Martin's, 1971.
Gary, Cassell, 1972.
Frank and Francesca, Thomas Nelson, 1972.
The Chinese Boy, Hodder & Stoughton, 1973.
The Cabby's Daughter, Hodder & Stoughton, 1974.
(With wife, Elizabeth Richenda Martin) *Katie,* Hodder & Stoughton, 1974.
Mister P and His Remarkable Flight, Hodder & Stoughton, 1975.
The Devilfish Mystery of the Flying Mum, Thomas Nelson, 1977.
The Mermaid Attack, Outback Press, 1978.
The Man in the Red Turban, Hutchinson, 1978.
Peppino Says Goodbye, Rigby, 1980.
The Girl Who Didn't Know Kelly, Hutchinson, 1984.

POETRY

Battlefields and Girls, Macmillan, 1942.
(With Hubert Nicholson and John Manifold) *Trident,* Fore, 1944.
(Editor) *Rhyme and Reason: Thirty-four Poems,* Fore, 1944.
From Life: Selected Poems, Current, 1953.
(Under pseudonym Spinifex) *Rob the Robber: His Life and Vindication,* J. Waters, 1954.
Poems, 1938-1958, Edwards & Shaw, 1958.
Spiegel the Cat: A Story-Poem Based on a Tale by Gottfried Keller, F. W. Cheshire, 1961, C. N. Potter, 1971.
The Gift: Poems, 1959-1965, Jacaranda, 1966.
The Idealist, Jacaranda, 1968.
I Rhyme My Time (juvenile), Jacaranda, 1980.

OTHER

The Shepherd and the Hunter (three-act play; first produced in London, 1945), Wingate, 1946.
The Shoes Men Walk In (short stories), Pilot Press, 1946.
(With F. E. Emery) *Psychological Effects of the "Western" Film: A Study in Television Viewing* (nonfiction), University of Melbourne, 1957.
Television Tension Programmes: A Study Based on a Content Analysis of Western, Crime, and Adventure Programmes Televised by Melbourne Stations, 1960-61 (nonfiction), Australian Broadcasting Control Board, 1963.
"The Young Wife" (play; adaptation of Martin's own novel), first produced in Melbourne, 1966.
On the Road to Sydney (travel), Thomas Nelson, 1970.
Foreigners, Rigby, 1981.
Armed/Neutrality for Australia, Dove Communications, 1984.

Also author of *I'll Take Australia.*

SIDELIGHTS: David Martin told *CA:* "I was described by the *Times Literary Supplement* as 'Australia's outstanding literary acquisition from post-war immigration.' I am one of my adopted country's most prolific writers. Having first won a reputation as a poet (though my mother language is German), I also became a novelist. My most widely read work of fiction is *The Young Wife,* which tells of a Greek migrant woman in

Melbourne. I have also written 'young' novels. They, too, deal mainly with the insider-outsider theme, often using Australia's colorful background.''

* * *

MARTIN, Philip (John Talbot) 1931-

PERSONAL: Born March 28, 1931, in Melbourne, Victoria, Australia; son of Henry Martin (a public servant) and Lorna (Talbot) Martin. *Education:* University of Melbourne, B.A., 1958. *Religion:* Roman Catholic.

ADDRESSES: Office—Department of English, Monash University, Clayton, Victoria 3168, Australia.

CAREER: University of Melbourne, Melbourne, Victoria, Australia, publications officer, 1956-60, tutor in English, 1960-62; Australian National University, Canberra, Australian Capital Territory, lecturer in English, 1963; Monash University, Clayton, Victoria, lecturer, 1964-70, senior lecturer in English, 1971—. Visiting lecturer at University of Amsterdam, 1967; visiting lecturer in Australian literature, University of Venice, 1976; visiting professor of English, Carleton College, 1983. Free-lance broadcaster for Australian Broadcasting Commission, 1962—.

MEMBER: Amnesty International, PEN, Fellowship of Australian Writers, Association for the Study of Australian Literature, American Association of Australian Literary Studies, Poets' Union of Australia.

WRITINGS:

Voice Unaccompanied (poems), Australian National University Press, 1970.
Shakespeare's Sonnets: Self, Love and Art (criticism), Cambridge University Press, 1972.
A Bone Flute (poems), Australian National University Press, 1974.
From Sweden (poems), Monash University, 1979.
(Editor with others) *Directory of Australian Poets 1980,* Poets' Union of Australia, 1980.
(Translator and author of introduction) *Lars Gustafsson: Selected Poems,* Quarterly Review of Literature, 1982.
A Flag for the Wind (poems), Longman Cheshire, 1982.
New and Selected Poems, Longman Cheshire, 1987.

CONTRIBUTOR

Douglas Stuart, editor, *Modern Australian Poetry,* Angus & Robertson (Sydney), 1963.
Bruce, Dawe, editor, *Dimensions,* McGraw, 1973.
Antologia della poesia australiana contemporanea (title means "Anthology of Contemporary Australian Poetry"), Nuova Academia (Milan), 1977.
Les A. Murray, editor, *New Oxford Book of Australian Verse,* Oxford University Press (Melbourne), 1986.
Murray, editor, *Anthology of Australian Religious Poetry,* Collins Dove, 1986.

OTHER

Also author and presenter of numerous programs for Australian radio and television, including programs of poems broadcast on BBC-3. Also contributor to *Australian Poetry* (annual anthology), 1957-72. Contributor of poems, articles, and reviews to many Australian, British, and American journals.

WORK IN PROGRESS: A book on the Australian poet A. D. Hope; a collection of essays on poetry; a new book of poems, *Love Music.*

SIDELIGHTS: Philip Martin writes *CA* that he "regards broadcasting and translating as extensions" of his roles of poet and university professor. "There is one comment on my work that I especially prize," he continues. "It came from the Hungarian poet and theatre-director Gyula Urban: 'These poems are crystal, but if you cut the crystal it would bleed.' I suppose they could also be described as modern-traditional (closer in form to Yeats and Rilke than to Pound or William Carlos Williams) and in the broad sense as religious. A few years back I wrote a good deal about continuities between the past and the present, and like countless other poets I wrote then, and I write now, of love and death. Lately the emphasis has been on love, the *good* news about love (we've heard a lot about the anguish). And more and more I write narrative-dramatic poems. All my work is for the voice, often for several voices, and next I want to write verse for the theatre. This century we've had plenty of poetry there, but few good plays in verse; I'd like to help change this."

BIOGRAPHICAL/CRITICAL SOURCES:

PERIODICALS

Monash Reporter, July, 1983.

* * *

MARX, Arthur 1921-

PERSONAL: Born July 21, 1921, in New York, N.Y.; son of Groucho (a comedian) and Ruth (a dancer; maiden name, Johnson) Marx; married Irene Kahn, February 27, 1943 (divorced June 26, 1961); married Lois Goldberg (an interior decorator), June 27, 1961; children: Steven, Andy. *Education:* Attended University of Southern California, 1939-40. *Politics:* "That depends on who's running." *Religion:* Jewish.

ADDRESSES: Home—Los Angeles, Calif. *Agent*—Scott Meredith Literary Agency, Inc., 845 Third Ave., New York, N.Y. 10022.

CAREER: Tournament tennis player, 1934-51; advertising copy writer, 1941; joke writer for Milton Berle's radio programs, 1942; Metro-Goldwyn-Mayer, Culver City, Calif., reader, 1948, writer of "Pete Smith Specialties," 1949-50; free-lance magazine writer, 1950-58; television writer, 1958—. Executive story consultant and script writer for "Alice," a series on CBS-TV, 1977-81. Producer and writer of Mickey Rooney's television show, 1964. *Military service:* U.S. Coast Guard, 1942-45; served in Pacific theater.

AWARDS, HONORS: Straw Hat Award from Council of Stock Theatres, 1970, for best new play of the summer season, "The Chic Life."

WRITINGS:

The Ordeal of Willie Brown (novel), Simon & Schuster, 1950.
Life with Groucho (biography), Simon & Schuster, 1954.
Not as a Crocodile (family stories), Harper, 1958.
Son of Groucho (autobiography), McKay, 1972.
Everybody Loves Somebody Sometime (about Dean Martin and Jerry Lewis), Hawthorn, 1974.
Goldwyn: A Biography of the Man behind the Myth, Norton, 1976.
Red Skelton, Dutton, 1979.
The Nine Lives of Mickey Rooney, Stein & Day, 1986.

FEATURE FILMS

"Blondie in the Dough," Columbia, 1947.

"Global Affair," Seven Arts, 1964.
"I'll Take Sweden," United Artists, 1965.
"Eight on the Lam," United Artists, 1967.
"Cancel My Reservation," Warner Bros., 1972.

Also co-wrote twelve "Pete Smith Specialties" for Metro-Goldwyn-Mayer, 1949-50.

PLAYS

(With Robert Fisher) "The Impossible Years" (two-act comedy), produced on Broadway at the Playhouse, October 13, 1965.
"Minnie's Boys" (two-act musical), first produced in New York City at Imperial Theater, March 26, 1970.
(With Fisher; also director) "Groucho: A Life in Revue" (two-act comedy), produced on Broadway at the Lucille Lortel Theater, October 8, 1986.

Also author of "My Daughter's Rated X," a comedy.

OTHER

Television writer for major network series, including "All in the Family," "Maude," "The Jeffersons," "McHale's Navy," and "Alice." Contributor of articles and photographs to popular national magazines, including *Saturday Evening Post, Esquire, Redbook, Cosmopolitan, Good Housekeeping*, and *Parade*.

WORK IN PROGRESS: "For Better or Worse," a play.

SIDELIGHTS: Arthur Marx told *CA:* "My first novel, *The Ordeal of Willie Brown*, was drawn directly from my experiences as an amateur tennis player during my high school and college years before going into the service in 1942. I was ranked as high as number five in the eighteen and under category, holding a major victory over the then current boy wonder, Jack Kramer. My novel attempted to expose the corrupt world of 'amateur' tennis, where the players were allegedly amateurs, but were actually taking great sums, in the form of expense money, under the table. The book suggested, in a comic way, that there should be an open tennis tournament, where the players could make an honest living doing what they did best. The open tennis tournament eventually came to pass, and I consider myself partially responsible for it.

"In my biographies of show business figures I felt it important to show them as real people and not the cardboard cutouts of publicity men's imaginations.

"My biography of my father, *Life with Groucho*, which was serialized in eight parts in the *Saturday Evening Post*, was one of the first of the biographies of show business luminaries to attract important critical acclaim. *New York Times* labeled it 'great,' and *New Yorker* called it 'an excellent piece of work.' I believe it started the trend of relatives writing objective biographies of famous figures."

MEDIA ADAPTATIONS: "The Impossible Years" was produced as a feature film.

BIOGRAPHICAL/CRITICAL SOURCES:

BOOKS

Marx, Arthur, *Life with Groucho*, Simon & Schuster, 1954.
Marx, Arthur, *Son of Groucho*, McKay, 1972.

PERIODICALS

Los Angeles Times Book Review, May 25, 1986.
New York Times, January 5, 1973, October 9, 1986.

New York Times Book Review, December 24, 1972.
Times Literary Supplement, May 18, 1973.
Washington Post Book World, December 24, 1972.

*   *   *

MASON, Nicholas (Charles Sheppard)   1938-

PERSONAL: Born December 30, 1938, in Harrow, England; son of Ronald Charles (a lecturer and writer) and Margaret Violet (a civil servant; maiden name, Coles) Mason; married Jane Nankivell (a health visitor), April 28, 1962; children: Peter Charles Christopher, Robert James, Anthony Alexander, Rosalind Jane. *Education:* Mansfield College, Oxford, B.A. (with honors), 1961.

ADDRESSES: Home—89 Lusted Lane, Tatsfield, Westerham, Kent, England. *Office—London Daily News,* Orbit House, New Fetter Lane, London E.C.4, England.

CAREER: Newcastle Evening Chronicle, Newcastle upon Tyne, England, reporter, 1961-65, reviewer, 1962-66, sub-editor, 1965-66; *London Sunday Times,* London, England, sub-editor, 1966-67, chief sub-editor, 1967-69, production editor, 1969-73, assistant editor, 1973-77, deputy sports editor, 1977-86; *London Daily News,* London, sports editor, 1986—.

WRITINGS:

(Editor) *The Olympics,* Times Newspapers, 1972.
(Editor with George Perry) *Rule Britannia: The Victorian World,* Times Books, 1974.
Football: The Story of All the World's Football Games, Temple Smith, 1974.
(Editor with John Lovesey and Edwin Taylor) *The Sunday Times Sports Book,* World's Work, 1979.
(With Sebastian Coe) *The Olympians,* Pavillion Books, 1984.

*   *   *

MASON, Ronald (Charles)   1912-

PERSONAL: Born July 30, 1912, in Thames Ditton, Surrey, England; son of Charles (a government official) and Mary (Canter) Mason; married Margaret Violet Coles, September 8, 1936; children: Nicholas Charles Sheppard, George Humphrey Paul, Elizabeth Mary. *Education:* University of London, B.A. (with first class honors), 1947. *Politics:* Socialist.

ADDRESSES: Home—Woodmans Cottage, Park Rd., Banstead, Surrey, England. *Agent*—David Higham Associates Ltd., 5-8 Lower John St., London W1R 4HA, England.

CAREER: H. M. Inland Revenue, Estate Duty Office, London, England, 1931-69, became senior examiner. Called to the Bar, Lincoln's Inn, 1935. University of London, London, England, part-time tutor, 1948-69, staff tutor in literature, extra-mural department, 1969-79.

MEMBER: Marylebone Cricket Club, Surrey County Cricket Club, Cricket Society.

WRITINGS:

Timbermills (novel), Sampson Low, Marston & Co., 1938.
The Gold Garland (novel), Sampson Low, Marston & Co., 1939.
Cold Pastoral (novel), Sampson Low, Marston & Co., 1946.
The House of the Living (novel), Sampson Low, Marston & Co., 1947.
The Spirit above the Dust: A Study of Herman Melville, Lehmann, 1951.

Batsman's Paradise: An Anatomy of Cricketomania, Hollis & Carter, 1955.
Jack Hobbs, Hollis & Carter, 1960.
Walter Hammond: A Biography, Hollis & Carter, 1962.
Sing All a Green Willow, Epworth, 1967.
Plum Warner's Last Season, Epworth, 1970.
Warwick Armstrong's Australians, Epworth, 1971.
(With Geoffrey Bush) *Songs from a Summer School* (songs), Department of Extramural Studies, University of London, 1975.
(With Bush) *More Songs from a Summer School* (songs), Department of Extramural Studies, University of London, 1979.
Ashes in the Mouth: The Story of the Bodyline Tour, 1932-1933, Hambledon, 1982.

Contributor to *Penguin, New Writing, Horizon, Voices, The Wind and the Rain, Adelphi, Friend,* and other anthologies and periodicals. Regular contributor to *Cricketer.*

AVOCATIONAL INTERESTS: Playing, watching, and studying cricket, reading, travel.

*   *   *

MATTISON, Judith   1939-

PERSONAL: Born December 9, 1939, in Milwaukee, Wis.; daughter of Arthur D. (a salesman) and Junice (Magnuson) Nelson; married John K. Mattison (a minister), August 25, 1962 (divorced January, 1982); children: Theodore John, Michael Andrew. *Education:* University of Minnesota, B.S., 1961; Luther Northwestern Seminary, M.Div., 1985.

ADDRESSES: Home—5029 Oakland Ave. S., Minneapolis, Minn. 55417. *Office*—Mount Olivet Lutheran Church, Minneapolis, Minn. 55419.

CAREER: Ordained minister of Evangelical Lutheran Church in America, 1985. Elementary school teacher in public schools in Hopkins, Minn., 1961-62, 1963-65, and in East Hartford, Conn., 1962-63; Minneapolis Public Schools, Minneapolis, Minn., volunteer, 1968-73, radio writer and producer, 1973-76; program director at Mount Olivet Retreat Center, 1977-79; Richfield Lutheran Church, Minneapolis, director of social ministries, 1979-85; Mount Olivet Lutheran Church, Minneapolis, associate pastor, 1986—. Member of Centennial District school board, 1971-75; member of board, Luther Northwestern Seminary, 1980-82, and Office for Communications Management Committee, Lutheran Church in America, 1982—. Member of Commission for Communications and dean of South Minneapolis Conference of West Metro Synod, Evangelical Lutheran Church in America, 1987—. Member of Minneapolis Aquatennial, 1960-61, and Minnesota Chorale, 1975-78.

MEMBER: Alpha Gamma Delta.

WRITINGS:

From a Woman's Heart, Augsburg, 1969.
Prayers from a Woman's Heart, Augsburg, 1972.
Prayers from a Mother's Heart, Augsburg, 1975.
Who Will Listen to Me?, Augsburg, 1977.
I'm Worried about Your Drinking, Augsburg, 1978.
Facing Up, Fortress, 1979.
Beginnings, Augsburg, 1980.
Mom Has a Second Job, Augsburg, 1980.
Help Me Adapt, Lord, Augsburg, 1981.
Divorce: The Pain and the Healing, Augsburg, 1985.

Life Is Good, Life Is Hard, Augsburg, 1987.

Contributor to *Lutheran, Lutheran Standard, Lutheran Women,* and *Scope.*

WORK IN PROGRESS: Devotions for women.

SIDELIGHTS: Judith Mattison told *CA:* "I write about feelings. . . . This brief, usually poetic form is a way of painting pictures of life. People see the event through words, and live it in their own feelings. We share the event, and hopefully come to know ourselves and others better."

*　　*　　*

MAZURSKY, Paul   1930-

PERSONAL: Birth-given name, Irwin; born April 25, 1930, in Brooklyn, N.Y.; son of David and Jean (Gerson) Mazursky; married Betsy Purdy, March 14, 1953; children: Meg, Jill. *Education:* Brooklyn College (now of the City University of New York), B.A., 1951.

ADDRESSES: Home—New York, N.Y.; and Beverly Hills, Calif.

CAREER: Screenwriter, actor, director, and producer of motion pictures. Writer and performer with Herb Hartig in comedy act, "Igor and H," and with Larry Tucker in semi-improvisational revue, "Second City"; writer with Tucker for television series, "The Danny Kaye Show"; actor in plays, including "The Seagull" and "Major Barbara," and motion pictures, including "Fear and Desire," 1953, "Blackboard Jungle," 1955, "Deathwatch," 1967, "Alex in Wonderland," 1971, "Blume in Love," 1973, "A Star Is Born," 1976, "An Unmarried Woman," 1978, "A Man, a Woman and a Bank," 1979, "Tempest," 1982, "Moscow on the Hudson," 1984, and "Down and Out in Beverly Hills," 1986.

AWARDS, HONORS: Nominated for best screenplay with Larry Tucker, Writers Guild, 1968, for "I Love You, Alice B. Toklas!"; Writers Guild Award, 1969, for "Bob & Carol & Ted & Alice"; nominated by Academy of Motion Picture Arts and Sciences for best screenplay with Tucker, 1969, for "Bob & Carol & Ted & Alice," for best screenplay with Josh Greenfield, 1974, for "Harry and Tonto," which was also nominated for best film, and for best screenplay, 1978, for "An Unmarried Woman," which was also nominated for best film; "Harry and Tonto" was named one of the *New York Times*'s eleven best films of 1974; recipient of other film awards.

WRITINGS:

SCREENPLAYS

(With Larry Tucker) "I Love You, Alice B. Toklas," Warner Brothers, 1968.
(With Tucker, and director) "Bob & Carol & Ted & Alice," Columbia, 1969.
(With Tucker, and director) "Alex in Wonderland," Metro-Goldwyn-Mayer, 1970.
(And director) "Blume in Love," Warner Brothers, 1973.
(With Josh Greenfield, and director) *Harry and Tonto* (released by Twentieth Century-Fox, 1974), Dutton, 1974.
(And director) "Next Stop, Greenwich Village," Twentieth Century-Fox, 1976.
(And director and co-producer) "An Unmarried Woman," Twentieth Century-Fox, 1978.
(And director) "Willie and Phil," Twentieth Century-Fox, 1980.

(With Leon Capetanos, and director and producer) "Tempest," Columbia, 1982.
(With Capetanos, and director and producer) "Moscow on the Hudson," Columbia, 1984.
(With Capetanos, and director and producer) "Down and Out in Beverly Hills," Buena Vista, 1986.

Also author with Capetanos of screenplay "Moon over Parador," 1987.

SIDELIGHTS: As the director of all but the first of his screenplays and the producer of several of them, Paul Mazursky exercises rare artistic control over his popular and often critically acclaimed filmwork. Mazursky's talent is especially recognized in films that focus satirically upon the urban middle class and the trendiness that frequently epitomizes its upwardly mobile lifestyle. David Ansen writes in *Newsweek* that Mazursky's "fond satires . . . have an uncanny capacity to send shivers of recognition through a middle class audience." His satiric perspective, however, does not aim at ridicule or scorn; his obvious affection for those who struggle toward self-discovery softens the satire that permeates his work. Calling him a "meticulous craftsman who values hard work and consistency," James Moore adds in a *Dictionary of Literary Biography* essay that "Mazursky has created a remarkably coherent body of work." This work, according to Richard Corliss in a *New Times* profile of Mazursky, is "unmatched in contemporary American cinema for its originality and cohesiveness."

Mazursky's early experience in acting, improvisational comedy, and television gag-writing figures prominently in both his screenwriting and directorial styles. "Mazursky's background as an actor and acting teacher helped him develop a remarkable sensitivity to actors, and an ability to extract the best and most natural performances," says Corliss. "As a director, he's no dictator; he's more like a fond co-conspirator, assisting actors in their fight against stereotype." Reviewers concur that few directors cast actors as shrewdly and impeccably as Mazursky. Noting that Mazursky has appeared in several of his own films, Pauline Kael observes in the *New Yorker* that there is an improvisational touch to his style of directing, "based on the actors' intuitively taking off from each other." Kael believes that this distinguishes Mazursky's uniqueness as an American director: "He writes, shapes, and edits the sequences to express the performing rhythm—to keep the actors' pulse. As a result, the audience feels unusually close to the characters—feels protective toward them." And "Mazursky's films are comic in the best sense," says Corliss. "They show an understanding of life as a comic joke . . . and a generous response to modern man and woman in their infinite variety."

Mazursky acknowledges to Henry Bromell in an *Atlantic* interview that the idea of two people actually living together fascinates him: "How is that possible? Who made that up? My movies are fantasies about what it would be like if certain things happened." For instance, Mazursky's first commercial success, "Bob & Carol & Ted & Alice," which granted him artistic freedom in the rest of his filmwork, explores the relationships between two married couples who experiment with open marriage; and his critically acclaimed "An Unmarried Woman" examines the struggles toward independence of a woman whose comfortable, sixteen-year marriage ends when her husband confesses his love for a woman he has met at Bloomingdale's. In a *Time* review of "An Unmarried Woman," Frank Rich calls it one of Mazursky's "bulletins from a combat zone," adding: "The battlefield is affluent urban America; the war is the sexual revolution of the 1970s. Mazursky describes the skirmishes in all their neurotic glory, tots up the emotional casualties and tries to identify the survivors. He does so with both compassion and dark wit, and the result has been a remarkable string of films that document the changing mores of an exasperating decade." Corliss, who feels that "Mazursky is likely to be remembered as *the* filmmaker of the seventies," maintains, "No screenwriter has probed so deep under the pampered skin of this fascinating, maligned decade; no director has so successfully mined it for home-truth humor and quirky revelations."

Although social comedy predominates in his filmmaking, Mazursky frequently draws upon his own personal experience as well. "Alex in Wonderland," for example, is about a director who, following the success of his first film, has trouble deciding the subject of his second. The film portrays the impediments to independent filmmaking and the compromises that creativity sometimes makes to the trendiness and pretension of a southern California lifestyle. Critics consider "Next Stop, Greenwich Village" Mazursky's most personal film. Not only does it represent the first film produced, directed, and written exclusively by Mazursky, but it dramatizes autobiographically the struggles of an aspiring young actor during the 1950s.

Moore notes that as a gesture of admiration Mazursky occasionally imitates the styles of other directors such as Federico Fellini and Francois Truffaut. While "Alex in Wonderland" and "Next Stop, Greenwich Village" recall the work of Fellini, "Willie and Phil" adapts "Jules and Jim" for a film about two men who meet at a revival of the Truffaut classic, become friends and then fall in love with the same woman. Noting the similarities between Mazursky and Truffaut, Corliss suggests that "the two filmmakers share a critical, but ultimately optimistic, view of life, approached from an oblique, metacomic angle." Mazursky has "shifted the period from the heroic era of the modern arts to the banal American seventies, a time when personal rebellion and aesthetic experimentation collapsed into universal spiritual diddling," observes David Denby in *New York*. Denby suggests that where Truffaut celebrates the freedom of his three "literary bohemians," Mazursky intentionally banalizes his threesome as "American neurotics, endlessly explaining, doubting, defending, deferring." However, Mazursky explains to Larry Kart in the *Chicago Tribune Book World* that despite the humor in the movie, he "tried desperately not to mock the characters, not to demean their plight—their not knowing what to do with their freedom."

Mazursky satirizes all his leading characters "with the most affectionate tolerance," states Denby, who finds that although they "may appear indecisive, deluded, or foolish . . . they never appear ugly, they never lose the possibility of grace." Believing, however, that Mazursky may satirize with too much affection for his subjects, some critics feel that at times he tends toward sentimentality. While appreciative of the humor in Mazursky's work, such critics seek a greater toughness beneath that humor. In a *Newsweek* review of "Willie and Phil," for instance, Jack Kroll notes that Mazursky's "style is deceptive; you have to look hard to see that beneath a jokey, facile surface he touches live nerves. The hard look also shows you that he goes soft a little too often for someone with his talent." Bromell, however, relates Mazursky's response to critical assessments of sentimentality in his films: "'I've been accused of being sentimental,' Mazursky said when I mentioned this problem. 'I've always defended myself by saying my movies aren't sentimental, they just have sentiment. I feel pity for my characters.'"

Corliss considers Mazursky to be "one of the new generation of gifted directors who have brought a vaguely European concern with what Mazursky has called 'inner journeys'—character studies, really—back home to traditional American genres and concerns." Mazursky's films often center on the possibility of change and on what John Simon defines in the *National Review* as the "arduous process of self-discovery." For instance, Mazursky's popular and critically successful "Harry and Tonto" focuses on "a limping old man with a buoyant spirit who buys cheap food for himself and good liver for Tonto, a cat . . . with a complicated temperament inclining audiences to anthropomorphism," as Penelope Gilliatt describes them in the *New Yorker*. Forced to vacate when the house in which Harry occupies a small room is scheduled for demolition, "this mild Lear begins to travel," writes Gilliatt. "He finds his children insufficient, one by one, and a rope on liberty, strung across the country." In *America*, Moira Walsh calls the film a "series of wacky incidents and encounters that defy adequate description but somehow maintain a modicum of plausibility, as well as a decent respect for the strivings of flawed humanity."

Mazursky's films "almost always end at the beginning," says Terry Curtis Fox in a *Film Comment* interview with him. Mazursky's protagonists frequently opt for the uncertainties of freedom rather than the comfortable but subtle restraints of security. Noting that his films usually culminate in a crisis, Fox perceives this to be "almost a process of regeneration." Mazursky acknowledges to Fox that it's something he deliberately tries to achieve, "It's definitely a mark in my films. I try for it, I want it, I believe in it." In films like "An Unmarried Woman" and "Harry and Tonto," says Fox, Mazursky is "dramatizing an internal state, . . . [something] difficult to do. It could easily fall off into something overly explicit." Mazursky replies: "Between 'Mary Hartman' and Ingmar Bergman. It hovers. But what I've seen works, I must say. I feel very good about it. . . . To me, inner journeys are much more exciting."

According to Bromell, Mazursky "sees life as a series of quixotic adventures. His heroes are all slightly confused and well-meaning innocents looking for happiness. This disease, rightly identified by Mazursky as a middle-class affliction, is both painful and funny, for the quest . . . can lead nowhere but home." And Bromell points out that Mazursky's commercial hits have allowed him to continue to make the type of film he enjoys—"modest, personal, filled with a sly, forgiving wit and autobiographical affection for the urban middle class of New York or Los Angeles, those two polar versions of the American Dream, one rooted in the Old World, a confusion of immigrants and intellectuals, the other a baffling, intoxicating, brave new world where displaced citizens pursue their ever-illusive pleasures." Ansen believes that Mazursky, who keeps an apartment in Greenwich Village and a house in Beverly Hills, is able in his films to "bridge two urban cultures that have been generally locked in mutual antipathy—New York and Los Angeles." Ansen continues, "He loves the energy and stimulation of the East, 'which keeps you in touch with the mob,' but he also loves the 'perpetual feeling of walking around in your underwear' that the West supplies. 'You can become a banana in L.A., sitting in your tub and watching "Hawaii Five-O,"' he says. 'The thing is, I *like* being a banana.' More accurately, Mazursky may be a banana split—between satire and celebration, shtick and seriousness, the two coasts."

Two of Mazursky's recent films exemplify this coastal ambivalence. "Moscow on the Hudson" is a patriotic film about a Russian musician who, while on tour in New York City with the Moscow circus, decides to defect during a shopping excursion to Bloomingdale's. He is welcomed into the home of a family who is no better off materially than the family he has left behind, and he must adapt to a new life in which practically everyone he meets seems to originate from someplace else. Mazursky has made a "comedy about a tragedy—about going away forever, about not being able to go home," says Kael in the *New Yorker*. On the other hand, "Down and Out in Beverly Hills" is about a homeless American who, having lost his canine companion, attempts suicide, only to be rescued and taken in by the materially wealthy but spiritually impoverished owner of the posh Beverly Hills swimming pool into which he jumps. The film concerns having everything and yet having nothing. Observing in the *Chicago Tribune Book World* that this film "casts a cold eye on conspicuous consumption and the vacuum that tends to rest in its core," Jeff Silverman calls it "a thinking person's funny movie with some basic profundities beneath the veneer." But the *New York Times*'s Vincent Canby writes that "my problem with the film is one I've had with a lot of earlier Mazursky comedies: I keep wanting it to be tougher, nastier and more seriously, more inventively cruel than . . . Mazursky has any intention of making it. Somewhere inside this softhearted film maker, there's a vicious social satirist waiting to break loose."

Nonetheless, Corliss finds that "Mazursky is his own man, and his films are not only very much *his*, they're completely *him*. And he, as any middle-class moviegoer will see from his films is us . . . trying to make connections with the world and ourselves—and, if we're lucky, laughing with sweet understanding at the whole cockeyed caravan of modern life." Although finding Mazursky "adept at lancing the excesses and improbabilities of the American culture," Jay Cocks indicates in a *Time* review of "Next Stop, Greenwich Village" that "what is best about Mazursky's work . . . comes from his affectionate kind of satire, always clear-eyed and almost never derisive." An inherent optimism hallmarks Mazursky's filmwork. "I know there are some wonderful filmmakers with really tragic views of life," Mazursky tells Bromell. "But for me, absurdity is always just around the corner. I see it all the time. I think life is a combination of awesome joy and a lot of pain, no matter how well adjusted you are, no matter how well organized. You're born and you know you're going to die, and so you start with an absurdity. You don't know whether to laugh or cry." Silverman believes that "for Mazursky, reflecting has a way of becoming tantamount to burlesquing and satirizing. They are his tools, the tools of a social commentator who can sting and hearten with equal facility. 'I seem to have a natural bent toward humor,' he'll remind you when the conversation takes a serious turn, 'and I seem to make people laugh, but I think there is in me a duality. I like to make people cry also, or at least to make people be aware of things. I like to deal with relationships. The perfect picture for me does all that.'"

BIOGRAPHICAL/CRITICAL SOURCES:

BOOKS

Dictionary of Literary Biography, Volume XLIV: *American Screenwriters*, Gale, 1986.
Monaco, James, *American Film Now*, New American Library, 1979.

PERIODICALS

America, September 21, 1974, April 1, 1978.
American Film, July-August, 1980.
Atlantic, September, 1980.
Chicago Tribune, September 26, 1980, April 6, 1984, February 5, 1986.
Chicago Tribune Book World, October 5, 1980, January 26, 1986.
Christian Century, May 9, 1984.
Commonweal, May 18, 1984.
Film Comment, March, 1978, February, 1986, April, 1986.
Life, September 4, 1970.
Los Angeles Times, December 30, 1977, July 8, 1979, January 31, 1986.
Maclean's, April 9, 1984.
Ms., March, 1978, October, 1980.
Nation, March 25, 1978, September 20, 1980.
National Review, May 14, 1976, April 14, 1978, June 1, 1984.
New Republic, September 14, 1974, February 21, 1976, March 11, 1978, May 28, 1984.
New Statesman, October 5, 1984.
Newsweek, September 2, 1974, February 16, 1976, March 13, 1978, April 10, 1978, August 25, 1980, April 16, 1984.
New Times, April 3, 1978.
New York, August 25, 1980.
New Yorker, August 26, 1974, February 2, 1976, March 6, 1978, September 1, 1980, April 16, 1984.
New York Times, October 8, 1968, September 17, 1969, December 23, 1970, January 17, 1971, June 18, 1973, August 12, 1973, September 9, 1973, September 30, 1973, August 13, 1974, December 31, 1974, March 5, 1978, August 15, 1980, August 13, 1982, April 6, 1984, January 17, 1986, January 31, 1986, February 13, 1986, February 16, 1986.
People, April 23, 1984.
Saturday Review, February 7, 1976, March 18, 1978, August, 1980.
Time, September 9, 1974, February 9, 1976, March 6, 1978, August 18, 1980, April 23, 1984, January 27, 1986.
Times (London), February 11, 1983.
Village Voice, February 16, 1976, March 6, 1978.
Washington Post, April 6, 1984, January 31, 1986.†

—*Sketch by Sharon Malinowski*

*   *   *

McCLUSKEY, John (A.), Jr. 1944-

PERSONAL: Born October 25, 1944, in Middletown, Ohio; son of John A. (a truck driver) and Helen (Harris) McCluskey; married Audrey Louise Thomas (a college instructor), December 24, 1969; children: Malik Douglass, Jerome Patrice, John Toure. *Education:* Harvard University, B.A. (cum laude), 1966; Stanford University, M.A., 1972.

ADDRESSES: Home—3527 Roxbury Circle, Bloomington, Ind. 47401. *Office*—Department of Afro-American Studies, Indiana University, Bloomington, Ind. 47405.

CAREER: Miles College, Birmingham, Ala., instructor in English, 1967-68; Valparaiso University, Valparaiso, Ind., lecturer in humanities and writer in residence, 1968-69; Case Western Reserve University, Cleveland, Ohio, coordinator of Afro-American studies, 1969-70, lecturer in Afro-American studies, 1970-72, assistant professor of American studies, 1972-74, assistant professor of English, 1974-77; Indiana University—Bloomington, associate professor, 1977-84, professor of Afro-American studies, 1984—, adjunct professor of English, 1984—, associate dean of graduate school, 1984—. Director, C.I.C. Minorities Fellowships Program, Indiana University, 1983—. Consultant, black studies pilot project, East Cleveland elementary school district, 1971; member of board of directors, Independent School of East Cleveland, 1972. Member of executive board, Bell Neighborhood Center, 1972; member of board of trustees, Goodrich Social Settlement, 1972. Member of advisory council, Karamu House Writers Conference, 1970; member of Cleveland planning committee, World Festival of Black Arts (Nigeria), 1974; director of black drama troupes in Birmingham and Cleveland. Consultant and editor, New Day Press, 1973-77. Has presented papers at numerous universities and on WJMO-Radio, Cleveland.

MEMBER: Modern Language Association of America, American Association of University Professors, National Council for Black Studies, Midwest Modern Language Association.

AWARDS, HONORS: Citation from Outstanding Educators of America, 1976; faculty research grants from Indiana University, 1977 and 1978; Yaddo residence fellowships, 1984 and 1986.

WRITINGS:

Look What They Done to My Song (novel), Random House, 1974.
(Editor) *Blacks in History, Volume II* (McCluskey was not associated with first volume), New Day Press, 1975.
(Editor) *Stories from Black History: Nine Stories,* five volumes, New Day Press, 1975.
(Editor) Ebraska Ceasor and others, *Blacks in Ohio: Seven Portraits,* New Day Press, 1976.
(Author of introduction) Robert Southgate, *Black Plots and Black Characters,* Gaylord, 1979.
(Contributor) Mari Evans, editor, *Black Women Writers (1950-1980): A Critical Evaluation,* Doubleday, 1983.
Mr. America's Last Season Blues (novel), Louisiana State University Press, 1983.
(Editor) *City of Refuge: Collected Stories of Rudolph Fisher,* University of Missouri Press, 1987.

CONTRIBUTOR TO ANTHOLOGIES

Orde Coombs, editor, *What We Must See: Young Black Storytellers,* Dodd, 1974.
Katharine Newman, editor, *Ethnic American Short Stories,* Simon & Schuster, 1975.
Martha Foley, editor, *Best American Short Stories,* Houghton, 1976.
William O'Rourke, editor, *On the Job,* Vintage, 1977.

OTHER

Contributor of poetry and short stories to magazines, including *Negro Digest, Obsidian, Black Review, Iowa Review, Seattle Review,* and *Choice;* contributor of reviews and articles to magazines and newspapers, including *Juju, Cleveland Magazine, Plain Dealer, Louisville Courier-Journal,* and *Black American Literature Forum.* Editor of *Juju,* 1974-77.

WORK IN PROGRESS: The River People (a novel) and short stories.

SIDELIGHTS: The fiction of John McCluskey, Jr., "reveals a strong awareness of history and an equally strong feeling for black cultural traditions," writes Frank E. Moorer in the *Dictionary of Literary Biography.* McCluskey's first novel, *Look*

What They Done to My Song, is the story of a young travelling black musician (Mack) who, Moorer writes, "wants to preach a message of love with his music, . . . an evangelist with a horn spreading a message of love and understanding." As Mack travels across the country—"his pilgrimage to self-understanding," according to Moorer—he encounters a diverse cast of characters, including an old Southern couple who treat him like a son, a frustrated hustler, and a young woman who denies her black heritage, claiming she is Portuguese. James C. Kilgore writes in *Black World* that these minor characters represent people "trying to make it in the America of the late Sixties," at the same time Mack himself is "seeking [and] running" in search of a "standing place." A reviewer in the *New Yorker* comments that McCluskey "illuminates brilliantly" his characters, adding that "youngish blacks who have lived through the anguish of the sixties rarely [have had] a better spokesman." Kilgore concludes that *Look What They Done to My Song* "is a novel whose vision reflects deep insight. . . . [It is] a lyrical novel which sings of justice, of love, of freedom, of survival."

"For McCluskey," writes Moorer, "the Afro-American cultural experience has been a heroic one—one that has nurtured the individual and the group." His 1983 novel, *Mr. America's Last Season Blues,* tells the story of a middle-aged former star athlete (Roscoe) who seeks to regain the hero status he once assumed in the small black community of Union City, Ohio. A former professional football player whose brief career ended with injuries, Roscoe has "settle[d] into a life of vague dissatisfaction, plagued by his regret over the stardom he never achieved," writes Jim Haskins in the *New York Times Book Review.* Moorer adds that Roscoe is continually "haunted by the black community's constant reminders of what he used to be and by his father's ghost which asks Roscoe if he still has the 'fighting spirit'." To prove himself, Roscoe initially becomes involved in a series of irresponsible actions, including a brief stint with the local semiprofessional football team and an extramarital affair with a former lover. However, he eventually finds himself trying to determine the truth behind a crime that his lover's son has wrongfully been charged with. "In doing so," observes Haskins, "he recognizes the cowardice and lying endemic to the declining black community of Union City and begins to assume greater responsibility for reversing that direction." It is at this point that the true nature of Roscoe's drive emerges, which Moorer describes as "regaining for the blacks in Union City a sense of identity, unity, and purpose." Don Johnson praises McCluskey in *Southern Humanities Review* for depicting Roscoe's struggles not as vain glory-seeking, but "as a mature man's attempt to comprehend and deal with the suffering wrought by time, love, and death."

McCluskey once commented: "As a writer, my commitment is to that level of creative excellence so ably demonstrated by Afro-American artists as diverse as Ralph Ellison, Romare Bearden, and Miles Davis. Hoping to avoid any fashionable ambiguity and pedantry, I want my fiction and essays to heighten the appreciation of the complexities of Afro-American literature and life."

AVOCATIONAL INTERESTS: Playing saxophone and bass clarinet, photography, swimming, jogging, and sailing; (McCluskey also coaches Little League football and Boys Club soccer).

BIOGRAPHICAL/CRITICAL SOURCES:

BOOKS

Dictionary of Literary Biography, Volume XXXIII: *Afro-American Fiction Writers after 1955,* Gale, 1984.

PERIODICALS

Black World, July, 1975.
New Yorker, November 25, 1974.
New York Times Book Review, November 17, 1974, April 1, 1984, December 20, 1987.
Southern Humanities Review, fall, 1984.

*   *   *

McDARRAH, Fred W(illiam)   1926-

PERSONAL: Born November 5, 1926, in Brooklyn, N.Y.; son of Howard Arthur and Elizabeth (Swahn) McDarrah; married Gloria Schoffel, November 5, 1960; children: Timothy Swann, Patrick James. *Education:* New York University, B.A., 1954.

ADDRESSES: Home—505 La Guardia Pl., New York, N.Y. 10012. *Office*—842 Broadway, New York, N.Y. 10003.

CAREER: Writer and photojournalist. Worked for advertising and publishing firms during 1950s; *Village Voice*, New York, N.Y., staff photographer, 1958-71, picture editor, 1971—. Photographs have been exhibited at galleries and museums, including Soho Photo Gallery, 1973, Whitney Museum, 1974, Dallas Museum, 1974, Lightworks Gallery, Syracuse University, Syracuse, N.Y., 1981, International Ausstellung, Cologne, West Germany, 1981, Galleria di Franca Mancini, Pesaro, Italy, 1983, and Musee du Quebec, 1987. *Military service:* U.S. Army, paratrooper, 1944-47; became staff sergeant.

MEMBER: American Society of Magazine Photographers, Authors Guild, Authors League of America, American Society of Picture Professionals, Photographic Society of America, National Press Photographers Association, Society for Photographic Education, New York Press Club, Photographic Historical Society of New York, New York Press Photographer's Association, Municipal Art Society (member of awards committee, 1978).

AWARDS, HONORS: Awards from New York Press Association, 1964, 1965, 1967, 1968, 1970, all for spot news photography, 1965 and 1967, both for feature photography, and 1969 and 1970, both for picture stories; first place awards from National Newspaper Association, 1966, for best pictorial series, and 1971, for spot news photography; Page One Award from New York Newspaper Guild, 1971 and 1981, both for best spot news photography; John Simon Guggenheim Memorial Foundation Award in photography, 1972; second place for Edward Steichen Memorial Award in newspaper photography, 1976.

WRITINGS:

(With commentary by wife, Gloria Schoffel McDarrah) *The Artist's World in Pictures*, Dutton, 1961.
Greenwich Village, Corinth Books, 1963.
New York, New York: A Photographic Tour of Manhattan Island from Battery Park to Spuyten Duyvil, Corinth Books, 1964.
Museums in New York, Dutton, 1967, 4th edition, Simon & Schuster, 1983.
(Editor) *Photography Market Place*, R. R. Bowker, 1975, revised edition, 1977.
(Editor) *Stock Photo and Assignment Source Book: Where to Find Photographs Instantly*, R. R. Bowker, 1977, 2nd edition, Photographic Arts Center, 1984.
(Compiler) *Kerouac and Friends: A Beat Generation Album*, Morrow, 1984.

PHOTOGRAPHIC ILLUSTRATOR

Elias Wilentz, editor, *The Beat Scene*, Corinth Books, 1960.
Art U.S.A. Now, two volumes, C. J. Boucher, 1962.
John Gruen, *The New Bohemia: The Combine Generation*, Shorecrest, 1966.
Sculpture in Environment, New York City Parks Department, 1967.
James J. Young, editor, *Bring Us Together: 3D Living Room Dialogues*, Friendship Press, 1970.
Summer Catalogue, New School, 1973.
The Beat Book (portfolio), Unspeakable Visions, 1974.
Poets of the Cities (catalogue), Dutton, 1974.
The Beat Diary (portfolio), Dutton, 1977.
Big Sky Anthology (portfolio), Big Sky Publishers, 1978.
The Beat Journey (portfolio), Unspeakable Visions, 1978.
How'm I Doing? The Wit and Wisdom of Ed Koch, Lion Books, 1981.
Beat Angels (portfolio), Unspeakable Visions, 1982.

OTHER

Regular contributor, *New York* magazine; book critic, *Infinity* magazine, 1972-73; book reviewer, *Photo District News*, 1985. Editor of *Executive Desk Diary* for *Saturday Review*, 1962-64.

SIDELIGHTS: Fred McDarrah's pictures of Robert F. Kennedy, George Segal, Allen Ginsberg, Jean Shepherd, Bob Dylan, Andy Warhol and many others have been published as posters and post cards.

BIOGRAPHICAL/CRITICAL SOURCES:

PERIODICALS

Archives of American Art, July, 1971.
Camera 35, November, 1972.
Cue, March 5, 1960, March 31, 1975.
Family Weekly, October 2, 1960.
Herald Tribune, May 1, 1960.
Invitation to Photography, spring, 1976.
New York Times Magazine, April 17, 1960.
Popular Photography, March, 1976.
35MM Photography, winter, 1977.
Time, February 15, 1960.
Village Voice, May 14, 1970, August 29, 1974.

*   *   *

McGUANE, Thomas (Francis III)   1939-

PERSONAL: Born December 11, 1939, in Wyandotte, Mich.; son of Thomas Francis (a manufacturer) and Alice (Torphy) McGuane; married Portia Rebecca Crockett, September 8, 1962 (divorced, 1975); married Margot Kidder (an actress), August, 1976 (divorced May, 1977); married Laurie Buffett, September 19, 1977; children: (first marriage) Thomas Francis IV; (second marriage) Maggie; (third marriage) Anne Buffett, Heather Hume McGuane (stepdaughter). *Education:* Attended University of Michigan and Olivet College; Michigan State University, B.A., 1962; Yale University, M.F.A., 1965; additional study at Stanford University, 1966-67.

ADDRESSES: Home—Box 25, McLeod, Mont. 59052. *Agent*—John Hawkins Associates, 71 West 23rd St., Suite 1600, New York, N.Y. 10010.

CAREER: Full-time writer.

AWARDS, HONORS: Wallace Stegner fellowship, Stanford University, 1966-67; Richard and Hinda Rosenthal Foundation Award in fiction from American Academy, 1971, for *The Bushwacked Piano;* National Book Award fiction nomination, 1974, for *Ninety-Two in the Shade.*

WRITINGS:

NOVELS

The Sporting Club, Simon & Schuster, 1969.
The Bushwacked Piano, Simon & Schuster, 1971.
Ninety-two in the Shade (also see below), Farrar, Straus, 1973.
Panama, Farrar, Straus, 1977.
Nobody's Angel, Random House, 1982.
Something to Be Desired, Random House, 1984.

SCREENPLAYS

"Rancho Deluxe," United Artists, 1975.
(Also director) "Ninety-two in the Shade" (adapted from his novel of the same title), United Artists, 1975.
The Missouri Breaks (produced by United Artists, 1976), Ballantine, 1976.
(With Bud Shrake) "Tom Horn," Warner Brothers, 1980.

OTHER

An Outside Chance: Essays on Sport, Farrar, Straus, 1980.
In the Crazies: Book and Portfolio (signed limited edition), Winn Books, 1984.
To Skin a Cat (short stories), Dutton, 1986.

Special contributor to *Sports Illustrated,* 1969-73.

WORK IN PROGRESS: A novel.

SIDELIGHTS: Thomas McGuane's first three novels established his reputation as a flamboyant stylist and satirist. *The Sporting Club, The Bushwacked Piano* and *Ninety-two in the Shade* juxtapose the ugly materialism of modern America against the beauty and power of the natural world. According to *Detroit* magazine writer Gregory Skwira, this trio of books perfectly captures "the hip disillusionment and general disorientation of the late 1960s." Although his early work had earned him high praise from the literary establishment, McGuane temporarily abandoned the novel in the early 1970s for work in the film industry. The personal chaos he experienced during that time is reflected in such later novels as *Panama* and *Something to Be Desired.* In these books, emotional depth and honesty take precedence over stylistic flamboyance, and many critics regard them as McGuane's finest.

McGuane grew up in an Irish family where storytelling was a natural art. When he announced his intention to become a writer, however, his parents disapproved of his ambition as hopelessly impractical. To counter their skepticism, McGuane devoted himself almost exclusively to his artistic efforts. While his university classmates enjoyed traditional college parties and diversions, McGuane wrote, read voraciously, studied the novel, or engaged in esoteric discussions with fellow students and contemporary novelists Jim Harrison and William Hjortsberg. McGuane's sober disposition earned him the nickname "The White Knight." His singlemindedness paid off: *The Sporting Club* was published when he was nearly thirty, and *The Bushwacked Piano* and *Ninety-two in the Shade* followed in quick succession.

The plots of these three novels are very different, but they are closely linked in style, theme, and tone. Each is written in what R. T. Smith calls in *American Book Review* "ampheta-mine-paced, acetylene-bright prose." "All present a picture of an America which has evolved into a 'declining snivelization' (from *Bushwacked*), a chrome-plated, chaotic landscape which threatens to lead right-thinking men to extremes of despair or utter frivolity," explains Larry McCaffrey in *Fiction International.* "Each of them presents main characters . . . who have recognized the defiled state of affairs around them, and who are desperately seeking out a set of values which allows them, as Skelton [the protagonist of *Ninety-two in the Shade*] puts it, 'to find a way of going on.'" In McCaffrey's estimation, the most remarkable thing about McGuane's writing is that with it, the author is "able to take the elements of this degraded condition and fashion from them shocking, energetic, and often beautiful works of prose—works which both mirror and comment upon our culture and which, yet, in their eloquence, transcend it."

McGuane's intense approach to his art was altered forever in 1972. Driving at 120 miles per hour on a trip from Montana to Key West, he lost control of his car and was involved in a serious accident. He walked away from it physically unharmed, but so profoundlly shaken that he was unable to speak for some time thereafter. After this brush with death, his relentless concentration on writing seemed misguided to him. McCaffrey quotes McGuane in the *Dictionary of Literary Biography Yearbook:* "After the accident, I finally realized I could stop pedaling so intensely, get off the bike and walk around the neighborhood. . . . It was getting unthinkable to spend another year sequestered like that, writing, and I just dropped out." McGuane was also finding it increasingly difficult to support his family on a novelist's income; while his books had received critical acclaim, none had been best-sellers. Accordingly, when movie producer Elliot Kastner asked him if he would be interested in a film project, McGuane eagerly accepted. Over the next few years he wrote several screenplays, and directed the screen version of *Ninety-two in the Shade.*

Changes were not limited to the author's work; his personal life was undergoing a transformation as well. Together with the other members of "Club Mandible"—a loosely-structured group of friends including singer Jimmy Buffett—McGuane began to enjoy a hedonistic lifestyle. He explained to Thomas Carney in *Esquire,* "I had paid my dues. . . . Enough was enough. In 1962 I had changed from a sociopath to a bookworm and now I just changed back. Buffett was in the same shape. We both heard voices telling us to do something." Accordingly, writes Carney, "McGuane the straight arrow who had spent years telling his friends how to live their lives while he lived his like a hermit became McGuane the boogie chieftain, rarely out of full dance regalia. The White Knight began staying out all night, enjoying drugs and drink in quantities. And women other than his wife."

McGuane's name began appearing in tabloids when he became romantically involved with actress Elizabeth Ashley during the shooting of his first film, "Rancho Deluxe." Ashley also starred in "Ninety-two in the Shade"; while still linked with her, McGuane began an affair wth another cast member, Margot Kidder. When McGuane and his first wife, Becky, divorced, Becky married the male lead of "Ninety-two in the Shade," Peter Fonda, and Tom married Margot Kidder, already the mother of his second child. McGuane and Kidder divorced several months later. The unexpected deaths of his father and sister compounded the confusion in McGuane's life. He told Skwira that the media depiction of his activities at that time was "overblown," but admitted, "I had a lot of fun drinking and punching people out for a short period of time."

The turmoil of that interval was clearly reflected in *Panama,* McGuane's first novel in four years. It is a first-person description of the disintegrating life of rock star Chester Hunnicutt Pomeroy, an overnight sensation who is burning out on his excessive lifestyle. In McCaffrey's words, *Panama* "in many ways appears to be a kind of heightened, surreal portrayal of McGuane's own suffering, self-delusion, and eventual self-understanding—a book which moves beyond his earlier novels' satiric and ironic stances." The book drew strong reactions, both favorable and unfavorable. Many reviewers who had unreservedly praised McGuane's earlier work received *Panama* coolly, with some implying that the author's screenwriting stint had ruined him as a novelist. A *Washington Post Book World* essay by Jonathan Yardley dismisses *Panama* as "a drearily self-indulgent little book, a contemplation of the price of celebrity that was, in point of fact, merely an exploitation of the author's new notoriety." Richard Elman complains in the *New York Times Book Review* that *Panama* "is all written up in a blowsy, first-person prose that goes in all directions and winds up being, basically, a *kvetch.*" He states that McGuane, "who was once upon a time wacky and droll [and who] is now sloppy and doleful," suffers from an inability to recognize "good" versus "bad" writing. "Everything of craft that must be done right is done wrong. . . . This book isn't written; it is hallucinated. The reader is asked to do the writer's work of imagining."

Other reviewers applaud *Panama* as the novel that finally joins McGuane's stylistic brilliance with an emotional intensity lacking in his earlier efforts. Susan Lardner suggests in a *New Yorker* review that McGuane's work as a director perhaps enriched the subsequent novel: "Maybe as a result of the experience, he has added to his store of apprehensions some dismal views of fame and the idea that life is a circus performance. . . . Whatever risk McGuane may have sensed in attempting a fourth novel with a simultaneous plunge into first person narration, the feat proves successful. The audience is left dazzled by the ingenuity of his turn, somewhat aghast at the swagger, hungry for more." Writing in the *Washington Post Book World,* Philip Caputo calls it McGuane's "most relentlessly honest novel. . . . Although *Panama* is as well written as its predecessors, its first-person point of view endows it with a greater directness; and the book not only gives us a look at the void, it takes us down into it. . . . *Panama* also contains some of the finest writing McGuane has done so far." *Village Voice* contributor Gary L. Fisketjon notes, "*Panama* is more ambitious if less slick than the earlier novels, which were restrained and protected by the net of a hotwired style and a consummate mockery; the humor here is not as harsh, and the objectivity is informed more by empathy than disdain. . . . Moving beyond satire, McGuane has achieved something difficult and strange, a wonderfully written novel that balances suffering and understanding." And in a Toronto *Globe & Mail* essay, Thad McIlroy deems *Panama* "one of the best books to have been published in the United States in the last 20 years. It's minimal, mad, disjointed at times, and consistently brilliant, terrifying and exhilarating. McGuane's use of language, and his ever-precise ear for dialogue, raise the novel out of the actual and into the universal, the realm of our finest literature."

McGuane's life stabilized considerably after his 1977 marriage to Laurie Buffett, sister of his friend Jimmy Buffett. He told *CA:* "Laurie and I share everything. She deserves a lot of

credit for my sanity and happiness." Living on his Montana ranch, the author perfected his riding and roping techniques and became a serious rodeo competitor. He commented to Carney in *Esquire,* "I've come to the point where art is no longer as important as life. Dropping six or seven good colts in the spring is just as satisfying as literature." McGuane's new down-to-earth attitude carried over to his prose style, as he explained to a *Detroit* magazine interviewer: "I'm trying to remove the *tour de force* or superficially flashy side of my writing. I'm trying to write a cleaner, plainer kind of American English. . . . I feel I have considerably better balance than I have ever had in my life and I don't care to show off; I just want to get the job done." Christopher Lehmann-Haupt refers favorably to McGuane's new direction in his *New York Times* review of the novel *Nobody's Angel:* "Both the author's affection for his characters and the strength of his narrative seem to matter even more to him than his compulsion to be stylistically 'original.'"

While *Nobody's Angel* echoes the dark tone of *Panama,* McGuane's next novel marks the first time that one of his restless protagonists finds fulfillment. *Something to Be Desired* revolves around Lucien Taylor and his two loves, Emily and Suzanne. When Emily, the more seductive and mysterious of the two, drops Lucien to marry a doctor, Lucien marries the virtuous Suzanne. The newlyweds go to work in Central America, where Lucien finds himself unable to forget Emily. When he hears she has murdered her husband, he deserts his wife and child to bail her out. He moves to Emily's ranch and becomes her lover, but she soon jumps bail, leaving him the ranch. Lucien converts it into a resort and finds happiness in a reconciliation with his family. Ronald Varney comments in the *Wall Street Journal* that "the somewhat bizarre plot twists of Mr. McGuane's story occasionally seem implausible. . . . And yet Mr. McGuane manages to pull this story off rather well, giving it, as in his other novels, such a compressed dramatic style that the reader is constantly entertained and diverted." *New York Times Book Review* critic Robert Roper names McGuane's sixth novel "his best, a remarkable work of honest colors and fresh phrasings that deliver strong, earned emotional effects."

Thomas McGuane's work has drawn comparisons to many famous authors, including William Faulkner, Albert Camus, Thomas Pynchon, F. Scott Fitzgerald, and most especially to Ernest Hemingway. Both McGuane and Hemingway portray virile heroes and anti-heroes vibrantly aware of their own masculinity; each author explores themes of men pitted against themselves and other men; each passionately loves game fishing and the outdoors. Discussing *Ninety-two in the Shade,* Thomas R. Edwards of the *New York Times Book Review* claims: "Clearly this is Hemingway country. Not just the heman pleasures of McGuane's men but even the locales of the novels . . . recapitulate Hemingway's western-hemisphere life and works." McCaffrey concurs in a *Fiction International* piece: "If [the set of value-systems of McGuane's protagonists] sounds very familiar to Hemingway's notion of a 'code' devised to help one face up to an empty universe, it should; certainly McGuane's emphasis on male aggressions, his ritualized scenes involving fishing, . . . and even the locales (Key West, the upper Rockies, up in Michigan) suggest something of Papa's influence, though with a distinctly contemporary, darkly humorous flavor."

When asked by Carter in *Fiction International* about the numerous Hemingway comparisons, McGuane replied: "I admire him, of course, and share a lot of similar interests, but I really don't write like him. . . . We have totally different styles. His world view was considerably more austere than mine. His insistence on his metaphysical closed system was fanatical. And he *was* a fanatic. But it gave him at his best moments a very beautiful prose style. And anyone who says otherwise is either stupid or is a lying sack of snake shit. We have few enough treasures in this twerp-ridden Republic to have to argue over Ernest Hemingway's greatness." To John Dorschner of the *Miami Herald* he speculated, "I can only agree that [my life and Hemingway's] appear to be similar, but that's all. What might be more pertinent is to think how my father was influenced by Hemingway. Places like the Keys and northern Michigan, those were places I was taken by my father."

Discussing his writing habits with Skwira in the *Detroit* magazine, McGuane noted, "I find it to my advantage to show up for work in an extremely regular, quite uninterrupted way." He averages eight to ten hours of work a day, six or seven days a week. He credits his temperate lifestyle with giving him a keener awareness of his craft, admitting that in earlier years "I really didn't quite know how I was achieving the effects I was achieving in literature. . . . But I know *exactly* how [*Something to Be Desired*] was written: long hours and a sore a--, in a state of clarity. And at the end, I remembered how I did all of it. With that behind me, as I sit down to start again, I start with a sort of optimism, with some expectation of achieving a certain level of results. . . . The thing that's most exciting to me now is that I feel that, barring illness, I think I'm looking at a long stretch of time where I can concentrate longer and harder on what I do best, more so than I've ever done before. And feeling that in itself produces kind of a glow."

MEDIA ADAPTATIONS: The Sporting Club was adapted by Lorenzo Semple, Jr., for a full-length film released by Avco Embassy Pictures in 1971.

CA INTERVIEW

CA interviewed Thomas McGuane by telephone on July 16, 1987, at his ranch in McLeod, Montana.

CA: You've said that you grew up among storytellers. Who were the early ones, the ones who made you want to tell stories too?

McGUANE: They were my mother and my uncle and my maternal grandfather, all Irish Catholics from the Boston area, where storytelling was a cultivated art.

CA: You were already writing seriously at Michigan State University, and after graduation went on to the Yale School of Drama, where you continued to write and graduated with a Masters in Fine Arts. How did your work at Yale fit into your writing plans?

McGUANE: I was at that time interested in all fictional writing, including dramatic writing. I remember in the late 1950s and early sixties there was a wonderful creative turbulence Off-Broadway, and I was excited about that. I just wanted to write; I wanted to write plays, novels, short stories—whatever I could do. It seemed that starting in one place was as good as starting in another. But I was and am very interested in plays. At Yale I was a playwriting major, which meant that I was substantially an English major. I did a lot of work in Elizabethan literature and eighteenth-century English drama.

CA: Two novels were rejected before The Sporting Club *was bought by Simon & Schuster. What were the lessons in the writing of those first two books?*

McGUANE: As in making anything, you get a better and better feel towards the material that you're working in, whether it's wood or words, through sheer gross exposure. I learned in the course of those two books that it was not enough just to blacken pages, that you must sense a curve in the material, a tendency towards closure and fruition. I found after a certain point that I could bring those things to it. I'm sure that writing novels that didn't work out had a lot to do with that education.

CA: Reviewers have made the inevitable comparison of your work with Hemingway's—based in large part on your mutual locales and themes—and compared you to a lesser degree with other writers. Are there influences or inspirations you can name among other writers?

McGUANE: I only know who my favorites have been. It's always hard to say whether or not your favorites have had very much to do with your own practice. I never could see the conflict between liking Hemingway and liking Faulkner. I guess that's now an official conflict, just as the conundrum Tolstoy-or-Dostoevski is an obligatory one. I always liked Hemingway *and* Faulkner; I liked Fitzgerald; I liked Tolstoy, Dostoevski, Turgenev. Probably my biggest influences were Sherwood Anderson, Scott Fitzgerald, Ivan Turgenev, Anton Chekhov, Henry Fielding, Mark Twain, Stephen Crane. I once said to Peter Taylor, "You know, I'd really rather be a reader than a writer." He said, "Me too!" I kind of feel that way, but there's a point in reading at which a sort of frustration develops and you want to do it yourself. That's the interest for me.

CA: Writers who've read voraciously probably have many influences they aren't even aware of.

McGUANE: I really like to read, and I've read some pretty unprepossessing stuff, too. I love to read semi-anthropological memoirs, diaries and chronicles of old cowboys or Aran Islanders or Indians. Sometimes you can read stuff that's really not literary in nature but has the same sort of magic that you wish you could put into your own work. The surface of literature that we try to control is one thing, but there's this mercurial, living thing down at the center that's a mystery.

CA: From the beginning, your characters have spoken and thought in a very hip, wise-cracking kind of way that gives your stories a special snap. In a favorite example of mine, Chester Hunnicutt Pomeroy, in Panama, *considers at one point that his life is "the best omelet you could make with a chain saw." How hard is it to achieve in the writing?*

McGUANE: Again, it probably goes back to the Celtic ambience that I grew up in. You look, for example, at Malcolm Lowry's *Under the Volcano.* It's a wonderful book, and it's always maldescribed by critics and reviewers as an altogether tragic book. One of the things that I think is at the core of its power is its wittiness. It's a sort of extreme gallows humor. If you just allow yourself to see that when you look back at the book, though its topics are dire in the extreme, it's on the verge of hilarious. I've always been fascinated by the tension of trench humor or gallows humor—inappropriate humor, a kind of intensification using a comic form of language in the presence of danger or mortality or sadness. I've found those situations more approachable for my particular abilities in that way rather than trying to write something that's really on the nose. I couldn't write morosely about death, for example; I wouldn't know how to do it.

CA: Ninety-two in the Shade was the book that got you into screenwriting (and, for that film, directing). Also among your screenwriting credits are "Rancho Deluxe," "The Missouri Breaks," and "Tom Horn." Do you feel the movie work has strengthened the fiction, or the process of writing it, in any way?

McGUANE: I think all writing strengthens the process of writing fiction. A genuine fictional talent should be a robust thing capable of taking on challenges from journalism, screenwriting, or any place that it finds itself. I remember reading an interview with Howard Hawks in which he talked about what a rapid, solid resourceful screenwriter William Faulkner was. In fact, Faulkner was Hawks's favorite screenwriter because if you were out on the set in an emergency and you could find a folding chair for Faulkner, you could get a new scene. It's good to know those things. Young writers especially are encouraged to think that their talents are these ineffably delicate things that can be damaged and destroyed by a light breeze from the wrong quarter. I think that's not true. I don't think screenwriting ever destroyed the talent of anybody who was meant to survive.

But there's something behind what I'm talking about. After hearing for years about how I'd gone to Hollywood and therefore sold out, I came to think that at bottom journalists and reviewers are frequently envious people, and while they would rarely say that you had injured yourself or your talent through, say, heroin addiction, one trip to Hollywood and you're destroyed beyond recovery. The only thing that explains that is envy because you were highly paid, you were in the company of people in places where *they* weren't welcome. It makes them mad, and it's kind of like class warfare. They write with a certain kind of respect and reverence about someone who's been acquitted for crimes of violence and been in clinics for narcotics addiction. They'll all say what a wonderful thing it is for the book at hand. But about somebody else they'll say, This man was in Hollywood last year, and his present book shows it.

CA: Could you be lured back to movies, or to writing for television?

McGUANE: I could be. I remember when I was young seeing great television programs—"Playhouse 90," for example; they did original screenplays. It would be fun to be invited to do something like that. I'd love Stanley Kubrick to say that he wanted me to do an edgy contemporary Western. But these are very unlikely things. And I'm now in a situation where I don't have to do it. I used to have to; I had no other way of surviving. *Ninety-two in the Shade* was reviewed everywhere in the nation ninety-five percent positively. It was nominated for a National Book Award, it was on the front page of the *New York Times Book Review*, it had two or three full-page ads, and it sold ten thousand copies. I made about $12,000 on it. I never saw anything beyond my advance. In fact, I probably still owe the publisher money for that book. The piety with which the literary bystanders tell you that you must not do movies is hard to accept in the face of the requirements that a family can impose on you.

CA: Your novels have attracted some academic attention, including treatment in a 1986 book called The New American Novel of Manners by Jerome Klinkowitz. How do you feel about the critical attention?

McGUANE: That one, for example, I saw and read. It fascinated me in the same way you would be fascinated if you wrote something and someone intelligent came over to your house and said, "Would you mind if I spoke to you for forty-five minutes about what you've done?" Other people have perspectives on what you've done that you would like to have yourself but can't have because you did it. Sometimes I'll look at that sort of thing and actually wonder whether I intended all the things that are being ascribed to me. At other times I feel that my work is being misread. But my feelings are never hurt by that kind of critic because they're always trying hard to come to grips with what you've written; it's not something that's dashed off. It seems to me that earns them some respect.

CA: There's sometimes the criticism that your female characters don't seem as real, as fully developed, as the male ones. Do you find them considerably harder to write?

McGUANE: Anything that's not me is harder to write than something that's like me. I wonder what Ellen Gilchrist would say if she were asked the same question about the men in her work. I find them to be more wooden than the women in Hemingway's novels. But the question rarely comes up that way because it's not currently the subject of sexual politics. For me it's harder to understand women than to understand men. I have lots of women in my family; I have three daughters, and as they get older I find out more about them. But I've always been a sort of typical male. I've always liked to be with other men; I have the same pack instincts. I probably *am* a more reliable observer of men's activities than women's. So I'd say that the criticism is probably true.

I would like to think, though, that I'm getting better. I did a fishing story for *Harper's* that came out this last spring, and the editor for it was a woman who told me that she was a feminist and that she had been warned not to read me because of the two-dimensional female characters in my books. Because she was doing the piece, she felt she should read more of my work, which she did, and she said she didn't find the criticism to be true at all. It's going away, thank God. But you can get framed, too. A book reviewer came up to me at a writers' conference where I spoke and said that a woman had asked him to review my last book for her paper. She said to him, "Do you know this fellow's work?" He said yes. And she said, "He's a male chauvinist pig novelist. Whatever you think of this book, you are to give it a bad review." Well, I don't think that's fair. Even if I *am* a male chauvinist pig novelist, that's not cricket.

CA: Setting is very prominent in your writing. One feels the steamy atmosphere of Key West reading Ninety-two in the Shade and sees the colors and shapes of the Western landscape reading Something to Be Desired. How much effect does your own location during the writing of a book have on the writing process? Can you write better in one place than in another?

McGUANE: When I used to wander back and forth between Key West and Montana, which I did when having the children in school didn't prevent me from doing it, I noticed that I'd do most of my writing in Montana and most of my living in Key West. Also, places that are heightened the way Key West is, the way New Orleans is, the way New York is, are intriguing to novelists. The novel is basically a social form. A novel is always being strained outside of its contours when it's made to portray a kind of solitude or nakedness. Knut Hamsun was able to do it beautifully, but it's rarely done very successfully. In fact, Chekhov, who wrote some very rural-looking stories, was careful to populate them as densely as a ghetto. I love places as such, though strangely enough I don't like to travel. But my wife is from Alabama, and the last ten years I've spent quite a lot of time in the Deep South. I like being a stranger. I like seeing a scene as though I were a floating camera, trying to guess what happened and who's there. I'm really sensitive to that, no matter where it is. If I went to Pittsburgh, I think I'd feel that force of lives lived in a very peculiar way in particular places, and what effect the setting had had on them.

CA: Reviewing Panama *for the* Washington Post Book World, *Phil Caputo said that you had done in that book "something unusual for authors in midcareer: written an autobiographical novel." Do you consider the book more or less autobiographical than your other novels?*

McGUANE: I think it's more autobiographical, although if you were to try to track that idea down to the actual incidents of the novel, it wouldn't meet with much success. In that it was a howl of ludicrous despair, it was autobiographically sincere.

CA: Was Panama *a personal triumph for you even though it didn't do well in sales?*

McGUANE: I've been all over the compass about that. It's got a funny history for me. For a long time I was sure it was the best thing I'd written. Now I think it's kind of an interesting book on the shelf, but I'm not sure it's the best thing I've written; it operates from too narrow a base to satisfy me right now. But it was such a crazy stroke from where I stood that it had a way of widening the possibilities, and I'm still very grateful for that. A progression had been seen in my first three books, and there were a lot of people who liked that progression and had imagined in their own minds what book four would be like. I had even done that. And so I saw to it that the fourth book was a complete departure from the earlier books. I think I really needed a departure. It takes ten years to get through three books, and that's a long time to be doing anything with something like a pattern in it. I wanted to stretch my wings a little bit. From that point of view, I look back on *Panama* as a great refresher, and I still like it a lot. I probably have more vociferous fans of that book than anything else I've written. While it got some of the worst reviews I ever got, it also got the best reviews I ever got. It got a great review in the *New Yorker,* where I had never gotten much attention before. There was no middle ground in the reviews: the negative ones were so outraged. I think Jonathan Yardley said it was proof that I should never write again.

CA: Was it pleasing in a way to have done a book that stirred much emotion, pro and con?

McGUANE: Looking at it from some altitude, I can say yes. At the time it was like being in a gang fight. It was so unpleasant. There was always something in the mail that was insulting and hurting. It was really painful to go through that. But there was something good about that too, because once I had survived it, I cared a lot less about what they thought. That was another freeing up.

CA: To Skin a Cat, a book of short stories, was published in 1986. Was doing the stories a challenge you deliberately set for yourself?

McGUANE: Not in a strict sense. I had some things that had accumulated in my mind over a period of years that weren't novels, and I wanted to write them. Superimposed on that was the feeling that I wasn't sure how to write short stories, though I'd read them all my life and read critically about them and loved them. That book took much longer than any novel I've written. With a short story, you can start out with a forty- or fifty-page manuscript and end up with an eight-page manuscript. There are at least two stories in there that took longer to write than my first two novels. Short stories are hard, but when they're right, they're so wonderful. They've got something that poetry can have, a vision much beyond their physicality.

CA: You are also a polished essayist, as the pieces collected in An Outside Chance *attest. Have your essays attracted a new set of readers, people who aren't so much fans of fiction?*

McGUANE: They are my contact with average people, people who are not interested in experimental fiction or whatever. One of the pleasures of my career is that I have never had a book out of print. I've never had a best-seller, except when *Ninety-Two* made the bottom of the best-seller list for one week, probably through a skew in the graph. I've never had big sales, and I've always had to do other things to make a living besides just write fiction. But the books have never gone out of print. The nice thing about that is that, after almost twenty years, each of them has acquired a readership and I hear from those readers. It's kind of like having a grocery store: you have your clients out there, and some of them like their beef well marbled and are glad that you keep what they want. It gives me a good feeling having those readers. But *An Outside Chance* has readers completely different from the readers of my fiction, sporting people who are frustrated by the things they read in *Sports Illustrated* and *Field & Stream* and wish somebody would take their activities more seriously, which I do. I'm glad I have that book out. Most of my friends are very nonliterary; they're ranchers, people who live around here, commercial fishermen down South, farmers. Sooner or later they'll say, "Tom, just what is it you write, anyway?" And believe me, I don't give them *Panama,* especially if they've been letting me hunt quail on their farm. I give them *An Outside Chance.*

CA: The pieces of your life seem to have settled well into place since the personal turmoil of the 1970s. Would it be accurate to say that writing, however important to you, is one part of a whole that includes ranching, travel, family?

McGUANE: Writing is really the keystone. I do too many other things. In fact, I'm guilty about that. But I'm really incapable of being happy or even making a normal contribution to my personal and family life unless writing is a daily thing I do. That's what I am, a writer. I may be a lousy one, I may be a great one, but I am a writer. Sometimes things happen—we'll travel, or this summer we've had endless house guests—and I'll go for a couple of weeks without writing. I'm just miserable then. I've ranched now for sixteen years, and I don't know whether I'm a rancher or not. I've ridden cutting horses for twenty years, and I don't know whether I'm a cowboy or not. But I do know I'm a writer, and knowing that one little thing is a kind of ballast. I'd hate to be without it. It's very important not to let the literary stockbrokers get to you too much, or they can take that away from you. John Steinbeck died having won the Nobel Prize but feeling that he was a fraud, that his life had been a waste and he had not left anything to his family or his country. That was because book reviewers had decided he was an idiot, and they told him that in all the newspapers right toward the end of his career. He believed it, and he died in misery. *Travels with Charlie*, which was a sweetly charming travel book, was his gravestone, critically. The reviewers savaged it. When Melville died, his wife put on his gravestone, underneath his name and the dates, *Writer*. And everyone thought it was so touching that there was someone still around who thought he was a writer. The only people who can take that away from you are reviewers, and you dare not give them that power.

CA: What would you like to do in the future, in the writing or otherwise?

McGUANE: I'm working on a novel now that appears to be longer and, I hope, better than anything I've ever done. You're always in the position you were in when you first started: you're not sure another page will come, you're not sure you can finish it, you're not sure it will be any good. At the same time, the exhilaration of occasionally glimpsing that it might be *very* good is an excitement that never diminishes. I just want to keep doing what I've been doing. I just want to be better at it. I'm as excited about writing fiction as I was twenty years ago. It's the only thing I'm absolutely sure I have any ability at—and I haven't been fired.

BIOGRAPHICAL/CRITICAL SOURCES:

BOOKS

Authors in the News, Volume II, Gale, 1976.
Contemporary Literary Criticism, Gale, Volume III, 1975, Volume VII, 1977, Volume XVIII, 1981, Volume XLV, 1987.
Dictionary of Literary Biography, Volume II: *American Novelists since World War II*, Gale, 1978.
Dictionary of Literary Biography Yearbook: 1980, Gale, 1981.
Klinkowitz, Jerome, *The New American Novel of Manners: The Fiction of Richard Yates, Dan Wakefield, and Thomas McGuane*, University of Georgia Press, 1986.

PERIODICALS

America, May 15, 1971.
American Book Review, May-June, 1983.
Atlantic, September, 1973.
Book World, May 2, 1971.
Chicago Tribune, November 5, 1978, April 12, 1985, November 3, 1986.
Chicago Tribune Book World, February 15, 1981.
Commonweal, October 26, 1973.
Crawdaddy, February, 1979.
Critique: Studies in Modern Fiction, August, 1975.
Detroit (Sunday supplement to *Detroit Free Press*), January 27, 1985.
Detroit News, April 25, 1982, November 18, 1984.
Detroit News Magazine, August 17, 1980.
Esquire, June 6, 1978.
Feature, February, 1979.
Fiction International, fall/winter, 1975.
Globe & Mail (Toronto), January 26, 1985, April 4, 1987.
Hudson Review, winter, 1973-74.
Miami Herald, October 13, 1974.

Nation, January 31, 1981, March 20, 1982.
New Mexico Humanities Review, fall, 1983.
New Republic, August 18, 1979.
Newsweek, April 19, 1971, July 23, 1973.
New Statesman, July 26, 1974.
New Yorker, September 11, 1971, June 23, 1973, April 19, 1979.
New York Review of Books, December 13, 1973.
New York Times, November 21, 1978, May 23, 1980, March 4, 1982, December 10, 1984, October 11, 1986.
New York Times Book Review, March 14, 1971, July 29, 1973, November 19, 1978, October 19, 1980, February 8, 1981, March 7, 1982, December 16, 1984.
Partisan Review, fall, 1972.
People, September 17, 1979, November 3, 1980.
Saturday Review, March 27, 1971.
Spectator, July 13, 1974.
Time, August 6, 1973, June 30, 1980.
Times Literary Supplement, May 24, 1985.
Village Voice, September 15, 1975, December 11, 1978.
Virginia Quarterly Review, spring, 1981.
Wall Street Journal, December 24, 1984.
Washington Post, December 30, 1980, October 2, 1986.
Washington Post Book World, November 19, 1978, February 28, 1982, December 16, 1984.

—*Interview by Jean W. Ross*

—*Sketch by Joan Goldsworthy*

*   *   *

McHANEY, Thomas L(afayette)   1936-

PERSONAL: Born October 17, 1936, in Paragould, Ark.; son of Thomas L. (a lawyer) and Maxine (Brown) McHaney; married Karen Honigmann (a cartographer), May 29, 1962 (divorced April, 1986); married Pearl Amelia Schmidt, May 5, 1986; children (from first marriage): Sudie Ann, Jessie Wynne, Molly Josephine. *Education:* Attended Christian Brothers College, 1954-56; Mississippi State University, B.A., 1959; University of North Carolina at Chapel Hill, M.A., 1963; University of South Carolina, Ph.D., 1968. *Politics:* Democrat.

ADDRESSES: Home—450 Clairmont Ave., Decatur, Ga. 30030. *Office*—Department of English, Georgia State University, University Plaza, Atlanta, Ga. 30303.

CAREER: University of Mississippi, Oxford, instructor in English, 1963-65; Georgia State University, Atlanta, assistant professor, 1968-73, associate professor, 1973-79, professor of English, 1979—. Fulbright lecturer, University of Bonn, 1976.

MEMBER: Modern Language Association of America, American Association of University Professors, South Atlantic Modern Language Association.

AWARDS, HONORS: Woodrow Wilson fellowship, 1960; fiction awards from *Reflections*, 1965, *Atlanta*, 1969, and *Prairie Schooner*, 1973; special award for fiction from Henry Bellaman Foundation, 1970, for short stories.

WRITINGS

(Contributor) Matthew J. Bruccoli, editor, *The Chief Glory of Every People*, Southern Illinois University Press, 1973.
William Faulkner's The Wild Palms: A Study, University Press of Mississippi, 1975.
William Faulkner: A Reference Guide, G. K. Hall, 1976.
(Editor) *Faulkner Studies in Japan*, University of Georgia Press, 1985.

(Editor) *William Faulkner Manuscripts,* forty-four volumes, Garland Publishing, 1986-87.

PLAYS

"Last of the Civil War Orphans," produced in Atlanta, Ga., by Atlanta New Play Project, 1981.
"A Place Where They Cried," produced in Atlanta by Alliance Theatre Company, 1983.
"A Spell of Dry Weather," produced by Atlanta New Play Project, 1984.
(Adaptor) "The Man That Corrupted Hadleyburg," produced by DeKalb College and Dunwoody Stage Door Players, 1985.

OTHER

Contributor of articles and short stories to journals, including *PMLA, Mississippi Quarterly, Transatlantic, Prairie Schooner, Georgia Review,* and *Cimarron Review.* Member of editorial board of *The Faulkner Journal,* 1985—.

*   *   *

McHARGUE, Georgess 1941-
(Alice Chase, Margo Scegge Usher)

PERSONAL: Born in 1941, in Norwalk, Conn.; daughter of W. R. (in advertising) and Georgess (Boomhower) McHargue; married Michael E. Roberts; children: Mairi Kathleen; stepchildren: Traci A. Roberts, Kelly Roberts Richardson. *Education:* Radcliffe College, B.A., 1963. *Politics:* Radical-Independent. *Religion:* None.

ADDRESSES: Home and office—51 Hollis St., Groton, Mass. 01450.

CAREER: Golden Press, New York City, various staff work, 1963-65; Doubleday & Co., Inc., New York City, associate editor, 1965-68, editor, 1968-70; free-lance writer, 1970—.

MEMBER: American Civil Liberties Union, Amnesty International, Phi Beta Kappa.

AWARDS, HONORS: Book World's Spring Festival Award, 1972, for *The Impossible People;* National Book Award nomination, 1973, for *The Impossible People;* MacDowell Colony fellow, 1984.

WRITINGS:

JUVENILES

The Beasts of Never: A History Natural and Un-natural of Monsters Mythological and Magical, Bobbs-Merrill, 1968, revised edition, Delacorte, 1988.
The Baker and the Basilisk, Bobbs-Merrill, 1970.
The Wonderful Wings of Harold Harrabescu, Delacorte, 1971.
The Impossible People: A History Natural and Unnatural of Beings Terrible and Wonderful, Holt, 1972.
Facts, Frauds and Phantasms: A Survey of the Spiritualist Movement, Doubleday, 1972.
Mummies, Lippincott, 1972.
Elidor and the Golden Ball, Dodd, 1973.
The Mermaid and the Whale, Holt, 1973.
Private Zoo, Viking, 1975.
Stoneflight, Viking, 1975.
Funny Bananas, Holt, 1975.
Meet the Werewolf, Lippincott, 1976.
The Talking Table Mystery, Doubleday, 1977.
Meet the Vampire, Lippincott, 1979.

The Horseman's Word, Delacorte, 1981.
The Turquoise Toad Mystery, Delacorte, 1982.
Meet the Witches, Harper, 1983.
See You Later, Crocodile!, Delacorte, 1988.

COMPILER

The Best of Both Worlds: An Anthology of Short Stories for All Ages, Doubleday, 1968.
Little Victories, Big Defeats, Delacorte, 1974.
Hot and Cold Running Cities, Holt, 1974.

OTHER

(With Michael Roberts) *A Field Guide to Conservation Archaeology in North America,* Lippincott, 1977.

Also author of mass-market juveniles under the pseudonyms Alice Chase and Margo Scegge Usher.

WORK IN PROGRESS: Beastie, a short novel, for Delacorte; adult nonfiction on an urban archaeological project, for Morrow; *Lands of Elsewhere,* nonfiction, for Delacorte.

SIDELIGHTS: Georgess McHargue has a "flair for combining research with an eminently readable style," believes *Horn Book* reviewer Paul Heins. McHargue has written several books exploring aspects of folklore, the occult, and related subjects. In *The Beasts of Never: A History Natural and Un-natural of Monsters Mythological and Magical,* McHargue presents the probable origins of mythical animals such as the dragon and the unicorn. "She proves that what does not exist can nevertheless seem real," notes Barbara Wersba in the *New York Times Book Review,* and in doing so, McHargue "actually illuminates mankind." In *The Impossible People: A History Natural and Unnatural of Beings Terrible and Wonderful,* the author takes a look at mermaids, pixies, brownies, and other mythical races. Wersba states, "Like the author's previous work, 'The Beasts of Never,' [*The Impossible People*] is a rare blend of scholarship, entertainment, wisdom, gravity and grace."

AVOCATIONAL INTERESTS: Mythical beings, monsters, politics, art, pseudoscience, theater, arcana, conservation, field archaeology, Renaissance history, gardening, embroidery, hiking, and horseback riding.

BIOGRAPHICAL/CRITICAL SOURCES:

BOOKS

Children's Literature Review, Volume II, Gale, 1976.

PERIODICALS

Christian Science Monitor, May 4, 1972.
Horn Book, August, 1972, October, 1972, April, 1973.
New York Times Book Review, July 28, 1968, May 31, 1970, April 2, 1972, May 25, 1975, September 7, 1975.
School Library Journal, May, 1972, October, 1972, November, 1972, May, 1973, January, 1974.
Washington Post Book World, May 7, 1972.

*   *   *

McLAREN, Ian Francis 1912-

PERSONAL: Born March 30, 1912, in Launceston, Australia; son of Alexander Morrison (a draper) and Elsie Elizabeth (Gibbins) McLaren; married Eileen Adele Porter, April 16, 1941; children: Andrew Forbes, Ailsa Louise McLaren McLeary, Neil Stuart, Ian Hugh. *Education:* University of Melbourne, Dip.Com., 1954.

ADDRESSES: Home—237 Waverley Rd., East Malvern, Victoria 3145, Australia.

CAREER: Chartered accountant, 1930-36; associated with Argus & Australasian Ltd., 1936-38; secretary of Davies Coop. N.S.W. Ltd., 1939-41; Victorian Legislative Assembly, Independent member of assembly for Glen Iris, 1945-47; chartered accountant, 1947-65; Victorian Legislative Assembly, Liberal member of assembly for Caulfield, 1965-67, and for Bennettswood, 1967-79, deputy speaker, 1973-79, chairman of Parliamentary Liberal Federal Affairs Committee, delegate to Australian Constitutional Convention, 1973-79; director of Nicholas Kiwi Ltd., 1981-83. Writer, 1954—. President of Caulfield Technical College, 1951-52. Chairman of Victoria Federation of Co-operative Housing Societies, 1946-49, Wyperfeld National Park, 1946-57, Australian Institute of Political Science, 1953-54, Good Neighbour Council of Victoria, 1955-58, Estate Agents Committee, 1956-65; Australian Wool Testing Authority, member, 1956-65, chairman, 1964-65. Member of board of directors of Kiwi International Co. Ltd., 1958-81, Gas and Fuel Corp. of Victoria, 1958-65, Power Corp. Australia Ltd., and Victoria Portland Cement Co. Commissioner for Taking Declarations and Affidavits, 1946—; member of Malvern City Council, 1951-53; council of University of Melbourne, 1977-79, National Fitness Council of Victoria, and Youth Advisory Council of Victoria. *Military service:* Royal Australian Naval Volunteer Reserve, active duty, 1940-45; served in Papua New Guinea, Dutch New Guinea, and the Philippines; became lieutenant.

MEMBER: World Council of Young Men's Christian Associations (vice-president, 1961-69), International Association of Y's Men's Clubs (director-at-large, 1938-39; vice-president, 1952-54), Royal Institute of Public Administration (fellow), Bibliographical Society of Australia and New Zealand, Institute of Chartered Accountants, Chartered Institute of Secretaries (associate), Private Libraries Association, Australian Young Men's Christian Association (national president, 1948-65; member of national council, 1958-62; member of board of governors, 1978), Royal Historical Society of Victoria (fellow; president, 1956-59), Book Collectors' Society of Victoria (president, 1965, fellow, 1986), Victorian Parliamentary Members Association, Youth Hostels Association of Victoria (president, 1947-48).

AWARDS, HONORS: Officer of Order of the British Empire, 1959; honorary bibliographer of library at University of Melbourne, 1975.

WRITINGS:

Local History in Australia, R.H.S.V. (Melbourne), 1954.
History of Latrobe Valley, R.H.S.V., 1957.
Como, R.H.S.V., 1957.
Australian Aviation: A Bibliographical Survey, Ballarat, 1958.
(Author of introduction) Henry Lawson, *The Ghosts of Many Christmases,* Hawthorn Press, 1958.
All Saints, St. Kilda,[Melbourne], 1958.
The Burke and Wills Tragedy, R.H.S.V., 1960.
McEvoy Mine Disaster, R.H.S.V., 1962.
William Wills, R.H.S.V., 1963.
Edward Edgar Pescott, 1872-1954, R.H.S.V., 1965.
How Victoria Began, R.H.S.V., 1968.
In the Wake of Flinders, R.H.S.V., 1974.
C. J. Dennis Contributions to Literary Magazines, State Library of South Australia, 1976.

C. J. Dennis: A Comprehensive Bibliography Based on the Collection of the Compiler, Libraries Board of South Australia, 1979.
C. J. Dennis in the Herald, Dalriada Press, 1981.
Marcus Clarke, State Library of Victoria, 1981.
Talking about C. J. Dennis, Monash University English Department, 1982.
Annotated Bibliography of Marcus Clarke, State Library of Victoria, 1982.
Whitcombe's Story Books: A Trans-Tasman Survey, Melbourne University Library, 1984.
The Chinese in Victoria: Official Reports and Documents, Red Rooster Press, 1985.
John Dunmore Lang, Turbulent Australian Scot: A Comprehensive Bibliography, Melbourne University Library, 1985.
Mary Gaunt, a Cosmopolitan Australian: An Annotated Bibliography, Melbourne University Library, 1986.
Grace Jennings Carmichael: From Croajingolong to London, Melbourne University Library, 1986.
Index to the Weekly Times Annual, 1911-1934: With a Bibliography of Charles Leslie Barrett, Melbourne University Library, 1986.
Cabinet Photographs and Postcards Relating to A. L. Gordon, Melbourne University Library, 1986.
Adam Lindsay Gordon: A Comprehensive Bibliography, Melbourne University Library, 1986.
Towards a Comprehensive Bibliography of Henry Kendall: John A. Ferguson Memorial Address, 1986, Royal Australian Historical Society, 1987.
Visit to Geelong and the Western District of Victoria in 1846 by John Dunmore Lang, Melbourne University Library, 1987.
Henry Kendall: A Comprehensive Bibliography, Melbourne University Library, 1987.

Also author of *Publishers' Author Advertisements,* Bibliographical Society, 1984, and *The Melbourne Public Library in 1888,* 1986.

WORK IN PROGRESS: Research on Irish rebellions that resulted in transportation to Australia.

SIDELIGHTS: Ian Francis McLaren's forty-thousand-volume library, now housed at the University of Melbourne, was begun in 1943 and grew rapidly during the collector's years in political office. McLaren's collection focuses on Australian history, particularly events such as the industrial revolution, and riots and rebellions that led to transportation or immigration to Australia.

BIOGRAPHICAL/CRITICAL SOURCES:

BOOKS

The Library of Ian F. McLaren, Hawthorn Press, 1974.

PERIODICALS

Age, January 26, 1963.

*   *   *

McPHERSON, James Alan   1943-

PERSONAL: Born September 16, 1943, in Savannah, Ga.; son of James Allen and Mable (Smalls) McPherson. *Education:* Attended Morgan State University, 1963-64; Morris Brown College, B.A., 1965; Harvard University, LL.B., 1968; University of Iowa, M.F.A., 1969.

ADDRESSES: Office—Department of English, University of Iowa, Iowa City, Iowa 52242.

CAREER: University of Iowa, Iowa City, instructor in writing at Law School, 1968-69, instructor in Afro-American literature, 1969; University of California, Santa Cruz, faculty member, 1969-70; Morgan State University, Baltimore, Md., faculty member, 1975-76; University of Virginia, Charlottesville, faculty member, 1976-81; University of Iowa, Writers Workshop, Iowa City, professor, 1981—.

MEMBER: Authors League of America.

AWARDS, HONORS: First prize, *Atlantic* short story contest, 1965, for "Gold Coast"; grant from Atlantic Monthly Press and Little, Brown, 1969; National Institute of Arts and Letters award in literature, 1970; Guggenheim fellow, 1972-73; Pulitzer Prize, 1978, for *Elbow Room: Stories;* MacArthur fellowship, 1981.

WRITINGS:

Hue and Cry: Short Stories, Atlantic-Little, Brown, 1969.
(Editor with Miller Williams) *Railroad: Trains and Train People in American Culture,* Random House, 1976.
Elbow Room: Stories, Atlantic-Little, Brown, 1977.
(Author of foreword) Breece D'J Pancake, *The Stories of Breece D'J Pancake,* Atlantic-Little, Brown, 1983.

CONTRIBUTOR

J. Hicks, editor, *Cutting Edges,* Holt, 1973.
Nick A. Ford, editor, *Black Insights: Significant Literature by Afro-Americans, 1760 to the Present,* Wiley, 1976.
Llewellyn Howland and Isabelle Storey, editors, *Book for Boston,* Godine, 1980.
Kimberly W. Benson, editor, *Speaking for You,* Howard University Press, 1987.
Alex Harris, *A World Unsuspected,* [Chapel Hill], 1987.

OTHER

Also contributor to *New Black Voices,* New American Library. Contributor to *Atlantic, Esquire, New York Times Magazine, Playboy, Reader's Digest,* and *Callaloo.* Contributing editor, *Atlantic,* 1969—; editor of special issue, *Iowa Review,* winter, 1984.

SIDELIGHTS: James Alan McPherson's stories of ordinary, working class people, though often concerning black characters, are noted for their ability to confront universal human problems. "His standpoint," Robie Macauley explains in the *New York Times Book Review,* "[is] that of a writer and a black, but not that of a black writer. [McPherson] refused to let his fiction fall into any color-code or ethnic code." Because of this stance, McPherson's characters are more fully rounded than are those of more racially-conscious writers. As Paul Bailey writes in the *Observer Review,* "the Negroes and whites [McPherson] describes always remain individual people—he never allows himself the luxury of turning them into Problems." Explaining his approach to the characters in his stories, McPherson is quoted by Patsy B. Perry of the *Dictionary of Literary Biography* as saying: "Certain of these people [his characters] happen to be black, and certain of them happen to be white; but I have tried to keep the color part of most of them far in the background, where these things should rightly be kept." McPherson has published two collections of short stories, *Hue and Cry: Short Stories* and *Elbow Room: Stories.* In 1978 he was awarded the Pulitzer Prize for fiction.

McPherson was born and raised in Savannah, Georgia, a city in which several cultures—including the French, Spanish, and Indian—have been uniquely blended. He cites this rich cultural heritage as a determining factor in his own ability to transcend racial barriers. The McPherson family also influenced his development of values. His father, at one time the only licensed black master electrician in Georgia, and his mother, a domestic in a white household, had important contacts in both the white and black communities. Through their efforts, McPherson obtained work as a grocery boy in a local supermarket and as a waiter on a train. These experiences have formed the basis for several later stories. McPherson's train employment also allowed him to travel across the country. Perry notes that McPherson "affirms the importance of both white and black communities in his development as an individual and as a writer of humanistic ideas."

McPherson's writing career began in the 1960s while he was still attending law school. His story "Gold Coast" won first prize in a contest sponsored by the *Atlantic* magazine and was later published in the magazine as well. The *Atlantic* was to play a pivotal role in McPherson's career. After earning a bachelor's degree, a law degree, and a master's degree in creative writing, McPherson became a contributing editor of the *Atlantic* in 1969. And the magazine, in conjunction with Little, Brown, also published his two collections of short stories.

McPherson's first collection, *Hue and Cry,* deals with characters whose lives are so desperate that they can only rage impotently against their situations. "The fact that these characters . . . ," writes Perry, "know nothing else to do except to sink slowly into madness, scream unintelligibly, or seek refuge . . . provides reason enough for McPherson's hue and cry." The *Times Literary Supplement* critic points to the book's "mostly desperate, mostly black, mostly lost figures in the urban nightmare of violence, rage and bewilderment that is currently America."

Despite the grim nature of his stories, McPherson manages to depict the lives of his characters with sympathy and grace. Bailey allows that McPherson's "powers of observation and character-drawing are remarkable, displaying a mature novelist's understanding of the vagaries and inconsistencies of human affairs." Writing in *Harper's,* Irving Howe maintains that McPherson "possesses an ability some writers take decades to acquire, the ability to keep the right distance from the creatures of his imagination, not to get murkily involved and blot out his figures with vanity and fuss." Granville Hicks of *Saturday Review* notes that McPherson "is acutely aware of the misery and injustice in the world, and he sympathizes deeply with the victims whether they are black or white."

Among the most prominent admirers of *Hue and Cry* is novelist Ralph Ellison. In a statement he contributed to the book's dust jacket, Ellison speaks of the difference between McPherson's writing and that of most other black writers. "McPherson," Ellison claims, "promises to move right past those talented but misguided writers . . . who take being black as a privilege for being obscenely second-rate and who regard their social predicament as Negroes as exempting them from the necessity of mastering the craft and forms of fiction. . . . McPherson will never, as a writer, be an embarrassment to such people of excellence as Willie Mays, Duke Ellington, Leontyne Price—or, for that matter, Stephen Crane or F. Scott Fitzgerald."

Elbow Room, McPherson's second collection, won even more critical praise than its predecessor. Again concerned with characters in desperate situations, the stories of *Elbow Room* are nonetheless more optimistic than McPherson's earlier works, the characters more willing to struggle for some measure of success. They "engage in life's battles with integrity of mind and spirit," as Perry explains. This optimism is noted by several critics. Robert Phillips of *Commonweal,* for example, finds the stories in *Elbow Room* to be "difficult struggles for survival, yet [McPherson's] sense of humor allows him to dwell on moments which otherwise might prove unbearable." Writing in *Newsweek,* Margo Jefferson calls McPherson "an astute realist who knows how to turn the conflicts between individual personalities and the surrounding culture into artful and highly serious comedies of manners."

McPherson's ability to create believable characters, and his focus on the underlying humanity of all his characters, is praised by such critics as Phillips. McPherson's stories, Phillips believes, "ultimately become not so much about the black condition as the human condition. . . . *Elbow Room* is a book of singular achievement." Macauley explains that McPherson has been able "to look beneath skin color and cliches of attitude into the hearts of his characters. . . . This is a fairly rare ability in American fiction." The *New Yorker* reviewer lists several other characteristics of McPherson's stories that are worthy of attention, calling him "one of those rare writers who can tell a story, describe shadings of character, and make sociological observations with equal subtlety."

Speaking of the obstacles and opportunities facing black writers, McPherson writes in the *Atlantic:* "It seems to me that much of our writing has been, and continues to be, sociological because black writers have been concerned with protesting black humanity and racial injustice to the larger society in those terms most easily understood by nonblack people. It also seems to me that we can correct this limitation either by defining and affirming the values and cultural institutions of our people for their education or by employing our own sense of reality and our own conception of what human life should be to explore, and perhaps help define, the cultural realities of contemporary American life."

BIOGRAPHICAL/CRITICAL SOURCES:

BOOKS

Contemporary Literary Criticism, Volume XIX, Gale, 1981.
Dictionary of Literary Biography, Volume XXXVIII: *Afro-American Writers after 1955: Dramatists and Prose Writers,* Gale, 1985.

PERIODICALS

Antioch Review, winter, 1978.
Atlantic, December, 1970, February, 1977.
Chicago Tribune Book World, May 25, 1969.
Christian Science Monitor, July 31, 1969.
CLA Journal, June, 1979.
Commonweal, September 19, 1969, September 15, 1978.
Ebony, December, 1981.
Harper's, December, 1969.
Iowa Journal of Literary Studies, 1983.
Nation, December 16, 1978.
Negro Digest, October, 1969, November, 1969.
Newsweek, June 16, 1969, October 17, 1977.
New Yorker, November 21, 1977.
New York Review of Books, November 10, 1977.

New York Times Book Review, June 1, 1969, September 25, 1977, September 2, 1979, February 13, 1983, May 13, 1984.
Observer Review, December 7, 1969.
Saturday Review, May 24, 1969.
Spectator, November 22, 1969.
Studies in American Fiction, autumn, 1973.
Times Literary Supplement, December 25, 1969.
Washington Post Book World, October 30, 1977, March 6, 1983.

—*Sketch by Thomas Wiloch*

*   *   *

McQUAID, Kim   1947-

PERSONAL: Born November 2, 1947, in Norwalk, Conn.; son of Francis Walter (an antiquarian bookseller) and Margaret Fitzgerald (Phelan) McQuaid. *Education:* Antioch College, B.A., 1970; graduate study at University of British Columbia, 1970-71; Northwestern University, M.A., 1973, Ph.D., 1975.

ADDRESSES: Home—Modockawando Farm, North Edgecomb, Me. 04556. *Office*—Department of History, Lake Erie College, Painesville, Ohio 44077.

CAREER: Worked as arts and crafts teacher and social worker, 1965-69, as illustrator, 1969, and as antiquarian bookseller, 1974-75; Antioch College, Yellow Springs, Ohio, instructor in history, 1975; Northwestern University, Evanston, Ill., part-time instructor in history, 1976-77; Lake Erie College, Painesville, Ohio, assistant professor, 1977-84, associate professor of history, 1984—. Mary Ball Washington Visiting Professor of U.S. History, University College, Dublin, 1985-86.

MEMBER: Economic History Association, Business History Conference.

AWARDS, HONORS: Woodrow Wilson fellowship, 1970.

WRITINGS:

(Contributor) Paul Uselding, editor, *Research in Economic History: An Annual Compilation of Research,* Volume I, JAI Press, 1976.
(With Edward Berkowitz) *Creating the Welfare State: The Political Economy of Twentieth-Century Reform,* Praeger, 1980, 2nd edition, revised and expanded, 1988.
Big Business and Presidential Power, Morrow, 1982.
A Response to Industrialism, Garland Publishing, 1986.
The Anxious Years: America in the Vietnam-Watergate Era, Basic Books, in press.

Contributor to history, business, economics, and law journals.

SIDELIGHTS: Kim McQuaid told *CA:* "As an Irishman from the state of Maine, I see my task as one of maintaining a healthy skepticism about the polysyllabic professional evasions of the day: rigorously examining the claims of the present in terms of the experiences of the past; avoiding the pomposity that afflicts so much of American academic life; remembering that history is about people as they are or were, rather than as intellectuals would have them be; and keeping what I hope is a caustic Down East sense of humor more or less intact."

*   *   *

MEIGHAN, Donald Charles   1929-
(Donald Charles)

PERSONAL: Born March 15, 1929, in San Francisco, Calif.;

son of Charles (a writer) and Lucille (Mellin) Meighan; married Shirley Blakeslee (an artist), March 4, 1950; children: Kathleen, Matthew, Timothy. *Education:* Attended University of California, Berkeley, 1945-47, and Art League School, 1950-54.

ADDRESSES: Home—412 North Ninth St., Murphysboro, Ill. 62966.

CAREER: San Francisco Chronicle, San Francisco, Calif., feature writer and artist, 1948-50; also worked as a truck driver, longshoreman, and ranch hand; creative director of Flair Merchandising Agency (advertising agency), 1956-65; free-lance illustrator and writer, 1965—. *Military service:* U.S. Army, 1947-50; editor of weekly newspaper.

MEMBER: Authors Guild, Authors League of America, Art Institute of Chicago.

AWARDS, HONORS: Gold medal from National Point of Purchase Advertising Institute, 1960, for ''Old Time Train'' construction; awards of merit for illustrations from San Francisco Advertising Club, 1961, Graphic Arts Council of Chicago, 1965, and Artists Guild of Chicago, 1979; silver medal from Printworld, 1976.

WRITINGS—Under name Donald Charles:

SELF-ILLUSTRATED

Busy Beaver's Day, Children's Press, 1972.
Count on Calico Cat, Children's Press, 1974.
Letters from Calico Cat, Children's Press, 1974.
Calico Cat Looks Around, Children's Press, 1975.
Calico Cat's Rainbow, Children's Press, 1975.
Fat, Fat Calico Cat, Children's Press, 1977.
Calico Cat Meets Bookworm, Children's Press, 1978.
Time to Rhyme with Calico Cat, Children's Press, 1978.
The Jolly Pancake, Children's Press, 1979.
Shaggy Dog's Animal Alphabet, Children's Press, 1979.
Shaggy Dog's Tall Tale, Children's Press, 1980.
Calico Cat at School, Children's Press, 1981.
Calico Cat's Exercise Book, Children's Press, 1982.
Shaggy Dog's Halloween, Children's Press, 1984.
Calico Cat's Year, Children's Press, 1984.
Shaggy Dog's Christmas, Children's Press, 1985.
Shaggy Dog's Birthday, Children's Press, 1986.

ILLUSTRATOR

D. L. Hubbard, *The Dragon Comes to Admela: Another Book about Admela and Its Royal Family,* Reilly & Lee, 1967.
Hubbard, *Dragons, Dragons: A Story,* Reilly & Lee, 1967.
Derlyne Gibson, *How Far Can It Go?,* Reilly & Lee, 1970.
Virginia Poulet, *Blue Bug and the Bullies,* Children's Press, 1971.
Gibson, *How Big Can It Grow?,* Reilly & Lee, 1971.
Illa Podendorf, *Tools for Observing,* Children's Press, 1971.
Poulet, *Blue Bug's Safety Book,* Children's Press, 1973.
Poulet, *Blue Bug's Vegetable Garden,* Children's Press, 1973.
Margaret Hillert, *The Little Cookie,* Follet, 1980.

WORK IN PROGRESS: ''I stockpile manuscripts for four or five years before rewriting and developing appropriate illustrations. Currently, I have about twenty picture stories waiting for that critical second look.''

SIDELIGHTS: Donald Charles Meighan told *CA:* ''In school, I showed an early proclivity for art, and received encouragement from a succession of wonderful teachers. There was never any doubt in my mind that I wanted to be a book illustrator.

In addition to art work, I wrote for school publications, and composed poems and stories for my own amusement.

''Although I started late in the children's book field, it seems as though everything I've done has prepared me for what I'm doing now. I have no problem searching for ideas. They flow so easily that I can dream up far more work than I can ever produce. The real challenge is not what to do, but how to do it. Many people think that the creative person starts with nothing, like God, and assembles something full-blown out of the cosmos. Actually, we are more like sculptors confronted with blocks of stone: we must painstakingly remove the unneeded material in order to expose the masterpieces that lie within.

''Most of the books I've had published so far have a rather didactic bent because they are intended for school libraries. I hope to do more trade books in the future, and I have a whole closet full of nonsense and whimsy waiting for me to give it pictorial life. I have some strong beliefs about the content of children's books. It may sound trite to say that I believe in entertainment, information, and enlightenment, but my prejudices may also define my beliefs: I detest mannered or 'precious' writing and illustration which I feel is condescending and therefore demeaning to the child. 'Sophisticated' children's books should be published as adult picture books since they are really for the amusement of adults and generally baffle children.

''Writing and illustrating children's books is not the most lucrative thing I've ever done, but it's rewarding in more important ways. When I get a letter from a reader, I remember when I was small, and how the distress of the moment was so often set aside by the magic of a book. I hope I can continue to repay that debt to the authors and illustrators who preceded me.''

*   *   *

MELLIN, Jeanne 1929-

PERSONAL: Born February 3, 1929, in Stamford, Conn.; daughter of Kenneth B. (a restaurateur) and Marjorie (Bates) Mellin; married Frederick Herrick (a professional horseman), October 23, 1955; children: Nancy Jeanne. *Education:* Rhode Island School of Design, B.F.A., 1948. *Politics:* Republican. *Religion:* Methodist.

ADDRESSES: Home and office—Saddleback Farm, R.D. #1, Hamilton, N.Y. 13346.

CAREER: Rides, trains, and shows horses professionally; portrait painter of horses and other animals; illustrator.

MEMBER: American Horse Show Association, American Morgan Horse Association, New York Morgan Horse Society.

WRITINGS:

Horses across America, Dutton, 1953.
Horses across the Ages, Dutton, 1954.
Pidgy's Surprise (juvenile), Dutton, 1955.
The Morgan Horse (also see below), Stephen Greene, 1961, revised edition, 1986.
America's Own Horse Breeds (prints), Stephen Greene, 1962.
Ponies on Parade (prints), Stephen Greene, 1966.
Ride a Horse, Sterling, 1970.
(Illustrator) Sarah Swift, *My Own Horse Book,* Stephen Greene, 1971.
The Morgan Horse Handbook (also see below), Stephen Greene, 1973.

Illustrated Horseback Riding for Beginners, Wilshire, 1974.
The Complete Morgan Horse (derived from *The Morgan Horse* and *The Morgan Horse Handbook*), Stephen Greene, 1986.

Author of script for American Morgan Horse Association movie, 1963, narrated by James Cagney.

WORK IN PROGRESS: A book of her own drawings and paintings of horses.

*   *   *

MERKL, Peter H(ans)   1932-

PERSONAL: Born January 29, 1932, in Munich, Germany (now in West Germany); son of Robert Joseph (a businessman) and Berta (Mitterer) Merkl; married Elisa M. Cruz (a writer), August 28, 1954; children: Jacqueline Susan. *Education:* Attended University of Munich, 1951-52, 1953-54; University of Minnesota, M.A., 1953; University of California, Berkeley, Ph.D, 1959.

ADDRESSES: Home—6543 Camino Venturoso, Goleta, Calif. 93117. *Office*—Department of Political Science, University of California, Santa Barbara, Calif. 93106.

CAREER: University of California, Santa Barbara, 1958—, began as assistant professor, currently professor of political science, acting chairman of department, 1972-73.

MEMBER: International Political Science Association, American Political Science Association, Western Political Science Association, Conference Group on German Politics (president, 1984-86).

AWARDS, HONORS: A. B. Jordan fellow, 1954; Haynes Foundation fellow, 1960; Social Science Research Council grant, 1962; University of California faculty fellow, 1963; Rockefeller Foundation grant, 1964; National Endowment for the Humanities grant, 1967, 1970, and 1980-84; Ford Foundation fellow, 1974; Ford Foundation and National Institute for Mental Health grant, 1976; Volkswagen Foundation grant, 1979-82; Japan Society for the Promotion of Science grant, 1980-83; Toyota Foundation grant, 1980-83; Institute for Global Conflict and Cooperation grant, 1984-86.

WRITINGS:

The Origin of the West German Republic, Oxford University Press, 1963.
Germany: Yesterday and Tomorrow, Oxford University Press, 1965.
Political Continuity and Change, Harper, 1967.
Rechtsradikalismus und Rassenfrage in den USA, Colloquim Verlag (Berlin), 1967.
Political Continuity and Change, Harper, 1967, 2nd edition, 1972.
Modern Comparative Politics, Holt, 1970, 2nd edition, Dryden, 1977.
German Foreign Policies, West and East: On the Threshold of a New European Era, Clio Press, 1974.
Political Violence under the Swastika: 581 Early Nazis, Princeton University Press, 1975.
Politische Soziologie der USA: Die konservative Demokratie, [Wiesbaden], 1977.
The Making of a Stormtrooper, Princeton University Press, 1980.
(Editor) *Western European Party Systems: Trends and Prospects,* Free Press, 1980.

(Co-editor) *Who Were the Fascists?: Social Roots of European Fascism,* Norwegian University Press, 1980.
(Editor with N. Smart) *Religion and Politics in the Modern World,* New York University Press, 1983.
(Editor) *West German Foreign Policy: Dilemmas and Directions,* Chicago Council on Foreign Relations, 1983.
(Editor) *New Local Centers in Centralized States,* University Press of America, 1985.
(Editor) *Political Violence and Terror: Motifs and Motivations,* University of California Press, 1986.

Also author of *American Democracy in World Perspective,* Harper, and *Introduction to Comparative Politics,* Holt. Contributor to journals in the United States and Germany.

WORK IN PROGRESS: Small Town in Bavaria; The Political Management of Economic Change in Postwar Japan and Germany; When Parties Fail: Emerging Alternative Organizations.

SIDELIGHTS: Peter H. Merkl told *CA* that he believes social scientists "have a special obligation to contribute to the understanding of our generation, both of itself and of other groups, nations, and civilizations."

BIOGRAPHICAL/CRITICAL SOURCES:

PERIODICALS

New York Review of Books, October 26, 1967.
New York Times Book Review, January 16, 1966, November 9, 1980.
Times Literary Supplement, April 28, 1966.

*   *   *

MEVES, Christa   1925-

PERSONAL: Born March 4, 1925, in Neumuenster, Germany (now West Germany); daughter of Carl and Else (Rohweder) Mittelstaedt; married Harald Meves (a doctor), December 18, 1946; children: two daughters. *Education:* Received degrees from University of Breslau, 1943, University of Kiel, 1948, University of Hamburg, 1949, and Psychotherapeutic Institute of Hannover and Goettingen, 1955. *Religion:* Catholic.

ADDRESSES: Home—Albertstrasse 14, 3110 Uelzen 1, West Germany.

CAREER: Child psychotherapist in private practice, Uelzen, Germany, 1960—. Co-editor of weekly magazine, *Rheinischer Merkur* (title means "Rhenanian Gazette").

AWARDS, HONORS: Wilhelm Boelsche medal; Prix Amade; gold medal of Herderbuecherei; Niedersaechsischer Verdienstorden first class; Konrad-Adenauer prize; Bundesverdienstkreuz first class.

WRITINGS:

Die Schulnoete unserer Kinder: Wie Eltern ihnen vorbeugen und abhelfen koennen, Furche-Verlag, 1969, 6th edition, Guetersloher Verlagshaus Mohn, 1981.
Mut zum Erziehen: Erfahrungen aus der psychagogischen Praxis, Furche-Verlag, 1970, reprinted as *Mut zum Erziehen: Seelische Gusundheit; Wie koennen wir sie unseren Kindern vermitteln?,* Gueterslohe Verlagshaus, 1976.
(With Joachim Illies) *Lieben, was ist das? Ein Grenzgespraech zwischen Biologie und Psychologie* (title means "Love—What Does It Mean?: Biological and Physical Aspects"), Herder-Verlag, 1970, reprinted, 1986.

Manipulierte Masslosigkeit: Psychsche Gefahren im technistierten Leben (title means "Manipulated Uncontrollability: Psychic Dangers in Technological Life"), Herder-Verlag, 1971, revised edition, 1975.

Erziehen lernen aus tiefenpsychologischer Sicht (title means "Learning to Educate"), Bayrischer Schulbuch-Verlag, 1971, revised edition, 1973, reprinted as *Erziehen lernen aus tiefenpsychologischer Sicht: Ein Kursbuch fuer Ellern und Erzieher*, Herder-Verlag, 1985.

Erziehen und Erzaehlen: Ueber Kinder und Maerchen (title means "Educating and Telling"), Kreuz-Verlag, 1971.

Verhaltensstoerungen bei Kindern (title means "Behavioral Disturbances in Children"), Piper-Verlag, 1971.

Wunschtraum und Wirklichkeit (title means "Illusion and Reality"), Herder-Verlag, 1972.

Ich reise fuer die Zukunft: Vortragserfahrungen und Erlebnisse einer Psychagogin (title means "I Travel for the Future: Life of a Psychagogin"), Herder-Verlag, 1973, reprinted as *Ich reise fuer die Zukunft: Ernste und heitere Vortragserlebnisse*, Herder-Verlag, 1982.

Die Bibel antwortet uns in Bildern: Tiefenpsychologische Textdeutungen im Hinblick auf Lebensfragen heute, Herder-Verlag, 1973, translation by Hal Taussig published as *The Bible Answers Us with Pictures*, Westminster Press, 1977.

Ehe-Alphabet (title means "Alphabet of Marriage"; also see below), Herder-Verlag, 1973.

Ermutigung zum Leben: Bilder und Betrachtungen (title means "Encouragement for Life"), Kreuz-Verlag, 1974.

Ich will leben: Briefe an Martina; Probleme des Jugendalters (title means "I Want to Live!"), Verlag Weisses Kreuz, 1974.

Wer passt zu mir? Der Lebenspartner—Wahl oder Qual? (title means "Who Is Suited to Me?"), Verlag Weisses Kreuz, 1974.

Kinderschicksal in unserer Hand: Erfahrungen aus der psychagogie (title means "Children's Fate in Our Hand: Experiences in a Psychagogian Practice"), Herder-Verlag, 1974.

Freiheit will gelernt sein (title means "Freedom Must Be Learned"), Herder-Verlag, 1975.

(With Illies) *Mit der Aggression leben: Ein Grenzgespraech zwischen Psychologie und Biologie* (title means "To Live with Aggressions"), Herder-Verlag, 1975.

Unser Leben muss anders werden: Glueck durch seelische Gesundheit (title means "Out Life Must Change"), Herder-Verlag, 1976.

Lange Schatten—helles Licht: Aus dem Tagebuch einer Psychagogin (title means "Long Shadows—Bright Light"), Herder-Verlag, 1976.

Ninive darf nicht untergehen: Verantwortung fuer die Zukunft (title means "Ninive Must Not Die!"), Verlag Weisses Kreuz, 1977.

Erziehung zur Reife und Verantwortung: Lustprinzip, Konsumverhalten und Aufklaerungsdiktatur kritisch betrachtet (title means "Education for Maturity and Responsibility"), Verlag Weisses Kreuz, 1977.

Wer wirft den ersten Stein? Am Leben lernen im Leiden reifen; Seelische Hilfe fuer Nachdenkliche (title means "Who Throws the First Stone?"), Verlag Weisses Kreuz, 1977.

Chancen und Krisen der modernen Ehe: Um unsere Grundwerte (title means "Chances and Crises of Modern Marriage"), Verlag Weisses Kreuz, 1977.

Antrieb—Charakter—Erziehung: Werden wir ein Volk von Neurotikern? (title means "Shall We Become a Nation of Neurotics?"), Fromm-Verlag, 1977.

Antworten Sie gleich!: Lebenschilfe in Briefen (title means "Please Answer Soon"), Herder-Verlag, 1977.

(Contributor) *Ursachen des Terrorismus in der Bundesrepublik Deutschland*, Verlag de Gruyter, 1978.

Typisch Mutter!: Ueber Muttertypen und ihre Kinder (title means "Typical Mother"), Herderbucherei, 1978.

(With Heinz D. Ortlieb) *Macht Gleichheit glueklich?* (title means "Does Equality Make You Happy?"), Herderbucherei, 1978.

Seelische Gesundheit und biblisches Heil (title means "Psychic Healthiness and Biblical Salvation"), Herder-Verlag, 1979.

Bedrohte Jugend—gefaehrdete Zukunft: Anmerkungen eines engagierten Christen zum Zietgeschehen, Verlag Weisses Kreuz, 1979.

So ihr nicht werdet wie die Kinder, Kreuz-Verlag, 1979.

(With Edelgard von Buddenbrock) *Denem im Dunkeln*, Verlag Weisses Kreuz, 1979.

(With Jutta Schmidt) *Anima-Verletzte Maedchenseele: Die Frau zwischen Verfremdung und Entfaltung*, Verlag Weisses Kreuz, 1979.

(Contributor) *Gymnasiale Erziehung*, Adamas-Verlag, 1980.

Der Weg zum sinnerfuellten Leben, Herder-Verlag, 1980.

Erziehung zur Frau, Adamas-Verlag, 1980.

Kleines ABC fuer Seelenhelfer: Grundregeln fuer die Begegnung mit Ratsuchenden und Patienten, Herder-Verlag, 1980.

Familie in der Zerreissprobe der Gesellschaft, Arbeitgeberverband-Metallindustrie, 1980.

(With Illies) *Unterwegs: Ein Briefwechsel in der Not unserer Zeit*, Herder-Verlag, 1980.

Unsere Kinder wachsen heran: Wie wir ihnen halfen koennen, Herder-Verlag, 1981.

Ich will mich aendern: Geschichte einer Genesung, Herder-Verlag, 1981.

Sein wie Gott?: Der Mensch zwischen Verwirklichung und Selbstzerstoerung, Verlag Weisses Kreuz, 1981.

Das grosse Fragezeichen: Merkwuerdige Erlebnisse von Astrid, Andreas, Monika, Peter, Maria, Thomas und Alexander, Verlag Weisses Kreuz, 1981.

Das Geringste gilt: Ansprachen und Aufsaetze, Verlag Weisses Kreuz, 1981.

(With Illies) *Giliebte Gefaehrten: Tiere als Hausgenossen und Miterzieher*, Herder-Verlag, 1981.

(With Illies) *Dienstanweisungen fuer Oberteufel*, Herder-Verlag, 1982.

(Contributor) *Frauen im Wehrdienst*, Herder-Verlag, 1982.

(With Ortlieb) *Die ruinierte Generation*, Herder-Verlag, 1982.

(Contributor) *Die Verwirklichung des Erziehungsauftrages der Schule angesichts bestehender Erziehungsprobleme*, Auer-Verlag, 1982.

Das Grosseltern-ABC: Was man wissen mus, um mit Kindern und Enkeln gluecklich zu werden (also see below), Herder-Verlag, 1983.

Bist du David? Junge Menschen von heute erleben biblische Schicksale, Herder-Verlag, 1983.

Was unsere Liebe vermag: Eine Lebenskunde, Herder-Verlag, 1983, reprinted as *Was unsere Liebe vermag: Hilfe fuer bedraengte Eltern*, Herder-Verlag, 1984.

Wohin gehen wir?: Orientierungspunkte, Herder-Verlag, 1984.

Problemkinder brauchen Hilfe: ABC der Verhaltensstoerungen fuer Eltern (also see below), Herder-Verlag, 1981.

Sexuelle Freiheit und neue Moral: Wir wollen warten, Verlag Weisses Kreuz, 1984.

Wer einem Kinde begegnel: Beitraege zu aktuellen Erziehungsfragen, Verlag Weisses Kreuz, 1984.

Ich habe ein Problem: Lebensfragen junger Menschen, Verlag Weisses Kreuz, 1984.

(Contributor) *Sterbehilfe—Mitleid oder Mord?,* Coprint-Verlag, 1984.

Der Mensch hinter seiner Maske: Aufsaetze zu seelischen Grundphaenomenen (title means "Men after Their Masks"), Verlag Weisses Kreuz, 1985.

Lebensrat von A-Z: Ehepartner, Kinder, Grosseltern (contains *Ehe-Alphabet, Grosseltern-ABC,* and *Problemkinder brauchen Hilfe*), Herder-Verlag, 1985.

Nussschalen im Ozean: Von der Hoffnung, ans Ufer zu kommen, Verlag Weisses Kreuz, 1985.

Ohne Familie geht es nicht: Ihr Sinn und ihre Gestaltung, Verlag Weisses Kreuz, 1985.

Aus Vorgeschichten lernen: Vom Massenelend vermeidbarer seelischer Erkrankungen, Herder-Verlag, 1985.

Plaedoyer fuer das Schamgefuehl: Und weitere aktuelle Beitraege, Verlag Weisses Kreuz, 1985.

Kraft, aus der Du leben kannst: Geburtstagsbriefe an die Enkel, Herder-Verlag, 1986.

Also coauthor with Lothar Kaiser, *Zeitloses Mass in massloser Zeit* (title means "Timeless Measure in Measureless Time"), 1976. Contributor of numerous articles to journals.

*   *   *

MICKIEWICZ, Ellen Propper   1938-

PERSONAL: Surname is pronounced Mits-*Keh*-vich; born November 6, 1938, in Hartford, Conn.; daughter of George K. and Rebecca (Adler) Propper; married Denis Mickiewicz (a professor), June 2, 1963; children: Cyril. *Education:* Wellesley College, B.A., 1960; Yale University, M.A., 1961, Ph.D., 1965.

ADDRESSES: Home—1555 Rainier Falls Dr., Atlanta, Ga. 30329. *Office*—Department of Political Science, Emory University, Atlanta, Ga. 30322.

CAREER: Yale University, New Haven, Conn., lecturer in political science, 1965-67; Michigan State University, East Lansing, assistant professor, 1967-69, associate professor, 1969-73, professor of political science, 1973-80, associate professor in Computer Institute for Social Science Research, 1972-73, academic administrative intern in Office of Provost, 1976-77; Emory University, Atlanta, Ga., Dean of Graduate School of Arts and Sciences, 1980-85, professor of political science, 1980—. Kathryn W. Davis Visiting Professor of Wellesley College, 1978; associate at Harvard University Russian Research Center, 1978; fellow of Carter Center, 1986—. Founder and first chairman of the board of directors, Opera Guild of Greater Lansing.

MEMBER: International Studies Association (vice-president for North America, 1983—), American Political Science Association, American Association for the Advancement of Slavic Studies (vice-president and president-elect, 1986-87, president, 1987-88).

AWARDS, HONORS: Guggenheim fellowship, 1973-74; Sigma Xi grant, 1973-74; Ford Foundation grant, 1979-80; Markle Foundation grants, 1984-86; Rockefeller Foundation grant, 1986-87; W. Alton Jones Foundation grant, 1987-88.

WRITINGS:

Soviet Political Schools, Yale University Press, 1967.

(Contributor with Frederick C. Barghoorn) *Communication in International Politics,* University of Illinois Press, 1972.

(Editor and contributor) *Handbook of Soviet Social Science Data,* Free Press, 1973.

Media and the Russian Public, Praeger, 1981.

(Co-editor) *Soviet Calculus of Nuclear War,* D. C. Heath, 1986.

(Co-editor) *International Security and Arms Control,* Praeger, 1986.

Split Signals: Television and Politics in the Soviet Union, Oxford University Press, 1987.

Contributor to Grolier's *Encyclopedia International,* 1969 and 1979. Contributor of articles and reviews to newspapers and journals, including *New York Times, Slavic Review, Corriere della sera, Journal of Communication,* and *Public Opinion Quarterly.* Editor of *Soviet Union,* 1980—.

WORK IN PROGRESS: Studies of mass media and communications in the Soviet Union.

*   *   *

MILLER, Donald Eugene   1929-

PERSONAL: Born December 2, 1929, in Dayton, Ohio; son of Daniel L. (a farmer) and Eliza Myrtle (Coning) Miller; married Phyllis Louise Gibbel, August 19, 1956; children: Bryan Daniel, Lisa Kathleen, Bruce David. *Education:* Attended Manchester College, 1947-49; University of Chicago, M.A., 1952; graduate study at United Theological Seminary, 1955-56; Bethany Theological Seminary, B.D., 1958; Harvard University, Ph.D., 1962; postdoctoral study at Yale University, 1968-69, and Cambridge University, 1975-76.

ADDRESSES: Office—Brethren General Offices, 1451 Dundee Ave., Elgin, Ill. 60120.

CAREER: Ordained minister of Church of the Brethren, 1958. Brethren Service Commission, Elgin, Ill., church service worker in Europe, 1952-54; high school teacher of social studies in Trotwood, Ohio, 1954-55; junior high school teacher in Chicago, Ill., 1957-58; Bethany Theological Seminary, Oak Brook, Ill., associate professor, 1961-70, professor of Christian education and ethics, 1970-86, director of graduate studies, 1976-86, Brightbill professor of ministry studies, 1982-86; Church of the Brethren, Elgin, general secretary of the general board, 1986—. Director of self-study for Chicago Cluster of Theological Schools, 1980-81.

MEMBER: Association of Professors and Researchers in Religious Education (president, 1968), Association for Professional Education for the Ministry (president, 1976—).

AWARDS, HONORS: Fellow of American Association of Theological Schools, 1968-69, and the association's Case Study Institute, 1972.

WRITINGS:

(With Warren F. Groff) *The Shaping of Modern Christian Thought,* World Publishing, 1968.

(With Graydon F. Snyder and Robert W. Neff) *Using Biblical Simulations,* Judson, Volume I, 1973, 2nd edition, 1974, Volume II, 1975.

A Self-Instruction Guide through Brethren History, Brethren Press, 1976.

The Wing-Footed Wanderer: Conscience and Transcendence, Abingdon, 1977.

Contemporary Approaches to Christian Education, Abingdon, 1982.

(With James N. Poling) *Foundations for a Practical Theology of Ministry,* Abingdon, 1985.
Story and Context, Abingdon, 1987.
The Gospel and Mother Goose, Brethren Press, 1987.

Editor of *Yearbook of Association for Professional Education for the Ministry,* 1972.

SIDELIGHTS: Donald Eugene Miller told *CA:* "My writings have all been directed to giving a contemporary expression to the Biblical message. On the one hand, they attempt to be deeply rooted in the Biblical tradition and Christian history. On the other hand, they attempt to be very much in touch with contemporary life and contemporary understanding."

*   *   *

MILNER, Ron(ald)   1938-

PERSONAL: Born May 29, 1938, in Detroit, Mich. *Education:* Attended Columbia University.

ADDRESSES: c/o New American Library, 1301 Sixth Ave., New York, N.Y. 10019.

CAREER: Playwright. Writer in residence, Lincoln University, 1966-67; teacher, Michigan State University, 1971-72; founder and director, Spirit of Shango theater company; director, "Don't Get God Started," 1986; led playwriting workshop, Wayne State University.

AWARDS, HONORS: Rockefeller grant; John Hay Whitney fellowship.

WRITINGS:

PLAYS

"Who's Got His Own" (three-act; also see below), first produced Off-Broadway at American Place Theatre, October 12, 1966.
"The Warning—A Theme for Linda" (one-act; first produced in New York with other plays as "A Black Quartet" at Chelsea Theatre Center, Brooklyn Academy of Music, April 25, 1969), published in *A Black Quartet: Four New Black Plays,* edited by Ben Caldwell and others, New American Library, 1970.
"The Monster" (one-act; first produced in Chicago at Louis Theatre Center, October, 1969), published in *Drama Review,* summer, 1968.
"M(ego) and the Green Ball of Freedom" (one-act; first produced in Detroit at Shango Theatre, 1971), published in *Black World,* April, 1971.
(Editor, author of introduction with Woodie King, Jr., and contributor) *Black Drama Anthology* (includes "Who's Got His Own"), New American Library, 1971.
What the Wine Sellers Buy (first produced in New York at New Federal Theatre, May 17, 1973), Samuel French, 1974.
"These Three," first produced in Detroit at Concept East Theater, 1974.
"Season's Reasons," first produced in Detroit at Langston Hughes Theatre, 1976.
"Work," first produced for Detroit Public Schools, January, 1978.
"Jazz-set," first produced in Los Angeles at Mark Taper Forum, 1980.
"Crack Steppin'," first produced in Detroit at Music Hall, November, 1981.

"Checkmates," produced in Los Angeles at Westwood Playhouse, July 17, 1987.
"Don't Get God Started," first produced on Broadway at Longacre Theatre, October, 1987.

Also author of "Life Agony" (one-act), first produced in Detroit at the Unstable Theatre and "The Greatest Gift," produced by Detroit Public Schools.

CONTRIBUTOR

Langston Hughes, editor, *Best Short Stories by Negro Writers,* Little, Brown, 1967.
Ahmed Alhamisi and Harun Kofi Wangara, editors, *Black Arts: An Anthology of Black Creations,* Black Arts, 1969.
Donald B. Gibson, editor, *Five Black Writers,* New York University Press, 1970.
Addison Gayle, Jr., editor, *The Black Aesthetic,* Doubleday, 1971.
William R. Robinson, editor, *Nommo: An Anthology of Modern Black African and Black American Literature,* Macmillan, 1972.
King, editor, *Black Short Story Anthology,* Columbia University Press, 1972.

Also contributor to *Black Poets and Prophets,* edited by King and Earl Anthony, New American Library.

OTHER

Contributor to *Negro Digest, Drama Review, Black World,* and other periodicals.

SIDELIGHTS: Ron Milner is "a pioneering force in the contemporary Afro-American theater," writes Beunyce Rayford Cunningham in the *Dictionary of Literary Biography.* Much of his work has involved growing beyond the theatre of the 1960s, where, as Milner told *Detroit News* reporter Bill Gray, "There used to be a lot of screaming and hate. . . . It was reacting to white racism and the themes were defiant directives at the white community. . . ." He continued, "We're no longer dealing with 'I am somebody' but more of who that 'somebody' really is." While not rejecting the revolutionary movements in black theatre, Milner represents a change in approach: a shift from combative performances to quieter dramas that still make a point. Comments Geneva Smitherman in *Black World,* "Those of us who were patient with our writers—as they lingered for what seems like an eternity in the catharsis/screaming stage—applaud this natural change in the course of theatrical events." Adds Cunningham, "Ron Milner's is essentially a theatre of intense, often lyrical, retrospection devoted primarily to illuminating the past events, personalities, and values which have shaped his struggling people."

Milner grew up in Detroit, on Hastings Street, also known as "'The Valley'—with the Muslims on one corner, hustlers and pimps on another, winos on one, and Aretha Franklin singing from her father's church on the other," reports Smitherman. It "was pretty infamous and supposedly criminal," Milner told David Richards of the *Washington Star-News.* But, he continued, "The more I read in high school, the more I realized that some tremendous, phenomenal things were happening around me. What happened in a Faulkner novel happened four times a day on Hastings Street. I thought why should these crazy people Faulkner writes about seem more important than my mother or my father or the dude down the street. Only because they had someone to write about them. So I became a writer."

Milner's work contains the constant appeal for stronger black families and tighter communities. According to Larry Neal in *The Black American Writer,* "Milner's main thrust is directed toward unifying the family around basic moral principles, toward bridging the 'generation gap.'" This has led some critics to label him a "preacher" and his dramas "morality plays." Not daunted by criticism, Milner told Betty DeRamus in the *Detroit Free Press* that art "has to educate as well as entertain. When people call me a preacher, I consider it a compliment . . . when you get an emotional response it's easier to involve the mind."

One of Milner's "morality plays" was very successful, both with the critics and with black audiences. *What the Wine-Sellers Buy* centers on the tempting of seventeen-year-old Steve by Rico, a pimp. Rico suggests that turning Steve's girlfriend into a prostitute is the easy way to make money. While Steve resists, future trials lay ahead. According to Cunningham, the play contains "many of the elements of Milner's previous family dramas: a young, innocent person forced to make a conscious decision about the direction of his or her life; a mother who retreats into the church; the figure of a male savior—this time a man of the church who befriends the mother and is determined to save her son. What is new here is the Faustian framework in which the menace to be dealt with is the seductions of street life represented by the pimp."

"As in all morality plays, good and the power of love" triumph, DeRamus notes, but adds, "what makes 'Wine Sellers' different is that the villain, Rico, is no cardboard figure who is easily knocked down. He is, in fact, so persuasive and logical that he seduces audiences as well as Steve." DeRamus reports that Milner patterned Rico after "the typical American businessman," and quotes Milner's comment that when Rico "talks about everything for profit, trading everything for money, he's talking about society. What he says about society is correct, but he is wrong in what he decides to trade. If you trade life, what do you buy?" In Rico, Milner did not create "simply the stereo-typical Black pimp," writes Smitherman. "Rather, Rico is the devious Seducer in our lives, moving to and fro, enticing us to compromise our morality, our politics and even our very souls." Still, the play leaves critics with a positive impression, as it focuses on young Steve triumphing over Rico's corruption. Edwin Wilson in the *Wall Street Journal* applauds the play's outlook: "the emphasis is not on past grievances and injustices, but on the future—on the problems and perils young people face growing up in broken homes and a hostile environment, and their determination to overcome these forces. . . . The play gives further evidence that black playwrights today . . . are determined to find their own way."

Much of Milner's energy in the 1970s was directed to defining and establishing a unique black theatre. "American theater was (and still is) the nut that few blacks are able to crack," Milner and his co-editor, Woodie King, Jr., observe in the introduction to *Black Drama Anthology.* They continue that "Black theater is, in fact, about the destruction of tradition, the traditional role of Negroes in white theater. . . . We say that if this theater is to be, it must—psychically, mentally, aesthetically, and physically,—go home." By "going home," Milner and King mean returning to the experiences that have given blacks their identity. Added Milner to Smitherman, "'Theater' and 'play' have always meant going to see somebody else's culture and seeing how you could translate it into your own terms. People always felt they were going to a foreign place for some foreign reason. But now there's a theater written to them, of them, for them and about them."

Milner believes that a local theatre can also help to unify the community. "Theater lifts a community in more ways than one," he said to Smitherman. "The idea of seeing yourself magnified and dramatized on stage gives you a whole perspective on who you are and where you are. You can isolate your emotions and thoughts and bring them to a place and ritualize them in an audience of people who empathize with you." Milner stresses the need for local theatre to communicate something valuable to its audience; he disapproves of creating art only for aesthetic reasons. "Theater for theater's sake is incest," he told Richards. "It gets thinner and thinner each time and drifts off into abstraction. But when it's directly involved in life, even when its badly done, it can cause people to argue, discuss, grow, or at least clarify where they stand. It's true, the aesthetic side can do something for you spiritually. But you can't let that prevent you from communicating on a basic level."

The play that "could thrust [Milner] into the role of the theater's primary chronicler of the contemporary black middle class," is "Checkmates," writes Don Shirley for the *Los Angeles Times.* "Checkmates," produced in 1987, examines the lives of an upwardly mobile couple in their thirties, who are coping with the stresses of marriage, two careers, and urban life. The pair is complemented by their landlords, an older couple with simpler lives, who remember the days when blacks worked in the fields, not offices. The landlords, despite their lack of sophistication, possess a steadiness that the younger, financially successful couple lack. Milner told Shirley, "It's dangerous to identify with [the younger couple], because you can't tell what they might say or do next. They aren't fixed. They can't say, 'These are the values I stand for.' The point of the older couple's lives was to build for the future. Now here is the future, and there are no rules left for the younger couple." Dan Sullivan, also writing for the *Los Angeles Times* enjoys the play's humor: Milner "knows his people so well that an equally big laugh will come on a quite ordinary remark, revealing more about the speaker than he or she realizes." But he also notes the underlying message. "'Checkmates' gives us a specific sense of today's corporate jungle and its particular risks for blacks, however hip, however educated."

While Milner finds the idea of the middle-class "one-dimensional," he is not hostile to the idea of writing to such an audience. "I was never a writer who said the middle class should be lined up against a wall and shot," he told Shirley. As different as it may seem from his previous work, "Checkmates" still falls in with Milner's basic philosophy toward black theatre, as he told Richards: "For a long time, black writers dwelled on our negative history. They could never see any real victory. For them, the only victory lay in the ability to endure defeat. I was consciously trying to break that. I function a great deal on what I intuitively feel are the needs of the time. And the needs of the time are for the positive."

BIOGRAPHICAL/CRITICAL SOURCES:

BOOKS

Alhamisi, Ahmed and Harun Kofi Wangara, editors, *Black Arts: An Anthology of Black Creations,* Black Arts, 1969.
Authors in the News, Volume I, Gale, 1976.
Bigsby, C. W. E., editor, *The Black American Writer,* Volume II: *Poetry and Drama,* Penguin Books, 1969.
Dictionary of Literary Biography, Volume XXXVIII: *Afro-American Writers after 1955: Dramatists and Prose Writers,* Gale, 1985.

Hill, Errol, editor, *The Theater of Black Americans,* Volume I: *Roots and Rituals: The Search for Identity* [and] *The Image Makers: Plays and Playwrights,* Prentice-Hall, 1980.

King, Woodie, Jr., editor, *Black Short Story Anthology,* Columbia University Press, 1972.

King, Woodie, Jr., and Ron Milner, editors, *Black Drama Anthology,* Columbia University Press, 1972.

Robinson, William R., editor, *Nommo: An Anthology of Black African and Black American Literature,* Macmillan, 1972.

PERIODICALS

Black World, April, 1971, April, 1976.
Detroit Free Press, January 5, 1975.
Detroit Free Press Magazine, June 24, 1979.
Detroit News, October 20, 1974.
Drama Review, summer, 1968.
Los Angeles Times, March 19, 1980, September 3, 1986, July 12, 1987, July 20, 1987.
New Yorker, November 9, 1987.
New York Times, July 21, 1982, October 31, 1987.
Wall Street Journal, February 21, 1974.
Washington Star-News, January 5, 1975.†

—*Sketch by Jani Prescott*

*   *   *

MOIR, Alfred   1924-

PERSONAL: Surname is pronounced Moy-er; born April 14, 1924, in Minneapolis, Minn.; son of William Wilmerding (a physician) and Blanche (Kummer) Moir. *Education:* Harvard University, A.B., 1948, M.A., 1949, Ph.D., 1953; University of Rome, graduate study, 1950-52.

ADDRESSES: Home—51 Seaview Dr., Santa Barbara, Calif. 93108. *Office*—Department of Art History, University of California, Santa Barbara, Calif. 93106.

CAREER: Harvard University, Harvard College, Cambridge, Mass., proctor, 1949-50; Tulane University of Louisiana, Newcomb College, New Orleans, instructor, 1952-54, assistant professor, 1954-59, associate professor of art history, 1959-63; University of California, Santa Barbara, associate professor, 1963-65, professor of art history, 1965—, chairman of department, 1963-69, director of Education Abroad Program in Italy, 1978-80, adjunct curator of drawings, University Museum, 1985—. Consultant, Isaac Delgado Museum of Art, New Orleans, 1954-57. Art historian in residence, American Academy in Rome, 1969-70, and 1980. *Military service:* U.S. Army, 1943-46; became master sergeant.

MEMBER: College Art Association, Society of Architectural Historians, Mediaeval Academy of America, Renaissance Society of America, Southern California Art Historians, Society of Fellows, American Academy in Rome.

AWARDS, HONORS: Fulbright fellow in Italy, 1950-51; honorary alumnus, Tulane University.

WRITINGS:

(Contributor) *Art in Italy, 1600-1700,* Detroit Institute of Arts, 1965.

The Italian Followers of Caravaggio, Harvard University Press, 1967.

(Editor) *Seventeenth-Century Italian Drawings from the Collection of Janos Scholz,* University of California, 1973.

Caravaggio and His Copyists, College Art Association of America, 1975.

European Drawings in the Santa Barbara Museum of Art, [Santa Barbara, Calif.], 1976.

(Editor) *Regional Styles of Drawing in Italy,* [Santa Barbara], 1977.

Caravaggio, Abrams, 1982.

(Editor and contributor) *Old Master Drawings from the Feitelson Collection,* University of Washington Press, 1983.

Also editor of *Old Master Drawings from the Collection of John and Alice Steiner,* 1986. Contributor to art journals.

*   *   *

MORRIS, Julian
See WEST, Morris L(anglo)

*   *   *

MORRISON, Dorothy Nafus

PERSONAL: Born in Nashua, Iowa; daughter of Roy A. (a merchant) and Edwinna (a teacher of Latin and German; maiden name, Bolton) Nafus; married Carl V. Morrison (a psychiatrist), April 25, 1936 (deceased, 1980); married Robert C. Hunter (an attorney), 1981; children: (first marriage) James, Anne (Mrs. John Feighner), David, John. *Education:* Attended University of Northern Iowa; University of Iowa, B.A.

ADDRESSES: Home—8600 Southwest 170th Ave., Beaverton, Ore. 97007.

CAREER: Music teacher in public schools in Iowa; teacher of stringed instruments in public schools in Beaverton, Ore., 1954-66; writer, 1965—.

WRITINGS:

JUVENILES

The Mystery of the Last Concert (fiction), Westminster, 1971.

(With husband, Carl V. Morrison) *Can I Help How I Feel?* (nonfiction), Atheneum, 1976.

Ladies Were Not Expected: Abigail Scott Duniway and Women's Rights (biography), Atheneum, 1977.

The Eagle and the Fort: The Story of John McLoughlin (biography), Atheneum, 1978.

Chief Sarah: Sarah Winnemucca's Fight for Indian Rights (biography), Atheneum, 1980.

(Contributor) William Gentz, editor, *Writing to Inspire,* Writer's Digest, 1982.

Under a Strong Wind: The Adventures of Jessie Benton Fremont (biography), Atheneum, 1983.

Whisper Goodbye (fiction), Atheneum, 1985, published in German as *Goodbye Whisper,* Albert Muller Verlag, 1987.

Somebody's Horse (fiction), Atheneum, 1986.

Whisper Again (fiction), Atheneum, 1987.

WORK IN PROGRESS: The Vanishing Trick.

SIDELIGHTS: Dorothy Nafus Morrison told *CA:* "I started writing when I was eight years old, with a 'novel' laid in a West I had never seen. Years later, when I moved to this area, I felt I had at last come to the place where I belonged.

"In several of my books I tried to picture the rich history of this area by writing biographies of its important citizens. I wrote about the fur trade, the Oregon trail, the heroic efforts to promote migration to the West, the growth of women's rights, the fight for Indian rights, and the gold rush. These were exciting events, which happened to real people. In exploring them I visited the places where they occurred, and made extensive use of primary sources, such as letters and journals. Rather than invent scenes or dialog, I quoted brief passages from my subjects' own writings.

"I have now moved into fiction—but I am still writing about the Northwest. I have laid two novels in the Columbia Gorge, one concerned with the problems which a high dam can cause when it floods a town, the other hinging on Indian petroglyphs. A third book takes place on a Wyoming ranch, and the one I am working on at present is about the Oregon Coast.

"One of the bonuses of writing is the focus it gives for travel. Besides doing research in Oregon, I have spent time on a Wyoming ranch, in the Mother Lode country of California, around Pyramid Lake in Nevada, in many parts of the state of Washington, and the fur country of Canada, especially that around Thunder Bay. I hope my books will stir young readers to greater understanding of the country in which they live, and the people who helped it grow."

BIOGRAPHICAL/CRITICAL SOURCES:

PERIODICALS

School Library Journal, November, 1977, September, 1979, November, 1980, November, 1983, May, 1985.

*   *   *

MOWAT, Farley (McGill)   1921-

PERSONAL: Born May 12, 1921, in Belleville, Ontario, Canada; son of Angus McGill and Helen (Thomson) Mowat; married Claire Angel Wheeler, 1965; children: (previous marriage) Robert Alexander, David Peter. *Education:* University of Toronto, B.A., 1949.

ADDRESSES: c/o McClelland & Stewart, 481 University Ave., Toronto, Ontario, Canada M5G 2E9.

CAREER: Self-employed author. *Military service:* Canadian Army, Infantry, 1939-45; became captain.

AWARDS, HONORS: President's Medal, University of Western Ontario, 1952, for best Canadian short story of 1952; Anisfield-Wolfe Award for contribution to interracial relations, 1954, for *People of the Deer;* Governor General's Medal, 1957, and Book of the Year Award, Canadian Association of Children's Librarians, both for *Lost in the Barrens;* Canadian Women's Clubs Award, 1958, for *The Dog Who Wouldn't Be;* Hans Christian Andersen International Award, 1958; Boys' Clubs of America Junior Book Award, 1962, for *Owls in the Family;* National Association of Independent Schools Award, 1963, for juvenile books; Hans Christian Andersen Honours List, 1965, for juvenile books; Canadian Centennial Medal, 1967; Leacock Medal, 1970, and L'Etoile de la Mer Honours List, 1972, both for *The Boat Who Wouldn't Float;* D.Lit., Laurentian University, 1970; Vicky Metcalf Award, 1970; Mark Twain Award, 1971; Doctor of Law from Lethbridge University, 1973, University of Toronto, 1973, and University of Prince Edward Island, 1979; Curran Award, 1977, for "contributions to understanding wolves"; Queen Elizabeth II Jubilee Medal, 1978; Knight of Mark Twain, 1980; Officer, Order of Canada, 1981; Doctor of Literature, University of Victoria, 1982, and Lakehead University, 1986.

WRITINGS:

NONFICTION

People of the Deer, Atlantic-Little, Brown, 1952, revised edition, McClelland & Stewart, 1975.
The Regiment, McClelland & Stewart, 1955, revised edition, 1973.
The Dog Who Wouldn't Be, Atlantic-Little, Brown, 1957.
(Editor) Samuel Hearne, *Coppermine Journey: An Account of a Great Adventure,* Atlantic-Little, Brown, 1958.
The Grey Seas Under, Atlantic-Little, Brown, 1958.
The Desperate People, Atlantic-Little, Brown, 1959.
(Editor) *Ordeal by Ice* (also see below), McClelland & Stewart, 1960.
The Serpent's Coil, McClelland & Stewart, 1961.
Owls in the Family (American Library Association Notable Book), Atlantic-Little, Brown, 1961.
Never Cry Wolf, Atlantic-Little, Brown, 1963, revised edition, McClelland & Stewart, 1973.
Westviking: The Ancient Norse in Greenland and North America, Atlantic-Little, Brown, 1965.
(Editor) *The Polar Passion: The Quest for the North Pole* (also see below), McClelland & Stewart, 1967, revised edition, McClelland & Stewart, 1973.
Canada North, Atlantic-Little, Brown, 1967.
(With John de Visser) *This Rock within the Sea: A Heritage Lost,* Atlantic-Little, Brown, 1969, new edition, McClelland & Stewart, 1976.
The Boat Who Wouldn't Float, McClelland & Stewart, 1969, Atlantic-Little, Brown, 1970.
The Siberians, Atlantic-Little, Brown, 1970 (published in Canada as *Sibir: My Discovery of Siberia,* McClelland & Stewart, 1970, revised edition, 1973).
A Whale for the Killing, Atlantic-Little, Brown, 1972.
(With David Blackwood) *Wake of the Great Sealers,* Atlantic-Little, Brown, 1973.
(Editor) *Tundra: Selections from the Great Accounts of Arctic Land Voyages* (also see below), McClelland & Stewart, 1973.
Top of the World Trilogy (includes *Ordeal by Ice, The Polar Passion: The Quest for the North Pole,* and *Tundra: Selections from the Great Accounts of Arctic Land Voyages*), McClelland & Stewart, 1976.
The Great Betrayal: Arctic Canada Now, Atlantic-Little, Brown, 1976 (published in Canada as *Canada North Now: The Great Betrayal,* McClelland & Stewart, 1976).
And No Birds Sang (memoir), Atlantic-Little, Brown, 1979.
The World of Farley Mowat: A Selection from His Works, edited by Peter Davison, Atlantic-Little, Brown, 1980.
Sea of Slaughter, Atlantic Monthly Press, 1984.
My Discovery of America, McClelland & Stewart, 1985.
Woman in the Mists: The Story of Dian Fossey and the Mountain Gorillas of Africa, Warner Books, 1987.

FICTION

Lost in the Barrens (juvenile novel), Atlantic-Little, Brown, 1956.
The Black Joke (juvenile novel), McClelland & Stewart, 1962.
The Curse of the Viking Grave (juvenile novel), Atlantic-Little, Brown, 1966.
The Snow Walker (short story collection), Atlantic-Little, Brown, 1975.

OTHER

Also author of television screenplays "Sea Fare" and "Diary

of a Boy on Vacation,'' both 1964. Contributor to magazines. A collection of Mowat's manuscripts is housed at McMaster University.

WORK IN PROGRESS: Two feature films; an autobiography.

SIDELIGHTS: Farley Mowat is Canada's most internationally recognized living writer. He has published over twenty-nine books, both fiction and nonfiction, many of which have been widely translated. Although he is frequently categorized as a nature writer, Mowat wishes to be considered a storyteller or ''saga man'' who is concerned about the preservation of all forms of life. Mowat's reputation is that of an outspoken advocate with an irreverent attitude toward bureaucracy and a love of the far Canadian North. He has aroused the ire of government officials many times in the course of his career with his harsh indictments of their treatment of endangered races of people and endangered species of animal life. With characteristic bluntness, Mowat once remarked in *Newsweek:* ''Modern man is such an arrogant cement head to believe that he can take without paying.''

Mowat first became aware of man's outrages against nature in the late 1940s when he accepted a position as a government biologist in the Barren Lands of northern Canada. He had accepted the assignment in part because it offered him a respite from civilization, since he had recently returned from serving in the Canadian Army where he had witnessed many injustices against his fellow man. ''I came back from the war rejecting my species,'' he told Cheryl McCall in *People* magazine. ''I hated what had been done to me and what I had done and what man did to man.''

Mowat's assignment in the Barrens was to study the area's wolves and their diet. The Canadian government suspected that the wolves were responsible for the dwindling caribou population, and they wanted evidence to corroborate their suspicions. After observing a wolf couple he named George and Angeline, however, Mowat found the wolves to be intelligent creatures who ate only what they needed. He learned that their diet consisted primarily of field mice and an occasional sickly caribou, and that by choosing the weak caribou, the wolves actually helped strengthen the herd.

Mowat fashioned his findings into an entertaining tale, *Never Cry Wolf,* where he also noted that his findings were ''not kindly received by ordained authority.'' A *Chicago Tribune Book World* reviewer calls Mowat's discovery ''a perfect example of the bureaucrats getting more than they bargained for.'' According to an *Atlantic* reviewer, ''the Canadian government . . . has never paid any discernible attention to the information it hired Mr. Mowat to assemble.''

The book's message was heeded by the reading public and by the governments of other countries, including Russia. Shortly after a translation of *Never Cry Wolf* appeared in Russian, government officials there banned the slaughter of wolves, whom they had previously thought to be arbitrary killers. In addition, *Los Angeles Time Book Review* contributor David Graber believes that ''by writing 'Never Cry Wolf,' [Mowat] almost single-handedly reversed the public's image of the wolf, from feared vermin to romantic symbol of the wilderness.''

Never Cry Wolf was welcomed by critics as well. *Christian Science Monitor* reviewer Harry C. Kenney notes that the book ''delightfully and instructively lifts one into a captivating animal kingdom,'' and Gavin Maxwell writes in *Book Week:* ''This is a fascinating and captivating book, and a tragic one, too, for it carries a bleak, dead-pan obituary of the wolf family

that Mr. Mowat had learned to love and respect. It is an epilogue that will not endear the Canadian Wildlife Service to readers. . . . Once more it is man who displays the qualities with which he has tried to damn the wolf.''

While in the Barrens, Mowat also befriended an Eskimo tribe called the Ihalmiut, nicknamed the People of the Deer because they depend almost solely on caribou for food, clothing, and shelter. While conversing with the Ihalmiut in a simplified form of their language that they had taught him, Mowat learned that the tribe had been dwindling for a number of years due to the decreasing availability of caribou. Mowat, enraged at the government's apathy toward preserving the tribe, began to write scathing letters to government officials, eventually losing his position as a result. He then decided to write a book entitled *People of the Deer* to help publicize the tribe's plight. *Saturday Review* contributor Ivan T. Sanderson observes: ''What [Mowat] learned by living with the pathetic remnants of this wonderful little race of Nature's most perfected gentlemen, learning their language and their history, and fighting the terrifying northern elements at their side, so enraged him that when he came to set down the record, he contrived the most damning indictment of his own government and country, the so-called white race and its Anglo-Saxon branch in particular, the Christian religion, and civilization as a whole, that had ever been written.''

Others express a similar admiration for *People of the Deer.* A *Times Literary Supplement* reviewer writes: ''The author traces with a beautiful clarity the material and spiritual bonds between land, deer and people, and the precarious ecological balance which had been struck between the forefathers of this handful of men and the antlered multitude.'' Observes Albert Hubbell in the *New Yorker:* ''It is not often that a writer finds himself the sole chronicler of a whole human society, even of a microcosmic one like the Ihalmiut, and Mowat has done marvellously well at the job, despite a stylistic looseness and a tendency to formlessness. Also, his justifiable anger at the Canadian government's neglect of the Ihalmiut, who are its wards, intrudes in places where it doesn't belong, but then, as I said, Mowat is something of a fanatic on this subject. His book, just the same, is a fine one.'' T. Morris Longstreth concludes in *Christian Science Monitor:* ''Mr. Mowat says of his book, 'This is a labor of love, and a small repayment to a race that gave me renewed faith in myself and in all men.' It will widen the horizons of many who are at the same time thankful that this explorer did the widening for them.''

Mowat's most bitter account of man's abuse of non-human life is *Sea of Slaughter,* published in 1984. ''Built of the accumulated fury of a lifetime,'' according to *Los Angeles Times Book Review* contributor David Graber, *Sea of Slaughter* is viewed by several critics to be his most important work to date. Tracy Kidder notes in the *Washington Post Book World* that compared to his earlier work *Never Cry Wolf,* this book ''is an out and out tirade.'' The book's title refers to the extinction and near-extinction of sea and land animals along the Atlantic seaboard of North America, extending from Cape Cod to Labrador. Mowat traces the area's history back to the sixteenth century when the waters teemed with fish, whales, walruses, and seals, and the shores abounded with bison, white bears (now known as polar bears because of their gradual trek northward), and other fur-bearing mammals. Currently, many of these species have been either greatly diminished or extinguished because of ''pollution, gross overhunting . . . , loss of habitat, destruction of food supplies, poachings and officially sanctioned 'cullings,''' writes Kidder.

The stark contrast between past and present is tremendously affecting, reviewers note. *Detroit News* contributor Lewis Regenstein, for example, writes that the book has several shortcomings, including some inaccuracies and a lack of footnoting, but claims that these "shortcomings pale in comparison to the importance of its message: We are not only destroying our wildlife but also the earth's ability to support a variety of life forms, including humans. As Mowat bluntly puts it, 'The living world is dying in our time.'" *Los Angeles Times Book Review* contributor David Graber believes that "the grandest anguish comes from Mowat's unrelenting historical accounts of the sheer *numbers* of whales, bears, salmon, lynx, wolves, bison, sea birds; numbers that sear because they proclaim what we have lost, what we have thrown away." Ian Darragh writes in *Quill & Quire:* "Mowat's description of the slaughter of millions of shorebirds for sport, for example, is appalling for what it implies about the aggression and violence apparently programmed into man's genetic code. There is little room for humour or Mowat's personal anecdotes in this epitaph for Atlantic Canada's once bountiful fish and wildlife." Concludes *Commonweal* critic Tom O'Brien: "*Sea of Slaughter* provides some heavier reading [than Mowat's other books]; the weight in the progression of chapters starts to build through the book like a dirge. Nevertheless, it may help to focus the burgeoning animal rights movement in this country and abroad. The cause has no more eloquent spokesperson."

Sea of Slaughter received some unintended but nevertheless welcome publicity in 1984 when Mowat was refused entrance into the United States, where he was planning to publicize the book. While boarding a plane at a Toronto airport, Mowat was detained by officials from the United States Immigration and Naturalization Service (INS) who acted on the information that Mowat's name appeared in the *Lookout Book,* a government document that lists the names of those individuals who represent a danger to the security of the United States.

Mowat later speculated in the *Chicago Tribune* about some possible reasons for his exclusion: "At first, . . . the assumption was that I was excluded because of the two trips I made to the Soviet Union [in the late 1960s]. . . . Then some guy at the INS supposedly said I was being kept out because I'd threatened the U.S. Armed Forces by threatening to shoot down American aircraft with a .22 caliber rifle. The fact is the Ottawa Citizen [where the story supposedly appeared in 1968] can't find any record of it, but that doesn't matter. I admit it, happily." Mowat added that more recently the suggestion has been that the "gun lobby and anti-environmentalists" might have wanted to prevent his publicizing *Sea of Slaughter.*

Although the United States Immigration and Naturalization Service later granted Mowat a month-long admittance for business purposes, Mowat refused the offer, demanding an as-yet undelivered apology. Instead, Mowat used the time he would have spent traveling to write *My Discovery of America,* where he describes in detail his attempts to determine why he was not allowed entry into the United States. *Los Angeles Times* contributor David Graber writes: "'My Discovery of America' is an entertaining chronicle offering useful and provocative insights about the American body politic, but it shouldn't be a book. Shame on Farley Mowat, customarily an economical wordsmith. Shame on Atlantic Monthly, which has a perfectly good outlet for the longish essay that this should have been."

The excitement caused by Mowat's experience and the subsequent book earned Mowat as much, or perhaps more, notoriety than he would have received in his scheduled tour.

Mowat, delighted by rising sales of *Sea of Slaughter,* told Jane Cawley in the *Chicago Tribune:* "I'm going to send a bouquet of roses to the INS . . . guy who stopped me, along with a note that says, 'Thanks for the publicity.'"

Mowat departs from his usual subject matter in *And No Birds Sang,* a memoir describing his experiences in the Canadian Army Infantry during World War II. The memoir, penned thirty years after Mowat's return from duty, was written in part to help refute the notion that it is sweet and honorable to die in service to one's country, a statement Mowat had seen gaining ground in the late 1970s. *And No Birds Sang* chronicles Mowat's initial enthusiasm and determination to fight and his gradual surrender to despair and a horrifying fear of warfare, a fear Mowat calls "The Worm That Never Dies." Contrary to the popular belief that each battle becomes increasingly easier, Mowat found that each attack on the enemy became more difficult as "The Worm" became more insidious. Christopher Lehmann-Haupt writes in the *New York Times:* "Bit by bit we begin to notice Mr. Mowat's growing preoccupation with what he will eventually name the Worm That Never Dies—gut-twisting fear. It doesn't bother him much at first, during a night landing on the southeast tip of Sicily, or during his platoon's initial victorious skirmishing with remnants of the German Army rapidly retreating to the north. But images of death accumulate in Mr. Mowat's mind—men cut in half, decapitated, blown to bits, or just driven mad—and the desire to fight steadily drains out of him."

Several reviewers believe that *And No Birds Sang* is a valuable addition to the literature of World War II. *Washington Post Book World* contributor Robert W. Smith calls the book "a powerful chunk of autobiography and a valuable contribution to war literature." *Time* critic R. Z. Sheppard writes: "*And No Birds Sang* needs no rhetoric. It can fall in with the best memoirs of World War II, a classic example of how unexploded emotions can be artfully defused."

Although other reviewers express reservations about the familiar nature of Mowat's theme, they add that Mowat nevertheless manages to bring a fresh perspective to the adage, "War is hell." David Weinberger remarks in *Macleans:* "Everybody knows that war is hell; it is the author's task to transform that knowledge into understanding. At times Mowat succeeds, at times the writing bogs down in adjectives and ellipsis." He adds, however, that "it takes a writer of stature—both as an author and as a moral, sensitive person—to make the attempt as valiantly as Mowat has." A similar opinion is expressed by Jean Strouse in *Newsweek:* "That war is hell is not news, but a story told this well serves, particularly in these precarious, saber-rattling days, as a vivid reminder."

In addition to his own memoirs, Mowat has authored a biography of the famed primatologist Dian Fossey. Shortly after Fossey was brutally murdered in 1985, Mowat was approached by Warner Books to write her biography. Although he initially refused—simply because he had never written a commissioned book—Mowat later accepted the offer after reading one of Fossey's *National Geographic* articles. Moved by "her empathy with the animal world, the impression that she had penetrated the barrier humans have erected," writes Beverly Slopen in *Publishers Weekly,* Mowat also thought "he could use her story as a vehicle for his message." Mowat told Slopen that while reading Fossey's letters and journals, though, "I began to realize that the importance of the book was her message, not my message. . . . I really became her collaborator.

It was the journals that did it. They weren't long, discursive accounts. They were short, raw cries from the heart.''

The biography, *Woman in the Mists: The Story of Dian Fossey and the Mountain Gorillas of Africa* was published in 1987. As Mowat indicated, the work relies heavily on Fossey's journal entries and letters to tell the story of her life. Fossey, originally a physical therapist, was invited by anthropologist Louis Leakey in 1967 to study primates in the Congo (now Zaire). Shortly thereafer Fossey's work was halted by political uprising, but the indomitable Fossey escaped armed soldiers to cross the border into Uganda. She established a research center on the Rwandan side of the Virunga Mountains, near the Parc National des Volcans, where she remained until her death.

Although the murder has not yet been solved, and thus Mowat is not able to say who killed Fossey, the book nevertheless "goes a long way toward revealing what it was about her that made a violent death seem inevitable," writes Eugene Linden in the *New York Times Book Review*. Fossey was known to stalk gorilla poachers, and she lived by the motto "An eye for an eye." When a man who had stoned her dog Cindy was captured, Fossey and her associates likewise stoned him. She also angered government officials by opposing "gorilla tourism" and the development of park land for agrarian purposes.

Some critics view Fossey's protective stance toward the apes as evidence of her misanthropy. Indeed, Stefan Kanfer relates in *Time* that Fossey once declared, "I feel more comfortable with gorillas than people. I can anticipate what a gorilla's going to do." *Washington Post Book World* contributor Mary Battiata writes: "Forced to choose between the needs of people and the survival of a threatened gorilla population, Fossey chose gorillas every time." Linden, on the other hand, maintains that "the diaries reveal a woman whose self-righteousness and sense of mission justified the kind of behavior that borders on madness."

Mowat's biography also reveals a side of Fossey that was generous, kind, witty, and romantic. She had a succession of affairs throughout her lifetime, including one with Louis Leakey, and longed for a stable, monogamous relationship. Thus Mowat, Battiata believes, "puts to rest—forever one hopes—the shopworn notion of Fossey as a misanthrope who preferred animals to her own species."

Several reviewers feel that more commentary from Mowat is needed in order to make sense of Fossey's controversial life and death. Mowat's self-appointed role as a "collaborator" rather than a biographer makes Battiata "uneasy," and she explains: "Though Mowat offers an intriguing and credible solution to the mystery of Fossey's unsolved murder, there is little else that is genuinely new here.... Mowat never really gets around to a clear-eyed evaluation of Fossey's scientific contributions or her conservation efforts. By failing to do so, he leaves a thin veil of romance over a life strong enough to stand unadorned." *Chicago Tribune* contributor Anita Susan Grossman similarly observes: "Farley Mowat has declined to do any serious analysis of his controversial subject. Instead, he limits himself to presenting excerpts from Fossey's own writings, strung together with the barest of factual narration. As a result, the central drama of Fossey's life remains as murky as the circumstances of her death. One awaits other, more comprehensive accounts of this extraordinary woman." Although Linden concurs that *Woman in the Mists* does have several problems, including a lack of footnotes, Mowat's "pedestrian" prose, and "interlocutory words [that] add little to

our understanding of Fossey or her world," he adds: "Despite these problems, this is a rare, gripping look at the tragically mingled destinies of a heroic, flawed woman and her beloved mountain gorillas amid the high mists of the Parc des Volcans."

Critical appraisal aside, Mowat states that the writing of Fossey's biography had a profound, sobering effect on him and that he will not undertake another biography. "It was a disturbing experience," he told Slopen. "It's almost as though I were possessed. I wasn't the master. I fought for mastery and I didn't win. It really was a transcendental experience and I'm uncomfortable with it."

Although Mowat has spent nearly a lifetime trying to convince man that he cannot continue to abuse nature without serious and sometimes irreversible repercussions, he believes that "in the end, my crusades have accomplished nothing." Mowat continues in *People* magazine: "I haven't saved the wolf, the whales, the seals, primitive man or the outport people. All I've done is to document the suicidal tendencies of modern man. I'm sure I haven't altered the course of human events one iota. Things will change inevitably, but it's strictly a matter of the lottery of fate. It has nothing to do with man's intentions."

MEDIA ADAPTATIONS: A Whale for the Killing was made into a movie and shown on ABC-TV in March, 1980; *Never Cry Wolf* was made into a film of the same title and released by Buena Vista in 1983. The National Film Board of Canada released a biographical film, "In Search of Farley Mowat," in May, 1981.

CA INTERVIEW

CA interviewed Farley Mowat by telephone on June 30, 1987, at his home in Nova Scotia, Canada.

CA: Your writing reflects a great sadness over what we've done to our fellow creatures, both human and nonhuman. When did the concern begin in earnest?

MOWAT: Probably soon after World War II. I was very concerned about what we were doing to our species and went to the other species for some solace. I discovered that we were treating them abominably too. The first book that concerned itself with other animals was *Never Cry Wolf*. But my experience in the Arctic in 1946-1947, where I became involved first of all with the Eskimos and then with the wolves and caribou, brought all three together.

CA: You became a controversial writer with your first book, People of the Deer. *In that book and its sequel,* The Desperate People, *you told the sad history of Eskimos whom you lived among for a while, and whom "civilization" has dealt with very harshly. Are all the Ihalmiut gone now?*

MOWAT: They have ceased to exist as a separate entity. There are survivors living on the west coast of Hudson Bay at Eskimo Point. They would be second and third generation now. But they are staging a bit of a revival, which is quite encouraging. Some of them have gone back just to visit the ancestral home grounds, not to live there. They're showing considerable interest in their own roots and collecting information about their past; I've been helping them with that. It may be a bit late, but still it's interesting that they're doing that.

CA: How are you helping them?

MOWAT: I've provided them with certain information. I had more information about the tribe than anybody else did, and my files still are available to them.

CA: It was amazing that the negative response to People of the Deer *even included a denial that the Ihalmiut tribe ever existed.*

MOWAT: Yes. That was from A. E. Porsild, the government spokesman. That's the way man has done consistently throughout history. We deny the abominations that we create; we simply say they don't exist. That's one way of dealing with them.

CA: "I am a storyteller, in the direct line of the old saga men," you told Cheryl McCall for People. *When did storytelling begin to coincide with your interest in wildlife to start you on your career as a writer?*

MOWAT: Well, you know, I'm interested in writing about wildlife, but that's secondary. I am basically a storyteller. That's my profession; it's my life. And that started when I was a little kid, I guess when I was six or seven or eight years old. I've always loved telling stories, and it seems to me that I've always been impelled to do it. Also, it gave me a marvelous opportunity to build a life of my own—I didn't have to work for anybody else; I didn't have to be at anybody's beck and call. But I notice in reading about myself the odd little bit that comes in, more and more I'm being categorized as a nature writer. That's nonsense. I'm not a nature writer. I write about life on this planet, and that includes human life and nonhuman life. I'm concerned about what's happening to all forms of life.

CA: Your parents seem to have been major influences in nurturing your talents. What would you give them special credit for?

MOWAT: For letting me go my own way, not interfering or interrupting or trying to direct me in ways of their choosing. Both my parents were extremely good about this. My mother permitted me to take risks that other mothers would have thought atrocious. And she didn't do it because she was thoughtless—it hurt her and bothered her, but she felt that it was only fair to me. My father helped by encouraging me to take other directions. He was never insistent that I should do what other boys were doing. For instance, I was no good at sports. He never put pressure on me to learn to be a sports-player, a team player. They were very permissive in the proper sense of the word. They disciplined me, in terms of moral strictures and that sort of thing, but in terms of letting me choose my own way of life, they were extremely permissive. I'm very grateful for that.

CA: One judges from the kilt stories told about you that you're especially proud of your Scottish heritage. Would you like to comment on that?

MOWAT: We're all nomads on this continent, and nomads who don't know who we are or where we came from, most of us. Every living form of social animal on this planet needs to belong somewhere. There's a phrase in Newfoundland. They don't ask you where you come from; they say, "Where do you belong?" We all have this urge. My desire to belong

somewhere is focused on my Scottish ancestry. Like everybody else in North America, I'm a bastard. God only knows how many bloodlines run in my veins. But the Scots one is the one that I have chosen.

CA: In several of your books—most recently Sea of Slaughter—*you've made an eloquent plea for animal conservation. What practical results have you seen from the books, in Canada or elsewhere?*

MOWAT: Nothing very specific. For instance, the wolf situation is getting worse, particularly in Alaska and the Yukon and British Columbia. In general, the people who are dedicated to witless killing of other forms of life seem to be carrying on pretty well unchanged. In fact, they're even making some gains. But what has happened is a change in the general attitude of Western man, of our society. More and more people are becoming fed up with the killer syndrome, and this is where the hope lies. We're not going to be able to reverse the killing process in the next decade, or perhaps two. But the indications are that in the very near future there will be such enormous pressure from the nonkilling members of the human species that the killers will be driven into a corner and disarmed. That's the hope.

CA: Canada gets a lot of negative publicity because of its annual seal slaughter. Do you see any indication that the government may be reconsidering its position?

MOWAT: Oh yes. It's flying kites right now to see whether they can start what they call a controlled cull. These are the gobbledygook words they use—they're going to "manage" the seals, have a "conrolled cull." They are definitely trying the waters to see if they can get away with having another massacre. The reaction from the real conservation groups—things like Greenpeace and the International Fund for Animal Welfare, the activists—is so strong that I think the government is backing down.

CA: You've traveled widely. Are there places where people seem to be more in tune with the natural world than we are in Canada and the U.S.?

MOWAT: The farther you get away from modern civilization, the more closely people are attuned to the natural world. They're a part of it. If you get far enough away, they are totally attuned to it; they don't kill anything unless there is need. They kill to eat, to keep themselves going, but they don't kill for fun, they don't kill for greed, they don't kill from any of the motivations that we have. So-called high civilization and conservation seem to be antipathetic. It's weird, and rather depressing. In terms of Western culture, the place that I know best that is reversing itself more strongly is the Soviet Union. There the conservation ethic has finally caught on. It took a long time, but having caught on, it's making enormous strides. It's moving much more rapidly there than it is here.

CA: Some of your books—for example, Owls in the Family, Lost in the Barrens, *and* The Curse of the Viking Grave—*are classified as juveniles. As a storyteller and a man who may still be a child in the best sense of the word, do you make a clear distinction between adult and juvenile?*

MOWAT: No, I don't make any distinction whatsoever. It depends on the tone of voice I hear in my head when I'm telling a story. I don't envisage my audience in these age groups—

ages six to twelve, or whatever. Some stories are best told in a childish way, and others you tell in a more complicated way. But I don't categorize those books as being juvenile or adult. They're not really novels either—I don't even like that. It's an arbitrary distinction made by cataloguers.

I've just heard, by the way, that *Never Cry Wolf* was banned in one of the Florida school districts on the grounds that it was obscene and indecent. I was quite flattered, actually. I'd prefer to be banned in Boston, but if I can't be banned in Boston, Florida will do.

CA: Never Cry Wolf may be your best-known book because of the movie based on it. Were you pleased with the way the movie portrayed the story?

MOWAT: Yes. Nobody should be foolish enough to expect the movie to be a mirror image of the book. But what happened with *Never Cry Wolf* as a movie was that it went on a parallel track to the book. The cargo carried on both tracks was the same. I was perfectly happy with the movie. Mind you, it made me look like a far worse nerd than I think I am. But that's OK. I became very good friends with Charles Martin Smith, who played the lead human role, as a result of the movie. In fact, he has become a Canadian as a result of making the film. We've traded first names: he's now Farley Martin Smith and I'm Charlie Mowat.

CA: You first wrote about World War II in The Regiment, *published in 1955, but there wasn't a memoir until* And No Birds Sang, *in 1979. Did you need the perspective of time to deal with your personal experiences in the war?*

MOWAT: No, it was simply my fears that another cataclysm was coming that made me write the memoir. This was a conservation book. I'm talking about the human species, not the other animals. It was an attempt to alert people of another, young generation to the reality of what war is all about. It's a memoir, but it's also a tract.

CA: In And No Birds Sang *you quote from a journal you kept during the war. How much of the experience came back from the journal, either directly or by having your memory triggered by the journal entries?*

MOWAT: I'd say three-quarters of it came back just through the triggering mechanism. I don't have a conscious memory; it's subconscious. I never know what's going to come out when I open that little trapdoor.

CA: Was it painful, writing the book?

MOWAT: Not terribly. It was a sorrowful episode. I cried a lot in my heart writing it. But it wasn't painful in the usual sense. It wasn't that I hated to go back and relive the events. I was so glad that I was alive, that I *could* go back and relive the events.

CA: In My Discovery of America, *published in 1985, you wrote about being kept from entering the United States for a promotion tour by U.S. Immigration and Naturalization, possibly because your name was in a "lookout book" of potentially dangerous characters. Has anything happened in this story since the book was published?*

MOWAT: My name is definitely in the so-called "Lookout Book," along with the names of about 40,000 other people.

This book grew out of the McCarran-Walter Act, passed in 1952. It had fallen into disuse during previous administrations as being simply a piece of idiocy, but the Reagan government resurrected it. I had a letter last week from your representative Barney Frank, who is fighting to get the McCarran-Walter Act changed. He said even the Reagan authorities are now so deeply embarrassed by what's been happening that they are making noises indicating they would be willing to see the act changed. That's good news.

CA: You seem to have been unusually lucky in your editors. Would you like to comment on them?

MOWAT: I've been extraordinarily lucky. In the United States it was Dudley Cloud at Atlantic Monthly Press and then Peter Davison at Atlantic. I went from one very good editor there to another very good editor. The same thing happened in Canada. It's interesting that I've only been published by the two publishing houses. All my books in Canada have been published by McClelland & Stewart, and in the States by Atlantic; I haven't moved around at all. Those days are gone, alas. Both those publishing houses have changed hands. But editors had a tremendously beneficial effect on my work, because I was lucky in having good editors who were literary men and women and understood exactly what I could do, which was tell stories. They didn't ask me to do anything else. They reinforced my strengths and didn't try to get me to fool around with my weaknesses. They're a vanished breed, though, I'm afraid.

CA: How do you see yourself in the context of Canadian letters?

MOWAT: I'm the best-selling Canadian writer of our time. That's bragging, but what the hell. A little braggadocio never hurt anybody. I am a current writer; I don't write for immortality or for the future. If my books are read after I'm dead, well and good. But I'll be gone, so I don't care. I want them to be read while I'm alive.

CA: Your wife, Claire Mowat, is also a writer. How much of a part does she play in your own books?

MOWAT: Not a very large part. She's in *Sibir* [*The Siberians* in the U.S.], and she's in *The Boat Who Wouldn't Float*. But that's about all. She's on her second book now. She also writes "subjective nonfiction" and is, I think, going to have a long career in her own right.

CA: Does she act as first reader for your work, or anything like that?

MOWAT: No. We don't interfere with each other's work.

CA: How do you divide your time now between your homes in Ontario and Nova Scotia?

MOWAT: It's variable. This year I'll probably be spending five or six months in Nova Scotia and the rest of the time in Ontario, with a fair amount of long-distance traveling. Now that I don't have to travel, I'm doing it more!

CA: You've been very busy recently writing a book about Dian Fossey. Would you tell me something about the inspiration and the sources for the book?

MOWAT: The original idea for the book came from Warner Books. They made contact with me through my Canadian publisher and asked me if I'd be interested. I said no, because I don't do commissioned books. But then I began thinking about it, and I began to remember what I had heard about Dian Fossey. I thought, My God, this could be interesting, so I did a little research and decided it would be a marvelous story, and I said I would do it. In the initial stages I didn't know what was going to happen, because I didn't know how much material was available about her. What was available publicly was pretty superficial. But I have a very good researcher, Wade Rowland. I sent Wade off to Africa to see what he could dig up, and he got on the trail of her archives and traced them back to Ithaca, New York, where he discovered them in a warehouse. She'd kept everything she had ever received, copies of everything she'd ever written—all her journals, all her diaries. It was incredible. It was too much good luck; it took six months just to look at the papers. It was more than we needed or wanted. There was so much material that I finally decided she didn't need a biographer. All she needed was somebody to put stuff together for her, and I decided I would be her amanuensis. So what I've written here is a posthumous autobiography; it's mostly in her words.

CA: Did any of your feelings about Fossey change through the writing of the book?

MOWAT: Not really, though I didn't realize that she was as much of an outsider, an outcast, as she turned out to be. I thought she was a bit of an Establishment type: she'd gone to Cambridge and taken her doctorate and so forth. But it turned out that she was a bloody rebel from the word go. She knuckled under at first because she felt she had to. Then her whole life developed into an enormous conflict between her concept of conservation, which was, to quote her, *active* conservation, and that of the Establishment conservation organizations. It ended up with her having an enormous battle to save the gorillas literally from physical death at the hands of poachers and sport hunters, and all the big Establishment conservation agencies trying to promote gorilla tourism as a means of providing a base for gorilla survival. She saved the gorillas single-handed despite what the conservation Establishment did.

CA: Do you have specific writing plans beyond the publication of the Fossey book?

MOWAT: Yes. This book was an interruption in my plans. My plans are to write a prolonged autobiography. I've been doing it all my life anyway, so I'm just going to continue that. It's going to be called, with apologies to Steinbeck, *Travels with Farley.*

BIOGRAPHICAL/CRITICAL SOURCES:

BOOKS

Egoff, Sheila, *The Republic of Childhood: A Critical Guide to Canadian Children's Literature in English,* Oxford University Press, 1975.
Mowat, Farley, *And No Birds Sang* (memoir), Atlantic-Little, Brown, 1979.

PERIODICALS

Atlantic, November, 1963.
Audubon, January, 1973.
Best Sellers, February, 1986.
Books in Canada, March, 1985, November, 1985.
Books of the Times, April, 1980.
Book Week, November 24, 1963.

Book World, December 31, 1972.
Canadian Children's Literature, No. 5 and 6, 1976.
Canadian Forum, July, 1974, March, 1976.
Canadian Geographical Journal, June, 1974.
Canadian Literature, spring, 1978.
Chicago Tribune, October 29, 1980, December 23, 1983, May 6, 1985, October 22, 1987.
Chicago Tribune Book World, November 13, 1983.
Christian Science Monitor, May 1, 1952, October 3, 1963, May 15, 1969, May 10, 1970, April 15, 1971, March 6, 1974.
Commonweal, September 6, 1985.
Contemporary Review, February, 1978.
Detroit News, April 21, 1985.
Economist, January 15, 1972.
Illustrated London News, September 20, 1952.
Los Angeles Times, December 13, 1985.
Los Angeles Times Book Review, March 16, 1980, April 28, 1985.
Macleans, October 8, 1979.
Nation, June 10, 1968.
New Republic, March 8, 1980.
Newsweek, February 18, 1980, September 30, 1985.
New Yorker, April 26, 1952, May 11, 1968, March 17, 1980.
New York Times, December 13, 1965, February 19, 1980.
New York Times Book Review, February 11, 1968, June 14, 1970, February 22, 1976, November 6, 1977, February 24, 1980, December 22, 1985, October 25, 1987.
Observer, March 4, 1973.
People, March 31, 1980.
Publishers Weekly, October 2, 1987.
Quill & Quire, December, 1984.
Saturday Evening Post, July 29, 1950, April 13, 1957.
Saturday Night, October 18, 1952, October 25, 1952, November, 1975.
Saturday Review, June 28, 1952, April 26, 1969, October 21, 1972.
Scientific American, March, 1964.
Sierra, September, 1978.
Spectator, November 21, 1952.
Time, February 18, 1980, May 6, 1985, October 26, 1987.
Times Literary Supplement, September 12, 1952, March 19, 1971, February 16, 1973.
Washington Post, October 9, 1983, April 25, 1985, October 25, 1985.
Washington Post Book World, February 24, 1980, May 12, 1985, October 25, 1987.

—*Sketch by Melissa Gaiownik*

—*Interview by Jean W. Ross*

*   *   *

MUHLENFELD, Elisabeth   1944-

PERSONAL: Born November 12, 1944, in Washington, D.C.; daughter of Merle Roberts (an insurance executive) and Cornelia (a teacher; maiden name, Herring) Showalter; married Edward F. Muhlenfeld, September 10, 1966 (divorced, 1975); married Laurin Arthur Wollan, Jr. (a criminologist and attorney), June 5, 1982; children: (first marriage) Allison Elisabeth Muhlenfeld, David Edward Muhlenfeld; (stepchildren) Ann Louise Wollan, Laurin Arthur Wollan III. *Education:* Goucher College, B.A., 1966; University of Texas at Arlington, M.A., 1973; University of South Carolina, Ph.D., 1978.

ADDRESSES: Home—1515 Hickory Ave., Tallahassee, Fla. 32303. *Office*—314 Westcott, Florida State University, Tallahassee, Fla. 32306.

CAREER: High school teacher in Virginia and Texas, 1968-70; Florida State University, Tallahassee, assistant professor, 1978-82, associate professor, 1982-87, professor of American and Southern literature, 1987—, dean of undergraduate studies, 1984—.

MEMBER: Modern Language Association of America, South Atlantic Modern Language Association, Society for the Study of Southern Literature (member of executive council, 1981-84, 1987-90).

WRITINGS:

Mary Boykin Chesnut: A Biography, Louisiana State University Press, 1981.
The Novels of William Faulkner: Absalom, Absalom!, Garland, 1983.
William Faulkner's "Absalom, Absalom!": A Critical Casebook, Garland, 1984.
(Editor with C. Vann Woodward) *The Private Mary Chestnut: The Unpublished Civil War Diaries,* Oxford University Press, 1984.
(Contributor) *A History of Southern Literature,* Louisiana State University Press, 1985.
Reading "Absalom, Absalom!", University Press of Mississippi, 1990.

Contributor of articles, essays, and reviews to journals, including *Southern Review, Mississippi Quarterly, Faulkner Journal, Southern World,* and *Journal of Southern History.*

SIDELIGHTS: Elisabeth Muhlenfeld's biography of Mary Boykin Chesnut, whose celebrated diary is one of the most vivid documents of the Civil War, was praised by P. J. Parish of the *Times Literary Supplement* for "its happy blend of sympathy and good sense." Walter Clemons of *Newsweek* commented: "Elisabeth Muhlenfeld's expert biography . . . satisfies our curiosity about the before-and-after of Chesnut's diary." Reid Beddow, in the *Washington Post Book World,* noted that the biography "happily complements" the diary and "rounds out the picture of this strong-minded woman and her family."

Muhlenfeld told *CA:* "My interests are in American literature and history—specifically Southern literature and history. I find the tasks of the biographer to be a happy conjunction of both interests, for one must hope to combine the stringent and objective attention to detail of the historian with that something which, for want of a better word, might as well be called insight that distinguishes the best critics, making all of their works creative accomplishments. Underneath all the 'scholarly' tasks I embark on is a delight in the human spirit, in the courage and perseverance with which individual men and women embrace the living of a life from day to day and decade to decade."

BIOGRAPHICAL/CRITICAL SOURCES:

PERIODICALS

Los Angeles Times Book Review, December 23, 1984.

Newsweek, April 13, 1981.
Times Literary Supplement, November 6, 1981.
Washington Post Book World, April 12, 1981.

*   *   *

MUNTON, Alan (Guy) 1945-

PERSONAL: Born May 3, 1945, in Winchester, England; son of Alexander John (a sailor and civil servant) and Marjorie (Tuffs) Munton; married Patricia Ann Fennell, November 3, 1976 (divorced 1986); children: Christopher, Louise. *Education:* University of Birmingham, B.A. (with honors), 1967, M.A., 1969; attended McGill University, 1969-70; Cambridge University, Ph.D., 1976.

ADDRESSES: Home—33 Connaught Ave., Plymouth, Devon PL4 7BT, England. *Office*—College of St. Mark and St. John, Derriford Rd., Plymouth, Devonshire PL6 8BH, England.

CAREER: University of Reading, Reading, England, lecturer in English literature, 1976-78; College of St. Mark and St. John, Plymouth, England, senior lecturer in English literature, 1978—.

WRITINGS:

(Editor) *Wyndham Lewis: Collected Poems and Plays,* Persea Books, 1979, revised edition, Humanities, 1981.
(Editor with Alan Young) *Seven Writers of the English Left: A Bibliography of Literature and Politics, 1916-1980,* Garland Publishing, 1981.
(Contributor) G. Cianci, editor, *Wyndham Lewis: Litteratura/Pittura,* Sellerio (Palermo), 1982.
(Contributor of bibliographical appendix) Boris Ford, editor, *The Cambridge Guide to the Arts,* Volume IX, Cambridge University Press, 1988.
English Fiction of the Second World War, Faber, 1988.

Contributor of articles and reviews to magazines and newspapers, including *PN Review.*

SIDELIGHTS: Alan Munton once wrote: "I want my work to be both scholarly and relevant to contemporary literary discussion. Attracted to Wyndham Lewis's fiction, criticism, and painting (but not to his politics), to the writers of the English Left of the 1930's, and to English war fiction, I have found three research areas in which there is a growing general interest, much work to be done, and much undervalued achievement to identify. I find bibliography difficult, depressing, and yet fascinating; it is an undervalued activity which can do as much as criticism to reestablish writers' reputations. I hope that my bibliography for *The Cambridge Guide to the Arts,* which includes all the arts (music, film, architecture, the crafts, etc.) for the years since 1945, will help readers to make sense of that period. To write as a critic is a release from the constraints of bibliography and editing; the constraint on the critic is that he should write well, or not at all."

N

NARVESON, Jan F(redric)   1936-

PERSONAL: Born June 15, 1936, in Erskine, Minn.; son of Carl Robert and Sophie (Krbechek) Narveson; children: Kaja Lee, Jascha, Julia. *Education:* University of Chicago, B.A., 1955, B.A., 1956; Harvard University, M.A., 1957, Ph.D., 1961; Oxford University, graduate study, 1959-60. *Politics:* "Mildly libertarian." *Religion:* None.

ADDRESSES: Home—57 Young St. W., Waterloo, Ontario, Canada N2L 2Z4. *Office*—Department of Philosophy, University of Waterloo, Waterloo, Ontario, Canada N2L 3G1.

CAREER: University of New Hampshire, Durham, instructor, 1961-62, assistant professor of philosophy, 1962-63; University of Waterloo, Waterloo, Ontario, assistant professor, 1963-66, associate professor, 1966-69, professor of philosophy, 1969—. Visiting professor at Johns Hopkins University, 1967, Stanford University, 1968, and University of Calgary, 1976. Founder and president, Kitchener-Waterloo Chamber Music Society. Member of board, Kitchener-Waterloo Symphony Orchestra, and Kitchener-Waterloo Community Orchestra.

MEMBER: American Philosophical Association, Canadian Philosophical Association, Canadian Civil Liberties Union, Phi Beta Kappa.

AWARDS, HONORS: Woodrow Wilson fellow, 1956-57; Frank Knox Memorial fellow at Oxford University, 1959-60.

WRITINGS:

Morality and Utility, Johns Hopkins Press, 1967.
Thinking about Ethics, Graphics Department, University of Waterloo, 1967.
Thinking about Politics, Graphics Department, University of Waterloo, 1968.
(Editor) *Moral Issues,* Oxford University Press (Toronto), 1983.
An Examination of Libertarianism, Temple University Press, in press.

CONTRIBUTOR

S. Gorovetz, editor, *Mill's Utilitarianism: Text and Commentary,* Bobbs-Merrill, 1971.
J. Rachels, editor, *Moral Problems,* Harper, 1971, 2nd edition, 1975.

M. Bayles, editor, *Ethics and Population,* Schenkman, 1976.
W. Shea and John King-Farlow, editors, *Contemporary Issues in Political Philosophy,* Science History Publications, 1976.
W. Aiken and H. LaFollette, editors, *World Hunger and Moral Obligation,* Prentice-Hall, 1977.
Obligations to Future Generations, Temple University Press, 1978.
Limits of Utilitarianism, University of Minnesota Press, 1982.
Ethics and Animals, Humana Press, 1982.
E. Regis, editor, *Gewirth's Ethical Rationalism,* University of Chicago Press, 1983.
R. G. Frey, editor, *Utility and Rights,* University of Minnesota Press, 1984.
Hardin, Mearsheimer, Dworkin, and Goodin, *Nuclear Deterrence,* University of Chicago Press, 1984.
D. Copp and D. Zimmerman, editors, *Morality, Reason and Truth,* Rowman & Allanheld, 1985.
M. Fox and L. Groarke, *Nuclear War: Philosophical Perspectives,* Peter Lang, 1985.
E. Regis, Jr., *Extraterrestrials: Science and Alien Intelligence,* Cambridge University Press, 1985.
Tom Regan, *Matters of Life and Death,* 2nd edition, Random House, 1986.
Philip Hanson, editor, *Environmental Ethics,* Institute for the Humanities, Simon Fraser University, 1986.
D. Copp, editor, *Nuclear Weapons, Deterrence and Disarmament,* University of Calgary Press, 1986.
Wil Waluchow and Deborah Poff, *Canadian Business Ethics,* Prentice-Hall, 1987.

Also contributor to *Morality and Universality: Essays on Ethical Universalizability,* edited by N. Potter and N. Timmins.

OTHER

Contributor to *Ethics, Analysis, Mind, Canadian Journal of Philosophy,* and other publications. Member of editorial boards of *Ethics, Philosophical Archives, Dialogue, Philosophy and Social Policy, Journal of Social Philosophy,* and *International Journal of Applied Ethics.*

AVOCATIONAL INTERESTS: "Major passion for music and audio equipment; minor passion for photography and motor cars."

NAYLOR, Phyllis (Reynolds)   1933-

PERSONAL: Born January 4, 1933, in Anderson, Ind.; daughter of Eugene S. and Lura (Schield) Reynolds; married second husband, Rex V. Naylor (a speech pathologist), May 26, 1960; children: Jeffrey Alan, Michael Scott. *Education:* Joliet Junior College, diploma, 1953; American University, B.A., 1963. *Politics:* Independent. *Religion:* Unitarian Universalist.

ADDRESSES: Home—9910 Holmhurst Rd., Bethesda, Md. 20817.

CAREER: Elementary school teacher in Hazelcrest, Ill., 1956; Montgomery County Education Association, Rockville, Md., assistant executive secretary, 1958-59; National Education Association, Washington, D.C., editorial assistant with *NEA Journal*, 1959-60; full-time writer, 1960—. Active in civil rights and peace organizations.

MEMBER: Society of Children's Book Writers, Authors Guild, Authors League of America, Children's Book Guild (Washington, D.C.; president, 1974-75, 1983-84).

AWARDS, HONORS: Golden Kite Award for nonfiction, Society of Children's Book Authors, 1978, and International Reading Association (IRA) Children's Choice citation, both for *How I Came to Be a Writer;* Child Study Award, Bank Street College, 1983, for *The Solomon System;* Edgar Allan Poe Award, Mystery Writers of America, 1985, for *Night Cry;* Young Adult Services Division (YASD) Best Book for Young Adults citation, American Library Association, American Library Association Notable Children's Book citation, Notable Children's Book in the Field of Social Studies citation, South Carolina Young Adult Book Award, 1985-86, all for *A String of Chances;* Notable Children's Book in the Field of Social Studies citation, for *The Dark of the Tunnel;* IRA Children's Choice citations, for *How Lazy Can You Get?* and *The Agony of Alice;* creative writing fellowship grant, National Endowment for the Arts, 1987.

WRITINGS:

Crazy Love: An Autobiographical Account of Marriage and Madness (nonfiction; Literary Guild selection), Morrow, 1977.
In Small Doses (humorous fiction), Atheneum, 1979.
Revelations (novel), St. Martin's, 1979.
Unexpected Pleasures (fiction), Putnam, 1986.
Maudie in the Middle, Atheneum, 1988.
The Christmas Surprise, Atheneum, in press.

FOR CHILDREN AND YOUNG ADULTS; NONFICTION

How to Find Your Wonderful Someone, How to Keep Him/ Her if You Do, How to Survive if You Don't, Fortress, 1972.
An Amish Family, J. Philip O'Hara, 1974.
Getting Along in Your Family, Abingdon, 1976.
How I Came to Be a Writer, Atheneum, 1978, revised edition, Aladdin Books, 1987.
Getting Along with Your Friends, Abingdon, 1980.
Getting Along with Your Teachers, Abingdon, 1981.

FOR CHILDREN AND YOUNG ADULTS: FICTION

The Galloping Goat and Other Stories (short stories), Abingdon, 1965.
Grasshoppers in the Soup: Short Stories for Teen-agers, Fortress, 1965.
Knee Deep in Ice Cream and Other Stories (short stories), Fortress, 1967.

What the Gulls Were Singing, Follett, 1967.
Jennifer Jean, the Cross-Eyed Queen, Lerner, 1967.
To Shake a Shadow, Abingdon, 1967.
The New Schoolmaster, Silver Burdett, 1967.
A New Year's Surprise, Silver Burdett, 1967.
When Rivers Meet, Friendship, 1968.
The Dark Side of the Moon (short stories), Fortress, 1969.
Meet Murdock, Follett, 1969.
To Make a Wee Moon, Follett, 1969.
The Private I and Other Stories (short stories), Fortress, 1969.
Making It Happen, Follett, 1970.
Ships in the Night, Fortress, 1970.
Wrestle the Mountain (Junior Literary Guild selection), Follett, 1971.
No Easy Circle, Follett, 1972.
To Walk the Sky Path (Weekly Reader Book Club selection), Follett, 1973.
Witch Sister (first volume of Witch trilogy), Atheneum, 1975.
Walking through the Dark (Junior Literary Guild selection), Atheneum, 1976.
Witch Water (second volume of Witch trilogy), Atheneum, 1977.
The Witch Herself (third volume of witch trilogy), Atheneum, 1978.
How Lazy Can You Get? (Weekly Reader Book Club selection), Atheneum, 1979.
A Change in the Wind, Augsburg Press, 1980.
Eddie, Incorporated, Atheneum, 1980.
Shadows on the Wall (first volume of York trilogy), Atheneum, 1980.
All Because I'm Older, Atheneum, 1981.
Faces in the Water (second volume in York trilogy), Atheneum, 1981.
Footprints at the Window (third volume of York trilogy), Atheneum, 1981.
The Boy with the Helium Head, Atheneum, 1982.
A String of Chances, Atheneum, 1982.
Never Born a Hero, Augsburg Press, 1982.
The Solomon System, Atheneum, 1983.
The Mad Gasser of Bessledorf Street, Atheneum, 1983.
A Triangle Has Four Sides, Augsburg Press, 1984.
Night Cry, Atheneum, 1984.
Old Sadie and the Christmas Bear, Atheneum, 1984.
The Dark of the Tunnel, Atheneum, 1985.
The Agony of Alice, Atheneum, 1985.
The Keeper, Atheneum, 1986.
The Bodies in the Besseldorf Hotel, Atheneum, 1986.
The Baby, the Bed, and the Rose, Atheneum, 1987.
The Year of the Gopher, Atheneum, 1987.
Beetles, Lightly Toasted, Atheneum, 1987.

WORK IN PROGRESS: Sang Spell; Loose Ties; Alice in Rapture, Sort of; Bernie and the Bessledorf Ghost; One of the Third-Grade Thonkers.

SIDELIGHTS: Phyllis Naylor told *CA:* "Two things that Willa Cather once wrote have stayed with me always: 'Let your fiction grow out of the land beneath your feet,' and 'The years from eight to fifteen are the formative period in a writer's life.' I first copied these sentences down without having any idea, really, of how they applied to me. It wasn't so much that there was nothing to write about back in the Midwest, as that we never seemed to stay in one place long enough to put down roots. My father was a traveling salesman; as he changed jobs, we changed houses, and by the time I entered high school, we had lived in eight different neighborhoods stretching across

Indiana, Illinois, and Iowa. The land beneath *my* feet was constantly changing.

"In those formative years that Cather wrote about, however, I frequently spent summers at either one of my grandparents' homes. If we drove west to Iowa, I found myself on a remote farm with my German-Scottish grandmother, where hugs were reserved for arrivals and departures, and in between was the practical no-nonsense business of the day to attend to. But if we went east to Maryland, where the terrain was rolling and the roads curving, I found myself in a world of southern relatives who had migrated from Mississippi, bringing the humid, suffocating climate of inbred warmth and gossip along with them.

"My grandfather was the minister of a small church, my grandmother the neighborhood midwife, and for the first time in my life I had a town I could encompass on foot, roads I could connect, faces that attached themselves to names I heard mentioned frequently over the supper table. It wasn't until years later that I realized just how much this small southern Maryland town had worked its way into my blood—its one-lane roads, canopied with trees which opened up occasionally for a tobacco field, past signs saying *Turkey Shoot, Every Sunday, Eleven Till Three,* or *Jesus Saves and Heals.*

"Four of my books have had their roots in this place or with these relatives: *Revelations, A String of Chances, Night Cry,* and *Unexpected Pleasures.* In the writing of them I can hear my grandparents' southern voices, the drawl of the hired man, the gossip, the complaints, the blessings. I would get quite sick of myself, of course, if all my books had their setting in the same place. But I find a certain replenishment when I dip back into southern Maryland. I experience that exhilarating rush of adrenalin I feel when I know that an idea is 'right.' And then I realize I'm home."

BIOGRAPHICAL/CRITICAL SOURCES:

BOOKS

Phyllis Naylor, *Crazy Love: An Autobiographical Account of Marriage and Madness,* Morrow, 1977.
Naylor, *How I Came to Be a Writer,* Atheneum, 1978, revised edition, Aladdin Books, 1987.

PERIODICALS

Chicago Tribune Book World, March 2, 1986.
Los Angeles Times, November 1, 1986.
New York Times Book Review, December 2, 1979, November 2, 1986.
Washington Post Book World, September 12, 1982, November 6, 1983, November 8, 1983, June 9, 1985, March 9, 1986, May 11, 1986, November 25, 1986, December 14, 1986, May 10, 1987.

*   *   *

NEIDER, Charles 1915-

PERSONAL: Surname rhymes with "rider"; born January 18, 1915, in Odessa, Russia (now U.S.S.R.); brought to United States in 1920, naturalized in 1927; son of Calman and Olga (Hornstein) Neider; married Joan Muriel Merrick, August 5, 1952; children: Susan Muriel. *Education:* City College (now of the City University of New York), B.S. (with honors), 1938.

ADDRESSES: Home—24 Southern Way, Princeton, N.J. 08540. *Office*—Stevenson College, University of California, Santa Cruz, Calif. 95064. *Agent*—Curtis Brown Ltd., 10 Astor Place, New York, N.Y. 10003.

CAREER: Free-lance writer and editor, 1938—.

AWARDS, HONORS: Mark Twain Scholar, 1956; Chapelbrook Foundation fellowship, 1970-71; grant from Grace Doherty Charitable Foundation, 1974; grant from National Science Foundation, 1976-77; Antarctic Service Medal of the United States, National Science Foundation, 1977; Guggenheim fellowship, 1977-78; National Endowment for the Humanities fellowship, 1977-78; Center for Advanced Study in Behavioral Sciences fellowship, 1977-78, summer, 1981; research associate in literature, 1978-79, and honorary fellow of Stevenson College, 1982—, both from University of California, Santa Cruz; resident fellowships (totalling thirteen) from Yaddo, MacDowell Colony, and Huntington Hartford Foundation.

WRITINGS:

The Frozen Sea: A Study of Franz Kafka, Oxford University Press, 1948, published in England as *Kafka: His Mind and Art,* Routledge & Kegan Paul, 1949.
(With Yan Bereznitsky) *Mark Twain and the Russians: An Exchange of Views* (letters between Neider and Bereznitsky), Hill & Wang, 1960.
Susy: A Childhood (biography of daughter, Susan Neider), Horizon, 1966.
Mark Twain (essays), Horizon, 1967.
Edge of the World: Ross Island, Antarctica; a Personal and Historical Narrative, color photographs by Neider, Doubleday, 1974.
Beyond Cape Horn: Travels in the Antarctic, color photographs by Neider, Sierra Books, 1980.

EDITOR

The Stature of Thomas Mann (anthology of commentary and criticism), New Directions, 1947, reprinted, Books for Libraries Press, 1968.
Great Short Stories from the World's Literature, Rinehart, 1950, revised edition, 1972.
Men of the High Calling (short stories), Abingdon, 1954.

EDITOR AND AUTHOR OF INTRODUCTION

Short Novels of the Masters, Rinehart, 1948.
Great Shipwrecks and Castaways: Authentic Accounts of Adventures at Sea, Harper, 1952.
The Fabulous Insects, Harper, 1953, reprinted, Books for Libraries Press, 1968.
Man against Nature: Tales of Adventure and Exploration, Harper, 1954.
Fanny Osbourne Stevenson (Mrs. Robert Louis) and Robert Louis Stevenson, *Our Samoan Adventure,* Harper, 1955.
Essays of the Masters, Rinehart, 1956.
The Complete Short Stories of Mark Twain, Hanover House, 1957, reprinted, Bantam Books, 1981, new edition, Doubleday, 1985.
Man against Woman: A Vade Mecum for the Weaker Sex and a Caution to Women, Harper, 1957.
Tolstoy's Tales of Courage and Conflict, Hanover House, 1958, new edition published as *Tolstoy: Tales of Courage and Conflict,* Carrol & Graf, 1985.
The Great West (annotated), Coward-McCann, 1958.
The Autobiography of Mark Twain (annotated), Harper, 1959, reprinted, 1975.

The Complete Humorous Sketches and Tales of Mark Twain, illustrations by Twain, Doubleday, 1961, new edition, 1985.

The Travels of Mark Twain (annotated), Coward-McCann, 1961.

Mark Twain: Life As I Find It; Essays, Sketches, Tales, and Other Material (annotated), Doubleday, 1961, new edition published as *Life As I Find It: Essays, Sketches, and Tales,* Harper, 1977.

The Complete Essays of Mark Twain, illustrations by Twain, Doubleday, 1963, new edition, 1985.

The Complete Novels of Mark Twain, Doubleday, 1963.

Mark Twain, *The Adentures of Colonel Sellers* (adaptation of *The Gilded Age,* co-authored by Twain and Charles Dudley Warner; annotated), Doubleday, 1965.

The Complete Travel Books of Mark Twain, two volumes, Doubleday, 1966.

The Complete Short Stories of Robert Louis Stevenson, Doubleday, 1969.

Antarctica: Authentic Accounts of Life and Exploration in the World's Highest, Driest, Windiest, Coldest, and Most Remote Continent (annotated), Random House, 1972.

The Complete Tales of Washington Irving, Doubleday, 1975.

Washington Irving, *George Washington: A Biography* (one-volume abridgment of Irving's original five-volume edition), Doubleday, 1976.

The Comic Mark Twain Reader: The Most Humorous Selections from His Stories, Sketches, Novels, Travel Books, and Speeches (annotated), Doubleday, 1977.

Twain, *A Tramp Abroad,* illustrations by Twain, Harper, 1977.

(Also author of commentary) *The Selected Letters of Mark Twain,* Harper, 1982.

(Also author of commentary) *Plymouth Rock and the Pilgrims and Other Salutary Platform Opinions* (Twain speeches), Harper, 1984.

Papa: An Intimate Biography of Mark Twain by Susy Clemens, His Daughter, Thirteen; with a Foreword and Copious Comments by Her Father, Doubleday, 1985.

Twain, *Adventures of Huckleberry Finn: Including the Omitted, Long, Brilliant Raft Chapter, with the Final "Tom Sawyer" Section, Abridged,* Doubleday, 1985.

Mark Twain at His Best: A Comprehensive Sampler, Doubleday, 1986.

The Outrageous Mark Twain, Doubleday, 1987.

NOVELS

The White Citadel, Twayne, 1954.

The Authentic Death of Hendry Jones (western), Harper, 1956.

Family Album, Hamish Hamilton, 1962, published as *Naked Eye,* Horizon, 1964.

Overflight, preface by Neider, New Horizon Press, 1986.

The Authentic Death of Hendry Jones has been published as *Guns Up.* Also author of *Mr. Burbank.*

OTHER

Contributor of articles to *New York Times.*

WORK IN PROGRESS: A novel set on an icebreaker in the Southern Ocean; the second and final volume of *Susy: A Childhood.*

SIDELIGHTS: Two very different subjects are predominant in the literary career of Charles Neider: the writings of American author Mark Twain (Samuel Langhorne Clemens) and the frozen continent of Antarctica, which Neider has visited on three separate occasions in the last twenty years. Although Neider has also authored several well-received novels, including *The White Citadel, The Authentic Death of Hendry Jones,* and *Naked Eye,* it is his groundbreaking work on Mark Twain and his more recent work on Antarctica for which he is best known. Neider has served as editor for numerous volumes of Twain's writings, beginning in 1957 with *The Complete Stories of Mark Twain,* which brought together Twain's stories in book form for the first time, and subsequent volumes that similarly collected Twain's essays and sketches. Over the last few years, however, Neider has also gained recognition for his writings about Antarctica, which focus on the region's unspoiled natural wonders and document the experiences of, as Neider explains in his *CA* interview, "a literary person who wanted to see what it was like to be a human being living and working on that remarkable continent." In a profile by Neil Baldwin for *Publishers Weekly,* Neider comments on the drawing power of both areas: "I call Antarctica the last great common on earth, the last great location of natural, public land, almost extraterrestrial in its pristine beauty and majesty.... And the same desire to preserve something endangered led me to collect Twain's work and save it from a scattered state of being."

Neider's enthusiasm for Twain took hold during the writing of his 1956 western *The Authentic Death of Hendry Jones,* which Lewis Nordyke in the *New York Times* called "an excellent dramatization of the myths that circulate around the deeds of bygone gunmen." To get a better grasp of authentic Old Southwest dialect, Neider reread Twain's *Roughing It* and *Life on the Mississippi.* In doing so, "[I] was struck by the way Twain had thrown entire yarns into his work, had made old tales come alive," Neider told Baldwin, and "went on a veritable Twain binge, read[ing] everything I could get my hands on." Neider discovered, however, that as late as the 1950s a majority of Twain's work had never been collected. Stories, essays, and sketches were scattered about in periodicals, limited editions, and unpublished manuscripts, a situation Neider "unabashedly" describes as "the consequence of 'a semi-literate democracy,'" Baldwin says. Realizing the need for a serious collection, Neider proposed to his agent that he initiate the project. Neider previously had edited a variety of literary collections, including anthologies of adventure literature and one of Thomas Mann criticism, in addition to publishing a critically praised original analysis of Franz Kafka entitled *The Frozen Sea.* When Neider's edition of *The Complete Short Stories of Mark Twain* was published in 1957, it was immediately recognized as a valuable contribution to Twain studies. Comprised of sketches, parodies, jokes, and anecdotes, Neider's volume was commended by Wallace Stegner on the front page of the *New York Times Book Review* for offering "a convenient basis for reappraisal; the sixty pieces which are here hospitably called short stories illustrate both the weaknesses and the strengths of Mark Twain as a writer of fiction."

Over the last thirty years, Neider has edited and annotated numerous collections of Twain's writing and "has steadily expanded the audience of Twain's readers by bringing out lively and attractive editions of his works," writes Shirley Horner in the *New York Times.* Neider particularly admires Twain the humorist, remarking to Baldwin that Twain's greatness lies in his being "a man who took the vernacular flow of our language and endowed it with profound and irresistible humor, lifted to the heights of pure literary style." Jeff Greenfield in the *New York Times Book Review* praises Neider's 1977 *The Comic Mark Twain Reader: The Most Humorous Selections from His Stories, Sketches, Novels, Travel Books, and Speeches* as a "splendid collection of Twain's humor....

The essays, tall tales, political gibes and general fulminations are not designed for wry smiles. They go for the belly laugh, and they hit.''

Neider has been lauded for the resource his Twain editions have provided readers, yet he has also been criticized for his selection of contents. In 1959 the *Literary Gazette* of Moscow attacked what they saw as suppression and censorship of Twain in Neider's edition of *The Autobiography of Mark Twain.* Neider subsequently appealed to Russian premier Nikita Kruschev and was granted an open rebuttal in the same publication. Neider told *CA:* ''I became perhaps the first Westerner to counterattack the Russians in their own press, and it's possible that I have a unique position in this regard, for I suspect the Russians didn't allow the precedent to be repeated.'' Apart from the *Literary Gazette* incident, some American reviewers have likewise been critical of Neider's selection criteria. Commenting on *The Selected Letters of Mark Twain* published in 1982, John Seelye writes in the *Chicago Tribune Book World:* ''The general reader interested in the details of Mark Twain's life will be grateful to Charles Neider for culling this selection from the two-volume edition of his correspondence, long out of print.'' Seelye adds, however, that ''scholars will be vexed, as they were by Neider's edition of Mark Twain's autobiography, published twenty years ago. Neider is cavalier to say the least with his texts, cutting and pasting as he goes, for as he warns us at the start, his is a very personal collection.'' Similarly, Walter Clemons in *Newsweek* remarks that Neider's introduction to *The Selected Letters* ''warns us that he has 'carefully avoided' making a representative selection of Mark Twain's letters.'' Neider maintains in his *CA* interview, however, that his major intent has been ''to share my enthusiasm for Mark Twain and to make him more available,'' rather than to present works of scholarship, since the academic world is ''often . . . beating a dead horse, or it's so pedantic.'' This spirit is particularly evident in Neider's own writings about Twain. In his introductions to the different volumes, Neider demonstrates, according to Baldwin, ''a sense of needing to place his own resolute, refreshingly unstuffy stamp of interpretation onto literature.''

This enthusiastic, personal approach to literature explores interesting terrain in Neider's writings about Antarctica. Since first visiting the isolated continent in 1969—fulfilling a lifelong fascination that began after meeting explorer Richard E. Byrd in 1931—Neider has authored two nonfiction accounts based on his experiences in Antarctica, in addition to *Overflight,* a novel inspired by a helicopter crash he survived on Mt. Erebus. Under the auspices of groups such as the U.S. Navy, National Science Foundation, New Zealand Antarctic Research Program, and British Antarctic Survey, Neider has visited the continent three times beween 1969 and 1977. ''I had a unique opportunity in the Antarctic—as a literary person and as a humanist, and with a global view of the place,'' Neider told a group at the University of California, Santa Cruz. ''I felt that my primary loyalty was not to any particular nation but to the planet itself. My job was to try to understand and convey what it's like to be a human being living and working in the Antarctic, and to accept the fact that I loved the place and needed to help protect it against the ravages of exploitation.'' Neider kept a journal and took notes on each of his trips, or when the extreme cold prevented his pen from working, used a tape recorder to log information. ''There were . . . times when I was under considerable strain because I was forced to choose between keeping abreast in my journal or having new experiences,'' Neider told the audience at Santa

Cruz. ''I felt that without the discipline of journal keeping I'd be merely an Antarctic beachcomber''; he adds, however, '''sometimes I felt I was in danger of being swamped by experiences.''

Neider's first book on his Antarctic travels, 1974's *Edge of the World: Ross Island, Antarctica; a Personal and Historical Narrative,* was praised by polar scientist Laurence McKinley Gould in *American Scholar* as ''one of the most absorbing and informative books yet written about the white continent.'' Containing photographs by Neider, along with accounts of the continent's early explorers, the book was likewise hailed by William F. Buckley, Jr., in the *New York Times Book Review:* ''[*Edge of the World*] can be read by [those] who love adventure, naturalists who want to know about the hidden spectaculars at the south tip of the earth, and casual readers who want a taste of everything down there in that mysterious, repellent, surrealistic world to which Neider gives a skeleton key.'' Gould concludes that ''no one has more precisely or more poetically caught the meaning of Antarctica in all its varied mystery and magnificence.''

In an effort to explore his Antarctic experiences at a deeper level, Neider wrote a second book of nonfiction entitled *Beyond Cape Horn: Travels in the Antarctic.* Neider notes in the book that his intent is to describe the continent ''for the first time in literary ways and to give an interior, an emotional, a psychological equivalent to the exterior places I have seen,'' adding that ''there are deprivations you experience in the Antarctic—sensory, perceptual, emotional, sexual—and there are fascinating interior consequences.'' According to some reviewers, however, Neider is only partly successful in conveying his intentions. Clive Sinclair remarks in the *Times Literary Supplement* that *Beyond Cape Horn* is ''a handsome book, full of beautiful observations, but it [is] also marked by a certain coldness that [has] nothing to do with the terrain.'' Sinclair elaborates that the interior landscape which Neider has set out to explain is somewhat obscure: ''Neider is prepared to take all manner of risks in getting to know Antarctica''; the result, however, ''is as though Neider has been moved by a great work of art but can't get others to share his feeling.'' Nonetheless, Sinclair praises Neider's detailed accounts of the external landscape. ''Neider's eye is a precision instrument,'' he writes. ''His descriptions are not impressions, but verbal equivalents of the scintillating colour photographs that illuminate the book.'' Likewise, Neider clearly stresses that Antarctica's ''awe-inspiring terrain should be left unexploited for the good of mankind.'' In his prologue to the book, Neider writes: ''In Antarctica man can view a truly primeval wilderness. It is essential to his psychic well-being that his feelings of awe, wonder, mystery, humility, his appreciation of incredible and unspoiled natural beauty on a tremendous scale, not be taken from him.''

Concerning his writings about Antarctica, Neider told the audience at Santa Cruz: ''I wrote nonfiction books first in order to pay off as promptly as possible my psychological debts to institutions and persons. Fiction seemed to need a longer time to mature.'' Neider's 1986 novel *Overflight* has been praised for its depiction of man's relationship to Antarctica and the demands imposed by the continent on those who venture there. *Overflight* extends from two actual events: the 1979 crash of an Air New Zealand tourist jet on volcanic Mt. Erebus, in which all 257 people aboard were killed, and a helicopter crash near the summit of the same mountain which Neider and three others survived in 1971. The theme of the novel, according to Sinclair, is ''behavior *in extremis*—of men and machines, and the elements,'' with Erebus existing as ''a malign thing of deceptive beauty, a deadly magnet, a reminder of those mysterious forces that can still outwit the fittest bodies and the sharpest machines.'' In *Overflight*, a tourist plane becomes engulfed in an Antarctic whiteout and crashes when the inexperienced pilot puts his faith in a clear radar screen—ignoring the main character's (Stevenson's) warning that the plane is at too low an altitude and headed straight for the volcano. ''The final impression [Neider] wants to convey,'' writes Sinclair, ''is that the ingenious plane and its trusting crew had been lured to destruction by the indigenous mountain.'' A second crash occurs in *Overflight* when Stevenson returns with three others to the original disaster site to scatter the ashes of two fellow passengers. Neider draws from the drama of his own helicopter crash, in which he was the only one of his party to be prepared with survival gear—a critical factor in the group's not freezing to death. Both crashes in *Overflight* depict, as Neider told the group at Santa Cruz, ''the hubris of high technology: the vain pride that leads human beings to trust technology too much, without being properly trained and without humility before complex machines.'' Dennis Drabelle in the *Washington Post* praises the novel for ''the vividness of Neider's scene painting, the authenticity of his crisis psychology . . . , and the intensity of his passion for Antarctica.''

Neider's respect and admiration for Antarctica is also manifested in his activism for worldwide cooperation in sanctioning part of Antarctica as an international park. In the prologue to *Beyond Cape Horn* Neider writes: ''What will protect this so-called savage place against the coming ravages of man if it is not a concordance of international opinion? Antarctica is an everyman's land, and any nation, however small, or any private firm, for that matter, if it has the capabilities, can go there to do its commercial will. . . . What more appropriate place for an international park than Antarctica where, although a number of nations claim sovereignty over various slices of the Antarctic pie, all such claims were shelved for the duration of the [Antarctic Treaty], which went into effect in June 1961 and whose life-span, without counting possible renewals, is thirty years. It should be agreed that no exploitation of any sort may take place in the proposed park. We owe it to our descendants, near and remote, to undertake this task before it is too late.''

MEDIA ADAPTATIONS: ''One-Eyed Jacks,'' a 1961 film adapted from Neider's novel *The Authentic Death of Hendry Jones,* was released by Paramount Pictures/Pennebaker; the film was produced and directed by Marlon Brando, who also starred in it. Recorded editions of *Edge of the World* and *Beyond Cape Horn* were released in 1988 by Books on Tape.

CA INTERVIEW

CA interviewed Charles Neider by telephone on July 17, 1987, at his home in Princeton, New Jersey.

CA: Since you met Admiral Richard E. Byrd and heard him speak after his return from the 1928-1930 Antarctic expedition, you'd wanted to go there yourself. Now you're becoming perhaps as much known for your writing about the Antarctic as for your work on Mark Twain. How did it all come about?

NEIDER: I was sixteen when I heard Byrd speak in Richmond, Virginia, where I grew up. Why I went to hear him in a public auditorium, I don't know. That's a mystery to me. I must have had an interest in the subject beforehand, or an interest in him

as a very appealing figure, one of the members of the famous Byrd family of Virginia. As I remember it, I was entranced with his speech. I went backstage and thanked him and shook his hand. I wanted to go to the Antarctic myself. But I was too young, and this was in the early '30s; the country was in pretty bad shape. Going to the Antarctic was out of the question. However, I didn't know that. I wrote to the National Geographic Society, the American Geographical Society, and other outfits. But Byrd's was an unusual Antarctic expedition, the first official American Antarctic expedition in almost a hundred years, since Charles Wilkes's expedition of 1838-1842. I got only polite letters in response.

Later on I would do things occasionally with the U.S. Navy, though not on an official basis. For instance, I took a submarine cruise with them for diving exercises in the North Atlantic because I was preparing the book called *Man against Nature,* a collection that Harper published in 1954. I was interested in what the Navy was doing, and I believe they were also somewhat aware of me as somebody who wanted to be involved in unusual experiences. Around September or October of 1969, I made a phone call to a Navy PR person in New York. It got relayed down to Washington, and lo and behold, I was notified officially by letter one day that I'd been chosen to go as the Navy's guest to visit American installations in the Antarctic. It was an august looking letter. It wasn't merely from the Navy, it was also on behalf of the State Department and the Department of the Interior. What these other organizations had to do with my forthcoming visit puzzled me. It was going to be a short, intensive trip. I remember I was alone in this house in Princeton where I am now, and I was so moved I got some bourbon to calm myself down and celebrate. It was an extraordinary moment for me, knowing I was actually going to the Antarctic.

Considering the great distance involved, it was a very brief trip. I flew to Christchurch, New Zealand, and then down to the Antarctic. I spent about six or seven days and was whirled around all over the place. At that time the Navy was in control of American activities in the Antarctic. Although our presence supposedly was for basic, not applied, scientific research, the Navy task force, which was the logistic supporter of our scientific effort, was nevertheless in charge. A rear admiral headed the task force, and I was treated in a special way. I found myself socializing too much with the admiral. That wasn't very good for a writer. I wanted access to the Antarctic, and above all, solitary access—I wanted to be alone there. But the admiral had nothing to gain by granting me such permission while having to take the blame if anything happened to me. Eventually, because I was intense about it and determined, we compromised.

That first trip opened my eyes. Still, I wasn't entirely surprised, for I'd fallen in love with Antarctica from the literature, and I was pretty well read about it. Laurence McKinley Gould, who was science leader and second in command of Byrd's first expedition, and who is now ninety and lives in Tucson, became a good friend of mine. He wrote in the *American Scholar* about my first Antarctic book, *Edge of the World,* that very probably nobody who had gone to the Antarctic had been better prepared than I was in terms of having read about it and knowing what to expect. In any event, I came back and I thought to myself, Well, it was a great introduction, but I can't do that again; it's too limited to have to beg the admiral for a helicopter flight, to have to be in his good graces, and to have a naval attache at my heels all the time. That's not what a writer is about. So the next time I went, it was under the aegis of the National Science Foundation, and I had many helicopter hours assigned to me as part of my program. Among other things, I did a lot of camping out. I did what I needed to do, with enthusiastic cooperation from the National Science Foundation. Shortly thereafer, a Presidential decision took the management of the Antarctic out of the Navy's hands and put it into the hands of the National Science Foundation. That made it much easier for me to do what I needed to do on the third expedition, where I was supported by the NSF but also, with their cooperation, became a visitor of the British, with the British Antarctic Survey. I believe I was the first and maybe the only official American visitor with the British.

I worked extremely hard in the Antarctic. I moved around a great deal and did many things, but above all I kept journals, and made tape recordings when it was impossible to write. It's a tough assignment to keep journals in rough terrain and severe climate. But I felt I had to. I felt a great sense of debt to the people and the institutions that made it possible for me to go there primarily as a humanistic observer. I believe I was the first such person, and I may still be the only person who went to the Antarctic not as an explorer, or a scientist, or a logistic supporter, or a government administrator or functionary, and not as a journalist, somebody who had a commitment to write an article for a newspaper or a magazine, but rather as a literary person who wanted to see what it was like to be a human being living and working on that remarkable continent.

CA: Robert Falcon Scott, Roald Amundsen, and Admiral Byrd, to name the best known explorers, were among your forbears and inspirations as travelers. Were there any literary models for what you set out to do in the writing about your travels?

NEIDER: No, there were none. I got a letter yesterday from Davida Kellogg, a scientist at the University of Maine at Orono, who, with her husband, has worked in the Antarctic. I haven't met her yet, but I'm going up there to visit her and her husband. In the letter she says there has been a kind of unwritten agreement among people who go to the Antarctic not to talk about their feelings about the place. She says that my *Beyond Cape Horn* "contained the first declaration of love for the place that I have ever read." She ends the letter by saying, "There's an awful lot of unxplored emotional territory [in the Antarctic], the stuff of literature," and urges me to go for it.

I'm not sure I agree entirely that there's a code of silence. It may be that the kind of person who normally goes to the Antarctic doesn't have the sensibility that Davida Kellogg misses. Or the people who go there may be so burdened by the difficulty of doing their tasks that they lack the opportunity to write about their feelings. One of the problems for a writer like me today, as compared to the time of Scott's first expedition, is the following. Scott would be based on a relatively luxurious ship—or at least his quarters were luxurious. He and his people would stay two years. He would keep extensive journals, other people would keep journals, Edward Wilson would make watercolors, and so on. Charles Darwin went as a young man on the *Beagle* and didn't return to England for almost five years. Today that's not possible—certainly not in the Antarctic. I've spent more time there than most people—two or three months at a clip, and that's a long time when you're being ferried around by icebreaker and C130s and helicopters.

The problem is that we don't have the time to take a great many notes. What we do have is photography, and this is what

I used, I believe pretty fruitfully. I took a lot of color photographs, which I use primarily as raw data, although I've published many for aesthetic reasons. There are times when you simply don't have the opportunity to write, such as on a rolling deck on an icebreaker in nasty weather. The photographs then become important raw data. I've just completed looking at several thousand slides of my last trip to the Antarctic in 1977 and doing what I call photodebriefing. I have a good viewer on my desk. I study each slide and note down by hand in a journal all the thoughts, memories, and ideas that come out of my looking at the pictures. They're not somebody else's photographs; these are scenes and events I've experienced myself, and so they're more meaningful to me than someone else's photographs would be. By using the photos as raw data, I try to make up for my lack of opportunities that people in the earlier times had when they spent a lot of time in the Antarctic.

CA: I'm fascinated by the photographs that appear in the Antarctic books. There's an amazing play of light, colors, textures. Doesn't the area present special photographic challenges?

NEIDER: Yes, many. In *Edge of the World* there's an appendix chapter that talks about those problems. One of them is that the Antarctic is so terribly dry, despite the fact that it has all this frozen water, so there's a lot of static electricity. If you were to rewind a roll of film at normal speed, it would be ruined by flashes of electricity inside the camera. You have to do it in slow motion. Also, it's so cold normally—particularly in continental Antarctica, as against maritime Antarctica, the Antarctic Peninsula area—that the film becomes extremely brittle. If you were to advance the frame in a normal way, very likely you would snap the film. Then there are problems of light leaks because there's so much intense light, plus the fact that cameras tend to freeze up. There are many, many problems like that.

Also, because I was trying to document the place, and because I love it so much, I did my best while taking the photographs to avoid interposing myself as a manipulator between the viewer and the Antarctic. Eliot Porter went to the Antarctic as an older man and did a book of photographs. Larry Gould and I agree it doesn't represent the Antarctic we know. It stylizes the Antarctic. I didn't fool with anything. I never cropped. I used the slowest possible color film, Kodachrome ASA 25, because of the great amount of light. Eventually I learned to use only one lens, the 50-millimeter lens, with rare exceptions, so I wouldn't be distracted by having to fiddle around with other lenses. The only filter I ever used was an ultraviolet filter. There's so much ultraviolet activity down there, the color of the sky would be affected otherwise. I think on the whole I stayed out of trouble. I was lucky. My percentage of loss was extremely low.

CA: A helicopter crash that you and the three other passengers survived, it would seem miraculously, was part of the impetus to write your Antarctic novel, Overflight, *published in 1986. Have you been pleased with the response to the book?*

NEIDER: On the whole I've been pleased. There have been some wonderful reviews. But, on the other hand, the *New York Times* and the Sunday *New York Times Book Review* have not reviewed the book. I don't know why. I can only speculate that they think it's phony or improbable or they're not prepared to deal with an Antarctic novel because they feel it's too remote. There was an article in the *New York Times* about *me,* and a nice comment about the book in it, but the article wasn't really about the book. One of the things that has saddened me about newspaper response to *Overflight* is that much more interest has been shown in me than in the book. I like to believe that *Overflight* has a life of its own. It would be comforting to have the child receive more attention than the parent.

CA: Overflight's ending sets the scene for a sequel. Is there one in the making?

NEIDER: I'm working on a novel now—I've been working on it since early December—that's set on an icebreaker on the Southern Ocean. I've been on two Coast Guard icebreakers. The last one was a fairly extensive trip, a thirteen-day voyage from the New Zealand sector of Antarctica to the South American sector, where I joined the British. Because I've had this exposure, this opportunity, I feel I should write a novel to try to capture a sense of this remarkable body of water. I don't know that I'll succeed. It's a very difficult, very demanding task, because I hope to include not merely human beings and a human story, but a real sense of this exotic body of water, the most exotic on the planet. It's notoriously rough. It's the coldest body of water on earth. It's the richest in terms of what's called biomass—the mass of life. It's fewer in species than other oceans, but the numbers of individuals are immense. It's also by far, I'm sure, the most beautiful body of water on earth. That's because of the remarkable ice forms, the tabular icebergs, and what happens to them as they weather. The tabular iceberg (the name means that it's shaped like a table) is unique to the Antarctic, and the Antarctic icebergs come in awesome sizes. One that was surveyed some years back turned out to be the size of the state of Connecticut. We're dealing with a scale that is very different from that of the temperate regions. The play of light and the extraordinary electric brilliance of the colors are unbelievable. This is a dream world. Most of the Antarctic is that way. Your eyes feel as if they're just freshly made. You feel as if these colors have just been minted. You never see colors like that in the temperate world. One of the reasons people want to go back is to check to see if they really *did* see all these things, if they weren't a figment of the imagination. It's hard to believe it after you leave it.

CA: We've talked only about the most recent of your varied interests, as expressed in the many books you've written or edited. Your first book was The Frozen Sea: A Study of Franz Kafka. *There's Thomas Mann and Robert Louis Stevenson. And one of your novels, a Western called* The Authentic Death of Hendry Jones, *led you to Mark Twain. Why do you find him "the greatest American writer"? What makes him wear so well?*

NEIDER: I think he's the most all-around human being, for one thing. He has limitations, true, but his humanity is broader and greater. And his language is the vernacular of the Mississippi Basin, what used to be called the Old Southwest. It's not the formal language of Hawthorne or Henry James, which doesn't stand up as well. The vernacular lasts longer. It's a more living language. Then, of course, there are very few writers in world literature, in my opinion, who excel Mark Twain as a humorist on all levels—just kidding around or being deadly serious and ironic, as in "The War Prayer." That alone makes him a giant. I've been with him a long, long time, and I still have belly laughs, still feel inspired by reading him. I know his limitations. He has many, particularly when

it comes to women. He idolizes women. He doesn't see them as human beings. But still he is an amazing and very vital force.

I have a new book coming out in September called *The Outrageous Mark Twain.* It's going to be important if for no other reason than that it brings out in book form five chapters on religion for his autobiography that he dictated in 1906 in New Hampshire. I call them "Reflections on Religion." The only time they've ever been published was in the *Hudson Review* in the fall of 1963. He didn't want them published, or he pretended he didn't. He censored them with a notation on the manuscript. Then his daughter Clara Clemens, whom I knew, sat on them. After she died, lawyers for the Mark Twain Estate censored them. It was only through perseverance over many, many years that I finally got permission to publish them in book form. They are devastating attacks on religion. He's particularly hard on Catholics. I think the Catholic community is going to be upset. When the chapters were published in the *Hudson Review,* the United Press International did a story that appeared in many newspapers, and numerous clergy were bitter about Mark Twain. I believe Mark Twain is so important a writer that anything he wrote—and these are magnificently written—deserves publication regardless of how we may feel about it.

There are other things in the book that will be rather shocking. One is "1601," the famous bawdy piece that he wrote in Elizabethan language, with all the four-letter words. Another is a speech he gave on masturbation before the Stomach Club in Paris. It's called "Science of Onanism," and it's hilariously funny. Then there's his long, amazing attack on Christian Science and Mary Baker Eddy, plus some wild bits of invective against Commodore Vanderbilt and other deserving gentlemen.

CA: You've had an interesting relationship with academia, a sort of friendship that never became a marriage, by your own choosing. Has being a non-academic in any way presented a handicap in your work on Mark Twain or other literary figures?

NEIDER: I don't think so. I think it's probably been good for me. Occasionally I've been invited to symposiums, but I have not wanted primarily to address other Mark Twain scholars. Academia is not my cup of tea. Often they're beating a dead horse, or it's so pedantic. I've tried to share my enthusiasm for Mark Twain and to make him more available and to do new things like the *Autobiography* and these "Reflections on Religion." I think I'm more comfortable with what I'm doing than I would be in an academic setting where I might have to worry about displeasing colleagues. But I am tangential in some connections. For example, I'm an honorary fellow of Stevenson College of the University of California at Santa Cruz. That means I feel comfortable about going to functions and using an office there frequently. But I don't have any duties. I don't teach. I'm happy with that kind of connection. I've had offices at Princeton University from time to time, but lately, maybe because of the nature of the work I'm doing now, I find I'm happier at home near my files and photographs and Antarctic maps.

CA: Your interests are so varied, though many of them are literary or can be expressed in a literary way. Do you see all of them as being tied together by other common threads?

NEIDER: Clive Sinclair, a critic who recently reviewed *Overflight* in the *Times Literary Supplement* also reviewed *Beyond Cape Horn* for the *TLS*. He made some startling connections in that earlier review, though how genuine they are is anybody's guess. He pointed out that here I am, really dedicated to the Antarctic, its well-being and its preservation, and long ago I wrote a book called *The Frozen Sea*. He pointed out that for a very long time I've lived on a street called *Southern Way*. I don't know what you can make of this, but as a child I spent some time in Siberia. Whether these connections make any sense, subliminally or otherwise, is not for me to say.

On the whole I think the main threads connecting my work are my enthusiasm and my willingness to go to some length to pursue those enthusiasms, to see where they lead me and then try to share them in literary form. And when great opportunities arise, to accept them as challenges. I feel it would be wrong for me to say to myself, OK, I had this voyage on the Southern Ocean and not to accept it as a challenge. You have to give back. I don't know where I got this ethos, but I feel it very strongly. It would be wrong for me to have been graced in that way and not try, somehow or other, to do something with it, to try to broaden it and share it. I also try to stay physically fit, not only because I feel better, but because I don't want my prose to become tired, I want it to continue to be economical and muscular, and I believe there's a strong connection between one's physical fitness and the prose one writes. Prose isn't something extraneous to the person.

BIOGRAPHICAL/CRITICAL SOURCES:

BOOKS

Neider, Charles, *Beyond Cape Horn: Travels in the Antarctic*, Sierra Books, 1980.

PERIODICALS

American Scholar, spring, 1975.
Chicago Sunday Tribune, February 17, 1957, March 5, 1961, November 26, 1961.
Chicago Tribune Book World, April 4, 1982.
Christian Science Monitor, May 26, 1982.
Los Angeles Times, March 26, 1982.
Los Angeles Times Book Review, January 18, 1987.
Newsweek, April 19, 1982.
New York Herald Tribune Weekly Book Review, February 1, 1948.
New York Times, January 25, 1948, May 23, 1948, January 6, 1952, February 28, 1954, August 29, 1954, August 26, 1956, February 17, 1957, April 26, 1975, May 19, 1977, December 14, 1986.
New York Times Book Review, February 10, 1957, January 17, 1965, June 23, 1974, April 10, 1977.
Publishers Weekly, October 4, 1985.
Saturday Review, April 27, 1963, January 9, 1965, February 11, 1967, April, 1982.
Times Literary Supplement, June 16, 1966, January 4, 1974, October 9, 1981, June 19, 1987.
Washington Post, January 9, 1987.
Yale Review, winter, 1949.

OTHER

Neider, Charles, lecture given at Stevenson College, University of California, Santa Cruz, March 2, 1987.

—*Sketch by Michael E. Mueller*

—*Interview by Jean W. Ross*

NEIDERMYER, Dan 1947-

PERSONAL: Born January 17, 1947, in Lancaster, Pa.; son of Paul D., Jr. (a farmer) and Margaret (Waidley) Neidermyer. *Education:* Philadelphia College of the Bible, B.S., 1968; graduate study at Temple University, 1966-71, Reformed Episcopal Seminary, 1968-71, and Millersville State College (now University), 1976—. *Politics:* Democrat. *Religion:* Protestant.

ADDRESSES: Home—R.D. 2, Ephrata, Pa. 17522. *Office*—Maranatha Productions, Inc., P.O. Box 124, Ephrata, Pa. 17522. *Agent*—Stephen Cogil, 5100 North Marine Dr., Chicago, Ill. 60640.

CAREER: Maranatha Productions (dramatic production organization), Ephrata, Pa., founder and executive producer, 1969—; Evangelical School of Theology, Myerstown, Pa., associate lecturer in communications, 1972—. Host of "The Dan Neidermyer Show," on D and E cable television, Ephrata, Pa.; writer for "Back to God Hour," Chicago, 1978—; director for Unicorn Theatre Company, Dixon, Ill., 1984—; writer-director for Crosslink Productions, Columbus, Ohio, 1984—.

WRITINGS:

Jonathan, Herald Press, 1973.

SCREENPLAYS

"Station to Freedom," Telerad Productions (Lancaster, Pa.), 1976.
"Greg: A Conflict of Love," Telerad Productions, 1979.
"Triumph in the Streets," International Society of Christian Endeavor (Columbus, Ohio), 1981.
"First Fruits," Gateway Films (Lansdale, Pa.)., 1983.
"Tough Choice," Nucleus Productions (Harlingen, Tex.), 1983.

Also author of "A Time to Love," 1978.

OTHER

Contributor to religious periodicals.

WORK IN PROGRESS: Several television screenplays; a play about John Calvin; several novels "concerning steroids, athletics, and professional sports."

*   *   *

NELSON, Geoffrey K(enneth) 1923-

PERSONAL: Born August 8, 1923, in Dereham, Norfolk, England; son of William John (a malthouse fireman) and Florence (Pitcher) Nelson; married Irene Griggs, July 31, 1955; children: Elizabeth, Christopher, Rosemary, David. *Education:* University of Liverpool, certificate in social science, 1950; Shoreditch College of Education, teacher's certificate, 1954; University of London, B.Sc., 1958, M.Sc., 1961, Ph.D., 1967.

ADDRESSES: Home—32 Clun Rd., Birmingham B31 1NU, England. *Office*—Department of Sociology, Birmingham Polytechnic, Birmingham, England.

CAREER: Westwood School, March, Cambridgeshire, England, teacher, 1956-62; Bournville College, Birmingham, England, assistant lecturer in sociology, 1962-64; Birmingham Polytechnic, Birmingham, lecturer, 1964-69, senior lecturer, 1969-75, principal lecturer in sociology, 1975—. Part-time tutor, Wolsey Hall, Oxford, 1961—. Besides teaching, has been employed in social work, agriculture, and civil service. Honorary fellow, Institute for the Study of Worship and Religious Architecture, University of Birmingham, 1969—. *Military service:* Home Guard, 1940-45.

MEMBER: British Sociological Association, American Sociological Association, Society for the Scientific Study of Religion, British Association for the Advancement of Science (secretary of sociology section, 1968-80), University of London Convocation (chairman of West Midland branch, 1967-82), Worcestershire Nature Conservation Trust (deputy chairman of Birmingham Group).

WRITINGS:

Spiritualism and Society, Schocken, 1969.
(With Rosemary A. Clews) *Mobility and Religious Commitment,* University of Birmingham, 1971.
(Contributor) A. Bryman, editor, *Religion in the Birmingham Area,* University of Birmingham, 1975.
History of Modern Spiritualism, Spiritualists' National Union, 1976.
Cults, New Religions and Religious Creativity, Routledge & Kegan Paul, 1987.

POETRY

Butterfly's Eye, G. K. Nelson, 1980.
A Poet's Reading, G. K. Nelson, 1980.

OTHER

Also author, with C. Hill and others, of *Video: Violence and Children* (a report of the Parliamentary Group Video Enquiry), 1984. Contributor to sociology journals and religion journals, including *British Journal of Sociology, Sociological Review, Journal for the Scientific Study of Religion, Review of Religious Research, Social Compass, Sociology and Social Research,* and *Reviewing Sociology;* contributor of articles on local history, religion, and natural history to newspapers and popular magazines, including *New Knowledge* and *Man, Myth, and Magic;* contributor of poetry to numerous magazines.

WORK IN PROGRESS: Unifying the Science of Humanity (a study of Victor Bradford); *Changing Patterns of Agricultural Life, 1930-1988;* a history of modern spiritualism; poetry.

SIDELIGHTS: Geoffrey K. Nelson told *CA:* "After a life devoted to teaching research and scholarship in sociology, which has been interspersed by the writing of poetry, I am looking forward to the development of my literary work. Those familiar with my work will detect a consistant attempt to synthesize poetry, mysticism, and science in the understanding of life and will consequently appreciate my interest in the life and work of Victor Bradford." Nelson's study of Bradford is to be published in his forthcoming work, *Unifying the Science of Humanity.*

BIOGRAPHICAL/CRITICAL SOURCES:

BOOKS

Yinger, J. Milton, *The Scientific Study of Religion,* Macmillan, 1970.

PERIODICALS

Times Literary Supplement, June 26, 1969.

*   *   *

NELSON, George (Carl) E(dward)   1900-1982

PERSONAL: Born August 4, 1900, in New York, N.Y.; died

February 20, 1982; son of Charles (a carpenter) and Christina (Gustafson) Nelson; married Lillian Gleissner, July 5, 1935 (died, 1959); married Mary Baronowski, February 18, 1966; married Jane Gallagher, June 1, 1979. *Education:* College of the City of New York (now City College of City University of New York), B.S., 1925, M.S., 1926; Columbia University, Ph.D., 1931; McGill University, librarian certificate, 1932.

ADDRESSES: Home—Oconomowoc, Wis.; Cuernavaca, Mexico.

CAREER: New York Public Library, New York City, assistant, 1917; College of the City of New York City (now City College of City University of New York), New York City, library assistant, 1921-25, instructor in biological sciences, 1925-31, assistant librarian, 1928, associate librarian, 1934-52; Fairleigh Dickinson University, Rutherford, N.Y., professor of library science and librarian, beginning 1952, director of Graduate School, 1954-55, director of library, beginning 1954, dean of libraries, 1958-62, dean of Graduate School, beginning 1960, director of Seminar on Mexico, 1968. Instituto de Arte y Literature de Cuernavaca, Cuernavaca, Mexico, director, beginning 1961; Centro Para Retirados Cuahnauac, Cuahnauac, Mexico, director, beginning 1966.

MEMBER: American Library Association, Special Libraries Association, American Institute of Management, American Management Association, American Society for Quality Control, American Association of University Professors, American Philatelic Society, American Topical Association, Phi Delta Kappa, Omega Epsilon Phi (national president, 1932).

WRITINGS:

The Introductory Biological Sciences in the Traditional Liberal Arts Colleges, Teachers College, Columbia University, 1931, reprinted, AMS Press, 1982.
(With Mary B. Nelson) *Retire on $65 a Week in Sunny Mexico: Sunny Cuernavaca,* Centro Para Retirados, 1966.
Live It up on $65 a Week in Sunny Mexico, Centro Para Retirados, 1968.
Historical Dictionary of Mexico, Scarecrow, 1972.
(With Mary B. Nelson) *Mexico A-Z: An Encyclopedia of Mexico,* Centro para Retirados (Cuernavaca), 1975.

Also author of *Omega Epsilon Directory,* 1932, and *Thomas Jefferson's Garden Book, Go Native in Mexico,* and *Guide to Selected Research Tools and Source Material for Graduate Students,* all 1958. Contributor to *Library Journal, School and Society,* and *School Science and Mathematics.*†

*   *   *

NICHOLSON, Norman (Cornthwaite)   1914-1987

PERSONAL: Born January 8, 1914, in Millom, Cumberland (now Cumbria), England; died May 30, 1987; son of Joseph (an outfitter) and Edith (Cornthwaite) Nicholson; married Yvonne Gardner (a teacher), July 5, 1956 (died, 1982). *Education:* Attended schools in Millom, England. *Religion:* Church of England.

ADDRESSES: Home—14 St. George's Ter., Millom, Cumbria, England. *Agent*—David Higham Associates Ltd., 5-8 Lower John St., Golden Square, London W1R 4HA, England.

CAREER: Poet, dramatist, novelist, biographer, critic, and topographer. Public lecturer and broadcaster on modern poetry, on the English Lake District, and on other subjects.

MEMBER: Royal Society of Literature (fellow), P.E.N.

AWARDS, HONORS: Heineman Prize for poetry, 1945, for *Five Rivers;* M.A., University of Manchester, 1958, and Open University, 1975; Cholmondeley Award for poetry, 1967; grants from Northern Arts Association, 1969, and Society of Authors, 1973; Queen's Gold Medal for poetry, 1977; Litt.D., Liverpool University, 1980, and University of Lancaster, 1984; Order of the British Empire, 1981.

WRITINGS:

POETRY

(With John Hall and Keith Douglas) *Selected Poems*, Bale & Staples, 1943.
Five Rivers, Faber, 1944, Dutton, 1945.
Rock Face, Faber, 1948.
The Pot Geranium, Faber, 1954.
Selected Poems, Faber, 1966.
A Local Habitation, Faber, 1972.
Stitch and Stone: A Cumbrian Landscape, Ceolfrith Press, 1975.
Cloud on Black Combe, illustrated by Rigby Graham, Cellar Press, 1975.
The Shadow of Black Combe, Mid-Northumberland Arts Group, 1978.
Sea to the West, Faber, 1981.
Selected Poems, 1940-82, Faber, 1982.
(With Frank Flynn and Gerda Mayer) *The Candy-Floss Tree*, Oxford University Press, 1984.

VERSE DRAMAS

The Old Man of the Mountains (three-act; first produced Off-Broadway at Mercury Theatre, 1945), Faber, 1946, revised edition, Macmillan, 1950.
Prophesy to the Wind (four scenes and prologue), Faber, 1950, Macmillan, 1951.
A Match for the Devil (four scenes), Faber, 1955.
Birth by Drowning, Faber, 1960.

Also author of the drama "This Way to the Tomb."

NOVELS

The Fire of the Lord, Nicholson & Watson, Dutton, 1946.
The Green Shore, Nicholson & Watson, 1947.

CRITICISM

Man and Literature (lectures), S.C.M. Press, 1943, Folcroft, 1974.
William Cowper, Lehmann, 1951, Folcroft, 1977.
William Cowper (pamphlet), Longmans, Green, 1960.

TOPOGRAPHY

Cumberland and Westmorland, R. Hale, 1949.
The Lakers: The Adventures of the First Tourists, R. Hale, 1955, Dufour, 1964.
Provincial Pleasures, R. Hale, 1959.
Portrait of the Lakes, R. Hale, 1963, Dufour, 1965, revised edition published as *The Lakes*, R. Hale, 1977.
Greater Lakeland, R. Hale, 1969, International Publications Service, 1970.

EDITOR OR COMPILER

An Anthology of Religious Verse Designed for the Times, Penguin, 1942.
(And author of introduction) *Wordsworth: An Introduction and Selection*, Transatlantic, 1949.
(And author of introduction) William Cowper, *Poems*, Grey Walls Press, 1951.

(And author of introduction) *A Choice of Cowper's Verse*, Faber, 1975.
The Lake District: An Anthology, R. Hale, 1977, Penguin, 1978.

OTHER

H. G. Wells (biography), Arthur Barker, 1950, Alan Swallow, 1951.
Enjoying It All, Waltham Forest Books, 1964.
(With others) *Writers on Themselves* (radio talks), introduction by Herbert Read, BBC Publications, 1964.
No Star on the Way Back: Ballads and Carols (radio script), Manchester Institute of Contemporary Arts, 1967.
Wednesday Early Closing (autobiography), Faber, 1975.

Contributor to *Horizon, Listener, Poetry, Spectator, Times Literary Supplement, Church Times, Stand*, and other periodicals.

SIDELIGHTS: Norman Nicholson wrote verse dramas, novels, literary biography, literary criticism, and topography, but he considered himself primarily a poet. Nicholson was born in the small mining town of Millom in Cumberland (now Cumbria), England, and lived there all of his life. According to Margaret B. McDowell in the *Dictionary of Literary Biography: Poets of Great Britain and Ireland, 1945-1960,* "[Nicholson's] writing reveals his conviction that an individual can find the wisdom of the universe in his hometown, and it emphasizes the value of community and nature in human development, as well as the need to center one's life in Christian faith and principle."

Nicholson's early adulthood conversion to Christianity, in addition to his intense feelings for the rugged landscape of his birth, inspired and pervaded most of his writing. His verse dramas, including *The Old Man of the Mountains* and *A Match for the Devil*, are rich with biblical symbolism and were written primarily for small gatherings in church halls; they were never as well-received by large, secular crowds. According to *Times Literary Supplement* reviewer William Scammell, Nicholson was a "regional poet *par excellence....* The sea of [Nicholson's poetry collection] *Sea to the West* is literally that part of the Irish Sea which washes up against the author's native Millom on the coast of Cumberland." Because Nicholson wrote consistently about the relationship between man and his environment, *Times Literary Supplement* critic Andrew Motion senses that whereas most authors hope to develop versatility in their writing, Nicholson was set on a poetry of restriction. For one, Motion noted that "relatives apart, . . . people are thin on the ground" of Nicholson's verse. In Motion's opinion, Nicholson "made a virtue of restraint, and its advantage is a poetry of impressive tact. Its disadvantage, though, is that it means he has to forgo the resonances, elevations and intensities which are produced by a sense of the egotistical sublime."

In the sense that Nicholson's poetry evolved from his love of nature and was written for ordinary people about everyday experiences and everyday strife, it has been likened to the romantic poetry of William Wordsworth and the poetry of other eighteenth-century poets, such as William Cowper, Thomas Gray, and Robert Burns. McDowell noted that "like Wordsworth, [Nicholson] is a romantic poet who writes about ordinary people as they are subject to the vagaries of nature. Yet his concern, more than Wordsworth's, extends the spoliation of the environment by modern industry, the effect of such misuse of nature upon ordinary people, and the responsibility of all individuals, in the light of Christian morality, to respect the creation of God on earth.'' The author of a London *Times* obituary on Nicholson professed that Nicholson's poetry was written ''under the influence but not in the shadow of Wordsworth . . . ; its humour and its reticent passion are both qualities very much Nicholson's own.'' As for Motion, he concluded that Nicholson's poetry, ''for all its incidental resemblances to Wordsworth, is really closer to Hardy; it is undeviatingly colloquial, anecdotal and empirical.'' Comparisons aside, to the *Times* writer, Nicholson ''was the most gifted English Christian provincial poet of his century; his work, in an age when poetry has become as much a matter of business and promotion as of literature, has not yet been properly evaluated.''

Collections of Nicholson's manuscripts are contained in the National Collection of Poetry Manuscripts, London, England, and in the Northern Arts Manuscript Collection, Newcastle upon Tyne, England.

BIOGRAPHICAL/CRITICAL SOURCES:

BOOKS

Dictionary of Literary Biography, Volume XXVII: *Poets of Great Britain and Ireland, 1945-1960,* Gale, 1984.
Gardner, Philip, *Norman Nicholson,* Twayne, 1973.
Morgan, Kathleen E., *Christian Themes in Contemporary Poets,* S.C.M. Press, 1965.
Nicholson, Norman, *Wednesday Early Closing* (autobiography), Faber, 1975.
Scammell, William, editor, *Between Comets: For Norman Nicholson at Seventy,* Taxvs, 1984.

PERIODICALS

Review of International English Literature, January, 1972.
Times Literary Supplement, July 3, 1981, December 10, 1982.

OBITUARIES:

PERIODICALS

Times (London), June 1, 1987.

*   *   *

NIXON, Joan Lowery   1927-

PERSONAL: Born February 3, 1927, in Los Angeles, Calif.; daughter of Joseph Michael (an accountant) and Margaret (Meyer) Lowery; married Hershell H. Nixon (a petroleum geologist), August 6, 1949; children: Kathleen Nixon Brush, Maureen Nixon Quinlan, Joseph Michael, Eileen Marie. *Education:* University of Southern California, B.A., 1947; California State College, Calif., certificate in elementary education, 1949. *Religion:* Roman Catholic.

ADDRESSES: Home—10215 Cedar Creek Dr., Houston, Tex. 77042. *Agent*—Amy Berkower, Writers House Inc., 21 West 26th St., New York, N.Y. 10010.

CAREER: Elementary school teacher in Los Angeles, Calif., 1947-50; Midland College, Midland, Tex., instructor in creative writing, 1971-73; University of Houston, Houston, Tex., instructor in creative writing, 1974-78.

MEMBER: Authors Guild, Authors League of America, Society of Children's Book Writers (former member of board of directors), Mystery Writers of America (regional vice-president, Southwest chapter), Western Writers of America, Kappa Delta Alumnae Association.

AWARDS, HONORS: Edgar Allan Poe Special Award, Mystery Writers of America, 1975, for *The Mysterious Red Tape Gang,* 1980, for *The Kidnapping of Christina Lattimore,* 1981, for *The Seance,* 1985, for *The Ghosts of Now: A Novel of Psychological Suspense,* and 1987, for *The Other Side of Dark;* Steck-Vaughn Award, Texas Institute of Letters, 1975, for *The Alligator under the Bed;* Outstanding Science Trade Book for children, National Science Teachers Association and Children's Book Council Joint Committee award, 1979, for *Volcanoes: Nature's Fireworks,* 1980, for *Glaciers: Nature's Frozen Rivers,* and 1981, for *Earthquakes: Nature in Motion;* Crabbery Award, Oxon Hill branch of Prince George's County Library (Maryland), 1984, for *Magnolia's Mixed-Up Magic.*

WRITINGS:

The Mystery of Hurricane Castle, Criterion, 1964.
The Mystery of the Grinning Idol, Criterion, 1965.
The Mystery of the Hidden Cockatoo, illustrated by Richard Lewis, Criterion, 1966.
The Mystery of the Haunted Woods, Criterion, 1967.
The Mystery of the Secret Stowaway, Criterion, 1968.
Delbert, the Plainclothes Detective, illustrated by Philip Smith, Criterion, 1971.
The Alligator under the Bed, illustrated by Jan Hughes, Putnam, 1974.
The Secret Box Mystery (Junior Literary Guild selection), illustrated by Leigh Grant, Putnam, 1974.
The Mysterious Red Tape Gang, illustrated by Joan Sandin, Putnam, 1974, paperback edition published as *The Adventures of the Red Tape Gang,* illustrated by Steven H. Stroud, Scholastic Inc., 1983.
(With others) *People and Me,* Benefic, 1975.
(With others) *This I Can Be,* Benefic, 1975.
The Mysterious Prowler, illustrated by Berthe Amoss, Harcourt, 1976.
Who Is My Neighbor?, Concordia, 1976.
Five Loaves and Two Fishes, Concordia, 1976.
(With husband, Hershell H. Nixon) *Oil and Gas: From Fossils to Fuels,* illustrated by Jean Day Zallinger, Harcourt, 1977.
The Son Who Came Home Again, Concordia, 1977.
Writing Mysteries for Young People, Writer, Inc., 1977.
The Boy Who Could Find Anything, illustrated by Syd Hoff, Harcourt, 1978.
Danger in Dinosaur Valley (Junior Literary Guild selection), illustrated by Marc Simont, Putnam, 1978.
(With H. Nixon) *Volcanoes: Nature's Fireworks,* Dodd, 1978.
Muffie Mouse and the Busy Birthday (Junior Literary Guild selection), illustrated by Geoffrey Hayes, Seabury, 1978.
When God Speaks, Our Sunday Visitor, 1978.
When God Listens, Our Sunday Visitor, 1978.
The Kidnapping of Christina Lattimore, Harcourt, 1979.
The Grandmother's Book, Abingdon, 1979.
The Butterfly Tree, Our Sunday Visitor, 1979.
Bigfoot Makes a Movie, illustrated by Hoff, Putnam, 1979.
The Seance, Harcourt, 1980.
Before You Were Born, illustrated by James McIlrath, Our Sunday Visitor, 1980.
Gloria Chipmunk, Star!, illustrated by Diane Dawson, Houghton, 1980.
If You Say So, Claude, illustrated by Lorinda Bryan Cauley, Warne, 1980.

(With H. Nixon) *Glaciers: Nature's Frozen Rivers*, Dodd, 1980.

Casey and the Great Idea, illustrated Amy Rowen, Dutton, 1980.

(With H. Nixon) *Earthquakes: Nature in Motion*, Dodd, 1981.

The Specter, Delacorte, 1982.

The Trouble with Charlie, Bantam, 1982.

The Gift, illustrated by Andrew Glass, Macmillan, 1983.

Magnolia's Mixed-Up Magic, illustrated by Linda Bucholtz-Ross, Putnam, 1983.

Days of Fear (for adults learning to read), photographs by Joan Menschenfreund, Dutton, 1983.

A Deadly Game of Magic, Harcourt, 1983.

The Ghosts of Now: A Novel of Psychological Suspense, Delacorte, 1984.

The House on Hackman's Hill, Scholastic Inc., 1985.

The Stalker, illustrated by Wendy Popp, Delacorte, 1985.

Maggie, Too, illustrated by Darrell Millsap, Harcourt, 1985.

(With H. Nixon) *Land under the Seas*, Dodd, 1985.

Beats Me, Claude (Junior Literary Guild selection), Viking, 1986.

The Other Side of Dark, Delacorte, 1986.

And Maggie Makes Three, Harcourt, 1986.

Haunted Island, Scholastic Inc., 1987.

Maggie Forevermore, Harcourt, 1987.

Fat Chance, Claude, Viking, 1987.

The Dark and Deadly Pool, Delacorte, 1987.

A Family Apart: The Orphan Train Quartet, Bantam, 1987.

If You Were A Writer, Macmillan, 1988.

The Island of Dangerous Dreams, Delacorte, 1988.

Silent Screams, Delacorte, in press.

"HOLIDAY MYSTERY" SERIES; ILLUSTRATED BY JIM CUMMINS

The New Year's Day Mystery, Albert Whitman, 1979.

The Halloween Mystery, Albert Whitman, 1979.

The Valentine's Day Mystery, Albert Whitman, 1979.

The Happy Birthday Mystery, Albert Whitman, 1979.

The Thanksgiving Day Mystery, Albert Whitman, 1980.

The April Fool Mystery, Albert Whitman, 1980.

The Easter Mystery, Albert Whitman, 1981.

The Christmas Eve Mystery, Albert Whitman, 1981.

"KLEEP: SPACE DETECTIVE" SERIES

Kidnapped on Astarr, illustrated by Paul Frame, Garrard, 1981.

Mysterious Queen of Magic, illustrated by Frame, Garrard, 1981.

Mystery Dolls from Planet Urd, illustrated by Frame, Garrard, 1981.

OTHER

Contributor to magazines, including *West Coast Review of Books, Writer, American Home, Woman's Day,* and *Ms.*

SIDELIGHTS: Joan Lowery Nixon told *CA:* "For many years I had written articles and short fiction for magazines for adults, and it was my own children who inspired me to write stories for children. Our eldest daughter said, 'If you're going to write a book, it has to be for children, and it has to be a mystery, and you have to put us in it.' That first book was *The Mystery of Hurricane Castle,* and the two main characters were named Kathy and Maureen. Our Eileen 'starred' in *The Mystery of the Grinning Idol,* and Joe was the main character in *The Mystery of the Secret Stowaway.*

"It was Kathy who asked me to teach her how to write, and this began seven years of volunteer teaching of creative writing to seventh and eighth graders. Eventually each of our children [was] in one of my classes and learned my own style of writing techniques and rules. Kathy is now a professional writer, too."

*   *   *

NOEL, Thomas Jacob   1945-

PERSONAL: Born May 6, 1945, in Cambridge, Mass.; son of Dix Webster (a professor of law) and Louise (a psychiatrist; maiden name, Jacob) Noel; married Violet Sumiko Kamiya (a visiting nurse coordinator), August 25, 1973. *Education:* University of Denver, B.A., 1966, M.A., 1969; University of Colorado, Ph.D., 1978. *Politics:* Democrat. *Religion:* Roman Catholic.

ADDRESSES: Home—1245 Newport St., Denver, Colo. 80220. *Office*—Department of History, University of Colorado, Denver, Colo. 80202.

CAREER: University of California, Riverside, librarian, 1969-70; Colorado Historical Society, Denver, artifacts technician, 1970-72; University of Colorado, Denver, instructor, 1972-79, assistant professor, 1979-82, associate professor of history, 1982—, director of Colorado Studies Center, 1981—. Tour guide for Smithsonian Institution Travel Associates. Member of board of directors of Historic Denver, Inc., 1982-85; Denver landmark commissioner, 1984—.

MEMBER: Colorado Authors League, Colorado Historical Society, Western History Association, Westerners (Denver Posse), Friends of the Denver Public Library (member of board, 1984—).

AWARDS, HONORS: Hafen Prize from Colorado Historical Society, 1975, for article "The Multi-Functional Frontier Saloon"; Top Hand Award from Colorado Authors League and Pursuit of Excellence Prize from University of Colorado, both 1981, for *Denver: Rocky Mountain Gold;* plaque from Downtown Denver, Inc., 1981, for books, tours, and classes; Colorado Authors League Award, 1981, for article "A Chat with Louis L'Amour," and 1984, for article "The Most Hated and Feared Man in America: Big Bill Haywood," in *Colorado Heritage;* Noel Park dedicated, 1984, in Larimer Square, Denver; grant from President's Fund for the Humanities, 1986—, to establish a public history program at University of Colorado, Denver.

WRITINGS:

Richthofen's Montclair: A Pioneer Denver Suburb, Pruett, 1978.

Denver: Rocky Mountain Gold, Continental Heritage, 1980.

Denver's Larimer Street: Main Street, Skid Row, and Urban Renaissance, Historic Denver, 1981.

The City and the Saloon: Denver, 1853-1916, University of Nebraska Press, 1982.

(With Fay Metcalf and Duane Smith) *A Colorado History*, Pruett, 1983.

Denver: Emergence of a Great City (television script), Denver Public Library, 1984.

The WPA Guide to 1930s Colorado, University Press of Kansas, 1987.

(With Barbara Norgren) *Denver: The City Beautiful and Its Architects,* Historic Denver, 1987.

Contributor to newspapers.

WORK IN PROGRESS: Books on the history of the Archdiocese of Denver; a guide to Denver architecture; a Colorado historical atlas.

SIDELIGHTS: Thomas J. Noel told *CA:* "I specialize in walking tours of Denver neighborhoods, cemeteries, churches, saloons, parks, and businesses as well as excursions to Colorado railroad and mining towns. There is a need for historical consciousness, particularly in glassy, gassy boomtowns like Denver. Colorado history, with its venerable Indian and Spanish roots, is fascinating. And the twentieth-century drama of those who stayed and tried to keep communities going after the gold and silver bursts remains largely untold."

*   *   *

NORMAN, C. J.
   See BARRETT, Norman (S.)

O

OBOJSKI, Robert 1929-

PERSONAL: Surname is pronounced O-*boy*-ski; born October 19, 1929, in Cleveland, Ohio; son of Thomas (a machinist) and Sophia (Sliwa) Obojski; married Danuta Galka (a librarian), March 6, 1965. *Education:* Western Reserve University (now Case Western Reserve University), A.B., 1951, A.M., 1952, Ph.D., 1955. *Politics:* Democrat. *Religion:* Polish National Catholic.

ADDRESSES: Home—58 Orchard Farm Rd., Port Washington, N.Y. 11050.

CAREER: Detroit Institute of Technology, Detroit, Mich., assistant professor, 1955-57, professor of English, 1957-60; *Coin World Weekly,* Sidney, Ohio, feature editor, 1961-62; Western Kentucky State University, Bowling Green, professor of English, 1963-64; Alliance College, Cambridge Springs, Pa., professor of English, 1964-69; Sterling Publishing Co., Inc., New York, N.Y., numismatic editor, 1969-70; free-lance writer, 1970—.

MEMBER: American Numismatic Association, Society for American Baseball Research.

WRITINGS:

Poland in Pictures, Sterling, 1969.
Ships and Explorers on Coins, Sterling, 1970.
(With Burton Hobson) *Illustrated Encyclopedia of World Coins,* Doubleday, 1970, 2nd edition, 1983.
Bush League: A History of Minor League Baseball (alternate Sports Illustrated Book Club selection), Macmillan, 1975.
The Rise of Japanese Baseball Power, Chilton, 1975.
All-Star Baseball since 1933, Stein & Day, 1980.
Coin Collector's Price Guide, Sterling, 1986.
Stamp Collector's Price Guide, Sterling, 1986.
Strange Baseball, Sterling, 1988.

EDITOR

Hobson, *Stamp Collector's Handbook,* Sterling, 1980.
Hobson, *Coin Collector's Handbook,* Sterling, 1980.
Hobson, *Coin Collecting as a Hobby,* Sterling, 1982.
Hobson, *Getting Started in Stamp Collecting,* Sterling, 1982.
Hobson and Fred Reinfeld, *Catalogue of the World's Most Popular Coins,* Sterling, 1983, 12th edition, 1986.

OTHER

Contributor to stamp and coin magazines. Contributing editor to *Guinness Book of World Records, Guinness Sports Record Book,* and *Collectors Editions Quarterly.*

SIDELIGHTS: Robert Obojski once told *CA:* "I wrote my first 'published' work for my junior high school mimeographed monthly, graduated to the senior high school type-set bi-weekly, wrote for the Western Reserve University weekly *Tribune* for four years, and then contributed a great deal of material gratis to various newspapers. After writing for hobby publications (mostly on baseball, stamps, and coins) for a number of years (and usually for very modest rates), I was finally invited by New York publishers to write and edit books.

"Evolving as a professional writer usually takes a great deal of time. I've seen too many young people who feel they're ready almost immediately to start writing for the major magazines and to produce books without going through the necessary apprenticeship process."

*   *   *

O'BRIEN, Saliee
See JANAS, Frankie-Lee

*   *   *

OLIVA, Leo E. 1937-

PERSONAL: Born November 5, 1937, in Woodston, Kan.; son of E. I. (a farmer) and Lela (Miller) Oliva; married Marlene Causey, August 31, 1958 (divorced, 1975); married Bonita M. Pabst, February 14, 1976; children: (first marriage) Eric, Stephanie, Rex. *Education:* Fort Hays State University, A.B., 1959; University of Denver, M.A., 1960, Ph.D., 1964.

ADDRESSES: Home—R.R. 1, Box 31, Woodston, Kan. 67675.

CAREER: Texas Wesleyan College, Fort Worth, assistant professor of history, 1962-64; Fort Hays State University, Hays, Kansas, assistant professor, 1964-67, associate professor, 1967-69, professor of history, 1969-78, acting chairman of department, 1966-67, chairman of department, 1967-75; self-employed, 1978—, as farmer, free-lance writer, and owner-operator of Type "O" (typesetting business), Heritage Tours, and Western Books (publisher). Visiting professor of history, Fort Hays State University, 1982—. Consultant to Fort Leavenworth Museum, 1975-76; tour guide for bus trips on the Santa Fe Trail.

MEMBER: American Association for State and Local History, Western History Association (charter member), Santa Fe Trail Association (charter member), Kansas State Historical Society (board of directors member, 1969—), Kansas Anthropological Association, Kansas History Teachers Association (executive board member, 1970-73; vice-president, 1975-76; president, 1976-77), Kansas Corral of the Westerners (sheriff, 1972; representative, 1974, 1977; Trail Boss, 1980-81; secretary-treasurer, 1982—), Fort Larned Historical Society, Rooks County Historical Society.

WRITINGS:

Soldiers on the Santa Fe Trail, University of Oklahoma Press, 1967.
(Contributor) Robin Higham and Carol Brandt, editors, *The United States Army in Peacetime: Essays in Honor of the Bicentennial,* Military Affairs, 1975.
(Contributor) *Kansas and the West: Bicentennial Essays in Honor of Nyle H. Miller,* Kansas State Historical Society, 1975.
Fort Hays: Frontier Army Post, 1865-1889, Kansas State Historical Society, 1980.
Fort Larned on the Santa Fe Trail, Kansas State Historical Society, 1982.
Ash Rock and the Stone Church: The History of a Kansas Rural Community, Sons and Daughters of Ash Rock, 1983.
Fort Scott on the Indian Frontier, Kansas State Historical Society, 1984.
Woodston: The Story of a Kansas Country Town, Western Books, 1985.
Santa Fe Trail Trivia, Western Books, 1985, enlarged edition with wife, Bonita M. Oliva, 1987.

Also author of *Stockton Heritage in Wood, Stone, and Brick: The Town and Its Historic Structures,* 1985; also contributor to *Brand Book of the Westerners,* 1960. Contributor of numerous articles to journals and other periodicals, including *American West, Kansas Historical Quarterly,* and *Journal of the West;* contributor of over 140 book reviews to numerous journals. Editor of newsletter, Santa Fe Trail Association; member of editorial board, Kansas Corral of the Westerners.

WORK IN PROGRESS: A revised edition of *Soldiers on the Santa Fe Trail;* a series on forts of Kansas for Kansas State Historical Society; historical research on western subjects, including the soldiers of Smoky Hill Trail, the Indian in American literature since 1890, historic churches of Kansas, General George A. Custer, and the location of the 1867 Medicine Lodge Peace Treaty negotiations.

AVOCATIONAL INTERESTS: Rafting western rivers; visiting the Grand Canyon, historic sites in Kansas and the West, and museums.

*   *   *

OLSON, Bernhard Emanuel 1910-1975

PERSONAL: Born February 27, 1910, in Winburne, Pa.; died September 22, 1975, in New York, N.Y.; son of John Frederick and Theresia Maria (Lilliestrom) Olson; married Frances M. Templin (a bookkeeper), November 23, 1947; children: Sandra Lee, Judith Anne, Terese Maria. *Education:* News-

paper Institute of America, New York, graduate, 1931; College of Emporia, A.B. (summa cum laude), 1938; Drew Theological Seminary, B.D. (magna cum laude), 1942; graduate study at Columbia University, 1943-44, and Yale University, 1945-47; Yale University, Ph.D., 1959. *Politics:* Democrat.

ADDRESSES: Home—799 Barth Dr., Baldwin, Long Island, N.Y. 11512.

CAREER: Clerk in insurance firm, then clerk at Rock Island Lines, New York City, 1925-31; *Queens Evening News,* Queens, N.Y., reporter, feature writer, music critic, and eventually night editor, 1931-34; licensed minister, Kansas Conference of Methodist Church, 1934-38; director of Christian education at Congregational church in Madison, N.J., 1940-42; ordained to ministry of Methodist Church as deacon, 1942, as elder, 1945; pastor of Methodist churches in Bangall-Pleasant Valley, Hillsdale and North Hillsdale, and Hancock, N.Y., 1942-51, and of churches in Waterbury, North Haven, New Haven, and Woodbury, Conn., 1951-60; Yale University, New Haven, Conn., director of intergroup project, 1952-60, research associate in religious education, 1957-60; Union Theological Seminary, New York City, instructor and research associate in Christian education and director of project in research and consultation in intergroup aspects of Christian education, 1960-63; National Council of Churches of Christ in the U.S.A., New York City, director of intergroup relations research, 1963-67; National Conference of Christians and Jews, New York City, national director of interreligious affairs and conductor of dialogues and conferences across the country, beginning 1967.

Lazrus Research Library, supervisor, beginning 1967; Lazrus Center for Interreligious Studies, executive director, beginning 1973. Nassau County Health and Welfare Council, member, 1961-66. Luther E. Woodward School for Emotionally Disturbed Children, member of board of directors, beginning 1961, president, 1961-66, honorary president, beginning 1966.

MEMBER: Religious Education Association (member of board of directors, New York Region), Religious Rsearch Association, National Association for Mental Health, American Academy of Religion, Academy of Ecumenists, American Swedish Historical Foundation, International Platform Association, Pennsylvania Society, Pi Gamma Mu, Phi Mu Alpha, Quill.

AWARDS, HONORS: Saturday Review Anisfield-Wolf Award ($1,000), 1963, and National Mass Media Brotherhood Award of National Conference of Christians and Jews, 1964, both for *Faith and Prejudice.*

WRITINGS:

(Author of introduction) Jules Isaac, *Has Anti-Semitism Roots in Christianity?,* National Conference of Christians and Jews, 1961.
The Crucifixion: The Jew and the Christian, Religious Education Association, 1963.
Faith and Prejudice, Yale University Press, 1963.
(Contributor) F. A. Meyer, editor, *Searching God's Word,* teacher's edition, Concordia, 1964.
(Contributor) Meyer and Douglass Burron, editors, *Learning about God,* teacher's edition, Concordia, 1965.

Author of manuals, published by National Conference of Christians and Jews, including "The Meaning and Conduct of Dialogue," 1970, "Homework for Christians," 1970, and "Public Aid for Nonpublic Education," 1971. Editor of National Conference of Christians and Jews publications, *Dia-*

logue, 1967-73, *Books for Brotherhood* (annual bibliography), and *Paperbacks on Intergroup Relations* (annual bibliography).

SIDELIGHTS: Bernhard Emanuel Olson, an ordained Methodist minister, was "a specialist in examining ways in which different religious communities misrepresent views of each other, and worked toward correcting those practices," according to a *Washington Post* obituary. Olson's book *Faith and Prejudice* is considered a leading work in this field.

AVOCATIONAL INTERESTS: Landscape painting, lecturing on music, writing poetry.

BIOGRAPHICAL/CRITICAL SOURCES:

PERIODICALS

Commentary, May, 1963.
Cosmopolitan, December, 1964.
Look, March 14, 1961, June 2, 1964.
Time, March 29, 1963.
Washington Post, September 24, 1975.

OBITUARIES:

PERIODICALS

New York Times, September 23, 1975.
Washington Post, September 24, 1975.†

*   *   *

OLSON, Richard Paul   1934-

PERSONAL: Born July 19, 1934, in Rapid City, S.D.; son of Ole (a minister) and Hazel (a county auditor; maiden name, Doty) Olson; married Mary Ann Edland, June 3, 1957; children: Julie, Lisa, Laurie. *Education:* Sioux Falls College, B.A. (with honors), 1956; Andover Newton Theological School, B.D., 1959, S.T.M. (with honors), 1960; Boston University, Ph.D., 1972.

ADDRESSES: Home—Overland Park, Kan. *Office*—Prairie Baptist Church, 7416 Roe Ave., Prairie Village, Kan. 66208.

CAREER: Ordained American Baptist minister in 1959; minister in Parker, S.D., 1960-63, and in Beaver Dam, Wis., 1963-67; associate minister in Lexington, Mass., 1967-71; First Baptist Church, Racine, Wis., senior pastor, 1971-80; First Baptist Church, Boulder, Colo., pastor, 1980-86; Prairie Baptist Church, Prairie Village, Kan., senior pastor, 1986—. Professor at Sioux Falls College, 1961-62; teacher at Beaver Dam Vocational Technical School, 1965-67; field education supervisor at Harvard Divinity School, 1970-71; lecturer at College of Racine, 1972-74, and Holy Redeemer College, 1973-74; counselor at Addiction Center of Racine, 1973-80. President of Downtown Cooperative Parish of Racine, 1974, 1979. Member of advisory committee on desegregation of Racine Unified School District, 1974-76, and of Funeral and Memorial Society of Racine and Kenosha, 1974-76.

MEMBER: American Association of Pastoral Counselors (fellow), Ministers Council of American Baptist Churches.

WRITINGS:

A Job or a Vocation, Thomas Nelson, 1973.
Mid-Life: A Time to Discover, a Time to Decide, Judson, 1980.
Changing Male Roles in Today's World, Judson, 1982.
(With Wayne G. Johnson) *Each Day a Gift,* Morrow, 1982.
(With Carole Della Pia-Terry) *Ministry with Remarried Persons,* Judson, 1984.
(With Pia-Terry) *Help for Remarried Couples and Families,* Judson, 1984.

Contributor to *Directions 80, Christian Home, Baptist Leader, Adult Class, High Call,* and *Foundations.*

WORK IN PROGRESS: With Helen Froyd, *Vocational Guidance That Families Can Offer Children;* with Joe Leonard, *Churches Ministry with Changing Families.*

P

PAGELS, Elaine Hiesey 1943-

PERSONAL: Born February 13, 1943, in Palo Alto, Calif.; daughter of William McKinley (a research biologist) and Louise Sophia (Boogaert) Hiesey; married Heinz R. Pagels (a theoretical physicist), June 7, 1969. *Education:* Stanford University, B.A., 1964, M.A., 1965; Harvard University, Ph.D., 1970. *Religion:* Episcopalian.

ADDRESSES: Home—27 West 87th St., New York, N.Y. 10024. *Office*—Department of Religion, Princeton University, Princeton, N.J. 08544. *Agent*—John Brockman Associates, Inc., 2307 Broadway, New York, N.Y. 10024.

CAREER: Barnard College, New York, N.Y., 1970-82, became professor of history of religion and head of department; Princeton University, Princeton, N.J., Harrington Spear Paine Professor of Religion, 1982—.

MEMBER: Society of Biblical Literature, American Academy of Religion.

AWARDS, HONORS: National Endowment for the Humanities grant, 1972-73; Mellon fellow, Aspen Institute of Humanistic Studies, 1974; Hazen fellow, 1975; Rockefeller fellow, 1978-79; National Book Critics Circle award for criticism, 1979, for *The Gnostic Gospels;* Guggenheim fellow, 1979-80; American Book Award, 1980, for *The Gnostic Gospels;* MacArthur Prize fellow, 1981—.

WRITINGS:

The Johannine Gospel in Gnostic Exegesis: Heracleon's Commentary on John, Abingdon, 1973.
The Gnostic Paul: Gnostic Exegesis of the Pauline Letters, Fortress, 1975.
The Gnostic Gospels, Random House, 1979.
The Gnostic Jesus and Early Christian Politics, Arizona State University, 1981.
(Contributor) *Nag Hammadi Codex III, 5: The Dialogue of the Savior,* Brill (Leiden), 1984.
Adam, Eve and the Serpent, Random House, 1987.

Member of editorial and translation board, *The Nag Hammadi Library in English,* Harper, 1978. Contributor to *Harvard Theological Review* and other journals.

SIDELIGHTS: In 1945, an Egyptian farmer near the town of Nag Hammadi came upon a cache of fifty-two ancient scrolls.

Examination by scholars in Cairo showed the scrolls to contain writings by the gnostics, an early heretical sect of Christians. It is surmised that the scrolls, written in the Coptic language, were hidden during the first or second century A.D. to prevent their destruction by the orthodox church as heretical texts. Because the find is one of the few examples of gnostic writing to have survived, it has been compared in importance to the Dead Sea Scrolls. An international team of scholars, including Elaine Hiesey Pagels, was established to study and translate the writings, which were published in 1978 as *The Nag Hammadi Library in English.* After this publication, Pagels decided to write a popular account of the scrolls to make the gnostic beliefs—often expressed in obscure, mystical language—more easily accessible to a general audience. Her book *The Gnostic Gospels* examines and explains some of the heretical beliefs of the gnostic sect and tells the story of its losing struggle against the orthodox Christian church.

At the time the gnostic scrolls were written, Christianity was a diverse and loosely-organized movement and the gnostic sect was one of several, each having its own interpretation of Christ's teachings. After an orthodox Christian church had been established in Rome, the gnostics and other sects were considered heretical and subsequently suppressed. Most gnostic writings were destroyed. Until recent discoveries of gnostic scrolls, including those at Nag Hammadi, scholars had no clear idea what the gnostics believed. With the actual writings available, scholars are now able to study gnostic teachings.

The religious beliefs of the gnostics differed in several important respects from the teachings adopted by the orthodox Christian church. A major belief was that direct communication with God was possible and that these communications were as valid as the teachings of the apostles or of Christ himself. Some gnostics even claimed to have received new teachings from Christ and the apostles. Gnostics believed that the death and resurrection of Christ was a metaphorical teaching story, not historic fact, while God was thought to be both male and female in nature.

Despite the theological differences, Pagels contends that the primary dispute between the gnostics and the orthodox church, and why the gnostics were finally branded as heretics, centered on a political difference. She points out that gnostic church structure was non-hierarchical, democratic, and allowed for the ordination of both men and women into the priesthood. In practice, by emphasizing the individual's relationship with God, the gnostics made any type of church organization virtually irrelevant to spiritual salvation. Gnostic claims of continuing contact with Christ and the apostles disputed the divine authority of the orthodox church and the exclusive validity of its scriptures. The gnostics' rejection of Christ's literal death and resurrection made them unwilling to die as martyrs for the faith, since they saw such a course as unnecessarily extreme. Orthodox believers, on the other hand, considering Christ's death an example to follow, thought the gnostic position insubordinate and cowardly. As Pagels explains in a *Publishers Weekly* interview: "Heresy turns out to be a lot of ideas not helpful in building an orthodox religion. That's really it. If you are constructing an institutional church, there are certain things you don't want Jesus to have said."

Critical reaction to *The Gnostic Gospels* has been divided, with some reviewers focusing their criticism on the gnostics' theological views rather than on Pagels' presentation of them. John Leonard, writing in the *New York Times,* finds that Pagels' reader is "made to listen to everybody who went sun-crazed out into the Middle Eastern desert and became prophetic." After comparing gnostic church structure to an "encounter group . . . a Studio 54," Leonard wonders: "Suppose these solipsists, instead of dreaming up excuses for not dying by example, as a witness for their faith, had joined the organization. Suppose they had declared a god, any god, after passing a resolution at the appropriate committee meeting." Raymond E. Brown of the *New York Times Book Review* notes that "from these works [the Nag Hammadi scrolls] we learn not a single verifiable new fact about Jesus' ministry, and only a few new sayings that might plausibly have been his. Professor Pagels recognizes this, for she does use the Coptic works correctly, not to describe Jesus but to describe the struggle within early Christianity."

According to the *Times Literary Supplement* reviewer Henry Chadwick, part of Pagels' intent in writing *The Gnostic Gospels* was to undermine what she sees as the Christian tradition's discrimination against women. "[Pagels] approaches gnosticism with very contemporary expectations: notably the hope that in these gnostic documents suppressed by ancient authority we may find an alternative Christianity sympathetic to Eastern and individualist mysticism, unencumbered by historical and miraculous events, emancipated if not from clergymen, at least from the notion that holy orders ought to be a male preserve." However, writes Chadwick, "the new material from Nag Hammadi offers only a few grains of encouragement to liberated women readers," partial evidence, Chadwick feels, of Pagels' failure to demonstrate how the exclusion of gnosticism left Christianity impoverished. Indeed, "Pagels may begin her book with the suggestion that the gnostic defeat was regrettable, but by the end she is explicitly inclined to the opinion that there is a lot to be said for something very like the main-line stuff."

From a different angle, Christopher Stead remarks in the *Chicago Tribune* that Pagels' "picture of the Gnostic movement in the early Church is reliable provided always one remembers that it was a minority movement. From the start [Gnosticism] showed features which made for disunion and disintegration. . . . Pagels gives us a fascinating picture of early Christian deviationists." Unlike the activist exponents of gnosticism today, the early gnostics were "mystics, symbolists, quietists . . . who could not have dominated the world of antiquity," offers Stead. For all that Pagels' exegesis may or may not do or be, declares Harold Bloom in the *Washington Post*

Book World, it is "always readable, always deeply informed, always richly suggestive of pathways her readers may wish to follow out for themselves."

BIOGRAPHICAL/CRITICAL SOURCES:

PERIODICALS

Atlantic, February, 1980.
Booklist, January 1, 1980.
Books of the Times, January, 1980.
Chicago Tribune, March 13, 1980.
Christian Century, June 9-16, 1976.
Christian Science Monitor, December 3, 1979.
Commonweal, November 9, 1979.
Critic, February 11, 1980.
Los Angeles Times, April 26, 1980.
Los Angeles Times Book Review, December 23, 1979.
Ms., April, 1980.
New York Times, December 14, 1979.
New York Times Book Review, January 20, 1980.
New Yorker, January 21, 1980.
Publishers Weekly, October 15, 1979.
Rolling Stone, March 6, 1980.
Spectator, March 15, 1980.
Times Literary Supplement, March 21, 1980.
Washington Post Book World, November 25, 1979.

* * *

PARGETER, Edith Mary 1913-
(Ellis Peters)

PERSONAL: Born September 28, 1913, in Horsehay, Shropshire, England; daughter of Edmund Valentine and Edith (Hordley) Pargeter. *Education:* Attended schools in England.

ADDRESSES: Home—Parkville, 14 Park Lane, Madeley, Telford, Shropshire TF7 5HF, England. *Agent*—Deborah Owen Ltd., 78 Narrow St., Limehouse, London E14 8BP, England.

CAREER: Pharmacist's assistant and dispenser in Dawley, Shropshire, England, 1933-40; full-time novelist and translator of prose and poetry from the Czech and Slovak. *Military service:* Women's Royal Naval Service, 1940-45; became petty officer; received British Empire Medal.

MEMBER: International Institute of Arts and Letters, Society of Authors, Authors League of America, Authors Guild, Crime Writers Association.

AWARDS, HONORS: Edgar Allan Poe Award for best mystery novel, Mystery Writers of America, 1961, for *Death and the Joyful Woman;* Gold medal, Czechoslovak Society for International Relations, 1968; Silver Dagger, Crime Writers Association, 1981, for *Monk's-Hood.*

WRITINGS:

Hortensius, Friend of Nero, Dickson, 1936.
Iron-Bound, Dickson, 1936.
The City Lies Foursquare, Reynal & Hitchcock, 1939.
Ordinary People, Heinemann, 1941, published as *People of My Own,* Reynal, 1942.
She Goes to War (novel), Heinemann, 1942.
The Eighth Champion of Christendom, Heinemann, 1945.
Reluctant Odyssey (sequel to *The Eighth Champion of Christendom*), Heinemann, 1946.
Warfare Accomplished, Heinemann, 1947.
The Fair Young Phoenix, Heinemann, 1948.

By Firelight, Heinemann, 1948, published as *By This Strange Fire,* Reynal & Hitchcock, 1948.

The Coast of Bohemia (travel), Heinemann, 1950.

Lost Children (novel), Heinemann, 1950.

Holiday with Violence, Heinemann, 1952.

This Rough Magic (novel), Heinemann, 1953.

Most Loving Mere Folly (novel), Heinemann, 1953.

The Soldier at the Door (novel), Heinemann, 1954.

A Means of Grace (novel), Heinemann, 1956.

The Assize of the Dying: 2 Novelletes (contains "The Assize of the Dying" and "Aunt Helen"), Doubleday, 1958 (published in England with an additional story, "The Seven Days of Monte Cervio," as *The Assize of the Dying: 3 Stories,* Heinemann, 1958).

The Heaven Tree, Doubleday, 1960.

The Green Branch, Heinemann, 1962.

The Scarlet Seed, Heinemann, 1963.

The Lily Hand and Other Stories, Heinemann, 1965.

A Bloody Field by Shrewsbury, Macmillan (London), 1972, published as *The Bloody Field,* Viking, 1973.

Sunrise in the West (first volume in "The Brothers of Gwynedd" sequence), Macmillan (London), 1974.

The Dragon at Noonday (second volume in "The Brothers of Gwynedd" sequence), Macmillan (London), 1975.

The Hounds of Sunset (third volume in "The Brothers of Gwynedd" sequence), Macmillan (London), 1976.

Afterglow and Nightfall (fourth volume in "The Brothers of Gwynedd" sequence), Macmillan (London), 1977.

The Marriage of Megotta, Viking, 1979.

UNDER PSEUDONYM ELLIS PETERS

Death Mask, Collins, 1959, Doubleday, 1960.

Where There's a Will, Doubleday, 1960 (published in England as *The Will and the Deed,* Collins, 1960), published as *The Will and the Deed,* Avon, 1966.

Funeral of Figaro, Collins, 1962, Morrow, 1964.

The Horn of Roland, Morrow, 1974.

Never Pick up Hitch-Hikers!, Morrow, 1976, bound with *Catch a Falling Spy* by Len Deighton and *More Tales of the Black Widowers* by Isaac Asimov, W. J. Black, 1978.

"FELSE FAMILY" DETECTIVE NOVELS SERIES

Fallen into the Pit, Heinemann, 1951.

(Under pseudonym Ellis Peters) *Death and the Joyful Woman,* Collins, 1961, Doubleday, 1962.

(Under pseudonym Ellis Peters) *Flight of a Witch,* Collins, 1964.

(Under pseudonym Ellis Peters) *Who Lies Here?,* Morrow, 1965 (published in England as *A Nice Derangement of Epitaphs,* Collins, 1965).

(Under pseudonym Ellis Peters) *The Piper on the Mountain,* Morrow, 1966.

(Under pseudonym Ellis Peters) *Black Is the Colour of My True-Love's Heart,* Morrow, 1967.

(Under pseudonym Ellis Peters) *The Grass Widow's Tale,* Morrow, 1968.

(Under pseudonym Ellis Peters) *The House of Green Turf,* Morrow, 1969.

(Under pseudonym Ellis Peters) *Mourning Raga,* Macmillan (London), 1969, Morrow, 1970.

(Under pseudonym Ellis Peters) *The Knocker on Death's Door,* Macmillan (London), 1970, Morrow, 1971.

(Under pseudnoym Ellis Peters) *Death to the Landlords!,* Morrow, 1972.

(Under pseudonym Ellis Peters) *City of Gold and Shadows,* Macmillan (London), 1973, Morrow, 1974.

(Under pseudonym Ellis Peters) *Rainbow's End,* Macmillan (London), 1978, Morrow, 1979.

"CHRONICLES OF BROTHER CADFAEL" MYSTERY SERIES; UNDER PSEUDONYM ELLIS PETERS

A Morbid Taste for Bones, Macmillan (London), 1977, Morrow, 1978.

One Corpse Too Many, Macmillan (London), 1979, Morrow, 1980.

Monk's-Hood, Macmillan (London), 1980, Morrow, 1981.

Saint Peter's Fair, Morrow, 1981.

The Leper of St. Giles, Macmillan (London), 1981, Morrow, 1982.

The Virgin in the Ice, Macmillan (London), 1982, Morrow, 1983.

The Sanctuary Sparrow, Morrow, 1983.

The Devil's Novice, Macmillan (London), 1983, Morrow, 1984.

Dead Man's Ransom, Morrow, 1984.

The Pilgrim of Hate, Macmillan (London), 1984, Morrow, 1985.

An Excellent Mystery, Morrow, 1985.

The Raven in the Foregate, Morrow, 1986.

The Rose Rent, Morrow, 1987.

The Hermit of Eyton Forest, Headline, 1987.

The Confession of Brother Haluin, Headline, 1988.

CONTRIBUTOR

Alfred Hitchcock Presents: Stories Not for the Nervous, Random House, 1965.

Alfred Hitchcock Presents: Stories That Scared Even Me, Random House, 1967.

George Hardinge, editor, *Winter's Crimes 1,* St. Martin's, 1969.

A. S. Burack, editor, *Techniques of Novel Writing,* The Writer, 1973.

Hilary Watson, editor, *Winter's Crimes 8,* St. Martin's, 1976.

Hardinge, editor, *Winter's Crimes 11,* St. Martin's, 1979.

Hardinge, editor, *Winter's Crimes 13,* St. Martin's, 1981.

TRANSLATIONS FROM THE CZECH

Jan Neruda, *Tales of the Little Quarter* (short stories), Heinemann, 1957, reprinted, Greenwood, 1977.

Frantisek Kosik, *The Sorrowful and Heroic Life of John Amos Comenius,* State Educational Publishing House (Prague), 1958.

A Handful of Linden Leaves: An Anthology of Czech Poetry, Artia (Prague), 1958.

Joseph Toman, *Don Juan,* Knopf, 1958.

Valja Styblova, *The Abortionists,* Secker & Warburg, 1961.

(With others) Mojmir Otruba and Zdenek Pesat, editors, *The Linden Tree: An Anthology of Czech and Slovak Literature, 1890-1960,* Artia (Prague), 1962.

Bozena Nemcova, *Granny: Scenes from Country Life,* Artia (Prague), 1962, reprinted, Greenwood, 1977.

Joseph Bor, *The Terezin Requiem,* Knopf, 1963.

Alois Jirasek, *Legends of Old Bohemia,* Hamlyn, 1963.

Karel Hynek Macha, *May,* Artia (Prague), 1965.

Vladislav Vancura, *The End of the Old Times,* Artia (Prague), 1965.

Bohumil Hrabel, *A Close Watch on the Trains,* J. Cape, 1968.

Josefa Slanska, *Report on My Husband,* Macmillan (London), 1969.

Ivan Klima, *A Ship Named Hope: Two Novels,* Gollancz, 1970.

Jaroslav Seifert, *Mozart in Prague*, Artia (Prague), 1970.

OTHER

Also author of *The Horn of Roland*, which was bound with *Danger Money* by Mignon G. Eberhart and *The Romanov Succession* by Brian Garfield for the Detective Book Club by W. J. Black. Contributor of short stories to magazines, including *The Saint* and *This Week*.

SIDELIGHTS: Edith Pargeter, writing as Ellis Peters, has "re-created the world of England in the first years of the High Middle Ages" in her chronicles of Brother Cadfael, according to Andrew M. Greeley in the *Armchair Detective*. A twelfth-century crusader turned monk and herbalist, Brother Cadfael is the protagonist of a series of novels which mix historical background, romance, and detection, and which Greeley describes as "a fascinating reconstruction of the religion, the history, the social structure, the culture, the politics, and the lifestyle of England in the twelfth century." Set on the Welsh border near Shrewsbury, where Peters lives today, the books take place during the tumultuous reign of Stephen of England, when fighting between the king and his cousin the Empress Matilda (or Maud) racked the realm.

Peters's Cadfael novels have been compared with Umberto Eco's best-seller *The Name of the Rose*, which tells the story of another crime-solving monk in fourteenth-century Italy. The resemblence, however, is only superficial; seven Cadfael chronicles preceeded Eco's book, and Peters does not expound a theory of semiotics as Eco does. Her books are, in fact, "closer in spirit to the heroics of *The Black Arrow* or *Men of Iron*," according to Geoffrey O'Brien in the *Village Voice*, and she lists Rudyard Kipling, Thomas Mallory and Helen Waddell among her literary influences. As Greeley points out, "Eco undoubtedly describes truth in his book. Ellis Peters, for her part, has only verisimilitude; and, as any storyteller knows, verisimilitude makes for a better story than truth and may, finally, at the level of myth and symbol, be even more true." Her interest is to tell a good story. Peters described herself to *CA* as "essentially a storyteller, and in my view no one who can't make that statement can possibly be a novelist, the novel being by definition an extended narrative reflecting the human condition, with the accent on the word 'narrative'."

Many of the books in this series have classic boy-meets-loses-gets-girl subplots which, in some reviewers' opinions, over-whelm the elements of detective fiction. For example, T. J. Binyon comments in the *Times Literary Supplement* that "to include not one, not two, but three separate romances" in *The Sanctuary Sparrow* seems excessive, and remarks that in *The Pilgrim of Hate*, "romance is gradually crowding out detection." Marcel Berlins states in the London *Times* that *An Excellent Mystery* has in fact "little mystery, though much chivalrous romance." Other commentators are not so troubled; the "twee little romances," as Margaret Cannon in the Toronto *Globe and Mail* calls them, are in her opinion used for effect, and do not interfere with the main story.

The "charmingly exotic (but not too exotic) background," as *Washington Post Book World* reviewer Joseph McLellan calls it, combined with Peters's grasp of characterization, forms a large part of the attraction these novels have for readers. Derrick Murdoch in the Toronto *Globe and Mail* defines their charm as "the manner in which the speech and usages of those ancient times are made to seem alive without unnecessary explanation." "Having read all the chronicles," Greeley states, "one feels that one has become part of a little section of En-

gland around Shrewsbury between 1137 and 1140, and that one knows the monks and the townsfolk and the squires and the nobility almost as though they were friends and neighbors." He continues, "Perhaps the greatest achievement of the Cadfael chronicles is Peters's ability to help us feel and accept the common humanity which links us to these inhabitants' world, so very different from our own."

Ellis Peters told *CA:* "Streams of consciousness and probings of the solitary, and usually uninteresting, human-soul-at-the-end-of-its-tether are not for me. Nor do I find vice and evil more interesting than virtue, and I hope my books go some way to defy and disprove that too easily accepted judgement. It gives me great satisfaction that many times people have written to me to tell me, in varying terms, that I have made them feel better, not worse, about being human. That's all the acknowledgment I need."

MEDIA ADAPTATIONS: The Assize of the Dying was filmed under the title "The Spaniard's Curse"; *Death and the Joyful Woman* was presented on "The Alfred Hitchcock Hour"; *Mourning Raga* and *The Heaven Tree* were adapted for radio in 1971 and 1975, respectively; Pargeter's short story "The Purple Children" was produced on television in Canada and Australia.

AVOCATIONAL INTERESTS: Music (especially opera and folk), theatre, art.

BIOGRAPHICAL/CRITICAL SOURCES:

PERIODICALS

Armchair Detective, summer, 1985.
Best Sellers, October 1, 1966, August 1, 1967, June 1, 1968, April 15, 1969, March 15, 1970, February, 1984, July, 1984, March, 1986, August, 1986, February, 1987.
Books and Bookmen, April, 1965, December, 1967, June, 1968, June, 1969, August, 1970.
Globe and Mail (Toronto), May 5, 1984, July 5, 1986, December 13, 1986.
Listener, May 19, 1983.
Los Angeles Times Book Review, January 31, 1982, February 26, 1984, October 27, 1985.
National Review, December 5, 1986.
New Yorker, November 5, 1984.
New York Times Book Review, May 9, 1965, November 6, 1966, August 13, 1967, May 26, 1968, September 26, 1982.
Observer, February 14, 1965, May 15, 1966, September 17, 1967, April 21, 1968, January 23, 1983, August 4, 1985.
Publishers Weekly, February 8, 1985.
Punch, May 29, 1968.
Spectator, March 5, 1965, June 3, 1966.
Time, August 17, 1987.
Times (London), January 21, 1983, July 11, 1985.
Times Literary Supplement, February 25, 1965, June 2, 1966, September 21, 1967, July 18, 1968, October 3, 1980, February 18, 1983, July 13, 1984, January 11, 1985, October 3, 1986, January 30, 1987.
Village Voice, July 16, 1985.
Washington Post Book World, January 31, 1981, June 21, 1981, May 16, 1982.
Wilson Library Bulletin, October, 1983.

*   *   *

PARKER, J(ohn) Carlyle   1931-

PERSONAL: Born October 14, 1931, in Ogden, Utah; son of

Levi C. (a farmer and guard) and Marietta (a seamstress; maiden name, Parkinson) Parker; married Janet C. Greene, May 31, 1956; children: Denise, Nathan, Bret. *Education:* Brigham Young University, B.A., 1957; University of California, Berkeley, M.L.S., 1958; Humbolt State College (now University), graduate study, 1959-60. *Politics:* Democrat. *Religion:* Church of Jesus Christ of Latter-day Saints.

ADDRESSES: Home—2115 North Denair Ave., Turlock, Calif. 95380. *Office*—Library, California State University, Stanislaus, 801 Monte Vista Ave., Turlock, Calif. 95380.

CAREER: Humboldt State College (now University), Arcata, Calif., librarian, 1958-60; Church College of Hawaii (now Brigham Young University, Hawaii), Laie, assistant and acting librarian, 1960-63; California State University, Stanislaus, Turlock, head of library public services, 1963-83, 1985—, assistant director, 1968-83, 1985—, acting director, 1983-84. Founder and librarian of Modesto California Branch Genealogical Library, 1968—. Secretary of Turlock Centennial Foundation Board, 1971-75; president of Turlock Community Concert Association, 1973-75. *Military service:* U.S. Army, 1953-55.

MEMBER: American Library Association, American Association of University Professors, National Education Association, Congress of Faculty Associations, California Teachers' Association, California Library Association, Stanislaus County Historical Society.

AWARDS, HONORS: American Library Association fellowship, 1965; Award of Merit, National Genealogical Society, 1984; fellow, Utah Genealogical Association, 1984; Meritorious Performance and Professional Promise Award, California State University, Stanislaus, 1986.

WRITINGS:

(Compiler) *An Annotated Bibliography of the History of Del Norte and Humboldt Counties,* Humboldt State College Library, 1960.
Sources of Californiana: From Padron to Voter Registration, Genealogical Society (Salt Lake City), 1969.
(Contributor) David F. Trask and Robert W. Pomeroy III, editors, *The Craft of Public History: An Annotated Select Bibliography,* Greenwood Press, 1983.
U.S. Genealogical Research, Marietta, 1987.

EDITOR

A Person Name Index to Orton's "Records of California Men in the War of the Rebellion, 1861 to 1867," Gale, 1978.
City, County, Town, and Township Index to the 1850 Federal Census Schedule, Gale, 1979.
An Index to the Biographees in 19th-Century California County Histories, Gale, 1979.
Library Service to Genealogists, Gale, 1979.
Genealogy in the Central Association of Libraries: A Union Catalog Based on Filby's "American and British Genealogy and Heraldry," Library, California State College, Stanislaus, 1981.
Dictionary of Archivist and Librarian Genealogical Instructors, Marietta, 1985.
Pennsylvania and Middle Atlantic States Genealogical Manuscripts: A User's Guide to the Manuscript Collections of the Genealogical Society of Pennsylvania, as Indexed in Its Manuscript Materials Index, Microfilmed by the Genealogical Department, Salt Lake City, Marietta, 1986.

(With wife, Janet G. Parker) *Nevada Biographical and Genealogical Sketch Index,* Marietta, 1986.

OTHER

Editor of "Genealogy and Local History" series, Gale, 1978-81. Contributor of articles and reviews to genealogy and library journals. Contributing editor, *Genealogy Journal,* 1980—.

SIDELIGHTS: J. Carlyle Parker told *CA:* "The majority of my early writing was an attempt to assist librarians in their understanding of how to help patrons in biographical, genealogical, and local history research; how to use and obtain these research materials; and to make some of these research materials easier to use and more accessible."

He adds, "Recently my attention has turned to helping genealogists to do their research through the preparation of indexes, guides, book and microform reviews, and how-to-do-it works."

AVOCATIONAL INTERESTS: Bicycling, ornithology, photography, travel, singing ("solos, duets, and in choirs").

*   *   *

PARKHILL, John
   See COX, William (Robert)

*   *   *

PATENT, Dorothy Hinshaw   1940-

PERSONAL: Born April 30, 1940, in Rochester, Minn.; daughter of Horton Corwin (a physician) and Dorothy (Youmans) Hinshaw; married Gregory Joseph Patent (a professor of zoology), March 21, 1964; children: David Gregory, Jason Daniel. *Education:* Stanford University, B.A., 1962; University of California, Berkeley, M.A., 1965, Ph.D., 1968; also studied at Friday Harbor Laboratories, University of Washington, 1965-67.

ADDRESSES: Home—5445 Skyway Dr., Missoula, Mont. 59801.

CAREER: Sinai Hospital, Detroit, Mich., post-doctoral fellow, 1968-69; Stazione Zoologica, Naples, Italy, post-doctoral researcher, 1970-71; University of Montana, Missoula, faculty affiliate in department of zoology, 1975—, acting assistant professor, 1977.

MEMBER: American Institute of Biological Sciences, American Society of Zoologists, American Association for the Advancement of Science, Authors Guild, Society of Children's Book Writers.

AWARDS, HONORS: The National Science Teachers Association has cited the following as outstanding science trade books: *Weasels, Otters, Skunks and Their Family,* 1973, *How Insects Communicate,* 1975, *Plants and Insects Together,* 1976, *The World of Worms,* 1978, *Animal and Plant Mimicry,* 1978, *Beetles and How They Live,* 1978, *Butterflies and Moths: How They Function,* 1979, *Sizes and Shapes in Nature: What They Mean,* 1979, *Raccoons, Coatimundis and Their Family,* 1979, *The Lives of Spiders,* 1980, *Bears of the World,* 1980, *Spider Magic,* 1982, *Arabian Horses,* 1982, *Germs!,* 1983, *Whales: Giants of the Deep,* 1984, *Farm Animals,* 1984, *Quarter Horses,* 1985, *The Sheep Book,* 1985, *Thoroughbred Horses,* 1985, *Buffalo: The American Bison Today,* 1986, *Draft Horses,* 1986, and *Mosquitoes,* 1986; Golden Kite Award in nonfiction, Society of Children's Book Writers, 1977, for *Evolution Goes on Every Day*, and 1980, for *The Lives of Spiders;* "Notable Book" citation, American Library Association, 1982, for *Spider Magic;* "Best Book for Young Adults" citation, American Library Association, 1986, for *The Quest for Artificial Intelligence;* Eva L. Gordon Award, American Nature Study Society, 1987.

WRITINGS:

JUVENILE NONFICTION; PUBLISHED BY HOLIDAY HOUSE

Weasels, Otters, Skunks and Their Family, 1973.
Microscopic Animals and Plants, 1974.
Frogs, Toads, Salamanders and How They Reproduce, 1975.
How Insects Communicate, 1975.
Fish and How They Reproduce, 1976.
Plants and Insects Together, 1976.
Evolution Goes on Every Day, 1977.
Reptiles and How They Reproduce, 1977.
(With Paul C. Schroeder) *Beetles and How They Live,* 1978.
Animal and Plant Mimicry, 1978.
The World of Worms, 1978.
Butterflies and Moths: How They Function, 1979.
Raccoons, Coatimundis and Their Family, 1979.
Sizes and Shapes in Nature: What They Mean, 1979.
Bacteria: How They Affect Other Living Things, 1980.
Bears of the World, 1980.
The Lives of Spiders, 1980.
Horses and Their Wild Relatives, 1981.
Hunters and the Hunted: Surviving in the Animal World, 1981.
Horses of America, 1981.
Arabian Horses, 1982.
Spider Magic, 1982.
A Picture Book of Cows, 1982.
A Picture Book of Ponies, photographs by William Munoz, 1983.
Germs!, 1983.
Farm Animals, photographs by Munoz, 1984.
Whales: Giants of the Deep, 1984.
Quarter Horses, photographs by Munoz, 1985.
Thoroughbred Horses, 1985.
Mosquitoes, 1986.
Draft Horses, photographs by Munoz, 1986.
All about Whales, 1987.
Dolphins and Porpoises, 1987.
Babies!, 1988.

OTHER JUVENILE NONFICTION

Where the Bald Eagles Gather, photographs by Munoz, Clarion Books, 1984.
Baby Horses, photographs by Munoz, Dodd, 1985.
The Sheep Book, photographs by Munoz, Dodd, 1985.
The Quest for Artificial Intelligence, Harcourt, 1986.
Maggie: A Sheep Dog (Junior Literary Guild selection), photographs by Munoz, Dodd, 1986.
Buffalo: The American Bison Today, Clarion Books, 1986.
The Way of the Grizzly, photographs by Munoz, Clarion Books, 1987.
Wheat: The Golden Harvest, photographs by Munoz, Dodd, 1987.
Christmas Trees (Junior Literary Guild selection), photographs by Munoz, Dodd, 1987.
A Horse of a Different Color, Dodd, 1988.
The Whooping Crane: A Comeback Story, Clarion Books, 1988.

OTHER

(With Diane E. Bilderback) *Garden Secrets* (adult nonfiction), Rodale Press, 1982.
(With Bilderback) *Backyard Fruits and Berries* (adult nonfiction), Rodale Press, 1984.

Contributor to gardening and farming magazines.

WORK IN PROGRESS: For Clarion Books, children's books on wild horses, on turkeys, and on wolves, all with photographs by Munoz; for Holiday House, *All about Dolphins and Porpoises,* and other children's books on Appaloosa horses, on humpback whales, and on ants; for Dodd, children's books on apple growing and on flower farming, both with photographs by Munoz; for Harcourt, a young adult book on animal intelligence; with Munoz, an adult book on grizzly bears.

SIDELIGHTS: Dorothy Hinshaw Patent told *CA:* "People want to know how authors pick topics to write about. I choose things I especially want to learn about myself, so I get paid for having fun. For the first few years of my career, I was a biologist who happened to write. This influenced my choice of topics— all were essentially translating scientific information into understandable form for children. But once I discovered that I had become a writer who happened to be trained as a scientist, the world of writing truly opened up for me. I discovered I could write about gardening and domesticated animals as well as about scientific subjects. Attitude means so much in how we build our lives.

"My main goals in my writing today are to give children a 'feel' for animals, to help them to respect other living things and to understand the need for conservation, wildlife management, and scientific research if we want to continue to share our crowded Earth with other living things."

BIOGRAPHICAL/CRITICAL SOURCES:

PERIODICALS

Missoulian, December 19, 1981, May 4, 1984.
San Rafael Independent-Journal, January 26, 1974.

*   *   *

PAWLIKOWSKI, John T. 1940-

PERSONAL: Surname is pronounced Paw-lee-*kov*-ski; born November 2, 1940, in Chicago, Ill.; son of Thaddeus John (a cork molder) and Anna (Mizera) Pawlikowski. *Education:* Attended Mount St. Philip, Milwaukee, Wis., 1958-60, and Servite Priory, Benburb, Northern Ireland, 1960-62; Loyola University, Chicago, Ill., A.B., 1963, graduate study, 1963-66; also attended Stonebridge Priory, Lake Bluff, Ill., 1963-66, and University of Wisconsin, 1965-67; College of Jewish Studies, Chicago, diploma, 1967; St. Mary of the Lake Seminary, Mundelein, Ill., S.T.B., 1967; University of Chicago, Ph.D., 1970. *Politics:* "Generally Democratic."

ADDRESSES: Home—1420 East 49th St., Chicago, Ill. 60615. *Office*—Catholic Theological Union, 5401 South Cornell Ave., Chicago, Ill. 60615-5698.

CAREER: Ordained Roman Catholic priest of Servite Fathers (O.S.M.), 1967; University of Chicago, Chicago, Ill., chaplain's assistant at Calvert House (Newman Club), 1967—; Catholic Theological Union, Chicago, 1968—, began as assistant professor, currently professor of ethics and acting president. Seminarian-Lay Apostolate Conference, executive chairman, 1964-65, member of executive committee, 1965-

66; chairman of National Council of Churches' Faith and Order Study Commission on Israel, 1972-73, and member of standing committee on Christian-Jewish relations, 1984—; chairman of Chicago Institute for Inter-religious Research, 1973; fellow, International Institute of Community service, 1975; member of United States Holocaust Memorial Council, 1980—; member of national board, Americans for Democratic Action, 1981—; also affiliated with Anti-Defamation League of B'nai B'rith, Inter-Seminary Movement, and Southern Christian Leadership Conference. Member of Advisory Committee, Secretariat for Catholic-Jewish Relations, National Conference of Catholic Bishops, 1971-73; vice-president, American Foundation for the Institute of Polish-Jewish Studies, 1986—; member of executive committee, National Polish-Jewish Dialogue, 1986—; vice-president, Chicago Clergy and Laity Concerned, 1987—.

MEMBER: American Society of Christian Ethics, Catholic Theological Society of America, American Academy of Religion.

AWARDS, HONORS: Fellowship to Institute of Jewish Studies, Wheeling College; Men of Achievement Award, 1973; Inter-faith Award, American Jewish Committee, 1973; Founder's Citation, National Catholic Conference Interracial Justice; Righteous among the Nations Award, Holocaust Museum (Detroit), 1986.

WRITINGS:

Epistle Homilies, Bruce Publishing, 1966.
Catechetics and Prejudice: How Catholic Teaching Materials View Jews, Protestants, and Racial Minorities, Paulist/Newman, 1973.
What Are They Saying about Christian-Jewish Relations?, Paulist Press, 1980.
The Holocaust: Its Implications for the Church and Society Problematic, Christian Theological Seminary, 1981.
Christ: In Light of the Christian-Jewish Dialogue, Paulist Press, 1982.
(Editor with Donald Senior) *Biblical and Theological Reflections on the Challenge of Peace,* M. Glazier, 1984.
(Author of general introduction and document introductions) *Justice in the Marketplace: Collected Statements of the Vatican and the United States Catholic Bishops on Economic Policy, 1891-1984,* Office of Publishing and Promotion Services, U.S. Catholic Conference, 1985.

Also author of *The Challenge of the Holocaust for Christian Theology,* Anti-Defamation League of B'nai B'rith, *Proposals for Church-Sponsored Housing,* 1971, *Sinai and Calvary, Social Ethics: Biblical and Theological Foundations, Church-State Relations: A Contemporary Catholic Perspective,* and *Housing Project for the Inner City: A Case Study.*

CONTRIBUTOR

Walter Wagoner, *The Seminary,* Sheed, 1966.
Michael Zeik and Martin Siegel, editors, *Root and Branch,* Roth, 1973.
Robert Heyer, editor, *Jewish/Christian Relations,* Paulist/Newman, 1975.
Clyde L. Manschreck and Barbara Brown Zikmund, editors, *The American Religious Experiment: Piety and Practicality,* Exploration Press, 1976.
Alan T. Davies, editor, *Antisemitism and the Foundations of Christianity,* Paulist Press, 1979.
Harry James Cargas, editor, *When God and Man Failed: Non-Jewish Views of the Holocaust,* Macmillan, 1981.

Henry Friedlander and Sybil Milton, editors, *The Holocaust: Ideology, Bureaucracy, and Genocide,* Kraus Reprint, 1981.
Eugene J. Fisher and Daniel F. Polish, editors, *Formation of Social Policy in the Catholic and Jewish Traditions,* University of Notre Dame Press, 1982.

Also contributor to *Auschwitz: Beginning of a New Era?,* edited by Eva Fleischner and Ktav, *Faith and Freedom,* edited by Richard Libowitz, *Genocide: Critical Issues of the Holocaust,* edited by Alex Grobman and Daniel Landes, *The Challenge of Shalom for Catholics and Jews,* edited by Annette Daum and Fisher, *Parish Path through Advent and Christmastime* and *Parish Path through Lent and Eastertime,* edited by Mary Anne Simcoe, *Anti-Semitism in the Contemporary World,* edited by Michael Curtis, *Cities of God: Faith, Politics and Pluralism in Judaism, Christianity and Islam,* edited by Nigel Biggar, Jamie S. Scott, and William Schweiker, *Christianity and Capitalism,* edited by Bruce Greele and David A. Krueger, *The Life of the Covenant!: The Challenge of Contemporary Judaism,* edited by Joseph A. Edelheit, and to *Selected Papers 1979: The American Society of Christian Ethics,* edited by Max L. Stackhouse.

OTHER

Also author of a monograph with Marc Tannenbaum, *Good Friday Worship: Jewish Concerns, Christian Response.* Contributor to journals, including *Furrow, Today, Journal of Ecumenical Studies, Cross Currents, Journal of Religion,* and *Ecumenist.*

SIDELIGHTS: John T. Pawlikowski speaks Polish and some German, modern Hebrew, and French; he reads Latin, French, German, Hebrew (biblical and modern), and Greek (classical and modern).

*   *   *

PAYNE, Donald Gordon   1924-
(Ian Cameron, Donald Gordon, James Vance Marshall)

PERSONAL: Born January 3, 1924, in London, England; son of Francis Gordon and Evelyn (Rogers) Payne; married Barbara Back, August 20, 1947; children: Christopher, Nigel, Adrian, Alison, Robin. *Education:* Corpus Christi College, Oxford, M.A., 1949. *Religion:* Church of England.

ADDRESSES: Home—Pippacre, Westcott Heath, near Dorking, Surrey RH4 3JZ, England. *Agent*—John Johnson, 45/47 Clerkenwell Green, London EC1R 0HT, England.

CAREER: Christopher Johnson Publishers Ltd., London, England, trainee, 1949-52; Robert Hale Ltd. (publishers), London, editor, 1952-56; full-time writer. *Military service:* Royal Naval Volunteer Reserve, Fleet Air Arm pilot, 1942-46; became lieutenant.

WRITINGS:

UNDER PSEUDONYM IAN CAMERON

The Midnight Sea, Hutchinson, 1958.
Red Duster, White Ensign (story of Malta convoys), Muller, 1959, Doubleday, 1960.
The Lost Ones, Hutchinson, 1961, Morrow, 1968.
Wings of the Morning (story of Fleet Air Arm in World War II), Hodder & Stoughton, 1962, Morrow, 1963.

Lodestone and Evening Star (history of sea exploration), Hodder & Stoughton, 1965, Dutton, 1966.
The Island at the Top of the World, Avon, 1970.
The Impossible Dream: Building of the Panama Canal, Morrow, 1971.
The Mountains at the Bottom of the World: Novel of Adventure, Morrow, 1972.
Magellan and the First Circumnavigation of the World, Saturday Review Press, 1973.
Antarctica: The Last Continent, Little, Brown, 1974.
The Young Eagles, St. Martin's, 1980.
To the Farthest Ends of the Earth, Dutton, 1980.
Mountains of the Gods, Facts on File, 1984.
Exploring Antarctica, Longman, 1984.
Exploring Africa, Longman, 1984.
Exploring the Himalaya, Longman, 1985.
Exploring Australia, Longman, 1985.
Lost Paradise, Salem House, 1987.

UNDER PSEUDONYM DONALD GORDON

Star-Raker, Morrow, 1962.
Flight of the Bat, Hodder & Stoughton, 1963, Morrow, 1964.
The Golden Oyster, Hodder & Stoughton, 1967, Morrow, 1968.
Leap in the Dark, Morrow, 1971.

UNDER PSEUDONYM JAMES VANCE MARSHALL

(Co-author) *The Children*, M. Joseph, 1959, published as *Walkabout*, Doubleday, 1961, reprinted, Sundance, 1984.
A River Ran Out of Eden, Morrow, 1963, published as *The Golden Seal*, Sundance, 1986.
My Boy John That Went to Sea, Hodder & Stoughton, 1966, Morrow, 1967.
A Walk to the Hills of the Dreamtime, Morrow, 1970.
The Wind at Morning, Morrow, 1973, new edition, G. K. Hall, 1974.
Still Waters, Morrow, 1982.

OTHER

(Contributor) *Into the Unknown*, National Geographic Society, 1987.

WORK IN PROGRESS: A book about the exploration of the Andes entitled *Kingdom of the Sun God*.

MEDIA ADAPTATIONS: The film "Walkabout" was produced by Twentieth Century-Fox in 1971; "Island at the Top of the World," based on the novel *The Lost Ones*, was filmed by Walt Disney Productions in 1974; "The Golden Seal" was released by Samuel Goldwyn in 1983.

AVOCATIONAL INTERESTS: Gardening, tennis, and writing.

*   *   *

PEARLMAN, Daniel (David)   1935-

PERSONAL: Born July 22, 1935, in New York, N.Y. *Education:* Brooklyn College (now Brooklyn College of the City University of New York), B.A., 1957; Columbia University, M.A., 1958, Ph.D., 1968.

ADDRESSES: Office—Department of English, University of Rhode Island, Kingston, R.I. 02881.

CAREER: Brooklyn College (now Brooklyn College of the City University of New York), Brooklyn, N.Y., instructor in English, 1958-60; University of Arizona, Tuscon, instructor in English, 1960-62; Brooklyn College of the City University

of New York, instructor in English, 1962-67; Monmouth College, West Long Branch, N.J., assistant professor of English, 1967-69; Mercer Community College, Trenton, N.J., professor of English and chairman of department, 1969-71; Columbus International College, Seville, Spain, director of academic affairs, 1972-73; Universidad de Sevilla, Seville, Spain, visiting professor of English, 1973-74; Herbert H. Lehman College of the City University of New York, Bronx, N.Y., assistant professor of academic skills, 1974-76; University of Idaho, Moscow, professor of English and chairman of department, 1976-80; University of Rhode Island, Kingston, professor of English and chairman of department, 1980—.

MEMBER: Science Fiction Writers of America.

AWARDS, HONORS: American Philosophical Society research grants, 1968 and 1971-72; American Council of Learned Societies research fellowship, 1971-72, for literary research abroad; National Endowment for the Arts grant, 1979; Idaho Research Foundation/University of Idaho Foundation grant, 1979; University of Rhode Island grant, 1981-82.

WRITINGS:

Guide to Rapid Revision, Odyssey, 1965, 4th edition, Macmillan, in press.
The Barb of Time: On the Unity of Ezra Pound's Cantos, Oxford University Press, 1969.
(Contributor) Grace Schulman, editor, *Ezra Pound: A Collection of Criticism*, McGraw, 1974.
(Translator with Luisa Campos) *Do caos a ordem: Visoes de sociedade nos Cantares de Ezra Pound*, Assirio e Alvim (Portugal), 1983.
Guide to Rapid Revision Workbook, Bobbs-Merrill, 1984, 2nd edition, Macmillan, in press.
(With Anita Du Bose) *Letter Perfect: An ABC for Business Writers*, Bobbs-Merrill, 1985.

Also author of a discussion guide to accompany film "Ezra Pound: Poet's Poet," 1971; author of unpublished novels *Astrobal*, *The Interview*, and *Look-out Man*. Contributor of short stories and novelettes to anthologies, including *Synergy*, Harcourt, and *Amazing Stories*, and to periodicals such as *New England Review* and *Bread Loaf Quarterly*. Contributor of articles and reviews to literary journals. Associate editor, *Paideuma* (journal of Ezra Pound scholarship).

WORK IN PROGRESS: Robert Frost and the New Deal; The Complete Correspondence between Ezra Pound and Senator William E. Borah; Black Flames, a novel about the Spanish Civil War.

BIOGRAPHICAL/CRITICAL SOURCES:

PERIODICALS

Criticism, fall, 1970.
Virginia Quarterly Review, spring, 1970.

*   *   *

PEARSALL, Derek (Albert)   1931-

PERSONAL: Born August 28, 1931, in Birmingham, England. *Education:* University of Birmingham, B.A., 1951, M.A., 1952.

ADDRESSES: Office—Department of English, Harvard University, Cambridge, Mass. 02138.

CAREER: University of London, King's College, London, England, assistant lecturer, 1959-61; lecturer in English, 1961-

65; University of York, Kings Manor, England, lecturer, 1965-68, senior lecturer, 1968-71, reader, 1971-76, professor of English, 1976-87, co-director of Centre for Medieval Studies, 1978-87; Harvard University, Cambridge, Mass., Gurney Professor of English, 1987—. Visiting professor at University of Toronto, 1963-64, University of Minnesota, spring, 1974, University of Connecticut, autumn, 1981-84, and Harvard University, 1985-87; lecturer at universities in the United States, Canada, Europe, England, and Australia.

MEMBER: New Chaucer Society (president, 1988), Early English Text Society (member of council).

WRITINGS:

(Editor) *The Floure and the Leafe and The Assembly of Ladies,* Thomas Nelson, 1962, reprinted, 1980.
(Contributor) D. S. Brewer, editor, *Chaucer and Chaucerians: Critical Studies in Middle English Literature,* Thomas Nelson, 1966.
(Editor with Elizabeth Salter) *Piers Plowman: Selections from the C-Text,* Edward Arnold, 1967.
Gower and Lydgate: Writers and Their Work, edited by Geoffrey Bullough, Longmans, Green, 1969.
(Editor with R. A. Waldron) *Medieval Literature and Civilization: Studies in Memory of G. N. Garmonsway,* Athlone Press, 1969.
(Contributor) W. F. Bolton, editor, *The Middle Ages,* Sphere Books, 1970.
John Lydgate, Routledge & Kegan Paul, 1970.
(With Salter) *Landscapes and Seasons of the Medieval World,* Elek, 1973.
(Contributor) George Watson, editor, *The New Cambridge Bibliography of English Literature,* Cambridge University Press, 1974.
Old English and Middle English Poetry, Routledge & Kegan Paul, 1976.
(Co-author of introduction) *The Auchinleck Manuscript,* Scolar Press, 1977.
Piers Plowman: An Edition of the C-Text, Edward Arnold, 1978.
(Contributor) Flemming G. Anderson and other editors, *Medieval Iconography and Narrative: A Symposium,* Odense University Press, 1980.
(Editor with A. S. G. Edwards) *Middle English Prose: Essays on Bibliographical Problems,* Garland Publishing, 1981.
(Contributor) Bernard S. Levy and Paul E. Szarmach, editors, *The Alliterative Tradition in the Fourteenth Century,* Kent State University Press, 1981.
(Contributor) Boris Ford, editor, *The New Pelican Guide to English Literature,* Penguin, 1982.
(Contributor) David Lawton, editor, *Middle English Alliterative Poetry and Its Literary Background,* D. S. Brewer, 1982.
(Editor) *Manuscripts and Readers in Fifteenth-Century England: The Literary Implications of Manuscript Study,* D. S. Brewer, 1983.
(Contributor) A. J. Minnis, editor, *Gower's Confessio Amantis: Responses and Reassessments,* D. S. Brewer, 1983.
(Editor) Geoffrey Chaucer, *The Nun's Priest's Tale* (variorum edition), University Press, 1983.
(Contributor) Paul G. Ruggiers, editor, *Editing Chaucer: The Great Tradition,* Pilgrim Books, 1984.
(Contributor) R. F. Yeager, editor, *Fifteenth-Century Studies: Recent Essays,* Archon Books, 1984.

(Editor with Nicolette Zeeman) Salter, *Fourteenth-Century English Poetry: Contexts and Readings,* Clarendon Press, 1984.
(Contributor) J. J. McGann, editor, *Textual Criticism and Literary Interpretation,* University of Chicago Press, 1985.
The Canterbury Tales: A Critical Study, Allen & Unwin, 1985.
(Contributor) David Aers, editor, *Medieval Literature: Criticism, Ideology and History,* Harvester Press, 1986.
(Contributor) Piero Boitani and Jill Mann, editors, *The Cambridge Chaucer Companion,* Cambridge University Press, 1986.
(Editor) *Manuscripts and Texts: Editorial Problems in Later Middle English Literature,* D. S. Brewer, 1987.

Contributor of articles and reviews to literature journals. Chairman of advisory committee of *Index of Middle English Prose;* member of advisory board of *Modern Language Review* and *Yearbook of English Studies.*

WORK IN PROGRESS: Editing *Publishing and Book-Production in England, 1375-1475* for Cambridge University Press.

SIDELIGHTS: In *Old English and Middle English Poetry,* Derek Pearsall surveys medieval English poetry. It is the first book in a six-volume *History of English Poetry* projected by Routledge & Kegan Paul. To write such a survey, *Times Literary Supplement* reviewer T. A. Shippey observes, "demands an implausible blend of knowledge, tact and boldness. All these qualities are shown to great advantage by Derek Pearsall."

Shippey notes that one of the book's greatest strengths is "its grasp of the different functions of poetry in pre-modern times." He also admires "the sense of abundance" that Pearsall evokes by elaborating not just on standard anthology pieces, but on others that never "quite made the grade." "No one is going to come away from this book without a note of something new to look up," the reviewer concludes. "*Old English and Middle English Poetry* does not aim at provoking total agreement . . . but it will educate the most learned on some points and stimulate the most ignorant on others."

BIOGRAPHICAL/CRITICAL SOURCES:

PERIODICALS

Times Literary Supplement, September 2, 1977.

*   *   *

PEHNT, Wolfgang 1931-

PERSONAL: Born September 3, 1931, in Kassel, Germany (now West Germany); son of Walter P. (an editor) and Herta P. (a journalist; maiden name, Roland); married Antje P. Dahl (a translator), November 11, 1962; children: Annette, Martin. *Education:* Attended Universities of Marburg, Munich, and Frankfort, 1951-56; received Dr.phil. from University of Frankfort.

ADDRESSES: Home—Goettinger Strasse 7, 5000 Cologne 40, West Germany. *Office*—Deutschlandfunk, Raderbergguertel 40, 5000 Cologne 51, West Germany.

CAREER: Deutschlandfunk (broadcasting company), Cologne, West Germany, editor of arts and architecture, 1963—.

WRITINGS:

NONFICTION; IN ENGLISH

(Editor) *Encyclopedia of Modern Architecture,* Thames & Hudson, 1964.

German Architecture: 1960-70, translated from German by E. Rockwell, Praeger, 1970.

Expressionist Architecture, translated from German by J. A. Underwood and E. Kuestner, Thames & Hudson, 1973.

Expressionist Architecture, in Drawings, translated from German by J. Gabriel, Thames & Hudson, 1985.

NONFICTION; IN GERMAN

Zeiterlebnis und Zeitdeutung in Goethes Lyrik, M. Niemeyer, 1957.

(With Suse Drost) *Bernhard Hoetger: Sein Leben und Schaffen,* H. M. Hauschild, 1974.

(Editor) *Die Stadt in der Bundesrepublik* (title means "The City in the Federal Republic of Germany"), Reclam Verlag, 1974.

(Contributor) G. C. Argan, editor, *Die Kunst des 20. Jahrhunderts* (title means "The Art of the Twentieth Century"), Propylaeen, 1977.

(Contributor) E. Stengraeber, editor, *Deutsche Kunst der 20er und 30er Jahre* (title means "German Art of the Twenties and Thirties"), Verlag F. Bruckmann, 1979.

Die Architektur des Expressionismus, G. Hatje, 1981.

Der Anfang der Bescheidenheit: Kritische Aufsaetze zur Architektur des 20. Jahrhunderts, Prestel, 1983.

Das Ende der Zuversicht: Architektur in diesem Jahrhundert, Siedler, 1983.

Architekturzeichnungen des Expressionismus, G. Hatje, 1985.

(Contributor) Juergen Joedicke, editor, *Architektur in Deutschland '85: Deutscher Architekturpreis 1985,* Kraemer (Stuttgart), 1985.

Hans Hollein; Museum in Moenchengladbach: Architektur als Collage, Fischer Taschenbuch, 1986.

SIDELIGHTS: An architectural historian, Wolfgang Pehnt studies modern architecture, most notably that of the expressionist movement. In *Expressionist Architecture,* Pehnt chronicles the background and development of the buildings of German-speaking countries from 1910 to 1923, a period about which little has been written. In discussing Rudolf Steiner, Bruno Taut, Hans Poelzig, and Erich Mendelsohn, as well as minor figures, Pehnt "makes up for the lack in this study of the movement and its makers," says a *New York Times Book Review* contributor. The reviewer adds that *Expressionist Architecture*'s "coverage is comprehensive and illuminating."

Pehnt told *CA* that he has "no message to humanity." He is "simply trying to find out how things happened."

BIOGRAPHICAL/CRITICAL SOURCES:

PERIODICALS

Choice, October, 1970, June, 1974.
New York Times Book Review, March 23, 1980.
Times Literary Supplement, April 19, 1974.

*   *   *

PEITCHINIS, Stephen G(abriel)   1925-

PERSONAL: Surname is pronounced *Pay*-chin-is; born October 12, 1925, in Macedonia, Greece; became Canadian citizen; married Jacquelyn A. Elliott (a psychologist), September 12, 1952. *Education:* University of Western Ontario, B.A. (honors), 1954, M.A., 1956; London School of Economics and Political Science, Ph.D., 1960.

ADDRESSES: Home—4155 Varsity Rd. N.W., Calgary, Alberta, Canada. *Office*—Department of Economics, University of Calgary, Calgary, Alberta F2N 1N4, Canada.

CAREER: University of Western Ontario, London, instructor in economics and political science, 1955-58, assistant professor, 1960-63, associate professor of labor and public finance, 1963-68; University of Calgary, Calgary, Alberta, professor of economics, 1968-73, currently head of department of economics, dean of Faculty of Business, 1973-76. Associate director, Human Resources Research Council of Alberta, 1969-70; director of research, Council of Ministers of Education of Canada, 1970-71.

MEMBER: Canadian Economics Association, Canadian Industrial Relations Research Institute, American Economic Association, Phi Delta Theta.

WRITINGS:

The Economics of Labour, McGraw (Canada), 1965.
Canadian Labour Economics, McGraw, 1970.
Labour-Management Relations in the Railway Industry, Queen's Printer, 1971.
The Canadian Labour Market, Oxford University Press, 1975.
The Effect of Technological Changes on Educational and Skill Requirements of Industry, Department of Industry, Trade, and Commerce, Ottawa, 1978.
Economic Implications of Computers and Telecommunications Technology, Department of Communications, Ottawa, 1980.
Computer Technology and Employment: Retrospect and Prospect, St. Martin's, 1983.
Issues in Management-Labour Relations in the 1990s, St. Martin's, 1985.

Contributor to journals in Canada, the United States, and Australia.

*   *   *

PENZL, Herbert   1910-

PERSONAL: Born September 2, 1910, in Neufelden, Austria; came to United States, 1936; naturalized U.S. citizen, 1944; son of Johann (an educator) and Hedwig (Schmdit) Penzl; married Vera Rothmueller, August 21, 1950. *Education:* Attended Brown University, 1932-34; University of Vienna, Ph.D., 1935.

ADDRESSES: Home—1125 Grizzly Peak Blvd., Berkeley, Calif. 94708. *Office*—Department of German, University of California, Berkeley, Calif. 94720.

CAREER: Rockford College, Rockford, Ill., assistant professor of German, 1936-38; University of Illinois at Urbana-Champaign, assistant professor of German, 1939-50; University of Michigan, Ann Arbor, associate professor, 1950-53, professor of German, 1953-63; University of California, Berkeley, professor of Germanic philology, 1963—. Smith-Mundt Professor of General Linguistics, University of Kabul, 1959; visiting professor at Tulane University, Georgetown University, 1951-53, Northwestern University, 1960, 1965, University of California, Irvine, 1966, University of Colorado, 1969, Australian National University, 1970, State University of New York at Buffalo, 1971, University of Vienna, 1980-81, University of Regensburg, 1981, University of Munich, 1982-83, and University of Klagenfurt, 1986, Arizona State University, 1988. *Military service:* U.S. Army, 1943-45.

MEMBER: Modern Language Association of America, Linguistic Society of America, American Name Society, American Dialect Society, Societos Linguistica Europaea.

AWARDS, HONORS: Guggenheim fellowship, 1967; Berkeley Citation, 1980.

WRITINGS:

A Grammar of Pashto, American Council of Learned Societies, 1955.
A Reader of Pashto, University of Michigan Press, 1965.
Geschichtliche deutsche Lautlehre, Hueber (Munich), 1969.
Lautsystem und Lautwandel in den althochdeutschen Dialekten, Hueber, 1971.
Methoden der germanischen Linguistik, Niemeyer (Tuebingen), 1972.
(With Marga Reis and Joseph B. Voyles) *Probleme der historischen Phonologie,* F. Steiner, 1974.
Vom Urgermanischen zum Nenhochdeutschen, E. Schmidt, 1975.
Linguistic Method (festschrift), edited by Irmengard Rauch and Gerald F. Carr, Mouton, 1979.
Fruhneuhochdeutsch, P. Lang, 1984.
Althochdeutsch: Eine Einfuehrung in Dialekte und Vorgeschlichte, P. Lang, 1986.

Contributor to linguistic journals.

WORK IN PROGRESS: Mittelhochdeutsch: Eine Einfuehrung in die Dialekte.

*   *   *

PETERS, Ellis
   See PARGETER, Edith Mary

*   *   *

PETERS, George W(illiam) 1907-

PERSONAL: Born September 3, 1907, in Cherson, Russia; came to United States, 1947; naturalized U.S. citizen, 1964; son of Wilhelm Bernhard and Anna (Baerg) Peters; married Susan Lepp, September 29, 1935; children: Mary Ann (Mrs. Ronald Wall), Arnold, Eldon, Lois-Grace (Mrs. Raymond Drever). *Education:* Herbert Bible Institute, Diploma, 1928; Winkler Bible Institute, Diploma, 1930; Tabor College, Th.B., 1939, A.B., 1943, St. Andrew's College, Saskatoon, B.D., 1945; University of Saskatchewan, A.B., 1945; Hartford Seminary, Ph.D., 1947; S.T.D., 1947.

ADDRESSES: Office—3909 Swiss Ave., Dallas Theological Seminary, Dallas, Tex. 75204.

CAREER: Clergyman of Mennonite Brethren Church; missionary in Canadian Northwest, 1930-32; Bethany Bible Institute, Hepburn, Saskatchewan, instructor, 1932-36, principal, 1937-42; Tabor College, School of Theology, Hillsboro, Kan., professor of theology, 1944-45; Pacific Bible Institute, Fresno, Calif., president, 1947-53, professor of theology and missions, 1953-55; Mennonite Brethren Biblical Seminary, Fresno, Calif., professor of theology and missions and dean, 1955-59; Mennonite Brethren Church, Buhler, Kan., pastor, 1959-61; Dallas Theological Seminary, Dallas, Tex., professor of world missions, 1961-78; Freie Hochschule fuer Mission, Stuttgart, West Germany, rector and professor of missiology and world cultures, 1978-87. Associate pastor of churches in Hepburn, Saskatchewan, 1933-42, Fresno, Calif., 1956-59; visiting professor at Winona Lake School of Theology, summers, 1966-68, and at Trinity Evangelical Divinity School, Deerfield, Ill., five summers. Member of Board of Missions and Services, Mennonite Brethren Churches, 1951—;

conductor of conferences and seminars in United States, Canada, New Zealand, Germany, Nigeria, Dahomy, Japan, Korea, and India.

MEMBER: Evangelical Theological Society (member of board of missions and services, 1951—), Association of Professors of Missions, Association of Evangelical Professors of Missions, International Association for Mission Studies, American Society of Missiology.

AWARDS, HONORS: Merit Award from Tabor College, 1971; named one of Outstanding Educators of America, 1972.

WRITINGS:

The Growth of Foreign Missions in the Mennonite Brethren Church, Board of Missions, Mennonite Brethren Church, 1952.
Into His Presence, privately printed, 1953.
The Call of God and the Missionary, privately printed, 1954.
Saturation Evangelism, Zondervan, 1970.
Divorce and Remarriage, Moody, 1972.
A Biblical Theology of Missions, Moody, 1972.
Indonesian Revival: Focus on Timor, Zondervan, 1973.
A Theology of Church Growth, Zondervan, 1981.
Foundations of Mennonite Brethren Missions, Kindred, 1984.

Contributor to church publications. Member of editorial staff, *Sunday School Quarterly* (Mennonite Brethren), 1950-70, and *Union Gospel Press Sunday School Quarterly,* 1965—.

WORK IN PROGRESS: Writing on revivalism in East Africa.

SIDELIGHTS: George W. Peters did missionary and anthropological research in Latin America, 1943-44, and at four other periods: in Australia and Fiji, 1950, Europe and the Near East, 1954, the Far East and India, 1964, Japan, 1965, Africa and Europe, 1968, 1969, Korea, Indonesia, and India, 1970, 1973.

*   *   *

PETERSON, Paul E(lliott) 1940-

PERSONAL: Born September 16, 1940, in Montevideo, Minn.; children: three. *Education:* Concordia College, Moorhead, Minn., B.A. (summa cum laude), 1962; University of Chicago, M.A., 1964, Ph.D., 1967.

ADDRESSES: Office—Department of Political Science, University of Chicago, 5828 South University Ave., Chicago, Ill. 60637.

CAREER: National Opinion Research Center, Chicago, Ill., research assistant, summer, 1964; University of Chicago, Chicago, assistant professor, 1967-72, associate professor, 1972-77, professor of education and political science, 1977—.

AWARDS, HONORS: Woodrow Wilson fellowships, 1962-63, 1966; North Atlantic Treaty Organization (NATO) post-doctoral fellowship, 1968-69; Guggenheim fellow, 1978-79; German Marshall fellow, 1978-79.

WRITINGS:

(With David Greenstone) *Race and Authority in Urban Politics,* Russell Sage, 1973.
School Politics, Chicago Style, University of Chicago Press, 1976.
City Limits, University of Chicago Press, 1981.
The Politics of School Reform, 1870-1940, University of Chicago Press, 1985.

(With Barry G. Rabe and Kenneth K. Wong) *When Federalism Works*, Brookings Institution, 1986.

EDITOR

(With S. M. David) *Urban Politics and Public Policy: The City in Crisis*, Praeger, 1973, 2nd edition, 1976.
Readings in American Democracy, Kendall/Hunt, 1979.
The New Urban Reality, Brookings Institution, 1985.
(With Jon E. Chubb) *The New Direction in American Politics*, Brookings Institution, 1985.

CONTRIBUTOR

James Q. Wilson, editor, *City Politics and Policy Outputs*, Wiley, 1968.
Duane Lockard, editor, *Governing the States and Localities*, Macmillan, 1969.
Frank Lutz, editor, *Toward Improved Urban Education*, Scribner, 1970.
Bryan T. Downes, editor, *Cities and Suburbs*, Wadsworth, 1970.
Robert Sigel, editor, *Political Socialization*, Random House, 1970.
Irving A. Spergel, editor, *Community Organizations*, Sage Publications, Inc., 1972.
Dale Rogers Marshall, editor, *Urban Policy Making*, Sage Publications, Inc., 1979.
Making the Grade, The Fund, 1983.

OTHER

Contributor to *American Political Science Review, Comparative Politics, Journal of Politics, Studies in Philosophy and Education, Discourse*, and *Administrator's Notebook*.†

*   *   *

PFAFF, William (Wendle III)   1928-

PERSONAL: Born December 29, 1928, in Council Bluffs, Iowa; son of William Wendle, Jr. (a businessman) and Adele (Keeline) Pfaff; married Carolyn Frances Cleary, May 1, 1964; children: Nicholas James William, Alexandra Frances Astley. *Education:* University of Notre Dame, B.A., 1949. *Politics:* Independent. *Religion:* Roman Catholic.

ADDRESSES: Home and office—60 Rue de Varenne, 75007 Paris, France. *Agent*—Harold Ober Associates, Inc., 40 East 49th St., New York, N.Y. 10017.

CAREER: Commonweal, New York City, associate editor and foreign correspondent, 1949-55; American Broadcasting Co., News and Public Affairs, New York City, writer, 1955-57; Free Europe Committee, Inc., New York City, executive, 1957-61; Hudson Institute, Inc., Croton-on-Hudson, N.Y., senior member, 1961-78; Hudson Research Europe Ltd., Paris, France, deputy director, 1971-78. *Military service:* U.S. Army, 1951-52; served in Infantry and Army Special Forces.

AWARDS, HONORS: Rockefeller Foundation grant in international studies as senior fellow, Russian Institute, Columbia University, 1962-63.

WRITINGS:

(With Edmund Stillman) *The New Politics: America and the End of the Postwar World*, Coward, 1961, reprinted, Greenwood Press, 1984.
(With Stillman) *The Politics of Hysteria: The Sources of Twentieth-Century Conflict*, Harper, 1964, reprinted, Greenwood Press, 1981.

(With Stillman) *Power and Impotence: The Failure of America's Foreign Policy*, Random House, 1966.
(With Frank E. Armbruster, Raymond Gastil, Herman Kahn, and Stillman) *Can We Win in Vietnam?*, Praeger, 1968.
(Contributor) Irving Howe, editor, *A Dissenter's Guide to Foreign Policy*, Praeger, 1968.
(Contributor) J. G. Kirk, editor, *America Now*, Atheneum, 1968.
(Contributor) Ned O'Gorman, editor, *Prophetic Voices: Ideas and Words on Revolution*, Random House, 1969.
Condemned to Freedom, Random House, 1971.
(Contributor) R. E. Meagher, *Toothing Stones: Rethinking the Political*, Swallow Press, 1972.

Political commentator, *New Yorker*, 1972—; columnist, *International Herald Tribune* and the *Los Angeles Times* syndicate, both 1978—.

BIOGRAPHICAL/CRITICAL SOURCES:

PERIODICALS

Salmagundi, spring-summer, 1986.

*   *   *

PFALTZGRAFF, Robert L., Jr.   1934-

PERSONAL: Born June 1, 1934, in Philadelphia, Pa.; son of Robert L. and Mary (Warriner) Pfaltzgraff; married Diane A. Kressler (an associate professor of political science), May 20, 1967; children: Suzanne Diane, Robert Louis III. *Education:* Swarthmore College, B.A., 1956; University of Pennsylvania, M.B.A., 1958, M.A., 1959, Ph.D., 1964.

ADDRESSES: Home—663 Wallace Dr., Strafford, Pa. 19087. *Office*—Institute for Foreign Policy Analysis, Inc., Central Plaza Bldg., Tenth Floor, 675 Massachusetts Ave., Cambridge, Mass. 02139.

CAREER: University of Pennsylvania, Philadelphia, research assistant, 1959-63, assistant professor of political science, 1964-71, Foreign Policy Research Institute, research associate, 1964-71, deputy director, 1971-73, director, 1973-76; Tufts University, Fletcher School of Law and Diplomacy, Medford, Mass., associate professor, 1971-77, professor of international politics, 1977-83, Shelby Cullom Davis Professor of International Security Studies, 1983—; Institute for Foreign Policy Analysis, Inc., Cambridge, Mass., president, 1976—. Visiting lecturer, Foreign Service Institute, U.S. Department of State, 1970-71; George C. Marshall Professor, College of Europe, 1971-72; guest professor, National Defense College, Tokyo, 1981. President, U.S. Strategic Institute, 1977-79.

MEMBER: International Institute for Strategic Studies (London), Council on Foreign Relations.

AWARDS, HONORS: Guggenheim fellowship, 1968-69; Relm fellow, 1969.

WRITINGS:

(Contributor) *Building the Atlantic World*, Harper, 1963.
Britain Faces Europe: 1957-1967, University of Pennsylvania Press, 1969.
The Atlantic Community: A Complex Imbalance, Van Nostrand, 1969.
(Editor) *Politics and the International System*, Lippincott, 1969, 2nd edition, 1972.
(Co-author) *Contending Theories of International Relations*, Lippincott, 1971, 2nd edition, Harper, 1981.

(Co-editor and contributor) *SALT: Implications for Arms Control in the 1970s*, University of Pittsburgh Press, 1973.

(Co-editor and contributor) *The Superpowers in a Multinuclear World*, Heath, 1974.

(Editor and contributor) *Contrasting Approaches to Strategic Arms Control*, Heath, 1974.

(Co-editor and contributor) *New Technologies and Non-Nuclear Conflict: The Other Arms Race*, Heath, 1975.

The Study of International Relations: A Guide to Information Sources, Gale, 1977.

(Co-author) *The Cruise Missile: Bargaining Chip or Defense Bargain?*, Institute for Foreign Policy Analysis, 1977.

(Co-author) *Soviet Theater Strategy in Europe: Implications for NATO*, U.S. Strategic Institute, 1978.

(Co-editor and contributor) *Arms Transfers to the Third World: The Military Buildup in Less Industrial Countries*, Westview, 1978.

(Co-editor and contributor) *The Atlantic Community in Crisis: Redefining the Atlantic Relationship*, Pergamon, 1979.

(Co-author) *SALT II and U.S.-Soviet Strategic Forces*, Institute for Foreign Policy Analysis, 1979.

Energy Issues and Alliance Relationships: The United States, Western Europe and Japan, Institute for Foreign Policy Analysis, 1980.

(Co-editor and contributor) *Intelligence Policy and National Security*, Macmillan, 1981.

(Co-author) *Power Projection and the Long-Range Combat Aircraft: Missions, Capabilities, and Alternative Designs*, Institute for Foreign Policy Analysis, 1981.

(Co-editor and contributor) *Projection of Power: Perspectives, Perceptions and Problems*, Archon Books, 1982.

(Co-editor and contributor) *The U.S. Defense Mobilization Infrastructure: Problems and Priorities*, Archon Books, 1982.

(Co-author) *The Greens of West Germany: Origins, Strategies and Transatlantic Implications*, Institute for Foreign Policy Analysis, 1983.

(Co-editor) *International Security Dimensions of Space*, Archon Books, 1984.

(Co-editor) *National Security Policy: The Decision-Making Process*, Archon Books, 1984.

(Co-editor) *Security Commitments and Capabilities: Elements of an American Global Strategy*, Archon Books, 1985.

(Co-editor) *Hydra of Carnage: International Linkages of Terrorism and Low-Intensity Operations*, Heath, 1985.

(Co-author) *Shattering Europe's Defense Consensus: The Antinuclear Protest Movement and the Future of NATO*, Pergamon-Brassey, 1985.

(Co-editor) *The Peace Movement in Europe and the United States*, St. Martin's Press, 1985.

(Co-author) *American Foreign Policy: FDR to Reagan*, Harper, 1985.

National Security: Ethics, Strategy and Politics, Pergamon, 1986.

(Co-author) *Strategic Defense and Extended Deterrence*, Institute for Foreign Policy Analysis, 1986.

(Co-editor) *Emerging Doctrines and Technologies: Implications for Global and Regional Political-Military Balances*, Lexington Books, 1987.

(Co-editor) *Selling the Rope to Hang Capitalism?: The Debate on West-East Trade and Technology Transfer*, Pergamon-Brassey, in press.

(Co-editor and contributor) *Protracted Warfare—The Third World Arena: A Dimension of U.S.-Soviet Conflict*, Lexington Books, in press.

Special editor and contributor, *Annals of the American Academy of Political and Social Science*, September, 1981. Contributor to *American Behavioral Scientist, Journal of Common Market Studies, New Republic, European Review, Air University Review, American Spectator, Arms Control and Security, Astronautics and Aeronautics, Atlantic Community Quarterly, Current History, Europa-Archiv, Europe-America Letter, Intercollegiate Review, International Affairs, International Security, International Studies Quarterly, International Security Review, Korea and World Affairs, Spettatore Internazionale, Orbis, Political Science Quarterly, Politique Internationale, Strategic Review*, and *The World and I*. Editor, *Orbis*, beginning, 1973.

WORK IN PROGRESS: Research in numerous areas, including: American foreign policy since World War II; U.S. national security interests in the years leading to the twentieth century; West European perspectives on deterrence, defense, and strategy; U.S. alliance policies in the 1990s; recent trends in international relations theory.

*   *   *

PHILLIPS, (Elizabeth Margaret Ann) Barty   1933-

PERSONAL: Born May 4, 1933, in Dorking, England; daughter of Henry Lloyd (a headmaster) and Margaret (Strawn) Brereton; married Pearson Phillips (a journalist), April 16, 1955 (divorced, 1965); children: John, Jane, Charles. *Education:* Educated in Scotland, England, and Germany.

ADDRESSES: Home and office—Cottage, Marden Hill, Hertford SG14 2NE, England. *Agent*—Curtis Brown, 162-168 Regent St., London W1R 5TA, England.

CAREER: Observer, London, England, home editor, 1968-83; free-lance writer for *Sunday Times, Observer*, and *Sunday Telegraph*, 1983—. Conducted occasional household television program, "Pebble Mill at One," for British Broadcasting Corp., 1975.

WRITINGS:

How to Decorate without Going Broke, Doubleday, 1974.

(With Eleanor Van Zandt) *Interior Decorating Made Simple*, Jupiter Books, 1974.

(Contributor) Beverley Hilton and Maria Kroll, editors, *The House Book*, Mitchell Beazley, 1975.

Wonder Worker: Barty Phillips' Book of Repairs and Renovations, Sidgwick & Jackson, 1977.

(With Nicholas Hills) *Setting up Home*, Design Council, 1978.

Wonder Worker's Complete Book of Cleaning, illustrated by Pat Birrell, Sidgwick & Jackson, 1980, published as *The Complete Book of Cleaning*, Hamlyn, 1981.

The Bargain Book: How Not to Pay the Full Retail Price for Almost Anything, Pan Books, 1982.

Conran and the Habitat Story, Weidenfeld and Nicolson, 1984.

Doing up a Dump, Macdonald, 1985.

(With Vernon Gibberd) *Kitchen Planning and Design*, Windward, 1986.

Your Baby Boy, Piatkus, 1987.

Your Baby Girl, Piatkus, 1987.

The Christopher Wray Book of Decorative Lighting, Webb & Bower, 1987.

House Sense, Macdonald, 1987.

Pay Less to Keep Warm, Macdonald, 1987.

Also consultant editor for *Reader's Digest Household Manual*, Reader's Digest Association, 1977.

PHILLIPS, Jayne Anne 1952-

PERSONAL: Born July 19, 1952, in Buckhannon, W.Va.; daughter of Russell R. (a contractor) and Martha Jane (a teacher; maiden name, Thornhill) Phillips; married Mark Brian Stockman (a physician), May 26, 1985; children: one son, two stepsons. *Education:* West Virginia University, B.A. (magna cum laude), 1974; University of Iowa, M.F.A., 1978.

ADDRESSES: Home—Brookline, Mass. *Agent*—Lynn Nesbit, International Creative Management, 40 West 57th St., New York, N.Y. 10019.

CAREER: Writer. Adjunct associate professor of English, Boston University, Boston, Mass., 1982—; Fanny Howe Chair of Letters, Brandeis University, Waltham, Mass., 1986-87.

MEMBER: Authors League of America, Authors Guild, PEN.

AWARDS, HONORS: Pushcart Prize, Pushcart Press, 1977, for *Sweethearts,* 1979, for short stories "Home" and "Lechery," and 1983, for short story "How Mickey Made It"; Fels Award in fiction, Coordinating Council of Literary Magazines, 1978, for *Sweethearts;* National Endowment for the Arts fellowship, 1978 and 1985; St. Lawrence Award for fiction, 1979, for *Counting;* Sue Kaufman Award for first fiction, American Academy and Institute of Arts and Letters, 1980, for *Black Tickets;* O. Henry Award, Doubleday & Co., 1980, for short story "Snow"; Bunting Institute fellowship, Radcliffe College, 1981, for body of work; National Book Critics Circle Award nomination, American Library Association Notable Book citation, and *New York Times* Best Books of 1984 citation, all 1984, all for *Machine Dreams.*

WRITINGS:

Sweethearts, Truck Press, 1976.
Counting, Vehicle Editions, 1978.
Black Tickets (short stories), Delacorte, 1979.
How Mickey Made It (short stories), Bookslinger, 1981.
Machine Dreams (novel), E. P. Dutton/Lawrence, 1984.
Fast Lanes (short stories), Vehicle Editions, 1984, reprinted, E. P. Dutton/Lawrence, 1987.

CONTRIBUTOR TO ANTHOLOGIES

Henderson, editor, *The Pushcart Prize II: Best of the Small Presses,* Pushcart Press, 1978.
Joyce Carol Oates and Shannon Ravenel, editors, *The Best American Short Stories 1979: Selected from U.S. and Canadian Magazines,* Houghton, 1979.
Abrams, editor, *The O. Henry Awards: Prize Stories 1980,* Doubleday, 1980.
Henderson, editor, *The Pushcart Prize IV: Best of the Small Presses,* Pushcart Press, 1980.
Cassill, editor, *The Norton Anthology of Short Fiction,* Norton, 1981.
Henderson, editor, *The Pushcart Prize VII: Best of the Small Presses,* Pushcart Press, 1983.
Wolff, editor, *Matters of Life and Death,* Wampeter Press, 1983.
Woodman, editor, *Stories About How Things Fall Apart and What Happens When They Do,* Word Beat Press, 1985.
Henry, editor, *Ploughshares Reader: Fiction for the Eighties,* Pushcart Press, 1985.
Hills and Jenks, editors, *Esquire Fiction Reader,* Wampeter Press, 1985.

Jenks, editor, *Soldiers and Civilians: Americans at War and at Home,* Bantam, 1986.
Solomon, editor, *American Wives,* Signet/New American Library, 1986.
Norris, editor, *New American Short Stories,* New American Library, 1986.
Forkner and Samway, editors, *Stories of the Modern South,* Penguin, 1986.
Chipps and Henderson, editors, *Love Stories for the Time Being,* Pushcart Press, 1987.
Carver and Jenks, editors, *American Short Story Masterpieces,* Delacorte, 1987.

OTHER

Contributor of short stories to magazines, including *Granta, Grand Street, Esquire,* and *Rolling Stone.*

SIDELIGHTS: Jayne Anne Phillips "stepped out of the ranks of her generation as one of its most gifted writers," writes Michiko Kakutani in the *New York Times.* "Her quick, piercing tales of love and loss [demonstrate] a keen love of language, and a rare talent of illuminating the secret core of ordinary lives with clearsighted unsentimentality," Kakutani continues. Phillips began as a poet, and that influence is apparent in her prose. Her "use of language is richly sensuous," says Carol Rumens in the *Times Literary Supplement.* "She takes street slang all the way to poetry and back.... Few enough writers at any time have the power to take language and polish it until it is sharp and gleaming again." David Wilk, Phillips' first publisher, is quoted by David Edelstein of *Esquire* as stating that her prose is enhanced by "the specificity of her language, the closely controlled writing on emotion."

The short stories in *Black Tickets,* Phillips' first effort for a commercial press, fall into three basic categories: short stylistic exercises, interior monologues by damaged misfits from the fringes of society, and longer stories about family life. In these stories, notes Michael Adams in the *Dictionary of Literary Biography Yearbook: 1980,* "Phillips explores the banality of horror and the horror of the banal through her examination of sex, violence, innocence, loneliness, illness, madness, various forms of love and lovelessness," and lack of communication. These stories were drawn, observes James N. Baker of *Newsweek,* "from observations she made in her rootless days on the road," in the mid-1970s when she wandered from West Virginia to California and back again, "then developed in her imagination."

"Most of the stories in *Black Tickets,*" states Thomas R. Edwards in the *New York Review of Books,* "examine the lives of people who are desperately poor, morally deadened, in some way denied comfort, beauty, and love." While some of these stories deal with alienation within families, others are "edgy, almost hallucinatory portraits of disaffected, drugged out survivors of the 60s," according to Kakutani in the *New York Times.* Stories of this genre in the collection include "Gemcrack," the monologue of a murderer driven by a voice in his head that he calls "Uncle," and "Lechery," the story of a disturbed teenaged girl who propositions adolescents. These are "brittle episodes of despair, violence and sex," declares *Harper's* reviewer Jeffrey Burke, characterized by "economy and fierceness [and] startling sexuality," in the words of Walter Clemons of *Newsweek.*

Other stories—the strongest of the collection, in some reviewers' opinions—focus on less unique individuals. They are about "more or less ordinary people, in families, who are trying to love each other across a gap," according to Edwards. Stories such as "Home," "The Heavenly Animal," and "Souvenir" all deal with the problems of grown-up children and their aging parents: a young woman's return home forces her divorced mother to come to terms with both her daughter's and her own sexuality; a father attempts to share his life—Catholic senior citizens meals, car repairs—with his daughter and fails; a mother slowly dying of cancer still has the courage to comfort her daughter. In them, Edwards states, "Phillips wonderfully captures the tones and gestures in which familial love unexpectedly persists even after altered circumstances have made [that love] impossible to express directly."

While some reviewers—like Rumens, who calls the dramatic monologues in *Black Tickets* "dazzling"—enjoy Phillips' richly sensuous language, others feel the author's best work is found in the more narrative stories concerning the sense of alienation felt by young people returning home. Stone calls them "the most direct and honest of the longer works in the collection" and states that "the language in these stories serves character and plot rather than the other way around." "The strength in these stories," says Mary Peterson in the *North American Review,* "is that even narrative gives way to necessity: honesty gets more time than forced technique; language is simple and essential, not flashy; and even the hard truth, the cruel one, gets telling."

In his review of *Black Tickets* which appeared in the *New York Times Book Review,* John Irving remarks, "I hope Miss Phillips is writing a novel because she seems at her deepest and broadest when she sustains a narrative, manipulates a plot, develops characters through more than one phase of their life or their behavior. I believe she would shine in a novel." *Machine Dreams,* the next book in Phillips' oeuvre, is indeed a novel. In it, the author uses the family in much the same way she had in some of the stories in *Black Tickets.* The novel tells the story of the Hampson family—Mitch, Jean, their daughter Danner and son Billy—focusing on the years between World War II and the Vietnam War, although it does show glimpses of an earlier, quieter time in Jean's and Mitch's reminiscences. Essentially, it is the story of the family's collapse, told from the point of view of each of the family members.

In a larger sense, however, *Machine Dreams* is about disorientation in modern life, tracing, in the words of Allen H. Peacock in the *Chicago Tribune Book World,* "not only [the Hampson's] uneasy truce with contemporary America but contemporary America's unending war with itself." Mitch and Jean were raised in the days of the Depression, hard times, "but characterized by community, stability and even optimism. You could tell the good guys from the bad ones in the war Mitch fought," says Jonathan Yardley in the *Washington Post Book World. Machine Dreams* is, he concludes, "a story of possibility gradually turning into disappointment and disillusionment," in which the Hampson family's dissolution mirrors "the simultaneous dissolution of the nation." Peacock echoes this analysis, declaring, "This is the stuff of tragedy: disintegration of a family, disintegration by association of a society." Toronto *Globe and Mail* contributor Catherine Bush points out that the machine dreams of the title, "the belief in technology as perpetual onward-and-upward progress; the car as quintessential symbol of prosperity; the glamor of flight . . . become nightmares. Literally, the dream comes crashing down when Billy leaps out of a flaming helicopter in Vietnam." Bush notes that Vietnam itself, however, is not the cause of

the dissolution; appropriately, she observes, Phillips "embeds the war in a larger process of breakdown."

Part of this tragedy lies in the characters' inability to understand or control what is happening to them. Kakutani explains: "Everywhere in this book there are signs that the old certainties, which Miss Phillips's characters long for, have vanished or drifted out of reach. Looking for love, they end up in dissonant marriages and improvised relationships; wanting safety, they settle for the consolation of familiar habits." For them, there are no answers, there is no understanding. "This fundamental inexplicability to things," states Nicholas Spice in the *London Review of Books,* "is compounded for Phillips's characters by their uncertainty about what it is exactly that needs explaining. Emerson's dictum 'Dream delivers us to dream, and there is no end to illusion' might aptly stand as the motto of the book."

In *Machine Dreams,* many reviewers recognize the strength and power of Phillips' prose. "'Black Tickets' posed a dilemma" for readers, states Anne Tyler in the *New York Times Book Review.* "Was it so striking because it was so horrifying, or because it was so brilliantly written? With 'Machine Dreams' we don't have to ask. Its shocks arise from small, ordinary moments, patiently developed, that suddenly burst out with far more meaning than we had expected. And each of these moments owes its impact to an assured and gifted writer." She also rises to the technical challenge of using more than one point of view. As John Skow of *Time* magazine declares, "Phillips . . . expresses herself in all four [character] voices with clarity and grace." Geoffrey Stokes writes in the *Voice Literary Supplement,* "That *Machine Dreams* would be among the year's best written novels was easy to predict," and Yardley calls the novel "an elegaic, wistful, rueful book."

A theme of discontinuity and isolation from the past, similar to that of *Machine Dreams,* is expressed in *Fast Lanes.* Like *Black Tickets,* it is a collection of short stories, whose "structural discontinuities," in the opinion of Paul Skenazy in the *San Francisco Chronicle,* "mirror the disassociated lives Phillips sets before us." The book begins with "stories of youthful drift and confusion and gradually moves, with increasing authority, into the past and what we might call home," comments Jay McInerney in the *New York Times Book Review.* Many of the characters "are joined more by circumstances than by relationships"; they "lack purpose and authority," says Pico Iyer of *Time* magazine. "Their world is fluid, but they do not quite go under. They simply float." These are people, adds Kakutani, for whom "rootlessness has become the price of freedom, alienation the cost of self-fulfillment."

In some reviewers' opinions, *Fast Lanes* suffers in comparison with *Machine Dreams.* For instance, Kakutani states that although "these [first] pieces remain shiny tributes to [the author's] skills—they rarely open out in ways that might move us or shed light on history the way that . . . *Machine Dreams* did." David Remnick, writing for the *Washington Post Book World,* does find that the last two stories in the book—the ones most reminiscent of the novel—are "such strong stories that they erase any disappointment one might have felt in the other five. They are among the best work of one of our most fascinating and gritty writers, and there can be little disappointment in that." Chicago *Tribune Books* contributor Alan Cheuse similarly says that in these stories "you can see [Phillips'] talent grow and flex its muscles and open its throat to reach notes in practice that few of us get to hit when trying our hardest at the height of our powers."

Some of Phillips' best writing, concludes Marianne Wiggins of the *Times Literary Supplement,* concerns "the near-distant, fugitive past—life in the great USA fifteen years ago," reflecting the unsettledness of that period in American life. In some ways her writing returns to themes first expounded by the poets and novelists of the Beat generation; *Los Angeles Times Book Review* contributor Richard Eder calls *Fast Lanes* "the closing of a cycle that began over three decades ago with Kerouac's 'On the Road,'" the novel about the post-World War II generation's journey in search of the ultimate experience. "It is the return trip," Eder concludes, "and Phillips gives it a full measure of pain, laced with tenderness." Mc-Inerney echoes this assessment, calling Phillips "a feminized Kerouac."

In an interview with Phillips for *Publishers Weekly,* Celia Gilbert remarks, "Phillips has always been obsessed by the rootlessness of her generation and the accommodations families have to make to changing times." She adds, "Writing about . . . people on the road and at loose ends, she reflected part of her generation's experience, the generation that was of college age in the '70s." Phillips herself summarized her vision in that same interview: "Unlike the people of the '60s, we didn't have a strong sense of goals, nor the illusion we could make a difference. They were very organized and considered themselves a community. Their enemy was an obvious one. By the '70s, people began to experience a kind of massive ennui. Kids dropping acid did it to obliterate themselves, not to have a religious experience. Only people with a strong sense of self came through. . . . In the '70s there was still enough security so that people felt they could be floaters. Now things are too shaky for that."

CA INTERVIEW

CA interviewed Jayne Anne Phillips by telephone on May 12, 1987, at her home in Brookline, Massachusetts.

CA: You were obviously writing seriously early on; your work began to be published while you were a student at the University of West Virginia. What made you want to be a writer?

PHILLIPS: I never made a decision to be a writer, I just evolved into one, I think because language and books were always a means of travel and a kind of enlarged experience for me.

CA: You started with poetry. Do you consider the very short prose pieces in Sweethearts *and* Counting, *some reprinted in* Black Tickets, *a kind of transition between the poetry and prose?*

PHILLIPS: They were a transition in that I think I taught myself to write fiction by writing extremely compressed fictions. There are a few pieces in *Sweethearts* that are more like prose poems, like "Happy" and "A Stranger in the Night." They're just paragraphs. But as I continued with that form, I really began to write fiction in that I was writing a whole story within a very compressed space. I think writing in that kind of compression means that images carry a tremendous amount of weight, and they also tell a great deal: they tell an entire story. But there's a great difference between the way the images work in fiction and the way image works in a poem.

Those stories have a beginning, middle, and end, but they are scrambled in such a way that time exists with a kind of synchronicity; the past, present, and future operate in the mind almost simultaneously. I'm interested in the way perception itself works, and I think I began to experiment with writing about perception in those very short pieces. As my work has developed, I hope that I have begun to explore the same thing in larger terms.

CA: It's interesting to look at how writing poetry first shapes the approach to fiction. Do you write the longer pieces now starting from a compressed point of view?

PHILLIPS: I don't think I'm working any longer with the compressed point of view. I think making the leap into novel-writing had to do with spinning out what may have begun as something compressed. But having started as a poet means that the writer continues to write line by line rather than by means of an outline. Each sentence is composed as a poet would compose a line of poetry; the words are stressed in a certain way, each word bears a certain weight, and there's a tendency not to use any word that doesn't have to be used.

CA: One of the things you did so well in Black Tickets, *the first book to have wide exposure, was to speak in the voices of what Michael Adams called in* Dictionary of Literary Biography Yearbook: 1980 *grotesques, such as the mass-murderer narrating "Gemcrack." How do you go about putting yourself into such a character, getting the voice?*

PHILLIPS: I think it has to do with ear, with listening in a particular way to how people talk and being able to expand on fragments of heard talk, staying with the sound and then enlarging it.

CA: Is your interest in such a character then primarily putting yourself into that voice and capturing the sound?

PHILLIPS: "Gemcrack" was inspired by media coverage of murderers, particularly the way it's done in America, in which the murderer, if he is that type of psychopath, is able to make his voice heard to millions of people. That's what that story is about. There must be many different kinds of murderers; some of them are insane and some of them probably aren't. It also has to do with an interest in life history, an interest in the beginning of the journey and how people arrive at a certain point.

I think the risky thing about a story like "Gemcrack" or "Lechery" is that, through the first-person voice, you take the reader in before the reader suspects where he or she is. Because they're reading in the first-person voice, readers begin to associate with the voice, and the voice begins to dip into their own experience. It's through taking on the voice that they may develop some understanding, some compassion, even for a grotesque, and some understanding that they might possibly have been this person if they had lived this history. That's where the fear comes in. I think when people read Benjy's monologue in *The Sound and the Fury,* the thing that's so effective is that they begin to take on that perception. It's the only way to really understand, or to truly empathize, to *become* that voice for a moment.

CA: Black Tickets *was first winner of the Sue Kaufman Prize for First Fiction, given by the American Academy and Institute of Arts and Letters, but you'd won other awards and fellowships for the earlier work. Was the Sue Kaufman Prize a kind of milestone?*

PHILLIPS: Yes. Because it was associated with the American Academy, it was momentous. Going to the ceremony and being with other admired writers was important.

CA: The family stories in Black Tickets *seem to have led to the novel* Machine Dreams, *in which you develop the Hampsons' story from the early years of this century into the Vietnam years. And those characters even go beyond the novel, into some of the stories in your new collection,* Fast Lanes. *Can you tell me something about their genesis and the way they continue in your mind?*

PHILLIPS: They are just fully rounded characters, and they are connected in my mind to some version of my hometown. And they are all part of a vanished world, because they are part of a place that no longer exists, a time that no longer exists. They continue to exist for me. I don't know if I'll write about them in the future; I don't like the idea of sequels. But they may appear in some other guise.

CA: In Machine Dreams *you captured not only the physical details of the changing times, but the great psychological difference between the time during and just after World War II and the time of Vietnam. Did the book start out to be political in that sense?*

PHILLIPS: I think good writing is intrinsically political. When I read a book, I like to have a sense of the outside world. But the sense of the world can be conveyed in a very interior fashion by some writers. Faulkner wasn't writing to fix the South in readers' minds; he was writing about people who were very rooted in where they were, and the South was defined by extension. I think the same thing is true of someone like Donald Barthelme: he surely doesn't set out to think about the urban New York consciousness, but that consciousness comes across in the jumps and leaps he makes, the fragmented way that he writes. So I believe that if you manage to convey a rounded character, you're conveying a whole history, not only of that person but of the place in which he developed. Part of what fascinated me about writing a book that ranged over time was just to find a way into those times by knowing the characters, by inhabiting the characters and trying to be in the vanished world.

CA: There are details in the book about such things as how an unused parlor was "dusted every day, spotless, and the floor was polished once a week with linseed rags fastened onto a broom." That's more than a fact; it tells something about a way of life. Did many such details come from talking with members of your own family?

PHILLIPS: Details like that may have been overheard, but that detail was invented. It just seemed to me like a good way to polish a floor.

CA: Jessica Lange bought the film rights to Machine Dreams. *Is there any movie news?*

PHILLIPS: There's a script that's been developing for the past year, and there's now a final version. A director has not yet been hired. The film might be quite good, though it's not trying to convey the whole book. It starts in the '40s, though it goes back farther than that in brief flashbacks. I'm just thinking of it as something totally separate from the book, because otherwise it'll seem like a reduction.

CA: In Fast Lanes *you pursue the drifters again, as well as the family characters. And as Jay McInerney pointed out in his review of the book in the* New York Times Book Review, *"the two worlds are not mutually exclusive." He concluded his review by saying that you appear "to be evolving into a regional writer and family chronicler, a cousin of Reynolds Price and Eudora Welty." Do you see your work taking that specific direction?*

PHILLIPS: What does "regional writer" mean? If anyone is a world-class writer, it's Eudora Welty. Her work is respected and emulated all over the world; her work will obviously last. If I can be a regional writer like Eudora Welty, I'll be very happy. But the term "regional writer" is such a silly one. I don't know who uses it except people who've never lived outside New York City. I was only glad that McInerney connected it to people like Reynolds Price and Eudora Welty. There's nothing regional about them—their work has to do with the world.

I appreciated Richard Eder's interesting review, which appeared in the *Los Angeles Times.* It was very perceptive, having to do with techniques in writing stories. And he talked about the first-person stories in *Fast Lane* being different in that they presumed a listener, so that there really were two people there—the speaker and also a listener. That was an aspect of the stories that struck me as true, one I hadn't considered.

CA: You've said that your work is autobiographical in the sense that method acting is autobiographical: "the feeling is real although the circumstances are very different." Could you talk a bit about how that works in the creation of a story or a novel? Does it begin with something very close to home and gain distance in the writing?

PHILLIPS: I think the compelling reason for writing, the risk the writer takes in becoming the characters, has to spring from something autobiographical in the sense that any family a writer creates is going to come in some way from what the writer experienced as a child, as a parent, or whatever. That is how you learn what family is. There may be very basic differences between what you write and what you lived, but I think the feeling, the experience of intimacy and the fear of loss of intimacy, springs directly from what people have experienced.

Likewise the political events that people live through are firmly felt in the way that they have influenced relationships. I think the reason American writers are said to write less politically than European writers is simply because most Americans, because of our system of government, are insulated from political events. Our basic daily lives are not turned inside-out as easily as the lives of Europeans. What happens in the news is what happens in the news. We read about the various revelations about the contras, but until there's an actual war in Central America, Americans will not start writing books about it, because it's not part of daily life, it's just something we hear about. We can be afraid about it, we can think about it, we can talk about it and organize against it or whatever, but until what we can buy in the grocery store is affected, until it hits home, it's not really part of our lives. But if the Italian government topples, people in France are very much affected. They feel it immediately.

If you write about politics in America, you have to deal in very subtle terms, because we are incredibly insulated by the supposed stability of our government, and we're also insulated from the effects of the government policy. The whole aim of our government is to keep things running smoothly here so that they'll all get re-elected, whereas the effects of a lot of their policies come down directly on the heads of people who are quite far away.

CA: You've said there are pauses between books. When you aren't actually writing anything, is the next work somehow cooking in your mind?

PHILLIPS: I hope so!

CA: Is it a conscious process of thought, or something that's happening more on a subconscious level?

PHILLIPS: I do a lot of thinking about it, but I'm not sure that the writing arises from my thinking. I think there's a breakthrough moment in which the writer hears the voice of the book, and the writer is working toward that moment. It's a totally mysterious process.

CA: Are you doing any teaching now?

PHILLIPS: I just taught at Brandeis this past semester, and I'm not teaching now. That was the first time I'd taught in three years. I find that I just don't have time to teach. I have a family, and I find that I just don't have time to teach.

CA: The Iowa Writers' Workshop seems to have been helpful to you. How do you feel about its effect on your development, and the advisability of the writing school experience for beginning writers generally?

PHILLIPS: The workshop was helpful in that it was a first experience within a community of writers; my development until then had been isolated. My first (small press) book had been published before I went to Iowa, and my sense of myself as a writer was firmly established. In that sense, I wasn't a "beginning writer." I advise my students not to go from one (undergrad) writing program to another, even more high-powered one, but to take some time to travel, work, be alone. The writer benefits from having been alone with the work. The commitment then is purely his.

CA: You don't seem to see a lot of other writers. When you've settled in new places, you've often chosen to live in surroundings in which you could be rather anonymous. Has that kind of isolation been important to you?

PHILLIPS: I find that writing, like any art, requires a certain amount of emotional space. I "hear" my work more intensely in relative quiet.

CA: Would you like to comment on your association with Sam Lawrence?

PHILLIPS: It's a tremendous luxury for a writer to have an ongoing relationship with a trusted publisher. It means that all you have to do is write the work. That's difficult enough in itself. But it's a great blessing to know that if you succeed at creating the book and making it powerful, you'll be able to trust that the publisher will then take it and publish it the best way possible.

BIOGRAPHICAL/CRITICAL SOURCES:

BOOKS

Contemporary Literary Criticism, Gale, Volume XV, 1980, Volume XXXIII, 1985.
Dictionary of Literary Biography Yearbook: 1980, Gale, 1981.

PERIODICALS

Books & Arts, November 23, 1979.
Books and Bookmen, December, 1984.
Books of the Times, January, 1980.
Boston Review, August, 1984.
Chicago Tribune, September 30, 1979.
Chicago Tribune Book World, June 24, 1984, July 22, 1984.
Commonweal, October 19, 1984.
Detroit News, January 27, 1980, December 13, 1984.
Elle, April, 1987.
Esquire, December, 1985.
Globe and Mail (Toronto), July 28, 1984.
Harper's, September, 1979.
Kirkus Reviews, February 15, 1987.
Listener, December 13, 1984.
London Review of Books, February 7, 1985.
Los Angeles Times Book Review, July 9, 1984, April 19, 1987.
Ms., June, 1984, June, 1987.
New Leader, December 3, 1979.
New Republic, December 24, 1984, September 2, 1985.
New Statesman, November 9, 1984.
Newsweek, October 22, 1979, July 16, 1984.
New York Review of Books, March 6, 1980.
New York Times, June 12, 1984, June 28, 1984, January 6, 1985, April 4, 1987, April 11, 1987.
New York Times Book Review, September 30, 1979, July 1, 1984, March 17, 1985, May 5, 1985, May 3, 1987.
North American Review, winter, 1979.
Observer, October 28, 1984.
Publishers Weekly, May 9, 1980, June 8, 1984, February 27, 1987.
Quill and Quire, September, 1984.
San Francisco Chronicle, July 22, 1984, April 5, 1987.
Spectator, November 3, 1984.
Threepenny Review, spring, 1981.
Time, July 16, 1984, June 1, 1987.
Times Literary Supplement, November 14, 1980, November 23, 1984, September 11, 1987.
Tribune Books (Chicago), April 19, 1987.
Village Voice, October 29, 1979.
Voice Literary Supplement, June, 1984, February, 1986.
Wall Street Journal, July 25, 1984.
Washington Post Book World, December 21, 1979, June 24, 1984, April 26, 1987.
West Coast Review of Books, November, 1984.

—*Sketch by Kenneth R. Shepherd*

—*Interview by Jean W. Ross*

*   *   *

PICCHIO, Riccardo 1923-

PERSONAL: Born September 7, 1923, in Alessandria, Italy; son of Carlo (a writer) and Maria (Fontana) Picchio; married Maria Simonelli (a university professor), September 8, 1968. *Education:* University of Rome, Doctorate in humanities, 1946, Libera Docenza, 1953; Ecole Nationale des Langues Vivantes, diploma, 1950.

ADDRESSES: Home—168 Westwood Rd., New Haven, Conn. 06515. *Office*—Hall of Graduate Studies, Box 11, Yale University, New Haven, Conn. 06520.

CAREER: Avanti (newspaper), Rome, Italy, member of editorial board, 1944-47; University of Warsaw, Warsaw, Poland, lecturer in Italian, 1947-49; University of Florence, Florence, Italy, Extraordinary Professor of Russian Literature, 1954-61; University of Rome, Rome, professor and director of Institute of Slavic Philology, 1961-68; Yale University, New Haven, Conn., professor of Slavic languages and literatures, 1968—. Visiting professor at University of Pisa, 1959-61, and Columbia University, 1965-66. *Military service:* Italian Army, 1943; active in underground, 1943-44.

MEMBER: International Committee of Slavists, Italian Association of Slavists (secretary-general, 1961-68), American Association for the Advancement of Slavic Studies, Mediaeval Academy of America, Academy Adam Mickiewicz (Bologna).

AWARDS, HONORS: Order of SS, Cyril and Methodius, first class (Bulgaria), 1963; M.A., Yale University, 1968.

WRITINGS:

Storia della letteratura russa antica, Nuova Accademia Editrice, 1959, 2nd edition, 1968.
I racconti di Cechov, Edizioni Radio Italiani, 1961.
La Letteratura russa antica, Sansoni, 1968.
L'Europa Orientale dal Rinascimento all'Illuminismo, Vallardi, 1970.
Studi sulla questione della lingua, Editrice Ateneo, 1971.
Etudes litterairs slavo-romanes, Licosa-Sansani, 1978.
(Editor with Harvey Goldblatt) *Aspects of the Slavic Language Question,* three volumes, Slavica, 1984.

Contributor to numerous periodicals. Editor, *Ricerche Slavistiche* (Rome), 1953, and *Studia Historica et Philologica.*

SIDELIGHTS: Riccardo Picchio told *CA* that he has devoted his work to international collaboration. He is antifascist and believes "in the humanistic heritage."

*   *   *

PINKERTON, James R(onald)   1932-

PERSONAL: Born December 1, 1932, in Milwaukee, Wis.; son of Adam Brownlie and Florence Louise (Korn) Pinkerton; married Marjorie Glass, June 29, 1957; children: Steven James, Kathryn Lynn. *Education:* Carroll College, Waukesha, Wis., B.A., 1954; University of Wisconsin—Madison, M.B.A., 1958, M.S., 1962, Ph.D., 1965. *Politics:* Independent. *Religion:* Presbyterian.

ADDRESSES: Home—1014 Westport Dr., Columbia, Mo. 65201. *Office*—Department of Rural Sociology, University of Missouri, Columbia, Mo. 65211.

CAREER: Eastern Michigan University, Ypsilanti, assistant professor of sociology, 1964-65; University of Missouri—Columbia, assistant professor, 1965-69, associate professor of rural sociology, 1969—, faculty research assistant, 1965-69, research associate, 1969-75. *Military service:* U.S. Army, personnel specialist, 1954-56; served in France.

MEMBER: American Sociological Association, Population Association of America, American Association of University Professors, Rural Sociological Society, Midwest Sociological Society, Gamma Sigma Delta.

AWARDS, HONORS: Faculty fellowships from Summer Manpower Research Institute of Iowa State University's Industrial Relations Center, 1968, 1969; research grant from U.S. Department of Labor, 1973.

WRITINGS:

The Relation of Socioeconomic Characteristics of Metropolitan Areas to Variations in the Mortality Rate of the Middle-Aged Population (monograph), Research Center, School of Business and Public Administration, University of Missouri—Columbia, 1967.
Projections of Socioeconomic Data to 1967, 1975, and 1990: Summary Report (monograph), Research Center, School of Business and Public Administration, University of Missouri—Columbia, 1968.
(With Rex R. Campbell and Floyd K. Harmston) *Projections of Socioeconomic Data to 1967, 1975, and 1990,* Research Center, School of Business and Public Administration, University of Missouri—Columbia, 1968.
Residential Patterns of Socioeconomic Strata in Missouri's Metropolitan Areas (monograph), Research Center, School of Business and Public Administration, University of Missouri—Columbia, 1969.
(Editor with wife, Marjorie J. Pinkerton) *Outdoor Recreation and Leisure: A Reference Guide and Selected Bibliography,* Research Center, School of Business and Public Administration, University of Missouri—Columbia, 1969.
Socioeconomic Determinants of Urban Poverty Area Workers' Labor Force Participation and Income, National Technical Information Service, 1978.
(With Rex. R. Campbell and Robert L. McNamara) *Social Assessment for Mark Twain National Forest* (monograph), Department of Rural Sociology, University of Missouri—Columbia, 1981.
(With Dana E. Gallup and Cathy A. Hughes) *Social Analysis of User and Local Attitudes toward Wilderness Management* (monograph), Department of Rural Sociology, University of Missouri—Columbia, 1985.
(With Edward Wesley Hassinger) *The Human Community,* Macmillan, 1986.

Contributor to proceedings. Contributor to *Rural Sociology, Land Economics, Demography, Urban Affairs Quarterly,* and *American Journal of Sociology.*

WORK IN PROGRESS: Research on changes in city-suburban differences in age structure and rural extension information centers; writing a study guide for a course entitled "Urban Sociology."

*   *   *

PISHKIN, Vladimir   1931-

PERSONAL: Born March 12, 1931, in Belgrade, Yugoslavia; came to United States in 1946, naturalized, 1951; son of Vasily (a physician) and Olga (Bartosh) Pishkin; married Dorothy Louise Martin, September 12, 1953; children: Gayle Ann, Mark Vladimir. *Education:* Attended Montana School of Mines (now Montana College of Mineral Science and Technology), 1947-48; Montana State University, B.A., 1951, M.A., 1955; University of Utah, Ph.D., 1958. *Politics:* Independent.

ADDRESSES: Home—3113 Northwest 62nd St., Oklahoma City, Okla. 73112. *Office*—Department of Psychology, University of Oklahoma, Box 26901, Oklahoma City, Okla. 73190; and 151A Veterans Administration Hospital, 921 Northwest 13th St., Oklahoma City, Okla. 73104.

CAREER: Montana State University, Missoula, instructor in psychology, 1954-55; Montana State Hospital, Warm Springs, clinical psychologist, 1955-56; University of Utah, Salt Lake City, senior clinical assistant, 1957-58; Veterans Administration Neuropsychiatric Hospital, Salt Lake City, intern in clinical psychology, 1957-59; Veterans Administration Hospital, Tomah, Wis., director of Neuropsychiatric Research Laboratories, 1959-62; University of Oklahoma, Oklahoma City, assistant professor, 1962-63, associate professor of medical psychology, 1963-67, associate professor of biological psychology, 1966-67, professor, 1967—, professor of research psychology, 1967—, adjunct associate professor at Norman campus, 1962-70, adjunct professor, 1970—; Veterans Administration Hospital, Oklahoma City, chief research psychologist in Behavioral Science Laboratories and associate director of laboratories, 1962—, associate chief of staff in medical research, 1970—.

Visiting professor of psychology, Oklahoma City University, 1963—, Interboro General Hospital, 1967, Montana State University, 1967, University of Florida, 1967, University of Colorado, 1968, and California State University, San Diego (now San Diego State University), 1972. Licensed by Oklahoma Board of Examiners of Psychologists, 1966. Member of board of directors, Psychology Press, 1963—; member of national merit review board in behavioral sciences, Veterans Administration Central Office, 1972—; consultant to U.S. Department of State and to Walter Reed Army Hospital. *Military service:* U.S. Air Force Reserve, 1952-54.

MEMBER: American Psychological Association (fellow), Psychonomic Society, American Association for the Advancement of Science (fellow), Midwestern Psychological Association, Southwestern Psychological Association (president, 1972—), Oklahoma Psychological Association, Wisconsin Psychological Association, New York Academy of Sciences, Sigma Xi, Imperial Council of the Ancient Arabic Order of the Nobles of the Mystic Shrine for North America.

AWARDS, HONORS: National Science Foundation grant to visit Science Institute of the Soviet National Committee, with International Programme of the Academy of Sciences in Moscow and Leningrad, 1972; distinguished service award from Junior Chamber of Commerce of America.

WRITINGS:

(With Frederick C. Thorne) *The Ideological Survey: A Study of Opinion and Belief,* Clinical Psychology Publishing, 1965.
(Contributor) J. P. Lysaught, editor, *Programmed Instruction in Medical Education,* Rochester Clearing House, 1965.
(With J. T. Shurley and A. Wolfgang) *A New Method for Assessing Drug Effects upon Human Decision Making and Stress: Hydrosyzine in Hospitalized Psychiatric Patients,* Medical Division, Pfizer Laboratories, Volume I, 1966.
(Contributor) James K. Dent, editor, *A Bibliographic Index of Evaluation in Mental Health,* National Institute of Mental Health, 1966.
(With J. L. Mathis and C. M. Pierce) *Basic Psychiatry: A Primer of Concepts and Terminology,* Appleton, 1968, 2nd edition, 1972.
(Contributor) *Biomedical and Behavioral Science Research in Antarctica,* National Academy of Science and National Research Council, 1971.
(With Thorne) *The Personal Development Study,* Clinical Psychology Publishing, 1977.

(With Thorne) *The Objective Measurement of Femininity,* Clinical Psychology Publishing, 1977.
(With Thorne) *The Measurement of Personal Health,* Clinical Psychology Publishing, 1978.

Contributor to transactions, proceedings, and bulletins. Contributor of more than one hundred-fifty articles to psychology journals including *Psychological Abstracts, Journal of Clinical Psychology, Journal of Biological Psychology, Journal of Abnormal Psychology, Psychonomic Science,* and *Diseases of the Nervous System. Journal of Clinical Psychology,* associate editor, 1969-74, editor-in-chief, 1974—.

WORK IN PROGRESS: Research on cognitive functioning, psychopathology, and sensory isolation.

*   *   *

PLATT, Charles 1945-
(Aston Cantwell, Robert Clarke, Charlotte Prentice; Blakely St. James, a house pseudonym)

PERSONAL: Born April 26, 1945, in London, England; son of Maurice and Marjorie (Hubbard) Platt; married Leah Wallach, 1971 (divorced); married Nancy Weber, 1976 (divorced); children: (second marriage) Rose. *Education:* Attended Cambridge University; London College of Printing, Higher Diploma in Printing Management. *Politics:* Libertarian.

ADDRESSES: Agent—Merrilee Heifetz, Writers House, 21 West 26th St., New York, N.Y. 10010.

CAREER: New Worlds (monthly magazine of speculative fiction), London, England, designer, 1966-68, production manager, 1969, editor, 1969-70, U.S. editor, 1974-75, editor and publisher (final issue), 1979; Zero Population Growth, New York City, copywriter and graphic designer, 1970; New School for Social Research, New York City, member of faculty, 1971—, instructor in contemporary science fiction, 1971-80, instructor in basic principles of technology, 1977-80, instructor in computer programming and use, 1983—. Adjunct assistant professor of creative writing, Staten Island Community College, 1972; instructor in writing and publishing, Apple Skills Exchange and International Skills Exchange, 1977-80. Personal assistant and book-jacket designer, Clive Bingley Ltd. (publisher), 1967-68; consulting editor in science fiction, Avon Books, 1972-74; science fiction editor, Condor Publishing, 1977-78; editor, Franklin Watts, Inc., 1986—; editor and publisher, Black Sheep Books, 1987—. Writer of documentation for computer software, Dwo Quong Fok Lok Sow, Inc., 1982-84; freelance computer programmer and computer consultant, 1984—.

AWARDS, HONORS: Locus Award for nonfiction, 1985, for *Dream Makers,* Volume II: *The Uncommon Men and Women Who Write Science Fiction.*

WRITINGS:

FICTION

Garbage World (science fiction), Berkley Publishing, 1967.
City Dwellers (near-future novel), Sidgwick & Jackson, 1970.
The Gas (science fiction and erotica), Ophelia Press, 1970, revised edition, Savoy Books, 1979.
The Image Job (suspense), Ophelia Press, 1971.
Planet of the Voles: A Science Fiction Novel, Putnam, 1971.
The Power and the Pain (erotica), Ophelia Press, 1971.
(Editor with Michael Moorcock) *New Worlds 5* (science fiction), Avon, 1974.

(Editor with Hilary Bailey) *New Worlds 6* (science fiction), Avon, 1975.

(Under pseudonym Blakely St. James) *A Song for Christmas* (erotica), Playboy Press, 1976.

Sweet Evil (suspense), Berkley Publishing, 1977.

Twilight of the City (near-future novel), Macmillan, 1977.

(Under pseudonym Blakely St. James) *Christina Enchanted* (erotica), Playboy Press, 1980.

(Under pseudonym Charlotte Prentice) *Love's Savage Embrace* (historical romance), Jove, 1981.

(Under pseudonym Blakely St. James) *Christina's Touch* (erotica), Playboy Press, 1982.

(Under pseudonym Aston Cantwell) *Double Delight* (novel), Warner Books, 1983.

(Under pseudonym Aston Cantwell) *Tease for Two* (novel), Warner Books, 1983.

(Under pseudonym Robert Clarke) *Less than Human* (science fiction satire), Avon, 1986 (published in England under own name, Grafton Books, 1987).

Plasm (science fiction), Signet, 1987.

Childhood's Troopers (science fiction satire), Avon, 1988.

SOMA (science fiction), Signet, 1988.

NONFICTION

T-Shirting: A Do-It-Yourself Guide to Getting It on Your Chest (crafts guide), Hawthorne, 1975.

Outdoor Survival (guide for young adults), F. Watts, 1976.

Using WP-6502 (technical reference), Dwo Quong Fok Lok Sow, 1980.

Dream Makers: The Uncommon People Who Write Science Fiction (profiles; also see below), Berkley Publishing, 1980, Volume II: *The Uncommon Men and Women Who Write Science Fiction*, 1983.

Graphics Guide to the Commodore 64 (computers), Sybex, 1984.

BASIC without Maths (computers), Zomba Books, 1984.

More from Your Micro (computers), Avon, 1985.

Artificial Intelligence in Action: Commodore 64 (computers), Trillium, 1985.

Dream Makers: Science Fiction and Fantasy Writers at Work (profiles; contains new material and selections from *Dream Makers* Volumes I and II), Ungar, 1987.

OTHER

(Contributor) Judith Merril, editor, *England Swings SF: Stories of Speculative Fiction*, Doubleday, 1968 (published in England as *Space-Time Journal*, Granada, 1972).

(With Thomas M. Disch and Marilyn Hacker) *Highway Sandwiches* (poetry), privately printed, 1970.

(Contributor) Richard C. Kostelanetz, editor, *Breakthrough Fictioneers*, Something Else Press, 1973.

(Author of introduction) R. A. Lafferty, *The Devil Is Dead*, Gregg, 1977.

(Author of introduction) A. E. Van Vogt, *The Players of Null-A*, Gregg, 1977.

(Author of introduction) Michael Moorcock, *The Condition of Muzak*, Gregg, 1978.

(Author of introduction) Philip K. Dick, *The Zap Gun*, Gregg, 1979.

The Whole Truth Computer Handbook (humor), Avon, 1984, (published in England with David Langford as *Micromania: The Whole Truth about Home Computers*, Gollancz, 1984).

How to Be a Happy Cat (humor), Main Street Press, 1987.

Also contributor to Samuel R. Delany, Jr., editor, *Quark*, Popular Library, to Damon Knight, editor, *Orbit*, Putnam, and to Jones, editor, *The New SF*. Also author of computer programs *Keyboard Command* and *Zippy Floppy*, both Trillium Press, and *Madelbrew, Life Forms, Cell Systems*, and *Cell Systems II*, all self-published. New York columnist for *Los Angeles Free Press;* columnist for *Interzone* (England), and *Hayakawa SF Magazine* (Japan); regular columnist for *The Fetish Times*, 1978-80. Contributor of criticism, short stories and reviews to periodicals, including *Harper's, Omni, Village Voice, Microcomputing, Magazine of Fantasy and Science Fiction, Foundation, Isaac Asimov's Science Fiction Magazine*, and *Science Fiction Review*. Editor and publisher, *Patchin Review*, 1981-85; editor and publisher, *REM Magazine*, 1985—.

SIDELIGHTS: *Dream Makers*, Charles Platt's collections of interviews with science fiction and fantasy authors, has been described by Barry N. Malzberg in the *Magazine of Fantasy and Science Fiction* as "one of the most important works about science fiction and its processes." "What *Dream Makers* is about," concludes Malzberg, "is nothing other than the effect the writing of science fiction has had upon a group of people who are otherwise as heterogeneous and scattered as any group might be." In the collections, Platt "experiments with the role of the critic," says Donald M. Hassler in the *Science Fiction and Fantasy Book Review*. He continues, "Platt's critical attempts to break old categories and establish new ones with regard to science fiction and fantasy and his astute diagnosis of the publishing and marketing impact on the literature . . . permeate the book."

AVOCATIONAL INTERESTS: Photography, music.

BIOGRAPHICAL/CRITICAL SOURCES:

BOOKS

Platt, Charles, *Dream Makers: The Uncommon People Who Write Science Fiction*, Berkley Publishing, 1980, Volume II: *The Uncommon Men and Women Who Write Science Fiction*, 1983.

PERIODICALS

Analog Science Fiction/Science Fact, October, 1983.
Booklist, February 1, 1981, June 1, 1983.
Chicago Tribune Book World, November 16, 1980.
Choice, March, 1981.
Magazine of Fantasy and Science Fiction, September, 1981, November, 1983.
Science Fiction and Fantasy Book Review, June, 1979, June, 1983.
Science Fiction Review, May, 1976, May, 1977, February, 1981, February, 1984, May, 1984.
Science Fiction Studies, November, 1981.
Voice of Youth Advocates, December, 1983.
Washington Post Book World, March 4, 1984, February 3, 1985, June 14, 1987.

*   *   *

PLESUR, Milton   1927-1987

PERSONAL: Born April 16, 1927, in Buffalo, N.Y.; died November 14, 1987, after a heart attack. *Education:* New York State College for Teachers (now State University of New York College at Buffalo), B.S., 1947; University of Buffalo (now State University of New York at Buffalo), M.A., 1949; University of Rochester, Ph.D., 1954.

ADDRESSES: *Home*—105 Wendover Ave., Kenmore, N.Y. 14223. *Office*—Department of History, State University of New York at Buffalo, Buffalo, N.Y. 14261.

CAREER: High school teacher of social studies in Buffalo, N.Y., and Niagara Falls, N.Y., 1949-50, 1953-55; State University of New York at Buffalo, instructor, 1952-56, assistant professor, 1956-64, associate professor, 1964-71, professor of history, 1971-87, assistant dean of University College, 1959-66; acting dean, 1965.

MEMBER: Organization of American Historians, Popular Culture Association, American Jewish Historical Society, American Film Institute, Alpha Sigma Lambda, Kappa Delta Pi, Phi Eta Sigma.

WRITINGS:

(Contributor) Isidore S. Meyer, editor, *Early History of Zionism in America*, American Jewish Historical Society and Theodor Herzl Foundation, 1958.
(Contributor) Raphael Patai, *Herzl Year Book Studies in the History of Zionism in America, 1894-1919*, Herzl Press, 1963.
(Contributor) H. Wayne Morgan, editor, *The Gilded Age: A Reappraisal*, Syracuse University Press, 1963.
(Editor) *The 1920s: Problems and Paradoxes*, Allyn & Bacon, 1969.
(Editor) *Intellectual Alienation in the 1920s*, Heath, 1970.
(Editor) *Creating an American Empire: 1865-1914*, Pitman-Ozer, 1971.
America's Outward Thrust: Approaches to Foreign Affairs, 1865-1890 (monograph), Northern Illinois University Press, 1971.
(Contributor) Rexford G. Tugwell and Thomas E. Cronin, editors, *The Presidency Reappraised*, Praeger, 1974.
(Contributor) Paul L. Murphy, editor, *Political Parties in American History*, Putnam, 1974.
(Contributor) *An American Historian: Essays to Honor Selig Adler*, State University of New York at Buffalo, 1980.
Jewish Life in Twentieth-Century America: Challenge and Accommodation, Nelson-Hall, 1982.

Contributor to *McGraw-Hill Encyclopedia of World Biography, Encyclopedia Hebraica, Herzl Year Book*, and *Encyclopedia Judaica*. Contributor of about fifty articles and reviews to periodicals and to professional journals, including *American Jewish Historical Quarterly, American History Illustrated, Review of Politics, African World, Pacific Historical Review, Journal of American History, Political Science Quarterly, American Political Science Review, Ohio History, Historian, Social Education, Journal of Popular Culture, American Classic Screen*, and *Journal of Popular Film*.

WORK IN PROGRESS: A book on the attitudes of selected motion picture personnel (i.e., actors, directors, producers, writers) toward the film industry from the 1920s through the 1940s.

[Death information provided by Kay Becker, Department of History, State University of New York at Buffalo]

*   *   *

PLUMPP, Sterling D(ominic)   1940-

PERSONAL: Born January 30, 1940, in Clinton, Miss.; son of Cyrus Hampton (a laborer) and Mary (Emmanuel) Plumpp; married Falvia Delgrazia Jackson (a registered nurse), December 21, 1968; children: Harriet Nzinga. *Education:* St. Benedict's College (now Benedictine College), student, 1960-62; Roosevelt University, B.A., 1968, graduate study, 1969-71.

ADDRESSES: *Home*—1212 S. Michigan Ave., Apt. 1210, Chicago, Ill. 60605. *Office*—Department of Black Studies, University of Illinois at Chicago Circle, P.O. Box 4348, Chicago, Ill. 60680.

CAREER: Main Post Office, Chicago, Ill., distribution clerk, 1962-64, 1966-69; North Park College, Chicago, Ill., counselor, 1969-71; University of Illinois at Chicago Circle, instructor, 1971-84, associate professor in Black Studies, 1984—. Poet in residence, Evanston School, Ill., and Youth Black Heritage Theater Ensemble Studio. Director of Young Writer's Workshop for Urban Gateways. *Military service:* U.S. Army, 1964-66.

MEMBER: National Association for the Advancement of Colored People, Operation PUSH.

AWARDS, HONORS: Illinois Arts Council Literary Award, 1975, for an excerpt from *Clinton;* Broadside Press Publishers Award, 1975; Illinois Arts Council Award, 1981, and Carl Sandburg Literary Award for Poetry, Friends of the Chicago Public Library, 1983, both for *The Mojo Hands Call, I Must Go.*

WRITINGS:

Portable Soul, Third World Press, 1969, revised edition, 1974.
Half Black, Half Blacker, Third World Press, 1970.
(Contributor) Patricia L. Brown, Don L. Lee, and Francis Ward, editors, *To Gwen with Love*, Johnson, 1971.
Muslim Men, Broadside Press, 1972.
Black Rituals, Third World Press, 1972.
Steps to Break the Circle, Third World Press, 1974.
Clinton (poems), Broadside Press, 1976.
(Editor) *Somehow We Survive: An Anthology of South African Writing*, illustrations by Dumile Feni, Thunder's Mouth Press, 1981.
(Contributor) Joyce Jones, Mary McTaggart, and Maria Mootry, editors, *The Otherwise Room*, The Poetry Factory Press, 1981.
The Mojo Hands Call, I Must Go (poems), Thunder's Mouth Press, 1982.
Blues: The Story Always Untold (poems), Another Chicago Press, in press.

Also contributor to all four volumes of *Mississippi Writers: Reflections of Childhood and Youth*, edited by Dorothy Abbott. Contributor to *Black World, Another Chicago Magazine, Black American Literature Forum, Black Scholar, AFRO-DIASPORA*, and *Journal of Black Poetry*. Editor for Third World Press, 1970—, and Institute for Positive Education; managing editor, *Black Books Bulletin*, 1971-73; poetry editor, *Black American Literature Forum*, 1982—.

WORK IN PROGRESS: *Superbad and the Hip Jesus;* research on black critics and on the work of Ernest Gaines and Henry Dumas; *Mighty Long Time*, a novel about a blues singer.

SIDELIGHTS: The contrast between Sterling D. Plumpp's early years in rural Mississippi and the "psychological maiming" that he sustained as an ambitious young student, postal worker, and draftee after coming to Chicago in 1962 "has provided a rich source of both verbal and psychological tension for his art," observes *Dictionary of Literary Biography* contributor James Cunningham. *Clinton*, a book of poetry named after the poet's birthplace, shows this most clearly, writes Cunningham:

"As readers follow the poet from one period, from one part of the country, from one area of experience to another, they witness a great deal of psychological maiming. With the exception of the black Southern church, the chief violators are seen to be the major institutions in the hero's life: the tenant farming system, the educational system, the federal government in the civilian and military guises of post office employer and army trainer. Their main violence against the protagonist is their concerted effort to have him trade his own vision for theirs.'' The forces of oppression, evident in this and other works, can in part account for Plumpp's movement toward writing as a defense, according to Cunningham. ''For the business of becoming a writer, . . . and its appeal for the besieged hero, are equivalent to achieving two forms of mastery: a personal point of view and the skill to express and preserve this vision through the medium of words.''

Plumpp, who had written four books of poetry and *Black Rituals* (a prose work of social psychology about behavior that supports oppression of the black community) by 1975, won the Illinois Arts Council Literary Award that year for *Clinton*. His next and most comprehensive work, *The Mojo Hands Call, I Must Go,* brought him even more acclaim, winning another Illinois Arts Council Award for Poetry and the Carl Sandburg Literary Award for Poetry from the Friends of the Chicago Public Library in 1983. The poem ''Fractured Dreams,'' says Cunningham, ''dramatizes the effort of a self-doubting and self-denouncing protagonist to keep faith with that reservoir of collective identity best articulated by the blues tradition,'' and, in the title poem, reports a *Choice* reviewer, the speaker returns ''to his rural origins via a reconversion to the mystical belief in the life force, the Mojo hands, that had sustained his people in the past.''

Regarding his role as a poet, Plumpp commented that although he has been working steadily on *Mighty Long Time,* a novel about a blues singer, he sees himself ''principally as a poet,'' and is reconciled to the fact ''that I was put here to recover, mold and discover the most private of public languages speaking to me from the Afro-American side of time. The novel is an extension of my quest for language in the blues; as my concept of poetry develops, the more urgent it becomes for me to devote time to its callings.'' Dorothy Abbott's profile on Plumpp for the *Southern Register* cites his statement that he speaks most often from his Mississippi experiences because it allows him to ''maneuver into the reservoir of my being without first having to plod through attacks against whites; I [can] see the survival lines of my people concealed in the many ways they did things. . . . When my work is read I would like you to think of what's behind a good blues song, behind the sweat and jubilation of a church rocking, or what's behind the laughter of old black women.''

While other poets of Plumpp's generation have spoken with a more militant urban tone, his writing does not rely heavily on the use of Black English vernacular, nor does he express his politics directly. ''He is not a street poet, like Don L. Lee [now Haki R. Madhubuti] or Carolyn Rodgers. . . . Plumpp is more of a poet's poet. He is somewhat more difficult [to read], condensed, cryptic, elliptic, general,'' comments Dudley Randall in a *Negro Digest* review. About Plumpp's distinctive voice, Cunningham suggests that the poet's ''work is remarkably free of the restrictions imposed by the black aesthetic movement on such matters as subject matter, diction, and aesthetic stance. In his poetry, for instance, and in his limited forays into fiction, the Southern rural experience is on an equal footing with that of the urban Midwest. . . . Indeed, the range

and complexity of statement, so characteristic of his poetry, can be viewed as significant correctives to the arbitrary biases of the black arts writer of the 1960s and early 1970s.''

If his politics are not highlighted in his poetics, they are evident in his activities as editor for the Third World Press and the Institute for Positive Education, two black cultural institutions run by the activist-poet Haki R. Madhubuti. Plumpp also makes an indirect attack on apartheid in his collection *Somehow We Survive: An Anthology of South African Writing.* Poems he gathered from three continents, some brought forward from obscure publications, ''focus . . . on life's complexities, not on apartheid, which is merely the ugliest part,'' says David Dorsey in *World Literature Today.* Plumpp has also worked to develop the skills of other writers as an associate professor at the University of Illinois at Chicago Circle since the 1970s.

Pieces written by Plumpp for *Another Chicago Magazine* and *Black American Literature Forum* during the 1980s, notes Cunningham, reflect ''an intensified preoccupation with improving the quality of life in America, especially for families.'' The essayist concludes, ''Plumpp's most ambitious recent efforts . . . have revealed not only a writer at the height of his current powers of illumination and eloquence but one who is intent on stretching himself to the utmost as an artist.''

The Sterling D. Plumpp Collection, containing works by African and Afro-American writers, resides at the University of Mississippi.

BIOGRAPHICAL/CRITICAL SOURCES:

BOOKS

Dictionary of Literary Biography, Volume XLI: *Afro-American Poets since 1955,* Gale, 1985.
Redmond, Eugene B., editor, *Drumvoices: The Mission of Afro-American Poetry, A Critical History,* Anchor/Doubleday, 1976.

PERIODICALS

American Book Review, January, 1983.
Black World, April, 1971.
Choice, March, 1983.
Negro Digest, February, 1970.
Reader (Chicago), October 17, 1986.
Southern Register, winter, 1984.
World Literature Today, winter, 1984.

—*Sketch by Marilyn K. Basel*

*   *   *

POOLE, Peggy 1925-
(Terry Roche)

PERSONAL: Born March 8, 1925, in Canterbury, Kent, England; daughter of Reginald and Barbara (Tate) Thornton; married Reginald Poole (an executive), August, 1949; children: Catherine, Barbara, Elizabeth. *Education:* Attended Benenden School in England.

ADDRESSES: Home—18 Townfield Rd., West Kirby, Wirral, Merseyside L48 7EZ, England. *Agent*—Dorothy Sharp, Flat 1, 111 Gloucester Avenue, Regent's Park, London NW1 8LB, England.

CAREER: Worked in the Bodleian Library, Oxford, England, 1946-47; secretary for physicians in London, 1947-49; writer.

Producer, hostess, and interviewer for national and local British Broadcasting Corp. programs, 1960—; editor and presenter of "First Heard" poetry program, B.B.C. Radio Merseyside, 1976—. *Military service:* Women's Royal Naval Service, 1943-45.

MEMBER: International Poetry Society, Poetry Society, Society of Women Writers and Journalists, Jabberwocky, VER Poets, Merseyside Arts Association.

WRITINGS:

Never a Put up Job (poetry), Quentin Nelson, 1970.
Cherry Stones and Other Poems, Headland, 1983.
No Wilderness in Them, Windows, 1984.
Midnight Walk and Other Poems, Envoi, 1986.

UNDER PSEUDONYM TERRY ROCHE

Brum (illustrated by Beryl Sanders), Dobson, 1978.
Shadows on the Sand, Dobson, 1979.
Your Turn to Put the Light Out, Dobson, 1980.

OTHER

Work has appeared in anthologies, including *All Made of Fantasy,* 1980. Columnist, *Deesider,* 1974-75. Contributor of short stories and articles to such publications as *Guardian, Liverpool Daily Post,* and *Woman's Weekly,* and of poetry to periodicals, including *Smoke, Orbis, Country Quest, New Poetry,* and *Poetry Nottingham.*

WORK IN PROGRESS: *Cowslips in the Chalkpit: A Kent Cameo; Sydney Sparrow,* another children's story.

SIDELIGHTS: Peggy Poole told *CA:* "In my children's books, fact mixes with fiction. Six successive holidays on the canals resulted in *Brum,* while *Shadows on the Sand* is set in Merseyside. The best part, for me as author, is when the fictional characters take over the story; the controversial ending in *Your Turn to Put the Light Out* was 'dictated' to me in the night.

"For sixteen years I was co-organiser of Jabberwocky, a monthly evening of poetry old and new, published and unpublished. Jabberwocky also produced four poetry collections and enjoyed readings from national poets including Stephen Spender, Ted Hughes, Seamus Heaney, Thom Gunn and Douglas Dunn."

Poole noted that *Midnight Walk and Other Poems* "contains several poems that have been prize-winners in national poetry competitions."

*   *   *

PORQUERAS-MAYO, Alberto 1930-

PERSONAL: Born January 13, 1930, in Lerida, Spain; naturalized U.S. citizen in 1973; son of Jose Maria (a physician) and Pilar (Mayo) Porqueras; children: Maria Teresa, Nicole Meritxell. *Education:* Attended University of Barcelona, 1947-50; University of Madrid, Licenciatura (master's degree), 1952, Ph.D., 1954; University of Bonn, post-doctoral study, 1954-55. *Religion:* Roman Catholic.

ADDRESSES: *Office*—4080 Foreign Language Building, 707 South Matthews, University of Illinois, Urbana, Ill. 61801.

CAREER: University of Madrid, Madrid, Spain, assistant professor of Spanish literature, 1953-54; University of Hamburg, Hamburg, Germany, lecturer in Spanish language and literature, 1955-58; Emory University, Atlanta, Ga., assistant professor of Spanish, 1958-60; University of Missouri—Colum-

bia, associate professor, 1960-64, professor of Spanish, 1964-68; University of Illinois at Urbana-Champaign, professor of Spanish literature, 1968—, associate member of Center for Advanced Studies, 1970-71, and 1981-82. Instructor in Spanish, International University of Santander, summers, 1952, 1953, 1957; co-director of seminar of Catalan dialectology, University of Bonn, summer, 1955; visiting professor at Western Reserve University (now Case Western Reserve University), summers, 1959, 1963, and University of Colorado, summer, 1961.

MEMBER: International Association of Hispanists, International Association of Catalan, American Comparative Literature Association, Asociacion Europea de Profesores de Espanol, North American Catalan Association (honorary president).

AWARDS, HONORS: Scholarship to study literary criticism in Germany, High Council of Scientific Research in Madrid, 1954-55; Menendez Pelayo Prize for research in literature, 1955; nominated Miembro Correspondiente of Instituto de Estudios Ilerdenses, 1964, in recognition of research on Lope de Vega and Lerida; American Philosophical Society grants for research in Spain, 1966-67, and 1976.

WRITINGS:

El Prologo como genero literario: Su estudio en el Siglo de Oro (title means "The Prologue as Literary Genre: Its Study in the Golden Age"), Consejo Superior de Investigaciones Cientificas, 1957.
(Editor) Alfonso de Carvallo, *El Cisne de Apolo* (title means "The Swan of Apolo"), two volumes, Consejo Superior de Investigaciones Cientificas, 1958.
El problema de la verdad poetica en el Siglo de Oro (monograph; title means "The Problem of Poetic Truth in the Golden Age"), Ateneo, 1961.
(With F. Sanchez Escribano) *Preceptiva dramatica espanola del Renacimiento y Barroco* (title means "Spanish Dramatic Theory in Renaissance and Baroque"), Gredos, 1965, 2nd edition, 1972.
El Prologo en el Renacimiento espanol (title means "The Prologue in Spanish Renaissance"), Consejo Superior de Investigaciones Cientificas, 1965.
El Prologo en el Manierismo y Barroco espanoles (title means "The Prologue in Spanish Mannerism and Baroque"), Consejo Superior de Investigationes Cientificas, 1968.
(Editor with C. Rojas) *Filologia y critica hispanica: Homenaje al Prof. F. Sanchez Escribano* (title means "Spanish Philology and Criticism: Homage to Prof. F. Sanchez Escribano"), Ediciones Alcala, 1969.
(With J. L. Laurenti) *Ensayo bibliografico del prologo en la literatura* (title means "Bibliographic Essay on the Prologues in Literature"), Consejo Superior de Investigaciones Cientificas, 1971.
Temas y Formas de la Literatura Espanola (title means "Themes and Forms in Spanish Literature"), Gredos, 1972.
(Editor) Pedro Calderon, *El Principe constante,* Espasa-Calpe, 1975.
(Author of introduction) Calderon, *La Vida es sveno* [and] *El alcalde de Zalamea,* Espasa-Calpe, 1977.
(With Laurenti) *The Spanish Golden Age (1472-1700): A Catalog of Rare Books Held in the Library of the University of Illinois and in Selected North American Libraries,* G. K. Hall, 1979.
(Editor with Jaume Marti i Olivella and Carme Rey i Grange) *Antologia de la narrativa catalana dels 70,* Publicacions

de L'Abadia de Montserrat, 1980, translation published as *The New Catalan Short Story: An Anthology*, University Press of America, 1983.

La Teoria poetica en el Renacimiento y Manierismo espanoles, Puoill, 1986.

Contributor of articles and reviews to *Revista de Literatura, Revista de Filologia Espanola, Boletin de Filologia Espanola, Hispanic Review, Revista Hispanica Moderna, Atlantida, Romance Notes, Segismundo, Bulletin Hispanique, Romanische Forschungen, Estudios Clasicos,* and many other journals.

* * *

PORTE, Joel (Miles) 1933-

PERSONAL: Born November 13, 1933, in Brooklyn, N.Y.; son of Jack and Frances (Derison) Porte; married Ilana d'Ancona, June 17, 1962 (divorced, 1976); married Helene Sophrin, October 18, 1985; children: (first marriage) Susanna Maria. *Education:* City College (now City College of the City University of New York), A.B.(magna cum laude), 1957; Harvard University, A.M., 1958, Ph.D., 1962.

ADDRESSES: Home—Ithaca, N.Y. *Office*—Goldwin Smith Hall, Cornell University, Ithaca, N.Y. 14853.

CAREER: Harvard University, Cambridge, Mass., instructor, 1962-64, assistant professor, 1964-68, associate professor, 1968-69, professor of English and American literature, 1969-82, Ernest Bernbaum Professor of Literature, 1982-87, chairman of department, 1985-87; Cornell University, Ithaca, N.Y., Frederic J. Whiton Professor of American Literature, 1987—. Visiting lecturer, City College (now City College of the City University of New York), summer, 1958 and 1959, and American Studies Research Center, Hyderabad, India, 1976. Scholar-in-residence, Rockefeller Foundation Study Center, Bellagio, Italy, 1979.

AWARDS, HONORS: Guggenheim fellow, 1981-82.

WRITINGS:

Emerson and Thoreau: Transcendentalists in Conflict, Wesleyan University Press, 1966, reprinted, AMS Press, 1985.
The Romance in America: Studies in Cooper, Poe, Hawthorne, Melville, and James, Wesleyan University Press, 1969.
Representative Man: Ralph Waldo Emerson in His Time, Oxford University Press, 1979.
(Author of introduction) Nathaniel Hawthorne, *The Scarlet Letter,* Dell, 1979.
(Author of introduction) Oliver Wendell Holmes, *Ralph Waldo Emerson,* Chelsea House, 1980.
(Editor) *Emerson in His Journals,* Harvard University Press, 1982.
(Editor) *Emerson: Prospect and Retrospect,* Harvard University Press, 1982.
(Editor) Ralph Waldo Emerson, *Essays and Lectures,* Literary Classics of the United States, 1983.
(Editor) *New Essays on "Portrait of a Lady,"* Cambridge University Press, 1988.

CONTRIBUTOR

Harry Levin, editor, *Veins of Humor,* Harvard University Press, 1972.
Monroe Engel, editor, *Uses of Literature,* Harvard University Press, 1973.

Matthew Bruccoli, editor, *The Chief Glory of Every People,* Southern Illinois University Press, 1973.
Richard Thompson, editor, *The Gothic Imagination,* Washington State University Press, 1974.
Daniel Aaron, editor, *Studies in Biography,* Harvard University Press, 1978.
(Author of introduction) George Santayana, *Interpretations of Poetry and Religion,* MIT Press, 1988.

OTHER

Contributor of articles and reviews to *New England Quarterly, Christian Science Monitor, New Leader, New Boston Review, Forum, American Literature, Studies in Romanticism, Journal of American History, Criticism, American Literary Realism, Harvard Magazine, Raritan Review,* and other periodicals and newspapers.

WORK IN PROGRESS: In Respect to Egotism: Studies in American Romantic Writing.

SIDELIGHTS: Joel Porte's *Representative Man: Ralph Waldo Emerson in His Time* "refracts the crucial events through the prism of Emerson's journals, letter and essays, concentrating on a selection of images and ideas that seem fused with the internal heat of the light they represent," according to Paul Zweig in the *New York Times Book Review.* "Each chapter centers on a series of textual analyses that Mr. Porte conducts with enormous precision but also with charm and wit. [He] seems to probe the very texture of Emerson's mind."

Books and Bookmen reviewer Harold Beaver expresses a different opinion. Although he sees Porte's work as "an admirably lucid introduction" to Emerson, he states, "Nowhere [does Porte consider Emerson's] notions in contemporary, structuralist terms. Nor is the language of nineteenth century idealism ever tested against its twentieth century, phenomenological counterpart." He believes that a twentieth century critical biography must use "the metalanguage of its own contemporaries: to use only Emerson's language in explicating Emerson runs the risk of marooning Emerson further in his own past."

Philip F. Gura suggests otherwise in the *Virginia Quarterly Review:* "As the title suggests, the vigor of this critical biography comes in good measure from a mind actively seeking to understand Emerson *in his time,* with tools well-tempered in the crucible of contemporary biographical and literary criticism." Such an approach allows Porte to exhibit "this great American before our eyes so that new colors are struck from each angle. He also succeeds in showing how Emerson in his time speaks to our own."

BIOGRAPHICAL/CRITICAL SOURCES:

PERIODICALS

Books and Bookmen, June, 1979.
Nation, March 31, 1979.
New Republic, February 24, 1979.
New York Times Book Review, February 11, 1979.
Sewanee Review, April, 1980.
Times Literary Supplement, August 27, 1982.
Virginia Quarterly Review, summer, 1979.
Washington Post Book World, July 25, 1982.

* * *

PORTER, Bern(ard Harden) 1911-

PERSONAL: Born February 14, 1911, in Porter Settlement,

Me.; son of Lewis Harden and Etta Flora (Rogers) Porter; married Helen Elaine Hendren (a poet), 1946 (divorced, August, 1947); married Margaret Eudine Preston (a writer), August 27, 1955 (died April 17, 1975); married Lula Mae Blom, September 9, 1976 (divorced November 25, 1986). *Education:* Colby College, Sc.B., 1932; Brown University, Sc.M., 1933; special courses at Da Vinci School, 1937, Convair School, 1957, University of Maine, 1960, and Federal School, 1963. *Politics:* Republican. *Religion:* Methodist.

ADDRESSES: Office—22 Salmond Rd., Belfast, Me. 04915. *Agent*—William Rutledge, 5228 Irvine Ave., North Hollywood, Calif.

CAREER: Bern Porter (publishing company), Belfast, Me., president, 1929—; Acheson Colloids Corp., Port Huron, Mich., physicist, 1935-40; Manhattan District Engineers, Princeton, N.J., Berkeley, Calif., and Oak Ridge, Tenn., physicist, 1940-45; Bern Porter, Inc., Belfast, chairman of board, 1945—; Institute of Advanced Thinking, Belfast, 1959—; Bern Porter International, Belfast, president, 1974—. Artist and illustrator; exhibited in Maine, New York, San Francisco, Japan, and Tasmania. Director of Contemporary Gallery, West Coast Design Guild, and Fund for Contemporary Expression, 1947-50. Consulting physicist, 1945—. Republican candidate for governor of Maine, 1969.

MEMBER: International Poetry Society (founding fellow), International Platform Association, International Academy of Poets (founder), Society for International Development, Technical Publishing Society (fellow), American Astronautical Society (associate fellow), Society of Technical Writers and Publishers (associate member), American Physical Society, Institute of Radio Engineers, American Rocket Society (associate member), American Society of Emeriti, National Society of Programmed Instruction, Phi Beta Kappa, Sigma Xi, Kappa Phi Kappa, Chi Gamma Sigma, Xi Epsilon Mu, Fenway Club (Boston), Algonquin Club, St. Andrew's Club.

AWARDS, HONORS: Sc.D., Institute of Advanced Thinking, 1959; recipient of awards from PEN, 1975, 1976, 1977, and 1987, and from Authors League, 1977; Carnegie Author, 1975; diploma merit, Centro Studi E Scambi Internazionale, Rome, 1976; National Endowment for the Arts literary award, 1979; scholarship, Visual Studies, 1986.

WRITINGS:

Colloidal Graphite: Its Properties and Applications, Acheson, 1939.
Map of Physics, Cenco, 1939.
Map of Chemistry, University of Pennsylvania, 1941.
(Self-illustrated) *Doldrums,* Al Press, 1941.
Map of Joyceana, Circle Editions, 1946.
(Editor) *Seashore Brochures,* Christian F. Ver Becke, 1947.
Art Techniques, Gillick Press, 1947.
The Union of Science and Art, Greenwood Press, 1948.
Commentary on the Relationship of Art and Science, Stanford University, 1956.
Rocket Data Book, Convair, 1956.
Dictionary of Rocket Terminology, Convair, 1956.
Circle: Reproductions of Art Work, 1944-1947, Circle Editions, 1963, reprinted, 1978.
Reporting and Preventive Maintenance Forms for the 465L Program, Federal Electric Corp., 1963.
I've Left (autobiographical essays), Marathon, 1963, reprinted, University Microfilms, 1978, 2nd edition, Marathon, 1969.

Applicable 465L Publications, Federal Electric Corp., 1963.
What Henry Miller Said and Why It Is Important (booklet), D. Turrell, 1964, 2nd edition, Bern Porter, 1969.
Dynamic Test Vehicle Instrumentation and Data System Criteria, Boeing, 1965.
Dynamic Test Vehicle Data Reduction and Correlation Requirements, Boeing, 1965.
The First Publication of F. Scott Fitzgerald (booklet), Quality Books, 1965.
Dynamic Test Program Requirements, Boeing, 1965.
Mathematics for Electronics, Prentice-Hall, 1965.
Art Productions: 1928-1965, D. Turrell, 1965.
Captive Firing of Flight State Reliability Study, Boeing, 1966.
System Methodologies and Their Utilization, Boeing, 1966.
Founds, Contemporary, 1966.
Summary Report of the Knox County Regional Comprehensive Plan: Phase III, [Rockland, Me.], 1969.
Found Poems, Something Else Press, 1972.
Eighty-Nine Offenses, Abyss Publications, 1974.
Selected Founds, Croissant, 1975.
The Last Acts of Saint FY, Xerox Sutra, 1976.
Isla Vista, Turkey Press, 1981.
The Book of Do's, Dog Ear Press, 1982.
Here Comes Everybody's Don't Book, Dog Ear Press, 1985.
Belfast Belfastia, Abstra, 1987.
Ciao-Ciao, Visual Studies, 1987.
Repertorio cronologico de legislacion, two volumes, Visual Studies, 1987.
Printing in Europe, Visual Studies, 1987.
Why My Left Leg Is Hot, Xerox Sutra, 1987.
Mothering Time, Abstra, 1988.

PUBLISHED BY BERN PORTER

Me, 1943.
(Compiler) *Henry Miller: A Bibliography,* 1943, revised edition, 1969.
Schillerhaus: 1947-1950, 1955.
Drawings: 1954-1955, 1956.
(Compiler) *H. L. Mencken: A Bibliography,* 1957.
Drawings: 1955-1956, 1959.
(Compiler) *F. Scott Fitzgerald: A Bibliography,* 1960.
Aphasia, 1961.
The Waste-Maker, 1926-1961, 1961.
Scandinavian Summer, 1961.
Charcoal Drawings, 1935-1937, 1963.
Assorted Art, 1928-1963, 1963.
Day Notes for Mother, 1964.
Native Alphabet, 1964.
Scigraffiti, 1964.
AL0110, 1964.
468B, 1966.
Moscow, 1966.
Cut Leaves, 1966.
The Box, 1968.
Dieresis, 1969.
Artifacts, 1969.
scda 19, 1969.
Oraison funebres de Bossuet, 1970.
OEye, 1970.
Reminiscences, 1927-1970, 1970.
PER Book, 1970.
Enry One, 1970.
Enry 2-5, 1970.
ULA, 1971.
Assorted Cuts, 1965-1970, five volumes, 1971.

b.p., 1971.
NEXA 914, 1971.
The 14th of February, 1972.
Trattoria Due Fermi, 1973.
Hand-Fashioned Chocolates, 1974.
Run-On, 1975.
Where to Go/What to Do/When in New York/Week of June 22, 1972, 1975.
American Strange, 1979.
I Ricordi di Firenze, 1981.

EDITOR; PUBLISHED BY BERN PORTER

Henry Miller, *The Plight of the Creative Artist in the U.S.A.*, 1944.
Miller, *Henry Miller Miscellanea*, 1945.
Miller, *Echolalia*, 1946.
Robert Carleton Brown, 1956.
Harry Kiakis, *The Watts Towers*, 1959.
Kiakis, *Venice: Beatnik Capitol*, 1961.
Dieter Rot, *Cutcards*, 1963.
Ray Johnson, *A Book about Death*, 1963.
Jack Roth, *The Exciting, Igniting World of Art*, 1964.
William B. Faulkner, Jr., *Man*, 1965.
Bay-Area Creators: 1945-1965, 1965.
B. P. at Schillerhaus, 1966.
Harry Bowden: His Studio and Work, 1966.
Wernher von Braun: A Bibliography and Selected Papers, 1966.
Art Scrapbook, 1967.
Art Prints, 1967.
Selected Articles by R. Buckminster Fuller, 1968.
The Private Papers of Wilhelm Reich, 1942-1954, 1969.
Philip Lloyd Ely, *Bernard Langlais*, 1969.
Contemporary Italian Poets, 1973.
Vestigia: Notes on the Life and Work of Janelle Viglini, 1975.
The Viglini Letters, two volumes, 1975.
Gee Whizzels, 1977.

EDITOR AND ILLUSTRATOR

Miller, *Semblance of a Devoted Past*, Bern Porter, 1944.
The Happy Rock: A Book about Henry Miller, Bern Porter, 1945, reprinted, Walton Press, 1970.
John Hoffman, *Journey to the End*, Bern Porter, 1956.
John G. Moore, *The Latitude and Longitude of Henry Miller*, Marathon, 1962.
William B. Faulkner, Jr., *Henry: An Anthology by World Poets*, Bern Porter, 1970.

ILLUSTRATOR

A. L. Blackwood, *General Physics Text*, Bern Porter, 1943.
Leonard Wolfe, *Hamadryad Hunted*, Bern Porter, 1947.
Antoine Artaud, *Judgement*, Bern Porter, 1955.
Dick Higgins, *What Are Legends*, Bern Porter, 1960.
Stephen Barry Kimble, *Henry Miller*, Bern Porter, 1965.
Michael Fraenkel, *Genesis*, Bern Porter, 1970.
James Joyce, *Poems Pennyeach*, Bern Porter, 1970.
Alfred, Lord Tennyson, *Lover's Tale*, Walton Press, 1971.
James Erwin Schevill, *Breakout*, Bern Porter, 1974.
Higgins, *City with All the Angels: A Radio Play*, Unpublished Editions, 1974.

Also illustrator of *Die fabelhafte Getraume von Taifen*, by Higgins, 1970, and *Origins, Initiations*, by Kirk Robertson, 1980. Illustrator of maps and posters; illustrator for more than twenty magazines and newspapers, 1926-82, including *Score* and *Velocity*.

OTHER

Also author of numerous booklets and pamphlets on art, technology, and literature. Editor of magazines, including *Colby White Mule*, 1929-32, *The Leaves Fall*, 1942-45, *Circle*, 1944-45, and *Broadside*, 1954-56.

WORK IN PROGRESS: Completion of a seven-volume visual study incorporating *Found Poems* (1972), *The Book of Do's* (1982), *Here Comes Everybody's Don't Book* (1985), *Sweet End, My Time, Bern's Turn, The Porter Book, Never Ends*, and *The Institute; Resume of Physics*, three volumes.

SIDELIGHTS: Bern Porter writes: "Travels in remote areas like Newfoundland, Tasmania, Russia, Venezuela, with extended living periods among cultures like the Laplanders, Ulithians, Guamanians, Balinese, and others, force me into a continuing search for ways the science of physics can promote a better life. My experiences with the development of the A-bomb and later pilgrimage to Hiroshima have already given rise to many creative forms like sciarch, sciart, et. al., discussed in my autobiographical work, *I've Left.* I enjoy a large correspondence with creative workers from all over the world. Current interests are centered on techniques and procedures for programed instruction, learning 'by machine' and experiments in visual expression of language structure. Additional and prolonged travels [include trips to] South America, Canada, Nepal, Greenland, and Spain, with five trips around the world by air and sea, always with a view for betterment in rural areas like Maine through written and art expression, artist exhibitions, poetry festivals, performances and shared living spaces."

BIOGRAPHICAL/CRITICAL SOURCES:

BOOKS

Dunbar, Margaret, *Bern! Porter! Interview!*, Dog Ear Press, 1982.
Porter, Bern, *I've Left*, Marathon, 1963, reprinted, University Microfilms, 1978, 2nd edition, Marathon, 1969.
Schevill, James Erwin, *The Roaring Market and the Silent Tomb* (biography), Abbey Press, 1957, updated edition, Dog Ear Press, 1988.
Schevill, James Erwin, *Lovecraft's Follies* (theater version), Swallow Press, 1971.

PERIODICALS

Maine Times, August 22, 1980.
Velocity (interview), November, 1985.
Voice Literary Supplement, October, 1984.

*   *   *

PORTER, Bernard (John) 1941-

PERSONAL: Born February 5, 1941, in Essex, England; son of Cyril George (a teacher) and Ruth (a teacher; maiden name, Rabbett) Porter; married Deirdre O'Hara (a state registered nurse), July 29, 1972; children: Zoe Caroline, Benedict Campion, Kate. *Education:* Corpus Christi College, Cambridge, B.A., 1963, M.A. and Ph.D., both 1967. *Religion:* "Agnostic, with Methodist upbringing."

ADDRESSES: Home—16 Newgate St., Cottingham, East Yorkshire HU16 4DT, England. *Office*—Department of History, University of Hull, Hull HU6 7RX, England.

CAREER: Cambridge University, Cambridge, England, research fellow at Corpus Christi College, 1966-68; University of Hull, Hull, England, lecturer, 1968-78, senior lecturer, 1978-87, reader in history, 1987—. Consultant to the Open University.

MEMBER: Association of University Teachers, Historical Association.

WRITINGS:

Critics of Empire: British Radical Attitudes to Colonialism in Africa, 1896-1914, Macmillan, 1968.
The Lion's Share: A Short History of British Imperialism, 1850-1970, Longman, 1976, 2nd edition published as *The Lion's Share: A Short History of British Imperialism, 1850-1983,* 1984.
The Refugee Question in Mid-Victorian Politics, Cambridge University Press, 1979.
Britain, Europe, and the World, 1850-1982, Allen & Unwin, 1983, 2nd edition published as *Britain, Europe, and the World, 1850-1986,* 1987.
The Origins of the Vigilant State: The London Metropolitan Police Special Branch before the First World War, Weidenfeld, 1987.

CONTRIBUTOR

Peter Warwick, editor, *The South African War,* Longman, 1980.
Donald Read, editor, *Edwardian England,* Croom Helm, 1982.
B. Pimlott, editor, *Fabian Essays in Socialist Thought,* Heinemann, 1984.

OTHER

Contributor to *Journal of Imperial and Commonwealth History, Immigrants and Minorities, Victorian Studies, Historical Journal, History Today, Times Higher Education Supplement, Intelligence and National Security, Bulletin of the Society for the Study of Labour History,* and *Encyclopedia International.* Editor of *Journal of Imperial and Commonwealth History,* 1979-82.

WORK IN PROGRESS: Research in the field of British domestic covert counter-subversion since the eighteenth century.

AVOCATIONAL INTERESTS: Art, architecture, classical music (especially nineteenth-century romantic music), cricket, science fiction.

*   *   *

PORTER, David L(indsey)   1941-

PERSONAL: Born February 18, 1941, in Holyoke, Mass.; son of Willis Hubert and Lora Frances (Bowen) Porter; married Marilyn Esther Platt (an elementary school teacher), November 28, 1970; children: Kevin, Andrea. *Education:* Franklin College, B.A. (magna cum laude), 1963; Ohio University, M.A., 1965; Pennsylvania State University, Ph.D., 1970. *Religion:* American Baptist.

ADDRESSES: Home—616 Fourth Ave. E., Oskaloosa, Iowa 52577. *Office*—Department of Social Science, William Penn College, Oskaloosa, Iowa 52577.

CAREER: Rensselaer Polytechnic Institute, Troy, N.Y., assistant professor of history, 1970-75, co-director of American Studies Program, 1972-74; State of New York Civil Service, Troy, educational administrative assistant, 1975-76; William Penn College, Oskaloosa, Iowa, assistant professor, 1976-77, associate professor of history, 1977-82, professor of history and political science, 1982-86, Louis Tuttle Shangle Professor

of history and political science, 1986—, supervisor of pre-law program, 1979—. Chairman of Troy Bicentennial Committee, 1975-76, Sperry & Hutchinson Foundation lectureship series, 1980-82, and annual assembly of Iowa State United Nations Association, 1982; supervisor of Iowa General Assembly legislative internship program, 1978—, Mahaska County records inventory project, 1978-79, and Washington Center internship program, 1985—.

MEMBER: North American Society for Sport History, American Historical Association, Organization of American Historians, American Association of University Professors, Society for the History of American Foreign Relations, Society for American Baseball Research, Popular Culture Association, Professional Football Researchers Association, College Football Researchers Association, State Historical Society of Iowa, Mahaska County Historical Society, Mahaska County United Nations Association, Alpha, Phi Alpha Theta, Kappa Delta Pi.

AWARDS, HONORS: National Science Foundation grant, 1967; Faculty travel grant, Rensselaer Polytechnic Institute, 1974; National Endowment for the Humanities grant, 1979; Eleanor Roosevelt Institute grant, 1981; United Nations Association distinguished service award, 1981; professional development grant, William Penn College, 1986.

WRITINGS:

The Seventy-sixth Congress and World War II, 1939-1940, University of Missouri Press, 1979.
Congress and the Waning of the New Deal, Kennikat, 1980.
(Editor and contributor) *The Biographical Dictionary of American Sports: Baseball,* Greenwood Press, 1987.
(Editor and contributor) *The Biographical Dictionary of American Sports: Football,* Greenwood Press, 1987.

CONTRIBUTOR

Warren F. Kuehl, editor, *The Biographical Dictionary of Internationalists,* Greenwood Press, 1983.
Ray B. Browne and Marshall W. Fishwick, editors, *The Hero in Transition,* Bowling Green University, 1983.
Carl E. Krog and William R. Tanner, editors, *Herbert Hoover and the Republican Era: A Reconsideration,* University Press of America, 1984.
History of Mahaska County, Curtis Media, 1985.
Otis L. Graham, Jr., and Meghan R. Wander, editors, *Franklin D. Roosevelt, His Life and Times: An Encyclopedia View,* G. K. Hall, 1985.
William O. Pederson and Ann M. McLaurin, editors, *The Rating Game in American Politics: An Interdisciplinary Approach,* Irvington, 1987.

OTHER

Contributor to *Directory of Teaching Innovations in History, Dictionary of American Biography, The Book of Lists #3, Sports History—Selected Syllabi,* edited by Noverr and Ziewacz, *Sports Encyclopedia North America,* edited by John D. Windhausen, and *Book of Days 1988.* Contributor to journals, including *Foundations, Filson Club History Quarterly, Aerospace Historian, Midwest Review, Palimpsest, American Heritage, Senate History, American Historical Association Perspectives,* and *North American Society for Sports History Proceedings,* and to various state historical journals. Contributor to newspapers, including *Chicago Tribune* and *Des Moines Register.* Contributor of commentary, National Public Radio. Contributor of reviews to the *Journal of American History,* the *Annals of Iowa, Chicago History, Midwest Review,* and the *Society for American Baseball Research Review of Books.*

WORK IN PROGRESS: Four books, *Congress and Foreign Policy, 1941; America's Greatest Figures; Representative Mary T. Norton of New Jersey;* and *Cap Anson: Baseball's First Superstar;* editing *Biographical Dictionary of American Sports: Other Major Outdoor Sports* and *Biographical Dictionary of American Sports: Major Indoor Sports* for Greenwood Press; contributions for *The Harry S. Truman Encyclopedia,* edited by Richard Kirkendall for G. K. Hall.

* * *

POYNTER, Dan(iel Frank) 1938-

PERSONAL: Born September 17, 1938, in New York, N.Y.; son of William Frank (a sales engineer) and Josephine (a newspaper columnist; maiden name, Thompson) Poynter. *Education:* Attended City College of San Francisco, 1956-57, University of the Pacific, 1957-59, and University of San Francisco, 1958-59; Chico State College (now California State University, Chico), B.A., 1960; graduate study at San Francisco Law School, 1961-62.

ADDRESSES: Home—Route 1, Goleta, Calif. 93117-9701. *Office*—Para Publishing, P.O. Box 4232-51, Santa Barbara, Calif. 93140-4232.

CAREER: Paladin Sport Parachutes, Oakland, Calif., manager, 1962-64; Tri-State Parachute Company, Flemington, N.J., general manager, 1964-65; Parachutes Incorporated, Orange, Mass., marketing manager and research and development director, 1965-66; Strong Enterprises, Inc., North Quincy, Mass., parachute design specialist, 1967-73; Para Publishing (formerly Parachuting Publications), owner, North Quincy, 1969-74, Santa Barbara, Calif., 1974—; writer. Federally licensed master parachute rigger with all ratings, back, seat, and chest; expert parachutist with highest class license and 1200 jumps; parachuting instructor and examiner. Licensed pilot, single engine land planes and gliders; hang gliding flight examiner. *Military service:* California National Guard, 1956-59; U.S. Army Reserve, 1959-64.

MEMBER: Commission Internationale de Vol Libre of the Federation Aeronautique Internationale (U.S. Delegate; past president; honorary lifetime president), International Frisbee Association, United States Hang Gliding Association (life member; past member of the board; chief of U.S. team delegation), Association of American Publishers, United States Parachute Association (life member; member of the board, 1966-79; secretary; chairman of the board; chief of U.S. team delegation), American Institute of Aeronautics and Astronautics (senior member of technical committee), National Aeronautics Association (past delegate), Computer Writers Association, Aviation/Space Writers Association, Committee of Small Magazine Editors and Publishers (past member of the board of directors; Santa Barbara chapter president, 1979-82), Parachute Equipment Industry Association (past secretary; chairman of technical committee), Society of Automotive Engineers (chairman of technical committee), Experimental Aircraft Association, Survival and Flight Equipment Association, Soaring Society of America, Museum of Parachuting and Air Safety (past director), Book Publicists of Southern California, Publishers Association of Southern California (member of the board, 1984—), Calistoga Skydivers (past secretary), North-

ern California Parachute Council (past secretary), Northeast Sport Parachute Council (past secretary; past president).

AWARDS, HONORS: Gold Parachutists Wings, United States Parachute Association, 1972, for 1000 freefall sport parachute dives; Diplome d'Honneur, Federation Aeronautique Internationale, 1979, for contributions to the sport of hang gliding; Achievement award, United States Parachuting Association, 1981, for contributions to the association and the sport of parachuting; Paul Tissandier Diploma, Federation Aeronautique Internationale, 1984; Meritorious Achievement award and certificate, Central Atlantic Sport Parachute Association, for parachute equipment advances and twenty years of membership; Bronze Otto Lillienthal Medal, U.S. Hang Gliding Association.

WRITINGS:

(Editor) *The Parachute Songbook,* Northeast Sport Parachute Council, 1967.
I-E Course for Parachuting Instructor/Examiner Candidates, Parachuting Publications, 1971, 3rd edition published as *Parachuting I-E Course: A Program of Study to Prepare the Expert Parachutist for the U.S.P.A. Instructor/Examiner Written Examination,* 1978.
The Parachute Manual: A Technical Treatise on the Parachute, Parachuting Publications, 1972, 3rd edition published as *The Parachute Manual: A Treatise on Aerodynamic Decelerators,* Para Publishing, 1984.
Hang Gliding: The Basic Book of Skysurfing, D. F. Poynter, 1973, 10th edition published as *Hang Gliding: The Basic Handbook of Ultralight Flying,* Para Publishing, 1981.
Manned Kiting: The Basic Handbook of Tow-Launched Hang Gliding, D. F. Poynter, 1974.
Hang Gliding Manual and Log: A Basic Text for the Novice, Parachuting Publications, 1976.
Parachuting Manual and Log: A Text for the Novice, Parachuting Publications, 1976.
Parachute Rigging Course: A Course Study for the FAA Senior Rigger Certificate, Parachuting Publications, 1977, revised edition, Para Publishing, 1981.
(With Martin Hunt and David Hunn) *Hang Gliding,* Arco, 1977.
Parachuting: The Skydiver's Handbook, Parachuting Publications, 1978.
(With Mark Danna) *Frisbee Player's Handbook,* Parachuting Publications, 1978.
The Self-Publishing Manual: How to Write, Print, and Sell Your Own Book, Parachuting Publications, 1979, 3rd edition, Para Press, 1984.
Publishing Short-Run Books: How to Paste Up and Reproduce Books Instantly Using Your Copy Shop, Parachuting Publications, 1980.
Toobee Player's Handbook: The Amazing Flying Can, Para Publishing, 1981.
Book Fairs: An Exhibiting Guide for Publishers, Para Publishing, 1981, 4th edition, 1986.
Business Letters for Publishers: Creative Correspondence Outlines, Para Publishing, 1981.
Word Processors and Information Processing: A Basic Manual on What They Are and How to Buy, Para Publishing, 1982.
Computer Selection Guide: Choosing the Right Hardware and Software—Business—Professional—Personal, Para Publishing, 1983.
Parachuting Manual for Square/Tandem Equipment, Para Publishing, 1985.

(With Mindy Bingham) *Is There a Book Inside You?: How to Successfully Author a Book Alone or Through Collaboration*, Para Publishing, 1985.

CONTRIBUTOR

Alwyn T. Perrin, editor, *The Explorers Ltd. Source Book*, Harper & Row, 1973.

Bob Anderson, editor, *Sport-Source*, Anderson World, 1975.

Frank Covino, editor, *Skier's Digest*, Follett, 1976.

Pat Works and Jan Works, editors, *Parachuting: United We Fall, a Relative Work Anthology*, RWU Parachuting, 1979.

Stewart Brand, editor, *The Next Whole Earth Catalog*, Alternatives, 1981.

Also contributor to Cesar H. Villanueva D., *Buen Salto*, and to Stewart Brand, editor, *The Whole Earth Catalog*.

OTHER

Contributor to the *Encyclopedia Americana*. Author of column, "Parachuting Poynters," in *Parachutist* magazine, 1963—. Contributor of aviation and other articles and photographs to a variety of publications, including *Parachutist, Skydiver, Success in Self-Publishing, Frisbee World, Hang Glider Weekly, Publishers Weekly,* and *Small Press*. Founder/editor of *Spotter*, parachuting's news magazine, 1965-74. Founder/editor of *Para-Newsbriefs*, the official publication of the Parachute Equipment Industry Association.

WORK IN PROGRESS: Books on parachutes and publishing.

SIDELIGHTS: Dan Poynter told *CA:* "My writing career began with magazine articles. The articles helped me to develop a writing style, bank materials for a later book, and establish a readership. The first book, *The Parachute Manual*, required eight years to research and draft. Since no publisher would be interested in such an obscure subject, it was self-published.

"This unique forty-five dollar treatise sells at the rate of one thousand copies per year and was revised in 1977 and 1984. In 1973, the sport of hang gliding was being reborn. Unable to find a book on the subject, I wrote *Hang Gliding*. So far, it has been through the press ten times for 130,000 [copies] in print, and there are two printings of a German edition. After *Hang Gliding* my book output accelerated to as many as two per year while all the other books were being revised as they came up for reprinting. All books were self-published except for the four translations and the sale of *Word Processors* to Prentice-Hall. Noting my successes in publishing, many people asked for the secrets. To comply with their demands, I wrote *The Self-Publishing Manual* in 1979; it was self-published, of course. Several other books on various aspects of publishing followed.

"My publishing success should be attributed to my marketing insight rather than to any particular literary ability. For years I wrote about aviation sports and served on the boards of the national and international sport aviation organizations. More recently, I've been applying all I have learned to the production and politics of publishing. Publishing is exciting and fun. Book marketing is stimulating—and easy, if you don't do it the traditional New York way.

"I enjoy publishing and marketing my written wares. The information I provide is useful and enjoyed by others while it provides a good living for me."

Dan Poynter is the grandnephew of poets Kathleen Norris and Frank Norris, and of novelist Stephen Vincent Benet. He holds a patent on a type of parachute pack.

AVOCATIONAL INTERESTS: Skydiving, aviation, traveling.

BIOGRAPHICAL/CRITICAL SOURCES:

PERIODICALS

ABA Booklist, December, 1979, January, 1984.

American Libraries, September, 1983.

Choice, December, 1978, January, 1980.

Library Journal, August 12, 1975, February 14, 1978, March 17, 1978, May 15, 1982.

New York Times Book Review, February 18, 1978.

Publishers Weekly, February 28, 1978, August 21, 1978.

Santa Barbara News and Review, January 12, 1983.

Santa Barbara News-Press, March 17, 1982.

Small Press Review, May, 1979, November, 1980, January, 1982.

West Coast Review of Books, July, 1982.

Western Publisher, October, 1980, January, 1981, February-March, 1982.

Writer's Digest, December, 1980, May, 1981.

*   *   *

PRENTICE, Charlotte
See PLATT, Charles

*   *   *

PRESSER, Janice   1946-
(Janice Presser Greene)

PERSONAL: Born February 14, 1946, in New York, N.Y.; daughter of Murray S. and Esther (maiden name, Friedman) Presser; married Sanford I. Greene, December 19, 1965 (divorced May, 1982); married Barry S. Perlman (an executive), June 25, 1982; children: Andrew, Marni. *Education:* City College of the City University of New York, B.A., 1967; Columbia University, B.S.N., 1978; Hunter College of the City University of New York, M.A., 1981. *Politics:* Independent. *Religion:* Lifespring Congregational Church.

ADDRESSES: Home and office—Box 598, Palmyra, N.J. 08065.

CAREER: New York City Department of Social Services, New York City, case manager, 1967-69, La Leche League of New York City, professional liaison, chapter president, and group leader, 1970-79; private practice as childbirth educator and family counselor, New York City, 1974-81; psychotherapist in private practice, Palmyra, N.J., 1981-85; Steininger Guidance Center of Camden County, Inc., Cherry Hill, N.J., crisis nurse therapist, 1985—. Lecturer, Seminars in Perinatal Education, Inc., 1981-84. Board member, LCC Health Project, 1980-82, Furniture Design Systems Corporation, 1984-85, and SanBar General Corporation, 1984—.

Professional advisory board member, Home Oriented Maternity Experience, 1977-80, Cooperative Childbirth Network, 1977-81, Scleroderma Society of Greater New York, 1980-82, Society for the Protection of the Unborn through Nutrition, 1980-82, Society for Patient Awareness, 1982-85 and 1987—, and Intact Education Foundation, 1982—.

MEMBER: American Association of Pastoral Counselors, Authors League of America, Authors Guild, Scleroderma Society of Greater New York (publications director, 1981—).

WRITINGS:

(Under name Janice Presser Greene; with Gail Storza Brewer) *Right From the Start*, Rodale Press, 1981.
(Editor of American edition) Sheila Kitzinger, *The Complete Book of Pregnancy and Childbirth*, Knopf, 1981.
(With Brewer and Julianna Freehand) *Breastfeeding*, Knopf, 1983.
When Two Become Three: The Couple's Book of Pregnancy, Doubleday, 1984.
Inspiring Parenthood, Ballantine/Epiphany, 1986.

Contributor of poems, books reviews, and articles to *Nursing Care, Mother's Manual, Soho Weekly News*, and to several childbirth organization newsletters.

WORK IN PROGRESS: An inspirational nonfiction book.

SIDELIGHTS: Janice Presser told *CA:* "I never set out to be a writer. My English course grades attest to that. But my curiosity overcame my education. My bywords are 'question authority' and 'embrace entropy'; my life may be chaotic at times, but it's never dull.

"*Breastfeeding* was a joy to work on. We were all breast-feeding mothers—even our editor!—and thus shared the desire to express, not only our knowledge, but our emotions.

"Being able to write about the spiritual side of life without fear of being edited was the nicest part of doing *Inspired Parenthood*. I've come to believe that there are five aspects that need to be examined to understand your life: the biological, the intrapsychic (i.e. your thoughts and feelings), the family you come from, the society you live in, and the spiritual. You need to understand them and integrate them."

When asked for her advice to fathers, Presser commented: "If you want to help your baby grow up secure, put your efforts into strengthening your marriage instead of wasting your life away as a workaholic. Really knowing your mate makes mutual parenting easier."

*   *   *

PRICE, Alfred   1936-

PERSONAL: Born August 3, 1936, in Cheam, Surrey, England; son of Lewis (a building contractor) and Augustine (Gefall) Price; married Jane Beaven, March 14, 1964; children: Fiona, Clare. *Education:* Educated at schools in Surrey, England; Ph.D., Loughborough University, 1985. *Religion:* Church of England.

ADDRESSES: Home—19 Bayley Close, Uppingham, Rutland, Leicestershire LE15 9TG, England. *Agent*—Campbell Thomson & McLaughlin Ltd., 31 Newington Green, London N16 9PU, England.

CAREER: Royal Air Force, 1952-74, specialized in electronic warfare, aircraft weaponry, and modern air fighting tactics; currently full-time writer.

MEMBER: Royal Historical Society (fellow).

AWARDS, HONORS: L. G. Groves Memorial Prize for aircraft safety, 1963.

WRITINGS:

Instruments of Darkness: The Struggle for Radar Supremacy, Kimber & Co., 1967, revised edition published as *Instruments of Darkness: The History of Electronic Warfare*, Macdonald & Jane's, 1977, Scribner, 1978.
German Air Force Bombers of World War II, Volume I, Doubleday, 1968, 2nd edition, Hylton-Lacey, 1971, Volume II, Hylton-Lacey, 1969.
Luftwaffe: Birth, Life, and Death of an Air Force, Macdonald & Co., 1970.
Aircraft versus Submarine: The Evolution of the Anti-Submarine Aircraft, 1912-1972, Kimber & Co., 1973, U.S. Naval Institute, 1974.
Battle over the Reich, Ian Allan, 1973, Scribner, 1974.
Spitfire at War, Ian Allan, 1974, Scribner, 1977.
World War II Fighter Conflict, Macdonald & Jane's, 1975, Hippocrene, 1979.
The Bomber in World War II, Macdonald & Jane's, 1976, Scribner, 1979.
Blitz on Britain: The Bomber Attacks on the United Kingdom, 1939-1945, Ian Allan, 1977.
Focke-Wulf 190 at War, International Publications Service, 1977.
Spitfire: A Documentary History, Macdonald & Jane's, 1977.
Luftwaffe Handbook, 1939-1945, Scribner, 1977.
Battle of Britain: The Hardest Day—August 18, 1940, Macdonald & Jane's, 1979, published as *The Hardest Day: 18 August 1940—The Battle of Britain*, Scribner, 1980.
(With Jeff Ethell) *The German Jets in Combat*, Jane's Publishing Co., 1980.
(With Ethell) *Target Berlin: Mission 250, 6 March 1944*, Jane's Publishing Co., 1981.
Luftwaffe: 1933-1945, Arms & Armour Press, Volumes I-II, 1981, Volumes III-IV, 1982.
The Spitfire Story, Jane's Publishing Co., 1982, Arms & Armour Press, 1985.
Harrier at War, Ian Allen, 1984.
(With Ethell) *Air War South Atlantic*, Macmillan, 1985.
Air Battle Central Europe, Free Press, 1987.

Also author of *History of U.S. Electronic Warfare*, Volume I: *Association of Old Crows*, 1984.

WORK IN PROGRESS: Volume II of *History of U.S. Electronic Warfare*.

SIDELIGHTS: Alfred Price told *CA:* "I never cease to be enthralled with the research for my books. There are so many fascinating people around, all one has to do is to ask the right questions. And if one looks around the various archives carefully enough, the required documentary evidence can usually be found. Fortunately other people seem to find historical research interesting too and buy my books, thus enabling me to continue in my chosen profession."

*   *   *

PRICE, Beverley Joan   1931-
(Beverley Randell)

PERSONAL: Born in 1931 in Wellington, New Zealand; daughter of William Harding and Gwendolyn Louise (Ryall) Randell; married Hugh Price (a book publisher), October 17, 1959; children: Susan. *Education:* Victoria University of Wellington, B.A., 1952; Wellington Teachers College, Diploma of Teaching, 1953.

ADDRESSES: Home and office—24 Glasgow St., Kelburn, Wellington, New Zealand.

CAREER: Free-lance writer. Teacher of junior classes at schools in Wellington, Raumati, and Marlborough, New Zealand, 1953-59, and London, England, 1957-58; Price Milburn & Co. Ltd., Wellington, editor, 1962-84.

MEMBER: International PEN, New Zealand Women Writers Society, Australian Society of Authors.

WRITINGS—Under name Beverley Randell:

JUVENILES

Tiny Tales, sixteen volumes, Wheaton, 1965.
PM Commonwealth Readers, sixteen volumes, A. H. & A. W. Reed, 1965.
John, the Mouse Who Learned to Read, Collins, 1966, reprinted, Penguin, 1986.
Methuen Number Story Caption Books, sixteen volumes, Methuen, 1967.
Methuen Caption Books, Volumes I-IV: *Blue Set,* Volumes V-VIII: *Green Set,* Volumes IX-XII: *Orange Set,* Volumes XIII-XVI: *Purple Set,* Volumes XVII-XX: *Red Set,* Volumes XXI-XXIV: *Yellow Set,* Methuen, 1967, 2nd edition, 1974.
(Editor) *Red Car Books,* six volumes, Methuen, 1967.
Instant Readers, sixteen volumes, Price Milburn, 1969-70.
(With Olive Harvey and Joy Cowley) *Bowmar Primary Reading Series: Supplementary to All Basic Reading Series,* sixty-six volumes, Bowmar, 1969.
Listening Skillbuilders, twenty-four volumes, Price Milburn, 1971.
(With Susanne Emanuel) *Mark and Meg Books,* nine volumes, Methuen, 1971.
Guide to the Ready to Read Series, and Supporting Books, Price Milburn, 1972.
Methuen Story Readers, one hundred two volumes, Methuen, 1972-76.
First Phonics, twenty-four volumes, Methuen, 1973.
PM Creative Workbooks, nine volumes, Price Milburn, 1973.
(With Robin Robilliard) *Country Readers,* eighteen volumes, Price Milburn, 1974.
(With Robilliard) *Methuen Country Books,* four volumes, Methuen, 1974.
(Editor) *People at Work,* fourteen volumes, Price Milburn, 1974.
(Editor) *Everyday Stories,* twenty-eight volumes, Price Milburn, 1976.
(With Clive Harper) *Animal Books,* sixteen volumes, Thomas Nelson, 1978.
(With James K. Baxter) *Readalongs,* thirty-six volumes, Price Milburn, 1979-81.
Phonic Blends, twenty-four volumes, Methuen, 1979.
Singing Games, Price Milburn, 1981.
(Co-author) *Joining-In Books,* eighteen volumes, Nelson, 1984.
Rhyme and Rhythm Books, four volumes, Heinemann, 1985.
Look and Listen, twenty-four volumes, Heinemann, 1985.

EDITOR OF SERIES

"PM Instant Readers," Price Milburn, 1969-70.
"PM Town Readers," Price Milburn, 1971.
"Dinghy Stories," Methuen, 1973.
"PM Everyday Stories," Price Milburn, 1973-80.
"PM Science Concept Books," Price Milburn, 1974.
"People at Work," Price Milburn, 1974.
"PM Seagulls," Price Milburn, 1980.

"Early Days," Price Milburn, 1982.

SIDELIGHTS: Beverley Joan Price, better known as Beverley Randell, once wrote: "In 1972 I traveled to England to lecture on reading at teachers' centers, and I have several times lectured in Australia, particularly in 1980. My interests are reading schemes, understanding how children learn to read, and writing the sort of books that can help them. The school books I dislike most are all those that are narrow and restricting—mere reading exercises (often 'based on linguistic principles'). But I like those that strike a spark—that are exciting, memorable, splendid."

Randell's books have been translated into several languages, including Italian, Greek, Chinese and Welsh, and aboriginal languages.

BIOGRAPHICAL/CRITICAL SOURCES:

BOOKS

Reading Is Everybody's Business, International Reading Association, 1972.

                              *   *   *

PRICE, Nelson Lynn 1931-

PERSONAL: Born August 24, 1931, in Osyka, Miss.; son of Robert S. and Genevieve (Dykes) Price; married Trudy Knight, February 12, 1956; children: Lynn (Mrs. Roger Hill), Sharon (Mrs. Randy Turner). *Education:* Southeastern Louisiana University, B.S., 1953; New Orleans Baptist Theological Seminary, Th.M., 1957; Emmanuel School of Theology, D.D., 1971; Mercer University, D.D., 1984.

ADDRESSES: Home—1400 Beaumont Dr., Kennesaw, Ga. 30144. *Office*—Roswell Street Baptist Church, 774 Roswell St., Marietta, Ga. 30060.

CAREER: Pastor in New Orleans, La., 1957-65; Roswell Street Baptist Church, Marietta, Ga., pastor, 1965—. Southern Baptist Convention, current president of Pastors' Conference and member of Home Mission Board, past president of Ministers in Broadcasting; former vice-president of Louisiana Baptist Convention; Georgia Baptist Convention, first vice-president, 1981, and past president. Former trustee of Louisiana College and New Orleans Baptist Theological Seminary; former national trustee of Fellowship of Christian Athletes; former member of Georgia Board of Human Resources. Broadcasts weekly over WXIA-TV, Atlanta, Ga., ACTS-TV Network, Liberty Broadcasting Network, and WFOM-Radio, Marietta; former daily commentator over WYNX-Radio, Marietta. Numerous speaking engagements, including the inaugural message before President Jimmy Carter, his cabinet and staff, on Inauguration Day morning, 1977.

MEMBER: New Orleans Baptist Theological Seminary Alumni Association (past president).

AWARDS, HONORS: Public service award from Cobb County Chamber of Commerce; Liberty Bell Award from Cobb County Bar Association; Cobb County Citizen of the Year Award from *Marietta Daily Journal;* "Best Sermon" citations from *Inside Cobb Magazine,* 1986 and 1987; commendation from General Assembly of Georgia, 1986, for twenty years of service to the State of Georgia.

WRITINGS:

Shadows We Run From, Broadman, 1975.
I've Got to Play on Their Court, Broadman, 1976.
How to Find Out Who You Are, Broadman, 1977.
Supreme Happiness, Broadman, 1979.
Only the Beginning, Broadman, 1980.
The Destruction of Death, Broadman, 1983.
Farewell to Fear, Broadman, 1983.
Called to Splendor, Broadman, 1984.
*Tenderness and Twenty-Four Other Ways to Make a Marriage
    Work,* Fleming Revell, 1986.
The Emmanuel Factor, Broadman, 1987.

Also author of *The Occult Is Lion Country.* Contributor of
weekly editorial to *Marietta Daily Journal,* 1966—.

SIDELIGHTS: Nelson Lynn Price once told *CA:* "When I
write, I begin at about 4:00 a.m. and crash on a topic until I
have exhausted it or me. My work, *The Destruction of Death,*
is related to the resurrection. The subject is approached as an
apologetic stance with the ambition of affording inspiration."

R

RAMANUJAN, A(ttipat) K(rishnaswami) 1929-

PERSONAL: First two "a's" in surname are long vowels; born March 16, 1929, in Mysore, India; son of Attipat Asuri (a professor) and Seshammal Krishnaswami; married Molly Daniels, June 7, 1962; children: Krittika (daughter), Krishnaswami (son). *Education:* Mysore University, B.A. (with honors), 1949, M.A., 1950; Deccan College, graduate diplomas, 1958 and 1959; Indiana University, Ph.D., 1963.

ADDRESSES: Home—5629 South Dorchester Ave., Chicago, Ill. 60637. *Office*—South Asia Language and Area Center, University of Chicago, 1130 East 59th St., Chicago, Ill. 60637.

CAREER: Lecturer in English at colleges in India, 1950-58, including University of Baroda, 1957-58; University of Chicago, Chicago, Ill., research associate in Tamil, 1961, assistant professor of linguistics (Tamil and Dravidian languages), 1962-65, associate professor, 1966-68, professor of linguistics and Dravidian studies, 1968—, professor on committee on social thought, 1972—, chairman of department of South Asian languages and civilizations, 1980-85, William E. Colvin Professor, 1983. Visiting professor, University of Wisconsin, 1965 and 1971, University of California at Berkeley, 1966 and 1973, University of Michigan, 1970, Carleton College, 1978 and 1982.

AWARDS, HONORS: Fulbright travel fellowship and Smith-Mundt fellowship for study in United States, 1959-60; faculty research fellowship, American Institute of Indian Studies, 1963-64; fellow, Indiana School of Letters, 1963; Poetry Society recommendation, 1964, for *The Striders;* Tamil Writers' Association Award, 1969; Fulbright fellowship, 1969; American Council of Learned Societies fellowship, 1973; National Book Award nomination, 1974, for *Speaking of Siva;* National Endowment for the Humanities fellowships, 1976 and 1982; named Padma Sri by Government of India, 1976; MacArthur Prize fellowship, 1983-88.

WRITINGS:

Proverbs (in Kannada), Karnatak University (Dharwar, India), 1955.
Fifteen Poems from a Classical Tamil Anthology, Writer's Workshop (Calcutta), 1965.
The Striders (poems), Oxford University Press, 1966.

No Lotus in the Navel (poems; in Kannada), Manohar Granthmala (Dharwar), 1969.
Relations (poems), Oxford University Press, 1972.
(With E. C. Dimock and others) *The Literatures of India: An Introduction,* University of Chicago Press, 1975.
And Other Poems (in Kannada), [Dharwar], 1977.
Selected Poems, Oxford University Press, 1977.
Mattobbana Atmakate (novel), [Dharwar], 1978.
Second Sight (poems), Oxford University Press, 1986.
(With S. Blackburn) *Another Harmony: New Essays in South Asian Folklore,* University of California Press, 1986.

TRANSLATOR

Shouri Ramanujan (pseudonym of wife, Molly Ramanujan) *Haladi Meenu* (translation into Kannada of her original English manuscript, *The Yellow Fish*), Manohar Granthmala, 1966.
The Interior Landscape: Love Poems from a Classical Tamil Anthology, Indiana University Press, 1967.
(With Michael Garman and Rajeev Taranath) M. Gopalakrishna Adiga, *The Song of the Earth and Other Poems,* Writer's Workshop, 1968.
(With others) *Selected Poems of G. Sankara Kurup,* Dialogue Calcutta, c. 1969.
Speaking of Siva, Penguin, 1973.
U. R. Anantha Murthy, *Samskara* (novel), Oxford University Press, 1976.
Hymns for the Drowning (medieval Tamil religious poems), Princeton University Press, 1981.
Poems of Love and War (classical Tamil poetry), Columbia University Press, 1985.

OTHER

Poems in English are represented in more than sixty anthologies and have been published in Indian, British, and American periodicals.

WORK IN PROGRESS: An anthology of Indian poetry; a book of poems; a book of Indian folktales.

BIOGRAPHICAL/CRITICAL SOURCES:

PERIODICALS

New York Times Book Review, November 20, 1966.
Poetry, March, 1967.

RAMANUJAN, Molly   1932-
(Shouri Ramanujan; Shouri Daniels)

PERSONAL: Born July 2, 1932, in Kerala, India; daughter of Chacko and Leah (Mikhail) Daniels; married Attipat Krishnaswami Ramanujan (a poet and professor of linguistics), June 7, 1962; children: Krittika (daughter), Krishnaswami (son). *Education:* University of Bombay, B.A. (with honors), 1955, M.A., 1957; Indiana University, graduate study, 1961-62, summer, 1964; University of Chicago, presently doctoral candidate.

ADDRESSES: Home—5629 Dorchester Ave., Chicago, Ill. 60637.

CAREER: Started out as a journalist and worked on *Deccan Herald* (English-langue newspaper), Bangalore, India, but "found it meaningless"; taught English literature at Sophia College, Bombay, India, 1957, Lady Shri Ram College, Delhi, India, 1958-64, Delhi University, Delhi, 1971-73, and at Kennedy-King College, Chicago, Ill., 1974-76.

AWARDS, HONORS: Smith-Mundt and Fulbright grants for study in United States, 1961-62; award for best fiction, Illinois Arts Council, 1978; award for best literary criticism, Illinois Arts Council, 1982.

WRITINGS:

(Under name Shouri Ramanujan) *Haladi Meenu* (in Kannada; translation by husband, A. K. Ramanujan, of her original English manuscript, *The Yellow Fish*), Manohar Granthmala (Dharwar), 1966.
(Under name Shouri Daniels) *Salt Doll*, Vikas, 1978.
G. V. Desani: Writer and Worldview, Arnold-Heinemann, 1984.

Portions of "The Yellow Fish" have been published in English in *Chicago Review*, 1968, and in *Experiments in Prose*, Swallow Press, 1969; portions of *Salt Doll* have been published in *Tri-Quarterly*, winter, 1974, *Primavera*, and *Femina*, January, 1976. Contributor to *Femina, Carleton Miscellany, Chicago Literary Review, Chicago Review, Journal of Literary Studies*, and *The Saul Bellow Journal*, and to newspapers in India; author of book reviews for Indian PEN, 1956-57.

WORK IN PROGRESS: Garden of the Morning Breeze, a romance set in India; *A City of Children,* a novella and six short stories; *Structure and Worldview in E. M. Forster's "A Passage to India".*

SIDELIGHTS: Molly Ramanujan told *CA:* "I am interested in 'characters,' my writing has to be about what it is to be some particular person. My earliest literary passion was for *Hamlet*. I tore the play out, bound it, tied it to my wrist, and was never seen without it. I have read very few books seriously, but these few I chew, digest, and make my own. I take the movies seriously. I am excited about anything that seems to be a new way of doing things, especially in narrative techniques. I have discovered that I am incurably sane. Not in the least bit mad.

"In 'The Yellow Fish,' I tried to present the point of view of both men and women, but in *Salt Doll* I tried to write exclusively from a woman's point of view. Now I am trying to work out a pre-Romantic neutral point of view. In the book of short stories, I hope to write exclusively from the point of view of an old-fashioned man. I wrote *Salt Doll* from 1968 to 1970, and revised it and rewrote it for another two years. I

originally wrote it for Saul Bellow who was kind enough to read several drafts. For four years after that I did nothing but teach. . . . I have now started spending several hours at the typewriter, and am turning out a short story each month. My new publisher, Vikas, distributes in the United States, and though I expect the book [of short stories] to be banned in India, I'm sure it will find many readers here."

Ramanujan described her "most pleasurable writing experience: I wrote a romance set in India, with British characters and Indian servants. While writing it I often found myself rolling with laughter on the carpet. It's called *The Garden of the Morning Breeze*. All those who have read the typescript say 'it's unputdownable.' The most painful experience: I wrote a serious book of fiction called *A City of Children*, and although four of the short stories have already been published in the United States, no publisher in India wants it."

Publication of *Haladi Meenu* caused something of a furor in Kannada, according to the *Chicago Review*. Mrs. Ramanujan, who sometimes uses the Indian name of Shouri instead of Molly, has also lived in Aden, Arabia. She and her husband return to India every other year.

    *   *   *

RAMANUJAN, Shouri
See RAMANUJAN, Molly

    *   *   *

RANDELL, Beverley
See PRICE, Beverley Joan

    *   *   *

RANDOM, Alan
See KAY, Ernest

    *   *   *

RASHKE, Richard L.   1936-

PERSONAL: Born April 23, 1936, in Milwaukee, Wis.; son of Guy and Angeline (Luksich) Rashke; married Paula Kaufmann, May 9, 1981. *Education:* American University, M.A., 1973.

ADDRESSES: Home and office—1411 F. St. NE, Washington, D.C. 20002.

CAREER: Writer.

WRITINGS:

The Deacon in Search of Identity, Paulist Press, 1975.
The Killing of Karen Silkwood: The Story behind the Kerr-McGee Plutonium Case, Houghton, 1981.
Escape from Sobibor (nonfiction), Houghton, 1982.
Stormy Genius: The Life of Aviation's Maverick, Bill Lear (nonfiction), Houghton, 1985.
(With Robert Parker) *Capitol Hill in Black and White* (nonfiction), Dodd, 1986.
Runaway Father (nonfiction), Harcourt, 1988.

SIDELIGHTS: The Killing of Karen Silkwood: The Story behind the Kerr-MeGee Plutonium Case is Richard L. Rashke's account of the facts and controversy regarding the death of a young nuclear technician. Karen Silkwood was killed in a car accident while en route to a meeting with a *New York Times* reporter in November of 1974. At this meeting, she was to hand over evidence of a safety and security crisis at the Kerr-McGee plutonium fuel rod manufacturing plant in Crescent, Oklahoma, where she was employed. Rashke works to prove that Silkwood's death was not accidental and that the events surrounding it were covered up by several law enforcement agencies.

Silkwood's safety concerns led her to collect evidence of violations at Kerr-McGee, which she initially planned to hand over to union officials. But a pending decertification vote which would have expelled the union from the plant threatened to block the effectiveness of this action. At the same time, Silkwood discovered that she had been exposed to a possibly lethal dose of radiation, and the source of this contamination was eventually traced to plutonium in her apartment refrigerator. After this discovery, Silkwood, with the aid of her union, arranged to meet a *New York Times* reporter with the evidence she had collected. She died before handing it over, and no documents were found at the site of her car accident.

Reviewers of *The Killing of Karen Silkwood* generally find it worth reading but express some reservations. Joseph Nocera of the *New Republic* feels that "though clear, concise, and understandable, Rashke's book leaves little doubt that he has been bitten by the conspiracy bug as much as anyone else who's ever written about the case. Although he is willing to separate the facts from the theories, it is clear that he finds the theories more intriguing." Gregg Easterbrook, in a *Washington Post Book World* review, approves of the book and is convinced by Rashke's arguments that Silkwood's death was not accidental but the result of a plot. He states: "Rashke has produced a chronicle that meets a demanding test of objectivity," but later expresses disappointment in the author's refusal to propose who might be behind the plot. In Easterbrook's view, Rashke's "objectivity gets in his way; because he cannot prove who did it, he does not even speculate." *Saturday Review* contributor Tamar Jacoby concedes that "the book's strength remains its informative discussion of the issues surrounding nuclear energy. . . . In places Rashke's argument is undermined by his crusading polemical tone, but with or without that melodrama, he tells a frightening story."

BIOGRAPHICAL/CRITICAL SOURCES:

PERIODICALS

Atlantic, March, 1981.
Los Angeles Times, April 16, 1981.
New Republic, May 16, 1981.
New York Times, November 7, 1985.
New York Times Book Review, June 14, 1981.
Saturday Review, March, 1981.
Washington Post, December 14, 1982.
Washington Post Book World, March 22, 1981.

*   *   *

REDGATE, John
   See KENNEDY, Adam

*   *   *

REED, Graham   1923-

PERSONAL: Born March 13, 1923, in Coventry, England; son of Fred (a teacher) and Winifred (Graham) Reed; married Jean Rutter, December 13, 1947; children: Lindsey (Mrs. Colin Bent). *Education:* Downing College, Cambridge, B.A. and

M.A., 1949; University of Durham, M.Litt., 1963; University of Manchester, Ph.D., 1966.

ADDRESSES: Home—1357 Mount Pleasant, Toronto, Ontario, Canada M4N 2T6. *Office*—Glendon College, York University, 4700 Keele St., Downsview, Ontario, Canada M3J 1P3.

CAREER: Educational psychologist in Kingston upon Hull, Yorkshire, England, 1949-59; University of Manchester, Manchester, England, lecturer in clinical psychology, 1959-66; University of Aberdeen, Aberdeen, Scotland, senior lecturer in psychology, 1966-69; York University, Downsview, Ontario, Atkinson College, professor of psychology, 1970-81, chairman of department, 1970-73, dean of faculty of graduate studies, 1973-81, Glendon College, professor of psychology and chairman of department, 1982—. Visiting professor, Clark Institute of Psychiatry, University of Toronto, 1981-82. *Military service:* British Army, 1942-47; became captain.

MEMBER: British Psychological Society, Royal Society of Health, Canadian Psychological Association.

WRITINGS:

Fisher's Creek, Dobson, 1963.
How to Read Faster under Water, Peter Wolfe, 1968.
The Psychology of Anomalous Experience: A Cognitive Approach, Hutchinson, 1972.
Magical Miracles You Can Do, Elsevier-Nelson, 1979.
Obsessional Experience and Compulsive Behaviour, Academic Press, 1985.

Contributor to learned journals.

WORK IN PROGRESS: A novel; a study of obsessional disorders.

AVOCATIONAL INTERESTS: Collecting seventeenth-century Dutch etchings and eighteenth-century porcelain tea-bowls; playing chamber music on the viola and jazz on the trombone.

*   *   *

REEVE, Joel
   See COX, William (Robert)

*   *   *

REICHERT, Herbert W(illiam)   1917-1978
   (Wilhelm Schad)

PERSONAL: Born June 5, 1917, in New York, N.Y., died March 15, 1978; son of William and Johanna (Schad) Reichert; married Irene Nassau (a free-lance artist), March 15, 1950; children: Susan Vanessa. *Education:* Columbia University, B.A., 1938, M.A., 1940; University of Tuebingen, additional study, 1938-39; University of Illinois, Ph.D., 1942. *Politics:* Democrat.

ADDRESSES: Home—2136 North Lake Shore Dr., Chapel Hill, N.C. 27514. *Office*—Department of German, University of North Carolina, Chapel Hill, N.C. 27514.

CAREER: U.S. Army Air Forces, Technical Training Command, civilian instructor in meteorology, 1942-44; University of Wisconsin, (now University of Wisconsin-Madison), Madison, instructor in German, 1944-45; Grinnell College, Grinnell, Iowa, assistant professor of German, 1945-47; University of North Carolina at Chapel Hill, assistant professor, 1947-53, associate professor, 1953-58, professor of German literature, 1959-78, head of department, 1965-70. Citizens' Committee for Chapel Hill Schools, member, 1959-64, chairman, 1963-64.

MEMBER: International Arthur Schnitzler Research Association (vice-president, 1963-78), Modern Langauge Association of America, American Association of Teachers of German, South Atlantic Modern Language Association, Delta Phi Alpha.

AWARDS, HONORS: Guggenheim fellow, 1958-59.

WRITINGS:

Basic Concepts in the Philosophy of Gottfried Keller, University of North Carolina Studies in German Language and Literature, 1949, reprinted, AMS Press, 1986.
(Editor) *Deutsche Horspiele* (four German radio plays), Appleton, 1959.
(Editor with Karl Schlechta) *International Nietzsche Bibliography,* University of North Carolina Comparative Literature Series, 1960, revised edition, 1968.
(Editor with Herman Salinger) *Studies in Arthur Schnitzler,* University of North Carolina Studies in German Language and Literature, 1963, reprinted, AMS Press, 1986.
The Impact of Nietzsche on Hermann Hesse, Enigma Press (Mt. Pleasant, Mich.), 1972.
Friedrich Nietzsche's Impact on Modern German Literature, University of North Carolina Press, 1975.

Translator, under pseudonym Wilhelm Schad. Contributor to *German Quarterly, Monatshefte, German Review, Modern Language Notes.*

AVOCATIONAL INTERESTS: Travel, sports, tennis, sailing, piano, swimming, photography.†

*   *   *

REINHARZ, Jehuda 1944-

PERSONAL: Born August 1, 1944, in Haifa, Palestine (now Israel); came to the United States, 1961, naturalized, 1966; son of Fred and Anita (Weigler) Reinharz; married Shulamit Rothschild (an associate professor). *Education:* Columbia University, B.S., 1967; Jewish Theological Seminary in America, B.R.E., 1967; Harvard University, M.A., 1968; Brandeis University, Ph.D., 1972.

ADDRESSES: Office—Department of Near Eastern and Judaic Studies, Brandeis University, Waltham, Mass. 02554.

CAREER: Hebrew College, Brookline, Mass., instructor in Jewish history, 1969-70; Brandeis University, Hiatt Institute, Jerusalem, Israel, instructor in Jewish history, autumn, 1970; University of Michigan, Ann Arbor, assistant professor, 1972-76, associate professor, 1976-80, professor of history, 1980-82, staff member of Center for Near Eastern and North African studies, 1972-82; Brandeis University, Waltham, Mass., Richard Koret Professor of Modern Jewish History, 1982—. Instructor at Boston University, 1969-70, and Clark University, spring, 1972; visiting professor at Hiatt Institute, Brandeis University, 1973.

MEMBER: Association for Jewish Studies (member of board of governors, 1974-84), Leo Baeck Institute, Conference on Jewish Social Studies, World Union of Jewish Studies, American Historical Association.

AWARDS, HONORS: Woodrow Wilson fellowship for research in Germany and Israel, 1970-71, 1973, 1975-76; Amer-

ican Council of Learned Societies fellowship, 1974; National Endowment for the Humanities grant, 1979-80; Leo Baeck Institute fellow, 1982; Kenneth B. Smilen Literary Award, 1985; *Present Tense*/Joel H. Cavior Literary Award, 1985, and National Jewish Book Award, 1986, both for *Chaim Weizmann: The Making of a Zionist Leader;* Lady Davis fellow, Hebrew University, 1987-88.

WRITINGS:

(Contributor) Herbert A. Strauss, editor, *Conference on Intellectual Policies in American Jewry,* American Federation of Jews from Central Europe, 1972.
(Contributor) Geoffrey Wigoder, editor, *Zionism,* Keter Publishing House, 1973.
(Contributor) Michael A. Fishbane and Paul R. Flohr, editors, *Texts and Studies: Essays in Honor of Nahum N. Glatzer,* E. J. Brill, 1975.
Fatherland or Promised Land?: The Dilemma of the German Jew, 1893-1914, University of Michigan Press, 1975.
(Co-editor) *The Jew in the Modern World,* Oxford University Press, 1980.
(Editor) *Dokumente zur Geschichte des deutschen Zionismus 1882-1933,* J. C. B. Mohr, 1981.
(Co-editor) *Philosophers, Mystics and Politicians,* Duke University Press, 1982.
Chaim Weizmann: The Making of a Zionist Leader, Oxford University Press, 1985.
(Editor with Walter Schatzberg) *The Jewish Response to German Culture: From the Enlightenment to World War II,* University Press of New England, 1985.
(Editor) *Living with Anti-Semitism,* University Press of New England, 1987.
Hashomer Hazair in Germany, 1928-1939, Sifriat Poalim, 1988.

Editor of *Letters and Papers of Chaim Weizmann,* Volume IX, Oxford University Press. Contributor to *Yearbook of the Leo Baeck Institute XXII,* edited by Robert Weltsch and Arnold Paucker.

WORK IN PROGRESS: As co-author, *The Emergence of the Jewish State 1880-1948;* as co-editor, *The Jews of Poland in the Interwar Period.*

SIDELIGHTS: Jehuda Reinharz, professor of modern Jewish history at Brandeis University, has won acclaim for his biography of Israel's first president, entitled *Chaim Weizmann: The Making of a Zionist Leader.* Writes *New York Times Book Review* contributor Chaim Raphael, "It was high time for something like an official biography to be written, if only to give the author, with access to a vast quantity of archives and unofficial sources, a chance to pinpoint the magic that singled Weizmann out among the European Zionists of the time." But Weizmann's "magic" is not easily discerned from the story of the years before he became a Zionist leader; his "character was full of paradox," explains Raphael, who also observes that Weizmann, who was a dedicated chemist, took "as many steps backward as forward" on the path to statesmanship. Reinharz's reliance on his subject's personal writings contributes to the confusion and redeems it at the same time, says Raphael. Patricia P. O'Connor notes in the same source that the only personal papers unavailable to the biographer were some letters the young Weizmann had written during a four-year courtship to a woman he later spurned. John Gross, writing in the *New York Times,* deems the biography "admirable," and "easily the most authoritative so far." Its value was also recognized by two literary awards, one from *Present Tense* in 1985, and the Jewish National Book Award in 1986.

Reinharz is proficient in Hebrew, German, French, Yiddish, and Aramaic.

BIOGRAPHICAL/CRITICAL SOURCES:

PERIODICALS

Globe & Mail (Toronto), August 22, 1987.
New York Times, May 7, 1985.
New York Times Book Review, June 30, 1985.
Times Literary Supplement, September 26, 1986.
Washington Post Book World, June 23, 1985.

*   *   *

REINKE, William A(ndrew)   1928-

PERSONAL: Born August 10, 1928, in Cleveland, Ohio; son of William Adolph (a manufacturer's agent) and Agnes (Stranberg) Reinke; married Charlene Pelton, January 30, 1960; children: Cheryl, Deborah, Cara, William. *Education:* Kenyon College, B.A., 1949; University of Pennsylvania, M.B.A., 1950; Western Reserve University (now Case Western Reserve University), Ph.D., 1961. *Religion:* Protestant.

ADDRESSES: Home—1212 Brixton Rd., Baltimore, Md. 21239. *Office*—School of Public Health, Johns Hopkins University, 615 North Wolfe St., Baltimore, Md. 21205.

CAREER: Western Reserve University (now Case Western Reserve University), Cleveland, Ohio, instructor in mathematics, 1959-61; Corning Glass Works, Corning, N.Y., senior researcher in mathematics, 1961-63; University of Maryland, School of Medicine, Baltimore, assistant professor of preventive medicine, 1963-64; Johns Hopkins University, School of Public Health, Baltimore, Md., associate professor, 1965-68; professor of international health, 1968—, assistant dean, 1974-76, associate dean, 1976-77. Consultant to World Health Organization. *Military service:* U.S. Army, 1953-55; became sergeant.

MEMBER: American Public Health Association, Operations Research Society of America, Institute of Management Sciences, American Statistical Association, Phi Beta Kappa.

WRITINGS:

Statistics for Decision Making, National Foremen's Institute, 1963.
The Planning of Health Services, School of Hygiene and Public Health, Johns Hopkins University, 1969.
(Editor) *Health Planning: Qualitative Aspects and Quantitative Techniques,* Johns Hopkins Press, 1972.
(With F. Grundy) *Health Practice Research and Formalized Managerial Methods,* World Health Organization, 1973.
Quantitative Decision Procedures for Health Workers, School of Hygiene and Public Health, Johns Hopkins University, 1975.

Contributor to journals.

*   *   *

REISS, Albert J(ohn), Jr.   1922-

PERSONAL: Born December 9, 1922, in Cascade, Wis.; son of Albert John and Erma Amanda (Schueler) Reiss; married Emma Lucille Hutto, June, 1953 (divorced August, 1986); children: Peter C., Paul Wetherington, Amy. *Education:* Marquette University, Ph.B., 1944; University of Chicago, M.A., 1948, Ph.D., 1949.

ADDRESSES: Home—600 Prospect St., Apt. A7, New Haven, Conn. 06511. *Office*—Department of Sociology, Yale University, 140 Prospect St., New Haven, Conn. 06520.

CAREER: Illinois Board of Public Welfare Commissioners, Springfield, social research analyst, 1946-47; University of Chicago, Chicago, Ill., instructor, 1947-49, assistant professor of sociology and administrative secretary of department, 1949-52, assistant director of Chicago Community Inventory, 1947-52, and acting director, 1951-52; Vanderbilt University, Nashville, Tenn., associate professor, 1952-54, professor of sociology, 1954-58, chairman of department of sociology and anthropology, 1952-58; University of Iowa, Iowa City, professor of sociology, 1958-60, chairman of department of sociology and anthropology, 1959-60, director of Iowa Urban Community Research Center, 1959-60; University of Wisconsin—Madison, professor of sociology and director of Wisconsin Survey Research Laboratory, 1960-61; University of Michigan, Ann Arbor, professor of sociology, 1961-70, chairman of department, 1964-70, director of Center for Research on Social Organization, 1961-70, lecturer in law, 1968-70; Yale University, New Haven, Conn., professor of sociology, 1970-77, William Graham Sumner Professor of Sociology, 1977—, chairman of department, 1972-78, 1985-89, lecturer in law, 1972—, professor of sociology in Institution for Social and Policy Studies, 1970—.

Visiting professor, University of Denver Law School, summers, 1970-72; visiting fellow, Cambridge University, 1974; George W. Beto Chair in Criminal Justice, Sam Houston State University, summer, 1985. Member of Mental Health Small Grants Committee, National Institutes of Health, 1960-63; member of advisory panel for sociology and social psychology, National Science Foundation, 1963-65; member of behavioral sciences panel to Wooldridge Committee, Executive Office of the President, Office of Science and Technology, 1964; consultant to President's Commission on Law Enforcement and Administration of Justice, 1966-67, and National Advisory Commission on Civil Disorders, 1967-68.

Member of National Advisory Committee for Juvenile Justice and Delinquency Prevention, 1975-78; chairman of advisory committee, Juvenile Justice and Delinquency Prevention in the state of Connecticut, 1976-79; member of Connecticut Justice Commission, 1977-79; member of advisory board, Police Decision Making Project, Center for Research in Criminal Justice, University of Illinois, 1978-79; member of advisory panel and technical committee, National Crime Survey Re-design Project, 1979-81; member of Governor's Task Force on Jail and Prison Overcrowding, state of Connecticut, 1980-81; member of Panel on Research on Criminal Careers, National Research Council, 1983-86; member of law and social sciences advisory panel, National Science Foundation, 1983-87; member of advisory board, Program Evaluation and Methodology Division, U.S. General Accounting Office, 1985—. *Military service:* U.S. Army Air Forces, 1943-44.

MEMBER: International Society of Criminology (member of executive council, 1983-85, 1985-89; president of scientific commission, 1985-89), International Sociological Association, American Society of Criminology (fellow; executive counselor, 1979-82; president, 1983-84), American Sociological Association (fellow; member of council, 1962-65; member of executive committee, 1963-65), American Association for the Advancement of Science (fellow), Society for the Study of Social Problems (member of council, 1965-67; vice-president, 1966-67; president, 1969), American Statistical Association (fellow), Law and Society Association, Sociological Research Association, Eastern Sociological Association, Ohio Valley Sociological Association (president, 1966).

AWARDS, HONORS: Bicentennial Medal, Columbia University, 1954; M.A. (privatim), Yale University, 1970; Bruce Smith, Sr., Award, Academy of Criminal Justice Sciences, 1981; Edwin H. Sutherland Award, American Society of Criminology, 1981; LL.D. (honoris causa), John Jay College of Criminal Justice of the City University of New York, 1981; fellow, Western Society of Criminology, 1982, American Academy of Arts and Sciences, 1983, and American Statistical Association, 1983; docteur honoris causa, University of Montreal, 1985.

WRITINGS:

(Editor) *Selected Readings in Social Pathology,* University of Chicago Bookstore, 1947.

A Survey of Probation Needs and Services in Illinois during 1946, State of Illinois Child Welfare Commission, 1947.

Chaplaincy in Illinois Mental Hospitals, State of Illinois Board of Public Welfare Commissioners, 1948.

(With E. W. Burgess, Louis Wirth, and Don T. Blackiston) *Survey of the Chicago Crime Commission,* Chicago Crime Commission, 1948.

(Editor with Paul K. Hatt) *Reader in Urban Sociology,* Free Press of Glencoe, 1951, revised edition published as *Cities and Society; A Reader in Urban Sociology,* 1957.

(With Evelyn M. Kitagawa) *Preliminary Report of Household Data for Chicago Workers,* Chicago Community Inventory Publications, 1951.

(With Leonard Z. Breen) *Geographic Distribution of Retail Trade in the Chicago Metropolitan Area,* Chicago Community Inventory Publications, 1952.

(With Kitagawa) *Estimates of Potential Work Force and Summary of the Population and Work Force in Six Cities,* Chicago Community Inventory Publications, 1952.

Patterns of Occupation Mobility for Workers in Four Cities, Chicago Community Inventory Publications, 1953.

A Review and Evaluation of Research on the Community: A Memorandum to the Committee on Social Behavior, Social Science Research Council, 1954.

(With Jay W. Artis and Albert Lewis Rhodes) *Population Handbook: Nashville, Tennessee,* Vanderbilt University, Institute of Research and Training in the Social Sciences, 1955.

(With Otis Dudley Duncan) *Social Characteristics of Urban and Rural Communities,* Wiley, 1956, reprinted, Russell, 1976.

(Editor with Elizabeth Wirth Marvick) *Community Life and Social Policy: Selected Papers by Louis Wirth,* University of Chicago Press, 1956.

A Socio-Psychological Study of Conforming and Deviating Behavior among Adolescents, University of Iowa Press, 1959.

(With Duncan, Hatt, and Cecil C. North) *Occupations and Social Status,* Free Press of Glencoe, 1961, reprinted, Arno, 1978, 2nd edition, Free Press, 1965.

Social Organizations and Socialization: Variations on a Theme about Generations, University of Michigan, Center for Research on Social Organization, 1963.

(Editor and author of introduction) *Louis Wirth on Cities and Social Life,* University of Chicago Press, 1964.

(Editor and author of introduction) *Schools in a Changing Society,* Free Press, 1965.

(With Rosemary Sarri and Robert Vinter) *Treating Youthful Offenders in the Community,* Correctional Research Associates, 1966.

Studies in Crime and Law Enforcement in Major Metropolitan Areas, two volumes, U.S. Government Printing Office, 1967.

(Editor) *Cooley and Sociological Analysis,* University of Michigan Press, 1968.

The Police and the Public, Yale University Press, 1971.

Methodological Studies in Crime Classification, Yale University Press, 1972.

(Author of foreword) Anthony E. Simpson, *The Literature of Police Corruption,* McGraw, 1977.

(Author of foreword with Lee Sechrest) William Bieck and others, *Response Time Analysis,* Board of Police Commissioners, Kansas City, Missouri, 1977.

(Author of foreword) Lawrence W. Sherman, *Scandal and Reform: Controlling Police Corruption,* University of California Press, 1978.

(Author of foreword) William M. Rhodes, *Plea Bargaining: Who Gains and Who Loses?,* Institute for Law and Social Research, 1978.

Deterrence and Incapacitation: Estimating the Effects of Criminal Sanctions on Crime Rates, National Academy of Sciences, 1978.

(Editor with Johannes Knutsson and Eckhart Kuhlhorn, and contributor) *Police and the Social Order: Contemporary Research Perspectives,* National Swedish Council for Crime Prevention (Stockholm), 1979.

(Editor with Stephen E. Fienberg, and contributor) *Indicators of Crime and Criminal Justice: Quantitative Studies,* Bureau of Justice Statistics, 1980.

(With Albert D. Biderman) *Data Sources on White-Collar Law Breaking,* National Institute of Justice, 1981.

(Author of foreword) F. Thomas Juster and Kenneth C. Land, editors, *Social Accounting Systems: Essays on the Status of the Art,* Academic Press, 1981.

Policing a City's Central District: The Oakland Story, National Institute of Justice, 1985.

(Editor with Michael H. Tonry, and contributor) *Communities and Crime,* University of Chicago Press, 1986.

Private Employment of Public Police, National Institute of Justice, 1987.

CONTRIBUTOR

The Municipal Yearbook, International City Management, 1952.

R. M. Fisher, editor, *The Metropolis in Modern Life,* Doubleday, 1955.

Education and Juvenile Delinquency, U.S. Government Printing Office, 1956.

Hans Zetterberg, editor, *Sociology in the United States of America,* UNESCO, 1956.

(With Duncan) William Dobriner, editor, *The Suburban Community,* Putnam, 1958.

Britannica Book of the Year, 1959, Encyclopaedia Britannica, 1959.

Hendrick M. Ruitenbeck, *The Problem of Homosexuality in Modern Society,* Dutton, 1963.

Ruth S. Caven, editor, *Readings in Juvenile Delinquency,* Lippincott, 1964.

Howard S. Becker, editor, *The Other Side: Perspectives on Deviance,* Free Press of Glencoe, 1964.

Julius Gould and William L. Kolb, editors, *A Dictionary of the Social Sciences,* Free Press of Glencoe, 1964.

Worterbuch der Soziologie, Ferdinand Enke Verlag (Stuttgart), 1965.

Rose Giallombardo, editor, *Juvenile Delinquency,* Wiley, 1966.

David J. Bordua, editor, *The Police: Six Sociological Essays,* Wiley, 1967.

(With Bordua) *The Uses of Sociology,* Basic Books, 1967.

New Catholic Encyclopedia, McGraw, 1967.

John Gagnon and William Simon, editors, *Sexual Deviance,* Harper, 1967.

Proceedings of Extension and Continuing Education Seminar, North Carolina State University Press, 1967.

Becker and others, editors, *Institutions and the Person,* Aldine, 1968.

A. F. Branstadter and Louis A. Radelet, editors, *Police and Community Relations,* Free Press, 1968.

International Encyclopedia of the Social Sciences, MacMillan, 1968.

Talcott Parsons, editor, *American Sociology: Perspectives, Problems, Methods,* Basic Books, 1968.

Crime against Small Business: A Report of the Small Business Administration, 1969, U.S. Government Printing Office, 1969.

Barbara N. McLennan, editor, *Crime in Urban Society,* Dunellen, 1970.

T. M. Stinnett, editor, *The Teacher Dropout,* F. E. Peacock, 1970.

Michael Lipsky, editor, *Law and Order: Police Encounters,* Trans-Action, 1970.

Leon Radzinowicz and Marvin E. Wolfgang, editors, *The Criminal in the Arms of the Law,* Basic Books, 1971.

Herbert Costner, editor, *Sociological Methodology,* Jossey-Bass, 1971.

(With Howard W. Aldrich) Harlan Hahn, editor, *Police in Urban Society,* Sage Publications, 1971.

Charles E. Reasons and Jack L. Kuykendall, editors, *Race, Crime and Justice,* Goodyear, 1972.

Agnus Campbell and Philip E. Converse, editors, *The Human Meaning of Social Change,* Russell Sage, 1972.

Lee Rainwater, editor, *Deviance and Liberty,* Aldine, 1974.

Daniel Glaser, editor, *Handbook of Criminology,* Rand McNally, 1974.

(With Marc LeBlanc and Guy Tardif) Denis Szabo, editor, *Police: Culture et Societe,* Les Presses de l'Universite de Montreal, 1974.

N. J. Demarath III, Otto Larsen, and Karl F. Schuessler, editors, *Social Policy and Sociology,* Academic Press, 1975.

A. Wallace Sinaiko and Laurie A. Broedling, editors, *Perspectives on Attitude Assessment: Surveys and Their Alternatives,* Smithsonian Institution Press, 1975.

Policy Development Seminars, 1974, Volume I, U.S. Department of Justice, Law Enforcement Assistance Administration, 1975.

Control and Authority in Institutions: Proceedings of the Fourth International Seminar in Comparative Clinical Criminology, University of Montreal Press, 1975.

Ronald Crelinsten and Danielle Laberge-Altemejd, editors, *Hostage Taking: Problem of Prevention and Control,* University of Maryland, Institute of Criminal Justice and Criminology, 1976.

James F. Short, Jr., editor, *Delinquency, Crime and Society,* University of Chicago Press, 1976.

The Belmont Report: Ethical Principles and Guidelines for the Protection of Human Subjects of Research, U.S. Government Printing Office, 1978.

Keith M. Wulff, editor, *Regulation of Scientific Inquiry: Societal Concerns with Research,* American Association for the Advancement of Science, 1979.

Susan Lustman Katz, editor, *Proceedings of the International Year of the Child Advocacy,* Yale University Press, 1979.

Carl B. Klockars and Finbar W. O'Connor, editors, *Deviance and Decency: The Ethics of Research with Human Subjects,* Sage Publications, 1979.

Malcolm W. Klein and Katherine S. Teilman, editors, *Handbook of Criminal Justice Evaluation,* Sage Publications, 1980.

Richard J. Lundman, *Police Behavior: A Sociological Perspective,* Oxford University Press, 1980.

Reflections of America: Commemorating the Statistical Abstract Centennial, U.S. Department of Commerce-Bureau of the Census, 1980.

Hans Joachim Schneider, editor, *Die Psychologie des 20. Jahrhunderts,* Volume XIV, Kindler Verlag (Zurich), 1981.

The Five-Year Outlook on Science and Technology, 1981, National Science Foundation, 1982.

Rita Donelan, editor, *The Maintenance of Order in Society,* Canadian Police College, 1982.

Maurice Punch, editor, *Control in the Police Organizations,* MIT Press, 1983.

Jose M. Rico, compiler, *Policia y sociedad democratica,* Aliana Editorial (Madrid), 1983.

R. Gassin and F. Boulan, editors, *Connaitre la Criminalite: Le Dernier Etat de la Question,* Presses Universitaires D'Aix Marseille, 1983.

Hans Juergen Kerner, editor, *Geharhlich oder Gefahrdet? Eine internationale Diskussion zur Sanktioneirung: Behandlung und gesicherten Unterbringung von schwer oder widerholt delinquenten Jugenlichen,* Ruprectt-Karls Universitat Heidelberg, 1983.

Keith Hawkins and John Thomas, editors, *Enforcing Regulation,* Kluwer-Nijhoff, 1984.

George J. McCall and George H. Weber, editors, *Social Science and Public Policy: The Roles of Academic Disciplines in Policy Analysis,* Associated Faculty Press, 1984.

Information Policy and Crime Control Strategies, Bureau of Justice Statistics, 1984.

Robert G. Lehnen and Wesley G. Skogan, editors, *The National Crime Survey: Working Papers,* Volume II: *Methodological Studies,* Bureau of Justice Statistics, 1984.

Criminal Justice Processes and Perspectives in a Changing World, Centro Nazionale di Prevenzione e Difesa (Milan), 1985.

Anthony N. Doob and Edward L. Greenspan, editors, *Perspectives in Criminal Law: Essays in Honor of John LL.J. Edwards,* Canada Law Book (Ontario), 1985.

Leigh Burstein, Howard E. Freeman, and Peter H. Rossi, editors, *Collecting Evaluation Data: Problems and Solutions,* Sage Publications, 1985.

William A. Geller, editor, *Police Leadership in America: Crisis and Opportunity,* Praeger, 1985.

Proceedings of the Attorney General's Crime Conference 85, California Department of Justice, 1985.

Neal Smelser and Dean R. Gerstein, editors, *Behavioral and Social Science: Fifty Years of Discovery,* National Academy Press, 1986.

Ezzat A. Fattah, editor, *From Crime Policy to Victim Policy,* Macmillan (London), 1986.

A. Blumstein, J. Cohen, J. Roth, and C. Visher, editors, *Criminal Careers and Career Criminals,* National Academy Press, 1986.

Michael Novak, editor, *Character and Crime: An Inquiry into the Causes of the Virtue of Nations*, Brownson Institute, 1986.
Clifford D. Shearing and Philip C. Stenning, editors, *Private Policing*, Sage Publications, 1987.

Also contributor to *Encyclopaedia Britannica*.

OTHER

Author of numerous book reviews in books and journals. Author of survey and crime reports. Contributor to sociology, law, and education periodicals, including *American Journal of Sociology*, *Stanford Law Review*, *Journal of Human Relations*, *Social Forces*, *Law and Contemporary Problems*, and *Journal of Criminal Law and Criminology*. Editor, "Arnold and Caroline Rose" monograph series, American Sociological Association, 1968-71; editor with Harold Wilensky, "Introduction to Modern Society" series, 1968-74. Associate editor, *American Journal of Sociology*, 1950-52, 1961-64, *Sociological Quarterly*, 1960-62, *Social Problems*, 1961-64, *Sociological Methods and Research*, 1971-73, and *Social Forces*, 1974-77. Book review editor, *Journal of Marriage and Family Living*, 1949-52; sociology editor, *Encyclopedia of the Social Sciences*, 1961-67; advisory editor, *Encyclopaedia Britannica*, 1969—, *American Journal of Sociology*, 1979-81, *Law and Society Review*, 1982-83, and *Howard Journal of Criminal Justice*, 1983—; member of editorial board, *Journal of Conflict Resolution*, 1972-75, *Current Sociology*, 1973-76, *Victimology: An International Journal*, 1976-79, *Sociometry*, 1977-79, *Criminology*, 1978-81, *Crime and Justice: An Annual Review of Research*, 1978-85, and *Journal of Quantitative Criminology*, 1984—.

*   *   *

RESNICK, Michael D(iamond)   1942-
(Mike Resnick)

PERSONAL: Born March 5, 1942, in Chicago, Ill.; son of William (a writer) and Gertrude (a writer; maiden name, Diamond) Resnick; married Carol Cain (a kennel owner), October 2, 1961; children: Laura. *Education:* Attended University of Chicago, 1959-61, and Roosevelt University, 1962-63. *Politics:* "Unaffiliated moderate." *Religion:* None.

ADDRESSES: Home—10547 Tanager Hills Dr., Cincinnati, Ohio 45249. *Agent*—Eleanor Wood, Spectrum Literary Agency, 432 Park Ave. S., Suite 1205, New York, N.Y. 10016.

CAREER: Santa Fe Railroad, Chicago, Ill., file clerk, 1962-65; *National Tattler*, Chicago, editor, 1965-66; *National Insider*, Chicago, editor, 1966-69; Oligarch Publishing Co., Chicago, editor and publisher, 1969; free-lance writer, 1969—.

MEMBER: Science Fiction Writers of America, Mystery Writers of America.

AWARDS, HONORS: Best short fiction award from the American Dog Writers Association, 1978, for "The Last Dog," and 1979, for "Blue."

WRITINGS:

The Goddess of Ganymede (novel), Grant, 1967.
Pursuit on Ganymede (novel), Paperback Library, 1968.
Redbeard (novel), Lancer, 1969.

UNDER NAME MIKE RESNICK

Official Guide to the Fantastics, House of Collectibles, 1976.

Official Guide to Comic Books and Big Little Books, House of Collectibles, 1977.
Gymnastics and You: The Whole Story of the Sport, Rand McNally, 1978.
Official Guide to Comic and Science Fiction Books, House of Collectibles, 1979.
(With Glenn A. Larson) *Battlestar Gallactica Number Five: Galactica Discovers Earth*, Berkley, 1980.
The Soul Eater, Signet, 1981.
Birthright: The Book of Man, Signet, 1982.
Walpurgis III, Signet, 1982.
The Branch, Signet, 1984.
Unauthorized Autobiographies and Other Curiosities, Misfit Press, 1984.
Adventures, Signet, 1985.
Santiago: A Myth of the Far Future, Tor Books, 1986.
Stalking the Unicorn: A Fable of Tonight, Tor Books, 1987.
The Dark Lady: A Romance of the Far Future, Tor Books, 1987.
Ivory: A Legend of Past and Future, Tor Books, 1988.
Paradise: A Chronicle of a Distant World, Tor Books, in press.

"TALES OF THE GALACTIC MIDWAY" SERIES; PUBLISHED BY SIGNET

Sideshow, 1982.
The Three-Legged Hootch Dancer, 1983.
The Wild Alien Tamer, 1983.
The Best Rootin' Tootin' Shootin' Gunslinger in the Whole Damned Galaxy, 1983.

"TALES OF THE VELVET COMET" SERIES

Eros Ascending, Phantasia Press, 1984.
Eros at Zenith, Phantasia Press, 1984.
Eros Descending, Signet, 1985.
Eros at Nadir, Signet, 1986.

OTHER

Contributor of about 200 reviews to periodicals.

WORK IN PROGRESS: Kenya, a "mainstream" novel.

SIDELIGHTS: Mike Resnick told *CA:* "For a dozen years, from 1964 until 1976, I was—I freely admit it—a pseudonymous hack writer. Hell, I was the *penultimate* pseudonymous hack writer. I wrote every word of seven monthly newspapers—that's about 175,000 words a month—in addition to the never-ending stream of more than two hundred junk books. Finally, the stream did end. (Looking back now, I truly don't know where I found the energy, or why I didn't die of exhaustion a couple of years into it.)

"In late 1976 I took my ill-gotten literary gains (and they were munificent) and invested them in the largest and most luxurious boarding and grooming kennel then extant. I stopped writing almost completely for about four years while turning the business around, and then, totally secure financially for the rest of my life, I returned to my typewriter, albeit at a far slower pace, to see what I could do now that my writing didn't have to put bread on the table.

"All those books which have appeared since mid-1981 have been written during this period, and it is on these that I would like to be judged. I am still getting used to the luxury of rewriting and polishing, of not having to churn out fifty pages a day, of occasionally not completing even one page in a day. I feel guilty about it—old habits die hard—but I suspect my books are about 3000 percent better for it, and for their author being completely free from the demands of the marketplace.

"Most of my recent output has been labelled science fiction, though I sometimes wonder if 'moral parable' isn't a more proper category. I am not concerned with aliens (I have never met one), telepaths (ditto), invading extra-terrestrial armadas (still ditto). I am concerned, to borrow from Mr. Faulkner, with the human heart in conflict with itself—and far from proving a hindrance to such a quest, science fiction, with all of time and space to draw from, seems especially fitting for it."

BIOGRAPHICAL/CRITICAL SOURCES:

PERIODICALS

Baltimore Sun, April 25, 1986, January 16, 1987.
Cincinnati, September, 1982.
Los Angeles Times Book Review, April 11, 1982, July 18, 1982.
South Bend Tribune, October 26, 1986.
Tri-State Gazette, November 15, 1986.

*   *   *

RESNICK, Mike
See RESNICK, Michael D(iamond)

*   *   *

RESTAK, Richard M(artin)   1942-

PERSONAL: Born February 4, 1942, in Wilmington, Del.; son of Lewis J. (a physician) and Alice (Hynes) Restak; married Carolyn Serbent, October 12, 1968; children: Jennifer, Alison, Ann. *Education:* Gettysburg College, A.B., 1962; Georgetown University, M.D., 1966.

ADDRESSES: Home—4737 Fulton St. N.W., Washington, D.C. 20007. *Office*—1800 R Street, N.W., Suite C-3, Washington, D.C. 20009. *Agent*—Sterling Lord Agency, Inc., 660 Madison Ave., New York, N.Y. 10021.

CAREER: Certified by American Board of Psychiatry and Neurology, 1977. St. Vincent's Hospital, New York City, intern, 1966-67; Mount Sinai Hospital, New York City, resident in psychiatry, 1967-68; Georgetown University Hospital, Washington, D.C., resident in psychiatry, 1968-69; George Washington University Hospital, Washington, D.C., resident in neurology, 1970-73. Private practices in Washington, D.C., in psychiatry, 1969-70, and in neurology and neuropsychiatry, 1973—. Georgetown University, Washington, D.C., 1975—, began as clinical instructor, became clinical associate professor of neurology and director of Adult Neurobehavioral Center; member of clinical faculty, St. Elizabeth's Hospital. Visiting lecturer at numerous colleges and universities, including Kenyon College, Ohio State University, Wright State University, National War College, University of Maryland, and Loyola University of Chicago, and at various governmental agencies, including the Department of State, Central Intelligence Agency, National Security Administration, and National Aeronautics and Space Administration (NASA). Consultant to the Council for Science and Society (London), the Kennedy Institute for the Study of Reproduction and Bioethics, and the Tokyo Broadcast System. Member of board of directors, Institute for Psychiatry and Foreign Affairs, 1984-87. Guest on several radio and television programs, including "The MacNeil-

Lehrer Report," "Larry King Show," "Good Morning, America," "Today," and the "Merv Griffin Show."

MEMBER: International Neuropsychological Society, International Platform Association, Royal Society of Medicine (London), American Academy of Neurology, American Academy of Psychiatry and the Law, American Psychiatric Association, Behavioral Neurology Society, Semiotic Society of America, National Book Critics' Circle, Cosmos Club, New York Academy of Sciences, Philosophical Society of Washington, Georgetown Clinical Society, International Brotherhood of Magicians.

AWARDS, HONORS: National Endowment for the Humanities fellowship, 1976; Claude Bernard Science Journalism Award, National Society for Medical Research, 1976; Distinguished Alumni Award, Gettysburg College, 1985.

WRITINGS:

Premeditated Man: Bioethics and the Control of Future Human Life, Viking, 1975.
(Contributor) James S. Ekenrod, *Who Controls the Controllers?*, Allyn & Bacon, 1975.
(Contributor) Albert Rosenfeld, editor, *Mind and Supermind*, Holt, 1976.
(Contributor) Charles M. Cobb, *The Shapes of Prose: A Rhetorical Reader for College Writing*, Holt, 1976.
The Brain: The Last Frontier; Explorations of the Human Mind and Our Future, Doubleday, 1979.
The Self Seekers, Doubleday, 1982.
(Contributor) Van Tassel and Van Tassel, *The Compleat Computer*, Science Research Associates, 1982.
(Contributor) Thomas Cooley, *Norton Sampler: Short Essays for Composition*, 2nd edition, Norton, 1982.
(Contributor) Lichtenberg, Bornstein, and Silver, editors, *Empathy I*, Analytic Press, 1984.
(Contributor) Lewis H. Lapham, editor, *High Technology and Human Freedom*, Smithsonian Institution Press, 1985.
The Infant Mind, Doubleday, 1986.
(Guest editor, and contributor) *The Psychiatric Clinics of North America: Neuropsychiatry*, W. B. Saunders, 1986.

Contributor of articles and reviews to professional journals and other periodicals, including *Newsday, New York Times, New York Times Book Review, Psychology Today, Reader's Digest, Saturday Review, Science Digest, Sciences, Semiotica, Smithsonian, Washington Post Book World, Wilson Quarterly*, and *Zygon Journal of Religion and Science*. Consultant to *The Encyclopedia of Bioethics* and member of editorial board of *Integrative Psychiatry: An International Journal for the Synthesis of Medicine and Psychiatry*, 1986.

WORK IN PROGRESS: Magazine articles.

SIDELIGHTS: Richard M. Restak "is a practicing neurologist who believes that science is too serious a business to be left to the scientists," says Gerald Jones in the *New York Times Book Review* about Restak's first book, *Premeditated Man: Bioethics and the Control of Future Human Life*. Concerned with the philosophical aspects of scientific research, Restak surveys the laboratories and journals of behavior modification, genetic engineering, and psychosurgery, and finds scientists remiss in considering the social implications of their work. "Restak argues that the decisions should not be left, as they usually are today, in the hands of some anonymous scientific-industrial elite (with the rest of us finding out about disasters only after the fact, as in the thalidomide case)," writes Jonas. The questions Restak raises in *Premeditated Man* are basically ideological, observes Maya Pines in the *Washington Post Book World.* "They affect not only our health but the length and quality of our lives—and these are matters over which we should have far more control."

Restak's best-selling and critically well-received *The Brain: The Last Frontier* was written to accompany a successful Public Broadcasting System television series on that subject. "It is rich in imagination and filled with lore about the brain as well as details about the history of brain research and up-to-date scientific insights into the brain's function," writes Harold M. Schmeck, Jr., in the *New York Times Book Review.* Although Israel Rosenfield concurs in the *New York Review of Books* that Restak "presents many interesting findings," he suggests that Restak's "philosophical comments are unhelpful." However, finding the book "most engaging . . . and pretty respectable from a scientific standpoint," David Graber concludes in the *Los Angeles Times Book Review:* "'The Brain' is excellent popular science: It's fun to read, high in information content, scientifically honest and should have broad appeal."

Regarding Restak's *The Self Seekers,* Joe Ashcroft writes in *Best Sellers* that this work "attempts to explore questions not usually considered within the realm of neurology." The book deals with what Restak perceives as the range of narcissism inherent in humanity and its behavioral manifestations. According to Bruce Mazlish in the *Washington Post Book World,* "A merit of Restak's book is that he documents the line leading from normal to disturbed narcissism, and then to the borderline condition, and over it to psychotic behavior." Paul Robinson states in *Psychology Today,* however, "It is not a work of serious scholarship or reflection, but the book makes for diverting reading." Similarly, Ashcroft suggests that while the book contains "a number of interesting case studies . . . [it] seems destined more for the 'pop' psychology bookshelf than for a graduate class reading list." And Mazlish, who considers the book "depressing but very informative," thinks that "Restak nevertheless offers as good or better a presentation of object relations and narcissistic theory for the general reader as one can find."

More recently, Restak studied the fetal and infant brain and drew evidence from such fields as genetics, embryology, neuroanatomy, and pathology for his book *The Infant Mind.* According to Edith Johnson in the *New York Times Book Review,* Restak "vividly if haphazardly documents his point that the baby's brain, no mere miniature, immature version of a grownup's, is ideally suited to the complex and surprisingly active state of being a baby." Robin Marantz Henig, who finds that the book suffers from poor editing, that it is "too wordy, too disorganized," suggests in the *Washington Post* that Restak should have employed more examples of experiments rather than speculations: "When he's describing studies of infant behavior, or explaining how brain cells communicate, Restak is at his best."

AVOCATIONAL INTERESTS: English literature.

BIOGRAPHICAL/CRITICAL SOURCES:

PERIODICALS

Best Sellers, September, 1982.
Los Angeles Times Book Review, December 2, 1984.
New York Review of Books, March 14, 1985.
New York Times Book Review, November 16, 1975, November 25, 1984, November 30, 1986.
Psychology Today, September, 1982.

Washington Post, June 21, 1979, December 2, 1986.
Washington Post Book World, March 14, 1976, June 20, 1982.

*   *   *

REX, John A(rderne) 1925-

PERSONAL: Born March 5, 1925, in Port Elizabeth, South Africa; son of Frederick Edward George (a postal worker) and Winifred Natalie (Arderne) Rex; married Pamela Margaret Rutherford, July 9, 1949 (divorced, 1963); married Margaret Ellen Biggs, June 5, 1965; children: (first marriage) Catherine Anne, Helen Joan; (second marriage) Frederick John, David Malcolm. *Education:* University of South Africa, B.A., 1948; Leeds University, Ph.D., 1956.

ADDRESSES: Home—33 Arlington Ave., Leamington Spa, England. *Office*—Research Unit on Ethnic Relations, St. Peter's College, University of Aston, College Rd., Birmingham B8 3TE, England.

CAREER: Leeds University, Leeds, England, lecturer in sociology, 1949-62; Birmingham University, Birmingham, England, lecturer, 1962-64; University of Durham, Durham, England, professor of social theory and institutions, 1964-70; University of Warwick, Coventry, England, professor of sociology, 1970-79; University of Aston, Birmingham, visiting professor and director of Research Unit on Ethnic Relations, 1979—. Visiting lecturer, University of Hull, 1960-61; visiting professor, University of Toronto, 1974-75. Member of housing panel, National Committee for Commonwealth Immigrants, 1966-68; member of various United Nations committees on minorities, race, and racial prejudice. *Military service:* South African and Royal Navies, 1963-65; served as able seaman.

MEMBER: International Sociological Association (president of committee on racial and ethnic minorities, 1974-82), British Sociological Association (chairman, 1969-71), British Association for the Advancement of Science, Association of University Teachers.

WRITINGS:

Key Problems of Sociological Theory, Routledge & Kegan Paul, 1961.
(With Robert Moore) *Race, Community and Conflict: Study of Sparkbrook,* Oxford University Press, 1967.
Race Relations in Sociological Theory, Weidenfeld & Nicolson, 1970.
Race, Colonialism and the City, Routledge & Kegan Paul, 1973.
Discovering Sociology: Studies in Sociological Theory and Method, Routledge & Kegan Paul, 1973.
(Editor, author of introduction, and contributor) *Approaches to Sociology: An Introduction to the Major Trends in British Sociology,* Routledge & Kegan Paul, 1974.
Sociology and the Demystification of the Modern World, Routledge & Kegan Paul, 1974.
(With Sally Tomlinson) *Colonial Immigrants in a British City: A Class Analysis,* Routledge & Kegan Paul, 1979.
Social Conflict, Longman, 1981.
(Editor) *Apartheid and Social Research,* UNESCO, 1981.
(Editor with D. Mason) *Theories of Race and Ethnic Relations,* Cambridge University Press, 1986.
Race and Ethnicity, Open University Press, 1986.

CONTRIBUTOR

R. Pahl, editor, *Readings in Urban Sociology,* Pergamon, 1968.

Burgess, editor, *Matters of Principle*, Penguin, 1968.
T. Raison, editor, *The Founding Fathers of Sociology*, Pelican, 1968.
S. Zubaida, editor, *Race and Racialism*, Tavistock, 1970.
Butterworth and Weir, *The Sociology of Modern Britain*, Fontana, 1970.
K. H. Tjaden, *Soziale Systeme*, Gluchterhand (Berlin), 1971.
A. Sahey, editor, *Max Weber and Modern Sociology*, Routledge & Kegan Paul, 1971.
Ethnies, Volume I, Mouton, 1971.
Richardson and Spears, editors, *Race, Culture and Intelligence*, Penguin, 1972.
Etniska Minoriteter 1, Norden (Lund), 1972.
Leftwich, editor, *South Africa: Economic Growth and Political Change*, Alison & Busby, 1974.
Giddens and Stanworth, editors, *Elites and Power in British Society*, Cambridge University Press, 1974.
B. Parekh, editor, *Colour, Consciousness and Culture: Immigrant Intellectuals in Britain*, Allen & Unwin, 1974.
Leo Kuper, editor, *Race, Science and Society*, UNESCO, 1975.
Lambert and Weir, editors, *Cities in Modern Britain*, Fontana, 1975.
Bowker and Carrier, editors, *Race and Ethnic Relations*, Hutchinson, 1976.
Race and Class in Post-Colonial Society, UNESCO, 1977.
Robert Miles and Annie Phizacklea, editors, *Racism and Political Action in Britain*, Routledge & Kegan Paul, 1979.
The Child's Right to Education, UNESCO (Paris), 1979.
Berting, Geyer, and Jurkovich, editors, *Problems in International Comparative Research in the Social Sciences*, Pergamon Press, 1979.
Kenneth Lunn, editor, *Hosts, Immigrants and Minorities: Historical Responses to Newcomers in British Society, 1870-1914*, Dawson & Sons, 1980.
Social Research and Public Policy: Three Perspectives, Social Research Association (London), 1980.
Social Theories: Race and Colonialism, UNESCO, 1980.
Ceri Peach, editor, *Ethnic Segregation in Cities*, Croom Helm, 1981.
Justin Wintle, editor, *Makers of Modern Culture*, Routledge & Kegan Paul, 1981.
Maurice Craft, editor, *Teaching in a Multi-Cultural Society*, Falmer Press, 1981.
J. Solomos, editor, *Migrant Workers in Metropolitan Cities*, European Science Foundation (Strasbourg), 1982.
Tom Bottomore, editor, *Sociology: The State of the Art*, Sage Publications, 1982.
Ernest Cashmore and Barry Troyna, editors, *Black Youth in Crisis*, Allen & Unwin, 1982.
Robert Ross, editor, *Racism and Colonialism*, M. Nijhoff (The Hague), 1982.
Iverson, editor, *Urbanism and Urbanization*, E. J. Brill (Leiden), 1983.
L. Fried, editor, *Minorities: Community and Identity*, Dahlem Foundation (Berlin), 1984.
J. Benyon, editor, *Scarman and After*, Pergamon Press, 1984.
Phillip Norton, editor, *Law and Order in British Politics*, Gower Publishing, 1985.
Peter Worsley and others, editors, *Introducing Sociology*, Penguin, 1986.
Urban Quality of Life: Social, Psychological and Physical Conditions, De Gruyter, 1986.
C. Brock, editor, *The Caribbean in Europe*, Cass & Company, 1986.

Also contributor to *Kryzys I Sahisma*, Volume II, edited by E. Mokrzycki, Pauswowy Institut Wydarzilzy (Warsaw).

OTHER

Editor of sociology series, Granada Books/MacGibbon & Kee, 1970-73; editor, "International Library of Sociology" series, Routledge & Kegan Paul, 1973. Contributor to *Enzyklopadie der geisteswissenschaftlichen Arbeitsmethoden*. Contributor to periodicals, including *Times* (London), *Times Literary Supplement*, *British Journal of Sociology*, *Sociological Review*, *Political Quarterly*, *Population Studies*, *New Statesman*, *Nation*, *New Society*, and *Sociology*. Consulting editor, *American Journal of Sociology*, 1974-76.

SIDELIGHTS: John A. Rex once commented: "My object in writing about sociological topics is to demystify them. Too much sociology mystifies social reality through the use of jargon and pretentious scientism. My main political concern, however, is justice for racial minorities, and I have sought to bring together arguments and evidence which will help this cause, particularly in South Africa and Britain. My hope is to live to see the day when a non-racial democracy is established in South Africa, now the most fully racialist state in the modern world."

A number of critics have singled out Rex's work for demonstrating sociological insight imbued with a genuine social concern regarding the issue of racism. "The appearance of a new book on race relations by John Rex is an event of some importance," writes a reviewer in the *Times Literary Supplement* regarding *Race, Colonialism and the City*. "Not only is [Rex] joint-author of one of the most important empirical studies of race relations in Britain *(Race, Community and Conflict)*: he was also, as he points out himself in [*Race, Colonialsm and the City*] 'one of the first to relate problems of race relations to a framework of urban sociology.' The reviewer adds that Rex is "a vigorous and determined polemicist, who has argued persistently for the importance of the topic against those social scientists of widely differing persuasions who would relegate it to a marginal position." Donald G. MacRae remarks in the *New Statesman* that Rex "is a man concerned to enlighten and to do good. His sociology is, among other things, a way of doing politics by other means, for sociology [quoting Rex] 'is a subject whose insights should be available to the great mass of the people.'"

BIOGRAPHICAL/CRITICAL SOURCES:

PERIODICALS

New Statesman, June 21, 1974.
Times Educational Supplement, May 25, 1984.
Times Literary Supplement, April 13, 1967, July 13, 1973, August 10, 1973, August 23, 1974, February 11, 1983.

*   *   *

REZNECK, Samuel   1897-1983

PERSONAL: Born August 4, 1897, in Poland; naturalized U. S. citizen; died June 11, 1983; son of Benjamin and Celia (Drazner) Rezneck; married Elizabeth Fishburne, August 20, 1933; children: Daniel A. *Education:* Harvard University, A.B., 1919, A.M., 1921, Ph.D., 1926. *Religion:* Jewish.

ADDRESSES: Home—4501 Connecticut Ave. N.W., Washington, D.C. 20008. *Office*—Department of History, Rensselaer Polytechnic Institute, Troy, N.Y. 12181.

CAREER: Ohio State University, Columbus, instructor in history, 1921-23; Rensselaer Polytechnic Institute, Troy, N.Y., professor of history, 1926-62, professor emeritus, 1962-83. President of Troy Public Library, 1968-69. *Military service:* U.S. Army, 1918.

MEMBER: American Historical Association, American Economic History Association (vice-president, 1957-59), New York State Historical Association, Phi Beta Kappa.

WRITINGS:

Education for a Technological Society: A Sesquicentennial History of Rensselaer Polytechnic Institute, Wiley, 1968.
Business Depressions and Financial Panics, Greenwood Press, 1968.
Profiles of the Past of Troy, New York, Chamber of Commerce (Troy, N.Y.), 1970.
Unrecognized Patriots: The Jews in the American Revolution, Greenwood Press, 1975.
The Saga of an American Jewish Family since the Revolution: The Family of Jonas Phillips, University Press of America, 1980.

Contributor to *American Historical Review, Journal of Modern History, Journal of Economic History, Journal of Political Economy, New York History, English Historical Review,* and *English Law Quarterly.* Member of editorial board of *Journal of Economic History,* 1953-56.

OBITUARIES:

PERIODICALS

Washington Post, June 12, 1983.

*   *   *

RICH, Elaine Sommers 1926-

PERSONAL: Born February 8, 1926, in Plevna, Ind.; daughter of Monroe and Effie (Horner) Sommers; married Ronald L. Rich (a chemistry professor), June 14, 1953; children: Jonathan, Andrew, Miriam, Mark. *Education:* Goshen College, B.A., 1947; Michigan State University, M.A., 1950. *Religion:* Mennonite.

ADDRESSES: Home—112 South Spring St., Bluffton, Ohio 45817.

CAREER: Goshen College, Goshen, Ind., instructor in speech and English, 1947-49, 1950-53; Bethel College, North Newton, Kan., instructor in speech, 1953-66; International Christian University, Tokyo, Japan, lecturer, 1971-78; Bluffton College, Bluffton, Ohio, advisor to international students, 1979—.

MEMBER: National Association for Foreign Student Affairs.

WRITINGS:

(Editor) *Breaking Bread Together,* Herald, 1958.
Hannah Elizabeth, Harper, 1964.
(Contributor) J. C. Wenger, editor, *They Met God,* Herald, 1964.
(Contributor) Helen Alderfer, editor, *A Farthing in Her Hand,* Herald, 1964.
(Contributor) Lisa Sergio, editor, *Prayers of Women,* Harper, 1965.
Tomorrow, Tomorrow, Tomorrow, Herald, 1966.
Am I This Countryside? (poems), Pinchpenny Press, 1981.

Mennonite Women, 1683-1983: A Story of God's Faithfulness, Herald, 1983.
Spiritual Elegance: A Biography of Pauline Krehbiel Raid, Bluffton College, 1987.
Golden Apples in Silver Bowls (a collection of prayers), Faith & Life, 1988.

Also author of *The Bridge Love Built* and of an unpublished play about Bertha Von Suttner, "Tough Dove." Author of fortnightly column, "Thinking with . . . ," in *Mennonite Weekly Review,* 1973—. Contributor to periodicals, including *Poet* and *Japan Christian Quarterly.*

WORK IN PROGRESS: A long poem, with the working title "Red Cherry Wonder."

SIDELIGHTS: Elaine Sommers Rich comments on her writing: "C. S. Lewis once said that some of the books he wanted to read did not exist. Therefore he had to write them. I feel that way about my own writing.

"I believe that Jesus Christ is Lord of history. He works in a wonder-inspiring way. (The Pennsylvania Dutch have a saying, 'It wonders me.') Some tremendous things that happen, happen quietly without making big headlines in the world's newspapers. That's exciting to me. Inner growth is exciting. Genuine goodness is exciting, and I'd rather try to portray growth and goodness than to try to write about 'cops 'n robbers and military victories.' *Hannah Elizabeth* tells of how a girl came to glimpse deeply the meaning of her own faith. *Tomorrow, Tomorrow, Tomorrow* shows a tiny seed of love that grew into a tree, improved treatment of the mentally ill. *The Bridge Love Built,* unfortunately never published, tells about a boy who came to understand that he belonged to two cultures, not just one, as most people do."

Rich later told *CA:* "For twenty years I had the privilege of living intimately with our own four children and their many friends, who were in and out of our home in North Newton, Kansas, and on the campus of the International Christian University in Tokyo. I have great respect for the intellect and spiritual sensitivity of these children and of my adult readers.

"I also have great hope for the future. Human beings can learn to use nuclear energy constructively rather than destructively. We could well be on the threshold of a great time in history, a time of worldwide peace when every human being has the good things of life, from food and music to the rights enumerated in the *Universal Declaration of Human Rights.* I hope these values conme through in what I write."

She adds: "Among contemporary writers I most admire Elizabeth Yates and Aleksandr Solzhenitsyn. I like Yates's inner independence and integrity. Throughout her long productive lifetime she has stood aloof from literary fads and fashions in her choice and treatment of subjects. Solzhenitsyn has attempted to tell the truth. Difficult! He has demonstrated the power of one lone voice telling the truth.

"From the preceding generation I like Virginia Woolf for her treatment of psychological time, Pearl Buck for her recognition that it is great but difficult to have been born female, and Willa Cather for her classical style and portrayal of the dignity and beauty inherent in everyday life.

"I also like *haiku* by Japanese masters (Basho, Issa). I like Selma Lagerlof, Sigrid Undset, Sarah Orne Jewett, Christina Rossetti, Robert Browning, Blake, Keats, Gerard Manley Hopkins, and Walt Whitman."

RICHARDS, Carl Edward, Jr. 1933-

PERSONAL: Born March 20, 1933, in Pittsburgh, Pa.; son of Carl Edward (a salesman) and Irene (Skirms) Richards; married Alecia Ann Stone, December 2, 1955; children: Kim, Tracey, Christine. *Education:* Ohio State University, D.D.S., 1958.

ADDRESSES: Home—7301 Belding Rd., Rockford, Mich. 49341. *Office*—3934 West River, Comstock Park, Mich. 49321.

CAREER: Private dental practice, Comstock Park, Mich., 1958—.

WRITINGS:

(With Doug Swisher) *Selective Trout*, Crown, 1971.
(With Doug Swisher) *Fly Fishing Strategy*, Winchester Press, 1975.
(With Swisher and Fred Arbona) *Stoneflies*, Lyons Books, 1980.
(With Swisher) *Tying the Swisher/Richards Flies*, Stackpole, 1980.

* * *

RICHIE, Donald (Steiner) 1924-

PERSONAL: Born April 17, 1924, in Lima, Ohio; son of Kent Hayes and Ona (Steiner) Richie; married Mary Evans (a writer), November, 1961 (divorced, 1965). *Education:* Attended Antioch College, 1942; Columbia University, B.S., 1953.

ADDRESSES: Home—304 Shato Nezo, Yanaka, 1, 1-18, Taito-ku, Tokyo 110, Japan.

CAREER: Japan Times, Tokyo, film critic, 1955-68; New York Museum of Modern Art, New York, N.Y., curator of film, 1968-73; literary critic, 1973—. Advisor to Uni-Japan, Film, 1961—. *Wartime service:* U.S. Maritime Service, 1942-45.

AWARDS, HONORS: Citations from Japanese government, 1963, 1970; citation from U.S. National Film Critics' Society, 1970.

WRITINGS:

(With Joseph L. Anderson) *The Japanese Film: Art and Industry,* Grove, 1959, expanded edition, Princeton University Press, 1982.
The Japanese Movie: An Illustrated History, Kodansha (England), 1965, revised edition, 1982.
The Films of Akira Kurosawa, University of California Press, 1965, revised edition, 1984.
Companions of the Holiday, Weatherhill (Tokyo), 1968.
(Editor) Akira Kurosawa, *Rashomon: A Film,* Grove, 1969, reprinted, Rutgers University Press, 1987.
George Stevens: An American Romantic, Museum of Modern Art, 1970, reprinted, 1985.
Japanese Cinema, Doubleday, 1971.
The Inland Sea, Weatherhill, 1971, reprinted, Century, 1987.
Three Modern Kyogen, C. E. Tuttle, 1972.
Ozu: The Man and His Films, University of California Press, 1974.
(With Mana Maeda) *Ji: Signs and Symbols of Japan,* Kodansha, 1975.
The Japanese Tatoo, photographs by Ian Buruma, Weatherhill, 1980.

Zen Inklings: Some Stories, Fables, Parables, Sermons and Prints with Notes and Commentaries, Weatherhill, 1982.
A Taste of Japan: Food Fact and Fable; What the People Eat; Customs and Etiquette, Kodansha, 1985.
Where Are the Victors?, C. E. Tuttle, 1986.
Introducing Tokyo, Kodansha, 1987.

Also author of *Different People: Portraits of Some Japanese,* 1987, and a novel, *Tokyo Nights,* 1988.

WORK IN PROGRESS: Kumagai, a historical novel.

SIDELIGHTS: Donald Richie told *CA:* "Living as I do in Japan, and having lived here well over half my life, I write mainly about this country and its people. It has become my subject, one which I seek to describe, understand, even perhaps to illuminate. The experience of attempting to limn an entire culture has given me, perhaps not so paradoxically, a deeper insight into my own and a consequent understanding of all cultures which I might not have otherwise had."

AVOCATIONAL INTERESTS: Music.

BIOGRAPHICAL/CRITICAL SOURCES:

PERIODICALS

Times Literary Supplement, July 3, 1987.

* * *

RICKERT, John E(arl) 1923-

PERSONAL: Born April 23, 1923, in Rutland, Vt.; son of John Blair and Florence (Borah) Rickert; married Ann Koriat, February 10, 1946; married Gertrude McGuire, December 23, 1968; children: Jon E., Anne Elizabeth. *Education:* Stanford University, A.B., 1951; American Institute of Foreign Trade, B.F.T., 1953; Rutgers University, M.A., 1958; Clark University, Ph.D., 1960. *Religion:* Unitarian Universalist.

ADDRESSES: Home—539 Boston Ave., Egg Harbor, N.J. 08215. *Office*—Department of Business and Economics, Rutgers University, Camden, N.J. 08102.

CAREER: Self-employed builder, 1953-57; Planning Department, Worcester, Mass., head of research section, 1959-60; University of Pittsburgh, Pittsburgh, Pa., assistant professor of geography, 1960-64, Urban Land Institute, Washington, D.C., project director, 1963-64; Kent State University, Kent, Ohio, associate professor of geography and associate director of Center for Urban Regionalism, 1965-71; Stockton State College, Pomona, N.J., dean of management science, 1971-75; Rutgers University, Camden, N.J., professor of marketing, 1975—. *Military service:* U.S. Army Air Forces, 1942-46; served in Pacific theater.

MEMBER: American Society of Information Science, American Association of University Professors, Association of American Geographers, National Recreation and Park Association, Urban and Regional Information Systems Association (vice-president, 1970—).

WRITINGS:

Urban Thesaurus: A Vocabulary for Indexing and Retrieving Urban Literature, Kent State University Press, 1968.
(Editor) *Urban and Regional Information Systems: Federal Activities and Specialized Programs,* Center for Urban Regionalism, Kent State University, 1969.

(Editor) *Urban and Regional Information Systems: Service Systems for Cities,* Center for Urban Regionalism, Kent State University, 1969.

(Editor) *Urban and Regional Information Systems: Information Systems and Political Systems,* Stockton State College, 1972.

Author of numerous monographs. Contributor to journals. Editor, *Proceedings from the Annual Conference of Urban and Regional Information Systems Association,* 1968-75.

WORK IN PROGRESS: Editing *Gale Information Guides* of the "Urban Studies Series"; research on relationship between the "family life cycle" and the physical deterioration in urban housing; a study of two thousand houses in Shaker Heights, Ohio.

*   *   *

RIEDEL, Walter E(rwin) 1936-

PERSONAL: Born August 3, 1936, in Germany; married Ingrid F. A. Wetklo (a nursing school instructor), 1963; children: Caroline, Jennifer. *Education:* University of Alberta, B.Ed., 1960, M.A., 1963; McGill University, Ph.D., 1966.

ADDRESSES: Home—340 Beach Dr., Victoria, British Columbia, Canada. *Office*—Department of Germanic Studies, Box 1700, University of Victoria, Victoria, British Columbia, Canada V8W 2Y2.

CAREER: University of Victoria, Victoria, British Columbia, instructor, 1962-64, assistant professor, 1964-70, associate professor of German, 1970—.

MEMBER: Canadian Association of University Teachers of German, Canadian Comparative Literature Association.

WRITINGS:

(With Armin Arnold) *Kanadische Erzaehler der Gegenwart,* Manesse, 1967.
(Editor) *Modern Canadian Short Stories,* Hueber, 1969.
Der neue Mensch, Bouvier, 1970.
Moderne Erzaehler der Welt Kanada, Erdmann, 1976.
Das literarische Kanadabild, Bouvier, 1980.
(Editor) *The Old World and the New: Literary Perspectives of German-Speaking Canadians,* University of Toronto Press, 1984.
(Co-editor) *Gute Wanderschaft, mein Bruder,* St. Benno Verlag, 1986.
(Editor with Peter Liddell) Carl Weiselberger, *Bridges, Sketches of Life, Artists . . . ,* Hyperion Press, 1987.

*   *   *

RIESELBACH, Leroy N(ewman) 1934-

PERSONAL: Born July 11, 1934, in Milwaukee, Wis.; son of L. LeRoy (a lawyer) and Lillian (Newman) Rieselbach; married Helen Funk, June 29, 1957; children: Erik, Kurt, Alice, Karen. *Education:* Harvard University, A.B., 1956; Yale University, M.A., 1958, Ph.D., 1964.

ADDRESSES: Home—108 Glenwood E., Bloomington, Ind. 47401. *Office*—Department of Political Science, Indiana University, Bloomington, Ind. 47405.

CAREER: Indiana University at Bloomington, lecturer, 1964, assistant professor, 1964-66, associate professor, 1966-70, professor of political science, 1970—, chairman of depart-

ment, 1971-77. Postdoctoral fellow, Mental Health Research Institute, University of Michigan, Ann Arbor, 1964-65; research associate, Center for International Affairs, Harvard University, 1969.

MEMBER: American Political Science Association, Midwest Political Science Association, Western Political Science Association, Southern Political Science Association.

WRITINGS:

The Roots of Isolationism, Bobbs-Merrill, 1967.
(Editor with George I. Balch) *Psychology and Politics: An Introductory Reader,* Holt, 1969.
(Editor) *The Congressional System: Notes and Readings,* Duxbury, 1970, 2nd edition, 1979.
(Contributor) Oliver Walter, editor, *Political Scientists at Work,* Duxbury, 1971.
Congressional Politics, McGraw, 1973.
(Editor) *People vs. Government: Essays on Institutional Responsiveness,* Indiana University Press, 1975.
Congressional Reform in the Seventies, General Learning Press, 1977.
(Editor) *Legislative Reform: The Policy Impact,* Lexington Books, 1978.
(Contributor) George Bishop, editor, *Presidential Debates of 1976,* Praeger, 1978.
(Contributor) Dennis Hale, editor, *The U.S. Congress,* Boston University, 1982.
(Contributor) Stuart Nagel, editor, *Encyclopedia of Policy Studies,* Dekker, 1982.
(Contributor) Ada W. Finifter, editor, *Political Science: The State of the Discipline,* American Political Science Association, 1983.
(With Joseph K. Unekis) *Congressional Committee Politics,* Praeger, 1984.
Congressional Reform, CQ Press, 1986.
(Editor with Gerald C. Wright and Lawrence C. Dodd; also contributor) *Congress and Policy Change,* Agathon, 1986.
(Contributor) Donald J. Calista, editor, *Public Policy and Political Institutions,* JAI Press, 1986.

Contributor of articles and reviews to professional journals.

*   *   *

RIKER, William H(arrison) 1920-

PERSONAL: Born September 22, 1920, in Des Moines, Iowa; son of Ben H. and Alice (Lenox) Riker; married Mary Elizabeth Lewis, April 15, 1943; children: Katharine, William, Mary, Benjamin (deceased). *Education:* De Pauw University, B.A., 1942; Harvard University, Ph.D., 1948. *Politics:* Nonpartisan. *Religion:* Presbyterian.

ADDRESSES: Home—75 Windemere Rd., Rochester, N.Y. 14610.

CAREER: Lawrence College (now University), Appleton, Wis., assistant professor, 1948-50, associate professor, 1950-58, professor of political science, 1958-62; University of Rochester, Rochester, N.Y., professor of political science, 1962-78, Wilson Professor of political science, 1978—, chairman of department, 1962-78, dean of graduate studies, 1978-83. Visiting professor, Washington University, St. Louis, 1983-84. Vice-chairman, Outagamie County (Wis.) Democratic Party, 1958-62. Member of the board of zoning appeals, Rochester, 1965-73.

MEMBER: International Political Science Association, American Academy of Arts and Sciences, National Academy of Sciences, American Political Science Association (president, 1982-83), Public Choice Society (chairman, 1965-67), Phi Beta Kappa.

AWARDS, HONORS: Fund for the Advancement of Education fellow, 1951-52; Rockefeller Foundation fellow, 1955-56; Center for Advanced Study in the Behavioral Sciences fellow, 1960-61; Uhrig Prize for excellence in teaching, 1962; Fairchild fellow, California Institute of Technology, 1973-74; L.H.D., Lawrence University, 1975, and State University of New York at Stony Brook, 1985; Ph.D., Uppsala University, 1977; Litt.D., De Pauw University, 1979; Guggenheim fellow, 1983-84; University prize for excellence in graduate teaching, 1987.

WRITINGS:

Democracy in the United States, Macmillan, 1953.
Soldiers of the States, Public Affairs Press, 1957, reprinted, Ayer Company, 1979.
The Study of Local Politics, Random House, 1958.
The Theory of Political Coalitions, Yale University Press, 1962, reprinted, Greenwood Press, 1984.
Federalism: Origin, Operation, Significance, Little, Brown, 1964.
(With Peter C. Ordeshook) *An Introduction to Positive Political Theory,* Prentice-Hall, 1972.
(With Steven M. Maser and Richard N. Rosett) *The Effects of Zoning and Externalities on the Price of Land in Monroe County, New York,* University of Rochester, 1974.
Liberalism against Populism: A Confrontation between the Theory of Democracy and the Theory of Social Choice, W. H. Freeman, 1982.
The Art of Political Manipulation, Yale University Press, 1986.
The Development of American Federalism, Kluwer Academic, 1987.

Contributor to professional journals.

WORK IN PROGRESS: A description of the rhetoric and her-esthetic of the ratification of the United States Constitution.

*   *   *

RINGER, Alexander L(othar)   1921-

PERSONAL: Born February 3, 1921, in Berlin, Germany; naturalized U.S. citizen; son of Abe (pronounced Ah-*bay;* a banker) and Anna (Prager) Ringer; married Claude Pouderoux, January 24, 1947; children: Miriam, Deborah. *Education:* College Francais, Berlin, Germany, abitur, 1938; attended Hollaender Conservatory of Music, 1936-38, and Amsterdam Muzieklyceum, 1940-42; University of Amsterdam, B.A., 1947; New School for Social Research, M.A., 1949; Columbia University, Ph.D., 1955. *Religion:* Jewish.

ADDRESSES: *Home*—11 Stanford Pl., Champaign, Ill. 61820. *Office*—4014 Music Building, Room 2136, 1114 West Nevada St., University of Illinois, Urbana, Ill. 61801.

CAREER: American Joint Distribution Committee, New York City, field representative in charge of World War II displaced persons in Germany and the Netherlands, 1945-47; City College (now City College of the City University of New York), New York City, instructor, 1948-51, lecturer in music, 1951-52; University of Pennsylvania, Philadelphia, assistant professor of music, 1952-55; University of California, Berkeley,

assistant professor of music, 1955-56; University of Oklahoma, Norman, associate professor of music, 1956-58; University of Illinois at Urbana-Champaign, associate professor, 1958-63, professor of musicology, 1963—, chairman of Division of Musicology, 1963-69. Fulbright visiting professor, Hebrew University, 1962-63, 1966-67; visiting professor, University of Heidelberg, 1983-84; has lectured at universities in Zurich, Marburg, Frankfurt, and Berlin, and at University of Amsterdam, University of Utrecht, University of Tehran, Kiel University, Weizmann Institute of Science, University of California, University of Colorado, University of Tel Aviv, University of North Carolina, Yale University, and Coe College. Cantor, organist, and choral director in synagogues in the United States and the Netherlands, 1941-58. Project director, Kodaly Fellowship Program, National Endowment for the Arts, 1968-73.

MEMBER: International Musicological Society, International Folk Music Council (member of executive board, 1967-70), American Musicological Society (member of council, 1952-55, 1957-60, and 1972-74; member of executive board, 1965-66), American Society for Jewish Music, College Music Society (member of council, 1958-63, 1967-70), American Professors for Peace in the Middle East (member of executive board and council, 1968—; chairman of Midwest Region, 1977-78), Musicological Society for the Netherlands, Israel Musicological Society, Federated Jewish Charities (member of board of directors of local branch, 1965—), Pi Kappa Lambda, Philomathean Society (honorary member).

AWARDS, HONORS: Distinguished service award from Philadelphia Jewish Music Council, 1955; grants from American Council of Learned Societies, Smithsonian Institution, Ford Foundation, National Endowment for the Arts, University of Oklahoma, and University of Illinois.

WRITINGS:

(Contributor) *The Cultural Heritage of the Twentieth Century,* Pennsylvania Literary Review, 1956.
(Editor) Edward Pierce, *For Hunting,* Theodore Presser, 1958.
(Contributor) *Contemporary Music in Europe,* Norton, 1965.
(Editor) *Yearbook of the International Folk Music Council,* University of Illinois Press, Volume I, 1970, Volume II, 1971.
An Experimental Program in the Development of Musical Literacy (monograph), ERIC and U.S. Department of Health, Education, and Welfare, 1970.
(Contributor) P. H. Lang, editor, *The Creative World of Beethoven,* Norton, 1971.
(Contributor) Beth Landis and Polly Carter, editors, *The Eclectic Curriculum in American Music Education: Contributions of Dalcroze, Kodaly, and Orff,* Music Educators National Conference, 1972.
Arnold Schoenberg and the Prophetic Image in Music, J. Arnold Schoenberg Institute, 1979.
Arnold Schoenberg and the Politics of Jewish Survival, J. Arnold Schoenberg Institute, 1979.
Schoenberg, Weill and Epic Theater, J. Arnold Schoenberg Institute, 1980.
(Contributor) Antonio Serravezza, editor, *La Sociologia della Musica,* Edizioni di Torino, 1983.
(Contributor) Ed Strainchamps and M. R. Maniates, editors, *Music and Civilization,* Norton, 1984.
(Contributor) Laszlo Vikar, editor, *Reflections on Kodaly,* International Kodaly Society, 1985.

(Contributor) Allan W. Atlas, editor, *Music in the Classic Era*, Pendragon, 1985.

(Contributor) Kim H. Kowalke, editor, *A New Orpheus: Essays on Kurt Weill*, Yale University Press, 1986.

(Contributor) Leroy R. Shaw, Nancy R. Cirillo, and Marion S. Miller, editors, *Wagner in Retrospect*, Rodolpi, 1987.

Author of program notes. Contributor to honorary volumes, yearbooks, and symposia, and to *Encyclopaedia Britannica, Encyclopedia of Music and Musicians, The Encyclopedia of Religion, Grove's Dictionary of Music*, and *Dictionary of Twentieth-Century Music*. Contributor of over one hundred articles and reviews to periodicals, including *Saturday Review, Musical Quarterly, Current Musicology, Studia Musicologica, Journal of the History of Ideas, Die Musik Forschung, Forum Musicologicum, Analecta Musicologica*, and *Studies in Medieval Culture*.

WORK IN PROGRESS: Three books, *A Language of Feeling: Studies in Nineteenth-Century Music, Arnold Schoenberg und seize Zeit*, and *Music Through Education: Report on an American Kodaly Experiment*.

*   *   *

RITCHIE, William A(ugustus)   1903-

PERSONAL: Born November 20, 1903, in Rochester, N.Y.; married Beatrice Fisher, 1933. *Education:* University of Rochester, B.S., 1936, M.S., 1938; Columbia University, Ph.D., 1944.

ADDRESSES: Home—21 Pine St., Delmar, N.Y. 12054.

CAREER: Rochester Museum of Arts and Sciences, Rochester, N.Y., assistant in archaeology, 1924-28, assistant archaeologist, 1929-38, archaeologist and curator of anthropology, 1938-49; New York State Museum, Albany, senior scientist, 1949-50, state archaeologist, 1950-71. Lecturer at University of Rochester, 1943-49; adjunct or visiting professor at Syracuse University, 1963-64, Harpur College (now State University of New York at Binghamton), 1964-65, and State University of New York at Albany, 1967-72. Research associate, Section of Man, Carnegie Museum, 1973—.

MEMBER: American Anthropological Association (fellow), Society for American Archaeology (president, 1956), American Association for the Advancement of Science (fellow), Eastern States Archeological Federation (director of research, 1946-50; president, 1950-54), New York State Archaeological Association (fellow; president, 1954-58), Phi Beta Kappa, Sigma Xi.

AWARDS, HONORS: A. Cressy Morrison Prize from New York Academy of Sciences, 1942; D.Sc. from Waynesburg College, 1950; Centennial Award from University of Rochester, 1950; Cornplanter Medal from Cayuga County Historical Society, 1966; LL.D. from Trent University, 1972; Distinguished Service Award from Society for American Archaeology, 1987; eight grants from various organizations.

WRITINGS:

The Lamoka Lake Site: The Type Station of the Archaic Algonkin Period in New York, New York State Archaeological Association, 1932, reprinted, Kraus, 1970.

The Pre-Iroquoian Occupations of New York State, Rochester Museum of Arts and Sciences, 1944.

The Archaeology of New York State, Natural History Press, 1965, 2nd revised edition, Harbor Hill, 1980.

The Archaeology of Martha's Vineyard, Natural History Press, 1969.

Dutch Hollow: An Early Historic Period, Rochester Museum, 1954, reprinted, Kraus, 1975.

(With Robert E. Funk) *Aboriginal Settlement Patterns in the Northeast*, New York State Museum and Science Service, 1973.

Contributor of more than 150 monographs, papers, and articles to journals. Society for American Archaeology, assistant editor, 1935-53, associate editor, 1953-55.

*   *   *

RITSCHL, Dietrich   1929-

PERSONAL: Born January 17, 1929, in Basel, Switzerland; son of Hans and Gertrud (Stoerring) Ritschl; married Rosemarie Courvoisier, April 18, 1952; children: Christian, Lucas, Stephan, Johannes, *Education:* Attended University of Tuebingen, University of Basel, and University of Bern, 1945-50; University of Edinburgh, Ph.D., 1957, D.D., 1976.

ADDRESSES: Home—4418 Reigoldswil, BL, Switzerland. *Office*—Ecumenical Institute, University of Heidelberg, 6900 Heidelberg, West Germany.

CAREER: Ordained to Presbyterian ministry, 1950; assistant minister in Zyfen, Switzerland, 1950-52; minister in Scotland, 1952-58, and in Wimberly, Tex., 1958-62; Austin Presbyterian Seminary, Austin, Tex., guest professor, 1958-60, associate professor of history of dogma and New Testament, 1960-63; Pittsburgh Theological Seminary, Pittsburgh, Pa., professor of history of doctrine and systematic theology, 1963-69; Union Theological Seminary, New York, N.Y., Harry Emerson Fosdick Professor, 1969-70; University of Mainz, Mainz, West Germany, professor of systematic theology, 1970-83; University of Heidelberg, Heidelberg, West Germany, professor of systematic theology, 1983—, director of International Center for the Interchange in Science, 1986—. Guest lecturer, Presbyterian College, Montreal, Quebec, 1957, Episcopal Seminary of the Southwest, Austin, 1959-61, and United Theological Faculty, Melbourne, Australia; guest professor, Knox College, Dunedin, New Zealand, 1970, 1972, 1974, 1977, 1979, 1982, and 1987. Special lecturer in Hungary, Czechoslovakia, the Soviet Union, India, and Mexico. President of theological commission, National Council of Churches, West Germany and West Berlin, 1979—.

WRITINGS:

Vom Leben in der Kirche, [Neukirchen], 1957, translation published as *Christ Our Life*, Oliver & Boyd, 1960.

Die homiletische Funktion der Gemeinde, EvZ (Zurich), 1960.

A Theology of Proclamation, John Knox, 1960.

Nur Menschen, Kathe Vogt Verlag (Berlin), 1962.

Athanasius, [Zurich], 1963.

Memory and Hope: An Inquiry into the Presence of Christ, Macmillan, 1967.

Konzepte, Volume I, P. Lang (Bern), 1976.

"Story" als Rohmaterial der Theologie, Kaiser (Munich), 1976.

Theologie in den neuen Welten, [Munich], 1981.

Zur Logik der Theologie, Kaiser (Munich), 1984, translation published as *The Logic of Theology*, S.C.M. Press, 1986.

Konzepte: Oekumene, Medizin, Ethik, gesammette Aufsaetze, Kaiser (Munich), 1986.

(With B. Luban-Plozza) *Die Familie: Risiken und Chancen, eine therapeutische Orientierung*, Birkhauser (Basel), 1987.

Contributor of articles on patristics, systematic theology, and medical ethics to theology journals in Switzerland, Germany, Great Britain, and the United States.

*   *   *

RIVERA, Feliciano (Moreno)   1932-

PERSONAL: Born November 24, 1932, in Morley, Colo.; son of Marcos A. and Maria Remedios (Moreno) Rivera. *Education:* Attended University of Maryland, 1956-57, Whitworth College, 1958-59, and University of New Mexico, 1959-60; University of Denver, B.A., 1961, M.A., 1964; University of Colorado, M.A., 1963; University of Southern California, Ph.D., 1970.

ADDRESSES: Office—Department of History, San Jose State University, Washington Square, San Jose, Calif. 95192.

CAREER: University of Denver, Denver, Colo., instructor in history and Latin American studies and instructor in Spanish and Latin American studies at Peace Corps Training Center, 1962-64; East Los Angeles College, Los Angeles, Calif., instructor, 1964-68; San Jose State University, San Jose, Calif., assistant professor, 1968-69, associate professor, 1969-70, professor of history, 1970—, director of Bilingual Institute in Social Studies, 1970-72, chairman of Department of Mexican American Studies, 1984—. Teacher of social studies and Spanish in public schools in Los Angeles, Calif., 1964-66. Lecturer at De Anza Community Forum, 1971; member of National Education Task Force de la Raza; member of board of directors of Santa Clara planning council and youth opportunities council; associate of Danforth Foundation. Consultant to Institute for Philosophical Research, U.S. Department of Health, Education, and Welfare, and International Technical Service, Inc.

MEMBER: American Historical Association (Pacific Coast branch), American Association of Teachers of Spanish and Portuguese, National Association of Mexican American Educators, National Association for Chicano Studies, American Association of University Professors, Western History Association, Rocky Mountain Council of Latin American Studies, Pacific Coast Council for Latin American Studies, California Historical Association, Chicano Teachers Association, Phi Sigma Iota, Sigma Delta Phi.

WRITINGS:

A Guide to the Study of the Mexican American, Fearson, 1969.
A Guideline for the Study of Mexican American History, Educational Consulting Associates, 1970.
(Co-editor) *Makers of America,* Encyclopedia Britannica, 1970.
(Editor) *A Documentary History of the Mexican American,* Praeger, 1971.
Voices of La Raza, Little, Brown, 1971.
A Selective Bibliography for the Study of Mexican American History, R. & E. Associates, 1972.
(Co-author with Matt S. Meier) *The Chicanos: A History of the Mexican American,* Hill & Wang, 1972.
(Co-editor with Meier) *Readings on La Raza: Twentieth Century,* Hill & Wang, 1973.
(With Meier) *Dictionary of Mexican American History,* Greenwood Press, 1981.

Also author of *Chicano Lives: Nineteenth and Twentieth Centuries,* and *An Encyclopedia: Chicano History and Culture.*

SIDELIGHTS: The Chicanos: A History of the Mexican American has been translated into Spanish.

RIVET, A(lbert) L(ionel) F(rederick)   1915-

PERSONAL: Surname is pronounced Reev-ay; born November 30, 1915, in England; son of Albert Robert and Rose (Bulow) Rivet; married Audrey Catherine Webb, April 8, 1947; children: Peter Leo, Anne Catherine. *Education:* Oriel College, Oxford, B.A., 1938, M.A., 1947. *Politics:* Social Democrat. *Religion:* Church of England.

ADDRESSES: Home—University of Keele, 7 Springpool, Keele, Staffordshire, England.

CAREER: Teacher in Hitchin, England, 1939-40; civil defense worker in London, England, 1939-40; bookseller in Cambridge, England, Norwich, England, and then Crowborough, England, 1946-51; Ordnance Survey Department, London and Edinburgh, Scotland, assistant archaeology officer, 1951-64; University of Keele, Keele, Staffordshire, England, lecturer, 1964-67, reader in Romano-British studies, 1967-74, professor of Roman provincial studies, 1974-81, Leverhulme Emeritus Fellow, 1981-83. Member of executive committee, British School at Rome, 1974-83; member of Royal Commission on Historical Monuments, 1979-85. *Military service:* British Army, Royal Artillery and Royal Signals, 1940-46; became major.

MEMBER: British Academy (fellow), Royal Archaeological Institute (member of council, 1955-59 and 1963-67), Society of Antiquaries (London), Society of Antiquaries of Scotland (member of council, 1960-64), Society for the Promotion of Roman Studies (president, 1977-80), Council for Name Studies in Great Britain and Ireland, German Archaeological Institute (honorary corresponding fellow).

WRITINGS:

(Compiler) *Ordnance Survey Map of Roman Britain,* 3rd edition, Ordnance Survey, 1956.
Town and Country in Roman Britain, Hutchinson, 1958, revised edition, 1964.
(Compiler) *Ordnance Survey Map of Southern Britain in the Iron Age,* Ordnance Survey, 1962.
(Editor) *The Iron Age in Northern Britain,* Edinburgh University Press, 1966.
(Editor and contributor) *The Roman Villa in Britain,* Praeger, 1969.
(With Colin Smith) *The Place-Names of Roman Britain,* Princeton University Press, 1979.
Rudyard Kipling's Roman Britain: Fact and Fiction, University of Keele, 1980.
(Compiler with S. S. Frere and N. H. H. Sitwell) *Tabula Imperii Romani,* sheet N30: *Britannia Septentrionalis,* Oxford University Press, 1987.
Gallia Narbonensis and Alpes Maritimae, Batsford, 1988.

CONTRIBUTOR

P. Corder, editor, *Romano-British Villas,* Council for British Archaeology, 1955.
Frere, editor, *Problems of the Iron Age in Southern Britain,* Institute of Archaeology (London), 1960.
J. S. Wacher, editor, *The Civitas Capitals of Roman Britain,* Leicester University Press, 1966.
M. Jesson and D. Hill, editors, *The Iron Age and Its Hill-Forts,* [Southampton], 1971.
R. Chevallier, editor, *Litterature greco-romaine et geographie historique,* [Paris], 1974.

H. Temporini, editor, *Aufstieg und Niedergang der Roemischen Welt,* Volume II, Part 3, de Gruyter, 1975.

W. Rodwell and T. Rowley, editors, *Small Towns of Roman Britain,* Britain Archaeological Reports, 1975.

R. Goodburn and P. Bartholomew, editors, *Aspects of the Notitia Dignitatum,* British Archaeological Reports, 1976.

M. I. Finley, editor, *Atlas of Classical Archaeology,* McGraw, 1977.

Paul-Marie Duval and E. Frezouls, editors, *Themes de recherche sur les villes antiques d'occident,* CNRS (Paris), 1977.

Haupt and H. G. Horn, editors, *Studien zu den Militaergrenzen Roms,* Volume II, [Bonn], 1977.

N. Coldstream and M. A. R. Colledge, editors, *Acta of the XI International Congress of Classical Archaeology,* [London], 1979.

N. G. L. Hammond, editor, *Atlas of the Greek and Roman World in Antiquity,* Noyes Press, 1981.

La citta antica come fatto di cultura, Como, 1983.

OTHER

Editor, *Proceedings* of the Society of Antiquaries of Scotland, 1961-64. Contributor to *Oxford Classical Dictionary* and *Princeton Dictionary of Classical Archaeology.* Contributor to *Britannia* and *Antiquity;* author of reviews on the subject of Roman Britain and Gaul.

BIOGRAPHICAL/CRITICAL SOURCES:

PERIODICALS

Times Literary Supplement, January 11, 1980.

*　　*　　*

ROBBINS, Wayne
    See COX, William (Robert)

*　　*　　*

ROBERTS, Mervin F(rancis) 1922-

PERSONAL: Born June 7, 1922, in New York, N.Y.; son of Gus R. (an inventor) and Esther N. (a school teacher) Roberts; married Edith May Foster, June, 1949; children: Edith, Robin (deceased), Martha, Nancy, Neel, William (deceased). *Education:* Alfred University, B.S., 1944. *Politics:* Republican. *Religion:* Baptist.

ADDRESSES: Home and office—Duck River Lane, Old Lyme, Conn. 06371.

CAREER: Writer; photographer of animal movements; consultant on animal behavior; consultant on fish behavior to Northeast Utilities, 1970—; councillor for marine resources to governor of Connecticut, 1971-72; shellfish commissioner. Chaplain of Old Lyme Fire Department, 1970—. *Military service:* U.S. Naval Reserve, active duty, 1942-46; became lieutenant junior grade.

MEMBER: National Rifle Association (life member), American Fisheries Society, Connecticut Association of Conservation Commissioners (past president).

WRITINGS:

Turtles as Pets, T. F. H. Publications, 1953.
Beginning the Aquarium, T. F. H. Publications, 1955.
Chameleons, T. F. H. Publications, 1956.
Parakeets in Your Home, Sterling, 1956.

How to Raise and Train a Pet Hamster, T. F. H. Publications, 1957, reprinted, 1973.

Guinea Pigs, T. F. H. Publications, 1957, published as *Guinea Pigs for Beginners,* 1972.

Snakes, T. F. H. Publications, 1958, published as *All about Boas and Other Snakes,* 1975.

A Camera Is Thrust upon You (manual), U.S. Navy, 1961.

Pigeons, T. F. H. Publications, 1962.

Tidal Marsh Plants of Connecticut, Connecticut Arboretum, 1970.

Tropical Fish, T. F. H. Publications, 1970.

Your Terrarium, T. F. H. Publications, 1972.

Teddy Bear Hamsters, T. F. H. Publications, 1974.

(With daughter, Martha Roberts) *All about Iguanas,* T. F. H. Publications, 1976.

All about Salamanders, T. F. H. Publications, 1976.

All about Chameleons and Anoles, T. F. H. Publications, 1977.

All about Ferrets, T. F. H. Publications, 1977.

All about Land Hermit Crabs, T. F. H. Publications, 1978.

Newts and Salamanders, T. F. H. Publications, 1979.

The Tidemarsh Guide, Dutton, 1979, 2nd edition, Peregrine Press, 1982.

Society Finches, T. F. H. Publications, 1979.

Breeding Society Finches, T. F. H. Publications, 1979.

Breeding Zebra Finches, T. F. H. Publications, 1980.

Turtles, T. F. H. Publications, 1980.

Zebra Finches, T. F. H. Publications, 1981.

The T. F. H. Book of Hamsters, T. F. H. Publications, 1981.

All about Breeding Canaries, T. F. H. Publications, 1982.

All about Breeding Lovebirds, T. F. H. Publications, 1983.

Gouldian Finches, T. F. H. Publications, 1984.

All about Breeding Budgerigars, T. F. H. Publications, 1984.

Pearlmakers, privately printed, 1984.

The Tidemarsh Guide to Fishes, privately printed, 1985.

A Complete Introduction to Snakes, T. F. H. Publications, 1987.

Associate editor of *Factory,* 1959.

WORK IN PROGRESS: Additional titles in the Tidemarsh Guide series and a terrarium book for T. F. H. Publications.

SIDELIGHTS: Mervin F. Roberts told *CA:* "Writing is not much easier than digging ditches but it does keep me out of the cold."

AVOCATIONAL INTERESTS: Duck hunting, trapshooting, working as a gunsmith, inventing (has invented glass bottle color sorter for the recycling industry and heaters and pumps for aquariums).

*　　*　　*

ROBINSON, Blackwell P(ierce) 1916-

PERSONAL: Born April 4, 1916, in Goldsboro, N.C.; son of William Smith O'Brien (a lawyer and superior court judge) and Annie W. (Pierce) Robinson; married Mary Hudson (a college professor), June 10, 1948; children: Anna Pierce, Norma Dunn, Margaret Dillon. *Education:* University of North Carolina, A.B., 1937, Ph.D., 1953; Duke University, A.M., 1939. *Politics:* Republican. *Religion:* Episcopal.

ADDRESSES: Home—211 West Bessemer Ave., Greensboro, N.C. 27401. *Office*—Department of History, University of North Carolina, Greensboro, N.C. 27412.

CAREER: High Point College, High Point, N.C., assistant professor, 1954-55, associate professor of history, 1955-57;

University of North Carolina, Greensboro, assistant professor, 1957-60, associate professor of history and political science, 1960—.

MEMBER: Historical Society of North Carolina (vice-president, 1967; president, 1978), Phi Beta Kappa.

AWARDS, HONORS: American Society of Local and County Historians Award, 1957, for *A History of Moore County, North Carolina, 1747-1847;* Peace Award, 1959, for best book on North Carolina history for the bienium, *William R. Davie.*

WRITINGS:

(Contributor) Hugh Lefler and Paul Wager, editors, *Orange County, 1752-1952*, Orange Printshop (Chapel Hill), 1953.
The History of Escheats to the University, University of North Carolina Press, 1955.
The North Carolina Guide, University of North Carolina Press, 1955, reprinted, Scholarly Press, 1978.
A History of Moore County, North Carolina, 1747-1847, Moore County Historical Association, 1956.
William R. Davie, University of North Carolina Press, 1957.
(Editor) *Battles and Engagements of the American Revolution in North Carolina*, Daughters of the American Revolution, 1961.
The Five Royal Governors of North Carolina, Carolina Charter Tercentenary Commission, 1963.
The North Carolina Adventure, Moore Publishing, 1969.
(Editor) *The Revolutionary War Sketches of William R. Davie*, North Carolina Department of Cultural Resources, 1976.
Three Decades of Devotion: The Story of the Tryon County Commission and the Tryon Palace Restoration, Tryon Palace Commission, 1978.
The History of Guilford County, North Carolina, U.S.A. to 1980 A.D., edited by Sydney M. Cone, Jr., Volume I: *Guilford County's First 150 Years* (bound with Volume II: *A Celebration of Guilford County since 1890*, by Alexander R. Stoeson), Guilford County Commissioners, 1981.

Also author of *The History of Holy Trinity Episcopal Church, Greensboro, N.C.*, 1982. Contributor to *North Carolina Historical Review, World Book Encyclopedia, Encyclopaedia Britannica*, and *Grolier's Encyclopedia.*

WORK IN PROGRESS: Chief Justice Thomas Ruffin.

*   *   *

ROBINSON, Nancy K(onheim) 1942-

PERSONAL: Born August 12, 1942, in New York, N.Y.; daughter of Norris David (in advertising) and Natalie (Barnett) Konheim; married Peter Beverley Robinson, May 6, 1966 (divorced, 1987); children: Kenneth Beverley, Alice Natalie. *Education:* Vassar College, A.B., 1964.

ADDRESSES: Home—New York, N.Y.

CAREER: Free-lance writer and researcher, 1972—.

MEMBER: Authors League of America, Authors Guild, Writers Guild of America East, PEN American Center, Mystery Writers of America.

AWARDS, HONORS: U.S. Customs Award, 1978, for historical article; Four Leaf Clover Award from Scholastic Book Services, 1981.

WRITINGS:

FOR JUVENILES

Jungle Laboratory: The Story of Ray Carpenter and the Howling Monkeys (nonfiction; illustrated by Bill Tinker), Hastings House, 1973.
Firefighters! (nonfiction), Scholastic Inc., 1979.
Wendy and the Bullies (fiction; illustrated by Ingrid Fetz), Hastings House, 1980.
Just Plain Cat (fiction), Scholastic Inc., 1981.
Mom, You're Fired (fiction; illustrated by Ed Arno), Scholastic Inc., 1981.
Veronica the Show-Off (illustrated by Sheila Greenwald), Scholastic Inc., 1982.
Oh Honestly, Angela! (illustrated by Richard Williams), Scholastic Inc., 1985.
Veronica Knows Best (illustrated by Rosanne Kaloustian), Scholastic Inc., 1987.

''T*A*C*K*'' SERIES; FOR JUVENILES

(With Marvin Miller) *T*A*C*K* to the Rescue* (illustrated by Alan Tiegreen), Scholastic Inc., 1982.
(With Miller) *T*A*C*K* Secret Service* (illustrated by Tiegreen), Scholastic Inc., 1983.
(With Miller) *T*A*C*K* into Danger* (illustrated by Tiegreen), Scholastic Inc., 1983.
(With Miller) *T*A*C*K* against Time* (illustrated by Tiegreen), Scholastic Inc., 1983.

''TRIPPER AND SAM'' SERIES; FOR JUVENILES

The Phantom Film Crew, Scholastic Inc., 1986.
Danger on the Sound Track, Scholastic Inc., 1986.
The Ghost Who Wanted to Be a Star, Scholastic Inc., 1987.

OTHER

Writer of ''Men of Bronze,'' a documentary broadcast by Public Broadcasting System (PBS-TV), February, 1978.

SIDELIGHTS: Nancy K. Robinson once told *CA:* ''When I write for children I always pick a subject that has puzzled me for a long time. I do not write any differently for children than for adults, but writing for children has become my first love. Children write letters. They ask very difficult questions. They put me on the spot. They do not let me get away with anything!''

*   *   *

ROBSON, Ernest (Mack) 1902-

PERSONAL: Born December 24, 1902, in Chicago, Ill.; son of Oscar (an industrialist) and Sarah (Frank) Robson; married Marion Mendelsohn, January 22, 1948; children: Robert Oscar. *Education:* Amherst College, A.B., 1924; additional study, Pratt Institute Chemical School, 1934-37.

ADDRESSES: Home and office—Primary Press, P.O. Box 105A, Parker Ford, Pa. 19457.

CAREER: Chicago Daily News, Chicago, Ill., reporter, 1925-26; Standard Varnish Works, New York, N.Y., advertising writer, 1927-30; industrial worker with various companies, 1933-36; fur trapper, 1937-41; detergent chemist in New York and New Jersey, 1942-57.

MEMBER: General Systems Research Society, Astronomic League, Speech Association of America, Acoustic Society of America.

WRITINGS:

The Orchestra of the Language, Yoseloff, 1959.

(Contributor) Louise Baughan Murdy, editor, *Sound and Sense in Dylan Thomas's Poetry,* Humanities, 1967.

Transwhichics (science and poetry), Primary Press, 1970.

Thomas Onetwo (pop literature about the 1920s), Something Else Press, 1971.

Choices (poems), calligraphy by wife, Marion Robson, Middle Earth Books, 1973.

(With M. Robson) *I Only Work Here: Five Decades of Poetry in Four Styles,* Dufour, 1975.

Poetry as Performance Art on and off the Page, Primary Press, 1976.

Vowel and Dipthong Tones: New Procedures for Sound Poets (study of whisper music), edited by Gloria Borden, Primary Press, 1977.

(Editor with Jet Wimp) *Against Infinity: An Anthology of Contemporary Mathematical Poetry,* Primary Press, 1979.

(With Larry Wendt) *Phonetic Music with Electronic Music* (book and cassette), Primary Press, 1981.

Freedom, Cannibalism, Creative Love and the Values of Cosmic Nonsense: A Philosophical Manifesto, Primary Press, 1986.

"Names in the Cosmic Ocean" (play), produced in Philadelphia at Painted Bride Art Center, January 5, 1986.

Also author of book and cassette *Shadows of the Voice,* 1982. Contributor of chapters to books on poetry. Contributor of articles and poems to magazines, including *Leonardo: Art Science and Technology.* Has recorded "Selected Poems of Ernest Robson," 1978, and "Names in the Cosmic Ocean."

WORK IN PROGRESS: Poetry collection to be titled *Cosmic Valentines.*

SIDELIGHTS: Ernest Robson writes: "My main interest has been the development of subjective dimensions of physics and astronomy that are compatible with poetry via information models . . . [, that is,] relations between the mechanical, recurrent and the non-mechanical, infrequent features of existence, . . . including a concept of emotions as survival vectors. This approach attaches much importance to interdependencies between micro and macro universes. I have concluded that survival of the species depends on a world-wide acceptance of the limitations of the human mind for solar information and the inadequacy of all codifications and social systems."

Robson's poems have been read on WNYC-Radio. *Transwhichics* has been translated into Spanish.

*   *   *

ROCHE, Terry
  See POOLE, Peggy

*   *   *

ROCHER, Guy 1924-

PERSONAL: Born April 20, 1924, in Berthierville, Quebec, Canada; son of Barthelemy (a civil engineer) and Jeanne (Magnan) Rocher; married Suzanne Cloutier, 1949 (divorced, 1981); married Claire-Emmanuelle Depocas, 1986; children: (first marriage) Genevieve, Anne-Marie, Isabelle, Claire. *Education:* University of Montreal, B.A., 1943, Laval University, M.A., 1950; Harvard University, graduate study, 1950-52, Ph.D., 1957.

ADDRESSES: Home—4670 De Grand-Pre, Montreal, Quebec, Canada H2T 2H7. *Office*—Law Faculty, University of Montreal, Montreal, Quebec, Canada H3C 3J7.

CAREER: Laval University, Quebec City, Quebec assistant professor, 1952-57, associate professor of sociology, 1957-60, director of School of Social Service, 1958-60; University of Montreal, Montreal, Quebec, professor of sociology, 1960—, director of department, 1960-65, assistant dean, Faculty of Social Sciences, 1962-67, affiliated with Center for Research into Public Law, Faculty of Law, 1979—. Member of Royal Commission of Inquiry on Education in Province of Quebec, 1961-65; governor of Canadian College of Workers, 1963-66; president of commission of inquiry on the New French University at Montreal, 1965; member of Canadian Broadcast Board, 1966-68; vice-president of Arts Council of Canada, 1969-74; deputy minister of cultural development, Quebec Government, 1976-79; president of administrative council of Radio-Quebec, 1979-81; deputy minister for social development, Quebec Government, 1981-83.

MEMBER: International Young Catholic Students (Canada; president, 1945-48), International Association of French-speaking Sociologists (treasurer, 1958-59), Canadian Association of Sociology (president, 1961-62), French-Canadian Association of Sociologists and Anthropologists (president, 1967-69), American Sociological Association, Canadian Economic Association, French-Canadian Association for the Advancement of Science.

AWARDS, HONORS: Carnegie Foundation fellow at Harvard University, 1951-52; research grants from Royal Society of Canada, 1957-58, and Arts Council of Canada, 1965-66, 1968-69; Companion of the Order of Canada, 1971, for contribution to Canadian education.

WRITINGS:

With P. H. Chombard de Lauwe and others) *Famille et habitation,* Centre National de la Recherche Scientifique (Paris), 1960.

(With others) *Rapport de la commission royale d'enquete sur l'enseignement,* Queen's Printer, Volume I, 1963, Volume II, 1964, Volume III, 1964, Volume IV, 1966, Volume V, 1966.

Introduction a la sociologie generale, three volumes, Editions H.M.H., 1968-69, translation by Peta Sheriff published as *A General Introduction to Sociology: A Theoretical Perspective,* St. Martin's, 1972.

(With Pierre W. Belanger) *Ecole et societe au Quebec,* Editions H.M.H., 1971, new edition, 1975.

Talcott Parsons et la sociologie americaine, Presses Universitaires de France, 1972, translation by Barbara and Stephen Mennell, with an introduction by Stephen Mennell, published as *Talcott Parsons and American Sociology,* Nelson, 1974, Barnes & Noble, 1975.

Le Quebec en mutation, Editions H.M.H., 1973.

(With others) *Ecole de demain,* Editions Delachaux, 1976.

(With Leon Bernier and Belanger) *Generation, maturation et conjoncture: Une Etude des changements d'attitude dans le Quebec des annees 1970,* Faculte des Sciences de l'Education, Universite Laval and Departement de Sociologie, Universite de Montreal, 1980.

(With others) *Continuite et rupture: Les Sciences sociales au Quebec,* Les Presses de Universite de Montreal, 1984.

CONTRIBUTOR

Situation de la recherche sur le Canada francais, Laval University Press, 1962.

L'Utilisation des ressources humaines, Institut Canadien des Affaires Publiques, 1965.

(Author of preface) Colette Moreux, *Fin d'une religion?,* University of Montreal Press, 1969.

Le Nouveau defi des valeurs, Editions H.M.H., 1969.

Perspectives on Revolution and Evolution, Duke University Press, 1979.

OTHER

Contributor to professional journals, committee reports, and to *Montreal Star.* Managing editor, *Service Social,* 1958-60; member of editorial board, *Recherches sociographiques, Sociologie et societes, Quebec-Science,* and *Maintenant.*

WORK IN PROGRESS: A book on the sociology of law; research on the legal dimensions of technological change.

SIDELIGHTS: Guy Rocher's *Introduction a la sociologie generale* has been translated into Spanish, Portuguese, Italian, and Persian; *Talcott Parsons et la sociologie americaine* has been translated into Italian, Dutch, and Japanese.

*   *   *

RODBERG, Leonard S(idney) 1932-

PERSONAL: Born December 14, 1932, in Baltimore, Md.; son of Milton and Esther (Vineburg) Rodberg; married Ruth Bloom, June 10, 1954; married Joanne Lukomnic, January 21, 1979; children: Lee, Elliot, Paul, Susan, Simon. *Education:* Attended Lehigh University, 1951-53; Johns Hopkins University, A.B., 1954; Massachusetts Institute of Technology, Ph.D., 1956.

ADDRESSES: Office—Public Resource Center, 1747 Connecticut Ave. N.W., Washington, D.C. 20009.

CAREER: Massachusetts Institute of Technology, Cambridge, research associate in physics, 1956-57; Research Institute for Advanced Study, Baltimore, Md., staff scientist, 1957; University of California, Berkeley, research associate, 1958-59; University of Maryland, College Park, assistant professor of physics, 1959-61; U.S. Arms Control and Disarmament Agency, Washington, D.C., science policy officer, 1961-63, office chief, 1963-66; University of Maryland, associate professor of physics, 1966-70; Institute for Policy Studies, Washington, D.C., resident fellow, 1970-77; Public Resource Center, Washington, D.C., director, 1977—. Consultant, Los Alamos Scientific Laboratory, 1959—.

MEMBER: American Public Health Association (member of task force on national health service plans, 1977-78; member of medical care committee on national health service proposals, 1978-79), Federation of American Scientists.

AWARDS, HONORS: Meritorious Honor Award, U.S. Arms Control and Disarmament Agency, 1966; named Distinguished Young Scientist of the Year, Maryland Academy of Sciences, 1967.

WRITINGS:

(With R. M. Thaler) *Introduction to the Quantum Theory of Scattering,* Academic Press, 1967.

(Editor with Derek Shearer) *The Pentagon Watchers,* Doubleday, 1970.

(With Meg Schachter) *State Conservation and Solar Energy Tax Programs: Incentives or Windfalls?,* Council of State Planning Agencies, 1980.

Contributor to scientific journals.

WORK IN PROGRESS: Economic Issues in a Technological Society; Community-Based Health Programs; Community and Labor Energy Policies.

*   *   *

ROMANO, Clare 1922-
(Clare Ross)

PERSONAL: Born in Palisade, N.J.; married John Ross (an artist, painter, and professor), November 23, 1943; children: Christopher, Timothy. *Education:* Attended Cooper Union School of Art, 1939-43, Ecole des Beaux Arts, Fontainebleau, France, 1949, and Instituto Statale d'Arte, Florence, Italy, 1958-59.

ADDRESSES: Home—Box 1122, Madison Square Station, New York, N.Y. 10159. *Office*—Department of Fine Arts, Pratt Institute, 200 Willoughby Ave, Brooklyn, N.Y. 11205.

CAREER: Artist. New School for Social Research, New York City, instructor in printmaking, 1960-73; Art Center of Northern New Jersey, Tenafly, instructor in painting and design, 1961-65; Pratt Graphic Art Center, New York City, began as instructor, became adjunct associate professor in printmaking, 1963-85; Manhattanville College, Purchase, N.Y., instructor in printmaking, 1964-65; Pratt Institute, Brooklyn, N.Y., 1964—, began as assistant professor, became associate professor in printmaking. U.S. Information Agency artist-in-residence at "Graphic Arts U.S.A.," an exhibition. Art has been exhibited in about sixty one-person shows (including Associated American Artists Gallery, 1967, 1982, and Boston Museum of Fine Arts, 1968), many permanent collections (including Metropolitan Museum of Art, Library of Congress, Smithsonian Institution, National Collection of Fine Arts, Museum of Modern Art, Whitney Museum of American Art, and more than a dozen U.S. embassies abroad), private galleries, and American and foreign group exhibitions; art work has been commissioned by Jewish Museum, Hilton Hotel, International Graphic Arts Society, Philadelphia Print Club, and Manufacturers Hanover Trust; lecturer for television, colleges, and universities.

MEMBER: Society of American Graphic Artists (president, 1970-72), American Color Print Society, National Academy of Design (academician), Print Club of Philadelphia, Boston Printmakers.

AWARDS, HONORS: Purchase awards from Brooklyn Museum, 1951, Library of Congress, 1951, 1966, New Jersey State Museum, 1967, 1970, Boston Printmakers, 1967, eighth national print exhibit of Silvermine Guild, 1970; Louis Comfort Tiffany grant for printmaking, 1952; awards from Society of American Graphic Artists, 1953, 1962, 1967, 1968, 1971; Fulbright grant for printmaking in Florence, Italy, 1958-59; awards from Philadelphia Print Club, 1960, 1971, Montclair Museum, 1962; *Sprints and Distances: Sports in Poetry and the Poetry in Sport* was named an American Library Association Notable Book in 1965; citation for professional achievement from Cooper Union School of Art, 1966; John Taylor Arms Memorial Prize from National Academy, 1967; presentation artist award from Boston Printmakers, 1967; selected Children's Books of the Year, Child Study Association of America, 1971, for *God Wash the World and Start Again,* and 1974, for *Conjure Tales;* MacDowell Colony Fellowships, 1974, 1976, 1978, 1982, 1987; Distinguished Teacher Award, Pratt Institute, 1979; New Jersey State Council Arts Grant, 1980.

WRITINGS:

WITH HUSBAND, JOHN ROSS

The Complete Printmaker, Free Press, 1972.
The Complete New Techniques in Printmaking, Free Press, 1974.
The Complete Intaglio Print, Free Press, 1974.
The Complete Relief Print, Free Press, 1974.
The Complete Screen Print and the Lithograph, Free Press, 1974.
The Complete Collograph: The Art and Technique of Printmaking from Collage Plates, Macmillan, 1980.

ILLUSTRATOR WITH J. ROSS

Edgar Lee Masters, *Spoon River Anthology*, Macmillan, 1963.
Walt Whitman, *Leaves of Grass*, edited by Lawrence G. Powell, Crowell, 1964.
James Marnell, *Labor Day*, Crowell, 1966.
Charles W. Chesnutt, *Conjure Tales*, retold by Ray A. Shepard, Dutton, 1973.
New Coasts and Strange Harbors: Discovering Poems, edited by Helen Hill and Agnes Perkins, Crowell, 1974.

UNDER NAME CLARE ROSS; ILLUSTRATOR WITH J. ROSS

(Contributor of woodcuts) May Garelick, *Manhattan Island*, Crowell, 1957.
Gerald Doan McDonald, editor, *A Way of Knowing: A Collection of Poems for Boys*, Crowell, 1959.
Sophia Cedarbaum, *Chanukah, the Festival of Lights*, Union of American Hebrew Congregations, 1960.
Cedarbaum, *Passover, the Festival of Freedom*, Union of American Hebrew Congregations, 1960.
Cedarbaum, *Purim, a Joyous Holiday*, Union of American Hebrew Congregations, 1960.
Cedarbaum, *Sabbath, a Day of Delight*, Union of American Hebrew Congregations, 1960.
Clyde R. Bulla, *The Ring and the Fire: Stories from Wagner's Nibelung Operas*, Crowell, 1962.
Whitman, *Poems of Walt Whitman*, Crowell, 1964.
Lillian Morrison, editor, *Sprints and Distances: Sports in Poetry and the Poetry in Sport*, Crowell, 1965.
Henry Wadsworth Longfellow, *Poems*, Crowell, 1967.
Mira Brichto, *God around Us*, Union of American Hebrew Congregations, 1969.
Molly Cone, *About God*, edited by Jack D. Spiro, Union of American Hebrew Congregations, 1973.

OTHER

(Author of introduction) Burton Wasserman, *Bridges of Vision*, New Jersey State Museum, 1969.
(Illustrator under name Clare Ross) Lorenz Graham, *God Wash the World and Start Again*, Crowell, 1971.

Also contributor to *Artist's Proof*, 1964 and 1966, and to *Encyclopedia Americana*, 1971.

BIOGRAPHICAL/CRITICAL SOURCES:

BOOKS

Eichenberg, Fritz, *The Art of the Print*, Abrams, 1977.
Faulkner, Ray and Edwin Ziegfeld, *Art Today*, Holt, 1969.
Gilmour, Pat, *Modern Prints*, Studio Vista, 1970.
Heller, Jules, *Printmaking Today*, Holt, 1972.
Kingman, Lee and others, editors, *Illustrator of Children's Books: 1957-1966*, Horn Book, 1968, *1967-1976*, 1978.

PERIODICALS

American Artist, August 16, 1981.
Art in America, fall, 1960, April, 1965.
Artist's Proof, Volume V, Pratt Graphic Art Center, 1964.
Art News, May, 1967.
Christian Science Monitor, November 24, 1967.
New York Times, October 24, 1965.
Pratt Alumnus, spring, 1967.

*   *   *

ROOD, Ronald (N.)   1920-

PERSONAL: Surname rhymes with "food"; born July 7, 1920, in Torrington, Conn.; son of Nellis Frost (a life insurance underwriter) and Bessie (Chamberlain) Rood; married Margaret Bruce (a teacher), December 21, 1942; children: Janice, Thomas Elliot, Alison, Roger Warren. *Education:* University of Connecticut, B.S., 1941, M.S., 1949.

ADDRESSES: Home and office—R. R. 1, Box 740, Lincoln, Vt. 05443.

CAREER: Writer. Long Island Agricultural and Technical Institute, Farmingdale, N.Y., instructor in biology, 1949-53; Grolier Enterprises, New York, N.Y., research editor, 1954-64; Middlebury College, Middlebury, Vt. instructor in biology, 1956-58. Church choir director. *Military service:* U.S. Army Air Forces, fighter pilot, World War II; received Air Medal.

MEMBER: Forest and Field, American Forestry Association, National Wildlife Federation, Outdoor Writers Association of America, League of Vermont Writers (president, 1965-67, 1975), Vermont Natural Resources Council.

WRITINGS:

The How and Why Wonder Book of Insects, Grosset, 1960.
The How and Why Wonder Book of Ants and Bees, Grosset, 1962.
Land Alive: The World of Nature at One Family's Door, Stephen Greene, 1962.
The How and Why Wonder Book of Butterflies and Moths, Grosset, 1963.
The Loon in My Bathtub, Stephen Greene, 1964, revised edition, New England Press, 1986.
The Sea and Its Wonderful Creatures, Whitman Publishing, 1965.
Bees, Bugs and Beetles: The Arrow Book of Insects, Four Winds, 1965.
Hundred Acre Welcome: The Story of a Chincoteague Pony, Stephen Greene, 1967.
Vermont Life Book of Nature, Stephen Greene, 1967.
How Do You Spank a Porcupine?, Trident, 1969, revised edition, New England Press, 1983.
Animal Champions, Grosset, 1969.
Answers about Insects, Grosset, 1969.
Animals Nobody Loves, Stephen Greene, 1971, revised edition, New England Press, 1987.
Who Wakes the Groundhog?, Norton, 1973.
May I Keep This Clam, Mother? It Followed Me Home, Simon & Schuster, 1973.
Good Things Are Happening, Stephen Greene, 1975.
It's Going to Sting Me, Simon & Schuster, 1976.
Possum in the Parking Lot, Simon & Schuster, 1977.
Elephant Bones and Lonely Hearts, Stephen Greene, 1977.
Laska, Norton, 1980.

Ron Rood's Vermont: An Easygoing Guide to the Outdoors in the Green Mountain State, New England Press, 1987.

Contributor to numerous periodicals, including *Reader's Digest, Coronet, Audubon Magazine, Christian Herald, New York Times, Pageant,* and *Vermont Life.*

SIDELIGHTS: Ronald Rood told *CA:* ''I paid $5.00 for my typewriter years ago. Now, two dozen books later, I'm still trying to get my money back!''

*   *   *

ROSENBERG, Jerry M. 1935-

PERSONAL: Born February 5, 1935, in New York, N.Y.; son of Frank (a businessman) and Esther (Gardner) Rosenberg; married Ellen Young, September 11, 1960; children: Lauren Monica, Elizabeth. *Education:* City College (now City College of the City University of New York), B.S., 1956; Ohio State University, M.A., 1957; Sorbonne, University of Paris, Certificate, 1958; New York University, Ph.D., 1962. *Religion:* Hebrew.

ADDRESSES: *Home*—515 Tulfan Ter., New York, N.Y. 10463. *Office*—Department of Business Administration, Rutgers University, Newark, N.J. 07102.

CAREER: Government Bureau of Automation, Paris, France, research psychologist, 1957-58; State University of New York, School of Industrial and Labor Relations at Cornell University, Ithaca, assistant professor, 1961-64; Columbia University, New York City, assistant professor, 1964-68; Polytechnic Institute of Brooklyn, Brooklyn, N.Y., professor of management and chairman of department, 1974-77; City University of New York, New York City, professor of management, 1977-80; Rutgers University, Newark, N.J., professor in graduate school of management and chairman of department of business administration, 1980—. Lecturer, Institute of Productivity, Tel-Aviv, summer, 1962; visiting professor, University of British Columbia, summer, 1967. Former conference director, American Foundation on Automation and Employment. Former member of New York Mayor's Committee on Youth and Work and of National Conference of Christians and Jews advisory committee for labor, management, and public interest.

MEMBER: Academy of Management.

AWARDS, HONORS: Grants from Fulbright Foundation and French government.

WRITINGS:

Automation, Manpower and Education, Random House, 1966.
The Death of Privacy, Random House, 1969.
The Computer Prophets, Macmillan, 1969.
Dictionary of Business and Management, Wiley, 1978, 2nd edition, 1983.
Dictionary of Banking and Finance, Wiley, 1982, 2nd edition published as *Dictionary of Banking and Financial Services,* 1985.
Inside the Wall Street Journal: The History and the Power of Dow Jones & Company and America's Most Influential Newspaper, Macmillan, 1982.
Dictionary of Computers, Data Processing and Telecommunications, Wiley, 1984, 2nd edition published as *Dictionary of Computers, Information Processing and Telecommunications,* 1987.
Dictionary of Artificial Intelligence and Robotics, Wiley, 1986.
The Investor's Dictionary, Wiley, 1986.

AVOCATIONAL INTERESTS: Tennis, travel, collecting antiquarian books.

*   *   *

ROSENFELD, Alvin H(irsch) 1938-

PERSONAL: Born April 28, 1938, in Philadelphia, Pa.; son of Max and Bertha (Cohen) Rosenfeld; married Erna Baber, August 2, 1966; children: Gavriel (son), Dalia. *Education:* Temple University, B.A., 1960; Brown University, M.A., 1962, Ph.D., 1967. *Religion:* Jewish.

ADDRESSES: *Home*—1026 East Wylie St., Bloomington, Ind. 47401. *Office*—Department of English, Indiana University, Bloomington, Ind. 47405.

CAREER: Brown University, Providence, R.I., instructor in English, 1967-68; Indiana University at Bloomington, assistant professor, 1968-72, associate professor, 1972-77, professor of English, 1977—, director of Jewish studies, 1974—. Visiting professor, University of Kiel, 1964-65, and at Hebrew University; research fellow, Hamburg University, 1985. Member of international committee of the Institute of Contemporary Jewry at Hebrew University.

MEMBER: Association of American Professors for Peace in the Middle East, United States Holocaust Memorial Council (special advisor to chairman), Association for Jewish Studies, Anti-Defamation League of B'nai B'rith, Phi Beta Kappa.

AWARDS, HONORS: Recipient of fellowship grants from American Council of Learned Societies, National Foundation of Jewish Culture, and National Endowment for the Humanities.

WRITINGS:

(Editor) *William Blake: Essays,* Brown University Press, 1969.
(Editor) *Collected Poetry of John Wheelwright,* New Directions, 1972.
(Editor with Irving Greenberg) *Confronting the Holocaust: The Impact of Elie Wiesel,* Indiana University Press, 1979.
A Double Dying: Reflections on Holocaust Literature, Indiana University Press, 1980.
(Translator with wife, Erna Rosenfeld) Guenther Schwarberg, *The Murders at Bullenhuser Damm,* Indiana University Press, 1984.
Imagining Hitler, Indiana University Press, 1985.

Editor of ''Jewish Literature and Culture'' book series. Author of numerous scholarly and critical articles on American poetry, Jewish writers, and the literature of the Holocaust. Contributing editor, *American Poetry Review,* 1973—. Member of editorial board, *Shoah: A Review of Holocaust Studies and Commemorations.*

WORK IN PROGRESS: Research in American poetry, Jewish-American literature, and literature of the Holocaust.

SIDELIGHTS: In his book *A Double Dying: Reflections on Holocaust Literature,* author Alvin H. Rosenfeld examines the effects of the Holocaust on post-World War II literature. Basing his study on the assumption that the Holocaust was ''a major turning point in history and [in] the history of consciousness,'' Rosenfeld concludes that the subsequent outpouring of ''literature without analogy'' presents both the reader and the critic with problems of interpretation and appraisal.

According to Irving Abrahamson of the *Chicago Tribune Book World,* Rosenfeld proves to be "a sure guide, knowledgeable and insightful" in his discussions of various first person accounts and novels that have appeared in English, German, or Yiddish since the end of the war. Abrahamson and Susan Jacoby of the *New York Times Book Review* agree that the most thought-provoking essay in the collection deals with what Jacoby terms the "misappropriation" of the Holocaust "as a personal and political metaphor by artists far removed from the cataclysm—in sensibility and experience if not in time." In this essay, Rosenfeld is especially critical of such writers as William Styron *(Sophie's Choice),* Peter Weiss *(The Investigation),* Sylvia Plath ("Daddy" and other poems), and Leslie Epstein *(King of the Jews)* for what he regards as their "deceptions and distortions that result from inauthentic responses to the Holocaust."

In the case of *Sophie's Choice,* for example, Rosenfeld condemns certain passages in which Styron links eroticism with life in the concentration camps, a connection Rosenfeld feels leads to the creation of "a new and singularly perverse type of sex object"—namely, the starved and mutilated woman. But his major criticism of the Holocaust-inspired works deals not with the instances of misplaced eroticism, but with what he views as a tendency on the part of the authors to either minimize "the terror of the camps by falsely generalizing or universalizing it" or to resort to "hyperbole or excessive strain [in] an invasion of history by hysteria." Jacoby, who describes Rosenfeld's study as "lucid enough for a general audience and detailed enough for academics," concludes: "Both the living and the dead deserve better from artists whose work arises from the unique hold the holocaust continues to exercise on the imagination of post-Auschwitz man."

In *Imagining Hitler,* Rosenfeld directs his attention to the image of Adolf Hitler in post-1945 American popular culture. According to Rosenfeld, fiction and film in America have continually trivialized National Socialism (Nazism) and the horror of Hitler; fiction in particular is inclined to portray Hitler as a man without victims, says Rosenfeld. In the opinion of *New York Times Book Review* critic Fritz Stern, Rosenfeld "writes out of moral outrage. . . . He is appalled to find that the Nazi 'aura of destructive power has been turned into sexual and political fantasies, religious allegories, pseudohistories, science fictions'. . . . He objects to 'fiction's infidelity to history,' and demonstrates that freedom from fact has not given us some kind of deeper understanding of Hitler's horror. . . . The danger includes the possibility that this ghost of Hitler can inspire mad would-be emulators." For John Gross in the *New York Times, Imagining Hitler* is a "forceful survey. . . . Few of the writers [Rosenfeld] considers this time emerge with much credit."

BIOGRAPHICAL/CRITICAL SOURCES:

BOOKS

Rosenfeld, Alvin H., *A Double Dying: Reflections on Holocaust Literature,* Indiana University Press, 1980.
Rosenfeld, Alvin H., *Imagining Hitler,* Indiana University Press, 1985.

PERIODICALS

Chicago Tribune Book World, June 15, 1980.
New York Times Book Review, December 21, 1980, May 12, 1985.

ROSS, Clare
See ROMANO, Clare

*   *   *

ROWLAND-ENTWISTLE, (Arthur) Theodore (Henry) 1925-
(John Briquebec, Lea Clarke, Anyon Ellis, James Hall-Clarke, T. E. Henry, J. T. Lawrence)

PERSONAL: Born July 30, 1925, in Clayton-le-Moors, Lancashire, England; son of Arthur (an author and journalist) and Sylvia Morton (a teacher; maiden name, Clarke) Rowland-Entwistle; married Jean Isobel Esther Cooke (a writer and editor), March 18, 1968. *Education:* Open University, B.A., 1977. *Religion:* Church of England.

ADDRESSES: Home—West Dene, Stonestile Lane, Hastings, East Sussex TN35 4PE, England. *Agent*—Rupert Crew Ltd., King's Mews, Gray's Inn Rd., London WC1N 2JA England.

CAREER: Daily Mail, Manchester and London, England, subeditor, 1944-55; *TV Times,* London, chief sub-editor, 1955-56, production editor, 1956-60, assistant editor, 1961; *World Book Encyclopedia,* London, senior editor, 1962-67; director, Leander Associates Ltd. (editorial consultants), 1967-69; director, First Features Ltd. (a newspaper features agency), 1972-79.

MEMBER: Royal Geographical Society (fellow), Zoological Society of London (fellow).

WRITINGS:

Teach Yourself the Violin (adult nonfiction), English University Press, 1967, published as *Violin,* McKay, 1974.
Insect Life: The World You Never See (adult nonfiction), Rand McNally, 1976.

JUVENILES

(Under pseudonym John Briquebec) *Winston Churchill,* McGraw, 1972.
Napoleon, Hart-Davis, 1973.
Facts and Records Book of Animals, Purnell, 1975.
The Restless Earth, Purnell, 1977.
Exploring Animal Homes, illustrations by Graham Allen and others, F. Watts, 1978.
Exploring Animal Journeys, illustrations by Allen and others, Ward, Lock, 1978.
Let's Look at Wild Animals, edited by Jennifer Justice, illustrations by Mike Atkinson, Ward, Lock, 1978.
Natural Wonders of the World, Octopus, 1980.
(Editor) *Pictorial Encyclopedia of Nature,* Purnell, 1980.
The Illustrated Atlas of the Bible Lands, Longman, 1981.
Ancient World, Galley Press, 1981.
(Under pseudonym John Briquebec) *Animals and Man,* Purnell, 1982.
(Under pseudonym Anyon Ellis) *Wild Animals,* illustrations by Bernard Robinson and Wendy Meadway, Granada, 1982.
(Under pseudonym John Briquebec) *Trees,* illustrated by David Salariya, Granada, 1982.
(Under pseudonym J. T. Lawrence) *Fossils,* Granada, 1982.
(Under pseudonym James Hall-Clarke), *Fishes,* Granada, 1983.
Insects, Granada, 1983.
(Under pseudonym T. E. Henry) *The Seashore,* Granada, 1983.
Heraldry, Granada, 1984.
Houses, Wayland, 1985.

Confucius, Wayland, 1986.
Stamps, Wayland, 1986.
Nebuchadnezzar, Wayland, 1986.
Rivers and Lakes, Wayland, 1986.
Focus on Rubber, Wayland, 1986.
Focus on Coal, Wayland, 1987.
The Royal Marines, Wayland, 1987.
The Secret Service, Wayland, 1987.
The Special Air Service, Wayland, 1987.
Jungles and Rainforests, Wayland, 1987.

WITH WIFE, JEAN COOKE

Animal Worlds, illustrations by Bernard Robinson and others, Sampson Low, 1974.
Famous Composers, David & Charles, 1974.
Famous Explorers, David & Charles, 1974.
Famous Kings and Emperors, David & Charles, 1976.
(Also with Ann Kramer) *World of History,* Hamlyn, 1977.
(Editors) *The Junior Encyclopedia of General Knowledge,* foreword by Magnus Magnusson, Octopus, 1978.
(Editors) *Purnell's Concise Encyclopedia of the Arts,* Purnell, 1979.
(Editors) *Purnell's Pictorial Encyclopedia,* Purnell, 1979.
(Editors) *Purnell's Pictorial Encyclopedia of Nature,* Purnell, 1980.
(Under pseudonym Lea Clarke) *The Beaver Book of Sporting Rules,* Hamlyn, 1980.
(Also with Kramer) *History Factfinder,* Ward, Lock, 1981.
Rainbow Fact Book of British History, W. H. Smith, 1984.

CONTRIBUTOR

Michael W. Dempsey, editor, *Everyman's Factfinder,* Dent, 1982.
Kramer and Lindy Newton, editors, *Quest for the Past,* Reader's Digest Association, 1984.
John Paxton, consultant editor, *New Illustrated Everyman's Encyclopedia,* Octopus Books, 1984.
Magnusson, consultant editor, *Reader's Digest Book of Facts,* Reader's Digest Association, 1985.
The Giant Book of Facts, Octopus, 1987.

OTHER

Contributor of articles and consultant to additional encyclopedias, including *New Junior World Encyclopedia, Apollo Encyclopedia, Modern Century Illustrated Encyclopedia, Encyclopedia of Wild Life, Encyclopedia of Africa, Encyclopedia of Inventions, Concise Encyclopedia of Geography, Concise Encyclopedia of History, Rainbow Encyclopedia, St. Michael Encyclopedia of Natural History,* and *Pictorial Encyclopedia of History.* Contributor of articles and consultant to atlases, including *St. Michael Atlas of World Geography, My First Picture Atlas,* and *Encyclopedic Atlas of the World.* Editor of *Hastings Talking Newspaper for the Blind,* 1981—. Contributor of articles to periodicals.

SIDELIGHTS: Theodore Rowland-Entwistle told *CA:* "Apart from my unpublished poetry, I am a non-creative writer; I produce reference material for young people and nonspecialist adults. Consequently, my main objectives are accuracy and clarity. I would recommend the discipline of sub-editing for a national newspaper as training for any writer, but don't stick at it too long. I am fortunate to be able to collaborate with my wife on most of my work."

ROZOVSKY, Lorne Elkin   1942-

PERSONAL: Born September 13, 1942, in Timmins, Ontario, Canada; son of Hyman (a mining engineer) and Gladys (Freiman) Rozovsky; married Fay Adrienne Frank (a lawyer and writer), December 16, 1979; children: Joshua, Aaron. *Education:* University of New Brunswick, B.A., 1963; University of Toronto, LL.B., 1966.

ADDRESSES: Home—1951 Parkwood Terrace, Halifax, Nova Scotia, Canada B3H 4G4. *Office*—P.O. Box 2471, Station M, Halifax, Nova Scotia, Canada B3J 3E4.

CAREER: Province of Nova Scotia, Department of Health, Halifax, legal counsel, 1967-79; private practice of law in Halifax, 1979—, associated with Patterson Kitz, 1985—. Appointed Queens Counsel, 1984. Adjunct associate professor at Dalhousie University, 1980—.

MEMBER: Canadian Bar Association, American Society of Hospital Attorneys, American Society of Law and Medicine, American College of Legal Medicine (honorary fellow, 1986), Nova Scotia Barristers Society, Nova Scotia Medical-Legal Society, Writers Federation of Nova Scotia.

WRITINGS:

Canadian Hospital Law: A Practical Guide, Canadian Hospital Association, 1974, 2nd edition, 1979.
Canadian Manual of Hospital By-Laws, Canadian Hospital Association, 1976.
The Canadian Patient's Book of Rights, Doubleday, 1980.
(With wife, F. A. Rozovsky) *Legal Sex,* Doubleday, 1982.
Consent to Treatment, Little, Brown, 1983.
(With F. A. Rozovsky) *Canadian Health Facilities Law Guide,* CCH Canadian, 1983.
(With F. A. Rozovsky) *Canadian Law of Patient Records,* Butterworths, 1984.
Canadian Dental Law, Butterworths, 1987.

Author of regular columns with F. A. Rozovsky, appearing in *Canadian Doctor, Health Care, Canadian Operating Room, Nursing Journal,* and *Canadian Critical Care Nursing Journal.* Also columnist for *Oral Health, Dental Practice Management,* and *Canadian Veterinary Journal.*

SIDELIGHTS: Lorne Elkin Rozovsky told *CA:* "Law is too important to be left to lawyers and politicians because it affects every member of society in the same way that medicine affects everyone. My wife and I write exclusively about health law. We explain American and Canadian law to health professionals and to the public in a way that everyone can understand. We try to prevent legal problems rather than solve them. We practice preventive law."

*   *   *

RUDE, George F. E(lliot)   1910-

PERSONAL: Born February 8, 1910, in Oslo, Norway; son of Jens Essendrop (an engineer) and Amy (Elliot) Rude; married Doreen de la Hoyde, March 16, 1940. *Education:* Cambridge University, B.A. (with honors), 1931; University of London, B.A. (with honors), 1948, Ph.D., 1950.

ADDRESSES: Home—24 Cadborough Cliff, Rye, East Sussex TN31 7EB, England.

CAREER: Schoolmaster, Stowe School, Buckingham, England, 1931-35, St. Paul's School, London, England, 1936-49, Sir Walter St. John's School, 1950-54, and Holloway

School, 1954-59; University of Adelaide, Adelaide, South Australia, senior lecturer, 1960-63, professor of history, 1964-67. Flinders University of South Australia, Bedford Park, professor of history, 1968-70; Concordia University, Montreal, Quebec, professor of history, 1970—.

MEMBER: Royal Historical Society (fellow), Australian Humanities Research Council (member of executive committee), Historical Association (London).

AWARDS, HONORS: Alexander Prize, Royal Historical Society, 1955, for essay "The Gordon Riots: The Rioters and Their Victims"; LL.D., University of Adelaide (now Flinders University of South Australia), 1967.

WRITINGS:

The Crowd in the French Revolution, Clarendon Press, 1959, new edition, Oxford University Press, 1972.
Wilkes and Liberty: A Social Study of 1763 to 1774, Clarendon Press, 1962.
Revolutionary Europe, 1783-1815, Meridian Books, 1964.
The Crowd in History: A Study of Popular Disturbances in France and England, 1730-1850, Wiley, 1964.
(Editor) *The Eighteenth Century,* Free Press, 1965.
(Author of introduction) Georges Duveau, *1848: The Making of a Revolution,* Pantheon, 1966.
(Editor) *Robespierre,* Prentice-Hall, 1967.
(With E. J. Hobsbawm) *Captain Swing: A Social History of the Great English Agricultural Uprising of 1830,* Pantheon, 1969, Norton, 1975.
Paris and London in the Eighteenth Century: Studies in Popular Protest, Collins, 1970, Viking, 1971.
Hanoverian London, 1714-1808, University of California Press, 1971.
Debate on Europe, 1815-1850, Harper, 1972.
Europe in the Eighteenth Century: Aristocracy and the Bourgeois Challenge, Weidenfeld & Nicolson, 1972, Praeger, 1973.
Robespierre: Portrait of a Revolutionary Democrat, Collins, 1975, Viking, 1976.
Protest and Punishment: The Story of the Social and Political Protesters Transported to Australia, 1788-1868, Oxford University Press, 1978.
Ideology and Popular Protest, Lawrence & Wishart, 1980, Pantheon, 1981.
Criminal and Victim: Crime and Society in Early Nineteenth-Century England, Oxford University Press, 1985.
The French Revolution after Two Hundred Years, Weidenfeld & Nicolson, 1987.

Contributor to professional journals in England, France, Italy, Germany, and Australia.

*   *   *

RUDOLF, Anthony 1942-

PERSONAL: Born September 6, 1942, in London, England; son of Henry Cyril (a certified public accountant) and Esther (Rosenberg) Rudolf; married Brenda Marshall (a book designer), March 15, 1970 (divorced, 1981); two children. *Education:* British Institute, Paris, France, certificate (with distinction), 1961; Trinity College, Cambridge, B.A., 1964. *Politics:* Labour Party. *Religion:* Jewish.

ADDRESSES: Home—8 The Oaks, Woodside Avenue, London N12, England.

CAREER: Junior executive with British Travel Association, London, England, and Chicago, Ill., 1964-66; teacher of English and French in London School Service, and private teacher of English as a foreign language, 1967-68; worked in London bookshops including a period as co-proprietor of own business, 1969-71; *European Judaism,* London, literary editor, 1970-72, managing editor, 1972-75. Member of Jury for Neustadt International Literature Prize, University of Oklahoma, 1986. Has broadcast for British Broadcasting Corp. Radio, British Broadcasting Corp. World Service, and French radio, and given poetry readings in Great Britain, France, and Yugoslavia. Patron, Nuclear Freeze Movement, 1987.

MEMBER: National Poetry Centre (member of general council, 1970-76), Cambridge Poetry Festival Society.

WRITINGS:

(Translator) *Selected Poems of Yves Bonnefoy,* J. Cape, 1968, Grossman, 1969.
The Manifold Circle (poems), Carcanet, 1971.
(Translator) Ana Novac, *The Soup Complex* (play), Stand, 1972.
(Editor with Richard Burns) Charles Tomlinson, *An Octave for Octavio Paz,* Menard, 1972.
(Translator) *Tyorkin and The Stovemakers: Selected Verse and Prose of Alexander Tvardovsky,* Carcanet, 1974.
(Compiler) *Edmund Jabes Bibliography,* Menard, 1974.
(Translator) Francaise Basch, *Relative Creatures: Victorian Women in Society and the Novel,* Allen Lane, 1974.
(Translator with Peter Jay) Petru Popescu, *Boxes, Stairs and Whistle Time* (poems), Omphalos, 1975.
(Editor) *Poems for Shakespeare IV,* Globe Playhouse Trust Publications, 1976.
(Translator, and author of introduction) Eugene Heimler, *The Storm: The Tragedy of Sinai* (verse play), Menard, 1976.
The Same River Twice (poems), Carcanet, 1976.
(Translator with Daniel Weissbort) Evgeny Vinokurov, *The War Is Over* (selected poems), Carcanet, 1976.
(Translator) *Poems of Edmond Jabes,* Menard, 1978.
(Editor with Howard Schwartz) *Voices within the Ark: The Modern Jewish Poets,* Avon, 1980.
After the Dream (poems), Cauldron, 1980.
(With others) *For David Gascoyne on His Sixty-fifth Birthday: 10 October, 1981* (poems), Enitharmon/Ampersand, 1981.

Also author of political pamphlet, *Byron's Darkness: Lost Summer and Nuclear Winter,* 1984. Contributor of translations of many French, Russian, and other poets to books and anthologies, including *The Random House Book of Twentieth Century French Poetry* and *The Penguin Book of Post-War Russian Poetry,* and to numerous periodicals, including *Times Literary Supplement, Nation,* and *Poetry Nation Review.* Contributor of poems, articles, and reviews to literary journals, including *Tree, Holy Beggars Gazette, Roy Rogers, Transatlantic Review, World Literature Today, Literary Review,* and *Contemporary Literature in Translation.*

London editor of *Stand.* Founder and co-editor of *Journals of Pierre Menard;* advisory editor of *Modern Poetry in Translation* and *Heimler Foundation Newsletter.* Guest editor of *Cambridge Opinion/Circuit,* 1968, *Workshop,* 1971, *Poetry Review,* 1971, *Modern Poetry in Translation,* 1973, *New Linguist,* 1973, *Books,* 1974, and *Roy Rogers,* 1974.

BIOGRAPHICAL/CRITICAL SOURCES:

PERIODICALS

New York Times Book Review, January 4, 1981.
Times Literary Supplement, September 26, 1986.

*   *   *

RUGGIERS, Paul G(eorge)   1918-

PERSONAL: Born April 29, 1918, in Paterson, N.J.; married
Ernestine Eddleman, May 29, 1948; children: Christopher.
Education: Washington and Jefferson College, A.B., 1940;
Cornell University, Ph.D., 1947. *Politics:* Democrat. *Religion:* Catholic.

ADDRESSES: Home—1035 Cruce St., Norman, Okla. 73069.
Office—Variorum Chaucer, University of Oklahoma, Norman, Okla. 73019.

CAREER: University of Oklahoma, Norman, instructor, 1946-
47, assistant professor, 1947-52, associate professor, 1952-
57, professor of English, 1957-64, David Ross Boyd Professor, 1964—, George Lynn Cross Research Professor of English, 1972—, director of honors program, 1963-69. *Military service:* U.S. Army, Military Intelligence, 1942-45; became
master sergeant.

MEMBER: Modern Language Association of America, Phi Beta
Kappa.

AWARDS, HONORS: Ford Foundation fellow, 1954-55; Guggenheim fellow, 1956-57; Fulbright research fellow in Italy,
1961-62.

WRITINGS:

Florence in the Age of Dante, University of Oklahoma Press,
    1964, reprinted, 1985.
The Art of the Canterbury Tales, University of Wisconsin Press,
    1965.

EDITOR

(And translator) Michele Barbi, *Life of Dante,* University of
    California Press, 1954.
Cultural Leadership in the Great Plains, University of Oklahoma Press, 1957.
(With Irving Ribner) *Modern American Reader,* American Book
    Co., 1958.
(With Jesse Elvin Burkett) *Bachelor of Liberal Studies: Development of a Curriculum at the University of Oklahoma,*
    Center for the Study of Liberal Education for Adults, Boston University, 1965.
(And contributor) *Versions of Medieval Comedy,* University
    of Oklahoma Press, 1977.
*The Canterbury Tales: A Facsimile and Transcription of the
    Hengwrt Manuscript with Variants from the Ellesmere
    Manuscript,* University of Oklahoma Press, 1979.
Editing Chaucer: The Great Tradition, University of Oklahoma Press, 1979.

General editor, *A Variorum Edition of the Works of Geoffrey
Chaucer* and the ''Variorum Facsimile'' series.

CONTRIBUTOR

Beryl Rowland, editor, *Oxford Companion to Chaucer Studies,* Oxford University Press, 1968, revised edition, 1979.
Jess B. Bessinger, Jr., and Robert R. Raymo, editors, *Medieval Studies in Honor of Lillian Herlands Hornstein,* New
    York University Press, 1976.
A Festschrift in Honor of Paul Beichner, Notre Dame University, 1977, published as *Chaucerian Problems and
    Perspectives: Essays Presented to Paul E. Beichner C.S.G.,*
    edited by Edward Vasta and Zacharias P. Thundy, University of Notre Dame Press, 1979.

OTHER

Contributor of articles and reviews to professional journals,
including *College English, Oklahoma Quarterly,* and the
Chaucer Review.

S

SAGE, Juniper
See HURD, Edith (Thacher)

* * *

St. JAMES, Blakely
See PLATT, Charles

* * *

SANCHEZ, Sonia 1934-

PERSONAL: Born September 9, 1934, in Birmingham, Ala.; daughter of Wilson L. and Lena (Jones) Driver; children: Anita, Morani Neusi, Mungu Neusi. *Education:* Hunter College (now Hunter College of the City University of New York), B.A., 1955; post-graduate study, New York University. *Politics:* "Peace, freedom, and justice."

ADDRESSES: Home—407 W. Chelten Ave., Philadelphia, Pa. 19144. *Office*—Department of English/Women's Studies, Temple University, Broad and Montgomery, Philadelphia, Pa. 19122.

CAREER: Staff member, Downtown Community School, New York City, 1965-67; San Francisco State College (now University), San Francisco, instructor, 1966-68; University of Pittsburgh, Pittsburgh, Pa., assistant professor, 1969-79; Rutgers University, New Brunswick, N.J., assistant professor, 1970-71; Manhattan Community College of the City University of New York, New York City, assistant professor of Black literature and creative writing, 1971-73; City College of the City University of New York, New York City, teacher of creative writing, 1972; Amherst College, Amherst, Mass., associate professor, 1972-75; University of Pennsylvania, Philadelphia, Pa., 1976-77; Temple University, Philadelphia, associate professor, 1977, professor, 1979—, faculty fellow in provost's office, 1986-87, presidential fellow, 1987-88. Member, Literature Panel of the Pennsylvania Council on the Arts.

AWARDS, HONORS: PEN Writing Award, 1969; National Institute of Arts and Letters grant, 1970; Ph.D., Wilberforce University, 1972; National Endowment for the Arts Award, 1978-79; Honorary Citizen of Atlanta, 1982; Tribute to Black Women Award, Black Students of Smith College, 1982; Lucretia Mott Award, 1984; American Book Award, Before Columbus Foundation, 1985, for *homegirls & handgrenades.*

WRITINGS:

Homecoming (poetry), Broadside Press, 1969.
We a BaddDDD People (poetry), with foreword by Dudley Randall, Broadside Press, 1970.
It's a New Day: Poems for Young Brothas and Sistuhs (juvenile), Broadside Press, 1971.
(Editor) *Three Hundred and Sixty Degrees of Blackness Comin' at You* (poetry), 5X Publishing Co., 1971.
A Sun Lady for All Seasons Reads Her Poetry (record album), Folkways, 1971.
Ima Talken bout the Nation of Islam, TruthDel, 1972.
Love Poems, Third Press, 1973.
A Blues Book for Blue Black Magical Women (poetry), Broadside Press, 1973.
The Adventures of Fat Head, Small Head, and Square Head (juvenile), Third Press, 1973.
(Editor and contributor) *We Be Word Sorcerers: 25 Stories by Black Americans,* Bantam, 1973.
I've Been a Woman: New and Selected Poems, Black Scholar Press, 1978.
A Sound Investment and Other Stories (juvenile), Third World Press, 1979.
Crisis in Culture—Two Speeches by Sonia Sanchez, Black Liberation Press, 1983.
homegirls & handgrenades (poems), Thunder's Mouth Press, 1984.
(Contributor) Mari Evans, editor, *Black Women Writers (1950-1980): A Critical Evaluation,* introduction by Stephen Henderson, Doubleday-Anchor, 1984.

PLAYS

"The Bronx Is Next," first produced in New York at Theatre Black, October 3, 1970 (included in *Cavalcade: Negro American Writing from 1760 to the Present,* edited by Arthur Davis and Saunders Redding, Houghton, 1971).
"Sister Son/ji," first produced with "Cop and Blow" and "Players Inn" by Neil Harris and "Gettin' It Together" by Richard Wesley as "Black Visions," Off-Broadway at New York Shakespeare Festival Public Theatre, 1972 (included in *New Plays from the Black Theatre,* edited by Ed Bullins, Bantam, 1969).
"Uh Huh; But How Do It Free Us?", first produced in Chicago at Northwestern University Theater, 1975 (included in *The New Lafayette Theatre Presents: Plays with Aes-*

thetic Comments by Six Black Playwrights, Ed Bullins, J. E. Gaines, Clay Gross, Oyamo, Sonia Sanchez, Richard Wesley, edited by Bullins, Anchor Press, 1974).

"Malcolm Man/Don't Live Here No More," first produced in Philadelphia at ASCOM Community Center, 1979.

"I'm Black When I'm Singing, I'm Blue When I Ain't," first produced in Atlanta, Georgia at OIC Theatre, April 23, 1982.

Also author of "Dirty Hearts," 1972.

CONTRIBUTOR TO ANTHOLOGIES

Robert Giammanco, editor, *Potero Negro* (title means "Black Power"), Giu. Laterza & Figli, 1968.

Le Roi Jones and Ray Neal, editors, *Black Fire: An Anthology of Afro-American Writing,* Morrow, 1968.

Dudley Randall and Margaret G. Burroughs, editors, *For Malcolm: Poems on the Life and Death of Malcolm X,* Broadside Press, 1968.

Walter Lowenfels, editor, *The Writing on the Wall: One Hundred Eight American Poems of Protest,* Doubleday, 1969.

Arnold Adoff, editor, *Black Out Loud: An Anthology of Modern Poems by Black Americans,* Macmillan, 1970.

Lowenfels, editor, *In a Time of Revolution: Poems from Our Third World,* Random House, 1970.

June M. Jordan, editor, *Soulscript,* Doubleday, 1970.

Gwendolyn Brooks, editor, *A Broadside Treasury,* Broadside Press, 1971.

Randall, editor, *Black Poets,* Bantam, 1971.

Orde Coombs, editor, *We Speak as Liberators: Young Black Poets,* Dodd, 1971.

Bernard W. Bell, editor, *Modern and Contemporary Afro-American Poetry,* Allyn & Bacon, 1972.

Adoff, editor, *The Poetry of Black America: An Anthology of the 20th Century,* Harper, 1973.

J. Chace and W. Chace, *Making It New,* Canfield Press, 1973.

Donald B. Gibson, editor, *Modern Black Poets,* Prentice-Hall, 1973.

Stephen Henderson, editor, *Understanding the New Black Poetry: Black Speech and Black Music as Poetic References,* Morrow, 1973.

J. Paul Hunter, editor, *Norton Introduction to Literature: Poetry,* Norton, 1973.

James Schevill, editor, *Breakout: In Search of New Theatrical Environments,* Swallow Press, 1973.

Lucille Iverson and Kathryn Ruby, editors, *We Become New: Poems by Contemporary Women,* Bantam, 1975.

Quincy Troupe and Rainer Schulte, editors, *Giant Talk: An Anthology of Third World Writings,* Random House, 1975.

Henry B. Chapin, editor, *Sports in Literature,* McKay, 1976.

Brooks and Warren, editors, *Understanding Poetry,* Holt, 1976.

Ann Reit, editor, *Alone amid All the Noise,* Four Winds/Scholastic, 1976.

Erlene Stetson, editor, *Black Sister: Poetry by Black American Women, 1746-1980,* Indiana University Press, 1981.

Amiri and Amina Baraka, editors, *Confirmation: An Anthology of African-American Women,* Morrow, 1983.

Burney Hollis, editor, *Swords upon this Hill,* Morgan State University Press, 1984.

Jerome Rothenberg, editor, *Technicians of the Sacred: A Range of Poetries from Africa, America, Asia, Europe and Oceana,* University of California Press, 1985.

Marge Piercy, editor, *Early Ripening: American Women's Poetry Now,* Pandora (London), 1987.

Poems also included in *Night Comes Softly, Black Arts, To Gwen With Love, New Black Voices, Blackspirits, The New Black Poetry, A Rock Against the Wind, America: A Prophecy, Nommo, Black Culture,* and *Natural Process.*

OTHER

Author of column for *American Poetry Review,* 1977-78, for *Philadelphia Daily News,* 1982-83. Contributor of poems to *Minnesota Review, Black World,* and other periodicals. Contributor of plays to *Scripts, Black Theatre, Drama Review,* and other theater journals. Contributor of articles to several journals, including *Journal of African Civilizations.*

WORK IN PROGRESS: Editing a book of critical essays on four women poets, Audre Lorde, Margaret Walker, Gwendolyn Brooks, and Sonia Sanchez; a play.

SIDELIGHTS: Sonia Sanchez is often named among the strongest voices of black nationalism, the cultural revolution of the 1960s in which many black Americans sought a new identity distinct from the values of the white establishment. C. W. E. Bigsby comments in *The Second Black Renaissance: Essays in Black Literature* that "the distinguishing characteristic of her work is a language which catches the nuance of the spoken word, the rhythms of the street, and of a music which is partly jazz and partly a lyricism which underlies ordinary conversation." Her emphasis on poetry as a spoken art, or performance, connects Sanchez to the traditions of her African ancestors, an oral tradition preserved in earlier slave narratives and forms of music indigenous to the black experience in America, as Bernard W. Bell demonstrates in *The Folk Roots of Contemporary Afro-American Poetry.* In addition to her poetry, for which she has won many prizes, Sanchez has contributed equally-well-known plays, short stories, and children's books to a body of literature called "The Second Renaissance," as Bigsby's title reflects.

Sanchez reached adulthood in Harlem, which only thirty years before had been the cradle of the first literary "renaissance" in the United States to celebrate the works of black writers. Political science and poetry were the subjects of her studies at Hunter College and New York University during the fifties. In the next decade Sanchez began to combine these interests into one activity, "the creat[ion] of social ideals," as she wrote for a section about her writings in *Black Women Writers (1950-1980): A Critical Evaluation,* edited by Mari Evans. For Sanchez, writing and performing poetry is a means of constructive political activism to the extent that it draws her people together to affirm pride in their heritage and build the confidence needed to accomplish political goals. Yet the terms of "black rhetoric," or words by themselves, are not enough, she says often in poems and interviews. Biographers cite her record of service as an educator, activist, and supporter of black institutions as proof of her commitment to this belief. Writing in the *Dictionary of Literary Biography,* Kalamu ya Salaam introduces Sanchez as "one of the few creative artists who have significantly influenced the course of black American literature and culture."

Before Sanchez became recognized as a part of the growing black arts movement of the 1960s, she worked in the Civil Rights movement as a supporter of the Congress of Racial Equality. At that time, she, like many educated black people who enjoyed economic stability, held integrationist ideals. But after hearing Malcolm X say that blacks would never be fully accepted as part of mainstream America despite their professional or economic achievements, she chose to base her identity on her racial heritage. David Williams reports that the title of her first book, *Homecoming*, announces this return to a sense of self grounded in the realities of her urban neighborhood after having viewed it for a time from the outside through the lens of white cultural values. In the title poem, "Sanchez presents the act of returning home as a rejection of fantasy and an acceptance of involvement," notes Williams in *Black Women Writers (1950-1980)*. For the same reasons, Sanchez did not seek a major publisher for the book. She preferred Dudley Randall's Broadside Press, a publisher dedicated to the works of black authors, that was to see many of her books into print. Reacting to the poems in *Homecoming*, Johari Amini's review in *Black World* warns that they "hurt (but doesn't anything that cleans good) and [the] lines are blowgun dartsharp with a wisdom ancient as kilimanjaro." Haki Madhubuti's essay in *Black Women Writers (1950-1980)* comments on this same effect, first remarking that "Sanchez . . . is forever questioning Black people's commitment to struggle," saying again later that she is "forever disturbing the dust in our acculturated lives."

One aspect of her stand against acculturation is a poetic language that does not conform to the dictates of standard English. Madhubuti writes, "More than any other poet, [Sanchez] has been responsible for legitimizing the use of urban Black English in written form. . . . She has taken Black speech and put it in the context of world literature." Salaam elaborates, "In her work from the 1960s she restructured traditional English grammar to suit her interest in black speech patterns"—a technique most apparent, he feels, in *We a BaddDDD People*. In one poem cited by Madhubuti which he says is "concerned with Black-on-Black damage," Sanchez predicts that genuine "RE VO LU TION" might come about "if moth- as programmed / sistuhs to / good feelings bout they blk / men / and i / mean if blk / fathas proved / they man / hood by fighten the enemy. . . ." These reviewers explain that by inserting extra letters in some word and extra space between lines, words, and syllables within a poem, Sanchez provides dramatic accents and other clues that indicate how the poem is to be said aloud.

The sound of the poems when read aloud has always been important to Sanchez. Her first readings established her reputation as a poet whose energetic performances had a powerful effect on her listeners. She has visited Cuba, China, the West Indies, Europe, and more than five hundred campuses in the United States to give readings, for which she is still in demand. Of her popularity, Salaam relates, "Sanchez developed techniques for reading her poetry that were unique in their use of traditional chants and near-screams drawn out to an almost earsplitting level. The sound elements, which give a musical quality to the intellectual statements in the poetry, are akin to Western African languages; Sanchez has tried to recapture a style of delivery that she felt had been muted by the experience of slavery. In her successful experimentation with such techniques, she joined . . . others in being innovative enough to bring black poetry to black people at a level that was accessible to the masses as well as enjoyable for them."

Sanchez is also known as an innovator in the field of education. During the sixties, she taught in San Francisco's Downtown Community School and became a crusader and curriculum developer for black studies programs in American colleges and universities. Materials on black literature and history had been absent from the schools she had attended, and she has worked to see that other young people are not similarly disenfranchised. Opposition to this goal has often complicated her

career, sometimes making it difficult for her to find or keep teaching positions; nevertheless, Sanchez has fought to remain in the academic arena to shape and encourage the next generation. She wrote two books for her children (*The Adventures of Fat Head, Small Head, and Square Head*, and *A Sound Investment and Other Stories*) for reasons she expressed to interviewer Claudia Tate in *Black Women Writers at Work*: "I do think that it's important to leave a legacy of my books for my children to read and understand; to leave a legacy of the history of black people who have moved toward revolution and freedom; to leave a legacy of not being afraid to tell the truth. . . . We must pass this on to our children, rather than a legacy of fear and victimization."

Because she takes action against oppression wherever she sees it, she has had to contend with not only college administrators, but also the FBI, and sometimes fellow-members of political organizations. Reviewers note that while her early books speak more directly to widespread social oppression, the plays she wrote during the seventies give more attention to the poet's interpersonal battles. For example, "Uh Huh; But How Do It Free Us?" portrays a black woman involved in the movement against white oppression who also resists subjection to her abusive husband. This kind of resistance, writes Salaam, was not welcomed by the leaders of the black power movement at that time.

Sanchez resigned from the Nation of Islam after three years of membership. She had joined the Nation of Islam in 1972 because she wanted her children to see an "organization that was trying to deal with the concepts of nationhood, morality, small businesses, schools. . . . And these things were very important to me," she told Tate. As Sanchez sees it, her contribution to the Nation was her open fight against the inferior status it assigned to women in relation to men. Believing that cultural survival requires the work of women and children no less than the efforts of men, Sanchez felt compelled to speak up rather than to give up the influence she could exert through public readings of her poetry. "It especially was important for women in the Nation to see that," stated Sanchez, who also told Tate that she has had to battle the "so-called sexism" of many people outside the Nation as well.

Thus Sanchez became a voice in what Stephen E. Henderson calls "a 'revolution within the Revolution'" that grew as black women in general began to reassess their position as ". . . the vicitms not only of racial injustice but of a sexual arrogance tantamount to dual colonialism—one from without, the other from within, the Black community," he writes in his introduction to Evans's book. This consciousness surfaces in works that treat politics in the context of personal relationships. Sanchez told Tate, "If we're not careful, the animosity between black men and women will destroy us." To avoid this fate, she believes, women must refuse to adopt the posture of victims and "move on" out of damaging relationships with men, since, in her words recorded in the interview, "If you cannot remove yourself from the oppression of a man, how in the hell are you going to remove yourself from the oppression of a country?"

Consequently, *A Blues Book for Blue Black Magical Women*, written during her membership in the Nation, examines the experience of being female in a society that "does not prepare young black women, or women period, to be women," as she told Tate. Another section tells about her political involvements before and after she committed herself to the establishment of ethnic pride. In this book, as in her plays and stories,

"Sanchez uses many of the particulars of her own life as illustrations of a general condition," writes Salaam. He offers that Sanchez "remains the fiery, poetic advocate of revolutionary change, but she also gives full voice to the individual human being struggling to survive sanely and to find joy and love in life." *Love Poems* contains many of the haiku Sanchez wrote during a particularly stressful period of her life. An interview she gave to *Black Collegian* disclosed that she had been beset by the problems of relocation, illness and poverty. Writing haiku allowed her to "compress a lot of emotion" into a few lines, which helped her to stay sane. Under the circumstances, she also felt that there was no guarantee she would have the time to finish longer works. The poems in these two books are no less political for their being more personal, say reviewers. "The haiku in her hands is the ultimate in activist poetry, as abrupt and as final as a fist," comments Williams. In Salaam's opinion, "No other poet of the 1960s and 1970s managed so masterfully to chronicle both their public and personal development with poetry of such thoroughgoing honesty and relevant and revelatory depth."

Madhubuti says of the poet, "Much of her work is autobiographical, but not in the limiting sense that it is only about Sonia Sanchez." For example, in her well-known story "After Saturday Night Comes Sunday," a woman on the verge of madness finds strength to break out of a painful liaison with a drug abuser without herself becoming trapped in self-pity or alcoholism. "It's not just a personal story," the poet, who has survived divorce, told Tate. "It might be a personal experience, but the whole world comes into it." Readers of all backgrounds can appreciate writings concerned with black identity and survival, she declares in *Black Women Writers at Work*, mentioning that her works have been translated into European languages and remarking that "you don't have to whitewash yourself to be universal." At another point in the interview, she explained why she deliberately pushes her writing beyond autobiography: "We must move past always focusing on the 'personal self' because there's a larger self. There's a 'self' of black people. And many of us will have to make a sacrifice in our lives to ensure that our bigger self continues." In her statement for *Black Women Writers (1950-1980)*, she presents her own life as an example of the price that must be paid to contribute to social change: "I see myself helping to bring forth the truth about the world. I cannot tell the truth about anything unless I confess to being a student. . . . My first lesson was that one's ego always compromised how something was viewed. I had to wash my ego in the needs/ aspiration of my people. Selflessness is key for conveying the need to end greed and oppression. I try to achieve this state as I write."

According to *Detroit News* contributor Carole Cook, the title of the American Book Award winner *homegirls & homegrenades* "underscores the creative tension between love and anger intrinsic to . . . young black women poets." Speaking in *Black Women Writers (1950-1980)* of the creative tension between protest and affirmation in her writing, Sanchez declared, "I still believe that the age for which we write is the age evolving out of the dregs of the twentieth century into a more humane age. Therefore I recognize that my writing must serve a dual purpose. It must be a clarion call to the values of change while it also speaks to the beauty of a nonexploitative age." Throughout her poems, Sanchez emphasizes the importance of strong family relationships, and exposes the dangers of substance abuse among people who hope to be the vital agents of change, relates Richard K. Barksdale in *Modern Black Poets:*

A Collection of Critical Essays. Her message, as he notes, is that the desired revolution will not come about through "violence, anger, or rage;" rather, "political astuteness and moral power" among black people are needed to build the new world. Commenting on the content of the poems as it has broadened over the years, Madhubuti observes that Sanchez "remains an intense and meticulous poet who has not compromised craft or skill for message."

"Her work has matured; she's a much better writer now than she was ten years ago. She has continued to grow, but her will has not changed," states critic Sherley Anne Williams, who told Tate that black women writers as a group have kept their commitment to social revolution strong, while others seem to be letting it die out. In the same book, Sanchez attributes this waning, in part, to the rewards that have been given to black writers who focus on themes other than revolution. "The greatness of Sonia Sanchez," believes Salaam, "is that she is an inspiration." Madhubuti shares this view, concluding, "Sanchez has been an inspiration to a generation of young poets. . . . Her concreteness and consistency over these many years is noteworthy. She has not bought refuge for day-to-day struggles by becoming a writer in the Western tradition. . . . Somehow, one feels deep inside that in a real fight, this is the type of black woman you would want at your side."

BIOGRAPHICAL/CRITICAL SOURCES:

BOOKS

Bankier, Joanna, and Deirdre Lashgari, editors, *Women Poets of the World*, Macmillan, 1983.
Bell, Bernard W., *The Folk Roots of Contemporary Afro-American Poetry*, Broadside Press, 1974.
Bigsby, C. W. E., editor, *The Second Black Renaissance: Essays in Black Literature*, Greenwood Press, 1980.
Contemporary Literary Criticism, Volume V, Gale, 1976.
Dictionary of Literary Biography, Volume LXI: *Afro-American Poets since 1955*, Gale, 1985.
Evans, Mari, editor, *Black Women Writers (1950-1980): A Critical Evaluation*, with introduction by Stephen E. Henderson, Doubleday-Anchor, 1984.
Gibson, Donald B., editor, *Modern Black Poets: A Collection of Critical Essays*, Prentice-Hall, 1973.
Randall, Dudley, *Broadside Memories: Poets I Have Known*, Broadside Press, 1975.
Redmond, Eugene B., *Drumvoices: The Mission of Afro-American Poetry, A Critical History*, Anchor, 1976.
Sanchez, Sonia, *We a BaddDDD People*, Broadside Press, 1970.
Tate, Claudia, editor, *Black Women Writers At Work*, Continuum, 1983.

PERIODICALS

Black Creation, fall, 1973.
Black Scholar, May, 1979, January, 1980, March, 1981.
Black World, August, 1970, April, 1971, September, 1971, April, 1972, March, 1975.
Book World, January 27, 1974.
CLA Journal, September, 1971.
Ebony, March, 1974.
Essence, July, 1979.
Indian Journal of American Studies, July, 1983.
Negro Digest, December, 1969.
New Republic, February 22, 1975.
Newsweek, April 17, 1972.
Phylon, June, 1975.

Poetry, October, 1973.
Poetry Review, April, 1985.
Publishers Weekly, October 1, 1973, July 15, 1974.
Time, May 1, 1972.

—Sketch by Marilyn K. Basel

*   *   *

SANDBERG, Peter Lars 1934-

PERSONAL: Born December 13, 1934, in Winchester, Mass.; son of Lars Josef (a management consultant) and Janice (Whittaker) Sandberg; married Nancy Bell (an English professor), September 8, 1956. *Education:* Florida Southern College, B.S., 1958; University of Colorado, M.A., 1959; graduate study at University of Iowa, 1959-61.

ADDRESSES: Home and office—Bow Lake, Strafford, N.H.; and Mt. Sidney, Va. *Agent*—McIntosh & Otis, Inc., 310 Madison Ave., New York, N.Y. 10017.

CAREER: Phoenix College, Phoenix, Ariz., instructor in English and creative writing, 1961-64; *Phoenix Point West,* Phoenix, editor, 1964-66; National Forge Co., Irvine, Pa., writer and researcher, 1966-68; Northeastern University, Boston, Mass., assistant professor of English, 1968-69, lecturer in fiction writing, 1969-76. Free-lance writer. Guest fiction writer, Holy Cross College, Worcester, Mass., 1978 and 1981. Document analyst, Acumenics Research and Technology Co., Fairfax, Va., 1985.

WRITINGS:

(With Robert Parker) *Order and Diversity: The Craft of Prose,* Wiley, 1973.
Dwight D. Eisenhower (juvenile), Chelsea House, 1986.

NOVELS

Wolf Mountain, Playboy Press, 1975.
King's Point, Playboy Press, 1978.
Stubb's Run, Houghton, 1979.
(With Mark Berent) *Brass Diamonds* (first novel in suspense trilogy), New American Library, 1980.

Also author of *The Honeycomb Bid* and *The Chinese Spur,* second and third novels in a suspense trilogy.

SHORT STORIES

(Contributor) Curt Johnson, editor, *Best Little Magazine Fiction 1970,* New York University Press, 1970.
(Contributor) DeLisle, Parker, Ridlon, and Yokelson, editors, *The Personal Response to Literature,* Houghton, 1971.
(Contributor) Martha Foley, editor, *Best American Short Stories,* Houghton, 1974.
(Contributor) *Playboy's Laughing Lovers,* edited by *Playboy* editors, Playboy Press, 1975.
(Contributor) Farrell, Pierce, Pittman, and Wood, editors, *Traits and Topics: An Anthology of Short Stories,* Scott, Foresman, 1976.
(Contributor) Jean S. Mullen, editor, *Outsiders: American Short Stories for Students of ESL,* Prentice-Hall, 1984.
Gabe's Fall and Other Climbing Stories, Birchfield, 1988.

OTHER

Also contributor to *Playboy, McCall's, Saturday Review, Good Housekeeping,* and literary journals. Former editor, *Reveille.* Former book reviewer for city magazine in Phoenix, Arizona.

WORK IN PROGRESS: A novel, tentatively entitled *The Last Ascent of Goodwillie Jones.*

SIDELIGHTS: Peter Lars Sandberg told *CA:* "I have always been intrigued with the ways in which a man can define his courage and/or cowardice in a confrontation with nature. The first story I wrote had to do with a young man climbing a mountain, and I suspect the last one will have to do with an old man climbing a mountain—though I hasten to add I do write about other things."

Sandberg's papers will be included in Boston University's Twentieth Century Archives collection. His novels have been printed in English, Dutch, Italian, Swedish, Norwegian, and Portuguese editions.

MEDIA ADAPTATIONS: The short story "Calloway's Climb" was produced by American Broadcasting Corp. as a television special in 1978.

BIOGRAPHICAL/CRITICAL SOURCES:

PERIODICALS

America, November 15, 1975.
New York Times Book Review, December 2, 1979.
Times Literary Supplement, April 23, 1976.

*   *   *

SAVARY, Louis M(ichael) 1936-

PERSONAL: First syllable of surname rhymes with "pave"; born January 17, 1936, in Scranton, Pa.; son of Louis Michael and Margaret (Nagy) Savary. *Education:* Fordham University, A.B., 1960; Woodstock College, Ph.L., 1961, S.T.L., 1968; Catholic University of America, M.A., 1963, Ph.D., 1965, S.T.D., 1970.

ADDRESSES: Home—623 Brielle Ave., Brielle, N.J. 08730. *Office*—5201 MacArthur Terrace, N.W., Washington, D.C. 20016.

CAREER: Ordained Roman Catholic priest, member of Society of Jesus (Jesuits), 1954; left Jesuits, 1984; Collins Associates, New York, N.Y., writer and senior editor, 1967-74; affiliated with Just for You Books, Brielle, N.J., 1974-80; affiliated with Inner Development Associates (specialists in interpersonal and spiritual growth), Washington, D.C., 1980—. Currently senior training analyst with Education Systems for the Future, Columbia, Md. Adjunct member of faculty of St. Joseph College, West Hartford, Conn., Loyola University, New Orleans, La., and Pacific School of Religion, Berkeley, Calif.

MEMBER: Mathematical Association of America, American Statistical Association, American Society of Composers, Authors and Publishers (ASCAP), American Teilhard Association, American Personnel and Guidance Association, Institute for Consciousness and Music.

AWARDS, HONORS: Christopher Book Award, 1970, for *Listen to Love.*

WRITINGS:

His World and His Work, Paulist Press, 1967.
The Kingdom of Downtown: Finding Teenagers in Their Music, Paulist Press, 1967.
(Co-author) *Christian Awareness,* four volumes, Christian Brothers Publications, 1968.
(Co-author) *Listen to Love,* Regina Press, 1968.

(Co-author) *Patterns of Promise*, St. Mary's College Press, 1968.

(Co-author) *Living with Christ*, with teacher's guides, four volumes, St. Mary's College Press, 1968-69.

(With Adrianne Blue) *Faces of Freedom*, St. Mary's College Press, 1969.

(With Blue) *Horizons of Hope*, St. Mary's College Press, 1969.

(With Maureen P. Collins) *Ritual and Life*, St. Mary's College Press, 1970.

(With Collins) *Shaping of a Self*, St. Mary's College Press, 1970.

(Co-author) *Teaching Your Child about God*, St. Mary's College Press, 1970.

(With Thomas J. O'Connor) *Finding Each Other*, Paulist/Newman, 1971.

(With O'Connor) *Finding God*, Paulist/Newman, 1971.

Getting High Naturally, Association Press, 1971.

Love and Hate in America Today, Association Press, 1971.

Popular Song and Youth Today, Association Press, 1971.

Touch with Love, Association Press, 1971.

Cycles, three volumes, Regina Press, 1971-73.

One Life Together: A Celebration of Love in Marriage, Regina Press, 1972.

A Time for Salvation, Regina Press, 1972.

Jesus: The Face of Man, Harper, 1972.

(With Marianne S. Andersen) *Passages: A Guide for Pilgrims of the Mind*, Harper, 1972.

(With Helen L. Bonny) *Music and Your Mind: Listening with a New Consciousness*, Harper, 1973.

Psychological Themes in the Golden Epistle of William of Saint Thierry, University of Salzburg, 1973.

(With Shirley Linde) *The Sleep Book*, Harper, 1974.

(With Muriel James) *The Power at the Bottom of the Well: Transactional Analysis and Religious Experience*, Harper, 1974.

Integrating Values: Theory and Exercises for Clarifying and Integrating Religious Values, Pflaum/Standard, 1974.

(With Bonny) *ASC and Music Experience: A Guide for Facilitators and Leaders*, ICM Press, 1974.

Creativity and Children: Stimulating Imaginative Responses to Music, ICM Press, 1974.

Who Has Seen the Wind?: The Holy Spirit in the Church and the World, Regina Press, 1975.

(With Muriel James) *The Heart of Friendship*, Harper, 1975.

(With Mary Paolini and George Lane) *Interpersonal Communication: A Worktext for Self-Understanding and Growth in Personal Relations*, Loyola University Press, 1975.

(With Paolini and William E. Frankhauser) *The Storyteller's Bible*, Regina, 1978.

(With Margaret Ehlen-Miller) *Mindways: A Guide for Exploring Your Mind*, Harper, 1978.

(With Patricia H. Berne) *Prayerways: For Those Who Feel Discouraged or Distraught, Frightened or Frustrated, Angry or Anxious, Powerless or Purposeless, Over-Extended or Under-Appreciated, Burned Out or Just Plain Worn Out*, Harper, 1980.

(With Theresa O'Callaghan Scheihing) *Our Treasured Heritage: Teaching Christian Meditation to Children*, Crossroad, 1981.

(With Berne) *Building Self-Esteem in Children*, Continuum, 1981.

(With Berne) *What Will the Neighbors Say?*, Continuum, 1982.

(With Berne and Stephron K. Williams) *Dreamswork and Spiritual Growth: A Christian Approach to Dreamwork*, Paulist Press, 1984.

(With Stephen Halpern) *Sound Health: The Music and Sounds That Make Us Whole*, Harper, 1985.

Welcome to the Wonderful World of the Somatron: A Manual for Its Uses, Somasonics, 1987.

(With Berne) *Kything: The Art of Spiritual Presence*, Paulist Press, 1988.

(With Berne) *Dream Symbol Work*, Paulist Press, 1988.

EDITOR

(With Thomas J. O'Connor) *The Heart Has Its Seasons*, Regina Press, 1971.

(With Paul Carrico) *Contemporary Film and the New Generation*, Association Press, 1971.

(With Maureen P. Collins) *Peace, War and Youth*, Association Press, 1971.

(With Thomas P. Collins) *A People of Compassion: The Concerns of Edward Kennedy*, Regina Press, 1972.

(With Paolini) *Moments with God: A Book of Prayers for Children*, Regina Press, 1975.

JUVENILES; PUBLISHED BY REGINA PRESS

The Life of Jesus for Children, 1979.

The Friends of Jesus for Children, 1979.

The Miracles of Jesus for Children, 1979.

The Prayers of Jesus for Children, 1980.

The Holy Spirit for Children, 1980.

The Rosary for Children, 1981.

The Stations of the Cross for Children, 1981.

The Mission of Catherine Laboure: The Miraculous Medal, 1981.

The Seasons of the Church Year for Children, 1982.

My First Prayer Book, 1982.

My First Book of Saints, 1982.

The Life of Mary for Children, 1982.

FILMSTRIPS

''Images of Christ,'' Thomas S. Klise, 1971.

''Images of Revelation,'' Thomas S. Klise, 1971.

''Images of Love,'' Thomas S. Klise, 1971.

''Images of the Future,'' Thomas S. Klise, 1971.

''Images of the New Man,'' Thomas S. Klise, 1972.

''A Time to Grow,'' Sisters of the Good Shepherd, 1972.

''Social Studies,'' W. H. Sadlier, 1972-73.

''Religious Awareness,'' (series), Thomas S. Klise, 1973.

''A Call to Consecration,'' Sisters of the Good Shepherd, 1973.

CASSETTES

''Self-Actualization I,'' NCR Cassettes, 1975.

''Self-Actualization II,'' NCR Cassettes, 1975.

''Biblical Meditations with Music I,'' NCR Cassettes, 1975.

''Biblical Meditations with Music II,'' NCR Cassettes, 1975.

''Meditations with Music: Cycle B,'' NCR Cassettes, 1976.

''Meditations with Music: Cycle C,'' NCR Cassettes, 1976.

''The Inner Me,'' NCR Cassettes, 1977.

''Carrying Out Life Decisions,'' NCR Cassettes, 1977.

''The Lord's Prayer: Integrating Eastern and Western Prayer'' (four cassettes), NCR Cassettes, 1977.

''You Are Called'' (twenty cassettes), NCR Cassettes, 1978.

''Psalms of Reconciliation,'' NCR Cassettes, 1978.

''Life at the Heart of the World,'' NCR Cassettes, 1979.

''Spiritual Growth through Dreams'' (six cassettes), NCR Cassettes, 1979.

''Prayers of Power: Mantra Chanting,'' NCR Cassettes, 1979.

''Body/Mind/Spirit Prayers: Twenty Ways to Stay Spiritually Alive'' (four cassettes), NCR Cassettes, 1980.

"Spirituality of Teilhard de Chardin" (four cassettes), NCR Cassettes, 1980.
"Gift of Life," NCR Cassettes, 1980.
"The Joyful Mysteries," NCR Cassettes, 1981.
"The Sorrowful Mysteries," NCR Cassettes, 1981.
"The Glorious Mysteries," NCR Cassettes, 1982.
"Healing through Mary," NCR Cassettes, 1982.
"Praying with the Right Brain," (four cassettes), NCR Cassettes, 1983.
"Affirmations for Personal Power" (two cassettes), NCR Cassettes, 1986.
"Healing and Wholeness: Meditations with Music" (three cassettes), NCR Cassettes, 1986.
"Hail, Mary!," NCR Cassettes, 1987.
"The Life of Mary: Meditations with Music" (three cassettes), NCR Cassettes, 1987.

INSTRUCTIONAL MODULES

(With Peter Esseff and Mary Esseff) *The Future of Christianity in Lebanon,* Educational Systems for the Future, 1986.
(With P. Esseff and M. Esseff) *The Management of Training,* Educational Systems for the Future, 1986.
(With P. Esseff and M. Esseff) *Interactive Teaching Skills,* revised edition, Educational Systems for the Future, 1987.
(With P. Esseff and M. Esseff) *Advanced Interactive Teaching Skills,* Educational Systems for the Future, 1987.
(With P. Esseff and M. Esseff) *Master Instructor Training,* Educational Systems for the Future, 1987.
(With P. Esseff and M. Esseff) *How to Develop and Instruct People-to-People Machine Demonstrations,* Educational Systems for the Future, 1987.
(With P. Esseff and M. Esseff) *How to Develop and Instruct People-to-People Role Plays,* Educational Systems for the Future, 1987.
(With P. Esseff and M. Esseff) *How to Develop and Instruct People-to-Paper Case Studies,* Educational Systems for the Future, 1987.
(With P. Esseff and M. Esseff) *Instructional Development Learning System: Pro Trainer I* (seven instructional modules), Educational Systems for the Future, 1987.
Orientation for New General Motors Salaried Employees (eight instructional modules), General Motors Education and Training, 1987.

OTHER

(Co-author) *Religious Awareness Teaching Program,* six volumes with teaching guide, St. Mary's Press, 1970.
(Ghostwriter) Mary Conway Kohler, *Young People Learning to Care: Making a Difference through Youth Participation,* Seaburg, 1983.
(Ghostwriter) Robert Fritz, *The Path of Least Resistance: Principles for Creating What You Want to Create,* DMA, 1984.

Author of two recordings for the Institute for Consciousness and Music, "Creative Listening: Music and Imagination Experiences for Children," and, with M. Trinitas Bochini, "A New Way to Music: Altered States of Consciousness and Music." Also author of four booklets for Just For You Books, including *Getting to Know You: A Funbook for Families,* 1974, and *Side by Side: Another Funbook for Couples,* 1975. Contributor to *Religious Book Guide, Review for Religious Praying,* and *Sisters Today.*

SIDELIGHTS: Louis M. Savary told *CA:* "I see myself as a specialist in interpersonal and spiritual growth, a 'technician of the sacred,' sharing with the ordinary reader practical ways of expanding consciousness and developing the whole person. My vision is to introduce people to powerful psychological techniques and spiritual practices in order to help society evolve through the inner transformation of individuals and relationships."

*　　*　　*

SCANNELL, Vernon 1922-

PERSONAL: Born January 23, 1922, in Lincolnshire, England; married Josephine Higson, October, 1954; children: Jacob, John, Tobias, Nancy, Jane. *Education:* Attended University of Leeds, 1946-47. *Politics:* "Romantic Radical."

ADDRESSES: Home—51 North St., Otley, West Yorkshire LS21 1AH, England.

CAREER: Author. Professional boxer for brief period; teacher of English, Hazelwood School, Limpsfield, Surrey, England, 1955-62. Broadcasts talks and poetry. *Military service:* British Army, 1941-46.

MEMBER: Royal Society of Literature (fellow).

AWARDS, HONORS: Heinemann Award for Literature from the Royal Society of Literature, 1960, for *The Masks of Love;* Cholmondoley Poetry Prize, 1974, for *The Winter Man.*

WRITINGS:

POEMS

Graves and Resurrections, Fortune Press, 1948.
A Mortal Pitch, Villiers Publications, 1957.
(Contributor) Howard Sergeant and Dannie Abse, editors, *Mavericks: An Anthology,* Editions Poetry and Poverty (London), 1957.
The Masks of Love, Putnam, 1960.
A Sense of Danger, Putnam, 1962.
Walking Wounded: Poems 1962-1965, Eyre & Spottiswoode, 1965.
Epithets of War: Poems 1965-1969, Eyre & Spottiswoode, 1969.
(Contributor with Jon Silkin) Dennis Butts, editor, *Pergamon Poets 8* (anthology), Pergamon, 1970.
The Dangerous Ones, Pergamon, 1970.
Mastering the Craft (for young adults), Pergamon, 1970.
(Contributor) Jeremy Robson, editor, *Corgi Modern Poets in Focus: 4* (anthology), Corgi Books, 1971.
Selected Poems, Allison & Busby, 1971.
The Winter Man, Allison & Busby, 1971.
The Apple-Raid and Other Poems (for young adults), Chatto & Windus, 1974.
The Loving Game, Robson Books, 1975.
A Lonely Game, Wheaton, 1979.
New and Collected Poems: 1950-1980, Robson Books, 1980.
Winterlude, Robson Books, 1982.
(With Gregory Harrison and Laurence Smith) *Catch the Light* (for children), Oxford University Press, 1983.
Funeral Games and Other Poems, Robson Books, 1987.

NOVELS

The Fight, Nevill, 1953.
The Wound and the Scar, Nevill, 1954.
The Big Chance, John Long, 1960.
The Shadowed Place, John Long, 1961.
The Face of the Enemy, Putnam, 1961.

The Dividing Night, Putnam, 1962.
The Big Time, Longmans, Green, 1965.
Ring of Truth, Robson Books, 1983.

OTHER

(Editor with Patricia Beer and Ted Hughes) *New Poems 1962: A PEN Anthology of Contemporary Poetry,* Hutchinson, 1962.
Edward Thomas (criticism), Longmans, Green, for the British Council, 1963.
The Tiger and the Rose (autobiography), Hamish Hamilton, 1971.
Not without Glory: Poets of the Second World War, Woburn, 1976.
A Proper Gentleman (autobiography), Robson Books, 1977.
(Editor) *Sporting Literature: An Anthology,* Oxford University Press, 1987.

Also author of radio scripts "A Man's Game" and "A Door with One Eye," and of radio opera "The Cancelling Dark," with music by Christopher Whellen, performed December 5, 1965. Contributor to *Listener, Encounter, London Magazine, Spectator,* and *Times Literary Supplement.*

SIDELIGHTS: "For more than thirty years [Vernon] Scannell has written poems that meet the challenges of established forms while drawing on his vivid experiences as soldier, boxer, lover, husband and father, tutor and lecturer, broadcaster, drinker, and general survivor," writes John H. Schwartz in the *Dictionary of Literary Biography: Poets of Great Britain and Ireland, 1945-1960.* A versatile writer who is also recognized for his novels and autobiographies, Scannell is frequently referred to as a "melancholy poet" because of the frequency with which he writes about danger and death, says Schwartz. Reviewing Scannell's *Winterlude* in the *Times Literary Supplement,* though, Geroge Szirtes indicates that Scannell "is rarely ungraceful, he can deal with complex and powerful emotions, he has a coherent view of the world and an impeccable understanding of his social and historical milieu. . . . He is, in short, a very fine poet." Schwartz observes that "Scannell remains a discerning observer of the walking wounded, himself included, of modern urban and suburban life." And although his poetry is "sometimes uninspired . . . more often his poems successfully direct the reader's eye afresh to the pathos and humor in an imperfect world." Schwartz believes that Scannell's poetry reveals "a likeable personality speaking in a distinctive voice. Reviewers more often than not have applauded Scannell's work, and he has a loyal following of readers."

BIOGRAPHICAL/CRITICAL SOURCES:

BOOKS

Dictionary of Literary Biography, Volume XXVII: *Poets of Great Britain and Ireland, 1945-1960,* Gale, 1984.
Hay, Phillip, and Angharad Wynn-Jones, *Three Poets, Two Children: Leonard Clark, Vernon Scannell, Dannie Abse Answer Questions by Two Children,* edited by Desmond Badham-Thornhill, Thornhill Press, 1975.
Morrish, Hilary, *The Poet Speaks: Interviews with Contemporary Poets,* edited by Peter Orr, Routledge & Kegan Paul, 1966.
Robson, Jeremy, editor, *Corgi Modern Poets in Focus: 4,* Corgi Books, 1971.

PERIODICALS

New Statesman, October 21, 1977.

Times (London), July 23, 1987.
Times Literary Supplement, August 1, 1980, October 15, 1982, July 22, 1983, November 11, 1983, April 10, 1987.

*   *   *

SCANZONI, John H.   1935-

PERSONAL: Born March 25, 1935, in Chicago, Ill.; son of Victor and Ida Scanzoni; children: Stephen, David. *Education:* Wheaton College, Wheaton, Ill., A.B., 1958; University of Oregon, Ph.D., 1964. *Politics:* Independent. *Religion:* Independent.

ADDRESSES: *Home*—1114 Northwest Sixth St., Gainesville, Fla. 32601. *Office*—Department of Sociology, University of Florida, Gainesville, Fla. 32611.

CAREER: Indiana University at Bloomington, assistant professor, 1964-68, associate professor, 1968-72, professor of sociology, 1972-78; University of North Carolina at Greensboro, professor of family relations and sociology, 1978-87; University of Florida, Gainesville, professor of sociology, 1987—.

MEMBER: American Sociological Association, National Council on Family Relations, Southeast Council on Family Relations.

WRITINGS:

Readings in Social Problems: Sociology and Social Issues, Allyn & Bacon, 1967.
Opportunity and the Family, Free Press, 1970.
The Black Family in Modern Society, University of Chicago Press, 1971, 2nd edition, 1977.
Sexual Bargaining: Power Politics in American Marriage, University of Chicago Press, 1972, 2nd edition, 1982.
Sex Roles, Life-Styles and Childbearing: Changing Patterns in Marriage and the Family, Free Press, 1975.
(With Letha Scanzoni) *Men, Women and Change: A Sociology of Marriage and Family,* McGraw, 1976, 3rd edition, 1988.
Sex Roles, Women's Work, and Marital Conflict, Lexington Books, 1978.
Love and Negotiate: Creative Conflict in Marriage, Word, Inc., 1979.
(With Maximiliane Szinovacz) *Family Decision Making: A Developmental Sex Role Model,* Sage Publications, 1980.
Shaping Tomorrow's Family: Theory and Policy for the Twenty-first Century, Sage Publications, 1983.
Sexually-Based Close Relationships: Rethinking Families and Marriages, Sage Publications, 1988.

Contributor to professional journals and anthologies.

*   *   *

SCHAD, Wilhelm
See REICHERT, Herbert W(illiam)

*   *   *

SCHMIDT, Dorothea
See WENDER, Dorothea

*   *   *

SCHMIDT, Stanley (Albert)   1944-

PERSONAL: Born March 7, 1944, in Cincinnati, Ohio; son

of Otto E. W. (an electrical engineer) and Georgia (Metcalf) Schmidt; married Joyce Tokarz, June 9, 1979. *Education:* University of Cincinnati, B.S. (with high honors), 1966; Case Western Reserve University, M.A., 1968, Ph.D., 1969.

ADDRESSES: Office—*Analog,* 380 Lexington Ave., New York, N.Y. 10017. *Agent*—Scott Meredith Literary Agency Inc., 845 Third Ave., New York, N.Y. 10022.

CAREER: Heidelberg College, Tiffin, Ohio, assistant professor of physics, 1969-78, also taught courses in astronomy, science fiction, and biology; Davis Publications, Inc., New York, N.Y., editor of *Analog Science Fiction/Science Fact,* 1978—; free-lance writer, musician, and photographer.

MEMBER: American Association of Physics Teachers, Science Fiction Writers of America, National Space Society (member of board of advisors), American Federation of Musicians, Appalachian Trail Conference, Phi Beta Kappa, Sigma Xi.

WRITINGS:

SCIENCE FICTION NOVELS

Newton and the Quasi-Apple, Doubleday, 1975.
The Sins of the Fathers (first serialized in *Analog,* 1973-74), Berkley Publishing, 1976.
Lifeboat Earth, Berkley Publishing, 1981.
Tweedlioop, Tor Books, 1986.

EDITOR

(And contributor) *Analog's Golden Anniversary Anthology,* Dial, 1980.
Analog Yearbook II, Ace Books, 1981.
Analog: Readers' Choice, Davis Publications, 1982.
Analog's Children of the Future, Dial, 1982.
Analog's Lighter Side, Dial, 1982.
Analog's Writers' Choice, Dial, Volume I, 1983, (and contributor) Volume II, 1984.
War and Peace: Possible Futures from Analog, Dial, 1983.
(And contributor) *Aliens from Analog,* Dial, 1983.
From Mind to Mind: Tales of Communication from Analog, Dial, 1984.
(And contributor) *Analog's Expanding Universe,* Longmeadow, 1986.

CONTRIBUTOR

Martin H. Greenberg and others, editors, *Anthropology through Science Fiction,* St. Martin's, 1974.
Greenberg and others, editors, *Sociology through Science Fiction,* St. Martin's, 1974.
Joseph Olander and others, editors, *American Government through Science Fiction,* Rand McNally, 1974.
Jack Williamson, editor, *Teaching Science Fiction: Education for Tomorrow,* Mirage Press, 1975.
Thomas D. Clareson, editor, *Many Futures, Many Worlds,* Kent State University Press, 1976.
Greenberg and Isaac Asimov, editors, *Election Day 2084,* Prometheus Books, 1984.
Susan Shwartz, editor, *Habitats,* DAW, 1984.

OTHER

Contributor to science fiction, writing, camping, and physics journals.

WORK IN PROGRESS: One novel; one anthology; short stories; articles.

SIDELIGHTS: Stanley Schmidt wrote to *CA:* "Most of my writing is science fiction, with equal emphasis on both words of the name, and an even stronger emphasis on intellectually stimulating entertainment. It is not realistic to try to think about either the 'scientific' or the 'humanistic' part of our future without considering how it will interact with the other. It's also relatively easy to imagine ways the future can be horrible; it's much harder to suggest ways we can make it *better*—but in the long run, the latter is vastly more worthwhile."

Schmidt reads Spanish, German, Russian, Portuguese, French, Italian, Dutch, Polish, Catalan, and Swahili.

AVOCATIONAL INTERESTS: Music (Schmidt plays several instruments and composes music), travel, camping, hiking, backpacking, photography, flying, cooking, linguistics.

BIOGRAPHICAL/CRITICAL SOURCES:

PERIODICALS

Analog Science Fiction/Science Fact, December, 1977.
Toledo Blade, January 31, 1975.

* * *

SCHNEIDER, Myra 1936-
(Sarah Grovelands)

PERSONAL: Born June 20, 1936, in London, England; daughter of Isaac (a researcher for the British navy and a scientist) and Louise (a teacher; maiden name, Green) Fagelston; married Erwin Schneider (a computer consultant), November 10, 1963; children: Benjamin Philip. *Education:* Bedford College, London, B.A. (with honors), 1959. *Politics:* Socialist. *Religion:* Pantheist.

ADDRESSES: Home—130 Morton Way, London N14 7AL, England.

CAREER: British Broadcasting Corp. (BBC), London, England, secretary, 1960; worked as secretary and assistant to educational manager of Ginn & Co. Ltd.; Clapton Park Secondary School, Hackney, London, teacher of English, 1964; Woodberry Down Comprehensive School, Manor House, London, teacher of English, 1964-66; Flightways Day Centre (activities center for handicapped adults), Colindale, London, teacher, 1974—; free-lance writer.

WRITINGS:

Marigold's Monster (juvenile), illustrations by Thelma Lambert, Heinemann, 1977.
If Only I Could Walk (young adult), Heinemann, 1978.
Will the Real Pete Roberts Stand Up? (young adult), Heinemann, 1979.
Fistful of Yellow Hope (poems), Littlewood Press, 1984.
Cat Therapy (poems), Littlewood Press, 1986.
The Cathedral of Birds, Littlewood Press, 1988.

UNDER PSEUDONYM SARAH GROVELANDS

The Man Behind the Mask (romance), R. Hale, 1986.

CONTRIBUTOR TO ANTHOLOGIES

Chaos of the Night, Virago, 1984.
Worlds Apart, Mary Glasgow, 1986.

OTHER

Contributor of poems to periodicals, including *Pick, Pennine Platform, Orbis, Staple,* and *Other Poetry.*

WORK IN PROGRESS: The Sunflowers, an adult novel; "many poems."

SIDELIGHTS: Myra Schneider once told *CA* that the severe recession in England which began in 1979 adversely affected the publishers of children's fiction such that "very little good fiction (or any fiction for children) has been published in England" since then. More recently, Schneider wrote: "Because the market for novels for children and teenagers is still limited (the increase in novels for teenagers in the last couple of years [1985-87] is mainly in fiction with romance-based plots) I began to write more poetry and think more about writing fiction for adults. By 1984 I realized writing poetry was my true metier and John Killick, the editor of the Littlewood Press which had just started publishing booklets, was sufficiently interested in my work to want to make my *Fistful of Yellow Hope* his first full-length collection."

Since being published by Littlewood Press, Schneider says, "I am beginning to be known in parts of the poetry world and have become more and more committed to poetry. This has led to other activities including giving poetry readings, talks, occasionally judging competitions—and I have started to review poetry.

"I have also had a chance to participate in or help run poetry workshops and I am very interested in doing much more of this with all kinds of groups, especially in schools. I am extremely interested in unlocking people so that they can write therapeutic writing. I also like to spread the message that it is not possible to write good poetry without reading good poets in depth. Therapeutic writing links in with some of my teaching work with disabled adults.

"I am extremely interested in teaching disabled people [who have] acute learning and/or emotional problems (and have had many different insights into language from doing this). There is now a much greater awareness of the needs of disabled people but much still needs to be done to enable them to integrate in society and live as independently and normally as possible. Deaf people and others with communication difficulties are the most cut off in our society and much needs to be done to improve both methods and materials in teaching these people."

AVOCATIONAL INTERESTS: Friends, reading poetry, novels, theatre, art, music, walking, visiting the countryside and old buildings, travelling, growing fruit and vegetables.

*   *   *

SCHOEPS, Karl-Heinz 1935-

PERSONAL: Born December 8, 1935, in Dinslaken, Germany (now West Germany); son of Karl G. (a teacher) and Ella (Gruhl) Schoeps; married Dorothy Sturdivant, August, 1965. *Education:* University of Bonn, Staatsexamen, 1962; attended University of London, 1958-59; University of Wisconsin—Madison, Ph.D., 1971.

ADDRESSES: Office—Department of Germanic Languages and Literature, 3072 Foreign Languages Building, University of Illinois at Urbana-Champaign, Urbana, Ill. 61801.

CAREER: Gymnasium Wipperfurth and Wuppertal, Wuppertal, West Germany, English teacher, 1964-67; University of Illinois at Urbana-Champaign, assistant professor, 1971-76; Mount Holyoke College, South Hadley, Mass., assistant professor, 1977; University of Illinois at Urbana-Champaign, associate professor of German, 1977—.

MEMBER: International Brecht Society (secretary-treasurer, 1979—), Modern Language Association of America, American Association of Teachers of German.

WRITINGS:

(Contributor) John Fuegi and others, editors, *Brecht Heute/ Brecht Today: Yearbook of the International Brecht Society,* Athenaeum (Frankfurt-am-Main), 1973.
Bertolt Brecht und Bernard Shaw, Bouvier, 1974.
(Contributor) Siegfried Mews and Herbert Knust, editors, *Essays on Brecht: Theatre and Politics,* University of North Carolina Press, 1974.
Bertolt Brecht, Ungar, 1977.
(Contributor) Kurt Otten and Gerd Rohmann, editors, *George Bernard Shaw,* Wisserschaftliche Buchgessellschaft, 1978.
(Contributor) Helmut Koopmann, editor, *Handbuch des deutschen Romans,* Bagel, 1983.
(With Richard Zipser) *DDR-Literatur in Tauwetter* (anthology), three volumes, Peter Lang, 1985.
(Contributor) Donald C. Haberman, compiler and editor, *G. B. Shaw: An Annotated Bibliography of Writings about Him,* Northern Illinois University Press, 1986.
(Contributor) Heinz D. Osterle, editor, *Amerika! New Images in German Literature,* Pennsylvania State University Press, 1987.
(With Knust) *Literatur im Dritten Reich,* Peter Lang, in press.

Contributor of articles on Bertolt Brecht and East German literature to periodicals, including *Germanic Review, Comparative Literature Studies, Books Abroad, Monatshefte,* and *German Quarterly.*

SIDELIGHTS: Karl-Heinz Schoeps told *CA:* "Apart from the aesthetics of literature, I am very interested in the interaction of literature with society, history, and politics. My other professional interests are modern German literature (including East Germany), drama, and comparative literature, especially the relationships among English, American, and German literature. Besides my native German and English, I have some Latin, French, and Spanish."

AVOCATIONAL INTERESTS: Travel, classical music, opera, tennis, skiing, soccer.

BIOGRAPHICAL/CRITICAL SOURCES:

PERIODICALS

German Quarterly, November, 1977, March, 1979.
Modern Language Review, July, 1977.
New Boston Review, April/May, 1979.

*   *   *

SCHWARTZ, Alvin 1927-

PERSONAL: Born April 25, 1927, in Brooklyn, N.Y.; son of Harry (a taxi-driver) and Gussie (Younger) Schwartz; married Barbara Carmer (a learning consultant), August 7, 1954; children: John, Peter, Nancy, Elizabeth. *Education:* Attended City College (now City College of the City University of New York), 1944-45; Colby College, A.B., 1949; Northwestern University, M.S. in Journalism, 1951. *Politics:* Independent.

ADDRESSES: Home and office—505 Prospect Ave., Princeton, N.J. 08540. *Agent*—Marilyn Marlow, Curtis Brown Ltd., 10 Astor Place, New York, N.Y. 10003.

CAREER: Newspaper reporter, 1951-55; writer for nonprofit and commercial organizations, 1955-59; Opinion Research

Corp., Princeton, N.J., director of communications, 1959-64; free-lance writer and author of books for adults and children, 1963—. Adjunct professor of English, Rutgers University, 1962-78. Trustee, Joint Free Library of Princeton, 1972-74. Member of national council, Boy Scouts of America, 1972-74. *Military service:* U.S. Navy, 1945-46.

MEMBER: Authors League of America, Authors Guild.

AWARDS, HONORS: American Library Association notable book, 1967, for *Museum: The Story of America's Treasure Houses,* 1982, for *The Cat's Elbow and Other Secret Languages,* 1983, for *Unriddling: All Sorts of Riddles to Puzzle Your Guessery,* 1984, for *In a Dark, Dark Room and Other Scary Stories;* National Council of Teachers of English citation, 1972, for *A Twister of Twists, a Tangler of Tongues,* 1975, for *Whoppers: Tall Tales and Other Lies; New York Times* best children's book of the year citation, 1972, for *A Twister of Twists, a Tangler of Tongues,* 1973, for *Tomfoolery: Trickery and Foolery with Words;* American Library Association and National Endowment for the Humanities bicentennial book, 1972, for *The Unions: What They Are, How They Came to Be, How They Affect Each of Us,* 1973, for *Central City/Spread City: The Metropolitan Regions Where More and More of Us Spend Our Lives;* National Council for the Social Studies citation, 1975, for *Whoppers; School Library Journal* best book of the year citation, 1976, for *Kickle Snifters and Other Fearsome Critters;* Colorado Children's Book Award, 1986, for *In a Dark, Dark Room;* Arizona Children's Book Award, 1986, for *Scary Stories to Tell in the Dark;* New Jersey Library Association Garden State Award, 1986, for *In a Dark, Dark Room.*

WRITINGS:

A Parent's Guide to Children's Play and Recreation, Collier, 1963.
How to Fly a Kite, Catch a Fish, Grow a Flower, and Other Activities for You and Your Child, Macmillan, 1965.
Evaluating Your Public Relations (pamphlet), National Public Relations Council of Health and Welfare Services, 1965.
America's Exciting Cities: A Guide for Parents and Children, Crowell, 1966.
The Night Workers, Dutton, 1966.
What Do You Think?: An Introduction to Public Opinion, How It Forms, Functions, and Affects Our Lives, Dutton, 1966.
The City and Its People: The Story of One City's Government, Dutton, 1967.
Museum: The Story of America's Treasure Houses, Dutton, 1967.
The People's Choice: The Story of Candidates, Campaigns, and Elections, Dutton, 1967.
To Be a Father: Stories, Letters, Essays, Poems, Comments, and Proverbs on the Delights and Despairs of Fatherhood, Crown, 1968.
Old Cities and New Towns: The Changing Face of the Nation, Dutton, 1968.
The Rainy Day Book, Trident Press, 1968.
University: The Students, Faculty, and Campus Life at One University, Viking, 1969.
Going Camping: A Complete Guide for the Uncertain Beginner in Family Camping, Macmillan, 1969, revised edition published as *Going Camping: A Complete Guide for the Family Camper,* 1972.
(Compiler) *A Twister of Twists, a Tangler of Tongues,* Lippincott, 1972.

Hobbies: An Introduction to Crafts, Collections, Nature Study, and Other Life-Long Pursuits, Simon & Schuster, 1972.
The Unions: What They Are, How They Came to Be, How They Affect Each of Us, Viking, 1972.
No Such Mirrors (novel), Writers' Cooperative (Montreal), 1972.
(Compiler) *Witcracks: Jokes and Jests from American Folklore,* Lippincott, 1973.
Tomfoolery: Trickery and Foolery with Words, Lippincott, 1973.
Central City/Spread City: The Metropolitan Regions Where More and More of Us Spend Our Lives, Macmillan, 1973.
Cross Your Fingers, Spit in Your Hat: Superstitions and Other Beliefs, Lippincott, 1974.
(Compiler) *Whoppers: Tall Tales and Other Lies,* Lippincott, 1975.
Kickle Snifters and Other Fearsome Critters, Lippincott, 1976.
Stores, Macmillan, 1977.
(Editor and compiler) *When I Grew Up Long Ago: Family Living, Going to School, Games and Parties, Cures and Deaths, a Comet, a War, Falling in Love, and Other Things I Remember; Older People Talk about the Days When They Were Young,* Lippincott, 1978.
(Compiler) *Chin Music: Tall Talk and Other Talk,* Lippincott, 1979.
Flapdoodle: Pure Nonsense from American Folklore, Lippincott, 1980.
(Editor) *Ten Copycats in a Boat and Other Riddles,* Harper, 1980.
(Compiler) *Scary Stories to Tell in the Dark,* Lippincott, 1981.
(Compiler) *The Cat's Elbow and Other Secret Languages,* Farrar, Straus, 1982.
Busy Buzzing Bumblebees and Other Tongue Twisters, Harper, 1982.
There Is a Carrot in My Ear and Other Noodle Tales, Harper, 1982.
Unriddling: All Sorts of Riddles to Puzzle Your Guessery, Lippincott, 1983.
In a Dark, Dark Room and Other Scary Stories, Harper, 1984.
(Compiler) *More Scary Stories to Tell in the Dark,* Lippincott, 1984.
Fat Man in a Fur Coat and Other Bear Stories, Farrar, Straus, 1984.
(Compiler) *Tales of Trickery from the Land of Spoof,* Farrar, Straus, 1985.
All of Our Noses Are Here and Other Noodle Tales, Harper, 1985.
Love Magic: Dream Signs and Other Ways to Learn the Future, Lippincott, 1987.
Telling Fortunes: Love Magic, Dream Signs and Other Ways to Learn the Future, Harper, 1987.

WORK IN PROGRESS: Various books for young people dealing with folklore and other subjects.

SIDELIGHTS: "If the current generation grows up with a knowledge of traditional humor, it may well be because of Alvin Schwartz's many volumes of humorous American folklore," comments a reviewer in the *Horn Book Magazine.* Humor plays an important role in many of Schwartz's books; William Cole, writing for the *New York Times Book Review,* says, "We can do with a little laughter. Thus a hearty welcome to Alvin Schwartz's [*Tomfoolery: Trickery and Foolery with Words*], a collection of verbal tricks from American folklore that can be as successful with adults as with children." Cole praises the author's sense of the absurd, and continues, "[With] this collection, his notes, sources and bibliography Mr. Schwartz has elevated foolishness to a form of art.''

In an article written for the *Horn Book Magazine*, Schwartz explains why he uses his particular brand of humor: ''I first became interested in folklore when most of us do, in childhood. But at that time I had no idea that the games, sayings, songs, rhymes, taunts, and jokes I knew; the things I wrote on walls; the superstitions I relied on; the tales I heard and learned; the customs we practiced at home; or the ways we had of doing things were all folklore. I also did not realize that much of this lore gave my life structure and continuity, that these games, songs, jokes, tales, and customs were often very old, that ordinary people like me had created them, and that all this had survived simply and remarkably because one person had told another.''

Schwartz stresses the need for tradition and continuity in modern society; he says, ''As our technology has advanced, we have come to rely increasingly on other people for goods, services, and entertainment and less on ourselves and on those we know. The extended family and the traditions it preserved have disappeared. . . . As a result of such changes, we have to a serious extent become alienated from our traditions and have lost a sense of place and a sense of self. If this perception is correct, we have altered the fabric of our society, and we are changing from something we were to something we have not yet become.''

BIOGRAPHICAL/CRITICAL SOURCES:

BOOKS

Children's Literature Review, Volume III, Gale, 1978.

PERIODICALS

Horn Book Magazine, June, 1977, August, 1977, February, 1984.
Kirkus Reviews, November 15, 1973.
New York Times Book Review, May 6, 1973, January 17, 1982.

*   *   *

SCHWARTZ, Pedro 1935-

PERSONAL: Born January 30, 1935, in Madrid, Spain; son of Juan (a diplomat) and Carmen (Giron) Schwartz; married Mercedes Juste (divorced); married Ana Bravo (a singer); children: (first marriage) Guillermo; (second marriage) Marco, Gregory, Sylvia. *Education:* University of Madrid, B.Iuris, 1957, Dr.Iuris, 1965; London School of Economics and Political Science, London, Ph.D., 1964, M.Sc.Econ., 1973.

ADDRESSES: Home—Gurtubay 3, 28001 Madrid, Spain. *Office*—Iberagentes, Rz de Alarcon 7, 28014 Madrid, Spain.

CAREER: Economist. Bank of Spain, Madrid, Spain, staff economist, 1968-75; Instituto de Economia de Mercado, Madrid, Spain, director, 1978-82; Conservative Coalition, Madrid, deputy for Madrid, 1982-86; Iberagentes (licensed stockbrokers), Madrid, director, 1986—. Professor of history of economic doctrines at Universidad Complutense de Madrid, Spain, 1969—.

MEMBER: Trilateral Commission, Mont Pelerin Society, History of Economic Thought Society.

WRITINGS:

La *''Nueva economia politica'' de John Stuart Mill*, Editorial Tecnos, 1968, translation published as *The New Political Economy of J. S. Mill*, Duke University Press, 1972.
El productivo nacional de Espana en el siglo XX (title means ''Spain's Gross National Product in the Twentieth Century''), Instituto de Estudios Fiscales, 1977.
(With Manuel-Jesus Gonzalez) *Una historia del Instituto Nacional de Industria, 1941-1976* (title means ''A History of the Spanish Institute of Nationalized Industries, 1941-1976''), Editorial Tecnos, 1978.
(Contributor) P. Salin, editor, *Currency Competition and Monetary Union*, Nijhoff, 1984.
(Contributor) R. D. C. Black, editor, *Ideas in Economics*, Macmillan, 1986.

Also author of *Bases filosoficas del Liberalismo*, Instituto de Espana; also author of radio productions for British Broadcasting Corp. (BBC-Radio). Contributor to scientific journals, to newspapers, and to popular magazines.

WORK IN PROGRESS: A History of Spanish Economic Thought.

SIDELIGHTS: Originally, *The New Political Economy of J. S. Mill* was Pedro Schwartz's thesis, which he presented at the University of London in 1964. Expounding on Mill's theory of economic and social policy, the book suggests that understanding the economist's views on policy illuminates the greater body of his work. Mill, as the preface of *The New Political Economy* noted, wanted to transport economics from ''a narrow science into an instrument for social progress.''

Praised by critics, this work has been called a ''thorough'' account of the economist's thinking, including some of the psychological influences on Mill, as well as an enlightening picture of his life. ''One of the virtues of Pedro Schwartz's timely and useful reassessment of Mill's work,'' said a *Times Literary Supplement* reviewer, ''is his careful account of just how it was that Mill's reputation declined, and how easily we are misled by hindsight.''

Schwartz told *CA:* ''My profession is that of a political economist. The institute I direct was set up in defense of economic freedom. Since I wrote my book on J. S. Mill, I have moved away from a 'liberal' position (in the U.S. sense) toward a 'conservative' stance because, as I learned from my teachers at the London School of Economics and Political Science, Keynesianism does not fit the facts.

''For many years, I worked in favor of a democracy in Spain. As soon as freedom had returned to my country, I felt I must work for its consolidation along Jeffersonian lines.

''But not all is politics in my life. My real ambitions are to discover a theorem in economics and to write good biographies. If I were rich, I would ride more, travel more, and listen to more operas.''

BIOGRAPHICAL/CRITICAL SOURCES:

PERIODICALS

American Historical Review, April 15, 1973.
Library Journal, April 15, 1973.
Times Literary Supplement, March 9, 1973.

*   *   *

SCOTT-HERON, Gil 1952-

PERSONAL: Born April 1, 1952, in Chicago, Ill.; son of Bobbie Scott (mother). *Education:* Attended Fieldston School of Ethical Culture and Lincoln University; Johns Hopkins University, M.A., 1972.

ADDRESSES: Home—Alexandria, Va. *Office*—c/o Mister E?, P.O. Box 11639, Alexandria, Va. 22312.

CAREER: Writer and musician. Teacher of creative writing at Federal City College in Washington, D.C., 1972-76.

WRITINGS:

The Vulture (novel), World Publishing, 1970.
Small Talk at 125th and Lenox (poems; also see below), photographs by Steve Wilson, World Publishing, 1970.
The Nigger Factory (novel), Dial, 1972.

Also author of a book of poetry, *So Far, So Good,* 1988.

RECORDINGS

"Small Talk at 125th and Lenox," Flying Dutchman, 1970.
"Pieces of a Man," Flying Dutchman, 1971.
"Free Will," Flying Dutchman, 1972.
"Winter in America," Strata East, 1973.
"The Revolution Will Not Be Televised," Flying Dutchman, 1974.
"The First Minute of a New Day," Arista, 1975.
"From South Africa to South Carolina," Arista, 1975.
"It's Your World," Arista, 1976.
"Bridges," Arista, 1977.
"The Mind of Gil Scott-Heron," Arista, 1979.
"1980," Arista, 1980.
"Real Eyes," Arista, 1980.
"No Nukes," M. V. S. E., 1980.
"Reflections," Arista, 1981.
"Moving Target," Arista, 1982.
"Sun City," Artists Against Apartheid, 1985.

Also recorded "Secrets," 1978, and "The Best of Gil Scott-Heron, 1984.

SIDELIGHTS: Recording artist Gil Scott-Heron's sixteen record albums "[have] overshadowed his writings to such a degree that, in the main, his audience is not aware of his early literary creations," writes Jon Woodson in the *Dictionary of Literary Biography.* While a college student during the turbulent late sixties and early seventies, Scott-Heron published two novels and a volume of poetry where he advocated revolution as a cure to the ills of society. These works, according to Woodson, "have taken on importance simply by being the literary outpourings of a figure better known as a public voice speaking out against oppression in the world."

In his first novel *The Vulture,* Scott-Heron depicts the corruption of a black neighborhood and the efforts of a revolutionary group, BAMBU, to rehabilitate the area. Woodson comments that *The Vulture* "reveals a corruption so basic to American society that even revolutionary groups that attempt to wrest power from their oppressors are finally included in the same destructive and parasitical patterns that drive the majority culture." *The Nigger Factory,* Scott-Heron's second novel, is set in southern Virginia at a fictional black college and describes how students' demands for meaningful change escalate into a three-day crisis. A *Book World* contributor observes that the novel contains some stylistic problems, but nevertheless concludes: "This is a young man's novel that can be read as much for its message as for its promise. Scott-Heron's prose will take care of itself—he has seen into the human heart, and that is what real novels are all about."

In subsequent years, Scott-Heron has devoted himself almost entirely to composing, performing, and recording music. His music includes elements of jazz, blues, and Latin rhythms and employs what *New York Times* social critic Janet Maslin describes as "tough, concise lyrics." Like his novels and poetry, Scott-Heron's music is concerned with issues such as social injustice, alcoholism, drug abuse, and political corruption, but Woodson notes that his earlier militancy has "moderated to the point where 'Third World Revolution' anthems can be balanced by such optimistic statements as 'Better Days Ahead' and 'A Prayer for Everybody.'"

BIOGRAPHICAL/CRITICAL SOURCES:

BOOKS

Dictionary of Literary Biography, Volume XLI: *Afro-American Poets since 1955,* Gale, 1985.

PERIODICALS

Book World, March 12, 1972.
Down Beat, January 25, 1979.
Ebony, July, 1975.
Newsweek, February 10, 1975.
New York Times, January 12, 1983.†

*   *   *

SEASHORE, Stanley E.   1915-

PERSONAL: Born September 4, 1915, in Wahoo, Neb.; son of August Theodore and Jennie Rose Seashore; married Eva Danielson, August 29, 1940; children: Karen Seashore Louis, Christine Sigrid. *Education:* University of Iowa, B.A., 1937; University of Minnesota, M.A., 1939; University of Michigan, Ph.D., 1954.

ADDRESSES: Home—2270 Manchester Rd., Ann Arbor, Mich. 48104. *Office*—Institute for Social Research, University of Michigan, Box 1248, Ann Arbor, Mich. 48106.

CAREER: Personnel manager, U.S. Steel Corp., 1939-45; A. T. Kearney & Co., Chicago, Ill., staff consultant, 1945-50; University of Michigan, Ann Arbor, assistant professor, 1956-60, associate professor, 1960-64, professor of psychology, 1964—, program director, Institute for Social Research, 1950—. Chairman, Commission for Certification of Psychologists, State of Michigan.

MEMBER: American Psychological Association (fellow; president of Division of Organizational and Industrial Psychology, 1968-69), American Sociological Association, Association for Applied Anthropology, American Board of Professional Psychologists, Sigma Xi.

AWARDS, HONORS: Fulbright fellow, 1956-57; Guggenheim fellow, 1965-66; NIAS fellow, 1972-73; citation for distinguished contributions, Academy of Management, 1984.

WRITINGS:

Group Cohesiveness in the Industrial Work Group, Institute for Social Research, University of Michigan, 1954.
(With David Bowers) *Changing the Structure and Functioning of an Organization,* Institute for Social Research, University of Michigan, 1963.
(Editor and contributor) *Assessing Organizational Performance with Behavioral Measurements,* Foundation for Research on Human Behavior, 1964.
(With Alfred Marrow and Bowers) *Management by Participation,* Harper, 1967.

(Editor with Robert McNeill) *Management of the Urban Crisis: Government and the Behavioral Sciences*, Free Press, 1971.

(With Lawler, Mirvis, and Cammann) *Assessing Organizational Change: A Guide To Methods, Measures and Practices*, Wiley, 1983.

(With E. M. Gramlich and G. H. Ross) *Proposed Plan of Activities Concerning Social, Economic Issues*, Industrial Technology Institute, 1983.

CONTRIBUTOR

(With R. Likert) W. Haber, editor, *Manpower Problems in the United States*, Harper, 1954.

Likert and S. P. Hayes, editors, *Some Applications of Behavioural Research*, UNESCO (Paris), 1957.

Research into Factors Influencing Human Relations, Paul Brand (Hilversum, Netherlands), 1959.

Bowers, editor, *Applying Modern Management Principles to Sales Organizations*, Foundation for Research on Human Behavior, 1963.

B. P. Indik and F. K. Berrien, editors, *People, Groups and Organizations*, Teachers College Press, 1968.

(With Bowers) Marrow, editor, *The Failure of Success*, American Management Association, 1972.

T. H. Hammar and S. B. Bacharach, editors, *Reward Systems and Power Distribution*, School of Industrial and Labor Relations, Cornell University, 1977.

Lawler, D. A. Nadler and Cammann, editors, *Organizational Assessment: Perspectives on the Measurement of Organizational Behavior and the Quality of Work Life*, Wiley, 1980.

(With M. K. Moch) S. P. Sethi and C. L. Swanson, editors, *Private Enterprise and Public Purpose*, Wiley, 1981.

W. M. Hoffman and T. J. Wyly, editors, *The Work Ethic in Business*, Oelschlager, Gunn & Hain, 1981.

A. H. Van de Ven and W. F. Joyce, editors, *Perspectives on Organization Design and Behavior*, Wiley, 1981.

(With Moch) P. C. Nystrom and W. H. Starbuck, editors, *Handbook of Organizational Design*, Volume I, Oxford University Press, 1981.

C. A. Bramlette, editor, *The Individual and the Future of Organizations*, Georgia State University, 1981.

J. E. Sieber, editor, *The Ethics of Social Research: Surveys and Experiments*, Springer-Verlag, 1982.

K. S. Cameron and D. A. Whetten, editors, *Organizational Effectiveness: A Comparison of Multiple Models*, Academic Press, 1983.

OTHER

Also principle investigator and coauthor of survey reports for government U.S. Office of Personnel Management, 1980-82. Contributor to proceedings of numerous conferences, including the Industrial Engineering Institute conference, 1956, the International Management Congress, 1963, the Industrial Relations Research Association conference, 1971, and the Annual U.S.-Polish Conference on the Management of Large-Scale Organizations, 1977 and 1978. Contributor of more than thirty articles to social science journals.

*   *   *

SELBY, Donald Joseph   1915-

PERSONAL: Born February 7, 1915, in Kansas City, Mo.; son of Benjamin Wood and Evelyn (Wharton) Selby; married Clarice Allene Beggs, 1939; children: Robert Wallace Donald Lee. *Education:* William Jewell College, A.B., 1946; Andover Newton Theological School, B.D. (cum laude), 1949; Boston University, Ph.D., 1954.

ADDRESSES: Home—204 Maupin Ave., Salisbury, N.C. 28144. *Office*—Catawba College, Salisbury, N.C. 28144.

CAREER: Ordained minister in United Church of Christ; Pilgrim Congregational Church, Merrimac, Mass., pastor 1948-56; Catawba College, Salisbury, N.C., professor of religion, 1956—. Part-time teacher, School of Theology, Boston University, 1955-56.

MEMBER: Society of Biblical Literature, American Academy of Religion, American Society for Oriental Research.

WRITINGS:

Toward the Understanding of St. Paul, Prentice-Hall, 1962.
Introduction to the New Testament: The Word Became Flesh, Macmillan, 1971.
(With J. King West) *Introduction to the Bible* (two volumes), Macmillan, 1971.†

*   *   *

SHINE, Ted   1931-

PERSONAL: Born April 26, 1931, in Baton Rouge, La.; son of Theodis Wesley and Bessie (Herson) Shine. *Education:* Howard University, B.A., 1953; Iowa State University of Science and Technology (now University of Iowa), M.A., 1958; University of California, Santa Barbara, Ph.D, 1971. *Politics:* Democrat. *Religion:* Baptist.

ADDRESSES: Home—10717 Cox Lane, Dallas, Tex. 75229. *Office*—P.O. Box 2082, Prairie View, Tex. 77445. *Agent*—Flora Roberts, Inc., 157 West 57th St., New York, N.Y. 10019.

CAREER: Dillard University, New Orleans, La., instructor in drama and English, 1960-61; Howard University, Washington, D.C., assistant professor of drama, 1961-67; Prairie View A & M University, Prairie View, Tex., professor and head of department of drama, 1967—. Board member, Texas Non-Profit Theatres, Inc. *Military service:* U.S. Army, 1955-57.

MEMBER: American Theatre Association, Southwest Theatre Conference, Texas Educational Theatre Association.

AWARDS, HONORS: Brook-Hines Award for Playwriting, Howard University, 1970, for "Morning, Noon, and Night."

WRITINGS:

PLAYS

Sho Is Hot in the Cotton Patch (one-act; first produced in Washington, D.C. at Howard University, 1950; produced as "Miss Weaver" in New York City at St. Mark's Playhouse, 1968), Encore, 1966.
Shoes (also see below), Encore, 1967.
"Morning, Noon, and Night" (three-act; first produced in Washington, D.C. at Howard University, 1964), published in *The Black Teacher and the Dramatic Arts*, edited by William Reardon and Thomas D. Pawley, Negro Universities Press, 1970.
"Plantation" (one-act; also see below), first produced in 1970.
Contributions: Three Short Plays (contains "Plantation," "Shoes," and "Contribution"), Dramatists Play Service, 1970. *Contribution* (one-act; first produced in New York City, 1967), Chilton, 1972.

(Editor with James V. Hatch, and contributor) *Black Theatre, U.S.A.: Forty-five Plays by Black Americans, 1847-1974* (includes "Herbert III " [one-act], first produced in Wichita Falls, Tex., at Midwestern State University, October, 1975), Free Press, 1974.

The Woman Who Was Tampered with in Youth (one-act; first produced at Fisk University, 1983), Sea Urchin Press, 1980.

Good Old Soul (one-act; first produced at Fisk University, 1983), Tennessee State University Press, 1984.

Going Berserk (one-act), National Association for Dramatic and Speech Arts, 1984.

UNPUBLISHED PLAYS

"Cold Day in August" (one-act), 1950.
"Dry August," 1952.
"Bat's Out of Hell," 1955.
"Good News," 1956.
"Entourage Royale" (musical), 1958.
"Epitaph for a Bluebird," 1958.
"A Rat's Revolt," 1959.
"Miss Victoria" (one-act), 1965.
"Pontiac" (one-act), 1967.
"Revolution," 1968.
"Jeanne West" (musical), 1968.
"The Coca-Cola Boys" (one-act), 1969.
"Comeback after the Fire" (full-length sequel to "Morning, Noon, and Night"), 1969.
"Flora's Kisses" (one-act), 1969.
"Hamburgers at Hamburger Haven Are Impersonal" (one-act), 1969.
"Idabel's Fortune" (one-act), 1969.
"The Night of Baker's End," 1974.
"Baby Cakes" (two-act), first produced in Austin, Tex. at the University of Texas at Austin, 1981.
"Old Grass," 1983.
"Ancestors" (three-act), first produced in Dallas, Tex., 1986.
"Deep Ellum Blues" (two-act ballet), first produced in Dallas, 1986.

OTHER

Also author of more than sixty scripts for television series "Our Street."

WORK IN PROGRESS: "Death Row," a documentary work concerning prisoners who find love on death row.

SIDELIGHTS: "Ted Shine continues a tradition established in American black theater by Langston Hughes—the use of humor as an incisive weapon and as a defense against weeping," writes Winona L. Fletcher in a *Dictionary of Literary Biography* essay. Noting that Shine "possesses microscopic insight and a finely tuned ear for dialogue and dialect, particularly that spoken by the rural Southerner," Fletcher finds that "his dramas work on stage and screen; his audiences, black or white, cannot escape from a sense of verity and from the messages Shine drives home to them." Fletcher considers Shine unique in his treatment of the thematic concerns he shares with other contemporary black playwrights, such as "the black family struggles, religion, a generation/communication gap caused by the 'new' thinking of the black revolution, and the need for love and acceptance." Says Fletcher, "Always there is serious meaning behind the laughter, and the route to self-determinism is clearly marked for those who wish to pursue it."

Shine commented: "Motivation for my work stems from life itself—a sad face, a broken heart, a trembling voice, a cry in the night. The purpose of drama for me continues to be to teach and to please, and hopefully my work will emerge realistically—uplifting the dignity of mankind."

BIOGRAPHICAL/CRITICAL SOURCES:

BOOKS

Dictionary of Literary Biography, Volume XXXVIII: *Afro-American Writers after 1955: Dramatists and Prose Writers,* Gale, 1985.

Harris, Trudier, *From Mammies to Militants: Domestics in Black American Literature,* Temple University Press, 1982.

PERIODICALS

Black American Literature Forum, summer, 1980.
Encore, number 12, 1969.†

*   *   *

SKINNER, Knute (Rumsey) 1929-

PERSONAL: Born April 25, 1929, in St. Louis, Mo.; son of George Rumsey (a salesman) and Lidi (a civil servant; maiden name, Skjoldvig) Skinner; married Jean Pratt, November, 1953 (divorced September, 1977); married Edna Faye Kiel, March 25, 1978; children: Frank, Dunstan, Morgan. *Education:* Attended Culver-Stockton College, Canton, Mo., 1947-49; Colorado State College (now University of Northern Colorado), A.B., 1951; Middlebury College, M.A., 1954; State University of Iowa (now University of Iowa), Ph.D., 1958.

ADDRESSES: Home—412 North State St., Bellingham, Wash. 98225; and Killaspuglonane, Lahinch, County Clare, Ireland (summer). *Office*—Department of English, Western Washington University, Bellingham, Wash. 98225.

CAREER: Boise Senior High School, Boise, Idaho, teacher of English, 1951-54; State University of Iowa (now University of Iowa), Iowa City, instructor in English, 1955-56, 1957-58, and 1960-61; Oklahoma College for Women (now University of Science and Arts of Oklahoma), Chickasha, assistant professor of English, 1961-62; Western Washington University, Bellingham, assistant professor, 1971-73, professor of English, 1973—. Poetry editor, Southern Illinois University Press, 1975-76; editor and publisher, *Bellingham Review* and Signpost Press, 1977—. Has given poetry readings at conferences, colleges, universities, and high schools, throughout the United States and Ireland.

MEMBER: Poetry Society of America, American Committee for Irish Studies, Washington Poets Association.

AWARDS, HONORS: Huntington Hartford Foundation fellowship, 1961; National Endowment for the Arts fellowship in creative writing, 1975; Millay Colony for the Arts fellowship, 1976.

WRITINGS:

POETRY

Stranger with a Watch, Golden Quill, 1965.
A Close Sky over Killaspuglonane, Dolmen Press (Dublin), 1968, 2nd edition, Burton International, 1975.
In Dinosaur Country, Pierian, 1969.
The Sorcerers: A Laotian Tale, Goliards Press, 1972.
Hearing of the Hard Times, Northwoods Press, 1981.
The Flame Room, Folly Press, 1983.
Selected Poems, Aquila Press, 1985.

CONTRIBUTOR TO ANTHOLOGIES

New Campus Writing #3, Grove, 1959.
Midland, Random House, 1961.
Doors into Poetry, Prentice-Hall, 1962.
Flame Annual, Different Press, 1965.
A Poet's Dozen: Fourteen Poems by Pacific Northwest Poets,
     Friends of the Market (Seattle), 1966.
The New Orlando Poetry Anthology, Volume III, New Or-
     lando Publications, 1967.
*Laudamus Te: A Cycle of Poems to the Praise and Glory of
     God*, Manifold Publications, 1967.
An Introduction to Poetry, 2nd edition, Little, Brown, 1971,
     6th edition, 1986.
New Generation: Poetry Anthology, Ann Arbor Review Books,
     1971.
Charles Angoff, editor, *The Diamond Anthology*, A. S. Barnes,
     1971.
Our Only Hope Is Humor: Some Public Poems, Ashland Po-
     etry Press, 1972.
Lewis Turco, editor, *Poetry: An Introduction through Writing*,
     Reston, 1973.
X. J. Kennedy, editor, *Messages: A Thematic Anthology of
     Poetry*, Little, Brown, 1973.
*Poets West: Contemporary Poems from the Eleven Western
     States*, Perivale, 1975.
Literature: An Introduction to Fiction, Poetry and Drama,
     Little, Brown, 1976, 4th edition, 1987.
Edward Field, editor, *A Geography of Poets*, Bantam, 1979.
The Poet's Choice, Tendril, 1980.
Sevrin Housen, editor, *Feathers and Bones: Ten Poets of the
     Irish Earth*, Halcyon Press, 1981.
Kennedy, editor, *Tygers of Wrath: Poems of Hate, Anger and
     Invective*, University of Georgia Press, 1981.
Light Year '84, Bits Press, 1983.
*Iron Age Anthology: A Selection of Work from Iron Magazine
     1973-83*, Iron Press, 1983.
Poets and Peace International, Arc Press, 1983.
*Rain in the Forest, Light in the Trees: Contemporary Poetry
     from the Northwest*, Owl Creek Press, 1983.
Light Year '85, Bits Press, 1984.
Poets on the Commons, City of Kent Arts Commission, 1984.
*Ketchup and Other Vegetables: American Poets on President
     Reagan*, Poetry Associates, 1984.
Light Year '86, Bits Press, 1985.
Poetry Doors One: A Poetry Workbook, Word and Action
     (Dorset), 1985.
Light Year '87, Bits Press, 1986.
*Strong Measures: Contemporary American Poetry in Tradi-
     tional Forms*, Harper, 1986.

OTHER

Contributor of poems to numerous periodicals, including *Ohio
Review, Colorado Quarterly, New Republic, New Letters, Mid-
American Review*, and *Chicago Review;* contributor of short
stories and reviews to *Limbo, Quartet, Midwest, Irish Press,
Northwest Review*, and *Hibernia*. Guest editor, *Pyramid*,
Number 13, 1973.

WORK IN PROGRESS: *Learning to Spell ''Zucchini,''* a book
of poetry.

SIDELIGHTS: Knute Skinner, who divides his time between
homes in Bellingham, Washington, and rural Ireland, told *CA*
that life in Ireland "exerts a strong influence on my work."
He has recorded his poetry for the British Council, for poetry
rooms at Harvard, Leeds, Hull and Durham universities, and

for radio programs in the United States and Ireland. His poetry
is also the subject of two videotapes, one made at the University of Wisconsin—La Crosse and the other at Triton College in Chicago, and of an educational television film made
at the State University of New York College at Brockport.

*   *   *

SMITH, Dwight L.   1918-

PERSONAL: Born April 11, 1918, in West Elkton, Ohio; son
of Clarence S. (a minister) and Mary (Barnhart) Smith; married Jane DeLeon, May 5, 1955; children: Gregory B. *Education:* Indiana Central College (now University of Indianapolis), A.B., 1940; Indiana University, A.M., 1941, Ph.D.,
1949. *Religion:* Presbyterian.

ADDRESSES: *Home*—409 Emerald Woods Dr., Oxford, Ohio
45056. *Office*—Department of History, Miami University,
Oxford, Ohio 45056.

CAREER: Indiana Central College (now University of Indianapolis), Indianapolis, instructor in history, 1942-43; Ohio
State University, Columbus, instructor in history, 1949-53;
Miami University, Oxford, Ohio, assistant professor, 1953-
56, associate professor, 1956-60, professor of history, 1960-
84, professor emeritus, 1984—. Visiting instructor in history,
Centre College of Kentucky, 1952; Carnegie Visiting Assistant
Professor of History, Columbia University, 1954-55; visiting
professor of history, Indiana University, 1962-63, University
of Alberta, 1964, Colorado College, 1965, University of British Columbia, 1967, and University of New Mexico, 1968.
Presbyterian Church, deacon, 1957-60, elder, 1961-66, 1978-
83, church historian, 1966-79. *Military Service:* U.S. Army
Air Corps, 1943-46; became staff sergeant.

MEMBER: American Historical Association, Association for
Canadian Studies, Canadian Historical Association, Organization of American Historians, Association for the Bibliography of History (president, 1980-81), American-Indian Eth-
nohistoric Conference (president, 1955-56), Western History
Association (member of council, 1982-85), Ohio Academy of
History (president, 1978-79), Ohio Historical Society (research historian, 1950-51), Indiana Central College Alumni
Association (member of board of directors, 1964-70; president, 1968-69), Oxford Museum Association (member of board
of trustees, 1956-60; president, 1957-58), Friends of the Miami
University Library Society (president, 1979-80).

AWARDS, HONORS: Newberry Library fellow, 1952, 1964;
Miami University research fellow, 1957, 1959, 1982; Lilly
Endowment fellow, 1962; Institute of Environmental Sciences
fellow, 1977; award of merit, American Bibliographical Center, 1980; Samuel Foster Haven fellow, American Antiquarian
Society, 1982; Huntington Library fellow, 1983; distinguished
service award, Ohio Academy of History, 1985; Litt.D., University of Indianapolis, 1987.

WRITINGS:

From Greene Ville to Fallen Timbers, Indiana Historical So-
     ciety, 1952.
(Editor) *The Western Journals of John May*, Historical and
     Philosophical Society of Ohio, 1961.
(Editor with C. Gregory Crampton) *The Hoskaninni Papers*,
     University of Utah Press, 1961.
Down the Colorado, University of Oklahoma Press, 1965.
Western Life in the Stirrups, Caxton Club, 1965.
The Photographer and the River, Stagecoach Press, 1967.

(Editor) *John D. Young and the Colorado Gold Rush,* Lakeside Press, 1969.

(Editor with Lloyd W. Garrison) *The American Political Process,* American Bibliographical Center-Clio Press, 1972.

Afro-American History: A Bibliography, American Bibliographical Center-Clio Press, 1974, Volume II, 1981.

Indians of the United States and Canada: A Bibliography, American Bibliographical Center-Clio Press, 1974, Volume II, 1983.

Era of the American Revolution, American Bibliographical Center-Clio Press, 1975.

The American and Canadian West, American Bibliographical Center-Clio Press, 1979.

The History of Canada, American Bibliographical Center-Clio Press, 1983.

The War of 1812, Garland Publishing, 1985.

(With C. Gregory Crampton) *The Colorado River Survey,* Howe Brothers, 1987.

CONTRIBUTOR

The Governors of Ohio, Ohio Historical Society, 1954.

K. Ross Toole and others, editors, *Probing the American West,* Museum of New Mexico Press, 1962.

1962 Brand Book, Denver Westerners, 1963.

John F. McDermott, editor, *Travelers on the Western Frontier,* University of Illinois Press, 1970.

The French, the Indians, and George Rogers Clark in the Illinois Country, Indiana Historical Society, 1977.

This Land of Ours: The Acquisition and Disposition of the Public Domain, Indiana Historical Society, 1978.

Ian MacPherson, editor, *Western Canada,* Sunflower University Press, 1985.

OTHER

Contributor to many professional journals, including *Historical Abstracts* and *America: History and Life.* Book review editor, *Ethnohistory,* 1954-60; editor, *Old Northwest,* 1974-87.

*   *   *

SPAETH, Gerold   1939-

PERSONAL: Born October 16, 1939, in Rapperswil, Switzerland; son of Josef (an organ builder) and Martha (Ruegg) Spaeth; married Anita Baumann, 1964; children: Veit, Salome. *Education:* Attended commercial schools in Switzerland and England.

ADDRESSES: Home—Sternengraben, Rapperswil 8640, Switzerland. *Agent*—Scott Meredith Literary Agency, Inc., 845 Third Ave., New York, N.Y. 10022.

CAREER: Held various positions in international trade and advertising in Zurich, Switzerland, Vevey, Switzerland, Fribourg, Switzerland, and London, England; free-lance writer, 1968—; part-time employee in family organ-building business, 1975—.

MEMBER: International P.E.N., Gruppe Olten.

AWARDS, HONORS: Conrad Ferdinand Meyer-Preis und Werkjahr der Stadt Zuerich, 1970; Werkauftrag der Stiftung Pro Helvetia, 1972; Werkjahr der Stiftung der Schweizerischen Landesausstellung, 1973; Werkjahr des Kantons Zuerich, 1975; Anerkennungsgabe der Stadt Zuerich, 1977; Traeger des erstmals verliehenen Alfred Doeblin-Preises, 1979; Stipendiat des DAAD Kuenstlerprogramms Berlin, 1980; Stipendiat des Istituto Svizzero Roma, 1980-82; Internationaler Pressepreis der Stadt Rom, 1983; Georg-Mackensen-Literaturpreis, 1984; Traeger des erstmal verliehenen Hoerspielpreises der Stiftung Radio Basel, 1987.

WRITINGS:

Unschlect (novel), Arche Verlag, 1970, translation by Rita Kimber and Robert Kimber published as *A Prelude to the Long Happy Life of Maximilian Goodman,* Little, Brown, 1975.

Stimmgaenge (novel), Arche Verlag, 1972.

Zwoelf Geschichten (short stories), Arche Verlag, 1973.

Die heile Hoelle (novel; title means ''The Hidden Hell''), Arche Verlag, 1974.

Kings Insel (novel; title means ''King's Island''), Arche Verlag, 1976.

Balzapf; oder, Als ich auftauchte (novel), Arche Verlag, 1977.

Ende der Nacht, Pfaffenweiler Presse, 1979.

Commedia, S. Fischer Verlag, 1980.

Vom Rom bis Kotzebue, Artemis Verlag Zuerich, 1982.

Sacramento, S. Fischer Verlag, 1983.

Sindbadland, S. Fischer Verlag, 1984.

RADIO PLAYS, PRODUCED IN SWITZERLAND, GERMANY, AND CANADA

Heisser Sonntag, Schweizerische Werbestelle fuer das Buch des Schweizerischen Buchhaendler- und Verlagsvereins, 1971.

''Mein Oktober: Hoellisch,'' 1972.

''Grund-Riss eines grossen Hauses,'' 1974.

''Schattentanz,'' 1976.

''Morgenprozession,'' 1977.

''Heisse Sunntig,'' 1978.

''Lange Leitung,'' 1978.

''In der Ferne eine Stadt,'' 1979.

''Kalter Tag,'' 1980.

''Masken,'' 1980.

''Eine alte Geschichte,'' 1982.

''Unser Wilhelm! Unser Tell!,'' first produced at Theatre Carouge-Geneve, 1986.

''Mein Besuch im Staedtchen am See,'' 1986.

''Der See am Morgen,'' 1986.

*   *   *

SPELLMAN, Roger G.
See COX, William (Robert)

*   *   *

SPINIFEX
See MARTIN, David

*   *   *

SPRIGEL, Olivier
See AVICE, Claude (Pierre Marie)

*   *   *

STACHYS, Dimitris
See CONSTANTELOS, Demetrios J.

STALLYBRASS, Oliver (George Weatherhead) 1925-1978

PERSONAL: Born March 11, 1925, in Heswall, Cheshire, England; died November 28, 1978; son of Clare Oswald (a doctor) and Irene (Weatherhead) Stallybrass; married Gunnvor Sannerud (a design consultant), July 8, 1948; children: Anne, Michael. *Education:* Attended School of Oriental and African Studies, London, 1943-44; Clare College, Cambridge, B.A. (second class honors), 1951; University College, London, Postgraduate Diploma in Librarianship, 1954. *Politics:* "No party loyalties." *Religion:* None (humanist).

ADDRESSES: Home and office—106 Westwood Hill, London S.E.26, England.

CAREER: Portsmouth Grammar School, Portsmouth, England, English master, 1951; London Library, London, England, staff, 1952-53, 1954-64, chief cataloger, 1958-61, deputy librarian, 1961-64; Secker & Warburg Ltd. (publishers), London, editor and advertising manager, 1964-66; Royal Institution of Great Britain, London, librarian and publications officer, 1966-67. *Military service:* British Army, 1944-47; became sergeant.

MEMBER: Translators Association, Society of Indexers, National Book League, Society of Authors, London Library.

WRITINGS:

EDITOR

(And contributor) *Aspects of E. M. Forster* (fifteen essays written for Forster's ninetieth birthday), Harcourt, 1969.
(With L. Pearce Williams and Rosemary Fitzgerald) *The Selected Correspondence of Michael Faraday,* Cambridge University Press, 1971.
The Manuscript of "Howard's End," Edward Arnold, 1973.
Yon Barna, *Eisenstein,* translated by Lise Hunder, Secker & Warburg, 1973.
E. M. Forster, *Howard's End,* Penguin, 1973.
Forster, *The Life to Come, and Other Stories,* Penguin, 1975.
Forster, *Two Cheers for Democracy,* Penguin, 1976.
(With Alan Bullock, and contributor) *The Harper Dictionary of Modern Thought,* Harper, 1977 (published in England as *The Fontana Dictionary of Modern Thought,* Fontana, 1977).
The Manuscripts of "A Passage to India," Edward Arnold, 1978.

Editor of "The Abinger Edition of E. M. Forster" series, Holmes & Meier, 1979.

TRANSLATOR

Axel Jensen, *Epp,* Chatto & Windus, 1967.
Knut Hamsun, *Victoria,* Farrar, Straus, 1969.
(With David Hamblyn) Milan Kundera, *The Joke,* Coward, 1969.
Four Screenplays ("The Passion of Joan of Arc," "Vampire," "Day of Wrath," "The Word"), Indiana University Press, 1970.
Rolf Doecker, *Marius,* Harcourt, 1970.
Sven Plovgaard, editor, *Public Library Buildings,* Library Association (London), 1971.
(With Roger Greaves) Pierre Leprohon, *The Italian Cinema,* Praeger, 1972.
Johan Borgen, *The Red Mist,* Calder & Boyars, 1973.
Niels Jensen, *Days of Courage,* Harcourt, 1973 (published in England as *When the Land Lay Waste,* Methuen, 1973).

(With wife, Gunnvor Stallybrass) Hamsun, *The Wanderer,* Farrar, Straus, 1975.
Erik Sletholt, *Wild and Tame: A View of Animals,* Duckworth, 1976.
(With G. Stallybrass) Hamsun, *The Women at the Pump,* Souvenir Press, 1978.

OTHER

(With Emil Gelenczei and Roland Sallay) *The Ben-Oni Defence,* British Chess Magazine, 1966.

Indexer of many books, including *The Collected Essays, Journalism and Letters of George Orwell,* four volumes, Harcourt, 1968. Contributor of poems, articles, and reviews to *Guardian, Listener, New Statesman, Indexer, Times Literary Supplement, Spectator, Correspondence Chess,* and other British journals and newspapers. Editor, *Link,* 1958-62, *Proceedings of the Royal Institution of Great Britain,* 1966-67, and *Asian Affairs: Journal of the Royal Central Asian Society,* 1969-70.

BIOGRAPHICAL/CRITICAL SOURCES:

PERIODICALS

Book World, February 2, 1969.
New Statesman, January 17, 1969.
New Yorker, February 15, 1969.
Saturday Review, February 15, 1969.†

*   *   *

STEPHAN, Leslie (Bates) 1933-

PERSONAL: Born May 1, 1933, in Boston, Mass.; daughter of Leslie Marriner (a dentist) and Ann (Gustafson) Bates; married Richard Allen Stephan (a consultant), January 22, 1955; children: John Eric, Johanna Marriner, Anne Christina, Mark David, Martin Jonathan, Maria Alvina. *Education:* Attended Skidmore College, 1951-52, Simmons College, 1952-54; Radcliffe College, B.A. (cum laude), 1957; Lesley College, Cambridge, Mass., elementary teachers certification, 1981, M.Ed. and special education certification, 1984.

ADDRESSES: Home—103 North Main St., Topsfield, Mass. 01983. *Agent*—Oscar Collier, Collier Associates, 2000 Flat Run Rd., Seaman, Ohio 45679.

CAREER: Director of nursery school in Harrison, N.Y., 1958-59; special education tutor, 1975-83; affiliated with Danvers High School, Danvers, Mass., 1984—.

WRITINGS:

A Dam for Nothing, Viking, 1966.
Murder R.F.D., Scribner, 1978 (published in England as *Murder in the Family,* R. Hale, 1979).
Murder or Not, R. Hale, 1981.
Murder Most Distressing, St. Martin's, 1986.

WORK IN PROGRESS: Another mystery novel.

SIDELIGHTS: Leslie Stephan lived in Iraq, 1955, in Switzerland, 1960-63, in Mexico, 1966-67, and in Algeria, 1968. She speaks German, French, and some Spanish.

AVOCATIONAL INTERESTS: Reading, gardening, swimming, cross-country skiing, walking, listening to music.

*   *   *

STEPHEN, R. J.
See BARRETT, Norman (S.)

STOKER, Alan 1930-
(Alan Evans)

PERSONAL: Born October 2, 1930, in Sunderland, Durham, England; son of Robert and Edith (Milne) Stoker; married Irene Evans, April 30, 1960; children: Neil Douglas, John Robert. *Education:* Attended schools in Sunderland, England, 1935-47.

ADDRESSES: Home—9 Dale Rd., Walton on Thames, Surrey, England. *Agent*—Murray Pollinger, 4 Garrick St., London WC2E 9BH, England.

CAREER: Civil servant in England, 1951—, currently as an executive officer. *Military service:* British Army, Royal Artillery, 1949-51. Army Reserve, 1951-73; became sergeant.

WRITINGS:

UNDER PSEUDONYM ALAN EVANS

The End of the Running, Cassell, 1966.
Mantrap, Cassell, 1967.
Bannon, Cassell, 1968.
Vicious Circle, R. Hale, 1970.
The Big Deal, R. Hale, 1971.
Running Scared, Brockhampton Press, 1975.
Kidnap, Hodder & Stoughton, 1976.
Thunder at Dawn, Hodder & Stoughton, 1978.
Escape at the Devil's Gate, Hodder & Stoughton, 1978.
Ship of Force, Hodder & Stoughton, 1979.
Dauntless, Hodder & Stoughton, 1980.
Seek out and Destroy!, Hodder & Stoughton, 1982.
Deed of Glory, Hodder & Stoughton, 1984.
Audacity, Hodder & Stoughton, 1985.
Eagle at Taranyo, Hodder & Stoughton, 1987.

WORK IN PROGRESS: Night Action, a naval adventure novel.

AVOCATIONAL INTERESTS: Rugby football, beer, "a willing but inept gardener; hate working about the house."

*   *   *

STRASSER, Susan 1948-

PERSONAL: Born March 27, 1948, in Pittsburgh, Pa.; daughter of Alexander (a physicist) and Maxine (Hochberg) Strasser. *Education:* Reed College, B.A., 1969; State University of New York at Stony Brook, M.A., 1971, Ph.D., 1977.

ADDRESSES: Home—6008 Athens Beach Dr. N.W., Olympia, Wash. 98502. *Office*—Evergreen State College, Olympia, Wash. 98505.

CAREER: Evergreen State College, Olympia, Wash., member of American history faculty, 1975—.

AWARDS, HONORS: Woodrow Wilson fellowship, 1969; Smithsonian Institution predoctoral fellowship, 1973-75; American Council of Learned Societies fellowship, 1984-85; Bunting Institute fellow, Radcliffe College, 1984-85; Harvard-Newcomen Fellowship in Business History, 1985-86.

WRITINGS:

Never Done: A History of American Housework, Pantheon, 1982.
(Co-author) *Washington: Images of a State's Heritage,* Melior Publications, 1988.

(Contributor) R. Jackson Wilson, editor, *American Culture* (tentative title), Dorsey, 1988.
Satisfaction Guaranteed: Branded Products and the National Market at the Turn of the Century (tentative title), Pantheon, in press.

SIDELIGHTS: Susan Strasser's 1982 book *Never Done: A History of American Housework* has been praised as a comprehensive and detailed analysis of how technological and economic developments of the last century have altered the nature of domestic work in America. Strasser begins by documenting how difficult and dangerous housework once was, and how technology has changed it. Advancements such as running water, for instance, have made laundry a much easier task: "One wash, one boiling, and one rinse used about fifty gallons of water," Strasser notes, ". . . which had to be moved from pump or well or faucet to stove and tub, in buckets and wash boilers that might weigh as much as forty or fifty pounds." With electricity, the need of indoor flame for heating and cooking became unnecessary, reducing the risk both of house fires and carbon monoxide poisoning—while also decreasing the presence of soot throughout home interiors. In conveying what housework once entailed, "Strasser's outstanding merit is detail," comments Naomi Bliven in the *New Yorker.* "Her research retrieves what history usually discards—the taken-for-granted minutiae of the everyday life of ordinary people—and her documentation enables us to visualize how nasty and unhealthful homes used to be." Bliven continues: "I know of no other writer who has explained so clearly what until just yesterday was the noisome reality of the American interior."

While housework has been made easier because of technological advances, on a social scale the changes have come somewhat as a mixed blessing, according to Strasser. As Jacqueline Jones points out in the *Nation,* "*Never Done* advances two main arguments: first, that as housework became less physically arduous, it intensified the isolation of women in their own homes, and second, that corporations have intruded further and further into domestic life." As a result of technological advances, a major change in domestic America has been the transition of the household from a private industry—the country's largest, according to Strasser—to a consumer market bombarded by outside producers. "When women ceased pickling and curing food and making soap, clothing and candles in their own homes," notes Jones, "and began to buy those things instead, they lost their hold on the productive economy, as it is traditionally defined." Carol Moldaw in the *Boston Review* adds that women "became passive, isolated consumers. . . . Furthermore, many of the home-based, independent ways in which women supported themselves were usurped and not immediately replaced, or were replaced by restrictive jobs." Carol Travis in *Psychology Today* points out that Strasser "does not romanticize the hard work that women did a century ago, but neither does she dismiss it as trivial or without value."

Some critics view this aspect of *Never Done* with caution, however. Bliven writes that at times the book lacks a "realistic sense of acceptable losses in exchange for substantial gains." Nonetheless, Bliven maintains that Strasser's "main argument—that homes and everybody in them are intimately involved with and profoundly affected by the world around them—is undeniable." Moldaw concludes that "whether or not one shares Strasser's perspective on the losses modern life has foisted on the household and the houseworker,. . . *Never Done* remains an absorbing book." Carolyn See in the *Los Angeles Times Book Review* praises the book for prompting discussion of even broader topics than the changing face of domestic life in America. *Never Done* ''sheds light on competitiveness, acquisitiveness, our strange ideas of 'leisure' and, above all, on our expenditure of energy. . . . Looking at housework shows us—amazingly,. . . how we live.'' See concludes that ''beneath the details of childrearing and root vegetables are the questions of what all of us must be doing.''

BIOGRAPHICAL/CRITICAL SOURCES:

BOOKS

Strasser, Susan, *Never Done: A History of American Housework*, Pantheon, 1982.

PERIODICALS

Boston Review, December, 1982.
Chicago Tribune Book World, July 18, 1982.
Choice, October, 1982.
Los Angeles Times Book Review, May 23, 1982.
Ms., May, 1982.
Nation, September 4, 1982.
New Yorker, September 6, 1982.
New York Times Book Review, December 12, 1982.
Psychology Today, July, 1982.

*   *   *

STRATTON, Thomas
    See COULSON, Robert S(tratton)
    and DeWEESE, Thomas Eugene

*   *   *

STROZIER, Charles B(urnett)   1944-

PERSONAL: Born February 16, 1944, in Athens, Ga.; son of Robert M. (a university president) and Margaret (an academic administrator; maiden name, Burnett) Strozier; married Carol A. Kelly (a medical administrator), September 4, 1965, divorced, 1983; married Cathryn C. Compton-Strozier, January 21, 1985; children: Michael, Matthew, Christopher. *Education:* Harvard University, B.A., 1966; University of Chicago, M.A., 1967, Ph.D., 1971; research candidate at Institute for Psychoanalysis, 1974-79.

ADDRESSES: Home—717 President St., Brooklyn, N.Y. 11215. *Office*—John Jay College, 444 West 56th, New York, N.Y. 10019.

CAREER: Sangamon State University, Springfield, Ill., assistant professor, 1972-76, associate professor, 1976-82, professor of history, 1982-86; John Jay College of Criminal Justice of the City University of New York, professor of history, 1986—, executive director of the Center on Violence and Human Survival, 1986—. Visiting assistant professor of psychiatry, Department of Psychiatry, Rush Medical School, Chicago, Ill., 1977-86; consultant to Department of Psychiatry, Michael Reese Hospital, Chicago, 1980-86.

MEMBER: American Historical Association (executive officer, Group for the Use of Psychology in History, 1972—).

AWARDS, HONORS: Named writer of the year by the Lincoln Library, Springfield, 1981.

WRITINGS:

(Editor with Cullom Davis, Rebecca Veach, and Geoffrey Ward) *The Public and Private Lincoln: Contemporary Perspectives*, Southern Illinois University Press, 1979.

Lincoln's Quest for Union: Public and Private Meanings, Basic Books, 1982.
(With Daniel Offer) *The Leader*, Plenum, 1985.
(Editor) *Self Psychology and the Humanities*, Norton, 1985.

Founding editor of *Psychohistory Review*, 1974-86. Contributor of articles to journals, including *American Heritage* and *Illinois Issues*.

SIDELIGHTS: In *Lincoln's Quest for Union: Public and Private Meanings*, Charles B. Strozier discusses Lincoln's emotional crises and relates them to decisions made in his public life. Among the emotional conflicts Strozier considers crucial are Lincoln's guilt over his mother's death and a period of upheaval that occurred between his two engagements to Mary Todd. Strozier states in his conclusion that ''after 1854 Lincoln discovered, remarkably enough, that his private concerns found reflection in the country as a whole. . . . In the idea of a house divided, Lincoln found a way of creatively enlarging his private concerns to fill the public space.''

In a *New York Times* article, Christopher Lehmann-Haupt finds that Strozier's psychohistorical work says ''some new and original things about one of the most exhaustively investigated subjects in human history. . . . His line of reasoning is sensitive, cautious, entirely free of psychiatric jargon, and surpassingly eloquent.'' Edwin M. Yoder, Jr., in a *Washington Post* review, was less enthusiastic about the book's psychohistorical approach but states, ''Strozier's treatment of Lincoln, while also 'psychobiographical' to a degree, shows a firmer command of the tangled political literature without which Lincoln's emerging purposes and politics, messianic or not, can hardly be understood. . . . He does not ignore . . . the grainy texture of events.''

Strozier told *CA:* ''Psychohistory blends the psychologist's concern for the universal in human experience with the historian's appreciation for the unique moment in the past. It is an approach that is *slowly* coming into acceptance.''

BIOGRAPHICAL/CRITICAL SOURCES:

PERIODICALS

Los Angeles Book Review, July 4, 1982.
New York Times, April 29, 1982.
Washington Post Book World, May 16, 1982.

*   *   *

STRUTZ, Henry   1932-

PERSONAL: Born October 31, 1932, in New York, N.Y.; son of Henry F. W. and Barbara (Laches) Strutz. *Education:* City College (now City College of the City University of New York), B.A., 1955; Brown University, M.A., 1961; doctoral study at Rutgers University.

ADDRESSES: Home—P. O. Box 250, Hornell, N.Y. 14843.

CAREER: New York College of Music, New York City, instructor in German, 1957-62, acting registrar, 1961; City College (now City College of the City University of New York), New York City, lecturer in German, 1958-62; Yeshiva University, New York City, instructor in German, 1960-61; Rutgers University, New Brunswick, N.J., instructor in German, 1962-65; Skidmore College, Saratoga Springs, N.Y., instructor in German, 1965-70; State University of New York Agricultural and Technical College at Alfred, associate professor of languages, 1970-76.

WRITINGS:

The Flower and the Flame, Terrier Press, 1960.
Moon Howls, Terrier Press, 1962.
(Contributor) *Autographs and Manuscripts,* Scribner, 1978.
Dancing with Shiva (poetry and short essays), Vega Press, 1981.
1001 Pitfalls in German, Barron's, 1981, 2nd revised edition, 1986.
German at a Glance, Barron's, 1984.
(Contributor) *The Traveler's Phrase Book,* Barron's, 1985.
(Contributor) *The Traveler's Dictionary,* Barron's, 1985.

Also author of *Consolations* and *Talking Business* (a German-English/English-German commercial dictionary); also author of audioscript for 90-minute cassette (which accompanies *German at a Glance*), Barron's, 1985.

EDITOR

201 German Verbs, Barron's, 1963, 2nd edition, 1965.
501 German Verbs, Barron's, 1972.
(With H. K. Thompson, Jr.) *Doenitz at Nuremberg: A Re-Appraisal,* Amber Publishing, 1976.
301 German Verbs, Barron's, 1981.

OTHER

Contributor of articles, short stories, and poetry to numerous periodicals, including *Third Eye, Kansas Quarterly, Vega, Golden Isis, Parnassus, Lapis,* and *Tempest.*

WORK IN PROGRESS: A Dictionary of Magical Animals; Wandering Words: Some Sexy Etymologies; ten-plus additional titles ("Some, I think, are progressing to real prospects for publication. Others are more problematical in their progress.")

SIDELIGHTS: Henry Strutz told *CA:* "I try to relate and integrate into language study as many aspects of human life as possible, particularly emphasizing music as a tool in language learning. I believe that in teaching a language, and most other things, an attempt should be made to convey cultural values as well as information about the human condition. Unfortunately, editors have not always been able to appreciate some of the more basic and racy aspects of the human condition which I felt should be included, and therefore the spectrum is not as broad as I would have wished.

"In literature, too, I admire a broad spectrum, such as the Renaissance fusion and confusion of Judeo-Christian myth with the classical tradition called 'pagan' by some. This fusion is fruitful as a source of literary material and metaphor, but it can be broadened. Islam should, of course, be included as the other branch of the Judeo-Christian complex it is. Perhaps all three can be subsumed into the far more vast, and to me esthetically and philosophically richer and more comprehensive, traditions of India and the Orient. The Trimurti can easily absorb the Trinity. Vishnu, for instance, has had so many interesting avatars (among them the Buddha, some say) that perhaps the prophets of the Judeo-Christian-Islamic systems should be counted among them.

"Although I am not committed to any one specific system, I do affirm the mythic impulse behind all of them. I find it vitalizing to create and craft out of the debris of the occidental myth system in which I was raised, while combining it with other mythologies. In a world 'yearning to be one', as Thomas Mann put it, I find this a revealing and rewarding approach. In my poems, short stories, and in the several novels I'm working on, I draw from this syncretistic mythmaking of my own. Thus, for example, the great god-bird Garuda can merge with the Holy Ghost dove, which can in turn become Aphrodite's doves. Poe's and Woden's ravens fly with the Phoenix. Various forms of the rook of the *Arabian Nights* consort with Pallas Athena's owls and Zeus's eagles, while whole flocks of very particular parakeets congregate with all kinds of comforting paracletes.

"This kaleidoscopic and constant recycling is not confined to an avian world but tries to embrace the whole (usually) beautifully evolutioning world, inside us and all around us. Chinese celestial dancers or 'apsaras' along with Mohammedan houris can traipse with Terpsichore and join Shiva for a schottische or for any dance he pleases in any number of possible configurations of choreographed atoms.

"I think I keep my writing from getting too exuberant, high-flown, Baroque, and 'poetic' (as the preceding might lead a reader to believe) by trying to touch all the bases, including the basic. As far as literary exploration and investigation is concerned, no taboos as to language or subject matter exist for me. Like other writers, I delight in the many surprising revelations granted to me concerning myself and the world, which occur during the course of creating characters or developing themes."

*   *   *

STUART-CLARK, Christopher (Anthony) 1940-

PERSONAL: Born December 1, 1940, in Steyning, Sussex, England; son of Arthur (a schoolmaster) and Peggy (Anthony) Stuart-Clark; married Jill Price, April 15, 1967; children: Michael Philip, Nicola Clare. *Education:* Pembroke College, Cambridge, B.A., 1963, M.A., 1967; University of London, certificate of education, 1967. *Religion:* Church of England.

ADDRESSES: Home—10/F, B1 South Bay Garden, 33 South Bay Close, Hong Kong. *Office*—Chinese International School, 7 Eastern Hospital Rd., Causeway Bay, Hong Kong.

CAREER: Cheam School, Newbury, Berkshire, England, teacher, 1963-68; Dragon School, Oxford, England, teacher of senior English, head of classics, and housemaster, 1968-83; Chinese International School, Hong Kong, principal, 1983—.

MEMBER: Schools Council of the United Kingdom, National Association for Gifted Children.

WRITINGS:

(Editor with Michael Harrison) *The New Dragon Book of Verse* (juvenile anthology), Oxford University Press, 1977.
(Editor with Harrison, *Poems* (juvenile anthology), with teacher's book, Oxford University Press, 1980.
(Editor with Harrison) *Poems 2* (juvenile anthology), with teacher's book, Oxford University Press, 1980.
(Editor with Harrison) *Narrative Poems,* Oxford University Press, 1981.
(Editor with Harrison) *Noah's Ark,* Oxford University Press, 1983.
(Editor with Harrison) *The Oxford Book of Christmas Poems,* Oxford University Press, 1983.
(Editor with Harrison) *Writing Poems,* Oxford University Press, 1986.

WORK IN PROGRESS: Peace and War, a poetry anthology, with Harrison; *The Oxford Treasury of Children's Poems,* with

Harrison; *The Junior Dragon Book of Verse,* with Harrison, all for Oxford University Press.

SIDELIGHTS: Christopher Stuart-Clark told *CA:* "Our aim with the poetry anthologies has been to present a mixture of modern and earlier poetry in an attractive combination for children of nine to fifteen years. *Poems* and *Poems 2* present anthologies to the pupils without any commentary, while the teacher's books contain suggestions for follow-up work of a centripetal rather than centrifugal nature. Thus, we avoid having pupils regard poems as writing 'with questions on it afterwards.'

"*The New Dragon Book of Verse* and *Narrative Poems* are both anthologies of new and early poems, chosen from our experiences of teaching English to nine-to-thirteen-year-old children. The illustrations, which in both books were commissioned from artists for the book, aim to give further stimulus to the child's imagination.

"*Writing Poems* completes a trilogy with *Poems* and *Poems 2* which introduces children to the skills and varied approaches needed in writing poems.

"*Noah's Ark* and *The Oxford Book of Christmas Poems* are both 'family books' rather than school books, with pictures and poems that we hope will appeal to all members of the family on the two themes concerned."

BIOGRAPHICAL/CRITICAL SOURCES:

PERIODICALS

Times Literary Supplement, July 18, 1980.

*   *   *

STUBER, Florian (Cy)   1947-

PERSONAL: Born March 1, 1947, in Buffalo, N.Y.; son of Florian George (a sheet metal worker) and Dorothy (a registered nurse; maiden name, Blatz) Stuber. *Education:* Columbia University, B.A. (cum laude), 1968, M.A. (with highest honors), 1969, M.Phil. (with distinction), 1971, Ph.D. (with distinction), 1980.

ADDRESSES: Home—134 West 93rd St., No. 3B, New York, N.Y. 10025. *Office*—Department of English, Fashion Institute of Technology, 227 West 27th St., New York, N.Y. 10001. *Agent*—Richard Horner, Richard Horner Associates Ltd., 165 West 46th St., No. 710, New York, N.Y. 10025.

CAREER: Hofstra University, Hempstead, N.Y., instructor, 1969; Columbia University, New York City, instructor in English, 1970-75, director of E.O.P. Writing Workshop, 1973-76, administrative coordinator of Conferences on Humanities and Public Policy Issues, 1974-76; Fashion Institute of Technology, New York City, assistant professor of English, 1977—; Barnard College, New York City, lecturer and instructor in English, 1979-85; free-lance editor, 1980—. Columbia University, lecturer, spring, 1980, visiting assistant professor of English, fall, 1986. Co-owner, Stuber-Doody Productions, 1984—.

MEMBER: Dramatists Guild, Authors League of America, Dance Theater Workshop, American Society for Eighteenth-Century Studies (ASECS), Society for Textual Scholarship, Northeast American Society for Eighteenth-Century Studies (NEASECS), Dickens Fellowship of New York (vice-president, 1972-75).

AWARDS, HONORS: Woodrow Wilson fellow, 1968-69; grants from Axe-Houghton Foundation, 1984 and 1985, for "Clarissa: A Theatre Work."

WRITINGS:

(Editor with Michael Mooney and author of introduction) *Small Comforts for Hard Times: Humanists on Public Policy,* Columbia University Press, 1977.

PLAYS

(With Margaret Doody and John Sgueglia) "Clarissa: The Encounter" (one-act), first produced in New York City at Circle Repertory Lab, May 26, 1983.
(With Doody) "Clarissa: A Theatre Work, Part One," first produced as three-act in New York City at Douglas Fairbanks Theater, March 12, 1984, produced as two-act in New York City at West End Theater, October 26, 1984.

OTHER

"Pamela's Wedding Day at F.I.T." (videotape), Stuber-Doody Productions for British Broadcasting Corp. (BBC-TV), 1985.
"Dramatizing 'Clarissa'" (videotape), Stuber-Doody Producitons, 1986.

Small Comforts for Hard Times: Humanists on Public Policy has been translated into Spanish. Also author, with Joshua Simon and Clark Piper, of "Foreign Affair" (screenplay), 1986, of introductory material and chapter summaries for the annual broadcast of *Ulysses,* WBAI-FM Radio, 1978-80, and, with Doody, of "Friends of Clarissa" (newsletter), 1983—; also manuscript editor of numerous books. Contributor of articles to *Modern Language Studies, TEXT: Transactions of the Society for Textual Scholarship,* and *Studies in English Literature;* contributor of reviews to *Johnsonian Newsletter.* Script consultant for "Open and Notorious," an American Broadcasting Corp. (ABC-TV) "Movie of the Week," produced by King-Hitzig Productions, 1977.

WORK IN PROGRESS: Clarissa and Her World for Cambridge University Press; editor-in-chief of a projected 10-volume edition of the "Clarissa" series for AMS Press; with Doody, "Clarissa: A Theater Work" (parts two and three).

*   *   *

STUHLMUELLER, Carroll   1923-

PERSONAL: Born April 2, 1923, in Hamilton, Ohio; son of William and Alma (Huesing) Stuhlmueller. *Education:* Attended Passionist seminaries in St. Louis, Mo., Detroit, Mich., Chicago, Ill., and Louisville, Ky., 1936-50; Catholic University of America, S.T.L., 1952; Pontifical Biblical Institute, Rome, Italy, S.S.L., 1954, S.S.D., 1968.

ADDRESSES: Office—Catholic Theological Union, 5401 S. Cornell Ave., Chicago, Ill. 60615.

CAREER: Roman Catholic priest of Passionist order; Passionist Seminary, Chicago, Ill., teacher of scripture and Hebrew, 1954-58; Viatorian Seminary, Evanston, Ill., assistant professor of scripture, 1955-58; Passionist Seminary, Louisville, Ky., professor of scripture, 1958-65; Loretto Junior College, Nerinx, Ky., assistant professor of scripture and history, 1959-65; St. Meinrad Seminary, St. Meinrad, Ind., professor of scripture and Hebrew, 1965-68; Catholic Theological Union, Chicago, professor of Old Testament, 1968—. Member of summer faculty, Graduate School of Theology, St. Mary's

College, Notre Dame, Ind., 1957-64; member of fall faculty, St. John's University, New York, N.Y., 1970-75. Visiting professor, Ecole Biblique et Archeologique, Jerusalem, 1973, Winter Theological School, South Africa, summer, 1973, University of San Francisco, summer, 1986, and University of Notre Dame, summer, 1987. Member of Ecumenical Scholars Dialogue of Roman Catholic Church and Southern Baptist Convention, 1985—.

MEMBER: Catholic Biblical Association of America (president, 1979), Catholic Theological Society of America, Society of Biblical Literature, National Council of Churches (Catholic member of Faith and Order Commission, 1970-73).

AWARDS, HONORS: Honorary Ph.D., Benedictine College, Atchison, Kan., 1970, and Rosary College, River Forest, Ill., 1987.

WRITINGS:

The Gospel of St. Luke, Liturgical Press, 1960, 2nd edition, 1964.
Leviticus, Paulist Press, 1960.
Postexilic Prophets, Paulist Press, 1961.
The Books of Aggai, Zacharia, Malachia, Jona, Joel, Abdia, with a Commentary, Paulist Press, 1961.
(Editor) Barnabas Ahern, New Horizons, Fides, 1963.
The Prophets and the Word of God, Fides, 1964, 2nd edition, 1966.
Book of Isaiah, Liturgical Press, 1964.
(Contributor) Jerome Biblical Commentary, Prentice-Hall, 1968.
Creative Redemption in Deutero-Isaiah, Biblical Institute Press, 1970.
The Books of Jeremiah and Baruch: Introduction and Commentary, Liturgical Press, 1971.
Prophets: Charismatic Men, Argus, 1972.
Biblical Inspiration: Divine-Human Phenomenon, Argus, 1972.
(Co-editor) The Bible Today Reader, Liturgical Press, 1973.

Reconciliation: A Biblical Call, Franciscan Herald, 1975.
Isaiah, Franciscan Herald, 1976.
Thirsting for the Lord: Essays in Biblical Spirituality, Alba House, 1977, 2nd edition, Doubleday, 1980.
The Psalms, Franciscan Herald, 1979.
Biblical Meditations for Lent, Paulist Press, 1979.
Biblical Meditations for the Easter Season, Paulist Press, 1980.
Biblical Meditations for Advent and the Christmas Season, Paulist Press, 1980.
Biblical Meditations for Ordinary Time, three volumes, Paulist Press, 1981.
(With Donald Senior) Biblical Foundations of Mission, Orbis, 1982.
The Psalms, two volumes, M. Glazier, 1983.
Amos, Hosea, Micah, Nahum, Habakkuk, Liturgical Press, 1986.

Also author of Haggai and Zechariah, 1988. Co-editor of Old Testament Reading Guide, Liturgical Press. Editor, with Martin McNamara, of "Old Testament Message" series, twenty-three volumes, Michael Glazier. Contributor to The New Catholic Encyclopedia, McGraw, 1966. Contributor to Catholic journals. Bible Today, member of editorial board, 1965-80, 85—, editor, 1980-84; member of editorial board, Catholic Biblical Quarterly, 1974-78, and Journal of Biblical Literature, 1987-91.

WORK IN PROGRESS: Introduction to the Old Testament; Bible for the Elderly; Sickness, Disability and Healing in Biblical Perspective.

SIDELIGHTS: Carroll Stuhlmueller told CA: "In getting older, my interest is shifting from more scientific, exegetical work to more popular writing on Biblical spirituality. In fact, as a long-term plan over the final years of my career with the Old Testament, a multi-volume piece on the Old Testament is being planned at a publisher's request."

T

TAYLOR, Bernard 1934-

PERSONAL: Born October 2, 1934, in Wiltshire, England; son of Albert Ernest (a cooper) and Edna (Tanner) Taylor. *Education:* Attended Swindon College of Art, 1956-58, and Chelsea College of Art, 1958-60; University of Birmingham, B.A. (honors), 1961.

ADDRESSES: Home—London, England. *Agent*—Curtis Brown Ltd., 162-168 Regent St., London W1R 5TA, England.

CAREER: Lived in the United States in the 1960s for six years, working as a teacher, a painter, a book illustrator, and then as an actor; since returning to England in 1969, has continued with his acting career; writer, 1969—. Playwright-in-residence at Queen's Theatre, Hornchurch, England, 1975-76. *Military service:* Royal Air Force, 1952-54.

AWARDS, HONORS: Most promising new playwright award, 1975, for "Mice on the First Floor"; *Cruelly Murdered: Constance Kent and the Killing at Road Hill House* was named one of the ten best books of 1979 by a *London Evening News* panel of critics; Gold Dagger Award for best nonfiction crime book, Crime Writers' Association, 1987, for *Perfect Murder: A Century of Unsolved Homicides*.

WRITINGS:

(Contributor) Mary Danby, editor, *Eighth Fontana Book of Horror*, Fontana, 1973.
(Contributor) Danby, editor, *Frighteners*, Fontana, 1974.
"Daughter of the Apaches" (two-act play), produced in Hornchurch, England, at Queen's Theatre, 1974.
"Mice on the First Floor" (three-act play), produced in Hornchurch at Queen's Theatre, 1975.
(Contributor) Richard Davis, editor, *Year's Best Horror Stories III*, DAW Books, 1975.
(Contributor) Danby, editor, *Frighteners II*, Fontana, 1976.
The Godsend (supernatural horror novel), St. Martin's, 1976.
Sweetheart, Sweetheart (supernatural horror novel), Souvenir Press, 1977, St. Martin's, 1978.
Cruelly Murdered: Constance Kent and the Killing at Road Hill House (nonfiction), Souvenir Press, 1979.
The Reaping, Souvenir Press, 1980.
The Moorstone Sickness (supernatural horror novel), St. Martin's, 1982.

(Contributor) Charles L. Grant, editor, *Dodd, Mead Gallery of Horror* (short story anthology), Dodd, 1983.
The Kindness of Strangers (psychological horror novel), St. Martin's, 1985.
(Contributor) Grant, editor, *After Midnight* (short story anthology), Tor Books, 1986.
Madeleine (psychological horror novel), Severn House, 1987.
(With Stephen Knight) *Perfect Murder: A Century of Unsolved Homicides* (nonfiction), Grafton & Co., 1987.
Mother's Boys (psychological horror novel), St. Martin's, 1988.
(With Kate Clarke) *Murder at the Priory: The Mysterious Poisoning of Charles Bravo* (nonfiction), Grafton & Co., 1988.
Wild Card (novel of the supernatural), Grafton & Co., in press.

Author of scripts for comedy series, "Maggie, It's Me!," for the British Broadcasting Corporation (BBC-TV). Contributor of illustrations to children's books and women's magazines, including *Harper's;* designer of cover for Dutch edition of own novel *The Godsend* and British edition of own novel *Sweetheart, Sweetheart.*

*　　*　　*

TEMPLE, Paul
See DURBRIDGE, Francis (Henry)

*　　*　　*

THOMAS, Anna (Irena) 1948-

PERSONAL: Born July 12, 1948, in Stuttgart, Germany (now West Germany); daughter of Jan and Aniela (Kozerski) Thomas; married Gregory Nava (a filmmaker). *Education:* University of California, Los Angeles, B.A., 1972.

ADDRESSES: Home—Ojai, Calif. *Agent*—International Creative Management, 40 West 57th St., New York, N.Y. 10019.

CAREER: Writer, director, and producer of films.

AWARDS, HONORS: Academy Award nomination for best original screenplay, 1985, for "El Norte."

WRITINGS:

SCREENPLAYS

(With husband, Gregory Nava) "The Confessions of Amans," Bauer International, 1977.

(With Nava; also producer) "El Norte," Cinecom International/Island Alive, 1984.

Also author, director, and producer of "The Haunting of M," 1979; also author of several other feature screenplays and of "An Old and Dear Friend" (short film).

OTHER

The Vegetarian Epicure, Knopf, Book I, 1972, Book II, 1978.

WORK IN PROGRESS: Writing and producing a new dramatic feature film, "Destiny" (tentative title).

SIDELIGHTS: "El Norte," co-written by Anne Thomas with her husband Gregory Nava (also the film's director), won critical acclaim in 1984 as a moving and authentic dramatization of the plight of a Guatemalan brother and sister who flee to the United States in search of a better life. The film follows the journey of the Guatemalans as they leave their politically oppressed native village, maneuver through the corrupt and dangerous atmosphere of a Mexican border town, and finally arrive in Southern California, which, as Annette Insdorf notes in the *New York Times,* is presented in the film as offering "exhilarating, confusing and often dehumanizing possibilities for illegal immigrants." The film examines the adjustment of the Guatemalans to their new life in America, ultimately focusing on their acceptance of what Kevin Thomas in the *Los Angeles Times* identifies as "the treacherousness of the American dream, where, in the struggle for survival, the individual is tempted increasingly to think only of himself." Vincent Canby in the *New York Times* states that "the real and most poignant point of 'El Norte' is . . . the ease and the eagerness with which, after their initial homesickness, [the Guatemalans] adapt themselves to the gringo world." While the film takes several opportunities to satirize American society, it also shows, according to Canby, how "the plastic society enchants." Nonetheless "El Norte" centers on the perspective of the immigrants in relating their experiences. Insdorf observes that "El Norte" is distinguished from many other American films that deal with Latin America, in that "Americans are peripheral to the action, and the United States is a foreign and exotic locale—traditional land of promise rather than the center and the point of reference."

"El Norte" was also noted for weaving together authentic cultural details such as native Indian dress, language, and religion, with various narrative techniques, approaching what Janet Maslin in the *New York Times* identified as "'the hallucinogenic realism' of modern Latin American fiction." Thomas elaborated on the cultural basis for this aspect of the film, telling Insdorf that "we didn't want 'El Norte' to look like a docu-drama, or have any stylistic elements that would remind people of journalism or 'rough-around-the-edges' documentary. The style we aimed for is the dream realism that comes from the Mayan culture." Thomas's and Nava's achievements in "El Norte" were noted by Gary Arnold in the *Washington Post* as revealing "filmmaking talent in the process of finding a distinctive look, voice and subject matter." Maslin also remarked that "a small, independently made film with the sweep of 'El Norte,' with solid, sympathetic performances by unknown actors and a visual style of astonishing vibrancy, must be regarded as a remarkable accomplishment." A number of reviewers named "El Norte" one of the best films of 1984.

In addition to her success as a filmmaker, and while enrolled in the film school of U.C.L.A., Thomas authored *The Vegetarian Epicure* cookbooks, the first of which was a bestseller

in the United States. Regarding these areas of her experience, Thomas once told *CA:* "I've been tremendously lucky to be able to make a living doing things that I really enjoy. My film work was a pure labor of love for some years, and is now paying dividends monetarily as well as aesthetically. But I was doubly fortunate: I was able to turn an avocation into a second career by writing cookbooks. My interest in food has provided me not only with many pleasant hours at the table with my friends, but through my books has also supported me during those rough early years of breaking into a film career. The success of these books has delighted me!" The first volume of *The Vegetarian Epicure* has been translated into Spanish, Dutch, and Japanese. Both volumes have been translated into German.

BIOGRAPHICAL/CRITICAL SOURCES:

PERIODICALS

Los Angeles Times, March 8, 1984.
New York Times, November 18, 1977, January 8, 1984, January 11, 1984, January 22, 1984.
Washington Post, April 7, 1984.

*　　*　　*

THOMAS, Jane Resh   1936-

PERSONAL: Born August 15, 1936, in Kalamazoo, Mich.; daughter of Reed Beneval (in sales) and Thelma (a teacher; maiden name, Scott) Resh; married Richard Thomas (a copywriter), November 13, 1961; children: Jason. *Education:* Bronson School of Nursing, R.N., 1957; attended Michigan State University, 1959-60; University of Minnesota, B.A. (summa cum laude), 1967, M.A., 1971.

ADDRESSES: Home—Minneapolis, Minn.

CAREER: Worked as registered nurse, 1957-60; University of Minnesota at Minneapolis, instructor in English composition, 1967-80; free-lance writer, 1972—. Instructor in writing children's fiction for various arts programs, 1983—; frequent guest lecturer, 1984—.

MEMBER: Phi Beta Kappa.

WRITINGS:

JUVENILE FICTION

Elizabeth Catches a Fish (juvenile), illustrated by Joseph Duffy, Seabury, 1977.
The Comeback Dog (Junior Literary Guild selection), illustrated by Troy Howell, Clarion, 1981.
Courage at Indian Deep, Clarion, 1984.
Wheels, illustrated by Emily McCully, Clarion, 1986.
Fox in a Trap, illustrated by Howell, Clarion, 1987.
Saying Good-bye to Grandma, Clarion, 1988.

Also author of "Children's Books," a regular column in the *Minneapolis Tribune.* Contributor of articles and reviews to periodicals, including *Hornbook Magazine* and *New York Times Book Review.*

SIDELIGHTS: Jane Resh Thomas's first book, *Elizabeth Catches a Fish,* is a simple story focusing on seven-year-old Elizabeth, who hooks a large bass while on a fishing outing with her father. According to Barbara Karlin of the *New York Times Book Review,* Thomas tells Elizabeth's story with "vivid clarity and precision."

The subject of Thomas's second book is of a more serious nature than her first. Daniel, a nine-year-old, is forced to deal with the death of Captain, his family's dog and the closest friend of Daniel, an only child growing up in the country. When Daniel finds an injured dog, he nurses it to health, but remains coolly aloof, afraid to get emotionally attached. The healed dog runs away, leaving Daniel daunted. But when the dog returns, Daniel resolves to adopt and care for it, despite the risk of being hurt once again. The *New York Times Book Review*'s Marjorie N. Allen wrote: "Mrs. Thomas has written a middle reader with substance—a rare achievement."

Thomas once told *CA:* "When I was a child in Kalamazoo, Michigan, my father bought an adult English setter named Bill, who flinched at every move we made as if he expected us to kick him. He couldn't be friendly to us until one day he came imploringly to my mother with pronged seeds in his eyes and sat patiently while she removed them with tweezers. After that he forgave us whatever wrongs others had done him and became one of the best dogs we ever had.

"Bill sometimes went with us to our grandparents' farm, a peach orchard and tree nursery near Lake Michigan. A creek, where Mother had hunted snakes when she was a girl, meandered across the meadow. One spring, after a flood had subsided, I found enough blue crayfish claws on the ground to fill a strawberry box. I kept them under our porch for a long time, even though they smelled bad, because they were beautiful.

"We spent weekends at a cottage on Big Cedar Lake, where our parents owned ten acres of land. In the swamp that bordered the lake, wild ladyslippers and rattlesnakes grew among poison sumac and watercress. One oak tree was so big that my brother and I couldn't reach around it, and so old it must have been growing when Indians lived nearby. I often fished with my father, who taught me to see what I looked at—the herons and loons that nested in the reeds, the mist that clung to the water at dawn, the dogwood and cattails, and the deer drinking at the spring at the first morning light that had appeared, it seemed, between one blink and another.

"When we were at home in Kalamazoo, my favorite place was the Washington Square Library, with its stone entryway, its fireplace and leaded windows, and what seemed like miles of books. I wrote to Maud Hart Lovelace once and received an answer. Busy though my mother was, raising four children with little except financial support from my father, she found time to read to us. I learned to love literature at her side. My family were uncommunicative people, and I relied on books, as I did on nature, not only to entertain but to sustain myself. For a brief, blissful time, we had a membership we could ill afford in the Junior Literary Guild. I remember my utter joy when books like *Big Tree* and *Bonnie's Boy* arrived in the mail.

"I have wanted to be a writer at least since I was seven years old, but was much discouraged by the conventional responses of adults to the things I wrote. The world has always been a wonder and a mystery to me. I write, as I read, in order to understand it and to find out what I think and feel. The dog, Bill, the farm, the crayfish claws, and the dawn-lit lake have come back to me in the stories that are in my head and on paper, even though I now live six hundred miles and twenty-five years from home. And although my father and grandparents died years ago, they have come back too. The oak tree fell in a storm a few years ago, but it lives again in my mind. They are all transformed, mixed with things and people that

never happened and never were, and blended with present events, like my son Jason's long effort to make friends with Rosie, the standoffish poodle we bought at the pound. Transformed though we are, I recognize all of us and the magical places I love in the stories that make my past present and my present comprehensible."

Thomas later wrote *CA:* "I find in retrospect that I have repeatedly been trying to say in most of my books what Dylan Thomas said in a poem: 'death shall have no dominion.'"

BIOGRAPHICAL/CRITICAL SOURCES:

Bulletin of the Center for Children's Books, November, 1977.
Horn Book, August, 1977, August, 1981.
Ms., December, 1978.
New York Times Book Review, May 1, 1977, May 10, 1981.
Publishers Weekly, February 28, 1977.

*   *   *

THOMAS, Victoria
See DeWEESE, Thomas Eugene

*   *   *

THOMSON, David (Robert Alexander)   1914-1988

PERSONAL: Born February 17, 1914, in Quetta, India (now Pakistan); died February, 1988; son of Alexander G. (an army officer) and Annie W. (a nurse; maiden name, Finlay) Thomson; married Martina Mayne (an art therapist); children: three sons. *Education:* Lincoln College, Oxford, B.A., 1936.

ADDRESSES: Home—22 Regent's Park Ter., London N.W. 1, England.

CAREER: Private tutor of history and English in County Roscommon, Ireland, 1932-43; British Broadcasting Corp., London, England, writer and producer in features department, 1943-69; writer, 1969-88.

MEMBER: Royal Society of Literature (honorary fellow), Society of Authors, Association on Broadcasting Standards, Zoological Society (London; associate), United Arts Club (Dublin), Chelsea Arts Club (London).

AWARDS, HONORS: McVities Award for Scottish Book of the Year, 1987, for *Nairn in Darkness and Light.*

WRITINGS:

The People of the Sea: A Journey in Search of the Seal Legend, Turnstile Press, 1954, John Day, 1955, 3rd edition, Granada, 1980.
Daniel (novel), Barrie & Rockliff, 1962.
Break in the Sun (novel), Barrie & Rockliff, 1965.
(With George Ewart Evans) *The Leaping Hare,* Faber, 1972.
Woodbrook, Barrie & Jenkins, 1974, Universe Books, 1976.
(Editor with Moyra McGusty) *The Irish Journals of Elizabeth Smith, 1840-1850: A Selection,* Oxford University Press, 1979.
In Camden Town (nonfiction), Hutchinson, 1983.
Dandiprat's Days (novel), Dent & Sons, 1983.
Nairn in Darkness and Light, Hutchinson, 1987.

FOR CHILDREN

Danny Fox, illustrated by Gunvor Edwards, Penguin, 1966.
Danny Fox Meets a Stranger, illustrated by Edwards, Penguin, 1968.

Danny Fox at the Palace, illustrated by Edwards, Puffin Books, 1976.
Ronan and Other Stories, Macmillan, 1984.

SIDELIGHTS: David Thompson once told *CA:* "My interests are in traditional lore, including folklore, storytelling, ballads and songs; in natural history and legends about animals; and in international culture, especially the literature of the U.S.S.R. and of czarist Russia, of France, Italy, Greece, and certain Latin American countries.

"My special love and knowledge is of Irish history, politics, and literature—perhaps because I know them better than and more intimately than I do anything else.

"The only literary prize I shall ever win was in 1921, when I was seven years old, for a short story in *Little Folks.*"

Thomson's interest in Ireland is particularly evident in *Woodbrook,* an account of his years as a family tutor on a decaying Irish estate (named Woodbrook) in County Roscommon. The book revolves around Thomson's love affair with one of the family daughters, Phoebe, in whom the author "loves the whole essence of Woodbrook," writes Roy Foster in the *Times Literary Supplement.* On this larger scale, Foster notes that *Woodbrook* "transmits . . . an almost painful nostalgia . . . [and] an extraordinarily vivid and particular picture of life in the Irish countryside a generation ago." Thomson draws heavily from various historical sources to accentuate his descriptions; in doing so, he "demonstrate[s] how attitudes and events from the past continue to affect the Irish present," remarks Caroline Blackwood in the *Listener.* "[Thomson] very brilliantly succeeds," Blackwood continues, "in making the reader feel that something personal and fresh is being said by an Englishman about that now rather over-covered subject, Ireland." Foster concludes that "*Woodbrook* is in many ways an admirable book, conveying an almost impossible *congeries* of autobiography, experience, pain and history."

Thomson's 1983 book *In Camden Town* likewise displays an affinity for history, although the setting is in the London district of Camden Town, Thomson's residence since 1956. A collection of journal entries that covers the period from August, 1980 to April, 1982, the book provides items of social commentary that offer glimpses into the district's working-class history. Thomson's sources are varied; in addition to citing historical information from books, he quotes a number of Camden Town's current inhabitants, in particular those on the margins of society. J. K. L. Walker notes in the *Times Literary Supplement* that "Thomson writes of the poor, the destitute, the disreputable, among whom he moves on easy terms, not with the bright professional concern of the social worker, but with [a] never-flagging curiosity and forbearance." Walker goes on to praise Thomson for the portrait he creates of Camden Town. "[The book] is characterized by precise observation of place and people and a tone of gentle, almost dreamy humanism that avoids sentimentality by a just adequate margin. . . . It is a distinguished addition to the literature of London."

BIOGRAPHICAL/CRITICAL SOURCES:

PERIODICALS

Choice, April, 1968.
Listener, December 12, 1974, October 13, 1983, October 20, 1983.

New Statesman, January 10, 1975, October 14, 1983.
Saturday Review, October 30, 1976.
Spectator, December 28, 1974, October 1, 1983.
Times Educational Supplement, December 30, 1983.
Times Literary Supplement, February 7, 1975, October 21, 1983.

OBITUARIES:

PERIODICALS

Times (London), March 1, 1988.†

*   *   *

THORNE, Nicola
   See ELLERBECK, Rosemary (Anne L'Estrange)

*   *   *

(al-)TIBAWI, A(bdul-)L(atif)   1910-1981

PERSONAL: Born April 29, 1910, in Taibeh, Palestine (now Israel); died in an accident, October 16, 1981, in London, England. *Education:* American University of Beirut, B.A., 1939, Ph.D., 1952, D.Lit., 1962.

ADDRESSES: Home—Sakeena, 7 Cranbrook Dr., Esher, Surrey, England. *Office*—Institute of Education, University of London, Malet St., London W.C.1, England.

CAREER: Held various administrative and academic posts in Palestine; worked for British Broadcasting Corp. (BBC) Arabic service; lecturer at University of London, Harvard University, and Institute of Education, University of London.

MEMBER: Arab Academy (Damascus).

WRITINGS:

Arab Education in Mandatory Palestine, Luzac, 1956.
British Interests in Palestine, 1800-1901, Oxford University Press, 1961.
Muhadarat fi Tarikh al-Arab wa al-Islam (lectures on the history of the Arabs and Islam), Dar al-Andalus (Beirut), Volume I, 1963, Volume II, 1966.
English-Speaking Orientalists, Islamic Centre (Geneva), 1965.
American Interests in Syria, 1800-1901, Clarendon Press, 1966.
A Modern History of Syria, Including Lebanon and Palestine, Macmillan, 1969.
Jerusalem: Its Place in Islam and Arab History (monograph), Institute of Palestinian Studies, 1969.
Islamic Education: Its Traditions and Modernization into the Arab National Systems, Luzac, 1972.
Arabic and Islamic Themes: Historical, Educational, and Literary Studies, Luzac, 1976.
Anglo-Arab Relations and the Question of Palestine, 1914-1921, Luzac, 1977.
The Islamic Pious Foundations in Jerusalem: Origins, History and Usurpation by Israel, Islamic Cultural Centre, 1978.
Second Critique of English-Speaking Orientalists: Their Approach to Islam and the Arabs, Islamic Cultural Centre, 1979.

Author of three pamphlets published by Luzac for Islamic Cultural Centre and Royal Central Asian Society; contributor to *American University of Beirut Festival Book,* 1967; contributor of more than forty articles and ninety reviews to British, European, American, and Middle Eastern journals.

OBITUARIES:

PERIODICALS

Muslim World, January 1, 1982.
Times (London), October 29, 1981.†

*   *   *

TICKLE, P(hyllis) A(lexander)   1934-

PERSONAL: Born March 12, 1934, in Johnson City, Tenn.; daughter of Philip Wade (an educator) and Katherine (Porter) Alexander; married Samuel Milton Tickle (a physician), June 17, 1955; children: Nora Katherine Cannon, Mary Gammon Clark, Laura Lee Goodman, John Crockett II, Philip Wade (deceased), Samuel Milton, Jr., Rebecca Rutledge. *Education:* Shorter College, student, 1951-54; East Tennessee State University, B.A., 1955; Furman University, M.A., 1961. *Religion:* Episcopalian.

ADDRESSES: Home—3522 Lucy Road S., Lucy, Tenn. 38053. *Office*—Suite 401, Mid-Memphis Tower, 1407 Union Ave., Memphis, Tenn. 38104.

CAREER: Furman University, Greenville, S.C., instructor in psychology, 1960-62; Southwestern at Memphis, Memphis, Tenn., instructor in English, 1962-65; Memphis Academy of Arts, Memphis, Tenn., teacher and dean of humanities, 1965-71; writer, 1971—. Poet in residence, Brooks Memorial, 1977—; poetry co-ordinator for Cumberland Valley Writers' Conference, 1977—. Member of Literary panel and artist-in-education panel, Tennessee Arts Commission; member of board of directors of Upward Bound at LeMoyne-Owen College, 1968-70, and Sunshine Day Care Center, 1970-71; member of board of trustees of Grace-St. Luke's Episcopal School, 1970-76; member of bishop's committee on abortion, 1987—.

MEMBER: Tennessee Humanities Council (member of executive board, 1987—), Tennessee Literary Arts Association (former vice-president for western Tennessee), Publishers Association of the South (president, 1984-85; member of executive board, 1985—), Committee of Small Magazine Editors and Publishers.

AWARDS, HONORS: Tickle's narrative poem "American Genesis" was selected by Tennessee's American Bicentennial Commission as a bicentennial poem for the state, 1976; individual fellowship in literature, Tennessee Arts Commission, 1984; Polly Bond Award, 1985.

WRITINGS:

An Introduction to the Patterns of Indo-European Speech, Memphis Academy of Arts, 1968.
Figs and Fury (a chancel play; first produced in Memphis, Tenn. at Grace-St. Luke Episcopal Church), St. Luke's Press, 1974, 2nd edition, 1976.
It's No Fun to Be Sick (juvenile), St. Luke's Press, 1976.
The Story of Two Johns (for children facing the loss of a loved one), St. Luke's Press, 1976.
On Beyond Koch, Brooks Memorial, 1980.
On Beyond Ais, Tennessee Arts Commission, 1982.
Puppeteers for Our Lady, St. Michael's Church, 1982.
The City Essays, Dixie Flyer Press, 1982.
What the Heart Already Knows, Upper Room, 1985.
Final Sanity, Upper Room, 1987.
Ordinary Times, Upper Room, 1988.
Growing Up Tickled, Abingdon, in press.

CONTRIBUTOR TO ANTHOLOGIES

Contemporary Poets of the New South, Brevity Press, 1977.
The Good People of Gomorrah, St. Luke's Press, 1979.
Tigris and Euphrates, St. Luke's Press, 1979.
Windflower Almanac, Windflower Press, 1980.
Womanblood, Continuing Saga, 1981.

OTHER

Columnist for *Dixie Flyer* and *Feminist Digest*, 1975-78, and for *Church News;* poetry editor, *Chaff*, 1978; founding editor, St. Luke's Press, managing editor, 1975-83, senior editor, 1983—; member of editorial board, *Church News*, 1986—; secretary of the board, Raccoon Books, a tax-exempt sister house to St. Luke's Press. Has contributed poems to periodicals, including *Images, Nexus*, and *Velvet Wings*. Contributor of articles and reviews to magazines.

WORK IN PROGRESS: A young adult fantasy; a book of nonfiction on aging; a series of murder mysteries.

SIDELIGHTS: P. A. Tickle writes: "I lecture a great deal and find this a most satisfying experience. I think of myself as a poetess by trade, but having had seven children has also given me some kind of background for enjoying children's literature and I am finding that rewarding also. Spanish is my language of choice and all things Mexican and/or Spanish are as natural to me as breathing.

"The women's movement comes at a time when being a wife, mother, and writer is no longer regarded as natural, but rather as a social statement or a private protest. Within the framework of all these factors, I find myself drawn more and more toward the ancients—to the works and values of Sappho and Catullus—to Cavafy and Rilke in our own time, and always, to Eliot."

*   *   *

TIEDT, Iris M(cClellan)   1928-

PERSONAL: Surname rhymes with "bead"; born February 3, 1928, in Dayton, Ohio; daughter of Raymond Hill (an engineer) and Ermalene (Swartzel) McClellan; married Sidney W. Tiedt (a college professor), September 17, 1949 (divorced, 1978); children: Pamela Lynne, Ryan Sidney. *Education:* Northwestern University, B.S., 1950; University of Orgeon, M.A., 1961; Stanford University, Ph.D., 1972. *Politics:* Democrat.

ADDRESSES: Home—1654 Fairorchard Ave., San Jose, Calif. 95125. *Office*—San Jose State University, San Jose, Calif. 95192.

CAREER: Language arts teacher in Chicago, Ill., 1950-51, Kenai, Alaska, 1951-52, and Anchorage, Alaska, 1953-57; University of Oregon, Eugene, teaching fellow and supervisor of student teaching, 1959-61; Roosevelt Junior High School, Eugene, English teacher, 1961; University of Santa Clara, Santa Clara, Calif., director of teacher education, 1968-72, director of graduate reading program, 1972-75; San Jose State University, San Jose, Calif., director of South Bay Writing Project, 1977—.

MEMBER: American Association of University Women (life membership), Modern Language Association, National Council of Teachers of English, National Organization for Women, National Women's Political Caucus, Sierra Club (life membership), Stanford Alumni Association (life membership), California Association of Teachers of English, Pi Lambda, Sigma Delta Pi.

WRITINGS:

Bulletin Board Captions, Contemporary Press, 1964, revised edition, 1965.

Opening Classrooms and New Ways with Individualization, National Council of Teachers of English, 1973.

Women and Girls, National Council of Teachers of English, 1973.

(Editor) *Drama in Your Classroom,* National Council of Teachers of English, 1974.

(Editor) *What's New in Reading,* National Council of Teachers of English, 1974.

Sexism in Education, General Learning Press, 1974.

Books/Literature/Children, Houghton, 1975, third edition published as *The Language Arts Handbook,* 1981.

Effective English (sixth grade textbook), Silver Burdett, 1978.

Exploring Books with Children, Houghton, 1979.

(With daughter, Pamela Tiedt) *Multicultural Teaching: A Handbook of Activities, Information, and Resources,* Allyn & Bacon, 1979.

The Writing Process: Composition and Applied Grammar (tenth grade textbook), Allyn & Bacon, 1981.

Elements of English (tenth grade textbook), Allyn & Bacon, 1982.

The Time Has Come . . . to Focus on Writing, Prentice-Hall, 1982.

Writing Strategies for 1-8 Classrooms, Fearon, 1982.

(With Suzanne Bruemmer, Sheila Lane, Patricia Stelwagon, Kathleen Watanabe, and Mary Young Williams) *Teaching Writing in K-8 Classrooms,* Prentice-Hall, 1983.

The Language Arts Handbook, Prentice-Hall, 1983.

(With Nora Ho, Lisa Johnson, and Williams) *Lessons from a Writing Project,* three volumes, David Lake, 1987.

Catching the Writing Express, David Lake, 1987.

Enjoying the Written Word, David Lake, 1987.

Learning to Use Written Language, David Lake, 1987.

(With Jo Ellen Carlson, Bert Howard, and Watanabe) *Teaching Thinking across the Grades: A Handbook of Activities, Information, and Resources,* Allyn & Bacon, 1988.

Reading, Thinking, and Writing: A Holistic Language and Literacy Program, Allyn & Bacon, 1988.

Evaluating Writing: A Student-centered Approach, Allyn & Bacon, 1988.

(With P. Tiedt) *Discovering English Grammar* (teacher's handbook and student textbooks, grades 1-8), David Lake, 1988.

(With Carlson, Shirley Haymond, Josephine Lugo, and Mary Ann Simpson) *Making Connections,* Houghton, in press.

WITH SIDNEY W. TIEDT

Unrequired Reading: An Annotated Bibliography for Teachers and School Administrators, Oregon State University Press, 1963, 2nd edition, 1967.

Creative Writing Ideas, Contemporary Press, 1963, revised edition, 1964.

Exploring Words, Contemporary Press, 1963, published as *Exciting Reading Activities,* c. 1975.

Imaginative Social Studies Activities for the Elementary School, Prentice-Hall, 1964.

Selected Free Materials, Contemporary Press, 1964.

Elementary Teacher's Complete Ideas Handbook, Prentice-Hall, 1965.

Contemporary English in the Elementary School, Prentice-Hall, 1967, 2nd edition, 1975.

(Compilers) *Readings on Contemporary English in the Elementary School,* Prentice-Hall, 1967.

Language Arts Activities for the Classroom, Allyn & Bacon, 1978, 2nd edition, 1987.

Language Arts Activities: A Handbook of Activities, Information, and Resources, Allyn & Bacon, 1987.

OTHER

Co-editor, "Contemporary Classics" series, Contemporary Press. Author of syndicated column, "An Open Letter to Women," 1981—. Contributor to professional journals, including *Instructor, Childhood Education,* and *Elementary English.* Editor, *Language Arts,* 1972-76, and *Elementary English,* 1972—.

SIDELIGHTS: Iris M. Tiedt told *CA:* "I write because I want to have an impact on what is happening in the world today. I am concerned, for example, about the role of women, the politics of feminism, and the values that are imposed on girls from birth.

"I grew up with an 'I can' attitude, and I wonder why. I am working toward developing that kind of attitude for all children as they discover their potential. Children need self-esteem in order to learn. It is we adults who injure that self-esteem when children are quite young, so it is we adults who must change our ways of relating to children. This is the kind of thing I write about.

"I learned to write by writing, and I did not begin seriously until I was thirty-five. I see writing as a wonderful form of therapy, and I recommend keeping journals and writing about experiences that may be painful. I also recommend sharing these writings with others who are also writing as a way of expressing and relating these emotions and gaining support from understanding human beings. I teach a course called 'Women by the Sea' which meets at Asilomar, a resort by the ocean in California, where we spend the weekend writing and sharing our writing. It is exhilarating!

"We need to know much more about teaching writing in order to encourage students to write effectively. We still have many misperceptions that get in the way of really communicating through writing. We focus on error avoidance—grammar, spelling, and penmanship—and think we are teaching writing. Writing begins with ideas. We need to begin with thinking and talking about ideas. Communicating these ideas will lead children to write and to savor the excitement of turning out a well-stated argument or describing a peak experience in poetry."

AVOCATIONAL INTERESTS: The arts, writing poetry and stories, designing original rugs, wordplay, swimming, skiing.

*   *   *

TIEDT, Sidney W(illis) 1927-

PERSONAL: Surname rhymes with "bead"; born August 15, 1927, in Chicago, Ill; son of Harry W. and Jeanette U. (Ryan) Tiedt; married Iris McClellan (a professor), September 17, 1949 (divorced); children: Pamela Lynne, Ryan Sidney. *Education:* Northwestern University, B.S., 1950, M.A., 1953; University of Oregon, Ed.D., 1961. *Politics:* Democrat.

ADDRESSES: Office—San Jose State University, San Jose, Calif. 95192.

CAREER: Teacher in Illinois and Alaska, 1950-56; commercial salmon fisherman in Alaska, summers, 1953-55; Anchorage (Alaska) Independent School District, principal, 1956-59; with University of Orgeon, Eugene, 1959-61; San Jose State University, San Jose, Calif., professor of education, 1961—. Director, National Defense Education Act Contemporary English Institute, 1965. Consultant and evaluator of English programs, Fresno School District and Oakland, Calif., 1968; consultant, Department of Education, Commonwealth of the North Marianas Islands, Saipan. *Military service:* U.S. Navy, 1945-46.

MEMBER: American Educational Research Association, National Council of Teachers of English, Phi Delta Kappa.

WRITINGS:

Quotes for Teaching, Contemporary Press, 1964.
The Role of the Government in Education, Oxford University Press, 1966.
(With Lowell G. Kieth) *Contemporary Curriculum in the Elementary School,* Harper, 1968, 2nd edition, 1974.
(Editor) *Teaching the Disadvantaged Child,* Oxford University Press, 1968.
Creativity in the Classroom, General Learning, 1974.

WITH IRIS M. TIEDT

Unrequired Reading: An Annotated Bibliography for Teachers and School Administrators, Oregon State University Press, 1963, 2nd edition, 1967.
Creative Writing Ideas, Contemporary Press, 1963, revised edition, 1964.
Exploring Words, Contemporary Press, 1963, published as *Exciting Reading Activities,* c. 1975.
Imaginative Social Studies Activities for the Elementary School, Prentice-Hall, 1964.
Selected Free Materials, Contemporary Press, 1964.
Elementary Teacher's Complete Ideas Handbook, Prentice-Hall, 1965.
Contemporary English in the Elementary School, Prentice-Hall, 1967, 2nd edition, 1975.
(Compilers) *Readings on Contemporary English in the Elementary School,* Prentice-Hall, 1967.
Language Arts Activities for the Classroom, Allyn & Bacon, 1978, 2nd edition, 1987.
Language Arts Activities: A Handbook of Activities, Information, and Resources, Allyn & Bacon, 1987.

OTHER

Co-editor, ''Contemporary Classroom Series,'' Contemporary Press, ''The Elementary Teacher's Ideas and Materials Workshop'' series, Parker Publishing, 1968—, and ''Contemporary Education Foundation Series,'' General Learning, 1974. Contributor to *Instructor, Clearing House,* and other professional journals.

WORK IN PROGRESS: New editions of *The Elementary Teacher's Complete Ideas Handbook,* Prentice-Hall, and *Language Arts Activities for the Classroom,* Allyn & Bacon; ''presently working on a book in the field of reading for Scott Foresman.''

SIDELIGHTS: Sidney W. Tiedt told *CA:* ''Some of the best writing being done is in the area of nonfiction. People are interested in how things work. I am interested in how our language works and most of my writing has been in that field. I also feel strongly that writing, research and teaching go together. I see writing as a way of extending my teaching. My major goals in life are to become a better teacher and to enjoy life as long as possible.''†

*   *   *

TOOLEY, M. J.
    See TOOLEY, Michael J(ohn)

*   *   *

TOOLEY, Michael J(ohn)   1942-
    (M. J. Tooley)

PERSONAL: Born December 17, 1942, in Barnstaple, England; son of William Alfred (a chartered structural engineer) and Lynda Isis (Bedford) Tooley; married Rosanna Mary Mellor (an artist), September 5, 1973; children: Nicholas William, Anna Catharina Mary. *Education:* University of Birmingham, B.A., 1965; attended Columbia University, 1965-66; University of Lancaster, Ph.D., 1969. *Religion:* Church of England.

ADDRESSES: Home—The Old Vicarage, Witton-le-Wear, County Durham DL14 0AN, England. *Office*—Department of Geography, University of Durham, South Rd., Durham DH1 3LE, England.

CAREER: University of Durham, Durham, England, lecturer, 1969-79, tutor at St. Aidan's College, 1973—, senior lecturer in geography, 1979—, reader in geography, 1987—. British representative to UNESCO's International Geological Correlation Programme Project, 1976—. Trustee of the Durham Research Trust.

MEMBER: Royal Geographical Society (fellow), British Ecological Society, Friends of Durham University Botanic Garden (chairman).

AWARDS, HONORS: Fulbright fellow in the United States, 1965-66.

WRITINGS:

(Editor with Clarence Kidson) *The Quaternary History of the Irish Sea,* Wiley, 1977.
(Under name M. J. Tooley) *Sea-Level Changes,* Clarendon Press, 1978.
(Editor, under name M. J. Tooley, with I. G. Simmons) *The Environment in British Prehistory,* Cornell University Press, 1981.
(With wife, Rosanna M. Tooley) *The Gardens of Gertrude Jekyll in Northern England,* Michaelmas, 1982.
(Editor with Gillian M. Sheail) *The Climatic Scene,* Allen & Unwin, 1984.
Gertrude Jekyll: Artist, Gardener, Craftswoman, Michaelmas, 1985.

Editor of information bulletin of UNESCO's International Geological Correlation Programme Project; editor of *Journal of Durham University Botanic Garden.*

SIDELIGHTS: Michael J. Tooley told *CA:* ''My work, writings, and interests are eclectic. It was perhaps inevitable that I developed an interest in coastal and sea-level changes because I was born and brought up close to the coast of North Devon, England, and went to school on the Lancashire coast at a site only a few meters above sea-level. The coast and the sea have made a strong impression on me, as they have on countless generations of this island people—from Great Tooley of Ipswich onwards. My work on coastal and sea-level changes [has] both an academic and a practical value: the former to know the position of sea-levels and the dilation and contraction of the seas; the latter to know man's response and adaption to these changes in prehistoric, historic, and present times. Human settlements are densely concentrated along estuaries and the world's coastlines: what would the impact be on them of a rise in sea-level of five meters?

"I am interested in the history of landscapes and the impact of prehistoric and historic man on the biosphere. Time and space perspectives have largely been forgotten, and we need to regain a sense of time and place that history, prehistory, and geography teach us. Landscape history can be brought right up to the present century, and the life and work of Gertrude Jekyll has been a continuing inspiration: she was concise and economical in her use of language, inventive and innovative in her craftwork and gardening, and full of wit and a joy for life and living things."

BIOGRAPHICAL/CRITICAL SOURCES:

PERIODICALS

Times Literary Supplement, December 23, 1983.

*   *   *

TRACY, Honor (Lilbush Wingfield) 1913-

PERSONAL: Born October 19, 1913, in Bury St. Edmunds, East Anglia, England; daughter of Humphrey Ernest Wingfield (a surgeon) and Christabel May Clare (Miller) Tracy. *Education:* Educated privately in London, England.

ADDRESSES: Home—The Flat, Walmer Lodge, Hanley Swan, Worcester, England.

CAREER: Simpkin Marshall Ltd. (publishers), London, England, general assistant, 1934-37; free-lance writer, 1937-39; Ministry of Information, London, Japanese specialist, 1941-45; *Observer,* London, special correspondent, 1946, 1947-48 (from Japan in 1947); *Sunday Times,* London, Dublin correspondent, 1950; British Broadcasting Corp., Third Programme, contributor of talks and features, 1950-68, roving correspondent, 1951-52; novelist, 1954—. *Military service:* British Women's Auxiliary Air Force, Intelligence, 1939-41; became sergeant.

AWARDS, HONORS: Award from British Writers Guild, 1968, for radio feature script "Sorrows of Ireland."

WRITINGS:

(Translator) B. de Ligt, *The Conquest of Violence,* Dutton, 1937.
Kakemono: A Sketch Book of Post-War Japan, Methuen, 1950.
Mind You, I've Said Nothing!: Forays in the Irish Republic (essays), Methuen, 1953, British Book Centre, 1958, reprinted, White Lion, 1973.
Silk Hats and No Breakfast: Notes on a Spanish Journey, Methuen, 1957, Random House, 1958.
Spanish Leaves, Random House, 1964.
Winter in Castille, Methuen, 1973, Random House, 1975.
The Heart of England, Hamish Hamilton, 1983.

FICTION

The Deserters, Methuen, 1954.
The Straight and Narrow Path, 1956, Random House, 1957, reprinted, White Lion, 1971.
The Prospects Are Pleasing, Random House, 1958, reprinted, White Lion, 1973.

A Number of Things, Random House, 1960.
A Season of Mists, Random House, 1961.
The First Day of Friday, Random House, 1963.
Men at Work, Methuen, 1966, Random House, 1967.
The Beauty of the World, Methuen, 1967, published as *Settled in Chambers,* Random House, 1968.
The Butterflies of the Province, Random House, 1970.
The Quiet End of Evening, Random House, 1972.
In a Year of Grace, Random House, 1975.
The Man from Next Door, Random House, 1977.
The Ballad of Castle Reef, Random House, 1979.

Contributor of short stories to anthologies, including *Winter Tales 22* and *Best Love Stories,* and to periodicals, including *Atlantic, Harper's Bazaar, Mademoiselle, Horizon, Lilliput, Queen,* and *New Statesman.* Contributor to *Daily Telegraph,* 1973—.

WORK IN PROGRESS: A novel entitled *Darling Buds.*

SIDELIGHTS: Honor Tracy is well known as both a novelist and a travel writer. She has written extensively about traveling in Spain, much to the delight of critics who praise the wit and charm of these nonfiction accounts. Of her fictive efforts, however, reviewers are more critical. Though she aims at satire, critics maintain that she frequently misses her mark, particularly in her later novels which poke fun at British-Irish antagonisms.

A case in point is Tracy's tenth novel, *The Man from Next Door.* Set in London, the story pits a naive English schoolmistress against an unscrupulous Irishman. "The result," observes *America* reviewer Terrence A. McVeigh, "is a totally uneven contest and a nasty little story of victim and victimizer. So biased is the characterization that it is difficult not to interpret the tale as blatant chauvinism." Valerie Boylan, however, suggests in the *Dictionary of Literary Biography* that the novel satirizes both "a romantic genre of writing and . . . the types of Englishness and Irishness that are most annoying and baffling to the Irish and the English respectively." McVeigh concludes that the stereotyping of the Irish bank clerk as "instinctively hostile to all things British," including his hapless victim, works against the novel's early promise of suspense. Instead of satire, the result is pathos that evokes "pity rather than amusement or scorn." Boylan observes, though, that "as well as providing in her Irish novels a satirical view of Ireland as a corrective to the patriotic romantic works of the Anglo-Irish renaissance, perhaps the greatest contribution of [Tracy's] other novels lies in the guide that they offer the sensible person to the bewildering England of the post-World War II era."

AVOCATIONAL INTERESTS: International travel, music, wildlife, gardening.

BIOGRAPHICAL/CRITICAL SOURCES:

BOOKS

Dictionary of Literary Biography, Volume XV: *British Novelists, 1930-1959,* Gale, 1983.
Ginden, James, *Postwar British Fiction: New Accents and Attitudes,* University of California Press, 1962.

PERIODICALS

America, March 4, 1978, February 2, 1980.
National Observer, August 12, 1968.
New York Times, December 26, 1979.

New York Times Book Review, March 10, 1968, May 8, 1977. *Time,* April 5, 1968.

*   *   *

TRUBY, J(ohn) David 1938-

PERSONAL: Born April 17, 1938, in Bellefonte, Pa.; son of John H.(a bank executive) and Mable (Fiscus) Truby; married Nancy Berg (a teacher), June 11, 1962; children: Christopher Scott. *Education:* Pennsylvania State University, B.A., 1960, M.A., 1962, Ph.D., 1970. *Politics:* Republican.

ADDRESSES: Home—P.O. Box 163, Shelocta, Pa. 15774. *Office*—Department of Journalism, Indiana University of Pennsylvania, Indiana, Pa. 15705.

CAREER: Centre Film Laboratory, State College, Pa., advertising director, 1959-60; WMAJ-Radio, State College, member of news staff, 1961-62; Clarion State College, Clarion, Pa., director of public relations, 1962-65; Barash Advertising, State College, senior copywriter, 1965-67; free-lance writer, 1967-69; Indiana University of Pennsylvania, Indiana, associate professor, 1969-73, professor of journalism, 1973—; editor for National News Service, 1984—. *Military service:* U.S. Army, Intelligence, 1960-61; became sergeant.

MEMBER: Alpha Delta Sigma, Alpha Phi Gamma, Sigma Delta Chi.

AWARDS, HONORS: Pennsylvania Newspaper Publishers Association Press Column Award, 1971; *Fifth Estate* writing awards, 1971, 1974; First Place Writing Award from Foreign Policy Council of Washington, 1982.

WRITINGS:

Advertising for You, MacMurray Publishers, 1965.
(With Elwood Murray and Gerald M. Phillips) *Speech: Science/Art,* Bobbs-Merrill, 1969.
Silencers, Snipers and Assassins: An Overview of Whispering Death, Paladin Press, 1972.
The Quiet Killers, Paladin Press, 1972.
Improvised-Modified Firearms, Paladin Press, 1974.
Paladin's Pictorial History of the Lewis Gun, Paladin Press, 1976.
Women at War: A Deadly Species, Paladin Press, 1977.
How Terrorists Kill: The Complete Terrorist Arsenal, Paladin Press, 1978.
Quiet Killers II: Silencer Update, edited by Devon Christensen, Paladin Press, 1979.
Silencers in the 1980s: Great Designs, Great Designers, Paladin Press, 1984.

Also author of books under various pseudonyms. Contributor of nearly five hundred articles to magazines.

WORK IN PROGRESS: A book on American POW/MIAs in the Soviet Union.

*   *   *

TRYPANIS, C(onstantine) A(thanasius) 1909-

PERSONAL: Born January 22, 1909, in Chios, Greece; son of Athanasius G. and Maria (Zolota) Trypanis; married Aliki Macris, April 6, 1941; children: Marilena. *Education:* University of Athens, M.A., 1930, D. Phil., 1937; graduate study at University of Berlin, 1933-35, and University of Munich, 1935-38; Oxford University, M.A., 1946. *Religion:* Greek Orthodox.

ADDRESSES: Home—3 George Nikolaou, Kefisia, Athens, Greece.

CAREER: University of Athens, Athens, Greece, lecturer in classics, 1939-47; Oxford University, Oxford, England, Bywater and Southeby Professor of Byzantine and Modern Greek Literature and Language and fellow of Exeter College, 1947-68, emeritus fellow, 1968—; University of Chicago, Chicago, Ill., University Professor of Classics, 1968-74; Government of Greece, Athens, Minister of Culture and Science, 1974-77. Archon Hieromnemon of Oecumenical Patriarchate, 1964—. Visiting professor at Hunter College of the City University of New York, 1963, Harvard University, summer, 1963, 1964, University of Chicago, 1965-66, University of Vienna, 1971, and University of Sydney, 1979. Member of Institute for Advanced Study, Princeton University, 1959-60. *Military service:* Greek Army, Infantry, 1939-41; became lieutenant.

MEMBER: International Poetry Society (fellow), Royal Society of Literature (fellow), Oxford Philological Society, British Classical Association, British Academy (fellow), Medieval Academy of America, Institute for Balkan Studies, Academy of Athens (president), Athenaeum Club (London), Athens Lawn Tennis Club, Oxford University Lawn Tennis and Croquet Club.

AWARDS, HONORS: Koraes Prize, Academy of Athens, 1933; Heinemann Award, 1959, for *Cocks of Hades;* Herter Prize from University of Vienna; D.Litt., Oxford University, 1972; D.H.L. from Assumption College and MacMurray College; Ordre des Arts et Lettres; Ordre National du Merite.

WRITINGS:

The Influence of Hesiod upon the Homeric Hymn on Hermes, Leones (Athens), 1939.
The Influence of Hesiod upon the Homeric Hymn on Apollo, Leones (Athens), 1939.
Alexandria Poetry, Garouphalias (Athens), 1943.
(Compiler) *Medieval and Modern Greek Poetry,* Clarendon Press, 1951, reprinted, 1968.
Callimachus, Loeb, 1958, 2nd edition (with Thomas Gelzer), 1975.
(Editor with Paul Maas) *Sancti Romani Melodi Cantica,* Volume I: *Cantica Genuina,* Clarendon Press, 1963, Volume II: *Cantica Dubia,* Walter de Gruyter (Berlin), 1970, both volumes published as *Cantica,* Clarendon Press, 1970.
(Compiler) *Fourteen Early Byzantine Cantica,* Boehlau in Kommission, 1968.
(Editor and author of introduction) *The Penguin Book of Greek Verse,* Penguin, 1971.
The Homeric Epics, International Scholarly Book, 1977.
Greek Poetry: From Homer to Seferis, University of Chicago Press, 1982.
Sophocles' Three Theban Plays, Aris & Phillips, 1986.

POETRY

Tartessos, Aetos (Athens), 1945.
Pedasus, School of Art, University of Reading, 1955.
Stones of Troy (also see below; Poetry Book Society selection), Faber, 1956.
Cocks of Hades (also see below), Faber, 1958.
Grooves in the Wind (includes *Stones of Troy* and *Cocks of Hades*), Chilmark Press, 1964.
Pompeian Dog (Poetry Book Society selection), Faber, 1964, Chilmark Press, 1965.
The Elegies of a Glass Adonis (long poem), Chilmark Press, 1967.

The Glass Adonis, Faber, 1972, Chilmark Press, 1973.
Skias Onar, Hestia, 1986.

OTHER

Also author of plays *Prosfiges*, 1984. Translator of Aeschylus's *Persians* and Sophocles's *Oedipus Rex, Oedipus at Colonus*, and *Electra* for British Broadcasting Corp. Contributor to *Encyclopaedia Britannica, Chambers's Encyclopaedia, Encyclopaedia Hebraica, Encyclopaedia of Poetry and Poetics, Oxford Classical Dictionary*, and *Die Religion in Geschichte und Gegenwart*. Contributor of articles and reviews to periodicals, including *Times Literary Supplement, Classical Review, Greece and Rome, Hermes, Byzantinische Zeitschrift, Journal of Hellenic Studies, Gnomon, Medium Aevum, Balkan Studies, Athena, Oxford Magazine*, and *Studies in Eastern Chant*.

SIDELIGHTS: C. A. Trypanis told *CA:* "I work for many hours every day, but I never 'sit down to write poetry.' That urge comes suddenly and unexpectedly—a picture, a tune, a memory, practically anything can produce it—and I have to put aside no matter what I am doing and write my lines. Later I correct them, but nearly never change them completely."

A native of Greece who writes poetry in English, Trypanis "has an impeccable ear for the rhythms of a language that is not his own," writes Charles Higham in the *Sydney Morning Herald*. According to E. G. Burrows in *Poetry*, it was "this care for his adopted language, his fine control of line and the form of a poem, which, undoubtedly, prompted Theodore Roethke to recommend Trypanis to the [student of poetry]." His poems, notes William Jay Smith in *Harper's*, "have the discipline and surface simplicity of those of Robert Graves, but one is conscious always of a sharp and subtle mind at work." Reviewing *Pompeian Dog* in *Books Abroad*, Guy Owen believes that Trypanis reminds one of the Greek masters "in his compression, lucidity, and balance, as well as in his epigrammatic quality."

Owen points out that though Trypanis's work is not yet widely known in America, it should be, "now that American poetry seems to be given over to a cult of personality, to poems about personal crisis." A *Cambridge Review* critic explains: "[Trypanis] does not allow the harsher preoccupations of the twentieth-century West to intrude into his lovely Aegean world. . . . If [he] is influenced by Nietzsche or Freud or Sartre, he is very skillful in concealing the fact. His only purpose is to describe, for his own enjoyment and ours, the enchanting things with which memory or his reading fills his mind. He is intoxicated by beauty. He almost gives us too much of it, like one who has come into possession of a vast treasure and scatters it abroad with prodigal generosity."

Calling Trypanis's more recent book, *Greek Poetry: From Homer to Seferis* "a massive and memorable work of original character," Michael Grant observes in the *New York Times Book Review*, "It covers the achievements of the ancient, medieval and modern Greeks in a single volume and as a single field of study." Because neither ancient nor modern Greek is a widely-known language, Grant indicates that while a verse translation is superior to a prose translation in conveying "to some extent, the breathtaking excitement that Greek poetry of many periods generates," the reader must rely upon "description and explanation" in order to understand the meaning of these poems. "And in this book," says Grant, "there is an abundance of both, judiciously selected and presented."

AVOCATIONAL INTERESTS: Walking, tennis, painting.

BIOGRAPHICAL/CRITICAL SOURCES:

PERIODICALS

Books Abroad, winter, 1967.
Cambridge Review, June 5, 1965.
Harper's, August, 1965.
New York Times Book Review, January 9, 1983.
Partisan Review, summer, 1968.
Poetry, December, 1964.
Sydney Morning Herald, October 12, 1952.
Times (London), December 31, 1981.
Times Literary Supplement, October 14, 1955, November 5, 1964, May 21, 1982.

*   *   *

TUCHMAN, Barbara (Wertheim) 1912-

PERSONAL: Born January 30, 1912, in New York, N.Y.; daughter of Maurice (a banker) and Alma (Morgenthau) Wertheim; married Lester R. Tuchman (a physician), 1940; children: Lucy, Jessica, Alma. *Education:* Radcliffe College, B.A., 1933.

ADDRESSES: Agent—Timothy Seldes, Russell & Volkening, Inc., 50 West 29th St., New York, N.Y. 10001.

CAREER: Institute of Pacific Relations, New York City, research and editorial assistant, 1933-35; *Nation*, New York City, staff writer and foreign correspondent, 1935-37, correspondent in Madrid, 1937, correspondent in the United States, 1939; Office of War Information, New York City, editor, 1943-45. Trustee, Radcliffe College, 1960-72. Appointed Jefferson Lecturer for the National Endowment for the Humanities, 1980. Lecturer at Harvard University, University of California, U.S. Naval War College, and other institutions.

MEMBER: Society of American Historians (president, 1970-73), Authors Guild (treasurer), Authors League of America (member of council), American Academy of Arts and Letters (president, 1979—), American Academy of Arts and Sciences, Cosmopolitan Club.

AWARDS, HONORS: Pulitzer Prize, 1963, for *The Guns of August*, and 1972, for *Stilwell and the American Experience in China, 1911-1945;* gold medal for history, American Academy of Arts and Sciences, 1978; Regent Medal of Excellence, University of the State of New York, 1984; Sarah Josepha Hale Award, 1985; Abraham Lincoln Literary Award, Union League Club, 1985; received Order of Leopold from the Kingdom of Belgium; D.Litt. from Yale University, Columbia University, New York University, Williams College, University of Massachusetts, Smith College, Hamilton College, Mount Holyoke College, Boston University, Harvard University, and other schools.

WRITINGS:

The Lost British Policy: Britain and Spain since 1700, United Editorial, 1938.
Bible and Sword: England and Palestine from the Bronze Age to Balfour, New York University Press, 1956.
The Zimmermann Telegram, Viking, 1958, new edition, Macmillan, 1966.
The Guns of August (Book-of-the-Month Club selection), Macmillan, 1962 (published in England as *August, 1914*, Constable, 1962).

The Proud Tower: A Portrait of the World before the War, 1890-1914 (Book-of-the-Month Club selection), Macmillan, 1966.

Stilwell and the American Experience in China, 1911-1945 (Book-of-the-Month Club selection), Macmillan, 1971 (published in England as *Sand against the Wind: Stilwell and the American Experience in China, 1911-1945*, Macmillan [London], 1971).

Notes from China, Collier Books, 1972.

A Distant Mirror: The Calamitous Fourteenth Century, Knopf, 1978.

Practicing History: Selected Essays, Knopf, 1981.

The March of Folly: From Troy to Vietnam, Knopf, 1984.

Contributor to *Harper's, Atlantic, New York Times, American Scholar, Foreign Affairs*, and other publications.

SIDELIGHTS: Barbara Tuchman writes narrative histories that are strongly literary in nature, believing that the work of most historians is often too obscure for the average reader. "Historians who stuff in every item of research they have found, every shoe-lace and telephone call of a biographical subject, are not doing the hard work of selecting and shaping a readable story," she tells *CA.* "And besides, they seem not to have an ear for clear lucid prose, are not thinking of their readers." Tuchman favors the literary arpproach. "There should be a beginning, a middle, and an end," she states, "plus an element of suspense to keep a reader turning the pages." Her approach to history has won her two Pulitzer Prizes. Tuchman is also "a bestselling author and America's foremost popular historian," as Wendy Smith writes in *Publishers Weekly.*

Although not trained as a historian, Tuchman does not see that as a disadvantage. "I never took a Ph.D.," she admits. "It's what saved me, I think. If I had taken a doctoral degree, it would have stifled any writing capacity." To prepare for her books, Tuchman first researches the available information and then visits the appropriate historical sites. For *The Guns of August,* she walked the battlefields of World War I; for *A Distant Mirror: The Calamitous Fourteenth Century,* she crossed the same mountains the Crusaders of the fourteenth century crossed.

Tuchman explains to Jim Miller of *Newsweek* that it was difficult for her to become a writer of history. "It was a struggle," she states. "I had three small children and no status whatever." Tuchman's ambitions seemed out of place in a family prominent in politics and banking. Her grandfather had been U.S. ambassador to Turkey and Mexico under President Woodrow Wilson. Her father was a banker and an owner of the *Nation* magazine. An uncle served as the secretary of the treasury under President Franklin D. Roosevelt. "To come home, close a door and feel that it was your place to work," Tuchman tells Miller, "that was very difficult, particularly when you were—well, just a Park Avenue matron."

It wasn't until her third book, *The Zimmermann Telegram,* that Tuchman achieved success as a writer. A best-seller, the book concerns the infamous German telegram to Mexico during World War I which promised the Mexican government portions of the American Southwest if it would enter the war on Germany's behalf. The exposure of the telegram was instrumental in bringing the United States into the war against Germany. As Ferdinand Kuhn explains in *Saturday Review,* "the blundering telegram was important in history, and for this reason the story is worth telling." Tuchman's account of the pivotal affair is singled out for its remarkable detail. "There can only be praise," writes the *Times Literary Supplement*

critic, "for the writer's mastery of a mass of documents treating all sides of this amazing affair." Ernest S. Pisko of the *Christian Science Monitor* notes Tuchman's "stupendous knowledge of all the facts and all the persona even remotely involved in the dramatic story."

The Guns of August, a look at the opening days of World War I, was Tuchman's next best-seller and winner of her first Pulitzer Prize. It is, Bruce Blivenn, Jr. writes in the *New Yorker,* a "neatly perfect literary triumph." Focusing on the opening strategies and battles of the war, Tuchman argues that errors on all sides in the conflict led to the stalemate of trench warfare—a four-year period of enormous and largely pointless casualties. "There is much of battle orders, of tactical, strategic, and logistical problems in the pages of 'The Guns of August,'" Pisko writes. "But such is the skill of the author that these technical issues become organic parts of an epic never flagging in suspense." Although Cyril Falls of the *New York Times Book Review* finds that "the errors and omissions of 'The Guns of August' mount to a formidable total," he judges the book to be "a lucid, fair, critical and witty account." Bliven claims that "Tuchman leans toward seeing issues as black and white, but her control of her material is so certain and her opinions are so passionate that it would be risky to argue with her."

With *The Proud Tower: A Portrait of the World before the War, 1890-1914,* Tuchman turned to an examination of society before the First World War and of the events and forces which led to the war. World War I, she writes in the book, "lies like a band of scorched earth dividing that time from ours. In wiping out so many lives which would have been operative on the years that followed, in destroying beliefs, changing ideas, and leaving incurable wounds of disillusion, it created a physical as well as psychological gulf between two epochs." In eight chapters, each covering a different topic, Tuchman provides varied glimpses of pre-war society. "*The Proud Tower,*" Oscar Handlin comments in the *Atlantic,* "is consistently interesting. [Tuchman] is a skillful and imaginative writer. She has the storyteller's knack for getting the maximum dramatic effect out of the events which crowd her pages."

Tuchman won her second Pulitzer Prize for the 1971 book *Stilwell and the American Experience in China, 1911-1945.* It follows the career of Joseph Warren Stilwell, an American military officer who served in China in various capacities from 1911 to 1944. Stilwell's years in China saw that country's transformation from a feudal society to a communist state. The book is, Anthony Grey writes in the *Washington Post Book World,* "an extremely creditable compendium of the mightiness, the miseries, the personalities, the perversities, the facts and frustrations of China in the past half-century seen through unhappy American eyes." O. Edmund Clubb, writing in the *Saturday Review,* finds *Stilwell and the American Experience in China* to be "an admirably structured work that is excellent as narrative and fascinating as history," while Allen S. Whiting, in a review for the *Nation,* calls it "the most interesting and informative book on U.S.-China relations to appear since World War II."

Although Tuchman's most popular books had dealt with twentieth-century history, in 1978 she published a book about the Middle Ages, *A Distant Mirror: The Calamitous Fourteenth Century.* Her interest in the period stemmed from what she saw as similarities between the fourteenth century and our own time; the book's title refers to this similarity. David Benson, writing in the *Spectator,* lists the "resemblances between that period and our own'' as ''almost continual warfare, both civil and international, widespread political instability and popular uprisings, a crisis of confidence in almost all institutions, especially the Church, and a rise of individualism combined with a general decline in authority.'' The central event of the fourteenth century was the bubonic plague, which swept across Europe and Asia, killing nearly a third of the population. Tuchman compares the plague to the possible devastation a nuclear war might cause in our own century.

Following the career of Enguerrand de Coucy VII, a French knight and nobleman, *A Distant Mirror* becomes an ''ambitious, absorbing historical panorama,'' as Naomi Bliven writes in the *New Yorker*. De Coucy was related to both the French and English royal families and owned land near the troublesome Flemish border, so his life touched upon many key events and personalities of the time. Tuchman's narrative brings these events and personalities to vivid life. Despite the book's several drawbacks, Laurence Stone of the *New York Review of Books* finds it ''beautifully written, careful and thorough in its scholarship, extensive in the range of topics peripherally touched upon, and enlivened by consistently intelligent comment. What Mrs. Tuchman does superbly is to tell *how* it was, to convey a sense of time and place.'' This ability to recreate the texture of fourteenth-century life is also noted by Brian Tierney of the *Washington Post Book World*. Tuchman's ''special gift,'' Tierney writes, ''is to bring a past age to life by the accumulation of countless concrete details, lovingly collected and deftly presented. . . . The result is a kind of brilliant, dazzling, impressionistic picture of the surface of medieval life.''

In *The March of Folly: From Troy to Vietnam*, Tuchman ranges over Western history from the mythical Trojan horse of ancient Greece to the Vietnam War, examining in depth four episodes where governmental ''folly'' is most evident: the Trojans' decision to bring the wooden horse into their city; the corruption of the Renaissance popes, which helped to provoke the Protestant Reformation; the English policy towards the rebellious American colonies; and the American involvement in the Vietnam War. These episodes were similar, Michael Howard explains in the *Washington Post Book World*, in that ''the actors involved pursued a course of action which was not only foolish but seen at the time to be foolish; which was the responsibility of an entire group or class rather than a single misguided individual, and to which a sensible and feasible alternative was quite obviously available.'' *The March of Folly* is a change in approach for Tuchman. ''I've done what I always said I would never do,'' she told Smith, ''and that is to take a theory before I wrote a book. My other books were narrative, and I tried not to adopt a thesis except what emerged from the material. It's what I don't believe in when writing history, actually.''

Some critics took exception to the thesis of *The March of Folly*. Jack Lessenberry of the *Detroit News*, speaking of the four historic events that Tuchman discusses, asks: ''What common thread links these events? I can't tell, and I read the book.'' Christopher Lehmann-Haupt of the *New York Times* believes that much of what Tuchman discusses in the book has been better handled by other writers: ''Any way one approaches 'The March of Folly,' it is unsatisfying. . . . Better books have been written about Vietnam, the American Revolution, the Renaissance Popes and the Trojan Horse. Better things have been said about human folly.''

But, as H. J. Kirchhoff of the Toronto *Globe and Mail* maintains, ''there are many good reasons to recommend'' *The March of Folly*. Kirchhoff believes that ''Tuchman writes well about the major players in turbulent times. She researches her subjects with exemplary thoroughness, and discusses them with imagination and clear good sense. And her analysis of political folly . . . offers valuable (and sobering) insights into the political process.'' Writing in the *New York Times Book Review*, John Keegan states that Tuchman identifies political folly ''with precision, dissects it with delicacy and dismisses it with contempt.'' Theodore Draper of the *New Republic* finds that ''one admires Tuchman's ability to assimilate, organize, and dramatize enormous gobs of disparate material. She never ceases to be vivid and vigorous. Most readers will be carried along by her storytelling art.''

In her collection *Practicing History: Selected Essays*, Tuchman presents her own ideas on how history should best be written. Divided into three parts—''The Craft,'' ''The Practice,'' and ''Learning from History''—the book reveals many of the assumptions and concerns which have made Tuchman one of the most popular historians in the country. She particularly emphasizes the importance of narrative writing. ''The historian's basic mode,'' Marcus Cunliffe explains in his review of the book for the *Washington Post Book World*, ''is that of narration: movement through time, so as to disclose to the reader in a clear, compelling sequence a set of significant events.''

Tuchman's emphasis on narrative has helped to make her books best-sellers, though it is in sharp contrast to the approach taken by academic historians. ''Most academics,'' Miller writes, ''lack the talent or inclination to write for a general audience. Into this vacuum has stepped Tuchman. . . . Her imaginative choice of topics and flair for words have enabled her to satisfy the popular hunger for real history spiced with drama, color and a dash of uplifting seriousness.'' Writing in the *New Republic*, Jack Beatty maintains that ''Tuchman's books provide [her readers] with examples that lift the level of their lives. Before the academic deluge this was what history was supposed to do—to teach philosophy by example—and few writers have performed this office more inspiritingly than Barbara Tuchman.''

Despite some criticism of her work by the academic world—Walter Kendrick of the *Village Voice* reports that ''academic historians disdain her work now and always will''—few observers doubt the sheer power of Tuchman's writing. ''Tuchman may not be a historian's historian,'' Laurence Freedman admits in the *Times Literary Supplement*, ''but she is a pleasure for the layman to read.'' ''Whatever her subject,'' Smith writes, ''Tuchman brings to it a flair for the dramatic, a striking ability to combine narrative sweep with individual character analysis, and a vividly entertaining prose style.'' Because of her ability to turn ''complex historical muddles into narrative that preserves an air of complexity but can be simply read . . . ,'' Kendrick argues, Tuchman will be remembered ''as an entertainer, one who made the past palatable to millions of readers.''

MEDIA ADAPTATIONS: The Guns of August was filmed in 1964.

BIOGRAPHICAL/CRITICAL SOURCES:

BOOKS

Bowman, Kathleen, *New Women in Social Sciences*, Creative Education Press, 1976.
Contemporary Issues Criticism, Volume I, Gale, 1982.
Tuchman, Barbara, *The Proud Tower: A Portrait of the World before the War, 1890-1914*, Macmillan, 1966.

Tuchman, Barbara, *Practicing History: Selected Essays*, Knopf, 1981.

PERIODICALS

America, February 5, 1966.
American Historical Review, July, 1966.
American Political Science Review, June, 1972.
Atlantic, February, 1966, October, 1978, April, 1984.
Books and Bookmen, May, 1979.
Book Week, January 9, 1966.
Book World, February 28, 1971.
Boston Globe, March 4, 1984.
Business Week, September 25, 1978.
Chicago Tribune Book World, March 4, 1984.
Christian Century, May 14, 1975.
Christian Science Monitor, October 2, 1958, February 1, 1962, March 24, 1971, September 18, 1978.
Chronicle Review, October 2, 1978.
Commentary, December, 1978.
Contemporary Review, April, 1982.
Cosmopolitan, January, 1967.
Critic, April-May, 1966.
Current History, May, 1966.
Detroit News, March 25, 1984.
Economist, February 26, 1966.
Esquire, June, 1971.
Globe and Mail (Toronto), April 21, 1984.
Harper's, February, 1966.
Journal of American History, September, 1966, December, 1971.
Life, February 19, 1971.
Listener, January 6, 1972, March 29, 1979.
Los Angeles Times Book Review, March 18, 1984.
Ms., July, 1979.
Nation, February 14, 1966, April 26, 1971.
National Review, February 8, 1966, December 8, 1978.
New Leader, October 9, 1978.
New Republic, March 27, 1971, October 28, 1978, October 21, 1981, March 26, 1984.
New Statesman, June 22, 1962.
Newsweek, February 15, 1971, September 25, 1978, March 12, 1984.
New Yorker, April 14, 1962, February 5, 1966, November 13, 1978.
New York Review of Books, February 3, 1966, July 22, 1971, August 9, 1973, September 28, 1978, March 29, 1984.
New York Times, February 15, 1971, February 27, 1979, September 29, 1981, September 7, 1982, March 7, 1984.
New York Times Book Review, January 28, 1962, January 9, 1966, February 7, 1971, April 22, 1973, November 12, 1978, September 27, 1981, March 11, 1984, March 24, 1985.
Observer, July 15, 1979.
Progressive, June, 1971.
Publishers Weekly, March 2, 1984.
Punch, March 9, 1966.
Saturday Review, October 18, 1958, January 27, 1962, January 15, 1966, February 20, 1971, October 28, 1978.
Spectator, March 31, 1979, July 21, 1984.
Time, February 9, 1962, January 14, 1966, February 15, 1971, March 26, 1984.
Times (London), May 17, 1984.
Times Literary Supplement, March 20, 1959, June 8, 1962, December 10, 1971, June 22, 1984.
Village Voice, June 19, 1978, September 30, 1981.

Virginia Quarterly Review, summer, 1966.
Wall Street Journal, January 14, 1966.
Washington Post, October 5, 1978.
Washington Post Book World, February 13, 1972, October 8, 1978, September 27, 1981, February 2, 1984.

—*Sketch by Thomas Wiloch*

*   *   *

TURBAYNE, Colin Murray   1916-

PERSONAL: Born February 7, 1916, in Tanny Morel, Queensland, Australia; came to United States, 1947; naturalized 1957; son of David Livingstone and Rene (Lahey) Turbayne; married Alisa Margaret Krimmer, June 22, 1940; children: Ronald Murray, John Garvald. *Education:* University of Queensland, B.A., 1940, M.A., 1947; University of Pennsylvania, Ph.D., 1950.

ADDRESSES: Home—185 Highland Pkwy., Rochester, N.Y. 14620. *Office*—Department of Philosophy, University of Rochester, Rochester, N.Y. 14627.

CAREER: University of Pennsylvania, Philadelphia, instructor, 1947-50; University of Washington, Seattle, assistant professor, 1950-55; University of California, Berkeley, assistant professor, 1955-57; University of Rochester, Rochester, N.Y., associate professor, 1957-62, professor of philosophy, 1962-81, professor emeritus, 1981—. *Military service:* Australian Military Forces, Infantry, 1940-45; became captain.

MEMBER: American Philosophical Association, American Association of University Professors.

AWARDS, HONORS: Fulbright fellowship, University of Melbourne, 1963; Guggenheim fellowship, 1965-66; National Endowment for the Humanities senior fellowship, 1974.

WRITINGS:

(Editor) George Berkeley, *Three Dialogues Between Hylas and Philonous*, Bobbs-Merrill, 1954, reprinted, Macmillan, 1984.
(Editor) Berkeley, *Treatise Concerning the Principles of Human Knowledge*, Bobbs-Merrill, 1957.
(Editor) Berkeley, *Principles*, Bobbs-Merrill, 1958, reprinted, Macmillan, 1984.
The Myth of Metaphor, Yale University Press, 1962, 2nd revised edition, University of South Carolina Press, 1970.
(Editor) Berkeley, *Works on Vision*, Bobbs-Merrill, 1963, reprinted, Greenwood, 1981.
(Editor) Berkeley, *Principles, Dialogues, and Philosophical Correspondence with Samuel Johnson*, Bobbs-Merrill, 1965, reprinted, Macmillan, 1984.
(Editor) Berkeley, *A Treatise Concerning the Principles of Human Knowledge: Text and Critical Essays*, Bobbs-Merrill, 1970.
(Editor and contributor) *Berkeley: Critical and Interpretive Essays*, University of Minnesota Press, 1982.

Contributor to professional journals.

WORK IN PROGRESS: Metaphor and Mind; a book on Plato's procreation model and its influence on later philosophies of mind, especially in Aristotle, Berkeley, and Kant, based on the articles "Plato's 'Fantastic Appendix': The Procreation Model of the *Timaeus*," in *Paideia: Special Plato Issue* (1976), and "Aristotle's Androgynous Mind," in *Paideia: Special Aristotle Issue* (1979); "Kant's Passive and Active Mind," unpublished.

SIDELIGHTS: The Myth of Metaphor has been translated into Spanish by Celia Paschero and published in Mexico.

AVOCATIONAL INTERESTS: Tennis, surfing.

*   *   *

TURCO, Lewis (Putnam) 1934-
(Wesli Court)

PERSONAL: Born May 2, 1934, in Buffalo, N.Y.; son of Luigi (a minister) and May (Putnam) Turco; married Jean Houdlette (a music librarian), June 16, 1956; children: Melora Ann, Christopher Cameron. *Education:* University of Connecticut, B.A., 1959; State University of Iowa, M.A., 1962.

ADDRESSES: Home—Box 362, Oswego, N.Y. 13126. *Office*—39B Swetman Hall, State University of New York College, Oswego, N.Y. 13126. *Agent*—Arthur Orrmont, Author Aid Associates, 340 East 52nd St., New York, N.Y. 10022 (literary); Bill Thompson, Lordly & Dame, Inc., 51 Church St., Boston, Mass. 02116 (booking).

CAREER: Fenn College (now Cleveland State University), Cleveland, Ohio, instructor in English, 1960-64, founder and director of Poetry Center, 1961-64; Hillsdale College, Hillsdale, Michigan, assistant professor of English, 1964-65; State University of New York, College at Oswego, assistant professor, 1965-68, associate professor, 1968-71, founder and director of program in writing arts, 1969—, professor of English, 1971—. Visiting professor, State University of New York at Potsdam, 1968-69; faculty exchange scholar, State University of New York system, 1975—; Bingham Poet in Residence, University of Louisville, 1982. Mathom Press, Oswego, chief editor, 1977-84, editor and publisher, 1984—. Honorary trustee, Theodore Roethke Memorial Foundation. *Military service:* U.S. Navy, 1952-56.

MEMBER: PEN American Center, Poetry Society of America, Modern Language Association, Northeastern Modern Language Association.

AWARDS, HONORS: Yaddo Foundation resident fellow, 1959 (poetry), and 1977 (fiction); Academy of American Poets prize, 1960; Bread Loaf Poetry Conference fellow, 1961; American Weave Press Chapbook Award, 1962; State University of New York Research Foundation faculty fellow, 1966, 1967, 1969, 1971, 1973, and 1978; first prize in fiction, *The Miscellany*, 1969; Helen Bullis Prize, *Poetry Northwest*, 1972; winner, National Endowment for the Arts/PEN Syndicated Fiction Project, 1983; First Poetry Award, *Kansas Quarterly*/Kansas Arts Commission, 1985, for a poem written under the pseudonym Wesli Court; President's Award, S.U.N.Y. College at Oswego, 1985, for scholarly and creative activity and research; Melville Cane Award, Poetry Society of America, 1987, for *Visions and Revisions of American Poetry.*

WRITINGS:

"Dreams of Stone and Sun" (play; originally titled "The Dark Man"), first produced in Storrs, Conn., at the University of Connecticut's Jorgensen Little Theater, May, 1959.

First Poems (Book Club for Poetry selection), Golden Quill Press, 1960.

The Sketches and Livevil: A Mask (poems), American Weave Press, 1962.

The Book of Forms: A Handbook of Poetics, Dutton, 1968, expanded edition published as *The New Book of Forms: A Handbook of Poetics,* University Press of New England, 1986.

Awaken, Bells Falling: Poems, 1959-67, University of Missouri Press, 1968.

"The Elections Last Fall," first produced in Oswego, N.Y. at Tyler Hall Experimental Theater, December, 1969.

The Inhabitant: Poems, with Prints by Thom. Seawell, Despa, 1970.

Creative Writing in Poetry, State University of New York, 1970.

The Literature of New York: A Selective Bibliography of Colonial and Native New York State Authors, New York State English Council, 1970.

Pocoangelini: A Fantography and Other Poems, Despa, 1971.

Poetry: An Introduction through Writing, Reston, 1973.

The Weed Garden (poems), Peaceweed, 1973.

Freshman Composition and Literature, State University of New York, 1974.

A Cage of Creatures (poems), Banjo Press, 1978.

Seasons of the Blood (poems; chapbook), Mammoth, 1980.

American Still Lifes (poems), Mathom, 1981.

The Compleat Melancholick; Being a Sequence of Found, Composite, and Composed Poems, Based Largely upon Robert Burton's "Anatomy of Melancholy," Bieler Press, 1985.

A Maze of Monsters (poems), Livingston University Press, 1986.

Visions and Revisions of American Poetry, University of Arkansas Press, 1986.

"The Fog" (libretto for a closet opera), with music by Dutch composer Walter Heckster, first produced in the Netherlands, 1988.

Speaking Fictively (a Socratic dialogue), Writers Digest Books, in press.

UNDER PSEUDONYM WESLI COURT

Courses in Lambents, Mathom, 1977.

Curses and Laments, Song Magazine, 1978.

Murgatroyd and Mabel (juvenile), Mathom, 1978.

The Airs of Wales, Temple University Poetry Newsletter, 1981.

CONTRIBUTOR TO ANTHOLOGIES

New Campus Writing 3, Grove, 1959.

Poetry for Pleasure, Doubleday, 1960.

Midland: Twenty-Five Years of Fiction and Poetry from the University of Iowa Writers' Workshop, Random House, 1961.

Anthology of Contemporary American Poetry (a record album), Folkways, 1961.

Doors into Poetry, Prentice-Hall, 1962.

Of Poetry and Power, Basic Books, 1964.

Best Poems of 1965: Borestone Mountain Poetry Awards, Pacific Books, 1966.

The Kennedy Reader, Bobbs-Merrill, 1967.

The New Yorker Book of Poems, Viking, 1969.

The Best Poems of 1971: Borestone Mountain Poetry Awards, Pacific Books, 1972.

Contemporary Poetry in America, Random House, 1973.

America Is Not All Traffic Lights, Little-Brown, 1976.

William Heyen, editor, *American Poets in 1976,* Bobbs-Merrill, 1976.

Realms of Light, photographs by Ernst Haas, Walker, 1978.

Poets Teaching: The Creative Process, Longman, 1980.

Beowulf to Beatles and Beyond, Macmillan, 1981.

Tygers of Wrath, University of Georgia, 1981.

A Green Place, Delacorte, 1982.

Poeti Italo-Americani/Italo-American Poets, Antonio Carello Editore (Catanzaro, Italy), 1985.
Available Press/PEN Short Story Collection, Ballantine, 1986.
Strong Measures, Harper, 1986.
Seems Like Old Times, Iowa Writers' Workshop, 1986.
Patterns of Poetry, Louisiana State University, 1986.
John Ciardi: Measure of the Man, University of Arkansas, 1987.
Ecstatic Occasions, Expedient Forms, Macmillan, 1987.

OTHER

Also author of *A Sampler of Hours: Poems from Lines in Emily Dickinson's Letters; The Book of Beasts: An Alphabestiary of Fabulous Creatures* (poems); *Ancient Music: Modern Versions of Medieval British Poems; Letters to the Dead: A Sequence* (poems); *The Shifting Web* (poems); *A Book of Proverbs* (poems); *The Devil's Disease: A Narrative of the Age of Witchcraft in England and New England, 1580-1697* (nonfiction); *Contemporaries* (criticism); and *Talk about Poetry: Collected Interviews,* all unpublished. Editor, *The Poetry of Manoah Bodman,* also unpublished. Author of "While the Spider Slept," a dance scenario for a ballet first produced in Stockholm, Sweden, by the Royal Swedish Ballet, 1965. Contributor to *Dictionary of Literary Biography Yearbook,* 1983-87, *Contemporary Literary Criticism, First Printings of American Authors, Colliers Encyclopedia,* and the revised edition of *Princeton Encyclopedia of Poetry and Poetics.* Contributor of poems, stories, essays and reviews to many literary journals and periodicals, including *New Yorker, Poetry, Nation, New Republic,* and *Sewanee Review.*

WORK IN PROGRESS: Selected Poems; Voices in an Old House, poems; *Guinevere's Quest,* a comic novel; and "an as yet untitled book of short stories and a collection of memoirs."

SIDELIGHTS: "Those who frequent the small world of the little poetry magazines know Lewis Turco as a champion of the classical virtues of form and craftsmanship," writes David G. McLean in an *Agora* review. Turco's commitment to technique is also grounded in *The Book of Forms: A Handbook of Poetics* and its expanded version, *The New Book of Forms.* Widely considered indispensible for an appreciation of poetry, the handbook contains definitions of poetic terms and "a wealth of technical information," says a *Booklist* reviewer. Turco's "form finder" catalogues examples of verse forms used by poets from many countries and time periods. "Turco seems to have the whole of the English lyric tradition at his fingertips" when composing poetry as well, believes Felix Stefanile. Writing in *Italian Americana,* Stefanile cites an enviable "precision of language" in poems he trusts more readily than the "'spontaneous' mutter" offered by the "studiously untutored poets of the confessional school." The poet, however, wants readers to see more than formalism in his verse. As he once told *CA,* "It appears [that people] think, because I am the author of *The Book of Forms,* that I believe everyone ought to write sonnets, or villanelles. That is very far from the truth, as anyone who looks at my poetry can tell: no two [poems] are alike, either in form or in content. There is no joy in doing over and over what you know you can do."

William Heyen and other critics trace a development in Turco's verse from exhibitions of technical skill in the early works to a lesser emphasis on virtuoso effects in later books. In Turco's *First Poems,* as Heyen remarks in a *Modern Poetry Studies* survey, the poet's fondness for traditional forms and unusual, antique words sometimes results in poems that are "too stiff, metrically, or too pretty, or too ingenious." *Dic-*

tionary of Literary Biography Yearbook, 1984 contributor Mary Doll suggests, "Perhaps in response to these comments, Lewis Turco created an alter ego, 'Wesli Court,' an anagram of his own name. As a traditional versifier, Court could publish as many metrically 'correct,' formalistically clever works as Turco desired." Works published under the Wesli Court pseudonym include two chapbooks, one book of poetry, and one book for children.

Though "an infatuation with verbal dance" still can be traced in the later poems, says Doll, they reveal a growing "consciousness of objects and nature." Heyen expresses a similar view, pointing out that the poems in *Awaken, Bells Falling: Poems, 1959-1967,* represent "a great step forward" for Turco, who increasingly permits his subjects to present their own being as objects apart from what the poet or reader may want them to signify. "In his best work, Turco shows us what it is to 'see through a glass darkly' from the other side," Doll notes. As in Zen poetry, she observes, "the *It* rather than the *I* is evoked" in poems that make imagistic statements. For example, a set of illustrations by Thomas Seawell in *The Inhabitant* help "to draw the reader's eye ever more into focus on the things of life," and Japanese forms such as the haiku (a three-line form used often in Turco's chapbook *Seasons of the Blood*) further pare the poet's reflections down to "imagery and sensory impression," writes Doll. A number of critics feel that this progress culminates in the 1981 volume *American Still Lifes,* a series of poems that scans New World history from Colonial times to the present. "Turco's achievement," believes Doll, "is in bringing an Eastern prosody of the senses to bear on the familiar themes and things of Western culture. . . . In the forms of Eastern culture Turco's poetry reached a new level: not *his* command, but language's depths were plumbed, and archetypes surfaced."

Turco's literary criticism defends his conviction that a poet is first of all a craftsman or maker and only secondarily a visionary or prophet, relates McLean. *Visions and Revisions of American Poetry,* according to *Times Literary Supplement* contributor Mark Ford, constitutes "a fiercely formalist rejection of organic poetry as it derives from [Ralph Waldo] Emerson." In the ongoing debate between "professionals" and "amateurs," Turco favors poets who master patterns of rhythm, rhyme and syllable count over Walt Whitman and others who use a more relaxed, speech-oriented mode of expression, Ford elaborates. The reviewer's remark that *Visions and Revisions* is "brilliantly written, continually challenging, and almost always wrong" is tempered by his comment that "it is possible to disagree with everything Turco says and still find this book superbly engrossing."

"The critic Donald Davie, speaking in his capacity as a judge for the Poetry Society of America, had similar words when he awarded *Visions and Revisions* the society's 1987 Melville Cane Award for 'the best prose book about poetry published during the years 1985-1986,'" Turco told *CA.* He added, "Davie wrote in his citation that 'Mr. Turco's book offers not revisions but one thorough-going and far-reaching revision—of the course of American poetry through centuries as commonly understood. It is polemical, but good-humored, lightly and racily written but with passion, deeply serious, disconcerting and timely.'"

BIOGRAPHICAL/CRITICAL SOURCES:

BOOKS

Contemporary Literary Criticism, Volume XI, Gale, 1979.

Dictionary of Literary Biography Yearbook, 1984, Gale, 1985.
Heyen, William, *American Poets in 1976*, Bobbs-Merrill, c. 1976.
Moore, Marianne, Howard Nemerov, and Alan Swallow, editors, *Riverside Poetry 3*, Twayne, 1958.
Turco, Lewis, *The Book of Forms: A Handbook of Poetics*, Dutton, 1968, expanded edition published as *The New Book of Forms: A Handbook of Poetics*, University Press of New England, 1986.
Turco, Lewis, *Visions and Revisions of American Poetry*, University of Arkansas Press, 1986.

PERIODICALS

Agora, spring, 1972.
Centennial Review, spring, 1987.
Concerning Poetry, fall, 1969.
Cream City Review, Volume XIII, numbers 1 and 2, 1983.
Italian Americana, spring, 1975.
Modern Poetry Studies, Volume II, number 3, 1971, winter, 1974.
Poetry, March, 1969, March, 1973.
Sewanee Review, January, 1982.
Times Literary Supplement, May 22, 1987.
Virginia Quarterly Review, autumn, 1968.

—*Sketch by Marilyn K. Basel*

*   *   *

TURNER, George W(illiam)   1921-

PERSONAL: Born October 26, 1921, in Dannevirke, New Zealand; son of Albert George (a farmer) and Elinor Jessie (a dressmaker; maiden name, Anderson) Turner; married Beryl Horrobin (an academic), April 18, 1949; children: Anton Eric, Neil Thurstan. *Education:* University of New Zealand, M.A., 1948; University of London, Diploma in English Linguistic Studies, 1964.

ADDRESSES: Home—3 Marola Ave., Rostrevor, South Australia 5073.

CAREER: Teacher of science and agriculture at a high school in Dannevirke, New Zealand, 1944, and Auckland Teachers' College in Auckland, New Zealand, 1945; teacher of languages at Wellington College, Wellington, New Zealand, 1946; University of Canterbury, Canterbury, New Zealand, University Library, head of orders department, 1949-52; Canterbury Public Library, Canterbury, New Zealand, head of reference department, 1953-54; University of Canterbury, lecturer, 1955-64, senior lecturer in English, 1964; University of Adelaide, Adelaide, Australia, reader in English, 1965—, chairman of department, 1975-77. Lecturer in Germany, Sweden, England, France, Yugoslavia, and Canada. *Military service:* Served in New Zealand Army, 1942.

MEMBER: Australia and New Zealand Association for Medieval and Renaissance Studies, Linguistic Society of Australia, Australian Universities Language and Literature Association, Academy of the Humanities (fellow).

WRITINGS:

The English Language in Ausralia and New Zealand, Longmans, Green, 1966, 2nd edition, 1972, reprinted, 1987.
(Author of introduction) Joseph Furphy, *Ribgy's Romance*, Ribgy, 1972.
German for Librarians, Massey University, 1972.
Stylistics, Penguin, 1973.

(Editor) *Good Australian English and Good New Zealand English*, illustrations by Daphne Howie, A. H. & A. W. Reed, 1973.
Linguistics in Australia since 1958, Sydney University Press for the Australian Academy of the Humanities, 1976.
(Editor) *The Australian Pocket Oxford Dictionary*, 2nd edition, Oxford University Press, 1984.
(Editor) *The Australian Concise Oxford Dictionary*, Oxford University Press, in press.

Contributor of "A Supplement of Australian Words" to Australian edition of *Oxford Paperback Dictionary*.

WORK IN PROGRESS: With Frances Devlin Glass and P. R. Eaden, an annotated edition of *Such Is Life*, by Joseph Furphy.

SIDELIGHTS: George W. Turner wrote: "In my early years I worked in a cheese factory, as a builder's laborer and shop assistant, in a radio factory, and as a meter reader. I became interested in books and language early.

"My writing has owed much—really everything—to academic colleagues. My main books have been commissioned for series; unprompted, I, a New Zealand country boy, would not have had the temerity to write them.

"I have two opposite ambitions in writing. In one mood I would simply like to establish a fact, however minute, that was not known before. This ambition comes nearest to fulfillment in the work I do as a consultant for the *Oxford English Dictionary* (second supplement) checking entries for Australian and New Zealand words, in which it is sometimes possible to fill in the earlier history of a word with quotations of earlier date than those collected by previous informants. The opposite ambition is symoptic, a desire to break down barriers between academic subjects. Articles I have written link linguistics with science or logic, or journalism or history. Especially important in this connection is an ambition to heal the old feud between linguistic and literary study.

"My habit when writing a book is to plan the outline in about eight or ten chapters, setting aside a folder for each chapter and putting all quotations, ideas, and facts into the appropriate folder as they come to hand. The book then organizes itself around the material. Quotations and illustrative examples often seem to come in very aptly this way, because in fact they precede the connecting text they illustrate."

*   *   *

TY-CASPER, Linda   1931-

PERSONAL: Surname is pronounced Tee-*Cas*-per; born September 17, 1931, in Manila, Philippines; came to the United States in 1956; daughter of Francisco Figueroa (a civil engineer) and Catalina (an educator and writer; maiden name, Velasquez) Ty; married Leonard R. Casper (a professor and writer), July 14, 1956; children: Gretchen, Kristina. *Education:* University of the Philippines, A.A., 1951, LL.B., 1955; Harvard University, LL.M., 1957. *Politics:* Independent. *Religion:* Roman Catholic.

ADDRESSES: Home—Saxonville, Mass. *Agent*—Bonnie Crown, International Literature and Arts Agency, 50 East 10th St., No. R5, New York, N.Y. 10003.

CAREER: Conducted writers' workshop at Ateneo de Manila University, 1978, 1980; writer-in-residence at University of the Philippines, 1980, 1982.

MEMBER: PEN Women (Wellesley branch), Society of Radcliffe Fellows, Boston Authors.

AWARDS, HONORS: Fellow at Silliman University, 1963, and Radcliffe Institute, 1974-75; Djerassi writing fellowship, 1984; literature award, Filipino-American Women's Network, 1985; *Awaiting Trespass* chosen as one of five fiction titles in twenty selected for 1986, Feminist Book Fortnight of Britain and Ireland.

WRITINGS:

The Transparent Sun and Other Stories, Peso Book, 1963.
The Peninsulars (historical novel), Bookmark, 1964.
The Secret Runner and Other Stories, Florentino, 1974.
The Three-Cornered Sun (historical novel), New Day, 1979.
Dread Empire (novella), Heinemann, 1980.
Hazards of Distance (novella), New Day, 1981.
Fortress in the Plaza (novella), New Day, 1985.
Awaiting Trespass (novella), Readers International, 1985.
Wings of Stone, Readers International, 1986.
Ten Thousand Seeds, Ateneo, 1987.
A Small Garden Party, New Day, 1988.

Also author of *Dream Eden*.

Work represented in anthologies, including *Best American Short Stories of 1977*, edited by Martha Foley. Contributor of articles and stories to magazines and newspapers in the United States and abroad, including *Asia, Descant, Nantucket Review, Prairie Schooner, Manila Review*, and *Solidarity*.

WORK IN PROGRESS: The Stranded Whale, about the Philippine-American War to 1901; completion expected in 1991.

SIDELIGHTS: Linda Ty-Casper told *CA:* "I have always let life carry me along. I trained as a lawyer because my parents wanted either a doctor or a lawyer. After graduation, one was expected to attend graduate school abroad, take a government appointment, or work for law firms. I went to Harvard because my husband took a teaching position at Boston College.

"As early as four years of age, I had seen myself as a writer. I had written stories in the Philippines while waiting for the results of bar examinations. After my last examination at Harvard, I wrote a story immediately.

"Then I began reading books on Philippine history. It was to correct their misjudgments that I wrote my first historical novel, *The Peninsulars*. The positive comments of its critics encouraged me to think about writing novels set in other critical periods of Philippine history. I began research on the revolution of 1896. It took me fifteen years to research, write, rewrite (when the manuscript was lost), and revise that project.

"Still, I did not think of myself as a writer, only as someone who was writing. During visits to the Philippines, where people at home waited for me to make use of my legal training and my law class of 1955 affectionately considered me a 'deviant,' I felt apologetic. But I knew even then that I could not wake up daily with the attitudes proper to a lawyer and those proper to a writer; nor could I alternate between them. The fact that I work best by myself further predisposed me to write. For me, writing became both a refuge and a way of being in the world; it was also compatible with raising a family in the fifties and with adjusting to a different country.

"In 1980, I first accepted myself as a writer. That year I was asked to be resident fictionist at the University of the Philippines Creative Writing Center. I was finally convinced when

I was introduced, on separate occasions, to a national artist, a senator, and a leading architect, and they recognized me as 'the novelist.' Up to that time I was always somebody's wife, daughter, or mother.

"I write on impulse. The first lines of stories come to me in the midst of other things. I work steadily in one sitting until the story needs only to be revised. I do not work every day, for that would make writing a drudgery for me. With novels and novellas, I write one scene at a time, much like short stories.

"Events shape each chapter of my novels. I know the event and its public outcome, but I don't know what my characters will do as they re-enact it. I research exhaustively, until I can see the place and feel the time: newspapers, songs, letters to editors, all manner of accounts, including telephone directories, are among my sources. I read novels from the period to get the rhythm of words and sentences as distinguished from the rhythm of life which the details of daily living recreate. Inspired by contemporary crises, my novellas are more like extended short stories.

"As I write, I have to make discoveries to be surprised. In a sense, each book is a first book. I try to write each one differently, as if it were being written during the period when the events took place. I try to present a portrait of the country, hence the variety of characters and points of view; and the minimal reference to 'historical' figures who are already much written about.

"Although I do not write regularly, I am always ready to write when the temptation comes. In between I deliberately occupy myself with what can be readily put aside, with what does not linger in the mind or compete for attention. I write in English, rather than Pilipino, because that was the language of instruction when I was growing up. It is a matter of being able to write down my thoughts quickly before they flee. But I hope to write more seriously in Pilipino, or, failing in that, to translate my writings. I find English precise and objective, while Pilipino allows me to locate feelings better. Cultural affinities and common language allow a writer to implicate his country more deeply in his work, but our lives are not so small and restricted that they should be expressed only in one language. Instead of dividing us, the languages we use will define our variousness and complexity.

"I believe writing provides alternatives, by adding still other 'selves' to literature, that house of our many selves. Because a writer writes, history cannot be entirely rewritten according to the specifications of politicians."

BIOGRAPHICAL/CRITICAL SOURCES:

BOOKS

Casper, Leonard R., *New Writing from the Philippines*, Syracuse University Press, 1966.
Schwartz, Norda Lacey, *Articles on Women Writers, 1960-1975*, American Bibliographical Center—Clio Press, 1977.

PERIODICALS

AmerAsia Journal, Volume XIII, number 1, 1986-87.
Asiaweek, February 16, 1986.
Belles Lettres, spring, 1987.
Booklist, January, 1986.
Boston Globe, November 24, 1985, January 25, 1987.
Bulletin Today, September 11, 1986.
City Life, 1986.

Everywoman, June, 1986.
Feminist Bookstore News, January, 1987.
Filipinas II, 1981, 1983.
Globe and Mail (Toronto), December 6, 1986.
Heritage, 1967.
Hudson Review, March, 1986.
In These Times, February, 1985.
Journal of Asian Studies, August, 1981.
Kirkus Reviews, August 15, 1985, September 15, 1986.
Library Journal, October 15, 1985.
Los Angeles Times, February 9, 1986.
Los Angeles Times Book Review, February 2, 1986.
Manila (Los Angeles), 1972.
Manila Chronicle, June 3, 1971.
Manila Times, February 16, 1987.
MetroWest (Middlesex News), February 6, 1986.
Middlesex News, November 12, 1985, November 28, 1985,
    January 15, 1987, February 4, 1987, April 5, 1987.
Morning Star, 1986.
New Statesman, October 18, 1985.
New York Times Book Review, October 27, 1985.
Observer, March 16, 1985.
Pacific Affairs, summer, 1983.
Panorama, March 18, 1979, August 9, 1981.
Philippine Collegian, summer, 1968.
Philippine News, March 26, 1985, April 2, 1985, October 1,
    1985.
Philippine Studies, Volume XXX, 1982, Volume XXXII, 1984,
    Volume XXXIV, 1986.
Pilot, March 21, 1986, February 27, 1987.
Publishers Weekly, October 10, 1985, October 10, 1986.
Radcliffe Quarterly, June, 1975, December 1980, June, 1983,
    March, 1986.
Saint Louis University Research Journal, Volume II, number
    2, 1974.
San Francisco Chronicle, May 25, 1986, December 4, 1986.
South, April, 1987.
Spare Rib, December, 1986.
Tribune, June 6, 1986.
Who, December 9, 1978.
Women's Review of Books, July, 1986.
World Literature Today, autumn, 1982, winter, 1987.

*   *   *

TYLER, Richard W(illis) 1917-

PERSONAL: Born January 7, 1917, in Willington, Conn.; son of Frederic Spencer (a banker) and Jessie (Reed) Tyler; married Elizabeth McKenzie, September 4, 1946; children: Ann Elizabeth, Jane Margaret. *Education:* Connecticut State College (now University of Connecticut), B.A., 1938; Brown University, Ph.D., 1946.

ADDRESSES: Home—5815 North 8th Place, Phoenix, Ariz. 85014-2102.

CAREER: University of Iowa, Iowa City, visiting lecturer in Romance languages, 1944-46; University of Texas, Main Uni-

versity (now University of Texas at Austin), assistant professor, 1946-52, associate professor of Romance languages, 1952-65; University of Nebraska, Lincoln, professor of modern languages and literatures, 1965-87, professor emeritus, 1987—.

MEMBER: Asociacion Internacional de Hispanistas, Modern Language Association of America, American Association of Teachers of Spanish and Portuguese, American Association of University Professors, Comediantes, Spanish Heritage Association, National Trust for Historic Preservation, American Civil Liberties Union, American Association of Retired Persons, National Retired Teacher Association, National Wildlife Federation, Humane Society of the United States, Smithsonian Associates, Midwest Modern Language Association, Rocky Mountain Modern Language Association, Arizona Center for Medieval and Renaissance Studies, Sons of the American Revolution, Maiwand Jezails (propaganda minister, 1967—).

WRITINGS:

(With D. K. Barton and Pedro N. Trakas) *Beginning Spanish
    Course*, Heath, 1954, 3rd edition, 1972.
(With S. G. Morley) *Los nombres de personajes en las co-
    medias de Lope de Vega*, University of California Press,
    1961.
(Editor) Lope de Vega, *La corona de Hungria*, University of
    North Carolina, 1972.
(With Sergio D. Elizondo) *The Characters, Plots and Settings
    of Calderon's Comedias*, Society of Spanish and Spanish-
    American Studies, 1981.

CONTRIBUTOR

*Lope de Vega Studies: A Critical Survey and Annotated Bib-
    liography*, University of Toronto Press, 1964.
Homenaje a Rodriguez-Monino, Castalia (Madrid), 1966.
*Calderon de la Barca Studies: A Critical Survey and Anno-
    tated Bibliography*, University of Toronto Press, 1971.
Homenaje a William L. Fichter . . . , Castalia, 1971.
Frans Amelinckx and Joyce Megay, editors, *Travel Quest and
    Pilgrimage as a Literary Theme: Studies in Honor of Reino
    Virtanen*, Society of Spanish and Spanish-American Stud-
    ies, 1978.
William McCrary and Jose A. Madrigal, editors, *Studies in
    Honor of Everett W. Hesse*, Society of Spanish and Span-
    ish-American Studies, 1981.
*Estudios sobre el siglo de oro en homenaje a Raymond R.
    MacCurdy*, Catedra (Madrid), 1983.

OTHER

Editor of *Los comendadores de Cordoba* by de Vega.

WORK IN PROGRESS: Editing collected works of Antonio Mira de Amescua; research on settings of de Vega's plays; compiling, with E. J. Mickel, a book on great baseball players.

AVOCATIONAL INTERESTS: Travel (Europe, especially Spain), professional sports.

U

UNDERWOOD, Lewis Graham
See WAGNER, C(harles) Peter

*   *   *

UNDERWOOD, Tim (Edward)   1948-

PERSONAL: Born January 12, 1948, in Sault Sainte Marie, Mich.; son of John Norman (a chemist) and Johanna Wilma (a teacher; maiden name, Able) Underwood. *Education:* Attended Michigan State University, 1965-67, and College of Marin, 1973.

ADDRESSES: Home—P.O. Box 481130, Los Angeles, Calif. 90048. *Office*—Underwood/Miller, 515 Chestnut St., Columbia, Pa. 17512.

CAREER: East-West Musical Instrument Co., San Francisco, Calif., assistant production manager, 1972-76; Underwood/Miller (publishers), Columbia, Pa., and Los Angeles, Calif., vice-president, 1976—.

WRITINGS:

(With Daniel J.H. Levack) *Fantasms,* Underwood/Miller, 1979.
(Editor with Chuck Miller) *Jack Vance,* Taplinger, 1980.
(Editor with Miller) *The Book of the Sixth World Fantasy Convention,* Underwood/Miller, 1980.
(Editor wth Miller) *Fear Itself: The Horror Fiction of Stephen King,* Underwood/Miller, 1982.
(Editor with Miller and contributor) *Kingdom of Fear: The World of Stephen King,* Underwood/Miller, 1986.
(Compiler with Miller) Jeff Conner, *Stephen King Goes to Hollywood,* New American Library, 1987.
(Editor with Miller) *Bare Bones,* McGraw, 1988.

Also author of *Creators of Another World,* 1988.

SIDELIGHTS: Tim Underwood told *CA:* "Moral fantasy is the most important and significant genre of fiction today. So I enjoy publishing it as well as writing about it. The modern myths of our contemporary society can be understood through images uncovered in the 'underground' genres of film and fiction: fantasy, science fiction, horror and crime. These are darkside reflections, the dreams of our time."

URDANG, Constance (Henriette)   1922-

PERSONAL: Born December 26, 1922, in New York, N.Y.; daughter of Harry Rudman (a teacher) and Annabel (Schafran) Urdang; married Donald Finkel (a writer and poet), August 14, 1956; children: Liza, Thomas Noah, Amy Maria. *Education:* Smith College, A.B., 1943; University of Iowa, M.F.A., 1956.

ADDRESSES: Home—6943 Columbia Pl., St. Louis, Mo. 63130. *Agent*—Georges Borchardt Inc., 136 East 57th St., New York, N.Y. 10022.

CAREER: Free-lance writer and editor. U.S. Department of the Army, Washington, D.C., military intelligence analyst, 1944-46; National Bellas Hess, Inc., New York City, copy editor, 1947-51; P. F. Collier & Son, New York City, editor, 1952-54. Coordinator of The Writers' Program, Washington University, St. Louis, Mo., 1977-84. Visiting lecturer, Princeton University, spring, 1985.

AWARDS, HONORS: Carleton Miscellany's First Centennial Award for prose, for *Natural History;* National Endowment for the Arts fellow, 1976; Delmore Schwartz Memorial Poetry Award, 1981.

WRITINGS:

(Editor with Paul Engel) *Prize Short Stories, 1957: The O. Henry Awards,* Doubleday, 1957.
(Editor with Engle and Curtis Harnack) *Prize Short Stories, 1959: The O. Henry Awards,* Doubleday, 1959.
Charades and Celebrations (poems), October House, 1965.
Natural History (novel), Harper, 1969.
The Picnic in the Cemetery (poems), Braziller, 1975.
The Lone Woman and Others (poems), University of Pittsburgh Press, 1980.
Only the World (poems), University of Pittsburgh Press, 1983.
Lucha (novella), Coffee House Press, 1986.
American Earthquakes (novella), Coffee House Press, 1988.

Contributor of poetry and prose to anthologies and to numerous periodicals.

SIDELIGHTS: Poet and novelist Constance Urdang's poem "The Moon Tree," from her first poetry collection, *Charades and Celebrations,* has been praised by Raymond Roseliep in a *Poetry* article as "the kind of thing Stephen Vincent Benet had in mind when he defined poetry as magic." Roseliep feels that another poem from this collection, "The Old Woman," is "achievement of the same caliber... and so is 'In the Junkshop,' which proves that poems can be written about anything." *Saturday Review* critic W. T. Scott explains that "by sheer force of style [Urdang] can make mythological figures out of aunts and grandparents, and she can deal with historical figures in exciting livelier ways than we usually get these days. She is a fine poet with a sardonic eye trained to real values."

As a novelist, Urdang has fared rather well also, though *Natural History* is, according to its author as quoted in *Saturday Review:* "Not a novel. A series of images in the form of prose episodes. Their meaning, if any, to emerge when at the end one can look back to try and make out the 'significant patterns. . . .'" Muriel Haynes in that same *Saturday Review* article likens *Natural History* to a journal, or "thought book," in which literally, though not in other regards, "nothing happens; a succession of everyday people, men and women, old and young, dead and alive, move in and out, serving as metaphors for ways-of-being-in-the-world." These everyday people who represent "ways-of-being-in-the-world" include the narrator, her family, and three of her female friends, and emphasis is placed on the age-old concerns of "time, birth, generation, old age, love, [and] death," as defined by *New York Times Book Review* critic Jay Neugeboren. Neugeboren believes, despite Urdang's "anti-fiction pattern," that *Natural History* "seems quite old-fashioned. . . . [Its] concerns remain fundamental, traditional." And he adds that "in spite of the book's fragmented surface, in spite of its disclaimers ('Not a novel . . .'), it becomes, due to its sure and singular voice, a coherent, evocative and real object in its own right." Whereas a contributor to the *Virginia Quarterly Review* says Urdang's structural strategy in *Natural History* fails, the same contributor praises the book's narrative for its "honest, moving, and intelligent questioning of what a woman's role is, and can be, in our society. [It] . . . has the fascination of a brilliant journal." As for Haynes, she believes "the effect of *Natural History* is a bit like that of a speculative talk with a sharp-minded friend of fine sensibility. There is a similar intimate ease,. . .there is intellectual exhilaration."

With three poetry collections in between, Urdang followed her first fiction, *Natural History,* with a novella entitled *Lucha.* Courtney Weaver writes in the *San Francisco Chronicle* that *Lucha* is a "literary mural of three generations of Mexican women which, despite its brevity, sacrifices neither beauty nor relevance." This mural paints the life history of Luz Filomena whose nickname, "Lucha," means to "struggle." Weaver focuses on the contrast Urdang develops between Lucha, a believer in urbanization and the idea of progress for women and for Mexico, and her niece, Nieves, a woman content to be mother and housekeeper—"[Nieves] is the icon of Mexico herself: Fertile, impassive, silent," offers Weaver. Whereas Lucha is rather accepting of Mexico's passivity in the first two sections of the book, she is, writes Weaver, "continually trying, continually struggling toward a new ideal of femininity and of herself." *New York Times Book Review* commentator Susan Wood judges that "in this spare, often elegant tale[,] . . . Urdang obviously knows Mexico and she writes about the country and its people with feeling and understanding. But . . . one feels something is curiously missing." Weaver, in turn, says *Lucha,* "like an effective painting, . . . may be praised for its capture of time and character. . . . It is a novel not about struggling dialectics but rather about the interweaving of sorrow, fulfillment, beauty and change."

BIOGRAPHICAL/CRITICAL SOURCES:

PERIODICALS

Book World, August 17, 1969.
Gargoyle, June, 1983.
New York Times Book Review, July 29, 1969, January 11, 1987.
Poetry, April, 1966.
San Francisco Chronicle, March 8, 1987.
Saturday Review, October 9, 1965, July 19, 1969.
Virginia Quarterly Review, autumn, 1969.

*   *   *

USHER, Margo Scegge
   See McHARGUE, Georgess

V

VANDENBUSCHE, Duane (Lee) 1937-

PERSONAL: Born August 4, 1937, in Detroit, Mich.; son of George C. (a farmer) and Ruby (Briggs) Vandenbusche. *Education:* Northern Michigan College (now University), B.S., 1959; Oklahoma State University, M.A., 1960, Ed.D., 1964. *Politics:* Democrat. *Religion:* Roman Catholic.

ADDRESSES: Home—West of Gunnison, Gunnison, Colo. 81230. *Office*—Department of History, Western State College of Colorado, Gunnison, Colo. 81230.

CAREER: Western State College of Colorado, Gunnison, instructor, 1962-63, assistant professor, 1963-67, associate professor, 1967-73, professor of history, 1973—.

MEMBER: Western History Association, Rocky Mountain Social Science Association.

AWARDS, HONORS: National Association for State and Local History research grants, 1967 and 1970; Boettcher Foundation grant, 1978; named Cross-Country Coach of the Year by National Association of Intercollegiate Athletics, 1986, and Professor of the Year by Western State College of Colorado, 1986-87.

WRITINGS:

Marble, Colorado: City of Stone, Golden Bell, 1970.
Early Days in the Gunnison Country, B & B Publishing, 1974.
The Gunnison Country, privately printed, 1980.
(With Duane Smith) *A Land Alone: Colorado's Western Slope,* Pruett, 1981.

Also author, with Walter Borneman, of *The Lake City Railroad* (Colorado Rail Annual Number 14), 1979. Contributor of articles to *Colorado,* and other periodicals.

AVOCATIONAL INTERESTS: Fishing, hiking, boating, tennis, skiing, golf, running.

*   *   *

VAUGHAN WILLIAMS, Ursula Wood 1911-
(Ursula Wood)

PERSONAL: Born March 15, 1911, in Valletta, Malta; daughter of Sir Robert Ferguson (an army officer) and Beryl (Penton) Lock; married Michael Forrester Wood (an army officer), May 24, 1933 (died, 1942); married Ralph Vaughan Williams (a composer), February 7, 1953 (died, 1958). *Education:* Attended private schools in England and Brussels, Belgium.

ADDRESSES: Home—66 Gloucester Crescent, London N.W.1, England.

CAREER: Writer and lyricist. Member of British Music Information Centre; member of committee, Musicians Benevolent Fund.

MEMBER: National Folk Music Library.

AWARDS, HONORS: Named fellow of Royal Academy of Music, 1974, and of Royal College of Music, 1976; elected member of Royal Northern College of Music, 1980.

WRITINGS:

(Editor with Imogen Holst) Ralph Vaughan Williams and Gustav Holst, *Heirs and Rebels: Letters Written to Each Other and Occasional Writings on Music,* Oxford University Press, 1959, reprinted, Greenwood Press, 1980.
(Editor with Holst) *A Yacre of Land: Sixteen Folk-Songs from the Manuscript Collection of Ralph Vaughan Williams,* Oxford University Press, 1961.
(Author of preface) R. Vaughan Williams, *National Music and Other Essays,* Oxford University Press, 1963.
R.V.W.: A Biography of Ralph Vaughan Williams, Oxford University Press, 1964.
Metamorphoses (novel), Duckworth, 1966.
Set to Partners (novel), Duckworth, 1968.
(With John Lunn) *A Picture Biography of Ralph Vaughan Williams,* Oxford University Press, 1971.
Aspects (verse), Autolycus Publications, 1984.
The Yellow Dress (novel), Kensal Press, 1984.

AUTHOR OF LYRICS FOR MUSICAL COMPOSITIONS

(Under name Ursula Wood) R. Vaughan Williams, *The Sons of Light: A Cantata for Chorus and Orchestra,* Oxford University Press, 1951.
R. Vaughan Williams, *Four Last Songs: For Medium Voice and Piano,* Oxford University Press, 1960.
Charles Camillieri, *Melita* (opera), Novello, 1968.

Malcolm Williamson, *The Brilliant and the Dark: An Operatic Sequence,* Weinberger, 1969.
Williamson, *The Icy Mirror,* Weinberger, 1972.
Williamson, *Ode to Music,* Weinberger, 1972.
Phyllis Tate, *Compassion,* Oxford University Press, 1979.
Elizabeth Lutyens, *Variations,* Oxford University Press, 1979.

Also author of lyrics for "The Sofa," music by Elizabeth Maconchy, 1959, "David and Bathsheba," music by David Barlow, 1969, "Serenade," music by Anthony Scott, 1972, "Stars and Shadows," music by Brian Hughes, 1976, "Aspects," music by Roger Steptoe, 1978, "King of Maledon," music by Steptoe, 1979, "The Looking Glass," music by Steptoe, 1980, and "The Inheritor," music by Steptoe, 1980, "Echoes," music by Ronald Jenalir, 1986.

UNDER NAME URSULA WOOD

No Other Choice (verse), Basil Blackwell, 1941.
Fall of Leaf (verse), Basil Blackwell, 1943.
(Translator) Engel Lund, *A Second Book of Folk Songs,* C. Fischer, 1947.
Need for Speech (verse), Basil Blackwell, 1948.
Wandering Pilgrimage (verse), Hand & Flower Press, 1952.
Silence and Music (verse), Essential Books, 1959.

AVOCATIONAL INTERESTS: The theatre, travel, and gardening.

*   *   *

VELLA, Walter F(rancis)   1924-

PERSONAL: Born July 13, 1924, in San Francisco, Calif.; son of Noah J. and Gabrielle (Lavoie) Vella; married Dorothy Burgeson (an assistant professor of English), June 16, 1951; children: Eric Nelson, Paul Laurence. *Education:* University of California, Berkeley, B.A., 1947, M.A., 1950, Ph.D., 1954.

ADDRESSES: Home—2621 Laau St., #9, Honolulu, Hawaii 96826. *Office*—Department of History, University of Hawaii, Honolulu, Hawaii 96822.

CAREER: Cleveland Public Library, Cleveland, Ohio, curator of John G. White collection, 1957-62; University of Hawaii, Honolulu, associate professor, 1962-65, professor of history, 1965—, chairman of Southeast Asian Studies, 1970-75. *Military service:* U.S. Army, 1943-46; served in China-Burma-India theater; received Bronze Star and distinguished unit citation.

MEMBER: Association for Asian Studies (member of board of directors, 1971-74), Asian Perspectives (member of board of directors, 1969—).

AWARDS, HONORS: Foreign Area fellow, 1956-57; ACLS/SSRC fellow, 1969-70; Ford Foundation fellow, 1975-76.

WRITINGS:

Impact of the West on Government in Thailand, University of California Press, 1955.
Siam under Rama III, J. J. Augustin, 1957.
Chaiyo! King Vajiravudh and the Development of Thai Nationalism, University Press of Hawaii, 1978.

EDITOR

G. Coedes, *The Indianized States of Southeast Asia,* East-West Center, 1967.
Aspects of Vietnamese History, University Press of Hawaii, 1972.

OTHER

Contributor to *Journal of Asian Studies* and *Journal of the Siam Society.*

WORK IN PROGRESS: Sunthorn Phu, Poet-Mirror of Thai Society.†

*   *   *

VERDUIN, John R(ichard), Jr.   1931-

PERSONAL: Born July 6, 1931, in Muskegon, Mich.; son of John Richard (a salesman) and Dorothy (Eckman) Verduin; married Janet M. Falk, January 26, 1963; children: John Richard III, Susan E. *Education:* University of Albuquerque, B.S., 1954; Michigan State University, M.A., 1959, Ph.D., 1962.

ADDRESSES: Home—107 North Lark Ln., Carbondale, Ill. 62901. *Office*—Department of Educational Administration and Foundations, Southern Illinois University, Carbondale, Ill. 62901.

CAREER: Public school teacher in Muskegon, Mich., 1954-56, and Greenville, Mich., 1956-59; State University of New York College at Geneseo, assistant professor, 1962-64, associate professor of education, 1964-67; Southern Illinois University at Carbondale, associate professor, 1967-70, professor in department of educational administraion and foundations, 1970—, assistant dean, 1967-73. State of Illinois Gifted program, member of advisory council, 1968—, chairman, 1973—. Special consultant to American Association of Colleges for Teacher Education, 1966-67; member of teacher education committee, Illinois Association of Supervision and Curriculum Development. Member and chairman of education commission, First United Methodist Church, Carbondale. Member of Carbondale Model Cities committee and of Goals for Carbondale committee. *Military service:* U.S. Marine Corps, 1951.

MEMBER: Association for Supervision and Curriculum Development, American Educational Research Association, Illinois Adult and Continuing Education Association, Phi Delta Kappa, Kappa Delta Phi.

WRITINGS:

Cooperative Curriculum Improvement, Prentice-Hall, 1967.
Conceptual Models in Teacher Education, American Association of Colleges for Teacher Education, 1967.
(Co-author) *Pre-Student Teaching Laboratory Experiences,* Kendall/Hunt, 1970.
(Contributor) William Joyce, Robert Oana, and W. Robert Houston, editors, *Elementary Education in the Seventies,* Holt, 1970.
(Co-author) *Project Follow Through,* State of Illinois, 1971.
(Co-author) *Adults Teaching Adults: Principles and Strategies,* Learning Concepts, 1977.
(Contributor) James R. Gress and David Purpel, editors, *Curriculum: An Introduction to the Field,* McCutchan, 1978.
(Co-author) *The Adult Educator: A Handbook for Staff Development,* Gulf Publishing, 1979.
Curriculum Building for Adult Learning, Southern Illinois University Press, 1980.
(Co-author) *Adults and Their Leisure: The Need for Lifelong Learning,* C. C Thomas, 1984.
(Co-author) *Differential Education of the Gifted: A Taxonomy of 32 Key Concepts,* Southern Illinois University Press, 1986.
(Co-author) *The Lifelong Learning Experience: An Introduction,* C. C Thomas, 1986.

Also author of reports on educational research and projects for the State of Illinois. Contributor of articles to education journals.

WORK IN PROGRESS: Co-authoring *Instrumentation of Factor III: The Demands of Knowledge* and *Distance Education.*

AVOCATIONAL INTERESTS: Woodworking, gardening, golfing, and tennis.

*   *   *

VIOLI, Paul   1944-

PERSONAL: Born July 20, 1944; son of Joseph T. and Irma (Francesconi) Violi; married Carol Ann Boylston (a teacher), June, 1969; children: Helen, Alexander. *Education:* Boston University, B.A., 1966.

ADDRESSES: Home—23 Cedar Ledges, Putnam Valley, N.Y. 10579.

CAREER: Architectural Forum, New York City, managing editor, 1972-74. Adjunct assistant professor at New York University.

AWARDS, HONORS: Poetry award, New York State Council on the Arts, 1978; Ingram Merrill Foundation Poetry Award, 1979; National Endowment for the Arts grant, 1980, 1986; New York Foundation for the Arts grant, 1987.

WRITINGS:

POETRY

Automatic Transmissions, Swollen Magpie Press, 1970.
Waterworks, Toothpaste Press, 1972.
In Baltic Circles, Kulchur Press, 1973.
Some Poems, Swollen Magpie Press, 1976.
Harmatan: Poem, drawings by Paula North, Sun Press, 1977.
Splurge: Poems, Sun Press, 1981.
American Express, J.S.C. Publications (London), 1982.
Likewise, Hanging Loose Press, 1987.

AVOCATIONAL INTERESTS: Travel (West Africa, Europe, Asia).

BIOGRAPHICAL/CRITICAL SOURCES:

PERIODICALS

Newsday, December 19, 1982.
Voice Literary Supplement, May, 1983.
Washington Post Book World, January 1, 1978.

W

WAGNER, C(harles) Peter 1930-
(Epafrodito, Lewis Graham Underwood)

PERSONAL: Born August 15, 1930, in New York, N.Y.; son of C. Graham (a buyer) and Mary (Lewis) Wagner; married Doris Mueller (a missionary), October 15, 1950; children: Karen, Ruth, Rebecca. *Education:* Rutgers University, B.S., 1952; Fuller Theological Seminary, B.D., 1955, M.A., 1968; Princeton Theological Seminary, Th.M., 1962; University of Southern California, Ph.D., 1977.

ADDRESSES: Home—135 North Oakland Ave., Pasadena, Calif. 91101.

CAREER: Congregational clergyman, 1955—; Instituto Biblico del Oriente, San Jose, Bolivia, director, 1956-61; Instituto Biblico Emaus, Cochabamba, Bolivia, professor and director, 1962-71; Andes Evangelical Mission (now S.I.M. International), Cochabamba, associate director, 1964-71; Fuller Theological Seminary, Pasadena, Calif., professor of church growth, 1971—. Senior field consultant, Fuller Evangelistic Association, Pasadena, 1971—.

MEMBER: Phi Beta Kappa.

WRITINGS:

(With Joseph S. McCullough) *The Condor of the Jungle,* Revell, 1966.
Defeat of the Bird God, Zondervan, 1967.
Latin American Theology, Eerdmans, 1969.
The Protestant Movement in Bolivia, William Carey Library, 1970.
(With Ralph Covell) *An Extension Seminary Primer,* William Carey Library, 1971.
A Turned-On Church in an Uptight World, Zondervan, 1971.
Frontiers in Missionary Strategy, Moody, 1972.
(Editor) *Church/Mission Tensions Today,* Moody, 1972.
Look Out! The Pentecostals Are Coming, Creation House, 1973.
Stop the World, I Want to Get On, Regal Books, 1974.
Your Church Can Grow: Seven Vital Signs of a Healthy Church, Regal Books, 1976.
Your Church and Church Growth (includes workbook and six cassette tapes), Fuller Evangelistic Association of Pasadena, 1976, revised edition published as *The Growing Church,* 1982.

(Editor with Edward R. Dayton) *Unreached Peoples '79,* David C. Cook, 1978.
Your Spiritual Gifts Can Help Your Church Grow, Regal Books, 1979.
Your Church Can Be Healthy, Abingdon, 1979.
Our Kind of People: The Ethical Dimensions of Church Growth in America, John Knox, 1979.
(Editor with Dayton) *Unreached Peoples '80,* David C. Cook, 1980.
(With Bob Waymire) *The Church Growth Survey Handbook,* Global Church Growth Bulletin, 1980.
(Editor with Dayton) *Unreached Peoples '81,* David C. Cook, 1981.
Church Growth and the Whole Gospel, Harper, 1981.
Effective Body Building: Biblical Steps to Spiritual Growth, Here's Life Publishers, 1982.
Helping Your Church Grow (includes workbook and cassette tapes), David C. Cook, 1982.
(Editor with Donald A. McGavran and James H. Montgomery) *Church Growth Bulletin: Third Consolidated Volume,* Global Church Growth Bulletin, 1982.
On the Crest of the Wave: Becoming a World Christian, Regal Books, 1983.
Leading Your Church to Growth, Regal Books, 1984.
Spiritual Power and Church Growth, Creation House, 1986.
Church Growth: State of the Art, Tyndale, 1986.
Strategies for Church Growth, Regal Books, 1987.
(Editor) *Signs and Wonders Today,* Creation House, 1987.

Contributor, sometimes under pseudonyms Epafrodito and Lewis Graham Underwood, to religious periodicals. Former editor of *Vision Evangelica* (Cochabamba, Bolivia), *Pensamiento Cristiano* (Cordoba, Argentina), and *Andean Outlook.*

*   *   *

WALKER, Dale L(ee) 1935-

PERSONAL: Born August 3, 1935, in Decatur, Ill.; son of Russell Dale (a career soldier) and Eileen M. (Guysinger) Walker; married Alice McCord, September 30, 1960; children: Dianne, Eric, Christopher, Michael, John. *Education:* Texas Western College (now University of Texas at El Paso), B.A., 1962. *Politics:* Democrat. *Religion:* Protestant.

ADDRESSES: Home—800 Green Cove, El Paso, Tex. 79932. *Office*—News and Publications Office, University of Texas, El Paso, Tex. 79968.

CAREER: KTSM-TV, El Paso, Tex., reporter, 1962-66; University of Texas at El Paso, director of News-Information Office, 1966—; director of Texas Western Press, 1985. *Military service:* U.S. Navy, 1955-59.

MEMBER: Western Writers of America, Texas Institute of Letters.

AWARDS, HONORS: Special Spur Award, Western Writers of America, 1986, for five year editorship of *The Roundup*.

WRITINGS:

(Author of introductory essay) George Sterling, *Wine of Wizardry*, Pinion Press, 1962.
(With Richard O'Connor) *The Lost Revolutionary: A Biography of John Reed*, Harcourt, 1967.
C. L. Sonnichsen: Grassroots Historian, Texas Western Press, 1972.
The Alien Worlds of Jack London (monograph), Wolf House Books, 1973.
(Editor) Howard A. Craig, *Sunward I've Climbed*, Texas Western Press, 1974.
Jack London, Sherlock Holmes, and Sir Arthur Conan Doyle (monograph), Alvin S. Fick, 1974.
(Contributor) W. Burns Taylor and Richard Santelli, editors, *Passing Through*, Santay Publishers, 1974.
Death Was the Black Horse: The Story of Rough Rider, Buckey O'Neill, Madrona Press, 1975.
(Editor and author of introduction) *Curious Fragments: Jack London's Tales of Fantasy Fiction*, Kennikat, 1975.
(Contributor) Howard Lamar, editor, *The Reader's Encyclopedia of the American West*, Crowell, 1977.
No Mentor but Myself: Jack London, the Writer's Writer, Kennikat, 1979.
Only the Clouds Remain: Ted Parsons of the Lafayette Escadrille, Alandale, 1980.
Jack London and Conan Doyle: A Literary Kinship, Gaslight, 1981.
(Author of introductory essay) *An American for Lafayette: The Diaries of E. C. C. Genet*, University of Virginia Press, 1981.
(Editor and author of introduction) *Will Henry's West*, Texas Western Press, 1984.
(Editor and author of introduction) *In a Far Country: Jack London's Western Tales*, Green Hill, 1986.
Januarius McGahan: The Life and Campaigns of an American War Correspondent, 1844-1878, Ohio University Press, 1988.

Contributor to newspapers and magazines. Books editor, *El Paso Times*, 1979-85; editor, *The Roundup*, 1980-85.

WORK IN PROGRESS: Disputed Barricades, a work on Americans in the French Foreign Legion, 1914-1918.

SIDELIGHTS: Dale L. Walker writes: "My principal areas of reading and writing interest are: 1) American and British biographical subjects, nineteenth century; 2) Victorian era, 1839-1900, military history; 3) Jack London studies."

*   *   *

WALKER, Stuart H(odge)   1923-

PERSONAL: Born April 19, 1923, in Brooklyn, N.Y.; son of Robert Osgood (an inventor) and Alice (Hodge) Walker; married Frances Taylor, March 10, 1945; children: Susan, Lee. *Education:* Middlebury College, A.B., 1942; New York University, M.D., 1945. *Politics:* Republican.

ADDRESSES: Home—Luce Creek Dr., Annapolis, Md. 21401. *Office*—Department of Pediatrics, Mercy Hospital, 301 St. Paul Place, Baltimore, Md. 21202.

CAREER: University of Maryland, Baltimore, professor of pediatrics, 1957—; Mercy Hospital, Baltimore, Md., head of department of pediatrics, 1961—. *Military service:* U.S. Army, Medical Corps, 1943-53; became major.

MEMBER: Academy of Pediatrics, Severn Sailing Association (commodore, 1958-63), Chesapeake Bay Yacht Racing Association (president, 1962-65).

WRITINGS:

Techniques of Small Boat Racing, Norton, 1961.
Tactics of Small Boat Racing, Norton, 1965.
Performance Advances in Small Boat Racing, Norton, 1969.
Wind and Strategy, Norton, 1973.
Advanced Racing Tactics, Norton, 1977.
Winning: The Psychology of Competition, illustrated by Thomas C. Price, Norton, 1980.
A Manual of Sail Trim, illustrated by Price, Norton, 1985.

Also author of "Wind and Weather" (audio-visual program), Audio Navigation Institute, 1979. Author of column "Tactics" in *Sailing World*, and of columns in *Modern Boating, Australian Sailing, Sailing: Inland and Offshore*, and *Seahorse*. Creator of "Marks to Port," a sailboat racing game.

WORK IN PROGRESS: Strategy and Tactics, for Norton; *Travels with Thermopylae*, a self-illustrated book of vignettes of European travel.

SIDELIGHTS: Stuart H. Walker has won the Prince of Wales Cup and Princess Elizabeth Cup in sailing. He was a member of the 1968 United States Olympic team and the 1979 United States Pan American Games sailing team.

BIOGRAPHICAL/CRITICAL SOURCES:

PERIODICALS

Books and Bookmen, December, 1967.
Times Literary Supplement, September 7, 1967.
Yacht, August, 1969, February, 1970, November, 1980.

*   *   *

WALLERSTEIN, Immanuel   1930-

PERSONAL: Born September 28, 1930, in New York, N.Y.; son of Lazar and Sally (Guensberg) Wallerstein; married Beatrice Morgenstern, May 25, 1964; children: Katharine Ellen. *Education:* Columbia University, A.B., 1951, M.A., 1954, Ph.D., 1959; Oxford University, graduate study, 1955-56. *Religion:* Jewish.

ADDRESSES: Office—Department of Sociology, State University of New York, Binghamton, N.Y. 13901.

CAREER: Columbia University, New York, N.Y., instructor, 1958-59, assistant professor, 1959-63, associate professor of sociology, 1963-71; McGill University, Montreal, Quebec, professor of sociology, 1971-76; State University of New York at Binghamton, distinguished professor of sociology and director of Fernand Braudel Center for the Study of Economies,

Historical Systems, and Civilizations, 1976—. *Military service:* U.S. Army, 1951-53.

MEMBER: International Sociological Association (vice-president, research commission, national movements and imperialism, 1972-90), International African Institute (member of executive council, 1978-84), Social Science Research Council (member of board of directors, 1980-86), African Studies Association (president, 1972-73), American Sociological Association (member of executive council, 1977-80).

WRITINGS:

Africa: The Politics of Independence, Random House, 1961.
The Road to Independence: Ghana and the Ivory Coast, Mouton, 1964.
(Editor) *Social Change: The Colonial Situation,* Wiley, 1966.
Africa: The Politics of Unity, Random House, 1967.
University in Turmoil: The Politics of Change, Atheneum, 1969.
(Editor with Paul Starr) *The University Crisis: A Reader,* two volumes, Random House, 1970.
The Modern World-System, Academic Press, Volume I: *Capitalist Agriculture and the Origins of the European World Economy in the Sixteenth Century,* 1974, Volume II: *Mercantilism and the Consolidation of the European World-Economy, 1600-1740,* 1980.
World Inequality, Black Rose Books (Montreal), 1975.
(Editor with Peter C. Gutkind) *Political Economy of Contemporary Africa,* Sage Publications, 1976.
The Capitalist World-Economy, Cambridge University Press, 1979.
(Editor with Terence K. Hopkins) *Processes of the World-System,* Sage Publications, 1980.
(With Hopkins and others) *World-System Analysis: Theory and Methodology,* Sage Publications, 1982.
(With Samir Amin, Giovanni Arrighi, and Andre Gunder Frank) *Dynamics of Global Crisis,* Macmillan, 1982.
(Editor with Aquinode Braganca) *The African Liberation Reader,* three volumes, Zed Press (London), 1982.
Historical Capitalism, Verso, 1983.
(Editor) *Labor in the World Social Structure,* Sage Publications, 1983.
The Politics of the World Economy, Cambridge University Press, 1984.
(Editor with Joan Smith and Hans-Dieter Evans) *Households and the World Economy,* Sage Publications, 1984.
Africa and the Modern World, African World Press, 1986.

Editor, *Review,* and *Political Economy of the World System Annuals.* Contributor to professional journals.

*   *   *

WALLIS, Kenneth F(rank) 1938-

PERSONAL: Born March 26, 1938, in Mexborough, England. *Education:* University of Manchester, B.Sc., 1959, M.Sc.Tech., 1961; Stanford University, Ph.D., 1966.

ADDRESSES: Office—Department of Economics, University of Warwick, Coventry CV4 7AL, England.

CAREER: Yale University, Cowles Foundation, New Haven, Conn., member of research staff, 1965-66; University of London, London School of Economics and Political Science, London, England, lecturer, 1966-72, reader in statistics and econometrics, 1972-77; University of Warwick, Coventry, England, professor of econometrics, 1977—, director, Economic and

Social Research Council Macroeconomic Modelling Bureau, 1983—. Governor, National Institute of Economic and Social Research, London, 1978—. Member, U.K. Treasury Academic Panel, 1980—, chairman, 1987—.

MEMBER: Econometric Society (fellow), Royal Economic Society, Royal Statistical Society (member of council, 1972-76).

WRITINGS:

Introductory Econometrics, Aldine, 1972, 2nd edition (with Mark B. Stewart), Halsted, 1981.
(Contributor) M. Parkin and M. T. Sumner, editors, *Incomes Policy and Inflation,* Manchester University Press, 1972.
Topics in Applied Econometrics, Gray-Mills, 1973, 2nd revised edition, University of Minnesota Press, 1979.
(Contributor) R. E. Lucas and T. J. Sargent, editors, *Rational Expectations and Econometric Practice,* University of Minnesota Press, 1981.
(Contributor with M. H. Salmon) G. C. Chow and P. Corsi, editors, *Evaluating the Reliability of Macroeconomic Models,* Wiley, 1982.
(Editor with David F. Henry) *Econometrics and Quantitative Economics,* Basil Blackwell, 1984.
(Editor with others) *Models of the U.K. Economy* (annual series of review volumes), Oxford University Press, 1984-87.

Contributor of articles to periodicals, including *Review of Economics and Statistics, Economica, Econometrica, Journal of Economic Literature, Journal of the American Statistical Association,* and *Journal of the Royal Statistical Society.* Member of editorial board, *Review of Economic Studies,* 1971-76. Joint editor, *Economica,* 1973-76. Co-editor, *Econometrica,* 1977-83.

*   *   *

WARD, Jonas
See COX, William (Robert)

*   *   *

WARE, Kallistos (Timothy Richard) 1934-
(Timothy Ware)

PERSONAL: Born September 11, 1934, in Bath, Somerset, England; son of Richard Fenwick and Evereld (Edwardes) Ware. *Education:* Magdalen College, Oxford, B.A., 1956, M.A., 1959, D.Phil., 1965. *Religion:* Eastern Orthodox.

ADDRESSES: Home—15 Staverton Rd., Oxford OX2 6XH, England. *Office*—Pembroke College, Oxford University, Oxford, England.

CAREER: Westminster Under School, London, England, classics master, 1958-59; Oxford University, Oxford, England, researcher in church history, Magdalen College, 1960-63, Spalding Lecturer in Eastern Orthodox Studies, 1966—, fellow of Pembroke College, 1970—. Priest of the Eastern Orthodox Church, 1966—; priest-in-charge, Greek Orthodox Parish of Holy Trinity, 1966—; member of the Monastic Brotherhood of St. John the Theologian, Patmos, 1966—; Anglican-Orthodox Joint Doctrinal Discussions, theological secretary, 1973-79, counsellor, 1979—; titular bishop of Diokleia, and assistant bishop in the Orthodox Archdiocese of Thyateira and Great Britain, 1982—.

WRITINGS:

(Under name Timothy Ware) *The Orthodox Church*, Penguin, 1963, 5th revised edition (under name Kallistos Ware), 1980.

(Under name Timothy Ware) *Eustratios Argenti: A Study of the Green Church under Turkish Rule*, Clarendon Press, 1964, Oxford University Press (New York), 1965.

(Author of introduction under name Timothy Ware) Chariton, editor, *The Art of Prayer: An Orthodox Anthology*, Faber, 1966.

(Co-translator) *The Festal Menaion*, Faber, 1969.

(Editor with Colin Davey) *Anglican-Orthodox Dialogue: The Moscow Statement Agreed by the Anglican-Orthodox Joint Doctrinal Commission 1976*, S.P.C.K., 1977.

(Co-translator) *The Lenten Triodion*, Faber, 1978.

(Co-translator) *The Philokalia*, Faber, Volume I, 1979, Volume II, 1981, Volume III, 1984.

The Orthodox Way, Mowbrays, 1979.

(Author of introduction) John Climacus, *The Ladder of Divine Ascent*, Paulist Press, 1982.

(Editor with George Every and Richard Harries) *Seasons of the Spirit: Readings through the Christian Year*, S.P.C.K., 1984.

Co-editor of *Eastern Churches Review*, 1967-78, and *Sobornost*, 1979—.

WORK IN PROGRESS: A history of Greek Orthodoxy since 1453; a study of the human person according to the Greek fathers.

*   *   *

WARE, Timothy
See WARE, Kallistos (Timothy Richard)

*   *   *

WARNER, James A(loysius)   1918-

PERSONAL: Born March 1, 1918, in Detroit, Mich.; son of Andrew Thomas Warner (a salesman); married Gloria J. Boyle, June 27, 1942; children: Gary, Dennis, Dawn. *Education:* Attended Detroit schools.

ADDRESSES: Home—4201 East Baker Ave., Abingdon, Md. 21009.

CAREER: Bata Shoe Co., Belcamp, Md., salesman, 1940-54; Contractors, Inc., Belcamp, Md., owner, 1954-69; J. A. Warner, Inc., Forrest Hill, Md., president, 1969—.

MEMBER: Baltimore Camera Club.

WRITINGS:

(With Donald Delinger)*The Gentle People: A Portrait of the Amish*, Grossman, 1969.

The Quiet Land, Grossman, 1970.

Songs That Made America, Grossman, 1972.

The Darker Brother, with photographs, edited by Styne M. Slade, Dutton, 1974.

(With Slade) *The Mormon Way*, with photographs, Prentice-Hall, 1976.

(With Margaret J. White) *Best Friends* (photographs), A & W Publishers, 1980.

(With White) *Chesapeake: A Portrait of the Bay Country*, E. R. Hostetler, 1982.

(With White) *The Decoy as Art: Waterfowl in a Wooden Soul* (photographs), Middle Atlantic Press, 1985.

(With White) *In the Footsteps of the Artist: Thoreau and the World of Andrew Wyeth*, Middle Atlantic Press, 1986.†

*   *   *

WARREN, James E(dward), Jr.   1908-

PERSONAL: Born December 11, 1908, in Atlanta, Ga.; son of James Edward (an attorney) and Jean (Mauck) Warren. *Education:* Emory University, A.B., 1930, M.A.T., 1941; attended Georgia State College (now University), Yale University, and Cambridge University. *Politics:* ''No party.'' *Religion:* Methodist.

ADDRESSES: Home—544 Deering Rd. N.W., Atlanta, Ga. 30309.

CAREER: Atlanta (Ga.) public schools, junior high and high school teacher of English, Latin, history, and journalism, 1933-59; Lovett School, Atlanta, Ga., head of English department, 1960-73, poet-in-residence, 1974-75, historian, 1980—. Part-time instructor in English at Georgia Institute of Technology, 1958-60. *Military service:* U.S. Army Air Force, 1942-45; became sergeant.

MEMBER: Poetry Society of America, Academy of American Poets, Georgia Poetry Society, Georgia Writers Association (trustee), Kappa Phi Kappa.

AWARDS, HONORS: Annual award, Poetry Society of America, 1937; literary achievement award for poetry, Georgia Writers Association, 1967, for *Selected Poems;* Excellence in Teaching Award, Georgia Association of Independent Schools, 1974; Governor's Award in poetry, Georgia Council for the Arts, 1980; Barrow Prize; Nathan Haskell Dole Prize; Fluvanna Prize; May Sinton Leitch Memorial Prize; Writer of the Year Award, Atlanta Writers Club.

WRITINGS:

This Side of Babylon (poetry), Banner Press, 1938.

Against the Furious Men (poetry), Banner Press, 1946.

The Teacher of English: His Materials and Opportunities, A. Swallow, 1956.

Altars and Destinations (chapbook), privately printed, 1964.

Trembling Still for Troy (chapbook), privately printed, 1965.

Greener Year, Whiter Bough (chapbook), privately printed, 1966.

Selected Poems, Branden Press, 1967.

The Winding of Clocks (chapbook), privately printed, 1968.

Listen, My Land (chapbook), privately printed, 1971.

(Contributor) V. R. Mollenkott, compiler, *Adam among the Television Trees*, Word, Inc., 1971.

(Contributor) Charles Angoff, editor, *The Diamond Anthology*, A. S. Barnes, 1971.

How to Write a Research Paper, Branden Press, 1972.

Mostly of Emily Dickinson (chapbook), privately printed, 1972.

Walking with Candles (chapbook), Print Shop, 1973.

A Kind of Fighting (chapbook), Colony Square, 1974.

Bequest/Request (chapbook), Print Shop, 1976.

Prieu-Dieu and Jubilee (chapbook), Print Shop, 1978.

Collected Poems, Dan Abrams, 1979.

The Elegance of God (chapbook), Print Shop, 1981.

Poems of Lovett, Lovett School, 1986.

Also author of *History of the Lovett School*, 1976. Contributor to numerous anthologies. Contributor of poetry and book reviews to periodicals, such as *Atlanta Journal, Atlantic, Christian Science Monitor, Good Housekeeping, New York Times, Prairie Schooner, Saturday Review, Sewanee Review,* and other publications in the United States, Canada, England, Belgium, Japan, France, and Greece. Contributor of educational articles and translations of Horace, Catullus, Propertius, Tibullus, and other classical writers to professional journals. Associate editor, *Versecraft,* 1933-46; editor, *Georgia English Counselor,* 1957-62.

SIDELIGHTS: James E. Warren, Jr., wrote to *CA:* "As a poet I have always agreed with Byron's statement: 'Didactic poetry is my abhorrence.' I am an art-for-its-own-sake person, writing poetry principally because I wish to be a poet, not because I wish to use verse to correct social matters. I leave the 'Me Generation' to add to the accumulation of dedicated scraps of free verse scribbled in an effort 'to make a statement.' Having grown up in love with meter and rhyme, I find less and less that I like, and feel poetry is losing its appeal to its former public by this very lack. Few outside of the writers themselves find anything of beauty and/or interest in the prosy little expressions of the untalented. I suspect our plethora of 'poetry workshops' for encouraging this easy and unimpressive rhetoric."

AVOCATIONAL INTERESTS: Family history.

BIOGRAPHICAL/CRITICAL SOURCES:

PERIODICALS

Georgia Magazine, October-November, 1967.

*   *   *

WARSH, Lewis   1944-

PERSONAL: Born November 9, 1944, in New York, N.Y.; married Bernadette Mayer (a poet), November, 1975; children: Marie Ray, Sophia Crystal, Max. *Education:* City College of the City University of New York, B.A., 1966, M.A., 1975.

ADDRESSES: Home and office—40 Clinton St., New York, N.Y. 10002.

CAREER: Poet. *Angel Hair* (magazine) and Angel Hair Books, New York City, co-founder and co-editor, 1966-77; *Boston Eagle,* Boston, Mass., co-editor, 1973-75; *United Artists* (magazine) and United Artists Books, New York City, co-founder and publisher, 1977—. Teacher in St. Marks in the Bowery Poetry Project, 1973-75; lecturer at Kerouac School of Disembodied Poetics, Boulder, Colo., 1978, New England College, 1979-80, Queens College, 1984-86, and Farleigh Dickinson University, 1987—. Adjunct associate professor at Long Island University, 1987—.

AWARDS, HONORS: Poet's Foundation Award, 1972; Creative Artists Public Service Award in fiction, 1977; National Endowment for the Arts grant in poetry, 1979; Coordinating Council of Literary Magazines editor's fellowship, 1981.

WRITINGS:

The Suicide Rates (poems), Toad Press, 1967.
Highjacking: Poems, Boke Press, 1968.
Moving through Air (poems), Angel Hair Books, 1968.
(With Tom Clark) *Chicago* (poems), Angel Hair Books, 1969.
Words, Staring (poems), Orange Bear Reader, 1971.
Dreaming as One: Poems, Corinth Books, 1971.
Long Distance (poems), Ferry Press, 1971.
Part of My History (autobiography), Coach House Press, 1972.

(Translator) Robert Desnos, *Night of Loveless Nights,* The Ant's Forefoot, 1973.
Immediate Surrounding (poems), Other Books, 1974.
Today (poems), Adventures in Poetry, 1974.
The Maharajah's Son (autobiography), Angel Hair Books, 1977.
Blue Heaven (poems), Kulchur, 1978.
Hives (poems), United Artists Books, 1979.
Methods of Birth Control (poems), Sun & Moon, 1982.
Agnes & Sally (fiction), The Fiction Collective, 1984.
The Corset (poems), In Camera, 1986.
Information from the Surface of Venus (poems), United Artists, 1987.

Contributor to *Poetry, Paris Review, Big Sky,* and other publications.

*   *   *

WASHBURN, Dorothy K(oster)   1945-

PERSONAL: Born May 17, 1945, in Cleveland, Ohio; daughter of E. Frederick (a pathologist) and Mary Jane (a librarian; maiden name, Miller) Koster; married William N. Washburn (a research chemist), September 20, 1969. *Education:* Oberlin College, B.A., 1967; Columbia University, Ph.D., 1972.

ADDRESSES: Home—1820 Mendon-Ionia Rd., Ionia, N.Y. 14475. *Office*—Department of Anthropology, University of Rochester, Rochester, N.Y. 14627.

CAREER: Harvard University, Cambridge, Mass., research fellow in North American archaeology at Peabody Museum of Archaeology and Ethnology, 1972-76; University of California, Berkeley, fellow of Miller Institute for Basic Research in Science, 1976-78; California Academy of Sciences, San Francisco, assistant curator, 1978-80, associate curator, 1980-84; University of Rochester, Rochester, N.Y., National Science Foundation Visiting Professor for Women in the Sciences, 1984-85, visiting associate professor, 1986—. Assistant director of San Jose State University's Hovenweep expedition, 1975-76.

MEMBER: American Anthropological Association (fellow), Society for American Archaeology, California Academy of Sciences (fellow).

WRITINGS:

A Symmetry Analysis of Upper Gila Area Ceramic Design, Peabody Museum of Archaeology and Ethnology, Harvard University, 1977.
(Editor) *Hopi Kachina: Spirit of Life,* California Academy of Sciences, 1980.
(Editor) *Structure and Cognition in Art,* Cambridge University Press, 1983.
(Editor and contributor) *The Elkus Collection: Southwestern Indian Art,* California Academy of Sciences, 1984.
(With Donald Crowe) *Symmetries of Culture: Handbook of Symmetry Analysis,* University of Washington Press, 1988.

Also author of *Categories of Material Culture: Bakuba Raffia Cloth Patterns* (manuscript).

SIDELIGHTS: Dorothy K. Washburn told *CA:* "My professional interest lies in problems of classification, categorization, and systematic analysis of material culture."

*   *   *

WASMUTH, William J.   1925-

PERSONAL: Born February 6, 1925, in St. Louis, Mo.; son

of William H. (a cabinetmaker) and Bertha (Koch) Wasmuth; married Norma Whittleman (a college instructor in health services), November 17, 1951; children: Craig, Scott, Toni. *Education:* Jefferson College, St. Louis, Mo., B.S., 1945; Washington University, M.B.A., 1955; Indiana University, D.B.A., 1961.

ADDRESSES: Home—381 The Parkway, Ithaca, N.Y. 14850. *Office*—Room 101, Industrial and Labor Relations Extension Building, New York State School of Industrial and Labor Relations, Cornell University, Ithaca, N.Y. 14853.

CAREER: Junior aeronautical engineer, McDonnell Aircraft, 1945-46; Rice-Stix, Inc., St. Louis, Mo., management analyst, 1947-51; Air Training Command, Scott Air Force Base, Belleville, Ill., management systems analyst, 1951-53; Business Collaborators, Inc., St. Louis, management consultant, 1953-54; Freund Baking Co., St. Louis, assistant to president, 1954-58, assistant in plant management, 1956-58; Cornell University, New York State School of Industrial and Labor Relations, Ithaca, N.Y., assistant professor, 1961-66, associate professor, 1966-71, professor of management and industrial relations, 1971—, chairman of department, Extension Division, and assistant to dean, 1978—. Visiting lecturer, Health Service Administration, Ithaca College, 1971—. President and treasurer, Organization Evaluation, Inc. (management consultants), Ithaca, 1971—. *Military service:* U.S. Army Air Forces, 1946-47.

MEMBER: Industrial Relations Research Association, Academy of Management, American Association of University Professors, Association of Educators of Rehabilitation Facility Personnel, Beta Gamma Sigma.

WRITINGS:

(With Rollin Simonds, Raymond Hilgert, and Hak Lee) *Human Resources Administration: Problems of Growth and Change*, Houghton, 1970.
(With George deLodzia) *Organization Cases and Intrigues: Dynamics of Supervision*, Grid, 1974.
(With Leonard Greenhalgh) *Effective Supervision: Developing Your Skills through Critical Incidents*, Prentice-Hall, 1979.

WORK IN PROGRESS: A study of open systems approach to examining a variety of health organizations, social nonprofit agencies, and hotel banquet facilities.

SIDELIGHTS: William J. Wasmuth comments: "In writing [*Effective Supervision*] we steered clear of dry, abstract 'principles' [and] routine situations. Rather, the focus was on handling twenty-five tough, make-or-break problems, called 'critical incidents,' where the abilities or shortcomings of a supervisor become very clear to higher-ups." Wasmuth and his colleagues find that this approach is quite successful with students. "Students became intrigued in finding out who succeeds and who fails, especially when their stereotypes of heroes are exploded or their predictions of villains are proven wrong. In short, *suspense* is still a great motivator for plowing through required reading and we intend to capitalize on it in future texts as well."

* * *

WASSERMAN, Pauline 1943-

PERSONAL: Born November 17, 1943, in Portland, Maine; daughter of Kenneth P. and S. Bernice (Coffin) MacKenzie; married Sheldon Wasserman (a writer), April 13, 1963. *Education:* Attended Rhode Island School of Design.

ADDRESSES: Home and office—16 Rutgers Rd., Piscataway, N.J. 08854.

CAREER: Writer.

MEMBER: Accademia Vitivinicola della Daunia, Amici del Vino, Commanderie du Bontemps de Medoc, New York Wine Writers Circle.

AWARDS, HONORS: Regione Toscana first prize for foreign journalists (with Sheldon Wasserman), 1981, for article "The Wines of Chianti"; first place among foreign journalists (with Sheldon Wasserman), 1985, Columbini contest on wines of Montalcino, for article "Brunello di Montalcino: Great Unheralded Reds from Italy."

WRITINGS:

WITH HUSBAND, SHELDON WASSERMAN

The Wines of the Cotes du Rhone, Stein & Day, 1977.
Don't Ask Your Waiter: A Dictionary of Dining Terms, Stein & Day, 1978.
White Wines of the World, Stein & Day, 1978, revised edition, 1980.
Guide to Fortified Wines, Marlborough Press, 1983.
(Contributor) *The Price Guide to Good Wine*, Addison-Wesley, 1983.
Sparkling Wine, New Century, 1984.
Italy's Noble Red Wines, New Century, 1985.
(Contributor) *The International Wine Review Buyer's Guide*, New American Library, 1987.

Also contributor to *Il Veronelli: Enciclopedia mondiale dei vine e della acquaviti*, Rizzoli Editori, 1983.

WORK IN PROGRESS: Pocket Guide to Wine; Pocket Guide to Italian Wine.

SIDELIGHTS: Pauline Wasserman wrote: "I'm looking forward to doing more writing in the fields of food and travel. These two subjects are naturally complementary to my work on wine. One day I'd also like to write a book on some aspect of the lyric stage."

AVOCATIONAL INTERESTS: Classical music (especially opera), fashion design, travel.

* * *

WASSERMAN, Sheldon 1940-

PERSONAL: Born December 17, 1940, in Boston, Mass.; son of Myer (a laborer) and Florence (Youngstein) Wasserman; married Pauline MacKenzie (a writer), April 13, 1963. *Education:* Attended schools in Providence, R.I.

ADDRESSES: Home and office—16 Rutgers Rd., Piscataway, N.J. 08854.

CAREER: Honeywell Co., programmer analyst in Massachusetts and Colorado, 1963-65; Technical Operations, Inc., Maryland, programmer analyst, 1965; Computer Applications, Inc., Massachusetts, programmer analyst, 1966-67; RCA Corp., worked in Massachusetts, New Jersey, and Germany as systems designer analyst, systems programmer analyst, and regional systems specialist, 1967-71; Delta Resources, senior programmer analyst in New York, 1972-75; free-lance programmer and systems analyst, 1975—. Lecturer on wine and wine consultant to restaurants, 1975—. *Military service:* U.S. Army Reserve, active duty, 1958-61.

MEMBER: Accademia Vitivinicola della Daunia, Club Paladini dei Vini di Sicilia, Compagnons de Beaujolais, Le Grand Conseil L'Academie du Vin de Bordeaux, Ordem dos Companheiros de Sao Vicente, New York Wine Writers Circle.

AWARDS, HONORS: Regione Toscana first prize for foreign journalists (with Pauline Wasserman), 1981, for article "The Wines of Chianti"; first place among foreign journalists (with Pauline Wasserman), Colombini contest on wines of Montalcino, 1985, for article "Brunello di Montalcino: Great Unheralded Reds from Italy."

WRITINGS:

The Wines of Italy: A Consumer's Guide, Stein & Day, 1976.

WITH WIFE, PAULINE WASSERMAN

The Wines of the Cotes du Rhone, Stein & Day, 1977.
Don't Ask Your Waiter: A Dictionary of Dining Terms, Stein & Day, 1978.
White Wines of the World, Stein & Day, 1978, revised edition, 1980.
Guide to Fortified Wines, Marlborough Press, 1983.
(Contributor) *The Price Guide to Good Wine,* Addison-Wesley, 1983.
Sparkling Wine, New Century, 1984.
Italy's Noble Red Wines, New Century, 1985.
(Contributor) *The International Wine Review Buyer's Guide,* New American Library, 1987.

Also contributor to *Il Veronelli: Enciclopedia mondiale dei vine e della acquaviti,* Rizzoli Editori, 1983.

OTHER

(Contributing editor) Henri Gault and Christian Millau, *The Best of Italy,* Crown, 1984.

Author of regular columns for *International Wine Review, Beverage Retailer Weekly,* and *Drinks International.* Contributor to periodicals, including *Quarterly Review of Wine, New York Wine Cellar,* and *Italian Wines and Spirits.*

WORK IN PROGRESS: Pocket Guide to Italy's Noble Red Wines; In Gold We Trust: Causes and Solution to the Current International Monetary Muddle.

SIDELIGHTS: "Economics is still a real interest," Sheldon Wasserman once told *CA,* "but wine has become a more compelling one. Speaking on wine to audiences of fellow and future wine-lovers is also a pleasure. Why wine? It is not only a fascination in itself but represents one of the few fields of endeavor today where quality and integrity are still valued over mediocrity."

AVOCATIONAL INTERESTS: "Travel and related research with respect to food, wine, the people and their customs, and history."

*   *   *

WATSON, David   1934-

PERSONAL: Born January 20, 1934, in Nashville, Tenn.; son of Manly Arthur (a lawyer) and Faye (Givens) Watson; married Joyce Frank (a librarian, editor, and writer), September 14, 1957; children: Daniel, Malia. *Education:* Vanderbilt University, B.A., 1959; Yale University, Ph.D., 1963.

ADDRESSES: Office—Department of Psychology, University of Hawaii, Honolulu, Hawaii 96822.

CAREER: University of Toronto, Toronto, Ontario, assistant professor, 1963-66, associate professor of psychology, 1966-67; Pierce College, Athens, Greece, Fulbright lecturer, 1967-68; University of Hawaii, Honolulu, associate professor, 1968-72, professor of psychology, 1972—.

WRITINGS:

Self-Directed Behavior, Brooks/Cole, 1972, 5th edition, 1989.
Here's Psychology, Ginn, 1977.
Psychology: What It Is, How to Use It, Canfield Press, 1978.
Social Psychology: Science and Application, Scott, Foresman, 1984.

WORK IN PROGRESS: An introduction to psychology.

*   *   *

WATSON, Ian   1943-

PERSONAL: Born April 20, 1943, in North Shields, England; son of John William (a postmaster) and Ellen (Rowley) Watson; married Judith Jackson, September 1, 1962; children: Jessica Scott. *Education:* Balliol College, Oxford, B.A. (first class honors), 1963, B.Litt., 1965, M.A., 1966.

ADDRESSES: c/o Victor Gollancz Ltd., 14 Henrietta St., London WC2E 8QJ, England.

CAREER: University of Dar es Salaam, Dar es Salaam, Tanzania, lecturer in literature, 1965-67; Tokyo University of Education and Keio University, Tokyo, Japan, lecturer in English, 1967-70; Birmingham Polytechnic, Birmingham, England, lecturer, 1970-75, senior lecturer in complementary studies (science fiction and futures studies) for School of the History of Art in Art and Design Center, 1975-76; writer, 1976—. Temporary lecturer, English department, Japan Women's University, Tokyo, 1968-69. Writer-in-residence, Nene College, Northamptonshire, England, 1984.

MEMBER: Science Fiction Writers of America, Science Fiction Foundation (London; member of governing council, 1974—).

AWARDS, HONORS: The Embedding was named runner-up for the John W. Campbell Memorial Award, 1974, in French translation won the Prix Apollo, 1975, and in Spanish translation won the Premios Zikkurath, 1978; guest of honor, Second French National Science Fiction Congress, 1975, and Leodicon (in Belgium), 1976; *The Jonah Kit* won the Orbit Award, 1976, and the British Science Fiction Association Award for best paperback book published in Britain, 1978; Southern Arts Association literary bursary, 1978; "The Very Slow Time Machine" was nominated for the Hugo Award for best short story, 1979; British guest of honor at the British National Science Fiction Convention, 1981; short story "The World SF Convention of 2080" was a runner-up for the British Science Fiction Award, 1981; "Slow Birds" was nominated for the Hugo and Nebula Awards for best novelette, 1984; Prix Europeen de Science Fiction, 1985, for work as a novelist; short story "Jingling Geordie's Hole" was a runner-up for the British Science Fiction Association Award, 1987.

WRITINGS:

SCIENCE FICTION NOVELS

The Embedding, Gollancz, 1973, Scribner, 1975.
The Jonah Kit, Gollancz, 1975, Scribner, 1976.

(With wife, Judith Jackson Watson) *Orgasmachine* (French translation of original English manuscript), Editions Champ-Libre, 1976.

Japan Tomorrow (juvenile), Bunken, 1977.

The Martian Inca, Scribner, 1977.

Alien Embassy, Gollancz, 1977, Ace Books, 1978.

God's World, Gollancz, 1979.

The Gardens of Delight, Gollancz, 1980, Pocket Books, 1982.

(With Michael Bishop) *Under Heaven's Bridge*, Gollancz, 1981, Ace Books, 1982.

Deathhunter, Gollancz, 1981, St. Martin's, 1986.

Chekhov's Journey, Gollancz, 1983.

Converts, Granada, 1984, St. Martin's, 1985.

The Book of the River (first volume in Yaleen trilogy), Gollancz, 1984, DAW Books, 1986.

The Book of the Stars (second volume in Yaleen trilogy), Gollancz, 1985, DAW Books, 1986.

The Book of Being (third volume in Yaleen trilogy), Gollancz, 1985, DAW Books, 1986.

Queenmagic, Kingmagic, Gollancz, 1986.

OTHER

Japan: A Cat's Eye View (juvenile), Bunken, 1969.

The Very Slow Time Machine (short stories), Ace Books, 1979.

(Editor) *Pictures at an Exhibition: A Science Fiction Anthology*, Greystoke Mobray, 1981.

Sunstroke and Other Stories (short stories), Gollancz, 1982.

(Editor with Bishop) *Changes*, Ace Books, 1982.

Slow Birds and Other Stories (short stories), Gollancz, 1985.

The Book of Ian Watson, Mark Ziesing, 1985.

(Editor with Pamela Sargent) *Afterlives: An Anthology of Stories about Life after Death*, Vintage Trade, 1986.

Evil Water (short stories), Gollancz, 1987.

The Power (horror), Headline, 1987.

Also contributor of stories to science fiction anthologies. Contributor of stories and articles to science fiction magazines and literary journals, including *Chicago Review, London Magazine, Ambit, Transition,* and *Transatlantic Review.* Features editor of *Foundation: The Review of Science Fiction,* 1975—. European editor of *Science Fiction Writers of America Bulletin.*

SIDELIGHTS: Ian Watson "may not be the best writer in British science fiction, but he is probably the best thinker," according to a reviewer for the *Washington Post Book World.* He presents new ideas and concepts of how the universe works and how we determine what is real. "I'm attempting to alter the states of mind of my readers, to make them more conscious of the operating programs that are running their brains—the sort of thing that John Lilly refers to as 'metaprogramming,'" Watson tells Charles Platt in *Dream Makers: The Uncommon People Who Write Science Fiction.* "I'm interested in ways of examining the structure of your thinking, and trying to present narratives that make people think a bit about the pattern and style of their thoughts, and what alternative thought-structures they could enter into. That is what I say science fiction ought to be about, presenting you with an alternative-reality paradigm, a different way of conceptualizing reality and the universe."

Watson's early books focus on reality, maintaining that it is defined by our perception of it and can, therefore, be altered. His first novel, *The Embedding,* involves the search for a primary language which, if discovered, may provide clues to understanding the nature of reality. Charles Platt in *Dream Makers* says, "The book suggests that an isolated group of

children, educated to think differently, would inhabit a different reality from ours, with different natural laws." Similar themes are explored in *The Jonah Kit,* in which the universe is discovered to have existed for only a few microseconds after its creation and a whale is imprinted with a human soul, and in *The Martian Inca,* in which an extraterrestrial microorganism accidently infects both a group of Andean natives and a couple of American astronauts. In each case, a character's perception of the universe which surrounds him changes, and, for that character at least, the universe itself changes correspondingly.

Watson's later works *God's World* and *The Gardens of Delight* are less about the evolution of consciousness than about the nature of God. *God's World* concerns a trip to heaven. Angels appear at sacred places all over the globe, inviting humanity to join God, who lives in a star system some distance away. A spaceship with neo-crusaders aboard sets out, using technology provided by the angels, but, on their arrival, the humans' expectations are shattered. They find themselves in a world with its own heaven, which can be reached by dreaming or death, but they discover that the struggle between good and evil is not nearly as simple as it seems. *The Gardens of Delight* is based on the painting "The Garden of Earthly Delights" by Hieronymus Bosch, a surrealistic vision of life after death, filled with outsized animals, bizarrely shaped vegetables, anthropomorphic minerals, and naked people. The novel tells the story of a spaceship crew's search for God against the backdrop of Bosch's allegorical work. Mysterious immortal beings, in an attempt to bring purpose to their existences, have been molding worlds to fit what they have learned about other forms of life. A chance encounter with colonists from Earth causes the aliens to transform one world into a living replica of Bosch's painting. When another spacecraft arrives some years later, its crew begins a search for the aliens, who fancy themselves "God."

In Watson's opinion, these two studies of the search for God, although alike, represent views from opposite angles. He told David Langford in *Science Fiction Review,* "*GW* and *Gardens* are mirror images in the sense that, in the former, the journey to an objective alien world is presented as a journey through *imaginative* space, the physical starship journey being also a journey through the imagination—whereas, in the latter, the creators (who are also the inhabitants) of the alien Bosch-world have to imagine (and create) a human starship arriving there, in order to understand their own reality."

This emphasis on ideas pervades Watson's fiction. Watson himself admits to Platt that "my fault is that I would tend to write philosophical, abstract books." In the opinion of Gerald Jonas, writing for the *New York Times Book Review,* Watson in his early novels "did not know when to stop: too many concepts, too many characters, too much plot." Eric Korn in the *Times Literary Supplement* notes that "Ian Watson certainly treats ideas as though there were plenty more where those come from," but he sees this as a strength rather than a weakness, saying, "he is one of the few esseffers who can afford to. . . . [He] juggles with more notions on a page than many writers have in a lifetime." Spider Robinson in *Analog Science Fiction/Science Fact* and Alex de Jonge in the *Spectator* both admit that Watson's books are not easy to read, but recommend them strongly anyway. Robinson in particular views the author's multiplicity of ideas as one of Watson's strong points; he says of *Miracle Workers,* Watson's novel about the origin of UFOs, "I report myself dubious, confused, mightily intrigued, and enormously impressed. Watson is groping along the edge of something important here, and knows it: essentially he is like a fish trying to write a science fiction novel for his fellows about the unseen but inferable air-breathers. Daring, heady stuff . . . not to be missed by the thoughtful, and not in a million years to be taken for light entertainment.''

Some critics feel that Watson's fascination with ideas interferes with the creation of effective prose. For example, a reviewer for the *Times Literary Supplement* calls the opening twenty pages of *The Embedding* ''superbly unreadable,'' and Korn says, ''Mr. Watson can postulate a meeting of minds across a conceptual gulf, but in the nature of things he cannot describe it.'' Kelvin Johnston says in the *Observer* that *Chekhov's Journey* ''is a clever little stunt, though it suffers from the common illusion, not confined to SF novelists, that to be obscure is to be mature. [The book is] too ingenious for its own good.''

Although Baird Searles and his co-editors in *A Reader's Guide to Science Fiction* call Watson's *The Embedding* ''a serious, difficult and fascinating book, one that assumes its reader's intelligence,'' other commenters find the author's output uneven, the quality of his work varying from novel to novel. Korn declares that *The Jonah Kit* was ''flawed in realization.'' He continues, ''Most of the characters exist only to break the exposition up into easy chunks of dialogue, and have human attributes stuck in them like feathers in a hat.'' However, he says of *Miracle Visitors,* ''There is, as usual, a richness of character and description.'' Jonas praises Watson's first two novels as being ''distinguished by an irresistible blend of narrative energy and intellectual interest''; but he says of *The Martian Inca,* ''the book fails to cohere. The ideas, while fascinating in themselves, are not really dramatized. . . . However, with all its faults, it is still superior to most contemporary sf.''

Reviewers disagree over Watson's ability to present ideas that have been treated elsewhere in art and literature. The themes of *God's World* and *The Gardens of Delight,* the questions of how we tell the difference between good and evil and what happens to us after death, have been examined by artists and philosophers many, many times over the years. Korn says, ''I am less enthusiastic about *God's World* than any of the previous novels; it seems, if not perfunctory, at least hurried in relation to its theme.'' Alex de Jonge, writing in the *Spectator,* holds a different opinion: he states that *God's World* ''is quite as good as [Watson's] earlier works . . . never for a moment do we feel the author has overreached himself,'' and he calls it ''a work of great distinction.'' Similar differences of opinion surround *The Gardens of Delight;* Gay Firth comments in the London *Times* that Watson is attempting in *Gardens* to retell a story which has been ''better described by Dante and Bunyan.'' Galen Strawson in the *Times Literary Supplement* indicates that ''Watson's fantasy is the puppet of Bosch's own . . . his Phantastic Faculty is much better off when left to its own devices than when it is forced to elaborate on someone else's.'' On the other hand, Tom Easton, writing for *Analog Science Fiction/Science Fact,* says, ''*Gardens* is a strange book, as strange as Bosch's original painting. But Watson has handled the imagery well, emerging with a story that could stand discussion in terms of Bunyan and Dante. It's an allegory that denies itself even as it says perfection of the soul is possible.''

Critical response to Watson, whether positive or negative, recognizes the writer's innovative approach to science fiction. As he told *CA,* ''The Science Fiction I am interested in should be scientific—in that it deals with the impact of scientific ideas

and discoveries; and however farfetched these ideas or discoveries may be, they should be dealt with from a standpoint of realism, not fantasy or magic. But at the same time, SF should be metaphorical—in that it functions as a tool for thinking about the world and its future, Man and the Universe, flexibly and boldly. . . . SF should be contradictory, in that it envisages a multiplicity of possible futures. SF should be rooted in a sense of Man (adequate characterization, not puppets; sense of real social milieu). Yet it should be this without being 'earthbound' (by refusing to consider the nature of Alien experience or the Universe at large). Indeed, it must try to tackle ultimate questions: about the nature of reality, about the origin and significance of the Universe, and of life within this Universe.''

BIOGRAPHICAL/CRITICAL SOURCES:

BOOKS

Platt, Charles, *Dream Makers: The Uncommon People Who Write Science Fiction,* Berkeley Publishing, 1980.
Pringle, David, *Science Fiction: The 100 Best Novels,* Xanadu, 1985.
Searles, Baird, Martin Last, Beth Meacham, and Michael Franklin, editors, *A Reader's Guide to Science Fiction,* Avon, 1979.
Staicar, Ted, editor, *Critical Encounters II: Writers & Themes in Science Fiction,* Ungar, 1982.

PERIODICALS

Analog Science Fiction/Science Fact, March, 1979, June, 1979, September, 1982, October, 1986.
Economist, August 20, 1983.
Fantasy Review, August, 1984, April, 1985, July, 1985, November, 1985, May, 1986, November, 1986.
New Statesman, April 24, 1987.
New York Times Book Review, July 20, 1975, September 12, 1976, November 27, 1977, September 21, 1986.
Observer, February 20, 1983, August 5, 1984, December 26, 1986, April 26, 1987.
Punch, June 13, 1984, December 12, 1984, November 6, 1985, June 4, 1986.
Science Fiction and Fantasy Book Review, January, 1982, July, 1983.
Science Fiction Review, spring, 1982, winter, 1982, summer, 1985, spring, 1986.
Spectator, August 26, 1978, January 12, 1980, September 13, 1980.
Times (London), February 3, 1980, March 3, 1983, October 31, 1985.
Times Literary Supplement, September 11, 1973, May 23, 1975, July 8, 1977, January 27, 1978, May 30, 1980, July 18, 1980, September 10, 1982.
Voice Literary Supplement, October, 1984, July, 1985.
Washington Post Book World, July 26, 1981, March 28, 1982, April 28, 1985.
West Coast Review of Books, July, 1979.

—*Sketch by Kenneth R. Shepherd*

*   *   *

WATSON, Lyall 1939-

PERSONAL: Born April 12, 1939, in Johannesburg, South Africa; son of Douglas (an architect) and Mary (Morkel) Watson. *Education:* University of Witwatersrand, B.S., 1958;

University of Natal, M.S., 1959; University of London, Ph.D., 1963. *Politics:* "Absolutely none." *Religion:* "Animist."

ADDRESSES: *Home*—Ballplehob, County Cork, Ireland. *Office*—BCM-Biologic, London WC1, England. *Agent*—Murray Pollinger, 4 Garrick St., London WC2E 9BH, England.

CAREER: Zoological Garden of Johannesburg, Johannesburg, South Africa, director, 1964-65; British Broadcasting Corp., London, England, producer of documentary films, 1966-67; BCM-Biologic (consultants), London, founder and director, 1967—. Expedition leader and researcher in Antarctica, Amazon River area, the Seychelles, and Indonesia, 1968-72.

WRITINGS:

The Omnivorous Ape, Coward, 1971.
Supernature, Doubleday, 1973.
The Romeo Error: A Meditation on Life and Death, Doubleday, 1974.
Gifts of Unknown Things, Simon & Schuster, 1977.
Lifetide: The Biology of the Unconscious, Simon & Schuster, 1978.
Sea Guide to Whales of the World, illustrated by Tom Ritchie, Dutton, 1981.
Lightning Bird: The Story of One Man's Journey into Africa (biography), Dutton, 1982.
Heaven's Breath: A Natural History of the Wind, Morrow, 1985.
The Dreams of Dragons: Riddles of Natural History, Morrow, 1987.
Supernature II (sequel to *Supernature*), Bantam, 1988.

Also author of screenplays for feature films "Gifts of Unknown Things" and "Lifetide: The Biology of the Unconscious." Contributor to Reader's Digest Services' "Living World of Animals" series, 1970. Contributor to professional journals.

WORK IN PROGRESS: Research toward the building of a bridge between scientific investigation and mystic revelation; *The Secret Life of Machines.*

SIDELIGHTS: "Since 1967 I have travelled constantly," writes biologist Lyall Watson, "looking and listening, collecting bits and pieces of apparently useless and unconnected information, stopping every two years to put the fragments together into some sort of meaningful pattern. Sometimes it works out. And so far, enough people have enjoyed the results to justify publishing several million copies in fourteen languages."

Gifts of Unknown Things is an account of Watson's brief visit to Nus Tarian, a small Indonesian island, and the seemingly supernatural occurrences he witnessed there. Many of the paranormal phenomena in the book center on a young girl named Tia, and several of the book's reviewers find the events incredible. John Naughton, for example, writes in the *New Statesman* that Watson's "chronicle of [Tia's] more spectacular exploits stretches the reader's credulity to breaking point and beyond." Christopher Lehmann-Haupt of the *New York Times* elaborates: "I don't believe that Tia, the young orphan girl of the island, learned to heal burns by touching them with her hand, to cure schizophrenia by drawing out bad chemicals, to raise a man from the dead, and, finally, when the Muslim natives begin to find Tia's powers too disturbing to their orthodoxy, to transform herself into a porpoise. . . . Now it may well be, as Mr. Watson argues, that my Western rationalism is woefully limited—that it fails to perceive what children and poets and Eastern mystics and with-it physicists see with the

greatest of ease, which is that 'There are levels of reality far too mysterious for totally objective common sense. There are things that cannot be known by exercise only of the scientific method.' Fair enough. But just because Newton has turned out to be wrong doesn't make *all* things possible. . . . Yet this is how Mr. Watson reasons."

In *Lifetide: The Biology of the Unconscious,* Watson attempts to construct a unified model of life and the universe that accounts for phenomena currently unexplained by modern science. Using a plethora of examples from biology—his own area of expertise—as well as such disciplines as physics, anthropology, medicine, psychology, and paleontology, Watson argues that evolution and everything else in the cosmos is deliberately directed by a kind of collective unconscious of all living things (including biological components). He calls this "contingent system" the Lifetide and describes it as "the whole panoply of hidden forces that shape life in all its miraculous guises,. . . the eddies and vortices of nature that flow together to form the living stream." Reviewing the book in the *Washington Post Book World,* Dan Sperling declares: "Watson builds an admirable case in favor of the existence of such a contingent system, and believes that the eventual discovery of its parameters and properties will reveal it to be the source of much that we now call the paranormal,. . . [though] even this, he feels, will not solve the underlying mysteries of the Lifetide." Sperling also points out that Watson's description of this system contains "language so rich and lively that at times the book seems as though it were written by a poet rather than a scientist."

BIOGRAPHICAL/CRITICAL SOURCES:

BOOKS

Watson, Lyall, *Lifetide: The Biology of the Unconscious,* Simon & Schuster, 1978.

PERIODICALS

Globe and Mail (Toronto), December 8, 1984, October 4, 1986.
New Statesman, July 2, 1976.
New York Times, April 13, 1977.
New York Times Book Review, June 3, 1979, April 18, 1982, May 10, 1987.
Spectator, October 26, 1974.
Times Literary Supplement, December 20, 1974, August 20, 1982.
Washington Post Book World, April 10, 1977, July 15, 1979, May 23, 1982.

*   *   *

WATTS, Meredith W(ayne, Jr.)   1941-

PERSONAL: Born April 14, 1941, in Bloomington, Ill.; son of Meredith Wayne, Sr. and Leah Lucille (Stiegman) Watts; married Elizabeth Anne Guthrie, November 1, 1969 (divorced, 1976); children: David, Christopher. *Education:* Attended University of Mainz, summer, 1961; Lawrence University, B.A., 1962; Northern Illinois University, graduate study, 1962-63; Northwestern University, M.A., 1964, Ph.D., 1967; University of Michigan, additional study, summer, 1964.

ADDRESSES: *Home*—2113 East Jarvis St., Milwaukee, Wis. 53211. *Office*—Department of Political Science, University of Wisconsin—Milwaukee, Milwaukee, Wis. 53201.

CAREER: Northwestern University, Evanston, Ill., instructor in political science, 1965-66; University of Wisconsin—Milwaukee, assistant professor, 1966-67, 1970-74, associate professor, 1974-78, professor of political science, 1978—, assistant to the chancellor, 1977-79, assistant chancellor for student services, 1979-81. *Military service:* U.S. Air Force, 1967-70.

MEMBER: International Communication Association, International Society for Human Ethology, International Political Science Association, International Society for Research on Aggression, American Political Science Association, Midwest Political Science Association.

AWARDS, HONORS: National Science Foundation research grant, 1965-66; University of Wisconsin—Milwaukee Graduate School research grant, 1972.

WRITINGS:

(With Lee F. Anderson and Allen R. Wilcox) *Legislative Roll Call Analysis,* Northwestern University Press, 1966.
(With Wilder Crane, Jr.) *State Legislative Systems,* Prentice-Hall, 1968.
(Contributor) Wilcox, editor, *Public Opinion and Political Attitudes: A Reader,* Wiley, 1973.
(Editor) *Biopolitics: Ethological and Physiological Approaches,* Jossey-Bass, 1981.
(Editor) *Biopolitics and Gender,* Haworth Press, 1984.

Contributor of articles and reviews to psychology, political science, and communications journals.

WORK IN PROGRESS: Research on political attitudes and behavior, psychophysiological approaches to sociopolitical behavior, and biopolitics.

*   *   *

WAYBURN, Peggy   1921-

PERSONAL: Born September 2, 1921, in New York, N.Y.; daughter of Thomas Ketchin (an electrical engineer) and Cornelia (Ligon) Elliott; married Edgar Wayburn (a physician), September 12, 1947; children: Cynthia, William, Diana, Laurie. *Education:* Barnard College, B.A. (cum laude), 1942.

ADDRESSES: Home—30 Sea View Ter., San Francisco, Calif. 94121.

CAREER: Western Electric Co., Kearny, N.J., project engineer, 1942-43; Conde Nast Publications, New York City, copy writer, 1943-45; *Country Book* (magazine), New York City, editor, 1943-45; J. Walter Thompson, San Francisco, Calif., copy writer, 1945-49. Director of numerous community groups and conservation organizations.

MEMBER: Sierra Club, Phi Beta Kappa.

AWARDS, HONORS: California Conservation Council award, 1961; Sierra Club special service award, 1967.

WRITINGS:

(Editor) *The Last Redwoods and Parkland of Redwood Creek,* Sierra Books, 1969.
Edge of Life: The World of the Estuary, Sierra Books, 1972.
(With Mike Miller) *Alaska: The Great Land,* Sierra Books, 1974.
Adventuring in Alaska: The Ultimate Travel Guide to the Great Land, Sierra Books, 1982.
Adventuring in the San Francisco Bay Area, Sierra Books, 1987.

Also author of "Circle of Life" film strip series, Random House, 1974, and "Alaska" film strip series, Scribner, 1975. Contributor to *Sierra Club Bulletin* and other conservation periodicals.

*   *   *

WEBB, Pauline M(ary)   1927-

PERSONAL: Born June 28, 1927, in London, England; daughter of Leonard F. (a Methodist minister) and Daisy (Barnes) Webb. *Education:* King's College, London, B.A. (with honors), 1948; London Institute of Education, teaching diploma, 1949; Union Theological Seminary, New York, N.Y., S.T.M., 1965.

ADDRESSES: 14 Paddocks Green, Salomon St., London NW9 8NH, England.

CAREER: Teacher and assistant mistress of grammar school in Twickenham, England, 1949-52; Methodist Missionary Society, London, England, youth officer, 1952-54, editor, 1954-64, director of lay training, 1967-73, executive secretary, 1973-79; British Broadcasting Corp. World Service, London, organizer of religious broadcasting, 1979-87. Became accredited local preacher of Methodist Church, 1953. Vice-president of Methodist Conference, 1965-66; member of World Methodist Executive Committee, 1966-74. Teacher at Adult Evening Institute of Westminster College of Commerce, 1952-54; member of Anglican-Methodist Negotiating Commission, 1965-68; World Council of Churches, vice-chairman of central committee, 1968-75, moderator of Assembly Preparation committee, 1981-83.

AWARDS, HONORS: Honorary doctorates, University of Brussels, 1985, University of Victoria, Toronto, 1986, University of Mt. St. Vincent, Nova Scotia, 1987.

WRITINGS:

Women of Our Company, Cargate, 1958.
Women of Our Time, Cargate, 1960.
Operation Healing: Stories of the Work of Medical Missions throughout the World, with Bible Links and Things to Do, Edinburgh House Press, 1964.
All God's Children, Oliphants, 1965.
Are We Yet Alive?: Addresses on the Mission of the Church in the Modern World, Epworth, 1966.
Agenda for the Churches, SCM Press, 1968.
(Contributor) Rupert E. Davies, editor, *We Believe in God,* Allen & Unwin, 1968.
Salvation Today, SCM Press, 1974.
(Contributor) David Haslam, editor, *Agenda for Prophets,* Bowerham Press, 1980.
Where Are the Women, Epworth, 1980.
Celebrating Friendship, SCM Press, 1986.
Evidence for the Power of Prayer, Mowbray, 1987.

Also author of pageants "Kingdoms Ablaze," 1958, "Set My People Free," 1960, and "Bring Them to Me," 1964, film scripts "Bright Diadem" (on southern India), "The Road to Dabou," "New Life in Nigeria," and "Beauty for Ashes," and television scripts "Man on Fire," "Let Loose in the World," "A Women's Place?," and "A Death Reported."

SIDELIGHTS: Pauline M. Webb told *CA* her primary concerns are "the mission and unity of the Church, the ministry of the laity, race relations, world poverty, and the contribution of women in Church and community." She has traveled in Sri

Lanka, India, Burma, Nigeria, Kenya, Zambia, the United States, the Caribbean, and most of western Europe.

*   *   *

WEBB, Peter B(randram)   1941-

PERSONAL: Born May 23, 1941, in Hove, England; son of Francis (an army officer) and Enid (Elliot-Heywood) Webb. *Education:* Cambridge University, B.A. (with honors), 1963, M.A., 1967; Courtauld Institute of Art, London, Academic Diploma in Art History, 1965; graduate study, University of East Anglia, beginning 1983.

ADDRESSES: Home—1, Muswell Ave., Muswell Hill, London N10 2EB, England. *Office*—Cat Hill, Cockfosters, Barnet, Hertfordshire, England.

CAREER: Coventry College of Art (now Lanchester Polytechnic), Coventry, England, lecturer in art history, 1965-70; Middlesex Polytechnic, London, England, senior lecturer in art history, 1970-85, principal lecturer in art history, 1985—. Visiting lecturer at more than sixty schools, including Cambridge University, Oxford University, University of London, University of Hong Kong, University of Houston, University of Texas at Austin, Concordia University, and New York University. Guest on British radio and television programs. Honorary member of Print Makers Council.

MEMBER: Association of Art Historians.

WRITINGS:

(With Grant Lewison and Rosalind Billingham) *Coventry New Architecture,* [Warwickshire, England], 1969.
(Contributor) Stephen Verney, editor, *Art and the Mind of Man,* University of Birmingham Press, 1970.
The Erotic Arts, Secker & Warburg, 1975, New York Graphic Society, 1976, 4th revised edition, Farrar, Straus, 1983.
The Erotic Drawings of the Marquis von Bayros, Amorini Press, 1976.
(Art editor) *The Visual Dictionary of Sex,* A & W Publishers, 1977.
(Author of introduction) Ron Serlin, *Ron Serlin,* Perrins Lane Gallery (London), 1978.
(Contributor) *Disabled Artists in History,* Round House Gallery (London), 1981.
(Contributor) Ashwin, editor, *The Art and Design Historian as Author,* Middlesex Polytechnic, 1982.
(Contributor) Maurice Yaffe, editor, *The Influence of Pornography on Behaviour,* Academic Press, 1982.
(Contributor) Alan Bold, editor, *The Sexual Dimension in Literature,* Barnes & Noble, 1983.
(Art editor) Roger Gregerson, *Sexual Practices: The Story of Human Sexuality,* Mitchell Beazley, 1983.
(Author of introduction) *Forbidden Images* (catalogue), Maclean Gallery (London), 1985.
Hans Bellmer, Abrams, 1985.
(Author of introduction) *The Forbidden Library,* Maclean Gallery, 1986.
David Hockney, McGraw, 1988.

Contributor to magazines and newspapers, including *Artscribe, Scorpio,* and *Christian Science Monitor.*

SIDELIGHTS: Peter B. Webb told *CA:* "My expertise as an art historian is in late nineteenth- and early twentieth-century painting. My writing and lecturing tend to concentrate on the world of erotic art. This is something of a crusade for me. I feel it is of great importance for people to realize the vital role that eroticism has played in the culture of almost every civilization, so that they can have a better understanding of the vital role that sex can and should play in their own lives and in their own society."

In a *Times Literary Supplement* review of Webb's book *Hans Bellmer,* Roger Cardinal writes: "Given the cloud of ignorance and prejudice which inhibits our Anglo-Saxon view of Bellmer, Peter Webb's buoyant and informative study, the first monograph in English, is welcome. It makes available enough biographical, critical and visual material to facilitate a thorough appraisal of the artist's contribution to Surrealism and to modern culture at large."

AVOCATIONAL INTERESTS: Travel, cinema (attending and making films), collecting books ("an uncontrollable passion, and the reason for continual moves to larger houses").

BIOGRAPHICAL/CRITICAL SOURCES:

PERIODICALS

Books & Bookmen, November, 1978.
Chicago Tribune Book World, June 15, 1986.
Times (London), February 17, 1971.
Times Literary Supplement, February 2, 1976, August 23, 1985.
Washington Post, December 5, 1976.

*   *   *

WECHMAN, Robert Joseph   1939-

PERSONAL: Born September 23, 1939, in New York, N.Y.; son of David Samuel (a businessman) and Blanche (Udell) Wechman; married Stephanie Helene Kellman, June 18, 1967; children: Craig Samuel, Evan Mitchell, Darren Max. *Education:* Hunter College of the City University of New York, B.A., 1961; City College of the City University of New York, M.A., 1964; Columbia University, M.A., 1966; Syracuse University, Ph.D., 1970; University of Pennsylvania, postdoctoral study, 1973.

ADDRESSES: Home—9 Verdin Dr., New City, N.Y. 10956.

CAREER: Board of Education, New York, N.Y., teacher of history, 1961-63; high school teacher of history and economics, Dobbs Ferry, N.Y., 1963-66; Elmira College, Elmira, N.Y., instructor in history and economics, 1966-70; Hartwick College, Oneonta, N.Y., assistant professor of history and coordinator of urban studies, 1970-74; Beavertown Mills, assistant vice president, 1977-80, vice president, 1980—. Adjunct professor of social science and business administration at New School for Social Research, State University of New York, Rockland Community College, 1974-80, Empire State College, 1974, Bergen Community College, 1976-80, and Berkeley Business Institute, 1979; adjunct associate professor of marketing at Pace University, 1980—; adjunct associate professor of economics and business administration at St. Thomas Aquinas College, 1981—, and Dominican College, summer, 1981; adjunct assistant professor of business management at City College of the City University of New York, 1981. Visiting lecturer, State University of New York, Corning, summers, 1967, 1970—. President of Verdin Associates, Inc., 1982—, and of Robert J. Wechman Consulting, 1984—. Member of Board of Ethics, City of Oneonta, 1971-74, Otsego County Bicentennial Commission, 1972-74, and Antipollution and Environmental Commission, Oneonta, 1972-74. Speech writer for political candidates. *Military service:* U.S. Army, 1959-60. U.S. Army Reserve, 1960-65.

MEMBER: American Association of University Professors, Council for Basic Education, University Centers for Rational Alternatives, Phi Alpha Theta, Delta Tau Kappa.

AWARDS, HONORS: Marcus Award for distinguished teaching, 1972; Outstanding Educators of America Award, 1972.

WRITINGS:

(Editor) *Readings and Interpretations of Critical Issues in Modern American Life*, Associated Educational Services, 1968.
(Editor with Albert Ovedovitz) *The Crisis in Population*, Stipes, 1969.
Urban America: A Guide to the Literature, Stipes, 1971.
(With David M. Zielonka) *The Eager Immigrants*, Stipes, 1972.
The Economic Development of the Italian-American, Stipes, 1983.
Encountering Management, Stipes, 1987.

Contributor of articles and reviews to journals in his field.

AVOCATIONAL INTERESTS: "Good books, good music, interesting conversation, and sports."

*   *   *

WECHSLER, Herbert 1909-

PERSONAL: Born December 4, 1909, in New York, N.Y.; son of Samuel and Anna (Weisberger) Wechsler; married Elzie Stern Stix, May 29, 1933 (divorced, 1957); married Doris L. Klauber, April 13, 1957. *Education:* City College (now City College of the City University of New York), A.B., 1928; Columbia University, LL.B., 1931. *Politics:* Democrat. *Religion:* Jewish.

ADDRESSES: Home—179 East 70th St., New York, N.Y. 10027. *Office*—American Law Institute, 435 West 116th St., New York, N.Y. 10027.

CAREER: Admitted to the Bar of New York State, 1933, and the Bar of the U.S. Supreme Court, 1937. Worked as a law clerk for Justice Harlan F. Stone, U.S. Supreme Court, 1932-33; Columbia University, New York, N.Y., instructor, 1931-32, assistant professor, 1933-38, associate professor, 1938-45, professor, 1945-78, Harlan Fiske Stone Professor of Constitutional Law, 1957-78, emeritus, 1978—. American Law Institute, chief reporter of *Model Penal Code*, 1952-62, director, 1963-84. Special Assistant to U.S. Attorney General, 1940-44; assistant U.S. attorney general in charge of War Division, U.S. Department of Justice, 1944-46. Harvard University, visiting professor, 1956-57, Holmes Lecturer, 1958; Rothgerber Professor, University of Colorado, 1987. Member of federal, state, and local commissions. Consultant to government agencies.

MEMBER: British Academy (fellow), American Bar Association, American Judicature Society, American Academy of Political and Social Science, American Law Institute (life member), Academy of Political Science, American Society of International Law, American Academy of Arts and Sciences (fellow), Association of the Bar of the City of New York (past vice-president), Century Association, Mid-Ocean Club (Bermuda), Eastward Ho Club (Chatham, Massachusetts).

AWARDS, HONORS: LL.D., University of Chicago, 1962, Harvard University, 1967, Columbia University, 1978, Georgetown University, 1984; Sutherland Medal, American Society of Criminology, 1963; American Bar Foundation Award,

1967; Townsend Harris Medal, City College alumni, 1969; Columbia Law Alumni Medal, 1971; Association of the Bar Medal, 1985; Learned Hand Award, Federal Bar Council, 1985.

WRITINGS:

(With Jerome Michael) *Criminal Law and its Administration: Cases, Statutes and Commentaries*, Foundation Press, 1940.
(With Henry M. Hart, Jr.) *The Federal Courts and the Federal System*, Foundation Press, 1953, 2nd edition (with others) published as *Hart and Wechsler's The Federal Courts and the Federal System*, 1973.
Toward Neutral Principles of Constitutional Law (monograph), Bobbs-Merrill, c. 1960.
Principles, Politics and Fundamental Law, Harvard University Press, 1961.
The Nationalization of Civil Liberties and Civil Rights, University of Texas at Austin, 1970.

Editor with Hart of *The Judicial Code and Rules of Procedure in the Federal Courts, with Excerpts from the Criminal Code* and of annual revision, Foundation Press, 1949-83. Contributor to numerous legal and other periodicals, including *Harvard Law Review*, *Columbia Law Review*, *Virginia Quarterly*, and *Fortune*. Editor of *Columbia University Law Review*, 1929-31; editorial board chairman, *Uniform Commercial Code*, 1965-84.

BIOGRAPHICAL/CRITICAL SOURCES:

PERIODICALS

Columbia Law Review, June, 1978.

*   *   *

WELLER, Allen Stuart 1907-

PERSONAL: Born February 1, 1907, in Chicago, Ill.; son of Stuart and Harriet (Marvin) Weller; married Rachel Fort, 1929; children: Judith (Mrs. Cyril H. Harvey), Ruth (Mrs. Zafar Khilji), John Marvin. *Education:* University of Chicago, Ph.B., 1927, Ph.D., 1942; Princeton University, A.M., 1929.

ADDRESSES: Home—412 West Iowa St., Urbana, Ill. 61801. *Office*—Krannert Art Museum, University of Illinois, Champaign, Ill. 61820.

CAREER: University of Missouri, Columbia, 1929-42, 1946-47, began as assistant professor, became associate professor; University of Illinois at Urbana-Champaign, professor of history of art, 1947-75, head of department of art, 1949-54, dean of College of Fine and Applied Arts, 1954-71, director, Krannert Art Museum, 1964-75. Visiting summer professor, University of Minnesota, 1947, University of Colorado, 1949, University of California, 1950, 1953, University of Rhode Island, 1963, and Aspen Institute for Humanistic Studies, 1963. Guest curator, Mitchell Museum, Mt. Vernon, Ill., 1978-80 and 1983. Consultant in humanities to Field Enterprises Educational Corp. *Military service:* U.S. Army Air Forces, 1942-46; became major; awarded Legion of Merit.

MEMBER: College Art Asssociation (board of directors, 1953-57, 1965-69), Society of Architectural Historians, National Association of Schools of Art (fellow), Royal Society of London (fellow), Midwestern College Art Conference (vice-president, 1952; president, 1953), Phi Beta Kappa, Phi Kappa Phi, Omicron Delta Kappa, Phi Gamma Delta, University Club (Urbana), Arts Club and Cliff Dwellers Club (both Chicago), Princeton Club (New York).

AWARDS, HONORS: LL.D., Indiana Central College (now University of Indianapolis), 1965; Benjamin Franklin fellowship, Royal Society of Arts, London, 1970; D.F.A., University of Florida, 1977.

WRITINGS:

Francesco di Giorgio, 1439-1501, University of Chicago Press, 1943.
Abraham Rattner, University of Illinois Press, 1956.
Art, U.S.A.: Now, Viking, 1962.
(Compiler and author of introduction) *Contemporary American Painting and Sculpture, 1963,* University of Illinois Press, 1963.
Contemporary American Painting and Sculpture, 1965, University of Illinois Press, 1965.
Contemporary American Painting and Sculpture, 1967, University of Illinois Press, 1967.
The Joys and Sorrows of Recent American Art, University of Illinois Press, 1968.
Watercolor U.S.A. National Invitational Exhibition, Springfield Art Museum, Springfield, Missouri, May 2-July 4, 1976, The Gallery, 1976.
Lorado in Paris: The Letters of Lorado Taft, 1880-1885, University of Illinois Press, 1985.

Contributor to *Encyclopedia Americana, Encyclopedia of World Art,* and *Encyclopaedia Britannica.* Contributor to art magazines and journals. Book review editor, *Arts Journal,* 1949-67; Chicago correspondent, *Arts,* 1952-58.

WORK IN PROGRESS: Lorado Taft: The Chicago Years.

SIDELIGHTS: Allen S. Weller is the former chairman of Festival of Contemporary Arts at the University of Illinois and member of jury selecting contemporary painting and sculpture for the festivals. His book *The Joys and Sorrows of Contemporary American Art* has been translated into Spanish, and *Art U.S.A.: Now* has been translated into German.

BIOGRAPHICAL/CRITICAL SOURCES:

PERIODICALS

Times Literary Supplement, September 21, 1967, June 5, 1969.

*   *   *

WENDER, Dorothea   1934-
(Dorothea Schmidt)

PERSONAL: Born August 28, 1934, in Dayton, Ohio; daughter of Werner B. (a commercial artist) and Margaret (a writer; maiden name, Chase) Schmidt; married Paul H. Wender (a psychiatrist; divorced); children: Jocelyn, Leslie, Melissa. *Education:* Radcliffe College, B.A. (magna cum laude), 1956; University of Minnesota, M.A., 1960; Harvard University, Ph.D,. 1964.

ADDRESSES: Home—Norton, Mass. *Office*—Department of Classics, Wheaton College, Norton, Mass. 02766.

CAREER: Dell Publishing Co., New York, N.Y., editorial assistant, 1956-57; Trinity College, Washington, D.C., lecturer in English composition and world literature, 1962-63; George Washington University, Washington, D.C., lecturer in classical literature, 1964-66; University of Maryland, College Park, lecturer in Latin, 1966-67; Trinity College, assistant professor of classics and chairman of department, 1967-70; Wheaton College, Norton, Mass., professor of classics, 1970—,

Howard Meneeley Resident Professor, 1974-75, chairman of department, 1971—.

MEMBER: American Philological Association, American Association of University Professors, Classical Association of New England.

WRITINGS:

Hesiod and Theognis (verse translation), Penguin, 1973.
(With Marcia Polese) *Frankie and the Fawn* (juvenile), Abingdon, 1975.
The Myth of Washington, Arion, 1976.
The Last Scenes of the Odyssey, E. J. Brill, 1978.
(Translator and author of introduction) *Roman Poetry from the Republic to the Silver Age,* Southern Illinois University Press, 1980.

Contributor of articles and reviews, sometimes under name Dorothea Schmidt, to *Classical Journal, American Journal of Philology, Book World,* and *Arethusa.*

WORK IN PROGRESS: The Will of the Beast: Sexual Imagery in the "Trachiniae."†

*   *   *

WESLAGER, C(linton) A(lfred)   1909-

PERSONAL: Surname pronounced Wes-law-ger, with a hard "g"; born April 30, 1909, in Pittsburgh, Pa.; son of Fred H. (a contractor) and Alice (Lowe) Weslager; married Ruth Hurst, June 9, 1933; children: Ann Tatnall, Clintòn, Jr., Thomas. *Education:* University of Pittsburgh, B.A., 1933.

ADDRESSES: Home—Old Public Rd., R.D. 2, Box 104, Hockessin, Del. 19707.

CAREER: Life Savers Corp., Port Chester, N.Y., sales promotion manager, 1933-37; E. I. du Pont de Nemours & Co., Inc., Wilmington, Del., beginning 1937, sales manager, 1959-66, automotive products marketing manager, 1966-68; Brandywine College, Wilmington, Del., visiting professor, 1968-83, professor emeritus, 1983—. Member of faculty of history department, Wesley College, 1964, and University of Delaware, 1965, 1967; lecturer to historical, archeological, and other learned societies. President of Richardson Park (Del.) Board of School Trustees, 1953-57. Editor, Archeological Society of Delaware, 1938-53, and Historic Red Clay Valley, Inc., 1960-66. Consultant to Smithsonian Institution on log cabins in the Delaware Valley.

MEMBER: Chemical Specialties Manufacturers Association (chairman of automotive division, 1959-60), Eastern States Archeological Federation (president, 1954-58), Archeological Society of Delaware (president, 1942-48, 1950-53), New Jersey Archeological Society (fellow), Holland Society of New York (fellow), Sigma Delta Chi.

AWARDS, HONORS: Award of Merit from American Association for State and Local History, 1965, 1968; Lindback Award, 1977; Archibald Crozier Award, Archeological Society of Delaware, 1978; L.H.D., Widener University, 1986; Medal of Distinction, University of Delaware, 1987.

WRITINGS:

Delaware's Forgotten Folk, University of Pennsylvania Press, 1943.
Delaware's Buried Past, University of Pennsylvania Press, 1944.

Delaware's Forgotten River, Hambleton, 1947.

(Contributor) H. Clay Reed, editor, *Delaware: A History of the First State*, three volumes, Lewis Historical Publishing Co., 1947.

The Nanticoke Indians, Pennsylvania Historical Commission, 1948.

Brandywine Springs, Knebels, 1949.

Indian Place-Names in Delaware, Archeological Society of Delaware, 1950.

(Contributor) Charles B. Clark, editor, *The Eastern Shore of Maryland and Virginia*, three volumes, Lewis Historical Publishing Co., 1950.

Red Men on the Brandywine, Knebels, 1953.

The Richardsons of Delaware, Knebels, 1957.

Dutch Explorers, Traders and Settlers in the Delaware Valley, University of Pennsylvania Press, 1961.

The Garrett Snuff Fortune, Knebels, 1965.

The English on the Delaware, Rutgers University Press, 1967.

The Log Cabin in America: From Pioneer Days to the Present, Rutgers University Press, 1969.

History of the Delaware Indians, Rutgers University Press, 1972.

Magic Medicines of the Indians, Middle Atlantic Press, 1973.

The Stamp Act Congress, University of Delaware Press, 1976.

The Delaware Indian Westward Migration, Middle Atlantic Press, 1978.

The Delaware: A Critical Bibliography, Indiana University Press, 1978.

The Nanticoke Indians, Past and Present, University of Delaware Press, 1983.

Swedes and Dutch at New Castle, Middle Atlantic Press, 1987.

Author of six monographs on regional history subjects, 1959-64; also author of historical essays and papers published by Columbia University Press and University of Delaware Press. Contributor of articles and book reviews to historical, archeological, and folklore journals. Editor, *Hole News* (Life Savers Corp.), 1936-37, *F&F Magazine* (Du Pont Co.), 1946-47; contributing editor, *Delaware Today*, 1965.

WORK IN PROGRESS: New Sweden on the Delaware for Middle Atlantic Press.

*   *   *

WEST, Morris L(anglo) 1916-
(Michael East, Julian Morris)

PERSONAL: Born April 26, 1916, in Melbourne, Australia; son of Charles Langlo and Florence Guilfoyle (Hanlon) West; married Joyce Lawford, August 14, 1952; children: Christopher, Paul, Melanie, Michael. *Education:* Studied with Christian Brothers Order, 1933, leaving before final vows, 1939; University of Melbourne, Australia, B.A., 1937.

ADDRESSES: Home and office—310 Hudson Parade, Clareville, New South Wales, Australia 2107. *Agent*—Maurice Greenbaum, Rosenman Colin, Freund Lewis & Cohen, 587 Madison Ave., New York, N.Y. 10022.

CAREER: Teacher of modern languages and mathematics in New South Wales, Australia, and Tasmania, 1933-39; secretary to William Morris Hughes, former prime minister of Australia, 1943; Australasian Radio Productions, managing director, 1943-53; film and dramatic writer for Shell Co. and Australian Broadcasting Network, 1954—; commentator and writer, 1954—. Publicity manager, Murdoch newspaper chain, Melbourne, 1945-46; chairman, National Book Council; chair-

man, Council of the National Library of Australia; fellow, World Academy of Art and Science. *Military service:* Australian Imperial Forces, 1939-43; became lieutenant.

MEMBER: Royal Society of Literature (fellow), Royal Prince Alfred Yacht Club (Sydney).

AWARDS, HONORS: William Heinemann Award of the Royal Society, 1959, National Brotherhood Award of the National Council of Christians and Jews, 1960, and James Tait Black Memorial Award, 1960, all for *The Devil's Advocate;* Bestsellers Paperback of the Year Award, 1965, for *The Shoes of the Fisherman;* D.Litt., University of Santa Clara, 1969; Dag Hammarskjoeld International Prize, Pax Mundi, Diplomatic Academy of Peace, 1978; Universe Literary Prize, 1981, for *The Clowns of God;* D.Litt., Mercy College, 1982; invested as member of Order of Australia, 1985 Honours List.

WRITINGS:

(Under pseudonym Julian Morris) *Moon in My Pocket*, Australasian Publishing, 1945.

Gallows on the Sand (also see below), Angus & Robertson, 1956, large print edition, Ulverscroft, 1971.

Kundu (also see below), Dell, 1956.

The Crooked Road, Morrow, 1957 (published in England as *The Big Story*, Heinemann, 1957).

Children of the Shadows: The True Story of the Street Urchins of Naples, Doubleday, 1957 (published in England as *Children of the Sun*, Heinemann, 1957, reprinted, Fontana, 1977).

Backlash, Morrow, 1958 (published in England as *The Second Victory* [also see below], Heinemann, 1958, second edition, Hodder & Stoughton, 1985).

(Under pseudonym Michael East) *McCreary Moves In*, Heinemann, 1958, published as *The Concubine* (also see below), New English Library, 1967, reprinted under real name and original title, Coronet Books, 1983.

The Devil's Advocate (also see below), Morrow, 1959.

(Under pseudonym Michael East) *The Naked Country* (also see below), Heinemann, 1960, reprinted, Coronet, 1983.

Daughter of Silence (novel; also see below), Morrow, 1961.

Daughter of Silence: A Dramatization of the Novel (play; first produced on Broadway by Richard Halliday, November, 1961), Morrow, 1962.

The Shoes of the Fisherman (also see below), Morrow, 1963, limited edition, Franklin Library, 1980.

The Ambassador, Morrow, 1965.

The Tower of Babel (Book-of-the-Month Club selection), Morrow, 1967, large print edition, Ulverscroft, 1986.

The Heretic: A Play in Three Acts, Morrow, 1969.

(With Robert Francis) *Scandal in the Assembly: The Matrimonial Laws and Tribunals of the Roman Catholic Church, 1970*, Morrow, 1970.

Summer of the Red Wolf, Morrow, 1971.

The Salamander (also see below), Morrow, 1973.

Harlequin, Morrow, 1974.

The Navigator, Morrow, 1976.

Selected Works, Heinemann Octopus, 1977.

The Devil's Advocate; [and] *The Second Victory;* [and] *Daughter of Silence;* [and] *The Salamander;* [and] *The Shoes of the Fisherman*, Heinemann, 1977.

Proteus, limited first edition, Franklin Library, 1979, Morrow, 1979.

The Clowns of God, Morrow, 1981.

A West Quartet: Four Novels of Intrigue and High Adventure (includes *The Naked Country, Gallows on the Sand, The Concubine,* and *Kundu*), Morrow, 1981.

The World Is Made of Glass, Avon, 1983.
Cassidy, Doubleday, 1986.

Also author of play "The World Is Made of Glass," 1984, adapted from his novel of the same title.

SIDELIGHTS: Since the mid-1950s, Australian novelist Morris L. West has written suspense novels that plunge the reader into political turmoil, world-wide governmental corruption, and the internal workings of the Catholic Church. West spent several years in a Roman Catholic monastery and worked for six months as the Vatican correspondent for the *London Daily Mail;* his experiences have contributed to a moral and ethical outlook on current events that permeates all his work. According to *New York Times Book Review* contributor Herbert Mitgang, "West is known for his theological thrillers that pose hard, frequently unanswerable questions about today's turbulent world—including the constraints on liberty imposed by democratic societies." West is also known for his high output. Having written over twenty novels, "Morris West invents stories as though the world were running out of them," comments Webster Schott in the *New York Times Book Review.* Says Diane Casselberry Manuel in the *Christian Science Monitor,* "at his best, author West is a skillful storyteller who knows how to build suspense into every twist of the plot."

Three of West's better known works—*The Devil's Advocate, The Shoes of the Fisherman,* and *The Clowns of God*—feature protagonists who are representatives of the Church. *The Devil's Advocate* concerns a dying Catholic priest who is sent to an Italian village to investigate the life of a proposed saint and who ends up making an important self-discovery: "He had kept the rules all his life: all the rules—except one; that sooner or later he must step beyond the forms and conventions and enter into a direct, personal relationship with his fellows and with his God." According to *Renascence* contributor Arnold L. Goldsmith, *The Devil's Advocate* is "a richly textured, finely constructed story with all of the ingredients of a literary classic.... West is able to blend the personal with the local and the universal, giving us not only the memorable portrait of a deeply disturbed theologian, but also a wider view of the troubled soul of a church, a country, and the world."

In *The Shoes of the Fisherman,* a humble Ukrainian pope finds himself the central negotiator in an attempt to prevent the United States and the Soviet Union from starting World War III. During the negotiations, the pope must confront the Russian who once tortured him. The work, a popular and critical success, demonstrates West's concern with modern man's inability to communicate with his brother. "We're not using the same words. We don't understand each other. We are not selecting, we aren't balancing ... simply because life is too risky, too tormenting.... I've been trying, therefore, to use what is a very old manner of story telling. To make this conflict of legitimate points of view *clear,* through the medium of the novel," West told Shari Steiner in an interview for *Writer's Digest.* "In *The Shoes of the Fisherman,* the idea of the central character was a man who believed that he was—and publicly claimed to be—the Vicar of Christ," West continued. "Now, theoretically, this is the man who must look at the world through the eye of God, and try to make some sense out of its complexity. He was therefore a natural character medium through which this hopeless attempt had to be made."

Eighteen years later, West again used a pope as a central character, this time in *The Clowns of God.* Pope Gregory is forced by the Church to abdicate his seat when he receives a vision of the Second Coming of Christ and decides to communicate this apocalyptic message to the rest of the world. *The Clowns of God* shows the Church in a harsher light than West's previous theological novels and reflects West's ambivalence with the institution as a governing unit. "West has great faith in the power of faith, but little tolerance for the bureaucratic wranglings that often seem to accompany organized religion," states Manuel. The ambivalence may have originated in West's experiences with the Christian Brothers monastery where he studied for six years. Intending to become a priest, he left before taking his final vows. "My education with the Christian Brothers ... was very strongly tinged with Jansenism, a restrictive, puritanical attitude to religion," West explained to Steiner. "This has probably produced in me an attitude of extreme tolerance and the desire to find out what the other man thinks first before we make any judgments."

Critics had varying responses to *The Clowns of God.* Walter Shapiro in the *Washington Post* dislikes West's description of Christ, who appears at the book's conclusion, "a handsome fellow in his early 30s." Robert Kaftan writes in the *Christian Century* that "the characters become so many pieces to be manipulated to propel the story forward." He applauds the novel's setting, however, saying that West's "portrait of the world at the edge is chilling and disquieting." Edmund Fuller agrees. "As a melodrama it is tautly absorbing in its doom-threat genre. Yet the book far transcends that aspect, for Mr. West is an intelligent, thoughtful writer with knowledge of the ecclesiastical and theological issues that are the essence of his tale," he states in the *Wall Street Journal.* And Richard A. Blake writes in *America* that "West has succeeded ... in raising the most significant questions of human survival in a very human and religious context."

A turning point in West's career came with the publication of *The World Is Made of Glass,* the imaginative expansion of a brief entry in Carl Jung's diary, where he records meeting with a woman: "A lady came to my office. She refused to give her name.... What she wanted to communicate to me was a confession." The lady, according to West, is Magda Liliane Kardoss von Gamsfeld, a horse breeder, physician, and the illegitimate offspring of an English Duchess and a Hungarian nobleman. Raised by her father, Magda was seduced by him at sixteen, which started her on a path of lesbianism, sado-masochism, and finally, murder. She comes to Jung in a state of suicidal depression.

The story deviates from West's usual fare in that it contains only two characters, Jung and Magda, who relate the plot in monologue form. "Within the course of a single day Jung has become the recipient of confessions that it would probably take the average psychoanalyst weeks, months or even years to elicit from a patient," writes Francis King in the *Spectator.* But Magda's confessions produce an unexpected reaction in the psychiatrist. "Jung himself is constantly and disturbingly aware of the parallel between his own situation, in which he is poised to attempt the symbolic murder of his beloved father-figure Freud, and that of this siren, who is guilty of real murder," King continues. Magda's honesty also leads Jung to more closely examine his broken marriage and affair with a former student, plus his suddenly remembered, unsavory memories from childhood. The impact of this forces him to conclude, "we are both imprisoned in a transparent world." And finally Magda asks, "Is it possible that Jung, not I, is the clown in this absurd circus?... Who here is the crazy one?"

Detroit News contributor Andrew Greeley believes that *The World Is Made of Glass* is one of West's finest works. "Morris West has done for Carl Gustav Jung what D. M. Thomas did for Sigmund Freud—written a novel which brings Jung and his milieu alive. In the process he has produced a story which is very unlike most of his previous work. . . . Jung's chaotic personal life is vividly portrayed." *New York Times Book Review* contributor Philippe Van Rjndt says "Magda von Gamsfeld is Mr. West's most impressive creation." And Patricia Olson comments in the *Christian Century* that while West is generally "known for his realistic narration, his sensitive character portrayal and his concern for modern religion, [he] has never before presented such melodrama, such passionate characters, or such a critique of conventional Christianity as he does here."

Some critics dislike the book's conclusion, in which the physician who initially sent Magda to Jung provides her with a solution by giving her a job as director of a refuge for fallen women. Mayo Mohs notes in *Time* that "the author kisses off this denouement in a scant few pages, barely hinting at the thoughts and feelings of the new Magda. Having built the novel on the spectacle of her corruption, West might have reflected a bit more on the drama of her return to grace." Beryl Lieff Benderly indicates in the *Washington Post* that "Magda functions not as a person but as a plot device to permit West's exploration of certain themes—the line between good and evil, the nature of guilt and obsession, the curative power of redemption. . . . But to touch deeply, a story about sin and redemption or madness and cure must involve real people in a palpable world, not made-to-order abstractions in a universe of concepts." Van Rjndt, however, finds Magda's new life believable. "For all the cruelty Magda inflicts and receives, her struggle towards redemption demands our respect and compels our fascination," she writes.

Greeley concludes that "so sharp is the departure from earlier stories that one wonders if West . . . has not reached an important and extremely fruitful turning point in his career as a storyteller." But West primarily sees himself as a communicator, and his stories as vehicles for his messages. He told Steiner he wants to be "the type of person who . . . causes other people to examine their lives . . . the kind of man who turns the world upside down and says, lookit, it looks different, doesn't it?"

MEDIA ADAPTATIONS: The Devil's Advocate, as dramatized by Dore Schary, was produced by the Theatre Guild at the Billy Rose Theatre in March, 1961; *The Shoes of the Fisherman* was filmed by M-G-M in 1968.

BIOGRAPHICAL/CRITICAL SOURCES:

BOOKS

Contemporary Literary Criticism, Gale, Volume VI, 1976, Volume XXXIII, 1985.
West, Morris L., *The Devil's Advocate,* Morrow, 1959.
West, Morris L., *The World Is Made of Glass,* Avon, 1983.

PERIODICALS

America, August 29-September 5, 1981.
Atlantic, April, 1968.
Best Sellers, March 1, 1968, April 1, 1970, June 1, 1970.
Books and Bookmen, April, 1968, April, 1979, August, 1983.
Catholic World, September, 1961, February, 1962.
Chicago Tribune Book World, December 25, 1983.
Christian Century, May 20, 1981, October 12, 1983.

Christian Science Monitor, August 10, 1981.
Detroit News, July 10, 1983.
International Fiction Review, January, 1975.
Jewish Quarterly, autumn, 1968.
Life, February 23, 1968.
Look, August 1, 1961.
Los Angeles Times Book Review, February 18, 1979, July 17, 1983, October 19, 1986.
Nation, December 16, 1961, May 17, 1965.
National Observer, March 11, 1968.
National Review, February 14, 1975.
Newsweek, December 11, 1961.
New Yorker, December 9, 1961.
New York Times, May 27, 1987.
New York Times Book Review, April 25, 1965, February 22, 1968, April 7, 1968, September 19, 1971, October 21, 1973, October 27, 1974, August 29, 1976, March 4, 1979, March 11, 1979, August 9, 1981, November 26, 1981, July 3, 1983, November 9, 1986, May 27, 1987.
Observer Review, March 3, 1968.
Plays and Players, September, 1970.
Punch, March 6, 1968.
Renascence, summer, 1962.
Reporter, January 4, 1962.
Saturday Review, April 24, 1965, February 24, 1968.
Spectator, March 8, 1968, October 5, 1974, July 23, 1983.
Stage, July 23, 1970.
Theatre Arts, February, 1962.
This Week, December 4, 1966.
Time, December 8, 1961, July 6, 1970, November 4, 1974, October 4, 1976, January 22, 1979, July 25, 1983.
Times (London), May 6, 1965, July 14, 1983, February 5, 1987.
Times Literary Supplement, May 6, 1965, July 16, 1970, August 3, 1973.
Wall Street Journal, August 24, 1981.
Washington Post, June 8, 1981, July 8, 1983, November 15, 1986.
Writer's Digest, February, 1971.

—Sketch by Jani Prescott

*   *   *

WHARMBY, Margot
(Alison Winn)

PERSONAL: Born in England; married Ewart Wharmby; children: David, Martin, Alison, Philip.

ADDRESSES: Home—Cherry Burton, 3 Powys Ave., Leicester, England.

WRITINGS—Under pseudonym Alison Winn:

JUVENILES

Roundabout, Hodder & Stoughton, 1961.
Swings and Things, illustrations by Jennie Corbett and Peggie Fortnum, Hodder & Stoughton, 1963, Rand McNally, 1965.
Helter Skelter, illustrations by Janina Ede, Hodder & Stoughton, 1966.
A First Cinderella, Hodder & Stoughton, 1966.
Aunt Isabella's Umbrella, illustrations by Gladys Ambrus, Hodder & Stoughton, 1976, Children's Press, 1977.
Charlie's Iron Horse, Hodder & Stoughton, 1979.
Patchwork Pieces, Hodder & Stoughton, 1980.
"*Hello God,*" Word Books, 1984.

INTERPRETER OF ENGLISH TEXTS FROM SWEDISH; ALL JUVENILES

Gunilla Wolde, "The Thomas Books" series, ten volumes, Hodder & Stoughton, 1971-75.

Ulf Loefgren, *Who Holds Up the Traffic?*, Hodder & Stoughton, 1973.

Loefgren, *One, Two, Three, Four*, Hodder & Stoughton, 1973.

Loefgren, *The Flying Orchestra*, Hodder & Stoughton, 1973.

Loefgren, *The Magic Kite*, Hodder & Stoughton, 1973.

Loefgren, *The Colour Trumpet*, Hodder & Stoughton, 1973.

Wolde, "The Emma Books" series, ten volumes, Hodder & Stoughton, 1975-77.

Loefgren, *Harlequin*, Hodder & Stoughton, 1978.

Babro Lindgren, *The Wild Baby*, Hodder & Stoughton, 1981.

Lindgren, *The Wild Baby's Boat Trip*, Hodder & Stoughton, 1983.

Also author of English text for *The Tale of Two Hands* by Loefgren, and *The Wild Baby's Dog* by Lindgren.

*   *   *

WHEELER, (Charles) Gidley 1938- (Charles Gidley)

PERSONAL: Born August 21, 1938, in Bristol, England; son of James Gidley (a soldier) and Joyce Mary (a nurse; maiden name, Marks) Wheeler; married Felicity Bull, April 28, 1962; children: Emma, Andrew. *Education:* Attended Royal Naval College, Dartmouth, 1954-58.

ADDRESSES: Home—Winchester, England. *Agent*—Curtis Brown, 162-168 Regent St., London W1R 5TA, England.

CAREER: Royal Navy, 1954-80, Fleet Air Arm pilot, minesweeper captain, senior pilot of Airborne Early Warning squadron, executive officer of frigate; became lieutenant commander. Author.

MEMBER: Society of Authors, Naval Records Society, Naval Review, Royal Naval Sailing Association, Association of Royal Navy Officers, Mensa.

WRITINGS—Under name Charles Gidley:

The River Running By (novel), St. Martin's, 1981.

The Raging of the Sea (novel), Andre Deutsch, 1984, Viking, 1985.

The Believer (novel), Andre Deutsch, 1986.

Armada (novel), Weidenfeld & Nicholson, 1987, Viking, 1988.

Contributor of seven stories to *Blackwood's Magazine*, 1966-75, and episodes to BBC-TV's "Warship" and "Wings" series and Yorkshire TV's "Thundercloud" and "The Sandbaggers" series, 1976-80.

WORK IN PROGRESS: "An historical novel about the events in Britain and France in 1939-40, culminating in the evacuation of 338,000 troops from the beaches of Dunkirk. I may use some of my father's experiences, as he fought at Boulogne and escaped aboard the last destroyer to leave the port."

SIDELIGHTS: Writing under the name Charles Gidley, Gidley Wheeler explores the realm of personal relationships. His first published novel, *The River Running By,* takes place from 1933 to 1974 and examines the lives of the Anglo-Portuguese Teape family, detailing the relationships of the family heir, Bobby Teape, with three women: a Portuguese peasant girl, an English woman, and an expatriate colonial. Writing in the *Times Literary Supplement* about this book, Peter Lewis finds it "an unusual and much better than average example of the type of fiction now almost always condescendingly labeled 'popular'—the family saga." Lewis believes that Wheeler, throughout his novel, "relates the lives of the many individuals he writes about to the wider context in which they are all enmeshed. . . . Yet the network of family and personal relationships predominates."

For his second novel, *The Raging of the Sea,* Wheeler draws on his vast experiences with the Royal Navy for a story about Steven and Alan Jannaway, brothers whose father died defusing a bomb during the second world war, and whose lives are closely linked to the British Royal Navy. "There are wonderful passages here about the navy, about the nuts and bolts of maneuvering ships, and about what it's like to be a pilot on an aircraft carrier," says Carolyn See in the *Times Literary Supplement*. Although See considers these passages "great fun," she believes that "it is in the sorting out of family relationships that Gidley excels, and in the conjuring up of that helpless impotence of the individual caught in the coils of a larger organization that cares nothing at all for the individuals in it."

Wheeler told *CA:* "I put a great deal of myself into my characters, but I don't think I am recognisable in any of them. All my novels are close to home and all my characters have something of me in them. So you will probably find out more about me by reading my books than anything I can write here. Like Kipling, I can only urge you to 'read the books, read the books.'"

BIOGRAPHICAL/CRITICAL SOURCES:

PERIODICALS

Newsday, January, 1985.

Times Literary Supplement, July 17, 1981, February 11, 1985.

*   *   *

WHELAN, Elizabeth M(urphy) 1943-

PERSONAL: Born December 4, 1943, in New York, N.Y.; daughter of Joseph F. (an attorney) and Marion (Barrett) Murphy; married Stephen Thomas Whelan (an attorney), April 3, 1971; children: Christine Barrett. *Education:* Connecticut College, B.A., 1965; Yale University, M.P.H., 1967; Harvard University, M.S., 1968, Sc.D., 1971.

ADDRESSES: Home—165 West End Ave., 11R, New York, N.Y. 10023. *Office*—American Council on Science and Health, 1995 Broadway, New York, N.Y. 10023. *Agent*—Pam Bernstein, William Morris Agency, 1350 Avenue of the Americas, New York, N.Y. 10019.

CAREER: New Haven Health Department, New Haven, Conn., member of staff, 1966-67; Massachusetts Department of Public Health, Boston, epidemiologist/vital statistician, 1968-71; Planned Parenthood-World Population, New York City, county study coordinator, 1971-72; American Council on Science and Health, New York City, executive director, 1975—. Moderator of nationally syndicated radio program "Healthline." Consultant to Cable News Network (CNN-TV), Child Welfare League of America, Population Council, and other organizations.

MEMBER: American Public Health Association, American Medical Writers Association, Population Association of America.

WRITINGS:

Sex and Sensibility: A New Look at Being a Woman, McGraw, 1974.

A Baby?—Maybe: A Guide to Making the Most Fateful Decision of Your Life, Bobbs-Merrill, 1975, revised edition, 1980.

(With father-in-law, Stephen T. Whelan) *Making Sense out of Sex: A New Look at Being a Man,* McGraw, 1975.

(With Frederick J. Stare) *Panic in the Pantry: Food Facts and Fallacies,* Atheneum, 1975.

Boy or Girl?: The Sex Selection Technique That Makes All Others Obsolete, Bobbs-Merrill, 1977.

The Pregnancy Experience: The Psychology of Expectant Parenthood, Norton, 1978.

Preventing Cancer, Norton, 1978.

(With Stare) *Eat OK Feel OK!: Food Facts and Your Health,* Christopher, 1978.

(With Stare) *The 100% Natural, Purely Organic, Cholesterol Free, Megavitamin Low Carbohydrate Nutrition Hoax,* Atheneum, 1984.

Toxic Terror, E. Jameson, 1986.

(With Stare) *The Harvard Square Diet,* Prometheus Books, 1987.

Contributor to numerous periodicals, including *Glamour, Cosmopolitan, National Review, Weight Watchers, American Baby,* and *Across the Board.* Member of editorial board, *Connecticut College Alumni News,* 1972—.

* * *

WHITE, James F(loyd)   1932-

PERSONAL: Born January 23, 1932, in Boston, Mass.; son of Edwin T. (an engineer) and Madeline (Rinker) White; wife's name, Susan J.; children: Louise, Robert, Ellen, Laura, Martin. *Education:* Harvard University, A.B., 1953; Union Theological Seminary, New York, N.Y., B.D., 1956; attended Cambridge University, 1956-57; Duke Univesity, Ph.D., 1960. *Religion:* United Methodist.

ADDRESSES: Home—17840 Ponader Dr., South Bend, Ind. 46635. *Office*—Department of Theology, University of Notre Dame, Notre Dame, Ind. 46556.

CAREER: Ordained minister of California-Nevada Conference of the United Methodist Church, 1961; Ohio Wesleyan University, Delaware, instructor in religion, 1959-61; Southern Methodist University, Dallas, Tex., assistant professor, 1961-65, associate professor, 1965-71, professor of Christian worship, 1971-83; University of Notre Dame, Notre Dame, Ind., professor of liturgy, 1983—.

MEMBER: North American Academy of Liturgy.

AWARDS, HONORS: Berakah Award from North American Academy of Liturgy, 1983.

WRITINGS:

The Cambridge Movement: The Ecclesiologists and the Gothic Revival, Cambridge University Press, 1962, revised edition, 1979.

(Contributor) Stuart Henry, editor, *A Miscellany of American Christianity,* Duke University Press, 1963.

Protestant Worship and Church Architecture: Theological and Historical Considerations, Oxford University Press, 1964.

(With H. G. Hardin and J. D. Quillian) *Celebration of the Gospel,* Abingdon, 1964.

Architecture at Southern Methodist University, Southern Methodist University Press, 1966.

The Worldliness of Worship, Oxford University Press, 1967.

New Forms of Worship, Abingdon, 1971.

(Editor) *Supplemental Worship Resources,* Abingdon, Volume I, 1972, Volume VI, 1979, Volume X, 1980.

Christian Worship in Transition, Abingdon, 1976.

Introduction to Christian Worship, Abingdon, 1980.

Sacraments as God's Self Giving, Abingdon, 1983.

John Wesley's Sunday Service, Abingdon, 1984.

(With wife, Susan J. White) *Church Architecture,* Abingdon, 1988.

Contributor to religious journals. Former editor, *Union Seminary Quarterly Review.*

WORK IN PROGRESS: A book on Protestant traditions of worship.

SIDELIGHTS: James F. White told *CA:* "Much of my work has revolved around giving guidance to the changes in Protestant worship since Vatican II. Through writing, speaking, training ministers, and now, at Notre Dame, training those who will teach worship courses, I have worked and continue to work for the reshaping of Christian worship in America."

AVOCATIONAL INTERESTS: Travel, hiking, music, nature.

* * *

WHITE, Laurence B(arton), Jr.   1935-

PERSONAL: Born September 21, 1935, in Norwood, Mass.; son of Laurence B. (an engineer) and Anna (a teacher; maiden name, Dewhurst) White; married Doris E. Pickard (a teacher aide), September 10, 1961; children: William Oliver, David Laurence. *Education:* University of New Hampshire, B.A., 1958.

ADDRESSES: Home—12 Rockland St., Stoughton, Mass. 02072. *Office*—Needham Science Center, Needham Public Schools, Needham, Mass. 02192.

CAREER: Museum of Science, Boston, Mass., supervisor of programs and courses, 1958-65, acting director of Theatre of Electricity, 1960-65; Needham Public Schools, Needham Science Center, Needham, Mass., assistant director, 1965-79, director, 1979—. *Military service:* U.S. Army, Signal Corps, combat photographer, 1958-59.

MEMBER: Society of American Magicians, Mycological Society, Beekeepers Association.

AWARDS, HONORS: Child Study Association of America selected *So You Want to Be a Magician?* as one of the children's books of the year, 1972.

WRITINGS:

JUVENILES

Life in the Shifting Dunes, Boston Museum of Science, 1960.

Investigating Science with Coins, Addison-Wesley, 1969.

Investigating Science with Rubber Bands, Addison-Wesley, 1969.

Investigating Science with Nails, Addison-Wesley, 1970.

Investigating Science with Paper, Addison-Wesley, 1970.

So You Want to Be a Magician?, Addison-Wesley, 1972.

Science Games, Addison-Wesley, 1975.

Science Puzzles, Addison-Wesley, 1975.

Science Toys, Addison-Wesley, 1975.

Science Tricks, Addison-Wesley, 1975.

The Great Mysto: That's You, Addison-Wesley, 1975.

(With Ray Broekel) *Now You See It,* Little, Brown, 1979.

(With Broekel) *The Trick Book,* Doubleday, 1979.
(With Broekel) *The Surprise Book,* Doubleday, 1981.
(With Broekel) *Abra-Ca-Dazzle: Easy Magic Tricks,* Albert Whitman, 1982.
(With Broekel) *Hocus-Pocus: Magic You Can Do,* Albert Whitman, 1984.
(With Broekel) *Optical Illusions,* F. Watts, 1986.
(With Broekel) *Razzle Dazzle: Magic Tricks for You,* Albert Whitman, 1987.

OTHER

Author of material for Eduquip-Macallaster Co. Contributor to children's magazines.

WORK IN PROGRESS: A sourcebook for teachers, detailing many of the "unusual and original" demonstrations and experiments developed at the Needham Science Center for elementary students.

SIDELIGHTS: "The Needham Science Center," Laurence B. White, Jr., told *CA,* "works with all the elementary schools in [Needham, Massachusetts.] This brings me into direct contact with some two thousand young children each year. It is their curiosity, excitement, and enthusiasm that *makes* me write books for them. Children so enjoy sharing the things they like with me [that] I can do no less than return the favor.... I would urge every children's author to visit a local elementary school. As the local 'resident' author in our school system, I am asked to do so regularly. The experience will make you want to rush right home and write another book.

"Children, tomorrow's adults, are a very special audience. Certainly any author could make considerably more money writing adult fiction, but somehow I cannot imagine the effects on the audience to be as far reaching. I would like to think that somewhere I might have planted the seeds deep in a young mind that one day may belong to a world famous scientist or renowned magician. The thought is a delicious one!"

BIOGRAPHICAL/CRITICAL SOURCES:

PERIODICALS

New York Times Book Review, August 20, 1972.

*   *   *

WHONE, Herbert 1925-

PERSONAL: Born June 4, 1925, in Bingley, England; son of Bannister (a textile designer) and Nellie (Stead) Whone; married Helen Margery Reed; children: Adam, Nicholas, Katrina, Helena, Hannah. *Education:* Victoria University of Manchester, B.Mus. (with honors), 1949; Royal College of Music, A.R.M.C.M., 1949.

ADDRESSES: Home—46 Duchy Rd., Harrogate, Yorkshire, England.

CAREER: Violinist with Royal Philharmonic Orchestra, London, England, 1950-51, and British Broadcasting Corp. Symphony Orchestra, London, 1952-56; Scottish National Orchestra, Glasgow, Scotland, deputy leader, 1957-65; Huddersfield Polytechnic, Huddersfield, England, teacher of violin, 1966—. *Military service:* Royal Air Force, 1943-46.

WRITINGS:

The Simplicity of Playing the Violin (self-illustrated), Gollancz, 1972, Drake Publishers, 1973.

The Hidden Face of Music (self-illustrated), Gollancz, 1974, Garden Studio, 1978, revised edition, 1979.
The Essential West Riding: Its Character in Words and Pictures, E. P. Publishers, 1975.
The Integrated Violinist (self-illustrated), Gollancz, 1976.
Church, Monastery, Cathedral: A Guide to the Symbolism of the Christian Tradition (drawings by Denys Baker, based on sketches by Whone), Enslow Publishers, 1977.
Nursery Rhymes for Adult Children, Tallis Press, 1985.
Fountains Abbey, Smith-Settle, 1987.

Contributor of six articles on violin technique to *Strad.*

SIDELIGHTS: Herbert Whone told *CA:* "Music books indicate the connection of music, and learning of a stringed instrument in particular, with the *whole man*—not simply an analytical technique. In this sense the message breaks academic limits. *Hidden Face of Music* is the symbology of the role of music in man's life—its power on all levels. Everything is simple once the veils of error have been removed.

"I am at present painting and am open to the movement of the spirit. All activities abide by the same laws and all help each other."

AVOCATIONAL INTERESTS: Art, photography, ancient religions.

*   *   *

WILCOX, Robert K(alleen) 1943-

PERSONAL: Born July 21, 1943, in Indianapolis, Ind.; son of Jacob Guire (a real estate broker) and Agnes (a real estate broker; maiden name, Kalleen) Wilcox; married Begona de Amezola; children: Robert Guire, Amaya Begona. *Education:* Attended University of Oklahoma, 1962-64, and Miami-Dade Junior College, 1964; University of Florida, B.S., 1966.

ADDRESSES: Home and office—4064 Woodman Ave., Sherman Oaks, Calif. 91423. *Agent*—(literary) Jet Literary Associates, 124 East 84th St., New York, N.Y. 10028; (film) Gary Salt, The Paul Kohner Agency, 9169 Sunset Blvd., Los Angeles, Calif. 90069.

CAREER: Gainesville Sun, Gainesville, Fla., part-time reporter, 1964-66; *Miami News,* Miami, Fla., police reporter, 1966-67, general assignments reporter, 1967-69, religion editor, 1970-73; free-lance writer, 1973—. Former features editor, *Voice;* stringer for *New York Times,* 1973-78. *Military service:* U.S. Air Force Reserve, 1967-73; became first lieutenant.

MEMBER: Authors Guild, Authors League of America, Writer's Guild of America, West, Sigma Delta Chi.

AWARDS, HONORS: Supple Memorial Award from Religion Newswriters Association, 1970; Creative Excellence Award, U.S. Industrial Film Festival, 1981, for "The S.S. Norway"; Council on International Nontheatrical Events Golden Eagle Certificate, 1981, for "The S.S. Norway," and 1982, for "Resource Recovery"; Gold Medal, Venice International Film Festival, 1983, for "Resource Recovery"; two William Randolph Hearst Awards for editorial writing, *Gainesville Sun.*

WRITINGS:

The Mysterious Deaths at Ann Arbor, Popular Library, 1977.
Shroud, Macmillan, 1977.
Fatal Glimpse, Leisure Books, 1981.
Japan's Secret War, Morrow, 1985.

Also author of television scripts, including "Mummy Talks," for "Simon and Simon," Universal Studios; a two-hour pilot and a one-hour episode for Mary Tyler Moore Productions; a half-hour series for Comworld. Author of documentary films, including "The S.S. Norway" and "Everglades Harvest" for Cinema East; "Resource Recovery" for Coronado Studios; "Safehouse" for Aims Media. Author of industrial sales/training films for Hanna International. Contributor to *Collier's Encyclopedia;* contributor to magazines and newspapers, including *New York Times, Times* (London), *National Geographic,* and *Catholic Digest.*

WORK IN PROGRESS: *Scream of Eagles: The True Story of Top Gun,* for Arbor House. Also films, television shows, and books.

SIDELIGHTS: Robert K. Wilcox wrote *CA:* "I'm inclined toward serious nonfiction, but basically am always just looking to tell a good story. I enjoy writing about different things and researching interesting subjects. My family benefits because I'm at home a lot. I benefit because I enjoy seeing my family."

Shroud has been translated into Spanish, German, Greek, Japanese, and Finnish; *Japan's Secret War* has been translated into French.

BIOGRAPHICAL/CRITICAL SOURCES:

PERIODICALS

Washington Post Book World, March 31, 1985.

*   *   *

WILDING, Michael 1942-

PERSONAL: Born January 5, 1942, in Worcester, England; son of Richard (an iron molder) and Dorothy Mary (Bull) Wilding. *Education:* Lincoln College, Oxford, B.A., 1963, M.A., 1967.

ADDRESSES: *Office*—Department of English, University of Sydney, Sydney, New South Wales 2006, Australia.

CAREER: Teacher at primary school in Spetchley, England, 1960; University of Sydney, Sydney, Australia, lecturer in English, 1962-66; University of Birmingham, Birmingham, England, assistant lecturer, 1967, lecturer in English, 1968; University of Sydney, senior lecturer, 1969-72, reader in English, 1972—. Director of Wild & Woolley Ltd. (publishers), 1974-79. Member of council of Literature Board of Australia, 1975-76.

AWARDS, HONORS: Senior fellowship from Literature Board of Australia, 1978.

WRITINGS:

Milton's "Paradise Lost," Sydney University Press, 1969.
(With Michael Green and Richard Hoggart) *Cultural Policy in Great Britain,* United Nations Educational, Scientific and Cultural Organization, 1970.
Aspects of the Dying Process (stories), University of Queensland Press, 1972.
Living Together (novel), University of Queensland Press, 1974.
The Short Story Embassy (novel), Wild & Woolley, 1975.
The West Midland Underground (stories), University of Queensland Press, 1975.
Scenic Drive (novel), Wild & Woolley, 1976.
Marcus Clarke, Oxford University Press, 1977.
The Phallic Forest (stories), Wild & Woolley, 1978.

Political Fictions (criticism), Routledge & Kegan Paul, 1980.
Pacific Highway (novel), Hale & Iremonger, 1981.
Reading the Signs (stories), Hale & Iremonger, 1984.
The Paraguayan Experiment (novel), Penguin Books, 1985.
The Man of Slow Feeling: Selected Short Stories, Penguin Books, 1985.
Dragon's Teeth: Literature in the English Revolution (criticism), Clarendon Press, 1986.

EDITOR

(With Charles Higham) *Australians Abroad,* F. W. Cheshire, 1967.
Henry James, *Three Tales,* Hicks Smith, 1967.
Marvell: Modern Judgements, Macmillan, 1969.
John Sheffield, *The Tragedy of Julius Caesar and Marcus Brutus,* Cornmarket, 1970.
(With Shirley Cass, Ros Cheney, and David Malouf) *We Took Their Orders and Are Dead: An Anti-War Anthology,* Ure Smith, 1971.
The Portable Marcus Clarke, University of Queensland Press, 1976.
(With Stephen Knight) *The Radical Reader,* Wild & Woolley, 1977.
The Tabloid Story Pocket Book, Wild & Woolley, 1978.
William Lane, *The Workingman's Paradise,* Sydney University Press, 1980.
Marcus Clarke, *Stories,* Hale & Iremonger, 1983.

OTHER

Also author of "The Phallic Forest" (film), released by Sydney Filmmakers Co-op, 1972. General editor of "Australia and Pacific Writing Series," University of Queensland Press, 1972-80. Editor of *Isis,* 1962, *Balcony,* 1965-66, *Tabloid Story,* 1972-75, and *Post-Modern Writing,* 1979-81. Australian editor of *Stand,* 1971—.

WORK IN PROGRESS: *Social Visions,* criticism.

BIOGRAPHICAL/CRITICAL SOURCES:

BOOKS

Dutton, Geoffrey, editor, *Literature of Australia,* revised edition, Penguin Books, 1976.
Hamilton, K. G., editor, *Studies in the Recent Australian Novel,* University of Queensland Press, 1978.

PERIODICALS

Age Monthly Review (Melbourne), September, 1985.
Aspect, spring, 1975.
Australian Literary Studies, Volume XI, 1983.
Caliban, Volume 14, 1977.
Cleo, June, 1975.
Kunapipi, Volume I, number 2, 1980.
Meanjin, Volume XL, 1981, Volume XLV, number 1, 1986.
Overland, Number 96, 1984.
Pacific Quarterly, Volume IV, number 4, 1979.
Southerly, Volume XXXIII, number 2, 1973.
Sydney Morning Herald, February 8, 1986.
Washington Post Book World, March 20, 1983.
Waves, Volume VII, number 4, 1979.

*   *   *

WILLIAMS, Paul O(sborne) 1935-

PERSONAL: Born January 17, 1935, in Chatham, N.J.; son of Naboth Osborne (an electrical engineer) and Helen (Chadwick) Williams; married Kerry Lynn Blau, March 14, 1985; children: (previous marriage) Anne Chadwick, Evan Osborne. *Education:* Principia College, B.A. (with highest honors), 1956; University of Pennsylvania, M.A., 1958, Ph.D., 1962. *Politics:* Independent.

ADDRESSES: Home—657 Duncan St., San Francisco, Calif. 94131.

CAREER: University of Pennsylvania, Philadelphia, assistant instructor in English, 1957-60; Duke University, Durham, N.C., instructor, 1961-62, assistant professor of English, 1962-64; Principia College, Elsah, Ill., assistant professor, 1964-68, associate professor, 1968-77, professor of English, 1977-81, Cornelius and Muriel Wood Chair in Humanities, 1981-86. Member of board of trustees of village of Elsah, 1969-75; member of Quarry-Elsah Volunteer Firefighters, 1973-86, president, 1980-81; director of Elsah Museum, 1978-85; founding member of board of directors of Historic Elsah Foundation, 1970-77. Member of board of chancellors of St. Louis Poetry Center, 1974-80, president, 1978-80; member of Illinois Humanities Council, 1977-81.

MEMBER: Modern Language Association of America, Thoreau Society (president, 1977), Science Fiction Research Association, Midwest Modern Language Association, Illinois Historical Society, Greater St. Louis Historical Association (president, 1975).

AWARDS, HONORS: John W. Campbell Award, World Science Fiction Convention, 1983, for body of work by a new writer.

WRITINGS:

(With Charles B. Hosmer) *Elsah: A Historic Guidebook,* Historic Elsah Foundation, 1967.
The McNair Family of Elsah, Illinois: Uncommon Common Men (monograph), Historic Elsah Foundation, 1982.
Frederick Oakes Sylvester: The Artist's Encounter with Elsah (monograph), Historic Elsah Foundation, 1986.
Only Apparently Real, Arbor House, 1986.

SCIENCE FICTION; "THE PELBAR CYCLE" SERIES

The Breaking of Northwall, Del Rey Books, 1981.
The Ends of the Circle, Del Rey Books, 1981.
The Dome in the Forest, Del Rey Books, 1981.
The Fall of the Shell, Del Rey Books, 1982.
An Ambush of Shadows, Del Rey Books, 1983.
The Song of the Axe, Del Rey Books, 1984.
The Sword of Forbearance, Del Rey Books, 1985.

CONTRIBUTOR

Lucy Hazelton, editor, *St. Louis Poetry Center: An Anthology, 1946-1976,* Sheba Press, 1978.

Work represented in anthologies, including *The Edge of the Woods: Fifty-Five Haiku,* 1968, and *Jack, Be Quick: Fifty Poems,* privately printed, 1971.

OTHER

Contributor of more than two hundred fifty articles, poems, and reviews to magazines, including *Sheba Review, Star Line, Webster Review, Thoreau Journal, Arts,* and *Christian Science Sentinel,* and to newspapers.

SIDELIGHTS: While also a writer on midwestern American history, Paul O. Williams is chiefly known for his Pelbar Cycle, a science-fiction series describing the slow growth of civilization after a nuclear holocaust. In *The Dome in the Forest,* the third book in the cycle, Williams describes the meeting of two dissimilar cultures: one technologically advanced but isolated from the world, the other a flourishing, warlike tribe. According to *Los Angeles Times Book Review* contributor Don Strachan, "With depth and precision, Williams examines the power of our fear and our love for each other."

Williams has also interviewed and written about Philip K. Dick, a science fiction novelist largely ignored in his lifetime whose reputation has grown since his death. *Only Apparently Real* is a collection of Williams's observations on, and interviews with, Dick. Gregory Frost observes in the *Washington Post Book World* that *Only Apparently Real* contains "somewhat fictionalized scenes," but that "the insights into [Dick's] novels are valuable."

AVOCATIONAL INTERESTS: Boating, jogging, gardening, photography, beekeeping, numismatics, reading.

BIOGRAPHICAL/CRITICAL SOURCES:

PERIODICALS

Christian Science Monitor, June 8, 1981, February 16, 1983.
Los Angeles Times Book Review, January 31, 1982.
Science Fiction Review, August, 1981, May, 1982.
Washington Post Book World, May 25, 1986.

*   *   *

WILLKE, John Charles   1925-

PERSONAL: Born April 5, 1925, in Maria Stein, Ohio; son of Gerard T. (a physician) and Marie (Wuennemann) Willke; married Barbara Jean Hiltz (a writer, lecturer, and professor of nursing), June 5, 1948; children: Marie Margaret (Mrs. Robert Meyers), Theresa Ann (Mrs. William Wilka), Charles Gerard, Joseph John, Anne Margaret (Mrs. Patrick Millea), Timothy Edward. *Education:* Attended Xavier University, Cincinnati, Ohio, and Oberlin College; University of Cincinnati, M.D., 1948. *Religion:* Roman Catholic.

ADDRESSES: Home—7634 Pineglen Dr., Cincinnati, Ohio 45224. *Office*—National Right to Life Committee, Suite 500, 419 Seventh St., N.W., Washington, D.C. 20004.

CAREER: Good Samaritan Hospital, Cincinnati, Ohio, intern, 1948-49, resident, 1949-51; private practice in family medicine and counseling, 1950—, and in obstetrics, 1950-65; National Right to Life Committee, Washington, D.C., member of founding board of directors, president, 1980-83, 1984—; International Right to Life Federation, president, 1985—. Certified sex educator. *Military service:* U.S. Air Force, Medical Corps, 1952-54; became captain.

MEMBER: World Federation of Physicians Who Respect Life (member of founding board of directors), International Birthright (member of founding board of directors), American Medical Association, American Academy of Family Practice, American Board of Family Practice, American Association of Sex Educators and Counselors, American Academy of Medical Ethics (secretary, treasurer, 1986—), National Alliance for Family Life (founding member), National Institute of Family Relations, Ohio Right to Life Society (past president), Ohio State Medical Association, Academy of Medicine of Cincinnati, Cincinnati Right to Life (co-chairman).

WRITINGS:

WITH WIFE, BARBARA WILLKE

The Wonder of Sex, Hiltz Publishing, 1964, published as *Wonder of Sex: How to Teach Children,* Hayes Publishing, 1983.
Sex Education: The How-To for Teachers, Hiltz Publishing, 1970.
Sex: Should We Wait?, Hiltz Publishing, 1970.
Handbook on Abortion, Hiltz Publishing, 1971, revised edition, 1973.
Sex and Love, Silver Burdett, 1972.
Marriage, Silver Burdett, 1972.
How to Teach the Pro-Life Story, Hiltz Publishing, 1973.
Abortion: How It Is, Hayes Publishing, 1975.
Sex Education in the Classroom, Hayes Publishing, 1977.
Abortion: As It Is, Hayes Publishing, 1981.
Abortion and Slavery: History Repeats, Hayes Publishing, 1984.
Abortion: Questions and Answers, Hayes Publishing, 1986.

Also author of *Human Life and Abortion: The Hard Questions,* 1987; contributor to more than fifty magazines and professional journals.

WORK IN PROGRESS: Continued research on fetology, complications of induced abortion, viability and premature baby survival, as well as teaching methods for all these areas.

SIDELIGHTS: John Charles Willke believes in preserving and enhancing family life. In his practice as a physician and counselor, he urges parents to love each other wholeheartedly and to raise responsible children, so as to lead young adults toward mature decisions regarding sex and marriage. As president of the National Right to Life Committee, Willke supports a human life amendment to the U.S. Constitution. He told *CA* he is convinced that if "the war on the unborn [is] won by the pro-abortionists, all other efforts at saving family life in America [are] doomed to failure."

*   *   *

WILTZ, Chris(tine)   1948-

PERSONAL: Born January 3, 1948, in New Orleans, La.; daughter of Adolphe Michael (an accountant) and Merle (an underwriter; maiden name, Hiers) Wiltz; married Kenneth McElroy, November 25, 1970 (divorced, 1976); married Joseph Pecot (a communications company president), February 13, 1976; children: (second marriage) Marigny Katherine. *Education:* Attended University of Southwestern Louisiana, 1965, Loyola University, New Orleans, La., 1966-67, and University of New Orleans, 1967; San Francisco State College, B.A., 1969.

ADDRESSES: Home—New Orleans, La. *Agent*—Barney Karpfinger, The Karpfinger Agency, 500 Fifth Ave., Suite 2800, New York, N.Y. 10010.

CAREER: Bowes Co. (advertising firm), Los Angeles, Calif., proofreader, 1969; Tulane University, New Orleans, La., secretary in School of Medicine, 1969-70; Maple Street Bookshop, New Orleans, in sales and orders, 1970-71; Tulane University, grant researcher in School of Medicine, 1971-72; *Dealerscope* (home elecronics trade journals), Waltham, Mass., staff writer, 1978; writer, 1978—.

WRITINGS:

"NEAL RAFFERTY" DETECTIVE SERIES

The Killing Circle, Macmillan, 1981.

A Diamond before You Die, Mysterious Press, 1987.
The Emerald Lizard, Mysterious Press, 1988.

SIDELIGHTS: Chris Wiltz told *CA:* "It's no mystery that I decided to write detective novels, since I wrote my first detective story when I was eight years old. But that story featured a girl detective. Now Neal Rafferty, a New Orleans-based male detective, tells the story, and that might seem like a puzzling choice since I'm a woman. With two Rafferty novels and a third almost completed, though, I find that one of the things I enjoy most about writing from a male point of view is viewing women. I like writing from a different perspective than my own.

"I also like writing about New Orleans. In a detective novel, place can become almost as important as character. New Orleans is full of interesting people and places to write stories about, which I'll continue to do in the Neal Rafferty series and in other writing as well."

BIOGRAPHICAL/CRITICAL SOURCES:

PERIODICALS

Gambit, September 12, 1981.
New Orleans, January, 1982.
Times-Picayune, January 3, 1982, May 25, 1986, March 22, 1987, March 29, 1987.

*   *   *

WINCH, Robert F(rancis)   1911-1977

PERSONAL: Born August 31, 1911, in Lakewood, Ohio; died April 19, 1977; son of Frank S. and Blanche (Welch) Winch; married Martha Brashares (a social worker), September 3, 1938. *Education:* Western Reserve University (now Case Western Reserve University), A.B., 1935; University of Chicago, A.M., 1939, Ph.D., 1942.

ADDRESSES: Home—Apt. 502, 128 N. Craig St., Pittsburgh, Pa. *Office*—Department of Sociology, Northwestern University, Evanston, Ill. 60201.

CAREER: University of Chicago, Chicago, Ill., instructor in sociology, 1941-42; Vanderbilt University, Nashville, Tenn., associate professor of sociology, 1946-48; Northwestern University, Evanston, Ill., associate professor, 1948-55, professor of sociology, 1955-77, chairman of department, 1967-70. *Military service:* U.S. Naval Reserve, active duty, 1942-45; became lieutenant.

MEMBER: American Sociological Association (fellow), American Psychological Association (fellow), American Statistical Association, Sociological Research Association, American Association for the Advancement of Science (fellow).

AWARDS, HONORS: Social Science Research Council fellowship, 1945-46; Guggenheim fellowship, 1955-56, 1974-75; E. W. Burgess Award of the National Council on Family Relations, 1968.

WRITINGS:

The Modern Family, Holt, 1952, 3rd edition, 1971.
(Editor with Robert McGinnis and contributor) *Selected Studies in Marriage and the Family,* Holt, 1953, 3rd edition (editor with Louis Wolf Goodman), 1968, 4th edition (editor with Graham B. Spanier), 1974.
(Contributor) Joseph B. Gittler, editor, *Review of Sociology: Analysis of a Decade,* Wiley, 1957.

Mate Selection: A Study of Complementary Needs, Harper, 1958.
Identification and Its Familial Determinants, Bobbs-Merrill, 1962.
(With Margaret T. Gordon) *Familial Structure and Function as Influence,* Lexington, 1974.
(With Rae Lesser Blumberg and others) *Familial Organization: A Quest for Determinants,* Free Press, 1977.

Contributor to *Encyclopedia of Sexual Behavior,* Hawthorn, 1961, *International Encyclopedia of the Social Sciences,* Crowell-Collier, 1968, and professional journals. Associate editor of *Sociometry,* 1956-61, *Journal of Marriage and Family,* 1965-69, and *Sociology Quarterly,* 1970—.

SIDELIGHTS: In a *Contemporary Sociology* review of Robert F. Winch's *Familial Organization: A Quest for Determinants,* W. R. Burr writes that this book "is a continuation of a century-old, evolving, and cumulative study of ways societal forces influence an important social institution—the family. . . . The volume is an important contribution to sociology and the science of the family."

BIOGRAPHICAL/CRITICAL SOURCES:

PERIODICALS

Contemporary Sociology, May, 1979.†

*　　*　　*

WINGATE, John (Allan) 1920-

PERSONAL: Born March 15, 1920, in Carbis Bay, Cornwall, England; son of Allan and Joyce (Heriz-Smith) Wingate; children: Susan Wingate Tuckett, Christopher. *Education:* Attended Royal Naval College, Dartmouth, England. *Politics:* "Paternal Capitalism."

ADDRESSES: c/o Lloyds Bank International, 43 boulevard des Capuchines, 75002 Paris, France.

CAREER: Horticulturist, 1947-51; schoolmaster at Fonthill, Sussex and Aysgarth, Yorkshire, and housemaster at Milton Abbey, Dorset, 1953-65; Calshot Activities Centre, Calshot, Hampshire, warden, 1965-70; free-lance writer, 1970—. *Military service:* Royal Navy, 1933-46, 1951-52; received Distinguished Service Cross; mentioned in dispatches.

MEMBER: Authors' Society, Naval Records Society, Army and Navy Club.

WRITINGS:

NONFICTION

HMS "Dreadnought" Battleship, 1906-1920, Profile Publications, 1970.
(Editor) *Warships in Profile,* three volumes, Doubleday, 1972-74.
HMS "Belfast": In Trust for the Nation, 1939-1971, Profile Publications, 1972.

FICTION

Below the Horizon (also see below), Arthur Barker, 1974, St. Martin's, 1975.
The Sea above Them, Arthur Barker, 1975, St. Martin's, 1976.
Oil Strike, St. Martin's, 1976.
Avalanche, St. Martin's, 1977.
Black Tide, Weidenfeld & Nicolson, 1977.
Red Mutiny: A Diary, St. Martin's, 1978.

Target Risk (also see below), Weidenfeld & Nicolson, 1978.
Seawaymen, Weidenfeld & Nicolson, 1979.
Frigate (first volume in trilogy), Weidenfeld & Nicolson, 1980.
Carrier (second volume in trilogy), Weidenfeld & Nicolson, 1981.
Submarine (third volume in trilogy), St. Martin's, 1982.
William the Conqueror: An Historic Novel, F. Watts, 1983.
Below the Horizon [and] *Target Risk,* New English Library, 1984.
Go Deep, St. Martin's, 1985.
The Wind Is Free, Weidenfeld & Nicolson, 1986.
The Man Called Mark, Weidenfeld & Nicolson, 1987.

"SUBMARINER SINCLAIR" SERIES

Submariner Sinclair, George Newnes, 1959.
Jimmy-the-One, George Newnes, 1960.
Sinclair in Command: A Submariner Sinclair Story, George Newnes, 1961.
Nuclear Captain: The Fourth Story of Submariner Sinclair, Macdonald & Co., 1962.
Sub-Zero: A Submariner Sinclair Story, Macdonald & Co., 1963.
Full Fathom Five: A Submariner Sinclair Story, Heinemann, 1967.
In the Blood: A Sinclair Story, Heinemann, 1973.

"ACTION" SERIES

Torpedo Strike, Macdonald & Co., 1964.
Never So Proud: Crete, May, 1941, the Battle and Evacuation, Meredith Press, 1966.
Last Ditch: The English Channel, 1939-1943, Heinemann, 1971.

WORK IN PROGRESS: A novel, for Weidenfeld & Nicolson.

SIDELIGHTS: John Wingate told *CA:* "Serenity is the secret to happiness in this life. Acceptance of whatever rung on the ladder one finds oneself is the key to serenity. Each man, therefore, to his own talents; exploit them fully, looking never backwards, fearing not the future but savouring the today, however bleak the dawn. Only thus can a man feel part of God's purpose, can he persevere along the course set for him. Though he is but a speck in the Cosmos, part of which he is now capable of splitting asunder, he must never forget that he is but the agent of the God who created him and certainly is not a god himself.

"However insidious the debate, nothing can be allowed to intervene between him and his faith; he must to himself *first* always be true, whatever convention may ordain or however cruel the judgement of his fellows. Only through self-control and national discipline can a man or nation survive the pestilence of cynical materialism. For these qualities, he must turn back to the example of the saints, now so largely forgotten or derided.

"We are murdering our youth on the altar of 'educational' claptrap, a futile system dolloped out by too many second-rate citizens euphemistically dubbed 'Teachers' and 'Education Officers.' These men and women, in whose hands lie the future of the world, should be the most highly rewarded public servants in the land, subject to their being trained to educate youth specifically for the battle of life; discipline and the Christian virtues are the only essential qualities with which a young man or woman need to be equipped after schooling. Only if the teachers themselves are forged of such metal, as of yesteryear, can there be hope for the future of our nation and world. The appalling length of time it now takes to 'educate' an individual saps initiative, destroys purpose and ideals; this criminal waste destabilizes society.

"There's a lot to do on our beautiful planet. Let's harness the energy of our young people, so that they can go out and help their opposite numbers throughout the world. Then the barriers will come crashing down. A United States of Europe with a common currency; a World Government with its international police force . . . is the dream so *very* distant?"

Never So Proud: Crete, May, 1941, the Battle and Evacuation was translated into French in 1968.

* * *

WINN, Alison
See WHARMBY, Margot

* * *

WISEMAN, B(ernard) 1922-

PERSONAL: Born August 26, 1922, in Brooklyn, N.Y.; son of Abraham Z. and Yetta (Goldstein) Wiseman; married second wife, Susan Nadine Levin Cranis, May 9, 1970; children: Michael Avram, Andrew Lee; Peter Franklin Cranis (stepson). *Education:* Attended Art Students League, 1946. *Politics:* "Independent with conservative bias." *Religion:* Hebrew.

ADDRESSES: Home—2640 Lake Hill Rd., West Eau Gallie, Melbourne, Fla. 32935.

CAREER: Cartoonist, writer, and illustrator of books for children and adults, 1948—. Contract cartoonist for *New Yorker* (magazine), New York City, 1948-56, and *Punch* (magazine), London, England, 1948-59; cartoonist for Spadea Syndicate, 1965-66, and for McNaught Syndicate, 1967-69; became partner and art director of Crown Syndicate. Creator of cartoons and comic illustrations for *Saturday Evening Post, True, Look, This Week, Playboy, Rogue, Cosmopolitan,* and other periodicals; creator of advertising illustrations for American Airlines, New York Transport Authority, Woolite, and other companies and organizations. *Military service:* U.S. Coast Guard, 1941-46.

MEMBER: Young Men's Hebrew Association, New York Dojo Club, Mas Oyama's Karate Dojo.

WRITINGS:

SELF-ILLUSTRATED

Cartoon Countdown (cartoon book), Ballantine, 1959.
Morris the Moose, Harper, 1959, reprinted, Scholastic Book Services, 1973.
Morris Is a Cowboy, a Policeman, and a Baby Sitter, Harper, 1960.
The Log and Admiral Frog, Harper, 1961.
Irwin the Intern (cartoon book), Dell, 1962.
Boatniks (cartoon book), Dell, 1962.
(With Sandy Brier) *Sadness Is a Back View* (cartoon book), Citadel, 1964.
(With Brier) *Since I Quit Smoking I Don't Know What to Do with My Hands,* Citadel, 1964.
The Hat That Grew (cartoon book), E. M. Hale, 1967.
Morris Goes to School, Harper, 1970, published as *Morris the Moose Goes to School,* Scholastic Book Services, 1972.
Ninety-Six Cats, E. M. Hale, 1970.
Sex-Ed, Dell, 1971.
Little New Kangaroo, Macmillan, 1973.

Morris and Boris: Three Stories, Dodd, 1974, published as *Three Stories about Morris and Boris,* Scholastic Book Services, 1976.
Halloween with Morris and Boris, Dodd, 1975.
Billy Learns Karate, Holt, 1976.
Iglook's Seal, Dodd, 1977.
Bobby and Boo, the Little Spaceman, Holt, 1978.
Morris Has a Cold, Dodd, 1978.
The Lucky Runner, Garrard, 1979.
Morris Tells Boris Mother Moose Stories and Rhymes, Dodd, 1979.
My Googoo, Holt, 1979.
Quick Quackers, Garrard, 1979.
Hooray For Patsy's Oink!, Garrard, 1980.
Oscar Is a Mama!, Garrard, 1980.
Penny's Poodle Puppy, Pickle, Garrard, 1980.
Tails Are Not for Painting, Garrard, 1980.
Don't Make Fun!, Houghton, 1982.
Very Bumpy Bus Ride, Parents Magazine Press, 1982.
Doctor Duck and Nurse Swan, Dutton, 1985.
Cats! Cats! Cats!, Parents Book Club, 1985.
Christmas with Morris and Boris, Scholastic Book Services, 1986.
Dolly Dodo, Scholastic Book Services, 1987.
Barber Bear, Little, Brown, 1987.

"FUN TO LEARN" SERIES

The Nutty Nature Book, Platt & Munk, 1971.
The Silly Science Book, Platt & Munk, 1971.
Detective Dog, Platt & Munk, 1971.
Hats and Coats, Cows and Goats, Platt & Munk, 1971.

OTHER

(Illustrator) Frank Asche, *George's Store,* Parents Book Club, 1985.

Also author and illustrator of over twelve stories for educational publishers, Harcourt, Ginn, and Heath. Illustrator of stories, including "The Boy Who Found Xmas," 1966, by James A. Michener. Contributor of "Sir Nervous Norman" stories to *Boy's Life,* 1968—; contributor of numerous cartoons to periodicals in the United States and England.

WORK IN PROGRESS: Handy Hound, for Little, Brown; "a Harper and Row I-Can-Read book called *Morris and Boris at the Circus,* and an Early-I-Can-Read book called *Morris the Moose* that is a redoing of the very first Morris book. With my wife and stepson I am forming a company to produce videos for children. We have acquired the rights to many of my books and will begin with those, then go on to do videos of books by other author/artists."

SIDELIGHTS: Booklets that Bernard Wiseman illustrated for Radio Free Europe were dropped by balloons in Communist satellite countries.

* * *

WITTKOWSKI, Wolfgang 1925-

PERSONAL: Born August 15, 1925, in Halle, Germany; came to the United States in 1963; son of Gerhard (an economist) and Margarete (Linckelmann) Wittkowski; married Maria Jokiel (divorced, 1972); married Charlotte Koerner, 1977; children: (first marriage) Mechtild, Ute, Isa, Albrecht. *Education:* Attended University of Goettingen, 1945-50; University of Frankfurt, Staatsexamen, 1953, Ph.D., 1954.

ADDRESSES: Office—Department of German, State University of New York, Albany, N.Y. 12222.

CAREER: Assistant master of secondary school in Bad Nauheim, Germany, 1956-63; Ohio State University, Columbus, associate professor, 1963-66, professor of German, 1966-77; State University of New York at Albany, professor of German, 1977—. Organizer of biannual international symposia on Goethezeit, 1980—. *Military service:* German Army, 1943-45.

MEMBER: Modern Language Association of America, American Association of Teachers of German, Kleist, Goethe und Lessing Gesellschaft.

WRITINGS:

(Contributor) H. Kreuzer, editor, *Hebbel in neuer Sicht*, Kohlhammer (Stuttgart), 1963.
Der Junge Hebbel, De Gruyter (Berlin), 1969.
(With Claude David and Lawrence Ryan) *Kleist und Frankreich*, E. Schmidt (Berlin), 1969.
(Contributor) Klaus Berghahn, editor, *Friedrich Schiller: Theorie und Praxis der Dramen*, Wege der Forschung (Darmstadt), 1972.
Heinrich von Kleist's "Amphitryon," Materialien zur Rezeption und Interpretation, De Gruyter, 1978.
Georg Buechner: Personlichkeit, Weltbild, Werk, Winter (Heidelberg), 1978.
(Editor) *Friedrich Schiller: Kunst, Humanitoet und Politik in der Spaeten Aufklaerung—Ein Symposium*, Niemeyer (Tubingen), 1982.
Goethe im Kontext, Niemeyer (Tubingen), 1984.
Verlorene Klassik, Niemeyer (Tubingen), 1986.
Verantwortung und Utopie, Niemeyer (Tubingen), 1988.

Also contributor of articles on Droste-Huelshoff, Lessing, Leaz, Goethe, Schiller, Kleist, Hebbel, Buechner, Hoffmann, Grillparzer, Stifter, Raabe, Fontane, S. Kirsch, and Hemingway to American and German literature journals, handbooks, and Festschriften.

WORK IN PROGRESS: Research on Goethe's and Schiller's dramas.

* * *

WOOD, Ursula
　　See VAUGHAN WILLIAMS, Ursula Wood

* * *

WOZNICKI, Andrew N(icholas) 1931-

PERSONAL: Born October 19, 1931, in Katowice, Poland; son of Stanislaw (a tailor) and Anna (Jednoszyniec) Woznicki. *Education:* Catholic University of Lublin, M.A., 1960; Pon-

tifical Institute of Mediaeval Studies, Toronto, M.S.L., 1965; University of Toronto, Ph.D., 1967.

ADDRESSES: Office—Department of Philosophy, University of San Francisco, Ignatian Heights, San Francisco, Calif. 94117.

CAREER: Major Seminary, Poznan, Poland, assistant professor of philosophy, 1960-62; University of San Francisco, San Francisco, Calif., assistant professor, 1967-74, associate professor, 1974-80, professor of philosophy, 1980—, acting head of department, 1969-70. Visiting scholar, Catholic University of Lublin, 1981-82. Producer of radio programs, "Polish Cultural Hour," 1969-71, and "Central European Hour," 1972-74, both for station KQED-FM, San Francisco.

MEMBER: International Society for Metaphysics, American Association of University Professors, American Catholic Philosophical Association, Societe des amis de la theologie et la philosophie chretienne, Polish Institute of Arts and Sciences, Polish American Congress.

AWARDS, HONORS: Public Radio Award from station KQED-FM, San Francisco, 1970; American Council of Learned Societies grant, 1975-76.

WRITINGS:

Socio-Religious Principles of Migration Movements, Polish Research Institute in Canada (Toronto), 1968.
Teologia spoleczna ruchu mi gracyjnego, Towarzystwo Naukowe Polskiego Uniwersytetu Lubelskiego (Lublin), 1978.
A Christian Humanism: Karol Wojtyla's Existential Humanism, Mariel Publications, 1980.
Journey to the Unknown: Catholic Doctrine on Ethnicity and Migration, Golden Phoenix, 1982.
(Editor) Mieczyslaw Krapiec, *I—Man: An Outline of Philosophical Anthropology*, Mariel Publications, 1983, revised edition, 1985.
The Dignity of Man as a Person: Essays on the Christian Humanism of His Holiness, John Paul II, Society of Christ Publications, 1987.
Na Skalach, Przez Morza i Lady, Glob, 1988.

Contributor of numerous articles to journals and periodicals in North America and Europe. Editor and publisher, *San Francisco Echo*, 1969-71, *Migrant Echo*, 1972-81, member of editorial group, *Migration Today*, 1975.

WORK IN PROGRESS: Philosophical inquiry into the relationship between culture and religion; systematical studies of the cultural and religious changes in Poland; conducting a comparative study of metaphysics of St. Thomas and Heidegger; research on the philosophical implication of the Copernican system; a study of contemporary Polish Christian philosophy.

AVOCATIONAL INTERESTS: Mountain climbing, travel.

Y-Z

YORK, Amanda
See DIAL, Joan

*   *   *

YORKE, Katherine
See ELLERBECK, Rosemary (Anne L'Estrange)

*   *   *

YOUNG, David P(ollock)   1936-

PERSONAL: Born December 14, 1936, in Davenport, Iowa; son of Cecil T. (a businessman) and Mary (Pollock) Young; married Chloe Hamilton (a museum curator), June 17, 1963 (died February, 1985); children: Newell Hamilton, Margaret Helen. *Education:* Carleton College, A.B., 1958; Yale University, M.A., 1959, Ph.D., 1965.

ADDRESSES: Home—220 Shipherd Circle, Oberlin, Ohio 44074. *Office*—Department of English, Rice Hall, Oberlin College, Oberlin, Ohio 44074.

CAREER: Oberlin College, Oberlin, Ohio, instructor, 1961-65, assistant professor, 1965-69, associate professor, 1969-73, professor, 1973-86, Longman Professor of English, 1986—.

MEMBER: Modern Language Association of America, American Association of University Professors, PEN.

AWARDS, HONORS: Tane Prize for poetry, *Massachusetts Review,* 1965; National Endowment for the Humanities fellow in England, 1967-68; U.S. Award, International Poetry Forum, 1968; Guggenheim fellow, 1978-79; National Endowment for the Arts fellow, 1981-82.

WRITINGS:

Something of Great Constancy: The Art of "A Midsummer Night's Dream," Yale University Press, 1966.
(Editor) *Twentieth-Century Interpretations of "Henry IV, Part 2,"* Prentice-Hall, 1968.
Sweating Out the Winter (poetry), University of Pittsburgh Press, 1969.
(Contributor) *The Major Young Poets,* World Publishing, 1971.
(Contributor) *Just What the Country Needs: Another Poetry Anthology,* Wadsworth, 1971.

The Heart's Forest: Shakespeare's Pastoral Plays, Yale University Press, 1972.
Boxcars (poetry), Ecco Press, 1972.
Work Lights (prose poems), Cleveland State University Press, 1977.
The Names of a Hare in English (poetry), University of Pittsburgh Press, 1979.
(Editor with Stuart Friebert) *A Field Guide to Contemporary Poetry and Poetics,* Longman, 1980.
(Editor with Friebert and Richard Zipser) *Contemporary East German Poetry: A Special Issue of "Field,"* Oberlin College, 1980.
(Editor with Friebert) *The Longman Anthology of Contemporary American Poetry,* Longman, 1983.
Foraging (poetry), Wesleyan University Press, 1986.
Troubled Mirror: A Study of Yeats's "The Tower," University of Iowa Press, 1987.
Earthshine (poetry), Wesleyan University Press, in press.

Also editor, with Keith Holliman, of *Magical Realist Fiction, 1984.*

TRANSLATOR

Rainer M. Rilke, *Duino Elegies,* Norton, 1978.
Four T'ang Poets, Field, Oberlin College, 1980.
(With Friebert and Walker) *Valuable Nail: Selected Poems of Guenter Eich,* Field, Oberlin College, 1981.
Miroslav Holub, *Interferon; or, On Theater,* Field, Oberlin College, 1982.
Rainer M. Rilke, *Sonnets to Orpheus,* Wesleyan University Press, 1987.
Pablo Neruda, *The Heights of Macchu Picchu,* Songs before Zero Press, 1987.

OTHER

Contributor to *Criticism* and other periodicals. Editor, *Field: Contemporary Poetry and Poetics,* 1969—.

WORK IN PROGRESS: A new collection of poems; a study of Yeats and Stevens; an anthology of "magical realist fiction."

*   *   *

ZASLOW, Morris   1918-

PERSONAL: Born December 22, 1918, in Rosthern, Saskatchewan, Canada; son of Isaac (a grocer) and Bessie (Hardin) Zaslow; married Betty Winifred Stone, October 3, 1945; children: Jonathan Philip. *Education:* University of Alberta, B.A., 1940, B.Ed., 1942; University of Toronto, M.A., 1948, Ph.D., 1957.

ADDRESSES: Home—838 Waterloo St., London, Ontario, Canada N6A 3W6.

CAREER: High School teacher in Canada, 1941-42, 1945-47; Carleton University, Ottawa, Ontario, lecturer in history, 1950-52; University of Toronto, Toronto, Ontario, lecturer, 1952-59, assistant professor, 1959-64, associate professor of history, 1964-65; University of Western Ontario, London, professor of history, 1965-84, professor emeritus, 1984—. Visiting professor of Canadian studies, University of Calgary, 1979-80. Member of historical advisory committee, Metropolitan Toronto and Region Conservation Authority, 1958-65, and Archaeological and Historic Sites Board of Ontario, 1966-67. *Military service:* Royal Canadian Air Force, 1942-45.

MEMBER: Royal Society of Canada (fellow of Academy of Humanities and Social Sciences), Canadian Historical Association, Champlain Society (honorary vice president), Arctic Institute of North America (fellow), Ontario Historical Society (member of executive board, 1956-68; president, 1966-67).

AWARDS, HONORS: Rockefeller Foundation grants, 1955, 1956; Canada Council fellowships, 1960, 1968; Nuffield Foundation fellowship, 1960-61; Killam Foundation fellowship, 1973-74.

WRITINGS:

(Editor with W. B. Turner) *The Defended Border: Upper Canada and the War of 1812*, Macmillan, 1965.
The Opening of the Canadian North 1870-1914, McClelland & Stewart, 1971.
Reading the Rocks: The Story of the Geological Survey of Canada, 1842-1972, Macmillan, 1975.
(Editor) *A Century of Canada's Arctic Islands, 1880-1980*, Royal Society of Canada, 1981.
The Northwest Territories, 1905-1980, Canadian Historical Association, 1984.
The Northwest Expansion of Canada, 1914-1967, McClelland & Stewart, 1988.

Supervising editor of "General Series," eight volumes, Champlain Society, 1962-72; supervising editor, "Issues in Canadian History," eight volumes, Copp, 1966-68. Editor, *Ontario History* (quarterly journal), 1956-62.

WORK IN PROGRESS: The Correspondence of William Duncan of Metlakatla to the Church Missionary Society, London, 1856-1884, for the Champlain Society.

*   *   *

ZAWADSKY, Patience   1927-
(Patience Hartman; Becky Lynne, a pseudonym)

PERSONAL: Surname is pronounced Za-*wad*-sky; born March 30, 1927, in Trenton, N.J.; daughter of William C. and Mabel (Leicht) Hartman; married John P. Zawadsky (chairman of philosophy department at University of Wisconsin—Stevens Point), September 8, 1948; children: John, Paul, Rebecca, Elizabeth. *Education:* Douglass College, Rutgers University, B.A., 1948. *Politics:* Democrat.

ADDRESSES: Home—3900 Jordan Ln., Stevens Point, Wis. 54481.

CAREER: WTNJ, Trenton, N.J., writer, producer, and actor for radio series, "Teen-Age," 1943-44; Harvard University, Cambridge, Mass., research assistant and secretary, 1949-51; self-employed editor and researcher, Cambridge, 1951-54; Kilmer Job Corps, Edison, N.J., writing consultant, 1966; University of Wisconsin—Stevens Point, lecturer in English, 1967-72, 1980—. Free-lance writer for magazines. President of Children's Art Program, Stevens Point, 1980-81.

MEMBER: International Society of Dramatists, Dramatists Guild, American Association of University Women, Wisconsin Children's Theatre Association (vice-president, 1979-80), Phi Beta Kappa.

AWARDS, HONORS: Author's Award, New Jersey Association of English Teachers, 1968, for *The Mystery of the Old Musket;* plays selected for merit by Wisconsin Children's Theatre Association, 1976-78, 1980.

WRITINGS:

(Co-author) *Datebook of Popularity*, Prentice-Hall, 1960.
(Co-author) *Are These the Wonderful Years?*, Abbey Press, 1965.
The Mystery of the Old Musket (juvenile), Putnam, 1968.
Welcome to Longfellow, Transition, 1969.
Stand-In for Murder, Transition, 1969.
Demon of Raven's Cliff, Belmont-Tower, 1971.
The Man in the Long Black Cape, Scholastic Book Services, 1972.
How Much Is That in Rubles?, University of Wisconsin—Stevens Point, 1973.
From Peacehaven to Peace Haven, University of Wisconsin—Stevens Point, 1974.
The Devil's Chapel, Perfection Form Co., 1985.

MUSICALS

"Heavens to Bacchus," first produced at Douglass College, Rutgers University, 1945.
"Navy Blues," first produced at Douglass College, Rutgers University, 1946.
"Rest upon the Wind," first produced at Douglass College, Rutgers University, 1948.
"Hey, Mr. Time," first produced by University of Florida Sandspurs, 1949.
The Toys in the Haunted Castle (juvenile; first produced in 1977) I. E. Clark, 1979.
The Secret in the Toyroom (juvenile; produced nearly fifty times in Wisconsin), I. E. Clark, 1984.
"Milady," showcased on Broadway by Roger Hendricks Simm, 1987.

Also author of the following juvenile musicals produced in the United States: "Goldilocks and the Three Bears: A Moral Musical," 1973, "The Princess and the Frog," 1974, "The Bunny with the Lopsided Ear," 1975, "The Twelve Dancing Princesses," 1976, "Kitty Cat Blue," 1977, "The All New Jack," 1979, "Captain Meano and the Magic Song," 1979, "From Poland with Love," 1980, "The New Cinderella," 1981, "The Little Troll Who Wasn't," 1981, "Sleeping Beauty," 1982, "The Firebird (Chaybarashka)," 1982.

OTHER

Also author of radio play, "Christmas Fantasy," 1944; also author of screenplays, "The Beach House," and "The Second Coming of Charlie Beezle," both 1987, both under option. Contributor, under pseudonym Becky Lynne, of about forty articles and stories to *Teen;* contributor to *Datebook* under name, Patience Hartman; also contributor to ten other teen and juvenile magazines; in adult field, contributor of verse to *Saturday Evening Post, Life Today, Empire, Soviet Life,* and *Laugh Book,* and of articles to numerous periodicals, including *Coronet, Discovery, Personal Romances, Chatelaine, Family Digest, Ford Times,* and *Ladies Home Journal.*

WORK IN PROGRESS: Screenplay, ''Death of a Sex Symbol.''

SIDELIGHTS: ''After decades of writing books and articles for money,'' Patience Zawadsky once wrote, ''I felt I had paid my dues. I returned to my first love, musical comedy—but this time, musical comedy for children. I found there is little or no money in children's theater. Those who act in it are looked down upon by other actors; those who write for it are looked down upon by other playwrights. But the children's laughter and applause, and sometimes tears, are more of a reward than any other form of writing has to offer. What a shame that America has so little regard, on television and in the theaters, for the enrichment of its children.''

121080

121080